FamAI	Famous Author-Illustrators for Young People		
FamAYP	Famous Authors for Young People		
FamMS	Famous Modern Storytellers for Young People	*PoCH*	Poets of the Church
		PoIre	Poets of Ireland
FamPYP	Famous Poets for Young People	*PoLE*	Poets Laureate of England
FamSYP	Famous Storytellers for Young People	*Prof*	Profiles
FemPA	Female Poets of America	*PueRA*	Puerto Rican Authors
ForIl	Forty Illustrators & How They Work	*RAdv*	Reader's Adviser
ForWC	Foremost Women in Communications	*RCom*	Reader's Companion to World Literature
HsB&A	The House of Beadle & Adams		
IlBYP	Illustrators of Books for Young People	*REn*	Reader's Encyclopedia
IlCB	Illustrators of Children's Books	*REnAL*	Reader's Encyclopedia of American Literature
IndAu	Indiana Authors & Their Books		
IntMPA	International Motion Picture Almanac	*REnWD*	Reader's Encyclopedia of World Drama
IntWW	International Who's Who		
JBA	Junior Book of Authors	*RGAfL*	Reader's Guide to African Literature
LBAA	Living Black American Authors	*SenS*	A Sense of Story
LE	Leaders in Education	*SingR*	The Singing Roads
LFWS	Living Female Writers of the South	*SixAP*	Sixty American Poets
LongC	Longman Companion to 20th Century Literature	*SmATA*	Something about the Author
		St&VC	Story & Verse for Children
McGWD	McGraw-Hill Encyclopedia of World Drama	*TelT*	Tellers of Tales
		TexW	Texas Writers of Today
MnBBF	The Men behind Boys' Fiction	*ThBJA*	Third Book of Junior Authors
MnnWr	Minnesota Writers	*TwCA*	Twentieth Century Authors
ModAL	Modern American Literature	*TwCW*	Twentieth Century Writing
ModBL	Modern British Literature	*WEAL*	Webster's New World Companion to English & American Literature
ModGL	Modern German Literature		
ModRL	Modern Romance Literatures	*WNAA*	Who Was Who Among North American Authors
ModSL	Modern Slavic Literatures		
ModWD	Modern World Drama	*WW*	Who's Who
MorBMP	More Books by More People	*WWA*	Who's Who in America
MorJA	More Junior Authors	*WWAA*	Who's Who in American Art
MouLC	Moulton's Library of Literary Criticism	*WWAW*	Who's Who of American Women
		WWBWI	Who's Who of Boys' Writers & Illustrators
NCHEL	New Century Handbook of English Literature	*WWCan*	Who's Who in Canada
NYTBE	New York Times Biographical Edition	*WWCL*	Who's Who of Children's Literature
NYTBS	New York Times Biographical Service	*WWE*	Who's Who in the East
Newb	Newbery Medal Books	*WWGA*	Who's Who in Graphic Arts
NewbC	Newbery-Caldecott Medal Books	*WWLA*	Who's Who Among Living Authors
OhA&B	Ohio Authors & Their Books	*WWMW*	Who's Who in the Midwest
OxAm	Oxford Companion to American Literature	*WWMus*	Who's Who in Music & Musicians
		WWPNA	Who's Who Among Pacific Northwest Authors
OxCan	Oxford Companion to Canadian History & Literature	*WWS*	Who's Who in the South & Southwest
OxEng	Oxford Companion to English Literature	*WWT*	Who's Who in the Theatre
		WWTwL	Who's Who in 20th Century Literature
OxFr	Oxford Companion to French Literature	*WWW*	Who's Who in the West
		WWWor	Who's Who in the World
OxGer	Oxford Companion to German Literature	*WWWorJ*	Who's Who in World Jewry
		WisW	Wisconsin Writers
Pen Am	Penguin Companion to American Literature	*WorAu*	World Authors
		WrD	Writers Directory
Pen Cl	Penguin Companion to Classical, Oriental & African Literature	*YABC*	Yesterday's Authors of Books for Children
Pen Eng	Penguin Companion to English Literature		

CHILDREN'S AUTHORS AND ILLUSTRATORS:

AN INDEX TO
BIOGRAPHICAL DICTIONARIES

CHILDREN'S AUTHORS AND ILLUSTRATORS:

AN INDEX TO BIOGRAPHICAL DICTIONARIES

SECOND EDITION

Gale Biographical Index Series
Number 2

Adele Sarkissian, Editor

Gale Research Company   Book Tower   Detroit, Michigan 48226

Editor:	Adele Sarkissian
Assistant Editors:	D. Jayne Higo, Susan L. Stetler
Consultant:	Dennis La Beau
Production Supervisor:	Laura Bryant
Production Manager:	Michaeline Nowinski
Cover Design:	Arthur Chartow

Special thanks to Miranda Herbert and Barbara McNeil.

Computerized photocomposition by Computer Composition Corporation
Madison Heights, Michigan

Library of Congress Cataloging in Publication Data

Sarkissian, Adele.
   Children's authors and illustrators.

   (Gale biographical index series ; no. 2)
   Earlier ed. by D. La Beau.
   Includes index.
   1. Authors--Biography--Indexes.   2. Illustrators
--Biography--Indexes.   3. Children's literature
--Indexes.   I. La Beau, Dennis. Children's
authors and illustrators.   II. Title.
Z1037.A1L2   1978   016.809   78-16868
ISBN 0-8103-1079-1

Introduction

The second edition of *Children's Authors and Illustrators* updates and augments the first edition published in 1976.

A pioneer reference work of its kind, the first edition of *Children's Authors and Illustrators* indexed thirty-two biographical sources, most of which dealt solely with creators of children's literature. Aiming to increase its usefulness as a research tool, the editors of the second edition have made substantial additions to both the number of listees and the number of sources indexed.

Scope of the Second Edition

The men and women who write and illustrate for children are often also recognized scholars, artists, teachers, journalists, writers for adults, etc. Their biographies are found in literary, professional, and geographic biographical sources as diverse as *Who's Who of American Women, A Dictionary of Contemporary American Artists, American Men and Women of Science, Contemporary Authors,* and *Something about the Author. CA&I* now provides access to this broad range of biographical information, drawing upon all the reference sources contained in Gale's *Author Biographies Master Index* and *Biographical Dictionaries Master Index* and indexes yet unpublished. These master indexes are an ever-growing storehouse which currently includes nearly two million entries from over 400 biographical sources. *CA&I* now covers approximately 15,000 authors and illustrators who are cited in about 150 reference sources.

The writers and artists listed in *CA&I* represent a broad range of children's literature that is suitable for reading levels from pre-school through junior high school.

Authors listed also include those whose works have been adapted for the younger reader, or whose work has been included in children's anthologies. For example, Geoffrey Chaucer is represented in the *Anthology of Children's Literature* (where his biography also appears) and several adaptations of his writings are available for children.

Reading a Citation

Each citation gives the author's or illustrator's name, birth and death dates (if known), and an alphabetically-arranged list of reference sources in which biographical information may be found.

The reference sources cited are given in an abbreviated code form based upon the title of the book. The key to these book codes will be found on the endpapers. Full bibliographic citations, including the codes, will be found on pages vii to xxiii.

Since slight name variations inevitably occur from one reference source to another, the editors have attempted to correlate all listings for a given author by standardizing the name. In most cases the fullest form of the name has been used. The listing within a particular reference book may differ slightly from that given in this index, but standardization of the name will not interfere with locating the entry.

Cross references have been added to this edition of *CA&I* in order to alert the reader to:

1) Name variations in sources cited that do not allow for standardization

> For example, De Brunhoff, Laurent and Brunhoff, Laurent de

2) The use of pseudonyms

> For example, Charles Hamilton wrote under some twenty-six pen names, and twenty-five different authors wrote under the name "Frank Richards."

Any comments or suggestions regarding *CA&I* will be most welcome.

KEY TO BOOK CODES

CODE	BOOK INDEXED
AfA	*African Authors: A Companion to Black African Writing.* Volume 1: 1300-1973. By Donald E. Herdeck. Washington, D.C.: Black Orpheus Press, 1973.
Alli	Allibone, S. Austin: *A Critical Dictionary of English Literature and British and American Authors Living and Deceased from the Earliest Accounts to the Latter Half of the Nineteenth Century.* Containing over forty-six thousand articles (authors) with forty indexes of subjects. Three volumes. Philadelphia: J.B. Lippincott & Co., 1858-1871. Reprinted by Gale Research Co., Detroit, 1965. Also available from Gale on microfiche.
	Most entries are biographical. There are some blind cross-references.
Alli Sup	*A Supplement to Allibone's Critical Dictionary of English Literature and British and American Authors.* Containing over thirty-seven thousand articles (authors), and enumerating over ninety-three thousand titles. Two volumes. By John Foster Kirk. Philadelphia: J.B. Lippincott & Co., 1891. Reprinted by Gale Research Co., Detroit, 1965. Also available from Gale on microfiche.
AmA	*American Authors, 1600-1900: A Biographical Dictionary of American Literature.* Edited by Stanley J. Kunitz and Howard Haycraft. New York: H.W. Wilson Co., 1938.
AmA&B	*American Authors and Books, 1640 to the Present Day.* Third revised edition. By W.J. Burke and Will D. Howe. Revised by Irving Weiss and Anne Weiss. New York: Crown Publishers, Inc., 1972.
	Provides dates of birth and death, occupation and brief bibliographies.
AmLY	*The American Literary Yearbook.* A biographical and bibliographical dictionary of living North American authors; a record of contemporary literary activity; an authors' manual and students' text book. Volume 1, 1919. Edited by Hamilton Traub. Henning, Minnesota: Paul Traub, Publisher, 1919. Republished by Gale Research Co., Detroit, 1968. Also available from Gale on microfiche.
	Biographical dictionary begins on page 57. A list of pen names and pseudonyms begins on page 49, and is cited in this index by the code *"XR"*.
AmMWS 12 P	*American Men and Women of Science: The Physical and Biological Sciences.* 12th edition. Six volumes. Edited by the Jaques Cattell Press. New York: R.R. Bowker Co., 1971-1973.
AmMWS 12 S	*American Men and Women of Science: The Social and Behavioral Sciences.* 12th editon. Two volumes. Edited by the Jaques Cattell Press. New York: R.R. Bowker Co., 1973.
AmNov	*American Novelists of Today.* By Harry R. Warfel. New York: American Book Co., 1951. Reprinted by Greenwood Press, Westport, Conn., 1976.
	The *Index of Married Names and Pseudonyms* begins on page 477, and is cited in this index by the code *"XR"*.

Key to Book Codes

AmPB
American Picturebooks from Noah's Ark to The Beast Within. By Barbara Bader. New York: Macmillan Publishing Co., Inc. and London: Collier Macmillan Publishers, 1976.

AmSCAP 66
The ASCAP Biographical Dictionary of Composers, Authors and Publishers. 1966 edition. Compiled and edited by the Lynn Farnol Group, Inc. New York: American Society of Composers, Authors and Publishers, 1966.

This dictionary contains information on many writers and poets who have contributed to the music and theater worlds.

AmWr
American Writers: A Collection of Literary Biographies. Edited by Leonard Unger. Four volumes. New York: Charles Scribner's Sons, 1974.

Originally published as *The University of Minnesota Pamphlets on American Writers.*

AnCL
Anthology of Children's Literature. Fourth edition. Compiled and edited by Edna Johnson, Evelyn R. Sickels, and Frances Clarke Sayers. Boston: Houghton Mifflin Co., 1970.

Biographies begin on page 1217.

AnMV 1926
Anthology of Magazine Verse for 1926 and Yearbook of American Poetry. Edited by William Stanley Braithwaite. Freeport, New York: Books for Libraries Press (Granger Index Reprint Series), 1972. Reprinted from the 1926 edition.

A Biographical Dictionary of Poets in the United States is found in Part IV, at the back of this edition.

ArizL
Arizona in Literature: A Collection of the Best Writings of Arizona Authors from Early Spanish Days to the Present Time. By Mary G. Boyer. Ann Arbor: Gryphon Books, 1971. Reprinted from the 1935 edition published by the Arthur H. Clark Co., Glendale, Calif. Also available from Gale on microfiche.

Use the Index that begins on page 569 to find any given author.

ArtCS
The Art of the Comic Strip. By Judith O'Sullivan. College Park: University of Maryland, Department of Art, 1971.

Biographies are found on pages 60-87.

ArtsCL
Artists of a Certain Line: A Selection of Illustrators for Children's Books. By John Ryder. London: The Bodley Head, 1960.

AtlBL
Atlantic Brief Lives: A Biographical Companion to the Arts. Edited by Louis Kronenberger. Boston: Little, Brown and Co., 1971. (An Atlantic Monthly Press Book).

Au&ICB
Authors and Illustrators of Children's Books: Writings on Their Lives and Works. By Miriam Hoffman and Eva Samuels. New York: R.R. Bowker Co., 1972.

Au&Wr 6
The Author's and Writer's Who's Who. Sixth edition. Darien, Conn.: Hafner Publishing Co., Inc. (Published and copyrighted by Burke's Peerage, Ltd., London, 1971).

AuBYP
Authors of Books for Young People. Second edition. By Martha E. Ward and Dorothy A. Marquardt. Metuchen, N.J.: Scarecrow Press, Inc. 1971.

AuNews
Authors in the News. A compilation of news stories and feature articles from American newspapers and magazines covering writers and other members of the communications media. Edited by Barbara Nykoruk. (Biography News Library). Detroit: Gale Research Co., 1976-1977.

AuNews 1 Volume 1, 1976
AuNews 2 Volume 2, 1977

     Many of the articles give some biographical information.

BbD   *The Bibliophile Dictionary.* A biographical record of the great authors, with bibliographical notices of their principal works from the beginning of history. Originally published as Volumes 29 and 30 of *The Bibliophile Library of Literature, Art, and Rare Manuscripts.* Compiled and arranged by Nathan Haskell Dole, Forrest Morgan, and Caroline Ticknor. New York and London: International Bibliophile Society, 1904. Republished by Gale Research Co., Detroit, 1966. Also available from Gale on microfiche.

BbthC   *Bibliotheca Canadensis; or, A Manual of Canadian Literature.* By Henry J. Morgan. Ottawa: G.E. Desbarats, 1867. Reprinted by Gale Research Co., Detroit, 1968. Also available from Gale on microfiche.

BiD&SB   *Biographical Dictionary and Synopsis of Books Ancient and Modern.* Edited by Charles Dudley Warner. Akron, Ohio: Werner Co., 1902. Reprinted by Gale Research Co., Detroit, 1965. Also available from Gale on microfiche.

BiDL 5   *A Biographical Directory of Librarians in the United States and Canada.* Fifth edition. Edited by Lee Ash. Chicago: American Library Association, 1970.

BiDLA   *A Biographical Dictionary of the Living Authors of Great Britain and Ireland.* Comprising literary memoirs and anecdotes of their lives; and a chronological register of their publications, with the number of editons printed; including notices of some foreign writers whose works have been occasionally published in England. London: Printed for Henry Colburn; Public Library, Conduit Street, Hanover Square, 1816. Republished by Gale Research Co., Detroit, 1966. Also available from Gale on microfiche.

     A supplemental listing of authors begins on page 407, and is indicated in this index by the code *Sup.*

BiDPar   *Biographical Dictionary of Parapsychology, with Directory and Glossary, 1964-1966.* Edited by Helene Pleasants. New York: Garrett Publications, Helix Press, 1964.

BiDSA   *Biographical Dictionary of Southern Authors.* By Lucian Lamar Knight. Originally published as *Library of Southern Literature, Volume XV, Biographical Dictionary of Authors.* Atlanta: Martin & Hoyt Co., 1929. Reprinted by Gale Research Co., Detroit, 1978. Also available from Gale on microfiche.

BiEnAT   *The Biographical Encyclopaedia & Who's Who of the American Theatre.* First edition. Edited by Walter Rigdon. New York: James H. Heineman, Inc., 1966.

BiN   *Biography News.* Edited by Frank E. Bair. Detroit: Gale Research Co., 1974-1975.

BiN 1974 Volume 1, 1974
BiN 1975 Volume 2, 1975

BkC   *The Book of Catholic Authors.* Informal self-portraits of famous modern Catholic writers. Edited by Walter Romig. Detroit: Walter Romig & Co., 1942-?

BkC 1   First series, 1942
BkC 2   Second series, 1943
BkC 3   Third series, 1945
BkC 4   Fourth series (n.d.)
BkC 5   Fifth series (n.d.)
BkC 6   Sixth series (n.d.)

BkCL — *A Book of Children's Literature*. Third edition. By Lillian Hollowell. New York and Chicago: Holt, Rinehart and Winston, Inc., 1966.

Biographies of authors begin on page 553.

BkIE — *Book Illustrators in Eighteenth-Century England*. By Hanns Hammelmann. Edited and completed by T.S.R. Boase. New Haven and London: Yale University Press (for the Paul Mellon Centre for Studies in British Art, London), 1975.

BkP — *Books Are by People: Interviews with 104 Authors and Illustrators of Books for Young Children*. Edited by Lee Bennett Hopkins. New York: Citation Press, 1969.

BlkAW — *Black American Writers Past and Present: A Biographical and Bibliographical Dictionary*. Two volumes. By Theressa Gunnels Rush, Carol Fairbanks Myers, and Esther Spring Arata. Metuchen, N.J.: Scarecrow Press, Inc., 1975.

Br&AmS — *British and American Sporting Authors: Their Writings and Biographies*. By A. Henry Higginson. London: Hutchinson & Co., Ltd., 1951.

Use index in back of book to locate authors.

BrAu — *British Authors before 1800: A Biographical Dictionary*. Edited by Stanley J. Kunitz and Howard Haycraft. New York: H.W. Wilson Co., 1952.

BrAu 19 — *British Authors of the Nineteenth Century*. Edited by Stanley J. Kunitz. New York: H.W. Wilson Co., 1936.

BrCA — *British Children's Authors: Interviews at Home*. By Cornelia Jones and Olivia R. Way. Chicago: American Library Association, 1976.

Cald 1938 — *Caldecott Medal Books: 1938-1957*. With the artist's acceptance papers & related material chiefly from the *Horn Book Magazine*. Edited by Bertha Mahony Miller and Elinor Whitney Field. Horn Book Papers, Volume II. Boston: The Horn Book, Inc., 1957.

CanNov — *Canadian Novelists, 1920-1945*. By Clara Thomas. Toronto: Longmans, Green & Co., 1946. Reprinted by Folcroft Library Editions, Folcroft, Pa., 1970.

CanWW 12 — *The Canadian Who's Who*, Volume 12, 1970-1972. Toronto: Who's Who Canadian Publications, 1972.

CanWr — *Canadian Writers: A Biographical Dictionary*. Edited by Guy Sylvestre, Brandon Conron, and Carl F. Klinck. New edition, revised and enlarged. Toronto: Ryerson Press, 1960.

Biographies of Quebec authors are in French.

CarSB — *The Carolyn Sherwin Bailey Historical Collection of Children's Books: A Catalogue*. Edited and compiled by Dorothy R. Davis. New Haven: Southern Connecticut State College, 1966.

Some listings are not in strict alphabetical sequence. There is no index.

CasWL — *Cassell's Encyclopaedia of World Literature*. Edited by S.H. Steinberg in two volumes. Revised and enlarged in three volumes by J. Buchanan-Brown. New York: William Morrow & Co., Inc., 1973.

Biographies are found in Volumes 2 and 3.

CatA 1930 — *Catholic Authors: Contemporary Biographical Sketches, 1930-1947*. Edited by Matthew Hoehn. Newark: St. Mary's Abbey, 1957 (c1948).

CatA 1952 — *Catholic Authors: Contemporary Biographical Sketches*. Edited by Matthew Hoehn. Newark: St. Mary's Abbey, 1952.

CelR 3   *Celebrity Register.* Third edition. Earl Blackwell, editor-in-chief. New York: Simon & Schuster, 1973.

Chambr 1-3   *Chambers' Cyclopaedia of English Literature.* Edited by David Patrick. Revised by J. Liddell Geddie. Three volumes: Volume 1, 7th-17th century; Volume 2, 18th century; Volume 3, 19th-20th century. Philadelphia and New York: J.B. Lippincott Co., 1938. To be reprinted by Gale Research Co. Also available from Gale on microfiche.

    Use the indexes found at the back of the three volumes to locate authors.

ChFB   *The Child's First Books: A Critical Study of Pictures and Texts.* By Donnarae MacCann and Olga Richard. New York: H.W. Wilson Co., 1973.

ChFB A   Author biographies (pages 96-104)
ChFB I   Illustrator biographies (pages 47-71)

ChLR   *Children's Literature Review.* Excerpts from reviews, criticism, and commentary on books for children and young people. Detroit: Gale Research Co., 1976-1978.

ChLR 1   Volume 1, 1976
ChLR 2   Volume 2, 1976
ChLR 3   Volume 3, 1978

ChP   *The Children's Poets: Analyses and Appraisals of the Greatest English and American Poets for Children.* By Walter Barnes. Yonkers-on-Hudson: World Book Co., 1924.

ChPo   *Childhood in Poetry.* A catalogue, with biographical and critical annotations, of the books of English and American poets comprising the Shaw Childhood in Poetry Collection in the Library of the Florida State University, with lists of the poems that relate to childhood. By John Mackay Shaw. Four volumes. Detroit: Gale Research Co., 1967. Also available from Gale on microfiche.

    There are some blind cross-references.

ChPo S1   *Childhood in Poetry...Supplement (One).* By John Mackay Shaw. Three volumes. Detroit: Gale Research Co., 1972. Also available from Gale on microfiche.

ChPo S2   *Childhood in Poetry...Second Supplement.* By John Mackay Shaw. Detroit: Gale Research Co., 1976. Also available from Gale on microfiche.

ClDMEuL   *Columbia Dictionary of Modern European Literature.* Edited by Horatio Smith. New York and London: Columbia University Press, 1947. Also published as *A Dictionary of Modern European Literature.* London: Oxford University Press, 1947.

CnDAL   *Concise Dictionary of American Literature.* Edited by Robert Fulton Richards. New York: Philosophical Library, Inc., 1955. Reprinted by Greenwood Press, New York, 1969.

CnE&AP   *The Concise Encyclopedia of English and American Poets and Poetry.* Edited by Stephen Spender and Donald Hall. New York: Hawthorn Books, Inc., 1963.

CnMD   *The Concise Encyclopedia of Modern Drama.* By Siegfried Melchinger. Translated from the German by George Wellwarth. Edited by Henry Popkin. New York: Horizon Press, 1964.

    Biographies begin on page 159. A supplemental list of 21 playwrights with short biographical notices begins on page 287, and is cited in this index by the code *Sup.*

CnMWL   *The Concise Encyclopedia of Modern World Literature.* Edited by Geoffrey Grigson. Hutchinson of London, 1963.

    Biographical entries begin on page 29.

CnThe	*A Concise Encyclopedia of the Theatre.* By Robin May. Reading, England: Osprey Publishing, Ltd., 1974.
	Use the index at the back of the book to locate biographies.
ConAmA	*Contemporary American Authors: A Critical Survey and 219 Bio-Bibliographies.* By Fred B. Millett. New York: Harcourt, Brace & World, Inc., 1940. Reprinted by AMS Press, Inc., New York, 1970.
	Author biographies begin on page 207.
ConAmL	*Contemporary American Literature: Bibliographies and Study Outlines.* By John Matthews Manly and Edith Rickert. Revised by Fred B. Millett. New York: Harcourt, Brace, 1929. Reprinted by Haskell House Publishers, Ltd., New York, 1974.
	Biographical section begins on page 101.
ConAu	*Contemporary Authors.* A bio-bibliographical guide to current authors and their works. Detroit: Gale Research Co., 1962-1978. Also available from Gale on microfiche.
ConAu 1R	Volume 1-4, 1st revision, 1967
ConAu 5R	Volume 5-8, 1st revision, 1969
ConAu 9R	Volume 9-12, 1st revision, 1974
ConAu 13	Volume 13-14, 1965
ConAu 13R	Volume 13-16, 1st revision, 1975
ConAu 15	Volume 15-16, 1966
ConAu 17	Volume 17-18, 1967
ConAu 17R	Volume 17-20, 1st revision, 1976
ConAu 19	Volume 19-20, 1968
ConAu 21	Volume 21-22, 1969
ConAu 21R	Volume 21-24, 1st revision, 1977
ConAu 23	Volume 23-24, 1970
ConAu 25	Volume 25-28, 1971
ConAu 25R	Volume 25-28, 1st revision, 1977
ConAu 29	Volume 29-32, 1972
ConAu 33	Volume 33-36, 1973
ConAu 37	Volume 37-40, 1973
ConAu 41	Volume 41-44, 1974
ConAu 45	Volume 45-48, 1974
ConAu 49	Volume 49-52, 1975
ConAu 53	Volume 53-56, 1975
ConAu 57	Volume 57-60, 1976
ConAu 61	Volume 61-64, 1976
ConAu 65	Volume 65-68, 1977
ConAu 69	Volume 69-72, 1978
ConAu XR	Index to Volumes 1-72, found in back of Volume 69-72. This code refers to pseudonym entries which appear only as cross references in the cumulative index to *Contemporary Authors.*
ConAu P	*Contemporary Authors, Permanent Series.* A bio-bibliographical guide to current authors and their works. Detroit: Gale Research Co., 1975-1978. Also available from Gale on microfiche.
ConAu P-1	Volume 1, 1975
ConAu P-2	Volume 2, 1978
ConDr 1	*Contemporary Dramatists.* Edited by James Vinson. London: St. James Press and New York: St. Martin's Press, 1973.
	Biographies are given in the following sections: *Contemporary Dra-*

matists, page 7; Screen Writers, page 847; *Radio Writers,* page 857; *Television Writers,* page 867; *Musical Librettists,* page 875; *The Theatre of Mixed Means,* page 889.

ConICB   *Contemporary Illustrators of Children's Books.* Compiled and edited by Elinor Whitney and Bertha E. Mahony. Boston: The Bookshop for Boys and Girls, Women's Educational and Industrial Union, 1930. To be reprinted by Gale Research Co. Also available from Gale on microfiche.

ConLC   *Contemporary Literary Criticism.* Excerpts from criticism of the works of today's novelists, poets, playwrights, and other creative writers. Detroit: Gale Research Co., 1973-1976.

ConLC 1   Volume 1, 1973
ConLC 2   Volume 2, 1974
ConLC 3   Volume 3, 1975
ConLC 4   Volume 4, 1975
ConLC 5   Volume 5, 1976
ConLC 6   Volume 6, 1976

A series of collected criticism.

ConNov 1972   *Contemporary Novelists.* Edited by James Vinson. London: St. James Press and New York: St. Martin's Press, 1972.

ConNov 1976   *Contemporary Novelists.* Second edition. Edited by James Vinson and D.L. Kirkpatrick. London: St. James Press and New York: St. Martin's Press, 1976.

Deceased authors are listed in the appendix, which begins on page 1565.

ConP 1970   *Contemporary Poets.* Edited by Rosalie Murphy. London: St. James Press and New York: St. Martin's Press, 1970.

ConP 1975   *Contemporary Poets.* Second edition. Edited by James Vinson and D.L. Kirkpatrick. London: St. James Press and New York: St. Martin's Press, 1975.

Deceased poets are listed in the appendix, which begins on page 1745.

CrCAP   *Crowell's Handbook of Contemporary American Poetry.* By Karl Malkoff. New York: Thomas Y. Crowell Co., 1973.

Biographical entries begin on page 43.

CrCD   *Crowell's Handbook of Contemporary Drama.* By Michael Anderson, Jacques Guicharnaud, Kristin Morrison, Jack D. Zipes, and others. New York: Thomas Y. Crowell Co., 1971.

CrE&SL   *Crowell's Handbook of Elizabethan & Stuart Literature.* By James E. Ruoff. New York: Thomas Y. Crowell Co., 1975.

CriT   *The Critical Temper.* A survey of modern criticism on English and American Literature from the beginnings to the twentieth century. Three volumes. Edited by Martin Tucker. New York: Frederick Ungar Publishing Co., 1969.

CriT 1   Volume 1: From Old English to Shakespeare.

CriT 2   Volume 2: From Milton to Romantic Literature.

CriT 3   Volume 3: Victorian Literature and American Literature.

Authors are listed alphabetically within each period or division of literature.

CurB   *Current Biography,* 1940-February, 1975. New York: H.W. Wilson Co.

CyAL 1-2 *Cyclopaedia of American Literature.* Embracing personal and critical notices of authors, and selections from their writings, from the earliest period to the present day. By Evert A. Duyckinck and George L. Duyckinck. Two volumes. Philadelphia: Wm. Rutter & Co., 1875. Republished by Gale Research Co., Detroit, 1965. Also available from Gale on microfiche.

Use index in back of Volume 2 to locate authors.

CyWA *Cyclopedia of World Authors.* Edited by Frank N. Magill and Dayton Kohler. New York: Harper & Row, 1958. Originally published as *Masterplots Cyclopedia of World Authors.*

DcAmA *A Dictionary of American Authors.* By Oscar Fay Adams. Fifth edition, revised and enlarged. Boston and New York: Houghton Mifflin Co., 1904. Reprinted by Gale Research Co., Detroit, 1969. Also available from Gale on microfiche.

DcBiA *A Dictionary of Biographies of Authors Represented in the Authors Digest Series.* With a supplemental list of later titles and a supplementary biographical section. Edited by Rossiter Johnson. New York: Authors Press, 1927. Reprinted by Gale Research Co., Detroit, 1974. Also available from Gale on microfiche.

DcCAA 2 *A Dictionary of Contemporary American Artists.* Second edition. By Paul Cummings. New York: St. Martin's Press, 1971.

DcCLA *A Dictionary of Contemporary Latin American Authors.* Compiled by David William Foster. Tempe: Center for Latin American Studies, Arizona State University, 1975.

DcEnA *A Dictionary of English Authors, Biographical and Bibliographical.* New edition, revised with an appendix bringing the whole up to date and including a large amount of new matter. By R. Farquharson Sharp. London: Kegan Paul, Trench, Trubner & Co., Ltd., 1904. Reprinted by Gale Research Co., Detroit, 1978. Also available from Gale on microfiche.

Biographies found in the Appendix are indicated by the code *Ap.*

DcEnL *Dictionary of English Literature.* A comprehensive guide to English authors and their works. Second edition. By W. Davenport Adams. London: Cassell Petter & Galpin, (n.d.). Reprinted by Gale Research Co., Detroit, 1966. Also available from Gale on microfiche.

DcEuL *A Dictionary of European Literature.* Designed as a companion to English studies. By Laurie Magnus. Second, revised edition. London: George Routledge & Sons, Ltd. and New York: E.P. Dutton & Co., 1927. Republished by Gale Research Co., Detroit, 1974. Also available from Gale on microfiche.

DcLEnL *A Dictionary of Literature in the English Language, from Chaucer to 1940.* Two volumes. Compiled and edited by Robin Myers. Oxford and London: Pergamon Press, 1970.

Biographical entries are found in Volume 1. An author-title index is provided in Volume 2.

DcNAA *A Dictionary of North American Authors Deceased before 1950.* Compiled by W. Stewart Wallace. Toronto: Ryerson Press, 1951. Reprinted by Gale Research Co., Detroit, 1968. Also available from Gale on microfiche.

This is an index to biographical material found in standard reference sources, many of which are not included in this index.

DcOrL *Dictionary of Oriental Literatures.* Three volumes. Jaroslav Prusek, general editor. New York: Basic Books, Inc., 1974.

DcOrL 1	Volume 1: East Asia. Edited by Zbigniew Slupski.
DcOrL 2	Volume 2: South and South-East Asia. Edited by Dusan Zbavitel.
DcOrL 3	Volume 3: West Asia and North Africa. Edited by Jiri Becka.

DcRusL Dictionary of Russian Literature. By William E. Harkins. New York: Philosophical Library, Inc., 1956. Reprinted by Greenwood Press, Westport, Conn., 1971.

This book gives biographies of authors and appraises each author's contribution to Russian letters.

DcSpL Dictionary of Spanish Literature. By Maxim Newmark. New York: Philosophical Library, Inc., 1956. Republished by Littlefield, Adams & Co., Totowa, N.J., 1970.

DrAF 1976 A Directory of American Fiction Writers. 1976 edition. Names and addresses of more than 800 contemporary fiction writers whose work has been published in the United States. New York: Poets & Writers, Inc., 1976.

Provides addresses with mention of writer's latest published works. Use index which begins on page 123 to find author listings.

DrAP 1975 A Directory of American Poets. 1975 edition. Names and addresses of more than than 1,500 contemporary poets whose work has been published in the United States. New York: Poets & Writers, Inc., 1975.

Provides addresses with mention of poet's latest work. Use index, which begins on page vii, to find listings.

DrAS Directory of American Scholars. Sixth edition. Four volumes. Edited by Jaques Cattell Press. New York: R.R. Bowker Co., 1974.

DrAS 6E	Volume 2: *English, Speech, & Drama*
DrAS 6F	Volume 3: *Foreign Languages, Linguistics, & Philology*
DrAS 6H	Volume 1: *History*
DrAS 6P	Volume 4: *Philosophy, Religion, & Law*

DrLC 1969 Directory of Library Consultants. Edited by John N. Berry, III. New York: R.R. Bowker Co., 1969.

EarAB Early American Book Illustrators and Wood Engravers, 1670-1870. Volume 1, Main Catalogue. A catalogue of a collection of American books illustrated for the most part with woodcuts and wood engravings in the Princeton University Library. By Sinclair Hamilton. Princeton, N.J.: Princeton University Press, 1968 (c1958).

Use the index in the back of the book to locate entries.

EarAB Sup Early American Book Illustrators and Wood Engravers, 1670-1870. Volume 2, Supplement. By Sinclair Hamilton. Princeton, N.J.: Princeton University Press, 1968.

Use the index in the back of this volume to locate entries.

EncFCW 1969 Encyclopedia of Folk, Country and Western Music. By Irwin Stambler and Grelun Landon. New York: St. Martin's Press, 1969.

EncM&D Encyclopedia of Mystery and Detection. Edited by Chris Steinbrunner, Otto Penzler, Marvin Lachman, and Charles Shibuk. New York: McGraw-Hill, 1976.

EncWL Encyclopedia of World Literature in the 20th Century. Three volumes. Edited by Bernard Fleischmann. An enlarged and updated edition of the *Herder Lexikon der Weltliteratur im 20. Jahrhundert*. New York: Frederick Ungar Publishing Co., 1967.

Key to Book Codes

EncWL Sup *Encyclopedia of World Literature in the 20th Century.* Volume 4, Supplement. Edited by Frederick Ungar and Lina Mainiero. New York: Frederick Ungar Publishing Co., 1975.

EuAu *European Authors, 1000-1900: A Biographical Dictionary of European Literature.* Edited by Stanley J. Kunitz and Vineta Colby. New York: H.W. Wilson Co., 1967.

EvEuW *Everyman's Dictionary of European Writers.* By W.N. Hargreaves-Mawdsley. London: J.M. Dent & Sons, Ltd. and New York: E.P. Dutton & Co., 1968.

EvLB *Everyman's Dictionary of Literary Biography, English & American.* Revised edition. Compiled after John W. Cousin by D.C. Browning. London: J.M. Dent & Sons, Ltd. and New York: E.P. Dutton & Co., Inc., 1960.

FamAI *Famous Author-Illustrators for Young People.* By Norah Smaridge. New York: Dodd, Mead & Co., 1973.

FamAYP *Famous Authors for Young People.* By Ramon P. Coffman and Nathan G. Goodman. New York: Dodd, Mead & Co., 1943.

FamMS *Famous Modern Storytellers for Young People.* By Norah Smaridge. New York: Dodd, Mead & Co., 1969.

FamPYP *Famous Poets for Young People.* By Laura Benet. New York: Dodd, Mead & Co., 1964.

FamSYP *Famous Storytellers for Young People.* By Laura Benet. New York: Dodd, Mead & Co., 1968.

FemPA *The Female Poets of America.* With portraits, biographical notices, and specimens of their writings. By Thomas Buchanan Read. Seventh edition, revised. Philadelphia: E.H. Butler & Co., 1857. To be reprinted by Gale Research Co. Also available from Gale on microfiche.

ForIl *Forty Illustrators and How They Work.* By Ernest W. Watson. Cincinnati: Watson-Guptill Publications, Inc., 1946. Reprinted by Books for Libraries Press, Freeport, N.Y., 1970.

ForWC 1970 *Foremost Women in Communications.* New York: Foremost Americans Publishing Corp. in association with R.R. Bowker Co., 1970.

HsB&A *The House of Beadle and Adams and Its Dime and Nickel Novels: The Story of a Vanished Literature.* By Albert Johannsen. Norman: University of Oklahoma Press, 1950.

Biographical entries are found in Volume 2, beginning on page 6.

HsB&A Sup *The House of Beadle and Adams and Its Dime and Nickel Novels...* Volume 3, Supplement, Addenda, Corrigenda. By Albert Johannsen. Norman: University of Oklahoma Press, 1962.

Corrections and additions to the biographies in Volume 2 begin on page 15.

IlBYP *Illustrators of Books for Young People.* Second edition. By Martha E. Ward and Dorothy A. Marquardt. Metuchen, N.J.: Scarecrow Press, Inc., 1975.

IlCB 1744 *Illustrators of Children's Books, 1744-1945.* Compiled and edited by Bertha E. Mahony, Louise P. Latimer, and Beulah Folmsbee. Boston: The Horn Book, Inc., 1945, reprinted, 1970.

IlCB 1946 *Illustrators of Children's Books, 1946-1956.* Compiled and edited by Ruth Hill Viguers, Marcia Dalphin, and Bertha Mahony Miller. Boston: The Horn Book, Inc., 1958.

IICB 1957	*Illustrators of Children's Books, 1957-1966.* Compiled and edited by Lee King-man, Joanna Foster, and Ruth Giles Lontoft. Boston: The Horn Book, Inc., 1968.
IndAu 1816	*Indiana Authors and Their Books, 1816-1916:* Biographical sketches of authors who published during the first century of Indiana statehood with lists of their books. Compiled by R.E. Banta. Crawfordsville, Ind.: Wabash College, 1949.
IndAu 1917	*Indiana Authors and Their Books, 1917-1966:* A continuation of Indiana Authors and Their Books, 1816-1916, and containing additional names from the earlier period. Compiled by Donald E. Thompson. Crawfordsville, Ind.: Wabash College, 1974.
IntMPA 1975	*International Motion Picture Almanac.* 1975. Edited by Richard Gertner. New York: Quigley Publishing Co., 1975.
	In the "Who's Who in Motion Pictures and Television" section. The listings here are identical with those in the *International Television Almanac.*
IntWW 38	*The International Who's Who.* 38th edition, 1974-75. London: Europa Publications Ltd., 1974.
JBA 1934	*The Junior Book of Authors:* An introduction to the lives of writers and illustrators for younger readers from Lewis Carroll and Louisa Alcott to the present day. Illustrated with 260 photographs and drawings. Edited by Stanley J. Kunitz and Howard Haycraft. New York: H.W. Wilson Co., 1934 (first edition).
	The 1934 edition contains many biographies that were not carried over into the second edition.
JBA 1951	*The Junior Book of Authors.* Second edition, revised. Edited by Stanley J. Kunitz and Howard Haycraft. New York: H.W. Wilson Co., 1951.
LBAA	*Living Black American Authors: A Biographical Dictionary.* By Ann Allen Shockley and Sue P. Chandler. New York and London: R.R. Bowker Co., 1973.
LE 5	*Leaders in Education.* Fifth edition. Edited by Jaques Cattell Press. New York: R.R. Bowker Co., 1974.
LFWS	*The Living Female Writers of the South.* Edited by the author of *Southland Writers.* Philadelphia: Claxton, Remsen & Haffelfinger, 1872. To be reprinted by Gale Research Co. Also available from Gale on microfiche.
LongC	*Longman Companion to Twentieth Century Literature.* By A.C. Ward. London: Longman, 1970.
McGWD	*McGraw-Hill Encyclopedia of World Drama.* An international reference work in four volumes. New York: McGraw-Hill Book Co., 1972.
MnBBF	*The Men behind Boys' Fiction.* By W.O.G. Lofts and D.J. Adley. London: Howard Baker, 1970.
	Most entries are biographical.
MnnWr	*Minnesota Writers.* A collection of autobiographical stories by Minnesota prose writers. Edited and annotated by Carmen Nelson Richards. Minneapolis: T.S. Denison & Co., Inc., 1961.
	Use the table of contents to locate authors.
ModAL	*Modern American Literature.* A Library of Literary Criticism. Fourth enlarged edition. Three volumes. Compiled and edited by Dorothy Nyren Curley,

Maurice Kramer, and Elaine Fialka Kramer. New York: Frederick Ungar Publishing Co., 1969.

A book of collected criticism.

ModAL Sup   *Modern American Literature.* A Library of Literary Criticism. Volume IV, Supplement to the fourth edition. Compiled and edited by Dorothy Nyren, Maurice Kramer, and Elaine Fialka Kramer. New York: Frederick Ungar Publishing Co., 1976.

A book of collected criticism.

ModBL   *Modern British Literature.* A Library of Literary Criticism. Three volumes. Compiled and edited by Ruth Z. Temple and Martin Tucker. New York: Frederick Ungar Publishing Co., 1966.

A book of collected criticism.

ModBL Sup   *Modern British Literature.* A Library of Literary Criticism. Volume IV, Supplement. Compiled and edited by Martin Tucker and Rita Stein. New York: Frederick Ungar Publishing Co., 1975.

A book of collected criticism.

ModGL   *Modern German Literature.* A Library of Literary Criticism. Two volumes. Compiled and edited by Agnes Korner Domandi. New York: Frederick Ungar Publishing Co., 1972.

A book of collected criticism.

ModRL   *Modern Romance Literatures.* A Library of Literary Criticism. Compiled and edited by Dorothy Nyren Curley and Arthur Curley. New York: Frederick Ungar Publishing Co., 1967.

A book of collected criticism.

ModSL 1   *Modern Slavic Literatures. Volume 1: Russian Literature.* A Library of Literary Criticism. Compiled and edited by Vasa D. Mihailovich. New York: Frederick Ungar Publishing Co., 1972.

A book of collected criticism.

ModSL 2   *Modern Slavic Literatures. Volume 2: Bulgarian, Czechoslovak, Polish, Ukrainian and Yugoslav Literatures.* A Library of Literary Criticism. Compiled and edited by Vasa D. Mihailovich, Igor Hajek, Zbigniew Folejewski, Bogdan Czaykowski, Leo D. Rudnytzky, and Thomas Butler. New York: Frederick Ungar Publishing Co., 1976.

A book of collected criticism. Authors listed alphabetically by country or language. Use the alphabetical listing on page vii to locate authors.

ModWD   *Modern World Drama: An Encyclopedia.* By Myron Matlaw. New York: E.P. Dutton & Co., Inc., 1972.

MorBMP   *More Books by More People.* Interviews with sixty-five authors of books for children. By Lee Bennett Hopkins. New York: Citation Press, 1974.

MorJA   *More Junior Authors.* Edited by Muriel Fuller. New York: H.W. Wilson Co., 1963.

MouLC   *Moulton's Library of Literary Criticism of English and American Authors.* Through the beginning of the twentieth century. Four volumes. Abridged, revised and with additions by Martin Tucker. New York: Frederick Ungar Publishing Co., 1966.

MouLC 1   Volume 1: The Beginnings to the Seventeenth Century.

Alphabetical listing of authors begins on page xv.

MouLC 2	Volume 2: Neo-Classicism to the Romantic Period.
	Alphabetical listing of authors begins on page vii.
MouLC 3	Volume 3: The Romantic Period to the Victorian Age.
	Alphabetical listing of authors begins on page vii.
MouLC 4	Volume 4: The Mid-Nineteenth Century to Edwardianism.
	Alphabetical listing of authors begins on page vii.
NCHEL	*The New Century Handbood of English Literature.* Revised edition. Edited by Clarence L. Barnhart with the assistance of William D. Halsey. New York: Appleton, Century, Crofts, 1967.
NYTBE 1-4	*The New York Times Biographical Edition.* Volumes 1-4, 1970-1973. New York: Arno Press.
	Continued by *The New York Times Biographical Service* (NYTBS).
NYTBS 5	*The New York Times Biographical Service.* Volume 5, 1974. New York: Arno Press.
	Continues *The New York Times Biographical Edition* (NYTBE).
Newb 1922	*Newbery Medal Books, 1922-1955.* With their author's acceptance papers & related material chiefly from the *Horn Book Magazine.* Edited by Bertha Mahony Miller and Elinor Whitney Field. Horn Book Papers, Volume 1. Boston: The Horn Book, Inc., 1955.
NewbC 1956	*Newbery and Caldecott Medal Books, 1956-1965.* With acceptance papers, biographies & related material chiefly from the *Horn Book Magazine.* Edited by Lee Kingman. Boston: The Horn Book, Inc., 1965.
NewbC 1966	*Newbery and Caldecott Medal Books, 1966-1975.* Edited by Lee Kingman. Boston: The Horn Book, Inc., 1975.
OhA&B	*Ohio Authors and Their Books:* Biographical data and selective bibliographies for Ohio authors, native and resident, 1796-1950. Edited by William Coyle. Cleveland and New York: World Publishing Co., 1962.
OxAm	*The Oxford Companion to American Literature.* Fourth edition. By James D. Hart. New York: Oxford University Press, 1965.
OxCan	*The Oxford Companion to Canadian History and Literature.* By Norah Story. Toronto: Oxford University Press, 1967.
OxCan Sup	*Supplement to the Oxford Companion to Canadian History and Literature.* Edited by William Toye. Toronto: Oxford University Press, 1973.
	Most entries are biographical.
OxEng	*The Oxford Companion to English Literature.* Compiled and edited by Sir Paul Harvey. Fourth edition revised by Dorothy Eagle. Oxford and New York: Oxford University Press, 1967.
OxFr	*The Oxford Companion to French Literature.* Compiled and edited by Sir Paul Harvey and J.E. Heseltine. Oxford: Clarendon Press, 1959; corrected edition, 1966.
OxGer	*The Oxford Companion to German Literature.* By Henry and Mary Garland. Oxford: Clarendon Press, 1976.
Pen Am	*The Penguin Companion to American Literature.* ("The Penguin Companion to World Literature" series). Edited by Malcolm Bradbury, Eric Mottram, and

Jean Franco. New York: McGraw-Hill Book Co., 1971.

In two alphabetical sections. One is for the USA, the other for Latin America.

Pen Cl   *The Penguin Companion to Classical, Oriental & African Literature.* ("The Penguin Companion to World Literature" series). Edited by D. M. Lang and D. R. Dudley. New York: McGraw-Hill Book Co., 1969.

In four alphabetical sections by period and/or region.

Pen Eng   *The Penguin Companion to English Literature.* ("The Penguin Companion to World Literature" series). Edited by David Daiches. New York: McGraw-Hill Book Co., 1971.

Pen Eur   *Penguin Companion to European Literature.* ("The Penguin Companion to World Literature" series). Edited by Anthony Thorlby. New York: McGraw-Hill Book Co., 1969.

Pip   *The Pied Pipers: Interviews with the Influential Creators of Children's Literature.* Edited by Justin Wintle and Emma Fisher. New York: Paddington Press Ltd.-Two Continents Publishing Group, n.d.

PoCh   *The Poets of the Church: A Series of Biographical Sketches of Hymn-Writers with Notes on Their Hymns.* By Edwin F. Hatfield. New York: Anson D.F. Randolph & Co., 1884. To be reprinted by Gale Research Co. Also available from Gale on microfiche.

PoIre   *The Poets of Ireland: A Biographical and Bibliographical Dictionary of Irish Writers of English Verse.* By D.J. O'Donoghue. Dublin: Hodges Figgis & Co., Ltd. and London: Henry Frowde, Oxford University Press, 1912. Reprinted by Gale Research Co., Detroit, 1968. Also available from Gale on microfiche.

Has two biographical sections. The main section begins on page 5. The appendix starts on page 495.

PoLE   *The Poets Laureate of England.* Being a history of the office of poet laureate, biographical notices of its holders, and a collection of the satires, epigrams, and lampoons directed against them. By Walter Hamilton. London: Elliot Stock, 1879. Republished by Gale Research Co., Detroit, 1968. Also available from Gale on microfiche.

Use the index to locate entries.

Prof   *Profiles.* (Articles from *In Review: Canadian Books for Children,* published quarterly by the Ontario Provincial Library Service.) Revised edition. Edited by Irma McDonough. Ottawa: Canadian Library Association, 1975.

PueRA   *Puerto Rican Authors: A Biobibliographic Handbook.* By Marnesba D. Hill and Harold B. Schleifer. Translations of entries into Spanish by Daniel Maratos. Metuchen, N.J.: Scarecrow Press, 1974.

A bilingual edition.

RAdv 1   *The Reader's Adviser: A Layman's Guide to Literature.* 12th edition. Volume 1: *The Best in American and British Fiction, Poetry, Essays, Literary Biography, Bibliography, and Reference.* Edited by Sarah L. Prakken. New York and London: R.R. Bowker Co., 1974.

See the index for locations of author biographies and bibliographies.

RCom   *The Reader's Companion to World Literature.* Edited by Lillian Herlands Hornstein. Second edition, revised and updated by Lillian Herlands Hornstein, Leon Edel, and Horst Frenz. New York: New American Library, 1973.

REn	*The Reader's Encyclopedia.* Second edition. By William Rose Benet. New York: Thomas Y. Crowell Co., 1965.
REnAL	*The Reader's Encyclopedia of American Literature.* By Max J. Herzberg. New York: Thomas Y. Crowell Co., 1962.
REnWD	*The Reader's Encyclopedia of World Drama.* Edited by John Gassner and Edward Quinn. New York: Thomas Y. Crowell Co., 1969.
RGAfL	*A Reader's Guide to African Literature.* Compiled and edited by Hans M. Zell and Helene Silver. New York: Africana Publishing Corp., 1971.
	Biographies begin on page 113.
SenS	*A Sense of Story: Essays on Contemporary Writers for Children.* By John Rowe Townsend. London: Longman Group, Ltd., 1971.
SingR	*The Singing Roads: A Guide to Australian Children's Authors and Illustrators.* Arranged and edited by Hugh Anderson. Surry Hills: Wentworth Books.
SingR 1	Part 1, fourth edition, 1972
SingR 2	Part 2, 1970
SixAP	*Sixty American Poets, 1896-1944.* Selected, with preface and critical notes by Allen Tate. Washington: Library of Congress, 1954. Reprinted by Gale Research Co., Detroit, 1969. Also available from Gale on microfiche.
	A bibliographical study of major American poets.
SmATA	*Something about the Author.* Facts and pictures about contemporary authors and illustrators of books for young people. Edited by Anne Commire. Detroit: Gale Research Co., 1971-1978.
SmATA 1	Volume 1, 1971
SmATA 2	Volume 2, 1971
SmATA 3	Volume 3, 1972
SmATA 4	Volume 4, 1973
SmATA 5	Volume 5, 1973
SmATA 6	Volume 6, 1974
SmATA 7	Volume 7, 1975
SmATA 8	Volume 8, 1976
SmATA 9	Volume 9, 1976
SmATA 10	Volume 10, 1976
SmATA 11	Volume 11, 1977
SmATA 12	Volume 12, 1977
SmATA 13	Volume 13, 1978
SmATA XR	Index to Volumes 1-13, found in back of Volume 13. This code refers to pseudonym entries which appear only as cross references in the cumulative index to *Something about the Author.*
St&VC	*Story and Verse for Children.* Third edition. By Miriam Blanton Huber. New York: Macmillan Co., 1965.
	Biographies are located on pages 793-856.
TelT	*Tellers of Tales: British Authors of Children's Books from 1800 to 1964.* Revised edition. By Roger Lancelyn Green. New York: Franklin Watts, Inc., 1964.
TexW	*Texas Writers of Today.* By Florence Elberta Barns. Ann Arbor: Gryphon Books, 1971 (reprinted from the 1935 edition). Also available from Gale on microfiche.
ThBJA	*Third Book of Junior Authors.* Edited by Doris De Montreville and Donna Hill. New York: H.W. Wilson Co., 1972.

TwCA   *Twentieth Century Authors: A Biographical Dictionary of Modern Literature.* Edited by Stanley J. Kunitz and Howard Haycraft. New York: H.W. Wilson Co., 1942.

TwCA Sup   *Twentieth Century Authors.* First Supplement. Edited by Stanley J. Kunitz and Vineta Colby. New York: H.W. Wilson Co., 1955.

TwCW   *Twentieth Century Writing: A Reader's Guide to Contemporary Literature.* Edited by Kenneth Richardson. Levittown, N.Y.: Transatlantic Arts, Inc., 1969.

WEAL   *Webster's New World Companion to English and American Literature.* Edited by Arthur Pollard. New York: World Publishing, 1973.

WNAA   *Who Was Who among North American Authors, 1921-1939.* Two volumes. Gale Composite Biographical Dictionary Series, Number 1. Detroit: Gale Research Co., 1976. Originally published as *Who's Who among North American Authors,* Volumes 1-7, by the Golden Syndicate Publishing Co., Los Angeles, 1929-1939. Also available from Gale on microfiche.

WW 1974   *Who's Who.* 126th year of issue, 1974-1975. London: A. &C. Black, Ltd. New York: St. Martin's Press, 1974.

WWA 38   *Who's Who in America.* 38th edition, 1974-1975. Two volumes. Chicago: Marquis Who's Who, 1974.

WWAA 1973   *Who's Who in American Art.* 1973. Edited by the Jaques Cattell Press. New York: R.R. Bowker Co., 1973.

WWAW 8   *Who's Who of American Women.* Eighth edition, 1974-1975. Chicago: Marquis Who's Who, 1973.

WWBWI   *Who's Who of Boys' Writers and Illustrators, 1964.* Edited and compiled by Brian Doyle. London: published by the author, 1964.

    WWBWI A   Author biographies (begin on page 5)
    WWBWI I   Illustrator biographies (begin on page 79)

WWCan 1973   *Who's Who in Canada.* 62nd year of issue, 1973-74. Toronto: International Press, Ltd., 1973.

    Not arranged alphabetically; to locate names use the index at the front of the book.

WWCL   *The Who's Who of Children's Literature.* By Brian Doyle. New York: Schocken Books, 1968

WWE 14   *Who's Who in the East.* 14th edition, 1974-1975. Chicago: Marquis Who's Who, 1973.

WWGA   *Who's Who in Graphic Art.* An illustrated book of reference to the world's leading graphic designers, illustrators, typographers and cartoonists. Zurich: Amstutz & Herdeg Graphis Press, 1962.

    Use the index, which begins on page 576, to locate citations.

WWLA   *Who's Who Among Living Authors of Older Nations.* Covering the living authors and writers of all countries of the world except the United States of America, Canada, Mexico, Alaska, Hawaii, Newfoundland, the Philippine Islands, the West Indies, and Central America. Volume 1, 1931-1932. Edited by A. Lawrence. Los Angeles: Golden Syndicate Publishing Co., 1931. Republished by Gale Research Co., Detroit, 1966. Also available from Gale on microfiche.

WWMW 14   *Who's Who in the Midwest.* 14th edition, 1974-1975. Chicago: Marquis Who's Who, 1974.

WWMus 6   *Who's Who in Music and Musicians' International Directory.* Sixth edition. London: Burke's Peerage, Ltd. and New York: Hafner Publishing Co., Inc. 1972.

WWPNA   *Who's Who Among Pacific Northwest Authors.* Second edition. Edited by Frances Valentine Wright. Pacific Northwest Library Association, Reference Division, 1969.

    Biographies are alphabetical by state. Use the index, which begins on page 103, to locate citations.

WWS 13   *Who's Who in the South and Southwest.* 13th edition, 1973-1974. Chicago: Marquis Who's Who, 1973.

WWT 15   *Who's Who in the Theatre.* 15th edition, 1972. London: Sir Isaac Pitman and Sons, Ltd., 1972.

WWTwL   *Who's Who in Twentieth Century Literature.* By Martin Seymour-Smith. New York: Holt, Rinehart and Winston, 1976.

WWW 14   *Who's Who in the West.* 14th edition, 1974-1975. Chicago: Marquis Who's Who, 1974.

WWWor 2   *Who's Who in the World.* Second edition, 1974-1975. Chicago: Marquis Who's Who, 1973.

WWWorJ 1972   *Who's Who in World Jewry.* 1972. I.J. Carmin Karpman, chief editor. New York: Pitman Publishing Corp., 1972.

WisW   *Wisconsin Writers: Sketches and Studies.* By William A. Titus. Detroit: Gale Research Co., 1974 (reprinted from the 1930 edition published in Chicago). Also available from Gale on microfiche.

    Use the table of contents to locate authors.

WorAu   *World Authors, 1950-1970.* A companion volume to *Twentieth Century Authors.* Edited by John Wakeman. New York: H.W. Wilson Co., 1975.

WrD 1976   *The Writers Directory, 1976-78.* London: St. James Press and New York: St. Martin's Press, 1976.

YABC   *Yesterday's Authors of Books for Children.* Facts and pictures about authors and illustrators of books for young people, from early times to 1960. Edited by Anne Commire. Detroit: Gale Research Co., 1977-1978.

    YABC 1   Volume 1, 1977
    YABC 2   Volume 2, 1978
    YABC XR   Index to Volumes 1-2, found in back of Volume 2. This code refers to pseudonym entries which appear only as cross references in the cumulative index to *Yesterday's Authors of Books for Children.*

A

A L O E *Chambr 3, ChPo, DcEnL, NCHEL, WWCL*
A L O E *see* Tucker, Charlotte Maria
Aardema, Verna 1911- *ConAu 5R, SmATA 4, WrD*
Aaron, Chester 1923- *ConAu 21R, SmATA 9*
Aaseng, Rolf E 1923- *ConAu 49*
Abbey, Joseph 1889- *WWBWI I*
Abbott, Alice *ConAu XR, SmATA 8*
Abbott, Alice *see* Borland, Kathryn Kilby
Abbott, Alice *see* Speicher, Helen Ross
Abbott, Berenice 1898- *AmA&B, CurB 42*
Abbott, Cynthia 1908- *ArtsCL*
Abbott, Frank Frost 1860-1924 *AmLY, DcAmA, DcNAA*
Abbott, Henry, Manager *ConAu XR*
Abbott, Henry, Manager *see* Stratemeyer, Edward L
Abbott, Jacob 1803-1879 *Alli, Alli Sup, AmA, AmA&B, BbD, BiD&SB, CarSB, CnDAL, CyAL 2, DcAmA, DcEnL, DcNAA, JBA 1934, OxAm, REnAL*
Abbott, John Stevens Cabot 1805-1877 *Alli, Alli Sup, AmA, AmA&B, BbD, BiD&SB, CarSB, ChPo, ChPo S1, CyAL 2, DcAmA, DcEnL, DcNAA, EvLB, REnAL*
Abbott, Lawrence *MnBBF*
Abbott, Lawrence *see* Lawrence, Christopher George Holman
Abbott, R Tucker 1919- *ConAu 9R*
Abdul, Raoul 1929- *ChPo S2, ConAu 29, SmATA 12*
Abdullah, Ahmed, Sheikh *MnBBF*
Abdullah, Ahmed, Sheikh *see* Shah Ali Ikbal
Abeita, Louise 1926- *AmPB, AnCL*
Abeita, Louise *see* E-Yeh-Shure
Abel, Raymond 1911- *SmATA 12*
Abell, Kathleen 1938- *ConAu 49, SmATA 9*
Abernethy, Robert G 1927- *ConAu 21R, SmATA 5, WWA 38*
Abisch, Roslyn Kroop 1927- *ConAu 21R, SmATA 9, WWAW 8*
Abisch, Roslyn Kroop *see* Abisch, Roz
Abisch, Roslyn Kroop *see* McGillicuddy, Mr.
Abisch, Roslyn Kroop *see* Roche, A K
Abisch, Roslyn Kroop *see* Sniff, Mr.
Abisch, Roz *ChPo S1, ConAu XR, SmATA XR*
Abisch, Roz *see* Abisch, Roslyn Kroop
Abodaher, David J 1919- *ConAu 17R*
Abrahall, C H *SmATA XR*

Abrahall, C H *see* Hoskyns-Abrahall, Clare
Abrahall, Clare Hoskyns *ChPo S1, ConAu XR, SmATA XR*
Abrahall, Clare Hoskyns *see* Hoskyns-Abrahall, Clare
Abrahams, Hilary Ruth 1938- *IlBYP, IlCB 1957*
Abrahams, Robert David 1905- *AmA&B, AuBYP, ConAu P-2, SmATA 4, WWA 38, WWE 14, WWWorJ 1972*
Abrams, Lester *IlBYP*
Achebe, Chinua 1930- *AfA, Au&Wr 6, CasWL, ConAu 1R, ConLC 1, ConLC 3, ConLC 5, ConNov 1972, ConNov 1976, ConP 1975, EncWL, IntWW 38, LongC, Pen Cl, Pen Eng, RGAfL, TwCW, WEAL, WW 1974, WWTwL, WWWor 2, WorAu, WrD*
Acheson, Patricia Castles 1924- *AuBYP, ConAu 1R*
Acker, Helen *AuBYP*
Ackerman, Eugene 1888-1974 *SmATA 10*
Adair, Cecil *WWCL*
Adair, Cecil *see* Everett-Green, Evelyn
Adair, Ian 1942- *ConAu 69*
Adair, Margaret Weeks d1971 *ConAu P-1, SmATA 10*
Adam, Ruth Augusta 1907- *Au&Wr 6, WrD*
Adams, Adrienne 1906- *AmPB, BkP, ChPo, ChPo S1, ChPo S2, ConAu 49, IlBYP, IlCB 1946, IlCB 1957, SmATA 8, ThBJA*
Adams, Adrienne *see* Anderson, Adrienne Adams
Adams, Andy 1859-1935 *AmA&B, AmLY, BiDSA, CnDAL, DcAmA, DcLEnL, DcNAA, IndAu 1816, JBA 1934, JBA 1951, OxAm, REnAL, TexW, WNAA, YABC 1*
Adams, Clifton 1919- *ConAu 13R*
Adams, Clifton *see* Gant, Jonathon
Adams, Edward C *MnBBF*
Adams, Florence 1932- *ConAu 49*
Adams, Frederick K *MnBBF*
Adams, Gerald Drayson *MnBBF*
Adams, H C *MnBBF*
Adams, Harriet S *AmA&B, AuNews 2, ConAu 17R, EncM&D, SmATA 1*
Adams, Harriet S *see* Appleton, Victor, II
Adams, Harriet S *see* Barton, May Hollis
Adams, Harriet S *see* Dixon, Franklin W
Adams, Harriet S *see* Hope, Laura Lee
Adams, Harriet S *see* Keene, Carolyn

Adams, Harrison *see* Stratemeyer, Edward L
Adams, Harry *MnBBF*
Adams, Hazard 1926- *ConAu 9R, DrAS 6E, SmATA 6*
Adams, Henry Brooks 1838-1918 *Alli Sup, AmA&B, AmWr, AtlBL, BbD, BiD&SB, CasWL, CnDAL, CyWA, DcAmA, DcBiA, DcLEnL, DcNAA, EvLB, LongC, ModAL, ModAL Sup, OxAm, OxEng, Pen Am, RAdv 1, RCom, REn, REnAL, TwCW, WEAL, WWTwL*
Adams, J Verney *MnBBF*
Adams, John *MnBBF*
Adams, John 1750?-1814 *CarSB*
Adams, John *see* McLaren, J A
Adams, Julia Davis 1900- *AmA&B, JBA 1934, JBA 1951*
Adams, Julia Davis *see* Davis, Julia
Adams, Katharine *AmA&B, JBA 1934, JBA 1951*
Adams, Laurie 1941- *ConAu 53*
Adams, Laurie *see* Schneider, Laurie
Adams, Lawrence *MnBBF*
Adams, M P *MnBBF*
Adams, Pauline Batchelder *IlBYP*
Adams, Richard 1920- *AuNews 1, AuNews 2, ChPo S2, ConAu 49, ConLC 4, ConLC 5, PiP, SmATA 7, WrD*
Adams, Ruth Joyce *AuBYP*
Adams, Samuel Hopkins 1871-1958 *AmA&B, AmLY, AmNov, AuBYP, CnDAL, EncM&D, OxAm, REn, REnAL, TwCA, TwCA Sup, WNAA*
Adams, William Taylor 1822-1897 *Alli Sup, AmA, AmA&B, BbD, BiD&SB, CarSB, ChPo, ChPo S2, CnDAL, CyAL 2, DcAmA, DcEnL, DcNAA, HsB&A, HsB&A Sup, OxAm, REn, REnAL*
Adamson, Cecil *MnBBF*
Adamson, Gareth *WrD*
Adamson, Gareth 1925- *ConAu 13R*
Adamson, George Worsley 1913- *ChPo S1, ChPo S2, IlBYP, IlCB 1946, IlCB 1957*
Adamson, Graham *ConAu XR, SmATA XR*
Adamson, Graham *see* Groom, Arthur William
Adamson, Joy 1910- *Au&Wr 6, ConAu 69, CurB 72, SmATA 11, WWA 38, WWAW 8*
Adamson, Wendy Wriston 1942- *ConAu 53*
Adare, Allen *MnBBF*
Addams, Charles 1912- *AmA&B, CelR 3, ConAu 61, CurB 54*
Addiscombe, John *MnBBF*
Addison, Captain *MnBBF*
Addison, G Douglas *MnBBF*
Addy, Ted *ConAu XR, SmATA XR*
Addy, Ted *see* Winterbotham, R R
Adelberg, Doris *ChPo S1, ConAu XR, SmATA 7*
Adelberg, Doris *see* Orgel, Doris
Adelberg, Roy P 1928- *ConAu 17R*
Adelman, Bob 1930- *ConAu 69, WWE 14*
Adelson, Leone 1908- *AuBYP, ConAu 61, SmATA 11*
Adkins, Jan 1944- *ConAu 33, SmATA 8*
Adler, Bill 1929- *ConAu XR, WWE 14*
Adler, Bill *see* Adler, William
Adler, David A 1947- *ConAu 57*

Adler, Helmut E 1920- *AmMWS 12S, ConAu 33, WWWorJ 1972*
Adler, Irene *ConAu XR, SmATA XR*
Adler, Irene *see* Storr, Catherine
Adler, Irving 1913- *AmA&B, Au&Wr 6, AuBYP, ConAu 5R, SmATA 1, ThBJA*
Adler, Irving *see* Irving, Robert
Adler, Peggy *AuBYP*
Adler, Ruth 1915-1968 *AuBYP, ConAu 5R, ConAu 25R, SmATA 1, ThBJA*
Adler, Samuel 1928- *AmSCAP 66*
Adler, Warren 1927- *ConAu 69*
Adler, William 1929- *ConAu 9R*
Adler, William *see* Adler, Bill
Adoff, Arnold 1935- *AuBYP, AuNews 1, ChPo S1, ChPo S2, ConAu 41, MorBMP, SmATA 5*
Adorjan, Carol 1934- *ConAu 41, SmATA 10*
Adrian, Mary *AuBYP, ConAu XR, ForWC 1970, WWAW 8*
Adrian, Mary *see* Venn, Mary Eleanor
Adshead, Gladys L 1896- *AmA&B, ConAu 29, MorJA, SmATA 3*
Adshead, Mary 1904- *IlCB 1946, WW 1974*
Aeby, Jacquelyn *ConAu 29*
Aesop 620?BC-564?BC *AnCL, AtlBL, BiD&SB, CarSB, CasWL, ChPo, ChPo S1, ChPo S2, CyWA, DcEnL, NCHEL, OxEng, Pen Cl, RCom, REn, WWCL*
Afonsky, N *ArtCS*
Agapida, Antonio, Fray *YABC XR*
Agapida, Antonio, Fray *see* Irving, Washington
Agassi, Joseph 1927- *ConAu 41, DrAS 6P, WWA 38*
Agent '55' *MnBBF*
Agent '55' *see* Longhurst, Percy William
Agle, Nan Hayden 1905- *AuBYP, ConAu 1R, SmATA 3, WrD*
Agnew, Edith J 1897- *ConAu P-1, SmATA 11*
Agnew, Edith J *see* Marcelino
Agnew, Stephen Hamilton d1915 *MnBBF, WWBWI A*
Agnew, Stephen Hamilton *see* Allyne, Roy
Agnew, Stephen Hamilton *see* Stephens, Arthur
Agnew, Stephen Hamilton *see* Stephens, Kenneth
Agnew, Stephen Hamilton *see* Summers, Colin
Agostinelli, Maria Enrica 1929- *ConAu 33*
Agree, Rose H 1913- *BiDL 5, ChPo S1, ConAu 21R, WWAW 8*
Ahern, Margaret McCrohan 1921- *ConAu 13R, SmATA 10*
Ahern, Margaret McCrohan *see* O'Connell, Peg
Ahnstrom, Doris N 1915- *AuBYP*
Ahrenhold, Novie Moffat *IlBYP*
Aichinger, Helga 1937- *ConAu 25R, IlBYP, SmATA 4*
Aiken, Clarissa Lorenz 1899- *ConAu P-2, SmATA 12*
Aiken, Conrad Potter 1889-1973 *AmA&B, AmLY, AmLY Xr, AmWr, AnCL, AuBYP, CasWL, ChPo, ChPo S1, ChPo S2, CnDAL, CnE&AP, CnMD, CnMWL, ConAmA, ConAmL, ConAu 5R, ConAu 45, ConLC 1, ConLC 3, ConLC 5, ConNov 1972, ConP 1970, CurB 70, CurB 73, DcLEnL, EncWL, EvLB, LongC, ModAL, ModAL Sup, ModWD, NYTBE 4,*

OxAm, OxEng, Pen Am, RAdv 1, REn,
REnAL, SixAP, SmATA 3, TwCA,
TwCA Sup, TwCW, WEAL, WNAA,
WWA 38, WWE 14, WWTwL,
WWWor 2
Aiken, Conrad Potter *see* Jeake, Samuel, Jr.
Aiken, Joan 1924- *Au&Wr 6, AuBYP, BrCA,*
ChLR 1, ConAu 9R, SenS, SmATA 2,
ThBJA, WrD
Aimard, Gustave 1818-1883 *BiD&SB, EvEuW,*
HsB&A, MnBBF, OxAm
Ainsworth, Harriet *ConAu 57*
Ainsworth, Harriet *see* Cadell, Elizabeth
Ainsworth, Norma *ConAu 13R, SmATA 9*
Ainsworth, Norma *see* Ruedi, Norma Paul
Ainsworth, Ruth Gallard 1908- *Au&Wr 6,*
ChPo, ChPo S1, ConAu XR, SmATA 7,
WWCL, WrD
Ainsworth, William Harrison 1805-1882 *Alli,*
Alli Sup, BbD, BiD&SB, BrAu 19,
CasWL 19, Chambr 3, ChPo, ChPo S1,
CyWA, DcBiA, DcEnA, DcEnA Ap,
DcEnL, DcEuL, DcLEnL, EvLB,
MnBBF, NCHEL, OxEng, Pen Eng,
REn, TelT, WEAL, WWCL
Aistrop, Jack Bentley 1916- *Au&Wr 6,*
AuBYP, ConAu 1R
Aitchison, Janet 1962- *ConAu 57*
Aitken, A Donnelly 1892-1962 *MnBBF,*
WWBWI A
Aitken, A Donnelly *see* Donnelly, A
Aitken, A Donnelly *see* Shannon, A Donnelly
Aitken, B W *MnBBF*
Aitken, Dorothy 1916- *ConAu 49, SmATA 10*
Aitmatov, Chingiz 1928- *Au&Wr 6,*
IntWW 38, WWWor 2
Akbar *MnBBF*
Akens, David S 1921- *ConAu 25R*
Akens, Floyd *AmA&B, ThBJA*
Akens, Floyd *see* Baum, Lyman Frank
Akers, Floyd *AuBYP, DcNAA*
Akers, Floyd *see* Baum, Lyman Frank
Akino, Fuku 1908- *ChPo S2, IlBYP,*
IlCB 1957
Akiyama, Kazuo *AuBYP*
Aksenov, Vassily 1932- *ConAu 53*
Akutagawa, Ryunosuke 1892-1927 *CasWL Cl,*
DcOrL 1, Pen Cl, REn, WorAu
Alain 1868-1951 *AmA&B, CasWL,*
ClDMEuL, EncWL, EuAu, EvEuW,
IlBYP, IlCB 1957, OxFr, Pen Eur, REn
Alain *see* Brustlein, Daniel
Alais, Ernest W 1864-1922 *MnBBF,*
WWBWI A
Alais, Ernest W *see* Miller, Lawrence
Alais, Ernest W *see* Wolfe, Cedric
Alajalov, Constantin 1900- *CurB 42, ForIl,*
IlBYP, IlCB 1744, IlCB 1946, WWA 38,
WWAA 1973
Albert, Burton, Jr. 1936- *ConAu 61*
Albert, Louise 1928- *ConAu 69*
Albert, Marvin H *AuBYP*
Alberts, Frances Jacobs 1907- *ConAu 5R,*
ForWC 1970
Albinson, Jack *ConAu 57*
Albinson, Jack *see* Albinson, James P
Albinson, James P 1932- *ConAu 57*
Albinson, James P *see* Albinson, Jack
Albion, Lee Smith *IlBYP, IlCB 1957*

Albion, Lee Smith *see* Smith, Lee
Albrecht, Lillie 1894- *ConAu 5R, SmATA 12*
Alcorn, John 1935- *ChPo, ChPo S1, IlBYP,*
IlCB 1957, ThBJA
Alcott, Louisa May 1832-1888 *Alli Sup, AmA,*
AmA&B, AtlBL, AuBYP, BbD,
BiD&SB, CarSB, CasWL, Chambr 3,
ChLR 1, ChPo, CnDAL, CriT 3,
CyAL 2, CyWA, DcAmA, DcBiA,
DcEnL, DcLEnL, DcNAA, EvLB,
FamAYP, JBA 1934, MouLC 4, OxAm,
OxEng, Pen Am, REn, REnAL, St&VC,
WWCL, YABC 1
Aldan, Daisy 1923- *AmA&B, ConAu 13R,*
DrAP 1975, ForWC 1970
Aldcroft, Arthur *MnBBF, WWBWI A*
Alden, Carella *ConAu XR*
Alden, Carella *see* Remington, Ella-Carrie
Alden, Isabella Macdonald 1841-1930 *Alli Sup,*
AmA&B, AmLY, BbD, BiD&SB, CarSB,
DcAmA, DcNAA, LongC, OhA&B,
OxAm, YABC 2
Alden, Raymond Macdonald 1873-1924 *Alli Sup,*
AmA&B, AmLY, ChPo, DcAmA,
DcNAA
Alden, William Livingston 1837-1908 *Alli Sup,*
AmA, AmA&B, BbD, BiD&SB, CarSB,
ChPo, ChPo S2, DcAmA, DcNAA
Alder, Francis A 1937- *ConAu 61*
Alderman, Clifford Lindsey 1902- *AuBYP,*
ConAu 1R, SmATA 3
Alderson, William Thomas, Jr. 1926- *BiDL 5,*
ConAu 9R, DrAS 6H, WWA 38,
WWS 13
Aldin, Cecil Charles Windsor 1870-1935
Br&AmS, ChPo S1, ChPo S2, ConICB
Aldis, Dorothy 1897?-1966 *AmA&B, AnCL,*
AuBYP, BkCL, ChPo, ChPo S1,
ConAu 1R, JBA 1934, JBA 1951,
SmATA 2, St&VC, WNAA
Aldiss, Brian Wilson 1925- *Au&Wr 6,*
ConAu 5R, ConLC 5, ConNov 1972,
ConNov 1976, IntWW 38, TwCW 1976,
WW 1974, WWWor 2
Aldon, Adair *AuBYP, ConAu XR,*
SmATA 6
Aldon, Adair *see* Meigs, Cornelia Lynde
Aldous, Allan *SingR 1*
Aldrich, Bess Streeter 1881-1954 *AmA&B,*
AmNov, OxAm, REn, REnAL, TwCA,
TwCA Sup, WNAA
Aldrich, Thomas Bailey 1836-1907 *Alli,*
Alli Sup, AmA, AmA&B Sup, BbD,
BiD&SB, CarSB, CasWL, Chambr 3,
ChPo, ChPo S1, ChPo S2, CnDAL,
CyAL 2, CyWA, DcAmA, DcBiA,
DcEnA Ap, DcEnL, DcLEnL, DcNAA,
EncM&D, EvLB, JBA 1934, OxAm,
OxEng, Pen Am, REn, REnAL
Aldridge, Adele 1934- *ConAu 49, DrAP 1975*
Aldridge, James 1918- *Au&Wr 6, ConAu 61,*
ConNov 1972, ConNov 1976, CurB 43,
TwCA Sup, WW 1974, WrD
Aldridge, Josephine Haskell *AuBYP*
Alegria, Ricardo E 1921- *AmMWS 12S,*
ConAu 25R, PueRA, SmATA 6,
WWWor 2
Aleichem, Sholem 1859-1916 *CasWL, EncWL,*
REn

Alexander, Anna Barbara Cooke 1913-
  ConAu 57, SmATA 1
Alexander, Anna Barbara Cooke see Alexander,
  Anne
Alexander, Anna Barbara Cooke see Cooke,
  Barbara
Alexander, Anne ConAu 57
Alexander, Anne 1913- AuBYP
Alexander, Anne see Alexander, Anna Barbara
  Cooke
Alexander, Arthur 1927- ChPo S1, ConAu 5R
Alexander, Mrs. Cecil Frances 1818-1895
  Alli Sup, BiD&SB, BkCL, BrAu 19,
  Chambr 3, ChPo, ChPo S1, ChPo S2,
  DcEnL, EvLB, PoCh, PoIre
Alexander, Frances 1888- AnCL, ConAu 25R,
  SmATA 4, TexW, WrD
Alexander, Janet 1907- Au&Wr 6, WrD
Alexander, Jocelyn Anne Arundel 1930- AuBYP,
  ConAu 1R
Alexander, Linda Lewann 1935- ConAu 21R,
  ForWC 1970, SmATA 2, WrD
Alexander, Lloyd Chudley 1924- AnCL,
  Au&Wr 6, AuBYP, ChLR 1, ConAu 1R,
  MorBMP, PiP, NewbC 1966, SmATA 3,
  ThBJA, WWA 38, WWE 14
Alexander, Louis George 1932- Au&Wr 6,
  WrD
Alexander, Marge ConAu XR
Alexander, Marge see Edwards, Roselyn
Alexander, Martha 1920- SmATA 11
Alexander, Martha Kathleen 1910- Au&Wr 6,
  IlBYP
Alexander, Marthann 1907- ConAu 53
Alexander, Sue 1933- ConAu 53, SmATA 12
Alfriston, Louis MnBBF
Alger, Horatio 1834?-1899 AmA, AmA&B,
  BbD, BiD&SB, CarSB, CasWL, ChPo,
  ChPo S1, ChPo S2, CnDAL, CyAL 2,
  DcAmA, DcNAA, EvLB, OxAm,
  Pen Am, REn, REnAL, WEAL, WWCL
Alger, Leclaire Gowans 1898-1971 AuBYP,
  ThBJA
Alger, Leclaire Gowans see Nic Leodhas.
  Sorche
Aliki AmPB. AuBYP, ConAu XR
  IlCB 1957, SmATA 2, ThBJA
Aliki see Brandenberg, Aliki Liacouras
Alimayo, Chikuyo ConAu 57
Alimayo, Chikuyo see Franklin, Harold L
Alkema, Chester Jay 1932- ConAu 53,
  SmATA 12
Allamand, Pascale 1942- ConAu 69,
  SmATA 12
Allan, Elizabeth Preston 1848-1933 Alli Sup,
  AmA&B, BiDSA, CarSB, DcNAA
Allan, F Carney MnBBF
Allan, F Carney see MacDonald, Eric
Allan, F Carney see Neish, Duncan
Allan, John MnBBF
Allan, Mabel Esther 1915- Au&Wr 6, AuBYP,
  ConAu 5R, SmATA 5, WrD
Allan, Mabel Esther see Estoril, Jean
Allan, Mabel Esther see Hagon, Priscilla
Allan, Mabel Esther see Pilgrim, Anne
Allee, Marjorie Hill 1890-1945 AmA&B,
  DcNAA, IndAu 1917, JBA 1934,
  JBA 1951, WNAA
Allen, A B 1903-1975 ConAu P-2

Allen, Adam AuBYP, ConAu XR, MorJA,
  SmATA 1
Allen, Adam see Epstein, Beryl
Allen, Adam see Epstein, Samuel
Allen, Agnes d1959 WWCL
Allen, Allyn AuBYP, ConAu XR, SmATA 2
Allen, Allyn see Eberle, Irmengarde
Allen, Betsy AuBYP, ConAu XR, CurB 50,
  SmATA 1
Allen, Betsy see Cavanna, Betty
Allen, Carl ConAu 69
Allen, Cecil J 1886-1973 ConAu P-2
Allen, Chris MnBBF
Allen, Chris 1929- ConAu 29
Allen, Durward L 1910- AmMWS 12P,
  ConAu 41, WWA 38
Allen, Ethan 1904- CurB 54, OhA&B
Allen, Frederick Lewis 1890-1954 AmA&B,
  CnDAL, OxAm, REn, REnAL, TwCA,
  TwCA Sup
Allen, George J MnBBF
Allen, Gertrude E 1888- ConAu 61, SmATA 9
Allen, Gina 1918- AmA&B, ConAu 1R,
  WWA 38, WWAW 8
Allen, Henry AmA&B
Allen, Henry see Fisher, Clay
Allen, Hugh WWBWI A
Allen, Hugh see Gibbons, Harry Hornaby
  Clifford
Allen, James Lane 1849?-1925 AmA, AmA&B,
  AmLY, BbD, BiD&SB, BiDSA, CarSB,
  CasWL, ChPo S1, ChPo S3, CnDAL,
  ConAmL, DcAmA, DcBiA, DcLEnL,
  DcNAA, LongC, OxAm, REn, REnAL
Allen, Jules Verne 1883- TexW
Allen, Kenneth S 1913- Au&Wr 6, WrD
Allen, Lee 1915- AuBYP, ConAu 1R,
  OhA&B
Allen, Leroy 1912- ConAu 65, SmATA 11
Allen, Lewis MnBBF
Allen, Marie Louise AuBYP, ChPo
Allen, Marjorie 1931- ConAu 69
Allen, Mark MnBBF
Allen, Maury 1932- ConAu 17R
Allen, Mel 1913- AuBYP, CurB 50,
  IntMPA 1975, WWA 38, WWWorJ 1972
Allen, Merritt Parmelee 1892-1954 AuBYP,
  JBA 1951, WNAA
Allen, Oswald 1816- MnBBF
Allen, Richard J AuBYP
Allen, Robert ConAu XR
Allen, Robert see Garfinkel, Bernard
Allen, Robert Day 1927- AmMWS 12P,
  WWA 38, WWWor 2
Allen, Rodney F 1938- ConAu 61
Allen, Samuel 1917- BlkAW, ChPo S2,
  ConAu 49, DrAP 1975, LBAA,
  SmATA 9
Allen, Samuel see Vesey, Paul
Allen, T D 1908- AmA&B, ConAu XR
Allen, T D see Allen, Terril Diener
Allen, Terril Diener 1908- ConAu 5R,
  WWW 14
Allen, Terril Diener see Allen, T D
Allen, Willis Boyd 1855-1938 Alli Sup,
  AmA&B, BiD&SB, CarSB, ChPo,
  ChPo S1, ChPo S2, DcAmA, DcNAA,
  WNAA
Allerton, Mary ConAu XR, SmATA XR

Allerton, Mary *see* Govan, Christine Noble
Allfrey, Katherine *AuBYP*
Allingham, Claude *MnBBF*
Allingham, H J *WWBWI A*
Allingham, H J *see* Allingham, Herbert John
Allingham, Herbert John 1867-1935 *MnBBF,*
WWBWI A
Allingham, Herbert John *see* Allingham, H J
Allingham, John W *MnBBF*
Allingham, John W *see* Rollington, Ralph
Allingham, Margery 1904-1966 *ConAu 5R,*
ConAu 25R, DcLEnL, EncM&D, EvLB,
LongC, MnBBF, NCHEL Sup, TwCA,
TwCA Sup, TwCW
Allingham, William 1824?-1889 *Alli Sup,*
AnCL, BbD, BiD&SB, BrAu 19, CasWL,
Chambr 3, ChPo, ChPo S1, ChPo S2,
DcEnL, DcLEnL, EvLB, FamPYP,
NCHEL, Pen Eng, PoIre, REn, St&VC,
WEAL
Allinson, Beverly 1936- *ConAu 49, Prof*
Allison, Bob *AuBYP*
Allmendinger, David Frederick, Jr. 1938-
ConAu 61, DrAS 6H
Allred, Gordon Thatcher 1930- *ConAu 17R,*
DrAS 6E, SmATA 10
Allsop, Kenneth 1920-1973 *Au&Wr 6,*
ConAu 1R, WWWor 2, WorAu
Allward, Maurice 1923- *ConAu 5R*
Allyn, Paul *ConAu XR*
Allyn, Paul *see* Schosberg, Paul A
Allyne, Roy *MnBBF*
Allyne, Roy *see* Agnew, Stephen Hamilton
Almedingen, E M 1898-1971 *Au&Wr 6,*
ConAu 1R, LongC, SmATA 3, ThBJA,
WorAu
Almedingen, E M *see* VonAlmedingen, Martha
Edith
Almedingen, Martha Edith Von 1898-1971
SmATA 3
Almquist, Don 1929- *ChPo, IlBYP,*
SmATA 11
Aloise, Frank *IlBYP*
Alpenfels, Ethel J *WWAW 8*
Alsop, Mary O'Hara 1885- *ConAu 9R,*
SmATA 2
Alsop, Mary O'Hara *see* O'Hara, Mary
Alsop, Reese Fell *AuBYP*
Alter, Robert Edmond 1925-1965 *AuBYP,*
ConAu 1R, SmATA 9
Alter, Robert Edmond *see* Raymond, Robert
Alter, Robert Edmond *see* Retla, Robert
Altman, Frances 1937- *ConAu 65, WrD*
Altsheler, Joseph Alexander 1862-1919 *AmA&B,*
AuBYP, BiDSA, DcAmA, DcNAA,
JBA 1934, REnAL, TwCA, TwCA Sup,
YABC 1
Alvarez, Joseph A 1930- *ConAu 33*
Amacher, Richard Earl 1917- *ConAu 1R,*
DrAS 6E
Amadio, Nadine *SingR 2*
Amadon, Dean 1912- *AmMWS 12P,*
ConAu 61, WWA 38
Amaral, Anthony 1930- *ConAu 21R*
Ambler, Christopher Gifford 1886- *IlBYP,*
IlCB 1946, WWBWI 1
Ambler, Eric 1909- *AmA&B, Au&Wr 6,*
CnMWL, ConAu 9R, ConLC 4,
ConLC 6, ConNov 1972, ConNov 1976,

DcLEnL, EncM&D, LongC, NCHEL,
REn, TwCA Sup, TwCW, WW 1974,
WWWor 2
Ambrose, Stephen Edward 1936- *ConAu 1R,*
DrAS 6H
Ambrus, Gyozo Laszlo 1935- *ConAu 25R*
Ambrus, Gyozo Laszlo *see* Ambrus, Victor G
Ambrus, Victor G 1935- *BrCA, ChPo S1,*
ChPo S2, ConAu XR, IlBYP, IlCB 1957,
SmATA 1, ThBJA, WWCL
Ambrus, Victor G *see* Ambrus, Gyozo Laszlo
Amerman, Lockhart 1911-1969 *AuBYP,*
ConAu P-2, SmATA 3
Ames, Delano 1906- *Au&Wr 6, MnBBF,*
WWBWI A
Ames, Evelyn 1908- *ConAu 57, SmATA 13*
Ames, Gerald 1906- *BkP, SmATA 11,*
ThBJA
Ames, Lee Judah 1921- *AuBYP, ConAu 1R,*
IlCB 1946, IlCB 1957, SmATA 3,
WWAA 1973
Ames, Lee Judah *see* David, Jonathan
Ames, Mildred 1919- *ConAu 69*
Ames, Rose Wyler *ThBJA*
Ames, Rose Wyler *see* Thayer, Peter
Ames, Rose Wyler *see* Wyler, Rose
Amoaku, J K 1936- *ConAu 45*
Amon, Aline 1928- *ConAu 61, SmATA 9*
Amory, Cleveland 1917- *AmA&B, AuNews 1,*
BiN 1975, CelR 3, ConAu 69, REnAL,
TwCA Sup, WWA 38, WWWor 2
Amoss, Berthe 1925- *ConAu 21R, SmATA 5*
Amundsen, Richard E *IlBYP*
Anand, Mulk Raj 1905- *Au&Wr 6, CasWL,*
ConAu 65, ConNov 1972, ConNov 1976,
DcOrL 2, IntWW 38, Pen Eng, REn,
WEAL, WWWor 2, WorAu, WrD
Anckarsvard, Karin Inez Maria 1915-1969
AuBYP, ConAu 9R, SmATA 6, ThBJA
Ancona, George 1929- *ConAu 53, SmATA 12*
Andersen, Hans Christian 1805-1875 *AnCL,*
AtlBL, AuBYP, BbD, BiD&SB, CarSB,
CasWL, ChPo, ChPo S1, ChPo S2,
CyWA, DcBiA, DcEnL, DcEuL, EuAu,
EvEuW, FamAYP, FamSYP, JBA 1934,
JBA 1951, NCHEL, OxEng, Pen Eur,
RCom, REn, St&VC, WWCL, YABC 1
Andersen, Hans Christian *see* Walter, Villiam
Christian
Andersen, Yvonne 1932- *ConAu 29*
Anderson, Adrienne Adams *ThBJA*
Anderson, Adrienne Adams *see* Adams, Adrienne
Anderson, Brad 1924- *WWAA 1973*
Anderson, C W 1891-1971 *BkP, JBA 1951,*
SmATA 11, St&VC, ThBJA
Anderson, C W *see* Anderson, Clarence William
Anderson, Carl Thomas 1865-1948 *AmA&B,*
ArtCS
Anderson, Catherine Corley 1909- *ConAu 1R*
Anderson, Chester Grant 1923- *ConAu 25R,*
DrAS 6E
Anderson, Chuck 1933- *ConAu 49*
Anderson, Clarence William 1891-1971 *AuBYP,*
ConAu 29, IlCB 1744, IlCB 1946,
IlCB 1957
Anderson, Clarence William *see* Anderson, C W
Anderson, Clary *NYTBE 3*
Anderson, Dave *AuNews 2*
Anderson, Doug 1919- *WWAA 1973*

Anderson, Edna A *MnnWr*
Anderson, Eloise Adell 1927- *ConAu 53,*
SmATA 9
Anderson, Erica 1914- *ConAu 57, CurB 57,*
ForWC 1970, WWA 38, WWAW 8
Anderson, Ethel Todd *AuBYP, OhA&B*
Anderson, Frank *MnBBF*
Anderson, Frank *see* Dan, Uncle
Anderson, G J B *MnBBF, WWBWI A*
Anderson, G J B *see* Dangerfield, Captain
Anderson, G J B *see* Fielding, Howard
Anderson, G J B *see* Lynn, Max
Anderson, G J B *see* Whyte, Melton
Anderson, G J B *see* Y, Viscount
Anderson, George *ConAu XR, SmATA XR*
Anderson, George *see* Groom, Arthur William
Anderson, Gunnar *IlBYP*
Anderson, J R L 1911- *ConAu 25R*
Anderson, Jean 1930- *ConAu 41,*
ForWC 1970
Anderson, John 1909- *WrD*
Anderson, John L 1905- *ConAu 25R*
Anderson, John L *see* Anderson, Lonzo
Anderson, John Richard Lane 1911- *WrD*
Anderson, Joy 1928- *ConAu 25R, SmATA 1*
Anderson, Linsay *MnBBF*
Anderson, Lonzo *BkP, ConAu XR,*
SmATA 2, ThBJA
Anderson, Lonzo *see* Anderson, John L
Anderson, Lucia 1922- *AmMWS 12P,*
ConAu 41, SmATA 10
Anderson, Lucia *see* Lewis, Lucia Z
Anderson, Madeleine Paltenghi 1899-
ConAu P-1
Anderson, Madeleine Paltenghi *see* Paltenghi,
Madeleine
Anderson, Madelyn Klein *ConAu 69*
Anderson, Margaret J 1931- *ConAu 69*
Anderson, Mary 1939- *ConAu 49, SmATA 7*
Anderson, Neil *AuBYP*
Anderson, Neil *see* Beim, Jerrold
Anderson, Norman Dean 1928- *ConAu 33,*
LE 5
Anderson, Paul Lewis 1880- *WNAA*
Anderson, Poul 1926- *AmA&B, ConAu 1R,*
WWA 38, WorAu
Anderson, Ruth Irene 1919- *AuBYP,*
ConAu 1R, ForWC 1970, LE 5
Anderson, Sydney 1927- *AmMWS 12P*
Anderson, Warwick *MnBBF*
Anderson, William Robert 1921- *ConAu 5R,*
IntWW 38, WWA 38, WWS 13
Andom, R *MnBBF, WWBWI A*
Andom, R *see* Barrett, Alfred Walter
Andre, Evelyn M 1924- *ConAu 69*
Andrew, Prudence Hastings 1924- *Au&Wr 6,*
ConAu 1R, WrD
Andrews, Benny 1930- *ChPo S1, IlBYP,*
WWA 38, WWAA 1973, WWE 14
Andrews, F Emerson 1902- *AmA&B,*
ConAu 1R, WWA 38
Andrews, J S 1934- *ConAu 29, SmATA 4*
Andrews, J S *see* Andrews, James Sydney
Andrews, Jack *MnBBF*
Andrews, James Sydney 1934- *Au&Wr 6*
Andrews, James Sydney *see* Andrews, J S
Andrews, Jane 1833-1887 *Alli Sup, AmA&B,*
BiD&SB, CarSB, DcAmA, DcNAA,
OxAm, REnAL

Andrews, John *MnBBF, WWBWI A*
Andrews, Julie 1935- *BiEnAT, CelR 3,*
ConAu 37, CurB 56, IntMPA 1975,
IntWW 38, SmATA 7, WWA 38,
WWAW 8, WWT 15, WWWor 2, WrD
Andrews, Julie *see* Edwards, Julie
Andrews, Mary Raymond Shipman 1865?-1936
AmA&B, ChPo, ConAmL, DcNAA 1,
JBA 1934, REnAL, TwCA, WNAA
Andrews, Mervyn *MnBBF*
Andrews, Peter 1931- *ConAu 17R*
Andrews, Roy Chapman 1884-1960 *AmA&B,*
AuBYP, CurB 41, CurB 53, CurB 60,
EvLB, REnAL, TwCA, TwCA Sup,
WNAA
Andriola, Alfred 1912- *ArtCS*
Andrist, Ralph K 1914- *ConAu 9R*
Angas, John *MnBBF*
Angel, Heather 1941- *ConAu 69*
Angel, Marie 1923- *ChPo S1, ChPo S2,*
ConAu 29, IlBYP
Angeli, Marguerite De *JBA 1951*
Angeli, Marguerite De *see* DeAngeli, Marguerite
Angell, Madeline 1919- *ConAu 65*
Angell, Tony 1940- *ConAu 53*
Angelo, Valenti 1897- *AmA&B, AuBYP,*
BkC 6, CatA 1952, ChPo, IlCB 1744,
IlCB 1946, IlCB 1957, JBA 1951
Angier, Bradford *ConAu 5R, SmATA 12*
Angle, Paul McClelland 1900-1975 *AmA&B,*
ConAu 57, ConAu P-2, CurB 55,
DrAS 6H, NCHEL, REnAL, TwCA Sup,
WWA 38
Anglund, Joan Walsh 1926- *AmA&B,*
Au&Wr 6, AuBYP, ChLR 1, ChPo S1,
ChPo S2, ConAu 5R, FamAI, IlCB 1957,
SmATA 2, ThBJA, WWA 38,
WWAW 8
Angrist, Stanley W 1933- *AmMWS 12P,*
ConAu 25R, SmATA 4
Annett, Cora *AuBYP, ConAu XR,*
SmATA XR
Annett, Cora *see* Scott, Cora Annett
Annixter, Jane *AuBYP, ConAu XR,*
ForWC 1970, SmATA 1
Annixter, Jane *see* Sturtzel, Jane Levington
Annixter, Paul *ConAu XR, SmATA 1*
Annixter, Paul *see* Sturtzel, Howard A
Anno, Mitsumasa 1920?- *ChLR 2, ConAu 49,*
IlBYP, SmATA 5
Anrooy, Frans Van *SmATA 2*
Anrooy, Frans Van *see* VanAnrooy, Frans
Anson, Piers *MnBBF*
Anson, Piers *see* Dell, Draycot Montagu
Anstey, F 1856-1934 *Alli Sup, BiD&SB,*
Chambr 3, ChPo, ChPo S2, DcBiA,
DcEnA Ap, DcLEnL, EvLB, LongC,
MnBBF, ModBL, NCHEL, OxEng, REn,
TelT, TwCA, TwCA Sup, WWBWI A,
WWCL
Anstey, F *see* Guthrie, Thomas Anstey
Antell, Will 1935- *LE 5*
Anthondyke, Harry *MnBBF*
Anthony, C L *Chambr 3, ConAu XR,*
DcLEnL, LongC, NCHEL, SmATA 4
Anthony, C L *see* Smith, Dodie
Anthony, Edward 1895-1971 *AmA&B, AuBYP,*
BkCL, ChPo, ConAu 33, REnAL
Anthony, Evelyn *Au&Wr 6, ConAu XR*

Anthony, Evelyn *see* Ward-Thomas, Evelyn
Bridget Patricia S
Anticaglia, Elizabeth 1939- *ConAu 45*,
SmATA 12
Anton, Michael J 1940- *ConAu 57*,
SmATA 12
Antonacci, Robert J 1916- *ConAu 5R*
Antoncich, Betty 1913- *AuBYP, ConAu 13R*
Apilado, Tony *IlBYP*
Apion d048 *AnCL*
Appel, Benjamin 1907- *AmA&B, AmNov*,
ConAu 13R, DcLEnL, OxAm, TwCA,
TwCA Sup, WWA 38
Appel, David *AuBYP*
Appelbee, A S *MnBBF*
Appiah, Peggy 1921- *Au&Wr 6, ConAu 41*,
WrD
Appleton, Cecil *MnBBF*
Appleton, Victor *AmA&B, ConAu P-2*,
SmATA 1
Appleton, Victor *see* Stratemeyer, Edward L
Appleton, Victor, II *AmA&B, ConAu 17R*,
SmATA 1
Appleton, Victor, II *see* Adams, Harriet S
Appleton, Victor, II *see* Stratemeyer, Edward L
Appleyard, Dev *IlBYP*
Applin, Arthur G T 1883-1948? *MnBBF*
Apsler, Alfred 1907- *ConAu 5R, SmATA 10*,
WWPNA, WrD
Arason, Steingrimur *AuBYP*
Arbuckle, Wanda Rector Samson 1910-
ConAu 41, WWAW 8, WWW 14
Arbuthnot, May Hill 1884-1969 *AuBYP, ChPo*,
ChPo S2, ConAu 9R, OhA&B,
SmATA 2
Arch, E L *ConAu 49*
Arch, J *WWBWI 1*
Archer, Frank *ConAu XR*
Archer, Frank *see* O'Connor, Richard
Archer, Jules 1915- *AuBYP, ConAu 9R*,
SmATA 4
Archer, Marion Fuller 1917- *ConAu 5R*,
ForWC 1970, SmATA 11
Archer, Sellers G 1908- *ConAu 17R*
Archibald, C M *MnBBF*
Archibald, Joe 1898- *AuBYP, ConAu XR*
Archibald, Joe *see* Archibald, Joseph S
Archibald, Joseph S 1898- *ConAu 9R*,
SmATA 3
Archibald, Joseph S *see* Archibald, Joe
Arden, Barbi *ConAu XR, SmATA 3, ThBJA*
Arden, Barbi *see* Stoutenburg, Adrien
Arden, William *EncM&D*
Ardizzone, Edward 1900- *ArtsCL, Au&ICB*,
Au&Wr 6, AuBYP, BrCA, ChLR 3,
ChPo, ChPo S1, ChPo S2, ConAu 5R,
CurB 64, IlCB 1744, IlCB 1946,
IlCB 1957, IntWW 38, LongC, MorJA,
PiP, SmATA 1, WWCL, WWWor 2,
WrD
Arehart-Treichel, Joan 1942- *ConAu 57*
Aresty, Esther Bradford *ConAu 9R*,
ForWC 1970, WWAW 8, WrD
Argus, Arabella *Alli, CarSB*
Ariane *AmPB*
Ariane *see* Duplaix, Georges
Arkhurst, Joyce Cooper 1921- *BlkAW*,
ConAu 17R, ForWC 1970, LBAA, WrD
Arkin, Alan 1934- *AmSCAP 66, BiEnAT*,

CelR 3, CurB 67, EncFCW 1969,
IntMPA 1975, NYTBE 1, WWT 15
Arkin, David 1906- *AmSCAP 66, ConAu 21R*,
WrD
Arkley, Arthur James *WrD*
Arlandson, Leone 1917- *ConAu 29*
Arlandson, Leone *see* Ryland, Lee
Arlen, Michael J 1930- *AmA&B, ConAu 61*,
WWA 38, WWE 14
Armer, Alberta Roller 1904- *ConAu 5R*,
ForWC 1970, IndAu 1917, SmATA 9
Armer, Laura Adams 1874-1963 *AmA&B*,
AuBYP, ConAmA, ConAu 65, IlCB 1744,
JBA 1934, JBA 1951, Newb 1922,
SmATA 13
Armer, Sidney 1871- *IlCB 1744*
Armfield, Maxwell 1881?- *Au&Wr 6*,
ChPo S1, IlCB 1744
Armitage, Alfred *MnBBF, WWBWI A*
Armitage, Alfred *see* Graydon, W Murray
Armitage, Angus 1902- *Au&Wr 6*,
ConAu P-1, WrD
Armitage, Vincent *MnBBF*
Armitage, Vincent *see* Wheway, John W
Armour, Margaret d1943 *CarSB, ChPo S2*
Armour, R Coutts *MnBBF, WWBWI A*
Armour, R Coutts *see* Brisbane, Coutts
Armour, R Coutts *see* Tremayne, Hartley
Armour, R Coutts *see* Whitley, Reid
Armour, Richard Willard 1906- *AmA&B*,
AnCL, Au&Wr 6, AuBYP, ChPo,
ChPo S1, ChPo S2, ConAu 1R, CurB 58,
DrAS 6E, REnAL, WWA 38,
WWWor 2
Armstrong, Anthony 1897- *Au&Wr 6*,
DcLEnL, EncM&D, EvLB, IntWW 38,
LongC, MnBBF, WWWor 2
Armstrong, Anthony *see* Willis, Anthony
Armstrong
Armstrong, Edward Allworthy 1900- *Au&Wr 6*,
ConAu 5R
Armstrong, George D 1927- *SmATA 10*
Armstrong, Gerry 1929- *ConAu 13R*,
SmATA 10
Armstrong, Jack *MnBBF*
Armstrong, Jack *see* Felton, Frederick A
Armstrong, Richard 1903- *Au&Wr 6, AuBYP*,
SmATA 11, ThBJA, WWCL
Armstrong, Tom *IlBYP*
Armstrong, William H 1914- *AuBYP*,
AuNews 1, ChLR 1, ConAu 17R,
MorBMP, NewbC 1966, SmATA 4,
ThBJA
Armstrong, William Howard 1914- *WWA 38*,
WWE 14
Armytage *MnBBF*
Arndt, Ursula *ChPo S1, IlBYP*
Arnett, Caroline *SmATA XR*
Arnett, Caroline *see* Cole, Lois Dwight
Arno, Enrico 1913- *ChPo S1, ChPo S2*,
IlBYP, IlCB 1946, IlCB 1957
Arnold, Arnold 1921- *ChPo S2, ConAu 17R*
Arnold, Blake *MnBBF*
Arnold, Clement *MnBBF*
Arnold, Clement *see* Panting, Arnold Clement
Arnold, Eben *MnBBF*
Arnold, Edgar *MnBBF*
Arnold, Edmund C 1913- *ConAu 1R*,
WWWor 2

Arnold, Edwin Lester 1856- *Alli Sup, BiD&SB,*
  MnBBF, TelT, WWLA
Arnold, Elliott 1912- *AmA&B, AmNov,*
  Au&Wr 6, AuBYP, ConAu 17R,
  SmATA 5, TwCA Sup, WWA 38,
  WWW 14, WWWor 2, WrD
Arnold, Francena H 1888- *ConAu P-1*
Arnold, Frank *MnBBF*
Arnold, Frank *see* Young, Fred W
Arnold, Harry Loren, Jr. 1912- *WWA 38,*
  WWWor 2
Arnold, J E *MnBBF*
Arnold, Malcolm, Captain *MnBBF,*
  WWBWI A
Arnold, Malcolm, Captain *see* Murray, Andrew
  Nicholas
Arnold, Mary Ann 1918- *ConAu 65*
Arnold, Oren 1900- *ConAu 5R, SmATA 4*
Arnold, Pauline 1894- *ConAu 1R*
Arnold, Peter 1943- *ConAu 49*
Arnold, Ralph 1875- *AuBYP, WNAA*
Arnold, Rex *MnBBF*
Arnold, Rollo Davis *WrD*
Arnoldy, Julie *ConAu XR, SmATA XR*
Arnoldy, Julie *see* Bischoff, Julia Bristol
Arnosky, Jim 1946- *ConAu 69*
Arnothy, Christine 1930?- *Au&Wr 6,*
  ConAu 65, REn
Arnott, Kathleen 1914- *ConAu 57*
Arnov, Boris, Jr. 1926- *AuBYP, ConAu 1R,*
  SmATA 12
Arnow, Harriette Simpson 1908- *AmA&B,*
  AmNov, ConLC 2, ConNov 1976,
  CurB 54, WorAu, WrD
Arnstein, Helene S 1915- *ConAu 57,*
  SmATA 12
Arntson, Herbert E 1911- *ConAu 17R*
Arntson, Herbert Edward 1911- *DrAS 6E*
Arntson, Herbert E 1911- *SmATA 12,*
  WWPNA
Aronsten, Joan *SingR 1*
Arora, Shirley Lease 1930- *ConAu 1R,*
  DrAS 6F, SmATA 2
Arquette, Lois S 1934- *SmATA 1*
Arquette, Lois S *see* Cardoza, Lois S
Arquette, Lois S *see* Duncan, Lois
Arquette, Lois S *see* Kerry, Lois
Arre, Helen *ConAu XR*
Arre, Helen *see* Ross, Zola Helen
Arre, John *ConAu XR*
Arre, John *see* Holt, John Robert
Arriola, Gus 1917- *ArtCS*
Arter, Elmer K *MnBBF*
Arter, Wallace E *MnBBF*
Arter, Wallace E *see* Kay, Wallace
Artes, Dorothy Beecher 1919- *ConAu 57*
Arthur, Bruce *MnBBF*
Arthur, Harry *MnBBF*
Arthur, Harry *see* Base, A H
Arthur, Ruth Mabel 1905- *Au&Wr 6, BrCA,*
  ChPo, ConAu 9R, SmATA 7
Arthur, Timothy Shay 1809-1885 *Alli, Alli Sup,*
  AmA, AmA&B, BbD, BiD&SB, CarSB,
  CasWL, ChPo, ChPo S1, ChPo S2,
  CyAL 2, DcAmA, DcBiA, DcEnL,
  DcNAA, OxAm, Pen Am, REn, REnAL
Arthur, William *MnBBF, WWBWI A*
Arthur, William *see* Baker, William Arthur
  Howard

Arthurs, Harry *MnBBF*
Arthurs, Harry *see* Base, A H
Artis, Vicki Kimmel 1945- *ConAu 53,*
  SmATA 12
Artzybasheff, Boris Mikhailovic 1899-1965
  AmA&B, AmPB, AnCL, AuBYP,
  ChPo S2, ConICB, CurB 45, CurB 65,
  ForIl, IlCB 1744, JBA 1934, JBA 1951,
  St&VC
Aruego, Ariane *ConAu XR, SmATA 7*
Aruego, Ariane *see* Dewey, Ariane
Aruego, Jose 1932- *ChPo S2, ConAu 37,*
  IlBYP, SmATA 6
Arundel, Anne, Countess Of d1630 *AuBYP*
Arundel, Anne *see* Arundel, Jocelyn
Arundel, Honor 1919-1973 *Au&Wr 6,*
  ConAu 41, ConAu P-2
Arundel, Honor Morfydd 1919-1973 *SmATA 4*
Arundel, Jocelyn 1930- *ConAu XR, AuBYP*
Arundel, Jocelyn *see* Arundel, Anne
Arundel, Louis *CarSB*
Asare, Meshack 1945- *ConAu 61*
Asbjornsen, Peter Christen 1812-1885 *AnCL,*
  CarSB, CasWL, DcEuL, EuAu, EvEuW,
  St&VC, WWCL
Asch, Frank 1946- *AmPB, ConAu 41,*
  SmATA 5, WrD
Aschmann, Helen Tann *ConAu 13R*
Ascott, Adele *WWBWI A*
Ascott, Adele *see* Bobin, John William
Ascott, John *MnBBF, WWBWI A*
Ascott, John *see* Bobin, John William
Ash, Derek *MnBBF*
Ash, Derek *see* Bolton, F T
Ash, Fenton *MnBBF, WWBWI A*
Ash, Fenton *see* Atkins, A J
Ash, Fenton *see* Atkins, Frank A
Ash, Mark *MnBBF*
Ashabranner, Brent 1921- *ConAu 5R,*
  SmATA 1
Ashby, Gwynneth Margaret 1922- *Au&Wr 6,*
  ConAu 25R, WrD
Ashe, Arthur 1943- *BiN 1974, CelR 3,*
  ConAu 65, CurB 66, WWA 38,
  WWS 13
Ashe, Geoffrey 1923- *ConAu 5R*
Ashe, Gordon *ConAu XR, EncM&D, LongC,*
  WWBWI A, WorAu
Ashe, Gordon *see* Creasey, John
Ashey, Bella *ConAu XR, SmATA XR*
Ashey, Bella *see* Breinburg, Petronella
Ashford, Daisy 1881?-1972 *CarSB, ConAu 33,*
  DcLEnL, EvLB, LongC, NYTBE 3,
  Pen Eng, REn, SmATA XR, WWCL
Ashford, Daisy *see* Ashford, Margaret Mary
Ashford, Jeffrey 1926- *Au&Wr 6, AuBYP,*
  ConAu 1R, ConAu XR, EncM&D, WrD
Ashford, Jeffrey *see* Jeffries, Roderic
Ashford, Margaret Mary 1881?-1972 *NCHEL,*
  SmATA 10
Ashford, Margaret Mary *see* Ashford, Daisy
Ashley, Elizabeth *ConAu XR, SmATA XR*
Ashley, Elizabeth *see* Salmon, Annie Elizabeth
Ashley, Fred *MnBBF*
Ashley, Robert Paul, Jr. 1915- *AuBYP,*
  ConAu 17R, DrAS 6E, LE 5, WWA 38
Ashmead, Gordon *AuBYP*
Ashmun, Margaret Eliza d1940 *AmA&B,*
  CurB 40, DcNAA, JBA 1934, JBA 1951,

WNAA, WisW
Ashton-Warner, Sylvia 1908- *ConAu 69,
ConNov 1972, ConNov 1976, LongC,
Pen Eng, RAdv 1, TwCW, WorAu*
Ashworth, Chadwick *MnBBF*
Ashworth, Mae Hurley *IndAu 1917*
Asimov, Isaac 1920- *AmA&B, AmMWS 12P,
Au&Wr 6, AuBYP, CasWL, CelR 3,
ConAu 1R, ConLC 1, ConLC 3,
ConNov 1972, ConNov 1976, CurB 53,
CurB 68, DrAF 1976, EncM&D,
IntWW 38, LongC, Pen Am, REn,
REnAL, SmATA 1, ThBJA, TwCW,
WEAL, WWA 38, WWE 14, WWWor 2,
WorAu*
Asimov, Isaac *see* French, Paul
Asinof, Eliot 1919- *ConAu 9R, SmATA 6*
Asmussen, Des *IlBYP*
Aspin, Jehoshaphat *Br&AmS, CarSB*
Aspinwall, Alicia *CarSB, ChPo, DcAmA*
Asquith, Herbert 1881-1947 *BkCL, ChPo,
ChPo S1, ChPo S2, LongC, NCHEL,
St&VC, WWLA*
Aston, James *LongC, SmATA XR*
Aston, James *see* White, Terence Hanbury
Asturias, Miguel Angel 1899-1974 *CasWL,
ConAu 49, ConLC 3, CurB 68, CurB 74,
EncWL, IntWW 38, NYTBS 5, Pen Am,
TwCW, WW 1974, WWTwL,
WWWor 2, WorAu*
Atene, Ann *SmATA XR*
Atene, Ann *see* Atene, Anna
Atene, Anna 1922- *SmATA 12*
Atene, Anna *see* Atene, Ann
Atkey, Philip *EncM&D, MnBBF,
WWBWI A*
Atkey, Philip *see* Perowne, Barry
Atkins, A J *WWBWI A*
Atkins, A J *see* Ash, Fenton
Atkins, F J *MnBBF*
Atkins, Frank A *MnBBF*
Atkins, Frank A *see* Ash, Fenton
Atkins, Frank A *see* Aubrey, Frank
Atkinson, Eleanor 1863-1942 *AmA&B,
CurB 43, DcNAA, IndAu 1816,
JBA 1934, TwCA, TwCA Sup, WNAA*
Atkinson, M E *ConAu XR, SmATA 4*
Atkinson, M E *see* Frankau, Mary Evelyn
Atkinson
Atkinson, Margaret Fleming *AuBYP*
Atkinson, Mary Evelyn 1899- *Au&Wr 6,
SmATA 4, WWCL*
Atkinson, Reginald *MnBBF*
Atkinson, Reginald *see* Carlton, Lewis
Atkinson, W A *MnBBF*
Atticus *ConAu XR, DcEnL, SmATA XR*
Atticus *see* Fleming, Ian
Attwell, Mabel Lucie 1879-1964 *ChPo,
ChPo S1, WWCL*
Atwater, Florence Hasseltine *MorJA*
Atwater, Montgomery Meigs 1904- *AuBYP,
MorJA, WWPNA*
Atwater, Richard Tupper 1892-1948 *AmA&B,
BkCL, ChPo S1, MorJA*
Atwood, Ann Margaret 1913- *ConAu 41,
SmATA 7, WWA 38, WWAW 8*
Aubrey, Frank *MnBBF*
Aubrey, Frank *see* Atkins, Frank A
Aubry, Claude 1914- *OxCan Sup, Prof*

Audley, Captain *MnBBF*
Audubon, John James 1785?-1851 *Alli, AmA,
AmA&B, AtlBL, BbD, BiD&SB, BiDSA,
CnDAL, CyAL 1, DcAmA, DcLEnL,
DcNAA, MouLC 3, OhA&B, OxAm,
OxCan, OxEng, Pen Am, REn, REnAL*
Auerbach, Marjorie 1932- *ConAu 9R,
IlCB 1957*
Aulaire, Edgar Parin D' *AmPB, AnCL,
CurB 40, JBA 1934, JBA 1951*
Aulaire, Edgar Parin D' *see* D'Aulaire, Edgar
Parin
Aulaire, Ingri D' *AmPB, AnCL, JBA 1934,
JBA 1951*
Aulaire, Ingri D' *see* D'Aulaire, Ingri
Aulnoy, Marie-Catherine, Comtesse D'
1650?-1705 *BiD&SB, CarSB, CasWL,
DcEuL, OxFr*
Ault, Norman 1880-1950 *ChPo, ChPo S1,
ConICB, IlCB 1744*
Ault, Phillip H 1914- *WWA 38, WWMW 14*
Aunt Irene *NewbC 1966*
Austen, Jane 1775-1817 *Alli, AtlBL, BbD,
BiD&SB, BrAu 19, CasWL 19,
Chambr 2, CriT 2, CyWA, DcBiA,
DcEnA, DcEnL, DcEuL, DcLEnL, EvLB,
MouLC 2, NCHEL, OxEng, Pen Eng,
RAdv 1, RCom, REn, WEAL*
Austen, John 1886- *ChPo, ChPo S1,
ChPo S2, IlCB 1744*
Austin, Elizabeth S 1907- *ConAu P-2,
SmATA 5*
Austin, Frank *WWBWI A*
Austin, Frank *see* Faust, Frederick
Austin, Frederick Britten 1885-1941 *MnBBF,
NCHEL, WWLA*
Austin, Jane Goodwin 1831-1894 *Alli Sup,
AmA, AmA&B, BbD, BiD&SB, CarSB,
DcAmA, DcBiA, DcNAA, JBA 1934,
OxAm, REnAL*
Austin, Linda 1943- *ConAu 29*
Austin, Margot *AuBYP, ConAu P-1, MorJA,
SmATA 11*
Austin, Mary Hunter 1868-1934 *AmA&B,
AmLY, AnCL, BkCL, ChPo, ChPo S1,
ChPo S2, CnDAL, ConAmA, ConAmL,
DcAmA, DcLEnL, DcNAA, OxAm,
REnAL, St&VC, TwCA, TwCA Sup,
WNAA*
Austin, Mortimer *MnBBF, WWBWI A*
Austin, Mortimer *see* Rowe, John Gabriel
Austin, Oliver Luther, Jr. 1903- *AmMWS 12P,
ConAu 49, SmATA 7, WWS 13*
Austin, Phil 1910- *IlBYP, WWAA 1973*
Austin, Stanley E d1950? *MnBBF,
WWBWI A*
Austin, Stanley E *see* Clifford, Martin
Austin, Stanley E *see* Conquest, Owen
Austin, Stanley E *see* Richards, Frank
Austin, Stella *Alli Sup, TelT*
Averill, Esther Holden 1902- *AmA&B, AmPB,
AuBYP, BkCL, ConAu 29, ForWC 1970,
IlCB 1946, IlCB 1957, JBA 1934,
SmATA 1, WWAW 8, WrD*
Averill, Naomi *AmPB*
Avery, Al *AmA&B, AuBYP, ConAu XR,
SmATA 3*
Avery, Al *see* Montgomery, Rutherford George
Avery, Gillian Elise 1926- *AuBYP, ConAu 9R,*

SmATA 7, WWCL
Avery, Harold 1867-1943 MnBBF,
   WWBWI A, WWCL
Avery, Kay 1908- ConAu 1R, SmATA 5
Avery, Lynn AuBYP, ConAu XR,
   SmATA XR
Avery, Lynn see Cole, Lois Dwight
Avi ConAu XR
Avi see Wortis, Avi
Avi-Yonah, Michael 1904- WWWorJ 1972
Avinoff, Andrey 1884- IlCB 1744
Avison, George 1885- ConICB, IlBYP,
   IlCB 1744, IlCB 1946
Avrett, Robert 1901- ConAu 1R, WWS 13
Awdry, Wilbert Vere 1911- Au&Wr 6, WrD,
   WWCL
Axeman, Lois IlBYP
Ayars, Albert Lee 1917- AmMWS 12S,
   ConAu 29, LE 5, WWA 38, WWWor 2
Ayars, James Sterling 1898- AuBYP,
   ConAu 5R, SmATA 4, WWMW 14,
   WrD
Ayer, Jacqueline 1930- ConAu 69, IlBYP,
   IlCB 1957, SmATA 13
Ayer, Jacqueline Brandford 1930- ThBJA
Ayer, Margaret ConAu 65, ForWC 1970,
   IlBYP, IlCB 1946, MorJA
Aylesworth, Thomas Gibbons 1927-
   AmMWS 12P, ConAu 25R, IndAu 1917,
   LE 5, SmATA 4, WWE 14
Aylward, William James 1875- IlCB 1744
Aymar, Brandt 1911- ConAu 1R, WNAA
Aymar, Gordon Christian 1893- Au&Wr 6,
   ConAu 5R, WWA 38, WWAA 1973,
   WrD
Ayme, Marcel 1902-1967 BiEnAT, CasWL,
   ClDMEuL, CnMD, CnThe, EncWL,
   EvEuW, LongC, McGWD, ModRL,
   ModWD, OxFr, Pen Eur, REn,
   TwCA Sup, TwCW
Aynesworth, Cecil MnBBF
Aynesworth, Cecil see Childs, Edmund Burton
Ayre, Robert Hugh 1900- AuBYP,
   CanWW 12, ConAu 1R, OxCan,
   OxCan Sup, WWAA 1973

B

B B 1905- *Br&AmS, ConAu XR, LongC,*
SmATA 6, ThBJA, WWCL
B B see Watkins-Pitchford, Denys James
Baastad, Babbis Friis *ConAu XR, SmATA 7*
Baastad, Babbis Friis see Friis-Baastad, Babbis
Ellinor
Babbis, Eleanor *ConAu XR, SmATA 7,*
ThBJA
Babbis, Eleanor see Friis-Baastad, Babbis Ellinor
Babbitt, Natalie 1932- *ChLR 2, ChPo S2,*
ConAu 49, MorBMP, SmATA 6, WrD
Babcock, Dennis Arthur 1948- *ConAu 61*
Bach, Richard David 1936- *AuNews 1,*
BiN 1974, ConAu 9R, CurB 73,
SmATA 13
Bacharach, Herman Ilfeld 1899- *ConICB*
Bacheller, Irving 1859-1950 *AmA&B, BiD&SB,*
Chambr 3, ChPo, ChPo S1, ChPo S2,
ConAmL, DcAmA, DcBiA, DcLEnL,
JBA 1934, OxAm, REn, TwCA Sup,
WNAA S1
Bachman, Fred 1949- *ConAu 53, SmATA 12*
Back, William d1920? *MnBBF, WWBWI A*
Bacmeister, Rhoda W 1893- *ChPo, ConAu P-1*
Bacmeister, Rhoda Warner 1893- *ForWC 1970*
Bacmeister, Rhoda W 1893- *SmATA 11*
Bacon, Elizabeth 1914- *ConAu 29, SmATA 3*
Bacon, Elizabeth see Morrow, Betty
Bacon, Frances Atchinson 1903- *ConAu 1R*
Bacon, Josephine Dodge Daskam 1876-1961
AmA&B, ChPo, ChPo S2, DcAmA,
REnAL, St&VC, TwCA, TwCA Sup,
WNAA
Bacon, Margaret Hope 1921- *ConAu 25R,*
SmATA 6, WrD
Bacon, Martha *ChLR 3*
Bacon, Paul 1913- *AuBYP*
Bacon, Peggy 1895- *AmA&B, AmPB, ChPo,*
ChPo S2, ConAu P-2, ConICB, CurB 40,
IlBYP, IlCB 1744, IlCB 1946, IlCB 1957,
OxAm, REnAL, SmATA 2, St&VC,
WWA 38, WWAA 1973, WWAW 8
Bacon, Phillip 1922- *AmMWS 12S,*
ConAu 41, WWA 38, WWS 13,
WWWor 2
Bacot, J T W *MnBBF*
Baden-Powell, Sir Robert 1857-1941 *LongC,*
MnBBF, WWBWI A, WWCL, WWLA
Bader, Barbara *ChPo S2*
Badmin, Stanley Roy 1906- *IlCB 1946,*
WW 1974
Baerg, Harry John 1909- *ConAu 9R*

Baerg, Harry J 1909- *SmATA 12*
Baerg, Harry John 1909- *WrD*
Bagley, John Joseph 1908- *Au&Wr 6*
Bagnold, Enid 1889- *AuBYP, BiEnAT,*
ChPo S2, CnMD, ConAu 5R, ConDr 1,
ConNov 1976, CurB 64, DcLEnL, EvLB,
LongC, ModWD, NCHEL, OxEng, REn,
SmATA 1, TwCA, TwCA Sup, TwCW,
WW 1974, WWAW 8, WWCL,
WWT 15, WWWor 2
Bagnold, Enid see Lady Of Quality, A
Bagshotte, Annerley *MnBBF*
Bahadur, K P 1924- *ConAu 57*
Bahlke, Valerie Worth 1933- *ConAu 41*
Bahlke, Valerie Worth see Worth, Valerie
Bahti, Tom *IlBYP*
Bailey, Alice Cooper 1890- *ConAu P-1,*
ForWC 1970, SmATA 12, WWAW 8
Bailey, Bernadine Freeman 1901- *AuBYP,*
ConAu 5R, ForWC 1970, WWAW 8
Bailey, Carolyn Sherwin 1875-1961 *AmA&B,*
AnCL, AuBYP, BkCL, CarSB, ChPo,
ChPo S1, ChPo S2, CurB 48, JBA 1951,
Newb 1922, St&VC
Bailey, Charles W, II 1929- *ConAu 1R,*
WWA 38
Bailey, Flora *AuBYP*
Bailey, Jane H 1916- *ConAu 53, SmATA 12*
Bailey, John *AuBYP*
Bailey, Maralyn Collins 1941- *ConAu 53,*
SmATA 12
Bailey, Matilda *ConAu XR, SmATA 6*
Bailey, Matilda see Radford, Ruby Lorraine
Bailey, Maurice Charles 1932- *ConAu 53,*
SmATA 12
Bailey, Ralph Edgar 1893- *ConAu P-1,*
SmATA 11
Bailey, Robert Ernest *MnBBF*
Bailey-Jones, Beryl 1912- *IlBYP, IlCB 1946*
Bailey-Jones, Beryl see Jones, Beryl Bailey
Bain, Edward Ustick *AuBYP*
Bain, R Nisbet 1854-1909 *St&VC*
Baine, Colin T *MnBBF, WWBWI A*
Baines, R Read *MnBBF*
Baird, Bil 1904- *BiEnAT, BiN 1974, CelR 3,*
ChPo S2, CurB 54
Baird, G *MnBBF*
Baity, Elizabeth Chesley 1907- *AmA&B,*
AnCL, ConAu 29, MorJA, SmATA 1
Bakacs, George *IlBYP*
Bakeless, John Edwin 1894- *AmA&B,*
Au&Wr 6, AuBYP, ConAu 5R,

DrAS 6E, REnAL, SmATA 9, TwCA,
TwCA Sup, WNAA, WWA 38,
WWWor 2
Bakeless, Katherine Little 1895- *Au&Wr 6,*
ConAu 5R, SmATA 9, WWE 14
Baker, A *MnBBF*
Baker, Augusta 1911- *BiDL 5, BlkAW,*
ConAu 1R, LBAA, SmATA 3,
WWAW 8
Baker, Augustus *MnBBF, WWBWI A*
Baker, Augustus *see* Baron, Anthony
Baker, Augustus *see* Baron, John
Baker, Betty 1928- *AmA&B, AuBYP,*
ConAu XR, SmATA 5, ThBJA,
WWAW 8, WWW 14
Baker, Betty *see* Venturo, Betty Lou Baker
Baker, Charlotte 1910- *AuBYP, ConAu 17R,*
IlCB 1946, SmATA 2
Baker, Denys Val 1917- *ConAu 9R*
Baker, Elizabeth 1923- *ConAu 1R, WrD*
Baker, Elizabeth *see* Baker, Mary Elizabeth
Gillette
Baker, Emilie Kip *AmA&B, St&VC*
Baker, H S *MnBBF*
Baker, Harriette Newell 1815?-1893 *Alli Sup,*
AmA&B, BbD, BiD&SB, CarSB,
DcAmA, DcNAA
Baker, J S 1872?- *WWBWI I*
Baker, James Lawrence 1941- *ConAu 53*
Baker, Janice E 1941- *ConAu 57*
Baker, Jeffrey John Wheeler 1931-
AmMWS 12P, ConAu 49, SmATA 5
Baker, Jerry *AuNews 2*
Baker, Johnny *MnBBF*
Baker, Laura Nelson 1911- *Au&Wr 6,*
AuBYP, ConAu 5R, ForWC 1970,
MnnWr, SmATA 3, WrD
Baker, Liva 1930- *ConAu 29*
Baker, Lucinda 1916- *ConAu 65*
Baker, Margaret 1890- *Au&Wr 6, ChPo S2,*
ConAu 13R, JBA 1934, JBA 1951,
SmATA 4
Baker, Margaret Joyce 1918- *Au&Wr 6,*
AuBYP, ConAu 13R, MorJA,
SmATA 12, WrD
Baker, Mary 1897- *ConICB, IlCB 1744,*
IlCB 1946, JBA 1934, JBA 1951
Baker, Mary Elizabeth Gillette 1923-
SmATA 7
Baker, Mary Elizabeth Gillette *see* Baker,
Elizabeth
Baker, Mary Gladys Steel 1892-1974
ConAu P-1, SmATA 12
Baker, Mary Gladys Steel *see* Stuart, Sheila
Baker, Michael 1938- *ConAu 25R, SmATA 4,*
WrD
Baker, Nina Brown 1888-1957 *AmA&B,*
AuBYP, CurB 47, CurB 57, JBA 1951
Baker, Olaf *JBA 1934, JBA 1951, MnBBF*
Baker, Rachel 1904- *AuBYP, BkCL,*
ConAu 5R, MorJA, SmATA 2
Baker, Ray Stannard 1870-1946 *AmA&B,*
AmLY, CarSB, ChPo S2, ConAmL,
CurB 40, CurB 46, DcAmA, DcLEnL,
DcNAA, EvLB, LongC, OxAm, REn,
REnAL, TwCA, TwCA Sup, TwCW,
WNAA, WisW
Baker, Richard St. Barbe 1889- *Au&Wr 6,*
ConAu P-1, WW 1974

Baker, Robert H 1883- *WNAA*
Baker, Samm S 1909- *ConAu 5R, SmATA 12*
Baker, Sir Samuel White 1821-1893 *Alli Sup,*
BbD, BiD&SB, BrAu 19, Chambr 3,
DcEnL, EvLB, MnBBF, NCHEL, OxEng
Baker, Sarah Schoonmaker 1824-1906 *Alli Sup,*
CarSB, ChPo, DcAmA, DcNAA
Baker, Tom *MnBBF*
Baker, W Howard 1925- *WWBWI A*
Baker, W Howard *see* Baker, William Arthur
Howard
Baker, William Arthur Howard 1925- *MnBBF*
Baker, William Arthur Howard *see* Arthur,
William
Baker, William Arthur Howard *see* Baker, W
Howard
Baker, William Arthur Howard *see* Ballinger,
William A
Baker, William Arthur Howard *see* Saxon, Peter
Baker, William Arthur Howard *see* McNeilly,
Wilfred
Baker, William Arthur Howard *see* Williams,
Richard
Baker, William C 1891- *AuBYP*
Balaam *ConAu XR, SmATA XR*
Balaam *see* Lamb, G F
Balch, Glenn 1902- *AmA&B, AuBYP,*
ConAu 1R, MorJA, SmATA 3,
WWA 38, WWPNA, WWW 14
Balderson, Margaret *ConAu 25R*
Baldridge, Cyrus LeRoy 1889- *IlBYP,*
IlCB 1744, IlCB 1946, WNAA
Balducci, Carolyn 1946- *ConAu 33,*
SmATA 5
Baldwin, Anne Norris 1938- *ConAu 29,*
SmATA 5, WWAW 8, WrD
Baldwin, Arthur H *AuBYP*
Baldwin, Basil *MnBBF*
Baldwin, Basil *see* Ritchie, Balfour
Baldwin, Clara *ConAu 61, ForWC 1970,*
SmATA 11
Baldwin, Gordo *ConAu XR, SmATA XR*
Baldwin, Gordo *see* Baldwin, Gordon C
Baldwin, Gordon C 1908- *ConAu 1R,*
SmATA 12
Baldwin, Gordon C *see* Baldwin, Gordo
Baldwin, Gordon C *see* Gordon, Lew
Baldwin, James 1841-1925 *Alli Sup, AmA&B,*
AmLY, AnCL, AuBYP, CarSB, ChPo,
DcNAA, IndAu 1816, JBA 1934,
JBA 1951, REnAL
Baldwin, James 1924- *AmA&B, BlkAW,*
CasWL, CelR 3, ConAu 1R, ConDr 1,
ConLC 1, ConLC 2, ConLC 3, ConLC 4,
ConLC 5, ConNov 1972, ConNov 1976,
CrCD, CurB 59, CurB 64, DrAF 1976,
EncWL, LBAA, LongC, McGWD,
ModAL, ModAL Sup, ModWD,
NYTBE 3, OxAm, Pen Am, RAdv 1,
REn, REnAL, SmATA 9, TwCW,
WEAL, WW 1974, WWA 38, WWE 14,
WWTwL, WWWor 2, WorAu
Baldwin-Ford, Pamela *IlBYP*
Bales, Carol Ann 1940- *ConAu 45*
Balet, Jan B 1913- *AuBYP, IlCB 1946,*
SmATA 11, ThBJA
Balfour, David S *MnBBF*
Balian, Lorna 1929- *ChPo, ConAu 53,*
SmATA 9, WrD

Ball, B N *ConAu XR*
Ball, B N *see* Ball, Brian N
Ball, Brian N 1932- *ConAu 33*
Ball, Brian N *see* Ball, B N
Ball, Brian N *see* Kinsey-Jones, Brian
Ball, John 1911- *Au&Wr 6, AuBYP, ConAu 5R, EncM&D*
Ball, Robert *IIBYP, IICB 1946*
Ball, Zachary *AuBYP, ConAu XR, CurB 53, SmATA 3*
Ball, Zachary *see* Masters, Kelly Ray
Ballantine, Bill *AmPB*
Ballantine, Jack *MnBBF*
Ballantyne, Robert Michael 1825-1894 *Alli Sup, BbD, BbthC, BiD&SB, BrAu 19, CarSB, CasWL, Chambr 3, ChPo, ChPo S1, DcEnL, DcLEnL, EvLB, MnBBF, NCHEL, OxCan, OxEng, Pen Eng, TelT, WWBWI A, WWCL*
Ballard, Eric Alan *MnBBF*
Ballard, Eric Alan *see* Harrison, Edwin
Ballard, Lowell Clyne 1904- *ConAu P-1, SmATA 12*
Ballard, Martin 1929- *Au&Wr 6, ConAu 25R, SmATA 1*
Ballinger, William A *ConAu XR, MnBBF, WWBWI A*
Ballinger, William A *see* Baker, William Arthur Howard
Ballinger, William A *see* McNeilly, Wilfred
Ballou, Arthur W 1915- *ConAu 25R*
Balmer, Edwin 1883-1959 *AmA&B, EncM&D, REnAL, WNAA*
Balogh, Penelope 1916-1975 *Au&Wr 6, ConAu P-2, SmATA 1*
Balow, Tom 1931- *ConAu 45, SmATA 12*
Baltzer, Hans 1900- *IIBYP, IICB 1957*
Bambara, Toni Cade 1939- *BlkAW, LBAA*
Bambara, Toni Cade *see* Cade, Toni
Bamfylde, Walter *YABC XR*
Bamfylde, Walter *see* Bevan, Tom
Bamman, Henry A 1918- *ConAu 5R, LE 5, SmATA 12*
Bancks, G W *MnBBF*
Bancroft, Griffing 1907- *AuBYP, AuNews 1, ConAu 29, SmATA 6*
Bancroft, Laura *ThBJA*
Bancroft, Laura *see* Baum, L Frank
Bandel, Betty 1912- *DrAS 6E*
Bander, James Wynne *MnBBF*
Banel, Joseph 1943- *ConAu 45*
Baner, Skulda Vanadis 1897-1964 *ConAu P-1, SmATA 10*
Banfield, F *MnBBF*
Bangham, Mary Dickerson 1896- *ChPo, ConAu P-2*
Bangs, John Kendrick 1862-1922 *AmA&B, BbD, BiD&SB, CarSB, ChPo, ChPo S1, ChPo S2, DcAmA, DcLEnL, DcNAA, EncM&D, OxAm, REnAL, St&VC, TwCA, TwCA Sup*
Bangs, Robert Babbitt 1914- *AmMWS 12S, ConAu 37, WrD*
Banister, Manly 1914- *ConAu 41*
Bank-Jensen, Thea *ConAu XR*
Bank-Jensen, Thea *see* Ottesen, Thea Tauber
Banks, Lynne Reid *ConNov 1972, ConNov 1976, TwCW*
Banks, Marsh *MnBBF*

Banner, Angela *ConAu XR, SmATA XR*
Banner, Angela *see* Maddison, Angela Mary
Bannerman, Helen Brodie Cowan 1862?-1946 *CarSB, IICB 1744, JBA 1951, TelT, WWCL*
Banning, Evelyn I 1903- *ConAu 17R*
Bannon, Laura May d1963 *AuBYP, ConAu 1R, IICB 1744, IICB 1946, IICB 1957, MorJA, SmATA 6*
Barany, Stefan *WWBWI I*
Barbary, James *ConAu XR, SmATA XR*
Barbary, James *see* Baumann, Amy
Barbary, James *see* Beeching, Jack
Barbe, Walter Burke 1926- *ConAu 13R, LE 5, WWA 38*
Barbe, Wren 1913- *ConAu 13R*
Barber, D F 1940- *ConAu 61*
Barber, D F *see* Fletcher, David
Barber, Richard 1941- *ConAu 33*
Barberis, Franco 1905- *ConAu 25R*
Barbour, Ralph Henry 1870-1944 *AmA&B, AuBYP, CarSB, ChPo, CurB 44, DcAmA, DcNAA, JBA 1934, JBA 1951, REnAL*
Barclay, Barbara 1938- *ConAu 29*
Barclay, Isabel *ConAu XR, SmATA XR*
Barclay, Isabel *see* Dobell, I M B
Barclay, William 1907- *Au&Wr 6, WW 1974*
Bard, Bernard 1927- *ConAu 25R*
Bardsley, John *MnBBF*
Bardwell, Denver *MnBBF*
Bardwell, Denver *see* Sayers, James Denson
Bare, Arnold Edwin 1920- *IIBYP, IICB 1744, IICB 1946*
Barfoot, Audrey Ilma 1918-1964 *ConAu 5R*
Barham, Richard Harris 1788-1845 *Alli, BbD, BiD&SB, BrAu 19, CarSB, CasWL, Chambr 3, ChPo, ChPo S1, ChPo S2, DcEnA, DcEnL, DcEuL, DcLEnL, EvLB, NCHEL, OxEng*
Baring-Gould, Sabine 1834-1924? *BbD, BiD&SB, BrAu 19, CarSB, CatA S2, Chambr 3, ChPo, ChPo S1, DcBiA, DcEnA, DcEnA Ap, DcEnL, DcLEnL, EvLB, LongC, NCHEL, OxEng, Pen Eng, WEAL*
Barish, Matthew 1907- *ConAu 57, SmATA 12*
Barker, A J 1918- *ConAu 13R*
Barker, Albert W 1900- *SmATA 8*
Barker, Albert W *see* King, Reefe
Barker, Albert W *see* Macrae, Hawk
Barker, C Hedley *MnBBF*
Barker, Carol 1938- *ArtsCL*
Barker, Carol Minturn 1938- *ChPo S1, IIBYP, IICB 1957*
Barker, Cicely Mary *ChPo, ChPo S1, ChPo S2*
Barker, E M *ConAu XR*
Barker, E M *see* Barker, Elsa
Barker, Elsa 1906- *ConAu P-2*
Barker, Elsa *see* Barker, E M
Barker, Melvern J 1907- *ConAu P-1, IICB 1946, SmATA 11*
Barker, S Omar 1894- *ConAu P-2, SmATA 10, WNAA*
Barker, S Omar *see* Canusi, Jose
Barker, S Omar *see* Scott, Dan
Barker, S Omar *see* Squires, Phil

Barker, Will 1913- *Au&Wr 6, AuBYP,*
  ConAu 9R, SmATA 8
Barker, Will *see* Demarest, Doug
Barkley, James Edward 1941- *IIBYP,*
  SmATA 6
Barksdale, Lena *AmA&B, AuBYP*
Barlow, Roger *ConAu XR*
Barlow, Roger *see* Leckie, Robert
Barnaby, Ralph S 1893- *ConAu 61,*
  SmATA 9
Barnard, Alfred J 1878- *MnBBF, WWBWI A*
Barnard, Alfred J *see* Clifford, Martin
Barnard, Alfred J *see* Hart, Leonard
Barnard, C D *MnBBF*
Barnard, Frederick 1847?-1896 *ChPo S1,*
  WWBWI 1
Barnard, Peggy *SingR 1*
Barnard, Richard Innes *MnBBF*
Barnard, Richard Innes *see* Richards, Frank
Barnard, Robert J *MnBBF*
Barnard, Wilfred *MnBBF*
Barne, Kitty 1883-1957 *JBA 1951, WWCL*
Barnes, Catherine J 1918- *ChPo, IIBYP,*
  IICB 1946
Barnes, Eric Wollencott 1907-1962 *AmA&B,*
  AuBYP
Barnes, G G *MnBBF*
Barnes, Gregory Allen 1934- *ConAu 25R*
Barnes, Herbert *MnBBF*
Barnes, John *MnBBF*
Barnes, John *see* O'Donnell, Peter
Barnes, Leola Christie 1889- *TexW*
Barness, Richard 1917- *ConAu 65*
Barnett, John *MnBBF*
Barnett, John *see* Stagg, J R
Barnett, Moneta *IIBYP*
Barney, Maginel Wright 1881- *IICB 1744*
Barnhart, Clarence Lewis 1900- *AmA&B,*
  ConAu 13R, CurB 54, DrAS 6F,
  WWA 38, WWWor 2
Barnhart, Nancy 1889- *ChPo, IIBYP,*
  IICB 1744, IICB 1946
Barnouw, Adriaan Jacob 1877- *AuBYP,*
  ChPo S1, WNAA
Barnouw, Victor 1915- *AmMWS 12S,*
  WWA 38
Barnstone, Aliki 1956- *ChPo S1*
Barnstone, Willis 1927- *ConAu 17R,*
  DrAP 1975, DrAS 6F
Barnum, Jay Hyde *AuBYP, IICB 1946*
Barnum, P T *MnBBF*
Barnum, Richard *ConAu P-2, SmATA 1*
Barnum, Richard *see* Stratemeyer, Edward L
Barnwell, D Robinson 1915- *ConAu 17R*
Baron, Anthony *MnBBF, WWBWI A*
Baron, Anthony *see* Baker, Augustus
Baron, John *MnBBF, WWBWI A*
Baron, John *see* Baker, Augustus
Baron, Virginia Olsen 1931- *ConAu 25R*
Barr, Donald 1921- *ConAu 9R, WWA 38*
Barr, George 1907- *AmA&B, AuBYP,*
  ConAu 1R, SmATA 2
Barr, Jene 1900- *AmA&B, AuBYP,*
  ConAu 5R, WWAW 8
Barr, Nat *MnBBF, WWBWI A*
Barr, Nat *see* Goddard, Norman
Barr, Stephen 1904- *ConAu P-1*
Barradale-Smith, William *MnBBF*
Barradale-Smith, William *see* Bird, Richard

Barratt, Alfred W *WWBWI A*
Barratt, Alfred W *see* Barrett, Alfred Walter
Barrett, Alan *IIBYP*
Barrett, Alfred Walter 1869- *MnBBF*
Barrett, Alfred Walter *see* Andom, R
Barrett, Alfred Walter *see* Barratt, Alfred Walter
Barrett, Anne Mainwaring 1911- *Au&Wr 6,*
  ConAu P-2, WWAW 8, WrD
Barrett, Joseph *MnBBF*
Barrett, Judi *WrD*
Barrett, Marvin 1920- *ConAu 69*
Barrett, Ron *IIBYP*
Barrett, William Edmund 1900- *AmA&B,*
  Au&Wr 6, BkC 5, CatA 1952,
  ConAu 5R, REnAL, WWA 38,
  WWWor 2
Barrie, Alexander 1923- *Au&Wr 6,*
  ConAu 1R, WrD
Barrie, Donald C 1905- *ConAu 17R*
Barrie, Sir James Matthew 1860-1937 *Alli Sup,*
  AtlBL, BbD, BiD&SB, CarSB, CasWL,
  Chambr 3, ChPo, ChPo S1, ChPo S2,
  CnMD, CnThe, CyWA, DcBiA, DcEnA,
  DcEnA Ap, DcLEnL, EncWL, EvLB,
  FamAYP, JBA 1934, LongC, McGWD,
  ModBL, ModWD, NCHEL, OxEng,
  Pen Eng, RAdv 1, REn, REnWD, TelT,
  TwCA, TwCA Sup, TwCW, WEAL,
  WWCL, WWTwL, YABC 1
Barrie, S *MnBBF*
Barrie, S *see* Richards, Frank
Barrios, David *IIBYP*
Barron, A Elton *MnBBF*
Barron, A Elton *see* Burrage, Edwin Harcourt
Barrow, Frances Elizabeth 1822-1894 *Alli Sup,*
  AmA&B, BiD&SB, BiDSA, CarSB,
  DcAmA, DcNAA
Barrow-North, H *MnBBF, WWBWI A*
Barrows, Marjorie *AmA&B, AuBYP, ChPo,*
  ChPo S1, ConAu 21R, WNAA,
  WWA 38, WWAW 8
Barry, Arthur *MnBBF*
Barry, Dan 1923- *ArtCS*
Barry, Gerald R 1887- *MnBBF*
Barry, James E *IIBYP*
Barry, James P 1918- *ConAu 37, WrD*
Barry, Katharina Watjen 1936- *AuBYP, ChPo,*
  ConAu 9R, IICB 1957, SmATA 4
Barry, Lucy 1934- *ConAu 17R*
Barry, Robert Everett 1931- *AuBYP,*
  ConAu 5R, IICB 1957, SmATA 6, WrD
Barry, Seymour 1928- *ArtCS*
Barry, Wolfe *MnBBF*
Barsis, Max 1894?-1973 *ConAu 41*
Barss, William 1916- *ChPo S1, IIBYP,*
  IICB 1957
Barth, Edna 1914- *ConAu 41, SmATA 7*
Barthelme, Donald 1931- *AmA&B, CelR 3,*
  ConAu 21R, ConLC 1, ConLC 2,
  ConLC 3, ConLC 5, ConLC 6,
  ConNov 1972, ConNov 1976, DrAF 1976,
  ModAL Sup, Pen Am, RAdv 1,
  SmATA 7, WWA 38, WorAu, WrD
Bartlett, Charles C *MnBBF*
Bartlett, Evelyn *SingR 1*
Bartlett, J Allen *MnBBF*
Bartlett, Margaret Farrington 1896- *ConAu 5R*
Bartlett, Philip A *ConAu P-2, SmATA 1*
Bartlett, Philip A *see* Stratemeyer, Edward L

Bartlett, Robert Merrill 1899- *AmA&B,*
ConAu 5R, IndAu 1917, SmATA 12,
WWA 38
Bartlett, Ruth *ConAu 17R*
Bartlett, Vernon 1894- *Au&Wr 6, ConAu 61,*
IntWW 38, LongC, NCHEL, TwCA,
TwCA Sup, WW 1974, WWLA
Barton *MnBBF*
Barton, Byron 1930- *ConAu 57, SmATA 9*
Barton, May Hollis *ConAu P-2, SmATA 1*
Barton, May Hollis *see* Adams, Harriet S
Barton, May Hollis *see* Stratemeyer, Edward L
Barton, Thomas Frank 1905- *ConAu 45,*
WWA 38, WWWor 2
Bartos-Hoeppner, Barbara 1923- *Au&Wr 6,*
ConAu 25R, SmATA 5
Bartram, G B *MnBBF*
Bartsch, Jochen 1906- *IIBYP, IICB 1957*
Baruch, Dorothy Walter 1899- *AmA&B,*
AmPB, ChPo, St&VC
Base, A H *MnBBF*
Base, A H *see* Arthur, Harry
Base, A H *see* Arthurs, Harry
Bashevis, Isaac *ConAu XR, SmATA 3*
Bashevis, Isaac *see* Singer, Isaac Bashevis
Basho 1644-1694 *CasWL, DcOrL 1, Pen Cl,*
REn
Basile, Giambattista 1575?-1632 *CarSB,*
CasWL, EuAu, EvEuW, Pen Eur, REn
Basilevsky, Helen 1939- *IIBYP*
Baskin, Leonard 1922- *CurB 64, DcCAA 2,*
WWA 38, WWAA 1973, WWGA,
WWWor 2
Baskin, Wade 1924- *ConAu 21R*
Bason, Lillian 1913- *ConAu 69*
Bass, Virginia W 1905- *ConAu 61*
Basser, Veronica *SingR 1*
Bassermann, Lujo *ConAu XR*
Bassermann, Lujo *see* Schreiber, Hermann
Basset, Arthur Ward *MnBBF*
Bassett, John Keith *AuBYP, ConAu XR*
Bassett, John Keith *see* Keating, Lawrence A
Batchelor, Richard A C *MnBBF*
Batchelor, Richard A C *see* Henton, Collett
Batchelor, Richard A C *see* Mayne, Arthur
Bate, Lucy 1939- *ConAu 69*
Bate, Norman Arthur 1916- *AuBYP,*
ConAu 1R, IICB 1946, SmATA 5,
WWAA 1973, WrD
Bateman, Frederick *MnBBF*
Bateman, H *MnBBF*
Bateman, Henry Mayo 1887- *IICB 1744,*
WWBWI I
Bateman, Robert 1922- *Au&Wr 6, ConAu 5R*
Bateman, Walter L 1916- *ConAu 29*
Bates, Arlo 1850-1918 *Alli Sup, AmA,*
AmA&B, BbD, BiD&SB, CarSB, ChPo,
DcAmA, DcBiA, DcNAA, OxAm,
REnAL
Bates, Barbara S 1919- *ConAu 17R,*
ForWC 1970, SmATA 12, WWAW 8
Bates, Barbara S *see* Cuyler, Stephen
Bates, Barbara S *see* Roberts, Jim
Bates, Gordon *CarSB*
Bates, Harriet Leonora 1856-1886 *Alli Sup,*
AmA&B, BiD&SB, CarSB, DcAmA,
DcNAA
Bates, Katharine Lee 1859-1929 *Alli Sup,*
AmA&B, AmLY, AnMV 1926, BiD&SB,

CarSB, ChPo, ChPo S1, ChPo S2,
CnDAL, DcAmA, DcNAA, EvLB,
JBA 1934, OxAm, REnAL, TwCA,
TwCA Sup, TwCW, WNAA
Bates, Lieutenant *MnBBF*
Bates, Marston 1906-1974 *AmA&B,*
AmMWS 12P, ConAu 5R, ConAu 49,
CurB 56, CurB 74, NYTBS 5, WWA 38,
WWWor 2
Bath, Philip Ernest 1898- *Au&Wr 6,*
ConAu P-1
Batiuk, Thomas M 1947- *ConAu 69*
Batson, Larry 1930- *ConAu 57*
Battaglia, Aurelius *IIBYP*
Batten, Harry Mortimer 1888- *MnBBF,*
WWBWI A, WWCL, WWLA
Batten, Mary 1937- *ConAu 41, SmATA 5*
Batten, Peter W 1893- *MnBBF*
Batterberry, Ariane Ruskin 1935- *ConAu 69,*
SmATA 13
Battle, Gerald N 1914- *ConAu 57*
Battles, Edith 1921- *ConAu 41, SmATA 7*
Baudouy, Michel-Aime 1909- *ConAu P-2,*
SmATA 7, ThBJA
Bauer, E Charles 1916- *ConAu 9R*
Bauer, Fred 1934- *ConAu 29*
Bauer, Helen 1900- *ConAu 5R, ForWC 1970,*
SmATA 2
Bauer, Marion Dane 1938- *ConAu 69*
Bauernschmidt, Marjorie 1926- *IIBYP,*
IICB 1946
Baughman, Dorothy 1940- *ConAu 65*
Baum, Allyn Z 1924- *ConAu 17R, WWE 14*
Baum, Betty *AuBYP*
Baum, Lyman Frank 1856-1919 *AmA&B,*
AuBYP, CarSB, ChPo, ChPo S2,
CnDAL, DcAmA, DcNAA, FamSYP,
LongC, OxAm, Pen Am, REn, REnAL,
ThBJA, TwCA, WWCL
Baum, Lyman Frank *see* Akens, Floyd
Baum, Lyman Frank *see* Akers, Floyd
Baum, Lyman Frank *see* Bancroft, Laura
Baum, Lyman Frank *see* Fitzgerald, Hugh,
Captain
Baum, Lyman Frank *see* Metcalf, Suzanne
Baum, Lyman Frank *see* Stanton, Schuyler
Baum, Lyman Frank *see* VanDyne, Edith
Baum, Thomas 1940- *ConAu 65*
Baum, Willi 1931- *ConAu 29, SmATA 4*
Bauman, Elizabeth Hershberger 1924-
IndAu 1917
Bauman, M J *MnBBF*
Baumann, Amy 1922- *SmATA 10*
Baumann, Amy *see* Barbary, James
Baumann, Amy *see* Brown, Alexis
Baumann, Hans 1914- *Au&Wr 6, ConAu 5R,*
SmATA 2, ThBJA, WWWor 2
Baumer, Lewis 1870- *ChPo, IICB 1744*
Baumhauer, Hans 1913- *IIBYP, IICB 1946*
Baur, John E 1922- *ConAu 9R, DrAS 6H*
Bausch, William J 1929- *ConAu 29*
Bawden, Edward 1903- *IICB 1946, IntWW 38,*
WW 1974, WWGA, WWWor 2
Bawden, Nina 1925- *Au&Wr 6, BrCA,*
ChLR 2, ConAu XR, ConNov 1972,
ConNov 1976, SmATA 4, WrD
Bawden, Nina *see* Kark, Nina Mary
Bax, Arthur H *MnBBF*
Baxter, George Owen *MnBBF, WWBWI A*

Baxter, George Owen *see* Faust, Frederick
Baxter, Horlyor *MnBBF*
Baxter, W G 1856-1880? *WWBWI I*
Bayfield, William John 1871-1958 *MnBBF, WWBWI A*
Bayfield, William John *see* Blair, Allan
Bayfield, William John *see* Carr, George
Bayfield, William John *see* Carr, Gordon
Bayfield, William John *see* Dayle, Malcolm
Bayfield, William John *see* Dene, Hampton
Bayfield, William John *see* Gray, Gilbert
Bayfield, William John *see* Jardine, Warwick
Bayfield, William John *see* Maxwell, Allan
Bayfield, William John *see* Osborne, Mark
Bayfield, William John *see* West, Edgar
Bayley, Dorothy *ChPo*
Baylor, Byrd *ChLR 3*
Bayly, George *MnBBF*
Bayne, Charles S 1876- *MnBBF*
Bayne, Peter *MnBBF*
Bayne, Peter *see* Brindle, Ernest
Bayne-Jardine, C C 1932- *ConAu 25R*
Baynes, Ernest Harold 1868-1925 *AmLY, DcNAA, JBA 1934, JBA 1951, St&VC*
Baynes, Pauline Diana 1922- *ChPo, ChPo S2, IlBYP, IlCB 1946, IlCB 1957, ThBJA, WWCL*
Beach, Charles Amory *CarSB, ConAu P-2, SmATA 1*
Beach, Charles Amory *see* Stratemeyer, Edward L
Beach, Edward Latimer 1918- *Au&Wr 6, ConAu 5R, SmATA 12*
Beach, Stewart 1899- *AmA&B, AuBYP*
Beaglehole, J C 1901-1971 *ConAu P-2*
Beal, George *MnBBF*
Bealer, Alex W 1921- *ConAu 45, SmATA 8*
Beals, Carleton 1893- *AmA&B, Au&Wr 6, AuBYP, ConAu 1R, CurB 41, DcLEnL, IntWW 38, OxAm, REnAL, SmATA 12, TwCA, TwCA Sup, WNAA, WWA 38, WWWor 2*
Beals, Frank Lee 1881- *ConAu 5R*
Beaman, Joyce Proctor 1931- *ConAu 29*
Beaman, S G Hulme *WWCL*
Beame, Rona 1934- *ConAu 45, SmATA 12*
Bean, E A *MnBBF*
Beaney, Jan *ConAu XR, SmATA XR*
Beaney, Jan *see* Udall, Jan Beaney
Beard, Charles Austin 1874-1948 *AmA&B, ConAmA, CurB 41, CurB 48, DcLEnL, DcNAA, EvLB, IndAu 1816, LongC, OxAm, Pen Am, REn, REnAL, TwCA, TwCA Sup, WEAL*
Beard, Daniel Carter 1850-1941 *Alli Sup, AmA&B, AmLY, BiD&SB, CarSB, ChPo, CurB 41, DcAmA, DcNAA, JBA 1934, OhA&B, OxAm, REnAL, TwCA, TwCA Sup, WNAA*
Beard, Lina d1933 *DcNAA, WNAA*
Beard, William 1907- *AmA&B, WWA 38*
Bearden, Romare 1914- *CurB 72, DcCAA 2*
Beardmore, George 1908- *ConAu 69*
Beardsley, Aubrey Vincent 1872-1898 *AtlBL, BrAu 19, ChPo, ChPo S2, DcLEnL, NCHEL, REn, WEAL*
Beattie, Jessie Louise 1896- *Au&Wr 6, CanNov, CanWW 12, ConAu 5R, OxCan,*

Prof, WNAA
Beatty, Elizabeth *ConAu XR*
Beatty, Elizabeth *see* Holloway, Teresa
Beatty, Hetty Burlingame 1907?-1971 *AuBYP, ConAu 1R, IlCB 1946, IlCB 1957, MorJA, SmATA 5*
Beatty, Jerome, Jr. 1918- *AuBYP, ConAu 9R, SmATA 5*
Beatty, John 1922-1975 *ConAu 5R, ConAu 57, SmATA 6, ThBJA*
Beatty, Patricia Robbins 1922- *AuBYP, ConAu 1R, ForWC 1970, SmATA 1, ThBJA*
Beaty, Janice Janowski 1930- *ConAu 13R, ForWC 1970*
Beaty, John Yocum 1884- *AuBYP*
Beaumont, Brenchley *MnBBF*
Beaumont, Brenchley *see* Viles, Walter
Beausay, Florence Edith 1911- *ConAu 21R, WWAW 8, WrD*
Beaver, Barrington *MnBBF*
Bebb, Fisher *MnBBF*
Bebell, Mildred Hoyt 1909- *ConAu P-1*
Bebenroth, Charlotta M 1890- *OhA&B*
Bechtel, Louise Seaman 1894- *AmPB, ChPo, ChPo S1, ConAu P-2, SmATA 4*
Bechtel, Louise Seaman *see* Seaman, Louise
Beck, Ashley *MnBBF*
Beck, Barbara L 1927- *ConAu 17R, SmATA 12*
Beck, Christopher *MnBBF, WWBWI A, WWCL*
Beck, Christopher *see* Bridges, Thomas Charles
Becke, Louis 1850- *BbD, BiD&SB, Chambr 3, MnBBF*
Beckel, Graham 1913- *ConAu 1R*
Beckenham, John *MnBBF*
Becker, Beril 1901- *ConAu P-1, SmATA 11*
Becker, Charlotte *ChPo, WWAA 1973, WWAW 8*
Becker, John Leonard 1901- *AuBYP, ChPo, ChPo S2, ConAu P-1, SmATA 12*
Becker, May Lamberton 1873-1958 *AmA&B, ChPo, ChPo S1, CurB 41, CurB 58, REnAL, TwCA, TwCA Sup, WNAA*
Becker, Paula Lee 1941- *ConAu 17R, ForWC 1970, WWAW 8*
Becker, Ruby Wirt 1915- *ConAu 33*
Beckerley, L C *MnBBF*
Beckett, Sheilah *ChPo S1*
Beckhard, Arthur J *AuBYP*
Beckles Willson, Robina Elizabeth 1930- *Au&Wr 6, WrD*
Beckman, Gunnel 1910- *ConAu 33, SmATA 6*
Beckman, Kaj 1913- *IlCB 1946*
Beckman, Per 1913- *IlCB 1946*
Beckwith, Lillian *ConAu XR, WrD*
Beckwith, Lillian *see* Comber, Lillian
Beckwith, Yvonne 1936?- *ForWC 1970, WWAW 8*
Beddall, Barbara G 1919- *ConAu 33*
Beddington, Roy *WrD*
Beddoe, Ellaruth *ConAu XR*
Beddoe, Ellaruth *see* Elkins, Ella Ruth
Bedford, A N *ConAu XR, SmATA 3*
Bedford, A N *see* Watson, Jane Werner
Bedford, Annie North *ConAu XR, SmATA 3*
Bedford, Annie North *see* Watson, Jane Werner

Bedford, Francis Donkin 1864-1950 *ChPo,*
ChPo S1, ChPo S2, ConICB, IlCB 1744,
WWCL
Bedford, Lee *MnBBF*
Bedford, Ruth 1882- *SingR 1*
Bee, Clair 1900- *AuBYP, ConAu 1R*
Beebe, Ann 1919- *BiDL 5, ConAu 41*
Beebe, B F 1920- *ConAu 1R, SmATA 1,*
WrD
Beebe, B F *see* Beebe, Burdetta Faye
Beebe, Burdetta Faye 1920- *ForWC 1970*
Beebe, Burdetta Faye *see* Beebe, B F
Beebe, William 1877-1962 *AmA&B, AmLY,*
ConAmA, ConAmL, CurB 41, CurB 62,
DcLEnL, EvLB, OxAm, REnAL, St&VC,
TwCA, TwCA Sup, WNAA
Beech, Webb *ConAu XR, SmATA 5*
Beech, Webb *see* Butterworth, W E
Beeching, Jack *ConAu 21R*
Beeching, Jack *see* Barbary, James
Beecroft, John William Richard 1902-1966
AmA&B, AuBYP, ConAu 5R
Beeding, Francis 1885-1944 *CurB 43, DcLEnL,*
EncM&D, EvLB, LongC, MnBBF,
NCHEL, TwCA, TwCA Sup, TwCW
Beeding, Francis *see* Palmer, John Leslie
Beeding, Francis *see* Saunders, Hilary Aidan St.
George
Beeks, Graydon 1919- *ConAu 65*
Beeler, Nelson Frederick 1910- *AuBYP,*
ConAu 69, MorJA, SmATA 13
Beer, Kathleen Costello 1926- *ConAu 25R,*
WrD
Beer, Richard *IlBYP, IlCB 1957*
Beers, Dorothy Sands 1917- *ConAu 49,*
SmATA 9
Beers, Lorna 1897- *ConAu 49*
Beers, V Gilbert 1928- *ConAu 49, SmATA 9*
Beery, Mary 1907- *ConAu 5R, ForWC 1970,*
WrD
Beeston, L J *MnBBF, WWBWI A*
Beeston, L J *see* Camden, Richard
Beeston, L J *see* Davies, Lucian
Beetles, Peggy *ChPo S1*
Beeton, Samuel Orchart 1831-1877 *Alli Sup,*
ChPo S1, HsB&A, HsB&A Sup, MnBBF,
WWBWI A
Begay, Harrison *IlBYP*
Behn, Harry 1898-1973 *AmPB, AnCL, ArizL,*
AuBYP, BkCL, ChPo, ChPo S1,
ChPo S2, ConAu 5R, ConAu 53,
IlCB 1946, IlCB 1957, MorBMP, MorJA,
SmATA 2, St&VC
Behnke, Frances L *ConAu 33, SmATA 8*
Behnke, John 1945- *ConAu 69*
Behrens, June York 1925- *AuBYP,*
ConAu 17R, ForWC 1970
Behrman, Carol H 1925- *ConAu 61*
Beiler, Edna 1923- *ConAu 1R, IndAu 1917*
Beim, Jerrold 1910-1957 *AuBYP, JBA 1951*
Beim, Jerrold *see* Anderson, Neil
Beim, Lorraine 1909-1951 *JBA 1951*
Beiser, Arthur *AuBYP*
Beiser, Germaine 1931- *AuBYP, SmATA 11*
Beith, Sir John Hay 1876-1952 *Chambr 3,*
DcLEnL, EvLB, LongC, MnBBF,
NCHEL, REn, TwCA, TwCA Sup
Beitler, Ethel Jane 1906- *ConAu 5R*
Beitler, Stanley 1924- *AuBYP, ConAu 5R*

Belbin, Harry *MnBBF, WWBWI A*
Belbin, Harry *see* Garrish, Harold J
Belden, Shirley *AuBYP*
Belfield, Eversley 1918- *ConAu 25R*
Belfield, Harry Wedgwood *MnBBF,*
WWBWI A
Belfield, Harry Wedgwood *see* Drake, Rupert
Belfield, Harry Wedgwood *see* Grimshaw, Mark
Belfield, Harry Wedgwood *see* Wroxham, Cecil
Belknap, B H *YABC 1*
Belknap, B H *see* Ellis, Edward S
Bell, Anthea *ChPo S1*
Bell, Catherine Douglas d1861 *Alli Sup,*
CarSB, DcEnL
Bell, Corydon Whitten 1894- *AuBYP, ChPo,*
ConAu 5R, IlBYP, IlCB 1946,
IlCB 1957, OhA&B, SmATA 3, ThBJA
Bell, Eileen *ConAu 33*
Bell, Emily Mary *ConAu XR, SmATA XR*
Bell, Emily Mary *see* Cason, Mabel Earp
Bell, Gail Winther 1936- *ChPo S2, ConAu 41*
Bell, George *MnBBF*
Bell, Gertrude 1911- *ConAu 13R, SmATA 12*
Bell, Gina *ConAu XR, SmATA 7*
Bell, Gina *see* Iannone, Jeanne Koppel
Bell, Janet *ConAu XR, SmATA XR*
Bell, Janet *see* Clymer, Eleanor
Bell, John Keble 1875-1928 *ChPo, MnBBF,*
WWBWI A
Bell, John Keble *see* Howard, Keble
Bell, John Keble *see* Methuen, John
Bell, Joseph Newton 1921- *AuBYP,*
ConAu 5R, IndAu 1917, WWW 14
Bell, Kensil 1907- *AuBYP*
Bell, Lettice *CarSB*
Bell, Louise Price *ConAu P-1*
Bell, Margaret Elizabeth 1898- *AmA&B,*
AuBYP, ConAu 1R, CurB 52, MorJA,
SmATA 2
Bell, Norman 1899- *ConAu 61, SmATA 11*
Bell, Raymond Martin 1907- *AmMWS 12P,*
ConAu 29, SmATA 13
Bell, Robert Stanley Warren 1871-1921 *ChPo,*
MnBBF, WWBWI A, WWCL
Bell, Robert Stanley Warren *see* Brett, Hawksley
Bell, Robert Stanley Warren *see* Old Fag
Bell, Thelma Harrington 1896- *AuBYP, ChPo,*
ConAu 1R, OhA&B, SmATA 3, ThBJA
Bell, Whitfield Jenks, Jr. 1914- *DrAS 6H,*
WWA 38
Bell-Zano, Gina *ConAu XR, SmATA 7*
Bell-Zano, Gina *see* Iannone, Jeanne Koppel
Bellairs, John 1938- *ConAu 21R, SmATA 2,*
WrD
Bellamy, R L *MnBBF*
Bellasis, Brian *MnBBF*
Beller, William Stern 1919- *ConAu 5R,*
WWE 14
Bellingham, Cathel *MnBBF*
Belloc, Hilaire 1870-1953 *AnCL, AtlBL,*
AuBYP, BkC 5, CarSB, CasWL,
CatA 1930, Chambr 3, ChPo, ChPo S1,
ChPo S2, CnE&AP, CnMWL, CyWA,
DcLEnL, EvLB, FamPYP, LongC,
ModBL, ModBL Sup, NCHEL, OxEng,
Pen Eng, RAdv 1, REn, TwCA,
TwCA Sup, TwCW, WEAL, WWCL,
WWLA, YABC 1
Belmont, Claude *MnBBF*

Belpre, Pura *AuBYP, BkP*
Belshaw, Michael 1928- *ConAu 21R*
Belting, Natalia Maree 1915- *AuBYP,*
ChPo S2, ConAu 1R, DrAS 6H,
SmATA 6, ThBJA
Belton, John Raynor 1931- *ConAu 69*
Beltran, Alberto 1923- *IlBYP, IlCB 1957,*
WWGA, WWS 13
Belvedere, Lee *ConAu XR, SmATA 7*
Belvedere, Lee *see* Grayland, Valerie Merle
Bemelmans, Ludwig 1898-1962 *AmA&B,*
AmNov, AmPB, Au&ICB, AuBYP,
Cald 1938, ChPo, ChPo S1, ChPo S2,
ChFB 1, CnDAL, CurB 41, CurB 62,
DcLEnL, EncWL, IlBYP, IlCB 1744,
IlCB 1946, IlCB 1957, LongC, MorJA,
OxAm, Pen Am, REn, REnAL, TwCA,
TwCA Sup, TwCW, WWCL, WWGA
Benagh, Jim 1937- *ConAu 57*
Benarde, Melvin Albert 1923?- *AmMWS 12P,*
ConAu 25R, WWE 14
Benary-Isbert, Margot 1889- *AnCL, AuBYP,*
ConAu 5R, MorJA, SmATA 2
Benasutti, Marion 1908- *ConAu 21R,*
SmATA 6
Benchley, Nathaniel Goddard 1915- *AmA&B,*
Au&Wr 6, CelR 3, ConAu 1R, CurB 53,
SmATA 3, WWA 38, WWWor 2,
WorAu, WrD
Benchley, Peter B 1940- *AuNews 2,*
ConAu 17R, ConLC 4, SmATA 3
Benda, Wladyslaw Theodore 1873- *ChPo,*
IlCB 1744
Bender, Lucy Ellen 1942- *ConAu 25R*
Bendick, Jeanne 1919- *AmPB, AuBYP, BkP,*
ConAu 5R, IlCB 1946, IlCB 1957,
MorJA, SmATA 2
Bendick, Robert L 1917- *AuBYP, ConAu 61,*
MorJA, SmATA 11
Benedict, Dorothy Potter 1889- *ConAu P-1,*
SmATA 11
Benedict, Lois Trimble 1902-1967 *ConAu P-2,*
SmATA 12
Benedict, Rex Arthur 1920- *ConAu 17R,*
SmATA 8, WWE 14, WrD
Benedict, Stewart H 1924- *ConAu 13R,*
WWE 14
Benenson, Lawrence A *AuBYP*
Benet, Laura 1884- *AmA&B, AuBYP, ChPo,*
ConAu 9R, JBA 1951, REn, REnAL,
SmATA 3, WWA 38, WWAW 8,
WWE 14
Benet, Rosemary 1898?-1962 *ChPo, FamPYP*
Benet, Stephen Vincent 1898-1943 *AmA&B,*
AnCL, BkCL, CasWL, Chambr 3, ChPo,
ChPo S1, ChPo S2, CnDAL, CnE&AP,
CnMWL, ConAmA, ConAmL, CurB 43,
CyWA, DcLEnL, DcNAA, EncWL,
EvLB, FamPYP, LongC, ModAL, OxAm,
OxEng, Pen Am, RAdv 1, REn, REnAL,
SixAP, St&VC, TwCA, TwCA Sup,
TwCW, WEAL, WNAA, WWTwL,
YABC 1
Benet, Sula 1903- *AmMWS 12S, AuBYP*
Benet, William Rose 1886-1950 *AmA&B,*
ChPo, ChPo S1, ChPo S2, CnDAL,
ConAmA, ConAmL, DcLEnL, LongC,
OxAm, OxEng, Pen Am, REn, REnAL,
TwCA, TwCA Sup, WNAA

Benett, L *WWBWI I*
Benezra, Barbara 1921- *ConAu 13R,*
SmATA 10
Benford, Gregory 1941- *ConAu 69*
Benford, Harry 1917- *AmMWS 12P*
Benham, Leslie 1922- *ConAu 9R*
Benham, Lois 1924- *ConAu 9R*
Benjamin, Nora *ConAu XR*
Benjamin, Nora *see* Kubie, Nora Gottheil
Benjamin
Bennett, Anna Elizabeth 1914- *ChPo,*
ConAu 17R
Bennett, C N *MnBBF*
Bennett, C N *see* Collier, Norman
Bennett, Charles Moon 1899- *Au&Wr 6,*
EarAB Sup, MnBBF, WWBWI A, WrD
Bennett, Dorothea *ConAu XR*
Bennett, Dorothea *see* Young, Dorothea Bennett
Bennett, Eve *AuBYP*
Bennett, Fred 1877- *WWBWI I*
Bennett, Geoffrey Martin 1909- *Au&Wr 6,*
WW 1974, WrD
Bennett, Hilda R *MnBBF*
Bennett, Jay 1912- *ConAu 69*
Bennett, John *MnBBF*
Bennett, John 1865-1956 *AmA&B, BlkAW,*
CarSB, ChPo, ChPo S1, ConICB,
DcAmA, IlCB 1744, JBA 1934,
JBA 1951, OhA&B, OxAm, REnAL,
YABC 1
Bennett, John 1920- *ConAu 29, DrAP 1975,*
DrAS 6E
Bennett, Rainey 1907- *IlBYP, IlCB 1957,*
IndAu 1917, WWA 38
Bennett, Richard 1899- *IlBYP, IlCB 1744,*
IlCB 1946, JBA 1951
Bennett, Rolfe 1882- *MnBBF*
Bennett, Russell Hoadley 1896- *WWA 38*
Bennett, Susan *IlBYP*
Benson, Edward Frederic 1867-1940 *BbD,*
BiD&SB, Chambr 3, CurB 40,
DcEnA Ap, DcLEnL, EvLB, LongC,
MnBBF, ModBL, NCHEL, OxEng,
Pen Eng, TwCA, TwCW, WWBWI A
Benson, Mildred W 1905?- *AuBYP,*
ForWC 1970, OhA&B
Benson, Richard *MnBBF*
Benson, Sally 1900-1972 *AmA&B, BiEnAT,*
CnDAL, ConAu P-1, CurB 41, CurB 72,
NYTBE 3, OxAm, REn, REnAL,
SmATA 1, TwCA Sup
Bentel, Pearl Bucklen 1901- *AuBYP,*
ConAu P-2
Bentley, Nicolas Clerihew 1907- *Au&Wr 6,*
ChPo, ChPo S1, ChPo S2, ConAu 65,
IlCB 1744, IntWW 38, LongC, NCHEL,
WW 1974, WWWor 2
Bentley, Phyllis Eleanor 1894- *Au&Wr 6,*
ConAu 1R, DcLEnL, EncM&D, EvLB,
IntWW 38, LongC, ModBL, NCHEL,
Pen Eng, RAdv 1, REn, SmATA 6,
TwCA, TwCA Sup, TwCW, WW 1974
Benton, Clive *MnBBF*
Benton, Patricia 1907- *ConAu 5R, WrD*
Benton, Robert 1932- *AmA&B, ConAu 1R,*
ConDr 1
Benton, Thomas Hart 1889-1975 *AmA&B,*
CelR 3, CurB 40, DcCAA 2, IlCB 1744,
IlCB 1946, IntWW 38, OxAm, REn,

*REnAL, WWA 38, WWAA 1973,
WWWor 2*
Bere, Rennie Montague 1907- *Au&Wr 6,
WW 1974, WrD*
Berelson, Howard 1940- *IlBYP, SmATA 5*
Berenstain, Janice 1923- *AmA&B,
ConAu 25R, SmATA 12, AuBYP*
Berenstain, Stanley 1923- *AmA&B, AuBYP,
ChPo S1, ConAu 25R, SmATA 12,
WWAA 1973*
Beresford, Elisabeth *SingR 1*
Beresford, John *MnBBF, WWBWI A*
Beresford, John *see* Rochester, George Ernest
Beresford, Leslie *MnBBF, WWBWI A*
Berg, Dave *ConAu XR*
Berg, Dave *see* Berg, David
Berg, David 1920- *ConAu 21R*
Berg, David *see* Berg, Dave
Berg, Hans 1877- *WWLA*
Berg, Jean Horton Lutz 1913- *ChPo S1,
ConAu 53, ForWC 1970, SmATA 6,
WWAW 8, WWE 14*
Berg, Joan *IlCB 1957*
Berg, Joan *see* Victor, Joan Berg
Bergaust, Erik 1925- *AmA&B, AuBYP,
WWA 38*
Berger, Josef 1903-1971 *AmA&B, ConAu 5R,
ConAu 33, NYTBE 2*
Berger, Josef *see* Digges, Jeremiah
Berger, Melvin H 1927- *AuBYP, ConAu 5R,
SmATA 5*
Berger, Phil 1942- *ConAu 61*
Berger, Terry 1933- *ConAu 37, SmATA 8,
WrD*
Berger, William Merritt 1872- *ChPo, ConICB*
Bergere, Richard *WWAA 1973*
Bergere, Thea Lindgren 1933- *AmA&B,
AuBYP*
Bergey, Alyce 1934- *ConAu 5R*
Bergstrom, Louise 1914- *ConAu 29*
Berk, Phyllis Lavine *ForWC 1970*
Berkebile, Fred D 1900- *ConAu 5R*
Berkeley, Anthony 1893-1970 *EncM&D,
LongC, MnBBF, TwCA, TwCA Sup*
Berkeley, Anthony *see* Cox, Anthony Berkeley
Berkey, Helen L 1898- *ConAu P-2*
Berkman, Edward O 1914- *ConAu 61*
Berkman, Edward O *see* Berkman, Ted
Berkman, Ted *ConAu XR*
Berkman, Ted *see* Berkman, Edward O
Berkowitz, Freda Pastor 1910- *AuBYP,
ConAu P-1, SmATA 12*
Berliner, Franz 1930- *ConAu 29, SmATA 13*
Berna, Paul 1910?- *Au&Wr 6, AuBYP,
ThBJA*
Bernadette *ConAu XR, SmATA 4*
Bernadette *see* Watts, Bernadette
Bernard, Jacqueline 1921- *ConAu 21R,
SmATA 8*
Bernays, Anne *ConAu XR, DrAF 1976*
Bernays, Anne *see* Kaplan, Anne Bernays
Bernays, Edward L 1891- *AmA&B,
ConAu 17R, CurB 42, CurB 60, REnAL,
WNAA, WWA 38, WWWor 2,
WWWorJ 1972*
Berndt, Walter *ArtCS*
Berne, Eric 1910-1970 *ConAu 5R,
ConAu 25R, NYTBE 1*
Bernhardsen, Bris *ConAu XR*

Bernhardsen, Bris *see* Bernhardsen, Christian
Bernhardsen, Christian 1923- *ConAu 29*
Bernhardsen, Christian *see* Bernhardsen, Bris
Bernheim, Evelyne 1935- *ConAu 21R*
Bernheim, Marc 1924- *ConAu 21R*
Bernstein, Leonard 1918- *AmA&B,
AmSCAP 66, BiEnAT, CelR 3,
ConAu 1R, CurB 44, CurB 60,
IntWW 38, McGWD, NYTBE 3,
NYTBE 3, OxAm, REn, REnAL,
WW 1974, WWA 38, WWE 14,
WWMus 6, WWT 15, WWWor 2,
WWWorJ 1972*
Bernstein, Margery 1933- *ConAu 57*
Bernstein, Ralph 1877- *WNAA*
Bernstein, Ralph 1921- *AuBYP*
Bernstein, Theodore M 1904- *ConAu 1R,
NYTBE 3, SmATA 12, WNAA,
WWA 38, WWWorJ 1972*
Bernstein, Zena *ChPo S1, IlBYP*
Berquin, Arnaud 1749-1791 *CarSB, ChPo,
ChPo S1, OxFr*
Berrien, Edith Heal *ConAu XR, SmATA 7,
ForWC 1970*
Berrien, Edith Heal *see* Heal, Edith
Berrill, Jacquelyn 1905- *AuBYP, ConAu 17R,
IlCB 1957, SmATA 12*
Berrill, N J 1903- *AmMWS 12P, ConAu 17R*
Berrington, John *ConAu XR, SmATA 6*
Berrington, John *see* Brownjohn, Alan
Berrisford, Judith Mary 1912- *Au&Wr 6,
AuBYP*
Berry, Barbara J 1937- *ConAu 33, SmATA 7,
WrD*
Berry, Erick 1892- *AmPB, AuBYP, ChPo,
ConAu XR, ConICB, DcNAA,
IlCB 1946, JBA 1934, JBA 1951,
SmATA 2*
Berry, Erick *see* Best, Allena Champlin
Berry, James 1932- *ConAu 21R*
Berry, James *see* Berry, Jim
Berry, Jim *ConAu XR*
Berry, Jim *see* Berry, James
Berry, Len *MnBBF, WWBWI A*
Berry, William David 1926- *AuBYP,
IlCB 1957*
Berson, Harold 1926- *ChPo, ConAu 33,
IlBYP, IlCB 1957, SmATA 4*
Bertelli, Luigi 1858-1920 *CarSB*
Bertie *MnBBF*
Bertin, Leonard M 1918- *Au&Wr 6,
ConAu 13R*
Berton, Pierre 1920- *Au&Wr 6, CanWW 12,
CanWr, ConAu 1R, OxCan, OxCan Sup,
WWE 14, WrD*
Berwick, Jean 1929- *ConAu 9R, SmATA XR*
Berwick, Jean *see* Meyer, Jean Shepherd
Besier, George *MnBBF*
Beskow, Elsa 1874- *AnCL, BkCL, ChPo S2,
ConICB, IlCB 1744, JBA 1934,
JBA 1951*
Besser, Marianne *ForWC 1970*
Best, Allena Champlin 1892-1974 *AuBYP,
ConAu P-2, IlCB 1744, IlCB 1946,
JBA 1934, JBA 1951, SmATA 2*
Best, Allena Champlin *see* Berry, Erick
Best, Allena Champlin *see* Maxon, Anne
Best, Herbert 1894- *AmA&B, AmNov,
AuBYP, ConAu P-2, JBA 1934,*

JBA 1951, SmATA 2
Bestall, A E *WWBWI 1*
Bester, Alfred 1913- *AmA&B, ConAu 13R*
Beston, Henry 1888-1968 *AmA&B, ConAu 25R, JBA 1934, JBA 1951, OxCan, REnAL, TwCA, TwCA Sup*
Beston, Henry *see* Sheahan, Henry Beston
Beth, Mary *ConAu XR, SmATA XR*
Bethancourt, T Ernesto 1932- *ChLR 3, ConAu XR, SmATA 11*
Bethancourt, T Ernesto *see* Paisley, Tom
Bethell, Jean 1922- *ConAu 9R, SmATA 8*
Bethers, Ray 1902- *Au&Wr 6, AuBYP, ConAu P-1, SmATA 6*
Bethune, J G *HsB&A, YABC 1*
Bethune, J G *see* Ellis, Edward S
Bettina 1903- *AuBYP, ConAu XR, IICB 1946, IICB 1957, MorJA, REn, SmATA 1*
Bettina *see* Ehrlich, Bettina Bauer
Bettmann, Otto L 1903- *BiEnAT*
Bettmann, Otto Ludwig 1903- *ConAu 17R, CurB 61, WWA 38, WWAA 1973, WWWor 2*
Betts, Ethel Franklin *ChPo, ChPo S1*
Betz, Betty 1920- *AuBYP, ConAu 1R, MorJA*
Betz, Eva Kelly 1897-1968 *BkC 5, ConAu P-1, SmATA 10*
Betz, Eva Kelly *see* Peters, Caroline
Bevan, Tom 1868-1930? *MnBBF, WWBWI A, WWCL, YABC 2*
Bevan, Tom *see* Bamfylde, Walter
Bevans, Margaret *AuBYP*
Bevans, Michael H *AuBYP*
Bewick, John 1760?-1795 *Alli, CarSB, ChPo S1*
Bewick, Thomas 1753-1828 *Alli, BkIE, CarSB, ChPo, ChPo S1, ChPo S2, DcLEnL, NCHEL, St&VC, WWCL*
Bewley, Christopher *MnBBF*
Bey, R R Hubbard *MnBBF*
Beyer, Audrey White 1916- *ConAu 13R, ForWC 1970, SmATA 9*
Beyer, Evelyn M 1907- *ConAu P-2*
Beynon, John *MnBBF, WorAu*
Beynon, John *see* Harris, John Wyndham Parkes Lucas Beynon
Bial, Morrison David 1917- *ConAu 61, WWWorJ 1972*
Bialk, Elisa 1912- *ConAu XR, CurB 54, ForWC 1970, MorJA, SmATA 1*
Bialk, Elisa *see* Krautter, Elisa
Bianco, Margery Williams 1881-1944 *AmA&B, AnCL, AuBYP, BkCL, DcNAA, JBA 1934, JBA 1951, NCHEL, St&VC, WWCL*
Bianco, Pamela 1906- *AuBYP, ChPo, ConICB, IICB 1744, IICB 1946, JBA 1934, JBA 1951, WWAW 8*
Bianki, Vitali *AuBYP*
Bibby, Cyril 1914- *Au&Wr 6, ConAu 13R, WW 1974*
Bibby, Dause Leveridge 1911- *WWA 38*
Bible, Charles 1937- *ConAu 69, IIBYP, SmATA 13*
Bice, Clare 1909- *AuBYP, CanWW 12, IICB 1946, Prof, WWA 38, WWAA 1973*

Bickham, Jack Miles 1930- *AmA&B, ConAu 5R, WWA 38*
Bidston, Lester 1884- *MnBBF, WWBWI A*
Bidston, Lester *see* Hotspur, Paul
Biegel, Paul 1925- *Au&Wr 6, WrD*
Bielski, Alison Joy Prosser 1925- *ConP 1970, WrD*
Bierhorst, John 1936- *ConAu 33, SmATA 6*
Biesterveld, Betty Parsons 1923- *ConAu 1R*
Bigelow, Robert S 1918- *Au&Wr 6, WrD*
Biggers, Earl Derr 1884-1933 *AmA&B, ChPo S1, DcNAA, EncM&D, EvLB, MnBBF, OhA&B, OxAm, Pen Am, REn, REnAL, TwCA, TwCW, WNAA*
Bileck, Marvin 1920- *AmPB, IIBYP, IICB 1946, IICB 1957, WWAA 1973*
Bill, Alfred Hoyt 1879- *AmA&B, JBA 1934, JBA 1951, MnnWr*
Billings, Buck *MnBBF*
Billings, Henry 1901- *AmA&B, IICB 1946, MorJA, WWAA 1973*
Billings, Peggy 1928- *ConAu 25R*
Billout, Guy Rene 1941- *SmATA 10*
Binder, Eando *AuBYP, ConAu XR*
Binder, Eando *see* Binder, Otto Oscar
Binder, Otto Oscar 1911-1974 *AuBYP, ConAu 1R, ConAu 53*
Binder, Otto Oscar *see* Binder, Eando
Binder, Pearl 1904- *Au&Wr 6, IICB 1744, IICB 1946*
Bindloss, Harold 1866-1945 *LongC, MnBBF, OxCan, TwCA, TwCA Sup, WWLA*
Bingham, Arthur, Major *MnBBF*
Bingham, Arthur, Major *see* Rowe, W
Bingham, Evangeline M L 1899- *ConAu 65*
Bingham, Evangeline M L *see* Elliot, Geraldine
Bingley, David Ernest 1920- *ConAu 45*
Bingley, David Ernest *see* Roberts, John
Bingley, Thomas *Alli Sup, CarSB*
Binks, Robert *ChPo S2*
Binn, Mark A *IIBYP*
Binns, Archie 1899- *AmA&B, AmNov, OxAm, REnAL, TwCA, TwCA Sup, WWPNA*
Birch, Cyril 1925- *DrAS 6F*
Birch, J Weedon *MnBBF*
Birch, Reginald Bathurst 1856-1943 *ChPo, ChPo S1, ChPo S2, ConICB, CurB 43, JBA 1951*
Birchwood, Reginald *MnBBF*
Bird, Alice *IIBYP*
Bird, Anthony 1917- *ConAu 13R*
Bird, Caroline 1915- *ConAu 17R, ForWC 1970, WWAW 8*
Bird, Dorothy Maywood 1899- *ConAu P-1, WrD*
Bird, Lewis *MnBBF, WWBWI A*
Bird, Lewis *see* Hayter, Cecil Goodenough
Bird, Maria *WWCL*
Bird, Richard *MnBBF, WWBWI A*
Bird, Richard *see* Barradale-Smith, William
Birmingham, Lloyd 1924- *SmATA 12*
Birnage, Derek A W *MnBBF*
Birnage, Derek A W *see* Birnage, Dick
Birnage, Derek A W *see* Windsor, Frank
Birnage, Dick *MnBBF*
Birnage, Dick *see* Birnage, Derek A W
Biro, B S 1921- *ConAu 25R*
Biro, B S *see* Biro, Val

Biro, Balint S 1921- *IICB 1946*

Biro, Val 1921- *Au&Wr 6, ConAu XR, IIBYP, IICB 1957, SmATA 1*

Biro, Val *see* Biro, B S

Bischoff, Ilse Marthe 1903?- *AuBYP, ChPo, ChPo S1, ChPo S2, ConICB, IICB 1744, IICB 1946, MorJA*

Bischoff, Julia Bristol 1909-1970 *AuBYP, ConAu P-2, SmATA 12*

Bischoff, Julia Bristol *see* Arnoldy, Julie

Bishop, Claire Huchet *AmPB, AuBYP, BkP, CatA 1952, FamMS, JBA 1951*

Bishop, Curtis Kent 1912-1967 *AuBYP, ConAu P-1, SmATA 6*

Bishop, Curtis Kent *see* Brandon, Curt

Bishop, Curtis Kent *see* Carroll, Curt

Bishop, Elizabeth 1911- *AmA&B, Au&Wr 6, CelR 3, ChPo, ChPo S1, CnE&AP, ConAu 5R, ConLC 1, ConLC 4, ConP 1970, ConP 1975, CrCAP, DrAP 1975, EncWL, IntWW 38, ModAL, ModAL Sup, OxAm, Pen Am, RAdv 1, , REn, REnAL, TwCA Sup, TwCW, WEAL, WWA 38, WWAW 8, WWE 14, WWWor 2*

Bishop, Grace *AuBYP*

Bishop, James Alonzo 1907- *ConAu 17R*

Bishop, Jim 1907- *AmA&B, AuNews 1, AuNews 2, CelR 3, ConAu XR, CurB 69, DrAP 1975, REnAL, WWA 38, WWS 13, WWWor 2*

Bishop, Julian Truitt *MnBBF*

Bishop, Percy Cook *MnBBF, WWBWI A*

Bishop, Percy Cook *see* Cooke, Percival

Biskin, Miriam 1920- *ConAu 21R*

Bisset, Donald 1910- *Au&Wr 6, ConAu 33, SmATA 7*

Bitter, Gary G 1940- *AmMWS 12P, LE 5, WWW 14*

Bixby, William Courtney 1920- *AmA&B, AuBYP, ConAu 1R, SmATA 6, WWA 38*

Bjorklund, Lorence F *IIBYP, IICB 1946, IICB 1957*

Black, Miss *CarSB*

Black, Algernon David 1900- *ConAu 1R, SmATA 12*

Black, Cyril Edwin 1915- *AmA&B, ConAu 1R, DrAS 6H, WWA 38, WWE 14, WWWor 2*

Black, Ian Stuart 1915- *MnBBF*

Black, Irma Simonton 1906-1972 *AuBYP, ConAu 1R, ConAu 37, SmATA 2*

Black, Ladbroke Lionel Day 1877-1940 *ChPo S1, MnBBF, WWBWI A*

Black, Ladbroke Lionel Day *see* Day, Lionel

Black, Ladbroke Lionel Day *see* Meech, Thomas Cox

Black, Ladbroke Lionel Day *see* Urquhart, Paul

Black, Mansell *ConAu XR*

Black, Mansell *see* Trevor, Elleston

Black, Margaret K 1921- *Au&Wr 6, ConAu 29*

Black, Margaret K *see* Howorth, M K

Blackburn, Edith H *AuBYP*

Blackburn, Joyce Knight 1920- *ConAu 17R, IndAu 1917, WWAW 8*

Blackett, Veronica Heath 1927- *Au&Wr 6, ConAu 53, SmATA 12, WrD*

Blackett, Veronica Heath *see* Heath, Veronica

Blackledge, William James 1886- *MnBBF*

Blackmore, Fred *MnBBF*

Blackmore, Richard Doddridge 1825-1900 *Alli Sup, BbD, BiD&SB, BrAu 19, Chambr 3, ChPo, ChPo S1, ChPo S2, CyWA, DcBiA, DcEnA, DcEnA Ap, DcEnL, DcEuL, DcLEnL, EvLB, JBA 1934, MouLC 4, NCHEL, OxEng, Pen Eng, REn, TelT, WEAL*

Blackstock, Charity 1888- *Au&Wr 6, TwCW*

Blackwood, Paul E 1913- *AmMWS 12P, LE 5*

Blackwood, William *MnBBF*

Blades, Ann *OxCan Sup, Prof*

Bladow, Suzanne Wilson 1937- *ConAu 61*

Blaikley, Ernest *MnBBF*

Blaiklock, E M *MnBBF*

Blain, W *MnBBF*

Blaine, John *ConAu XR, SmATA 6*

Blaine, John *see* Goodwin, Harold Leland

Blaine, John *see* Harkins, Philip

Blaine, Marge *ConAu XR, SmATA XR*

Blaine, Marge *see* Blaine, Margery Kay

Blaine, Margery Kay 1937- *ConAu 61, SmATA 11*

Blaine, Margery Kay *see* Blaine, Marge

Blair, Allan *MnBBF, WWBWI A*

Blair, Allan *see* Bayfield, William John

Blair, Anthony *MnBBF*

Blair, Anthony *see* Walker, Rowland

Blair, Clay, Jr. 1925- *AmA&B, AuNews 2*

Blair, David *WWBWI A*

Blair, David *see* Goyne, Richard

Blair, Edward *MnBBF*

Blair, Erskine *MnBBF*

Blair, Helen 1910- *IIBYP, IICB 1946, WWAA 1973*

Blair, Lucile *ConAu XR*

Blair, Lucile *see* Yeakley, Marjory Hall

Blair, Mary Robinson 1911- *IICB 1946*

Blair, Ruth VanNess 1912- *ConAu 21R, SmATA 12, WWAW 8, WrD*

Blair, Walter 1900- *AmA&B, AuBYP, ChPo, ConAu 5R, DrAS 6E, REnAL, SmATA 12, WWA 38*

Blaisdell, Elinore 1904- *IIBYP, IICB 1744, IICB 1946*

Blake, Bernard *MnBBF*

Blake, Bud *ConAu 65*

Blake, Bud *see* Blake, Julian Watson

Blake, C J *MnBBF*

Blake, C W *WWBWI I*

Blake, Julian Watson 1918- *ConAu 65*

Blake, Julian Watson *see* Blake, Bud

Blake, Paul *MnBBF, WWBWI A*

Blake, Paul *see* Paull, Harry Major

Blake, Quentin 1932- *ArtsCL, ChPo S1, ConAu 25R, IIBYP, IICB 1957, SmATA 9*

Blake, Robert *MnBBF*

Blake, Royston *MnBBF*

Blake, Royston *see* Childs, Edmund Burton

Blake, Sexton *MnBBF, WWBWI A*

Blake, Stacey 1878-1964 *MnBBF, WWBWI A*

Blake, Walker E *ConAu XR*

Blake, Walker E *see* Butterworth, W E

Blake, Walter E *SmATA 5*

Blake, William 1757-1827 *Alli, AnCL, AtlBL, BbD, BiD&SB, BiDLA, BkIE, BrAu 19,*

CarSB, CasWL, Chambr 2, ChP, ChPo,
ChPo S1, ChPo S2, CnE&AP, CriT 2,
CyWA, DcEnA, DcEnA Ap, DcEnL,
DcEuL, DcLEnL, EvLB, FamPYP,
MouLC 3, NCHEL, OxEng, Pen Eng,
RAdv 1, RCom, REn, St&VC, WEAL
Blake, Wilton, Captain *MnBBF, WWBWI A,*
WWCL
Blake, Wilton, Captain *see* Parry, David Harold
Blakeley, Phyllis 1922- *ConAu 61, OxCan*
Blakesley, Stephen *MnBBF, WWBWI A*
Blakesley, Stephen *see* Bond, F
Blance, Ellen 1931- *ConAu 57*
Blanchard, Amy Ella 1856-1926 *BiD&SB,*
BiDSA, CarSB, ChPo, ChPo S1,
ChPo S2, DcAmA, DcNAA
Blanco, Tomas 1900- *PueRA*
Bland, Edith Nesbit 1858-1924 *AuBYP, ChPo,*
ChPo S1, ChPo S2, EvLB, JBA 1934,
NCHEL, TwCA, TwCA Sup, YABC 1
Bland, Edith Nesbit *see* Nesbit, E
Bland, Fabian *LongC, YABC 1*
Bland, Fabian *see* Nesbit, E
Blanton, Catherine 1907- *AuBYP, ConAu 1R*
Blanzaco, Andre C 1934- *ConAu 29*
Blassingame, Wyatt Rainey 1909- *AuBYP,*
ConAu 1R, SmATA 1, WrD
Blathwayt, Jean 1918- *Au&Wr 6, WrD*
Blatter, Dorothy 1901- *ConAu P-1*
Blaushild, Babette 1927- *ConAu 29*
Blayne, Roger *MnBBF*
Blaze, Don *MnBBF*
Bleeker, Sonia 1909- *BkP, ConAu XR,*
ForWC 1970, MorJA, SmATA 2
Blegvad, Erik 1923- *ChPo, IlBYP, IlCB 1946,*
IlCB 1957, ThBJA
Blegvad, Lenore 1926- *ConAu 69, ThBJA*
Bleich, Alan R 1913- *ConAu 13R*
Bleiler, E F *ChPo S2*
Bligh, William 1754-1817 *Alli, BiDLA,*
NCHEL, REn
Blinders, Belinda *MnBBF, WWBWI A*
Blinders, Belinda *see* Coke, Desmond
Blish, James 1921-1975 *AmA&B, Au&Wr 6,*
ConAu 1R, ConNov 1976, WorAu, WrD
Blishen, Edward 1920- *Au&Wr 6, ChPo,*
ConAu 17R, SmATA 8, WrD
Bliss, Michael *OxCan Sup*
Bliss, Ronald G 1942- *ConAu 53, SmATA 12*
Blitch, Fleming Lee 1933- *ConAu 9R*
Blitzer, Charles 1927- *WWA 38*
Bliven, Bruce 1889- *AmA&B, Au&Wr 6,*
AuBYP, ConAu 37, CurB 41, IntWW 38,
TwCA, TwCA Sup, WW 1974, WWW 14
WWA 38, WWW 14
Bliven, Bruce, Jr. 1916- *ConAu 17R,*
SmATA 2, WWA 38
Bliven, Naomi 1925- *ConAu 33, WWA 38,*
WWAW 8
Bloch, Lucienne 1909- *IlBYP, IlCB 1744,*
IlCB 1946, SmATA 10
Bloch, Marie Halun 1910- *Au&Wr 6, AuBYP,*
ConAu 1R, ForWC 1970, SmATA 6,
WrD
Bloch, Robert 1917- *AmA&B, ConAu 5R,*
DrAF 1976, EncM&D, IntMPA 1975,
SmATA 12
Blochman, Lawrence G 1900-1975 *ConAu 53,*
ConAu P-2, EncM&D, WNAA,

WWWorJ 1972
Block, Eugene B 1890- *ConAu 5R,*
WWWorJ 1972
Block, Irvin 1917- *ConAu 17R, SmATA 12*
Bloomer, Jack *MnBBF*
Bloomer, Jack *see* Lynch, John Gilbert Bohun
Bloomer, Steve *see* Jones, J G
Bloomer, Steven *MnBBF*
Bloomfield, Diana *ChPo*
Bloomfield, Robert 1766-1823 *Alli, BbD,*
BiD&SB, BiDLA, BrAu 19, CarSB,
CasWL, Chambr 2, ChPo, ChPo S1,
ChPo S2, DcEnL, DcLEnL, EvLB,
NCHEL, OxEng, WEAL
Bloomstein, Morris J 1928- *ConAu 25R*
Blough, Glenn Orlando 1907- *AmA&B,*
AuBYP, ConAu P-1, LE 5, MorJA,
SmATA 1, WWA 38
Bloundelle-Burton, John Edward 1850- *MnBBF*
Blue, Rose 1931- *ConAu 41, SmATA 5,*
WWAW 8
Blue, Wallace *ConAu XR*
Blue, Wallace *see* Kraenzel, Margaret
Bluett, A T Q *MnBBF*
Blumberg, Rhoda 1917- *ConAu 65*
Blumberg, Stanley 1921- *AmMWS 12S*
Blume, Judy 1938- *ChLR 2, ConAu 29, PiP,*
SmATA 2, WrD
Blumenfeld, Harold 1908- *WWWorJ 1972*
Blumenthal, Lassor Agoos 1926- *ConAu 25R,*
WWE 14
Blunt, Don *ConAu XR*
Blunt, Don *see* Booth, Edwin
Blust, Earl R *IlBYP*
Blutig, Eduard *ConAu XR*
Blutig, Eduard *see* Gorey, Edward St. John
Blyth, Harry 1852-1898 *Alli Sup, EncM&D,*
MnBBF, WWBWI A, WWCL
Blyth, Harry *see* Daring, Major
Blyth, Harry *see* Meredith, Hal
Blyth, Harry *see* Paul, Policeman
Blyth, Harry *see* Sinclair, Captain
Blyth, Spencer R *MnBBF*
Blyton, Carey 1932- *ChPo S2, ConAu 49,*
SmATA 9, WWMus 6
Blyton, Enid Mary 1898?-1968 *AuBYP, ChPo,*
ChPo S1, ChPo S2, ConAu 25R, LongC,
WWCL
Boardman, Fon Wyman, Jr. 1911- *ConAu 1R,*
SmATA 6, WrD
Boardman, Gwenn R 1924- *ConAu 45,*
SmATA 12
Boatner, Mark Mayo, III 1921- *ConAu 21R*
Bobbe, Dorothie DeBear 1905-1975 *ConAu P-2,*
SmATA 1
Bobin, Donald E M *MnBBF, WWBWI A*
Bobin, Donald E M *see* Halliday, Shirley
Bobin, Donald E M *see* Lawson, Warren J
Bobin, John William d1935 *MnBBF,*
WWBWI A
Bobin, John William *see* Ascott, Adele
Bobin, John William *see* Ascott, John
Bobin, John William *see* Ironside, Matthew
Bobin, John William *see* Nelson, Gertrude
Bobin, John William *see* Nelson, Steve
Bobin, John William *see* Nelson, Victor
Bobin, John William *see* Osborne, Mark
Bobri, V 1898- *ForIl, IlBYP, IlCB 1946,*
IlCB 1957

Bobri, V see Bobritsky, Vladimir
Bobritsky, Vladimir 1898- IIBYP, IICB 1744,
   IICB 1946, IICB 1957
Bobritsky, Vladimir see Bobri, V
Boccaccio, Giovanni 1313-1375 AtlBL, BbD,
   BiD&SB, CasWL, CyWA, DcBiA,
   DcEnL, DcEuL, EuAu, EvEuW, NCHEL,
   OxEng, Pen Eur, RCom, REn
Bock, Hal ConAu XR, SmATA XR
Bock, Hal see Bock, Harold I
Bock, Harold I 1939- ConAu 29, SmATA 10
Bock, Harold I see Bock, Hal
Bock, Vera ChPo, ChPo S1, ChPo S2,
   ConICB, IIBYP, IICB 1744, IICB 1946,
   IICB 1957, MorJA, WWAA 1973
Bock, William Sauts IIBYP
Bock, William Sauts see Netamuxwe
Bode, Carl 1911- AmA&B, Au&Wr 6,
   ConAu 1R, DrAP 1975, DrAS 6E,
   WWA 38, WWWor 2
Bodecker, N M 1922- ConAu 49, WrD
Bodecker, Nils Mogens 1922- ChPo S1,
   ChPo S2, IIBYP, IICB 1946, IICB 1957,
   SmATA 8
Boden, Hilda ConAu XR, SmATA XR
Boden, Hilda see Bodenham, Hilda Morris
Bodenham, Hilda Morris 1901- ConAu 9R,
   SmATA 13
Bodenham, Hilda Morris see Boden, Hilda
Bodenham, Hilda Morris see Welch, Pauline
Bodie, Idella F 1925- ConAu 41, SmATA 12
Boeckman, Charles 1920- ConAu 13R,
   SmATA 12
Boegehold, Betty 1913- AuBYP, ChPo S1,
   ConAu 69
Boegehold, Betty see Doyle, Donovan
Boesch, Mark J 1917- ConAu 21R,
   SmATA 12, WWPNA
Boesen, Victor 1908- ConAu 37, IndAu 1917
Boff, Charles MnBBF
Bogan, Louise 1897-1970 AmA&B, AuBYP,
   ChPo, CnDAL, CnE&AP, ConAmA,
   ConAu 25R, ConLC 4, ConP 1970,
   DcLEnL, EncWL, ModAL, ModAL Sup,
   NYTBE 1, OxAm, Pen Am, RAdv 1,
   REn, REnAL, SixAP, TwCA,
   TwCA Sup, TwCW
Boggs, Ralph Steele 1901- AnCL, AuBYP,
   ConAu P-1, DcSpL, DrAS 6F,
   IndAu 1917, SmATA 7, WNAA
Bogue, J Russell WWBWI A
Bohannan, Paul 1920- ConAu 9R
Bohle, Bruce 1918- ConAu 21R
Bohr, Theophilus ConAu XR
Bohr, Theophilus see Thistle, Mel
Boker, Irving IIBYP
Boland, Charles Michael 1917- ConAu 9R
Boland, Lillian C 1919- ConAu 29
Bolden, Joseph IIBYP
Boldrewood, Rolf 1826-1915 Alli Sup,
   BiD&SB, CasWL, Chambr 3, ChPo,
   DcLEnL, EvLB, LongC, NCHEL,
   OxEng, Pen Eng, REn, SingR 2, WEAL
Boldrewood, Rolf see Browne, T A
Bolee, Harold MnBBF
Boles, Paul Darcy 1919- Au&Wr 6,
   ConAu 9R, CurB 56, IndAu 1917,
   SmATA 9, WWS 13
Bolian, Polly 1925- ConAu 33, IIBYP,

SmATA 4
Bolin, Mayne MnBBF
Bolingbroke, William MnBBF
Bolingbroke, William see Home-Gall, William
   Bolinbroke
Bollen, Roger 1942?- ArtCS, AuNews 1,
   BiN 1974
Bolliger, Max 1929- ConAu 25R, SmATA 7
Bolognese, Donald Alan 1934- ChPo S1,
   ChPo S2, IIBYP, IICB 1957
Bolton, Carole 1926- ConAu 49, SmATA 6
Bolton, Charles MnBBF
Bolton, Evelyn ConAu XR
Bolton, Evelyn see Bunting, Anne Evelyn
Bolton, F H MnBBF, WWBWI A
Bolton, F T MnBBF
Bolton, F T see Ash, Derek
Bolton, F T see Hammond, Wally
Bolton, Henry Carrington 1843-1903 Alli Sup,
   BiD&SB, ChPo S1, DcAmA, DcNAA,
   St&VC
Bolton, Hugh WWBWI A
Bolton, Hugh see Gibbons, Harry Hornaby
   Clifford
Bolton, Ivy May 1879- AuBYP
Bolton, Sarah Knowles 1841-1916 Alli Sup,
   AmA, AmA&B, BbD, BiD&SB, CarSB,
   ChPo, ChPo S1, ChPo S2, DcAmA,
   DcNAA, OhA&B
Bomans, Godfried Jan Arnold 1913-1971
   ConAu P-2, WWWor 2
Bombeck, Erma 1927- AuNews 1,
   ConAu 21R
Bond, F MnBBF
Bond, F see Blakesley, Stephen
Bond, Geoffrey 1924- Au&Wr 6, ConAu 29
Bond, Gladys Baker 1912- ConAu 5R,
   ForWC 1970, WWAW 8, WWPNA,
   WWW 14
Bond, Gladys Baker see Mendel, Jo
Bond, J Harvey ConAu XR, SmATA XR
Bond, J Harvey see Winterbotham, R R
Bond, Jean Carey BlkAW
Bond, Michael 1926- Au&Wr 6, BrCA,
   ChLR 1, ConAu 5R, MorBMP,
   SmATA 6, ThBJA, WW 1974, WWCL,
   WrD
Bond, Nancy 1945- ConAu 65
Bond, Raymond T AmA&B
Bond, Richard MnBBF
Bond, Ruskin 1934- ConAu 29
Bond, Stephen MnBBF
Bone, Stephen 1904-1958 IIBYP, IICB 1946,
   LongC
Bonehill, Ralph, Captain ConAu XR, DcNAA
Bonehill, Ralph, Captain see Stratemeyer,
   Edward L
Boney, Mary Lily 1918- ConAu 13R
Bonham, Barbara Thomas 1926- ConAu 17R,
   SmATA 7, WrD
Bonham, Frank 1914- AuBYP, ConAu 9R,
   MorBMP, SmATA 1, ThBJA
Boni, Margaret Bradford 1893?-1974 AmA&B,
   ConAu 53
Bonner, Mary Graham 1890-1974 AmA&B,
   AuBYP, CanNov, CarSB, ChPo,
   ConAu 49, CurB 50, ForWC 1970,
   WNAA
Bonsall, Crosby Barbara Newell 1921- IIBYP,

IlCB 1957, ThBJA
Bonsall, Crosby Barbara Newell *see* Newell,
  Crosby
Bonser, A E *MnBBF*
Bontemps, Arna Wendell 1902-1973 *AmA&B,
  AmNov, AnMV 1926, Au&Wr 6,
  AuBYP, BkCL, BlkAW, ChPo S1,
  ConAu 1R, ConAu 41, ConLC 1,
  ConP 1970, CurB 46, CurB 73,
  JBA 1951, MorBMP, NYTBE 4, OxAm,
  REnAL, SmATA 2, St&VC, WEAL,
  WWA 38, WWWor 2*
Bonzon, Paul Jacques 1908- *Au&Wr 6,
  AuBYP, WWWor 2*
Boog Watson, Elspeth Janet 1900- *Au&Wr 6,
  ConAu P-1*
Booker, Simeon Saunders 1918- *ConAu 9R,
  LBAA*
Boone, Pat 1934- *AmA&B, AmSCAP 66,
  CelR 3, ConAu 1R, CurB 59,
  IntMPA 1975, SmATA 7, WWA 38*
Boone, Silas K *CarSB*
Boorer, Wendy 1931- *ConAu 57*
Boorstin, Daniel J 1914- *AmA&B, AuNews 2,
  ConAu 1R, CurB 68, DrAS 6H,
  IntWW 38, WWA 38, WWS 13,
  WWWorJ 1972, WorAu*
Booth, Christopher B *MnBBF*
Booth, D E *MnBBF*
Booth, Edwin *ConAu 17R*
Booth, Edwin *see* Blunt, Don
Booth, Ernest Sheldon 1915- *AmMWS 12P,
  ConAu 53, WWW 14*
Booth, Graham Charles 1935- *IlBYP,
  IlCB 1957*
Booth, Martin 1944- *ConP 1970, ConP 1975,
  WrD*
Booth, Maud Ballington 1865-1948 *CarSB,
  DcAmA, NCHEL*
Booth, Ned *MnBBF*
Booth, Patrick *MnBBF*
Booth, Rosemary Frances 1928- *ConAu 53,
  WrD*
Booth, Rosemary Frances *see* Murray, Frances
Boothby, Guy Newell 1867-1905 *BrAu 19,
  Chambr 3, EncM&D, EvLB, LongC,
  MnBBF*
Boque, J Russell *MnBBF*
Borden, Charles A 1912-1968 *AuBYP,
  ConAu 5R*
Borden, M *ConAu XR*
Borden, M *see* Saxon, Gladys Relyea
Borek, Ernest 1911- *AmMWS 12P*
Boreman, Jean 1909- *ConAu P-2*
Borer, Mary Cathcart 1906- *Au&Wr 6,
  ConAu 9R, WrD*
Borg, Inga *AuBYP*
Borg, Jack *MnBBF*
Borhegyi, Suzanne C Sims De 1926- *AuBYP*
Borhegyi, Suzanne C Sims De *see* DeBorhegyi,
  Suzanne C Sims
Borja, Corinne *IlBYP*
Borja, Robert *IlBYP*
Borland, Hal 1900- *AmA&B, Au&Wr 6,
  ChPo, ConAu 1R, REnAL, SmATA 5,
  WWA 38, WWWor 2, WorAu*
Borland, Hal *see* Borland, Harold Glen
Borland, Hal *see* West, Ward
Borland, Harold Glen *ConAu XR, SmATA 5*

Borland, Harold Glen *see* Borland, Hal
Borland, Kathryn Kilby 1916- *ConAu 53,
  IndAu 1917, WWA 38*
Borland, Kathryn Kilby *see* Abbott, Alice
Borland, Kathryn Kilby *see* Land, Jane
Borland, Kathryn Kilby *see* Land, Ross
Borlase, Skip *MnBBF*
Borlase, Skip *see* Bradley, J J G
Bornschlegel, Ruth *IlBYP*
Bornstein, Ruth 1927- *ConAu 61*
Borowitz, Eugene Bernard 1924- *ConAu 49,
  WWWorJ 1972*
Borski, Lucia Merecka *AnCL*
Borten, Helen Jacobson 1930- *AmPB, AuBYP,
  ChPo S2, ConAu 5R, IlCB 1957,
  ForWC 1970, SmATA 5, WrD*
Borton, Elizabeth 1904- *SmATA 1, ThBJA*
Borton, Elizabeth *see* Borton DeTrevino,
  Elizabeth
Borton, Elizabeth *see* DeTrevino, Elizabeth
  Borton
Borton, Elizabeth *see* Trevino, Elizabeth Borton
  De
Borton DeTrevino, Elizabeth 1904-
  NewbC 1966, WWAW 8
Borton DeTrevino, Elizabeth *see* Borton,
  Elizabeth
Bortstein, Larry 1942- *ConAu 33*
Bosco, Jack *ConAu XR, SmATA XR*
Bosco, Jack *see* Holliday, Joseph
Boshell, Gordon *ChPo S2*
Boshinski, Blanche 1922- *ConAu 21R,
  SmATA 10*
Bosschere, Jean De 1878- *IlCB 1744*
Bostelmann, Else *IlCB 1744*
Boston, Lucy Maria 1892- *AnCL, Au&Wr 6,
  AuBYP, BrCA, ChLR 3, PiP, SenS,
  ThBJA, WWCL, WrD*
Boswell, Hazel 1882- *IlCB 1744, OxCan Sup,
  Prof*
Boswell, Hilda *ChPo S2*
Boswell, James *IlCB 1957, MnBBF*
Bosworth, J Allan *AuBYP*
Bothwell, Jean *AuBYP, ConAu 1R, CurB 46,
  JBA 1951, SmATA 2*
Botkin, Benjamin Albert 1901-1975 *AmA&B,
  Au&Wr 6, ConAu P-1, DrAS 6E,
  REnAL, TwCA Sup, WWA 38,
  WWWorJ 1972*
Bott, H L *MnBBF*
Bottel, Helen 1914- *ConAu 25R, WWAW 8,
  WrD*
Botting, Douglas 1934- *ConAu 45, WrD*
Bottner, Barbara 1943- *ConAu 61*
Bottom, Raymond 1927- *ConAu 33*
Bouchard, Lois Kalb 1938- *ConAu 25R*
Bouchard, William *MnBBF*
Bouchard, William *see* Wright, W George
Boucher, Alan 1918- *ConAu 5R*
Boucher, W d1906 *WWBWI I*
Bouchier, W W *MnBBF*
Boulle, Pierre 1912- *ConAu 9R*
Bounds, S J *MnBBF*
Bourdeaux, Michael 1934- *ConAu 33*
Bourgeois, Florence 1904- *IlCB 1744*
Bourne, Evelyn *ConAu XR*
Bourne, George *MnBBF*
Bourne, Lawrence R *MnBBF, WWBWI A*
Bourne, Lesley *ConAu XR, SmATA XR*

Bourne, Lesley see Marshall, Evelyn

Bourne, Miriam Anne 1931- *ConAu 21R*

Bourne, William Oland *Alli Sup, CarSB, ChPo, ChPo S1, ChPo S2, DcNAA*

Boutet DeMonvel, L M 1850-1913 *JBA 1934, JBA 1951*

Boutet DeMonvel, Maurice *AmPB*

Boutet DeMonvel, Maurice see Monvel, Maurice Boutet De

Bouton, Josephine *ChPo*

Bouvet, Marie Marguerite 1865-1915 *AmA, AmA&B, BiD&SB, CarSB, DcAmA, DcNAA*

Bova, Ben W 1932- *ChLR 3, ConAu 5R, SmATA 6*

Bow, Ross *MnBBF*

Bowen, Betty Morgan *ConAu XR, SmATA XR*

Bowen, Betty Morgan 1921- *AuBYP*

Bowen, Betty Morgan see West, Betty

Bowen, Catherine Drinker 1897-1973 *AmA&B, ConAu 5R, ConAu 45, CurB 44, CurB 73, NYTBE 4, OxAm, REn, REnAL, SmATA 7, TwCA Sup, WW 1974, WWA 38, WWAW 8, WWWor 2*

Bowen, Elizabeth 1899-1973 *Au&Wr 6, AuBYP, CasWL, ConAu 41, ConAu P-2, ConLC 1, ConLC 3, ConLC 6, ConNov 1972, CyWA, DcLEnL, EncWL, EvLB, LongC, ModBL, ModBL Sup, NCHEL, OxEng, Pen Eng, RAdv 1, REn, TwCA, TwCA Sup, TwCW, WEAL, WWTwL*

Bowen, Irene *AuBYP*

Bowen, John 1924- *CnThe, ConAu 1R, ConDr 1, ConNov 1972, ConNov 1976, CrCD, REn, TwCW, WWT 15, WorAu, WrD*

Bowen, Joshua David 1930- *AuBYP*

Bowen, Marjorie 1886-1952 *DcLEnL, EvLB, LongC, NCHEL, REn, TwCA, TwCA Sup, TwCW, WWLA*

Bowen, Olwen *WWCL*

Bowen, Richard M 1928- *ConAu 21R, WWE 14, WrD*

Bowen, Robert Sidney 1900- *AuBYP*

Bower, B M 1871-1940 *AmA&B, DcNAA, LongC, REnAL, TwCA, WNAA*

Bowes, Anne LaBastille *ConAu 57*

Bowes, Anne LaBastille see LaBastille, Anne

Bowie, Jim *ConAu XR*

Bowie, Jim see Stratemeyer, Edward L

Bowie, Walter Russell 1882-1969 *AmA&B, ConAu 5R, WNAA*

Bowker, John Westerdale *WrD*

Bowles, D Richard 1910- *ConAu 33*

Bowles, W M *WWBWI I*

Bowles, W M see Cyclops

Bowman, Alice Bertha *MnBBF*

Bowman, Anne *Alli Sup, CarSB, ChPo S1, DcEnL*

Bowman, Bruce 1938- *ConAu 65*

Bowman, Frederick H U 1894- *Alli Sup, MnBBF, WWBWI A*

Bowman, Gerald d1967 *MnBBF, WWBWI A*

Bowman, Gerald see Hawke, Robert, Captain

Bowman, Gerald see Lynk, Warder

Bowman, Gerald see Magnus, Gerald

Bowman, James Cloyd 1880-1961 *AmA&B, AnCL, AuBYP, JBA 1951, OhA&B, St&VC, WNAA*

Bowman, John Stewart 1931- *Au&Wr 6, ConAu 9R*

Bowman, Kathleen 1942- *ConAu 69*

Bowman, Marcelle 1914- *ConAu 25R*

Bowmans, Godfried J A 1913- *ConAu 29*

Bowne, Eliza Southgate 1783-1809 *CarSB*

Bownes, William E *MnBBF*

Bowood, Richard *ConAu XR*

Bowood, Richard see Daniell, Albert Scott

Bowring, Sir John 1792-1872 *Alli, Alli Sup, BbD, BiD&SB, BrAu 19, CarSB, CasWL, Chambr 3, ChPo, ChPo S1, ChPo S2, DcEnL, DcLEnL, EvLB, PoCh*

Boxall, Ernest *MnBBF*

Boxer, Devorah *AuBYP*

Boyce, George A 1898- *ConAu 53*

Boyd, Don *MnBBF*

Boyd, Frank 1893- *ConICB*

Boyd, James 1888-1944 *AmA&B, CnDAL, ConAmA, ConAmL, CurB 44, CyWA, DcLEnL, DcNAA, LongC, OxAm, Pen Am, REnAL, TwCA, TwCA Sup, WNAA*

Boyd, John *ConAu XR*

Boyd, John see Upchurch, Boyd

Boyd, Malcolm 1923- *AmA&B, Au&Wr 6, CelR 3, ConAu 5R, CurB 68, WWA 38, -WWE 14, WWWor 2*

Boyd, Waldo T 1918- *ConAu 29, WrD*

Boyd, William Clouser 1903- *AmMWS 12P, WWA 38*

Boyer, Sophia Ames 1907?-1972 *ConAu 37*

Boyes, Howard C *MnBBF*

Boyes, Megan 1923- *Au&Wr 6, WrD*

Boyesen, Hjalmar Hjorth 1848-1895 *Alli Sup, AmA, AmA&B, BbD, BiD&SB, CarSB, ChPo, ChPo S1, DcAmA, DcBiA, DcLEnL, DcNAA, JBA 1934, OhA&B, OxAm, REnAL*

Boyington, F W *WWBWI I*

Boyle, Ann 1916- *ConAu 29, SmATA 10, WrD*

Boyle, Frederick 1841- *MnBBF*

Boyle, Joyce 1901- *ConAu P-1*

Boyle, Kay 1903- *AmA&B, AmNov, CasWL, CnDAL, ConAmA, ConAu 13R, ConLC 1, ConLC 5, ConNov 1972, ConNov 1976, ConP 1970, ConP 1975, CurB 42, DcLEnL, DrAF 1976, DrAP 1975, EncWL, ForWC 1970, LongC, ModAL, OxAm, Pen Am, RAdv 1, REn, REnAL, TwCA, TwCA Sup, WW 1974, WWA 38, WWAW 8, WWTwL, WWWor 2, WrD*

Boyle, Robert *MnBBF*

Boylston, Helen Dore 1895- *AuBYP, CurB 42, JBA 1951, WWCL*

Boyten, H E *MnBBF*

Boyton, Neil 1884-1956 *AmA&B, AuBYP, BkC 1, CatA 1930, WNAA*

Boze, Calvin *IlBYP*

Bozzo, Frank *IlBYP*

Brabourne, Lord see Knatchbull-Hugessen, E H

Brabourne, Lord Edward Hugessen K-H 1829-1893 *Alli Sup, BiD&SB, WWCL*

Brace, Dudley *MnBBF*

Brace, Geoffrey 1930- *ConAu 69*
Bracegirdle, Cyril 1920- *Au&Wr 6,*
  ConAu 45, WrD
Bracken, Anne *SingR 1*
Bracker, Charles Eugene 1895- *IlCB 1744*
Bradbury, Bianca 1908- *AmA&B, AuBYP,*
  ConAu 13R, SmATA 3
Bradbury, Parnell 1904- *Au&Wr 6,*
  ConAu 13R, WrD
Bradbury, Peggy 1930- *ConAu 65*
Bradbury, Ray 1920- *AmA&B, Au&Wr 6,*
  AuNews 1, AuNews 2, BiN 1974,
  CasWL, CelR 3, CnMWL, ConAu 1R,
  ConLC 1, ConLC 3, ConNov 1972,
  ConNov 1976, CurB 53, DrAF 1976,
  LongC, OxAm, Pen Am, REn, REnAL,
  SmATA 11, TwCA Sup, TwCW, WrD
Bradby, Godfrey Fox 1863-1947 *ChPo,*
  ChPo S1, ChPo S2, LongC, MnBBF,
  WWBWI A
Braddy, Nella 1894- *AuBYP, ChPo S1*
Bradfield, Jolly Roger *ConAu XR*
Bradfield, Jolly Roger *see* Bradfield, Roger
Bradfield, Roger 1924- *ConAu 17R*
Bradfield, Roger *see* Bradfield, Jolly Roger
Bradford, Adam, M.D. *AuBYP, ConAu XR*
Bradford, Adam, M.D. *see* Wassersug, Joseph
  David
Bradford, Edwin Emmanuel 1860- *MnBBF,*
  WWLA
Bradford, L, Captain *MnBBF*
Bradford, L, Captain *see* Carson, L B
Bradford, William Castle 1910- *AmMWS 12S,*
  ConAu 9R
Bradish, J S *MnBBF*
Bradley, Albert W *MnBBF*
Bradley, Albert W *see* Wentworth, Charles
Bradley, Duane 1914- *ConAu XR, AuBYP*
Bradley, Duane *see* Sanborn, Duane
Bradley, J J G *MnBBF*
Bradley, J J G *see* Borlase, Skip
Bradley, J J G *see* Leslie, Captain
Bradley, William H 1868- *ChPo, IlCB 1744*
Bradshaw, Percy V *ChPo, MnBBF,*
  WWBWI A, WWBWI I
Brady, Cyrus Townsend 1861-1920 *AmA&B,*
  AmLY, BiD&SB, CarSB, DcAmA,
  DcNAA, OhA&B, OxAm, REn, REnAL
Brady, Frank 1934- *ConAu 61*
Brady, Irene 1943- *ConAu 33, SmATA 4*
Brady, Rita G *AuBYP*
Braenne, Berit 1918- *ConAu 21R*
Bragdon, Elspeth MacDuffie 1897- *ConAu 5R,*
  SmATA 6
Bragdon, Elspeth MacDuffie *see* Elspeth
Bragdon, Lillian Jacot *AuBYP*
Bragg, Charles *IlBYP*
Braider, Donald 1923- *ConAu 33, WrD*
Brailsford, Frances 1917- *ConAu 29, WrD*
Braimah, Joseph Adam 1916- *ConAu 61*
Brain, H D *MnBBF*
Brainerd, John W 1918- *AmMWS 12P*
Braithwaite, Carlton *WWBWI A*
Braithwaite, Carlton *see* Brown, G W
Braithwaite, Coulton *MnBBF*
Braithwaite, Coulton *see* Brown, G W
Braithwaite, E R 1912- *ConNov 1972*
Bram, Elizabeth 1948- *ConAu 65*
Brampton, Peter *MnBBF*

Brancato, Robin F 1936- *ConAu 69*
Brand, Charles E *MnBBF, WWBWI A*
Brand, Christianna 1907- *Au&Wr 6, ChPo,*
  EncM&D, WrD
Brand, Dudley *MnBBF*
Brand, Dudley *see* Hild, H
Brand, Max *WWBWI A*
Brand, Max 1892-1944 *AmA&B, CurB 44,*
  DcLEnL, DcNAA, EncM&D, LongC,
  MnBBF, REn, REnAL, TwCA,
  TwCA Sup
Brand, Max *see* Faust, Frederick
Brand, Oscar 1920- *AmA&B, AuBYP,*
  CanWW 12, ConAu 1R, CurB 62,
  EncFCW 1969, WWA 38, WWWor 2,
  WWWorJ 1972
Brande, Ralph T 1921- *ConAu 25R*
Brandenberg, Aliki Liacouras 1929- *AuBYP,*
  ChPo S1, ConAu 1R, IlCB 1957,
  SmATA 2, ThBJA, WrD
Brandenberg, Aliki Liacouras *see* Aliki
Brandenberg, Franz 1932- *ConAu 29,*
  SmATA 8, WrD
Brandhorst, Carl T 1898- *AmMWS 12P,*
  ConAu P-2
Brandon, Brumsic, Jr. 1927- *SmATA 9*
Brandon, Curt *AuBYP, ConAu XR,*
  SmATA 6
Brandon, Curt *see* Bishop, Curtis
Brandon, John Gordon 1879-1941 *Alli, MnBBF,*
  WWBWI A
Brandon, Roy *WWBWI A*
Brandon, Roy *see* Hooper, Stanley
Brandon, William *IndAu 1917*
Brandreth, Gyles 1948- *ConAu 65*
Brandt, Richard *MnBBF, WWBWI A*
Brandt, Sue R 1916- *ConAu 25R*
Brandys, Marian 1912- *ConAu 57,*
  WWWor 2
Branfield, John 1931- *ConAu 41, SmATA 11,*
  WrD
Branley, Franklyn M 1915- *AmMWS 12P,*
  Au&Wr 6, AuBYP, BkP, ConAu 33,
  MorJA, REnAL, SmATA 4, WWA 38
Brann, Esther *AuBYP, ConICB, JBA 1934,*
  JBA 1951
Branner, Martin 1888-1970 *ArtCS*
Branner, Robert 1927- *WWA 38,*
  WWAA 1973
Branscum, Robbie 1937- *ConAu 61*
Bransom, Paul 1885- *ChPo, ConICB, IlBYP,*
  IlCB 1744, IlCB 1946, MorJA,
  WWAA 1973
Branson, Margaret Stimmann 1922- *ConAu 49*
Brant, Irving 1885- *ConAu 9R*
Brash, M M *MnBBF*
Brashler, William 1947- *ConAu 45*
Brasier, Virginia Rossmore 1910- *St&VC*
Brathwaite, Errol 1924- *ConAu 65*
Bratton, Helen 1899- *ConAu 21R, SmATA 4*
Bratton, Karl Henry 1906- *AuBYP, WWA 38*
Braude, Michael 1936- *ConAu 17R*
Brauer, Earle William 1918- *WWE 14*
Braun *CarSB*
Braun, Fritz d1921? *WWBWI I*
Braun, Kathy *AuBYP*
Braun, Saul M *AuBYP*
Braun, Wernher Von 1912- *AuBYP, CurB 52,*
  IntWW 38, NYTBE 1

Brautigan, Richard 1935?- *AmA&B, CelR 3, ConAu 53, ConLC 1, ConLC 3, ConLC 5, ConNov 1972, ConNov 1976, ConP 1970, ConP 1975, DrAF 1976, DrAP 1975, ModAL Sup, Pen Am, WWA 38*

Braverman, Libbie Levin 1900- *OhA&B, WWWorJ 1972*

Bray, Warwick 1936- *ConAu 25R*

Brayley, Leonard *MnBBF*

Braymer, Marjorie Elizabeth 1911- *AnCL, ConAu 1R, SmATA 6, WWA 38, WWAW 8, WWW 14*

Brazil, Angela 1868-1947 *DcLEnL, EvLB, LongC, WWCL, WWLA*

Breakspear, Norman *MnBBF*

Brearley, John *MnBBF, WWBWI A*

Brearley, John *see* Garbutt, John L

Brecht, Bertolt 1898-1956 *AtlBL, CasWL, ClDMEuL, CnMD, CnMWL, CnThe, CrCD, CyWA, EncWL, EvEuW, LongC, McGWD, ModGL, ModWD, OxEng, OxGer, Pen Eur, RCom, REn, REnWD, TwCA, TwCA Sup, TwCW, WWTwL*

Brecht, Edith 1895- *ConAu P-2, SmATA 6, WrD*

Brecht, George 1926- *ConDr 1, DcCAA 2, WWWor 2*

Breck, Alan *MnBBF*

Breck, Vivian 1895- *AmA&B, AuBYP, ConAu XR, MorJA, SmATA 1*

Breck, Vivian *see* Breckenfeld, Vivian Gurney

Breckenfeld, Vivian Gurney 1895- *AmA&B, AuBYP, ConAu 5R, ForWC 1970, SmATA 1*

Breckenfeld, Vivian Gurney *see* Breck, Vivian

Breda, Tjalmar *ConAu XR, SmATA XR*

Breda, Tjalmar *see* DeJong, David C

Bredon, John *MnBBF*

Bredon, John *see* Taylor, W T

Breeden, Stanley 1938- *Au&Wr 6*

Breetveld, Jim Patrick 1925- *AuBYP, ConAu 1R*

Breihan, Carl W 1916- *Au&Wr 6, ConAu 1R*

Breinburg, Petronella 1927- *ConAu 53, SmATA 11, WrD*

Breinburg, Petronella *see* Ashey, Bella

Breinburg, Petronella *see* Totham, Mary

Breisky, William J 1928- *ConAu 53*

Brelis, Nancy 1929- *ConAu 21R*

Brendon, Frank *WWBWI A*

Brendon, Frank *see* Gibbons, Harry Hornaby Clifford

Brennan, Joseph Gerard 1910- *AuBYP, ConAu 1R, DrAS 6P, WWA 38*

Brennan, Joseph Lomas 1903- *ConAu 5R, SmATA 6*

Brennan, Joseph Lomas *see* Lomas, Steve

Brennan, Joseph Payne 1918- *ChPo S1, ConAu 1R, EncM&D*

Brennan, Louis Arthur 1911- *ConAu 17R, WWE 14*

Brennan, Matthew J 1917- *WWA 38*

Brenner, Anita 1905-1974 *AmPB, AnCL, ConAu 49, ConAu 53, NYTBS 5, TexW*

Brenner, Barbara Johnes 1925- *AuBYP, ConAu 9R, ForWC 1970, SmATA 4*

Brenner, Fred *IlBYP*

Brenning, L H *WWBWI A*

Brenning, L H *see* Hunter, John

Brent, Charlton *MnBBF, WWBWI A*

Brent, Charlton *see* Emmett Brothers

Brent, Ernest *MnBBF, WWBWI A*

Brent, Ernest *see* Emmett Brothers

Brent, Francis *MnBBF, WWBWI A*

Brent, Francis *see* Hunter, Alfred John

Brent, Stuart *AuBYP*

Brent-Dyer, Elinor Mary *WWCL*

Brereton, F S *WWBWI A*

Brereton, F S *see* Brereton, Frederick Sadler

Brereton, Frederick Sadler 1872-1957 *ChPo S1, SixAP, WWCL*

Brereton, Frederick Sadler *see* Brereton, F S

Breslin, Jimmy 1930- *AmA&B, AuNews 1, CelR 3, ConLC 4, CurB 73, WWA 38, WWE 14, WWWor 2*

Breton, Edwin James 1828-1895 *MnBBF*

Breton, Guy *MnBBF*

Breton, Pierre, Captain *MnBBF*

Brett, Edwin James 1828-1895 *WWBWI A*

Brett, Grace Neff 1900- *ConAu 9R*

Brett, Harold M 1880?- *ChPo, ConICB, IlCB 1744*

Brett, Hawksley *MnBBF, WWBWI A*

Brett, Hawksley *see* Bell, Robert Stanley Warren

Brett, Mary Elizabeth *Au&Wr 6, ConAu 9R*

Brett, Mary Elizabeth *see* Brett, Molly

Brett, Molly *ConAu XR, WrD*

Brett, Molly *see* Brett, Mary Elizabeth

Brevannes, Maurice 1904- *IlBYP, IlCB 1946*

Brewster, Benjamin *AuBYP, ConAu XR, CurB 41, SmATA 2, SmATA 5*

Brewster, Benjamin *see* Elting, Mary

Brewster, Benjamin *see* Folsom, Franklin

Brewton, John Edmund 1898- *BkP, ChPo, ChPo S1, ChPo S2, ConAu 5R, SmATA 5*

Brewton, Sara W *BkP*

Brey, Charles *IlBYP*

Brick, John 1922-1973 *AmA&B, AuBYP, ConAu 45, ConAu P-1, CurB 53, CurB 73, SmATA 10*

Brickdale, Eleanor Fortescue *ChPo S1, IlCB 1744*

Bridges, Robert Seymour 1844-1930 *Alli Sup, AnCL, AtlBL, CasWL, ChPo, ChPo S1, ChPo S2, CnE&AP, DcEnA, DcEnA Ap, DcLEnL, EncWL, EvLB, LongC, ModBL, NCHEL, OxEng, Pen Eng, REn, TwCA, TwCA Sup, TwCW, WEAL, WWTwL*

Bridges, Thomas Charles 1868-1944 *MnBBF, WWBWI A, WWCL*

Bridges, Thomas Charles *see* Beck, Christopher

Bridges, Thomas Charles *see* Shaw, Martin

Bridges, Thomas Charles *see* Stanton, John

Bridges, Victor *MnBBF*

Bridges, Victor *see* James, Vernon

Bridges, William Andrew 1901- *AmA&B, AuBYP, ConAu 33, IndAu 1917, SmATA 5, WWA 38*

Bridgman, Lewis Jesse 1857-1931 *CarSB, ChPo, ChPo S1, ChPo S2, DcNAA*

Bridwell, Norman 1928- *ConAu 13R*

Bridwell, Norman Ray 1928- *IndAu 1917, SmATA 4, WrD*

Brier, Howard Maxwell 1903-1969 *AuBYP, ConAu P-1, CurB 51, MorJA, SmATA 8, WWPNA*

Briggs, Austin 1908- *ArtCS, WWAA 1973*
Briggs, Barbara *AuBYP*
Briggs, Jean *WrD*
Briggs, Mitchell Pirie 1892- *AmA&B*
Briggs, Peter 1921- *ConAu P-2, WWE 14*
Briggs, Raymond Redvers 1934- *ArtsCL,*
  Au&Wr 6, BkP, ChPo, ChPo S1,
  ChPo S2, IIBYP, IICB 1957, ThBJA,
  WWCL
Brigham, Grace A *IIBYP*
Bright, C A *MnBBF*
Bright, James *MnBBF, WWBWI A*
Bright, James *see* Rowe, John Gabriel
Bright, Robert 1902- *AmA&B, AmNov,*
  IIBYP, IICB 1946, IICB 1957, MorJA
Brightly, Ben *MnBBF*
Brightwell, Leonard Robert 1889- *IICB 1744,*
  MnBBF, WWBWI I
Brimberg, Stanlee 1947- *SmATA 9, WrD*
Brin, Ruth Firestone 1921- *ConAu 17R*
Brinckloe, Julie 1950- *ConAu 65, IIBYP,*
  SmATA 13
Brindel, June 1919- *ConAu 49*
Brindel, June Rachuy 1919- *SmATA 7*
Brindle, Ernest *MnBBF, WWBWI A*
Brindle, Ernest *see* Bayne, Peter
Brindze, Ruth 1903- *AuBYP, MorJA*
Brings, Lawrence Martin 1897- *WWA 38*
Brink, Carol Ryrie 1895- *AmA&B, AnCL,*
  Au&Wr 6, AuBYP, ChPo S1,
  ConAu 1R, FamMS, JBA 1951, MnnWr,
  MorBMP, Newb 1922, REnAL,
  SmATA 1, St&VC, WWA 38,
  WWAW 8, WWPNA, WrD
Brinkerhoff, R M 1880-1958 *ArtCS*
Brinley, Bertrand R 1917- *ConAu 29*
Brinsmead, H F 1922- *ConAu 21R*
Brinsmead, H F *see* Brinsmead, Hesba Fay
Brinsmead, Hesba Fay 1922- *SenS, SingR 2,*
  WrD
Brinsmead, Hesba Fay *see* Brinsmead, H F
Brinton, Henry 1901- *Au&Wr 6, ConAu 1R*
Brion, Marcel 1895- *Au&Wr 6, IntWW 38,*
  WWWor 2
Brisbane, Coutts d1942? *MnBBF, WWBWI A*
Brisbane, Coutts *see* Armour, R Coutts
Brisco, Pat A *ConAu XR*
Brisco, Pat A *see* Matthews, Patricia
Brisco, Patty *ConAu XR*
Brisco, Patty *see* Matthews, Clayton
Brisco, Patty *see* Matthews, Patricia
Briscoe, Ernest Edward 1882-1956 *MnBBF,*
  WWBWI I
Brisley, Joyce Lankester 1896- *Au&Wr 6,*
  ChPo, ChPo S1, WrD
Brister, C W 1926- *ConAu 13R*
Bristowe-Noble, J C *MnBBF*
Britt, Dell 1934- *ConAu 25R, SmATA 1*
Brittan, Charles Edward 1870- *IICB 1744*
Brittany, Louis *MnBBF, WWBWI A*
Brittany, Louis *see* Teed, George Heber
Britten, Frank Curzon *ChPo, MnBBF*
Britton, Herbert *MnBBF, WWBWI A*
Britton, Herbert *see* Eves, Reginald T
Bro, Margueritte Harmon 1894- *CurB 52,*
  MorJA
Broadbent, Abel *MnBBF*
Broadbent, David *MnBBF*
Broadhurst, Alan *WrD*

Brock, Betty Carter 1923- *ConAu 29,*
  SmATA 4, SmATA 7, WrD
Brock, C E 1870-1938 *WWBWI I*
Brock, Charles Edmond 1870-1938 *ChPo,*
  ChPo S1, JBA 1934, JBA 1951, WWCL
Brock, Emma Lillian 1886-1974 *AuBYP, ChPo,*
  ConAu 5R, ConICB, IICB 1744,
  IICB 1946, JBA 1934, JBA 1951,
  MnnWr, SmATA 8, St&VC, WWPNA
Brock, H M 1875-1960 *WWBWI I*
Brock, Henry Matthew 1875-1960 *ChPo,*
  ChPo S1, ChPo S2, IICB 1744,
  JBA 1934, JBA 1951, WWCL
Brock, Stanley E 1936- *ConAu 57*
Brock, Stuart *ConAu XR*
Brock, Stuart *see* Trimble, Louis P
Brockett, Eleanor Hall 1913-1967 *ConAu P-1,*
  SmATA 10
Brockington, Alfred Allen 1872- *MnBBF*
Brocklehurst, Tyrer *MnBBF*
Brockman, C Frank 1902- *ConAu 5R*
Broderick, Dorothy M 1929- *AuBYP, BiDL 5,*
  ConAu 13R, SmATA 5
Broderick, Francis Lyons 1922- *DrAS 6H,*
  WWA 38, WWE 14
Brokamp, Marilyn 1920- *ConAu 49,*
  SmATA 10
Brokamp, Marilyn *see* Lynn, Mary
Bromhall, Winifred *ChPo, ConICB, IIBYP,*
  IICB 1744, IICB 1946, MorJA
Bronin, Andrew 1947- *ConAu 45*
Bronowski, Jacob 1908-1974 *AmA&B, AnCL,*
  ConAu 1R, ConAu 53, DcLEnL,
  IntWW 38, NYTBS 5, WW 1974,
  WWA 38, WWWor 2, WorAu
Bronson, Lynn *AuBYP, ConAu XR, MorJA,*
  SmATA 4
Bronson, Lynn *see* Lampman, Evelyn Sibley
Bronson, Wilfred Swancourt 1894- *AmA&B,*
  AuBYP, IICB 1744, IICB 1946,
  JBA 1934, JBA 1951, St&VC
Bronte, Charlotte 1816-1855 *Alli, AtlBL, BbD,*
  BiD&SB, BrAu 19, CasWL, Chambr 3,
  ChPo, ChPo S1, ChPo S2, CriT 3,
  CyWA, DcBiA, DcEnA, DcEnA Ap,
  DcEnL, DcEuL, DcLEnL, EvLB,
  HsB&A, MouLC 3, OxEng, Pen Eng,
  RAdv 1, RCom, WEAL
Bronte, Emily 1818-1848 *BbD, BiD&SB,*
  BrAu 19, CasWL, ChPo, CriT 3, CyWA,
  DcBiA, DcEuL, DcLEnL, EvLB,
  MouLC 3, OxEng, Pen Eng, RAdv 1,
  RCom, WEAL
Brood, Norman *MnBBF*
Brook, Eric *MnBBF*
Brooke, Arthur *MnBBF, WWBWI A*
Brooke, Arthur *see* Marshall, Arthur C
Brooke, Leonard Leslie 1862-1940 *AnCL,*
  ChPo, ChPo S1, ConICB, IIBYP,
  JBA 1934, JBA 1951, St&VC, WWCL
Brookes, Kenneth 1897- *WWBWI I*
Brookins, Dana 1931- *ConAu 69*
Brooks, Amy d1931 *AmA&B, AmLY, CarSB,*
  DcNAA, WNAA
Brooks, Anita 1914- *AuBYP, ConAu 17R,*
  SmATA 5
Brooks, Anne Tedlock 1905- *ConAu 1R*
Brooks, Anne Tedlock *see* Carter, Anne
Brooks, Anne Tedlock *see* Millburn, Cynthia

Brooks, Charlotte K *AuBYP, LBAA*
Brooks, Colin *MnBBF*
Brooks, Edwy Searles 1889-1965 *EncM&D,
  MnBBF, WWCL, WWBWI A*
Brooks, Edwy Searles *see* Browne, Reginald
Brooks, Edwy Searles *see* Clifford, Martin
Brooks, Edwy Searles *see* Comrade, Robert W
Brooks, Edwy Searles *see* Gosfield, H
  Heddingham
Brooks, Edwy Searles *see* Gray, Berkeley
Brooks, Edwy Searles *see* Greaves, Norman
Brooks, Edwy Searles *see* Gunn, Victor
Brooks, Edwy Searles *see* Halstead, E Sinclair
Brooks, Edwy Searles *see* Halstead, S B
Brooks, Edwy Searles *see* Richards, Frank
Brooks, Edwy Searles *see* Thornton, Edward
Brooks, Elbridge Streeter 1846-1902 *Alli Sup,
  AmA, AmA&B, BbD, BiD&SB, CarSB,
  ChPo, DcAmA, DcNAA, JBA 1934,
  REnAL*
Brooks, Gwendolyn 1917- *AmA&B,
  AuNews 1, BiN 1974, BkCL, BlkAW,
  CasWL, CelR 3, ChPo, ChPo S1,
  ChPo S2, ConAu 1R, ConLC 1,
  ConLC 2, ConLC 4, ConLC 5,
  ConP 1970, ConP 1975, CrCAP,
  CurB 50, DrAP 1975, IntWW 38, LBAA,
  ModAL, ModAL Sup, OxAm, Pen Am,
  RAdv 1, REnAL, SmATA 6, TwCA Sup,
  WWA 38, WWAW 8, WWWor 2*
Brooks, Jeremy 1926- *Au&Wr 6, ConAu 5R,
  ConNov 1972, ConNov 1976, WrD*
Brooks, Jerome 1931- *ConAu 49*
Brooks, Leonard Harold d1950 *MnBBF*
Brooks, Leonard Harold *see* Steele, Howard
Brooks, Lester 1924- *ConAu 33, SmATA 7*
Brooks, Noah 1830-1903 *Alli Sup, AmA,
  AmA&B, BbD, BiD&SB, CarSB,
  DcAmA, DcNAA, JBA 1934, OxAm,
  REnAL*
Brooks, Patricia K 1926- *ConAu 25R*
Brooks, Paul 1909- *ConAu 13R, WWA 38,
  WWE 14*
Brooks, Phillips 1835-1893 *Alli Sup, AmA&B,
  AnCL, BbD, BiD&SB, Chambr 3, ChPo,
  ChPo S1, ChPo S2, DcAmA, DcNAA,
  OxAm, REnAL*
Brooks, Polly Schoyer 1912- *ConAu 1R,
  SmATA 12*
Brooks, Stewart Marshall 1923- *ConAu 17R,
  WWE 14*
Brooks, Van Wyck 1886-1963 *AmA&B,
  AmLY, AmWr, AtlBL, CasWL,
  Chambr 3, CnDAL, ConAmA, ConAmL,
  ConAu 1R, CurB 41, CurB 63,
  DcLEnL, EvLB, LongC, ModAL, OxAm,
  Pen Am, RAdv 1, REn, REnAL, TwCA,
  TwCA Sup, TwCW, WEAL, WNAA*
Brooks, Walter Rollin 1886-1958 *AmA&B,
  ChPo, JBA 1951, WNAA*
Broome, Lady Mary Ann d1911 *Alli Sup,
  CasWL, MnBBF*
Broomfield, Robert 1930- *IlBYP, IlCB 1957*
Broster, Dorothy Kathleen 1877?-1950 *DcLEnL,
  JBA 1934, JBA 1951, TwCW, WWLA*
Broughton, A J *MnBBF*
Broun, Emily *ConAu XR*
Broun, Emily *see* Sterne, Emma Gelders
Broun, Heywood Campbell 1888-1939 *CurB 40*

Browder, Walter Everett 1939- *ConAu 53*
Brower, Millicent *ConAu 41, SmATA 8*
Browin, Frances Williams 1898- *AuBYP,
  ConAu P-1, SmATA 5*
Browin, Frances Williams *see* Williams, Frances
  B
Brown, Abbie Farwell 1872?-1927 *AmA&B,
  AmLY, AnCL, CarSB, ChPo, ChPo S1,
  ChPo S2, DcAmA, DcNAA, JBA 1934,
  TwCA Sup, TwCA Sup, WNAA*
Brown, Alexis *ConAu XR, SmATA XR*
Brown, Alexis *see* Baumann, Amy
Brown, Beatrice Curtis *ChPo, ChPo S1,
  ConAu XR*
Brown, Beatrice Curtis *see* Curtis Brown, Beatrice
Brown, Bert *WWBWI 1*
Brown, Beth *AmSCAP 66, ConAu P-2*
Brown, Beth *see* Retner, Beth A
Brown, Betty *ConAu XR*
Brown, Betty *see* Jones, Elizabeth B
Brown, Bill 1910-1964 *AuBYP, ConAu XR,
  SmATA 5*
Brown, Bill *see* Brown, William L
Brown, Buck 1936- *WWA 38*
Brown, Campbell *MnBBF, WWBWI A*
Brown, Campbell *see* Brown, G W
Brown, Charles Perry *MnBBF*
Brown, Claude 1937- *AmA&B, BlkAW,
  CurB 67, DrAF 1976, LBAA, WWA 38*
Brown, Conrad 1922- *AuBYP*
Brown, Dee Alexander 1908- *BiDL 5,
  ConAu 13R, SmATA 5, WWA 38,
  WWMW 14*
Brown, Douglas 1907- *ConAu 25R*
Brown, Duncan *MnBBF*
Brown, Duncan *see* Nelson, T
Brown, Edna Adelaide 1875-1944 *AmA&B,
  DcNAA, JBA 1934, JBA 1951, WNAA*
Brown, Eleanor Frances 1908- *AuBYP,
  ConAu 29, SmATA 3*
Brown, Elizabeth Myers 1915- *WWAW 8*
Brown, Emily *SmATA 6*
Brown, Eric *MnBBF*
Brown, G W *MnBBF, WWBWI A*
Brown, G W *see* Braithwaite, Carlton
Brown, G W *see* Braithwaite, Coulton
Brown, G W *see* Brown, Campbell
Brown, G W *see* Campbell, G Wells
Brown, G W *see* Graham, Alexis
Brown, George Earl 1883-1964 *ChPo S1,
  ConAu 5R, SmATA 11*
Brown, Helen E *AuBYP*
Brown, Howard *MnBBF*
Brown, Ida Mae *ConAu P-2*
Brown, Irene Bennett 1932- *ConAu 29,
  SmATA 3*
Brown, Ivor John Carnegie 1891-1974
  *Au&Wr 6, BiEnAT, ConAu 9R,
  ConAu 49, DcLEnL, EvLB, LongC,
  ModBL, NCHEL, NYTBS 5, Pen Eng,
  SmATA 5, TwCA Sup, WW 1974,
  WWT 15, WWWor 2*
Brown, Jeff *AuBYP*
Brown, John 1810-1882 *Alli Sup, BiD&SB,
  BiDLA, BrAu 19, CarSB, CasWL, ChPo,
  DcEnA, DcEnL, DcEuL, DcLEnL, EvLB,
  NCHEL, OxEng, Pen Eng, REn*
Brown, John Mason 1900-1969 *AmA&B,
  BiEnAT, CnDAL, ConAu 9R,*

ConAu 25R, CurB 42, CurB 69, LongC, OxAm, Pen Am, REnAL, TwCA, TwCA Sup

Brown, Joseph E 1929- *ConAu 53*

Brown, Judith Gwyn 1933- *AuBYP, ChPo S1, IlCB 1957*

Brown, LeRoy 1908- *DrAS 6E*

Brown, Lloyd Arnold 1907-1966 *AuBYP, ConAu P-1*

Brown, Marc Tolon 1946- *ConAu 69, SmATA 10*

Brown, Marcia 1918- *AmA&B, AmPB, AnCL, AuBYP, BkP, Cald 1938, ChPo, ChPo S2, ChFB 1, ConAu 41, FamAI, IlBYP, IlCB 1946, IlCB 1957, MorJA, NewbC 1956, SmATA 7, WWA 38, WWAW 8*

Brown, Marel *WrD*

Brown, Marel *see* Brown, Margaret Elizabeth

Brown, Margaret Elizabeth *WrD*

Brown, Margaret Elizabeth *see* Brown, Marel

Brown, Margaret Wise 1910-1952 *AmPB, AmSCAP 66, Au&ICB, AuBYP, ChPo, ChPo S1, JBA 1951, REnAL, YABC 2*

Brown, Margaret Wise *see* Hay, Timothy

Brown, Margaret Wise *see* MacDonald, Golden

Brown, Margaret Wise *see* Sage, Juniper

Brown, Margery *ConAu 25R, SmATA 5*

Brown, Marion Marsh 1908- *AuBYP, ConAu 1R, DrAS 6E, SmATA 6*

Brown, Michael 1931- *ConAu 33*

Brown, Myra Berry 1918- *Au&Wr 6, AuBYP, ConAu 1R, ForWC 1970, SmATA 6*

Brown, Palmer 1919- *AmPB, ChPo, IlBYP, IlCB 1946, IlCB 1957*

Brown, Pamela Beatrice 1924- *Au&Wr 6, AuBYP, ConAu 13R, IntMPA 1975, SmATA 5, TelT, WWCL*

Brown, Paul 1893- *AuBYP, BkCL, Br&AmS, IlCB 1744, IlCB 1946, JBA 1951*

Brown, Philip S *AuBYP*

Brown, Ralph Adams 1908- *ConAu 33, DrAS 6H, WrD*

Brown, Raymond Bryan 1923- *ConAu 17R, DrAS 6P, LE 5*

Brown, Raymond Lamont 1939- *Au&Wr 6*

Brown, Regina *AuBYP*

Brown, Rosalie Moore 1910- *ConAu 5R, SmATA 9*

Brown, Rosalie Moore *see* Moore, Rosalie

Brown, Rose 1883-1952 *AmA&B*

Brown, Roy 1921- *ConAu 65*

Brown, Slater 1896- *AmA&B*

Brown, Vinson 1912- *AuBYP, ConAu 1R, WWW 14*

Brown, Virginia 1924- *ConAu 69*

Brown, Walter Reed 1929- *AmMWS 12P, ConAu 45*

Brown, William L 1910-1964 *AuBYP, ConAu 1R, SmATA 5*

Brown, William L *see* Brown, Bill

Browne, Dik 1917- *AuNews 1*

Browne, Frances 1816-1879 *Alli Sup, BrAu 19, ChPo, DcEnL, DcLEnL, FamSYP, JBA 1934, St&VC, TelT, WWCL*

Browne, Gordon Frederick 1858-1932 *ChPo, ChPo S1, WWBWI I, WWCL*

Browne, Hablot Knight 1815-1882 *ChPo, ChPo S1, ChPo S2, HsB&A, NCHEL,*

WWBWI I

Browne, Hablot Knight *see* Phiz

Browne, Leslie *MnBBF*

Browne, Maggie *Alli Sup, TelT*

Browne, Maggie *see* Hamer, Margaret

Browne, Michael Dennis 1940- *ChPo S2, ConAu 29, ConP 1970, ConP 1975, DrAP 1975, WrD*

Browne, Noel *MnBBF*

Browne, Reginald *MnBBF, WWBWI A, WWCL*

Browne, Reginald *see* Brooks, Edwy Searles

Browne, T A *SingR 2*

Browne, T A *see* Boldrewood, Rolf

Browne, Thomas Alexander 1826-1915 *Alli Sup, BiD&SB, BrAu 19, CarSB, CasWL, Chambr 3, DcLEnL, EvLB, LongC, NCHEL, OxEng, Pen Eng, REn*

Browne, Tom 1872-1910 *WWBWI I, WWCL*

Browne, William *MnBBF*

Browning, Colleen 1929- *ChPo S1, DcCAA 2, WWA 38, WWAA 1973, WWAW 8*

Browning, Elizabeth Barrett 1806?-1861 *Alli, Alli Sup, AtlBL, BbD, BiD&SB, BrAu 19, CasWL, Chambr 3, ChPo, ChPo S1, ChPo S2, CnE&AP, CriT 3, CyWA, DcEnA Ap, DcEnL, DcEuL, DcLEnL, EvLB, MouLC 3, NCHEL, OxEng, Pen Eng, RAdv 1, RCom, REn, WEAL*

Browning, Robert 1812-1889 *Alli, Alli Sup, AnCL, AtlBL, BiD&SB, BrAu 19, CasWL, Chambr 3, ChPo, ChPo S1, ChPo S2, CnE&AP, CnThe, CriT 3, CyWA, DcEnA, DcEnA Ap, DcEnL, DcEuL, DcLEnL, EvLB, McGWD, MouLC 4, NCHEL, OxEng, Pen Eng, RAdv 1, RCom, REn, REnWD, St&VC, WEAL, YABC 1*

Brownjohn, Alan 1931- *Au&Wr 6, ChPo S1, ChPo S2, ConAu 25R, ConP 1970, ConP 1975, SmATA 6, WrD*

Brownjohn, Alan *see* Berrington, John

Brownmiller, Susan *ForWC 1970*

Bruce, David *MnBBF*

Bruce, Mary 1927- *ConAu 25R, SmATA 1*

Bruce, Mary Grant *SingR 1*

Bruce, W A *MnBBF*

Bruchac, Joseph, III 1942- *ConAu 33, DrAF 1976, DrAP 1975*

Brueghel, Pieter 1525?-1569 *REn*

Bruere, Martha B *ChPo, WNAA*

Bruller, Jean 1902- *EvEuW, IlCB 1744, LongC, ModRL, REn, TwCA Sup, WW 1974, WWWor 2*

Brumbaugh, Robert Sherrick 1918- *ConAu 5R, DrAS 6P, WWA 38*

Bruner, Richard W 1926- *ConAu 49*

Brunetti, Cledo 1910- *ConAu P-2*

Brunhoff, Jean De 1899-1937 *AuBYP, IlCB 1946, JBA 1951, WWCL*

Brunhoff, Jean De *see* DeBrunhoff, Jean

Brunhoff, Laurent De 1925- *AuBYP, IlCB 1946, IlCB 1957, MorJA, NYTBE 3, WWCL*

Brunhoff, Laurent De *see* DeBrunhoff, Laurent

Brunner, John 1934- *Au&Wr 6, ConAu 1R*

Brussel-Smith, Bernard 1914- *IlBYP, IlCB 1946, WWA 38*

Brustlein, Daniel 1904- *AmA&B, IIBYP, IICB 1957*
Brustlein, Daniel *see* Alain
Brustlein, Janice Tworkov *AuBYP, ConAu 9R*
Brustlein, Janice Tworkov *see* Janice
Bruton, J G 1914- *ConAu 9R*
Bruun, Bertel 1937- *Au&Wr 6, ConAu 45*
Bryan, Catherine 1907- *AnCL*
Bryan, Catherine *see* Madden, Mabra
Bryan, J, III 1904- *ConAu 61*
Bryan, Joseph, III 1904- *AmA&B, AuBYP, REnAL, WWA 38*
Bryant, Sir Arthur 1899- *IntWW 38, WW 1974, WWWor 2*
Bryant, Bernice 1908- *ConAu P-1, SmATA 11*
Bryant, Bruce *MnBBF*
Bryant, Bruce *see* Wright, W George
Bryant, Gertrude Thomson *AuBYP*
Bryant, Sara Cone 1873- *AmA&B*
Bryant, William Cullen 1794-1878 *Alli, Alli Sup, AmA, AmA&B, AtlBL, BbD, BiD&SB, CarSB, CasWL, Chambr 3, ChPo, ChPo S1, ChPo S2, CnDAL, CnE&AP, CriT 3, CyAL 1, CyWA, DcAmA, DcEnL, DcLEnL, DcNAA, EvLB, MouLC 3, OxAm, OxEng, Pen Am, PoCh, RAdv 1, REn, REnAL, St&VC, WEAL*
Bryce, William Alexander 1886- *MnBBF*
Bryson, Bernarda 1905?- *ChPo, ConAu 49, IIBYP, IICB 1946, IICB 1957, SmATA 9, ThBJA*
Bryson, Bernarda *see* Shahn, Bernarda Bryson
Buba, Joy Flinsch 1904- *IIBYP, IICB 1946, WWAA 1973*
Buban, Peter, Sr. 1920- *LE 5*
Buchan, Charles *MnBBF*
Buchan, Baron John Tweedsmuir 1875-1940 *CasWL, Chambr 3, ChPo, ChPo S1, ChPo S2, CnMWL, CurB 40, CyWA, DcLEnL, EncM&D, EvLB, JBA 1934, LongC, MnBBF, ModBL, NCHEL, OxCan, OxEng, Pen Eng, REn, TelT, TwCA, TwCA Sup, TwCW, WEAL, WWBWI A, YABC 2*
Buchan, Baron John Tweedsmuir *see* Tweedsmuir, Baron
Buchanan, Carl *MnBBF*
Buchanan, William *AuBYP, ConAu XR*
Buchanan, William *see* Buck, William Ray
Buchheimer, Naomi Barnett 1927- *ConAu 5R*
Buchman, Dian Dincin *ConAu 61*
Buchsbaum, Ralph 1907- *AmMWS 12P, WWA 38*
Buchwald, Art 1925- *AmA&B, AuNews 1, BiN 1974, CelR 3, ConAu 5R, CurB 60, IntWW 38, NYTBE 3, Pen Am, SmATA 10, WW 1974, WWA 38, WWS 13, WWWor 2, WorAu*
Buchwald, Emilie 1935- *ConAu 49, SmATA 7*
Buck, Frank 1882?-1950 *AmA&B, CurB 43, CurB 50, MnBBF, REnAL*
Buck, Margaret Waring 1910- *AuBYP, ConAu 5R, SmATA 3, WrD*
Buck, Pearl S 1892-1973 *AmA&B, AmNov, Au&Wr 6, AuBYP, AuNews 1, BiEnAT, CasWL, CnDAL, ConAmA, ConAu 1R, ConAu 41, ConNov 1972, CyWA,*

DcLEnL, EncWL, EvLB, LongC, ModAL, NYTBE 4, OxAm, Pen Am, REn, REnAL, SmATA 1, TwCA, TwCA Sup, TwCW, WNAA, WWAW 8
Buck, Pearl S *see* Sedges, John
Buck, William Ray 1930- *AuBYP, ConAu 1R, WrD*
Buck, William Ray *see* Buchanan, William
Buckels, Alec *ChPo, ChPo S2, IICB 1744*
Buckeridge, Anthony Malcolm 1912- *ConAu 49, SmATA 6, WWCL*
Buckingham, James 1932- *ConAu 29*
Buckingham, James *see* Buckingham, Jamie
Buckingham, Jamie *Au&Wr 6, ConAu XR*
Buckingham, Jamie *see* Buckingham, James
Buckley, F *MnBBF*
Buckley, Francis Joseph 1928- *ConAu 33, DrAS 6P, WrD*
Buckley, Helen E 1918- *ConAu 5R, ForWC 1970, SmATA 2*
Buckley, Jerome Hamilton 1917- *AmA&B, CanWW 12, ChPo, ChPo S2, ConAu 1R, DrAS 6E, WWA 38, WWWor 2*
Buckley, Richard *MnBBF*
Buckley, William F, Jr. 1925- *AmA&B, AuNews 1*
Buckmaster, Henrietta *AmA&B, AmNov, Au&Wr 6, ConAu XR, CurB 46, OhA&B, SmATA 6, WorAu*
Buckmaster, Henrietta *see* Henkle, Henrietta
Buday, George 1907- *Au&Wr 6, WW 1974*
Budberg, Moura 1892?-1974 *ConAu 53, NYTBS 5*
Budd, Lillian 1897- *AuBYP, ConAu 1R, SmATA 7, WrD*
Buddee, Paul Edgar 1913- *Au&Wr 6, WrD*
Budden, Maria E 1780?-1832 *CarSB*
Buehnau, Ludwig *ConAu XR*
Buehnau, Ludwig *see* Schreiber, Hermann
Buehr, Walter Franklin 1897-1971 *AuBYP, ConAu 5R, ConAu 33, IICB 1946, IICB 1957, SmATA 3, ThBJA*
Buell, Ellen Lewis *AuBYP, ChPo S1, ForWC 1970*
Buell, Lawrence 1939- *ConAu 49*
Buell, Robert Kingery 1908-1971 *ConAu P-2*
Bufalari, Giuseppe 1927- *ConAu 25R*
Bufano, Remo 1894-1948 *AuBYP*
Buff, Conrad 1886- *AuBYP, BkCL, IICB 1744, IICB 1946, IICB 1957, JBA 1951, St&VC, WWA 38, WWW 14*
Buff, Mary Marsh 1890- *AmA&B, AuBYP, BkCL, JBA 1951, St&VC*
Buffalo Bill *MnBBF*
Bugbee, Emma *AuBYP*
Buley, Bernard *MnBBF*
Buley, Bernard *see* MacRae, Roy
Buley, Bernard *see* Masters, Bat
Buley, E C 1869- *MnBBF*
Bulfinch, Thomas 1796-1867 *Alli, Alli Sup, AmA, AmA&B, BiD&SB, CarSB, ChPo, DcAmA, DcNAA, OxAm, REn, REnAL*
Bull, Albert E *ChPo, MnBBF*
Bull, Albert E *see* Cromwell, Victor
Bull, Charles Livingston 1874-1932 *ConICB, DcNAA*
Bull, Norman John 1916- *Au&Wr 6*
Bulla, Clyde Robert 1914- *Au&ICB, AuBYP, BkP, ConAu 5R, MorJA, SmATA 2,*

WWW 14
Bullard, Marion *ConICB*
Bullen, Frank Thomas 1857-1915 *BiD&SB,*
  Chambr 3, CyWA, DcEnA Ap, EvLB,
  JBA 1934, LongC, TwCA
Bullen, N Ravenor H *ChPo, MnBBF,*
  WWBWI A
Bullivant, Cecil Henry 1882- *EncM&D,*
  MnBBF, WWBWI A
Bullivant, Cecil Henry *see* Dixon, Robert W
Bullivant, Cecil Henry *see* Everard, Maurice
Bullivant, Cecil Henry *see* Grey, Carlton
Bullivant, Cecil Henry *see* Millard, Alice
Bullivant, Cecil Henry *see* North, Colonel
Bullivant, Cecil Henry *see* Turville, Henry
Bullock, Henry Morton 1902- *WWA 38,*
  WWWor 2
Bullock, L G *AuBYP*
Bullock, W A C *Au&Wr 6*
Bulman, B H *MnBBF*
Bunce, William Harvey 1903- *AuBYP, WNAA*
Bungay, E Newton *WWBWI A*
Bungay, E Newton *see* Lance, John
Bungay, E Newton *see* Richmond, H B
Buntain, Ruth Jaeger *AuBYP*
Bunting, A E *ConAu XR*
Bunting, A E *see* Bunting, Anne Evelyn
Bunting, Anne Evelyn 1928- *ConAu 53*
Bunting, Anne Evelyn *see* Bolton, Evelyn
Bunting, Anne Evelyn *see* Bunting, A E
Bunting, Anne Evelyn *see* Bunting, Eve
Bunting, Eve *ConAu XR*
Bunting, Eve *see* Bunting, Anne Evelyn
Buntline, Ned 1823?-1886 *Alli Sup, AmA,*
  AmA&B, DcAmA, DcNAA, HsB&A,
  MnBBF, OhA&B, OxAm, REn, REnAL,
  WWBWI A
Buntline, Ned *see* Judson, Edward Zane Carroll
Bunyan, John 1628-1668 *Alli, AtlBL, BbD,*
  BiD&SB, BrAu, CarSB, CasWL,
  Chambr 1, ChPo, ChPo S1, ChPo S2,
  CrE&SL, CriT 2, CyWA, DcEnA,
  DcEnL, DcEuL, DcLEnL, EvLB,
  MouLC 1, NCHEL, OxEng, Pen Eng,
  RAdv 1, RCom, REn, WEAL
Burack, Abraham S 1908- *AmA&B,*
  ConAu 9R, WWWorJ 9R
Burack, Sylvia 1916- *ConAu 21R*
Burack, Sylvia *see* Kamerman, Sylvia E
Burbank, Addison *see* Newcomb, Covelle
Burbank, Addison Bushnell 1895- *CatA 1930,*
  IlCB 1744, IlCB 1946, JBA 1951
Burch, Gladys 1899- *AuBYP*
Burch, Robert Joseph 1925- *AuBYP,*
  ConAu 5R, MorBMP, SmATA 1, ThBJA,
  WrD
Burchard, Peter Duncan 1921- *Au&Wr 6,*
  AuBYP, ConAu 5R, IlCB 1946,
  IlCB 1957, SmATA 5, ThBJA
Burchard, Sue 1937- *ConAu 53*
Burchardt, Nellie 1921- *ConAu 21R,*
  SmATA 7, WrD
Burchell, Mary *Au&Wr 6*
Burckmyer, Elizabeth *IlBYP*
Burd, Clara Miller *ChPo, ChPo S2, ConICB*
Burdick, Eugene 1918-1965 *AmA&B,*
  ConAu 5R, ConAu 25R, TwCW, WorAu
Burdick, Loraine 1929- *ConAu 57*
Burford, Eleanor *ConAu XR, EncM&D,*

SmATA 2, WW 1974, WorAu
Burford, Eleanor *see* Hibbert, Eleanor Burford
Burford, Lolah *ConAu 41*
Burg, Marie *Au&Wr 6*
Burger, Carl Victor 1888-1967 *ConAu P-2,*
  IlCB 1957, SmATA 9
Burger, Nash K 1908- *ConAu P-2*
Burgess, Anthony 1917- *Au&Wr 6,*
  AuNews 1, CasWL, CelR 3, ConAu 1R,
  ConLC 1, ConLC 2, ConLC 4, ConLC 5,
  ConNov 1972, ConNov 1976, CurB 72,
  DrAF 1976, EncWL, IntWW 38, LongC,
  ModBL, ModBL Sup, NCHEL, Pen Eng,
  RAdv 1, TwCW, WEAL, WW 1974,
  WWTwL, WWWor 2, WorAu
Burgess, Christopher Victor 1921- *Au&Wr 6,*
  ConAu 9R
Burgess, Gelett 1866-1951 *AmA&B, AmLY,*
  AnMV 1926, BiD&SB, ChPo, ChPo S1,
  CnDAL, ConAmL, ConICB, DcAmA,
  EncM&D, EvLB, IlCB 1744, IlCB 1946,
  LongC, OxAm, REn, REnAL, TwCA,
  TwCA Sup, TwCW, WNAA
Burgess, J R *WWBWI I*
Burgess, Robert F 1927- *ConAu 25R,*
  SmATA 4
Burgess, Thornton Waldo 1874-1965 *AmA&B,*
  AuBYP, CarSB, ChPo, JBA 1934,
  JBA 1951, OxAm, REn, REnAL,
  WNAA, WWCL
Burgess, Trevor *ConAu XR*
Burgess, Trevor *see* Trevor, Elleston
Burglon, Nora *JBA 1951*
Burgoyne, Leon E 1916- *AuBYP*
Burgwyn, Mebane Holoman 1914- *ConAu 49,*
  SmATA 7
Burian, Zdenek 1905- *WWWor 2*
Burke, Carl F 1917- *ConAu 25R*
Burke, Jack *MnBBF*
Burke, John *ConAu XR*
Burke, John *see* O'Connor, Richard
Burke, John Frederick 1922- *ConAu 5R*
Burke, John Frederick *see* Burke, Jonathan
Burke, Jonathan *ConAu XR, MnBBF,*
  WWBWI A
Burke, Jonathan *see* Burke, John Frederick
Burke, Lynn *AuBYP*
Burke, Thomas 1886?-1945 *ChPo, ChPo S1,*
  ChPo S2, CurB 45, EncM&D, EvLB,
  LongC, MnBBF, NCHEL, REn, TwCA,
  WWBWI A, TwCA Sup
Burke, Thomas *see* Rhodes, Oakmead
Burkert, Nancy Ekholm 1933- *ChPo S1,*
  IlBYP, IlCB 1957, ThBJA
Burkett, Molly 1932- *ConAu 53*
Burkholz, Herbert 1932?- *ConAu 25R,*
  Au&Wr 6
Burland, Brian Berkeley 1931- *AuBYP,*
  ConAu 13R, DrAF 1976, WrD
Burland, C A *ConAu XR, SmATA 5*
Burland, C A *see* Burland, Cottie Arthur
Burland, Cottie Arthur 1905- *Au&Wr 6,*
  AuBYP, ConAu 5R, SmATA 5
Burland, Cottie Arthur *see* Burland, C A
Burlingame, Roger 1889-1967 *AmA&B,*
  ConAu 5R, REn, REnAL, SmATA 2,
  TwCA, TwCA Sup
Burlingame, Virginia 1900- *ConAu P-2*
Burlingame, Virginia *see* Struble, Virginia

Burman, Ben Lucien 1895- *AmA&B, Au&Wr 6, ConAu 5R, OxAm, REnAL, SmATA 6, TwCA, TwCA Sup, WNAA, WWA 38, WWWor 2*
Burn, Doris 1923- *ConAu 29, IICB 1957, SmATA 1, WWPNA*
Burnes, Alan Jeffrey 1935- *AmMWS 12S, WWE 14*
Burness, Tad *ConAu XR*
Burness, Tad *see* Burness, Wallace B
Burness, Wallace 1933- *ConAu 69*
Burness, Wallace B *see* Burness, Tad
Burnett, Avis 1937- *ConAu 41*
Burnett, Constance Buel 1893- *AuBYP, ConAu 5R*
Burnett, Frances Eliza Hodgson 1849-1924 *Alli Sup, AmA&B, AuBYP, BbD, BiD&SB, BiDSA, CarSB, Chambr 3, ChPo, ChPo S2, ConAmL, DcAmA, DcBiA, DcLEnL, DcNAA, EvLB, FamSYP, JBA 1934, LongC, OxAm, OxEng, Pen Am, Pen Eng, REn, REnAL, TelT, TwCA, TwCA Sup, WWCL, YABC 2*
Burnett, Ruth 1919- *BiDL 5*
Burnett, Virgil *ChPo S1*
Burnett, Whit 1899-1973 *AmA&B, ConAu 41, ConAu P-2, CurB 41, CurB 73, NYTBE 4, REnAL, TwCA, TwCA Sup, WWA 38*
Burney, Eugenia 1913- *ConAu 29*
Burnford, S D *ConAu XR, SmATA 3*
Burnford, S D *see* Burnford, Sheila
Burnford, Sheila 1918- *Au&Wr 6, AuBYP, BkCL, ChLR 2, ConAu 1R, OxCan, Prof, SmATA 3, WrD*
Burnford, Sheila *see* Burnford, S D
Burnford, Sheila *see* Every, Philip Cochrane
Burningham, Helen Oxenbury *ThBJA*
Burningham, Helen Oxenbury *see* Oxenbury, Helen
Burningham, John Mackintosh 1936- *Au&Wr 6, IIBYP, IICB 1957, ThBJA, WW 1974, WWCL*
Burns, Aubrey *TexW*
Burns, Irene *IIBYP*
Burns, Joan Simpson 1927- *ForWC 1970, WrD*
Burns, Jock *MnBBF*
Burns, Paul C *ConAu 1R, LE 5, SmATA 5*
Burns, Ray *SmATA XR*
Burns, Raymond 1924- *SmATA 9*
Burns, Robert 1759-1796 *Alli, AtlBL, BiD&SB, BrAu, CasWL, ChPo, ChPo S1, ChPo S2, CnE&AP, CriT 2, CyWA, DcEnA, DcEnA Ap, DcEnL, DcEuL, DcLEnL, EvLB, FamAYP, MouLC 2, NCHEL, OxEng, Pen Eng, RAdv 1, RCom, REn, WEAL*
Burns, William A 1909- *ConAu P-1, SmATA 5, WW 1974, WWA 38, WWW 14*
Burow, Daniel Robert 1931- *ConAu 29, WWMW 14*
Burr, Samuel Engle, Jr. 1897- *WWS 13*
Burrage, Alfred McLelland 1889-1956? *MnBBF, WWBWI A*
Burrage, Alfred McLelland *see* Cooee
Burrage, Alfred McLelland *see* Lancaster, Jack

Burrage, Alfred McLelland *see* Lelland, Frank
Burrage, Alfred McLelland *see* Young, Stewart
Burrage, Alfred Sherrington *MnBBF, WWBWI A*
Burrage, Alfred Sherrington *see* Hatherway, Cyril
Burrage, Alfred Sherrington *see* Jackson, Philander
Burrage, Alfred Sherrington *see* Sherrington, Alf
Burrage, Athol Harcourt 1899- *MnBBF*
Burrage, Edwin Harcourt 1839-1916 *MnBBF, WWBWI A*
Burrage, Edwin Harcourt *see* Barron, A Elton
Burrage, Edwin Harcourt *see* Darrell, Walter
Burrage, Edwin Harcourt *see* Morland, Bart
Burris, Burmah *IIBYP*
Burroughs, Edgar Rice 1875-1950 *AmA&B, AmLY, EvLB, LongC, MnBBF, OxAm, Pen Am, REn, REnAL, TwCA, TwCA Sup, TwCW, WWBWI A*
Burroughs, Jean Mitchel 1908- *ConAu 65*
Burroughs, John 1837-1921 *Alli Sup, AmA, AmA&B, AmLY, AnCL, BbD, BiD&SB, CarSB, Chambr 3, ChPo, ConAmL, DcAmA, DcEnA Ap, DcLEnL, DcNAA, EvLB, JBA 1934, OxAm, Pen Am, REn, REnAL*
Burroughs, Margaret Taylor 1917- *ConAu 21R*
Burroughs, Margaret Taylor *see* Taylor, Margaret
Burroughs, Polly 1925- *ConAu 25R, SmATA 2*
Burrow, Diana Wynne *WrD*
Burroway, Janet Gay 1936- *Au&Wr 6*
Burroway, Janet 1936- *ConAu 21R*
Burroway, Janet Gay 1936- *ConNov 1976, DrAS 6E, WrD*
Burrows, Denys *SingR 1*
Burrows, Harold *MnBBF*
Burstein, John 1949- *ConAu 69*
Burt, Jesse Clifton 1921- *ConAu 9R*
Burt, Mary Elizabeth 1850-1918 *Alli Sup, AmA&B, AmLY, DcNAA*
Burt, Nathaniel 1913- *AuBYP, ConAu 17R, DrAS 6E, WWE 14*
Burt, Olive Woolley 1894- *AuBYP, ChPo S2, ConAu 5R, ForWC 1970, SmATA 4*
Burton, Alan *MnBBF*
Burton, Edmund *MnBBF*
Burton, Edmund *see* Childs, Edmund Burton
Burton, Elizabeth *Au&Wr 6, AuBYP*
Burton, Hester 1913- *Au&Wr 6, ChLR 1, ConAu 9R, SmATA 7, ThBJA, WWCL, WrD*
Burton, John Andrew 1944- *ConAu 65*
Burton, John Andrew *WrD*
Burton, Katherine 1887?- *AuBYP, BkC 3, CatA 1930, OhA&B*
Burton, Maurice 1898- *Au&Wr 6, ConAu 65, WW 1974*
Burton, Robert 1941- *ConAu 45*
Burton, Virginia Lee 1909-1968 *AmA&B, AmPB, AnCL, Au&ICB, AuBYP, Cald 1938, ChFB A, ConAu 25R, ConAu P-1, CurB 43, CurB 68, IIBYP, IICB 1744, IICB 1946, IICB 1957, JBA 1951, SmATA 2*
Burton, William H 1890-1964 *ConAu 1R, SmATA 11*

Busby, Edith *AuBYP*
Busby, F M 1921- *ConAu 65*
Busch, Wilhelm 1832-1908 *BiD&SB, CasWL,*
 ChPo, ChPo S1, ChPo S2, ClDMEuL,
 EuAu, EvEuW, OxGer, Pen Eur, REn
Bush, Douglas 1896- *AmA&B, CanWr,*
 ConAu 37, DcLEnL, DrAS 6E, LongC,
 RAdv 1, TwCA Sup, WW 1974
Bush-Brown, Louise 1896?-1973 *AuBYP,*
 ConAu 49
Bushmiller, Ernest Paul 1905- *ConAu 29*
Bushmiller, Ernie *ConAu XR*
Bushmiller, Ernie 1905- *ArtCS, WWA 38*
Buske, Morris Roger 1912- *ConAu 13R*
Busoni, Rafaello 1900- *AmA&B, AuBYP,*
 IICB 1744, IICB 1946, IICB 1957,
 JBA 1951
Bussieres, Simone 1918- *ConAu 53, Prof*
Butcher, Grace 1934- *ConAu 25R*
Butcher, Thomas Kennedy *WrD*
Butcher, Thomas Kennedy 1914- *Au&Wr 6,*
 ConAu P-1, WrD
Butler, Albert 1923- *ConAu 13R*
Butler, Beverly Kathleen 1932- *AuBYP,*
 ChPo S2, ConAu 1R, ForWC 1970,
 SmATA 7
Butler, David Jonathon 1946- *ConAu 69*
Butler, Ellis Parker 1869-1937 *AmA&B, ChPo,*
 DcNAA, EncM&D, JBA 1934, OxAm,
 REnAL, TwCA, WNAA
Butler, Hal 1913- *AuBYP, ConAu 57*
Butler, Horacio 1897- *IICB 1744*
Butler, Mildred Allen 1897- *ConAu 29,*
 WWPNA
Butler, Professor *MnBBF*
Butler, Walter C *EncM&D, WWBWI A*
Butler, Walter C see Faust, Frederick
Butters, Dorothy Gilman 1923- *AmA&B,*
 AuBYP, ConAu 1R, ForWC 1970,
 SmATA 5
Butters, Dorothy Gilman see Gilman, Dorothy
Butterworth, Hezekiah 1839-1905 *Alli Sup,*
 AmA, AmA&B, BbD, BiD&SB, CarSB,
 ChPo, DcAmA, DcNAA
Butterworth, Oliver 1915- *ConAu 1R,*
 SmATA 1, WWA 38
Butterworth, W E 1929- *ConAu 1R,*
 SmATA 5
Butterworth, W E see Beech, Webb
Butterworth, W E see Blake, Walker E
Butterworth, W E see Douglas, James McM
Butterworth, W E see Scholefield, Edmund O
Butterworth, W E see Williams, Patrick J
Butterworth, William Edmund, III 1929-
 WWS 13
Buttfield, Helen *ChPo S1*
Buzzacroft, John *MnBBF*
Buzzati, Dino 1906-1972 *CnMD, ConAu 33,*
 CrCD, EncWL, IICB 1946, NYTBE 3,
 Pen Eur, TwCW, WWTwL, WorAu
Byars, Betsy 1928- *AuBYP, ChLR 1,*
 ConAu 33, MorBMP, NewbC 1966,
 SmATA 4, ThBJA
Bye, Beryl Joyce Rayment 1926- *Au&Wr 6,*
 ConAu 61, WrD
Byers, Irene 1906- *ConAu 9R, WrD*
Byfield, Barbara Ninde 1930- *ConAu 1R,*
 IIBYP, SmATA 8
Byrd, Franklyn *MnBBF*

Byrd, Grady *IIBYP*
Byrne, Peter 1925- *ConAu 65*
Byrnes, Gene 1893- *ArtCS*
Byron, Lord George Gordon Noel 1788-1824 *Alli,*
 AtlBL, BbD, BiD&SB, BiDLA,
 BiDLA Sup, BrAu 19, CasWL,
 Chambr 3, ChPo, ChPo S1, ChPo S2,
 CnE&AP, CnThe, CyWA, DcEnA,
 DcEnL, DcEuL, DcLEnL, EvLB,
 HsB&A, McGWD, NCHEL, OxEng,
 Pen Eng, RAdv 1, RCom, REn, REnWD,
 WEAL

C

Cabassa, Victoria 1912- *ConAu 49*
Cable, Mary 1920- *ConAu 25R, DrAF 1976, SmATA 9*
Caddell, Foster 1921- *WWAA 1973*
Caddy, Alice *IICB 1946*
Cade, Toni *BlkAW, ConAu XR*
Cade, Toni *see* Bambara, Toni Cade
Cadell, Elizabeth 1903- *Au&Wr 6, ConAu 57, CurB 51*
Cadell, Elizabeth *see* Ainsworth, Harriet
Cadwallader, Sharon 1936- *ConAu 49, SmATA 7*
Cady, Harrison 1877?- *ForII, NYTBE 1, WNAA*
Cady, Walter Harrison 1877?- *ChPo, ChPo S1, IICB 1744*
Caen, Herb 1916- *AuNews 1, CelR 3, ConAu 1R, WWA 38, WWWor 2*
Caffrey, Nancy *AuBYP*
Cagle, Malcolm Winfield 1918- *WWA 38*
Cahill *MnBBF*
Cahn, William 1912- *ConAu 21R*
Caidin, Martin 1927- *AmA&B, AuNews 2, ConAu 1R*
Cain, Arthur H 1913- *ConAu 1R, SmATA 3*
Cain, Arthur H *see* King, Arthur
Cain, Christopher *ConAu XR, SmATA 8*
Cain, Christopher *see* Fleming, Thomas J
Caines, Jeannette *BlkAW*
Caird, Janet 1913- *ConAu 49, WrD*
Cairns, Trevor 1922- *ConAu 33*
Calapai, Letterio 1903- *IICB 1946, WWA 38, WWA 1973*
Calde, Mark 1945- *ConAu 69*
Caldecott, Randolph 1846-1886 *AnCL, CarSB, ChPo, ChPo S1, ChPo S2, IIBYP, JBA 1934, JBA 1951, St&VC, WWCL*
Calder-Marshall, Arthur 1908- *Au&Wr 6, ConAu 61, ConNov 1972, ConNov 1976, DcLEnL, WW 1974, WorAu, WrD*
Caldwell, Erskine 1903- *AmA&B, AmNov, AmWr, Au&Wr 6, AuNews 1, BiN 1974, CasWL, CelR 3, CnDAL, ConAmA, ConAu 1R, ConLC 1, ConNov 1972, ConNov 1976, CurB 40, CyWA, DcLEnL, DrAF 1976, EncWL, EvLB, IntWW 38, LongC, ModAL, ModAL Sup, OxAm, Pen Am, RAdv 1, REn, REnAL, TwCA, TwCA Sup, TwCW, WEAL, WNAA, WW 1974, WWA 38, WWS 13, WWTwL, WWWor 2, WrD*
Caldwell, John Cope 1913- *AuBYP,*

ConAu 21R, SmATA 7
Calhoun, Mary *see* Wilkins, Mary Huiskamp Calhoun
Calhoun, Mary Huiskamp 1926- *AuBYP, ConAu 5R, ForWC 1970, SmATA 2, ThBJA*
Calkins, Dick 1895-1962 *ArtCS*
Calkins, Franklin *ConAu XR*
Calkins, Franklin *see* Stratemeyer, Edward L
Calkins, Franklin Welles 1857-1928 *AmA&B, DcNAA, MnBBF, WNAA*
Call, Hughie Florence 1890-1969 *ConAu 5R, SmATA 1, WWPNA*
Callaghan, Morley 1903- *IntWW 38, WW 1974, WrD*
Callahan, Claire Wallis 1890- *AuBYP, ConAu 5R*
Callahan, Dorothy *AuBYP*
Callahan, Jack 1889-1954 *ArtCS*
Callahan, Philip S 1923- *AmMWS 12P*
Callam, Tex *MnBBF*
Calley, William L, Jr. *NYTBS 5*
Callum, Myles 1934- *ConAu 9R, WWA 38*
Calvert, Elinor H *ConAu 5R*
Calvert, Elinor H *see* Lasell, Fen H
Calvert, James *AuBYP*
Calvert, Mary *WrD*
Calvert, Robert, Jr. 1922- *ConAu 25R*
Calvert, William Robinson 1882- *MnBBF*
Calvert, William Robinson *see* Croft, Roy
Calvert, William Robinson *see* Dale, Austin
Cam 1913- *IICB 1946*
Cam *see* Campbell, Barbara
Camden, Richard *MnBBF, WWBWI A*
Camden, Richard *see* Beeston, L J
Cameron, Barbara *SingR 2*
Cameron, Brian *MnBBF*
Cameron, Captain *MnBBF*
Cameron, Clifford *MnBBF*
Cameron, Clifford *see* Garbutt, John L
Cameron, Edna M 1905- *ConAu P-1, SmATA 3*
Cameron, Eleanor 1912- *AuBYP, ChLR 1, ChPo, ConAu 1R, SmATA 1, ThBJA*
Cameron, Elizabeth *ConAu XR, SmATA XR*
Cameron, Elizabeth *see* Nowell, Elizabeth Cameron
Cameron, Elizabeth Jane 1910- *ConAu 1R, WrD*
Cameron, Elizabeth Jane *see* Duncan, Jane
Cameron, John *ChPo, ChPo S1, WWBWI I*
Cameron, Katharine *IICB 1744*

35

Cameron, Polly 1928- *AuBYP, ChPo, ConAu 17R, ForWC 1970, IlCB 1957, SmATA 2*
Cameron, V Lovett *MnBBF*
Cammaerts, Emile Leon 1878-1953 *CarSB, ChPo, ChPo S1, ChPo S2, DcLEnL, EvEuW, LongC, TwCA Sup, WWLA*
Cammaerts, Tita *CarSB*
Camp, Charles L 1893-1975 *ConAu 61*
Camp, Fred V 1911- *ConAu 49*
Camp, Norma Cournow 1939- *ForWC 1970*
Camp, Walter Chauncey 1859-1925 *AmA&B, AmLY, BiD&SB, ChPo, DcAmA, DcNAA, JBA 1934, JBA 1951, REnAL, WNAA, YABC 1*
Campanella, Roy 1921- *CelR 3, WWA 38*
Campbell, Alistair 1925- *ChPo S1, ChPo S2, ConP 1970, ConP 1975, WrD*
Campbell, Andrew C 1923- *AmMWS 12P*
Campbell, Angus *ConAu XR*
Campbell, Angus *see* Chetwynd-Hayes, R
Campbell, Ann R 1925- *ConAu 21R, SmATA 11*
Campbell, Barbara *IlCB 1946*
Campbell, Barbara *see* Cam
Campbell, Beatrice Murphy *ConAu XR*
Campbell, Beatrice Murphy *see* Murphy, Beatrice M
Campbell, Big Bill *MnBBF*
Campbell, Bruce *AuBYP, ConAu XR, MorJA, SmATA 1*
Campbell, Bruce *see* Epstein, Samuel
Campbell, Camilla 1905- *ConAu P-2*
Campbell, Donald *MnBBF*
Campbell, Elizabeth A *AuBYP*
Campbell, G Wells *MnBBF*
Campbell, G Wells *see* Brown, G W
Campbell, Sir Gilbert *MnBBF*
Campbell, Hannah *ConAu 9R*
Campbell, Harry *MnBBF*
Campbell, Harry *see* Smith, Bernard
Campbell, Hope *ConAu 61*
Campbell, Hope *see* Hughes, Virginia
Campbell, Hope *see* Wallis, G McDonald
Campbell, Jane *ConAu XR, SmATA XR*
Campbell, Jane *see* Edwards, Jane Campbell
Campbell, Judith *ConAu XR*
Campbell, Kenneth *MnBBF*
Campbell, Sir Malcolm *MnBBF*
Campbell, Peter 1926- *ConAu 13R*
Campbell, R W *ConAu XR, SmATA 1*
Campbell, R W *see* Campbell, Rosemae Wells
Campbell, Robert 1914- *CanWW 12*
Campbell, Rosemae Wells 1909- *AuBYP, ConAu 13R, SmATA 1*
Campbell, Rosemae Wells *see* Campbell, R W
Campbell, Sydney G *MnBBF*
Campbell, Sydney G *see* Lawrence, Chester
Campbell, Virginia 1914- *ChPo, IlBYP, IlCB 1946*
Campbell, Wanda Jay *AuBYP*
Campe, Joachim Heinrich 1746-1818 *BiD&SB, CarSB, DcEuL*
Campion, Nardi Reeder 1917- *AuBYP, ConAu 1R*
Campling, F Knowles d1940 *MnBBF, WWBWI A*
Campling, F Knowles *see* Wood, Eric
Camps *WWBWI 1*

Campson, Kaye *MnBBF*
Candell, Victor G 1903- *ConICB*
Candy, Robert 1920- *AuBYP, IlCB 1946*
Canfield, Dorothy 1879-1958 *AmA&B, AmNov, Chambr 3, CnDAL, ConAmA, ConAmL, DcBiA, DcLEnL, JBA 1934, LongC, OxAm, REn, REnAL, TwCA, TwCA Sup, WNAA, YABC 1*
Canfield, Dorothy *see* Fisher, Dorothy Canfield
Caniff, Milton 1907- *ArtCS, CelR 3*
Cannam, Peggie 1925- *AuBYP, ConAu 13R*
Cannan, Joanna 1898-1961 *LongC, TwCA, TwCA Sup, WWCL*
Canning, Victor 1911- *Au&Wr 6, ConAu 13R, EncM&D, LongC, MnBBF, WW 1974, WorAu*
Cannon, Beth 1951- *ConAu 69*
Cannon, Cornelia James 1876- *AmA&B, JBA 1934, TwCA, TwCA Sup, WNAA*
Cannon, J R *MnBBF*
Cannon, J R *see* Goddard, Norman Molyneux
Cansdale, George 1909- *ConAu 9R*
Cansford, John *MnBBF*
Cantle, G H *MnBBF, WWBWI A*
Cantwell, Mary *ForWC 1970, WWA 38*
Canusi, Jose *ConAu XR, SmATA XR*
Canusi, Jose *see* Barker, S Omar
Canziani, Estella L M 1887- *ChPo S1, IlCB 1744*
Cape, Peter Irwin *WrD*
Capizzi, Michael 1941- *ConAu 41*
Caplan, Gerald 1917- *AmMWS 12S, Au&Wr 6, ConAu 25R, WWA 38, WWE 14*
Capp, Al 1909- *AmA&B, ArtCS, CelR 3, CurB 47, REnAL, WWA 38, WWAA 1973, WWWor 2*
Capper, Cecil *MnBBF*
Capps, Benjamin 1922- *ConAu 5R, SmATA 9*
Captain, The *MnBBF*
Caras, Roger Andrew 1928- *AmA&B, ConAu 1R, SmATA 12, WWA 38, WWE 14, WWWor 2, WWWorJ 1972*
Caras, Roger Andrew *see* Sarac, Roger
Carbonnier, Jeanne *ConAu P-2, SmATA 3*
Carcupino, F N *WWBWI 1*
Carden, Priscilla *AuBYP*
Cardinal, John C *MnBBF*
Cardon, Guy *MnBBF*
Cardozo, Lois S 1934- *AuBYP, ConAu 1R*
Cardozo, Lois S *see* Arquette, Lois S
Cardozo, Lois S *see* Duncan, Lois
Cardozo, Lois S *see* Kerry, Lois
Cardozo, Peter 1916- *ConAu 61*
Carew, Burleigh *MnBBF, WWBWI A*
Carew, Burleigh *see* Cook, Fred Gordon
Carew, Conway *MnBBF*
Carew, Dorothy 1910?-1973 *ConAu 41, NYTBE 4*
Carew, Jack *MnBBF*
Carew, Jan Rynveld Alwin 1925- *CasWL, ConNov 1972, ConNov 1976, WrD*
Carew, Sidney *MnBBF*
Carew, Singleton *MnBBF*
Carey, Ernestine Gilbreth 1908- *Au&Wr 6, ConAu 5R, CurB 49, SmATA 2, WWA 38, WWAW 8, WWWor 2*
Carigiet, Alois 1902- *IlBYP, IlCB 1946, IlCB 1957, ThBJA, WWGA*

Carini, Edward 1923- *ConAu 61*, *SmATA 9*
Carins, Dixon *MnBBF*
Carle, Eric 1929- *ChPo S2*, *ConAu 25R*, *IlBYP*, *SmATA 4*, *WWE 14*
Carleton, Barbee Oliver 1917- *ConAu 21R*
Carleton, L C, Captain *HsB&A*, *YABC 1*
Carleton, L C, Captain *see* Ellis, Edward S
Carley, Royal V 1906-1976 *WrD*
Carley, V Royal 1906-1976 *ConAu P-2*
Carlisle, Clark *ConAu XR*, *SmATA 3*
Carlisle, Clark *see* Holding, James
Carlisle, Olga Andreyev 1930- *ConAu 13R*
Carloni, Giancarlo *IlBYP*, *IlCB 1957*
Carlsen, G Robert 1917- *ConAu 17R*
Carlsen, Ruth C 1918- *ConAu 17R*, *SmATA 2*, *WrD*
Carlson, Al *IlBYP*
Carlson, Bernice Wells 1910- *AuBYP*, *ConAu 5R*, *ForWC 1970*, *SmATA 8*, *WrD*
Carlson, Carl Walter 1907- *AmMWS 12P*, *ConAu 49*
Carlson, Dale Bick 1935- *ConAu 9R*, *SmATA 1*, *WWE 14*
Carlson, Esther Elisabeth 1920- *AuBYP*, *ConAu 5R*
Carlson, Natalie Savage 1906- *AmA&B*, *AnCL*, *Au&ICB*, *Au&Wr 6*, *AuBYP*, *ConAu 1R*, *ForWC 1970*, *MorBMP*, *MorJA*, *REnAL*, *SmATA 2*, *WWAW 8*, *WrD*
Carlson, Richard Stocks 1942- *ConAu 57*
Carlson, Vada F 1897- *ConAu 21R*
Carlson, Vada F *see* Rose, Florella
Carlton, Lewis 1886- *MnBBF*, *WWBWI A*
Carlton, Lewis *see* Atkinson, Reginald
Carlton, Lewis *see* Carlton, Louise
Carlton, Lewis *see* Clifford, Martin
Carlton, Louise *WWBWI A*
Carlton, Louise *see* Carlton, Lewis
Carlyle, Thomas 1795-1881 *Alli*, *Alli Sup*, *AtlBL*, *BbD*, *BiD&SB*, *BrAu 19*, *CasWL*, *ChPo*, *ChPo S1*, *ChPo S2*, *CriT 3*, *CyWA*, *DcEnA*, *DcEnL*, *DcEuL*, *DcLEnL*, *EvLB*, *FamAYP*, *MouLC 3*, *NCHEL*, *OxEng*, *Pen Eng*, *RAdv 1*, *RCom*, *REn*, *WEAL*
Carmer, Carl Lamson 1893- *AmA&B*, *Au&Wr 6*, *AuBYP*, *ChPo*, *ChPo S1*, *ChPo S2*, *ConAu 5R*, *OxAm*, *REn*, *REnAL*, *St&VC*, *TwCA*, *TwCA Sup*, *WWA 38*, *WWWor 2*
Carmer, Elizabeth Black 1904- *AuBYP*, *IlCB 1946*
Carmichael, Roy *MnBBF*
Carmichael, William Edward 1922- *ConAu 37*
Carnahan, Marjorie R *AuBYP*
Carol, Bill J *AmA&B*, *ConAu XR*, *SmATA 3*
Carol, Bill J *see* Knott, William Cecil, Jr.
Carona, Philip B 1925- *AuBYP*, *ConAu 1R*
Caroselli *WWBWI 1*
Carpelan, Bo 1926- *ConAu 49*, *Pen Eur*, *SmATA 8*
Carpenter, Allan 1917- *ConAu 9R*, *SmATA 3*, *WrD*
Carpenter, Frances 1890-1972 *AmA&B*, *Au&Wr 6*, *AuBYP*, *ConAu 5R*, *ConAu 37*, *ForWC 1970*, *MorJA*,

SmATA 3
Carpenter, Margaret Haley *AmA&B*, *ChPo S1*, *ConAu 5R*, *DrAS 6E*, *ForWC 1970*
Carpenter, Patricia 1920- *AmMWS 12S*, *ConAu 29*, *SmATA 11*
Carpenter, Patricia *see* Evans, Patricia Healy
Carpenter, R A *MnBBF*
Carpentier, Georges *MnBBF*
Carpozi, George, Jr. 1920- *ConAu 13R*
Carr, Adams *MnBBF*
Carr, Adams *see* Walshe, Douglas
Carr, Albert Z 1902-1971 *AmA&B*, *ConAu 1R*, *ConAu 33*, *NYTBE 2*
Carr, Andrew *MnBBF*
Carr, Archie 1909- *WWWor 2*
Carr, Frank *MnBBF*
Carr, Gene 1881-1959 *ArtCS*, *REnAL*
Carr, George *MnBBF*, *WWBWI A*
Carr, George *see* Bayfield, William John
Carr, Glyn *ConAu XR*, *SmATA XR*
Carr, Glyn *see* Styles, Frank Showell
Carr, Gordon *MnBBF*, *WWBWI A*
Carr, Gordon *see* Bayfield, William John
Carr, Gordon *see* Wescombe, Charles
Carr, Gordon *see* West, Edgar
Carr, Harriett Helen 1899- *Au&Wr 6*, *AuBYP*, *ConAu P-1*, *ForWC 1970*, *MorJA*, *SmATA 3*
Carr, Howard *MnBBF*, *WWBWI A*
Carr, Howard *see* Hamilton, Cecily
Carr, Jo Crisler 1926- *ConAu 21R*, *WrD*
Carr, Kent *MnBBF*, *WWBWI A*
Carr, Kent *see* Oliver, Gertrude Kent
Carr, Mary Jane 1899- *AuBYP*, *BkC 1*, *CatA 1952*, *ChPo S2*, *ConAu P-1*, *JBA 1951*, *SmATA 2*
Carr, Melton *MnBBF*
Carr, Philippa *ConAu XR*, *WW 1974*
Carr, Philippa *see* Hibbert, Eleanor Burford
Carr, Wallace 1890- *MnBBF*
Carr-Clements, J *MnBBF*
Carrick, Carol 1935- *ConAu 45*, *SmATA 7*
Carrick, Donald 1929- *ConAu 53*, *IlBYP*, *SmATA 7*
Carrick, Malcolm *WrD*
Carrick, Valery 1869-1948 *AnCL*, *ChPo*, *ConICB*, *IlCB 1744*, *JBA 1934*, *JBA 1951*
Carrighar, Sally *AnCL*, *OhA&B*
Carrillo, Lawrence Wilbert, Jr. 1920- *ConAu 13R*, *LE 5*
Carrington, Hepworth *MnBBF*
Carrington, J K *MnBBF*
Carrington, Molly *ConAu XR*
Carrington, Molly *see* Matthews, C M
Carrington, Richard 1921- *Au&Wr 6*, *ConAu 9R*
Carrison, Daniel J 1917- *ConAu 37*
Carroll, Archer Latrobe 1894- *SmATA 7*
Carroll, Curt *AuBYP*, *ConAu XR*, *SmATA 3*
Carroll, Curt *see* Bishop, Curtis
Carroll, Gladys Hasty 1904- *AmA&B*, *AmNov*, *Au&Wr 6*, *ConAu 1R*, *ForWC 1970*, *OxAm*, *REnAL*, *TwCA*, *TwCA Sup*, *WNAA*, *WWA 38*, *WWAW 8*, *WWE 14*, *WWWor 2*, *WrD*
Carroll, John Millar 1925- *AmMWS 12P*,

⸱ *ConAu 5R, WWMW 14*
Carroll, Joseph T 1935- *Au&Wr 6*
Carroll, Latrobe 1894- *ConAu 1R, MorJA*
Carroll, Laura *ConAu XR, SmATA XR*
Carroll, Laura *see* Parr, Lucy
Carroll, Lewis 1832-1898 *Alli Sup, AnCL,*
    AtlBL, AuBYP, BbD, BiD&SB,
    BrAu 19, CasWL, Chambr 3, ChLR 2,
    ChP, ChPo, ChPo S1, ChPo S2,
    CnE&AP, CriT 3, CyWA, DcEnA,
    DcEnL, DcEuL, DcLEnL, EvLB,
    FamAYP, FamPYP, JBA 1934, NCHEL,
    OxEng, Pen Eng, RAdv 1, REn, St&VC,
    TelT, WEAL, WWCL, YABC XR
Carroll, Lewis *see* Dodgson, Charles Lutwidge
Carroll, Ruth Robinson 1899- *ConAu 1R,*
    IlBYP, IlCB 1946, IlCB 1957, MorJA
Carruth, Estelle 1910- *ConAu 9R*
Carruth, Hayden 1862-1932 *AmA&B, AmLY,*
    CarSB, ChPo, ChPo S1, ChPo S2,
    REnAL
Carruthers, Pat *MnBBF*
Carryl, Charles Edward 1841?-1920 *AmA,*
    AmA&B, AnCL, BiD&SB, CarSB, ChPo,
    ChPo S2, DcNAA, EvLB, JBA 1934,
    OxAm, REn, REnAL, St&VC, TwCA
Carse, Robert 1902-1971 *ConAu 1R,*
    ConAu 29, NYTBE 2, SmATA 5
Carson, J Franklin 1920- *ConAu 13R*
Carson, James, Captain *ConAu XR*
Carson, James, Captain *see* Stratemeyer, Edward
    L
Carson, John Franklin 1920- *AuBYP,*
    ConAu 13R, IndAu 1917, SmATA 1
Carson, Julia Margaret Hicks 1899- *AuBYP,*
    OhA&B
Carson, Kit, Jr. *MnBBF*
Carson, L B *MnBBF*
Carson, L B *see* Bradford, L, Captain
Carson, Matt *MnBBF*
Carson, Rachel Louise 1907-1964 *AmA&B,*
    AnCL, EvLB, LongC, OxAm, REn,
    TwCA Sup, TwCW
Carstairs, Rod *MnBBF*
Carstairs, Rod *see* Dalton, Gilbert
Carswell, Evelyn Medicus 1919- *AuBYP, LE 5*
Carter, A B *MnBBF*
Carter, Ad 1895-1957 *ArtCS*
Carter, Alec *MnBBF*
Carter, Angela 1940- *ConAu 53, ConLC 5*
Carter, Anne *ConAu XR*
Carter, Anne *see* Brooks, Anne Tedlock
Carter, Bruce *AuBYP, ConAu XR,*
    WW 1974
Carter, Bruce *see* Hough, Richard Alexander
Carter, Dorothy Sharp 1921- *ConAu 49,*
    SmATA 8
Carter, Ernest Frank 1899- *Au&Wr 6*
Carter, Frances Tunnell 1922- *AmMWS 12S,*
    ConAu 37, LE 5, WWAW 8, WWS 13,
    WrD
Carter, Helene 1887-1960 *IlCB 1744,*
    IlCB 1946, MorJA
Carter, Herbert S *MnBBF*
Carter, Hodding 1907-1972 *AmA&B, AmNov,*
    AuBYP, ConAu 13R, ConAu 33,
    ConAu P-1, CurR 72, NYTBE 3,
    SmATA 2, TwCA Sup, WWS 13
Carter, James *AuBYP*

Carter, James *see* Mayne, William
Carter, John Thomas 1921- *AmMWS 12S,*
    ConAu 33, LE 5, WWS 13, WrD
Carter, Joseph 1912- *ConAu 49*
Carter, Katharine J 1905- *ConAu 5R,*
    SmATA 2
Carter, Peter 1929- *ConAu 69*
Carter, Phyllis Ann *AuBYP, ConAu XR,*
    SmATA 2
Carter, Phyllis Ann *see* Eberle, Irmengarde
Carter, Robert F 1930- *DrAS 6H*
Carter, Russell Gordon 1892-1957 *AmA&B,*
    WNAA
Carter, Val *MnBBF*
Carter, William E 1926?- *AmMWS 12S,*
    AuBYP, ConAu 17R, SmATA 1
Cartner, William Carruthers 1910- *SmATA 11*
Cartwright, A *MnBBF, WWBWI A*
Cartwright, A *see* Twyman, Harold William
Cartwright, Sally 1923- *ConAu 49, SmATA 9*
Carty, Leo *IlBYP*
Carvalho, Clare N *MnBBF*
Carver, Saxon Rowe 1905- *ConAu P-1*
Cary *IlBYP, SmATA XR*
Cary *see* Cary, Louis F
Cary, Alice 1820-1871 *Alli Sup, AmA,*
    AmA&B, BbD, BiD&SB, CarSB,
    Chambr 3, ChPo, ChPo S1, CyAL 2,
    DcAmA, DcNAA, EvLB, OhA&B,
    OxAm
Cary, Barbara Knapp 1912?-1975 *ConAu 61*
Cary, Louis F 1915- *SmATA 9*
Cary, Louis F *see* Cary
Caryl, Jean *AuBYP, ConAu XR,*
    SmATA XR
Caryl, Jean *see* Kaplan, Jean Caryl Korn
Case, Elinor Rutt 1914- *AuBYP, ConAu 1R*
Case, Marshal T 1941- *ConAu 57, SmATA 9*
Case, Michael *ConAu XR, SmATA 5*
Case, Michael *see* Howard, Robert West
Casewit, Curtis 1922- *ConAu 13R, SmATA 4*
Casewit, Curtis *see* Green, D
Casewit, Curtis *see* Vernor, D
Casewit, Curtis *see* Werner, K
Casey, Brigid 1950- *ConAu 49, SmATA 9*
Cash, S J *WWBWI I*
Cashin, Edward L 1927- *ConAu 21R*
Cason, Mabel Earp 1892-1965 *ConAu P-1,*
    SmATA 10
Cason, Mabel Earp *see* Bell, Emily Mary
Cass, Joan Evelyn *Au&Wr 6, AuBYP,*
    ConAu 1R, SmATA 1, WrD
Cass-Beggs, Barbara *OxCan Sup*
Cassel, Lili 1924- *ChPo, IlCB 1946,*
    SmATA XR
Cassel, Lili *see* Wronker, Lili Cassel
Cassell, Sylvia 1924- *ConAu 5R, WWAW 8,*
    WWMW 14
Casserley, Anne *JBA 1934, JBA 1951*
Cassiday, Bruce 1920- *ConAu 1R*
Cassidy, Martin *MnBBF*
Cassidy, Vincent H 1923- *ConAu 21R,*
    DrAS 6H
Cassilis, Ina Leon *Alli Sup, MnBBF*
Casson, Lionel 1914- *Au&Wr 6, ConAu 9R,*
    DrAS 6H
Casson, R T *MnBBF*
Castellanos, Jane Mollie Robinson 1913-
    ConAu 9R, SmATA 9

Castellon, Federico 1914- *DcCAA 2,*
IlCB 1946
Castillo, Edmund L 1924- *AuBYP, ConAu 29,*
SmATA 1, WrD
Castle, Lee *ConAu XR, SmATA XR*
Castle, Lee *see* Ogan, George F
Castle, Lee *see* Ogan, Margaret E
Castleton, A G *MnBBF*
Castor, Henry 1909- *AuBYP, ConAu 17R*
Caswell, Helen Rayburn 1923- *ConAu 33,*
OxCan Sup, SmATA 12, WWAA 1973
Catchpole, William Leslie 1900?- *MnBBF,*
WWBWI A
Catchpole, William Leslie *see* Clifford, Martin
Catchpole, William Leslie *see* Conquest, Owen
Catchpole, William Leslie *see* Hawkins, Johns
Catchpole, William Leslie *see* Howard, Rowland
Catchpole, William Leslie *see* Howard, Roland
Catchpole, William Leslie *see* Hunter, Rowland
Catchpole, William Leslie *see* Richards, Frank
Catcombe, George *MnBBF*
Cathel, E E *MnBBF*
Cather, Carolyn *IlBYP*
Cather, Willa Sibert 1873?-1947 *AmA&B,*
AmWr, AtlBL, CasWL, Chambr 3,
ChPo, ChPo Sl, CnDAL, ConAmA,
ConAmL, CyWA, DcBiA, DcLEnL,
DcNAA, EncWL, EvLB, JBA 1934,
LongC, ModAL, ModAL Sup, OxAm,
OxCan, OxEng, Pen Am, RAdv 1,
RCom, REn, REnAL, TwCA,
TwCA Sup, TwCW, WEAL, WNAA,
WWTwL
Catherall, Arthur 1906- *Au&Wr 6, AuBYP,*
ConAu 5R, MnBBF, SmATA 3, WrD
Catherall, Arthur *see* Channel, A R
Catherall, Arthur *see* Corby, Dan
Catherall, Arthur *see* Hallard, Peter J
Catherwood, Mary Hartwell 1847-1902 *Alli Sup,*
AmA, AmA&B, BbD, BiD&SB, DcAmA,
DcBiA, DcLEnL, DcNAA, IndAu 1816,
JBA 1934, OhA&B, OxAm, REnAL
Cathon, Laura E 1908- *BiDL 5, ConAu 5R*
Cathon, Laura Elizabeth 1908- *ForWC 1970*
Catlin, Wynelle 1930- *ConAu 65, SmATA 13*
Catling, G *MnBBF*
Catling, Patrick Skene *WrD*
Catling, Thomas G *MnBBF*
Catton, Bruce 1899- *Alli Sup, AmA&B,*
AuNews 1, BiN 1974, CelR 3,
ConAu 5R, CurB 54, IntWW 38, OxAm,
Pen Am, REn, REnAL, SmATA 2,
TwCA Sup, WW 1974, WWA 38,
WWWor 2
Catz, Max *ConAu XR, SmATA XR*
Catz, Max *see* Glaser, Milton
Caudill, Rebecca 1899- *AmA&B, AuBYP,*
ChPo Sl, ConAu 5R, CurB 50,
ForWC 1970, MorJA, SmATA 1,
WWA 38, WWAW 8, WrD
Cauldwell, H T *MnBBF, WWBWI A*
Cauman, Sam 1910-1971 *ConAu P-2*
Causley, Charles 1917- *Au&Wr 6, AuBYP,*
ChPo, ChPo Sl, ChPo S2, CnE&AP,
ConAu 9R, ConP 1970, ConP 1975,
LongC, NCHEL, SmATA 3, WEAL,
WorAu, WrD
Cavallo, Diana 1931- *AmA&B, ConAu 1R,*
SmATA 7, WWA 38, WWAW 8,

WWE 14
Cavanah, Frances 1899- *AuBYP, ConAu 13R,*
CurB 54, ForWC 1970, IndAu 1917,
MorJA, SmATA 1, WNAA, WWAW 8,
WWS 13
Cavanna, Betty 1909- *Au&Wr 6, AuBYP,*
ConAu 9R, CurB 50, MorJA, SmATA 1
Cavanna, Betty *see* Allen, Betsy
Cavanna, Betty *see* Headley, Elizabeth
Cavendish, Peter *WWBWI A*
Cavendish, Peter *see* Horler, Sydney
Cavin, Ruth 1918- *ConAu 61*
Cavin, Wilfred *MnBBF*
Cawley, Winifred 1915- *ConAu 69,*
SmATA 13
Cebulash, Mel 1937- *ConAu 29, SmATA 10,*
WrD
Cebulash, Mel *see* Farrell, Ben
Cebulash, Mel *see* Harlan, Glen
Cebulash, Mel *see* Jansen, Jared
Cebulash, Mel *see* Mara, Jeanette
Ceder, Georgiana Dorcas *AmA&B, ConAu 1R,*
SmATA 10
Ceder, Georgianna Dorcas *see* Dor, Ana
Cellini, Eva *IlBYP*
Cellini, Joseph 1924- *IlBYP, IlCB 1957*
Cerf, Bennett Alfred 1898-1971 *AmA&B,*
Au&Wr 6, AuBYP, BiEnAT, ConAu 29,
ConAu P-2, CurB 41, CurB 58, CurB 71,
NYTBE 2, REn, REnAL, SmATA 7
Cerf, Christopher 1941- *ConAu 25R,*
SmATA 2
Cervantes, Miguel S De 1547-1616 *AtlBL, BbD,*
BiD&SB, CasWL, CnThe, CyWA,
DcBiA, DcEuL, DcSpL, EuAu, EvEuW,
McGWD, NCHEL, OxEng, Pen Eur,
RCom, REn, REnWD
Cervon, Jacqueline *ConAu XR*
Cervon, Jacqueline *see* Moussard, Jacqueline
Cetin, Frank Stanley 1921- *ConAu 1R,*
SmATA 2
Chaconas, D J 1938- *ConAu 21R*
Chadwick, Doris *SingR 1*
Chadwick, Lester *ConAu P-2, SmATA 1*
Chadwick, Lester *see* Stratemeyer, Edward L
Chafetz, Henry 1916- *AuBYP, ConAu 1R*
Chaffee, Allen *AmA&B, ConAu P-1,*
MnBBF, SmATA 3, WNAA, WrD
Chaffin, Lillie D 1925- *ConAu 33, DrAF 1976,*
ForWC 1970, SmATA 4, WWAW 8,
WrD
Chai, Winberg 1934?- *AmMWS 12S,*
ConAu 5R
Chaikin, Miriam *ForWC 1970*
Chaillu, Paul B Du *see* DuChaillu, Paul B
Chaillu, Paul Belloni Du 1829- *Chambr 3,*
DcEnL, JBA 1934
Chalfont, Peter *MnBBF*
Chalmers, Audrey 1899?-1957 *AuBYP,*
IlCB 1744, IlCB 1946
Chalmers, Mary Eileen 1927- *AmPB, AuBYP,*
ChPo, ConAu 5R, IlCB 1946, IlCB 1957,
SmATA 6, ThBJA
Chalon, John *WrD*
Chamberlain, Christopher 1918- *ArtsCL,*
IlCB 1957
Chamberlain, Elinor 1901- *AuBYP,*
ConAu P-1
Chamberlain, Joseph Miles 1923- *AmMWS 12P,*

WWA 38
Chamberlin, Eric Russell 1926- *Au&Wr 6*
Chamberlin, Jo Hubbard *AuBYP*
Chambers, Aidan 1934- *Au&Wr 6, ChPo S2, ConAu 25R, SmATA 1*
Chambers, C Bosseron *ConICB*
Chambers, Derek *MnBBF, WWBWI A*
Chambers, Derek *see* Hyde, D Herbert
Chambers, Margaret Ada Eastwood 1911- *ConAu 9R, SmATA 2*
Chambers, Margaret Ada Eastwood *see* Chambers, Peggy
Chambers, Peggy 1911- *Au&Wr 6, ConAu XR, SmATA 2*
Chambers, Peggy *see* Chambers, Margaret Ada Eastwood
Chambers, Philip 1936- *MnBBF, WWBWI A*
Chambers, Rex *MnBBF*
Chambers, Robert Warner 1924- *AmMWS 12P, AuBYP*
Chambers, Robert William 1865-1933 *AmA&B, BbD, BiD&SB, CarSB, Chambr 3, ChPo, ChPo S2, DcAmA, DcBiA, DcLEnL, DcNAA, OxAm, REnAL, TwCA*
Chambers, Sydney *MnBBF*
Champ, Tom *MnBBF*
Champney, Elizabeth Williams 1850-1922 *AmA&B, BbD, BiD&SB, CarSB, ChPo, ChPo S1, DcAmA, DcNAA, OhA&B*
Chan, Plato 1931- *IICB 1744*
Chance, John Newton 1911- *MnBBF, WWBWI A*
Chance, John Newton *see* Drummond, John
Chance, John Newton *see* Newton, David C
Chance, Richard Newton d1957 *MnBBF, WWBWI A*
Chancellor, John *Au&Wr 6, MnBBF*
Chandler, Anna Curtis *ChPo*
Chandler, Caroline Augusta 1906- *AmA&B, AmMWS 12S, AuBYP, BkC 4, CatA 1930, ConAu 17R, WWA 38, WWAW 8*
Chandler, David Porter 1933- *ConAu 45*
Chandler, Edna Walker 1908- *AuBYP, ConAu 1R, SmATA 11*
Chandler, Ruth Forbes 1894- *AuBYP, ConAu 1R, SmATA 2, WrD*
Chandler, Thomas 1911- *Alli, AuBYP*
Chandos, Herbert *MnBBF*
Chandos, Herbert *see* Maitland, T G Dowling
Chaneles, Sol 1926- *AmMWS 12S, ConAu 41*
Chaney, Jill 1932- *ConAu 25R*
Chang, Isabelle Chin 1924- *BiDL 5, WWAW 8, WrD*
Channel, A R *ConAu XR, MnBBF, SmATA 3*
Channel, A R *see* Catherall, Arthur
Channing-Renton, E M *WrD*
Chanover, Hyman 1920- *ConAu 49, WWWorJ 1972*
Chapin, Henry 1893- *Au&Wr 6, AuBYP*
Chapman, A H 1924- *ConAu 25R*
Chapman, Abraham 1915- *ConAu 45, DrAS 6E*
Chapman, Allen *ConAu XR, ConAu P-2, SmATA 1*
Chapman, Allen *see* Stratemeyer, Edward L
Chapman, Arthur Edward *MnBBF*
Chapman, Charles Henry 1879- *WWBWI I,*

WWCL
Chapman, Elizabeth 1919- *ConAu P-1, SmATA 10, WrD*
Chapman, Frank Michler 1864-1945 *AmA&B, CurB 46, DcAmA, DcNAA, JBA 1934, REnAL, TwCA, TwCA Sup*
Chapman, Frederick Trench 1887- *ChPo, IICB 1946*
Chapman, G H Murray *MnBBF*
Chapman, Jean *SingR 2*
Chapman, John Stanton *see* Chapman, Maristan
Chapman, John Stanton *see* Selkirk, Jane
Chapman, John Stanton Higham 1891- *AmA&B, AuBYP, TwCA, TwCA Sup, WNAA*
Chapman, Maristan *AmA&B, AmNov, AuBYP, REnAL, TwCA, TwCA Sup, WNAA*
Chapman, Maristan *see* Chapman, John Stanton
Chapman, Maristan *see* Chapman, Mary Hamilton Illsley
Chapman, Mary Hamilton Illsley 1895- *AmA&B, AmNov X, AuBYP, WNAA*
Chapman, Mary Hamilton Illsley *see* Chapman, Maristan
Chapman, Peggy *IIBYP*
Chapman, S H *WWBWI I*
Chapman, Sydney 1888-1970 *CurB 57, CurB 70, NYTBE 1, WWLA*
Chapman, Victoria L 1944- *ConAu 57*
Chapman, Walker *ConAu XR, SmATA XR, ThBJA*
Chapman, Walker *see* Silverberg, Robert
Chapone, Hester 1727-1801 *Alli, BiD&SB, BrAu, CarSB, CasWL, Chambr 2, ChPo, DcEnL, DcLEnL, EvLB, NCHEL, WEAL*
Chappell, Warren 1904- *ConAu 17R, IIBYP, IICB 1744, IICB 1946, IICB 1957, SmATA 6, ThBJA, WWAA 1973, WWGA*
Charles, Donald *IIBYP*
Charles, Louis *ConAu XR*
Charles, Louis *see* Stratemeyer, Edward L
Charles, Nicholas *ThBJA*
Charles, Nicholas *see* Kuskin, Karla Seidman
Charlesworth, Marie Louisa 1819-1880 *WWCL*
Charlie *MnBBF*
Charlip, Remy 1929- *AmPB, AuBYP, ChPo S1, ConAu 33, IICB 1946, IICB 1957, SmATA 4, ThBJA, WrD*
Charlot, Jean 1898- *AmPB, CatA 1952, ConAu 5R, CurB 45, IIBYP, IICB 1744, IICB 1946, IICB 1957, MorJA, SmATA 8, WWA 38, WWAA 1973, WWW 14*
Charlson, David *ConAu XR*
Charlson, David *see* Holmes, David Charles
Charlton *MnBBF*
Charlwood, D E 1915- *ConAu 21R, SingR 2, WrD*
Charmatz, Bill 1925- *ConAu 29, SmATA 7*
Charnock, Joan 1903- *Au&Wr 6, ConAu P-2, WrD*
Charnock, Joan *see* Thomson, Joan
Charosh, Mannis 1906- *ConAu 29, SmATA 5, WWE 14*
Charry, Elias 1906- *WWWorJ 1972*
Charteris, F C *MnBBF*
Charteris, Leslie 1907- *AmA&B, Au&Wr 6,*

ConAu 5R, EncM&D, EvLB,
IntMPA 1975, IntWW 38, LongC,
MnBBF, NCHEL, REn, REnAL, TwCA,
TwCA Sup, TwCW, WW 1974,
WWA 38, WWBWI A, WWS 13
Charvat, William 1905- *ChPo*
Chase, Alice *ConAu XR, SmATA 4*
Chase, Alice *see* McHargue, Georgess
Chase, Alice Elizabeth 1906- *Au&Wr 6,*
AuBYP, ConAu P-1, DrAS 6H,
ForWC 1970, WWAA 1973
Chase, Mary Coyle 1907- *AmA&B, AuBYP,*
BiEnAT, CnDAL, CnMD, ConDr 1,
CurB 45, DcLEnL, LongC, McGWD,
ModWD, OxAm, REn, REnAL,
TwCA Sup, WWA 38, WWAW 8, WrD
Chase, Mary Ellen 1887-1973 *AmA&B,*
AmNov, AuBYP, ChPo, ConAmA,
ConAu 41, ConAu P-1, ConLC 2,
CurB 40, CurB 73, DcLEnL, LongC,
NYTBE 4, OxAm, Pen Am, REn,
REnAL, SmATA 10, TwCA, TwCA Sup,
WNAA, WW 1974, WWAW 8
Chase, Powell *ChPo, MnBBF*
Chase, Rhoda *ChPo S2, ConICB*
Chase, Richard 1904- *AmA&B, AnCL, BkCL,*
ChPo S1, ConAu 61, MorJA, WWA 38
Chase, Stuart 1888- *AmA&B, ChPo S2,*
ConAmA, CurB 40, DcLEnL, IntWW 38,
LongC, OxAm, REn, REnAL, TwCA,
TwCA Sup, WNAA, WW 1974,
WWA 38, WWWor '2
Chasefield, H Carlton *MnBBF*
Chaseton *MnBBF*
Chastain, Madye Lee 1908- *AmA&B,*
ConAu 5R, CurB 58, IlCB 1946, MorJA,
SmATA 4
Chatelain, Clara De 1807-1876 *Alli Sup,*
CarSB
Chatham, Frank *MnBBF, WWBWI A*
Chatham, Frank *see* Rochester, George Ernest
Chaucer, Geoffrey 1340?-1400? *Alli, AnCL,*
AtlBL, BbD, BiD&SB, BrAu, CasWL,
Chambr 1, ChPo, ChPo S1, ChPo S2,
CnE&AP, CriT 1, CyWA, DcEnA,
DcEnL, DcEuL, DcLEnL, EvLB,
MouLC 1, NCHEL, OxEng, Pen Eng,
PoLE, RAdv 1, RCom, REn, WEAL
Chauncy, Nan Masterman 1900-1970 *AuBYP,*
ConAu 1R, SingR 1, SmATA 6, ThBJA
Chaundler, Christine 1887-1972 *Au&Wr 6,*
ChPo, ChPo S1, ChPo S2, ConAu P-2,
SmATA 1, WWCL
Chaundler, Christine *see* Martin, Peter
Chaverton, Bruce *MnBBF, WWBWI A*
Chaverton, Bruce *see* Cook, Fred Gordon
Chaytor, Henry John 1871- *MnBBF, WWLA*
Cheetham, Tom *MnBBF*
Cheifetz, Dan 1926- *ConAu 69, DrAF 1976*
Chekenian, Jane Gerard *ConAu XR*
Chen, Anthony *WrD*
Chen, Tony 1929- *ConAu 37, SmATA 6*
Chenault, Nell *ConAu XR, SmATA 2*
Chenault, Nell *see* Smith, Linell Nash
Cheney, Cora 1916- *AuBYP, ConAu 1R,*
SmATA 3
Cheney, Richard Eugene 1921- *WWA 38,*
WWE 14
Cheney, Sheldon Warren 1886- *WWA 38,*

WWWor 2
Cheney, Ted *ConAu XR, SmATA XR*
Cheney, Ted *see* Cheney, Theodore Albert
Cheney, Theodore Albert 1928- *ConAu 61,*
SmATA 11
Cheney, Theodore Albert *see* Cheney, Ted
Cheng, Hou-Tien 1944- *ConAu 69*
Chermayeff, Ivan 1932- *AmPB, ChPo,*
IlCB 1957, WWA 38, WWAA 1973,
WWE 14
Chernoff, Dorothy A *ConAu XR*
Chernoff, Dorothy A *see* Ernst, John
Chernoff, Goldie Taub 1909- *ConAu 33,*
SmATA 10
Cherryholmes, Anne *AuBYP, ConAu XR,*
SmATA 8
Cherryholmes, Anne *see* Price, Olive
Cherub, The *MnBBF*
Cherub, The *see* Gerard, John
Chesher, Kim *WrD*
Cheshire, Clive *MnBBF*
Chesler, Bernice 1932- *ConAu 25R*
Chesnutt, Charles Waddell 1858-1932 *AmA&B,*
AmLY, BlkAW, CasWL, CnDAL,
CyWA, DcAmA, DcNAA, OhA&B,
OxAm, Pen Am, REn, REnAL, TwCA,
TwCA Sup, WNAA
Chess, Victoria *ChPo S1*
Chester, George, Captain *MnBBF*
Chester, Gilbert 1888-1958 *MnBBF,*
WWBWI A
Chester, Gilbert *see* Gibbons, Harry Hornaby
Clifford
Chester, Michael 1928- *AuBYP, ConAu 1R*
Chesterton, Gilbert Keith 1874-1936 *AnCL,*
AtlBL, BkC 6, CasWL, CatA 1930,
Chambr 3, ChPo, ChPo S1, ChPo S2,
DcLEnL, EvLB, OxEng, Pen Eng,
TwCA, TwCA Sup, TwCW, WWLA
Chesterton, Rupert *MnBBF, WWBWI A*
Chetin, Helen 1922- *ConAu 29, SmATA 6*
Chetwynd-Hayes, R 1919- *ConAu 61*
Chetwynd-Hayes, R *see* Campbell, Angus
Chew, Ruth 1920- *ConAu 41, SmATA 7*
Chew, Ruth *see* Silver, Ruth
Cheyney, Peter 1896-1951 *DcLEnL, EncM&D,*
EvLB, MnBBF, REn, TwCW,
WWBWI A
Cheyney, Peter *see* Cheyney, Reginald Southouse
Cheyney, Reginald Southouse 1896-1951
MnBBF
Cheyney, Reginald Southouse *see* Cheyney, Peter
Chiang, Yee 1903- *DrAS 6F, IlCB 1744,*
IlCB 1946, LongC, TwCA Sup,
WW 1974, WWA 38
Chicorel, Marietta *BiDL 5*
Chidsey, Donald Barr 1902- *AmA&B, AmNov,*
Au&Wr 6, ConAu 5R, REnAL,
SmATA 3, TwCA Sup
Child, Charles Jesse 1901- *ChPo, IlCB 1744*
Child, Lydia Maria 1802-1880 *Alli, Alli Sup,*
AmA, AmA&B, BbD, BiD&SB, CarSB,
CasWL, Chambr 3, ChPo, ChPo S1,
ChPo S2, CyAL 2, DcAmA, DcEnL,
DcLEnL, DcNAA, EvLB, OxAm,
REnAL, St&VC
Child, Richard Washburn 1881-1935 *AmA&B,*
DcNAA, EncM&D, MnBBF, WNAA
Childers, Erskine 1905- *BiN 1975, WW 1974*

Childress, Alice 1920- *BlkAW, ConAu 45, LBAA, SmATA 7, WWA 38, WWAW 8*
Childs, Edmund Burton 1887- *MnBBF*
Childs, Edmund Burton *see* Aynesworth, Cecil
Childs, Edmund Burton *see* Blake, Royston
Childs, Edmund Burton *see* Burton, Edmund
Childs, H Fay 1890-1971 *ConAu P-1, SmATA 1*
Childs, John Farnsworth 1909- *AuBYP, WWA 38*
Childs, Maryanna 1910- *ConAu 9R, DrAS 6E*
Chimaera *ConAu XR, SmATA 2*
Chimaera *see* Farjeon, Eleanor
Chipperfield, Joseph Eugene 1912- *Au&Wr 6, AuBYP, ConAu 9R, MorJA, SmATA 2*
Chipperfield, Joseph Eugene *see* Craig, John Eland
Chisholm, Matt *ConAu XR*
Chisholm, Matt *see* Watts, Peter Christopher
Chitham, Edward *WrD*
Chittenden, Elizabeth F 1903- *ConAu 61, SmATA 9*
Chittenden, Margaret 1935- *ConAu 53*
Chittum, Ida 1918- *ConAu 37, SmATA 7, WrD*
Choate, Florence *ConICB*
Chorao, Kay 1936- *ConAu 49, IlBYP, SmATA 8*
Choron, Jacques 1904-1972 *AuBYP, ConAu 33, ConAu P-1, WWA 38*
Chrisman, Arthur Bowie 1889-1953 *AmA&B, AnCL, AuBYP, JBA 1934, JBA 1951, Newb 1922, REnAL, YABC 1*
Christensen, Gardell Dano 1907- *AuBYP, ConAu 9R, IlCB 1946, SmATA 1*
Christensen, Haaken 1886- *IlCB 1946*
Christgau, Alice Erickson 1902- *SmATA 13*
Christian, Mary Blount 1933- *ConAu 45, WrD, SmATA 9*
Christian, Roy Cloberry *WrD*
Christian, Samuel Terry 1937- *AmMWS 12P*
Christie, Agatha 1890?-1976 *Au&Wr 6, AuBYP, AuNews 1, AuNews 2, BiEnAT, BiN 1974, CasWL, CelR 3, CnThe, ConAu 17R, ConAu 61, ConDr 1, ConLC 1, ConLC 6, ConNov 1972, ConNov 1976, CurB 40, CurB 64, DcLEnL, EncM&D, EvLB, IntWW 38, LongC, MnBBF, NCHEL, OxEng, Pen Eng, REn, TwCA, TwCA Sup, TwCW, WW 1974, WWT 15*
Christie, Ann Philippa *WrD*
Christie, Stephen *MnBBF*
Christie, Stephen *see* Kuruppu, D S C
Christopher, John 1922- *ChLR 2, SenS, WorAu*
Christopher, Matt 1917- *WrD*
Christopher, Matt *see* Martin, Frederic
Christopher, Matthew F 1917- *AuBYP, ConAu 1R, MorBMP, SmATA 2*
Christy, Howard Chandler 1873?-1952 *AmA&B, ChPo, ChPo S2, IlCB 1744*
Chroman, Eleanor 1937- *ConAu 45*
Chrystie, Frances Nicholson 1904- *AuBYP*
Chu, Daniel 1933- *ConAu 13R, SmATA 11*
Chubb, Thomas Caldecot 1899-1972 *AmA&B, Au&Wr 6, ChPo, ChPo S1, ChPo S2, ConAu 1R, ConAu 33, NYTBE 3, REn, REnAL, WNAA*

Chukovsky, Korney Ivanovich 1882-1969 *AmPB, AuBYP, CasWL, ChPo S1, ChPo S2, ConAu 5R, ConAu 25R, Pen Eur, SmATA 5, WorAu*
Church, A J 1829-1912 *CarSB*
Church, Alfred John 1829-1912 *Alli Sup, AuBYP, ChPo S2, JBA 1934, JBA 1951, TelT*
Church, Richard 1893-1972 *Au&Wr 6, ChPo, ChPo S1, ChPo S2, ConAu 1R, ConAu 33, ConNov 1972, ConP 1970, DcLEnL, EvLB, LongC, ModBL, MorJA, NCHEL, Pen Eng, REn, SmATA 3, TwCA, TwCA Sup, TwCW, WWCL*
Churchill, E Richard 1937- *ConAu 17R, SmATA 11*
Churchill, Linda Rivers Ruler 1938- *ConAu 21R, WWAW 8*
Churchill, Winston 1871-1947 *AmA&B, BbD, BiD&SB, BiDSA, CarSB, CasWL, CnDAL, ConAmA, ConAmL, CyWA, DcAmA, DcBiA, DcLEnL, DcNAA, EvLB, JBA 1934, LongC, OxAm, OxEng, Pen Am, REn, REnAL, TwCA Sup, TwCW, WEAL, WNAA*
Chute, B J 1913- *AmA&B, ConAu 1R, MnBBF, MorJA, SmATA 2, WWAW 8, WrD*
Chute, Marchette Gaylord 1909- *AmA&B, Au&Wr 6, AuBYP, BiEnAT, BkCL, ChPo, ChPo S1, ChPo S2, ConAu 1R, CurB 50, DrAS 6H, EvLB, MnnWr, MorJA, RAdv 1, REnAL, SmATA 1, TwCA Sup, WW 1974, WWA 38, WWAW 8, WrD*
Chwast, Jacqueline 1932- *ChPo, ChPo S2, ConAu 49, IlBYP, IlCB 1957, SmATA 6*
Chwast, Seymour *IlBYP*
Ciardi, John 1916- *AmA&B, AuBYP, BkCL, BkP, CasWL, CelR 3, ChPo, ChPo S1, ChPo S2, CnDAL, ConAu 5R, ConP 1970, ConP 1975, CurB 67, DrAP 1975, DrAS 6E, ModAL, OxAm, Pen Am, RAdv 1, REn, REnAL, SmATA 1, St&VC, ThBJA, TwCA Sup, WEAL, WWA 38, WWE 14, WWWor 2, WrD*
Cingoli, Giulio *IlBYP, IlCB 1957*
Cinnamond, H P *MnBBF*
Citron, Samuel J 1908- *WWWorJ 1972*
Clagett, John 1916- *AmA&B, AuBYP, ConAu 5R*
Claiborne, Craig 1920- *AmA&B, ConAu 1R, CurB 69, WWA 38, WWE 14*
Claiborne, Robert 1919- *ConAu 29*
Clair, Andree *ConAu 29*
Clapp, Patricia 1912- *ConAu 25R, SmATA 4, WrD*
Clare, Helen *AuBYP, ConAu XR, SmATA 3, ThBJA, WWCL*
Clare, Helen *see* Hunter Blair, Pauline
Clare, Ronald *MnBBF*
Clare, Vincent *MnBBF*
Clark, Alfred *MnBBF*
Clark, Ann Nolan 1898- *AmA&B, AmPB, AnCL, Au&ICB, AuBYP, ConAu 5R, JBA 1951, MorBMP, Newb 1922, SmATA 4, St&VC, WWA 38, WWAW 8*

Clark, Billy Curtis 1928- *ConAu 1R,*
WWS 13
Clark, Champ 1923- *WWA 38*
Clark, David *see* Hardcastle, Michael
Clark, David Allen *ConAu XR*
Clark, David Allen *see* Ernst, John
Clark, Denis d1950? *AuBYP*
Clark, Eleanor 1913- *AmA&B, ConAu 9R,*
ConLC 5, ConNov 1972, ConNov 1976,
DrAF 1976, REnAL, TwCA Sup,
WWA 38, WrD
Clark, Electa 1910- *ConAu 69*
Clark, Eric 1911- *Au&Wr 6, ConAu 13R,*
WrD
Clark, Frank 1922- *AuBYP*
Clark, Frederick Stephen 1908- *ConAu 21R,*
WrD
Clark, Geoffrey H *MnBBF*
Clark, H H *CarSB*
Clark, H R D *MnBBF*
Clark, Mrs. Henry *MnBBF*
Clark, Howard *ConAu XR*
Clark, Howard *see* Haskin, Dorothy Clark
Clark, Imogen d1936 *AmA&B, BiD&SB,*
CarSB, DcAmA, DcNAA, WNAA
Clark, Leonard 1905- *Au&Wr 6, ChPo,*
ChPo S1, ChPo S2, ConAu 13R,
ConP 1970, ConP 1975, WW 1974, WrD
Clark, Margaret Goff 1913- *AuBYP,*
ConAu 1R, ForWC 1970, SmATA 8
Clark, Margery *BkCL*
Clark, Maria Louisa Guidish 1926- *ConAu 5R,*
WWAW 8, WrD
Clark, Maria Louisa Guidish *see* Clark, Mary
Lou
Clark, Marjorie Agnes 1911- *Au&Wr 6,*
ConAu 33, WrD
Clark, Mary Lou *ConAu XR*
Clark, Mary Lou *see* Clark, Maria Louisa
Guidish
Clark, Mavis Thorpe *ConAu 57, SingR 1,*
SmATA 8
Clark, Mavis Thorpe *see* Latham, Mavis
Clark, Merle *ConAu XR*
Clark, Merle *see* Gessner, Lynne
Clark, Patricia 1929- *SmATA 11*
Clark, Ronald William 1916- *Au&Wr 6,*
AuBYP, ConAu 25R, SmATA 2
Clark, Sue C 1935- *ConAu 41*
Clark, Van D 1909- *ConAu P-1, SmATA 2*
Clark, Virginia *ConAu XR, SmATA 7*
Clark, Virginia *see* Gray, Patricia Clark
Clark, W Fordyce 1865- *MnBBF*
Clark, Walter VanTilburg 1909-1971 *AmA&B,*
AmNov, CnDAL, ConAu 9R, ConAu 33,
ConNov 1972, ConNov 1976, CyWA,
ModAL, OxAm, Pen Am, RAdv 1, REn,
REnAL, SmATA 8, TwCA Sup
Clarke, Arthur Charles 1917- *Au&Wr 6,*
AuBYP, CelR 3, ConAu 1R, ConLC 1,
ConLC 4, ConNov 1972, ConNov 1976,
CurB 66, EvLB, IntWW 38, LongC,
NCHEL, SmATA 13, TwCA Sup,
TwCW, WEAL, WW 1974, WWWor 2
Clarke, Arthur E d1911 *WWBWI I*
Clarke, Arthur G 1887- *ConAu P-2*
Clarke, C E *MnBBF*
Clarke, Caroline Cowles Richard 1842-1913
CarSB

Clarke, Clorinda 1917- *ConAu 25R,*
SmATA 7, WWAW 8, WrD
Clarke, E Lidner *MnBBF*
Clarke, G R Lidner *MnBBF*
Clarke, Harry 1890- *ConICB*
Clarke, J F Gates 1905- *ConAu P-1*
Clarke, Joan *WrD*
Clarke, John *ConAu XR, SmATA 5*
Clarke, John *see* Laklan, Carli
Clarke, John *see* Laughlin, Virginia Carli
Clarke, Machael *ConAu XR*
Clarke, Machael *see* Newlon, Clarke
Clarke, Marjorie E H *SingR 1*
Clarke, Mary Stetson 1911- *ConAu 21R,*
SmATA 5, WrD
Clarke, Maurice, Captain *MnBBF*
Clarke, Maurice, Captain *see* Hook, Samuel
Clarke
Clarke, Michael *SmATA 6*
Clarke, Mollie *ChPo S1*
Clarke, Pauline 1921- *AnCL, Au&Wr 6,*
AuBYP, BrCA, ChPo, ConAu XR,
SmATA 3, ThBJA, WWCL
Clarke, Pauline *see* Hunter Blair, Pauline
Clarke, Percy A *MnBBF, WWBWI A*
Clarke, Percy A *see* Frazer, Martin
Clarke, Percy A *see* Lander, Dane
Clarke, Percy A *see* Lytton, Jane
Clarke, Percy A *see* Neilson, Vernon
Clarke, Percy A *see* Nielson, Vernon
Clarke, Percy A *see* Rogers, Steve
Clarke, Percy A *see* Watson, Saint John
Clarke, Percy A *see* Wentworth, Charles
Clarke, Rebecca Sophia 1833-1906 *Alli Sup,*
AmA, AmA&B, BiD&SB, CarSB,
DcAmA, DcNAA
Clarke, S Dacre *MnBBF, WWBWI A*
Clarke, S Dacre *see* Rayner, Guy
Clarke, Silvey *MnBBF, WWBWI A*
Clarke, Tom E 1915- *ConAu 5R, WWPNA*
Clarke, Vincent *MnBBF*
Clarkson, E Margaret 1915- *ConAu 1R*
Clarkson, Ewan 1929- *ConAu 25R, SmATA 9*
Clarkson, Jan Nagel *ForWC 1970*
Clavel, Bernard 1923- *ConAu 45, IntWW 38,*
WWWor 2
Claveloux, Nicole *IlBYP*
Claymore, Tod *WWBWI A*
Claymore, Tod *see* Clevely, Hugh
Clayton, Barbara *ConAu XR*
Clayton, Barbara *see* Pluff, Barbara Littlefield
Cleary, Beverly 1916- *AmA&B, Au&ICB,*
AuBYP, ChLR 2, ConAu 1R, MorBMP,
MorJA, SmATA 2, WWA 38,
WWAW 8, WrD
Cleaver, Carole 1934- *ConAu 49, SmATA 6*
Cleaver, Eldridge 1935- *AmA&B, BlkAW,*
CelR 3, ConAu 21R, CurB 70, LBAA,
LBAA, Pen Am, WEAL
Cleaver, Elizabeth *OxCan Sup, Prof*
Cleaver, Hylton Reginald 1891-1961 *LongC,*
MnBBF, WWBWI A, WWCL
Cleaver, Hylton Reginald *see* Crunden, Reginald
Cleaver, Nancy *ConAu XR*
Cleaver, Nancy *see* Mathews, Evelyn Craw
Cleaver, Vera *AuBYP*
Cleaver, William *AuBYP*
Cleeve, Brian 1921- *ConAu 49*
Clegg, John 1909- *Au&Wr 6*

Cleghorn, C A *MnBBF*
Cleig, Charles *MnBBF*
Cleishbotham, Jebediah *YABC XR*
Cleishbotham, Jebediah *see* Scott, Sir Walter
Cleland, Mabel *ConAu XR, SmATA 5*
Cleland, Mabel *see* Widdemer, Mabel Cleland
Clemens, Samuel Langhorne 1835-1910 *Alli Sup,
   AmA, AmA&B, AnCL, ArizL, AuBYP,
   BbD, BiD&SB, BiDPar, BiDSA, CarSB,
   CasWL, Chambr 3, ChPo, ChPo S1,
   CnDAL, CyAL 2, DcAmA, DcEnA,
   DcEnL, DcLEnL, DcNAA, EncM&D,
   EncWL, EvLB, JBA 1934, LongC,
   OxAm, OxEng, Pen Am, RCom, REn,
   REnAL, TwCA, YABC 2*
Clemens, Samuel Langhorne *see* Mark Twain
Clemens, Samuel Langhorne *see* Snodgrass,
   Thomas Jefferson
Clemens, Samuel Langhorne *see* Twain, Mark
Clement, Charles 1921- *ChPo S1, IICB 1946*
Clement, Roland C 1912- *AmMWS 12P,
   ConAu 49*
Clements, Bruce 1931- *ConAu 53*
Clements, Frank *AuBYP*
Clements, Harry *MnBBF*
Clementson, W A B *MnBBF*
Clemons, Elizabeth *ConAu XR, ForWC 1970,
   SmATA XR*
Clemons, Elizabeth *see* Nowell, Elizabeth
   Cameron
Clepper, Irene E *ConAu 53*
Clerk, N W *SmATA XR*
Clerk, N W *see* Lewis, C S
Cleveland, Frank *MnBBF, WWBWI A*
Cleveland, Frank *see* Shaw, Frank H
Clevely, Hugh *MnBBF, WWBWI A*
Clevely, Hugh *see* Claymore, Tod
Cleven, Cathrine *ConAu XR, ForWC 1970,
   SmATA 2*
Cleven, Cathrine *see* Cleven, Kathryn Seward
Cleven, Kathryn Seward *ConAu 1R,
   SmATA 2*
Cleven, Kathryn Seward *see* Cleven, Cathrine
Clevin, Joergen 1920- *ConAu 29, SmATA 7*
Clevin, Jorgen *ConAu XR*
Clewes, Dorothy Mary 1907- *Au&Wr 6,
   AuBYP, ConAu 5R, SmATA 1*
Cliffe, Gunton *MnBBF*
Clifford, Carrie Williams *BlkAW*
Clifford, Eth *ConAu XR, SmATA 3*
Clifford, Eth *see* Rosenberg, Ethel
Clifford, Harold B 1893- *ConAu P-1,
   SmATA 10*
Clifford, Harold B *see* Farnham, Burt
Clifford, Lionel B *MnBBF*
Clifford, Lloyd *MnBBF*
Clifford, Margaret Cort 1929- *ConAu 25R,
   ForWC 1970, SmATA 1, WWAW 8*
Clifford, Margaret Cort *see* Clifford, Peggy
Clifford, Margaret Cort *see* Cort, M C
Clifford, Martin *LongC, MnBBF,
   SmATA XR, WWBWI A, WWCL*
Clifford, Martin *see* Austin, Stanley E
Clifford, Martin *see* Barnard, Alfred J
Clifford, Martin *see* Brooks, Edwy Searles
Clifford, Martin *see* Carlton, Lewis
Clifford, Martin *see* Catchpole, William Leslie
Clifford, Martin *see* Cook, Fred Gordon
Clifford, Martin *see* Down, C Maurice

Clifford, Martin *see* Eves, Reginald T
Clifford, Martin *see* Griffith, Percy
Clifford, Martin *see* Hamilton, Charles Harold
   St. John
Clifford, Martin *see* Harper, Harry
Clifford, Martin *see* Herman, Julius
Clifford, Martin *see* Hinton, Herbert Allan
Clifford, Martin *see* Hook, H Clarke
Clifford, Martin *see* Hutt, Hector
Clifford, Martin *see* Kirkham, Reginald S
Clifford, Martin *see* Lowe, Claud D
Clifford, Martin *see* Newman, Kenneth E
Clifford, Martin *see* O'Mant, Hedley Percival
   Angelo
Clifford, Martin *see* Orme, K
Clifford, Martin *see* Pentelow, John Nix
Clifford, Martin *see* Ransome, L E
Clifford, Martin *see* Russell, C
Clifford, Martin *see* Samways, George Richmond
Clifford, Martin *see* Warwick, Francis Alister
Clifford, Martin *see* Wood-Smith, Noel
Clifford, Mary Louise Beneway 1926-
   ConAu 5R, WrD
Clifford, Peggy *ConAu XR, SmATA 1*
Clifford, Peggy *see* Clifford, Margaret Cort
Clifford, Read *MnBBF*
Clifford, Mrs. W K d1929 *Chambr 3, LongC,
   TelT*
Clifton, Harry *SmATA XR*
Clifton, Harry *see* Hamilton, Charles Harold St.
   John
Clifton, Henry *MnBBF*
Clifton, Henry *see* Hamilton, Charles Harold St.
   John
Clifton, Lucille 1936- *BlkAW, ChPo S1,
   ConAu 49, ConP 1975, DrAP 1975,
   WrD*
Clifton, Richard *MnBBF*
Cline, C Terry, Jr. 1935- *ConAu 61*
Cline, Linda 1941- *ConAu 65*
Clinton, Garth *MnBBF*
Clinton, Harry *MnBBF*
Clithero, Myrtle E 1906- *ConAu P-2*
Clithero, Myrtle E *see* Clithero, Sally
Clithero, Sally *ConAu XR*
Clithero, Sally *see* Clithero, Myrtle E
Clive, Clifford *MnBBF, SmATA XR,
   WWBWI A*
Clive, Clifford *see* Hamilton, Charles Harold St.
   John
Clive, Clifford *see* Home-Gall, Edward Reginald
Clive, Keith *MnBBF*
Close, H P *MnBBF*
Cloudsley-Thompson, J L 1921- *ConAu 17R*
Clutesi, George 1909?- *OxCan Sup, Prof*
Clutha, Janet Paterson Frame 1924- *ConAu 1R*
Clutha, Janet Paterson Frame *see* Frame, Janet
Clymer, Eleanor 1906- *AuBYP, ConAu 61,
   SmATA 9, WrD*
Clymer, Eleanor *see* Bell, Janet
Clymer, Eleanor *see* Kinsey, Elizabeth
Clymer, Theodore 1927- *ConAu 17R*
Coakley, Mary Lewis 1907- *BkC 6,
   ConAu P-1, ForWC 1970, WrD*
Coalson, Glo *IlBYP*
Coates, Belle 1896- *ConAu 5R, ForWC 1970,
   SmATA 2*
Coates, Doreen Frances 1912- *Au&Wr 6,
   WrD*

Coates, Ruth Allison 1915- *ConAu 57,*
SmATA 11
Coats, Alice M 1905- *Au&Wr 6, ConAu 53,*
IlCB 1744, SmATA 11
Coatsworth, Elizabeth Jane 1893- *AmA&B,*
AmNov, AnCL, Au&ICB, AuBYP,
BkCL, ChLR 2, ChPo, ChPo S1,
ConAu 5R, FamMS, ChPo S2,
JBA 1934, JBA 1951, MorBMP,
Newb 1922, OxAm, REnAL, SmATA 2,
St&VC, TwCA, TwCA Sup, WWA 38,
WWAW 8, WWCL, WWWor 2
Cobb, Alice 1909- *ConAu 5R, IndAu 1917*
Cobb, G Belton *MnBBF*
Cobb, Thomas 1854- *Alli, MnBBF, WWLA*
Cobb, Vicki 1938- *ChLR 2, ConAu 33,*
SmATA 8, WrD
Cobbett, Richard *ConAu XR, SmATA XR*
Cobbett, Richard *see* Pluckrose, Henry
Cobbett, William 1762-1835 *Alli, AtlBL, BbD,*
BbthC, BiD&SB, BiDLA, BiDLA Sup,
BrAu 19, CarSB, CasWL, Chambr 2,
CnDAL, DcEnA, DcEnL, DcEuL,
DcLEnL, EvLB, MouLC 3, NCHEL,
OxAm, OxEng, Pen Eng, REn, WEAL
Cober, Alan Edwin 1935- *IlBYP, IlCB 1957,*
SmATA 7
Cobham, Sir Alan *MnBBF, SmATA XR*
Cobham, Sir Alan 1894- *WW 1974*
Cobham, Sir Alan *see* Hamilton, Charles Harold
St. John
Coblentz, Catherine Cate 1897-1951
AnMV 1926, ChPo, ChPo S1, JBA 1951
Coblentz, Stanton Arthur 1896- *AmA&B,*
AnMV 1926, Au&Wr 6, ChPo, ChPo S1,
ChPo S2, ConAu 5R, CurB 54, REnAL,
WNAA, WWA 38
Coburn, Frederick Simpson 1871- *ChPo,*
ChPo S1, ChPo S2, IlCB 1744
Coburn, John Bowen 1914- *AmA&B,*
ConAu 1R, DrAS 6P, WWA 38
Cocagnac, Augustin Maurice 1924- *ConAu 25R,*
SmATA 7
Cocagnac, Augustin Maurice *see* Warbler, J M
Cochran, Bobbye A 1949- *SmATA 11*
Cochran, Hamilton 1898- *AmA&B, AmNov,*
Au&Wr 6, ConAu 1R, WWA 38, WrD
Cochrane, Alfred Henry John 1865- *MnBBF,*
WWLA
Cochrane, Louise Morley 1918- *ConAu 9R*
Cockett, Mary 1915- *Au&Wr 6, ConAu 9R,*
SmATA 3
Cocking, Percy d1964 *WWBWI I*
Cockling, Thelma *SingR 1*
Cockrell, Marian 1909- *AmA&B, AmNov,*
ConAu P-2
Cocks, Myra *ConICB*
Cockton, Henry 1807-1853 *Alli, BrAu 19,*
Chambr 3, DcBiA, DcEnL, MnBBF,
NCHEL, WWCL, WWBWI A
Coconis, Ted *IlBYP*
Cody, Al *ConAu XR*
Cody, Al *see* Joscelyn, Archie L
Cody, Stone *MnBBF*
Cody, Stone *see* Landsborough, G H
Cody, William Frederick 1846-1917 *AmA&B,*
DcNAA, HsB&A, OxAm, REn, REnAL
Coe, Douglas *AuBYP, ConAu XR, OhA&B,*
SmATA 1

Coe, Douglas *see* Epstein, Beryl
Coe, Douglas *see* Epstein, Samuel
Coe, Lloyd 1899- *IlCB 1946*
Coe, Miriam 1902- *WWAW 8, WWS 13,*
WrD
Coe, Richard N 1923- *ConAu 25R*
Coen, Rena Neumann 1925- *ConAu 13R,*
ForWC 1970, WrD
Coens, Sister Mary Xavier 1918- *ConAu 21R,*
DrAS 6E, WWAW 8
Coerr, Eleanor 1922- *ConAu 25R, SmATA 1,*
WrD
Coerr, Eleanor *see* Hicks, Eleanor B
Coerr, Eleanor *see* Page, Eleanor
Coffin, Charles Carleton 1823-1896 *Alli Sup,*
AmA, AmA&B, BbD, BiD&SB, CarSB,
DcAmA, DcNAA, OxAm, REnAL
Coffin, Geoffrey *AuBYP, ConAu XR,*
EncM&D, SmATA 3
Coffin, Geoffrey *see* Mason, F Van Wyck
Coffin, Robert Peter Tristram 1892-1955
AmA&B, AnMV 1926, ChPo, ChPo S1,
ChPo S2, CnDAL, ConAmA, DcLEnL,
LongC, OxAm, Pen Am, REn, REnAL,
St&VC, TwCA, TwCA Sup, WNAA
Coffman, Ramon Peyton 1896- *AmA&B,*
Au&Wr 6, ConAu P-2, IndAu 1917,
SmATA 4
Coffman, Ramon Peyton *see* Uncle Ray
Cogger, Percy *MnBBF*
Coggins, Herbert *AuBYP*
Coggins, Jack Banham 1911- *AuBYP,*
ConAu 5R, MorJA, SmATA 2,
WWA 38
Coghill, Nevill 1899- *ConAu 13R, ConDr 1,*
NCHEL, REn
Cogswell, Coralie Norris 1930- *ConAu 13R*
Cogswell, Coralie Norris *see* Howard, Coralie
Cohen, Barbara 1932- *ConAu 53, SmATA 10*
Cohen, Daniel 1936- *ChLR 3, ConAu 45,*
SmATA 8
Cohen, Florence Chanock 1927- *ConAu 5R*
Cohen, Joan Lebold 1932- *ConAu 25R,*
SmATA 4, WWAW 8
Cohen, Morton N 1921- *Au&Wr 6,*
ConAu 1R, DrAS 6E, WrD
Cohen, Morton N *see* Moreton, John
Cohen, Peter Zachary 1931- *ConAu 33,*
SmATA 4, WrD
Cohen, Robert Carl 1930- *SmATA 8*
Cohn, Angelo 1914- *ConAu 5R*
Cohn, Nik 1946- *Au&Wr 6*
Coit, Margaret Louise 1919?- *AmA&B,*
Au&Wr 6, AuBYP, ConAu 1R, CurB 51,
DrAS 6H, ForWC 1970, OxAm, REnAL,
SmATA 2, TwCA Sup, WWA 38,
WWAW 8
Coke, Desmond 1879-1940? *MnBBF,*
WWBWI A, WWCL, WWLA
Coke, Desmond *see* Blinders, Belinda
Colabella, Vincent *IlBYP*
Colbeck, Alfred *Alli Sup, MnBBF,*
WWBWI A
Colbeck, Maurice 1925- *Au&Wr 6,*
ConAu 13R, WrD
Colbert, Edwin H 1905- *AmMWS 12P,*
ConAu 61, CurB 65, IntWW 38,
WWA 38
Colby, C B 1904- *ConAu 1R, SmATA 3*

Colby, C B *see* Colby, Carroll Burleigh
Colby, Carroll Burleigh 1904- *AuBYP, MorJA, SmATA 3, WWA 38*
Colby, Carroll Burleigh *see* Colby, C B
Colby, Jean Poindexter 1909?- *ChPo S1, ConAu 1R, ForWC 1970, WWAW 8, WrD*
Colchester, Captain *MnBBF*
Coldsmith, Donald Charles 1926- *WWMW 14*
Cole, Alan *MnBBF*
Cole, Ann 1937- *ConAu 65*
Cole, Annette *SmATA XR*
Cole, Davis *AuBYP, ConAu XR, SmATA 2*
Cole, Davis *see* Elting, Mary
Cole, Jackson *ConAu XR, SmATA XR*
Cole, Jackson 1901- *MnBBF*
Cole, Jackson *see* Schisgal, Oscar
Cole, Lois Dwight 1902- *AmA&B, AuBYP, ConAu 1R, SmATA 10*
Cole, Lois Dwight *see* Arnett, Caroline
Cole, Lois Dwight *see* Avery, Lynn
Cole, Lois Dwight *see* Dudley, Nancy
Cole, Lois Dwight *see* Dwight, Allan
Cole, Lois Dwight *see* Eliot, Anne
Cole, Margaret Alice *ConAu 9R*
Cole, Sheila R 1939- *ConAu 53*
Cole, Stephen *ConAu XR*
Cole, Walter 1891- *IlCB 1744*
Cole, William 1919- *AuBYP, BkP, ChPo, ChPo S1, ChPo S2, ConAu 9R, SmATA 9, WrD*
Coleman, Francis 1913- *Au&Wr 6*
Coleman, Lonnie 1920- *BiEnAT, CurB 58*
Coleman, Pauline Hodgkinson *AuBYP*
Coleman, Satis N 1878- *WNAA*
Coleridge, Samuel Taylor 1772-1834 *Alli, AtlBL, BbD, BiD&SB, BiDLA, BrAu 19, CasWL, Chambr 3, ChPo, ChPo S1, ChPo S2, CnE&AP, CriT 2, CyWA, DcEnA, DcEnL, DcEuL, DcLEnL, EvLB, MouLC 3, NCHEL, OxEng, Pen Eng, RAdv 1, RCom, REn, WEAL*
Coleridge, Sara 1802-1852 *Alli, BiD&SB, BrAu 19, CasWL, Chambr 3, ChPo, ChPo S1, ChPo S2, DcEnL, DcLEnL, EvLB, NCHEL, OxEng, St&VC*
Coles, Detective Inspector *MnBBF*
Coles, Detective Inspector *see* Sempill, Ernest
Coles, Robert 1929- *AmA&B, Au&Wr 6, CelR 3, ConAu 45, CurB 69*
Colinski, A J *MnBBF*
Colinski, A J *see* MacPherson, Angus, Captain
Colinski, A J *see* Scott, Angus, Captain
Collard, Derek *IlBYP*
Collett, Rosemary K 1931- *ConAu 69*
Collier, Basil 1908- *Au&Wr 6, ConAu 5R*
Collier, Christopher 1930- *ConAu 33, DrAS 6H*
Collier, Edmund *AuBYP*
Collier, Ethel 1903- *AuBYP, ConAu 65*
Collier, Eugenia W 1928- *BlkAW, ConAu 49, LBAA, WrD*
Collier, James Lincoln 1928- *ChLR 3, ConAu 9R, SmATA 8*
Collier, James Lincoln *see* Williams, Charles
Collier, John C *MnBBF*
Collier, Norman *MnBBF*
Collier, Norman *see* Bennett, C N
Collier, Zena *ConAu XR, WrD*

Collier, Zena *see* Shumsky, Zena Feldman
Collin, Hedvig *AuBYP, ConICB, IlCB 1946*
Collings, Ellsworth *AuBYP*
Collingwood, Harry 1851-1920? *Alli Sup, MnBBF, WWBWI A, WWCL*
Collingwood, Harry *see* Lancaster, William Joseph Cosens
Collins, Colin *MnBBF*
Collins, Colin *see* Merland, Oliver
Collins, Dale 1897?- *SingR 2, TwCA, TwCA Sup*
Collins, Dale *see* Copeland, Michael
Collins, Dale *see* Fennimore, Stephen
Collins, David R 1940- *ConAu 29, SmATA 7, WWMW 14, WrD*
Collins, E *MnBBF*
Collins, Freda *ConAu XR, WrD*
Collins, Henry Hill 1907-1961 *AuBYP*
Collins, Jim 1934- *WWAA 1973*
Collins, Kreigh 1908- *WWAA 1973*
Collins, Michael 1930- *AmMWS 12P, IntWW 38, WW 1974, WWA 38, WWS 13, WWWor 2*
Collins, Norman Richard 1907- *Au&Wr 6, DcLEnL, EvLB, IntWW 38, LongC, NCHEL, TwCA Sup, WW 1974, WWA 38, WWWor 2, WrD*
Collins, Ruth Philpott 1890-1975 *ConAu 1R, ConAu 53*
Collins, Stephen 1927- *AmMWS 12P*
Collins, Wilkie 1824-1889 *AtlBL, BrAu 19, CyWA, EncM&D, HsB&A, MnBBF, NCHEL, Pen Eng, RAdv 1, REn, WEAL*
Collodi, Carlo 1826-1890 *AnCL, AuBYP, BkCL, CasWL, ChPo S2, EuAu, EvEuW, JBA 1934, JBA 1951, St&VC, WWCL*
Collodi, Carlo *see* Lorenzini, Carlo
Colloms, Brenda 1919- *Au&Wr 6, ConAu 61, WrD*
Colman, Hila *AuBYP, ConAu 13R, MorBMP, SmATA 1, ThBJA*
Colman, Hila *see* Crayder, Teresa
Colo, Edwin *MnBBF*
Colonius, Lillian 1911- *ConAu 21R, SmATA 3*
Colorado, Antonio J 1903- *ConAu XR, PueRA*
Colorado, Antonio J *see* Colorado Capella, Antonio Julio
Colorado Capella, Antonio Julio 1903- *ConAu 17R*
Colorado Capella, Antonio Julio *see* Colorado, Antonio J
Colt, Martin *AuBYP, ConAu XR, SmATA 1*
Colt, Martin *see* Epstein, Samuel
Colton, Helen 1918- *WWAW 8*
Colton, Joel 1918- *ConAu 1R, DrAS 6H, WWA 38, WWWorJ 1972*
Colum, Padraic 1881-1972 *AmA&B, AmSCAP 66, AnCL, AuBYP, BkC 3, CarSB, CasWL, CatA 1930, ChPo, ChPo S1, ChPo S2, CnMD, ConAu 33, ConP 1970, DcLEnL, EncWL, EvLB, FamSYP, JBA 1934, JBA 1951, LongC, McGWD, ModBL, ModBL Sup, ModWD, NCHEL, NYTBE 2, NYTBE 3, Pen Eng, RAdv 1, REn, REnWD, St&VC, TwCA, TwCA Sup, TwCW,*

WEAL

Colver, Alice Ross 1892- *AmA&B, AmNov, AuBYP, WNAA*

Colver, Anne 1908- *AmA&B, AuBYP, ConAu 45, OhA&B, SmATA 7*

Colver, Anne *see* Graff, Polly Anne Colver

Colver, Anne *see* Harris, Colver

Colwell, Eileen 1904- *ChPo S1, ConAu 29, CurB 63, SmATA 2, WWCL*

Colwell, Robert 1931- *ConAu 33*

Colyer, Penrose 1940- *ConAu 65*

Comber, Dorothy 1902- *SingR 2*

Comber, Lillian 1916- *ConAu 9R*

Comber, Lillian *see* Beckwith, Lillian

Combs, Joseph Franklin 1892- *WWS 13*

Comenius, Johann Amos 1592-1670? *BbD, BiD&SB, CarSB, CasWL, ChPo, ChPo S1, DcEuL, EuAu, EvEuW, Pen Eur, St&VC*

Comfort, Barbara 1916- *IlCB 1946*

Comfort, Iris Tracy *ConAu 13R, WrD*

Comfort, Jane Levington 1903- *AuBYP, ConAu XR, SmATA 1*

Comfort, Jane Levington *see* Sturtzel, Jane Levington

Comfort, John *MnBBF*

Comfort, Mildred Houghton 1886- *ConAu 9R, MnnWr, SmATA 3*

Comins, Ethel M 1901- *ConAu 61, SmATA 11, WWAW 8*

Commager, Henry Steele 1902- *AmA&B, AuBYP, BiN 1974, ChPo S1, ConAu 21R, CurB 46, DcLEnL, DrAS 6H, IntWW 38, OxAm, Pen Am, REn, REnAL, TwCA Sup, WW 1974, WWA 38, WWE 14, WWWor 2*

Commins, Dorothy Berliner *AuBYP*

Commire, Anne *ChPo S2*

Comparetti, Alice 1907- *ConAu 37*

Compere, Janet *IlBYP*

Compere, Mickie *ConAu XR*

Compere, Mickie *see* Davidson, Mickie Compere

Compton, Herbert Eastwick *MnBBF*

Compton, Margaret *DcNAA*

Comrade, Robert W *MnBBF, WWBWI A*

Comrade, Robert W *see* Brooks, Edwy Searles

Comstock, Anna Botsford 1854- *WNAA*

Conan Doyle, Arthur 1859-1930 *EncM&D*

Conan Doyle, Arthur *see* Doyle, Arthur Conan

Condit, Martha Olson 1913- *BiDL 5*

Condon, Richard 1915- *WWA 38, WWWor 2*

Cone, Molly Lamken 1918- *AuBYP, ConAu 1R, ForWC 1970, SmATA 1, ThBJA, WrD*

Cone, Molly Lamken *see* More, Caroline

Cone, Sydney M, Jr. 1904- *WWA 38*

Conford, Ellen 1942- *ConAu 33, SmATA 6, WrD*

Conger, Lesley *ConAu XR*

Conger, Marion 1915- *AuBYP, IndAu 1917*

Conklin, Gladys Plemon 1903- *AuBYP, BiDL 5, ConAu 1R, ForWC 1970, SmATA 2*

Conklin, Groff 1904- *AmA&B, ConAu 1R*

Conkling, Fleur *AuBYP*

Conkling, Hilda 1910- *AmA&B, AnCL, BkCL, ChPo, ConAmL, REnAL, St&VC, TwCA, TwCA Sup, WNAA*

Conly, Robert L 1918-1973 *ConAu 41*

Conly, Robert L *see* O'Brien, Robert C

Connelly, John Peter 1926- *WWE 14, WWMW 14*

Conner, Henry *MnBBF*

Conner, Henry *see* Gilbert, H

Conner, Patrick Reardon 1907- *ConAu 17R*

Conner, Patrick Reardon *see* Conner, Rearden

Conner, Rearden 1907- *Au&Wr 6, ConAu XR, WW 1974, WrD*

Conner, Rearden *see* Conner, Patrick Reardon

Connolly, Jerome Patrick 1931- *IlBYP, IlCB 1957, SmATA 8, WWAA 1973*

Connor, Joyce Mary *WrD*

Conquest, Owen *LongC, MnBBF, SmATA XR, WWBWI A, WWCL*

Conquest, Owen *see* Austin, Stanley E

Conquest, Owen *see* Catchpole, William Leslie

Conquest, Owen *see* Down, C Maurice

Conquest, Owen *see* Eves, Reginald T

Conquest, Owen *see* Hamilton, Charles Harold St. John

Conquest, Owen *see* Newman, Kenneth E

Conquest, Owen *see* O'Mant, Hedley Percival Angelo

Conquest, Owen *see* Pike, William Ernest

Conquest, Owen *see* Wood-Smith, Noel

Conrad, Arthur S 1907- *IlCB 1946*

Conrad, Barnaby 1922- *AmA&B, CelR 3, ConAu 9R, CurB 59, REnAL, WWA 38, WorAu*

Conrad, Joseph 1857-1924 *AtlBL, BbD, BiD&SB, CasWL, Chambr 3, CnMD, CnMWL, CyWA, DcEnA Ap, DcEuL, DcLEnL, EncM&D, EncWL, EvLB, JBA 1934, LongC, ModBL, ModBL Sup, ModWD, NCHEL, OxEng, Pen Eng, RAdv 1, RCom, REn, TwCA, TwCA Sup, TwCW, WEAL, WWTwL*

Conrad, Sybil 1921- *AuBYP, ConAu 21R*

Conroy, Jack 1899- *AmA&B, AmNov, ConAu XR, ConNov 1972, ConNov 1976, OhA&B, OxAm, WNAA, WWA 38, WrD*

Conroy, Robert *ConAu XR*

Conroy, Robert *see* Goldston, Robert Conroy

Considine, Bob 1906-1975 *AmA&B, AuNews 2, CelR 3, ConAu XR, CurB 47, REnAL*

Considine, Robert 1906-1975 *ConAu 61, CurB 47*

Constant, Alberta Wilson 1908- *ConAu 1R*

Contreras, Jerry *IlBYP*

Converse, Florence 1871- *AmA&B, BiDSA, CarSB, ChPo, ChPo S1, ChPo S2, DcAmA, WNAA*

Conway, Gordon *MnBBF, SmATA XR, WWBWI A*

Conway, Gordon *see* Hamilton, Charles Harold St. John

Conway, Helene *AuBYP*

Conway, Richard *MnBBF*

Conyers, Captain *see* Home-Gall, William Benjamin

Cooee *MnBBF*

Cooee *see* Burrage, Alfred McLelland

Cook, Bernadine 1924- *SmATA 11*

Cook, Fred Gordon 1900- *MnBBF, WWBWI A*

Cook, Fred Gordon *see* Carew, Burleigh

Cook, Fred Gordon *see* Chaverton, Bruce
Cook, Fred Gordon *see* Clifford, Martin
Cook, Fred Gordon *see* Foy, Peter
Cook, Fred Gordon *see* Owen, Vincent
Cook, Fred Gordon *see* Richards, Frank
Cook, Fred Gordon *see* Smeaton, Fred
Cook, Fred James 1911- *AmA&B, AuBYP, ConAu 9R, DcAmA, SmATA 2, WWA 38, WWWor 2*
Cook, George S 1920- *ConAu 49*
Cook, Gladys Emerson *AmA&B, AuBYP, ConAu 5R, ForWC 1970, IlCB 1946, WWA 38, WWAA 1973, WWAW 8, WWE 14*
Cook, Gladys Moon 1907- *ConAu 33*
Cook, Howard 1901- *DcCAA 2, IlCB 1744*
Cook, J Gordon 1916- *ConAu 9R*
Cook, John Estes *ThBJA*
Cook, Joseph Jay 1924- *AuBYP, ConAu 1R, SmATA 8*
Cook, Lyn *ConAu XR, OxCan Sup, Prof, SmATA XR*
Cook, Lyn *see* Waddell, Evelyn Margaret
Cook, Marion Belden *AuBYP*
Cook, Olive Rambo 1892- *AuBYP, ConAu 13R*
Cook, Robert Carter 1898- *AmMWS 12P, WWA 38*
Cook, Sherman R *AuBYP*
Cooke, Barbara *AuBYP*
Cooke, Barbara *see* Alexander, Anna Barbara Cooke
Cooke, David Coxe 1917- *AuBYP, ConAu 1R, SmATA 2*
Cooke, Donald Ewin 1916- *AuBYP, ConAu 1R, SmATA 2, WWAA 1973*
Cooke, Edith Helena *ChPo S1*
Cooke, Noel *WWBWI 1*
Cooke, Percival *MnBBF, WWBWI A*
Cooke, Percival *see* Bishop, Percy Cook
Cooke, W Bourne *MnBBF, WWBWI A*
Cookson, Catherine 1906- *Au&Wr 6, ConAu 13R, SmATA 9, WrD*
Cookson, Catherine *see* Marchant, Catherine
Cookson, Catherine *see* McMullen, Catherine
Cooley, Lydia *IlBYP*
Coolidge, Archibald C, Jr. 1928- *ConAu 37, DrAS 6E*
Coolidge, Olivia Ensor 1908- *AuBYP, BkCL, ConAu 5R, MorJA, SmATA 1*
Coolidge, Susan 1835-1905 *Alli Sup, AmA, AmA&B, BbD, BiD&SB, Chambr 3, ChPo, ChPo S2, DcAmA, DcLEnL, DcNAA, EvLB, JBA 1934, OhA&B, REnAL, WWCL*
Coolidge, Susan *see* Woolsey, Sarah Chauncey
Coomaraswamy, Ananda Kentish 1877-1947 *DcLEnL, DcNAA, WNAA*
Coombs, Charles Ira 1914- *AuBYP, ConAu 5R, SmATA 3*
Coombs, Charles Ira *see* Coombs, Chick
Coombs, Chick *AuBYP, ConAu XR, SmATA 3*
Coombs, Chick *see* Coombs, Charles Ira
Coombs, Patricia 1926- *ConAu 1R, IlBYP, IlCB 1957, SmATA 3, WrD*
Coon, Martha Sutherland 1884- *ConAu P-2, WWAW 8, WrD*
Cooney, Barbara 1917- *AmA&B, AuBYP,*

BkP, ChPo, ConAu 5R, IlBYP, IlCB 1744, IlCB 1946, IlCB 1957, MorJA, NewbC 1956, SmATA 6, St&VC, WWA 38, WWAA 1973, WWAW 8
Cooney, Timothy J 1929- *WWE 14*
Cooper, Alfred Benjamin 1863- *MnBBF, WWLA*
Cooper, Charles Henry St. John 1869-1926 *MnBBF*
Cooper, Charles Henry St. John *see* Cooper, Henry St. John
Cooper, Charles Henry St. John *see* Holme, Gordon
Cooper, Charles Henry St. John *see* Hosken, Clifford
Cooper, Charles Henry St. John *see* LeFevre, P, Lieutenant
Cooper, Charles Henry St. John *see* Saint John, Henry
Cooper, E Fitzgerald *MnBBF*
Cooper, Elizabeth Keyser 1910- *ConAu 1R*
Cooper, Freemont *MnBBF*
Cooper, Freemont *see* Steffens, Arthur
Cooper, George 1840-1927 *BkCL*
Cooper, Gordon 1932- *ConAu 61, WrD*
Cooper, Henry St. John *WWBWI A*
Cooper, Henry St. John *see* Cooper, Charles Henry St. John
Cooper, J Lawrence *MnBBF*
Cooper, James A *ConAu XR*
Cooper, James A *see* Stratemeyer, Edward L
Cooper, James Fenimore 1789-1851 *Alli, AmA, AmA&B, AmWr, AtlBL, AuBYP, BbD, BiD&SB, CasWL, Chambr 3, CnDAL, CriT 3, CyAL 1, CyWA, DcAmA, DcBiA, DcEnA, DcEnL, DcLEnL, DcNAA, EvLB, HsB&A, MnBBF, MouLC 3, OxAm, OxEng, Pen Am, RAdv 1, RCom, REn, REnAL, WEAL, WWBWI A, WWCL*
Cooper, Jamie Lee *ConAu 9R, IndAu 1917*
Cooper, John R *ConAu P-2, SmATA 1*
Cooper, John R *see* Stratemeyer, Edward L
Cooper, Kay 1941- *ConAu 45, SmATA 11*
Cooper, Lee Pelham 1926- *AuBYP, ConAu 5R, SmATA 5, WrD*
Cooper, Lettice 1897- *Au&Wr 6, ConAu 9R, ConNov 1972, ConNov 1976, WrD*
Cooper, Margaret *ChPo S2*
Cooper, Paulette 1944- *ConAu 37*
Cooper, Susan 1935- *Au&Wr 6, ConAu 29, SmATA 4, WrD*
Cooper, W D *CarSB*
Cooper, Wendy 1919- *Au&Wr 6, ConAu 13R, WrD*
Coopersmith, Harry 1903- *AmSCAP 66, ConAu P-2*
Coopersmith, Stanley 1926- *AmMWS 12S, ConAu 21R*
Copeland, Frances Virginia *AuBYP*
Copeland, Helen 1920- *ConAu 25R, SmATA 4*
Copeland, Michael *SingR 2*
Copeland, Michael *see* Collins, Dale
Copeland, Paul Worthington *AuBYP, WWPNA*
Copley, Heather 1920?- *ArtsCL, IlCB 1957*
Copp, Andrew James 1916- *ConAu 25R, WrD*

Copp, Andrew James *see* Copp, Jim
Copp, Jim *ConAu XR*
Copp, Jim *see* Copp, Andrew James
Coppard, Alfred Edgar 1878-1957 *ChPo,*
  ChPo S1, ChPo S2, DcLEnL, EvLB,
  LongC, ModBL, NCHEL, OxEng,
  Pen Eng, REn, TwCA, TwCA Sup,
  TwCW, WWCL, WWTwL, YABC 1
Coppard, Audrey 1931- *ConAu 29*
Coppel, Alfred 1921- *ConAu 17R, DrAF 1976,*
  WrD
Copping, Harold 1863-1932 *ChPo S2,*
  WWBWI 1
Coppock, Charles 1906- *AuBYP*
Corbett, Mrs. George *MnBBF*
Corbett, Harry *WWCL*
Corbett, James Edward 1875-1955 *AuBYP,*
  CurB 46, CurB 55
Corbett, Scott 1913- *Au&Wr 6, AuBYP,*
  ChLR 1, ConAu 1R, SmATA 2
Corbett-Smith, A 1879- *MnBBF, WWLA*
Corbin, J A *MnBBF*
Corbin, John 1870-1959 *AmA&B, BiD&SB,*
  CarSB, DcAmA, WNAA
Corbin, William *AuBYP, ConAu XR*
Corbin, William 1916- *MorJA, SmATA 3*
Corbin, William *see* McGraw, William Corbin
Corby, Dan *ConAu XR, SmATA 3*
Corby, Dan *see* Catherall, Arthur
Corcoran, Barbara 1911- *ConAu 21R,*
  SmATA 3, WrD
Corcoran, Barbara *see* Dixon, Paige
Corcoran, Barbara *see* Hamilton, Gail
Corcoran, Brewer 1877- *MnBBF, WNAA*
Corcos, Lucille 1908-1973 *AmA&B, AuBYP,*
  ChPo, ConAu 21R, IlCB 1946,
  IlCB 1957, SmATA 10, WWA 38,
  WWAA 1973, WWAW 8
Cordell, Alexander *ConAu XR, SmATA 7,*
  WrD
Cordell, Alexander *see* Graber, Alexander
Cordry, Clem *MnBBF*
Cordwell, F C G *MnBBF*
Cordwell, Fred G *WWBWI A*
Cordwell, Miriam 1908- *WWAW 8, WWE 14*
Corey, Dorothy *ConAu 69*
Corey, Robert *IlBYP*
Corfe, Tom 1928- *Au&Wr 6*
Cork, Barry Joynson *MnBBF*
Cork, Barry Joynson *see* Joynson, Barry
Corkery, Daniel 1878-1964 *CasWL,*
  CatA 1930, NCHEL, TwCA Sup
Corkran, Alice *TelT*
Cormack, M Grant 1913- *ConAu 1R,*
  SmATA 11
Cormack, Maribelle 1902- *AuBYP, JBA 1951*
Cormier, Robert Edmund 1925- *ConAu 1R,*
  SmATA 10
Cormier, Robert Edmund *see* Fitch, John, IV
Cornell, J *SmATA XR*
Cornell, J *see* Cornell, Jeffrey
Cornell, James C, Jr. 1938- *ConAu 69*
Cornell, Jean Gay 1920- *ConAu 45*
Cornell, Jeffrey 1945- *SmATA 11*
Cornell, Jeffrey *see* Cornell, J
Corner, Miss *CarSB*
Cornier, Vincent 1898- *EncM&D, MnBBF*
Cornish, Samuel James 1935?- *BlkAW,*
  ConAu 41, ConP 1970, ConP 1975,

DrAP 1975, LBAA, WrD
Cornish, W H *MnBBF*
Corren, Grace *ConAu XR*
Corren, Grace *see* Hoskins, Robert
Correy, Lee *ConAu 65, SmATA XR*
Correy, Lee *see* Stine, G Harry
Corrigan, Adeline *BiDL 5*
Corrigan, Barbara 1922- *ChPo, SmATA 8*
Corriveau, Monique 1927- *ConAu 61,*
  OxCan Sup, Prof
Corson, Hazel W 1906- *ConAu 1R*
Cort, M C *ConAu XR, SmATA 1*
Cort, M C *see* Clifford, Margaret Cort
Cortiella, H *WWBWI 1*
Corwin, Judith Hoffman 1946- *SmATA 10*
Corwin, June Atkin 1935- *IlCB 1957*
Corydon, Paul *MnBBF*
Cosby, Bill 1937- *BiN 1974, CelR 3,*
  CurB 67, IntMPA 1975, WWA 38,
  WWW 14, WWWor 2
Cosgrave, John O'Hara, II 1908- *ConAu 1R,*
  IlBYP, IlCB 1744, IlCB 1946, IlCB 1957,
  MorJA
Cosgrove, Margaret 1926- *AuBYP, ConAu 9R,*
  IlCB 1957
Cosgrove, Stephen 1945- *AuNews 1,*
  ConAu 69
Coskey, Evelyn 1932- *ConAu 41, SmATA 7*
Costain, Thomas Bertram 1885-1965 *AmA&B,*
  AmNov, AuBYP, CanWr, ConAu 5R,
  ConAu 25R, CurB 53, CurB 65,
  DcLEnL, LongC, OxAm, OxCan, REn,
  REnAL, TwCA Sup, TwCW
Costello, David F 1904- *AmMWS 12P,*
  ConAu 33, WWPNA
Costley-White, Hope 1894- *Au&Wr 6, WrD*
Cothern, Fayly H 1926- *ConAu 1R,*
  ForWC 1970, WrD
Cott, Jonathan 1942- *ChPo S2, ConAu 53*
Cotten, Sallie Southall *BiDSA, ChPo,*
  ChPo S1
Cotteril, Grant *MnBBF*
Cottle, Thomas J 1937- *BbthC, ConAu 33*
Cottler, Joseph 1899- *ConAu P-2*
Cottman, Evans W 1901- *IndAu 1917*
Cotton, Nathaniel 1705-1788 *Alli, BiDLA,*
  BrAu, CarSB, Chambr 2, ChPo S1,
  ChPo S2, EvLB, NCHEL
Cottrell, Dorothy 1902-1957 *CurB 55,*
  CurB 57, SingR 2
Cottrell, Leonard 1913- *Au&Wr 6, AuBYP,*
  ConAu 5R, IntWW 38, TwCW,
  WW 1974, WWWor 2, WorAu
Couch, Sir Arthur Thomas Quiller *Alli Sup,*
  ChPo, EvLB, JBA 1934, OxEng
Couch, Helen F 1907- *ConAu P-2*
Couffer, Jack 1924- *ConAu 1R*
Coughlan, Robert 1914- *AmA&B, ConAu 65,*
  IndAu 1917
Coulsdon, John *MnBBF*
Coulsdon, John *see* Hincks, Cyril Malcolm
Counts, George Sylvester 1889-1974 *AmA&B,*
  Au&Wr 6, ConAu 5R, ConAu 53,
  CurB 41, CurB 75, NYTBS 5,
  TwCA Sup, WNAA, WWA 38
Courage, John *WWBWI A*
Courage, John *see* Goyne, Richard
Courlander, Harold 1908- *AnCL, AuBYP,*
  BkCL, ConAu 9R, IndAu 1917, MorJA,

SmATA 6

Cournos, John 1881-1966 *AmA&B, ConAmL, ConAu P-2, DcLEnL, LongC, OxAm, REnAL, TwCA, TwCA Sup, WWLA*

Courtney, Charles *MnBBF*

Courtney, Elizabeth *SingR 2*

Courtney, Gwendoline *Au&Wr 6, ConAu P-1, WrD*

Cousins, Margaret 1905- *AmA&B, Au&Wr 6, AuBYP, ConAu 1R, ForWC 1970, SmATA 2, TexW, WWA 38, WWAW 8, WWWor 2, WrD*

Cousins, Margaret *see* Johns, Avery

Cousins, Margaret *see* Masters, William

Cousins, Margaret *see* Parrish, Mary

Cousland, D C *MnBBF*

Cousteau, Jacques-Yves 1910- *AnCL, ConAu 65, IntWW 38, REn, WW 1974, WWWor 2*

Covarrubias, Miguel 1905?-1958 *CurB 40, CurB 57, IlCB 1744, IlCB 1946, REnAL*

Covici, Pascal, Jr. 1930- *ConAu 1R, DrAS 6E*

Cowan, C England *MnBBF*

Cowan, Edward *MnBBF*

Cowan, Edward *see* Cowan, Ted

Cowan, Francis *MnBBF*

Cowan, Ted *MnBBF*

Cowan, Ted *see* Cowan, Edward

Cowdy, Alan *MnBBF*

Cowell, Cyril 1888- *ChPo S2, ConAu P-2*

Cowell, Frank Richard 1897- *Au&Wr 6, AuBYP, WW 1974*

Cowell, Richard 1897- *ConAu 53*

Cowen, Frances *Au&Wr 6, ConAu XR, WrD*

Cowen, Frances *see* Munthe, Frances

Cowie, Evelyn Elizabeth 1924- *Au&Wr 6, ConAu 13R, WrD*

Cowie, Leonard Wallace 1919- *Au&Wr 6, ConAu 13R, SmATA 4*

Cowles, Fleur *AmA&B, Au&Wr 6, AuNews 1, BiN 1974, ConAu 9R, CurB 52*

Cowles, Ginny 1924- *ConAu 57*

Cowley, Joy 1936- *ConAu 25R, SmATA 4*

Cowley, Malcolm 1898- *AmA&B, Au&Wr 6, CelR 3, ChPo, CnDAL, ConAmA, ConAu 5R, ConP 1970, ConP 1975, DcLEnL, EncWL, IntWW 38, ModAL, ModAL Sup, OxAm, Pen Am, RAdv 1, REn, REnAL, SixAP, SixAP, TwCA, TwCA Sup, WNAA, WWA 38, WWWor 2*

Cowlin, Dorothy 1911- *Au&Wr 6, WrD*

Cowper, William 1731-1800 *Alli, AnCL, AtlBL, BbD, BiD&SB, BrAu, CarSB, CasWL, Chambr 2, ChPo, ChPo S1, ChPo S2, CnE&AP, CriT 2, CyWA, DcEnA, DcEnL, DcEuL, DcLEnL, EvLB, MouLC 2, NCHEL, OxEng, Pen Eng, PoCh, RAdv 1, REn, WEAL*

Cox, Anthony Berkeley 1893-1970 *EncM&D, LongC, MnBBF, TwCA, TwCA Sup*

Cox, Anthony Berkeley *see* Berkeley, Anthony

Cox, Donald William 1921- *ConAu 1R*

Cox, Douglas *MnBBF*

Cox, Douglas *see* Cox, H D

Cox, E Albert 1876- *IlCB 1744*

Cox, Edith Muriel *WrD*

Cox, H D *MnBBF*

Cox, H D *see* Cox, Douglas

Cox, Jack 1915- *Au&Wr 6, ConAu XR, MnBBF, SmATA XR, WWBWI A, WWCL*

Cox, Jack *see* Cox, John Roberts

Cox, James Roberts *MnBBF*

Cox, John Roberts 1915- *Au&Wr 6, ConAu 29, SmATA 9*

Cox, John Roberts *see* Cox, Jack

Cox, John Roberts *see* Havenhand, John

Cox, John Roberts *see* Roberts, David

Cox, Lee Sheridan 1916- *ConAu 25R, DrAS 6E, IndAu 1917*

Cox, Palmer 1840-1924 *Alli Sup, AmA, AmA&B, BbD, BiD&SB, CarSB, ChPo, ChPo S1, ChPo S2, DcAmA, DcNAA, JBA 1934, MnBBF, OxAm*

Cox, Reginald H W *MnBBF*

Cox, Wally 1924-1973 *ConAu 41, CurB 54, CurB 73, NYTBE 4*

Cox, William Robert 1901- *AuBYP, ConAu 9R*

Coxe, George Harmon 1901- *AmA&B, EncM&D, MnBBF, REnAL, WWA 38, WorAu*

Coy, Harold 1902- *AuBYP, ConAu 5R, SmATA 3, WrD*

Coyle, David Cushman 1887-1969 *ConAu 1R*

Crabb, Edmond William 1912- *ConAu P-1, WrD*

Cradock, Mrs. H C *WWCL*

Craig, Andrew *MnBBF*

Craig, Eric *MnBBF*

Craig, George 1920- *Au&Wr 6*

Craig, Jean Teresa 1936- *ConAu 5R, LE 5, WrD*

Craig, John Eland *ConAu XR, SmATA 2*

Craig, John Eland *see* Chipperfield, Joseph Eugene

Craig, John Ernest 1921- *Prof*

Craig, John Ernest 1921- *WWA 38*

Craig, M Jean *AuBYP*

Craig, Margaret Maze 1911-1964 *ConAu 1R, MorJA, SmATA 9*

Craig, Mary Francis 1923- *ConAu 1R, SmATA 6, ThBJA, WWAW 8, WrD*

Craig, Mary Francis *see* Shura, Mary Francis

Craigie, Dorothy M 1908- *IlCB 1946*

Craik, Mrs. *Chambr 3, DcEnL, OxEng, TelT, WWCL*

Craik, Dinah Maria Mulock 1826-1887 *Alli Sup, AnCL, BbD, BiD&SB, BrAu 19, CarSB, CasWL, ChPo, ChPo S1, ChPo S2, DcEnA, DcEnA Ap, DcEuL, DcLEnL, EvLB, FamSYP, HsB&A, JBA 1934, NCHEL, REn, St&VC*

Craik, Dinah Maria Mulock *see* Mulock, Dinah Maria

Craik, Georgiana Marion 1831-1895 *Alli Sup, BiD&SB, CarSB, Chambr 3, DcEnL, NCHEL*

Cram, L D 1898- *IlCB 1946*

Cramer, Richard S 1928- *ConAu 29, DrAS 6H, WWW 14*

Crandall, Joy *ConAu 57*

Crandall, Joy *see* Martin, Joy

Crane, Alan 1901- *AuBYP*

Crane, Berkeley *MnBBF*

Crane, Berkeley *see* Marshall, Arthur C
Crane, Caroline 1930- *ConAu 9R,*
    ForWC 1970, SmATA 11, WrD
Crane, Edna Temple *ConAu XR*
Crane, Florence *AuBYP*
Crane, Hart 1899-1932 *LongC, ModAL,*
    ModAL Sup, OhA&B, OxAm, OxEng,
    Pen Am, RAdv 1, REn, REnAL, TwCA,
    TwCA Sup, TwCW, WEAL, WWTwL
Crane, Irving *AuBYP*
Crane, Lucy 1842-1882 *Alli Sup, ChPo S1*
Crane, Roy 1901- *ArtCS, WWAA 1973*
Crane, Stephen 1871-1900 *AmA, AmA&B,*
    AmWr, AtlBL, BbD, BiD&SB, CasWL,
    Chambr 3, ChPo, CnDAL, CnE&AP,
    CriT 3, CyWA, DcAmA, DcLEnL,
    DcNAA, EvLB, LongC, ModAL, OxAm,
    OxEng, Pen Am, RAdv 1, RCom, REn,
    REnAL, WEAL, YABC 2
Crane, Stephen *see* Smith, Johnston
Crane, Thomas 1843- *CarSB, ChPo*
Crane, Walter 1845-1915 *Alli Sup, CarSB,*
    ChPo, ChPo S1, ChPo S2, IlBYP,
    JBA 1934, JBA 1951, NCHEL, St&VC,
    WWCL
Crane, William D 1892- *ConAu 5R,*
    SmATA 1
Crary, Margaret Coleman 1906- *AuBYP,*
    ConAu 5R, ForWC 1970, SmATA 9
Craven, Essex *MnBBF*
Craven, Thomas 1889-1969 *AmA&B, AuBYP,*
    CurB 44, CurB 69, REnAL, TwCA,
    TwCA Sup
Crawford, Charles P 1945- *ConAu 45*
Crawford, Deborah 1922- *ConAu 49,*
    SmATA 6
Crawford, Joanna 1941- *ConAu 9R*
Crawford, John E 1904-1971 *ConAu P-2,*
    SmATA 3
Crawford, Phyllis 1899- *CurB 40, JBA 1951,*
    SmATA 3
Crawford, Phyllis *see* Turner, Josie
Crawford, Thelmar Wyche 1905- *AuBYP,*
    ConAu 1R
Crawford, Will *ConICB*
Crawford, William 1929- *ConAu 1R*
Crayder, Dorothy 1906- *ConAu 33, SmATA 7*
Crayder, Teresa *SmATA 1*
Crayder, Teresa *see* Colman, Hila
Crayon, Geoffrey *Alli, AmA&B, CnDAL,*
    DcEnL, OxAm, OxEng, REn, REnAL,
    YABC XR
Crayon, Geoffrey *see* Irving, Washington
Craz, Albert G 1926- *AuBYP, ConAu 17R*
Creasey, John 1908-1973 *Au&Wr 6,*
    ConAu 5R, CurB 63, CurB 73,
    EncM&D, LongC, MnBBF, NYTBE 4,
    REn, TwCW, WWBWI A, WorAu
Creasey, John *see* Ashe, Gordon
Creasey, John *see* Deane, Norman
Creasey, John *see* Halliday, Michael
Creasey, John *see* Hunt, Kyle
Creasey, John *see* Manton, Peter
Creasey, John *see* Marric, J J
Creasey, John *see* Martin, Richard
Creasey, John *see* Morton, Anthony
Creasey, John *see* Ranger, Ken
Creasey, John *see* Reilly, William K
Creasey, John *see* Riley, Tex

Creasey, John *see* York, Jeremy
Crecy, Jeanne *ConAu XR, SmATA 5*
Crecy, Jeanne *see* Williams, Jeanne
Credle, Ellis 1902- *AmPB, AuBYP,*
    ConAu 13R, IlCB 1744, IlCB 1946,
    JBA 1951, SmATA 1, St&VC
Creekmore, Raymond 1905- *IlCB 1946*
Creighton, Donald *MnBBF*
Creighton, Luella Bruce 1901- *ConAu P-1,*
    OxCan, OxCan Sup, Prof
Crespi, Pachita 1900- *AuBYP*
Cresswell, Helen 1934?- *Au&Wr 6, AuBYP,*
    ConAu 17R, SenS, SmATA 1, WrD
Creswick, Maurice *MnBBF*
Creswick, Paul 1866- *MnBBF, WWLA*
Cretan, Gladys 1921- *ConAu 29, SmATA 2,*
    WWAW 8
Crew, Fleming H 1882- *AmA&B, JBA 1951,*
    OhA&B
Crew, Helen Coale 1866-1941 *AmA&B, ChPo,*
    ChPo S1, JBA 1934, JBA 1951,
    YABC 2
Crews, Donald *IlBYP*
Crichlow, Ernest T 1914- *IlBYP, IlCB 1957*
Crichton, Jack *MnBBF*
Crichton, Jack *see* Miln, H Crichton
Crichton, Michael 1942- *AmA&B, Au&Wr 6,*
    AuNews 2, CelR 3, ConAu 25R,
    ConLC 2, ConLC 6, ConNov 1976,
    IntMPA 1975, NYTBE 1, SmATA 9
Crichton, Michael *see* Douglas, Michael
Crichton, Michael *see* Hudson, Jeffrey
Crichton, Michael *see* Lange, John
Crichton, Steve *MnBBF*
Crick, Vernon *MnBBF*
Crimmins, James Custis 1935- *ConAu 5R*
Crispin, Edmund 1921- *Au&Wr 6, CurB 49,*
    EncM&D, WorAu
Criss, Mildred 1890- *AuBYP, BkC 3,*
    CatA 1930
Crist, Eda 1909- *AuBYP*
Crockett, Lindsay *MnBBF*
Crockett, Lucy Herndon 1914- *CurB 53,*
    IlCB 1744, IlCB 1946
Crockett, Samuel Rutherford 1860-1914 *BbD,*
    BiD&SB, BrAu 19, CarSB, CasWL,
    Chambr 3, ChPo, DcBiA, DcEnA Ap,
    DcLEnL, EvLB, LongC, NCHEL,
    Pen Eng, REn, TelT, TwCA, TwCA Sup,
    WWCL
Croft, Roy *MnBBF*
Croft, Roy *see* Calvert, William Robinson
Croman, Dorothy Young *ConAu XR*
Cromie, William J 1930- *ConAu 13R,*
    SmATA 4
Crommelynck, Landa *IlBYP*
Crompton, Anne Eliot 1930- *ConAu 33*
Crompton, Frances Eliza *TelT*
Crompton, Richmal 1890-1969 *ConAu XR,*
    LongC, MnBBF, NCHEL, SmATA 5,
    WWCL, WWBWI A
Crompton, Richmal *see* Lamburn, Richmal
    Crompton
Crompton, William *MnBBF*
Crompton, William *see* Lamburn, Richmal
    Crompton
Cromwell, Victor *MnBBF*
Cromwell, Victor *see* Bull, Albert E
Cronbach, Abraham 1882-1965 *ConAu 1R,*

IndAu 1917, OhA&B, SmATA 11
Crone, Ruth 1919- *AuBYP, ConAu 9R,*
　SmATA 4
Cronin, A J 1896- *Au&Wr 6, CasWL,*
　CatA 1930, Chambr 3, ConAu 1R,
　ConNov 1976, CurB 42, DcLEnL,
　EncWL, EvLB, LongC, ModBL, NCHEL,
　Pen Eng, RAdv 1, REn, TwCA,
　TwCA Sup, TwCW, WNAA
Cronin, Bernard *MnBBF*
Cropp, Ben 1936- *ConAu 33, WrD*
Crosbie, W J *MnBBF*
Crosby, Alexander L 1906- *AuBYP,*
　ConAu 29, MorBMP, SmATA 2
Crosby, John *IlBYP*
Crosby, Percy 1891-1964 *ArtCS*
Crosby, Phoebe *AuBYP*
Crosfield, H C *MnBBF*
Crosher, G R *ConAu 69*
Cross, Anthony Glenn 1936- *MnBBF*
Cross, Dennis *MnBBF, WWBWI A*
Cross, Dennis *see* Gibbons, William
Cross, Frank B 1925- *AmMWS 12P*
Cross, John *MnBBF*
Cross, John Keir 1914-1967 *AuBYP, WWCL*
Cross, John Keir *see* MacFarlane, Stephen
Cross, May *MnBBF*
Cross, Milton 1897-1975 *AmA&B, CelR 3,*
　ConAu 53, NYTBE 2, WWA 38
Cross, Pennington *MnBBF*
Cross, Thomson *MnBBF*
Cross, Thomson *see* Wood, Samuel Andrew
Cross, Wilbur Lucius, III 1918- *Au&Wr 6,*
　ConAu 1R, SmATA 2, WWE 14
Crossley-Holland, Kevin 1941- *ChPo S1,*
　ConAu 41, ConP 1970, ConP 1975,
　SmATA 5, WrD
Crothers, Samuel McChord 1857-1927 *AmA&B,*
　CarSB, ChPo S2, ConAmL, DcAmA,
　DcNAA, OxAm, REnAL, TwCA,
　TwCA Sup, WNAA
Crouch, D *MnBBF*
Crouch, Marcus 1913- *Au&Wr 6, ChPo,*
　ChPo S2, ConAu 9R, SmATA 4,
　WWCL, WrD
Crouse, Anna *AuBYP*
Crouse, Russel 1893-1966 *AmA&B, AuBYP,*
　BiEnAT, CnDAL, CnThe, CurB 41,
　CurB 66, McGWD, ModWD, OhA&B,
　OxAm, REn, REnAL, TwCA Sup
Crouse, William Harry 1907- *AmMWS 12P,*
　AuBYP, ConAu 5R, IndAu 1917
Crout, George C 1917- *ConAu 29, SmATA 11*
Crowder, Michael 1934- *Au&Wr 6,*
　ConAu 1R, WrD
Crowe, Bettina Lum 1911- *Au&Wr 6, AuBYP,*
　ConAu 9R, SmATA 6, WWA 38,
　WWAW 8, WrD
Crowe, Bettina Lum *see* Lum, Peter
Crowe, Jocelyn 1906- *IlCB 1744*
Crowe, Robert L 1937- *ConAu 69*
Crowell, Grace Noll 1877-1969 *AmA&B,*
　BkCL, ChPo, ChPo S1, ChPo S2,
　REnAL, TexW, WNAA
Crowell, Pers 1910- *ConAu 29, IlBYP,*
　IlCB 1946, MorJA, SmATA 2, WWPNA
Crowfield, Christopher *DcEnL, DcNAA,*
　OxAm, YABC 1

Crowfield, Christopher *see* Stowe, Harriet
Beecher
Crowley, Christine 1922- *Au&Wr 6*
Crownfield, Gertrude 1867-1945 *AmA&B,*
　AuBYP, ChPo, ChPo S1, CurB 45,
　DcNAA, JBA 1934, JBA 1951, OhA&B,
　WNAA, YABC 1
Crowther, Bosley 1905- *AmA&B, CurB 57,*
　IntMPA 1975, WWWor 2
Crowther, James Gerald 1899- *AuBYP*
Cruickshank, Helen 1907- *AuBYP*
Cruikshank, George 1792-1878 *Alli, CarSB,*
　ChPo, ChPo S1, ChPo S2, IlBYP,
　NCHEL, REn, St&VC
Crump, Fred H, Jr. 1931- *ConAu 9R,*
　SmATA 11
Crump, Irving 1887- *AmA&B, AuBYP,*
　JBA 1934, JBA 1951, MnBBF
Crundal, Anson *MnBBF*
Crunden, Reginald *MnBBF, WWBWI A*
Crunden, Reginald *see* Cleaver, Hylton Reginald
Cruz, Ray 1933- *IlBYP, SmATA 6*
Crystal, H Y *MnBBF*
Cudlip, Mrs. Pender *DcEnL, MnBBF*
Cudlip, Mrs. Pender *see* Thomas, Annie
Cuffari, Richard 1925- *ChPo S2, IlBYP,*
　SmATA 6
Cule, William Edward *ChPo, MnBBF,*
　WWBWI A
Cullen, Countee 1903-1946 *AmA&B, AnCL,*
　AnMV 1926, BlkAW, CasWL, ChPo,
　ChPo S1, ConAmA, ConAmL, CurB 46,
　DcLEnL, DcNAA, ModAL, ModAL Sup,
　OxAm, Pen Am, RAdv 1, REn, REnAL,
　TwCA, TwCA Sup, WEAL, WNAA
Culley, John J *MnBBF*
Cullum, Ridgwell 1867-1943 *EvLB, LongC,*
　MnBBF, OxCan, TwCA, TwCA Sup,
　WWBWI A
Culp, Louanna McNary 1901-1965 *ConAu P-1,*
　SmATA 2
Culshaw, W J *MnBBF*
Cumberland, A M *MnBBF*
Cumming, Primrose Amy 1915- *Au&Wr 6,*
　ConAu 33, WrD
Cumming-Skinner, Dugald Matheson 1902-
　MnBBF, WWBWI A
Cumming-Skinner, Dugald Matheson *see*
Cummings, Ken
Cumming-Skinner, Dugald Matheson *see* Dane,
Donald
Cumming-Skinner, Dugald Matheson *see*
DeBeauregard, Henri
Cumming-Skinner, Dugald Matheson *see* Dundee,
Douglas
Cumming-Skinner, Dugald Matheson *see* Moray,
Dugald
Cummings, E E 1894-1962 *AmA&B, AmWr,*
　AnCL, AtlBL, AuBYP, CasWL, ChPo,
　CnDAL, CnE&AP, CnMD, CnMWL,
　ConAmA, ConAmL, ConLC 1, ConLC 3,
　CyWA, DcLEnL, EncWL, EvLB, LongC,
　McGWD, ModAL, ModAL Sup,
　ModWD, OxAm, OxEng, Pen Am,
　RAdv 1, REn, REnAL, SixAP, SixAP,
　TwCA, TwCA Sup, TwCW, WEAL,
　WWTwL
Cummings, J Abney d1919 *WWBWI I*
Cummings, Ken *MnBBF*

Cummings, Ken *see* Cumming-Skinner, Dugald Matheson
Cummings, Parke 1902- *AmA&B, ConAu P-1, SmATA 2, WWA 38*
Cummings, Richard *AuBYP, ConAu XR*
Cummings, W T 1933- *ConAu 1R*
Cummins, Maria Susanna 1827-1866 *Alli Sup, AmA, AmA&B, BbD, BiD&SB, Chambr 3, ChPo, DcAmA, DcBiA, DcLEnL, DcNAA, EvLB, OxAm, REn, REnAL, WWCL, YABC 1*
Cumpston, Astrid Kate Oatelaye *IlBYP*
Cumpston, Astrid Kate Oatelaye *see* Walford, Astrid
Cundall, Joseph 1818-1895 *Alli Sup, CarSB*
Cuneo, Cyrus 1879-1916 *WWBWI I*
Cuneo, Terence 1907- *MnBBF, WWBWI I*
Cunliffe, John Arthur 1933- *Au&Wr 6, ConAu 61, SmATA 11*
Cunliffe, Marcus 1922- *ConAu 21R*
Cunningham, Aline *ConAu 57*
Cunningham, Chet 1928- *ConAu 49*
Cunningham, Dale S 1932- *ConAu 13R, DrAS 6F, SmATA 11, WWE 14*
Cunningham, David 1909- *WWA 38*
Cunningham, Dellwyn *ChPo*
Cunningham, E V *AuBYP, ConAu XR, ConNov 1972, ConNov 1976, SmATA 7*
Cunningham, E V *see* Fast, Howard
Cunningham, Julia Woolfolk 1916- *AmA&B, AuBYP, ConAu 9R, MorBMP, SmATA 1, ThBJA, WWA 38, WWAW 8*
Cunningham, Mary *AuBYP*
Cunningham, Mary *see* Pierce, Mary Cunningham
Cunningham, Virginia 1909- *AuBYP, BiDL 5, OhA&B*
Cunningham, Walter *SingR 1*
Cunnington, Phillis 1887-1974 *Au&Wr 6, BiEnAT, ConAu 53*
Cunnison, C V L *MnBBF*
Curie, Eve 1904- *AmA&B, AnCL, Au&Wr 6, ConAu P-1, CurB 40, SmATA 1, WW 1974, WWA 38, WWAW 8, WWWor 2*
Curren, Polly 1917- *ConAu 1R*
Curry, Jane Louise 1932- *AuBYP, ConAu 17R, SmATA 1*
Curry, John Steuart 1897-1946 *CurB 41, CurB 46, DcCAA 2, IlCB 1744, OxAm, REn, REnAL*
Curry, Peggy Simson 1911- *ConAu 33, CurB 58, DrAF 1976, SmATA 8*
Curtayne, Alice 1898- *Au&Wr 6, BkC 6, CatA 1930, ConAu 53*
Curtin, Jeremiah 1840?-1906 *AmA, AmA&B, BiD&SB, DcAmA, DcNAA, REnAL*
Curtis, Alice Bertha *AuBYP*
Curtis, Alice Turner 1860-1958 *AmA&B, AuBYP, CarSB, ChPo, WNAA*
Curtis, Anthony 1925- *WWA 38, WWWor 2, WrD*
Curtis, Arnold 1917- *ConAu 29*
Curtis, Elizabeth *ConICB*
Curtis, Patricia 1924- *ConAu 69*
Curtis, Peter *ConAu XR, LongC, SmATA 8*
Curtis, Peter *see* Lofts, Norah
Curtis, Rosemary Ann 1935- *ConAu 9R*

Curtis Brown, Beatrice 1901-1974 *ConAu P-2*
Curtis Brown, Beatrice *see* Brown, Beatrice Curtis
Curto, Josephine *WrD*
Curwood, James Oliver 1878-1927 *AmA&B, DcNAA, LongC, MnBBF, OxAm, OxCan, REnAL, TwCA, TwCA Sup, WNAA*
Cusack, Ellen Dymphna 1902- *Au&Wr 6, DcLEnL, WWWor 2, WrD*
Cusack, Michael J 1928- *ConAu 69*
Cushman, Jerome 1914- *BiDL 5, ConAu 1R, SmATA 2, WWA 38, WWWorJ 1972, WrD*
Custer, Claude *MnBBF*
Custer, Claude *see* Goddard, Norman Molyneux
Cutler, Ann *AuBYP*
Cutler, Ebbitt 1923- *ConAu 49, SmATA 9*
Cutler, Ivor 1923- *Au&Wr 6, ConAu 5R, ConP 1970, WWMus 6, WrD*
Cutler, Katherine Noble 1905- *ConAu 5R*
Cutler, Samuel *ConAu XR, SmATA 5*
Cutler, Samuel *see* Folsom, Franklin
Cutt, W Towrie 1898- *OxCan Sup, WrD*
Cuyler, Stephen *ConAu XR, SmATA XR*
Cuyler, Stephen *see* Bates, Barbara S
Cyclops *WWBWI I*
Cyclops *see* Bowles, W M
Czaja, Michael 1911- *ConAu 57*

D

Dace, Wallace 1920- *DrAS 6E*
Dachs, David 1922- *ConAu 69*
Dacre, Stanley, Captain *MnBBF*
Dacre, Stanley, Captain *see* Hyatt, Stanley Portal
Daggett, R M *Alli Sup*
Daglish, Eric Fitch 1892- *ConICB, IlCB 1744, IlCB 1946, JBA 1934, LongC, TwCA, TwCA Sup*
Dagnall, J Deveral *MnBBF*
Dahl, Borghild 1890- *AuBYP, ConAu 1R, MnnWr, SmATA 7, ThBJA, WrD*
Dahl, Roald 1916- *Au&Wr 6, AuBYP, BiN 1974, ChLR 1, ConAu 1R, ConLC 1, ConLC 6, ConNov 1972, ConNov 1976, DrAF 1976, MorBMP, NCHEL, PiP, RAdv 1, REn, REnAL, SmATA 1, ThBJA, WWA 38, WWWor 2, WorAu, WrD*
Dahlstedt, Marden 1921- *ConAu 45, SmATA 8, WrD*
Dain, Martin J 1924- *ConAu 13R*
Dakers, Manton *MnBBF*
Dale, Austin *MnBBF*
Dale, Austin *see* Calvert, William Robinson
Dale, Edwin *MnBBF, WWBWI A*
Dale, Edwin *see* Home-Gall, Edward Reginald
Dale, Jack *ConAu XR, SmATA XR*
Dale, Jack *see* Holliday, Joseph
Dale, Leonard *MnBBF*
Dale, Margaret J Miller 1911- *ConAu 5R*
Dale, Margaret J Miller *see* Miller, Margaret J
Dale, Martin *MnBBF*
Dale, Roland *MnBBF*
Dale, Roland *see* Dale, Rowland
Dale, Rowland *MnBBF*
Dale, Rowland *see* Dale, Roland
Dale, Ruth Bluestone *AuBYP*
Dale, Victor *MnBBF*
Dale, Winston *MnBBF*
Daley, Arthur 1904-1974 *AmA&B, ConAu 45, ConAu P-2, CurB 56, CurB 74, NYTBS 5*
Dalgliesh, Alice 1893- *AmA&B, AmPB, AnCL, AuBYP, ChPo, JBA 1934, JBA 1951, St&VC, WNAA*
Dallas, Oswald *MnBBF, WWBWI A*
Dallas, Ruth 1919- *ChPo S2, ConAu 65, ConP 1970, ConP 1975, LongC, WrD*
Dalton, Alene *ChPo*
Dalton, Gilbert *MnBBF*
Dalton, Gilbert *see* Carstairs, Rod
Dalton, Gilbert *see* Norton, Victor

Dalton, Richard 1930- *ConAu 57*
Daly, Anne 1896- *ConAu P-2*
Daly, Carroll John 1889-1958 *AmA&B, EncM&D, MnBBF, WNAA*
Daly, Donald F *ConAu 69*
Daly, Jim *ConAu XR*
Daly, Jim *see* Stratemeyer, Edward L
Daly, Maureen 1921- *AmA&B, AmNov, AuBYP, BkC 4, CatA 1930, ConAu XR, CurB 46, MorJA, REnAL, SmATA 2*
Daly, Sheila John 1927?- *AuBYP, CatA 1952*
Daly, Thomas Augustine 1871-1948 *AmA&B, AmLY, BkC 1, CatA 1930, ChPo, ChPo S2, CnDAL, ConAmL, DcNAA, FamPYP, OxAm, REn, REnAL, TwCA, TwCA Sup, WNAA*
Dalzell, Kathleen Elizabeth *WrD*
D'Amato, Janet 1925- *ConAu 49, SmATA 9*
Damrosch, Helen Therese *SmATA XR*
Damrosch, Helen Therese *see* Tee-Van, Helen Damrosch
Dan, Uncle *MnBBF*
Dan, Uncle *see* Anderson, Frank
Dana, Barbara 1940- *ConAu 17R, ForWC 1970*
Dana, Richard Henry, Jr. 1815-1882 *Alli, Alli Sup, AmA, AmA&B, BbD, BiD&SB, CarSB, CasWL, Chambr 3, CnDAL, CriT 3, CyAL 2, CyWA, DcAmA, DcEnL, DcLEnL, DcNAA, EvLB, MouLC 4, OxAm, OxEng, Pen Am, REn, REnAL, WEAL*
Danaher, Kevin 1913- *ConAu 33*
D'Andrea, Annette Cole *see* Steiner, Barbara A
D'Andrea, Kate *SmATA XR*
Dane, Arnold *MnBBF*
Dane, Donald *MnBBF, WWBWI A*
Dane, Donald *see* Cumming-Skinner, Dugald Matheson
Dane, Lawrence *MnBBF*
Dane, Merton *MnBBF*
Dane, Richard *MnBBF*
Dane, Rupert *MnBBF*
Danesford, Earle *MnBBF, WWBWI A*
Danesford, Earle *see* Symonds, Francis Addington
Dangerfield, Balfour *ConAu XR, SmATA 2*
Dangerfield, Balfour *see* McCloskey, Robert
Dangerfield, Captain *MnBBF*
Dangerfield, Captain *see* Anderson, G J B
Dangerfield, George 1904- *AmA&B, ConAu 9R, CurB 53, DrAS 6H, OxAm,*

Polre. *WWA 38, WWW 14, WWWor 2, WorAu*
Daniel, Anita *AuBYP, ForWC 1970*
Daniel, Anne *SmATA XR*
Daniel, Anne *see* Steiner, Barbara A
Daniel, Frank *WWBWI 1*
Daniel, Hawthorne 1890- *AmA&B, Au&Wr 6, ConAu 5R, JBA 1934, JBA 1951, SmATA 8, WNAA, WWA 38, WWWor 2, WrD*
Daniel, Roland *MnBBF, WWBWI A, WWLA*
Daniel, Vincent *WWBWI 1*
Daniell, Albert Scott 1906-1965 *ConAu 5R*
Daniell, Albert Scott *see* Bowood, Richard
Daniell, Albert Scott *see* Daniell, David Scott
Daniell, Albert Scott *see* Lewesdon, John
Daniell, David Scott *ConAu XR*
Daniell, David Scott *see* Daniell, Albert Scott
Daniels, Arthur James 1863- *MnBBF, WWBWI A*
Daniels, Guy 1919- *ChPo S1, ConAu 21R, SmATA 11, SmATA 7, WWE 14*
Daniels, Jonathan 1902- *AmA&B, Au&Wr 6, AuBYP, CnDAL, ConAu 49, CurB 42, OxAm, REn, REnAL, TwCA, TwCA Sup, WWS 13, WWWor 2*
Daniels, Roger *MnBBF*
Danish, Barbara 1948- *ConAu 57*
Dann, Jack 1945- *ConAu 49, DrAF 1976*
Dannay, Frederic 1905- *AmA&B, AuBYP, ConAu 1R, CurB 40, DcLEnL, EncM&D, EvLB, IntWW 38, LongC, Pen Am, REn, TwCA, TwCA Sup, WW 1974, WWA 38, WWWor 2*
Dannay, Frederic *see* Nathan, Daniel
Dannay, Frederic *see* Queen, Ellery
Dannay, Frederic *see* Queen, Ellery, Jr.
Dannay, Frederic *see* Ross, Branaby
Dannett, Sylvia G L 1909- *ConAu 1R, WWAW 8, WWWorJ 1972*
Danska, Herbert 1927?- *ConAu 29, IIBYP, IICB 1946, IICB 1957*
Dantzic, Cynthia Maris 1933- *WWAW 8*
Darby, Ada Claire 1883-1953 *AmA&B, AuBYP*
Darby, Gene Kegley 1921- *ConAu 5R*
Darby, J N *ConAu XR, SmATA XR*
Darby, J N *see* Govan, Christine Noble
Darby, Patricia *AuBYP*
Darby, Ray 1912- *AmSCAP 66, AuBYP, ConAu 17R, SmATA 7*
D'Arcy, Edgar *MnBBF*
Dare, Arthur C *MnBBF, WWBWI A*
Dare, Captain *MnBBF*
Dare, Captain *see* Shaw, Stanley Gordon
Dare, Eveline *SingR 2*
Dare, Franklyn *MnBBF*
Dare, Gordon *MnBBF*
Dare, Harold *MnBBF*
Dare, Roderick *MnBBF*
Dareff, Hal 1920- *AmA&B, AuBYP, ConAu 65, WWA 38, WWE 14*
Dareff, Hal *see* Foley, Scott
Daring, Major *MnBBF, WWBWI A*
Daring, Major *see* Blyth, Harry
Daring, Victor *MnBBF*
Daring, Victor *see* Gannon, E J
Daringer, Helen Fern 1892- *ConAu P-2,*

CurB 51, MorJA, SmATA 1
Darley, Felix Octavius Carr 1822-1888 *Alli Sup, AmA&B, BiD&SB, CarSB, ChPo, ChPo S1, DcAmA, DcNAA, EarAB, EarAB Sup, OxAm*
Darling, Dick *MnBBF*
Darling, Edward 1907-1974 *AmA&B, ConAu 53, WWA 38*
Darling, Kathy *ConAu XR, SmATA XR*
Darling, Kathy *see* Darling, Mary Kathleen
Darling, Lois MacIntyre 1917- *AmA&B, AuBYP, ConAu 5R, IICB 1957, SmATA 3, WWA 38, WWAW 8, WWE 14*
Darling, Louis 1916-1970 *AmA&B, AuBYP, ConAu 5R, IICB 1946, IICB 1957, MorJA, NYTBE 1, SmATA 3*
Darling, Mary Kathleen 1943- *ConAu 53, SmATA 9*
Darling, Mary Kathleen *see* Darling, Kathy
Darlow, Denys 1921- *WWMus 6*
Darran, Mark *MnBBF, WWBWI A*
Darran, Mark *see* Goddard, Norman Molyneux
Darrell, Guy *MnBBF*
Darrell, Walter *MnBBF, WWBWI A*
Darrell, Walter *see* Burrage, Edwin Harcourt
Darrell, Walter *see* Garrish, Henry J
Darrow, Whitney, Jr. 1909- *AmA&B, ConAu 61, CurB 58, SmATA 13, WWA 38, WWAA 1973, WWWor 2*
Darton, Frederick Joseph Harvey d1936 *CarSB, ChPo*
Darwin, Beatrice *IIBYP*
Darwin, Charles Robert 1809-1882 *Alli, Alli Sup, AtlBL, BbD, BiD&SB, BrAu 19, CarSB, CasWL, Chambr 3, CyWA, DcEnA, DcEnA Ap, DcEnL, DcEuL, DcLEnL, EvLB, MouLC 4, NCHEL, OxEng, Pen Eng, RCom, REn, WEAL*
Darwin, Desmond *MnBBF*
Darwin, Elinor May d1954 *ChPo, ConICB, IICB 1744, IICB 1946*
Darwin, Leonard 1850-1943 *CurB 43, IIBYP, WWLA*
Daryl, A J *Alli Sup, MnBBF*
Das, Kamala 1934- *CasWL, ConP 1970, ConP 1975, WrD*
Dasent, Sir George Webbe 1817-1896 *Alli Sup, AnCL, BbD, BiD&SB, BrAu 19, Chambr 3, DcEnA, DcEnL, DcEuL, EvLB, NCHEL, OxEng, St&VC, WWCL*
Dashwood, Percy *MnBBF*
Dashman, Raymond Frederic 1919- *AmMWS 12P*
Dashman, Raymond Frederic 1919- *WWA 38*
Dashman, Raymond Frederic 1919- *WWWor 2*
D'Attilio, Anthony *IIBYP*
Dauer, Rosamond 1934- *ConAu 65*
Daugherty, Charles Michael 1914- *AuBYP, IICB 1946*
Daugherty, Harry R 1883- *IICB 1946*
Daugherty, James Henry 1889-1974 *AmA&B, AmLY, AmPB, AnCL, AuBYP, BkP, ChPo, ChPo S1, ConAu 49, CurB 40, CurB 74, IICB 1744, IICB 1946, IICB 1957, JBA 1934, JBA 1951, NYTBS 5, Newb 1922, SmATA 13,*

St&VC, WWA 38, WWAA 1973
Daugherty, Richard Deo 1922- *AmMWS 12S,
WWA 38*
D'Aulaire, Edgar Parin 1898- *AmA&B, AmPB,
AnCL, AuBYP, BkCL, BkP, Cald 1938,
ChPo S2, ConAu 49, ConICB, CurB 40,
IlBYP, IlCB 1744, IlCB 1946, IlCB 1957,
JBA 1934, JBA 1951, SmATA 5,
St&VC, WWA 38, WWAA 1973*
D'Aulaire, Edgar Parin *see* Aulaire, Edgar Parin
D'
D'Aulaire, Ingri 1904- *AmA&B, AmPB,
AnCL, AuBYP, BkCL, BkP, Cald 1938,
ChPo S2, ConAu 49, CurB 40, IlBYP,
IlCB 1744, IlCB 1946, IlCB 1957,
JBA 1934, JBA 1951, SmATA 5,
St&VC, WWA 38*
D'Aulaire, Ingri *see* Aulaire, Ingri D'
D'Aulnoy, Marie-Catherine, Comtesse
1650?-1705 *St&VC*
D'Aulnoy, Countess 1650?-1705 *WWCL*
Daunt, Atherley *MnBBF, WWBWI A*
Daunt, Atherley *see* Evans, Frank Howel
Davar, Ashok *ConAu 69*
Daveluy, Paule Cloutier 1919- *ConAu 9R,
OxCan Sup, Prof, SmATA 11*
Davenport, Marcia 1903- *AmA&B, AmNov,
AuBYP, ConAu 9R, CurB 44, DcLEnL,
LongC, OxAm, REn, REnAL,
TwCA Sup, WWA 38, WWAW 8,
WWWor 2*
Davenport, Spencer *ConAu XR*
Davenport, Spencer *see* Stratemeyer, Edward L
Davenport, Tex *MnBBF*
Davenport, Tex *see* Tiltman, Hugh Hessell
Daves, Michael 1938- *ConAu 9R*
Davey, George *WWBWI I*
Davey, Gilbert 1913- *Au&Wr 6, ConAu P-1,
WrD*
Davey, John *ConAu XR*
Davey, John *see* Richey, David
David, Eugene *AuBYP*
David, Heather M 1937- *ConAu 37*
David, Ismar *ChPo S1*
David, Jonathan *SmATA 3*
David, Jonathan *see* Ames, Lee Judah
Davidson, Basil 1914- *AmA&B, Au&Wr 6,
ConAu 1R, SmATA 13, WWWor 2,
WorAu*
Davidson, Bill *AuBYP*
Davidson, Gladys *ChPo S1*
Davidson, Jessica 1915- *ConAu 41, SmATA 5*
Davidson, Margaret 1936- *ConAu 25R,
SmATA 5*
Davidson, Margaret *see* Davidson, Mickie
Davidson, Marion *SmATA XR*
Davidson, Marion *see* Garis, Howard Roger
Davidson, Mary R 1885-1973 *ConAu 5R,
SmATA 9*
Davidson, Mickie *ConAu XR*
Davidson, Mickie *see* Davidson, Margaret
Davidson, Mildred *WrD*
Davidson, Rosalie 1921- *ConAu 69*
Davidson, T Whitfield *NYTBS 5*
Davies *MnBBF, WWBWI A*
Davies, A W *MnBBF*
Davies, A W *see* Davis, A W
Davies, A W *see* Richards, Frank
Davies, Edward C *MnBBF*

Davies, Evelyn 1924- *ConAu 61*
Davies, Joan Howard *Au&Wr 6, WrD*
Davies, John *MnBBF*
Davies, L P 1914- *ConAu 21R*
Davies, Lucian *MnBBF*
Davies, Lucian *see* Beeston, L J
Davies, M C D *MnBBF*
Davies, Peter 1937- *ConAu 53, Prof*
Davies, Philip *WWBWI A*
Davies, Valentine 1905-1961 *AmA&B, AmNov*
Davis, A W *MnBBF*
Davis, A W *see* Davies, A W
Davis, Angela 1944- *BiN 1974, CelR 3,
CurB 72, NYTBE 2*
Davis, Arnold *MnBBF, WWBWI A*
Davis, Arthur Kennard 1910- *ConAu P-1*
Davis, Bette J *IlBYP*
Davis, Burke 1913- *AmA&B, AuBYP,
ConAu 1R, SmATA 4, WWA 38, WrD*
Davis, Caroline E 1831- *Alli Sup, CarSB,
DcAmA*
Davis, Christopher 1928- *Au&Wr 6,
ConAu 9R, DrAF 1976, SmATA 6, WrD*
Davis, Clive E 1914- *AuBYP, ConAu 17R*
Davis, Daniel S 1936- *ConAu 45, SmATA 12*
Davis, Dimitris 1905- *IlCB 1957*
Davis, Edwin Adams 1904- *ConAu P-2,
DrAS 6H, WWA 38*
Davis, Frederick Clyde 1902- *AmA&B,
MnBBF*
Davis, Harriet Eager 1892?-1974 *ConAu 49*
Davis, Julia 1904?- *AmA&B, ConAu 1R,
JBA 1951, SmATA 6, WWAW 8, WrD*
Davis, Julia *see* Adams, Julia Davis
Davis, Julia *see* Draco, F
Davis, Kenneth S 1912- *AmA&B, AmNov,
ConAu 13R*
Davis, Lavinia Riker 1909-1961 *AmA&B,
AuBYP, JBA 1951, WNAA*
Davis, Marguerite 1889- *ChPo, ChPo S2,
ConICB, IlCB 1744, IlCB 1946,
WWA 38, WWAW 8, WWS 13*
Davis, Marilyn K 1928- *ConAu 5R,
ForWC 1970*
Davis, Mary Gould 1882-1956 *AmA&B, AnCL,
AuBYP, ChPo, ChPo S1, JBA 1934,
JBA 1951*
Davis, Mary L 1935- *ConAu 49, SmATA 9*
Davis, Mary Octavia 1901- *ConAu 25R,
SmATA 6, TexW*
Davis, Mary Octavia *see* Dutz
Davis, Paxton 1925- *ConAu 9R*
Davis, Phil 1906-1964 *ArtCS*
Davis, Philip *MnBBF*
Davis, Reda *AuBYP*
Davis, Richard *ConAu 53*
Davis, Richard Harding 1864-1916 *AmA&B,
BbD, BiD&SB, CarSB, CasWL,
Chambr 3, CnDAL, DcAmA, DcBiA,
DcEnA Ap, DcLEnL, DcNAA, EncM&D,
EvLB, JBA 1934, LongC, OxAm,
Pen Am, REn, REnAL, TwCA,
TwCA Sup, WEAL*
Davis, Robert 1881-1949 *AmA&B, AnCL,
CurB 49, DcNAA, JBA 1951, YABC 1*
Davis, Roy Eugene 1931- *ConAu 9R*
Davis, Russell Gerard 1922- *ConAu 5R,
SmATA 3, WWA 38*
Davis, Sammy, Jr. 1925- *BiEnAT, BiN 1974,*

CelR 3, CurB 56, IntMPA 1975,
NYTBE 2, NYTBE 3, WWA 38,
WWT 15, WWWor 2
Davis, Verne Theodore 1889-1973 ConAu 1R,
SmATA 6
Davis, William Stearns 1877-1930 AmA&B,
CarSB, DcAmA, DcNAA, JBA 1934,
OxAm, TwCA, WNAA
Davison, Frank Dalby 1893-1970 CasWL,
DcLEnL, SingR 1, TwCW
Dawlish, John MnBBF
Dawson, A J 1872?-1951 BbD, BiD&SB,
NCHEL, WWCL
Dawson, A W MnBBF
Dawson, Arnold H MnBBF
Dawson, C T MnBBF
Dawson, Colin MnBBF
Dawson, Dagmar 1933- SingR 2
Dawson, Elmer A ConAu P-2, SmATA 1
Dawson, Elmer A see Stratemeyer, Edward L
Dawson, F Morton MnBBF
Dawson, Hugh MnBBF
Dawson, Mary 1919- ChPo S1, ConAu 21R,
SmATA 11
Dawson, Mitchell 1890- AuBYP
Dawson, Peter WWBWI A
Dawson, Peter see Faust, Frederick
Dawson, Ray MnBBF
Dawtrey, John MnBBF
Day, A Grove 1904- AmA&B, ConAu 21R,
WNAA
Day, Beth 1924- ChPo S2, ConAu 9R,
ForWC 1970
Day, Beth Feagles see Feagles, Elizabeth
Day, George MnBBF
Day, George see Howard, Bruce
Day, Lionel MnBBF, WWBWI A
Day, Lionel see Black, Ladbroke Lionel Day
Day, Maurice 1892- ConICB, IlCB 1744
Day, Thomas 1748-1789 Alli, BbD, BiD&SB,
BrAu, CarSB, CasWL, ChPo, CyWA,
DcEnA, DcEnL, DcEuL, EvLB, NCHEL,
OxEng, Pen Eng, WWCL, YABC 1
Dayle, Malcolm MnBBF, WWBWI A
Dayle, Malcolm see Bayfield, William John
Dayle, Malcolm see Hincks, Cyril Malcolm
Dayne, Clement MnBBF
Dazey, Agnes J ConAu P-2, SmATA 2
Dazey, Agnes J see Johnston, Agnes Christine
Dazey, Frank M ConAu P-2, SmATA 2
Deakin, Guy MnBBF
Dean, Anabel 1915- ConAu 37, SmATA 12,
WrD
Dean, Donald MnBBF, WWBWI A
Dean, Donald see Hope, William Edward Stanton
Dean, Graham M 1904- AmA&B, AuBYP,
WWA 38
Dean, Leon W 1889- MnBBF, WNAA
Dean, Nell Marr 1910- AuBYP, ConAu 21R
Dean, Nell Marr see Roberts, Virginia
Dean, Rhoda WWBWI A
Dean, Rhoda see Hope, Stanton
Dean, Yetive H 1909- ConAu P-1
Deane, Fannie A CarSB
Deane, Norman ConAu XR, EncM&D,
LongC, WWBWI A
Deane, Norman see Creasey, John
Deane, Shirley Joan 1920- AmA&B,
Au&Wr 6, ConAu 1R

Deane, Vesey WrD, MnBBF
Deane, Vesey see Murray, Andrew Nicholas
Deane, Wallace MnBBF
DeAngeli, Marguerite see Angeli, Marguerite De
DeAngeli, Marguerite Lofft 1889- AmA&B,
Au&ICB, Au&Wr 6, AuBYP, AuNews 2,
BkCL, ChLR 1, ChPo, ChPo S1,
ConAu 5R, ConICB, CurB 47, FamMS,
IlCB 1744, IlCB 1946, IlCB 1957,
JBA 1951, MorBMP, Newb 1922,
SmATA 1, WWA 38, WWAA 1973,
WWAW 8
DeArmand, Frances Ullmann AuBYP,
ConAu 5R, SmATA 10
Dearmin, Jennie Tarascou 1924- ConAu 5R,
ForWC 1970, WWAW 8
Deason, Hilary J 1903- AmMWS 12P,
BiDL 5, ConAu 21R
DeBanke, Cecile 1889-1965 ConAu P-1,
LongC, SmATA 11
DeBeauregard, Henri MnBBF, WWBWI A
DeBeauregard, Henri see Cumming-Skinner,
Dugald Matheson
DeBeck, Billy 1890-1942 ArtCS
DeBlumenthal, Verra CarSB
DeBono, Edward 1933- Au&Wr 6,
ConAu 21R
DeBorhegyi, Suzanne C Sims see Borhegyi,
Suzanne C Sims De
DeBorhegyi, Suzanne Sims 1926- AuBYP,
ConAu 5R, ForWC 1970, WWAW 8
DeBosschere, Jean ChPo
DeBrunhoff, Jean 1899-1937 ChFB A
DeBrunhoff, Jean see Brunhoff, Jean De
DeBrunhoff, Laurent 1925- Au&Wr 6, MorJA,
PiP
DeBrunhoff, Laurent see Brunhoff, Laurent De
DeBruyn, Monica G 1952- ConAu 65,
SmATA 13
DeCamp, Catherine Crook 1907- ConAu 21R,
SmATA 12, WWAW 8, WrD
DeCamp, L Sprague 1907- AuBYP,
ConAu 1R, SmATA 9, WorAu
DeCamp, L Sprague see Lyon, Lyman R
DeCamp, L Sprague see Wells, J Wellington
Decker, Duane 1910-1964 AuBYP, ConAu 5R,
SmATA 5
Decker, Duane see Wayne, Richard
DeConde, Alexander 1920- AmA&B,
ConAu 5R, DrAS 6H, WWA 38,
WWWor 2
Dedham, Richard MnBBF
DeDiego, Julio 1900- WWAA 1973
Dedmon, Emmett 1918- AmA&B, Au&Wr 6,
ConAu 9R, WWA 38, WWMW 14,
WWWor 2
Dee, Dare MnBBF
Dee, Dare see Steffens, Arthur
Dee, Ruby 1924?- BiEnAT, BlkAW, CelR 3,
ChPo S2, CurB 70, NYTBE 1,
WWA 38, WWAW 8, WWT 15
Deedy, John 1923- ConAu 33
Defoe, Daniel 1660?-1731 Alli, AtlBL, BbD,
BiD&SB, BrAu, CarSB, CasWL,
Chambr 2, ChPo S1, CriT 2, CyWA,
DcBiA, DcEnA, DcEnL, DcEuL,
DcLEnL, EvLB, HsB&A, MnBBF,
MouLC 2, NCHEL, OxEng, Pen Eng,
RAdv 1, RCom, REn, WEAL, WWCL

Deford, Frank 1938- *ConAu 33*
DeForest, Charlotte B 1879- *ConAu P-2,*
  WNAA
DeGaspari *WWBWI 1*
DeGering, Etta Fowler 1898- *AuBYP,*
  ConAu P-1, ForWC 1970, SmATA 7
DeGrazia, Ettore 1909- *ConAu 61*
DeGrazia, Ettore *see* DeGrazia, Ted
DeGrazia, Ted *ConAu XR*
DeGrazia, Ted *see* DeGrazia, Ettore
DeGroot, Lee *ChPo S1*
DeGross, J H *ConAu XR*
DeGrummond, Lena Young *AuBYP,*
  ConAu 1R, SmATA 6
DeHamel, Joan Littledale *WrD*
DeHartog, Jan 1914- *AmA&B, BiEnAT,*
  CnMD, ConAu 1R, CurB 70, WWA 38,
  WWWor 2
DeHartog, Jan *see* Hartog, Jan De
Dehn, Olive *ChPo S1*
Dehn, Paul 1912- *IntMPA 1975, WW 1974,*
  WWT 15, WrD
Deighton, Len 1929- *ConAu 9R, ConLC 4,*
  ConNov 1972, ConNov 1976, EncM&D,
  IntMPA 1975, IntWW 38, NCHEL,
  TwCW, WWWor 2, WorAu
Deiss, Joseph Jay 1915- *Au&Wr 6, ConAu 33,*
  SmATA 12, WWA 38, WWWor 2, WrD
DeJong, David C *see* Breda, Tjalmar
DeJong, David Cornel 1905-1967 *AmA&B,*
  AmNov, AuBYP, ConAu 5R, CurB 44,
  CurB 67, OxAm, REn, REnAL,
  SmATA 10, TwCA, TwCA Sup
DeJong, Dola 1911- *AuBYP, ConAu 5R,*
  CurB 47, MorJA, SmATA 7
DeJong, Meindert 1906- *AnCL, Au&ICB,*
  Au&Wr 6, AuBYP, BkCL, CasWL,
  ChLR 1, ConAu 13R, CurB 52, FamMS,
  MorBMP, MorJA, Newb 1922, SenS,
  SmATA 2
DeKay, James T 1930- *ConAu 25R*
DeKay, Ormonde, Jr. 1923- *ChPo S2,*
  ConAu 49, SmATA 7
DeKiriline, Louise *ConAu XR, SmATA XR*
DeKiriline, Louise *see* Lawrence, Louise
  DeKiriline
Dekker, Carl *ConAu XR*
Dekker, Carl *see* Laffin, John
Dekle, Bernard 1905- *ConAu 17R*
Dekovic, Gene 1922- *WWA 38*
DeKruif, Paul 1890-1971 *AmA&B, BiEnAT,*
  ConAu 9R, ConAu 29, CurB 42,
  CurB 63, CurB 71, JBA 1934, LongC,
  OxAm, REn, REnAL, SmATA 5, TwCA,
  TwCA Sup
DeLaboulaye, Edouard R L *JBA 1934*
DeLaboulaye, Edouard R L *see* Laboulaye,
  Edouard R L De
DeLaCroix, Robert *AuBYP*
DeLage, Ida 1918- *ConAu 41, SmATA 11*
DeLaguna, Grace A 1878- *ConAu P-1*
DeLaIglesia, Maria Elena 1936- *ConAu 29*
DeLaMare, Walter 1873-1956 *AnCL, AtlBL,*
  AuBYP, BkCL, CarSB, CasWL,
  Chambr 3, ChP, ChPo, ChPo S1,
  ChPo S2, CnE&AP, CnMWL, CyWA,
  DcLEnL, EncWL, EvLB, FamPG,
  JBA 1934, JBA 1951, LongC, ModBL,
  NCHEL, OxEng, Pen Eng, RAdv 1,

  REn, St&VC, TelT, TwCA, TwCA Sup,
  TwCW, WEAL, WWCL, WWTwL
DeLaMare, Walter *see* LaMare, Walter De
DeLaMare, Walter *see* Mare, Walter DeLa
Delaney, Bud *ConAu 57*
Delaney, Bud *see* Delaney, Francis, Jr.
Delaney, Francis, Jr. 1931- *ConAu 57*
Delaney, Francis, Jr. *see* Delaney, Bud
Delaney, Harry 1932- *ConAu 25R, SmATA 3*
Delaney, Lolo M 1937- *ConAu 57*
Delaney, Ned 1951- *ConAu 65*
Delano, Hugh 1933- *ConAu 65*
Delano, Isaac O 1904- *ConAu 25R*
DeLaRamee, Louise 1840-1908 *BrAu 19,*
  CarSB, JBA 1934, TelT
DeLaRamee, Louise *see* LaRamee, Louise De
DeLaRamee, Louise *see* Ouida
DeLaRamee, Louise *see* Ramee, Louise DeLa
DeLaRoche, Mazo 1885-1961 *CanNov, CanWr,*
  CasWL, Chambr 3, ConAmL, CyWA,
  DcLEnL, EvLB, JBA 1934, LongC,
  OxAm, OxCan, OxEng, Pen Eng, REn,
  REnAL, TwCA, TwCA Sup, TwCW
DeLarrea, Victoria *IlBYP*
DeLaTorre, Lillian 1902- *AmA&B, AuBYP,*
  ConAu XR, CurB 49, EncM&D, REnAL,
  TwCA Sup
DeLaTorre, Lillian *see* McCue, Lillian Bueno
Delaune, Jewel Lynn DeGrummond *SmATA 7*
Delaune, Lynn D *AuBYP, ConAu 1R*
DeLaurentis, Louise Budde 1920- *ConAu 5R,*
  ForWC 1970, SmATA 12
DelBarco, Lucy Salamanca *ConAu 17R,*
  WWAW 8
DelBarco, Lucy Salamanca *see* Salamanca, Lucy
Delderfield, Eric R 1909- *Au&Wr 6,*
  ConAu 53
Delderfield, Ronald Frederick 1912-1972
  Au&Wr 6, WWCL
Deldman, Herbert 1910- *ConAu 29*
Delear, Frank J 1914- *ConAu 21R, WrD*
DeLeeuw, Adele *see* Leeuw, Adele De
DeLeeuw, Adele Louise 1899- *AmA&B,*
  AuBYP, ChPo S1, ConAu 1R, JBA 1951,
  OhA&B, SmATA 1, WNAA
DeLeeuw, Adele Louise 1899- *WWAW 8*
DeLeeuw, Adele Louise 1899- *WrD*
DeLeeuw, Cateau *see* Hamilton, Kay
DeLeeuw, Cateau *see* Lyon, Jessica
DeLeeuw, Cateau Wilhelmina 1903- *Au&Wr 6,*
  AuBYP, ConAu 1R, ForWC 1970,
  JBA 1951, OhA&B, WWAA 1973,
  WWAW 8
Delessert, Etienne 1941- *ConAu 21R, IlBYP*
Delgado, Alan 1909- *ConAu 9R, WrD*
Delisle, Harcourt *MnBBF*
Dell, Draycot Montagu 1888- *ChPo S1,*
  ChPo S2, MnBBF
Dell, Draycot Montagu *see* Anson, Piers
Dell, Draycot Montagu *see* Thompson, Stephen
Dell, Draycott M *WWBWI A*
Delmere, F *MnBBF*
Deloria, Vine, Jr. 1933- *AmA&B, ConAu 53,*
  CurB 74
DelRey, Lester 1915- *AmA&B, AuBYP,*
  ConAu 65, ThBJA
DelRey, Lester *see* Rey, Lester Del
DelRey, Lester *see* Saint John, Philip
DelRey, Lester *see* VanLhin, Erik

Delton, Judy 1931- *ConAu 57*
DeLulio, John *IlBYP*
Delving, Michael *AmA&B, SmATA 3, WorAu*
Delving, Michael *see* Williams, Jay
Demage, G *MnBBF*
DeMare, Eric S 1910- *Au&Wr 6, ConAu 9R*
Demaree, Doris Clore 1903- *IndAu 1917*
Demarest, Doug *ConAu XR, SmATA 8*
Demarest, Doug *see* Barker, Will
DeMartelly, John Stockton 1903- *IlCB 1744*
Demas, Vida 1927- *ConAu 49, SmATA 9*
DeMaupassant, Guy *EuAu*
DeMaupassant, Guy *see* Maupassant, Guy De
Deming, Dorothy 1893- *AuBYP, CurB 43*
Deming, Edwin W 1860-1942 *CurB 42*
Deming, Richard 1915- *ConAu 9R*
Deming, Richard *see* Franklin, Max
DeMiskey, Julian 1908- *IlCB 1957*
DeMorgan, Mary *Alli Sup, TelT*
DeMorgan, William Frend 1839-1917 *CasWL, Chambr 3, CyWA, DcBiA, DcEuL, DcLEnL, EvLB, JBA 1934, LongC, ModBL, NCHEL, OxEng, Pen Eng, REn, TwCA, TwCA Sup, TwCW*
DeMuth, Flora Nash 1888- *IlCB 1946*
Denbigh, Maurice *MnBBF*
Denbigh, Maurice *see* Nutbrown, Maurice
Dene, Alan *MnBBF, WWBWI A*
Dene, Alan *see* Wignall, Trevor C
Dene, Hampton *MnBBF, WWBWI A*
Dene, Hampton *see* Bayfield, William John
Dene, Hampton *see* Hook, Samuel Clarke
Denetsosie, Hoke *AmPB*
Denholm, Therese Mary Zita White 1933- *ConAu 9R*
Denholm, Therese Mary Zita White *see* White, Zita
Denison, Carol *AuBYP*
Denison, Muriel *AuBYP*
Denman, Frank *AuBYP*
Denman, George *MnBBF*
Dennis, C J 1876-1938 *LongC, SingR 2, TwCW*
Dennis, C J *see* Dennis, Clarence Michael James
Dennis, Clarence Michael James 1876-1938 *CasWL, ChPo, DcLEnL, EvLB, SingR 2*
Dennis, Clarence Michael James *see* Dennis, C J
Dennis, Henry C 1918- *AmMWS 12S, ConAu 41, WWW 14*
Dennis, Hugh *MnBBF*
Dennis, Morgan 1892?-1960 *AmA&B, AuBYP, IlCB 1744, IlCB 1946, MorJA*
Dennis, Wesley 1903-1966 *AuBYP, IlCB 1744, IlCB 1946, IlCB 1957, MorJA*
Dennison, George 1925- *AmA&B*
Denny, Norman George 1901- *Au&Wr 6, MnBBF*
Densen-Gerber, Judianne 1934- *ConAu 37, NYTBE 1, WWAW 8, WWE 14*
Denslow, W W *AmPB*
Dent, C H *MnBBF, WWBWI A*
Dent, C H *see* Fanshaw, Cecil
Dent, C H *see* Hudleston, John
Dent, C H *see* Hudleston, Robert
Dent, Denis *MnBBF*
Dent, Denis *see* Williams, Graeme
Denton, George *MnBBF*
Denton, Pete *MnBBF*

Denver, Athol *MnBBF*
Denver, Bruce *MnBBF*
Denver, Bruce *see* Hope, William Edward Stanton
Denvers, Jake *MnBBF*
Denvers, Jake *see* Edgar, Alfred
Denville, Hugh *MnBBF*
Denvir, Joan 1925- *ArtsCL*
Denzel, Justin F 1917- *ConAu 53*
Denzer, Ann Wiseman *ConAu 65*
Denzer, Ann Wiseman *see* Wiseman, Ann
DeOsma, Lupe *AuBYP*
DePaola, Thomas Anthony 1934- *ConAu 49, SmATA 11*
DePaola, Thomas Anthony *see* DePaola, Tomie
DePaola, Tomie *ConAu XR, ConAu 49, IlBYP, IlCB 1957, SmATA XR*
DePaola, Tomie *see* DePaola, Thomas Anthony
DePauw, Linda Grant 1940- *ConAu 21R, DrAS 6H*
Depew, Arthur M *ConAu 41*
DePuy, Henry Walter 1820-1876 *Alli, BiD&SB, CarSB, DcAmA, DcNAA*
Derby, Pat 1942- *ConAu 69*
DeRegniers, Beatrice Schenk 1914- *AmA&B, Au&Wr 6, AuBYP, BkP, ChPo, ChPo S1, ConAu 13R, IndAu 1917, MorJA, SmATA 2, WWA 38, WWAW 8, WWE 14, WrD*
Derham, Arthur Morgan *WrD*
Dering, Richard *MnBBF*
Derleth, August 1909-1971 *AmA&B, AmNov, AuBYP, BkC 6, ChPo, ChPo S2, CnDAL, ConAu 1R, ConAu 29, ConNov 1972, DcLEnL, EncM&D, NYTBE 2, OxAm, REn, REnAL, SmATA 5, TwCA, TwCA Sup, WNAA*
Derleth, August *see* Grendon, Stephen
Derleth, August *see* Mason, Tally
Derman, Sarah Audrey 1915- *ConAu 1R, SmATA 11*
DeRopp, Robert S 1913- *Au&Wr 6, ConAu 17R*
DeRosa, Peter 1932- *ConAu 21R*
DeRossi, Claude 1942- *ConAu 53*
DeRoussan, Jacques 1929- *Prof*
Derrick, Thomas *ChPo S1, IlCB 1744*
Derwent, Lavinia *ConAu 69*
Derwent, Vernon *MnBBF*
Desai, Anita 1937- *CasWL, ConNov 1972, ConNov 1976, REn, WrD*
DeSaint Exupery, Antoine *ModRL*
DeSaint-Exupery, Antoine *see* Saint-Exupery, Antoine De
DeSantis, Mary Allen 1930- *ConAu 9R*
Desbarats, Peter 1933- *ConAu 17R, OxCan*
DeSchanschieff, Juliet Dymoke *WrD*
Deschin, Celia Spalter 1903- *WWAW 8*
DeSchweinitz, Karl 1887-1975 *ConAu 61*
DeSelincourt, Aubrey 1894-1962 *DcLEnL, LongC, WWCL*
DeSeta *WWBWI 1*
DeSeyn, Donna E 1933- *ConAu 21R, LE 5, WWAW 8, WrD*
DeShields, James Thomas 1891- *TexW*
Deslys, Charles 1821-1885 *BiD&SB, MnBBF*
Desmond, Alice Curtis 1897- *AmA&B, AuBYP, ConAu 1R, SmATA 8, WWA 38, WWAW 8, WWE 14*
Desmond, Frank *MnBBF*

Desmond, J Patrick 1910- *ConAu 9R*
DeSola, Ralph 1908- *ConAu 53*
Desoutter, Denis Marcel 1919- *Au&Wr 6*
D'Esque, Count Jean Louis *MnBBF*
DeTerra, Rhoda Hoff 1901- *ConAu 1R*
DeTessier, Isabelle Emily *WWBWI 1*
DeTessier, Isabelle Emily *see* Duval, Marie
Detine, Padre *ConAu XR*, *SmATA 6*
Detine, Padre *see* Olsen, Ib Spang
Detmold, Edward J 1883?- *ChPo S1*, *ConICB*
DeTrevino, Elizabeth Borton 1904- *Au&ICB*,
  ForWC 1970, *MorBMP*, *NewbC 1966*
DeTrevino, Elizabeth Borton *see* Borton,
  Elizabeth
Deucher, Sybil *MorJA*
Deutsch, Babette 1895- *AmA&B*, *AnCL*,
  Au&Wr 6, *ChPo*, *ChPo S1*, *ChPo S2*,
  ConAmL, *ConAu 1R*, *ConP 1970*,
  ConP 1975, *DcLEnL*, *DrAP 1975*,
  DrAS 6E, *EvLB*, *IntWW 38*, *LongC*,
  MorJA, *OxAm*, *Pen Am*, *RAdv 1*, *REn*,
  REnAL, *SmATA 1*, *TwCA*, *TwCA Sup*,
  TwCW, *WNAA*, *WWA 38*, *WWAW 8*,
  WWWor 2, *WWWorJ 1972*, *WrD*
DeValera, Sinead 1879?-1975 *CatA 1952*,
  ConAu 53
Devaney, John 1926- *ConAu 17R*, *SmATA 12*
DeVeaux, Alexis 1948- *ConAu 65*,
  DrAF 1976
Devereux, Frederick L, Jr. 1914- *ConAu 49*,
  SmATA 9
DeVeyrac, Robert 1901- *IlCB 1744*
DeVigne, H Rosier *MnBBF*
DeVinck, Antoine 1924- *ConAu 53*
Devlin, Harry 1918- *ChPo S2*, *ConAu 65*,
  IlBYP, *SmATA 11*
Devlin, Wende 1918- *ConAu 61*, *IlBYP*,
  SmATA 11
Devore, Irven 1934- *ConAu 21R*, *WWA 38*
DeVries, John 1915- *AmSCAP 66*
DeVries, Leonard 1919- *Au&Wr 6*, *ChPo S1*
DeVries, Peter 1910- *AmA&B*, *Au&Wr 6*,
  BiEnAT, *CelR 3*, *CnDAL*, *ConAu 17R*,
  ConLC 1, *ConLC 2*, *ConLC 3*,
  ConNov 1972, *ConNov 1976*, *CurB 59*,
  DrAF 1976, *EncWL*, *IntWW 38*, *ModAL*,
  ModAL Sup, *OxAm*, *Pen Am*, *REnAL*,
  WW 1974, *WWA 38*, *WWTwL*,
  WWWor 2, *WorAu*
DeWaard, Elliott John 1935- *ConAu 49*,
  SmATA 7
DeWalton, John 1874- *WWBWI 1*
Dewdney, Selwyn 1909- *ConAu 69*, *OxCan*
Dewey, Ariane 1937- *ConAu 49*, *IlBYP*,
  SmATA 7
Dewey, Ariane *see* Aruego, Ariane
DeWitt, Cornelius Hugh 1905- *AmPB*,
  ChPo S1, *IlCB 1744*, *IlCB 1946*
DeWitt, James *AuBYP*, *ConAu XR*
DeWitt, James *see* Lewis, Mildred D
Dewitz, Ludwig Richard Max 1916- *DrAS 6P*
Dexter, Mark *MnBBF*
Dexter, Philip *MnBBF*
Dexter, Ralph *MnBBF*
Dexter, Walter 1877-1950? *MnBBF*
Deyneka, Anita 1943- *ConAu 61*
D'Harnoncourt, Rene 1901-1968 *AmPB*,
  CurB 52, *CurB 68*, *IlCB 1744*
Dias, Earl Joseph 1916- *ConAu 21R*,

DrAS 6E
Diaz, Mrs. A M 1821-1904 *CarSB*
Dibdin, Charles 1745-1814 *Alli*, *BbD*,
  BiD&SB, *BiDLA*, *BiDLA Sup*, *BrAu*,
  CasWL, *Chambr 2*, *ChPo*, *ChPo S1*,
  ChPo S2, *DcEnL*, *DcEuL*, *DcLEnL*,
  EvLB, *NCHEL*, *OxEng*, *St&VC*
Dibner, Bern 1897- *WWA 38*
Dick, Trella Lamson 1889-1974 *AuBYP*,
  SmATA 9, *ConAu 5R*
Dickens, Charles 1812-1870 *Alli*, *Alli Sup*,
  AtlBL, *AuBYP*, *BbD*, *BiD&SB*,
  BrAu 19, *CarSB*, *CasWL*, *Chambr 3*,
  ChPo, *ChPo S1*, *ChPo S2*, *CriT 3*,
  CyWA, *DcBiA*, *DcEnA*, *DcEnA Ap*,
  DcEnL, *DcEuL*, *DcLEnL*, *EncM&D*,
  EvLB, *FamAYP*, *HsB&A*, *JBA 1934*,
  MnBBF, *MouLC 3*, *NCHEL*, *OxAm*,
  OxEng, *Pen Am*, *Pen Eng*, *RAdv 1*,
  RCom, *REn*, *St&VC*, *TelT*, *WEAL*,
  WWCL
Dickens, Frank 1899- *Au&Wr 6*, *IntWW 38*,
  WW 1974, *WWWor 2*
Dickens, Monica Enid 1915- *Au&Wr 6*,
  CatA 1930, *ConAu 5R*, *ConNov 1972*,
  ConNov 1976, *DcLEnL*, *EvLB*,
  ForWC 1970, *LongC*, *NCHEL*, *Pen Eng*,
  REn, *SmATA 4*, *TwCW*, *WW 1974*,
  WWAW 8, *WorAu*, *WrD*
Dickey, James 1923- *AmA&B*, *AnCL*,
  AuNews 1, *AuNews 2*, *CelR 3*,
  ConAu 9R, *ConLC 1*, *ConLC 2*,
  ConLC 4, *ConP 1970*, *ConP 1975*,
  CrCAP, *CurB 68*, *DrAF 1976*,
  DrAP 1975, *DrAS 6E*, *EncWL*,
  IntWW 38, *ModAL*, *ModAL Sup*, *OxAm*,
  Pen Am, *RAdv 1*, *WEAL*, *WWA 38*,
  WWS 13, *WWTwL*, *WWWor 2*, *WorAu*
Dickey, Robert Livingston 1861- *ConICB*
Dickie, Edgar Primrose 1897- *Au&Wr 6*,
  ConAu P-1, *WW 1974*, *WrD*
Dickinson, Emily 1830-1886 *AmA*, *AmA&B*,
  AmWr, *AnCL*, *AtlBL*, *BiD&SB*, *CasWL*,
  Chambr 3, *ChPo*, *ChPo S1*, *ChPo S2*,
  CnDAL, *CnE&AP*, *CriT 3*, *CyWA*,
  DcAmA, *DcLEnL*, *DcNAA*, *EvLB*,
  ModAL, *ModAL Sup*, *OxAm*, *OxEng*,
  Pen Am, *RAdv 1*, *RCom*, *REn*, *REnAL*,
  St&VC, *WEAL*
Dickinson, Patric Thomas 1914- *Au&Wr 6*,
  ChPo S1, *ChPo S2*, *ConAu 9R*,
  ConP 1970, *ConP 1975*
Dickinson, Peter 1927- *Au&Wr 6*, *ConAu 41*,
  EncM&D, *SmATA 5*, *WrD*
Dickinson, Susan 1931- *ConAu 57*, *SmATA 8*
Dickinson, William Croft 1897-1963
  SmATA 13, *WWCL*
Dickson, Gordon R 1923- *ConAu 9R*
Dickson, James Grierson *MnBBF*
Dickson, James Grierson *see* King, Hilary
Dickson, Marguerite 1873-1953 *AuBYP*,
  CurB 52, *CurB 54*, *MorJA*
Dickson, Naida 1916- *ConAu 37*, *SmATA 8*,
  WrD
Dickson, Naida *see* Richardson, Grace Lee
Dietrich, Wilson G 1916- *ConAu 25R*
Dietz, Betty Warner *AuBYP*, *ConAu XR*
Dietz, David Henry 1897- *AmMWS 12P*,
  Au&Wr 6, *ConAu 1R*, *CurB 40*,

CurB 40, OhA&B, REnAL, SmATA 10,
WWA 38, WWWorJ 1972
Dietz, Elisabeth H 1908- ConAu 29, LE 5,
WWAW 8
Dietz, Elisabeth H see Dietz, Betty Warner
Dietz, Howard 1896- AmA&B, AmSCAP 66,
BiEnAT, CelR 3, ChPo, ConAu 53,
ConDr 1, CurB 65, ModWD, REnAL,
WWA 38, WWT 15
Dietz, Lew 1907- AuBYP, ConAu 5R,
SmATA 11, WrD
DiFiori, Lawrence IlBYP
Digges, Jeremiah AmA&B, ConAu XR
Digges, Jeremiah see Berger, Josef
Diggins, Julia E AuBYP
DiGirolamo, Vittorio 1928- ConAu 45
Dignam, C B MnBBF
DiGrazia, Thomas IlBYP
Dillard, Annie 1945- ConAu 49, DrAP 1975,
SmATA 10
Dillard, Polly Hargis 1916- ConAu 9R
Diller, Angela AuBYP
Dillon, Corinne Boyd IlBYP, IlCB 1946
Dillon, Dixie MnBBF
Dillon, Eilis 1920- Au&Wr 6, AuBYP,
ConAu 9R, SmATA 2, ThBJA
Dillon, Eilis see O'Cuilleanain, Eilis Dillon
Dilnot, George 1883-1951 MnBBF,
WWBWI A
Dilson, Jesse 1914- ConAu 25R, WWE 14,
WrD
Dimmitt, Richard Bertrand 1925- ConAu 17R,
WWW 14
Dimmock, Frederick Hayden 1895-1955 MnBBF,
WWBWI A, WWCL
Dimson, Theo Aeneas 1930- CanWW 12,
IlCB 1957, WWAA 1973, WWGA
Dines, Glen 1925- AuBYP, ConAu 9R,
IlCB 1946, IlCB 1957
Dines, Harry Glen 1925- SmATA 7
Dingle, Aylward Edward 1876- MnBBF
Dingle, Aylward Edward see Sinbad
Dinhofer, Alfred D WrD
Dinneen, Betty 1929- ConAu 57
Dinsdale, Mary 1920- ArtsCL
Dinsdale, Tim 1924- ConAu 1R, SmATA 11,
WrD
Diole, Philippe V 1908- ConAu 53
DiPreta, Tony ArtCS
Dirks, Rudolph 1877-1968 ArtCS
Disch, Thomas M 1940- ConAu 21R,
WWE 14
Disney, Walt 1901-1966 ArtCS, ChPo,
ChPo S1, ChPo S2, CurB 40, CurB 52,
CurB 67, LongC, OxAm, REn, REnAL,
WWCL, WWGA
Disston, Harry 1899- ConAu 41, WWS 13
Ditmars, Raymond Lee 1876-1942 AmA&B,
AuBYP, CurB 40, CurB 42, DcNAA,
JBA 1934, JBA 1951, REnAL, TwCA,
TwCA Sup, WNAA
DiValentin, Maria Messuri 1911- ConAu 5R,
SmATA 7
Divine, Arthur Durham 1904- DcLEnL
Divine, Arthur Durham see Divine, David
Divine, David DcLEnL
Divine, David see Divine, Arthur Durham
Dix, Beulah Marie 1876- AmA&B, CarSB,
DcAmA, JBA 1934, JBA 1951, REnAL

Dix, Maurice Buxton 1889-1957 CanNov,
MnBBF, WWBWI A
Dixon, Conrad WrD
Dixon, Cross MnBBF
Dixon, Don MnBBF
Dixon, Don see Stein, J H
Dixon, Franklin W CarSB, ConAu 17R,
EncM&D, SmATA 1, SmATA 2
Dixon, Franklin W see Adams, Harriet S
Dixon, Franklin W see Stratemeyer, Edward L
Dixon, Franklin W see Svenson, Andrew E
Dixon, James MnBBF
Dixon, Marjorie 1887- AuBYP, ConAu P-2
Dixon, Marjorie see Mack, Marjorie
Dixon, Paige ConAu XR
Dixon, Paige see Corcoran, Barbara
Dixon, Peter L 1931?- ConAu 45, SmATA 6,
WWA 38
Dixon, Robert W MnBBF, WWBWI A
Dixon, Robert W see Bullivant, Cecil Henry
Dixon, Tom MnBBF
Dizenzo, Charles 1938- ConAu 25R, ConDr 1
Doane, Pelagie 1906-1966 AuBYP, ChPo,
ConAu 1R, IlCB 1744, IlCB 1946,
MorJA, SmATA 7
Doane, Pelagie see Hoffner, Pelagie Doane
Dobbins, Dorothy Wyeth 1929- ConAu 69
Dobbins, Marybelle King 1900- ConAu 41,
IndAu 1917
Dobbs, Rose AuBYP
Dobell, I M B 1909- ConAu P-1, SmATA 11
Dobell, I M B see Barclay, Isabel
Dobias, Frank 1902- AmPB, ConICB,
IlCB 1744
Dobkin, Alexander 1908-1975 ChPo S1,
DcCAA 2, IlCB 1946, WWAA 1973,
WWWorJ 1972
Dobler, Lavinia G 1910- ConAu 1R,
ForWC 1970, MorBMP, SmATA 6,
WWAW 8
Dobrin, Arnold Jack 1928- ConAu 25R,
IlCB 1957, SmATA 4, WWE 14
Dobson, W H MnBBF
Dobuzhinskii, Mstislav Valerianovich 1875-
IlCB 1744
Docktor, Irv 1918- IlCB 1946
Doctor A see Silverstein, Alvin
Doctor A ConAu XR, SmATA 8
Doctor Seuss AmPB, ConAu XR
Doctor Seuss see Geisel, Theodor Seuss
Dodd, Ed Benton 1902- ConAu 25R,
SmATA 4
Dodd, Wayne D 1930- ConAu 33, DrAP 1975,
DrAS 6E, WrD
Dodd, Wayne D see Wayne, Donald
Dodds, Andrew 1927- ArtsCL, ChPo,
ChPo S1
Dodds, John Wendell 1902- Au&Wr 6,
ConAu 5R, DrAS 6E, WWA 38
Dodge, Bertha Sanford 1902- AuBYP,
ConAu 5R, SmATA 8, WrD
Dodge, Dick 1918?-1974 ConAu 49
Dodge, Langdon ConAu XR
Dodge, Langdon see Wolfson, Victor
Dodge, Mary Elizabeth Mapes 1831?-1905
Alli Sup, AmA, AmA&B, AuBYP, BbD,
BiD&SB, CarSB, ChPo, ChPo S1,
ChPo S2, DcAmA, DcBiA, DcNAA,
FamAYP, FamSYP, JBA 1934, OxAm,

REn, REnAL, WWCL
Dodgson, Charles Lutwidge 1832-1898 *Alli Sup,*
AnCL, AtlBL, AuBYP, BiD&SB,
BrAu 19, CarSB, CasWL, Chambr 3,
ChPo, ChPo S1, DcEnA, DcEnA Ap,
DcEnL, DcEuL, DcLEnL, EvLB,
JBA 1934, MouLC 4, NCHEL, OxEng,
Pen Eng, RCom, REn, TelT, WWCL,
YABC 2
Dodgson, Charles Lutwidge *see* Carroll, Lewis
Dodshon, George Montieth 1870?- *WWBWI 1*
Dodson, Kenneth M 1907- *ConAu 1R,*
SmATA 11, WrD
Dodworth, Dorothy L *AuBYP*
Doherty, Charles Hugh 1913- *Au&Wr 6,*
ConAu 9R, SmATA 6
Doherty, Ivy R Duffy 1922- *ConAu 9R*
Doherty, Ivy R Duffy *see* Hardwick, Sylvia
Doherty, John Stephen *AuBYP*
Doherty, P J *MnBBF*
Dolan, Edward F, Jr. 1924- *ConAu 33*
Dolbier, Maurice 1912- *AmA&B, AuBYP,*
ConAu 65, CurB 56, MorJA, WWA 38
Dolezal, Carroll *IlBYP*
Dolim, Mary Nuzum 1925- *AuBYP,*
ConAu 17R
Dolphin, Rex *MnBBF, WWBWI A*
Dolson, Hildegarde 1908- *ConAu 5R,*
ForWC 1970, SmATA 5
Domanska, Janina *AuBYP, AuNews 1,*
ChPo S2, ConAu 17R, IlCB 1957,
SmATA 6, ThBJA, WWA 38,
WWAW 8
Domanska, Janina *see* Laskowski, Janina
Domanska
Dombrowski, Kathe Schonberger Von 1881-
IlCB 1744
Dominy, Eric 1918- *ConAu 9R*
Domjan, Joseph 1907- *AuBYP, ConAu 9R*
Donaghue, Derek *MnBBF*
Donahey, William 1883?-1970 *ArtCS, AuBYP,*
ChPo S2, OhA&B, WNAA
Donahoe, Barnard 1932- *ConAu 17R*
Donalds, Gordon *AuBYP, ConAu XR,*
SmATA XR
Donalds, Gordon *see* Shirreffs, Gordon D
Donaldson, Major *MnBBF*
Donkin, Nance *SingR 1*
Donna, Natalie 1934- *AuBYP, ConAu 9R,*
ForWC 1970, SmATA 9, WWE 14,
WrD
Donnelly, A *MnBBF*
Donnelly, A *see* Aitken, A Donnelly
Donovan, Dick 1843-1934 *Alli Sup, EncM&D,*
MnBBF, NCHEL
Donovan, Dick *see* Muddock, Joyce Emerson
Preston
Donovan, Frank Robert 1906-1975 *AuBYP,*
ConAu 1R, ConAu 61
Donovan, John *ChLR 3*
Donovan, Robert John 1912- *AmA&B,*
Au&Wr 6, ConAu 1R, WWA 38,
WWWor 2
Doob, Leonard William 1909- *AmA&B,*
AmMWS 12S, ConAu 5R, IntWW 38,
SmATA 8, WWA 38, WWWor 2
Dor, Ana *ConAu XR, SmATA XR*
Dor, Ana *see* Ceder, Georgianna Dorcas
Doray, Maya 1922- *ConAu 45*

Dore, Gustave 1832-1883 *AtlBL, ChPo,*
ChPo S1, ChPo S2, IlBYP, OxFr, REn
Doremus, Robert *IlBYP*
Dorgan, Tad 1877-1929 *ArtCS*
Dorian, Edith M 1900- *ConAu P-1,*
ForWC 1970, SmATA 5
Dorian, Harry *SmATA XR*
Dorian, Harry *see* Hamilton, Charles Harold St.
John
Dorian, Marguerite *ConAu 17R, SmATA 7*
Dorliae, Peter Gondro 1935- *ConAu 29*
Dorling, Henry Taprell *DcLEnL, LongC,*
MnBBF
Dorling, Henry Taprell *see* Taffrail
Dorman, Michael 1932- *ConAu 13R,*
SmATA 7
Dorning, Harold *ChPo, ChPo S2, MnBBF*
Dorrian, Harry *MnBBF, WWBWI A*
Dorrian, Harry *see* Hamilton, Charles Harold St.
John
Dorset, Catherine Ann 1750?-1817? *BrAu 19,*
CarSB, ChPo, ChPo S1
Dorset, Phyllis 1924- *ConAu 25R*
Dorson, Richard Mercer 1916- *DrAS 6H*
Dorst, Tankred 1925- *CnMD Sup, ConAu 41,*
CrCD, McGWD, ModWD, OxGer
Doskocilova, Hana 1936- *ConAu 61*
DosPassos, John 1896-1970 *AmA&B, AmNov,*
AmWr, AtlBL, Au&Wr 6, BiEnAT,
CasWL, Chambr 3, CnDAL, CnMD,
ConAmA, ConAmL, ConAu 29,
ConLC 1, ConLC 4, CurB 40, CurB 70,
CyWA, DcLEnL, EncWL, EvLB, LongC,
ModAL, ModAL Sup, ModWD,
NYTBE 1, OxAm, OxEng, Pen Am,
RAdv 1, REn, REnAL, TwCA,
TwCA Sup, TwCW, WEAL, WNAA,
WWTwL
DosPassos, John *see* Passos, John Dos
Doss, Helen 1918?- *AuBYP, ConAu 9R*
Doss, Margot Patterson 1922- *ConAu 29,*
SmATA 6
Dotey, Clara *CarSB*
Dotts, Maryann J 1933- *ConAu 33, WrD*
Doty, Jean Slaughter 1929- *ConAu 45*
Doty, Jean Slaughter *see* Slaughter, Jean
Doty, Roy 1922- *ConAu 53, IlBYP*
Dotzenko, Grisha *IlBYP*
Dotzenko, Grisha *see* Grisha
Doubtfire, Dianne Joan 1918- *Au&Wr 6, WrD*
Dougherty, Joanna Foster *ConAu XR*
Dougherty, Joanna Foster *see* Foster, Joanna
Doughtie, Charles *AuBYP*
Doughty, Wayne Dyre 1929-1968 *IndAu 1917*
Douglas, Amanda Minnie 1837?-1916 *Alli Sup,*
AmA, AmA&B, BbD, BiD&SB, CarSB,
ChPo S1, ChPo S2, DcAmA, DcNAA
Douglas, David *MnBBF*
Douglas, James *MnBBF*
Douglas, James McM *SmATA 5*
Douglas, James McM *see* Butterworth, W E
Douglas, John Scott 1905- *AuBYP, WNAA*
Douglas, Kathryn *ConAu XR*
Douglas, Kathryn *see* Ewing, Kathryn
Douglas, Leonard *MnBBF*
Douglas, Marg *MnBBF*
Douglas, Marjory Stoneman 1890- *AmA&B,*
AuNews 2, ConAu 1R, CurB 53,
SmATA 10

Douglas, Michael *ConAu XR, IntMPA 1975*
Douglas, Michael *see* Crichton, Michael
Douglas, William Orville 1898- *AmA&B,*
Au&Wr 6, AuBYP, CelR 3, ConAu 9R,
CurB 41, CurB 50, DrAS 6P, IntWW 38,
MnnWr, NYTBE 1, OxAm, REn,
REnAL, TwCA Sup, WW 1974,
WWA 38, WWPNA, WWS 13,
WWW 14, WWWor 2
Douglass, Frederick 1817-1895 *Alli Sup, AmA,*
AmA&B, BbD, BiD&SB, BiDSA,
BlkAW, Chambr 3, DcAmA, DcNAA,
OxAm, REn, REnAL, WEAL
Douglass, Ralph 1895- *IlCB 1744, IlCB 1946*
Douse, Anthony *MnBBF*
Douthwaite, Louis Charles 1878- *MnBBF,*
WWBWI A
Douty, Esther M 1911- *ConAu 5R, SmATA 8*
Dow, Emily R 1904- *ConAu P-1, SmATA 10*
Dowd, Victor *IlBYP*
Dowdell, Dorothy Karns 1910- *ConAu 9R,*
ForWC 1970, SmATA 12
Dowden, Anne Ophelia *see* Todd, Anne Ophelia
Dowden, Anne Ophelia Todd 1907- *AuBYP,*
ConAu 9R, SmATA 7, WWAA 1973
Dowdey, Landon Gerald 1923- *SmATA 11*
Dowds, Gertrude *AuBYP*
Dowdy, Mrs. Regera *ConAu XR*
Dowdy, Mrs. Regera *see* Gorey, Edward St. John
Dowell, Frank Richard 1897- *ConAu 53*
Dowling, Victor J 1906- *IlBYP, IlCB 1946*
Down, C Maurice *MnBBF, WWBWI A*
Down, C Maurice *see* Clifford, Martin
Down, C Maurice *see* Conquest, Owen
Down, C Maurice *see* Howard, Prosper
Down, C Maurice *see* Richards, Frank
Downer, Marion 1892?-1971 *AuBYP,*
ConAu 33
Downey, Fairfax Davis 1893- *AmA&B,*
AmSCAP 66, AuBYP, ChPo, ConAu 1R,
CurB 49, OxCan, REnAL, SmATA 3,
WNAA, WWA 38, WrD
Downey, Glanville 1908- *ConAu 1R,*
DrAS 6H, WWA 38
Downey, Thomas *MnBBF, WWBWI I*
Downie, John 1931- *AmMWS 12P,*
OxCan Sup
Downie, Mary Alice 1934- *ConAu 25R,*
OxCan Sup, SmATA 13, WrD
Downie, Mary Alice *see* Hunter, Dawe
Downing, Brownie *SingR 2*
Downing, Warwick 1931- *ConAu 53*
Doyle, Sir Arthur Conan 1859-1930 *Alli Sup,*
AtlBL, AuBYP, BbD, BiD&SB, BiDPar,
CarSB, CasWL, Chambr 3, ChPo,
ChPo S1, CyWA, DcBiA, DcEnA Ap,
DcLEnL, EncM&D, EvLB, JBA 1934,
LongC, MnBBF, ModBL, NCHEL,
OxEng, Pen Eng, PoIre, RAdv 1, REn,
TelT, TwCA, TwCA Sup, TwCW,
WEAL, WWBWI A, WWCL, WWTwL
Doyle, Sir Arthur Conan *see* Conan Doyle,
Arthur
Doyle, Brian 1930- *Au&Wr 6, ChPo S1,*
ConAu 53
Doyle, Donovan *ConAu XR*
Doyle, Donovan *see* Boegehold, Betty
Doyle, Drac *MnBBF*
Doyle, J E *MnBBF*

Doyle, Janet *ChPo S1*
Doyle, Richard 1824-1883 *Alli Sup, ChPo,*
ChPo S1, ChPo S2, DcEuL, NCHEL
Doyle, Stanton *MnBBF*
Dr. Seuss *see* Geisel, Theodor Seuss
Drackett, Phil 1922- *Au&Wr 6, ConAu 9R,*
WrD
Draco, F *ConAu XR, SmATA 6*
Draco, F *see* Davis, Julia
Dragonwagon, Crescent 1952- *SmATA 11*
Draham, William 1887- *WWLA*
Drake, Alan *MnBBF*
Drake, Dick *MnBBF*
Drake, Frank *MnBBF, SmATA XR,*
WWBWI A
Drake, Frank *see* Hamilton, Charles Harold St.
John
Drake, Joan Howard 1924- *Au&Wr 6,*
ConAu 13R
Drake, John *MnBBF*
Drake, Rodney *MnBBF*
Drake, Rupert *MnBBF*
Drake, Rupert *see* Belfield, Harry Wedgwood
Drake, Samuel Adams 1833-1905 *Alli,*
Alli Sup, AmA, AmA&B, BbD,
BiD&SB, ChPo S1, CyAL 2, DcAmA,
DcNAA
Drake, Stan 1921- *ArtCS*
Draper, Ben *MnBBF*
Draper, Ben *see* Roberts, Holt
Draper, Cena C 1907- *ConAu 17R, WrD*
Draper, Hastings *ChPo, ConAu XR, MnBBF*
Draper, Hastings *see* Jeffries, Roderic
Draper, Nancy *AuBYP*
Drave, Winston *MnBBF*
Drayson, A W *MnBBF*
Drayson, A W *see* Warwick, Sidney
Drayson, R A *MnBBF*
Drayton, Gigi 1877-1936 *ArtCS*
Dresser, Lawrence *IlBYP*
Drew, Gordon *MnBBF*
Drew, Melville *MnBBF*
Drew, Michael *MnBBF*
Drew, Reginald *MnBBF, WWBWI A*
Drew, Reginald *see* Home-Gall, William
Benjamin
Drew, Sidney 1878- *MnBBF, WWBWI A*
Drew, Sidney *see* Murray, Edgar Joyce
Drew, Vaughan *MnBBF*
Drewery, Mary 1918- *ConAu 25R, SmATA 6*
Driggs, Howard Roscoe 1873-1963 *AmA&B,*
WNAA
Drigin, Serge *WWBWI I*
Drinkwater, Hartley *MnBBF*
Drinkwater, John 1882-1937 *Alli, BiDLA,*
CasWL, Chambr 3, ChPo, ChPo S1,
ChPo S2, CnMD, CnThe, DcLEnL,
EvLB, JBA 1934, LongC, McGWD,
ModBL, ModWD, NCHEL, OxEng,
Pen Eng, REn, St&VC, TwCA,
TwCA Sup, WEAL, WWLA
Driscoll, Barry *IlCB 1957*
Driving Hawk, Virginia *ConAu XR*
Driving Hawk, Virginia *see* Sneve, Virginia
Driving Hawk
Drubert, John H 1925- *ConAu 45*
Druce, Kay *SingR 1*
Drummond, Anthony *WWBWI A*
Drummond, Anthony *see* Hunter, John

Drummond, John *MnBBF, WWBWI A*

Drummond, John *see* Chance, John Newton

Drummond, V H 1911- *ConAu 13R*

Drummond, Violet Hilda 1911- *Au&Wr 6, IIBYP, IICB 1946, IICB 1957, SmATA 6, ThBJA*

Drummond, Walter *AuBYP, ConAu XR, SmATA XR, ThBJA*

Drummond, Walter *see* Silverberg, Robert

Druon, Maurice Samuel Roger Charles 1918- *Au&Wr 6, CasWL, ConAu 13R, EncWL, IntWW 38, Pen Eur, REn, WW 1974, WWWor 2, WorAu*

Drury, C W C *MnBBF*

Drury, Clare Marie *ConAu XR*

Drury, Clare Marie *see* Hoskyns-Abrahall, Clare

Drury, Maxine Cole 1914- *ConAu 5R, ForWC 1970, WrD*

Drury, Roger W 1914- *ConAu 65*

Drysdale, William 1852-1901 *Alli Sup, BiD&SB, BiDLA, CarSB, DcAmA, DcNAA*

Dubkin, Lois Knudson 1911- *ConAu 5R*

DuBlane, Daphne *ConAu XR, SmATA XR*

DuBlane, Daphne *see* Groom, Arthur William

DuBois, Shirley Graham 1907- *WrD, BlkAW, IndAu 1917*

DuBois, Theodora McCormick 1890- *AmA&B, AuBYP*

DuBois, W E B 1868-1963 *AmA&B, ConLC 1, ConLC 2, CurB 40, CurB 63*

DuBois, William Pene 1916- *AmA&B, AmPB, AuBYP, ChLR 1, ChPo S1, ConAu 5R, IICB 1744, IICB 1946, IICB 1957, JBA 1951, Newb 1922, SmATA 4, St&VC, WWCL*

DuBois, William Pene *see* Pene DuBois, William

Dubos, Rene 1901- *AmA&B, AmMWS 12P, CelR 3, ConAu 5R, NYTBE 2, WWWor 2*

DuBose, LaRocque 1926- *ConAu 21R, SmATA 2*

Dubrovin, Vivian 1931- *ConAu 57*

Ducas, Dorothy 1905- *AuBYP, ConAu 5R, ForWC 1970, WWAW 8, WWE 14*

Duchacek, Ivo D 1913- *AmMWS 12S, ConAu 1R, WrD*

DuChaillu, Paul B *see* Chaillu, Paul B Du

DuChaillu, Paul Belloni 1835-1903 *Alli Sup, AmA, AmA&B, BbD, BiD&SB, BiDSA, CarSB, Chambr 3, DcAmA, DcEnL, DcNAA, JBA 1934, OxAm, REnAL*

Duchesne, Janet 1930- *ArtsCL, IICB 1957*

Duckett, Alfred 1917- *BlkAW, ConAu 45*

Duckham, Baron Frederick 1933- *Au&Wr 6, WrD*

Ducornet, Erica 1943- *ConAu 37, SmATA 7*

Dudley, Ernest 1908?- *Au&Wr 6, ConAu 13R, MnBBF, WWBWI A*

Dudley, Frank *MnBBF*

Dudley, Geoffrey A 1917- *Au&Wr 6, ConAu 13R*

Dudley, Nancy *AuBYP, ConAu XR, SmATA XR*

Dudley, Nancy *see* Cole, Lois Dwight

Dudley, Ruth H 1905- *ConAu 61, SmATA 11, WWW 14*

Dufek, George John 1903- *CurB 57, IntWW 38, WWA 38, WWS 13,*

WWWor 2

Duff, Annis *ChPo*

Duff, Maggie *ConAu XR*

Duff, Maggie *see* Duff, Margaret K

Duff, Margaret K *ConAu 37*

Duff, Margaret K *see* Duff, Maggie

Duffy, Michael Francis 1906- *MnBBF, WWBWI A*

Duffy, Michael Francis *see* Richards, Frank

Dugan, James 1912- *AnCL, ConAu 5R*

Duggan, Alfred Leo 1903-1964 *AnCL, AuBYP, LongC, ModBL, TwCA Sup, TwCW*

Duggan, Mary M 1921- *ConAu 25R*

Duggan, Maurice d1975 *ConAu 53*

DuJardin, Rosamond Neal 1902-1963 *AmA&B, ConAu 1R, CurB 53, MorJA, REnAL, SmATA 2*

Duke, Anita *WrD*

Duke, Derek *MnBBF*

Duke, Derek *see* Phillips, Horace

Duke, Madelaine *Au&Wr 6, WrD*

Dukert, Joseph M 1929- *AuBYP, ConAu 5R, WrD*

Dulac, Edmund 1882-1953 *CarSB, ChPo, ChPo S2, ConICB, IICB 1744, JBA 1951, WWCL*

Dulieu, Jean *ConAu XR*

Dulieu, Jean *see* VanOort, Jan

Dumas, Alexandre, Pere 1802-1870 *AtlBL, BbD, BiD&SB, CarSB, CasWL, CnThe, CyWA, DcEuL, EuAu, EvEuW, HsB&A, McGWD, MnBBF, NCHEL, OxEng, OxFr, Pen Eur, RCom, REn, REnWD, WWCL*

Dumas, Frederic 1913- *ConAu 69*

Dumas, Gerald J 1930- *BlkAW, ConAu 25R, DrAP 1975*

DuMaurier, Daphne 1907- *Au&Wr 6, BiEnAT, ConAu 5R, ConLC 6, ConNov 1972, ConNov 1976, CurB 40, CyWA, DcLEnL, EncM&D, EvLB, IntWW 38, LongC, ModBL, NCHEL, Pen Eng, RAdv 1, REn, TwCA, TwCA Sup, TwCW, WW 1974, WWAW 8, WWWor 2*

DuMaurier, Daphne *see* Maurier, Daphne Du

Dumbrille, Dorothy Martha 1897?- *Au&Wr 6, CanNov, WrD*

Dumm, Edwina 1893- *ArtCS*

Dunbar, Ernest 1927- *ConAu 25R, WWE 14*

Dunbar, Paul Laurence 1872-1906 *AmA, AmA&B, BiD&SB, BkCL, BlkAW, CasWL, Chambr 3, ChPo, ChPo S1, ChPo S2, CnDAL, DcAmA, DcNAA, OhA&B, OxAm, Pen Am, RAdv 1, REn, REnAL, WEAL*

Duncan, Alistair 1927- *ConAu 61*

Duncan, David 1913- *AmA&B, AmNov, Au&Wr 6, WWPNA*

Duncan, Francis *MnBBF*

Duncan, Gregory *ConAu XR, SmATA 3*

Duncan, Gregory *see* McClintock, Marshall

Duncan, James *MnBBF, WWBWI A*

Duncan, James *see* Hadath, John Edward Gunby

Duncan, Jane *Au&Wr 6, ConAu XR*

Duncan, Jane *see* Cameron, Elizabeth Jane

Duncan, Julia K *AmNov X, ConAu P-2, SmATA 1*

Duncan, Julia K *see* Stratemeyer, Edward L

Duncan, Leslie *MnBBF*
Duncan, Lois 1934- *AuBYP, ConAu XR, SmATA 1, WrD*
Duncan, Lois *see* Cardozo, Lois S
Duncan, Norman 1871-1916 *AmA&B, CanWr, DcAmA, DcLEnL, DcNAA, JBA 1934, JBA 1951, OhA&B, OxCan, REnAL, YABC 1*
Duncan, Sylvia 1916- *Au&Wr 6*
Duncan, William Murdoch 1909- *Au&Wr 6, MnBBF, WWBWI A*
Duncombe, Frances 1900- *ConAu 25R*
Dundee, Douglas *MnBBF, WWBWI A*
Dundee, Douglas *see* Cumming-Skinner, Dugald Matheson
Dunham, John Lee 1939- *ConAu 29, WWMW 14*
Dunkley, Jack *WWBWI 1*
Dunlap, Hope 1880- *ChPo, ConICB, IlCB 1744*
Dunleavy, Janet Egleson 1928- *ConAu 57, DrAS 6E*
Dunleavy, Janet Egleson *see* Egleson, Janet F
Dunleavy, Janet Egleson *see* Frank, Janet
Dunlop, Agnes M R *see* Kyle, Elisabeth
Dunlop, Agnes M R *see* Ralston, Jan
Dunlop, Agnes Mary Robinson *Au&Wr 6, AuBYP, ConAu 13R, SmATA 3, WW 1974*
Dunlop, M P *MnBBF*
Dunn, Eleanor *WWAW 8, WWMW 14*
Dunn, Harvey T 1884- *IlCB 1744*
Dunn, Hugh Patrick *WrD*
Dunn, Joseph Allan Elphinstone 1872-1941 *AmA&B, AmLY, CurB 41, DcNAA, MnBBF*
Dunn, Judy *ConAu XR, SmATA 5*
Dunn, Judy *see* Spangenburg, Judith Dunn
Dunn, Marion Herndon 1920- *ConAu 29*
Dunn, Mary Lois *BiDL 5*
Dunn, Mary Lois 1930- *SmATA 6*
Dunnahoo, Terry 1927- *ConAu 41, SmATA 7, WWA 38*
Dunne, Mary Collins 1914- *ConAu 41, SmATA 11*
Dunne, Mary Collins *see* Moore, Regina
Dunnett, Margaret Rosalind 1909- *Au&Wr 6, WrD*
Dunnett, R F *MnBBF*
Dunning, Stephen 1924- *ChPo S1, ConAu 25R, LE 5*
Dunnington, Tom *IlBYP*
Dunsany, Baron Edward J M Prax Plunkett 1878-1957 *Alli Sup, AtlBL, CasWL, ChPo, ChPo S1, ChPo S2, CnMD, CnThe, DcLEnL, EncM&D, EvLB, JBA 1934, LongC, McGWD, ModBL, ModWD, NCHEL, OxEng, Pen Eng, REn, REnWD, TwCA, TwCA Sup, TwCW*
Dunsheath, Percy 1886- *Au&Wr 6, IntWW 38, WW 1974*
Dunstan, Gregory *MnBBF, WWBWI A*
Dunstan, Gregory *see* Rowe, John Gabriel
Dunton, Mary Jane *ChPo S1*
Duplaix, Georges *AmPB*
Duplaix, Georges *see* Ariane
Duplaix, Georges *see* Nicole
Dupre, Catherine *Au&Wr 6, ConAu 25R*
Dupuy, R Ernest 1887- *ConAu 1R,*

WWWor 2
Dupuy, T N 1916- *ConAu 1R, SmATA 4*
Dupuy, Trevor Nevitt 1916- *AuBYP, DrAS 6H, SmATA 4, WWA 38, WWWor 2*
Durack, Elizabeth 1916- *SingR 1*
Durack, Mary 1913- *Au&Wr 6, SingR 1, WrD*
Durant, John 1902- *AmA&B, AuBYP, ConAu 9R, WWA 38, WWS 13*
Durell, Ann *AuBYP*
Durham, John 1925- *DrAS 6E*
Durham, Mae *ConAu 57*
Durham, Mae *see* Roger, Mae Durham
Durham, Mae J *AnCL, BiDL 5*
Durham, Philip 1912- *ConAu 9R, DrAS 6E*
Durlacher, Ed *AuBYP*
Durrant, Sheila *WrD*
Durrell, Donald D 1903- *ConAu 17R*
Durrell, Donald Dewitt 1903- *WWA 38*
Durrell, Gerald Malcolm 1925- *Au&Wr 6, AuBYP, ConAu 5R, IntWW 38, LongC, NCHEL, REn, SmATA 8, TwCW, WW 1974, WWWor 2, WorAu, WrD*
Durrell, Lawrence 1912- *Au&Wr 6, CasWL, ChPo, CnE&AP, CnMD, CnMWL, ConAu 9R, ConDr 1, ConLC 1, ConLC 4, ConLC 6, ConNov 1972, ConNov 1976, ConP 1970, ConP 1975, CurB 63, DcLEnL, EncWL, EvLB, LongC, ModBL, ModBL Sup, ModWD, NCHEL, OxEng, Pen Eng, RAdv 1, REn, TwCA Sup, TwCW, WEAL, WWTwL*
DuSoe, Robert C 1892-1958 *MorJA, WNAA, YABC 2*
Dutton, Geoffrey Piers Henry 1922- *Au&Wr 6, CasWL, ConAu 45, ConNov 1972, ConNov 1976, ConP 1970, ConP 1975, WrD*
Dutton, Maude Barrows 1880- *CarSB*
Dutz *ConAu XR, SmATA 6*
Dutz *see* Davis, Mary Octavia
Duval, Marie 1850- *WWBWI 1*
Duval, Marie *see* DeTessier, Isabelle Emily
Duvall, Evelyn Millis 1906- *AmA&B, AmMWS 12S, ConAu 1R, CurB 47, ForWC 1970, SmATA 9, WWA 38, WWAW 8, WWWor 2*
Duvoisin, Roger Antoine 1904-1968 *AmA&B, AmPB, Au&ICB, Au&Wr 6, AuBYP, BkP, Cald 1938, ChPo, ChPo S1, ChPo S2, ConAu 13R, FamAI, IlBYP, IlCB 1744, IlCB 1946, IlCB 1957, JBA 1951, SmATA 2, St&VC, WWA 38, WWAA 1973, WWCL, WWGA, WrD*
D'vys, George Whitefield 1860-1941 *AmLY, CarSB, WNAA*
Dwiggins, Don 1913- *ConAu 17R, SmATA 4*
Dwiggins, William Addison 1880-1956 *AmA&B, IlCB 1744, IlCB 1946, OhA&B, OxAm, REnAL*
Dwight, Allan *ConAu XR, SmATA XR*
Dwight, Allan *see* Cole, Lois Dwight
Dwyer, Bill *ArtCS*
Dwyer, Vera *SingR 1*
Dyce, E Archer *MnBBF*
Dyer, James *WrD*

Dyke, Henry Van *Chambr 3, JBA 1934*
Dyke, John 1935- *ConAu 25R*
Dynely, James *AuBYP*
Dynely, James *see* Mayne, William
Dyson, Edward 1896- *SingR 2*

E

E-Yeh-Shure *AmPB*
E-Yeh-Shure *see* Abeita, Louise
Eady, K M *MnBBF, WWBWI A*
Eady, R *MnBBF, WWBWI A*
Eagar, Frances 1940- *SmATA 11*
Eager, Edward 1911-1964 *AmSCAP 66, AnCL,*
  AuBYP, ChPo, MorJA, WWCL
Eagle, Mike 1942- *SmATA 11*
Eames, Genevieve Torrey *AuBYP*
Earl, Frank *MnBBF*
Earle, Alice Morse 1853?-1911 *AmA&B, BbD,*
  BiD&SB, ChPo S1, DcAmA, DcLEnL,
  DcNAA, OxAm, REnAL
Earle, Ambrose *MnBBF, WWBWI A*
Earle, Ambrose *see* Jones, J G
Earle, Enid *WWBWI A*
Earle, Enid *see* Jones, J G
Earle, Eyvind 1916- *IlCB 1946*
Earle, Michael *MnBBF*
Earle, Olive Lydia *Au&Wr 6, ConAu 21R,*
  IlBYP, IlCB 1946, IlCB 1957, MorJA,
  SmATA 7
Earle, Vana 1917- *IlCB 1946*
Earnshaw, Brian 1929- *ConAu 25R*
Earnshaw, Harold *ChPo, WWBWI I*
Eastlake, William 1917- *AmA&B, Au&Wr 6,*
  ConAu 5R, ConNov 1972, ConNov 1976,
  DrAF 1976, ModAL Sup, OxAm,
  Pen Am, REnAL, WorAu
Eastman, Charles Alexander 1858-1939
  AmA&B, AmLY, ConAmL, DcAmA,
  JBA 1934, JBA 1951, OxAm, REnAL,
  YABC 1
Eastman, P D 1909- *IlCB 1957*
Eastman, Philip D *AuBYP*
Easton, Robert 1915- *ConAu 13R*
Eastwick, Ivy Olive 1905- *AuBYP, BkCL,*
  ChPo, ChPo S1, ConAu 5R, SmATA 3,
  WrD
Eaton, Anne Thaxter 1881-1971 *AmPB,*
  AmA&B, ChPo, ChPo S1, NYTBE 2
Eaton, Evelyn 1902- *ConAu 53*
Eaton, George L *AuBYP, SmATA XR*
Eaton, George L *see* Verral, Charles Spain
Eaton, Jeanette 1885-1968 *AmA&B, AnCL,*
  JBA 1934, JBA 1951, OhA&B, St&VC
Eaton, John 1942- *IlBYP*
Eaton, Tom 1940- *ConAu 41, IlBYP*
Eaton, Walter Prichard 1878-1957 *AmA&B,*
  CarSB, ChPo, ChPo S2, ConAmL,
  REnAL, TwCA, TwCA Sup, WNAA
Ebbutt, Phil *WWBWI I*

Ebel, Alex 1927- *SmATA 11*
Eberle, Irmengarde 1898- *AmA&B, AuBYP,*
  BkCL, ConAu 1R, CurB 46, JBA 1951,
  SmATA 2, WWA 38, WWAW 8,
  WWWor 2
Eberle, Irmengarde *see* Allen, Allyn
Eberle, Irmengarde *see* Carter, Phyllis Ann
Eberstadt, Frederick *AuBYP*
Eberstadt, Isabel 1934?- *AuBYP*
Eby, Lois Christine 1908- *AuBYP,*
  IndAu 1917
Eby, Lois Christine *see* Lawson, Patrick
Eccles, Frank *WrD*
Eckblad, Edith Berven 1923- *ConAu 17R,*
  ForWC 1970, WrD
Eckert, Allan W 1931- *ConAu 13R, WWA 38,*
  WWS 13
Eckert, Horst 1931- *ConAu 37, SmATA 8*
Eckert, Horst *see* Janosch
Eckstein, Gustav 1890- *AmA&B, ConAu 57,*
  CurB 42, OhA&B, TwCA Sup, WNAA
Economakis, Olga *AuBYP*
Ed, Carl 1890-1959 *ArtCS*
Eddy, Daniel Clarke 1823-1896 *Alli, Alli Sup,*
  AmA&B, BiD&SB, CarSB, DcAmA,
  DcNAA
Ede, Detective Inspector *MnBBF*
Ede, Janina 1937- *ArtsCL*
Edell, Celeste *ConAu 1R, SmATA 12*
Edelman, Lily 1915- *AuBYP, ConAu 61*
Edelson, Edward 1932- *ConAu 17R,*
  WWE 14
Eden, Charles H *MnBBF*
Edey, Maitland A 1910- *ConAu 57*
Edgar, Alfred 1896- *MnBBF, WWBWI A*
Edgar, Alfred *see* Denvers, Jake
Edgar, Alfred *see* Fowey, Roger
Edgar, Alfred *see* Gregory, Hylton
Edgar, Alfred *see* Hendren, Patsy
Edgar, Alfred *see* Lyndon, Barre
Edgar, Alfred *see* Rogers, Tom
Edgar, Alfred *see* Ryder, Steve
Edgar, Alfred *see* Sayers, Edgar
Edgar, Alfred *see* Steele, Howard
Edgar, Ken 1925- *ConAu 49*
Edgar, Lewis *MnBBF*
Edgarton, Miss S C 1819-1848 *CarSB*
Edgeworth, Maria 1767-1849 *Alli, AtlBL,*
  BbD, BiD&SB, BiDLA, BrAu 19, CarSB,
  CasWL, Chambr 2, ChPo, CriT 2,
  CyWA, DcBiA, DcEnA, DcEnL, DcEuL,
  DcLEnL, EvLB, MouLC 3, NCHEL,

OxEng, Pen Eng, PoIre, RAdv 1, REn,
TelT, WEAL, WWCL
Edgun 1913- IlBYP, IlCB 1946
Edgun see Wulff, Edgun Valdemar
Edlin, Herbert Leeson 1913- Au&Wr 6,
ConAu 61
Edmonds, Frank MnBBF
Edmonds, Harry 1891- Au&Wr 6, MnBBF
Edmonds, I G 1917- ConAu 33, SmATA 8
Edmonds, Percy MnBBF
Edmonds, Richard W AuBYP
Edmonds, Walter Dumaux 1903- AmA&B,
AmNov, AuBYP, CnDAL, ConAmA,
ConAu 5R, CurB 42, CyWA, DcLEnL,
ModAL, MorBMP, MorJA, Newb 1922,
OxAm, Pen Am, REn, REnAL,
SmATA 1, TwCA, TwCA Sup,
WWA 38, WrD
Edmund, Sean SmATA 4
Edmund, Sean see Pringle, Laurence
Edsall, Marian S 1920- ConAu 49, SmATA 8
Edson, Gus 1901-1966 AmA&B, ArtCS
Edwardes, Charles MnBBF
Edwardes, Michael 1923- ConAu 57
Edwards, Al ConAu XR
Edwards, Al see Nourse, Alan Edward
Edwards, Alan MnBBF, WWBWI A
Edwards, Anne 1927- Au&Wr 6, ConAu 61
Edwards, Bertram ConAu XR, SmATA XR
Edwards, Bertram see Edwards, Herbert Charles
Edwards, Bronwen Elizabeth ConAu XR,
SmATA XR
Edwards, Bronwen Elizabeth see Rose, Wendy
Edwards, Cecile Pepin 1916- AuBYP,
ConAu 5R
Edwards, David Lawrence 1929- Au&Wr 6,
ConAu 5R, WW 1974
Edwards, Don 1905- SingR 1
Edwards, Dorothy Au&Wr 6, ConAu 25R,
SmATA 4, WrD
Edwards, George Wharton 1859?-1950 Alli Sup,
AmA&B, AmLY, BbD, BiD&SB, ChPo,
ChPo S2, DcAmA, IlCB 1744, WNAA
Edwards, Harvey 1929- ConAu 25R,
SmATA 5, WrD
Edwards, Herbert Charles 1912- Au&Wr 6,
ConAu 9R, SmATA 12
Edwards, Herbert Charles see Edwards, Bertram
Edwards, Jane Campbell 1932- ConAu 13R,
ForWC 1970, SmATA 10
Edwards, Jane Campbell see Campbell, Jane
Edwards, Johnson MnBBF
Edwards, Johnson see Shute, Walter
Edwards, Julie 1935- ConAu XR, MorBMP,
SmATA 7
Edwards, Julie see Andrews, Julie
Edwards, Julie see Stratemeyer, Edward L
Edwards, Kate F 1877- WWAA 1973,
WWAW 8
Edwards, Lionel Dalhousie Robertson 1878-
Br&AmS, ChPo, IlCB 1744
Edwards, Margaret 1902- ConAu P-2
Edwards, Margaret Royalty 1895- ChPo S2
Edwards, Monica LeDoux Newton 1912-
Au&Wr 6, ConAu 9R, SmATA 12,
WWCL, WrD
Edwards, Peter 1934- IlBYP
Edwards, R M ConAu XR
Edwards, R M see Edwards, Roselyn

Edwards, R W K MnBBF
Edwards, Robert Hamilton 1872-1932 MnBBF,
WWBWI A
Edwards, Robert Hamilton see Grant, E Gordon
Edwards, Robert Hamilton see Sapte, W
Edwards, Roselyn 1929- ConAu 25R
Edwards, Roselyn see Alexander, Marge
Edwards, Roselyn see Edwards, R M
Edwards, Sally 1929- ConAu 25R, SmATA 7
Edwards, Walter d1940 MnBBF, WWBWI A
Edwards, Walter see Shute, Walter
Edy-Legrand 1893- IlCB 1946
Edy-Legrand see Legrand, Edy
Eells, Elsie Spicer 1880-1963 AmA&B
Efron, Alexander 1897- ConAu P-2
Egan, E W 1922- ConAu 21R
Egan, Pierce 1814-1880 Alli Sup, BbD,
BiD&SB, Chambr 3, DcEnA, DcEnL,
HsB&A, MnBBF, NCHEL, OxEng,
WWBWI A
Egermeier, Elsie E 1890- ChPo S1, ConAu 5R,
WNAA
Eggenberger, David 1918- ConAu 9R,
SmATA 6
Eggenhofer, Nicholas IlBYP
Eggleston, Edward 1837-1902 Alli Sup, AmA,
AmA&B, BbD, BiD&SB, CarSB,
CasWL, Chambr 3, ChPo, ChPo S1,
CnDAL, CyAL 2, CyWA, DcAmA,
DcBiA, DcNAA, DcRusL, EvLB,
IndAu 1816, JBA 1934, OxAm, OxEng,
Pen Am, REn, REnAL, WEAL
Egielski, Richard 1952- SmATA 11
Egleson, Janet F ConAu XR
Egleson, Janet F see Dunleavy, Janet Egleson
Egliston, E H MnBBF
Egypt, Ophelia Settle 1903- LBAA
Ehlert, Lois Jane 1934- IlCB 1957
Ehre, Edward 1905- ConAu 9R
Ehret, Walter 1918- AmSCAP 66
Ehrhardt, Reinhold 1900- ConAu 29
Ehrlich, Amy 1942- ConAu 37
Ehrlich, Bettina Bauer 1903- AuBYP,
ConAu P-1, IlCB 1946, IlCB 1957,
MorJA, SmATA 1
Ehrlich, Bettina Bauer see Bettina
Eichenberg, Fritz 1901- AnCL, ChPo S2,
ConAu 57, IlBYP, IlCB 1744, IlCB 1946,
IlCB 1957, MorJA, SmATA 9, St&VC,
WWA 38, WWAA 1973, WWGA
Eichler, Margrit 1942- AmMWS 12S
Eichner, James A 1927- ConAu 13R,
SmATA 4
Eicke, Edna ChPo, IlBYP
Eifert, Virginia Snider 1911-1966 AmA&B,
Au&Wr 6, AuBYP, ConAu 1R,
SmATA 2
Eiloart, Mrs. 1830- DcEnL, MnBBF
Eimerl, Sarel 1925- ConAu 21R
Einsel, Naiad SmATA 10
Einsel, Walter 1926- AuBYP, SmATA 10
Einstein, Charles 1926- ConAu 65
Einzig, Susan 1922- ArtsCL, IlCB 1957
Eipper, Paul 1891- JBA 1934, JBA 1951
Eisenberg, Azriel 1903- AuBYP, ConAu 49,
LE 5, SmATA 12, WWWorJ 1972
Eisenhower, Julie Nixon BiN 1974, NYTBE 2
Eisenstat, Jane Sperry 1920- ConAu 1R
Eisenstat, Jane Sperry see Sperry, J E

Eisenstein, Judith K 1909-　*WWWorJ 1972*
Eisgruber, Elsa　*ChPo S1, IICB 1744*
Eisner, Will 1917-　*AmA&B, WWA 38*
Eitzen, Allan 1928-　*IIBYP, SmATA 9*
Eitzen, Ruth 1924-　*ConAu 41, SmATA 9*
Eke, G S　*MnBBF*
Eksell, Olle 1918-　*WWGA*
Ekwensi, Cyprian 1921-　*AfA, Au&Wr 6,*
　CasWL, ConAu 29, ConLC 4,
　ConNov 1972, ConNov 1976, EncWL,
　IntWW 38, LongC, Pen Cl, RGAfL,
　TwCW, WEAL, WWTwL, WorAu, WrD
Elam, Richard M 1920-　*ConAu 61, SmATA 9*
Elbert, Virginie Fowler 1912-　*ConAu 61*
Elder, Michael Aiken 1931-　*Au&Wr 6,*
　ConAu 33, WrD
Eldred, Vince 1924-　*ConAu 69*
Eldridge, Mildred E 1909-　*ChPo, IICB 1946*
Elegant, Robert Sampson 1928-　*AmA&B,*
　ConAu 1R, WWA 38, WWW 14,
　WWWor 2
Eleska, Elena　*AmPB*
Elfman, Blossom 1925-　*ConAu 45, SmATA 8*
Elgin, Kathleen 1923-　*ConAu 25R, IIBYP,*
　IICB 1946, IICB 1957, WWAW 8
Elias, Frank　*MnBBF, WWBWI A*
Eliot, Anne　*ConAu XR, SmATA XR*
Eliot, Anne see Cole, Lois Dwight
Eliot, Frances 1901-　*IICB 1744*
Eliot, George　*MnBBF*
Eliot, George 1819-1880　*Alli Sup, AtlBL,*
　BbD, BiD&SB, BrAu 19, CasWL,
　Chambr 3, ChPo, ChPo S2, CriT 3,
　CyWA, DcBiA, DcEnA, DcEnA Ap,
　DcEnL, DcEuL, DcLEnL, EvLB,
　HsB&A, MouLC 3, NCHEL, OxEng,
　Pen Eng, RAdv 1, RCom, REn, WEAL
Eliot, George Fielding 1894-1971　*AmA&B,*
　ConAu 29, CurB 40, CurB 71, MnBBF,
　NYTBE 2, REnAL, TwCA, TwCA Sup
Eliot, T S 1888-1965　*AmA&B, AmWr, AnCL,*
　AtlBL, BiEnAT, CasWL, Chambr 3,
　ChPo, ChPo S1, ChPo S2, CnDAL,
　CnE&AP, CnMD, CnMWL, CnThe,
　ConAmL, ConAu 5R, ConAu 25R,
　ConLC 1, ConLC 2, ConLC 3, ConLC 6,
　CrCD, CyWA, DcLEnL, EncWL, EvLB,
　LongC, McGWD, ModAL, ModAL Sup,
　ModBL, ModBL Sup, ModWD, NCHEL,
　OxAm, OxEng, Pen Am, Pen Eng,
　RAdv 1, RCom, REn, REnAL, REnWD,
　SixAP, TwCA, TwCA Sup, TwCW,
　WEAL, WNAA, WWCL, WWTwL
Eliscu, Frank 1912-　*WWA 38, WWAA 1973,*
　WWWorJ 1972
Elisofon, Eliot 1911-1973　*AmA&B, ConAu 41,*
　CurB 72, NYTBE 4, WWAA 1973
Elkin, Benjamin 1911-　*Au&Wr 6, AuBYP,*
　ConAu 1R, SmATA 3, WWMW 14,
　WWWorJ 1972, WrD
Elkington, W M　*MnBBF*
Elkins, Dov Peretz 1937-　*AuBYP, ConAu 29,*
　SmATA 5, WrD
Elkins, Ella Ruth 1929-　*ConAu 25R*
Elkins, Ella Ruth see Beddoe, Ellaruth
Elkins, Ella Ruth see Wren, Ellaruth
Elkon, Juliette　*ConAu 57*
Elkon, Juliette see Elkon-Hamelecourt, Juliette
Elkon-Hamelecourt, Juliette 1912-　*ConAu 57*

Elkon-Hamelecourt, Juliette see Elkon, Juliette
Ellacott, S E 1911-　*ConAu 5R*
Ellbar, George　*MnBBF*
Ellen, Barbara 1938-　*AuBYP, ConAu 5R*
Ellin, E M 1905-　*ConAu P-2*
Elliot, Ian 1925-　*ConAu 69*
Elliott, Elizabeth Shippen Green　*IICB 1744*
Elliott, Geraldine　*ConAu XR*
Elliott, Geraldine see Bingham, Evangeline M L
Elliott, Gertrude　*ChPo*
Elliott, Harley 1940-　*ConAu 49, DrAP 1975*
Elliott, J Arthur　*MnBBF*
Elliott, Janice 1931-　*ConAu 13R, WrD*
Elliott, Mary　*Alli, CarSB, ChPo, ChPo S1,*
　ChPo S2
Elliott, Michael　*MnBBF*
Elliott, Robert　*ConAu XR*
Elliott, Robert see Garfinkel, Bernard
Elliott, Robert Cowell　*MnBBF, WWBWI A*
Elliott, Sarah M 1930-　*ConAu 41*
Elliott, William James　*MnBBF, WWBWI A*
Ellis, Edward S see Belknap, B H
Ellis, Edward S see Bethune, J G
Ellis, Edward S see Carleton, L C, Captain
Ellis, Edward S see Gordon, H R, Colonel
Ellis, Edward S see Hawthorne, R M, Captain
Ellis, Edward S see Jayne, R H, Lieutenant
Ellis, Edward S see Lassalle, C E
Ellis, Edward S see Lisle, Seward D
Ellis, Edward S see Muller, Billex
Ellis, Edward S see Randolph, J H, Lieutenant
Ellis, Edward S see Robins, Seelin
Ellis, Edward S see Rodman, Emerson
Ellis, Edward S see Wheeler, Captain
Ellis, Edward Sylvester 1840-1916　*Alli Sup,*
　AmA, AmA&B, BbD, BiD&SB, CarSB,
　DcAmA, DcNAA, HsB&A, OhA&B,
　OxAm, REnAL, WWCL, YABC 1
Ellis, Ella Thorp 1928-　*ConAu 49, SmATA 7,*
　WrD
Ellis, Frank　*MnBBF*
Ellis, Harry Bearse 1921-　*AmA&B, AuBYP,*
　ConAu 1R, SmATA 9, WWA 38,
　WWWor 2, WrD
Ellis, L Ethan 1898-　*ConAu 5R*
Ellis, Leo R 1909-　*ConAu 9R*
Ellis, Mary Jackson 1916-　*ConAu 1R,*
　ForWC 1970, MnnWr
Ellis, Mary Leith 1921-　*ConAu 21R,*
　WWAW 8
Ellis, Melvin Richard 1912-　*ConAu 13R,*
　SmATA 7
Ellis, R Hobart, Jr. 1918-　*AmMWS 12P*
Ellison, Dick　*MnBBF*
Ellison, Ellis　*MnBBF*
Ellison, Ellis see Snell, E L
Ellison, Harlan 1934-　*ConAu 5R, ConLC 1,*
　DrAF 1976
Ellison, Virginia Howell 1910-　*ConAu 33,*
　SmATA 4, WrD
Ellison, Virginia Howell see Howell, Virginia Tier
Ellison, Virginia Howell see Mapes, Mary A
Ellison, Virginia Howell see Mussey, Virginia H
Ellison, Virginia Howell see Soskin, V H
Ellison, Virginia Howell see Yung, Leong Gor
Ellsberg, Edward 1891-　*AmA&B, AmNov,*
　Au&Wr 6, AuBYP, ConAu 5R, CurB 42,
　JBA 1934, JBA 1951, REnAL,
　SmATA 7, TwCA, TwCA Sup,

WWA 38
Ellson, Ellis *MnBBF*
Ellson, Ellis *see* Snell, E L
Elman, Robert 1930- *ConAu 45*
Elmer, Irene 1937- *AuBYP, ConAu 1R*
Elrod, Jack *ArtCS*
Elsasser, Albert B 1918- *AmMWS 12S,
ConAu 69*
Elspeth *ConAu XR, SmATA 6*
Elspeth *see* Bragdon, Elspeth MacDuffie
Elston, Allan Vaughan 1887- *AmA&B,
Au&Wr 6, ConAu 1R, MnBBF*
Elting, Mary 1906- *AuBYP, ConAu 9R,
MorJA, SmATA 2*
Elting, Mary *see* Brewster, Benjamin
Elting, Mary *see* Cole, Davis
Elting, Mary *see* Gorham, Michael
Elting, Mary *see* Tatham, Campbell
Elwart, Joan Potter 1927- *ConAu 25R,
SmATA 2*
Elwell, Felicia Rosemary 1912- *Au&Wr 6,
AuBYP*
Elwood, Roger 1943- *ConAu 57*
Ely, George Herbert *MnBBF, WWBWI A*
Ely, George Herbert *see* Strang, Herbert
Emberley, Barbara A 1932- *BkP, ChPo,
ChPo S1, ConAu 5R, SmATA 8, ThBJA*
Emberley, Ed 1931- *Au&ICB, AuBYP, BkP,
ChPo, ChPo S1, ConAu 5R, IlBYP,
IlCB 1957, NewbC 1966, SmATA 8,
ThBJA*
Embry, Margaret Jacob 1919- *ConAu 1R,
ForWC 1970, SmATA 5*
Emerson, Alice B *AmA&B, CarSB,
ConAu P-2, SmATA 1*
Emerson, Alice B *see* Stratemeyer, Edward L
Emerson, Caroline Dwight 1891-1973 *AuBYP,
ConAu 45, ChPo, ConAu P-1*
Emerson, Ralph Waldo 1803-1882 *Alli,
Alli Sup, AmA, AmA&B, AmWr, AnCL,
AtlBL, BbD, BiD&SB, CasWL,
Chambr 3, ChPo, ChPo S1, CnDAL,
CnE&AP, CriT 3, CyAL 2, CyWA,
DcAmA, DcEnA, DcEnA Ap, DcEnL,
DcLEnL, DcNAA, EvLB, MouLC 4,
OxAm, OxEng, Pen Am, RAdv 1,
RCom, REn, REnAL, St&VC, WEAL*
Emerson, Sybil 1895- *IlCB 1744*
Emerson, William Keith 1925- *AmMWS 12P,
ConAu 41, WWA 38, WWE 14,
WWWor 2*
Emery, Anne 1907- *AuBYP, ConAu 1R,
CurB 52, MorJA, SmATA 1*
Emery, Russell Guy 1908- *AuBYP*
Emett, Rowland 1906- *IlCB 1946, WW 1974,
WWGA*
Emmet, Eric Revell 1909- *Au&Wr 6*
Emmett, Bruce 1949- *ConAu 57*
Emmett Brothers *MnBBF, WWBWI A*
Emmett Brothers *see* Brent, Charlton
Emmett Brothers *see* Brent, Ernest
Emmett Brothers *see* Lawrence, W E
Emmons, Della Gould 1890- *WWAW 8*
Emrich, Duncan 1908- *ChPo S1, ChPo S2,
ConAu 61, CurB 55, SmATA 11*
Emrich, Duncan *see* Macdonald, Blackie
Emrick, Harry Dale 1932- *WWMW 14*
Enderby, W D *MnBBF*
Engdahl, Sylvia Louise 1933- *ChLR 2,*

ConAu 29, SmATA 4, WrD
Engebrecht, P A 1935- *ConAu 57*
Engel, Leonard 1916-1964 *AmA&B*
Engel, Marian 1933- *CanWW 12,
ConAu 25R, ConNov 1976, OxCan Sup,
WrD*
Engelhardt, Sister Mary Veronice 1912- *WrD*
Engeman, John T 1901- *AuBYP*
England, Allan *MnBBF*
Engle, Eloise 1923- *ConAu 1R, SmATA 9,
WrD*
Englebert, Victor 1933- *ConAu 57, SmATA 8*
Englefield, Cicely 1893- *IlCB 1744*
Engler, Larry 1949- *ConAu 53*
English, Don *MnBBF*
English, Don *see* Owen, Miss D E
English, James W 1915- *ConAu 21R*
Engvick, William *AuBYP, ChPo*
Enright, Elizabeth 1909-1968 *AmA&B, AnCL,
AuBYP, BkCL, ConAu 25R, ConAu 61,
CurB 47, FamMS, IlCB 1744, IlCB 1946,
JBA 1951, Newb 1922, SmATA 9*
Enten, Harry *MnBBF, WWBWI A*
Epp, Margaret A 1913- *ConAu 9R,
WWAW 8, WWW 14*
Epp, Margaret A *WrD*
Epp, Margaret A *see* Goossen, Agnes
Epple, Anne Orth 1927- *ConAu 33, WrD*
Epps, Francis *MnBBF*
Epstein, Beryl *see* Allen, Adam
Epstein, Beryl *see* Coe, Douglas
Epstein, Beryl *see* Williams, Beryl
Epstein, Beryl Williams 1910- *AuBYP,
ConAu 5R, MorJA, OhA&B, SmATA 1*
Epstein, June Sadie *WrD*
Epstein, Morris 1921-1973 *ConAu 45,
NYTBE 4, WWWorJ 1972*
Epstein, Perle S 1938- *ConAu 65*
Epstein, Samuel 1909- *AuBYP, ConAu 9R,
MorJA, SmATA 1, WWWorJ 1972*
Epstein, Samuel *see* Allen, Adam
Epstein, Samuel *see* Campbell, Bruce
Epstein, Samuel *see* Coe, Douglas
Epstein, Samuel *see* Colt, Martin
Epstein, Samuel *see* Strong, Charles
Erdman, Loula Grace *AmA&B, AmNov,
AuBYP, ConAu 5R, DrAS 6E,
ForWC 1970, MorJA, SmATA 1, TexW*
Erdoes, Richard 1912- *IlBYP, IlCB 1957*
Erhard, Walter 1920- *IlCB 1957*
Erickson, Phoebe 1907- *AuBYP, ConAu 1R,
IlCB 1946*
Erickson, Sabra Rollins 1912- *ConAu 5R*
Erickson, Sabra Rollins *see* Holbrook, Sabra
Ericson, Dick 1916- *WWAA 1973*
Ericson, Ian *MnBBF*
Ericson, Walter *AuBYP, ConAu XR,
SmATA 7, TwCA Sup*
Ericson, Walter *see* Fast, Howard
Erikson, Eric *MnBBF*
Erikson, Mel *IlBYP*
Erlich, Lillian 1910- *AuBYP, ConAu 1R,
ForWC 1970, SmATA 10*
Ernest, Brother 1897- *AuBYP, BkC 3,
CatA 1930*
Ernst, John 1940- *ConAu 45*
Ernst, John *see* Chernoff, Dorothy A
Ernst, John *see* Clark, David Allen
Ernst, Kathryn F 1942- *ConAu 61*

Ernst, Ken 1918- *ArtCS*
Errym, Malcolm J *HsB&A, MnBBF,*
 WWBWI A
Errym, Malcolm J *see* Merry, Malcolm James
Ervin, Janet Halliday 1923- *ConAu 29,*
 ForWC 1970, SmATA 4, WWAW 8
Esherick, Joseph 1914- *WWA 38, WWWor 2*
Eskenazi, Gerald 1936- *ConAu 61*
Esmark, Dorrien *MnBBF*
Espinasse, Bernard *MnBBF*
Esses, Emma *MnBBF*
Essex, Captain *MnBBF*
Essex, Captain *see* Starr, Richard
Essex, Lewis *MnBBF, WWBWI A*
Essex, Lewis *see* Isaacs, Levi
Essex, Lewis *see* Starr, Richard
Essex, Louis *MnBBF*
Essex, Louis *see* Isaacs, Levi
Essex, Richard *MnBBF, WWBWI A*
Essex, Richard *see* Starr, Richard
Essrig, Harry 1912- *WWWorJ 1972*
Estel, P G *MnBBF*
Estep, Irene Compton *ConAu 1R, SmATA 5*
Estes, Eleanor 1906- *AmA&B, AmNov,*
 AnCL, AuBYP, BkCL, ChLR 2,
 ConAu 1R, CurB 46, IICB 1946,
 JBA 1951, MorBMP, Newb 1922,
 REnAL, SenS, SmATA 4, SmATA 7,
 St&VC, WWA 38, WWAW 8
Estoril, Jean *AuBYP, ConAu XR,*
 SmATA 5
Estoril, Jean *see* Allan, Mabel Esther
Estrada, Doris 1923- *ConAu 17R*
Etherton, P T 1879- *MnBBF, WWLA*
Ets, Marie Hall 1895- *AnCL, AmPB,*
 Au&ICB, Au&Wr 6, AuBYP, BkP,
 ChPo, ConAu 1R, FamAI, ForWC 1970,
 IIBYP, IICB 1744, IICB 1946, IICB 1957,
 JBA 1951, NewbC 1956, SmATA 2,
 St&VC, WWA 38, WWAA 1973,
 WWAW 8, WrD
Etter, Les 1904- *ConAu 25R*
Eubank, Nancy 1934- *ConAu 41*
Euller, John E 1926- *ConAu 9R*
Eunson, Dale 1904- *AmA&B, AmNov,*
 BiEnAT, ConAu 41, SmATA 5
Eustis, Helen 1916- *CurB 55, EncM&D,*
 OhA&B
Evanoff, Vlad 1916- *ConAu 5R*
Evans, A Eurule *MnBBF*
Evans, Sir Anthony 1922- *Au&Wr 6,*
 WW 1974
Evans, B E *MnBBF*
Evans, B J *MnBBF*
Evans, C S *CarSB*
Evans, Constance May 1890- *ConAu 9R, WrD*
Evans, E Estyn 1905- *ConAu 5R*
Evans, Edmund 1826-1905 *CarSB, ChPo,*
 ChPo S1, ChPo S2
Evans, Edna Hoffman 1913- *AuBYP,*
 ForWC 1970
Evans, Ernestine *AmPB*
Evans, Eubule *MnBBF*
Evans, Eva Knox 1905- *AuBYP, MorJA*
Evans, Evan *WWBWI A*
Evans, Evan *see* Faust, Frederick
Evans, Frank Howel *MnBBF, WWBWI A*
Evans, Frank Howel *see* Daunt, Atherley
Evans, Frank Howel *see* Payne, Crutchley

Evans, Gwyn 1899?-1938 *MnBBF,*
 WWBWI A
Evans, Gwyn *see* Gwynne, Arthur
Evans, Gwyn *see* Western, Barry
Evans, Henry 1918- *WWAA 1973*
Evans, Hubert *MnBBF*
Evans, I O 1894- *ConAu 13R*
Evans, Julia 1913- *Au&Wr 6, AuBYP,*
 ConAu 13R, WrD
Evans, Julia *see* Hobson, Polly
Evans, Katherine Floyd 1901-1964 *AuBYP,*
 ConAu 5R, IICB 1957, SmATA 5
Evans, Mari 1923- *BlkAW, ConAu 49,*
 ConP 1975, CrCAP, DrAP 1975, LBAA,
 SmATA 10, WrD
Evans, Mark *ConAu 65*
Evans, Mary Ann 1819-1880 *BiD&SB,*
 BrAu 19, CarSB, DcLEnL, EvLB,
 NCHEL, OxEng, Pen Eng, REn
Evans, Max 1925- *Au&Wr 6, ConAu 1R*
Evans, Patricia Healy *AuBYP, ConAu XR,*
 SmATA XR
Evans, Patricia Healy *see* Carpenter, Patricia
Evans, Rear Admiral *MnBBF*
Evans, Shirlee 1931- *ConAu 61*
Evans, Vice Admiral *MnBBF*
Evansen, Virginia Besaw 1921- *ConAu 13R,*
 WrD
Evarts, Hal G 1915- *ConAu 49, SmATA 6*
Evatt, Harriet 1895- *CurB 59*
Evelyn, A W *MnBBF*
Evelyn, A W *see* Wilkes, W
Evens, George Bramwell 1884-1943 *WWCL*
Evens, George Bramwell *see* Romany
Everard, Maurice *MnBBF, WWBWI A*
Everard, Maurice *see* Bullivant, Cecil Henry
Everard, Walter *MnBBF, WWBWI A*
Everard, Walter *see* Garrish, Harold J
Everett, Bernard *MnBBF, WWBWI A*
Everett, Michael *ChPo S2*
Everett, Percy W 1870- *MnBBF, WWBWI A*
Everett-Green, Evelyn 1856-1932 *CarSB,*
 MnBBF, TelT, WWBWI A, WWCL
Everett-Green, Evelyn *see* Adair, Cecil
Everett-Green, Evelyn *see* Ward, Evelyn
Evernden, Margery 1916- *ConAu 5R,*
 SmATA 5, WrD
Evers, Alf 1905- *AuBYP*
Eversley, David Edward Charles 1921-
 ConAu 1R
Eversley, David Edward Charles *see* Small,
 William
Everson, Dale Millar 1928- *ConAu 17R*
Everson, William Keith 1929- *AuBYP,*
 ConAu 1R, IntMPA 1975, WWA 38
Every, Philip Cochrane *AuBYP*
Every, Philip Cochrane *see* Burnford, Sheila
Eves, Reginald T *MnBBF, WWBWI A*
Eves, Reginald T *see* Britton, Herbert
Eves, Reginald T *see* Clifford, Martin
Eves, Reginald T *see* Conquest, Owen
Evslin, Bernard 1922- *ConAu 21R*
Ewen, David 1907- *AmA&B, Au&Wr 6,*
 AuBYP, BiEnAT, ConAu 1R, REnAL,
 SmATA 4, WWA 38, WWMus 6,
 WWS 13, WWWor 2, WWWorJ 1972
Ewen, Robert B 1940- *AmMWS 12S,*
 ConAu 37
Ewers, John C 1909- *OxCan, OxCan Sup*

Ewers, John K *SingR 1*
Ewing, Juliana Horatia 1841-1885 *Alli Sup,*
 BbD, BiD&SB, BrAu 19, CarSB,
 CasWL, ChPo, ChPo S1, ChPo S2,
 DcLEnL, EvLB, FamSYP, JBA 1934,
 NCHEL, OxEng, St&VC, TelT, WWCL
Ewing, Kathryn 1921- *ConAu 61*
Ewing, Kathryn *see* Douglas, Kathryn
Ex Constable Y *MnBBF*
Ex Private *MnBBF*
Eyerly, Jeannette Hyde 1908- *ConAu 1R,*
 ForWC 1970, SmATA 4, WWA 38,
 WWAW 8
Eyerly, Jeannette Hyde *see* Griffith, Jeannette
Eyles, D C *WWBWI 1*
Eyre, Katherine Wigmore 1901-1970 *AmA&B,*
 CurB 49, CurB 57, MorJA
Ezekiel, Nissim 1924- *CasWL, WrD,*
 ConP 1970, ConP 1975, REn, WEAL,
 WWWorJ 1972

F

Fabell, Walter *AuBYP*
Faber, Doris 1924- *AuBYP, ConAu 17R, SmATA 3*
Faber, Harold 1919- *AuBYP, ConAu 13R, SmATA 5*
Fabre, Jean Henri 1823-1915 *AnCL, JBA 1934, JBA 1951, LongC, OxFr, REn*
Fabres, Oscar 1900- *ChPo S1, IlBYP, IlCB 1946*
Fabricius, Johan Wigmore 1899- *Au&Wr 6, CasWL, ConAu 53, EvEuW, IlCB 1744, IntWW 38, TwCA, TwCA Sup, WWWor 2*
Fabun, Don 1920- *ConAu 45*
Fadiman, Clifton 1904- *AmA&B, CelR 3, ChPo S2, ConAu 61, CurB 41, CurB 55, IntMPA 1975, RAdv 1, REnAL, SmATA 11, TwCA, TwCA Sup, WWA 38, WWW 14, WWWor 2*
Fadiman, Edwin, Jr. 1925- *ConAu 29*
Fair, James Rutherford, Jr. 1920- *AmMWS 12P, ConAu 29, WWMW 14*
Fair, Sylvia 1933- *ConAu 69, SmATA 13*
Fairbanks, Nat *MnBBF*
Fairbanks, Nat *see* Pearce, Charles Louis St. John
Fairfax-Lucy, Brian 1898- *ConAu P-2, SmATA 6*
Fairfield, Charles *MnBBF*
Fairley, Peter 1930- *ConAu 29*
Fairlie, Gerard 1889- *Au&Wr 6*
Fairly, T S *MnBBF*
Fairman, Joan Alexandra 1935- *ConAu 33, SmATA 10, WrD*
Faithfull, Gail 1936- *ConAu 57, SmATA 8*
Faithfull, Gail *see* Keller, Gail Faithfull
Falconer, James *ConAu XR, SmATA XR*
Falconer, James *see* Kirkup, James
Falconer, Pearl *ArtsCL, IlCB 1957*
Falk, Irving A 1921- *ConAu 21R*
Falk, Lee *ArtCS*
Falkner, John Meade 1858-1932 *CnMWL, DcLEnL, EvLB, LongC, REn, WWCL, WorAu*
Falkner, Leonard 1900- *ConAu 21R, MnBBF, OhA&B, SmATA 12, WNAA*
Fall, Thomas *AuBYP*
Fallow, Burnett *ChPo, MnBBF*
Falls, C B *AmPB*
Falls, C B *see* Falls, Charles Buckles
Falls, Charles Buckles 1874-1960 *AuBYP, ChPo, ChPo S2, ConICB, IlCB 1744, IlCB 1946, IndAu 1917, JBA 1934,*
JBA 1951
Falls, Charles Buckles *see* Falls, C B
Falls, Cyril Bentham 1888- *ConAu P-1*
Falstein, Louis 1909- *AmA&B, WWA 38, WWWorJ 1972*
Falter, John 1910- *WWAA 1973*
Fancourt, Mary St. John 1898- *Au&Wr 6, WrD*
Fane, Essex *MnBBF*
Fane, Rupert *MnBBF*
Fanning, Leonard M 1888-1967 *ConAu 5R, SmATA 5*
Fanshaw, Cecil *MnBBF, WWBWI A*
Fanshaw, Cecil *see* Dent, C H
Faralla, Dana 1909- *AmA&B, AmNov, ConAu 49, SmATA 9*
Faralla, Dana *see* Faralla, Dorothy W
Faralla, Dana *see* Wilma, Dana
Faralla, Dorothy W *ConAu XR, SmATA XR*
Faralla, Dorothy W *see* Faralla, Dana
Farb, Peter 1929- *AmA&B, Au&Wr 6, ConAu 13R, SmATA 12, WWA 38, WWE 14, WWWor 2*
Fargo, Lucille Foster 1880- *AuBYP, OhA&B*
Faris, John Thomson 1871-1949 *AmA&B, CarSB, DcNAA, WNAA*
Farjeon, Annabel 1919- *ConAu 53, SmATA 11*
Farjeon, Annabel *see* Jefferson, Sarah
Farjeon, Eleanor 1881-1965 *AnCL, AuBYP, BkCL, CasWL, CatA 1952, ChPo, ChPo S1, ChPo S2, ConAu P-1, DcLEnL, FamMS, FamPYP, JBA 1934, JBA 1951, LongC, NCHEL, SmATA 2, St&VC, TelT, TwCA, TwCA Sup, TwCW, WWCL*
Farjeon, Eleanor *see* Chimaera
Farjeon, Eleanor *see* Tomfool
Farjeon, Joan Jefferson 1913- *IlCB 1946*
Farjeon, Joseph Jefferson 1883-1955 *MnBBF, NCHEL, TwCA, TwCA Sup, WWBWI A*
Farley, C R L *MnBBF*
Farley, Carol *ConAu XR, SmATA 4, WrD*
Farley, Carol *see* McDole, Carol
Farley, Harriet 1817-1907 *Alli, Alli Sup, AmA, AmA&B, BbD, BiD&SB, CarSB, CyAL 2, DcAmA, DcNAA, OxAm, REnAL*
Farley, Walter 1915- *AuBYP, ConAu 17R, CurB 49, JBA 1951, MorBMP, SmATA 2*

Farman, Ella 1843-1907 *Alli Sup, AmA&B, BiD&SB, CarSB, ChPo, ChPo S1, DcAmA*

Farmer, Henry *MnBBF, WWBWI A*

Farmer, Henry *see* Wright, Franklin

Farmer, Penelope 1939- *AuBYP, BrCA, ConAu 13R, WrD*

Farmer, Philip Jose 1918- *ConAu 1R*

Farmer, Robert Allen 1938- *ConAu 21R*

Farmer, Wendell *AuBYP*

Farnham, Burt *ConAu XR, SmATA XR*

Farnham, Burt *see* Clifford, Harold B

Farnol, Jeffrey 1878-1952 *LongC, TelT, TwCW*

Farnworth, Warren *WrD*

Farquhar, George G *MnBBF*

Farquhar, Margaret C 1905- *ConAu 69, SmATA 13*

Farquharson, Martha 1828-1909 *Alli Sup, AmA, AmA&B, BiDSA, DcAmA, DcNAA, OhA&B, OxAm, WWCL*

Farquharson, Martha *see* Finley, Martha

Farr, Diana Pullein-Thompson *ConAu 13R*

Farr, Diana Pullein-Thompson *see* Pullein-Thompson, Diana

Farr, Finis 1904- *ConAu 1R, SmATA 10*

Farrant, Leda 1927- *ConAu 21R*

Farrar, Frederick William 1831-1903 *Alli Sup, BbD, BiD&SB, BrAu 19, CasWL, Chambr 3, ChPo, DcEnA, DcEnA Ap, DcEnL, EvLB, NCHEL, Pen Eng, TelT, WWCL*

Farrar, John Chipman 1896-1974 *AmA&B, ChPo, ChPo S1, ChPo S2, NYTBS 5, REnAL, St&VC, WWA 38*

Farrar, Richard B, Jr. 1939- *ConAu 65*

Farre, Rowena *Au&Wr 6*

Farrell, Alan 1920- *Au&Wr 6, ConAu 13R*

Farrell, Anne A 1916- *ConAu 25R*

Farrell, Ben *ConAu XR, SmATA XR*

Farrell, Ben *see* Cebulash, Mel

Farrington, Selwyn Kip, Jr. 1904- *AmA&B, AuBYP*

Farris, Herbert *MnBBF*

Farrow, George Edward 1866-1920? *ChPo, ChPo S1, ChPo S2, MnBBF, TelT, WWCL*

Farthing, Alison *WrD*

Fassler, Joan 1931- *ConAu 61, SmATA 11*

Fast, Howard 1914- *AmA&B, AmNov, Au&Wr 6, AuBYP, CnDAL, ConAu 1R, ConNov 1972, ConNov 1976, CurB 43, DcLEnL, IntWW 38, ModAL, OxAm, Pen Am, REn, REnAL, SmATA 7, TwCA Sup, TwCW, WEAL, WWA 38, WWWor 2, WWWorJ 1972*

Fast, Howard *see* Cunningham, E V

Fast, Howard *see* Ericson, Walter

Fatchen, Max 1920- *Au&Wr 6, ConAu 25R, SingR 2*

Fatio, Louise 1904- *BkP, ConAu 37, MorJA, SmATA 6, WrD*

Faulhaber, Martha 1926- *ConAu 33, SmATA 7*

Faulkner, Anne Irvin 1906- *AuBYP, ConAu 1R, ForWC 1970*

Faulkner, Anne Irvin *see* Faulkner, Nancy Irvin

Faulkner, Elsie 1905- *ConAu 65*

Faulkner, Georgene 1873- *AmA&B, AuBYP,*

Faulkner, John *IIBYP*

Faulkner, Nancy *Au&Wr 6, AuBYP, ConAu XR, CurB 56*

Faulkner, Nancy Irvin *see* Faulkner, Anne Irvin

Faulkner, William 1897-1962 *AmA&B, AmNov, AmWr, AtlBL, AuNews 1, BiN 1974, CasWL, Chambr 3, CnDAL, CnMD, CnMWL, ConAmA, ConLC 1, ConLC 3, ConLC 6, CrCD, CurB 51, CurB 62, CyWA, DcLEnL, EncM&D, EncWL, LongC, ModAL, ModAL Sup, ModWD, OxAm, OxEng, Pen Am, RAdv 1, RCom, REn, REnAL, TwCA, TwCA Sup, TwCW, WEAL, WWTwL*

Faulknor, Clifford Vernon 1913- *ConAu 17R, OxCan Sup, Prof, WWW 14, WrD*

Faust, Frederick 1892-1944 *AmA&B, ChPo, CurB 44, DcLEnL, DcNAA, EncM&D, LongC, MnBBF, REn, REnAL, TwCA, TwCA Sup, WWBWI A*

Faust, Frederick *see* Austin, Frank

Faust, Frederick *see* Baxter, George Owen

Faust, Frederick *see* Brand, Max

Faust, Frederick *see* Butler, Walter C

Faust, Frederick *see* Dawson, Peter

Faust, Frederick *see* Evans, Evan

Faust, Frederick *see* Frederick, John

Fava, Rita 1932- *ChPo, ChPo S1, IICB 1946, IICB 1957*

Fava, Rita *see* Fegiz, Rita Fava

Favelli *WWBWI I*

Fawcett, Captain *MnBBF*

Fawcett, F Dubrez 1891-1968 *ConAu P-1, MnBBF, WWBWI A*

Fax, Elton Clay 1909- *ConAu 13R, LBAA, WWAA 1973*

Faxon, Lavinia *ConAu XR*

Faxon, Lavinia *see* Russ, Lavinia

Fay, Frederic L 1890- *ConAu P-2*

Feagles, Anita MacRae 1926- *AuBYP, ConAu 1R, ForWC 1970, SmATA 9*

Feagles, Anita MacRae *see* MacRae, Travis

Feagles, Elizabeth *ConAu XR*

Feagles, Elizabeth *see* Day, Beth Feagles

Feague, Mildred H 1915- *ConAu 29*

Fear, Duncan *MnBBF*

Fearn, C Eaton *MnBBF, WWBWI A*

Fearn, C Eaton *see* Lang, Peter

Fearn, C Eaton *see* Macrae, Herbert

Fearn, C Eaton *see* Merrick, Jim

Feaser, Daniel David 1920- *IIBYP, IICB 1957*

Fecher, Constance 1911- *Au&Wr 6, ConAu 49, SmATA 7*

Fecher, Constance *see* Heaven, Constance

Fedder, Ruth 1907- *ConAu 5R, LE 5*

Feelings, Thomas 1933- *ConAu 49, SmATA 8*

Feelings, Thomas *see* Feelings, Tom

Feelings, Tom *BkP, ConAu XR, IIBYP, LBAA, SmATA 8, ThBJA*

Feelings, Tom *see* Feelings, Thomas

Feerick, John David 1936- *ConAu 13R*

Fegiz, Rita Fava 1932- *IIBYP, IICB 1957*

Fegiz, Rita Fava *see* Fava, Rita

Feher, Joseph 1908- *WWAA 1973*

Fehrenbach, T R 1925- *ConAu 1R, WWS 13*

Feibleman, Peter S 1930- *REnAL*

Feiffer, Jules 1929- *AmA&B, ArtCS,*

Au&Wr 6, CelR 3, CnThe, ConAu 17R,
ConDr 1, ConLC 2, CrCD, CurB 61,
IntWW 38, McGWD, SmATA 8,
WWA 38, WWT 15, WWWor 2
Feil, Hila 1942- *ConAu 37, SmATA 12*
Feilen, John *SmATA XR*
Feilen, John *see* May, Julian
Feingold, S Norman 1914- *AmMWS 12S,*
ConAu 13R, LE 5, WWS 13,
WWWorJ 1972
Feininger, Lyonel 1871-1956 *ArtCS, AtlBL,*
CurB 55, CurB 56, DcCAA 2, OxGer,
REn
Feinstein, Alan Shawn 1931- *WWE 14*
Feis, Ruth 1892- *ConAu P-2*
Feist, Aubrey 1903- *Au&Wr 6, ConAu 41*
Feldman, Herbert 1910- *ConAu 29*
Felkin, Alfred Laurence 1856- *CarSB, WWLA*
Felkin, Ellen Thorneycroft 1860-1929 *CarSB,*
NCHEL, WWLA
Feller, Bob *CurB 41*
Feller, Bob *see* Feller, Robert William Andrew
Feller, Robert William Andrew 1918- *AuBYP*
Feller, Robert William Andrew *see* Feller, Bob
Fellner, Rudolph 1913- *AuBYP, WWMus 6*
Fellows, Lawrence 1924- *ConAu 49*
Fellows, Muriel H *AuBYP, ConAu 53,*
SmATA 10
Felsen, Gregor 1916- *JBA 1951*
Felsen, Henry Gregor 1916- *AuBYP,*
ConAu 1R, SmATA 1
Felsen, Henry Gregor *see* Vicker, Angus
Felt, Sue 1924- *IICB 1946*
Felton, Bruce 1946- *ConAu 65*
Felton, Frederick A *MnBBF*
Felton, Frederick A *see* Armstrong, Jack
Felton, Harold William 1902- *AuBYP,*
ChPo S2, ConAu 1R, MorJA, SmATA 1
Felton, Ronald Oliver 1909- *Au&Wr 6,*
ConAu 9R, SmATA 3
Felton, Ronald Oliver *see* Welch, Ronald
Fenn, Clive Robert 1870?- *MnBBF,*
WWBWI A
Fenn, Lady Eleanor 1743-1813 *CarSB, ChPo,*
DcEnL
Fenn, George Manville 1831-1909 *Alli Sup,*
BbD, BiD&SB, BrAu 19, Chambr 3,
ChPo, ChPo S2, DcBiA, DcEnL, EvLB,
HsB&A, MnBBF, NCHEL, WWBWI A,
WWCL
Fenn, George Manville *see* Manville, George
Fenn, W W *MnBBF*
Fennell, Hugh Wordsworth d1956 *MnBBF,*
WWBWI A
Fennell, Hugh Wordsworth *see* Leonard, Henry
Fenner, Carol Elizabeth 1929- *ConAu 5R,*
IICB 1957, SmATA 7
Fenner, Phyllis Reid 1899- *AuBYP, ConAu 5R,*
ForWC 1970, SmATA 1, WWAW 8
Fenner, Ralph *MnBBF*
Fennes, Clinton *MnBBF*
Fennimore, Stephen *SingR 2*
Fennimore, Stephen *see* Collins, Dale
Fenten, Barbara D 1935- *ConAu 53*
Fenten, D X 1932- *ConAu 33, SmATA 4,*
WrD
Fenton, Carroll Lane 1900-1969 *AmA&B,*
AuBYP, ConAu 1R, ConAu 29, MorJA,
SmATA 5

Fenton, Edward 1917- *Au&Wr 6, AuBYP,*
ConAu 9R, SmATA 7, ThBJA
Fenton, Mildred Adams 1899- *Au&Wr 6,*
MorJA
Fenton, Roderick *MnBBF*
Fenton, Sophia Harvati 1914- *ConAu 33*
Feravolo, Rocco Vincent 1922- *AuBYP,*
ConAu 1R, SmATA 10
Ferber, Edna 1887-1968 *AmA&B, AmNov,*
AuNews 1, BiEnAT, Chambr 3, CnDAL,
CnMD, CnThe, ConAmA, ConAmL,
ConAu 5R, ConAu 25R, DcLEnL,
EncWL, EvLB, LongC, McGWD,
ModAL, ModWD, OxAm, Pen Am, REn,
REnAL, SmATA 7, TwCA, TwCA Sup,
TwCW, WNAA, WisW
Ferguson, A *MnBBF*
Ferguson, Bob *SmATA XR*
Ferguson, Bob *see* Ferguson, Robert Bruce
Ferguson, Charles W 1901- *AmA&B,*
ConAu 13R, REnAL, TexW, WWA 38
Ferguson, Evelyn *WrD*
Ferguson, Robert Bruce 1927- *SmATA 13*
Ferguson, Robert Bruce *see* Ferguson, Bob
Ferguson, Walter W 1930- *IIBYP, IICB 1946*
Fergusson, Erna 1888-1964 *AmA&B,*
ConAu P-1, CurB 55, SmATA 5
Fermi, Laura Capon 1907- *AmA&B, AuBYP,*
ConAu 1R, CurB 58, SmATA 6,
WWA 38, WWAW 8, WWWor 2, WrD
Fern, Eugene A 1919- *ConAu 1R, SmATA 10*
Ferns, Ronald George 1925- *IICB 1957*
Ferrar, W J *MnBBF*
Ferris, Arthur *WWBWI A*
Ferris, Arthur *see* Rowe, John Gabriel
Ferris, Helen Josephine 1890-1969 *AmA&B,*
AuBYP, ChPo, JBA 1934, JBA 1951,
REnAL, WNAA
Ferris, James Cody *AmNov X, ConAu P-2,*
SmATA 1
Ferris, James Cody *see* Stratemeyer, Edward L
Ferro, Walter *WWAA 1973*
Fessenden, Katherine 1896?-1974 *ConAu 53*
Fetz, Ingrid 1915- *ChPo S1, IIBYP,*
IICB 1957
Feuerlicht, Roberta Strauss 1931- *ConAu 17R*
Feveril, Hubert *MnBBF*
Feveril, Hubert *see* Murray, A C
Fiammenghi, Gioia 1929- *IIBYP, IICB 1946,*
IICB 1957, SmATA 9
Fiarotta, Noel 1944- *ConAu 69*
Fiarotta, Phyllis 1942- *ConAu 69*
Fichter, George S 1922- *ConAu 17R,*
SmATA 7, WWS 13
Fichter, George S *see* Warner, Matt
Fidler, Kathleen *Au&Wr 6, ConAu 25R,*
SmATA 3, WrD
Fiedler, Jean *ConAu 17R, ConAu 29,*
SmATA 4
Field, Edward 1924- *AmA&B, ConAu 13R,*
ConP 1970, ConP 1975, CrCAP,
DrAP 1975, SmATA 8
Field, Eugene 1850-1895 *Alli Sup, AmA,*
AmA&B, AmSCAP 66, AuBYP, BbD,
BiD&SB, BiDSA, CarSB, CasWL,
Chambr 3, ChP, ChPo, ChPo S1,
ChPo S2, CnDAL, DcAmA, DcLEnL,
DcNAA, EvLB, FamPYP, JBA 1934,
OxAm, OxEng, Pen Am, RAdv 1, REn,

REnAL, St&VC
Field, Marcus MnBBF
Field, Michael 1915-1971 ConAu 29,
  NYTBE 2
Field, Peter MnBBF
Field, Rachel 1894-1942 AmA&B, AnCL,
  AuBYP, BkCL, CarSB, ChPo, ChPo S1,
  ChPo S2, CnDAL, ConAmA, ConICB,
  CurB 42, DcNAA, FamPYP, JBA 1934,
  JBA 1951, LongC, Newb 1922, OxAm,
  REnAL, St&VC, TwCA, TwCA Sup,
  TwCW
Field, Wilford E MnBBF
Fielder, Mildred 1913- ConAu 13R, WrD
Fielding, Howard MnBBF
Fielding, Howard see Anderson, G J B
Fielding, Lola 1930- ArtsCL
Fielding, Sarah 1710-1768 Alli, BbD,
  BiD&SB, BrAu, CarSB, CasWL,
  Chambr 2, DcEnA, DcEnL, DcEuL,
  DcLEnL, EvLB, NCHEL Eng, OxEng,
  Pen Eng
Fielding, Vernon MnBBF
Figes, Eva 1932- Au&Wr 6, ConAu 53,
  ConNov 1976, WrD
Figueroa, John L 1936- ConAu 65,
  DrAF 1976
Figueroa, Pablo 1938- ConAu 61, SmATA 9
Figuerola, Carmen SingR 2
Fijan, Carol 1918- ConAu 53, SmATA 12
Fillmore, Parker Hoysted 1878-1944 AmA&B,
  DcNAA, JBA 1934, JBA 1951, OhA&B,
  YABC 1
Filson, Floyd Vivian 1896- AmA&B,
  ConAu 61, WWA 38
Finch, Bernard MnBBF
Finch, Donald George 1937- ConAu 53
Finger, Charles Joseph 1869?-1941 AmA&B,
  AnCL, AuBYP, BkCL, CurB 41,
  DcNAA, JBA 1934, Newb 1922,
  OhA&B, REnAL, TwCA, WEAL
Fink, Augusta 1916- ConAu 33, WrD
Fink, Sam 1916- WWAA 1973
Fink, William Bertrand 1916- ConAu 41,
  DrAS 6H
Finke, Blythe Foote 1922- ConAu 65
Finkel, George 1909-1975 Au&Wr 6,
  ConAu P-2, SmATA 8, SingR 2
Finkel, George see Pennage, E M
Finlay, Ian F 1924- Au&Wr 6
Finlay, Ian Hamilton 1925- ChPo S2,
  ConP 1970, ConP 1975, WEAL, WorAu,
  WrD
Finlay, Winifred Lindsay Crawford 1910-
  Au&Wr 6, ConAu 9R, WWAW 8,
  WWWor 2, WrD
Finlayson, Ann 1925- ConAu 29, SmATA 8
Finley, Martha see Farquharson, Martha
Finley, Martha Farquharson 1828-1909 Alli Sup,
  AmA, AmA&B, BiD&SB, BiDSA,
  CarSB, CnDAL, DcAmA, DcNAA,
  IndAu 1816, OhA&B, OxAm, REnAL,
  WWCL
Finn, Jack M MnBBF
Finnemore, Hilda 1891- MnBBF
Finnemore, John E MnBBF, WWBWI A
Finnemore, Joseph 1860-1939 WWBWI I
Finney, Escott MnBBF
Finney, Gertrude Elva 1892- AuBYP,

ConAu P-1, CurB 57, IndAu 1917,
  WWPNA
Finnin, Mary ConP 1970, WWWor 2, WrD
Finocchiaro, Mary 1913- ConAu 29, DrAS 6F
Finta, Alexander 1881- IlCB 1744
Firdausi 935?-1020? AnCL, BiD&SB,
  NCHEL, REn
Firdousi 935?-1020? AnCL, NCHEL, REn
Firdusi 935?-1020? AnCL, BbD, BiD&SB,
  NCHEL, REn
Fischbach, Julius 1894- ConAu 5R,
  SmATA 10, WWMW 14
Fischer, Ann A IlBYP
Fischer, Anton Otto 1882- IlCB 1744,
  IlCB 1946
Fischer, Hans Erich 1909-1958 ChFB I, IlBYP,
  IlCB 1946, IlCB 1957, MorJA
Fischtrom, Harvey 1933-1974 ConAu 53,
  ThBJA
Fischtrom, Harvey see Zemach, Harve
Fischtrom, Margot Zemach ThBJA
Fischtrom, Margot Zemach see Zemach, Margot
Fish, Byron 1908- ConAu 45
Fish, Helen Dean 1890-1953 AmA&B, ChPo
Fisher, Aileen Lucia 1906- AuBYP, BkCL,
  BkP, ChPo, ChPo S1, ChPo S2,
  ConAu 5R, ForWC 1970, MorJA,
  SmATA 1
Fisher, Anne Benson 1898- AmA&B, AmNov
Fisher, Bud 1885-1954 AmA&B, ArtCS
Fisher, Clavin C 1912- ConAu 65
Fisher, Clay AmA&B
Fisher, Clay see Allen, Henry
Fisher, David AuBYP
Fisher, Dorothy Canfield 1879-1958 AmA&B,
  AmNov X, CarSB, Chambr 3, ChPo,
  ChPo S1, ChPo S2, CnDAL, ConAmA,
  ConAmL, LongC, ModAL, OhA&B,
  OxAm, REn, REnAL, TwCA,
  TwCA Sup, WNAA, YABC 1
Fisher, Dorothy Canfield see Canfield, Dorothy
Fisher, Dudley 1890-1951 ArtCS
Fisher, Ham 1901-1955 ArtCS
Fisher, Harvey Irvin 1916- AmMWS 12P,
  WWA 38
Fisher, John 1909- Au&Wr 6
Fisher, Laura Harrison 1934- ConAu 13R,
  ForWC 1970, SmATA 5
Fisher, Leonard Everett 1924- AuBYP,
  ConAu 1R, IlCB 1946, IlCB 1957,
  MorBMP, SmATA 4, ThBJA,
  WWAA 1973, WWE 14, WWWorJ 1972,
  WrD
Fisher, Lois Jeannette 1909- ConAu 5R
Fisher, M MnBBF
Fisher, Margery 1913- Au&Wr 6, AuBYP,
  ChPo, WWCL
Fisher, Murray MnBBF
Fisher, Thomas Henry WWBWI I
Fisher, Thomas Henry see Henry, Thomas
Fisher, W MnBBF
Fishman, Isidore 1908- Au&Wr 6
Fisk, Nicholas 1923- ConAu 65, IlBYP
Fison, Roger MnBBF
Fitch, Bob 1938- ConAu 21R
Fitch, Clarke AuBYP, ConAmA, ConAu XR,
  SmATA XR
Fitch, Clarke see Sinclair, Upton Beall
Fitch, Clyde 1865-1909 AmA, AmA&B,

CarSB, Chambr 3, CnDAL, CnMD,
CnThe, DcLEnL, DcNAA, McGWD,
ModAL, ModWD, OxAm, Pen Am,
REnAL, REnWD
Fitch, Florence Mary 1875-1959 AmA&B,
AuBYP, MorJA, OhA&B
Fitch, George Helgeson 1877-1915 AmA&B,
CarSB, DcNAA, REnAL
Fitch, John, IV SmATA XR
Fitch, John, IV see Cormier, Robert Edmund
Fitchett, William Henry MnBBF
Fitter, Richard Sidney Richmond 1913-
Au&Wr 6, ConAu 65, WW 1974
Fitts, James Franklin 1840-1890 AmA&B,
BiD&SB, CarSB, DcAmA, DcNAA
Fitzalan, Roger ConAu XR
Fitzalan, Roger see Trevor, Elleston
Fitzgerald, Cathleen 1932- ConAu 33
Fitzgerald, Charles Patrick 1902- Au&Wr 6,
WW 1974
Fitzgerald, Ed 1898- CurB 47
Fitzgerald, Edward Earl 1919- AmA&B,
AuBYP, WWA 38
Fitzgerald, Gerald MnBBF
Fitzgerald, Gerald see Green, Gerald B
Fitzgerald, Hugh, Captain ThBJA
Fitzgerald, Hugh, Captain see Baum, L Frank
Fitzgerald, John D 1907- ChLR 1
Fitzgibbon, Constantine 1919- AmA&B,
Au&Wr 6, IntWW 38, WW 1974,
WWWor 2, WorAu
Fitzhardinge, Joan Margaret 1912- Au&Wr 6,
AuBYP, ConAu 13R, SmATA 2, ThBJA
Fitzhardinge, Joan Margaret see Phipson, Joan
Fitzhugh, Louise 1928-1974 AuBYP, ChLR 1,
ConAu P-2, ConAu 53, SmATA 1,
ThBJA
Fitzpatrick, Sir James Percy 1862-1931 DcLEnL,
Pen Eng, WWCL
Fitzsimmons, Robert AuBYP
Fitzsimons, Ruth Marie AmMWS 12S,
ConAu 53, WWE 14
Flack, Marjorie 1897-1958 AmA&B, AmPB,
AuBYP, ChPo, IICB 1744, IICB 1946,
JBA 1934, JBA 1951, St&VC, YABC 2
Flammonde, Paris ConAu 17R
Flanders, Michael 1922-1975 Au&Wr 6,
AuBYP, BiEnAT, ChPo, ChPo S1,
ChPo S2, ConAu 5R, CurB 70,
IntWW 38
Flash Flood SmATA 6
Flanders, Michael 1922-1975 WW 1974,
WWT 15, WWWor 2
Flaxman, E MnBBF
Flaxman, E see Grey, Gordon
Flaxman, Traudl 1942- ConAu 25R
Flaxman, Traudl see Traudl
Flayderman, Phillip C 1930-1969 ConAu P-2
Fleet, Maxwell MnBBF
Fleischer, Max 1888- ArtCS, NYTBE 3
Fleischman, Albert Sidney 1920- AuBYP,
ConAu 1R
Fleischman, Albert Sidney see Fleischman, Sid
Fleischman, Sid AnCL, ChLR 1, ConAu XR,
SmATA 8, ThBJA
Fleischman, Sid see Fleischman, Albert Sidney
Fleischmann, Glen Harvey 1909- ConAu 33,
WWA 38, WWE 14, WWWor 2
Fleishman, Seymour 1918- IIBYP, IICB 1946,

IICB 1957
Fleming, Thomas J 1927- WWA 38
Fleissner, Else Mentz 1900- DrAS 6F
Fleming, Alice Carew Mulcahey 1928- AuBYP,
ConAu .1R, ForWC 1970, SmATA 9,
WWAW 8, WWE 14, WrD
Fleming, Elizabeth AuBYP, ChPo, ChPo S1,
ChPo S2, St&VC
Fleming, Ian 1908-1964 AuBYP, ConAu 5R,
ConLC 3, CurB 64, EncM&D, LongC,
NCHEL, Pen Eng, REn, SmATA 9,
SmATA 9, TwCW, WorAu
Fleming, Ian see Atticus
Fleming, Ronald MnBBF
Fleming, Thomas J 1927- AmA&B,
ConAu 5R, SmATA 8, WWWor 2
Fleming, Thomas J see Cain, Christopher
Fleming, Thomas J see James, T F
Fleming, Thomas J see Thomas, J F
Flender, Harold 1924- ConAu 49, DrAF 1976
Fletcher, Adele 1898- ConAu 17R
Fletcher, Alan Mark WrD
Fletcher, Andrew MnBBF
Fletcher, Beale AuBYP
Fletcher, Charles Seton MnBBF
Fletcher, Charlie May Hogue 1897- AuBYP,
ConAu 9R, SmATA 3
Fletcher, Charlie May Hogue see Simon, Charlie
May
Fletcher, Colin 1922- AuNews 1, ConAu 13R,
WWA 38
Fletcher, David ConAu XR
Fletcher, David see Barber, D F
Fletcher, Frank ArtCS, ChPo S2
Fletcher, Helen Jill 1911- AuBYP, ConAu 9R,
ForWC 1970, SmATA 13
Fletcher, Helen Jill see Lee, Carol
Fletcher, Helen Jill see Morey, Charles
Fletcher, Jane A SingR 1
Fletcher, John Gould 1886-1950 AmA&B,
AmLY, AnCL, CasWL, Chambr 3,
ChPo, CnDAL, ConAmA, ConAmL,
DcLEnL, EncWL, EvLB, LongC,
ModAL, OxAm, Pen Am, REn, REnAL,
SixAP, TwCA, TwCA Sup, WNAA
Fletcher, W CarSB, ChPo S1
Flettrich, Terry WWAW 8
Fleur, Anne IIBYP, IICB 1946
Fleur, Anne see Sari
Flexner, James Thomas 1908- AmA&B,
Au&Wr 6, ConAu 1R, SmATA 9,
WNAA, WWA 38, WWWA 1973,
WWE 14
Flint, Timothy 1780-1840 Alli, AmA,
AmA&B, BbD, BiD&SB, BiDSA,
CnDAL, CyAL 1, DcAmA, DcEnL,
DcLEnL, DcNAA, OhA&B, OxAm,
REnAL
Flintoff, Kit H MnBBF
Flitner, David Perkins, Jr. 1949- ConAu 45,
SmATA 7
Floethe, Louise Lee 1913- AuBYP, ConAu 1R,
ForWC 1970, SmATA 4
Floethe, Richard 1901- ChPo S2, ConAu 33,
IICB 1744, IICB 1946, IICB 1957,
MorJA, SmATA 4, WWAA 1973
Floherty, John Joseph 1882-1964 AmA&B,
AuBYP, JBA 1951
Flood, Flash see Robinson, Jan M

Flood, Paul *MnBBF*

Flora, James 1914- *ChFB A, ConAu 5R,
IIBYP, IICB 1946, IICB 1957, SmATA 1,
ThBJA*

Floren, Lee *ConAu 5R*

Floren, Lee *see* Nelson, Marguerite

Florence *IIBYP*

Florence *see* Wabbes, Maria

Flory, Jane Trescott 1917- *ConAu 9R*

Flory, Julia McCune 1882-1971 *ConAu P-2,
ConAu 29*

Flower, Desmond 1907- *ConAu 9R*

Flower, Sir Walter Newman 1897- *MnBBF*

Flowerdew, Herbert *MnBBF*

Flowerdew, Phyllis *WrD*

Floyd, Gareth *ChPo S1, IIBYP*

Floyd, Gilbert *MnBBF, WWBWI A*

Floyd, Gilbert *see* Grenfell, John

Floyd, Gilbert *see* Revel, Harry

Floyd, Gilbert *see* Shand, Captain

Floyd, Gilbert *see* Storm, Duncan

Flynn, Barbara 1928- *SmATA 9*

Flynn, Hamilton *MnBBF*

Flynn, Jackson *ConAu XR, SmATA XR*

Flynn, Jackson *see* Shirreffs, Gordon D

Flynn, James Joseph 1911- *ConAu 21R,
DrAS 6H, WWE 14*

Flynn, Robert 1932- *ConAu 29*

Fodor, Eugene 1905- *AmA&B, ConAu 21R,
WWA 38, WWWor 2*

Fodor, Ronald V 1944- *ConAu 65*

Foley, Bernice Williams 1902- *ConAu 29,
ForWC 1970*

Foley, Daniel Joseph 1913- *AuBYP,
ConAu 5R, WWE 14*

Foley, Louise Munro 1933- *ConAu 37, WrD*

Foley, Scott *ConAu 65*

Foley, Scott *see* Dareff, Hal

Folkard, Charles James 1878-1963 *ChPo,
ChPo S1, ConICB, IICB 1744,
WWBWI I, WWCL*

Follen, Eliza Lee 1787-1860 *Alli, AmA,
AmA&B, BiD&SB, ChPo, ChPo S1,
ChPo S2, DcAmA, DcNAA, FemPA,
St&VC*

Follett, Helen d1970 *AmA&B, AuBYP*

Follett, Robert John Richard 1928- *ConAu 21R,
WWA 38*

Folsom, Franklin 1907- *AuBYP, ConAu 1R,
SmATA 5*

Folsom, Franklin *see* Brewster, Benjamin

Folsom, Franklin *see* Cutler, Samuel

Folsom, Franklin *see* Gorham, Michael

Folsom, Franklin *see* Hopkins, Lyman

Folsom, Franklin *see* Nesbit, Troy

Folsom, Franklin Brewster *WrD*

Folsom, Michael Brewster 1938- *AuBYP*

FonEisen, Anthony T 1917- *ConAu 13R*

Fontana, Vincent James 1923- *AmMWS 12P,
ConAu 13R*

Fontane, Theodor 1819-1898 *BiD&SB, CasWL,
ChPo S2, ClDMEuL, CyWA, EuAu,
EvEuW, OxGer, Pen Eur, REn*

Fontenot, Mary Alice 1910- *ConAu 37,
ForWC 1970, WrD*

Foote, Darby Mozelle 1942- *ConAu 61*

Foote, Samuel 1720?-1777 *Alli, AnCL,
BiD&SB, BrAu, CasWL, Chambr 2,
ChPo, DcEnA, DcEnL, EvLB, McGWD,*

*MouLC 2, NCHEL, OxEng, Pen Eng,
REn, WEAL*

Forberg, Ati 1925- *AuBYP, ChPo, ChPo S1,
ChPo S2, IICB 1957*

Forbes, Athol *MnBBF*

Forbes, Athol *see* Phillips, Forbes A

Forbes, Bert *WWBWI I*

Forbes, Colin 1923- *Au&Wr 6*

Forbes, E Howard *MnBBF*

Forbes, Elliot 1917- *ConAu 9R, DrAS 6H,
WWA 38*

Forbes, Esther 1894?-1967 *AmA&B, AmNov,
AnCL, AuBYP, ChPo S2, ConAu 25R,
ConAu P-1, CyWA, DcLEnL, MorJA,
Newb 1922, OxAm, REn, REnAL,
SmATA 2, TwCA, TwCA Sup*

Forbes, Graham B *ConAu P-2*

Forbes, Graham B *see* Stratemeyer, Edward L

Forbes, Kathryn 1909-1966 *AmA&B, AmNov,
CurB 44, CurB 66, REn, REnAL*

Forbes, Kathryn *see* McLean, Kathryn

Forbus, Ina B *ConAu 1R, ForWC 1970*

Ford, Albert Lee *see* Stratemeyer, Edward L

Ford, Barry *see* Whitford, Joan

Ford, Elbur *EncM&D, WW 1974*

Ford, Elbur *see* Hibbert, Eleanor Burford

Ford, Ford Madox 1873-1939 *AtlBL, CasWL,
ChPo, ChPo S1, CnMWL, CyWA,
DcLEnL, EncWL, EvLB, LongC, ModBL,
ModBL Sup, NCHEL, OxEng, Pen Eng,
RAdv 1, REn, REnAL, TwCA,
TwCA Sup, TwCW, WEAL, WWTwL*

Ford, George *ChPo S2*

Ford, Hildegarde *ConAu XR*

Ford, Hildegarde *see* Morrison, Velma Ford

Ford, Lauren 1891- *AuBYP, IICB 1744,
IICB 1946*

Ford, Lee 1936- *ConAu 25R*

Ford, Marcia *ConAu XR, SmATA 6*

Ford, Marcia *see* Radford, Ruby Lorraine

Ford, Mary Forker 1905- *ConAu 9R,
ForWC 1970*

Ford, Nancy K *AuBYP*

Ford, Paul Leicester 1865-1902 *Alli Sup, AmA,
AmA&B, BbD, BiD&SB, CarSB,
Chambr 3, ChPo S1, CnDAL, DcAmA,
DcBiA, DcLEnL, DcNAA, EvLB,
JBA 1934, OxAm, REn, REnAL*

Ford, Quentin *MnBBF, WWBWI A*

Ford, Quentin *see* Pothecary, Raymond

Ford, T Murray 1854- *MnBBF*

Ford, T Murray *see* LeBreton, Thomas

Fordcliffe, W G *MnBBF*

Forde, R Asheton *MnBBF*

Forder, Walter *MnBBF*

Fordwych, Jack *MnBBF, WWBWI A*

Fordwych, Jack *see* Garrish, Harold J

Fordwych, John Edmund *MnBBF,
WWBWI A*

Fordwych, John Edmund *see* Garrish, Harold J

Foreman, Michael 1938- *ConAu 21R,
SmATA 2*

Forer, Lois Goldstein 1914- *ConAu 29,
WWA 38, WWAW 8, WWE 14*

Forest, Antonia *WrD*

Forester, Cecil Scott 1899-1966 *AmA&B,
ConAu 25R, CyWA, DcLEnL, EncM&D,
EvLB, LongC, MnBBF, ModBL,
NCHEL, RAdv 1, REn, REnAL,*

SmATA 13, TwCA, TwCA Sup, TwCW,
WEAL, WWCL
Forge, John MnBBF
Forge, John see Twyman, Harold William
Forman, Brenda 1936- Au&Wr 6, AuBYP,
ConAu 9R, ForWC 1970, SmATA 4
Forman, Harrison 1904- AmA&B, Au&Wr 6,
ConAu 5R, WWA 38, WWE 14,
WWWor 2
Forman, Leona S 1940- ConAu 25R
Forman, Werner OxCan Sup
Forrest, Geoffrey MnBBF
Forrest, George MnBBF
Forrest, R E WWBWI I
Forrest, Sybil AuBYP, ConAu XR
Forrest, Sybil see Markun, Patricia Maloney
Forrester, Charles Robert 1803-1850 CarSB,
NCHEL
Forrester, Edwin MnBBF, WWBWI A
Forrester, Frank H AuBYP
Forrester, Izola L 1878- AmA&B, CarSB
Forsee, Aylesa ConAu 1R, SmATA 1,
WWA 38, WWAW 8
Forsee, Aylesa WrD
Forsey, Peter Q MnBBF
Forsey, Peter Q see Garbutt, John L
Forsyth, Anne 1933- ConAu 29
Forsyth, Gloria AuBYP
Fortnum, Peggy 1919- ArtsCL, ChPo, IlBYP,
IlCB 1946, IlCB 1957
Fortune, Neil MnBBF
Fosdick, Charles Austin 1842-1915 Alli Sup,
AmA, AmA&B, BbD, BiD&SB, CarSB,
DcAmA, DcNAA, OxAm, REnAL
Fosdick, Harry Emerson 1878-1969 AmA&B,
AuBYP, ConAu 25R, CurB 40, CurB 69,
REnAL, TwCA Sup, WNAA
Foss, William O 1918- AuBYP, ConAu 17R
Foster, Alfred Edye Manning MnBBF,
WWLA
Foster, Celeste K MnnWr
Foster, Doris VanLiew 1899- ConAu 1R,
SmATA 10
Foster, Elizabeth 1905-1963 ConAu 1R,
SmATA 10
Foster, Elizabeth C 1902- ConAu 53,
SmATA 9
Foster, Elizabeth Vincent 1902- SmATA 12
Foster, Ernest 1852- Alli Sup, MnBBF,
WWBWI A
Foster, F Blanche 1919- BiDL 5, ConAu 61,
SmATA 11
Foster, Francis WWBWI A
Foster, Francis see Foster, Reginald F
Foster, G Allen 1907- ConAu 9R
Foster, Genevieve WrD
Foster, Genevieve 1893- AmA&B, AnCL,
Au&ICB, AuBYP, ConAu 5R,
IlCB 1946, IlCB 1957, JBA 1951,
MorBMP, SmATA 2
Foster, George Allen 1927- AuBYP
Foster, Grant MnBBF
Foster, Grant see Garrish, Harold J
Foster, Harold 1892- ArtCS
Foster, Joanna 1928- ChPo S1, ConAu 5R,
ForWC 1970
Foster, Joanna see Dougherty, Joanna Foster
Foster, John T 1925- ConAu 33, SmATA 8
Foster, Laura Louise 1918- ConAu 17R,

SmATA 6
Foster, Malcolm Burton 1931- Au&Wr 6,
CanWW 12, DrAS 6E, WrD
Foster, Marcia Lane 1897- IlCB 1744,
IlCB 1946
Foster, Marian Curtis 1909- AuBYP,
IlCB 1946, IlCB 1957, ThBJA
Foster, Marian Curtis see Mariana
Foster, Reginald F 1896- Au&Wr 6, MnBBF,
WW 1974, WWBWI A
Foster, Reginald F see Foster, Francis
Foster, Walter MnBBF
Foster VanLiew, Doris WrD
Fotheringham, E M MnBBF
Foulds, Elfrida Vipont 1902- ConAu 53, WrD
Foulds, Elfrida Vipont see Vipont, Charles
Foulds, Elfrida Vipont see Vipont, Elfrida
Fouque, Friedrich Heinrich K DeLaMotte
1777-1843 BbD, BiD&SB, CarSB, CasWL,
DcBiA, DcEuL, EuAu, EvEuW, HsB&A,
NCHEL, OxEng, OxGer, Pen Eur, REn,
WWCL
Fournier, Catharine 1908- WWA 38,
WWAW 8
Fowey, Roger MnBBF
Fowey, Roger see Edgar, Alfred
Fowke, Edith Margaret Fulton 1913-
CanWW 12, ChPo S1, ChPo S2,
ConAu 37, DrAS 6E, OxCan,
OxCan Sup, Prof, WrD
Fowler, Ethel Louise ChPo S1, ChPo S2
Fowler, H W 1858-1933 LongC, Pen Eng
Fowler, H W see Fowler, Henry Watson
Fowler, Helen SingR 1
Fowler, Henry Watson 1858-1933 DcLEnL,
EvLB, NCHEL, REn, TwCA,
TwCA Sup
Fowler, Henry Watson see Fowler, H W
Fowler, Mark 1949- ConAu 65
Fowler, Tom H MnBBF
Fowles, John 1926- Au&Wr 6, CelR 3,
ConAu 5R, ConLC 1, ConLC 2,
ConLC 3, ConLC 4, ConLC 6,
ConNov 1972, ConNov 1976, EncWL,
IntWW 38, ModBL Sup, NCHEL,
NYTBS 5, RAdv 1, TwCW, WEAL,
WWWor 2, WorAu
Fox, Aileen 1907- Au&Wr 6, ConAu 5R,
WrD
Fox, Charles MnBBF, WWBWI A
Fox, Charles Philip 1913- ConAu 1R,
SmATA 12
Fox, Dorothea Warren 1914- ConAu 61
Fox, Dorothy AuBYP
Fox, Eleanor ConAu XR, SmATA XR
Fox, Eleanor see Saint John, Wylly Folk
Fox, Fontaine 1884-1964 ArtCS
Fox, Franklin MnBBF
Fox, Freeman MnBBF, SmATA XR,
WWBWI A
Fox, Freeman see Hamilton, Charles Harold St.
John
Fox, Henry WWBWI I
Fox, John, Jr. 1863?-1919 AmA&B, BbD,
BiD&SB, BiDSA, CarSB, CnDAL,
ConAmL, DcAmA, DcBiA, DcLEnL,
DcNAA, EvLB, OxAm, REn, REnAL,
TwCA, TwCA Sup, TwCW
Fox, Lorraine SmATA 11

Fox, M W *WrD*
Fox, Mary Virginia 1919- *AuBYP, ConAu 29*
Fox, Mona Alexis 1915- *Au&Wr 6, WrD*
Fox, Norman A *MnBBF*
Fox, Paula 1923- *ChLR 1, ConLC 2, DrAF 1976, SenS, NewbC 1966, WWA 38, WrD*
Fox, Robert J 1927- *ConAu 45*
Fox, Sonny 1925- *ConAu 41*
Fox, William Wellington 1909- *AuBYP, ConAu 1R*
Foxwell, H S *WWBWI 1*
Foy, Peter *MnBBF*
Foy, Peter *see* Cook, Fred Gordon
Fozdar, Jamshed K 1926- *ConAu 49*
Frace, Charles *IlBYP*
Fradin, Dennis Brindell 1945- *ConAu 69*
Frahm, Anne B Schwerdt 1927- *ConAu 9R, WWAW 8*
Frame, Janet 1924- *CasWL, ConAu XR, ConLC 2, ConLC 3, ConLC 6, ConNov 1972, ConNov 1976, ConP 1975, IntWW 38, LongC, NCHEL, Pen Eng, RAdv 1, TwCW, WEAL, WorAu, WrD*
Frame, Janet *see* Clutha, Janet Paterson Frame
Frame, Paul 1913- *IlBYP, IlCB 1957*
Frampton, H F *MnBBF*
Frances, Miss 1908- *SmATA XR*
Frances, Miss *see* Horwich, Frances
Frances, Esteban 1915- *IlCB 1957*
Frances, S D *WWBWI A*
Frances, S D *see* Francis, Stephen D
Frances, S D *see* Janson, Hank
Francis, Saint 1182?-1226 *CarSB, NCHEL, Pen Eur*
Francis, Dee *ConAu XR*
Francis, Dee *see* Haas, Dorothy F
Francis, Dorothy Brenner 1926- *ConAu 21R, SmATA 10, WWAW 8, WrD*
Francis, Frank *ChPo S2*
Francis, Helen Dannefer 1915- *ConAu 13R, ForWC 1970, WrD*
Francis, Henry S 1925- *AuBYP*
Francis, Pamela 1926- *ConAu 29, SmATA 11, WrD*
Francis, Stephen D *MnBBF*
Francis, Stephen D *see* Frances, S D
Francis, Stephen D *see* Williams, Richard
Francis, T M *MnBBF*
Franco, Jean 1924- *ConAu 21R, DrAS 6F*
Franco, Johan 1908- *WWA 38, WWMus 6, WWS 13*
Francois, Andre 1915- *AmPB, Au&Wr 6, ChFB I, IlBYP, IlCB 1946, IlCB 1957, ThBJA, WWGA*
Francoise 1900?-1961 *AmPB, AnCL, IlBYP, IlCB 1946, IlCB 1957, MorJA*
Francoise *see* Seignobosc, Francoise
Frandsen, Maude Linstrom 1908- *WWAW 8, WrD*
Franes, S O *MnBBF*
Frank, Anne 1929-1944 *REn, TwCW*
Frank, Janet *ConAu 57*
Frank, Janet *see* Dunleavy, Janet Egleson
Frank, Josette 1893- *AuBYP, ChPo, ChPo S2, ConAu P-1, SmATA 10*
Frank, Mary 1933- *DcCAA 2, WWAA 1973*
Frank, Pat 1907-1964 *AmNov, ConAu 5R*

Frankau, Mary Evelyn Atkinson 1899- *ConAu P-1, SmATA 4*
Frankau, Mary Evelyn Atkinson *see* Atkinson, M E
Frankel, Bernice *ConAu 61, SmATA 9*
Frankel, Edward 1910- *AuBYP, LE 5*
Frankenberg, Lloyd 1907-1975 *AmA&B, ChPo S1, ConAu 1R, REnAL, TwCA Sup, WWA 38*
Frankenberg, Robert Clinton 1911- *IlBYP, IlCB 1946, IlCB 1957*
Frankenstein, Alfred 1906- *WWA 38, WWW 14, WWWor 2*
Franklin, Benjamin 1706-1790 *Alli, AmA, AmA&B, AmWr, AtlBL, BbD, BiD&SB, CasWL, ChPo, ChPo S1, ChPo S2, CnDAL, CriT 3, CyAL 1, CyWA, DcAmA, DcEnL, DcLEnL, DcNAA, EvLB, MouLC 2, NCHEL, OxAm, OxEng, Pen Am, RCom, REn, REnAL, WEAL*
Franklin, George Cory 1872- *MorJA*
Franklin, Harold 1920- *ConAu 29, SmATA 13*
Franklin, Harold L 1934- *ConAu 57*
Franklin, Harold L *see* Alimayo, Chikuyo
Franklin, Josephine *CarSB*
Franklin, Max *ConAu XR*
Franklin, Max *see* Deming, Richard
Franklin, Steve *ConAu XR, SmATA 6*
Franklin, Steve *see* Stevens, Franklin
Franzen, Nils-Olof 1916- *ConAu 29, SmATA 10*
Frascino, Edward *IlBYP*
Frasconi, Antonio 1919- *AmA&B, AmPB, AnCL, AuBYP, ChFB I, ConAu 1R, CurB 72, DcCAA 2, IlCB 1946, IlCB 1957, SmATA 6, ThBJA, WWA 38, WWAA 1973, WWE 14, WWGA, WWWor 2*
Fraser, Antonia 1932- *CurB 74, IntWW 38, WW 1974, WWAW 8, WWWor 2, WrD*
Fraser, Arvonne S 1925- *ConAu 33*
Fraser, Beatrice *AuBYP*
Fraser, Betty M 1928- *ChPo S1, IlBYP, IlCB 1957*
Fraser, Claude Lovat 1890-1921 *ChPo, ChPo S1, ChPo S2, JBA 1951*
Fraser, Conon 1930- *Au&Wr 6, ConAu P-1, WrD*
Fraser, Edith Emily Rose Oram 1903- *Au&Wr 6, ConAu P-1*
Fraser, Ella J *MnBBF*
Fraser, Eric 1902- *IlCB 1946*
Fraser, Ferrin *AuBYP*
Fraser, Kathleen 1937- *ConP 1970, DrAP 1975*
Fraser, W A *MnBBF*
Fraser Darling, Frank 1903- *Au&Wr 6, ConAu 61, IntWW 38, WW 1974*
Frazar, Douglas 1836-1896 *Alli Sup, CarSB, DcAmA, DcNAA*
Frazer, Allison *WWBWI A*
Frazer, Allison *see* Rochester, George Ernest
Frazer, Andrew *AuBYP, ConAu XR*
Frazer, Andrew *see* Lesser, Milton
Frazer, Sir James George 1854-1941 *Alli Sup, AtlBL, CasWL, Chambr 3, DcEnA Ap, DcLEnL, EvLB, LongC, NCHEL,*

OxEng, Pen Eng, REn, TwCA,
TwCA Sup, WEAL
Frazer, Martin MnBBF, WWBWI A
Frazer, Martin see Clarke, Percy A
Frazer, R H MnBBF
Frazer, R M MnBBF
Frazier, Claude A 1920- ConAu 29
Frazier, Neta Lohnes 1890- AuBYP,
ConAu 1R, ForWC 1970, SmATA 7,
WWPNA, WrD
Frazier, Walt 1945- CelR 3, CurB 73,
NYTBE 3, NYTBS 5, WWA 38
Freas, Lenwood IlBYP
Frederick, J George MnBBF
Frederick, John MnBBF
Frederick, John see Faust, Frederick
Fredericks, Arnold AmA&B, AuBYP,
DcNAA
Fredericks, Arnold see Kummer, Frederic Arnold
Fredericks, Fred 1929- ArtCS
Freed, Alvyn M 1913- AmMWS 12S,
ConAu 61
Freed, Stanley Arthur 1927- AmMWS 12S,
WWA 38
Freedgood, Lillian 1911- ConAu 13R
Freedman, Barnett 1901- IlCB 1744,
IlCB 1946
Freedman, Benedict 1919- AmA&B, AmNov,
ConAu 69, CurB 47, WWA 38
Freedman, Florence Bernstein 1908- ChPo S2,
LE 5
Freedman, Harold 1915- SingR 1
Freedman, Nancy 1920- AmA&B, AmNov,
ConAu 45, CurB 47
Freedman, Russell 1929- AuBYP, ConAu 17R
Freehof, Solomon B 1892- WWWorJ 1972
Freeman, Alfred S MnBBF
Freeman, Barbara Constance 1906- Au&Wr 6,
WrD
Freeman, Don 1908- AmPB, AuBYP, BkP,
IlCB 1946, IlCB 1957, MorJA
Freeman, Miss E MnBBF
Freeman, Miss E see Freeman, Jack
Freeman, Eugene 1906- AuBYP, ConAu 41,
DrAS 6P
Freeman, Gillian 1929- Au&Wr 6, ConAu 5R,
ConNov 1972, ConNov 1976, WrD
Freeman, Godfrey AuBYP
Freeman, Ira Maximilian 1905- AmA&B,
AmMWS 12P, AuBYP, MorJA
Freeman, Jack MnBBF
Freeman, Jack see Freeman, Miss E
Freeman, Jean Todd 1929- ConAu 25R
Freeman, Mrs. John MnBBF
Freeman, Mrs. John see Haynes, Nancy M
Freeman, John Henry Gordon 1903- MnBBF
Freeman, Lewis Ransome 1878- MnBBF
Freeman, Lucy 1916- AmA&B, ConAu 5R,
CurB 53, ForWC 1970, WWA 38,
WWAW 8, WWWorJ 1972
Freeman, Lydia 1907- MorJA
Freeman, Mae Blacker 1907- MorJA
Freeman, Margaret 1893- ChPo, ConICB,
IlCB 1744
Freeman, Mary E Wilkins 1852-1930 AmA&B,
AmLY, CarSB, CasWL, ChPo, ChPo S1,
ChPo S2, CnDAL, ConAmL, DcAmA,
DcEnA Ap, DcLEnL, DcNAA, LongC,
OxAm, OxEng, Pen Am, REn, REnAL,

TwCA
Freeman, Serge Herbert AuBYP
Freeman, Terence Reginald 1909- IlCB 1946
Freeman, William MnBBF
Fregosi, Claudia 1946- ConAu 69
Freidel, Frank 1916- ConAu 1R, DrAS 6H
Fremantle, Anne 1910- AmA&B, BkC 5,
CatA 1952, ConAu 13R, LongC, REnAL,
TwCA Sup
Fremlin, Victor MnBBF, WWBWI A
Fremlin, Victor see Philips, George Norman
French, Alice 1850-1934 Alli Sup, AmA,
AmA&B, AmLY, BbD, BiD&SB,
BiDSA, CarSB, DcAmA, DcNAA,
LongC, OxAm, REn, REnAL
French, Allen 1870-1946 AmA&B, CarSB,
ChPo, DcAmA, JBA 1934, JBA 1951,
MnBBF, REnAL, YABC 1
French, Dorothy Kayser 1926- AuBYP,
ConAu 9R, ForWC 1970, SmATA 5
French, Fiona 1944- ConAu 29, SmATA 6
French, Kathryn ConAu XR
French, Kathryn see Mosesson, Gloria R
French, Marion Flood 1920- AuBYP,
ConAu 33, ForWC 1970
French, Paul AmA&B, AuBYP, ConAu XR,
LongC, SmATA 1, ThBJA
French, Paul see Asimov, Isaac
Freschet, Berniece 1927- ConAu 17R
Frese, Dolores Warwick 1936- ConAu 5R
Frese, Dolores Warwick see Warwick, Dolores
Freuchen, Peter 1886-1957 AuBYP, Pen Eur,
TwCA, TwCA Sup
Freund, Rudolf 1915- IlBYP, IlCB 1744,
IlCB 1946
Frewer, Glyn 1931- Au&Wr 6, AuBYP,
ConAu 13R, SmATA 11, WrD
Frey, Shaney AuBYP
Fribourg, Marjorie G 1920- AuBYP,
ConAu 1R
Frick, C H ConAu XR, SmATA 6
Frick, C H see Irwin, Constance Frick
Frick, Constance ConAu XR, SmATA 6
Frick, Constance see Irwin, Constance Frick
Fried, John J 1940- ConAu 33
Friedland, Ronald Lloyd 1937-1975 ConAu 57,
ConAu P-2
Friedland, Ronald Lloyd see Lloyd, Ronald
Friedlander, Joanne K 1930- ConAu 61,
SmATA 9
Friedman, Estelle Ehrenwald 1920- AuBYP,
ForWC 1970, ConAu 5R, SmATA 7
Friedman, Eve Rosemary Tibber 1929-
ConAu 5R
Friedman, Eve Rosemary Tibber see Tibber,
Robert
Friedman, Frieda 1905- MorJA
Friedman, Ina R 1926- ConAu 53
Friedman, Judi 1925- AuNews 2, ConAu 65
Friedrich, Otto 1929- AmPB, ConAu 5R
Friedrich, Priscilla AmPB
Friend, Patrick MnBBF
Friendlich, Dick AuBYP, ConAu XR,
SmATA XR
Friendlich, Dick see Friendlich, Richard J
Friendlich, Richard J 1909- ConAu P-1,
SmATA 11
Friendlich, Richard J see Friendlich, Dick
Friermood, Elisabeth Hamilton 1903- AuBYP,

ConAu 1R, ForWC 1970, IndAu 1917,
MorJA, SmATA 5, WrD
Friers, Rowel Boyd 1920- IICB 1946
Friis, Babbis ConAu XR, SmATA 7, ThBJA
Friis, Babbis see Friis-Baastad, Babbis Ellinor
Friis-Baastad, Babbis Ellinor 1921-1970
ConAu 17R, SmATA 7, ThBJA
Friis-Baastad, Babbis Ellinor see Baastad, Babbis
Friis
Friis-Baastad, Babbis Ellinor see Babbis, Eleanor
Friis-Baastad, Babbis Ellinor see Friis, Babbis
Frimmer, Steven 1928- ConAu 33
Frisbee, Lucy Post AuBYP
Frisch, Otto Robert 1904- AuBYP, ConAu 9R,
IntWW 38, WW 1974, WWWor 2
Friskey, Margaret Richards 1901- AuBYP,
ConAu 5R, ForWC 1970, SmATA 5
Friskey, Margaret Richards see Sherman,
Elizabeth
Friston, D H WWBWI 1
Frith, Henry 1840- Alli Sup, CarSB,
ChPo S1, MnBBF
Frith, Michael IIBYP
Fritz, Jean Guttery 1915- AuBYP, ChLR 2,
ChPo S2, ConAu 1R, ForWC 1970,
MorBMP, SmATA 1, ThBJA
Froboess, Harry 1899- ConAu 17R
Froissart, Sir John 1337?-1410? WWCL
Froman, Elizabeth Hull 1920-1975 ConAu 53,
ConAu P-1, SmATA 10
Froman, Robert 1917- AuBYP, ConAu 1R,
SmATA 8
Fromm, Lilo IIBYP
Frost, Arthur Burdett 1851-1928 AmA&B,
AmPB, ChPo, ChPo S1, ChPo S2,
DcAmA, DcNAA, OxAm, REnAL,
St&VC
Frost, C Vernon EncM&D, MnBBF,
WWBWI A
Frost, Conrad MnBBF
Frost, Erica ConAu XR
Frost, Erica see Supraner, Robyn
Frost, Frances Mary 1905-1959 AmA&B,
AmNov, BkCL, ChPo, ChPo S1,
ChPo S2, CurB 50, CurB 59, MorJA,
REnAL, St&VC, WNAA
Frost, Lesley ConAu 21R
Frost, Robert 1874?-1963 AmA&B, AmLY,
AmWr, AnCL, AtlBL, CasWL,
Chambr 3, ChPo, ChPo S1, ChPo S2,
CnDAL, CnE&AP, CnMWL, ConAmA,
ConAmL, ConLC 1, ConLC 3, ConLC 4,
CurB 42, CurB 63, CyWA, DcLEnL,
EncWL, EvLB, FamPYP, LongC,
ModAL, ModAL Sup, NYTBE 3,
NYTBS 5, OxAm, OxEng, Pen Am,
RAdv 1, RCom, REn, REnAL, SixAP,
St&VC, TwCA, TwCA Sup, TwCW,
WEAL, WNAA, WWTwL
Frost, Thomas 1821-1908 Alli Sup, CarSB,
MnBBF
Frost, William Henry 1863-1904? CarSB,
DcNAA
Fry, Charles Burgess 1872-1956 MnBBF,
WWBWI A
Fry, Christopher 1907- Au&Wr 6, AuBYP,
BiEnAT, CasWL, CnMD, CnMWL,
CnThe, ConAu 17R, ConDr 1, ConLC 2,
ConP 1970, ConP 1975, CrCD, CurB 51,

CyWA, DcLEnL, EncWL, EvLB,
IntWW 38, LongC, McGWD, ModBL,
ModBL Sup, ModWD, NCHEL, OxEng,
Pen Eng, REn, TwCA Sup, TwCW,
WEAL, WW 1974, WWT 15,
WWWor 2
Fry, Guy 1903- ChPo, WWA 38
Fry, Reginald C MnBBF
Fry, Rosalie Kingsmill 1911- Au&Wr 6,
AuBYP, ChPo S1, ConAu 9R,
IICB 1946, IICB 1957, SmATA 3,
ThBJA, WrD
Fryars, Austin 1865- MnBBF
Fryars, Austin see Waters, Eddie
Fryatt, Norma R AuBYP, ConAu 57
Frye, Dean AuBYP
Frye, John 1910- ConAu 49
Fryer, Judith 1939- ConAu 69
Fuchs, Erich 1916- ConAu 29, SmATA 6
Fufuka, Karama ConAu XR
Fufuka, Karama see Morgan, Sharon A
Fujikawa, Gyo IIBYP, IICB 1957
Fujita, Tamao 1905- ConAu 37, SmATA 7
Fulke, Commissioner MnBBF
Fulke, Commissioner see Lomax, W J
Fullarton, Nan SingR 1
Fuller, Alice Cook AuBYP
Fuller, Anna 1853-1916 BiD&SB, CarSB,
DcAmA, DcNAA
Fuller, Catherine Leuthold 1916- ConAu 29,
SmATA 9
Fuller, Edmund 1914- AmA&B, AuBYP,
ChPo S1, ConNov 1972, ConNov 1976,
DrAS 6E, WorAu
Fuller, Iola 1906- AmNov, ConAu XR,
ForWC 1970, REnAL, SmATA 3
Fuller, Iola see McCoy, Iola Fuller
Fuller, Lois Hamilton 1915- ConAu 1R,
SmATA 11
Fuller, Miriam Morris 1933- BiDL 5,
ConAu 37
Fuller, R B 1890-1963 ArtCS
Fuller, Raymond Tifft 1889- AuBYP
Fuller, Roy Broadbent 1912- Au&Wr 6,
CasWL, ChPo S1, ChPo S2, CnE&AP,
ConAu 5R, ConLC 4, ConNov 1972,
ConNov 1976, ConP 1970, ConP 1975,
IntWW 38, LongC, ModBL, ModBL Sup,
NCHEL, Pen Eng, RAdv 1, REn,
TwCA Sup, TwCW, WEAL, WW 1974,
WWCL, WWTwL, WWWor 2, WrD
Fullerton, Hubert MnBBF
Fults, John Lee 1932- ConAu 53
Funai, Mamoru R 1932- ChPo S1, IICB 1957
Funderburk, Thomas R 1928- ConAu 17R,
IndAu 1917
Fung, Paul 1897-1944 ArtCS
Funk, Thompson 1911- ConAu 49, SmATA 7
Funk, Thompson see Funk, Tom
Funk, Tom ConAu XR, IIBYP, SmATA 7
Funk, Tom see Funk, Thompson
Funke, Lewis 1912- AmA&B, BiEnAT,
ConAu 49, SmATA 11, WWA 38,
WWE 14
Furer, Howard B 1934- ConAu 33, DrAS 6H
Furlong, Monica 1930- Au&Wr 6
Furnas, Clifford Cook 1900-1969 AmA&B,
Au&Wr 6, CurB 56, CurB 69,
IndAu 1917

Furneaux, Rupert 1908- *ConAu 1R*
Furness, Edna L 1906- *ConAu 37, DrAS 6E,
ForWC 1970*
Furniss, Harry 1854-1925 *ChPo, ChPo S1,
ChPo S2, WWCL*
Furniss, L M *MnBBF*
Furrer, Juerg 1939- *ConAu 69*
Furukawa, Toshi 1924- *ConAu 45*
Furukawa, Toshi *see* Kanzawa, Toshiko
Furze, Barton *MnBBF, WWBWI A*
Furze, Barton *see* Rochester, George Ernest
Fyleman, Rose 1877-1957 *AnCL, BkCL, ChPo,
ChPo S1, ChPo S2, EvLB, JBA 1934,
JBA 1951, LongC, St&VC, TwCA,
TwCA Sup, WWCL, WWLA*
Fyson, J G 1904- *ConAu P-2*

G

Gabel, Margaret 1938- *BiDL 5, ConAu 33*
Gaboriall, Emile 1833-1873 *MnBBF*
Gabriel, John *MnBBF*
Gabriel, John *see* Rowe, John Gabriel
Gabriel, Juri *WrD*
Gabrielson, Ira N 1889- *AmMWS 12P*
Gabrielson, Ira Noel 1889- *WWA 38,*
WWWor 2
Gaddis, Vincent H 1913- *ConAu 13R*
Gadson, W H *MnBBF*
Gaeddert, Lou Ann *BkP*
Gaer, Joseph 1897- *AmA&B, AuBYP,*
ConAu 9R, CurB 51, MorJA, WWA 38,
WWWorJ 1972
Gaer, Joseph *see* Gaer, Yossef
Gaer, Yossef *ConAu XR*
Gaer, Yossef *see* Gaer, Joseph
Gag, Flavia 1907- *AuBYP, ConAu 5R,*
IlCB 1744, IlCB 1946, MnnWr, MorJA
Gag, Wanda 1893-1946 *AmA&B, AmPB,*
AnCL, AuBYP, ChPo S2, ConICB,
CurB 46, DcNAA, FamAI, IlCB 1744,
JBA 1934, JBA 1951, REnAL, TwCA,
TwCA Sup, YABC 1
Gage, Wilson *AuBYP, ConAu XR,*
SmATA 3, ThBJA
Gage, Wilson *see* Steele, Mary Quintard Govan
Gagliardo, Ruth *AuBYP*
Gaines, Charles Kelsey 1854-1944? *AmA&B,*
DcNAA, WNAA
Gaines, Ernest J 1933- *AuNews 1, BlkAW,*
ConAu 9R, ConLC 3, ConNov 1972,
ConNov 1976, DrAF 1976, LBAA,
WWA 38
Galantiere, Lewis 1895- *AmA&B, WWA 38*
Galbraith, Jean *ConAu 37, WrD*
Galbraith, John Kenneth 1908- *AmA&B,*
AmMWS 12S, CanWW 12, CelR 3,
ConAu 21R, CurB 59, LongC, NYTBE 4,
REnAL, WW 1974, WorAu
Galdone, Paul 1914- *AuBYP, BkP, ChPo,*
ChPo S1, ChPo S2, IlCB 1946,
IlCB 1957, ThBJA
Gale, Alan *MnBBF*
Gale, Alan *see* Sempill, Ernest
Gale, H Winter *MnBBF*
Gale, H Winter *see* Maitland, T G Dowling
Gale, John *MnBBF*
Gale, John *see* Openshaw, G H
Galinsky, Ellen 1942- *ConAu 65*
Gall, Alice Crew 1878-1949 *AmA&B, AuBYP,*
JBA 1951, OhA&B

Gall, Morris 1907- *ConAu 45, DrAS 6H*
Gallant, Roy Arthur 1924- *AuBYP,*
ConAu 5R, SmATA 4, WrD
Gallico, Paul 1897-1976 *AmA&B, AmNov,*
Au&Wr 6, AuNews 1, ConAu 5R,
ConLC 2, ConNov 1972, ConNov 1976,
CurB 46, DcLEnL, EvLB, REnAL,
SmATA 13, TwCA Sup, TwCW, WrD
Gallu, Samuel *AuNews 2*
Galoway, Trevor *MnBBF*
Galster, Robert Miller 1928- *IlBYP,*
IlCB 1957
Galsworthy, John 1867-1933 *AtlBL, CasWL,*
Chambr 3, ChPo, ChPo S1, ChPo S2,
CnMD, CnMWL, CnThe, CyWA, DcBiA,
DcLEnL, EncWL, EvLB, LongC,
McGWD, ModBL, ModBL Sup, ModWD,
NCHEL, OxEng, Pen Eng, RAdv 1,
RCom, REn, REnWD, TwCA,
TwCA Sup, TwCW, WEAL, WWLA,
WWTwL
Galt, Thomas Franklin, Jr. 1908- *ConAu 5R,*
SmATA 5
Galt, Thomas Franklin, Jr. *see* Galt, Tom
Galt, Tom *ConAu XR, MorJA, SmATA 5*
Galt, Tom *see* Galt, Thomas Franklin, Jr.
Gammage, Allen Z 1917- *AmMWS 12S,*
ConAu 5R
Gammon, D J *MnBBF*
Gammon, D J *see* Robins, Fenton
Gamoran, Mamie Goldsmith 1900-
ForWC 1970, WWAW 8
Gamow, George 1904-1968 *AmA&B, CurB 51,*
CurB 68, REnAL, TwCA Sup
Gann, Ernest Kellogg 1910- *AmA&B, AmNov,*
AuNews 1, ConAu 1R, TwCW,
WWA 38, WWPNA, WWW 14, WorAu
Gannett, Ruth Chrisman Arens 1896-
IlCB 1946, MorJA
Gannett, Ruth Stiles 1923- *AuBYP, BkCL,*
ConAu 21R, SmATA 3
Gannon, E J *MnBBF, WWBWI A*
Gannon, E J *see* Daring, Victor
Gannon, E J *see* Kent, Beverley
Gannon, Robert Haines 1931- *ConAu 9R,*
SmATA 8
Ganpat *MnBBF*
Ganpat *see* Gompertz, M L G
Gans, Carl 1923- *AmMWS 12P*
Gant, Jonathan *ConAu XR*
Gant, Jonathan *see* Adams, Clifton
Gantos, Jack *ConAu 65*

Gantos, Jack *see* Gantos, John, Jr.
Gantos, John, Jr. 1951- *ConAu 65*
Gantos, John, Jr. *see* Gantos, Jack
Garagiola, Joe 1926- *BiN 1974, CelR 3, WWA 38, WWE 14*
Garbutt, Bernard 1900- *IlCB 1946*
Garbutt, John *WWBWI A*
Garbutt, John L *MnBBF*
Garbutt, John L *see* Brearley, John
Garbutt, John L *see* Cameron, Clifford
Garbutt, John L *see* Forsey, Peter Q
Garbutt, John L *see* Templar, John
Gard, Joyce 1911- *Au&Wr 6, AuBYP, BrCA*
Gard, Robert Edward 1910- *AuBYP, BiEnAT, OxCan, WWA 38*
Gardam, Jane 1928- *ConAu 49*
Garden, Nancy 1938- *ConAu 33, SmATA 12, WrD*
Garden, Robert Hal 1937- *ConAu 69*
Gardner, Dic *AuBYP, ConAu XR*
Gardner, Erle Stanley 1889-1970 *AmA&B, ConAu 5R, ConAu 25R, CurB 44, CurB 70, EncM&D, EvLB, LongC, MnBBF, NYTBE 1, OxAm, Pen Am, REn, REnAL, TwCA, TwCA Sup, TwCW, WNAA*
Gardner, Gerald 1929- *ConAu 1R*
Gardner, Horace John 1896- *WNAA*
Gardner, Jeanne LeMonnier 1925- *ConAu 17R, ForWC 1970, SmATA 5*
Gardner, Jeanne LeMonnier 1925- *WWAW 8*
Gardner, John Champlin, Jr. 1933- *ConAu 65, WWA 38*
Gardner, Joseph L 1933- *ConAu 29*
Gardner, Lillian Soskin 1907- *AuBYP*
Gardner, Martin 1914- *AmA&B, ChPo, ChPo S1, ChPo S2, WWE 14*
Gardner, Richard 1931- *AmA&B, ConAu 21R, WrD*
Gardner, Richard Alan 1931- *ConAu 33, SmATA 13, WWA 38, WrD*
Gardonyi, Geza 1863-1922 *CasWL, CIDMEuL, Pen Eur*
Garelick, May 1910- *AuBYP, BkP*
Garfield, Brian Wynne 1939- *ConAu 1R*
Garfield, Brian Wynne *see* O'Brian, Frank
Garfield, James B 1881- *SmATA 6*
Garfield, Leon 1921- *Au&Wr 6, ConAu 17R, PiP, SenS, SmATA 1, WWCL, WrD*
Garfinkel, Bernard 1929- *ConAu 25R*
Garfinkel, Bernard *see* Allen, Robert
Garfinkel, Bernard *see* Elliott, Robert
Garfinkel, Bernard *see* Martin, Janet
Garis, Howard Roger 1873-1962 *AmA&B, CarSB, REnAL, SmATA 13*
Garis, Howard Roger *see* Davidson, Marion
Garis, Lillian C 1873-1954 *CarSB, OhA&B*
Garland, Hamlin 1860-1940 *AmA&B, AmLY, AtlBL, BbD, BiD&SB, BiDPar, CasWL, Chambr 3, ChPo, CnDAL, ConAmA, ConAmL, CurB 40, CyWA, DcAmA, DcBiA, DcLEnL, DcNAA, EvLB, LongC, ModAL, OxAm, OxCan, OxEng, Pen Am, RAdv 1, REn, REnAL, St&VC, TwCA, TwCA Sup, WEAL, WNAA, WisW*
Garland, Rosemary *Au&Wr 6*
Garner, Alan 1935- *Au&Wr 6, BrCA, CasWL, ChPo S1, PiP, SenS, TelT,*

ThBJA, WWCL, WrD
Garner, Claud Wilton 1891- *ConAu 9R*
Garner, Elvira 1895- *IlCB 1744*
Garnett, Eve C R *Au&Wr 6, AuBYP, ConAu 1R, IlCB 1744, IlCB 1946, SmATA 3, WWCL, WrD*
Garnett, Henry 1905- *Au&Wr 6*
Garnett, Peter *MnBBF*
Garnett, Richard Duncan Carey 1923- *ConAu 5R, WrD*
Garratt, J Hilary *MnBBF*
Garraty, John Arthur 1920- *ConAu 1R, DrAS 6H, WWA 38, WWWor 2*
Garret, Maxwell R 1917- *WWWorJ 1972*
Garrett, Helen 1895- *AuBYP*
Garrett, Randall *ThBJA*
Garrick, John *MnBBF*
Garrigue, Sheila 1931- *ConAu 69*
Garrish, George *WWBWI A*
Garrish, George *see* Garrish, Henry J
Garrish, Harold J d1956 *MnBBF*
Garrish, Harold J *see* Belbin, Harry
Garrish, Harold J *see* Everard, Walter
Garrish, Harold J *see* Fordwych, Jack
Garrish, Harold J *see* Fordwych, John Edmund
Garrish, Harold J *see* Foster, Grant
Garrish, Harold J *see* Garrish, Henry J
Garrish, Harold J *see* Gerrish, George
Garrish, Harold J *see* Morrell, Wallace
Garrish, Henry J d1956 *WWBWI A*
Garrish, Henry J *see* Darrell, Walter
Garrish, Henry J *see* Garrish, George
Garrish, Henry J *see* Garrish, Harold J
Garrison, Christian 1942- *ConAu 65*
Garrison, Frederick *AuBYP, ConAmA, ConAu XR, SmATA XR*
Garrison, Frederick *see* Sinclair, Upton Beall
Garrison, Theodosia Pickering 1874-1944 *AmA&B, ChPo, ChPo S2, ConAmL, DcNAA, REnAL, St&VC*
Garrison, Webb B 1919- *ConAu 1R*
Garrison, Webb B *see* Webster, Gary
Garson, Eugenia *ChPo S1*
Garst, Doris Shannon 1894?- *ConAu 1R, ForWC 1970, SmATA 1*
Garst, Doris Shannon *see* Garst, Shannon
Garst, Shannon *AuBYP, ConAu XR, CurB 47, JBA 1951, SmATA 1*
Garst, Shannon *see* Garst, Doris Shannon
Garstin, A *MnBBF*
Garten, Jan *AuBYP*
Garthwaite, Marion Hook 1893- *AuBYP, ConAu 5R, SmATA 7*
Garthwaite, Wymond Bradbury 1895- *ChPo, ConICB*
Gartland, Robert Aldrich 1927- *ConAu 17R*
Gartman, Louise 1920- *ConAu 17R*
Gasbarri, Bodolpho *WWBWI 1*
Gascoigne, Eric *MnBBF*
Gascoigne, Eric *see* Mowbray, W J
Gask, Lillian *CarSB*
Gaskell, Thomas F 1916- *ConAu 17R*
Gaskin, Catherine 1929- *AmA&B, Au&Wr 6, ConAu 65, TwCW, WW 1974*
Gass, Irene *AuBYP*
Gaster, Theodor Herzl 1906- *DrAS 6P, WWA 38, WWWor 2, WWWorJ 1972*
Gatcombe, George *WWBWI 1*
Gatenby, Rosemary 1918- *ConAu 21R*

Gates, Clifford *MnBBF, WWBWl A*
Gates, Doris 1901- *AnCL, Au&ICB, AuBYP,
ConAu 1R, JBA 1951, SmATA 1*
Gates, Eleanor 1875-1951 *AmA&B, CarSB,
REnAL, WNAA*
Gathorne-Hardy, Jonathan G 1933- *Au&Wr 6,
WrD*
Gatti, Attilio 1896- *AmA&B, AuBYP,
JBA 1951*
Gatti, Ellen Morgan *AuBYP*
Gatty, Horatia Katherine Frances 1846-
*Alli Sup, CarSB, ChPo,
ChPo S1*
Gatty, Margaret Scott 1809-1873 *Alli Sup,
BiD&SB, CarSB, ChPo, ChPo S1,
ChPo S2, DcEnA, DcEnL, DcEuL,
DcLEnL, EvLB, NCHEL, TelT, WWCL
WWCL*
Gauch, Patricia Lee 1934- *ConAu 57*
Gaul, Albro T *AuBYP*
Gaulden, Ray 1914- *ConAu 17R*
Gault, Frank 1926- *ConAu 69*
Gault, William Campbell 1910- *AuBYP,
ConAu 49, EncM&D, SmATA 8*
Gaunt, Hardy *MnBBF*
Gaunt, Jeffrey *MnBBF*
Gaunt, Jeffrey see Rochester, George Ernest
Gaunt, M B *MnBBF*
Gaunt, Michael *ConAu 65*
Gaunt, Michael see Robertshaw, Denis
Gaunt Wolf *MnBBF*
Gavin, Wilfred *MnBBF*
Gay, John 1685?-1732 *Alli, AtlBL, BiD&SB,
BrAu, CarSB, CasWL, Chambr 2, ChPo,
ChPo S1, ChPo S2, CnE&AP, CnThe,
CriT 2, CyWA, DcEnA, DcEnA Ap,
DcEnL, DcEuL, DcLEnL, EvLB,
McGWD, MouLC 2, NCHEL, OxEng,
Pen Eng, REn, REnWD, WEAL*
Gay, Kathlyn Ruth McGarrahan 1930-
ConAu 21R, SmATA 9
Gay, Kathlyn Ruth McGarrahan *WWAW 8*
Gay, Kathlyn Ruth McGarrahan 1930- *WrD*
Gay, Peter 1923- *AmA&B, ConAu 13R,
DrAS 6H, WWA 38, WWE 14,
WWWor 2*
Gay, Zhenya 1906- *AuBYP, BkCL, ChPo,
ChPo S2, IlCB 1744, IlCB 1946, MorJA,
WWA 38, WWAW 8*
Gay-Kelly, Doreen 1952- *ConAu 61*
Geach, Patricia Sullivan 1916- *ConAu 29*
Geary, Clifford N 1916- *IlBYP, IlCB 1946*
Geary, Stanley *MnBBF*
Gee, Osman *MnBBF*
Gee, Osman see Hincks, Cyril Malcolm
Geer, Charles 1922- *IlBYP, IlCB 1946,
IlCB 1957*
Gehr, Mary *WWAA 1973, WWMW 14*
Geis, Darlene Stern *AuBYP, ConAu 1R,
SmATA 7*
Geis, Darlene Stern see Kelly, Ralph
Geis, Darlene Stern see London, Jane
Geis, Darlene Stern see Stevens, Peter
Geisel, Theodor Seuss 1904- *AmA&B, AmPB,
AmSCAP 66, Au&ICB, AuBYP,
ChLR 1, ChPo, ChPo S1, ChPo S2,
ChFB A, ConAu 13R, CurB 68, FamAI,
IlCB 1744, IlCB 1946, IlCB 1957, REn,
REnAL, SmATA 1, TwCA, TwCA Sup,*

WWA 38, WWW 14, WWWor 2
Geisel, Theodor Seuss see Doctor Seuss
Geisel, Theodor Seuss see LeSieg, Theo
Geisel, Theodor Seuss see Seuss, Dr.
Geismar, Maxwell 1909- *AmA&B, Au&Wr 6,
ConAu 1R, RAdv 1, REnAL, TwCA Sup*
Gekiere, Madeleine 1919- *ChPo, ChPo S1,
IlBYP, IlCB 1946, IlCB 1957, ThBJA,
WWAA 1973*
Geldart, Peter *MnBBF*
Gelinas, Paul J 1911- *ConAu 41, SmATA 10*
Gell, Frank *ConAu 57*
Gell, Frank see Kowet, Don
Geller, Allen 1941- *ConAu 25R*
Gellibrand, Emma *CarSB*
Gelman, Steve 1934- *ConAu 25R, SmATA 3,
WWE 14*
Gemme, Francis Robert 1934- *ConAu 21R,
WWE 14*
Gemmill, Jane Brown 1898- *ConAu 1R*
Gemming, Elizabeth 1932- *ConAu 65,
SmATA 11*
Genia *IlBYP*
Genia 1930- *IlCB 1957*
Genia see Wennerstrom, Genia Katherine
Gentleman, David William 1930- *ArtsCL,
Au&Wr 6, ChPo S1, ConAu 25R, IlBYP,
SmATA 7, WW 1974, WWGA*
Gentry, Helen 1897- *AmA&B, AmPB,
ForWC 1970*
George, Ernest *MnBBF*
George, Fairfax *MnBBF*
George, Jean Craighead 1919- *AmA&B, AnCL,
Au&Wr 6, AuBYP, ChLR 1, ConAu 5R,
IlCB 1946, MorBMP, MorJA,
NewbC 1966, SmATA 2*
George, John L 1916- *AmA&B, AmMWS 12P,
AnCL, AuBYP, BiDLA, BkCL,
ConAu 5R, SmATA 2*
George, Renee 1924- *IlCB 1946*
George, S C 1898- *ConAu 53, SmATA 11*
George, W Lloyd 1900?-1975 *ConAu 53*
Georgiady, Nicholas Peter 1921- *LE 5*
Georgiou, Constantine 1927- *ConAu 13R,
SmATA 7*
Gerard, Francis *MnBBF*
Gerard, John *MnBBF*
Gerard, John see Cherub, The
Gerassi, John 1931- *ConAu 5R*
Gerber, William 1908- *ConAu 37, DrAS 6P,
WWA 38, WWWorJ 1972*
Gere, Charles March 1869- *IlCB 1744*
Gergely, Tibor 1900- *AmPB, IlBYP,
IlCB 1744, IlCB 1946*
Germar, Herb *ConAu XR*
Germar, Herb see Germar, William H
Germar, William H 1911- *ConAu 21R*
Germar, William H see Germar, Herb
Gerrard, Peter *MnBBF*
Gerrard, Robert *MnBBF*
Gerrish, George *MnBBF*
Gerrish, George see Garrish, Harold J
Gerry, Margarita Spaulding 1870- *AmA&B,
CarSB*
Gersh, Harry 1912- *ConAu 1R,
WWWorJ 1972*
Gerson, Noel Bertram 1914- *AmA&B,
Au&Wr 6, AuBYP, WWA 38, WWE 14,
WWWor 2*

Gerson, Thomas Isaac 1906- *WNAA*
Gerson, Virginia *CarSB, ChPo, ChPo S1, IICB 1744*
Gervasi, Frank H 1908- *AmA&B, ConAu 13R, ConAu P-1*
Gervis, Ruth S 1894- *IICB 1744*
Gesch, Roy G 1920- *ConAu 21R*
Gesner, Clark 1938- *AmSCAP 66*
Gesner, Elsie Miller 1919- *ConAu 17R, ForWC 1970, WrD*
Gessner, Lynne 1919- *ConAu 25R, WrD*
Gessner, Lynne *see* Clark, Merle
Gezi, Kalil I 1930- *ConAu 25R*
Ghikas, Panos 1923- *IICB 1946*
Gianakoulis, Theodore *AuBYP*
Gibb, Spencer J *MnBBF*
Gibbings, Robert 1889-1958 *CurB 48, CurB 58, DcLEnL, EvLB, IICB 1744, IICB 1946, LongC, TwCA Sup*
Gibbon, F P *MnBBF*
Gibbons, Gail 1944- *ConAu 69*
Gibbons, H Clifford *WWBWI A*
Gibbons, Harry Hornaby Clifford 1888-1958 *MnBBF*
Gibbons, Harry Hornaby Clifford *see* Allen, Hugh
Gibbons, Harry Hornaby Clifford *see* Bolton, Hugh
Gibbons, Harry Hornaby Clifford *see* Brendon, Frank
Gibbons, Harry Hornaby Clifford *see* Chester, Gilbert
Gibbons, Harry Hornaby Clifford *see* Kempster, Bert
Gibbons, Harry Hornaby Clifford *see* Murray, Agatha
Gibbons, Harry Hornaby Clifford *see* Murray, Andrew
Gibbons, Harry Hornaby Clifford *see* Warwick, Clifford
Gibbons, Helen *WWBWI A*
Gibbons, Helen *see* Gibbons, William
Gibbons, Orlando 1583-1625 *Alli, NCHEL*
Gibbons, William 1900- *MnBBF, WWBWI A*
Gibbons, William *see* Cross, Dennis
Gibbons, William *see* Gibbons, Helen
Gibbons, William *see* Richards, Frank
Gibbs, Alonzo 1915- *AuBYP, ConAu 5R, SmATA 5, WrD*
Gibbs, Evelyn 1905- *IICB 1946*
Gibbs, May *SingR 1*
Gibney, Somerville *Alli Sup, ChPo, ChPo S2, MnBBF*
Gibson, Althea 1927- *CurB 57, WWA 38, WWAW 8*
Gibson, Charles Edmund 1916- *Au&Wr 6, ConAu 5R, WrD*
Gibson, Gertrude Hevener 1906- *ConAu 5R*
Gibson, Gwen *ForWC 1970*
Gibson, Josephine *ConAu XR, SmATA 2, ThBJA*
Gibson, Josephine *see* Hine, Sesyle Joslin
Gibson, Katharine 1893- *AmA&B, JBA 1951, OhA&B, St&VC*
Gibson, Walter Brown 1897- *EncM&D, WNAA*
Gibson, William 1914- *BiEnAT, ConAu 9R, ConDr 1, McGWD, ModAL, ModWD, Pen Am, REnAL, WWA 38, WWE 14,*

WWT 15, WWWor 2, WorAu
Gidal, Sonia Epstein 1922- *Au&Wr 6, AuBYP, ConAu 5R, SmATA 2*
Gidal, Tim N 1909- *ConAu 5R, SmATA 2*
Giegling, John A 1935- *ConAu 29, WrD*
Gielgud, Val Henry 1900- *Au&Wr 6, DcLEnL, EncM&D, IntWW 38, MnBBF, WW 1974, WWLA, WWWor 2*
Gies, Frances 1915- *ConAu 25R*
Gies, Joseph Cornelius 1916- *ConAu 5R*
Giffen, Daniel H 1938- *WWE 14, WWMW 14*
Gifford, Tom *MnBBF*
Gift, Theo *Alli Sup, MnBBF*
Giggah, K *MnBBF*
Giggah, K *see* Kenny, Stan
Gilbert, Alice *ChPo S2*
Gilbert, Ellen *ChPo S2*
Gilbert, H *MnBBF*
Gilbert, H *see* Conner, Henry
Gilbert, Helen Earle *AnMV 1926, AuBYP*
Gilbert, Joan 1931- *ConAu 21R, SmATA 10*
Gilbert, Miriam *ConAu XR, WWAW 8, WWE 14*
Gilbert, Miriam *see* Presberg, Miriam Goldstein
Gilbert, Nan *ConAu XR, SmATA 2*
Gilbert, Nan *see* Gilbertson, Mildred Geiger
Gilbert, Sara 1943- *ConAu 57, SmATA 11*
Gilbert, Sir William Schwenck 1836-1911 *Alli Sup, AtlBL, BbD, BiD&SB, BrAu 19, CasWL, Chambr 3, ChPo, ChPo S1, ChPo S2, CnE&AP, CnThe, CyWA, DcEnA, DcEnA Ap, DcEnL, DcEuL, DcLEnL, EvLB, McGWD, ModWD, MouLC 4, NCHEL, OxEng, Pen Eng, REn, REnWD, St&VC, WEAL*
Gilberts, Helen Ilene *WrD*
Gilbertson, Mildred Geiger 1908- *ConAu 5R, ForWC 1970, SmATA 2, WrD*
Gilbertson, Mildred Geiger *see* Gilbert, Nan
Gilborn, Alice 1936- *ConAu 69*
Gilbreath, Alice 1921- *ConAu 25R, SmATA 12*
Gilbreth, Frank Bunker, Jr. 1911- *AmA&B, ConAu 9R, CurB 49, SmATA 2, WWA 38, WWS 13, WWWor 2*
Gilchrist, S D *MnBBF*
Giles, Carl H 1935- *ConAu 29*
Gilfond, Henry *ConAu 21R, SmATA 2*
Gilforde, Robert *MnBBF*
Gilge, Jeanette 1924- *ConAu 61*
Gilkison, Grace *ConICB*
Gill *MnBBF*
Gill *see* Mordaunt, Wilton
Gill, Bob 1931- *ConAu 1R*
Gill, Derek L T 1919- *ConAu 49, SmATA 9*
Gill, Lawrence *MnBBF*
Gill, Margery Jean 1925- *ArtsCL, ChPo, ChPo S1, IIBYP, IICB 1957*
Gill, Richard Cochran 1901-1958 *AmA&B, AuBYP*
Gillander, H *MnBBF*
Gillanders, W R *MnBBF*
Gillelan, George Howard 1917- *AuBYP*
Gillespie, John Thomas 1928- *BiDL 5, LE 5*
Gillespie, M *MnBBF*
Gillett, Mary Bledsoe *ConAu P-2, SmATA 7*
Gillette, Henry Sampson 1915- *ConAu 5R, WrD*

Gillham, Charles Edward 1898- *AnCL*
Gillies, Margaret 1803-1887 *ChPo S1*
Gillon, Diana 1915- *Au&Wr 6, ConAu 13R*
Gillon, Meir Selig 1907- *Au&Wr 6, ConAu 13R*
Gillsater, Sven 1921- *Au&Wr 6*
Gillum, Helen L 1909- *ConAu 69*
Gilman, Dorothy *Au&Wr 6, ConAu XR, SmATA 5*
Gilman, Dorothy *see* Butters, Dorothy Gilman
Gilmore, David H *SingR 1*
Gilmore, Edith Spacil 1920- *ConAu 1R*
Gilmore, Horace Herman 1903- *AuBYP*
Gilmore, Iris *AuBYP*
Gilmore, Mary 1865-1962 *CasWL, DcLEnL, LongC, SingR 2, TwCW*
Gilroy, Frank D 1925- *AmA&B, ConDr 1, ConLC 2, CrCD, CurB 65, DrAF 1976, McGWD, ModWD, OxAm, WWE 14, WWT 15, WWWor 2, WrD*
Gilroy, Frank Daniel 1925- *WWA 38*
Gilson, Barbara *WWCL, YABC XR*
Gilson, Barbara *see* Gilson, Charles James Louis
Gilson, Charles James Louis 1878-1943 *MnBBF, WWBWI A, WWCL, WWLA, YABC 2*
Gilson, Charles James Louis *see* Gilson, Barbara
Gilstrap, Robert Lawrence 1933- *ConAu 9R, LE 5*
Gimpel, Herbert J 1915- *ConAu 17R*
Ginsburg, Mirra 1919- *ConAu 17R, SmATA 6, WWAW 8*
Ginter, Maria 1922- *Au&Wr 6, WrD*
Giovanni, Nikki 1943- *AuNews 1, BiN 1975, BlkAW, CelR 3, ChPo S2, ConAu 29, ConLC 2, ConLC 4, ConP 1975, CrCAP 2, CurB 73, DrAP 1975, LBAA, RAdv 1, WWA 38, WrD*
Giovanopoulos, Paul Arthur 1939- *ChPo S1, IIBYP, SmATA 7, WWE 14*
Gipson, Frederick Benjamin 1908-1973 *AmA&B, AuBYP, ConAu 1R, ConAu 45, CurB 57, NYTBE 4, SmATA 2, ThBJA*
Girvan, Helen 1891- *AuBYP, MorJA*
Gittings, Christine *Au&Wr 6, WrD*
Gittings, Jo Manton 1919- *Au&Wr 6, AuBYP, ConAu 5R, SmATA 3*
Gittings, Jo Manton *see* Manton, Jo
Gittings, Robert William Victor 1911- *Au&Wr 6, ChPo S2, ConAu 25R, ConP 1970, ConP 1975, SmATA 6, WW 1974, WWWor 2*
Giusti, George 1908- *WWA 38, WWAA 1973, WWGA*
Gladstone, Gary 1935- *ConAu 29, SmATA 12*
Gladstone, M J 1923- *ConAu 53*
Gladwin, Peter *MnBBF*
Gladych, B Michael 1910- *ConAu 5R*
Glanckoff, Samuel 1894- *ChPo, ConICB, IICB 1744*
Glanville, Brian 1931- *ConAu 5R*
Glanville, H L *MnBBF*
Glanzman, Louis S 1922- *IIBYP, IICB 1957*
Glaser, Milton 1929- *ChPo S2, ConAu 17R, IIBYP, IICB 1957, SmATA 11*
Glaser, Milton *see* Catz, Max
Glasgow, Ellen *CurB 46*
Glaspell, Susan 1882-1948 *AmA&B, AmNov, Chambr 3, CnDAL, CnMD, ConAmA, ConAmL, DcLEnL, DcNAA, LongC,*

McGWD, ModWD, OxAm, REn, REnAL, TwCA, TwCA Sup, WNAA, YABC 2
Glass, Malcolm *DrAP 1975*
Glass, Marvin *NYTBS 5*
Glattauer, Ned *IIBYP*
Glauber, Uta 1936- *ConAu 29*
Glaus, Marlene A *WrD*
Glazer, Tom 1914- *AmSCAP 66, ConAu 61, EncFCW 1969, SmATA 9*
Gleasner, Diana 1936- *ConAu 65*
Gleason, Judith 1929- *ConAu 61*
Gleick, Beth Youman *AuBYP*
Glemser, Bernard 1908- *Au&Wr 6*
Glen, Rowan *MnBBF*
Glendinning, Richard 1917- *ConAu 21R, WWS 13*
Glendinning, Sally *ConAu XR*
Glendinning, Sally *see* Glendinning, Sara W
Glendinning, Sara W 1913- *ConAu 49*
Glendinning, Sara W *see* Glendinning, Sally
Glenn, John Herschel, Jr. 1921- *AnCL, BiN 1974, CurB 62, IntWW 38, NYTBE 3, WW 1974, WWA 38, WWS 13, WWWor 2*
Gles, Margaret Breitmaier 1940- *ConAu 57*
Glick, Carl 1890- *ConAu 5R*
Glick, Virginia Kirkus 1893- *ConAu P-2*
Glick, Virginia Kirkus *see* Kirkus, Virginia
Glieg, Charles *MnBBF*
Gliewe, Unada G 1927- *ConAu 29, SmATA 3, WrD*
Gliewe, Unada G *see* Unada
Glines, Carroll V, Jr. 1920- *ConAu 1R*
Globe, Leah Ain 1900- *WWWorJ 1972*
Glossop, Cecil *WWBWI I*
Glossop, Reginald *MnBBF*
Gloucester, Vernon *MnBBF*
Glovach, Linda 1947- *ConAu 37, SmATA 7, WrD*
Glover, Bruce *MnBBF*
Glover, C Clabon *WWBWI A*
Glover, G Clabon d1934? *MnBBF*
Glover, G Clabon *see* Glover, Mark
Glover, Mark *MnBBF*
Glover, Mark *see* Glover, G Clabon
Glubok, Shirley 1933- *AuBYP, ChLR 1, ConAu 5R, ForWC 1970, MorBMP, SmATA 6, ThBJA*
Gluck, Herb 1925- *ConAu 45*
Glut, Donald F 1944- *ConAu 33*
Glyn, Anthony 1922- *Au&Wr 6, MnBBF, WW 1974*
Glyn, Harrison *MnBBF*
Glyn, Harrison *see* Steffens, Arthur
Glynne-Jones, William 1907- *Au&Wr 6, ConAu 5R, SmATA 11*
Gnagey, Thomas D 1938- *ConAu 49*
Gnoli, Count Domenico 1838-1915 *CasWL, CIDMEuL, IICB 1957*
Goad, W Arthur *MnBBF*
Goaman, Muriel *Au&Wr 6*
Gobbato, Imero 1923- *IIBYP, IICB 1957*
Goble, Warwick *ChPo S1, ConICB, IICB 1744, WWBWI I*
Gockel, Herman W 1906- *ConAu 1R*
Goddard, Ernest Hope 1879-1939 *MnBBF, WWBWI A*
Goddard, Ernest Hope *see* Hamilton, Ernest

Goddard, Norman Molyneux 1881-1917 *MnBBF,*
  WWBWI A
Goddard, Norman Molyneux *see* Barr, Nat
Goddard, Norman Molyneux *see* Cannon, J R
Goddard, Norman Molyneux *see* Custer, Claude
Goddard, Norman Molyneux *see* Darran, Mark
Goddard, Norman Molyneux *see* Haviland,
  Fergus, Captain
Goddard, Norman Molyneux *see* Pergarth, Peter
Goddard, Norman Molyneux *see* Rich, Henry K
Godden, Rumer 1907- *AnCL, Au&Wr 6,*
  AuBYP, ChPo, ChPo S1, ChPo S2,
  ConAu 5R, ConNov 1972, ConNov 1976,
  DcLEnL, FamMS, IntWW 38, LongC,
  ModBL, MorJA, NCHEL, PiP, RAdv 1,
  REn, SmATA 3, TwCA, TwCA Sup,
  TwCW, WW 1974, WWAW 8, WWCL,
  WWWor 2, WrD
Gode, Alexander *ConAu XR, NYTBE 1*
Gode, Alexander *see* Gode VonAesch, Alexander
Gode VonAesch, Alexander 1906-1970
  ConAu P-1
Gode VonAesch, Alexander *see* Gode, Alexander
Godey, John 1912- *AuNews 1, EncM&D*
Godwin, Edward Fell 1912- *IlCB 1946*
Godwin, Frank *MnBBF, WWBWI A*
Godwin, Frank *see* Starr, Richard
Godwin, Stephanie Mary *IlCB 1946*
Goethe, Johann Wolfgang Von 1749-1832 *AtlBL,*
  BbD, BiD&SB, CasWL, ChPo, ChPo S1,
  ChPo S2, CnThe, CyWA, DcBiA,
  DcEnL, DcEuL, EuAu, EvEuW,
  McGWD, NCHEL, OxEng, OxFr,
  OxGer, Pen Eur, RCom, REn,
  REnWD
Goettel, Elinor 1930- *ConAu 29, SmATA 12*
Goetz, Delia 1898- *AuBYP, CurB 49*
Goetz, Lee Garrett 1932- *ConAu 25R*
Goff, Charles *MnBBF*
Goff, Lloyd Lozes 1919- *WWAA 1973*
Goffstein, M B 1940- *ChLR 3, ConAu 21R,*
  SmATA 8
Going, V L *MnBBF*
Golann, Cecil Paige 1921- *ConAu 33,*
  SmATA 11
Gold, D J *WWBWI I*
Gold, Doris Bauman 1919- *ConAu 21R,*
  WWWorJ 1972
Gold, Herbert 1924- *AmA&B, ConAu 9R,*
  ConLC 4, ConNov 1972, ConNov 1976,
  CurB 55, DrAF 1976, ModAL, OxAm,
  Pen Am, RAdv 1, REnAL, TwCW,
  WWA 38, WWWor 2, WWWorJ 1972,
  WorAu, WrD
Gold, Phyllis *ConAu 57*
Gold, Phyllis *see* Goldberg, Phyllis
Gold, Sharlya *ConAu 61, SmATA 9*
Goldberg, Herbert S 1926- *AmMWS 12P,*
  ConAu 5R
Goldberg, Lazer 1920- *LE 5*
Goldberg, Martha 1907- *AuBYP*
Goldberg, Nathan 1924- *DrAS 6F*
Goldberg, Phyllis 1941- *ConAu 57*
Goldberg, Phyllis *see* Gold, Phyllis
Goldberg, Reuben L 1883-1970 *ConAu 5R*
Goldberg, Reuben L *see* Goldberg, Rube
Goldberg, Rube *ArtCS, ConAu XR,*
  CurB 48, CurB 71, NYTBE 1
Goldberg, Rube *see* Goldberg, Reuben L

Goldberg, Stan J 1939- *ConAu 49*
Golden Gorse *St&VC, WWCL*
Goldenson, Robert Myar 1908- *AmMWS 12S,*
  ConAu 29, WWA 38
Goldfeder, Cheryl *SmATA XR*
Goldfeder, Cheryl 1949- *ConAu 53*
Goldfeder, Cheryl *see* Paz, Zan
Goldfeder, James 1943- *ConAu 53*
Goldfeder, James *see* Goldfeder, Jim
Goldfeder, James *see* Paz, A
Goldfeder, Jim *ConAu XR, SmATA XR*
Goldfeder, Jim *see* Goldfeder, James
Goldfrank, Helen Colodny 1912- *AuBYP,*
  ConAu 1R, ForWC 1970,
  SmATA 6
Goldfrank, Helen Colodny *see* Kay, Helen
Goldin, Augusta Reider 1906- *ConAu 17R,*
  ForWC 1970, LE 5, SmATA 13,
  WWAW 8, WrD
Golding, Harry *CarSB, ChPo S2*
Golding, Morton J 1925- *ConAu 21R*
Golding, William 1911- *CasWL, CnMWL,*
  ConAu 5R, ConLC 1, ConLC 2,
  ConLC 3, ConNov 1972, ConNov 1976,
  CurB 64, EncWL, IntWW 38, LongC,
  ModBL, ModBL Sup, ModWD, NCHEL,
  Pen Eng, RAdv 1, REn, TwCW, WEAL,
  WW 1974, WWTwL, WorAu
Goldman, Alex J 1917- *ConAu 49,*
  WWWorJ 1972
Goldman, Phyllis W 1927- *ConAu 29*
Goldman, Susan 1939- *ConAu 65*
Goldman, William 1931- *AmA&B, BiEnAT,*
  BiN 1975, ConDr 1, ConLC 1,
  ConNov 1972, ConNov 1976, DrAF 1976,
  Pen Am, WEAL, WWA 38, WWE 14,
  WWWor 2, WrD
Goldner, Jameson Charles 1938- *WWW 14*
Goldsmith, Maurice 1913- *Au&Wr 6*
Goldsmith, Oliver 1728?-1774 *Alli, AtlBL,*
  BbD, BiD&SB, BrAu, CarSB, CasWL,
  Chambr 2, ChPo, ChPo S1, ChPo S2,
  CnE&AP, CnThe, CriT 2, CyWA,
  DcBiA, DcEnA, DcEnA Ap, DcEnL,
  DcEuL, DcLEnL, EvLB, HsB&A,
  McGWD, MouLC 2, NCHEL, OxEng,
  Pen Eng, PoIre, RAdv 1, REn, REnWD,
  WEAL
Goldstein, Nathan 1927- *ConAu 45, IlBYP*
Goldstein, Philip 1910- *ConAu 53*
Goldstein, Rose B 1904- *WWWorJ 1972*
Goldston, Robert Conroy 1927- *AmA&B,*
  Au&Wr 6, ConAu 17R, SmATA 6,
  WWA 38
Goldston, Robert Conroy *see* Conroy, Robert
Goldston, Robert Conroy *see* Stark, James
Goll, Reinhold Weimar 1897- *AuBYP,*
  ConAu 5R, WrD
Gollomb, Joseph 1881-1950 *AmA&B, AnCL,*
  AuBYP, JBA 1934, JBA 1951, REnAL,
  TwCA, TwCA Sup
Golombek, Harry 1911- *WW 1974*
Golsworthy, Arnold *MnBBF*
Gompertz, M L G *MnBBF*
Gompertz, M L G *see* Ganpat
Gonzalez, Gloria 1940- *ConAu 65*
Gonzalez, Xavier 1898- *DcCAA 2, IlBYP,*
  WWA 38, WWAA 1973
Gooch, Stanley J 1894-1958 *MnBBF,*

WWBWI A
Good, Stafford 1890- *ConICB*
Goodacre, Elizabeth Jane 1929- *Au&Wr 6,
WrD*
Goodall, John Strickland 1908- *ConAu 33,
IICB 1946, SmATA 4*
Goode, John 1927- *Au&Wr 6*
Goodenough, Nat *MnBBF*
Goodenow, Earle 1913- *IICB 1946*
Goodenow, Girard 1912- *IIBYP, IICB 1946*
Gooders, John 1937- *Au&Wr 6, ConAu 57*
Goodfellow, E J H 1843- *ChPo, WNAA*
Goodfellow, Thomas MacKey 1907- *WWA 38,
WWS 13*
Goodheart, Barbara 1934- *ConAu 33, WrD*
Goodman, Elaine 1930- *ConAu 37, SmATA 9*
Goodman, Linda *CelR 3, WWA 38,
WWAW 8*
Goodman, Nathan Gerson 1899-1953 *AmA&B,
REnAL*
Goodman, Walter 1927- *ConAu 9R,
SmATA 9, WWA 38, WWE 14*
Goodrich, Samuel Griswold 1793-1860 *Alli,
AmA, AmA&B, BbD, BbthC, BiD&SB,
CarSB, ChPo, ChPo S1, ChPo S2,
CyAL 2, DcAmA, DcEnL, DcNAA,
OxAm, REn, REnAL, WWCL*
Goodwin, Charles *MnBBF*
Goodwin, David 1878-1940? *MnBBF,
WWBWI A*
Goodwin, David *see* Gowing, Sydney
Goodwin, Hal *ConAu XR, SmATA XR*
Goodwin, Hal *see* Goodwin, Harold Leland
Goodwin, Harold 1919- *ConAu 57, IIBYP*
Goodwin, Harold Leland 1914- *ConAu 1R,
SmATA 13*
Goodwin, Harold Leland *see* Blaine, John
Goodwin, Harold Leland *see* Goodwin, Hal
Goodwin, Harold Leland *see* Gordon, Hal
Goodwin, Harold Leland *see* Savage, Blake
Goodwin, John *WWBWI A*
Goodwin, John *see* Goodwin, David
Goodwin, Maud Wilder 1856-1935 *AmA&B,
BiD&SB, CarSB, DcAmA, DcNAA,
REnAL*
Goodyear, Robert Arthur Hanson 1877?-1948
MnBBF, WWBWI A, WWCL, WWLA
Gookin, M B *MnBBF*
Goolagong, Evonne 1951- *BiN 1974, CelR 3,
CurB 71, NYTBE 2, WWAW 8,
WWWor 2*
Goossen, Agnes *ConAu XR*
Goossen, Agnes *see* Epp, Margaret A
Gordon, Bernard Ludwig 1931- *AmMWS 12P,
ConAu 29, DrLC 1969, WWE 14*
Gordon, Dorothy 1893- *AmA&B, AuBYP,
ChPo S1, CurB 55, CurB 70,
ForWC 1970, NYTBE 1, WWA 38*
Gordon, Elizabeth 1866-1922 *AmLY, CarSB,
ChPo, ChPo S1, DcNAA*
Gordon, Esther Saranga 1935- *ConAu 53,
SmATA 10*
Gordon, Ethel Edison 1915- *ConAu 53*
Gordon, Frederick *CarSB, ConAu P-2,
SmATA 1*
Gordon, Frederick *see* Stratemeyer, Edward L
Gordon, Geoffrey *MnBBF*
Gordon, Geoffrey *see* Jones, J G
Gordon, George N 1926- *ConAu 1R*

Gordon, Giles Alexander Esme 1940-
ConP 1970, WrD, ConP 1975
Gordon, Gordon 1912- *Au&Wr 6, ConAu 5R,
EncM&D, IndAu 1917*
Gordon, H R, Colonel *AmA&B, YABC 1*
Gordon, H R, Colonel *see* Ellis, Edward S
Gordon, Hal *SmATA XR*
Gordon, Hal *see* Goodwin, Harold Leland
Gordon, John 1925- *ConAu 25R, SmATA 6,
WrD*
Gordon, Lew *ConAu XR, SmATA XR*
Gordon, Lew *see* Baldwin, Gordon C
Gordon, Margaret Anna 1939- *ChPo S2,
IIBYP, IICB 1957, SmATA 9*
Gordon, Mildred 1912- *Au&Wr 6, ConAu 5R,
EncM&D, WWAW 8*
Gordon, Richard 1921- *MnBBF*
Gordon, Richard *see* Murray, Adrian
Gordon, S S *MnBBF, WWBWI A*
Gordon, S S *see* Shaw, Stanley Gordon
Gordon, Selma *ConAu XR, SmATA 3*
Gordon, Selma *see* Lanes, Selma Gordon
Gordon, Sol 1923- *AmMWS 12S, ConAu 53,
LE 5, SmATA 11*
Gordon, Stanley *MnBBF, WWBWI A*
Gordon, Stanley *see* Shaw, Stanley Gordon
Gordon, Stewart *AuBYP, ConAu XR,
SmATA XR*
Gordon, Stewart *see* Shirreffs, Gordon D
Gordon, Sydney 1914- *Au&Wr 6, ConAu 29,
WrD*
Gordon, Tom *MnBBF*
Gordon, W J *ChPo, MnBBF*
Gordon, W Murray *MnBBF*
Gordon, W Murray *see* Graydon, William
Murray
Gorelick, Molly Chernow 1920- *ConAu 21R,
SmATA 9, WWAW 8*
Gorey, Edward St. John 1925- *AmPB, ChPo,
ChPo S1, ConAu 5R, IIBYP, IICB 1957,
NYTBE 4*
Gorey, Edward St. John *see* Blutig, Eduard
Gorey, Edward St. John *see* Dowdy, Mrs. Regera
Gorey, Edward St. John *see* Grode, Redway
Gorey, Edward St. John *see* Mude, O
Gorey, Edward St. John *see* Weary, Ogdred
Gorey, Edward St. John *see* Wodge, Dreary
Gorfain, A D *WWBWI A*
Gorham, Charles Orson 1911-1975 *AmA&B,
AmNov, ConAu 61*
Gorham, Michael *AuBYP, ConAu XR,
SmATA 5*
Gorham, Michael *see* Elting, Mary
Gorham, Michael *see* Folsom, Franklin
Gorman, T J *MnBBF*
Gorman, Terry *IIBYP, IICB 1946*
Gorman, Terry *see* Powers, Richard M
Gorsline, Douglas Warner 1913- *AmA&B,
ChPo S1, ConAu 61, IIBYP, IICB 1946,
IICB 1957, SmATA 11, WWA 38,
WWAA 1973*
Gosfield, C Hedingham *WWBWI A*
Gosfield, H Heddingham *MnBBF*
Gosfield, H Heddingham *see* Brooks, Edwy
Searles
Goshorn, Elizabeth 1953- *ConAu 61*
Goss, Clay 1946- *BlkAW, ConAu 57*
Goss, Warren Lee 1835-1925 *Alli Sup,
AmA&B, AmLY, CarSB, DcAmA,*

DcNAA, WNAA

Gosse, Sir Edmund William 1849-1928 *Alli Sup, BbD, BiD&SB, CarSB, CasWL, Chambr 3, ChPo, ChPo S1, ChPo S2, CnMWL, DcEnA, DcEnA Ap, DcEnL, DcLEnL, EvLB, LongC, ModBL, NCHEL, OxEng, Pen Eng, TwCA, TwCA Sup, TwCW, WEAL*

Gossett, Margaret *AuBYP*

Gottlieb, Gerald 1923- *AuBYP, ConAu 5R, SmATA 7*

Gottlieb, Robin 1928- *AuBYP, ConAu 1R*

Gottlieb, William P *AuBYP*

Gottschalk, Alfred 1930- *LE 5, WWA 38, WWWor 2, WWWorJ 1972*

Goudey, Alice E 1898- *AuBYP, ThBJA*

Goudge, Elizabeth 1900- *Au&Wr 6, AuBYP, ChPo, ConAu 5R, CurB 40, LongC, NCHEL, REn, SmATA 2, ThBJA, TwCA, TwCA Sup, TwCW, WWCL, WrD*

Gough, Catherine 1931- *ConAu 25R*

Gough, Irene *SingR 2*

Gough, Philip 1908- *ChPo, IlCB 1946*

Goulart, Ron 1933- *ConAu 25R, SmATA 6*

Goulart, Ron *see* Lee, Howard

Goulart, Ron *see* Robeson, Kenneth

Goulart, Ron *see* Shawn, Frank S

Goulart, Ron *see* Steffanson, Con

Gould, Chester 1900- *ArtCS, CurB 71, EncM&D, WWA 38, WWMW 14*

Gould, Elizabeth Lincoln d1914 *CarSB, ChPo, DcNAA*

Gould, Harrison *MnBBF*

Gould, Jean Rosalind 1919?- *AuBYP, ConAu 5R, OhA&B, SmATA 11, WWA 38, WWAW 8, WWE 14, WrD*

Gould, Lilian 1920- *ConAu 49, SmATA 6*

Gould, Nathaniel 1857-1919 *Br&AmS, DcLEnL, EvLB, MnBBF, OxEng*

Goulding, Dorothy Jane *Prof*

Goulding, Francis Robert 1810-1881 *Alli, Alli Sup, AmA&B, BiD&SB, BiDSA, CarSB, DcAmA, DcNAA, REnAL*

Govan, Christine Noble 1898?- *AmNov, AuBYP, ConAu 1R, ForWC 1970, SmATA 9, WrD*

Govan, Christine Noble *see* Allerton, Mary

Govan, Christine Noble *see* Darby, J N

Govern, Elaine 1939- *ConAu 53*

Gower, Craven *MnBBF*

Gower, Craven *see* Hosken, Ernest Charles Heath

Gowing, Sydney 1878- *MnBBF, WWBWI A*

Gowing, Sydney *see* Goodwin, David

Gowing, Sydney *see* Tregellis, John

Goyne, Richard 1902-1957 *MnBBF, WWBWI A*

Goyne, Richard *see* Blair, David

Goyne, Richard *see* Courage, John

Goyne, Richard *see* Renin, Paul

Goyne, Richard *see* Standish, Evelyn

Goyne, Richard *see* Standish, Richard

Graber, Alexander 1914- *ConAu 1R, SmATA 7*

Graber, Alexander *see* Cordell, Alexander

Grabianski, Janusz 1929?- *ConAu 45, IlBYP, IlCB 1957, ThBJA*

Graboff, Abner 1919- *IlBYP, IlCB 1957*

Grace, Joseph *ConAu XR*

Grace, Joseph *see* Hornby, John

Gracie, L C *MnBBF*

Gracza, Margaret Young 1928- *ConAu 13R, ForWC 1970*

Graeme, Bruce 1900- *Au&Wr 6, EncM&D, MnBBF, WW 1974, WWBWI A*

Graeme, Bruce *see* Jeffries, Graeme Montagu

Graeme, Roderic *Au&Wr 6, ConAu XR, EncM&D*

Graeme, Roderic *see* Jeffries, Roderic

Graff, Polly Anne Colver *ConAu XR, SmATA 7*

Graff, Polly Anne Colver *see* Colver, Anne

Graff, S Stewart 1908- *AuBYP, ConAu 49, SmATA 9*

Grafton, Ann *ConAu XR*

Grafton, Ann *see* Owens, Thelma

Graham, Ada 1931- *ConAu 29, SmATA 11, WrD*

Graham, Al 1897- *AuBYP, ChPo, ChPo S1*

Graham, Alberta *AuBYP*

Graham, Alexis *MnBBF, WWBWI A*

Graham, Alexis *see* Brown, G W

Graham, Armitage *MnBBF, WWBWI A*

Graham, Armitage *see* Pentelow, John Nix

Graham, Billy *BiN 1974, CelR 3, ChPo S1, ConAu XR, CurB 51, CurB 73, IntWW 38, WW 1974, WWA 38*

Graham, Billy *see* Graham, William Franklin

Graham, Clarence R 1907- *AuBYP, BiDL 5, CurB 50, WWA 38, WWS 13*

Graham, Edward Harrison 1902- *Au&Wr 6*

Graham, Eleanor 1896- *Au&Wr 6, ChPo, ChPo S1, ChPo S2, WWCL*

Graham, Frank 1894-1965 *AmA&B*

Graham, Frank, Jr. 1925- *AuBYP, ConAu 9R, WWE 14*

Graham, Harold *MnBBF*

Graham, Harry Jocelyn Clive 1874-1936 *ChPo, ChPo S1, ChPo S2, CnMWL, EvLB, LongC, NCHEL, WWCL, WWLA*

Graham, Helen Holland *AuBYP*

Graham, John 1926- *ConAu 33, DrAS 6E, SmATA 11, WrD*

Graham, Jory 1925- *ConAu 29, WWAW 8, WWMW 14*

Graham, Lorenz B 1902- *BlkAW, ConAu 9R, LBAA, MorBMP, REnAL, SmATA 2, ThBJA*

Graham, Margaret Bloy 1920- *AmPB, IlBYP, IlCB 1946, IlCB 1957, MorJA, SmATA 11*

Graham, Robert *ConAu XR*

Graham, Robert *see* Haldeman, Joe

Graham, Robin Lee 1949- *ConAu 49, SmATA 7*

Graham, Shirley Lola 1907?- *AmA&B, AuBYP, BkCL, BlkAW, CurB 46, LBAA, MorJA, St&VC, TwCA Sup, WWA 38, WWAW 8*

Graham, William *MnBBF*

Graham, William Franklin 1918- *AmA&B, ConAu 9R*

Graham, William Franklin *see* Graham, Billy

Grahame, Arnold *MnBBF, WWBWI A*

Grahame, Kenneth 1859-1932 *AnCL, AtlBL, AuBYP, BkCL, CarSB, CasWL, Chambr 3, ChPo, ChPo S1, CnMWL, CyWA, DcLEnL, EvLB, FamSYP,*

*JBA 1934, LongC, ModBL, NCHEL,
OxEng, Pen Eng, REn, St&VC, TelT,
TwCA, TwCA Sup, TwCW, WWCL,
YABC 1*
Grainger, F E *see* Hill, Headon
Grainger, Francis Edward *EncM&D, MnBBF*
Gramatky, Hardie 1907- *AmA&B, AmPB,
AnCL, Au&ICB, AuBYP, AuNews 1,
BiN 1974, BkP, ConAu 1R, IlCB 1744,
IlCB 1946, IlCB 1957, JBA 1951,
SmATA 1, St&VC, WWA 38,
WWAA 1973, WWWor 2*
Gramet, Charles *AuBYP, ConAu 1R*
Granberg, Wilber J 1906- *ConAu 5R*
Granby, Phil *MnBBF*
Grand, Samuel 1912- *WWWorJ 1972*
Granda, Julio *IlBYP*
Grange, Peter *ConAu XR, ConNov 1972,
ConNov 1976, SmATA 5*
Grange, Peter *see* Nicole, Christopher Robin
Granstaff, Bill 1925- *SmATA 10*
Grant, A R *MnBBF*
Grant, Alistair 1925- *ArtsCL*
Grant, Anson *MnBBF*
Grant, Bruce 1893- *AuBYP, ConAu 1R,
SmATA 5*
Grant, Denby *MnBBF*
Grant, Douglas *MnBBF*
Grant, Douglas *see* Merland, Oliver
Grant, E Gordon *MnBBF*
Grant, E Gordon *see* Edwards, Robert Hamilton
Grant, Eva 1907- *ConAu 49, SmATA 7*
Grant, Gordon H 1875-1962 *AmA&B,
CurB 53, CurB 62, IlCB 1744,
IlCB 1946*
Grant, Harry *MnBBF*
Grant, Howard *MnBBF, WWBWI A*
Grant, Howard *see* Wright, Harold Tomlinson
Grant, Howard *see* Wright, W George
Grant, J B 1940- *ConAu 57*
Grant, James *MnBBF*
Grant, Leigh 1947- *IlBYP, SmATA 10*
Grant, Leslie *MnBBF*
Grant, Madeleine Parker 1895- *AuBYP*
Grant, Matthew G *SmATA XR*
Grant, Matthew G *see* May, Julian
Grant, Maxwell *MnBBF*
Grant, Maxwell *see* Richardson, Gladwell
Grant, Myrna 1934- *ConAu 53*
Grant, Neil 1938- *ConAu 33, WrD*
Gratton, Herbert J *MnBBF*
Graveny, Cecil *MnBBF*
Graves, Charles Parlin 1911-1972 *AuBYP,
ConAu 5R, ConAu 37, SmATA 4*
Graves, Charles Parlin *see* Parlin, John
Graves, John 1920- *ConAu 13R*
Graves, Mortimer *MnBBF*
Graves, Robert 1895- *AnCL, AuBYP,
CnE&AP, CnMWL, ConAu 5R,
ConLC 1, ConLC 2, ConLC 6,
ConNov 1972, ConNov 1976, ConP 1970,
ConP 1975, CyWA, EncWL, LongC,
ModBL, ModBL Sup, NCHEL, RAdv 1,
REn, TwCA, TwCA Sup, TwCW,
WEAL, WWTwL, WWWor 2*
Gray, Miss A A *CarSB, ChPo*
Gray, Alice *AuBYP, WWAW 8*
Gray, Andrew *MnBBF, WWBWI A*
Gray, Andrew *see* Murray, A C

Gray, Anne 1931- *ConAu 65*
Gray, Berkeley *EncM&D, MnBBF,
WWBWI A*
Gray, Berkeley *see* Brooks, Edwy Searles
Gray, Cecil *MnBBF*
Gray, Charles A 1938- *AmMWS 12P,
ConAu 17R*
Gray, Clarence 1902-1957 *ArtCS*
Gray, Dane *MnBBF*
Gray, Don *MnBBF*
Gray, Don *see* Graydon, Robert Murray
Gray, Elizabeth Janet 1902- *AmA&B, AnCL,
AuBYP, ConAu XR, CurB 43, JBA 1934,
JBA 1951, Newb 1922, SmATA 6*
Gray, Elizabeth Janet *see* Vining, Elizabeth Gray

Gray, Genevieve S 1920- *ConAu 33,
SmATA 4*
Gray, Genevieve S *see* Gray, Jenny
Gray, Geoffrey *MnBBF*
Gray, Geoffrey *see* Murray, C Geoffrey
Gray, George Hugh 1922- *ConAu 17R*
Gray, George Hugh *see* Gray, Tony
Gray, Gilbert *MnBBF, WWBWI A*
Gray, Gilbert *see* Bayfield, William John
Gray, Gilbert *see* Margerison, John S
Gray, Harold 1894-1968 *AmA&B, ArtCS,
REnAL, WNAA*
Gray, Henry *MnBBF*
Gray, J A *MnBBF*
Gray, Jenny *ConAu XR, SmATA 4*
Gray, Jenny *see* Gray, Genevieve S
Gray, Kay *MnBBF*
Gray, Malcolm *MnBBF*
Gray, Marian *ConAu XR*
Gray, Marian *see* Pierce, Edith Gray
Gray, Murray *MnBBF*
Gray, Nicholas Stuart 1922?- *ConAu 21R, PiP,
SmATA 4, WWT 15, WrD*
Gray, Noel 1926- *DrAS 6H*
Gray, Patricia Clark *AuBYP, ConAu 29,
SmATA 7*
Gray, Patricia Clark *see* Clark, Virginia
Gray, Patricia Clark *see* Gray, Patsey
Gray, Patsey *ConAu XR, SmATA 7*
Gray, Patsey *see* Gray, Patricia Clark
Gray, Professor *MnBBF*
Gray, R E *MnBBF*
Gray, R E *see* Ronald, Grayling
Gray, Rockwell 1912- *WWA 38*
Gray, Roland *MnBBF*
Gray, Tony *ConAu XR*
Gray, Tony *see* Gray, George Hugh
Gray, Walter *MnBBF*
Gray, William Dudley 1912- *IndAu 1917*
Graydon, H Murray *MnBBF*
Graydon, Mark *MnBBF*
Graydon, Mark *see* Graydon, Robert Murray
Graydon, Robert Murray 1891?-1937 *MnBBF,
WWBWI A*
Graydon, Robert Murray *see* Gray, Don
Graydon, Robert Murray *see* Graydon, Mark
Graydon, Robert Murray *see* Hamilton, Murray
Graydon, Robert Murray *see* Murray, Robert
Graydon, Robert Murray *see* O'Flynn, Jimmy
Graydon, Robert Murray *see* Roberts, Murray
Graydon, William Murray 1864-1946 *CarSB,
MnBBF, WWBWI A*
Graydon, William Murray *see* Armitage, Alfred

Graydon, William Murray *see* Gordon, W Murray

Graydon, William Murray *see* Murray, William

Graydon, William Murray *see* Olliver, Tom

Grayland, V Merle *ConAu XR*

Grayland, V Merle *see* Grayland, Valerie Merle

Grayland, Valerie Merle *Au&Wr 6, ConAu 9R, SmATA 7, WrD*

Grayland, Valerie Merle *see* Belvedere, Lee

Grayland, Valerie Merle *see* Grayland, V Merle

Grayland, Valerie Merle *see* Subond, Valerie

Grayson, Hubert *MnBBF*

Grayson, Marion F 1906- *AuBYP, ConAu 5R*

Grazia, Thomas Di *IlBYP*

Great Comte, The *SmATA XR*

Great Comte, The *see* Hawkesworth, Eric

Greaves, Griselda *ChPo S2*

Greaves, H B *MnBBF*

Greaves, Margaret 1914- *Au&Wr 6, ConAu 25R, SmATA 7, WrD*

Greaves, Norman *MnBBF*

Greaves, Norman *see* Brooks, Edwy Searles

Greeley, Andrew Moran 1928- *AmMWS 12S, ConAu 5R, CurB 72, LE 5, WWA 38*

Green, Adam *ConAu XR, REnAL, SmATA 2*

Green, Adam *see* Weisgard, Leonard Joseph

Green, Chaile *MnBBF*

Green, D *SmATA 4*

Green, D *see* Casewit, Curtis

Green, Elisabeth Sara *WrD*

Green, Elizabeth Shippen *ChPo, ConICB*

Green, Fitzhugh 1888-1947 *AmA&B, CarSB, DcNAA, WNAA*

Green, Gerald B *MnBBF*

Green, Gerald B *see* Fitzgerald, Gerald

Green, Jane 1937- *ConAu 61, SmATA 9*

Green, Margaret Murphy 1926- *AuBYP, ConAu 1R, ForWC 1970*

Green, Mary McBurney 1896- *AmPB, AuBYP, ConAu P-2*

Green, Mary Moore 1906- *ConAu P-1, SmATA 11*

Green, Morton 1937- *ConAu 57, SmATA 8*

Green, Norma B 1925- *ConAu 41, SmATA 11*

Green, Oliver *MnBBF*

Green, Phyllis 1932- *ConAu 45*

Green, Roger Lancelyn 1918- *Au&Wr 6, AuBYP, ChPo, ChPo S1, ChPo S2, ConAu 1R, SmATA 2, ThBJA, WWCL*

Green, Sheila Ellen 1934- *ConAu 1R, SmATA 8*

Green, Sheila Ellen *see* Greenwald, Sheila

Greenaway, Kate 1846-1901 *AnCL, AuBYP, CarSB, ChPo, ChPo S1, ChPo S2, FamAI, JBA 1934, JBA 1951, NCHEL, OxEng, WWCL, YABC 2*

Greenbaum, Louise G 1919- *ConAu 69*

Greenberg, Daniel A 1934- *ConAu 5R*

Greenberg, Eliezer 1896- *CasWL, WWWorJ 1972*

Greenberg, Harvey R 1935- *ConAu 33, SmATA 5*

Greenberg, Joanne Goldenberg 1932- *ConAu 5R*

Greenberg, Martin Harry 1941- *AmMWS 12S, ConAu 49*

Greenberg, Saul Norman 1923- *WWE 14*

Greenberg, Sidney 1917- *ConAu 9R,*

WWWorJ 1972

Greenberg, Sylvia S *AmMWS 12P*

Greenblatt, Augusta 1912- *ConAu 57*

Greenburg, Dan 1936- *AmA&B, ConAu 13R, WWA 38, WWE 14, WWWorJ 1972*

Greene, Mrs. *CarSB*

Greene, A C 1923- *ConAu 37, WWA 38*

Greene, Bette 1934- *ChLR 2, ConAu 53, SmATA 8, WrD*

Greene, Carla 1916- *AuBYP, ConAu 1R, ForWC 1970, SmATA 1, WrD*

Greene, Constance C 1924- *ConAu 61, SmATA 11*

Greene, Frances Nimmo *AmA&B, BiDSA, CarSB*

Greene, Graham 1904- *Au&Wr 6, AuNews 2, BiEnAT, BiN 1974, CasWL, CatA 1930, CelR 3, ChPo S2, CnMD, CnMWL, CnThe, ConAu 13R, ConDr 1, ConLC 1, ConLC 3, ConLC 6, ConNov 1972, ConNov 1976, CrCD, CurB 69, CyWA, EncM&D, EncWL, IntWW 38, LongC, McGWD, ModBL, ModBL Sup, ModWD, NCHEL, NYTBE 2, OxEng, Pen Eng, RAdv 1, REn, TwCA, TwCA Sup, TwCW, WEAL, WW 1974, WWCL, WWT 15, WWTwL, WWWor 2, WrD*

Greene, Sir Hugh 1910- *IntWW 38, WW 1974*

Greene, L Patrick *MnBBF*

Greene, W T *MnBBF*

Greene, Wade 1933- *SmATA 11*

Greenfield, Eloise 1929- *BlkAW, ConAu 49, LBAA, WrD*

Greenfield, Jeff 1943- *ConAu 37*

Greenhalgh, W S *WWBWI 1*

Greenhood, David 1895- *ConAu 1R*

Greenhood, David *see* Sawyer, Mark

Greening, Hamilton *MnBBF, SmATA XR, WWBWI A*

Greening, Hamilton *see* Hamilton, Charles Harold St. John

Greenlaw, John *MnBBF*

Greenleaf, Barbara Kaye 1942- *ConAu 29, SmATA 6*

Greenlee, William Purdy 1928- *DrAS 6P, WWS 13*

Greenwald, Sheila *ChPo, ConAu XR, IlBYP, IlCB 1957, SmATA 8*

Greenwald, Sheila *see* Green, Sheila Ellen

Greenwood, Edward Alister 1930- *ConAu 29*

Greenwood, Edward Alister *see* Greenwood, Ted

Greenwood, James *Alli Sup, DcEnL, MnBBF, TelT*

Greenwood, Robin *MnBBF*

Greenwood, Ted *ConAu XR*

Greenwood, Ted *see* Greenwood, Edward Alister

Greer, Terence 1929- *ArtsCL*

Greet, W Cabell *NYTBE 3*

Greey, Edward 1835-1888 *Alli Sup, BbD, BiD&SB, CarSB, DcAmA, DcNAA*

Gregg, Ernest *BlkAW*

Gregg, James R 1914- *AmMWS 12P, ConAu 21R*

Gregg, Martin *see* McNeilly, Wilfred Glassford

Gregg, Mary Kirby 1817-1893 *CarSB*

Gregor, Arthur 1923- *ConAu 25R, ConP 1970, ConP 1975, DrAP 1975, WWA 38, WrD*

Gregor, Elmer Russell 1878-1954 *AmA&B,*

MnBBF, WNAA
Gregory, Dave MnBBF
Gregory, Dave see Taylor, W T
Gregory, Duncan MnBBF
Gregory, Harry MnBBF
Gregory, Horace 1898- AmA&B, ChPo,
   ChPo S1, ChPo S2, CnDAL, ConAmA,
   ConAu 5R, ConP 1970, ConP 1975,
   DcLEnL, DrAP 1975, ModAL, OxAm,
   Pen Am, RAdv 1, REn, REnAL, SixAP,
   TwCA, TwCA Sup
Gregory, Hylton MnBBF, WWBWI A
Gregory, Hylton see Edgar, Alfred
Gregory, Hylton see Hill, Harry Egbert
Gregory, James Stothert 1912- Au&Wr 6,
   WrD
Gregory, Stephan ConAu XR
Greig, Gustav MnBBF
Grendon, Stephen SmATA 5
Grendon, Stephen see Derleth, August
Grenfell, John MnBBF
Grenfell, John see Floyd, Gilbert
Grenier, Mildred 1917- ConAu 29
Gresham, Ivor MnBBF
Gresham, Ivor see Grosvenor, Mrs. Ian
Gretz, Susanna 1937- ConAu 29, SmATA 7
Gretzer, John IlBYP
Grey, Carlton MnBBF
Grey, Carlton see Bullivant, Cecil Henry
Grey, Elizabeth 1917- Au&Wr 6, AuBYP
Grey, Elizabeth see Hogg, Beth
Grey, Frank R WWBWI 1
Grey, Gordon MnBBF
Grey, Gordon see Flaxman, E
Grey, Ivor MnBBF
Grey, Jerry 1926- AmMWS 12P, ConAu 53,
   SmATA 11, WWA 38, WWE 14,
   WWWor 2
Grey, John MnBBF
Grey, Vivian ConAu 17R
Grey, Zane 1875?-1939 AmA&B, ArizL,
   DcLEnL, DcNAA, EvLB, LongC,
   MnBBF, OhA&B, OxAm, Pen Am, REn,
   REnAL, TwCA, TwCA Sup, TwCW,
   WEAL, WNAA
Grey Owl 1888-1938 CanWr, DcLEnL,
   DcNAA, OxCan, WWCL
Gribble, Leonard Reginald 1908- Au&Wr 6,
   ConAu 53, EncM&D, LongC, MnBBF,
   WW 1974
Grice, Frederick 1910- Au&Wr 6, ConAu 9R,
   SmATA 6, WrD
Grice, Mary ChPo S2
Grider, Dorothy ChPo, IlCB 1946
Gridley, Marion Eleanor 1906- ConAu 45,
   ForWC 1970
Grieder, Walter 1924- ConAu 41, SmATA 9
Grierson, Elizabeth Wilson ChPo S2,
   JBA 1934, JBA 1951
Grierson, Francis Durham MnBBF
Griese, Arnold Alfred 1921- ConAu 49, LE 5,
   SmATA 9
Grieve, Alison MnBBF
Grifalconi, Ann 1929- BkP, ChPo S1,
   ConAu 5R, ForWC 1970, IlBYP,
   IlCB 1957, SmATA 2, ThBJA
Griffin, Ella AuBYP
Griffin, George MnBBF
Griffin, Gillett Good 1928- AuBYP, ChPo,

IlCB 1946
Griffin, Judith Berry BlkAW
Griffin, Sercombe MnBBF
Griffin, Velma AuBYP
Griffis, William Elliot 1843-1928 Alli Sup,
   AmA, AmA&B, AmLY, BbD, BiD&SB,
   CarSB, DcAmA, DcNAA, WNAA
Griffith, Jeannette ConAu XR, SmATA 4
Griffith, Jeannette see Eyerly, Jeannette Hyde
Griffith, Percy MnBBF, WWBWI A
Griffith, Percy see Clifford, Martin
Griffiths, Aileen Esther Au&Wr 6, WrD
Griffiths, Arthur MnBBF
Griffiths, Charles Tom Watson 1919-
   Au&Wr 6, WrD
Griffiths, G D 1910-1973 ConAu P-2
Griffiths, Helen 1939- ConAu 17R, SmATA 5
Griffiths, Maurice MnBBF
Griffiths, Maurice see Lowe, Claud D
Griffiths, R Boscowen MnBBF
Griffiths, Trevor 1935- ConDr 1, WrD
Grigson, Geoffrey Edward Harvey 1902-
   Au&Wr 6, AuBYP, ChPo, ChPo S1,
   ChPo S2, ConAu 25R, ConP 1970,
   ConP 1975, DcLEnL, EvLB, IntWW 38,
   LongC, ModBL, ModBL Sup, NCHEL,
   Pen Eng, REn, TwCA Sup, WW 1974,
   WWTwL, WWWor 2, WrD
Grigson, Jane 1928- ConAu 49
Grill, Nanette L 1935- ConAu 65
Grimley, Vivian Edmund MnBBF
Grimm, Jakob Ludwig Karl 1785-1863 AnCL,
   AtlBL, AuBYP, BbD, BiD&SB, CarSB,
   CasWL, ChPo, DcEuL, EuAu, EvEuW,
   FamSYP, NCHEL, OxEng, OxGer,
   Pen Eur, REn, St&VC, WWCL
Grimm, Wilhelm Karl 1786-1859 AnCL, AtlBL,
   AuBYP, BiD&SB, CarSB, CasWL, ChPo,
   ChPo S2, DcEuL, EuAu, EvEuW,
   FamSYP, OxEng, OxGer, Pen Eur, REn,
   St&VC
Grimm, William C 1907- ConAu 49
Grimmond, David MnBBF
Grimshaw, Mark ConAu XR, MnBBF,
   WWBWI A
Grimshaw, Mark see Belfield, Harry Wedgwood
Grimshaw, Mark see McKeag, Ernest L
Grimsley, Gordon ConAu XR, SmATA XR
Grimsley, Gordon see Groom, Arthur William
Gringhuis, Dirk ConAu XR, SmATA 6
Gringhuis, Dirk see Gringhuis, Richard H
Gringhuis, Richard H 1918- AuBYP,
   ConAu 1R, SmATA 6, WWMW 14
Gringhuis, Richard H see Gringhuis, Dirk
Grinnell, David AuBYP, ConAu XR
Grinnell, David see Wollheim, Donald Allen
Grinnell, George Bird 1849-1938 AmA&B,
   AmLY, BbD, BiD&SB, CarSB, DcAmA,
   DcNAA, JBA 1934, JBA 1951, OxAm,
   REnAL, St&VC, WNAA
Gripari, Pierre 1925- ConAu 29
Gripe, Maria 1923- ConAu 29, SmATA 2,
   ThBJA
Grisha IlBYP
Grisha see Dotzenko, Grisha
Grishina Givago, Nadejda J ConICB
Griswold, Frances Irene Burge 1826-1900
   Alli Sup, AmA&B, CarSB, ChPo,
   DcAmA, DcNAA

Groch, Judith 1929- *AuBYP, ConAu 9R, ForWC 1970*

Grode, Redway *ConAu XR*

Grode, Redway *see* Gorey, Edward St. John

Grodin, Adams John 1913- *IICB 1744*

Grohskopf, Bernice 1921- *ChPo, ConAu 5R, ForWC 1970, SmATA 7, WrD*

Grol, Lini Richards 1913- *ConAu 61, SmATA 9*

Grollman, Earl Alan 1925- *ConAu 21R, WWE 14*

Gronowicz, Antoni 1913- *Au&Wr 6, AuBYP, ConAu 25R, DrAF 1976, DrAP 1975, WWA 38, WWE 14, WWWor 2*

Groom, Arthur William 1898-1964 *ConAu 1R, SmATA 10*

Groom, Arthur William *see* Adamson, Graham

Groom, Arthur William *see* Anderson, George

Groom, Arthur William *see* DuBlane, Daphne

Groom, Arthur William *see* Grimsley, Gordon

Groom, Arthur William *see* Pembury, Bill

Groom, Arthur William *see* Stanstead, John

Groom, Arthur William *see* Templar, Maurice

Groom, Arthur William *see* Toonder, Martin

Groom, Coleman *MnBBF*

Gropper, William 1897- *AmA&B, AmPB, Au&Wr 6, CurB 40, DcCAA 2, IICB 1946, IntWW 38, REnAL, WW 1974, WWA 38, WWAA 1973, WWWor 2, WWWorJ 1972*

Grose, Helen Mason 1880- *IICB 1744*

Groser, Horace George *Alli Sup, ChPo S1, ChPo S2, MnBBF*

Gross, Milt 1895-1953 *AmA&B, ArtCS, REnAL*

Gross, Sarah Chokla 1906- *ConAu 61, ForWC 1970, SmATA 9*

Grosse, Charles *MnBBF*

Grossinger, Tania 1937- *ConAu 53, WrD*

Grossman, Nancy S 1940- *IIBYP, IICB 1957, WWAA 1973*

Grossman, Robert 1940- *SmATA 11*

Grosvenor, Donna Kerkam 1938- *WWAW 8*

Grosvenor, Mrs. Ian *MnBBF*

Grosvenor, Mrs. Ian *see* Gresham, Ivor

Grosvenor, Mrs. Ian *see* King, Reginald

Groth, John 1908- *CurB 43, WWA 38*

Grousset, Paschal 1844-1909 *CarSB*

Grover, Eulalie Osgood 1873-1958 *AmA&B, AuBYP, ChPo, ChPo S1, OhA&B, WNAA*

Groves, Ernest Rutherford 1877-1946 *AmA&B, CurB 43, CurB 46, DcNAA, WNAA*

Groves, Paul 1930- *Au&Wr 6*

Groves, William E *MnBBF*

Groves, William E *see* Scott, Ernest

Groves-Raines, Antony 1913- *IICB 1957*

Groves-Raines, Ralph Gore Anton 1913- *AuBYP*

Gruber, Ruth *ConAu 25R, ForWC 1970, WWWorJ 1972*

Gruber, Ruth *see* Michaels, Ruth Gruber

Gruelle, Johnny 1880?-1938 *AmA&B, AmSCAP 66, ChPo, REnAL*

Gruenberg, Ben C 1875-1965 *ConAu 13R*

Gruenberg, Sidonie Matsner 1881-1974 *AmA&B, AuBYP, ChPo, ConAu 13R, ConAu 49, ConAu P-1, CurB 40, CurB 74, NYTBS 5, SmATA 2, WNAA, WWAW 8*

Grumbine, E Evalyn 1900- *AuBYP*

Grumbine, E Evalyn *see* McNally, E Evalyn Grumbine

Guarcello, Giovanni *ChPo*

Guck, Dorothy 1913- *ConAu 49*

Gudmundson, Shirley M *AuBYP*

Guerber, Helene Adeline 1859-1929 *AmLY, BiD&SB, DcAmA, DcNAA, WNAA*

Guggenheim, Hans 1924- *IICB 1957*

Gugliotta, Bobette 1918- *ConAu 41, SmATA 7*

Guillaume, Jeanette G Flierl 1899- *ConAu 1R, SmATA 8*

Guillet, Edwin Clarence 1898-1975 *CanWW 12, OxCan, Prof*

Guillot, Rene 1900-1969 *AuBYP, ConAu 49, MorJA, SmATA 7, WWCL*

Guinness, Bryan *WW 1974, WrD*

Guiterman, Arthur 1871-1943 *AmA&B, AmLY, ChPo, ChPo S1, ChPo S2, CnDAL, CurB 43, DcNAA, EvLB, OxAm, REn, REnAL, St&VC, TwCA, TwCA Sup, WNAA*

Guizot, Madam 1773-1827 *CarSB*

Gulick, Bill *ConAu XR*

Gulick, Bill *see* Gulick, Grover C

Gulick, Grover C 1916- *ConAu 33, WWPNA*

Gulick, Grover C *see* Gulick, Bill

Gulick, Peggy 1918- *AuBYP*

Gull, Cyril Ranger 1875- *MnBBF*

Gullahorn, Genevieve *AuBYP*

Gulliver, Lemuel *ConAu XR*

Gulliver, Lemuel *see* Hastings, Macdonald

Gumley, F W *MnBBF*

Gumpertz, Robert 1925- *ConAu 69*

Gundrey, Elizabeth 1924- *ConAu 13R*

Gunn, Mrs. Aeneas 1870- *SingR 1*

Gunn, Mrs. Aeneas *see* Gunn, Jeannie

Gunn, Geoffrey *MnBBF*

Gunn, Jeannie *SingR 1*

Gunn, Jeannie *see* Gunn, Mrs. Aeneas

Gunn, Victor *MnBBF, WWBWI A*

Gunn, Victor *see* Brooks, Edwy Searles

Gunning, Monica Olwen 1930- *ConAu 65*

Gunnis, Louis *WWBWI 1*

Gunston, Bill *Au&Wr 6, ConAu XR, SmATA XR*

Gunston, Bill *see* Gunston, William Tudor

Gunston, David *Au&Wr 6*

Gunston, William Tudor 1927- *ConAu 49, SmATA 9*

Gunston, William Tudor *see* Gunston, Bill

Gunther, John 1901-1970 *AmA&B, AmNov, AuBYP, ConAu 9R, ConAu 25R, CurB 41, CurB 61, CurB 70, EvLB, LongC, NYTBE 1, OxAm, Pen Am, REn, REnAL, SmATA 2, TwCA, TwCA Sup*

Guralnik, David Bernard 1920- *DrAS 6F, WWWorJ 1972*

Gurdon, John Everard 1898- *MnBBF*

Gurko, Leo 1914- *ConAu 5R, DrAS 6E, SmATA 9, ThBJA, WWA 38*

Gurko, Miriam *ConAu 1R, SmATA 9, ThBJA*

Gurney, Eric *ChPo S2*

Gurney, Gene 1924- *ConAu 5R*

Gurney, J Eric 1910- *AuBYP, ConAu 1R*

Gurney, Nancy Jack 1915?-1973 *AuBYP,*

ConAu 45
Gurr, Robin Joy 1934- *SingR 2*
Gurr, Thomas Stuart *MnBBF*
Gustafson, Elton T *AuBYP*
Gustafson, Sarah R *SmATA 1*
Gustafson, Sarah R *see* Riedman, Sarah Regal
Gustaitis, Rasa 1934- *ConAu 25R*
Guthrie, A B, Jr. 1901- *ConAu 57, CurB 50,
   WrD*
Guthrie, Anne 1890- *AuBYP, ConAu 5R*
Guthrie, Archibald *MnBBF*
Guthrie, Archibald *see* Shaw, Frank H
Guthrie, Thomas Anstey 1856-1934 *Alli Sup,
   BiD&SB, Chambr 3, ChPo, ChPo S1,
   ChPo S2, DcEnA Ap, DcLEnL, EvLB,
   LongC, MnBBF, NCHEL, OxEng, TelT,
   TwCA, TwCA Sup, WWBWI A, WWCL*
Guthrie, Thomas Anstey *see* Anstey, F
Guthrie, Vee *ChPo, ChPo S2*
Gutnik, Martin J 1942- *ConAu 49*
Guy, Anne W *ConAu 5R*
Guy, Rosa 1925- *BlkAW, ConAu 17R*
Gwyne, Reginald *MnBBF*
Gwynne, Arthur *MnBBF*
Gwynne, Arthur *see* Evans, Gwyn
Gwynne, Fred *IlBYP*
Gwynne, John Harold 1899- *AuBYP*

H

Haaren, John Henry 1855-1916 *CarSB, DcNAA*

Haas, Carolyn Buhai 1926- *ConAu 65*

Haas, Dorothy F 1926- *ConAu 5R, ForWC 1970*

Haas, Dorothy F *see* Francis, Dee

Haas, Irene 1929- *ChPo S2, IlBYP, IlCB 1946, IlCB 1957, ThBJA*

Haas, James E 1943- *ConAu 61*

Habberton, John 1842-1921 *Alli Sup, AmA, AmA&B, BbD₁ BiD&SB, CarSB, Chambr 3, DcAmA, DcBiA, DcEnL, DcNAA, EvLB, OxAm, REnAL, WWCL*

Habberton, William *AuBYP*

Habel, Norman Charles 1932- *ConAu 17R, DrAS 6P*

Habenstreit, Barbara 1937- *ConAu 29, SmATA 5*

Haber, Heinz 1913- *AuBYP, CurB 52*

Haber, Louis 1910- *ConAu 29, SmATA 12*

Habig, Marion Alphonse 1901- *BkC 2, CatA 1930, ConAu 5R, DrAS 6H*

Hackett, Albert 1900- *AmA&B, AuBYP, BiEnAT, CurB 56, ModWD, OxAm, REnAL, WWA 38*

Hackett, Frances *AuBYP*

Hackney, Frances *SingR 1*

Hadath, Gunby 1880?-1954 *ChPo, WWBWI A, WWCL, WWLA*

Hadath, Gunby *see* Hadath, John Edward Gunby

Hadath, John Edward Gunby *MnBBF*

Hadath, John Edward Gunby *see* Duncan, James

Hadath, John Edward Gunby *see* Hadath, Gunby

Hadath, John Edward Gunby *see* Mowbray, John

Hadath, John Edward Gunby *see* O'Grady, Felix

Hadath, John Edward Gunby *see* Pearson, Shepperd

Hader, Berta 1890?-1976 *AmA&B, AmPB, Au&ICB, AuBYP, BkP, Cald 1938, ConAu 65, ConICB, IlBYP, IlCB 1744, IlCB 1946, IlCB 1957, JBA 1934, JBA 1951, St&VC*

Hader, Elmer Stanley 1889- *AmA&B, AmPB, Au&ICB, AuBYP, BkP, Cald 1938, ConICB, IlBYP, IlCB 1744, IlCB 1946, IlCB 1957, JBA 1934, JBA 1951, St&VC, WWA 38, WWAA 1973*

Hadfield, Alice Mary 1908- *Au&Wr 6*

Hadfield, Robert L *MnBBF, WWBWI A*

Hadley, Franklin *ConAu XR, SmATA XR*

Hadley, Franklin *see* Winterbotham, R R

Hadley, Leila 1926- *Au&Wr 6, ConAu 41*

Hafner, Marilyn 1925- *ChPo S1, IlBYP, SmATA 7*

Hafner, Marilyn *see* Reyna, Marilyn De

Hageman, Howard Garberich 1921- *ConAu 1R, DrAS 6P, WWA 38*

Hager, Alice Rogers 1894- *AmA&B, AuBYP, ConAu 5R, WWS 13*

Haggard, Sir Henry Rider 1856-1925 *Alli Sup, BbD, BiD&SB, Chambr 3, CyWA, DcBiA, DcEnA Ap, DcEuL, DcLEnL, EvLB, LongC, MnBBF, ModBL, NCHEL, OxEng, Pen Eng, REn, TelT, TwCA, TwCA Sup, WEAL, WWBWI A, WWCL*

Haggerty, James Joseph 1920- *ConAu 41, SmATA 5, WWS 13*

Haggeston, Scrope *MnBBF*

Haggeston, Scrope *see* Richardson

Hagon, Priscilla *ConAu XR, SmATA 5*

Hagon, Priscilla *see* Allan, Mabel Esther

Hahn, Emily 1905- *AmA&B, AuBYP, ConAu 1R, CurB 42, LongC, REnAL, SmATA 3, TwCA Sup, WNAA, WWA 38, WWAW 8, WWE 14, WWWor 2*

Hahn, Hannelore 1926- *ConAu 5R, DrAP 1975, SmATA 8*

Hahn, James 1947- *SmATA 9*

Hahn, Lynn 1949- *SmATA 9*

Hahn, Phil 1932- *WWA 38*

Haiblum, Isidore 1935- *DrAF 1976*

Haig-Brown, Roderick 1908-1976 *ConAu 5R, CurB 50, SmATA 12, WWW 14, WrD*

Haight, Anne Lyon 1895- *ConAu 33, WrD*

Haile, Ellen *Alli Sup, CarSB*

Haines, Charles 1928- *ConAu 41*

Haines, E *MnBBF*

Haines, Francis 1899- *ConAu 5R*

Haines, Gail Kay 1943- *ConAu 37, SmATA 11, WrD*

Haining, Peter 1940- *ConAu 45*

Hakluyt, Richard 1552?-1616 *Alli, AnCL, AtlBL, BiD&SB, BiDSA, BrAu, CasWL, Chambr 1, CrE&SL, CyWA, DcEnA, DcEnL, DcEuL, DcLEnL, EvLB, NCHEL, OxAm, OxCan, OxEng, Pen Eng, REn, REnAL, WEAL*

Halacy, Daniel Stephen, Jr. 1919- *AuBYP, ConAu 5R*

Halas, John 1912- *IntMPA 1975, WWGA*

Haldane, Roger John 1945- *SmATA 13*

Haldeman, Joe 1943- *ConAu 53*

Haldeman, Joe *see* Graham, Robert
Hale, Arlene 1924- *AuBYP*, *ConAu 1R*,
   WWAW 8
Hale, Clement *MnBBF*, *WWBWI A*
Hale, Clement *see* Steffens, Arthur
Hale, Edward Everett 1822-1909 *Alli*, *Alli Sup*,
   AmA, *AmA&B*, *BbD*, *BiD&SB*, *CarSB*,
   Chambr 3, *ChPo*, *ChPo S1*, *ChPo S2*,
   CnDAL, *CyAL 2*, *CyWA*, *DcAmA*,
   DcEnL, *DcLEnL*, *DcNAA*, *EvLB*,
   JBA 1934, *OxAm*, *Pen Am*, *REn*,
   REnAL
Hale, Geoffrey *MnBBF*
Hale, Helen *AuBYP*, *ConAu XR*,
   SmATA XR
Hale, Helen *see* Mulcahy, Lucille Burnett
Hale, Innis *MnBBF*
Hale, Innis *see* Hook, Samuel Clarke
Hale, Janet Campbell 1947- *ConAu 49*,
   DrAF 1976
Hale, John Rigby 1923- *Au&Wr 6*
Hale, Kathleen 1898- *Au&Wr 6*, *ChPo*,
   IlBYP, *IlCB 1946*, *IlCB 1957*, *WW 1974*,
   WWCL
Hale, Linda 1929- *ConAu 5R*, *SmATA 6*
Hale, Lucretia Peabody 1820-1900 *Alli Sup*,
   AmA, *AmA&B*, *BiD&SB*, *CarSB*,
   ChPo S2, *DcAmA*, *DcNAA*, *FamSYP*,
   JBA 1934, *OxAm*, *REnAL*, *WWCL*
Hale, Martin *MnBBF*, *WWBWI A*
Hale, Martin *see* Rochester, George Ernest
Hale, William Harlan 1910-1974 *AmA&B*,
   ConAu 49, *REnAL*, *WWA 38*, *WWE 14*
Hales, A G 1870- *MnBBF*, *WWBWI A*
Hales, Andrew *MnBBF*
Hales, C L *MnBBF*
Haley, Gail Einhart 1939- *ConAu 21R*, *IlBYP*,
   NewbC 1966, *ThBJA*, *WWA 38*
Halifax, Dick *MnBBF*
Hall, Adam *ConAu XR*, *EncM&D*
Hall, Adam *see* Trevor, Elleston
Hall, Adele 1910- *AuBYP*, *ConAu 1R*,
   SmATA 7
Hall, Anna Gertrude 1882-1967 *ConAu P-1*,
   SmATA 8
Hall, Anna Maria 1800-1881 *Alli*, *Alli Sup*,
   BbD, *BiD&SB*, *CarSB*, *DcEnL*, *DcLEnL*,
   EvLB, *NCHEL*, *Polre*
Hall, Anson *MnBBF*
Hall, Brian P 1935- *ConAu 61*
Hall, Carolyn Vosburg 1927- *ConAu 61*
Hall, Donald Andrew 1928- *AmA&B*, *AuBYP*,
   ChPo, *ChPo S1*, *CnE&AP*, *ConAu 5R*,
   ConLC 1, *ConP 1970*, *ConP 1975*,
   DrAF 1976, *DrAP 1975*, *OxAm*, *Pen Am*,
   RAdv 1, *REn*, *REnAL*, *WWA 38*,
   WorAu, *WrD*
Hall, Douglas 1931- *IlCB 1957*
Hall, Douglas Kent 1938- *ConAu 33*
Hall, Elvajean 1910- *AuBYP*, *BiDL 5*,
   ConAu 13R, *DrLC 1969*, *ForWC 1970*,
   SmATA 6, *WWAW 8*, *WWE 14*
Hall, Esther Greenacre *AuBYP*
Hall, Gordon Langley *Au&Wr 6*, *AuBYP*,
   ConAu XR
Hall, Gordon Langley *see* Simmons, Dawn
   Langley
Hall, Herman *MnBBF*
Hall, J Tillman 1916- *ConAu 1R*, *LE 5*

Hall, James Norman 1887-1951 *AmA&B*,
   AmNov, *AuBYP*, *CyWA*, *DcLEnL*,
   JBA 1934, *MnBBF*, *OxAm*, *Pen Am*,
   REn, *REnAL*, *TwCA*, *TwCA Sup*,
   WNAA
Hall, Jennie 1875-1921 *AmLY*, *DcNAA*
Hall, Lynn 1937- *ConAu 21R*, *SmATA 2*
Hall, Malcolm 1945- *ConAu 49*, *SmATA 7*
Hall, Marjory *AuBYP*, *ConAu XR*, *CurB 57*,
   WWAW 8, *WWE 14*, *WrD*
Hall, Marjory *see* Yeakley, Marjory Hall
Hall, Melville *MnBBF*
Hall, Natalie Watson 1923- *ConAu 5R*,
   IlCB 1957
Hall, Percy *MnBBF*
Hall, Richard *MnBBF*
Hall, Richard *see* Holton, Walter H
Hall, Rosalys Haskell 1914- *AuBYP*,
   ConAu 9R, *ForWC 1970*, *MorJA*,
   SmATA 7
Hall, Rupert *MnBBF*, *WWBWI A*
Hall, Rupert *see* Home-Gall, Edward Reginald
Hall, Ruth 1858-1934 *AmA&B*, *BiD&SB*,
   CarSB, *ChPo S1*, *DcAmA*, *DcNAA*,
   WNAA
Hall, Mrs. Samuel Carter 1800-1881 *Alli*,
   BrAu 19, *CarSB*, *Chambr 3*, *ChPo*,
   ChPo S1, *ChPo S2*
Hall, Saville *MnBBF*
Hall, Susan 1940- *ConAu 57*
Hall, William Norman 1915-1974 *AuBYP*,
   ConAu 53
Hall, Willis 1929- *CnMD*, *CnThe*, *ConDr 1*,
   CrCD, *LongC*, *ModWD*, *Pen Eng*,
   WW 1974, *WWT 15*, *WrD*
Hall-Quest, Olga Wilbourne 1899- *Au&Wr 6*,
   AuBYP, *ConAu 5R*, *ForWC 1970*,
   SmATA 11
Hallard, Peter J *MnBBF*, *SmATA 3*
Hallard, Peter J *see* Catherall, Arthur
Haller, Adolf 1897- *AuBYP*
Halliburton, Richard 1900-1939 *AmA&B*,
   CnDAL, *DcNAA*, *EvLB*, *OxAm*, *REnAL*,
   TwCA, *TwCA Sup*, *WNAA*
Halliburton, Warren J 1924- *ConAu 33*,
   LBAA
Halliday, E M 1913- *ConAu 1R*
Halliday, Michael *ConAu XR*, *EncM&D*,
   LongC, *WWBWI A*
Halliday, Michael *see* Creasey, John
Halliday, Shirley *WWBWI A*
Halliday, Shirley *see* Bobin, Donald E M
Hallin, Emily Watson 1919- *ConAu 25R*,
   SmATA 6, *WrD*
Hallinan, P K 1944- *ConAu 69*
Halliwell, James Orchard 1820-1889 *Alli*,
   CarSB, *DcEnA*, *OxEng*, *St&VC*
Hallstead, William Finn, III 1924- *ConAu 5R*,
   SmATA 11, *WWE 14*
Hallward, Michael 1889- *ConAu 49*,
   SmATA 12
Halse, Harold *MnBBF*
Halsell, Grace 1923- *AuBYP*, *AuNews 1*,
   ConAu 21R, *SmATA 13*
Halsman, Philippe 1906- *AmA&B*, *Au&Wr 6*,
   AuBYP, *ConAu 21R*, *CurB 60*,
   WWWor 2
Halstead, E Sinclair *MnBBF*, *WWBWI A*
Halstead, E Sinclair *see* Brooks, Edwy Searles

Halstead, S B *MnBBF, WWBWI A*

Halstead, S B *see* Brooks, Edwy Searles

Halsted, Anna Roosevelt 1906-1975 *ConAu 61*

Halter, Jon C 1941- *ConAu 61*

Ham, Olive Mary 1918- *Au&Wr 6, WrD*

Hamada, Hirosuke 1893- *ConAu 45*

Hamberger, John F 1934- *ConAu 69, IlBYP, IlCB 1957*

Hambleton, Jack *AuBYP*

Hamblin, Dora Jane 1920- *AuBYP, ConAu 37, ForWC 1970, WWAW 8*

Hamer, Margaret *TelT*

Hamer, Margaret *see* Browne, Maggie

Hamer, Sam Hield 1869- *ChPo, ChPo S2, MnBBF*

Hamerstrom, Frances 1907- *ConAu 69*

Hamerton, Philip Gilbert 1834-1894 *Alli Sup, BbD, BiD&SB, BrAu 19, CarSB, Chambr 3, ChPo, ChPo S1, DcBiA, DcEnL, EvLB, NCHEL*

Hamil, Thomas Arthur 1928- *AuBYP*

Hamill, Ethel *ConAu XR*

Hamill, Ethel *see* Webb, Jean Francis

Hamilton, Buzz *ConAu XR*

Hamilton, Buzz *see* Hemming, Roy

Hamilton, Cecily 1872-1952 *LongC, MnBBF, WWBWI A*

Hamilton, Cecily *see* Carr, Howard

Hamilton, Cecily *see* Hamilton, Max

Hamilton, Cecily *see* Herrod, Walter

Hamilton, Cecily *see* Howard, Frank

Hamilton, Cecily *see* Maitland, T G Dowling

Hamilton, Cecily *see* Monck, Tristan K

Hamilton, Cecily *see* Osborne, Adrian T

Hamilton, Cecily *see* Rae, Scott

Hamilton, Charles 1913- *ChPo S2, ConAu 5R*

Hamilton, Charles Harold St. John 1875?-1961 *LongC, MnBBF, OxEng, SmATA 13, WWBWI A, WWCL*

Hamilton, Charles Harold St. John *see* Clive, Clifford

Hamilton, Charles Harold St. John *see* Clifford, Martin

Hamilton, Charles Harold St. John *see* Clifton, Henry

Hamilton, Charles Harold St. John *see* Clifton, Harry

Hamilton, Charles Harold St. John *see* Cobham, Sir Alan

Hamilton, Charles Harold St. John *see* Conquest, Owen

Hamilton, Charles Harold St. John *see* Conway, Gordon

Hamilton, Charles Harold St. John *see* Dorrian, Harry

Hamilton, Charles Harold St. John *see* Dorian, Harry

Hamilton, Charles Harold St. John *see* Drake, Frank

Hamilton, Charles Harold St. John *see* Fox, Freeman

Hamilton, Charles Harold St. John *see* Greening, Hamilton

Hamilton, Charles Harold St. John *see* Herbert, Cecil

Hamilton, Charles Harold St. John *see* Howard, Prosper

Hamilton, Charles Harold St. John *see* Jennings, Robert

Hamilton, Charles Harold St. John *see* Jones, Gillingham

Hamilton, Charles Harold St. John *see* Llewelyn, T Harcourt

Hamilton, Charles Harold St. John *see* Owen, Clifford

Hamilton, Charles Harold St. John *see* Redway, Ridley

Hamilton, Charles Harold St. John *see* Redway, Ralph

Hamilton, Charles Harold St. John *see* Richards, Frank

Hamilton, Charles Harold St. John *see* Richards, Hilda

Hamilton, Charles Harold St. John *see* Robbins, Raleigh

Hamilton, Charles Harold St. John *see* Rodway, Roland

Hamilton, Charles Harold St. John *see* Rogers, Robert

Hamilton, Charles Harold St. John *see* Stanley, Robert

Hamilton, Charles Harold St. John *see* Stanhope, Eric

Hamilton, Charles Harold St. John *see* Wallace, Nigel

Hamilton, Charles Harold St. John *see* Wynyard, Talbot

Hamilton, Charles Harold St. John *see* Wynard, Talbot

Hamilton, Clive *CurB 44, CurB 64, EvLB, LongC, NCHEL, SmATA XR, TwCA Sup*

Hamilton, Clive *see* Lewis, C S

Hamilton, Dorothy 1906- *ConAu 33, SmATA 12*

Hamilton, Edith 1867-1963 *AmA&B, AnCL, CurB 63, REn, REnAL, TwCA, TwCA Sup, WNAA*

Hamilton, Ernest *MnBBF*

Hamilton, Ernest *see* Goddard, Ernest Hope

Hamilton, Gail *ConAu XR*

Hamilton, Gail *see* Corcoran, Barbara

Hamilton, George *MnBBF, WWBWI A*

Hamilton, George *see* Teed, George Heber

Hamilton, Kay *AuBYP, ConAu XR, OhA&B*

Hamilton, Kay *see* DeLeeuw, Cateau

Hamilton, Max *MnBBF, WWBWI A*

Hamilton, Max *see* Hamilton, Cecily

Hamilton, Murray *MnBBF*

Hamilton, Murray *see* Graydon, Robert Murray

Hamilton, Murray *see* Teed, George Heber

Hamilton, Robert W *ConAu XR*

Hamilton, Robert W *see* Stratemeyer, Edward L

Hamilton, Russel *AuBYP*

Hamilton, Virginia 1936- *Au&ICB, AuBYP, AuNews 1, BlkAW, ChLR 1, ChPo S2, ConAu 25R, MorBMP, NewbC 1966, SmATA 4, WWAW 8*

Hamley, Dennis 1935- *ConAu 57*

Hamlin, V T 1900- *ArtCS*

Hamm, Jack 1916- *ConAu 5R*

Hammer, Jeanne-Ruth 1912- *ConAu 9R*

Hammer, Richard 1928- *ConAu 25R, SmATA 6*

Hammerman, Gay M 1926- *ConAu 33, SmATA 9*

Hammerton, Grenville *MnBBF, WWBWI A*

Hammerton, Grenville *see* Shaw, Frank H

Hammett, Samuel Dashiell 1894-1961 *AmA&B,*
AuNews 1, DcLEnL, EvLB, MnBBF
Hammond, Ralph *AuBYP, ConAu XR,*
MnBBF
Hammond, Ralph *see* Hammond Innes, Ralph
Hammond, Wally *MnBBF*
Hammond, Wally *see* Bolton, F T
Hammond, Wally *see* Hammond, Walter
Hammond, Walter *MnBBF*
Hammond, Walter *see* Hammond, Wally
Hammond, Winifred Graham 1899-
IndAu 1917
Hammond Innes, Ralph 1913- *Au&Wr 6,*
AuBYP, ConAu 5R, CurB 54, LongC,
WW 1974, WWWor 2, WrD
Hammond Innes, Ralph *see* Hammond, Ralph
Hammontree, Marie 1913- *ConAu 5R,*
SmATA 13, WrD
Hamori, Laszlo Dezso 1911- *ConAu 9R*
Hampden, John 1898- *Au&Wr 6, WW 1974*
Hample, Stoo 1926- *ChPo*
Hampshire, Michael Allen *IlBYP*
Hampson, Alfred Leete *ChPo*
Hampton, Christopher Martin 1929- *ConAu 53,*
ConP 1975, WrD
Hamre, Leif 1914- *Au&Wr 6, ConAu 5R,*
SmATA 5, WrD
Hanaford, Phebe Ann 1829-1921 *Alli Sup,*
AmA&B, BbD, BiD&SB, CarSB,
DcAmA
Hancock, Alice VanFossen 1890- *ConAu 1R*
Hancock, Mary A 1923- *ConAu 37*
Hancock, Sibyl 1940- *ConAu 49, SmATA 9*
Handford, Nourma *SingR 1*
Handforth, Thomas S 1897-1948 *AmA&B,*
AuBYP, Cald 1938, IlBYP, IlCB 1744,
IlCB 1946, JBA 1951
Hanes, Frank Borden 1920- *AmA&B,*
ConAu 1R, WWS 13
Haney, Lynn 1941- *ConAu 49*
Hanff, Helene *ConAu 5R, SmATA 11*
Hankey, William Lee 1869- *ChPo S2,*
IlCB 1744
Hankinson, C J *see* Holland, Clive
Hankinson, Charles James 1866- *MnBBF,*
WWLA
Hanna, Geneva R *AuBYP*
Hanna, Paul Robert 1902- *ConAu 45, LE 5,*
SmATA 9
Hannum, Sara *AuBYP, ChPo S1*
Hano, Arnold 1922- *AuBYP, ConAu 9R,*
SmATA 12, WWW 14
Hansberry, Lorraine 1930-1965 *AmA&B,*
AuNews 2, BiEnAT, BlkAW, CasWL,
CnMD Sup, ConAu 25R, CrCD,
CurB 59, CurB 65, McGWD,
ModAL Sup, ModWD, REnAL, WorAu
Hansen, Harry 1884- *AmA&B, AuBYP,*
CurB 42, REnAL, TwCA, TwCA Sup,
WW 1974, WWA 38
Hansen, Mary Lewis 1933- *ConAu 17R*
Hanser, Richard 1909- *ConAu 5R,*
SmATA 13
Hanson, Charles Henry *Alli Sup, CarSB*
Hanson, Joan 1938- *ConAu 33, SmATA 8,*
WrD
Hanson, Michael James 1942- *ConAu 61,*
WrD
Hanson, V J *MnBBF, WWBWI A*

Hansor, Joyce *MnBBF*
Hapgood, Charles Hutchins 1904- *Au&Wr 6,*
ConAu 17R
Harcourt, George *MnBBF*
Hardcastle, Michael 1933- *ConAu 25R, WrD*
Hardcastle, Michael *see* Clark, David
Harden, Oleta Elizabeth 1935- *ConAu 37,*
WrD
Hardendorff, Jeanne B *ChPo S2*
Harder, Eleanor 1925- *ConAu 37*
Hardie, W Auchterlonie 1897- *MnBBF*
Harding, Charlotte 1873- *IlCB 1744*
Harding, James 1929- *Au&Wr 6, ConAu 33*
Harding, Robert 1897- *ChPo S1, WWBWI A*
Harding, S Graham *MnBBF*
Hardinge, Rex 1904- *MnBBF, WWBWI A*
Hardinge, Rex *see* Quintin, Rex
Hardinge, Rex *see* Wrexe, Charles
Hardwick, Michael 1924- *Au&Wr 6,*
ConAu 49
Hardwick, Mollie *Au&Wr 6, ConAu 49*
Hardwick, Richard 1923- *SmATA 12*
Hardwick, Richard *see* Holmes, Rick
Hardwick, Sylvia *ConAu XR*
Hardwick, Sylvia *see* Doherty, Ivy R Duffy
Hardy, A S *MnBBF*
Hardy, A S *see* Steffens, Arthur
Hardy, Alice Dale *ConAu P-2, SmATA 1*
Hardy, Alice Dale *see* Stratemeyer, Edward L
Hardy, Arthur Steffens 1875?-1940? *MnBBF,*
WWBWI A
Hardy, Arthur Steffens *see* Steffens, Arthur
Hardy, David A 1936- *ConAu 61, SmATA 9*
Hardy, E S *MnBBF*
Hardy, E S *see* Steffens, Arthur
Hardy, Paul 1862- *ChPo, ChPo S1, ChPo S2,*
WWBWI I
Hardy, Philip *MnBBF*
Hardy, Philip *see* Lowe, Claud D
Hardy, Stuart *ConAu XR, SmATA XR*
Hardy, Stuart *see* Schisgal, Oscar
Hardy, Thomas 1840-1928 *Alli Sup, AnCL,*
AtlBL, BbD, BiD&SB, BrAu 19, CasWL,
Chambr 3, ChPo, ChPo S1, ChPo S2,
CnE&AP, CnMWL, CriT 3, CyWA,
DcBiA, DcEnA, DcEnA Ap, DcEnL,
DcEuL, DcLEnL, EncWL, EvLB, LongC,
ModBL, ModBL Sup, ModWD, NCHEL,
OxEng, Pen Eng, RAdv 1, RCom, REn,
TwCW, WEAL, WWCL, WWLA,
WWTwL
Hare, T Truxton 1878-1956 *CarSB*
Harewood, George H H Lascelles, Earl Of 1923-
CurB 65, IntWW 38, WW 1974
Harfield, Edmund *MnBBF, WWBWI A*
Hargens, Charles, Jr. *ConICB*
Hargis, Ed *ChPo*
Hargis, John Edwin 1914- *IlCB 1744*
Hargrave, Sandra 1945- *SingR 2*
Hargrave, Sidney *MnBBF*
Harington, Joy 1914- *IntMPA 1975, WrD*
Hark, Mildred *ConAu XR, SmATA XR*
Hark, Mildred *see* McQueen, Mildred Hark
Harkaway, Hal *ConAu XR*
Harkaway, Hal *see* Stratemeyer, Edward L
Harker, Herbert *OxCan Sup*
Harker, John *MnBBF*
Harkins, Philip 1912- *AuBYP, ConAu 29,*
MorJA, SmATA 6

Harkins, Philip *see* Blaine, John
Harlan, Glen *ConAu XR, SmATA XR*
Harlan, Glen *see* Cebulash, Mel
Harland, Henry 1861-1905 *Alli Sup, AmA,*
 AmA&B, BbD, BiD&SB, CarSB,
 Chambr 3, DcAmA, DcBiA, DcEnA Ap,
 DcNAA, EvLB, LongC, OxAm, OxEng,
 Pen Am, REnAL
Harley, Timothy *Alli Sup*
Harlow, Alvin Fay 1875-1963 *AmA&B,*
 AuBYP, WNAA
Harmelink, Barbara *ConAu 61, SmATA 9*
Harmer, Mabel 1894- *ConAu 9R*
Harmon, Margaret 1906- *EnAu 69*
Harms, Valerie 1940- *ConAu 49*
Harmsworth, Alfred Charles William 1865-1922
 LongC, MnBBF, NCHEL
Harnan, Terry 1920- *ConAu 45, SmATA 12*
Harnan, Terry *see* Hull, Eric Traviss
Harnden, Ruth *ChPo S2*
Harnett, Cynthia Mary 1893- *Au&Wr 6,*
 AuBYP, ConAu P-1, IlCB 1946,
 SmATA 5, ThBJA, WWCL, WrD
Harper, Gillis *MnBBF*
Harper, Gillis *see* Miln, H Crichton
Harper, Harry *MnBBF*
Harper, Harry *see* Clifford, Martin
Harper, Wilhelmina 1884-1973 *AmA&B,*
 AuBYP, ConAu P-1, SmATA 4, WNAA,
 WWAW 8
Harribance, Sean *BiN 1974*
Harrington, Lyn Davis 1911- *AuBYP,*
 ConAu 5R, OxCan, OxCan Sup, Prof,
 SmATA 5
Harrington, Mark Raymond 1882-1971
 ConAu P-2
Harrington, Michael 1928- *AmA&B, CelR 3,*
 ConAu 17R, CurB 69, WWA 38
Harris, Christie Irwin 1907- *ConAu 5R,*
 OxCan Sup, Prof, SmATA 6
Harris, Colver *ConAu XR, OhA&B,*
 SmATA 7
Harris, Colver *see* Colver, Anne
Harris, Dorothy Joan 1931- *ConAu 45,*
 SmATA 13
Harris, Ernest S *MnBBF*
Harris, G W *MnBBF*
Harris, Gene Gray 1929- *ConAu 17R*
Harris, George Lawrence 1910- *AmMWS 12S*
Harris, Janet 1932- *ConAu 33, SmATA 4*
Harris, Joel Chandler 1848-1908 *Alli Sup,*
 AmA, AmA&B, AnCL, AtlBL, AuBYP,
 BbD, BiD&SB, BiDSA, CarSB, CasWL,
 Chambr 3, ChPo, ChPo S1, ChPo S2,
 CnDAL, CyWA, DcAmA, DcBiA,
 DcEnA Ap, DcLEnL, DcNAA, EvLB,
 FamAYP, JBA 1934, OxAm, OxEng,
 Pen Am, RAdv 1, REn, REnAL,
 St&VC, WEAL, WWCL, YABC 1
Harris, John *Au&Wr 6, WrD*
Harris, John B *MnBBF*
Harris, John Wyndham Parkes Lucas Beynon
 WorAu
Harris, John Wyndham Parkes Lucas Beynon *see*
 Beynon, John
Harris, Julie 1925- *BiEnAT, BiN 1974,*
 CelR 3, CurB 56, IntMPA 1975,
 WWA 38, WWAW 8, WWT 15,
 WWWor 2

Harris, Leon A, Jr. 1926- *AmSCAP 66,*
 AuBYP, ConAu 9R, SmATA 4,
 WWAA 1973
Harris, MacDonald *ConAu XR*
Harris, MacDonald *see* Heiney, Donald
Harris, Marilyn *ConAu XR*
Harris, Marilyn *see* Springer, Marilyn Ha
Harris, Marion Rose 1925- *Au&Wr 6, WrD,*
 ConAu P-1
Harris, Mary K 1905-1966 *CatA 1952,*
 ConAu P-1
Harris, Ray *SingR 1*
Harris, Rosemary Jeanne 1923- *Au&Wr 6,*
 BiEnAT, ConAu 33, SmATA 4,
 WW 1974, WrD
Harris, Stephen LeRoy 1937- *ConAu 29,*
 DrAS 6E, WWW 14
Harrison, Bill *ConAu XR*
Harrison, Bill *see* Harrison, William C
Harrison, C William 1913- *AuBYP,*
 IndAu 1917
Harrison, Charles *WWBWI 1*
Harrison, Cynthia Ellen 1946- *BiDL 5*
Harrison, Deloris 1938- *ConAu 61, SmATA 9*
Harrison, Edwin *MnBBF, WWBWI A*
Harrison, Edwin *see* Ballard, Eric Alan
Harrison, Elizabeth Cavanna 1909-
 ForWC 1970, WrD
Harrison, F Bayford *Alli Sup, MnBBF*
Harrison, George Russell 1898- *AmMWS 12P,*
 ConAu 17R
Harrison, H *MnBBF*
Harrison, Harry 1925- *ConAu 1R, SmATA 4,*
 WrD
Harrison, J P *MnBBF*
Harrison, Molly 1909- *Au&Wr 6, WW 1974*
Harrison, William C 1919- *ConAu 25R*
Harrison, William C *see* Harrison, Bill
Harrop, John *MnBBF*
Harshaw, Ruth Hetzel *AuBYP, WNAA*
Harston, Ruth 1944- *ConAu 41*
Hart, Carolyn Gimpel 1936- *ConAu 13R,*
 ForWC 1970
Hart, Dick 1920- *ArtsCL, IlCB 1946*
Hart, Elizabeth Anna 1822-1886 *ChPo S1,*
 TelT
Hart, James *MnBBF*
Hart, James *see* Higgins, James Hart
Hart, Johnny 1931- *ArtCS, AuNews 1,*
 BiN 1974, ConAu 49
Hart, Leonard *MnBBF*
Hart, Leonard *see* Barnard, Alfred J
Hart, Sackville *MnBBF*
Hart, William S *MnBBF*
Harte, Bret 1836?-1902 *AmA, AmA&B,*
 AtlBL, AuBYP, BiD&SB, CasWL,
 CnDAL, CriT 3, CyWA, DcAmA,
 DcNAA, OxAm, Pen Am, RAdv 1, REn,
 REnAL, WEAL
Harte, Oliver *MnBBF*
Harte, Oliver *see* Stagg, J R
Hartland, Edwin 1848-1927 *CarSB*
Hartman, Gertrude 1876-1955 *AmA&B,*
 JBA 1951
Hartmann, Helmut Henry *WrD*
Hartog, Jan De 1914- *CasWL, EncWL,*
 IntWW 38, TwCA Sup
Hartog, Jan De *see* DeHartog, Jan
Hartshorn, Ruth M 1928- *SmATA 11*

Hartwell, J M *MnBBF*
Hartwell, Nancy *AuBYP, ConAu XR*
Harvey, Alick *MnBBF*
Harvey, C H Fox *MnBBF*
Harvey, H *MnBBF*
Harvey, Jack *MnBBF*
Harvey, Ross *MnBBF, WWBWI A*
Harvey, Ross *see* Hook, H Clarke
Harwin, Brian *AuBYP, ConAu XR, SmATA XR*
Harwin, Brian *see* Henderson, LeGrand
Harwood, David 1938- *Au&Wr 6, WrD*
Harwood, Pearl Augusta 1903- *ConAu 13R, SmATA 9*
Haskell, Arnold Lionel 1903- *Au&Wr 6,* · *ConAu 5R, IntWW 38, SmATA 6, WW 1974, WWWor 2*
Haskell, Helen Eggleston 1871- *AmA&B, JBA 1934, JBA 1951*
Haskin, Dorothy Clark 1905- *ConAu 5R, ForWC 1970, WWAW 8, WrD*
Haskin, Dorothy Clark *see* Clark, Howard
Haskins, Ilma 1919- *ConAu 45*
Haskins, James 1941- *ChLR 3, ConAu 33, SmATA 9*
Haskins, James *see* Haskins, Jim
Haskins, Jim *ConAu XR, LBAA, SmATA XR, WrD*
Haskins, Jim *see* Haskins, James
Haslar, John *MnBBF*
Hasler, Joan 1931- *ConAu 29*
Haslip, Joan 1912- *WW 1974*
Hassall, Joan 1906- *ChPo, ChPo S1, ChPo S2, IlCB 1946, WW 1974, WWGA*
Hassall, John 1868-1948 *ChPo, ChPo S1, LongC, WWBWI I*
Hasselriis, Else *ConICB, IlCB 1744*
Hastings, Graham *ConAu XR, EncM&D*
Hastings, Graham *see* Jeffries, Roderic
Hastings, Ian 1912- *ConAu 45*
Hastings, Macdonald 1909- *Au&Wr 6, ConAu 53, EncM&D, WrD*
Hastings, Macdonald *see* Gulliver, Lemuel
Hastings, Michael *MnBBF*
Hatch, Alden 1898-1975 *AmA&B, Au&Wr 6, AuBYP, ConAu 65, WWA 38*
Hatch, Eric *NYTBE 4*
Hatch, James V 1928- *BiEnAT, ConAu 41, DrAS 6E*
Hatch, Mary Cottam 1912- *AnCL, BiDL 5, St&VC*
Hatch, Richard Warren 1898- *AmA&B, WNAA, WWCL*
Hatfield, William 1892?- *SingR 1*
Hathaway, Lulu 1903- *BiDL 5, ConAu 13R*
Hatherley, Captain *MnBBF*
Hatherway, Cyril *MnBBF*
Hatherway, Cyril *see* Burrage, Alfred Sherrington
Hauff, Wilhelm 1802-1827 *AuBYP, BiD&SB, CasWL, DcBiA, EuAu, EvEuW, OxGer, Pen Eur, REn, WWCL*
Haugaard, Erik Christian 1923- *AuBYP, ConAu 5R, SmATA 4, ThBJA, WrD*
Haughton, Rosemary 1927- *Au&Wr 6, ConAu 5R, WrD*
Hauman, Doris 1897- *IlCB 1946*
Hauman, George 1890- *IlCB 1946*

Haupt, Enid Annenberg *ForWC 1970, WWAW 8*
Hauser, Margaret L 1909- *ConAu P-1, SmATA 10*
Hauser, Margaret L *see* Head, Gay
Hausman, Gerald 1945- *ConAu 45, DrAP 1975, SmATA 13*
Hausman, Gerald *see* Hausman, Gerry
Hausman, Gerry *SmATA XR*
Hausman, Gerry *see* Hausman, Gerald
Hautzig, Esther Rudomin 1930- *AuBYP, ConAu 1R, ForWC 1970, MorBMP, SmATA 4, ThBJA, WrD*
Hautzig, Esther Rudomin *see* Rudomin, Esther
Havant, H *MnBBF*
Havant, H *see* Hughes, Harry
Havenhand, John *ConAu XR, SmATA XR*
Havenhand, John *see* Cox, John Roberts
Havighurst, Marion Boyd d1974 *AuBYP, ConAu 49, ConAu P-1, MorJA, OhA&B*
Havighurst, Walter Edwin 1901- *AmA&B, AmNov, Au&Wr 6, AuBYP, CnDAL, ConAu 1R, DrAS 6E, MorJA, OhA&B, OxAm, REnAL, SmATA 1, TwCA Sup, WWA 38*
Haviland, Fergus, Captain *MnBBF*
Haviland, Fergus, Captain *see* Goddard, Norman Molyneux
Haviland, Virginia 1911- *BiDL 5, ChPo S1, ChPo S2, ConAu 17R, SmATA 6, WWA 38, WWAW 8, WWS 13*
Havilton, Jeffrey *MnBBF, WWBWI A*
Havrevold, Finn 1905- *IntWW 38, WWWor 2*
Hawes, Charles Boardman 1889-1923 *AmA&B, AuBYP, DcNAA, JBA 1934, Newb 1922, REnAL, TwCA*
Hawes, Evelyn *AuNews 1, ConAu 13R*
Hawes, Judy 1913- *AmPB, ConAu 33, SmATA 4, WrD*
Hawk, Sparrow *MnBBF*
Hawk, Virginia Driving *SmATA 8*
Hawke, David Freeman 1923- *DrAS 6H*
Hawke, G *MnBBF*
Hawke, Robert *WWBWI A*
Hawke, Robert, Captain *MnBBF*
Hawke, Robert, Captain *see* Bowman, Gerald
Hawke, Robert *see* O'Mant, Hedley Percival Angelo
Hawkes, Hester 1900- *AuBYP*
Hawkesworth, Eric 1921- *ConAu 29, SmATA 13, WrD*
Hawkesworth, Eric *see* Great Comte, The
Hawkins, Sir Anthony Hope 1863-1933 *BbD, BiD&SB, Chambr 3, DcEnA Ap, DcLEnL, EvLB, LongC, NCHEL, OxEng, REn, TelT, TwCA, TwCA Sup, WWCL*
Hawkins, Anthony Hope *see* Hope, Anthony
Hawkins, Arthur 1903- *ConAu 21R, IlBYP*
Hawkins, Irene Beatrice 1906- *IlCB 1946*
Hawkins, John *MnBBF*
Hawkins, John *see* Catchpole, William Leslie
Hawkins, K J *MnBBF*
Hawkins, Michael *MnBBF*
Hawkins, Quail 1905- *AuBYP, ConAu 17R, SmATA 6*
Hawkins, Sheila 1905- *IlCB 1744, SingR 1*
Hawkinson, John Samuel 1912- *AuBYP, ConAu 5R, ConAu 21R, SmATA 4,*

WWA 38, WWMW 14
Hawkinson, Lucy 1924- *AuBYP*
Hawks, Francis Lister 1798-1866 *Alli, Alli Sup,*
AmA, AmA&B, BiD&SB, BiDSA,
CarSB, ChPo, ChPo S1, ChPo S2,
CyAL 2, DcAmA, DcNAA
Hawley, George *MnBBF*
Hawley, Herbert *MnBBF*
Hawley, Mabel C *ConAu P-2, SmATA 1*
Hawley, Mabel C *see* Stratemeyer, Edward L
Hawthorne, Hildegarde 1871-1952 *AmA&B,*
AuBYP, ChPo, DcAmA, JBA 1934,
JBA 1951, REnAL, WNAA
Hawthorne, Jennie *WrD*
Hawthorne, Julian 1846-1934 *Alli Sup,*
AmA&B, BbD, BiD&SB, CarSB,
Chambr 3, ChPo, ChPo S2, DcAmA,
DcBiA, DcEnA, DcEnA Ap, DcEnL,
DcNAA, EncM&D, OxAm, REnAL,
TwCA, WNAA
Hawthorne, Nathaniel 1804-1864 *Alli, Alli Sup,*
AmA, AmA&B, AmWr, AtlBL, BbD,
BiD&SB, CarSB, CasWL, Chambr 3,
ChPo S1, ChPo S2, CnDAL, CriT 3,
CyAL 2, CyWA, DcAmA, DcBiA,
DcEnA, DcEnA Ap, DcEnL, DcLEnL,
DcNAA, EvLB, FamAYP, MouLC 3,
OxAm, OxEng, Pen Am, RAdv 1,
RCom, REn, REnAL, St&VC, WEAL,
WWCL, YABC 2
Hawthorne, R M, Captain *HsB&A, YABC 1*
Hawthorne, R M, Captain *see* Ellis, Edward S
Hawton, Hector 1901- *Au&Wr 6,*
ConAu 13R, MnBBF, WWBWI A, WrD
Hawton, Hector *see* Sylvester, John
Hay, Ian 1876-1952 *Chambr 3, DcLEnL,*
EvLB, LongC, NCHEL, REn, TwCA,
TwCA Sup, TwCW, WWBWI A
Hay, John 1915- *AmA&B, SmATA 13,*
WWA 38
Hay, Montague- *MnBBF*
Hay, Timothy *YABC XR*
Hay, Timothy *see* Brown, Margaret Wise
Hay, Will *WWBWI A*
Haycox, Ernest 1899-1950 *AmA&B, MnBBF,*
REnAL, TwCA Sup, WNAA
Haycraft, Howard 1905- *AmA&B, AuBYP,*
BiDL 5, ConAu 21R, CurB 41, CurB 54,
EncM&D, IntWW 38, REnAL,
SmATA 6, WWA 38
Haycraft, Molly Costain 1911- *ConAu 13R,*
SmATA 6
Hayden, Gwendolen Lampshire *WWAW 8*
Hayden, Howard K 1930- *ConAu 17R*
Hayden, Robert C, Jr. 1937- *ConAu 69, WrD*
Haydon, Arthur Lincoln 1872- *ChPo, ChPo S1,*
ChPo S2, MnBBF, OxCan, WWBWI A,
WWLA
Haydon, Harold 1909- *WWAA 1973*
Haydon, N G *MnBBF*
Haydon, N G *see* Pembury, Grosvenor
Haydon, Percy Montague 1895- *MnBBF,*
WWBWI A
Haydon, Rex *MnBBF*
Hayens, Herbert 1861- *MnBBF, WWBWI A*
Hayes, Carlton Joseph Huntley 1882-1964
AmA&B, AmLY, CatA 1930, ConAu 1R,
CurB 42, CurB 64, LongC, REnAL,
SmATA 11, TwCA Sup, WNAA

Hayes, Clair W *CarSB*
Hayes, Florence 1895- *AuBYP*
Hayes, Geoffrey 1947- *ConAu 65*
Hayes, Ivor *MnBBF*
Hayes, Ivor *see* Ransome, L E
Hayes, John F 1904- *CanWW 12, ConAu P-1,*
SmATA 11
Hayes, Nancy M *WWBWI A*
Hayes, Will *ConAu 5R, SmATA 7*
Hayes, William Dimitt 1913- *AuBYP,*
ConAu 5R, SmATA 8, WW 1974
Haynes, Betsy 1937- *ConAu 57*
Haynes, Nancy M *MnBBF*
Haynes, Nancy M *see* Freeman, Mrs. John
Haynes, Pat *ConAu XR, MnBBF,*
WWBWI A
Haynes, Pat *see* McKeag, Ernest L
Haynes, Robert *IIBYP, MnBBF*
Haynes, V A *MnBBF*
Hays, Hobe *AuBYP*
Hays, Wilma Pitchford 1909- *AuBYP,*
ConAu 1R, ForWC 1970, SmATA 1,
ThBJA, WWAW 8, WrD
Hayter, Cecil Goodenough 1871-1922 *MnBBF,*
WWBWI A
Hayter, Cecil Goodenough *see* Bird, Lewis
Hayter, Cecil Goodenough *see* Steel, Howard
Hayward, A E 1885-1939 *ArtCS*
Hayward, Arthur Lawrence 1885- *MnBBF,*
WWBWI A, WWLA
Hayward, Charles Harold 1898- *Au&Wr 6,*
ConAu 9R
Hayward, Dagney *MnBBF*
Hayward, Dagney *see* Major, J D
Hayward, William Stephens *Alli Sup, MnBBF*
Haywood, Carolyn 1898- *AmA&B, Au&ICB,*
AuBYP, ChPo, ConAu 5R, ForWC 1970,
JBA 1951, MorBMP, SmATA 1
Hazard, Buck *MnBBF*
Hazel, Harry *AmA&B, MnBBF*
Hazel, Harry *see* Jones, J
Hazeltine, Alice Isabel 1878- *AuBYP, ChPo*
Hazelwood, Rex *MnBBF, WWBWI A*
Hazlett, Edward Everett 1892- *AuBYP*
Head, Ann *ConAu XR*
Head, Ann *see* Morse, Anne Christensen
Head, Gay *ConAu XR, SmATA XR*
Head, Gay *see* Hauser, Margaret L
Headley, Elizabeth *AuBYP, ConAu XR,*
MorJA, SmATA 1
Headley, Elizabeth *see* Cavanna, Betty
Headstrom, Richard 1902- *AuBYP,*
ConAu 1R, SmATA 8
Heady, Eleanor Butler 1917- *ConAu 41,*
SmATA 7, SmATA 8, WrD
Heady, Harold Franklin 1916- *AmMWS 12P,*
ConAu 53, WWA 38, WrD
Heal, Edith 1903- *ConAu 1R, SmATA 7,*
WWE 14
Heal, Edith *see* Berrien, Edith Heal
Heal, Edith *see* Page, Eileen
Heal, Edith *see* Powers, Margaret
Heaps, Willard Allison 1909- *AuBYP*
Heard, J Norman 1922- *ConAu 9R*
Hearn, Lafcadio 1850-1904 *Alli Sup, AmA,*
AmA&B, AnCL, AtlBL, BbD, BiD&SB,
BiDSA, CasWL, Chambr 3, ChPo,
CnDAL, CriT 3, CyWA, DcAmA,
DcBiA, DcEuL, DcLEnL, DcNAA,

EvLB, ModAL, NCHEL, OhA&B,
OxAm, OxEng, Pen Am, Pen Eng, PoIre,
RAdv 1, REn, REnAL
Hearn, Stanley *MnBBF, WWBWI A*
Hearne, George Richard Mant *MnBBF*
Hearne, George Richard Mant *see* Mant, Richard
Hearne, Jack W *MnBBF*
Hearon, Shelby 1931- *AuNews 2, ConAu 25R*
Heath, Bernard *MnBBF*
Heath, Bernard *see* Smith, Bernard
Heath, Ernest Dudley *IICB 1744*
Heath, Monroe 1899-1966 *AmA&B,*
ConAu P-1
Heath, Royal Vale 1883- *WNAA*
Heath, Stockton *MnBBF*
Heath, Veronica *ConAu XR, SmATA XR*
Heath, Veronica *see* Blackett, Veronica Heath
Heathcote, Claude *MnBBF, WWBWI A*
Heathcote, Claude *see* Panting, James Harwood
Heaven, Constance *ConAu XR, SmATA 7,*
WrD
Heaven, Constance *see* Fecher, Constance
Heber, Austin *MnBBF*
Heber, Austin *see* Poole, Reginald Heber
Heber, Reginald *MnBBF*
Heber, Reginald *see* Poole, Reginald Heber
Hecht, Henri Joseph 1922- *ConAu 29,*
SmATA 9
Hecht, Henri Joseph *see* Maik, Henri
Heck, Bessie Holland 1911- *ConAu 5R,*
ForWC 1970
Heckelmann, Charles N 1913- *ConAu 49*
Heckelmann, Charles N *see* Lawton, Charles
Heddle, Enid Moodie 1904- *SingR 1*
Heddle, J F Moodie *SingR 2*
Hedges, Sidney George 1897- *Au&Wr 6,*
ChPo, ChPo S1, ConAu 9R, MnBBF,
WW 1974
Hedges, Ursula M 1940- *ConAu 29*
Heerwagen, Paul K 1895- *ConAu 29, WrD*
Heffernan, John Baptist 1894- *DrAS 6H,*
WWA 38
Heffron, Dorris 1944- *ConAu 49*
Hefley, James Carl 1930- *ConAu 13R*
Hegarty, Reginald Beaton 1906-1973 *AuBYP,*
ConAu 41, ConAu P-1, SmATA 10
Hegeler, Sten 1923- *Au&Wr 6, WrD*
Heide, Florence Parry *ChPo S1, ChPo S2*
Heiderstadt, Dorothy 1907- *AuBYP, BiDL 5,*
ConAu 1R, ForWC 1970, SmATA 6
Heilbroner, Joan Knapp 1922- *ConAu 1R*
Heilman, Grant 1919- *ConAu 53*
Heimann, Susan 1940- *ConAu 33*
Hein, Lucille Eleanor 1915- *ConAu 5R,*
ForWC 1970, WrD
Heiney, Donald 1921- *ConAu 1R*
Heiney, Donald *see* Harris MacDonald
Heinlein, Robert A 1907- *AmA&B, Au&Wr 6,*
AuBYP, ConAu 1R, ConLC 1, ConLC 3,
ConNov 1972, ConNov 1976, CurB 55,
DrAF 1976, MorJA, Pen Am, REnAL,
SmATA 9, TwCA Sup, TwCW, WEAL,
WWA 38
Heinlein, Robert A *see* MacDonald, Anson
Heinlein, Robert A *see* Monroe, Lyle
Heinlein, Robert A *see* Riverside, John
Heinlein, Robert A *see* Saunders, Caleb
Heinly, John *IIBYP*
Heins, Paul 1909- *ConAu 69, SmATA 13,*

WWE 14
Heintze, Carl 1922- *ConAu 57*
Heinz, W C 1915- *ConAu 5R*
Held, John, Jr. 1889-1958 *AmA&B, ArtCS,*
ChPo S1, OxAm, REnAL
Helfman, Elizabeth S 1911- *AuBYP,*
ConAu 5R, ForWC 1970, SmATA 3,
WrD
Helfman, Harry Carmozin 1910- *AuBYP,*
ConAu 25R, SmATA 3, WWE 14, WrD
Heller, David 1922-1968 *ConAu P-1*
Heller, Dean Fons 1924- *ConAu 9R,*
ForWC 1970
Hellman, Hal *ConAu XR, SmATA 4, WrD*
Hellman, Hal *see* Hellman, Harold
Hellman, Harold 1927- *ConAu 25R,*
SmATA 4
Hellman, Harold *see* Hellman, Hal
Helm, Everett 1913- *ConAu 49, WWA 38*
Helm, Thomas 1919- *ConAu 5R*
Helmer, Jean Cassels *IIBYP*
Helmer, John 1946- *ConAu 41*
Helms, Randel 1942- *ConAu 49*
Helps, Racey 1913-1971 *ConAu P-2,*
ConAu 29, SmATA 2
Helweg, Hans H 1917- *IICB 1946*
Hemans, Felicia Dorothea Browne 1793-1835
Alli, BbD, BiD&SB, BrAu 19, CarSB,
CasWL, ChPo S2, DcEnA, DcEnL,
DcEuL, DcLEnL, EvLB, NCHEL,
OxEng, PoCh, REn, WEAL
Hemming, Roy 1928- *ConAu 61, SmATA 11,*
WWE 14
Hemming, Roy *see* Hamilton, Buzz
Hemphill, Martha Locke 1904- *ConAu 37*
Hemschemeyer, Judith 1935- *ConAu 49,*
DrAP 1975
Hemyng, Bracebridge 1841-1901 *EncM&D,*
HsB&A, MnBBF, WWBWI A, WWCL
Hemyng, Philip B *MnBBF*
Henderley, Brooks *ConAu P-2, SmATA 1*
Henderley, Brooks *see* Stratemeyer, Edward L
Henderlite, Rachel 1905- *ConAu 1R,*
WWA 38, WWAW 8
Henderson, Bernard William 1871- *MnBBF*
Henderson, Dion 1921- *ConAu 9R*
Henderson, Harold Gould 1889-1974 *ChPo,*
ChPo S1, DrAS 6F
Henderson, Irving *MnBBF*
Henderson, James *MnBBF*
Henderson, Keith 1883- *IICB 1744, WW 1974*
Henderson, LeGrand 1901-1965 *AuBYP,*
ConAu 5R, IICB 1744, IICB 1946,
IICB 1957, JBA 1951, SmATA 9
Henderson, LeGrand *see* Harwin, Brian
Henderson, LeGrand *see* LeGrand
Henderson, Richard 1924- *ConAu 13R*
Henderson, Zenna 1917- *ConAu 1R,*
SmATA 5
Hendin, David 1945- *ConAu 41*
Hendren, Patsy *MnBBF*
Hendren, Patsy *see* Edgar, Alfred
Hendrick, Joe *IIBYP*
Hendrick, Thomas William 1909- *Au&Wr 6,*
WrD
Hendrickson, Walter Brookfield, Jr. 1936-
ConAu 1R, IndAu 1917, SmATA 9
Hendry, J F 1912- *ConAu 29*
Hendryx, James Beardsley 1880-1963 *AmA&B,*

MnBBF, OhA&B, WNAA, WWBWI A
Heninger, S K, Jr. 1922- *ConAu 1R*
Henkel, Stephen Charles 1933- *ConAu 37, WrD*
Henkle, Henrietta 1909- *AmA&B, ConAu 69, CurB 46, OhA&B*
Henkle, Henrietta *see* Buckmaster, Henrietta
Henley, P A *MnBBF*
Henley, P A *see* Protheroe, Ernest
Henley, Victor *MnBBF*
Henneberger, Robert G 1921- *IlBYP, IlCB 1946*
Henri, Florette *AmA&B*
Henrich, H R *MnBBF*
Henriod, Lorraine 1925- *ConAu 45*
Henry, A L *MnBBF*
Henry, Joanne Landers 1927- *ConAu 17R, IndAu 1917, SmATA 6*
Henry, Marguerite 1902- *AmA&B, Au&ICB, Au&Wr 6, AuBYP, BkCL, ConAu 17R, CurB 47, FamMS, JBA 1951, Newb 1922, SmATA 11, WWA 38, WWAW 8, WWWor 2, WrD*
Henry, O 1862-1910 *AmA&B, AtlBL, BiDSA, CasWL, Chambr 3, ChPo, CnDAL, CyWA, DcLEnL, DcNAA, EncWL, EvLB, LongC, ModAL, OxAm, OxEng, Pen Am, RAdv 1, REn, REnAL, TwCA, TwCA Sup, TwCW, WEAL, WWTwL, YABC XR*
Henry, O *see* Porter, William Sydney
Henry, Oliver *YABC XR*
Henry, Oliver *see* Porter, William Sydney
Henry, Robert Selph 1889- *WNAA*
Henry, T S *MnBBF*
Henry, Thomas 1879-1962 *WWBWI I, WWCL*
Henry, Thomas *see* Fisher, Thomas Henry
Henry, Vera *ConAu 21R, WrD*
Henry, Will *AmA&B*
Henson, Clyde Eugene 1914- *ConAu 5R, DrAS 6E*
Henstra, Friso 1928- *IlBYP, SmATA 8*
Hentoff, Nat 1925- *AuBYP, ChLR 1, ChPo S2, ConAu 1R, REnAL, ThBJA, WrD*
Henton, Collett *MnBBF*
Henton, Collett *see* Batchelor, Richard A C
Henty, George Alfred 1832-1902 *Alli Sup, BbD, BiD&SB, BrAu 19, CarSB, CasWL, Chambr 3, DcLEnL, EvLB, JBA 1934, LongC, MnBBF, NCHEL, OxEng, Pen Eng, TelT, WWBWI A, WWCL*
Hepler, Loren George 1928- *AmMWS 12P*
Heppenstall, Margit Strom 1913- *ConAu 21R*
Hepworth, Carrington *MnBBF*
Herald, Kathleen *ConAu XR, ThBJA*
Herald, Kathleen *see* Peyton, Kathleen Wendy
Herben, Beatrice Slayton *CarSB*
Herber, Harold 1929- *DrAS 6E*
Herbert, Cecil *MnBBF, SmATA XR, WWBWI A*
Herbert, Cecil *see* Hamilton, Charles Harold St. John
Herbert, Charles *MnBBF*
Herbert, Don 1917- *BiEnAT, CurB 56, AuBYP, ConAu 29, SmATA 2*
Herbert, Don *see* Wizard, Mr.

Herbert, Frank *MnBBF*
Herbert, Frank Patrick 1920- *AmA&B, ConAu 53, SmATA 9, WWA 38*
Herbert, John *MnBBF*
Herbert, Tom 1938- *ConAu 69*
Herbert, Wally *ConAu XR, WWWor 2*
Herbert, Wally *see* Herbert, Walter William
Herbert, Walter William 1934- *ConAu 69, WW 1974*
Herbert, Walter William *see* Herbert, Wally
Herbst, Robert L 1935- *ConAu 61*
Herde, Rossiter *MnBBF*
Hereford, Robert A 1902- *AuBYP*
Herford, Oliver 1863-1935 *AmA&B, BiD&SB, CarSB, ChPo, ChPo S1, ChPo S2, DcAmA, DcNAA, EvLB, LongC, NCHEL, OxAm, REnAL, TwCA, TwCA Sup*
Herge *ConAu XR, SmATA XR*
Herge *see* Remi, Georges
Heritage, John *MnBBF*
Heritage, John *see* Shaw, Stanley Gordon
Heritage, Martin *EncM&D, WWBWI A*
Heritage, Martin *see* Horler, Sydney
Heriteau, Jacqueline 1925- *ConAu 45*
Herman, Charlotte 1937- *ConAu 41*
Herman, George R 1925- *ConAu 5R, DrAS 6E, WrD*
Herman, Julius 1870?- *WWBWI A*
Herman, Julius 1894-1955 *MnBBF*
Herman, Julius *see* Clifford, Martin
Herman, Julius *see* Richards, Frank
Herman, Vic 1919- *WWAA 1973, WWW 14*
Hermanson, Dennis 1947- *SmATA 10*
Herndon, Venable *WWA 38*
Herold, J Christopher *CurB 59, CurB 65*
Herrera, Velino 1902- *AmPB, IlCB 1744*
Herrick, Robert 1591-1674 *Alli, AnCL, AtlBL, BbD, BiD&SB, BrAu, CasWL, Chambr 1, ChPo, ChPo S1, ChPo S2, CnE&AP, CrE&SL, CriT 1, CyWA, DcEnA, DcEnL, DcEuL, DcLEnL, EvLB, LongC, MouLC 1, NCHEL, OxEng, Pen Eng, RAdv 1, REn, WEAL*
Herriman, George 1880-1944 *ArtCS, ChPo, REnAL*
Herring, Paul *MnBBF, WWBWI A*
Herring, Paul *see* Raeburn, David
Herrmann, Frank 1927- *ConAu 21R*
Herrmanns, Ralph 1933- *ConAu 9R, SmATA 11, WrD*
Herrod, Walter *MnBBF, WWBWI A*
Herrod, Walter *see* Hamilton, Cecily
Herrod, Walter *see* Light, Walter H
Herron, Edward A 1912- *ConAu 5R, SmATA 4*
Hersey, John Richard 1914- *IntWW 38*
Hershfield, Harry 1885- *ArtCS, NYTBS 5*
Hershon, Robert 1936- *ConAu 33, DrAP 1975*
Herst, Herman, Jr. 1909- *ConAu 1R*
Hervey, Hedley *MnBBF*
Hervey, Hedley *see* Strong, James
Hervey, M H *MnBBF*
Herz, Martin Florian 1917- *ConAu 21R, WWA 38, WrD*
Herzberg, Max J 1886-1958 *AmA&B, REnAL, WNAA*
Herzka, Heinz 1935- *ConAu 37*

Herzog, Arthur, III 1927- ConAu 17R,
  WWE 14
Herzog, Emile Salomon Wilhelm 1885- AuBYP,
  ClDMEuL, LongC, NCHEL, TwCA,
  TwCA Sup
Herzog, Emile Salomon Wilhelm see Maurois,
  Andre
Herzog, George 1901- IntWW 38, WWA 38
Heslop, J W H MnBBF
Hess, Fjeril 1893- AmA&B, JBA 1934,
  JBA 1951
Hess, Lilo 1916- AmPB, ConAu 33,
  SmATA 4
Hesse, Hermann 1877-1962 AtlBL, CasWL,
  ClDMEuL, ConAu P-2, ConLC 1,
  ConLC 2, ConLC 3, ConLC 6, CurB 62,
  CyWA, EncWL, EvEuW, ModGL,
  OxGer, Pen Eur, RCom, REn, TwCA,
  TwCA Sup, TwCW, WWTwL
Hessell, Henry MnBBF
Hessell, Henry see Tiltman, Hugh Hessell
Hester, Kathleen B 1905- ConAu P-2
Hettlinger, Richard Frederick 1920-
  ConAu 17R, DrAS 6P
Heuck, Sigrid IlBYP
Heuer, John 1941- ConAu 69
Heuman, William 1912- AuBYP, ConAu 5R
Heward, May ChPo S1, MnBBF
Heward, William L 1949- ConAu 53
Hewes, Agnes Danforth AmA&B, AuBYP,
  JBA 1934, JBA 1951
Hewett, Anita 1918- AuBYP, ConAu 21R,
  SmATA 13
Hewitt, C Rawleston MnBBF
Hewitt, Jean 1929- Au&Wr 6
Hewitt, R C MnBBF
Hey, Nigel S 1936- ConAu 33
Heyduck-Huth, Hilde 1929- ConAu 57,
  SmATA 8
Heyer, Georgette 1902-1974 Au&Wr 6,
  ConAu 49, DcLEnL, EncM&D, LongC,
  NCHEL, NYTBS 5, REn, TwCA,
  TwCA Sup, TwCW, WW 1974,
  WWA 38, WWWor 2
Heyerdahl, Thor 1914- Au&Wr 6, CelR 3,
  ConAu 5R, CurB 47, CurB 72,
  IntWW 38, LongC, SmATA 2,
  TwCA Sup, TwCW, WW 1974,
  WWWor 2
Heyliger, William 1884-1955 AmA&B,
  AuBYP, CatA 1930, JBA 1934,
  JBA 1951, REnAL, YABC 1
Heyliger, William see Williams, Hawley
Heyman, Kent 1930- WWA 38, WWE 14
Heyneman, Anne 1910?- ChPo, IlCB 1744,
  IlCB 1946
Heyward, DuBose 1885-1940 AmA&B, AmPB,
  AmSCAP 66, ChPo, CnDAL, CnMD,
  ConAmA, ConAmL, CurB 40, CyWA,
  DcLEnL, DcNAA, EvLB, LongC,
  McGWD, ModAL, ModWD, OxAm,
  Pen Am, REn, REnAL, TwCA,
  TwCA Sup, TwCW
Hibbert, Christopher 1924- Au&Wr 6,
  ConAu 1R, LongC, OxCan, SmATA 4,
  WW 1974
Hibbert, Eleanor Burford 1906- ConAu 17R,
  EncM&D, SmATA 2, WorAu
Hibbert, Eleanor Burford see Burford, Eleanor

Hibbert, Eleanor Burford see Carr, Philippa
Hibbert, Eleanor Burford see Ford, Elbur
Hibbert, Eleanor Burford see Holt, Victoria
Hibbert, Eleanor Burford see Kellow, Kathleen
Hibbert, Eleanor Burford see Plaidy, Jean
Hibbert, Eleanor Burford see Tate, Ellalice
Hicken, Victor 1921- ConAu 21R, DrAS 6H,
  WWA 38
Hickey, Madelyn Eastlund WrD
Hickling, W MnBBF
Hickman, Janet 1940- ConAu 65, SmATA 12
Hickman, Martha Whitmore 1925- WWAW 8
Hickok, Lorena A AuBYP
Hicks, Clifford Byron 1920- AmA&B, AuBYP,
  ConAu 5R, WWA 38
Hicks, Eleanor B ConAu XR, SmATA 1
Hicks, Eleanor B see Coerr, Eleanor
Hicks, Harvey ConAu XR
Hicks, Harvey see Stratemeyer, Edward L
Hida, Keiko 1913- ChPo S1, IlBYP
Hieatt, Constance Bartlett 1928- ConAu 5R,
  DrAS 6E, SmATA 4, WrD
Hiebert, Ray Eldon 1932- AmA&B,
  ConAu 17R, DrAS 6E, SmATA 13,
  WWA 38, WWE 14
Higdon, Hal 1931- ConAu 9R, SmATA 4,
  WrD
Higdon, Hal see Smith, Lafayette
Higgins, Charlotte M Alli Sup, CarSB
Higgins, Don 1928- ArtsCL, ConAu 25R
Higgins, Helen Boyd 1892-1971 IndAu 1917
Higgins, James Hart 1911- MnBBF
Higgins, James Hart see Hart, James
Higgins, Lewis R d1916 MnBBF, WWBWI 1
Higgins, Lewis R see Nugent, Frank
Higgins, Margaret WWBWI 1
Higgins, Walter MnBBF
Higginson, John A MnBBF
Highland, Harold Joseph 1917- AmMWS 12S
Highsmith, Patricia 1921- Au&Wr 6,
  BiN 1974, ConAu 1R, ConLC 2,
  ConLC 4, ConNov 1972, ConNov 1976,
  EncM&D, WW 1974, WWTwL, WorAu,
  WrD
Hightower, Florence Cole 1916- Au&Wr 6,
  AuBYP, ConAu 1R, SmATA 4, ThBJA
Higson, Kit WWCL
Hild, H MnBBF
Hild, H see Brand, Dudley
Hilder, Rowland 1905- ChPo S2, IlCB 1744,
  WW 1974, WWCL
Hildick, E W ConAu XR, SmATA 2,
  WWCL
Hildick, E W see Hildick, Wallace
Hildick, Edmund Wallace 1925- Au&Wr 6,
  SmATA 2
Hildick, Wallace 1925- ConAu 25R
Hildick, Wallace see Hildick, E W
Hildreth, Richard 1807-1865 Alli, AmA,
  AmA&B, BbD, BiD&SB, Chambr 3,
  CyAL 2, DcAmA, DcLEnL, DcNAA,
  OxAm, REnAL
Hiles, Bartram 1873- WWBWI 1
Hilken, Annie Kathleen 1902- IlCB 1946
Hill, Arnold MnBBF
Hill, Dave ConAu XR
Hill, Dave see Hill, David Charles
Hill, David Charles 1936- ConAu 17R
Hill, David Charles see Hill, Dave

Hill, Donna *ConAu 13R*
Hill, Elizabeth Starr 1925- *ConAu 17R,*
ForWC 1970, WrD
Hill, Fitzmaurice 1898- *SingR 2*
Hill, Frank Ernest 1888-1970? *AuBYP*
Hill, George Canning 1825-1898 *Alli, Alli Sup,*
BiD&SB, CarSB, DcAmA, DcNAA,
HsB&A
Hill, Grace Brooks *ConAu P-2, SmATA 1*
Hill, Grace Brooks *see* Stratemeyer, Edward L
Hill, Grace Livingston 1865-1947 *AmA&B,*
ChPo, DcAmA, DcNAA, REnAL, TwCA,
TwCA Sup, WNAA, YABC 2
Hill, Grace Livingston *see* Macdonald, Marcia
Hill, H Gregory *MnBBF*
Hill, H Gregory *see* Hill, Harry Egbert
Hill, Harry Egbert *MnBBF, WWBWI A*
Hill, Harry Egbert *see* Gregory, Hylton
Hill, Harry Egbert *see* Hill, H Gregory
Hill, Harry Egbert *see* Hill, Harry Gregory
Hill, Harry Gregory *MnBBF*
Hill, Harry Gregory *see* Hill, Harry Egbert
Hill, Headon 1857-1924 *EncM&D, MnBBF*
Hill, Headon *see* Grainger, F E
Hill, Helen d1942 *CurB 42, DcNAA*
Hill, John W *MnBBF*
Hill, Kathleen Louise 1917- *ConAu 9R,*
SmATA 4, WWA 38, WWAW 8
Hill, Kathleen Louise *see* Hill, Kay
Hill, Kay *ConAu XR, OxCan Sup, Prof,*
SmATA 4
Hill, Kay *see* Hill, Kathleen Louise
Hill, L A 1918- *ConAu 21R, WrD*
Hill, Lorna 1902- *Au&Wr 6, AuBYP,*
ConAu P-1, SmATA 12, WrD
Hill, Margaret 1915- *AuBYP, ConAu 1R*
Hill, Monica *ConAu XR, SmATA 3*
Hill, Monica *see* Watson, Jane Werner
Hill, Ralph Nading 1917- *AuBYP, ConAu 1R*
Hill, Reuben Lorenzo, Jr. 1912- *AmMWS 12S,*
WWA 38, WWWor 2
Hill, Robert W 1919- *AuBYP, ConAu 9R,*
SmATA 12
Hill, Ruth A *ConAu XR, SmATA 6*
Hill, Ruth A *see* Viguers, Ruth Hill
Hill, Ruth Livingston *ConAu XR,*
SmATA XR
Hill, Ruth Livingston *see* Munce, Ruth Hill
Hillcourt, William 1900- *AmA&B, AuBYP,*
WWA 38
Hillerman, Tony 1925- *ConAu 29, SmATA 6*
Hillert, Margaret 1920- *AuNews 1, ConAu 49,*
SmATA 8
Hilles, Helen 1905- *AuBYP*
Hilliard, Noel 1929- *ConAu 9R,*
ConNov 1972, ConNov 1976
Hilliard, Robert L 1925- *DrAS 6E*
Hillis, Dave 1945- *ConAu 57*
Hillman, May *AuBYP*
Hills, Frances Elizabeth *WrD*
Hillyer, Virgil Mores 1875-1931 *AmA&B,*
AuBYP, DcNAA, JBA 1934, JBA 1951
Hilton, Irene Pothus 1912- *ConAu 1R,*
SmATA 7
Hilton, James 1900-1954 *ChPo S1, CurB 42,*
CurB 55, CyWA, DcLEnL, EncM&D,
EvLB, LongC, MnBBF, ModBL,
NCHEL, Pen Eng, REn, REnAL, TwCA,
TwCA Sup, TwCW, WWBWI A

Hilton, John Buxton 1921- *Au&Wr 6,*
ConAu 53, WrD
Hilton, John Buxton *see* Stanley, Warwick
Hilton, Ralph 1907- *ConAu 29, SmATA 8*
Hilton, Suzanne 1922- *ConAu 29, SmATA 4,*
WrD
Him, George 1900- *IlCB 1744, IlCB 1957,*
WW 1974, WWGA, WWWorJ 1972
Himler, Ann 1946- *ConAu 53, SmATA 8*
Himler, Ronald 1937- *ChPo S2, ConAu 53,*
IlBYP, SmATA 6
Himmelheber, Diana Martin 1938- *ConAu 17R*
Hinckley, Helen *AuBYP, ConAu XR, WrD*
Hinckley, Helen *see* Jones, Helen Hinckley
Hincks, Cyril Malcolm 1881-1954 *MnBBF,*
WWBWI A
Hincks, Cyril Malcolm *see* Coulsdon, John
Hincks, Cyril Malcolm *see* Dayle, Malcolm
Hincks, Cyril Malcolm *see* Gee, Osman
Hincks, Cyril Malcolm *see* Howard, John M
Hincks, Cyril Malcolm *see* Malcolm, Charles
Hind, J R *MnBBF*
Hindman, Jane Ferguson 1905- *ConAu 25R,*
ForWC 1970, WWAW 8
Hinds, E M *ConAu XR*
Hinds, E M *see* Hinds, Margery
Hinds, Margery *Au&Wr 6, ConAu 9R,*
OxCan, WrD
Hinds, Margery *see* Hinds, E M
Hine, Al 1915- *AuBYP, ChPo, ChPo S1,*
ConAu 1R, ThBJA
Hine, Sesyle Joslin 1929- *ConAu 13R, ThBJA*
Hine, Sesyle Joslin *see* Gibson, Josephine
Hine, Sesyle Joslin *see* Joslin, Sesyle
Hine, Sesyle Joslin *see* Kirtland, G B
Hines, Bob *IlBYP*
Hinkins, Virginia *AuBYP*
Hinkle, Thomas Clark 1876-1949 *AmA&B,*
AuBYP, DcNAA, REnAL
Hinkson, H A *MnBBF*
Hinton, Charles Louis 1869- *ChPo, ChPo S2,*
IlCB 1744
Hinton, Herbert Allan 1888-1945 *MnBBF,*
WWBWI A
Hinton, Herbert Allan *see* Clifford, Martin
Hinton, Herbert Allan *see* Howard, Prosper
Hinton, Herbert Allan *see* Richards, Frank
Hinton, Phyllis *Au&Wr 6*
Hinton, S E *ChLR 3*
Hintze, Naomi A 1909- *ConAu 45*
Hippel, Ursula Von *AuBYP*
Hippel, Ursula Von *see* VonHippel, Ursula
Hippopotamus, Eugene H *AuBYP, ThBJA*
Hippopotamus, Eugene H *see* Kraus, Robert
Hipshman, May 1919- *AuBYP*
Hirsch, S Carl 1913- *AnCL, ConAu 5R,*
SmATA 2, ThBJA, WrD
Hirsch, Thomas L 1931- *ConAu 49*
Hirsh, Marilyn 1944- *ConAu 49, SmATA 7*
Hirshberg, Albert Simon 1909-1973 *AuBYP,*
ConAu 1R, ConAu 41, WWE 14
Hiser, Iona Seibert 1901- *ConAu 1R,*
SmATA 4
Hitchcock, Alfred 1899- *Au&Wr 6, BiN 1974,*
CelR 3, CurB 41, CurB 60, EncM&D,
IntMPA 1975, NCHEL, NYTBE 3,
NYTBS 6, REnAL
Hitte, Kathryn 1919- *AuBYP, ConAu 21R*
Hitz, Demi 1942- *ConAu 61, SmATA 11*

Hnizdovsky, Jacques 1915- *IIBYP,*
WWAA 1973
Hoag, Edwin 1926- *AuBYP, ConAu 13R*
Hoare, Robert John 1921- *Au&Wr 6,*
ConAu 9R, WrD
Hoban, John Staveley *MnBBF*
Hoban, Lillian 1925- *AmPB, AuBYP,*
ChPo S1, ConAu 69, IICB 1957, ThBJA
Hoban, Russell C 1925- *AmPB, AuBYP,*
ChLR 3, ChPo S1, ChPo S2, ConAu 5R,
SmATA 1, ThBJA, WrD
Hoban, Walt 1890-1939 *ArtCS*
Hobart, Billie 1935- *ConAu 49*
Hobart, Lois Elaine *ConAu 5R, WrD,*
AuBYP, ForWC 1970, MnnWr,
SmATA 7
Hobbs, Jack *MnBBF*
Hobbs, Jack *see* Horler, Sydney
Hobden, Roger *MnBBF*
Hoberman, Mary Ann 1930- *BkCL, ChPo S1,*
ChPo S2, ConAu 41, SmATA 5
Hobley, Leonard Frank 1903- *Au&Wr 6,*
ConAu 13R, WrD
Hobson, Burton 1933- *ConAu 5R, WWA 38*
Hobson, Mrs. Carey *MnBBF*
Hobson, Julius *LBAA*
Hobson, Laura Zametkin 1900- *ConAu 17R,*
CurB 47, WWA 38, WWAW 8, WrD
WrD
Hobson, Polly *AuBYP, ConAu XR*
Hobson, Polly *see* Evans, Julia
Hobson, Stanley *MnBBF*
Hochman, Sandra 1936- *AmA&B, ConAu 5R,*
ConLC 3, ConP 1970, ConP 1975,
DrAF 1976, DrAP 1975, NYTBE 2,
WWAW 8, WWE 14, WrD
Hochschild, Arlie Russell 1940- *ConAu 57,*
SmATA 11
Hochstein, Rolaine *ConAu 45*
Hockley, Lewis *MnBBF, WWBWI A*
Hockley, Lewis *see* Longhurst, Percy William
Hodder, Edwin 1837?-1904 *Alli Sup, CarSB,*
ChPo S1, DcEnL
Hodge, Jane Aiken 1917- *Au&Wr 6, AuBYP,*
ConAu 5R
Hodge, P W 1934- *ConAu 33, SmATA 12*
Hodges, C Walter 1909- *ConAu 13R,*
SmATA 2
Hodges, Carl G 1902-1964 *AuBYP, ConAu 5R,*
SmATA 10
Hodges, Cyril Walter 1909- *AnCL, Au&Wr 6,*
AuBYP, ChPo S2, IICB 1744, IICB 1946,
IICB 1957, SmATA 2, ThBJA,
WW 1974, WWCL
Hodges, David *IIBYP*
Hodges, Elizabeth Jamison *AuBYP,*
ConAu 9R, ForWC 1970, SmATA 1,
WWAW 8
Hodges, Margaret Moore 1911- *BiDL 5,*
ConAu 1R, DrAS 6E, ForWC 1970,
IndAu 1917, SmATA 1, WWA 38,
WWAW 8, WrD
Hodgetts, James Frederick *MnBBF,*
WWBWI A
Hodgson, Ralph 1871-1962 *AnCL, AtlBL,*
Chambr 3, ChPo, ChPo S1, ChPo S2,
CnE&AP, DcLEnL, EvLB, LongC,
ModBL, NCHEL, OhA&B, OxEng,
Pen Eng, REn, TwCA, TwCA Sup,

WWBWI 1, WWTwL
Hodgson, Ralph *see* Yorick
Hodgson, W E *MnBBF*
Hoehling, Mary 1914- *AuBYP*
Hoest, Bill *ConAu XR*
Hoest, Bill *see* Hoest, William
Hoest, William 1926- *ConAu 69*
Hoest, William *see* Hoest, Bill
Hoexter, Corinne K 1927- *ConAu 49,*
SmATA 6
Hoff, Carol 1900- *ConAu P-2, SmATA 11*
Hoff, P J *WWA 38*
Hoff, Rhoda *ChPo S1*
Hoff, Syd 1912- *AmA&B, Au&Wr 6,*
AuBYP, ChPo S1, ConAu 5R,
IICB 1957, SmATA 9, ThBJA, WWA 38,
WWWor 2, WWWorJ 1972
Hoffman, Franz 1814-1882 *CarSB*
Hoffman, Gail 1896- *ConAu 5R*
Hoffman, Gloria *AuBYP*
Hoffman, Paul 1934- *ConAu 45*
Hoffman, Phyllis Miriam 1944- *ConAu 29,*
SmATA 4, WWAW 8
Hoffman, Professor *MnBBF*
Hoffman, Professor *see* Lewis, Angelo J
Hoffmann, Christine *IIBYP*
Hoffmann, Ernest Theodor Amadeus 1776-1822
BiD&SB, CyWA, EuAu, NCHEL, OxEng,
OxFr, OxGer, RCom, REn, WWCL
Hoffmann, Felix 1911-1975 *ChPo S1,*
ConAu 29, ConAu 57, IIBYP, IICB 1946,
IICB 1957, SmATA 9, ThBJA
Hoffmann, Heinrich 1809-1894 *BiD&SB,*
CarSB, ChPo S1, DcEuL, EvEuW,
OxEng, WWCL
Hoffmann, Hilde 1927- *ConAu 25R, IIBYP*
Hoffmann, Margaret Jones 1910- *AuBYP,*
ConAu 5R
Hoffmann, Margaret Jones *see* Hoffmann, Peggy
Hoffmann, Peggy *AuBYP, ConAu XR,*
ForWC 1970, WrD
Hoffmann, Peggy *see* Hoffmann, Margaret Jones
Hoffmeister, Donald Frederick 1916-
AmMWS 12P, ConAu 53, WWA 38
Hoffner, Pelagie Doane *AuBYP*
Hoffner, Pelagie Doane *see* Doane, Pelagie
Hofland, Mrs. W H 1770-1844 *CarSB*
Hofman, David 1908- *Au&Wr 6*
Hofsinde, Robert 1902-1973 *AuBYP,*
ConAu 45, IICB 1946, ThBJA
Hogan, Bernice Harris 1929- *ChPo,*
ConAu 13R, ForWC 1970, SmATA 12
Hogan, George *MnBBF*
Hogan, Inez 1895?- *AuBYP, ConAu 1R,*
IICB 1744, MorJA, SmATA 2
Hogarth, Jr. *ConAu XR, SmATA 6*
Hogarth, Burne 1911- *ArtCS*
Hogarth, Jr. *see* Kent, Rockwell
Hogarth, Paul 1917- *Au&Wr 6, ConAu 49,*
WWGA
Hogben, Lancelot 1895-1975 *ConAu 61,*
CurB 41, IntWW 38, WW 1974
Hogeboom, Amy 1891- *AuBYP*
Hogg, Beth 1917- *AuBYP, ConAu 5R*
Hogg, Beth *see* Grey, Elizabeth
Hogg, Garry 1902- *Au&Wr 6, ConAu 21R,*
SmATA 2, WWCL, WrD
Hogner, Dorothy Childs *AmA&B, AuBYP,*
ConAu 33, JBA 1951, OxCan, SmATA 4,

WNAA, WrD
Hogner, Nils 1893-1970 *AuBYP, IICB 1744,*
  IICB 1946, IICB 1957, JBA 1951
Hogrogian, Nonny 1932- *AuBYP, BkP,*
  ChLR 2, ChPo S2, ConAu 45, IIBYP,
  IICB 1957, NewbC 1966, SmATA 7,
  ThBJA, WWA 38, WWE 14
Hogwood, Mackenzie *MnBBF*
Hohn, Hazel *ConAu 5R, WrD*
Hoke, Helen L 1903- *AuBYP*
Hoke, Helen L *see* Sterling, Helen
Hoke, John Lindsay 1925- *ConAu 41,*
  SmATA 7
Hokusai *REn*
Holberg, Richard A 1889-1942 *AuBYP,*
  JBA 1951
Holberg, Ruth Langland 1889- *ConAu 5R,*
  CurB 49, JBA 1951, SmATA 1, WrD
Holbrook, David 1923- *ConAu 5R*
Holbrook, Sabra *ConAu XR, CurB 48*
Holbrook, Sabra *see* Erickson, Sabra Rollins
Holbrook, Stewart Hall 1893-1964 *AmA&B,*
  AuBYP, ConAu 9R, ConAu P-1, OxAm,
  REnAL, SmATA 2, ThBJA, TwCA Sup,
  WNAA, WWPNA
Holby, John *MnBBF*
Holden, Molly 1927- *ConAu 25R, ConP 1970,*
  ConP 1975, WrD
Holden, Raymond Peckham 1894-1972 *AmA&B,*
  AuBYP, REnAL, TwCA, TwCA Sup
Holder, Glenn 1906- *ConAu 41, DrAS 6E*
Holder, William G 1937- *ConAu 25R*
Holding, Carlisle B 1849-1929 *Alli Sup, CarSB,*
  OhA&B
Holding, James 1907- *AuBYP, ConAu 25R,*
  SmATA 3
Holding, James *see* Carlisle, Clark
Holding, James *see* Queen, Ellery, Jr.
Holding, Val *MnBBF*
Holdsworth, William Curtis *IIBYP*
Holiday, Henry 1839-1927 *ChPo, ChPo S2*
Holisher, Desider 1901-1972 *ConAu 37,*
  ConAu P-2, SmATA 6, WWWorJ 1972
Holl, Adelaide Hinkle 1910?- *AmA&B,*
  ConAu 1R, ForWC 1970, SmATA 8,
  WWAW 8
Holland, Cecilia Anastasia *WrD*
Holland, Clive 1866- *MnBBF, WWLA*
Holland, Clive *see* Hankinson, C J
Holland, Isabelle 1920- *ConAu 21R,*
  SmATA 8
Holland, Janice 1913-1962 *IIBYP, IICB 1946,*
  IICB 1957
Holland, John *MnBBF*
Holland, Joyce F 1921- *ConAu 5R*
Holland, Marion 1908- *AuBYP, ConAu 61,*
  SmATA 6
Holland, Rodney *MnBBF*
Holland, Rupert Sargent 1878-1952 *AmLY,*
  ChPo, JBA 1934, JBA 1951, REnAL,
  WNAA
Holland, Stephen Bainsbridge *MnBBF*
Holland, Thomas 1908- *Alli, Au&Wr 6, WrD*
Hollander, John 1929- *AmA&B, AuBYP,*
  ChPo, ChPo S1, ConAu 1R, ConLC 2,
  ConLC 5, ConP 1970, ConP 1975,
  DrAP 1975, DrAS 6E, OxAm, Pen Am,
  REnAL, SmATA 13, WWA 38,
  WWE 14, WWTwL, WorAu

Hollander, Paul *AuBYP*
Hollander, Zander 1923- *ConAu 65*
Hollander, Zander *see* Peters, Alexander
Holliday, Joe *Au&Wr 6, ConAu XR,*
  SmATA XR
Holliday, Joe *see* Holliday, Joseph
Holliday, Joseph 1910- *ConAu P-2,*
  SmATA 11
Holliday, Joseph *see* Bosco, Jack
Holliday, Joseph *see* Dale, Jack
Holliday, Joseph *see* Holliday, Joe
Hollindale, Peter *WrD*
Holling, Holling Clancy 1900- *AmA&B,*
  AmPB, Au&ICB, AuBYP, IIBYP,
  IICB 1946, IICB 1957, JBA 1951,
  St&VC
Holling, Lucille Webster 1900- *IIBYP,*
  IICB 1946, IICB 1957, JBA 1951
Hollings, F S *CarSB, ChPo S2*
Hollingsworth, Alvin *IIBYP*
Holloway, Brenda Wilmar 1908- *Au&Wr 6,*
  ConAu P-1
Holloway, Charlotte Molyneux *CarSB*
Holloway, John *MnBBF*
Holloway, Teresa 1906- *ConAu 17R*
Holloway, Teresa *see* Beatty, Elizabeth
Holloway, Teresa *see* McLeod, Margaret Vail
Holloway, Trevor *MnBBF*
Holly, J Hunter *ConAu XR*
Holly, J Hunter *see* Holly, Joan Carol
Holly, Joan Carol 1932- *ConAu 1R*
Holly, Joan Carol *see* Holly, J Hunter
Holm, Anne 1922- *AnCL, ConAu 17R,*
  SmATA 1
Holm, Hannebo *AuBYP*
Holman, Bill 1903- *ArtCS*
Holman, E S *MnBBF*
Holman, Felice 1919- *AuBYP, ChPo S2,*
  ConAu 5R, SmATA 7, WrD
Holme, Bryan 1913- *AuBYP*
Holme, Gordon *MnBBF, WWBWI A*
Holme, Gordon *see* Cooper, Charles Henry St.
  John
Holmes, Andrew *MnBBF*
Holmes, Angus *MnBBF*
Holmes, Con *MnBBF*
Holmes, David Charles 1919- *ConAu 9R*
Holmes, David Charles *see* Charlson, David
Holmes, Edward *MnBBF, WWBWI A*
Holmes, Edward *see* Holmes, George Edward
Holmes, Efner Tudor 1949- *ConAu 65*
Holmes, Fred *WWBWI I*
Holmes, George Edward *MnBBF*
Holmes, George Edward *see* Holmes, Edward
Holmes, Leonard *MnBBF*
Holmes, Marjorie Rose 1910- *AmA&B,*
  AmNov, Au&Wr 6, AuBYP, AuNews 1,
  ConAu 1R, ForWC 1970, WWAW 8
Holmes, Martin *MnBBF*
Holmes, Martin 1905- *ConAu 49*
Holmes, Oliver Wendell 1809-1894 *Alli,*
  Alli Sup, AmA, AmA&B, AtIBL, BbD,
  BiD&SB, BiD&SB, CasWL, Chambr 3,
  ChPo, ChPo S1, ChPo S2, CnDAL,
  CriT 3, CyAL 2, CyWA, DcAmA,
  DcBiA, DcEnA, DcEnL, DcLEnL,
  DcNAA, EvLB, MouLC 4, OxAm,
  OxEng, Pen Am, PoCh, RAdv 1, REn,
  REnAL, St&VC, WEAL

Holmes, Prescott *CarSB*
Holmes, Radcliffe *MnBBF*
Holmes, Rick *ConAu XR, SmATA XR*
Holmes, Rick *see* Hardwick, Richard
Holmes, T W 1872- *WWBWI I*
Holmes, William Kersley 1882- *ChPo,*
ChPo S1, ChPo S2, ConAu 9R,
ConAu P-1
Holmgren, Virginia Cunningham *OhA&B*
Holmquist, Eve 1921- *ConAu 53, SmATA 11*
Holmscliff, Captain *MnBBF*
Holmstrand, Marie Juline 1908- *ConAu 5R,*
MnnWr
Holsaert, Eunice d1974 *AuBYP, ConAu 53*
Holsinger, Jane Lumley *AuBYP, ConAu 17R,*
ForWC 1970, WrD
Holt, Geoffrey B A *MnBBF*
Holt, Henry *MnBBF*
Holt, Jack *MnBBF*
Holt, John Robert 1926- *ConAu 25R*
Holt, John Robert *see* Arre, John
Holt, Kare 1917- *CasWL*
Holt, Margaret *AuBYP, ConAu 17R,*
SmATA 4
Holt, Margaret *see* Parish, Margaret Holt
Holt, Michael 1929- *ConAu 53, SmATA 13,*
WrD
Holt, Rackham *CurB 44*
Holt, Richard *MnBBF*
Holt, Richard *see* Holton, Walter H
Holt, Stephen *AuBYP, SmATA XR*
Holt, Stephen *see* Thompson, Harlan H
Holt, Thelma Jewett 1913- *ConAu 29*
Holt, Victoria *AmA&B, Au&Wr 6,*
ConAu XR, EncM&D, SmATA 2,
WW 1974, WWA 38, WWAW 8,
WorAu
Holt, Victoria *see* Hibbert, Eleanor Burford
Holt, Walter J *MnBBF*
Holton, Leonard *AuBYP, ConAu XR,*
EncM&D, SmATA 2, WorAu
Holton, Leonard *see* Wibberley, Leonard
Holton, Walter H *MnBBF*
Holton, Walter H *see* Hall, Richard
Holton, Walter H *see* Holt, Richard
Holyer, Erna Maria 1925- *ConAu 29, WrD*
Holyer, Erna Maria *see* Holyer, Ernie
Holyer, Ernie *ConAu XR*
Holyer, Ernie *see* Holyer, Erna Maria
Holz, Loretta 1943- *ConAu 65*
Homar, Lorenzo 1913- *WWAA 1973,*
WWGA
Home, Andrew 1864- *MnBBF, WWBWI A*
Home, Athol *MnBBF*
Home, Edwin *MnBBF*
Home, Edwin *see* Home-Gall, William Benjamin
Home, T *MnBBF*
Home, T *see* Home-Gall, William Benjamin
Home-Gall, Edward Reginald 1899?- *MnBBF,*
WWBWI A
Home-Gall, Edward Reginald *see* Clive, Clifford
Home-Gall, Edward Reginald *see* Dale, Edwin
Home-Gall, Edward Reginald *see* Hall, Rupert
Home-Gall, Edward Reginald *see* Home-Gall,
Reginald
Home-Gall, Reginald *MnBBF*
Home-Gall, Reginald *see* Home-Gall, Edward
Reginald

Home-Gall, William Benjamin 1870?-1936
MnBBF, WWBWI A
Home-Gall, William Benjamin *see* Conyers,
Captain
Home-Gall, William Benjamin *see* Drew,
Reginald
Home-Gall, William Benjamin *see* Home, Edwin
Home-Gall, William Benjamin *see* Home, T
Home-Gall, William Benjamin *see* Wray,
Reginald
Home-Gall, William Bolinbroke 1894- *MnBBF,*
WWBWI A
Home-Gall, William Bolinbroke *see* Bolingbroke,
William
Home-Gall, William Bolinbroke *see* Young, Will
Home Goal *MnBBF*
Homer *AtlBL, BbD, BiD&SB, CasWL,*
ChPo, CyWA, DcBiA, DcEnL, DcEuL,
NCHEL, OxEng, Pen Cl, RCom
Homsher, Lola Mae 1913- *ConAu 1R,*
DrAS 6H, WWW 14
Homze, Alma C 1932- *ConAu 29*
Honig, Donald 1931- *ConAu 17R, DrAF 1976*
Honness, Elizabeth H 1904- *AuBYP,*
ConAu 25R, SmATA 2, WWAW 8
Honore, Paul 1885- *ChPo, ConICB,*
IlCB 1744
Hoobler, Thomas *ConAu 69*
Hood, Flora Mae 1898- *ConAu 5R,*
ForWC 1970
Hood, George W *ConICB*
Hood, Joseph F 1925- *ConAu 33, SmATA 4*
Hood, Robert *MnBBF*
Hood, Robert Eric 1926- *ConAu 21R,*
WWA 38
Hood, Stephen *MnBBF, WWBWI A*
Hood, Stephen *see* Lewis, Jack
Hood, Thomas 1799-1845 *Alli, AnCL, AtlBL,*
BbD, BiD&SB, Br&AmS, BrAu 19,
CarSB, CasWL, Chambr 3, ChPo,
ChPo S1, ChPo S2, CnE&AP, CriT 2,
DcEnA, DcEnL, DcEuL, DcLEnL, EvLB,
MouLC 3, NCHEL, OxEng, Pen Eng,
REn, St&VC, WEAL
Hood, Thomas 1835-1874 *Alli Sup, BiD&SB,*
BrAu 19, Chambr 3, ChPo, ChPo S1,
ChPo S2, DcEnL, EvLB, NCHEL,
OxEng, TelT
Hook, Clarke *MnBBF*
Hook, Clarke *see* Hook, H Clarke
Hook, Clarke *see* Hook, Samuel Clarke
Hook, H Clarke *MnBBF, WWBWI A*
Hook, H Clarke *see* Clifford, Martin
Hook, H Clarke *see* Harvey, Ross
Hook, H Clarke *see* Hook, Clarke
Hook, H Clarke *see* Paine, Hammond
Hook, H Clarke *see* Ravenglass, Hal
Hook, H Clarke *see* Richards, Frank
Hook, Samuel Clarke *MnBBF, WWBWI A*
Hook, Samuel Clarke *see* Clarke, Maurice,
Captain
Hook, Samuel Clarke *see* Dene, Hampton
Hook, Samuel Clarke *see* Hale, Innis
Hook, Samuel Clarke *see* Hook, Clarke
Hook, Samuel Clarke *see* Hope, Edgar
Hook, Samuel Clarke *see* Lancaster, Captain
Hook, Samuel Clarke *see* Merriman, Maurice
Hook, Samuel Clarke *see* Monteith, Ewen
Hook, Samuel Clarke *see* Monteith, Owen

WWBWI A
Horowicz, A 1898- *WWBWI I*
Horrabin, James Francis 1884-1962 *NCHEL, WWBWI I, WWCL*
Horseman, Elaine Hall 1925- *ConAu 13R*
Horsfall, Magdalene 1884-1936 *CarSB*
Horsfall, Robert Bruce 1869- *ChPo, ChPo S1, IlCB 1744, WNAA*
Horsley, Reginald Ernest 1863- *ChPo, MnBBF*
Horton, F *MnBBF*
Horton, Lance *MnBBF*
Horton, Louise 1916- *ConAu 49*
Horvath, Betty 1927- *ConAu 17R, ForWC 1970, SmATA 4, WrD*
Horvath, Ferdinand Huszti 1891- *ConICB, IlCB 1744*
Horwich, Frances *see* Frances, Miss
Horwich, Frances R 1908- *AmA&B, ConAu P-1, ForWC 1970, SmATA 11, WWA 38, WWWorJ 1972*
Horwitz, Carrie Norris *CarSB*
Hosford, Dorothy 1900-1952 *AnCL, BkCL, MorJA, St&VC*
Hosford, Jessie 1892- *ConAu 41, SmATA 5*
Hosken, Clifford *MnBBF*
Hosken, Clifford *see* Cooper, Charles Henry St. John
Hosken, Ernest Charles Heath 1875- *MnBBF, WWLA*
Hosken, Ernest Charles Heath *see* Gower, Craven
Hosking, Eric 1909- *WW 1974*
Hoskins, Robert 1933- *ConAu 29*
Hoskins, Robert *see* Corren, Grace
Hoskyns-Abrahall, Clare *Au&Wr 6, ConAu 29, SmATA 13*
Hoskyns-Abrahall, Clare *see* Abrahall, C H
Hoskyns-Abrahall, Clare *see* Abrahall, Clare Hoskyns
Hoskyns-Abrahall, Clare *see* Drury, Clare Marie
Hostetler, Marian 1932- *ConAu 65*
Hotspur, Paul *MnBBF, WWBWI A*
Hotspur, Paul *see* Bidston, Lester
Houblon, A G *MnBBF*
Hough, Charlotte 1924- *ChPo S2, ConAu 9R, IlCB 1946, SmATA 9, WrD*
Hough, Lewis *MnBBF*
Hough, Richard Alexander 1922- *ConAu 5R, Au&Wr 6, AuBYP, WW 1974*
Hough, Richard Alexander *see* Carter, Bruce
Houghton, Ellen *CarSB*
Houghton, Eric 1930- *Au&Wr 6, AuBYP, ConAu 1R, SmATA 7, WrD*
Houghton, Thomas *Alli*
Houlehen, Robert J 1918- *ConAu 49*
House, Boyce 1896-1961 *AmA&B*
House, Charles 1916- *ConAu 25R*
Household, Geoffrey 1900- *Au&Wr 6, ConNov 1972, ConNov 1976, EncM&D, LongC, NCHEL, TwCA, TwCA Sup, WWCL, WrD*
Houselander, Caryll *CatA 1930*
Houser, Allan C 1914- *AmPB, IlBYP, IlCB 1744, IlCB 1946, IlCB 1957*
Housman, A E 1859-1936 *AnCL, AtlBL, CnE&AP, CnMWL, CyWA, EncWL, LongC, ModBL, ModBL Sup, Pen Eng, RAdv 1, RCom, REn, St&VC, TwCW, WEAL, WWTwL*
Housman, Laurence 1865-1959 *Chambr 3,*

ChPo, ChPo S1, ChPo S2, CnMD, DcEnA Ap, DcLEnL, EvLB, IlCB 1744, JBA 1934, LongC, McGWD, ModBL, ModWD, NCHEL, OxEng, Pen Eng, REn, TwCA, TwCA Sup, WWLA
Houston, James *ChLR 3, OxCan Sup*
Houston, James Archibald 1921- *ConAu 65, IlCB 1957, SmATA 13, WWE 14*
Houston, Joan 1928- *AuBYP, ConAu 17R*
Houston, W Robert, Jr. 1928- *ConAu 5R, LE 5, WrD*
Hovell, Lucille A 1916- *AuBYP, ConAu 5R*
Hovell, Lucille A *see* Hovell, Lucy A
Hovell, Lucy A *AuBYP, ConAu XR*
Hovell, Lucy A *see* Hovell, Lucille A
Howard, Alan 1922- *ChPo S1, ChPo S2, IlBYP, IlCB 1946, IlCB 1957*
Howard, Alice Woodbury *CarSB, OhA&B*
Howard, Bruce *MnBBF, WWBWI A*
Howard, Bruce *see* Day, George
Howard, Bruce *see* Pearson, Alec George
Howard, Coralie *ChPo, ChPo S1, ConAu XR*
Howard, Coralie *see* Cogswell, Coralie Norris
Howard, Edward Grenville George 1792?-1841 *CasWL, WWCL*
Howard, Elizabeth *AuBYP, ConAu XR, CurB 51, MorJA, TexW*
Howard, Elizabeth *see* Mizner, Elizabeth Howard
Howard, Frank *MnBBF, WWBWI A*
Howard, Frank *see* Hamilton, Cecily
Howard, Herbert *ChPo, MnBBF*
Howard, Jane 1935- *BiN 1974, ConAu 29*
Howard, John M *MnBBF, WWBWI A*
Howard, John M *see* Hincks, Cyril Malcolm
Howard, Keble *MnBBF, WWBWI A*
Howard, Keble *see* Bell, John Keble
Howard, Langley *MnBBF*
Howard, Louis G Redmond *MnBBF*
Howard, Louis G Redmond *see* Redmond-Howard, Louis G
Howard, Matthew V *MnnWr*
Howard, Prosper *MnBBF, SmATA XR, WWBWI A*
Howard, Prosper *see* Down, C Maurice
Howard, Prosper *see* Hamilton, Charles Harold St. John
Howard, Prosper *see* Hinton, Herbert Allan
Howard, Rob *IlBYP*
Howard, Robert West 1908- *AmA&B, Au&Wr 6, ConAu 1R, SmATA 5, WWWor 2*
Howard, Robert West *see* Case, Michael
Howard, Roland *MnBBF, WWBWI A*
Howard, Roland *see* Catchpole, William Leslie
Howard, Rowland *MnBBF*
Howard, Rowland *see* Catchpole, William Leslie
Howard, Thomas 1930- *ConAu 37*
Howard, Vanessa 1955- *BlkAW*
Howard, Vernon Linwood 1918- *AuBYP*
Howard-Gibbon, Amelia Frances 1826-1874 *ChPo S1*
Howarth, David Armine 1912- *ConAu 13R, SmATA 6, WW 1974, WrD*
Howarth, James 1866- *MnBBF*
Howden, Marjorie *SingR 2*
Howe, Frank *MnBBF, WWBWI A*
Howe, Gertrude Herrick 1902- *IlCB 1946*
Howe, Irving 1920- *AmA&B, ConAu 9R,*

DrAS 6E, ModAL, RAdv 1, REnAL,
TwCA Sup, WWA 38, WWWor 2,
WWWorJ 1972
Howe, Jane Moore 1914- *IndAu 1917*
Howell, S *ConAu XR, SmATA XR*
Howell, S *see* Styles, Frank Showell
Howell, Virginia Tier *ConAu XR, SmATA 4*
Howell, Virginia Tier *see* Ellison, Virginia Howell
Howells, Mildred 1872- *ChPo, WNAA*
Howells, William Dean 1837-1920 *Alli Sup,*
AmA, AmA&B, AmWr, AtlBL, BbD,
BiD&SB, CarSB, CasWL, Chambr 3,
ChPo, ChPo S1, ChPo S2, CnDAL,
CriT 3, CyAL 2, CyWA, DcAmA,
DcBiA, DcEnA, DcEnA Ap, DcEnL,
DcLEnL, DcNAA, EncWL, EvLB,
McGWD, ModAL, ModAL Sup,
ModWD, OhA&B, OxAm, OxEng,
Pen Am, RAdv 1, RCom, REn, REnAL,
WEAL
Howes, Barbara 1914- *AmA&B, ChPo,*
ConAu 9R, ConP 1970, ConP 1975,
DrAP 1975, ForWC 1970, Pen Am,
REnAL, SmATA 5, WWA 38, WorAu
Howitt, Mary 1799-1888 *Alli, Alli Sup, BbD,*
BiD&SB, BrAu 19, CarSB, CasWL,
ChPo, ChPo S1, ChPo S2, DcEnA,
DcEnL, DcEuL, EvLB, HsB&A,
NCHEL, TelT
Howitt, William 1792-1879 *Alli, Alli Sup,*
BbD, BiD&SB, BrAu 19, CarSB,
CasWL, ChPo, ChPo S1, ChPo S2,
DcEnA, DcEnL, DcEuL, EvLB, NCHEL
Howorth, M K *ConAu XR*
Howorth, M K *see* Black, Margaret K
Hoyland, Rosemary Jean 1929- *IlCB 1946*
Hoyle, Fred 1915- *Au&Wr 6, ConAu 5R,*
ConNov 1972, CurB 60, IntWW 38,
TwCW, WW 1974, WWWor 2, WorAu
Hoyle, Geoffrey 1942- *Au&Wr 6, ConAu 53,*
WrD
Hoys, Dudley *MnBBF*
Hoyt, Edwin Palmer, Jr. 1923- *AuBYP,*
ConAu 1R
Hoyt, Mary Finch *AuBYP*
Hoyt, Murray 1904- *ConAu 9R*
Hoyt, Olga Gruhzit 1922- *ConAu 25R,*
WWAW 8
Hu, Chang-Tu 1921?- *DrAS 6H, LE 5*
Hubbard, Ernest *WWBWI 1*
Hubbard, Freeman 1894- *ConAu 5R, WrD*
Hubbard, Margaret Ann *BkC 4, CatA 1930,*
ConAu XR, CurB 58, MnnWr
Hubbard, Margaret Ann *see* Priley, Margaret
Hubbard
Hubbell, Harriet Weed 1909- *AuBYP,*
ConAu 5R
Hubbell, Patricia 1928- *BkCL, ChPo S1,*
ChPo S2, ConAu 17R, SmATA 8
Huber, Charlotte *St&VC*
Huber, Miriam Blanton *AmA&B*
Hubert, Frank *MnBBF*
Hubert, Frank *see* Shaw, Frank H
Hubka, Betty 1924- *ConAu 13R*
Hubler, H Clark 1910- *AmMWS 12P,*
WWMW 14
Hubley, Faith 1924- *ForWC 1970*
Huddleston, David R *MnBBF*
Huddy, Delia 1934- *ConAu 25R*

Hudleston, John *MnBBF*
Hudleston, John *see* Dent, C H
Hudleston, Robert *MnBBF*
Hudleston, Robert *see* Dent, C H
Hudson, Gossie Harold 1930- *DrAS 6H*
Hudson, J *MnBBF*
Hudson, James A 1924- *ConAu 33, WrD*
Hudson, Jeffery *ConAu XR, SmATA XR*
Hudson, Jeffrey *see* Crichton, Michael
Hudson, Peggy 1936- *ConAu 37*
Hudson, William Henry 1841-1922 *Alli Sup,*
AnCL, AtlBL, CarSB, CasWL,
Chambr 3, ChPo S1, ChPo S2, CyWA,
DcBiA, DcEuL, DcLEnL, EvLB, LongC,
ModBL, NCHEL, OxEng, Pen Eng,
RAdv 1, REn, TwCA, TwCA Sup,
TwCW, WEAL
Hudson, Wilma Jones 1916- *ConAu 33, WrD*
Hueston, Ethel 1887- *AmA&B, AmNov,*
CarSB, REnAL
Huether, Anne Frances *ConAu XR*
Huff, Afton W 1928- *ConAu 65*
Huff, Betty Tracy *ConAu 25R, WrD*
Huffaker, Clair *WWA 38*
Huffaker, Sandy 1943- *SmATA 10*
Huffard, Grace Thompson 1892- *ChPo,*
ConAu P-1, IndAu 1917
Huggins, Alice Margaret 1891-1971 *ConAu P-1*
Hughes, Arthur 1832-1915 *ChPo, ChPo S1,*
WWCL
Hughes, Cledwyn 1920- *Au&Wr 6,*
ConAu 13R, WrD
Hughes, Fiona 1954- *Au&Wr 6*
Hughes, Harry *MnBBF*
Hughes, Harry *see* Havant, H
Hughes, Langston 1902-1967 *AmA&B,*
AmSCAP 66, AnCL, AuBYP, BiEnAT,
BkCL, BlkAW, ChPo, CnDAL, CnMD,
ConAmA, ConAu 1R, ConAu 25R,
ConLC 1, ConLC 5, ConP 1975, CrCD,
CurB 40, CurB 67, EncWL, LongC,
McGWD, ModAL, ModAL Sup,
ModWD, OxAm, Pen Am, RAdv 1, REn,
REnAL, SixAP, SmATA 4, St&VC,
TwCA, TwCA Sup, WEAL, WWTwL
Hughes, Mary *CarSB*
Hughes, Mary Louise 1910- *ConAu 29*
Hughes, Pennethorne 1907-1967 *ConAu 21R*
Hughes, Richard Arthur Warren 1900-
Au&Wr 6, CasWL, ChPo, ChPo S2,
ConAu 5R, ConLC 1, ConNov 1972,
ConNov 1976, CyWA, DcLEnL, EncWL,
EvLB, IntWW 38, LongC, ModBL,
ModBL Sup, NCHEL, OxEng, Pen Eng,
RAdv 1, REn, SmATA 8, TwCA,
TwCA Sup, TwCW, WW 1974, WWCL,
WWLA, WWTwL, WWWor 2, WrD
Hughes, Sam *ConAu XR*
Hughes, Sam *see* Wilks, Brian
Hughes, Shirley 1929- *IlCB 1957, WrD*
Hughes, Ted 1930- *CasWL, ChLR 3, ChPo,*
ChPo S1, ChPo S2, CnE&AP,
ConAu 1R, ConLC 2, ConLC 4,
ConP 1970, ConP 1975, EncWL,
IntWW 38, LongC, ModBL, ModBL Sup,
NCHEL, Pen Eng, RAdv 1, TwCW,
WEAL, WW 1974, WWTwL,
WWWor 2, WorAu, WrD
Hughes, Thomas 1822-1896 *Alli Sup, BbD,*

BiD&SB, BrAu 19, CarSB, CasWL,
CyWA, DcBiA, DcEnA, DcEnL, DcEuL,
DcLEnL, EvLB, JBA 1934, MnBBF,
MouLC 4, NCHEL, OxEng, Pen Eng,
REn, TelT, WWBWI A, WWCL
Hughes, Virginia ConAu XR
Hughes, Virginia see Campbell, Hope
Hugill, R MnBBF
Hugo, Victor Marie 1802-1885 AtlBL, BbD,
BiD&SB, CasWL, ChPo, ChPo S1,
ChPo S2, CnThe, CyWA, DcBiA,
DcEnL, DcEuL, EncM&D, EuAu,
EvEuW, HsB&A, McGWD, MnBBF,
NCHEL, OxEng, OxFr, Pen Eur, RCom,
REn, REnWD
Hulbert, Lloyd MnBBF
Hulbert, Lloyd see Pope, F W
Hull, Eleanor 1913- ConAu 9R, WrD
Hull, Eric Traviss ConAu XR, SmATA XR
Hull, Eric Traviss see Harnan, Terry
Hull, H Braxton AmA&B, ConAu XR,
SmATA XR
Hull, H Braxton see Jacobs, Helen Hull
Hull, Katharine 1921- ConAu 29
Hulme, Kathryn 1900- WWAW 8
Hulme, William Edward 1920- ConAu 13R,
DrAS 6P
Hults, Dorothy Niebrugge 1898- ConAu P-1,
SmATA 6
Humber, B A MnBBF
Humber, W B MnBBF
Humble, Richard 1945- ConAu 45
Hume, David MnBBF, WWBWI A
Hume, David see Turner, John Victor
Hume, Fergus 1859-1932 Alli Sup, BbD,
BiD&SB, DcLEnL, EncM&D, LongC,
MnBBF, NCHEL, TwCA, TwCA Sup
Hume, Lotta Carswell ConAu P-1, SmATA 7
Hume, Oscar MnBBF
Hume, Ruth F 1922- AuBYP
Hume, Valentine MnBBF
Hummel, Lisl ChPo, ConICB, IlCB 1744
Humphreville, Frances Tibbetts 1909-
ConAu 9R
Humphrey, Mrs. F A CarSB
Humphrey, William 1924- AmA&B,
ConNov 1972, ConNov 1976, DrAF 1976,
Pen Am, REnAL, WWA 38, WorAu
Humphreys, Gordon MnBBF
Humphries, Helen Speirs Dickie 1915-
Au&Wr 6, ConAu P-1
Humphries, Rolfe 1894-1969 AmA&B, CnDAL,
ConAu 5R, ConAu 25R, OxAm, RAdv 1,
REnAL, TwCA, TwCA Sup
Humphrys, Leslie George Au&Wr 6, WrD
Hungerford, Edward Buell 1900- AuBYP,
ConAu 37, DrAS 6E
Hungerford, Harold Ralph 1928- ConAu 33,
LE 5
Hunkin, Tim Mark Trelawney WrD
Hunt, Clara Whitehill 1871-1958 AmA&B,
JBA 1934, JBA 1951
Hunt, Douglas 1918- ConAu 13R
Hunt, Francis ConAu P-2
Hunt, Francis see Stratemeyer, Edward L
Hunt, George Pinney 1918- AuBYP, WWA 38
Hunt, Gladys M 1926- ConAu 29, WrD
Hunt, Graham MnBBF
Hunt, Henry George Bonavia 1847- Alli Sup,

MnBBF
Hunt, Irene 1907- AuBYP, ChLR 1,
ConAu 17R, MorBMP, NewbC 1966,
SmATA 2, ThBJA, WWA 38,
WWAW 8
Hunt, J D S MnBBF
Hunt, Jack WWBWI A
Hunt, Kari 1920- AuBYP, ConAu 41,
WWAA 1973
Hunt, Kyle ConAu XR, EncM&D, LongC
Hunt, Kyle see Creasey, John
Hunt, Mabel Leigh 1892-1971 AmA&B,
AuBYP, ConAu P-1, CurB 51,
IndAu 1917, JBA 1951, SmATA 1
Hunt, Marigold 1905- CatA 1952
Hunt, Maurice MnBBF
Hunt, Maurice see Parsons, B
Hunt, Patricia Joan 1921- Au&Wr 6, WrD
Hunt, Sam 1946- ConP 1975, WrD
Hunter, A C MnBBF
Hunter, Alfred John 1891-1961 MnBBF
Hunter, Alfred John see Brent, Francis
Hunter, Alfred John see Hunter, John
Hunter, Alfred John see Meriton, Peter
Hunter, Christine ConAu XR, WrD
Hunter, Christine see Hunter, Maud Lily
Hunter, Dawe SmATA XR
Hunter, Dawe see Downie, Mary Alice
Hunter, Evan 1926- AmA&B, AmSCAP 66,
Au&Wr 6, AuBYP, ConAu 5R,
ConNov 1972, ConNov 1976, CurB 56,
DrAF 1976, EncM&D, IntWW 38,
Pen Am, REn, REnAL, WWA 38,
WWE 14, WWTwL, WWWor 2, WorAu,
WrD
Hunter, Evan see McBain, Ed
Hunter, H MnBBF
Hunter, Hilda 1921?- Au&Wr 6, ConAu 49,
SmATA 7, WWMus 6
Hunter, Jim 1939- Au&Wr 6, ConAu 9R,
ConNov 1972, ConNov 1976
Hunter, John 1891- MnBBF, WWBWI A
Hunter, John see Brenning, L H
Hunter, John see Drummond, Anthony
Hunter, John see Hunter, Alfred John
Hunter, Kristin 1931- Au&ICB, AuBYP,
AuNews 1, BlkAW, ChLR 3,
ConAu 13R, ConNov 1972, ConNov 1976,
DrAF 1976, ForWC 1970, LBAA,
SmATA 12, WrD
Hunter, Maud Lily 1910- ConAu 9R
Hunter, Maud Lily see Hunter, Christine
Hunter, Mollie AuBYP, ConAu XR,
SmATA 2, ThBJA
Hunter, Mollie see McIlwraith, Maureen Mollie
Hunter
Hunter, Norman George Lorimer 1899-
Au&Wr 6, ChPo S2, WWCL, WrD
Hunter, Rowland MnBBF
Hunter, Rowland see Catchpole, William Leslie
Hunter Blair, Pauline 1921- ConAu 29,
SmATA 3
Hunter Blair, Pauline see Clare, Helen
Hunter Blair, Pauline see Clarke, Pauline
Huntingdon, A MnBBF
Huntingdon, Harry MnBBF, WWBWI A
Huntingdon, Harry see Pentelow, John Nix
Huntington, Harriet Elizabeth 1909- AmA&B,
AmPB, AuBYP, ConAu 5R, MorJA,

SmATA 1, WrD

Huntsberry, William E 1916- *ConAu 1R,*
DrAS 6E, SmATA 5

Hurd, Clement 1908- *AmPB, AuBYP,*
ChPo S1, ConAu 29, IlCB 1744,
IlCB 1946, IlCB 1957, MorJA,
SmATA 2

Hurd, Edith Thacher 1910- *AmPB, AuBYP,*
ConAu 13R, ForWC 1970, MorJA,
SmATA 2, WrD

Hurd, Edith Thacher *see* Sage, Juniper

Hurd, Edith Thacher *see* Thacher, Edith

Hurd, Michael John 1928- *Au&Wr 6,*
ConAu 65, WWMus 6, WrD

Hurd, Peter 1904- *ConICB, CurB 57,*
IlCB 1744, WWA 38, WWAA 1973,
WWWor 2

Hurford, Ian *MnBBF*

Hurlbut, Jesse Lyman 1843-1930 *Alli Sup,*
DcAmA, DcNAA, TwCA

Hurley, Leslie J 1911- *AuBYP, ConAu 49*

Hurley, William James, Jr. 1924- *ConAu 9R,*
LE 5

Hurlimann, Bettina 1909- *ChPo S1, ThBJA*

Huron *MnBBF*

Hurrell, Marion Isobel *MnBBF*

Hurst, Alec *MnBBF*

Hurt, Freda Mary Elizabeth 1911- *Au&Wr 6,*
WrD

Hurwitz, Abraham B 1905- *ConAu 29*

Hurwitz, Johanna 1937- *ConAu 65*

Hurwood, Bernhardt J 1926- *ConAu 25R,*
SmATA 12

Hurwood, Bernhardt J *see* Knight, Mallory T

Hurwood, Bernhardt J *see* Wilde, D Gunther

Hurwood, Bernhardt J *see* Xavier, Father

Hurworth, Fred R *MnBBF*

Hustington, Harry *MnBBF*

Hustington, Harry *see* Pentelow, John Nix

Hutchens, Paul 1902- *ConAu 61*

Hutchings, Margaret 1918- *ConAu 9R*

Hutchins, Carleen Maley 1911- *ConAu 17R,*
SmATA 9, WWAW 8, WWE 14

Hutchins, Pat 1942- *AmPB, IlBYP, WrD*

Hutchins, Ross Elliott 1906- *AuBYP,*
ConAu 9R, SmATA 4, ThBJA,
WWA 38

Hutchinson, George Andrew d1913 *MnBBF,*
WWBWI 1

Hutchinson, J R *MnBBF*

Hutchinson, R *MnBBF*

Hutchinson, Veronica S 1895-1961 *ChPo S2,*
OhA&B

Hutchinson, W M L *AnCL*

Hutchinson, William M 1916- *IlBYP,*
IlCB 1957

Hutchison, Chester Smith 1902- *AmMWS 12P,*
ConAu P-2, WWMW 14

Hutchison, Paula 1905- *ChPo, IlBYP,*
IlCB 1946

Huthmacher, J Joseph 1929- *ConAu 21R,*
DrAS 6H, SmATA 5

Hutt, Hector *MnBBF*

Hutt, Hector *see* Clifford, Martin

Hutto, Nelson 1904- *ConAu P-1*

Hutton, Clarke 1898- *IlCB 1744, IlCB 1946,*
IlCB 1957

Huxley, Aldous 1894-1963 *AmA&B, AtlBL,*
BiDPar, CasWL, Chambr 3, ChPo,

ChPo S1, ChPo S2, CnMD, CnMWL,
ConLC 1, ConLC 3, ConLC 4, ConLC 5,
CyWA, DcLEnL, EncWL, EvLB, LongC,
ModBL, ModBL Sup, ModWD, NCHEL,
OxEng, Pen Eng, RAdv 1, REn, TwCA,
TwCA Sup, TwCW, WEAL, WWTwL

Hyams, Joe 1923- *AmA&B, ConAu 17R,*
WWA 38

Hyatt, Stanley Portal 1877-1914 *MnBBF*

Hyatt, Stanley Portal *see* Dacre, Stanley, Captain

Hyde, A G *MnBBF*

Hyde, D Herbert *MnBBF, WWBWI A*

Hyde, D Herbert *see* Chambers, Derek

Hyde, Dayton Ogden 1925- *ConAu 25R,*
SmATA 9, WWA 38

Hyde, Dayton Ogden *see* Hyde, Hawk

Hyde, Hawk *ConAu XR, SmATA XR*

Hyde, Hawk *see* Hyde, Dayton Ogden

Hyde, Laurence Evelyn 1914- *ConAu 17R,*
WWAA 1973, WrD

Hyde, Margaret Oldroyd 1917- *AuBYP,*
ConAu 1R, SmATA 1, ThBJA

Hyde, Marston *MnBBF*

Hyde, Michael 1908- *Au&Wr 6, WrD*

Hyde, Wayne Frederick 1922- *ConAu 1R,*
SmATA 7

Hyland, Ann *WrD*

Hylander, Clarence John 1897-1964 *AmA&B,*
AuBYP, ConAu 5R, SmATA 7

Hyman, Dick 1904- *ConAu 17R*

Hyman, Frieda Clark 1913- *ConAu 5R,*
ForWC 1970, WWWorJ 1972

Hyman, Robin P 1931- *ConAu 41,*
SmATA 12

Hyman, Trina Schart 1939- *ChPo S1,*
ChPo S2, ConAu 49, IlBYP, IlCB 1957,
SmATA 7

Hymes, Lucia Manley 1907- *ChPo, ChPo S1,*
ConAu 5R,, SmATA 7

Hynd, Alan 1904?-1974 *ConAu 45*

Hyndman, Jane 1912- *AuBYP, SmATA 1*

Hyndman, Jane Lee *see* Wyndham, Lee

Hyne, Charles John Cutcliffe Wright 1865?-1944
EncM&D, EvLB, LongC, MnBBF,
NCHEL, TwCA, TwCA Sup,
WWBWI A, WWLA

I

SmATA 11
Irwin, Wallace Admah 1875-1959 *AmA&B,*
ChPo S1, ChPo S2, CnDAL, ConAmL,
DcAmA, OxAm, REn, REnAL, St&VC,
TwCA, TwCA Sup
Isaac, Joanne 1934- *ChPo S1, ConAu 25R*
Isaacs, Jacob *ConAu 57*
Isaacs, Jacob *see* Kranzler, George G
Isaacs, Levi *MnBBF*
Isaacs, Levi *see* Essex, Lewis
Isaacs, Levi *see* Essex, Louis
Ish-Kishor, Judith 1892-1972 *SmATA 11*
Ish-Kishor, Sulamith 1897?-1977 *AuBYP,*
ConAu 69, WNAA
Isham, Charlotte H 1912- *LE 5*
Ishmael, Woodi 1914- *IICB 1744, IICB 1946*
Ishmole, Jack 1924- *ConAu 49*
Islay, Nicholas *WWBWI A*
Islay, Nicholas *see* Murray, Andrew Nicholas
Islington, Frank *MnBBF*
Israel, Charles Edward 1920- *Au&Wr 6,*
CanWr, ConAu 1R, ConNov 1972,
ConNov 1976, DrAF 1976, IndAu 1917,
OxCan
Israel, Elaine 1945- *ConAu 53, SmATA 12*
Israel, Marion Louise 1882- *ConAu 1R*
Issa *CasWL*
Issler, Anne Roller 1892- *ConAu 49,*
IndAu 1917, WrD
Ivan, Gustave *AuBYP*
Ivan, Gustave *see* Miller, Martha
Ivan, Martha Miller Pfaff 1909- *AuBYP,*
ConAu P-2, WWAW 8
Ivan, Martha Miller Pfaff *see* Tavo, Gus
Ivanovsky, Elizabeth 1910- *IICB 1744*
Iverson, Genie 1942- *ConAu 65*
Ivor, Roderick *MnBBF*
Iwamatsu, Jun 1908- *AuBYP*
Izant, Grace Goulder 1893- *ConAu P-1*

J

Jablonski, Edward 1922- *AuBYP*, *ConAu 1R*
Jacberns, Raymond *CarSB*
Jacker, Corinne Litvin 1933- *AuBYP*,
  ConAu 17R, *ForWC 1970*, *WWAW 8*,
  WrD
Jackman, Leslie 1919- *ConAu 29*
Jackson, A M *MnBBF*
Jackson, C Paul 1902- *AuBYP*, *ConAu 5R*,
  SmATA 6
Jackson, C Paul *see* Jackson, Caary
Jackson, C Paul *see* Jackson, O B
Jackson, C Paul *see* Lochlons, Colin
Jackson, C Paul *see* Paulson, Jack
Jackson, Caary *ConAu XR*, *SmATA 6*
Jackson, Caary *see* Jackson, C Paul
Jackson, Donald 1919- *ConAu 17R*
Jackson, Eric *MnBBF*
Jackson, Genevieve Vaughan *IlCB 1946*
Jackson, Genevieve Vaughan *see*
  Vaughan-Jackson, Genevieve
Jackson, Geoffrey 1915- *ConAu 61*,
  IntWW 38, *WW 1974*, *WrD*
Jackson, Harry *MnBBF*
Jackson, Harvey *MnBBF*
Jackson, Helen Hunt 1831-1885 *Alli Sup*,
  AmA, *AmA&B*, *BbD*, *BiD&SB*, *CarSB*,
  CasWL, *ChPo*, *ChPo S1*, *ChPo S2*,
  CnDAL, *DcAmA*, *DcBiA*, *DcLEnL*,
  DcNAA, *EvLB*, *JBA 1934*, *MouLC 4*,
  OxAm, *REn*, *REnAL*, *St&VC*
Jackson, Howard *MnBBF*
Jackson, Howard *see* McGraw, J H
Jackson, Jacqueline 1928- *ConAu 45*
Jackson, Jesse 1908- *AuBYP*, *BlkAW*,
  ConAu 25R, *LBAA*, *OhA&B*, *SmATA 2*
Jackson, Julian 1867-1932 *MnBBF*,
  WWBWI A
Jackson, Julian *see* Wilson, John Park
Jackson, Lewis d1950? *MnBBF*, *WWBWI A*
Jackson, Lewis *see* Lewis, Jack
Jackson, Mary Coleman *AuBYP*
Jackson, O B *AuBYP*, *SmATA 6*
Jackson, O B *see* Jackson, C Paul
Jackson, Orpha *AuBYP*
Jackson, Philander *MnBBF*
Jackson, Philander *see* Burrage, Alfred
  Sherrington
Jackson, Robert Blake 1926- *AuBYP*,
  ConAu 5R, *SmATA 8*
Jackson, Rosemary Elizabeth *WrD*
Jackson, Sally *ConAu XR*, *SmATA XR*
Jackson, Shirley 1919-1965 *AmA&B*, *AmNov*,

ConAu 1R, ConAu 25R, ConNov 1976,
  LongC, ModAL, OxAm, Pen Am,
  RAdv 1, REn, REnAL, SmATA 2,
  TwCA Sup
Jacob, Helen Pierce 1927- *ConAu 69*
Jacobs, Allan Duane 1934- *LE 5*
Jacobs, Beth *AuBYP*
Jacobs, Donald Martin 1937- *DrAS 6H*
Jacobs, Flora Gill 1918- *AuBYP*, *ConAu 1R*,
  ForWC 1970, *SmATA 5*
Jacobs, Francine 1935- *ConAu 49*
Jacobs, Frank 1929- *AuBYP*, *ConAu 13R*
Jacobs, Helen Hull 1908- *AmA&B*, *Au&Wr 6*,
  AuBYP, *ConAu 9R*, *SmATA 12*,
  WWA 38, *WWAW 8*, *WrD*
Jacobs, Helen Hull *see* Hull, H Braxton
Jacobs, John Kedzie 1918- *WWA 38*,
  WWS 13
Jacobs, Joseph 1854-1916 *Alli Sup*, *AmA&B*,
  AnCL, *BiD&SB*, *BrAu 19*, *CarSB*,
  Chambr 3, *DcAmA*, *DcNAA*, *JBA 1934*,
  REnAL, *St&VC*, *WWCL*
Jacobs, Leland B *AuBYP*, *ChPo*, *ChPo S1*,
  ChPo S2
Jacobs, Lou, Jr. 1921- *ConAu 21R*, *SmATA 2*,
  WWW 14
Jacobs, Louis 1920- *ConAu 1R*
Jacobs, T C H *ConAu XR*, *MnBBF*,
  WWBWI A
Jacobs, T C H *see* Pendower, Jacques
Jacobs, William Jay 1933- *ConAu 57*, *LE 5*
Jacobs, William Wymark 1863-1943 *BbD*,
  BiD&SB, *CasWL*, *Chambr 3*, *DcBiA*,
  DcEnA Ap, *DcLEnL*, *EncM&D*, *EvLB*,
  LongC, *MnBBF*, *ModBL*, *NCHEL*,
  OxEng, *Pen Eng*, *REn*, *TwCA*,
  TwCA Sup, *TwCW*, *WWBWI A*,
  WWLA
Jacobson, Daniel 1923- *AmMWS 12S*,
  ConAu 53, *SmATA 12*
Jacobson, Ethel *ConAu 37*
Jacobson, Morris K 1906- *ConAu 45*
Jacoby *WWBWI I*
Jacques, Faith *ChPo*, *IlBYP*
Jacques, Robin 1920- *ArtsCL*, *ChPo S1*,
  IlBYP, *IlCB 1946*, *IlCB 1957*, *ThBJA*,
  WWCL
Jaffe, Leonard 1926- *WWWorJ 1972*
Jaffe, Rona 1932?- *AmA&B*, *AuNews 1*,
  BiN 1975, *WrD*
Jagendorf, Moritz Adolf 1888- *AnCL*, *AuBYP*,
  ConAu 5R, *CurB 52*, *MorJA*, *SmATA 2*,

WNAA, WrD
Jago, William H *MnBBF, WWBWI A*
Jahoda, Gloria 1926- *ConAu 1R,*
ForWC 1970
Jakes, John W 1932- *ConAu 57, OxCan Sup*
Jakes, John W *see* Payne, Alan
Jakes, John W *see* Scotland, Jay
Jakubowski, Charles *IlBYP*
James, Alan 1943- *Au&Wr 6, WrD*
James, Andrew *ConAu XR, SmATA XR*
James, Andrew *see* Kirkup, James
James, Bernard R *MnBBF*
James, Bessie Rowland 1895- *AmA&B,*
WNAA
James, Bruce *MnBBF*
James, Cy *ConAu XR*
James, Cy *see* Watts, Peter Christopher
James, David *MnBBF*
James, Dynely *ConAu XR, SmATA 6,*
ThBJA
James, Dynely *see* Mayne, William
James, Ernest *MnBBF*
James, Ernest *see* Pike, William Ernest
James, G P R *MnBBF*
James, Gilbert *ChPo, IlCB 1744*
James, Harold L *IlBYP*
James, Harry Clebourne 1896- *ConAu 5R,*
SmATA 11, WWW 14
James, Henry 1843-1916 *Alli Sup, AmA,*
AmA&B, AmWr, AtlBL, BbD, BiD&SB,
CasWL, CnDAL, CnMD, CnMWL,
CnThe, CriT 3, CyWA, DcAmA, DcBiA,
DcEnA, DcEnA Ap, DcEnL, DcEuL,
DcLEnL, DcNAA, EncWL, EvLB,
LongC, McGWD, ModAL, ModAL Sup,
ModBL, ModBL Sup, ModWD, NCHEL,
OxAm, OxEng, Pen Am, Pen Eng,
RAdv 1, RCom, REn, REnAL, REnWD,
TwCW, WEAL, WWTwL
James, Herbert Wentworth *MnBBF,*
WWBWI A
James, Herbert Wentworth *see* Wentworth,
Herbert
James, Josephine *ConAu XR, SmATA 6*
James, Josephine *see* Sterne, Emma Gelders
James, Leonard F 1904- *ConAu 49*
James, Marquis 1891-1955 *AmA&B, OxAm,*
REnAL, TwCA, TwCA Sup, WNAA
James, Norma Wood *AuBYP*
James, S T *MnBBF*
James, T F *ConAu XR, SmATA 8*
James, T F *see* Fleming, Thomas J
James, Theodore, Jr. 1934- *ConAu 33*
James, Vernon *MnBBF*
James, Vernon *see* Bridges, Victor
James, Will 1892-1942 *AuBYP, CurB 42,*
DcNAA, JBA 1934, JBA 1951,
Newb 1922, OxAm, REnAL, TwCA,
TwCA Sup, WNAA
Jameson, Malcolm 1891-1945 *AuBYP*
Jameson, Robert *MnBBF, WWBWI A*
Jameson, Vic 1924- *ConAu 17R*
Jamison, Andrew 1948- *ConAu 29*
Jane, Mary Childs 1909- *AuBYP, ConAu 1R,*
ForWC 1970, SmATA 6
Janes, Edward C 1908- *AuBYP*
Janeway, Elizabeth 1913- *AmA&B, AmNov,*
Au&Wr 6, AuBYP, AuNews 1, ChPo,
ConAu 45, CurB 44, DrAF 1976,

REnAL, TwCA Sup, WWAW 8,
WWE 14, WWWor 2
Janice *AuBYP, ConAu XR*
Janice *see* Brustlein, Janice Tworkov
Janiver, Thomas A 1849-1913 *CarSB*
Janosch *ChPo S1, ConAu XR, IlBYP,*
SmATA 8
Janosch *see* Eckert, Horst
Jansen, Jared *ConAu XR, SmATA XR*
Jansen, Jared *see* Cebulash, Mel
Janson, Dora Jane *AuBYP*
Janson, Hank *WWBWI A*
Janson, Hank *see* Frances, S D
Janson, Hank *see* Williams, Richard
Janson, Horst Woldemar 1913- *AuBYP,*
DrAS 6H, SmATA 9, WWA 38,
WWAA 1973, WWWor 2
Jansson, Tove 1914- *Au&Wr 6, ChLR 2,*
ConAu 17R, IlCB 1957, SmATA 3,
ThBJA, WWCL
Japp, May P *MnBBF*
Jaques, Francis Lee 1887- *IlCB 1946*
Jardine, Warwick *MnBBF, WWBWI A*
Jardine, Warwick *see* Bayfield, William John
Jardine, Warwick *see* Warwick, Francis Alister
Jarman, Rosemary Hawley 1935- *ConAu 49,*
SmATA 7
Jarrell, Randall 1914-1965 *AmA&B, AmWr,*
AnCL, AuBYP, CasWL, ChPo, ChPo S1,
CnDAL, CnE&AP, ConAu 5R,
ConAu 25R, ConLC 1, ConLC 2,
ConLC 6, ConP 1975, CrCAP, EncWL,
ModAL, ModAL Sup, OxAm, Pen Am,
RAdv 1, REn, REnAL, SixAP,
SmATA 7, ThBJA, TwCA Sup, TwCW,
WEAL, WWTwL
Jaszi, Jean Yourd *AuBYP, BkCL, ChPo*
Jauss, Anne Marie 1907- *AuBYP, ConAu 1R,*
ForWC 1970, IlCB 1946, IlCB 1957,
SmATA 10, WWAA 1973, WrD
Jaworski, Irene D *AuBYP*
Jayne, R H, Lieutenant *AmA&B, YABC 1*
Jayne, R H, Lieutenant *see* Ellis, Edward S
Jaynes, Clare *AmA&B, AmNov, AuBYP,*
ConAu XR, CurB 54
Jaynes, Clare *see* Mayer, Jane Rothschild
Jaynes, Ruth 1899- *ConAu P-2*
Jeake, Samuel, Jr. *ConAu XR, SmATA 3*
Jeake, Samuel, Jr. *see* Aiken, Conrad Potter
Jeal, Tim 1945- *Au&Wr 6, ConAu 21R*
Jefferies, Richard 1848-1887 *BiD&SB,*
BrAu 19, CarSB, CasWL, Chambr 3,
DcEnA, DcEuL, DcLEnL, EvLB,
MouLC 4, NCHEL, OxEng, Pen Eng,
RAdv 1, REn, TelT, WEAL, WWCL
Jeffers, Harry Paul 1934- *AuBYP*
Jeffers, Susan *IlBYP*
Jefferson, Alan 1921- *ConAu 33*
Jefferson, R L *MnBBF*
Jefferson, Robert Louis 1929- *IlBYP*
Jefferson, Sarah *ConAu XR, SmATA XR*
Jefferson, Sarah *see* Farjeon, Annabel
Jeffery, W L *MnBBF*
Jeffrey, Adi-Kent Thomas 1916- *ConAu 37*
Jeffries, G M *WWBWI A*
Jeffries, G M *see* Jeffries, Graeme Montagu
Jeffries, Graeme Montagu 1900- *MnBBF*
Jeffries, Graeme Montagu *see* Graeme, Bruce
Jeffries, Graeme Montagu *see* Jeffries, G M

Jeffries, Roderic 1926- *Au&Wr 6, AuBYP,*
  ConAu 17R, EncM&D, SmATA 4
Jeffries, Roderic *see* Ashford, Jeffrey
Jeffries, Roderic *see* Draper, Hastings
Jeffries, Roderic *see* Graeme, Roderic
Jeffries, Roderic *see* Hastings, Graham
Jemne, Elsa Laubach 1888- *IlCB 1744*
Jenkins, Alan 1914- *Au&Wr 6, ConAu 57*
Jenkins, Alan Charles 1914- *Au&Wr 6,*
  MnBBF
Jenkins, Elizabeth 1907- *DcLEnL, IntWW 38,*
  WW 1974, WWA 38, WWAW 8,
  WorAu
Jenkins, Ernest *MnBBF*
Jenkins, Ferguson 1943- *WWA 38*
Jenkins, Marie M 1909- *AmMWS 12P,*
  ConAu 41, SmATA 7, WWAW 8
Jenkins, Marie M *see* Markins, W S
Jenkins, Marie M *see* Scholastica, Sister Mary
Jenkins, Ray *WrD*
Jenkins, William Atwell 1922- *DrAS 6E,*
  SmATA 9, WWA 38
Jenks, Tudor 1857-1922 *AmA&B, AmLY,*
  BiD&SB, CarSB, ChPo, DcAmA,
  DcNAA, REnAL
Jenkyns, Chris 1924- *IlBYP, IlCB 1946*
Jenner, H P *WWBWI I*
Jenness, Aylette 1934- *ConAu 25R*
Jennings, Elizabeth 1926- *Au&Wr 6, ChPo,*
  ChPo S1, ChPo S2, ConAu 61, ConLC 5,
  ConP 1970, ConP 1975, LongC, ModBL,
  ModBL Sup, NCHEL, Pen Eng, RAdv 1,
  TwCW, WEAL, WW 1974, WWTwL,
  WorAu
Jennings, Gary 1928- *AuBYP, ConAu 5R,*
  SmATA 9
Jennings, Jerry 1935- *ConAu 53*
Jennings, John Edward, Jr. 1906-1973 *AmA&B,*
  AmNov, AuBYP, ConAu P-1, REnAL,
  TwCA Sup, WWE 14
Jennings, Michael 1931- *ConAu 69*
Jennings, Robert *MnBBF, SmATA XR,*
  WWBWI A
Jennings, Robert *see* Hamilton, Charles Harold
  St. John
Jennings, S M *ConAu XR, SmATA 3*
Jennings, S M *see* Meyer, Jerome Sydney
Jennison, C S *AuBYP, ConAu XR,*
  SmATA 6
Jennison, C S *see* Starbird, Kaye
Jennison, Christopher 1938- *ConAu 53*
Jennison, Keith Warren 1911- *AmA&B,*
  AuBYP
Jensen, David Edward 1909- *AmMWS 12P,*
  AuBYP, WWE 14
Jensen, Niels 1927- *ConAu 49*
Jensen, Pauline Marie 1900- *ConAu P-2*
Jensen, Virginia Allen 1927- *ConAu 45,*
  SmATA 8
Jermyn, R Gordon *MnBBF*
Jerome, Irene Elizabeth 1858- *Alli Sup, CarSB,*
  ChPo
Jerome, Jerome Klapka 1859-1927 *Alli Sup,*
  BbD, BiD&SB, CasWL, Chambr 3,
  CyWA, DcBiA, DcEnA Ap, DcLEnL,
  EvLB, LongC, McGWD, MnBBF,
  ModBL, ModWD, NCHEL, OxEng,
  Pen Eng, REn, TwCA, TwCW,
  WWBWI A

Jerome, John 1932- *ConAu 45*
Jerr, William A *AuBYP*
Jersey, Countess Of 1849- *CarSB*
Jessop, Gilbert L *MnBBF*
Jeter, Jacky *ConAu XR*
Jeter, Jacky *see* Jeter, Jacquelyn I
Jeter, Jacquelyn I 1935- *ConAu 25R*
Jeter, Jacquelyn I *see* Jeter, Jacky
Jewell, Nancy 1940- *ConAu 61*
Jewett, Eleanore Myers 1890-1967 *ChPo,*
  ConAu 5R, MorJA, SmATA 5
Jewett, Sarah Orne 1849-1909 *Alli Sup, AmA,*
  AmA&B, AmWr, AtlBL, AuBYP, BbD,
  BiD&SB, CarSB, CasWL, Chambr 3,
  ChPo, ChPo S1, ChPo S2, CnDAL,
  CriT 3, CyWA, DcAmA, DcBiA,
  DcLEnL, DcNAA, EvLB, JBA 1934,
  ModAL, OxAm, OxEng, Pen Am,
  RAdv 1, REn, REnAL, WEAL
Jezard, Alison 1919- *ConAu 29*
Jimenez, Juan Ramon 1881-1958 *AnCL, AtlBL,*
  CasWL, ClDMEuL, CnMWL, CyWA,
  DcSpL, EncWL, EvEuW, ModRL,
  Pen Eur, REn, TwCW, WWTwL,
  WorAu
Jobson, Patrick 1919- *IlCB 1946*
Jocelyn, Noel *MnBBF*
Joerns, Consuelo *IlBYP*
Johannis, Theodore B, Jr. 1914- *AmMWS 12S,*
  ConAu 33
Johansen, Margaret Alison 1896- *AuBYP,*
  TexW
John, Betty *ConAu XR, WrD*
John, Betty *see* John, Elizabeth Beaman
John, Elizabeth Beaman 1907- *ConAu 5R*
John, Elizabeth Beaman *see* John, Betty
Johns, Avery *ConAu XR, SmATA 2*
Johns, Avery *see* Cousins, Margaret
Johns, Gilbert *MnBBF, WWBWI A*
Johns, Gilbert *see* Stagg, James
Johns, William Earl 1893-1968 *MnBBF,*
  WWBWI A, WWCL
Johnson, A *ConAu XR*
Johnson, A *see* Johnson, Annabel Jones
Johnson, A E *ConAu XR, SmATA 2*
Johnson, A E *see* Johnson, Annabel Jones
Johnson, A E *see* Johnson, Edgar Raymond
Johnson, Annabel Jones 1921- *AmA&B,*
  AuBYP, ConAu 9R, SmATA 2, ThBJA
Johnson, Annabel Jones *see* Johnson, A
Johnson, Annabel Jones *see* Johnson, A E
Johnson, Avery Fischer 1906- *IlCB 1744,*
  IlCB 1946, WWA 38, WWAA 1973
Johnson, Bertha French 1906- *ConAu 41*
Johnson, Burges 1877-1963 *AmA&B, AmLY,*
  ChPo, ChPo S1, ChPo S2, REnAL,
  WNAA
Johnson, Charles Frederick *AuBYP*
Johnson, Charles R 1925- *ConAu 65,*
  SmATA 11, WWMW 14
Johnson, Charles R *see* Johnson, Chuck
Johnson, Charlotte Buel 1918- *WWA 38,*
  WWAA 1973, WWAW 8
Johnson, Chuck *ConAu 65, SmATA XR*
Johnson, Chuck *see* Johnson, Charles R
Johnson, Crockett *AmPB, Au&Wr 6,*
  AuBYP, BkP, ConAu XR, CurB 43,
  IlCB 1946, IlCB 1957, SmATA 1,
  ThBJA, WWAA 1973

Johnson, Crockett see Leisk, David Johnson
Johnson, Dorothy Marie 1905- *Au&Wr 6,*
  ConAu 5R, ForWC 1970, SmATA 6,
  WWPNA
Johnson, Dudley Vaughan *MnBBF*
Johnson, Dudley Vaughan see Vaughan, Dudley
Johnson, Edgar 1901- *AmA&B, AuBYP,*
  DrAS 6E, REnAL, TwCA Sup,
  WWA 38, WWWor 2
Johnson, Edgar Raymond 1912- *ConAu 9R,*
  SmATA 2, ThBJA
Johnson, Edgar Raymond see Johnson, A E
Johnson, Elizabeth 1911- *ConAu 1R,*
  SmATA 7
Johnson, Enid 1892- *AuBYP, JBA 1934*
Johnson, Enid see Peck, Anne Merriman
Johnson, Eric W 1918- *ConAu 5R, LE 5,*
  SmATA 8, WrD
Johnson, Eugene Harper *IIBYP, IICB 1946,*
  IICB 1957
Johnson, Evelyne 1932- *ConAu 69*
Johnson, Fred *ArtCS*
Johnson, Gaylord 1884- *ConAu P-1,*
  SmATA 7
Johnson, George 1917- *ConAu 5R*
Johnson, George M *MnBBF*
Johnson, Gerald White 1890- *AmA&B, AnCL,*
  AuBYP, CnDAL, OxAm, REnAL,
  ThBJA, TwCA Sup, ,WNAA, WWA 38,
  WWWor 2
Johnson, Helen Louise Kendrick 1843-1917
  Alli Sup, AmA, AmA&B, BiD&SB,
  CarSB, ChPo S1, DcAmA, DcNAA
Johnson, Henry T 1858-1920? *MnBBF,*
  WWBWI A
Johnson, Henry T see Thomson, Neil
Johnson, Humphrey Wynne 1925-1976
  ConAu 61
Johnson, James E 1927- *DrAS 6H*
Johnson, James Ralph 1922- *AuBYP,*
  ConAu 1R, SmATA 1, WrD
Johnson, James Weldon 1871-1938 *AmA&B,*
  AmSCAP 66, AnCL, AnMV 1926,
  BlkAW, CasWL, ChPo, ChPo S1,
  ChPo S2, ConAmA, ConAmL, DcLEnL,
  DcNAA, ModAL Sup, OxAm, Pen Am,
  RAdv 1, REn, REnAL, SixAP, TwCA,
  TwCA Sup, WEAL, WNAA
Johnson, Jerry Mack 1927- *ConAu 53*
Johnson, Jerry Mack see Mack, Jerry
Johnson, John E 1929- *ChPo S1, IIBYP,*
  IICB 1957
Johnson, LaVerne B 1925- *ConAu 65,*
  SmATA 13
Johnson, Lois Smith 1894- *ConAu P-1,*
  SmATA 6
Johnson, Lois Walfrid 1936- *ConAu 57*
Johnson, Margaret 1926- *ConAu 37*
Johnson, Margaret Sweet 1893- *AuBYP,*
  JBA 1951
Johnson, Milton 1932- *IICB 1957*
Johnson, Osa Helen 1894-1953 *AmA&B,*
  AuBYP, REnAL
Johnson, Richard *ConAu 57*
Johnson, Richard 1734-1793 *CarSB*
Johnson, Richard see Richey, David
Johnson, Richard C 1919- *ConAu 33*
Johnson, Robert E *AuBYP*
Johnson, Robert Ivar 1933- *AmA&B,*

AmMWS 12P, ConAu 53, WWA 38,
  WWWor 2
Johnson, Rossiter 1840-1931 *AmA&B, BbD,*
  BiD&SB, CarSB, ChPo, ChPo S1,
  DcAmA, DcNAA, OxCan, REnAL,
  WNAA
Johnson, Ryerson 1901- *ConAu 5R,*
  SmATA 10
Johnson, S Lawrence 1909- *ConAu 29, WrD*
Johnson, Shirley King 1927- *ConAu 9R,*
  ForWC 1970, SmATA 10, WrD
Johnson, Siddie Joe 1905- *AuBYP, BiDL 5,*
  ChPo S1, JBA 1951, TexW
Johnson, William Weber 1909- *AmA&B,*
  AuBYP, ConAu 17R, SmATA 7,
  WWA 38, WWW 14, WrD
Johnson, Winifred 1905- *ConAu 5R*
Johnston, Agnes Christine *ConAu XR,*
  SmATA 2
Johnston, Agnes Christine see Dazey, Agnes J
Johnston, Annie Fellows 1863-1931 *AmA&B,*
  ArizL, BiDSA, CarSB, ChPo, DcAmA,
  DcNAA, IndAu 1816, JBA 1934, OxAm,
  REnAL, TwCA, TwCA Sup
Johnston, Brenda A 1944- *ConAu 57*
Johnston, Charles Haven Ladd 1877-1943
  AmA&B, AmLY, WNAA
Johnston, Dorothy Grunbock 1915- *ConAu 5R*
Johnston, Edith Constance Farrington 1890-
  IICB 1744, IICB 1946
Johnston, H A S 1913-1967 *ConAu P-2*
Johnston, H A S see Sturton, Hugh
Johnston, Johanna *AuBYP, ConAu 57,*
  SmATA 12
Johnston, Laurie *AuBYP*
Johnston, Louisa Mae *AuBYP*
Johnston, Mary 1870-1936 *AmA&B, BbD,*
  BiD&SB, BiDSA, Chambr 3, ChPo,
  CnDAL, ConAmL, CyWA, DcAmA,
  DcBiA, DcEnA Ap, DcNAA, LongC,
  OxAm, REn, REnAL, TwCA
Johnston, Ralph E 1902- *AuBYP*
Johnston, Richard James Humphreys 1910-
  AmA&B, WWA 38
Johnston, Smith see Crane, Stephen
Johnston, Tony 1942- *ConAu 41, SmATA 8*
Johnston, William 1856- *MnBBF*
Johnstone, Anne G *IIBYP*
Johnstone, Janet G *IIBYP*
Johnstone, Kathleen Yerger 1906- *ConAu 9R,*
  ForWC 1970
Jolling, Jack *MnBBF*
Jolling, Jack see Judd, Alfred
Jolly, Hugh Reginald 1918- *WW 1974, WrD*
Jonas, Arthur 1930- *ConAu 13R*
Jonas, Nita *AmSCAP 66, ChPo*
Jones, Adrienne 1915- *ConAu 33, SmATA 7,*
  WrD
Jones, Arthur d1939 *WWBWI 1*
Jones, Barry *MnBBF*
Jones, Beryl Bailey- *IICB 1946*
Jones, Beryl Bailey see Bailey-Jones, Beryl
Jones, C A *CarSB*
Jones, Candy *CurB 61*
Jones, Carol Ann 1942- *IICB 1957*
Jones, Christine 1937- *ConAu 61*
Jones, Daisy 1906- *ConAu 17R*
Jones, David 1895-1974 *CasWL, CnE&AP,*
  CnMWL, ConAu 9R, ConAu 53,

Jones, Diana Wynne 1934- *Au&Wr 6,*
 ConAu 49, SmATA 9
Jones, Dorothy Holder *ConAu 9R,*
 ForWC 1970
Jones, Edward H, Jr. 1922- *ConAu 13R*
Jones, Elizabeth B 1907- *ConAu 61*
Jones, Elizabeth B *see* Brown, Betty
Jones, Elizabeth Orton 1910- *AuBYP,*
 Cald 1938, ChPo, ChPo S1, IlBYP,
 IlCB 1744, IlCB 1946, JBA 1951,
 St&VC, WWA 38, WWAA 1973,
 WWAW 8
Jones, Evan 1915- *AmA&B, Au&Wr 6,*
 ConAu 9R, SmATA 3
Jones, Everett LeRoi 1934- *AmA&B, CurB 70,*
 IntWW 38, WorAu
Jones, Gerald Norman *MnBBF*
Jones, Gillingham *MnBBF, SmATA XR,*
 WWBWI A
Jones, Gillingham *see* Hamilton, Charles Harold
 St. John
Jones, Glyn 1905- *Au&Wr 6, CnMWL,*
 ConAu 9R, ConNov 1972, ConNov 1976,
 ConP 1970, ConP 1975, ModBL, WorAu
Jones, Gwyn 1907- *Au&Wr 6, CasWL,*
 ConNov 1972, ConNov 1976, LongC,
 ModBL, OxCan, WW 1974
Jones, H Bedford *MnBBF*
Jones, Harold 1904- *ChPo, IlBYP, IlCB 1744,*
 IlCB 1946, IlCB 1957, ThBJA, WWCL
Jones, Helen Hinckley 1903- *AuBYP,*
 ChPo S2, ConAu 5R
Jones, Helen Hinckley *see* Hinckley, Helen
Jones, Hortense P 1918- *ConAu 61,*
 SmATA 9
Jones, J *MnBBF*
Jones, J *see* Hazel, Harry
Jones, J G *MnBBF, WWBWI A*
Jones, J G *see* Bloomer, Steve
Jones, J G *see* Earle, Ambrose
Jones, J G *see* Earle, Enid
Jones, J G *see* Gordon, Geoffrey
Jones, J G *see* Trew, Dighton
Jones, John Jay *CarSB*
Jones, Juanita Nuttall 1912- *AuBYP*
Jones, Lloid 1908- *AuBYP*
Jones, Louis Clark 1908- *ConAu 5R,*
 DrAS 6H, WWA 38, WWAA 1973,
 WWE 14
Jones, Margaret Boone 1924- *ConAu 25R*
Jones, Mary Alice 1898?- *AuBYP,*
 ConAu 17R, ForWC 1970, MorJA,
 SmATA 6, WWAW 8
Jones, Mary Voell 1933- *ConAu 21R,*
 WWAW 8, WrD
Jones, Peter 1921- *Au&Wr 6, ConAu 5R*
Jones, Richard 1926- *ConAu 49*
Jones, Richard C 1910- *IlCB 1744, IlCB 1946*
Jones, Tom *MnBBF*
Jones, Weyman 1928- *AuBYP, ConAu 17R,*
 SmATA 4
Jones, Wilfred J 1888- *AmPB, ConICB,*
 IlCB 1744
Jones Minor Of St. Agnes School *MnBBF*

Jonk, Clarence 1906- *ConAu 5R, SmATA 10*
Jordan, Elizabeth Garver 1867-1947 *AmA&B,*
 BkC 2, CarSB, CatA 1930, DcAmA,
 DcNAA, REnAL, WNAA, WisW
Jordan, J A *MnBBF*
Jordan, June Meyer 1936- *BlkAW, ConAu 33,*
 ChPo S1, ChPo S2, ConLC 5,
 DrAF 1976, DrAP 1975, LBAA,
 SmATA 4, WrD
Jordan, June Meyer *see* Meyer, June
Jordan, Mildred A 1901- *AmA&B, AmNov,*
 ConAu P-2, CurB 51, SmATA 5,
 TwCA Sup
Jordan, Philip Dillon 1903- *AuBYP,*
 ConAu 9R, DrAS 6H, MnnWr, OhA&B
Jorgensen, Mary Venn *AuBYP, ConAu 1R*
Jorgensen, Mary Venn *see* Venn, Mary Eleanor
Jorgenson, Ivar *AuBYP, ConAu XR,*
 SmATA XR, ThBJA
Jorgenson, Ivar *see* Silverberg, Robert
Joscelyn, Archie L 1899- *ConAu 1R*
Joscelyn, Archie L *see* Cody, Al
Joseph, Alexander 1907- *AmMWS 12P,*
 AuBYP, ConAu 13R
Joseph, Franz *ConAu 5R*
Joseph, Franz *see* Schnaubelt, Franz Joseph
Joseph, Joan 1939- *ConAu 25R*
Joslin, Sesyle *Au&Wr 6, AuBYP,*
 ConAu XR, SmATA 2, ThBJA
Joslin, Sesyle *see* Gibson, Josephine
Joslin, Sesyle *see* Hine, Sesyle Joslin
Joslin, Sesyle *see* Kirtland, G B
Josling, Harold *MnBBF*
Joughlin, Clueas *MnBBF*
Joy, Charles Rhind 1885- *AuBYP*
Joy, Dickson *MnBBF*
Joyce, Ernest *MnBBF*
Joyce, J Avery *SmATA 11*
Joyce, James 1882-1941 *AtlBL, CasWL,*
 Chambr 3, ChPo, ChPo S1, CnMD,
 CnMWL, CurB 41, CyWA, DcLEnL,
 EncWL, EvLB, LongC, McGWD,
 ModBL, ModBL Sup, ModWD, NCHEL,
 OxEng, Pen Eng, PoIre, RAdv 1, RCom,
 REn, TwCA, TwCA Sup, TwCW,
 WEAL, WWTwL
Joyce, James Avery 1902- *Au&Wr 6,*
 CurB 59, WWA 38, WWWor 2
Joyner, Jerry *IlBYP*
Joynson, Barry *MnBBF*
Joynson, Barry *see* Cork, Barry Joynson
Jucker, Sita 1921- *ConAu 29, IlBYP,*
 SmATA 5
Judd, Alfred *MnBBF, WWBWI A, WWLA*
Judd, Alfred *see* Jolling, Jack
Judd, Alfred *see* Power, Nelson
Judd, Frances K *ConAu P-2, SmATA 1*
Judd, Frances K *see* Stratemeyer, Edward L
Judson, Clara Ingram 1879-1960 *AmA&B,*
 Au&ICB, AuBYP, CarSB, CurB 48,
 IndAu 1816, JBA 1951, OxCan, WNAA
Judson, Edward Zane Carroll 1823?-1886
 Alli Sup, AmA, AmA&B, DcAmA,
 DcNAA, HsB&A, MnBBF, OhA&B,
 OxAm, REn, REnAL, WWBWI A
Judson, Edward Zane Carroll *see* Buntline, Ned
Judson, Harry Pratt 1849-1927 *Alli Sup,*
 AmA&B, BiD&SB, DcNAA
Jukes, John 1902- *WWBWI 1*

Julian, Nancy R   *AuBYP*
Jullian, Philippe 1922-   *IICB 1946*
Jumpp, Hugo   *ConAu XR, SmATA 4,*
  WNAA
Jumpp, Hugo *see* MacPeek, Walter G
Jupo, Frank J 1904-   *AuBYP, ConAu 5R,*
  IICB 1946, SmATA 7, WrD
Jurgensen, Barbara 1928-   *ConAu 17R*
Juster, Norton 1929-   *Au&Wr 6, AuBYP,*
  ConAu 13R, SmATA 3, WWCL
Justus, May 1898-   *AmA&B, AuBYP, ChPo,*
  ChPo S1, ChPo S2, ConAu 9R,
  ForWC 1970, JBA 1951, SmATA 1

K

K O S 1881- *ConICB*
Kabdebo, Tamas *ConAu XR, SmATA XR*
Kabdebo, Tamas *see* Kabdebo, Thomas
Kabdebo, Thomas 1934- *ConAu 53,
SmATA 10*
Kabdebo, Thomas *see* Kabdebo, Tamas
Kabotie, Fred 1900- *AmPB, WWA 38*
Kadesch, Robert R 1922- *AmMWS 12P,
ConAu 57, WWA 38*
Kaestner, Erich 1899-1974 *ConAu 49,
NYTBS 5*
Kaestner, Erich *see* Kastner, Erich
Kafka, Sherry 1937- *ConAu 21R*
Kahiga, Samuel 1940?- *AfA*
Kahl, Virginia 1919- *AuBYP, BkP, ChPo,
ChPo S1, ConAu 49, IICB 1946,
IICB 1957, MorJA*
Kahler, Hugh MacNair 1883- *AmA&B,
MnBBF, REnAL, WNAA*
Kahm, Harold S *MnBBF*
Kahn, Ely Jacques, Jr. 1916- *AmA&B,
Au&Wr 6, TwCA Sup, WWA 38,
WWE 14*
Kahn, Roger 1927- *AuBYP, ConAu 25R*
Kaiser, Ernest 1915- *BlkAW, ConAu 49,
LBAA*
Kakacek, Gen *AuBYP*
Kakimoto, Kozo 1915- *SmATA 11*
Kalashnikoff, Nicholas 1888-1961 *AmA&B,
MorJA, REnAL*
Kalb, Jonah 1926- *ConAu 53*
Kalb, S William 1897- *ConAu 33,
WWWorJ 1972*
Kaler, James Otis 1848-1912 *Alli Sup,
AmA&B, BiD&SB, CarSB, DcAmA,
DcNAA, JBA 1934, JBA 1951, OxAm*
Kaler, James Otis *see* Otis, James
Kalina, Sigmund 1911- *ConAu 49*
Kalish, Lionel *ChPo S1*
Kalmenoff, Matthew *IIBYP*
Kalnay, Francis 1899- *AuBYP, BkCL,
ConAu 49, SmATA 7*
Kalusky, Rebecca *AuBYP*
Kamen, Gloria 1923- *IIBYP, SmATA 9*
Kamerman, Sylvia E *ConAu XR*
Kamerman, Sylvia E *see* Burack, Sylvia
Kamm, Herbert 1917- *ConAu 69, WWA 38*
Kamm, Josephine 1905- *ConAu 9R, WrD*
Kampen, Owen *IIBYP*
Kandell, Alice S 1938- *ConAu 33, WrD*
Kane, Basil G 1931- *ConAu 69*
Kane, Bob *ArtCS, EncM&D*

Kane, Henry Bugbee 1902- *AmPB, AuBYP,
ChPo, ChPo S1, ChPo S2, IICB 1744,
IICB 1946, IICB 1957*
Kane, Robert S 1925- *ConAu 9R*
Kane, Robert William 1910- *IICB 1946*
Kantor, MacKinlay 1904- *AmA&B, AmNov,
AuBYP, ChPo S1, CnDAL, ConAmA,
ConAu 61, ConNov 1972, ConNov 1976,
DcLEnL, EncM&D, ModAL, OxAm,
Pen Am, REn, REnAL, TwCA,
TwCA Sup, TwCW, WWA 38, WrD*
Kanzawa, Toshiko *ConAu XR*
Kanzawa, Toshiko *see* Furukawa, Toshi
Kaplan, Albert A *AuBYP*
Kaplan, Anne Bernays 1930- *ConAu 1R*
Kaplan, Anne Bernays *see* Bernays, Anne
Kaplan, Boche 1926- *ConAu 21R, IIBYP*
Kaplan, Boche *see* Roche, A K
Kaplan, Irma 1900- *ConAu 29, SmATA 10*
Kaplan, Jean Caryl Korn 1926- *ConAu 5R,
SmATA 10*
Kaplan, Jean Caryl Korn *see* Caryl, Jean
Kaplan, Margaret *AuBYP*
Kaplan, Philip 1916- *ConAu 13R*
Kaplan, Richard 1929- *WWA 38*
Kaplan, S Howard 1938- *ConAu 25R*
Kapp, Paul 1907- *AmSCAP 66, AuBYP,
ChPo, ChPo S1, ChPo S2*
Karasz, Ilonka 1896- *ChPo, IIBYP,
IICB 1946*
Karen, Ruth 1922- *AuBYP, ConAu 17R,
SmATA 9, WWAW 8*
Kark, Nina Mary 1925- *ConAu 17R,
SmATA 4, WW 1974, WWAW 8*
Kark, Nina Mary *see* Bawden, Nina
Karl, Jean Edna 1927- *ChPo S1, ConAu 29,
ForWC 1970, WWAW 8*
Karlin, Eugene 1918- *IIBYP, IICB 1957,
SmATA 10*
Karlin, Muriel Schoenbrun *WWAW 8*
Karney, Beulah Mullen *ConAu 13R*
Kashiwagi, Isami 1925- *IIBYP, IICB 1946,
SmATA 10*
Kassil, Lev 1905- *TwCW*
Kassirer, Norma *AuBYP*
Kastner, Erich 1899-1974 *AuBYP, CasWL,
CIDMEuL, CnMD, CurB 64, CurB 74,
EncWL, EvEuW, IntWW 38, ModGL,
ModWD, OxGer, Pen Eur, ThBJA,
WW 1974, WWCL, WWWor 2, WorAu*
Kastner, Erich *see* Kaestner, Erich
Kastner, Jonathan 1937- *ConAu 25R*

Kastner, Marianna 1940- *ConAu 25R*
Katchamakoff, Atanas 1898- *IlCB 1744*
Katchen, Carole 1944- *ConAu 61, SmATA 9*
Kathryn *ConAu XR, SmATA XR*
Kathryn *see* Searle, Kathryn Adrienne
Katz, Bobbi 1933- *ChPo S2, ConAu 37, SmATA 12, WrD*
Katz, Fred 1938- *ConAu 49, SmATA 6*
Katz, William Loren 1927- *ConAu 21R, SmATA 13, WWA 38, WWE 14*
Kauffer, Edward McKnight 1891- *IlCB 1744*
Kaufman, Bob 1925- *BlkAW, ConAu 41, ConP 1970, DrAP 1975, LBAA, Pen Am, RAdv 1*
Kaufman, Joe 1911- *WWAA 1973*
Kaufman, Joe *see* Kaufman, Joseph
Kaufman, Joseph *see* Kaufman, Joe
Kaufman, Mervyn D 1932- *ConAu 5R, SmATA 4*
Kaufmann, Helen L 1887- *ConAu 5R, WWMus 6*
Kaufmann, John 1931- *IlBYP, IlCB 1957*
Kaula, Edna Mason 1906- *AuBYP, ConAu 5R, SmATA 13*
Kavaler, Lucy 1930- *AuBYP, ConAu 57*
Kavanaugh, Bill *ArtCS*
Kavanaugh, James J 1929- *ConAu 13R*
Kavet, Robert 1924- *ConAu 37*
Kay, A K Clark *MnBBF*
Kay, Bernard *MnBBF*
Kay, Gertrude Alice 1884-1939 *AmA&B, ChPo, ConICB, DcNAA, OhA&B, WNAA*
Kay, Helen *AuBYP, ConAu XR, ForWC 1970, SmATA 6*
Kay, Helen *see* Goldfrank, Helen Colodny
Kay, Kenneth 1915- *ConAu 9R*
Kay, Mara *ConAu 5R, SmATA 13, WrD*
Kay, Ray *MnBBF*
Kay, Terence 1918- *ConAu 17R*
Kay, Terence *see* Kay, Terry
Kay, Terry *ConAu XR*
Kay, Terry *see* Kay, Terence
Kay, Wallace *MnBBF*
Kay, Wallace *see* Arter, Wallace E
Kaye, Anstey *MnBBF*
Kaye, Crawford *MnBBF*
Kaye, George 1911- *WWAA 1973*
Kaye, Geraldine Hughesdon 1925- *Au&Wr 6, ConAu 13R, SmATA 10, WrD*
Kaye-Cook, L *MnBBF*
Keane, Bil 1922- *ConAu 33, SmATA 4, WWAA 1973*
Keary, Annie 1825-1879 *BbD, BiD&SB, BrAu 19, CasWL, ChPo, ChPo S1, EvLB, St&VC, TelT*
Keary, Peter 1865-1915 *MnBBF*
Keating, Bern *ConAu XR, SmATA XR, WrD*
Keating, Bern *see* Keating, Leo Bernard
Keating, Lawrence A 1903-1966 *AuBYP, ConAu 5R*
Keating, Lawrence A *see* Bassett, John Keith
Keating, Lawrence A *see* Thomas, H C
Keating, Leo Bernard 1915- *ConAu 29, SmATA 10*
Keating, Leo Bernard *see* Keating, Bern
Keating, Norma *AuBYP*
Keats, Ezra Jack 1916- *AmPB, Au&ICB, AuBYP, AuNews 1, BiN 1974, BkP,*

ChLR 1, ChPo S1, ChPo S2, IlBYP, IlCB 1946, IlCB 1957, MorJA, NewbC 1956, WWA 38, WrD
Keats, John 1795-1821 *Alli, AnCL, AtlBL, BiD&SB, BrAu 19, CasWL, Chambr 3, ChPo, ChPo S1, ChPo S2, CnE&AP, CriT 2, CyWA, DcEnA, DcEnL, DcEuL, DcLEnL, EvLB, MouLC 2, NCHEL, OxEng, Pen Eng, RAdv 1, RCom, REn, St&VC, WEAL*
Kedzie, Daniel Peter 1930- *ConAu 17R*
Keegan, Marcia 1943- *ConAu 49, SmATA 9*
Keeler, Katherine 1887- *AuBYP*
Keen, Martin L 1913- *ConAu 33, SmATA 4*
Keenan, Deborah 1950- *ConAu 69*
Keene, Carolyn *AmA&B, ConAu XR, EncM&D, SmATA 1*
Keene, Carolyn *see* Adams, Harriet S
Keene, Carolyn *see* Stratemeyer, Edward L
Keene, Roy *MnBBF*
Keeping, Charles William James 1924- *ArtsCL, Au&Wr 6, BrCA, ConAu 21R, IlBYP, IlCB 1957, PiP, SmATA 9, ThBJA, WW 1974*
Keeshan, Robert J 1927- *ConAu 5R*
Keeton, Elizabeth B 1919- *ConAu 29*
Keiler, Ralph *MnBBF*
Keir, Christine *ConAu XR, SmATA 3*
Keir, Christine *see* Popescu, Christine
Keir, Christine *see* Pullein-Thompson, Christine
Keith, Adolphus 1939- *BlkAW*
Keith, Carlton *AuBYP, ConAu XR, SmATA 1*
Keith, Carlton *see* Robertson, Keith Charlton
Keith, Eros *ChPo S2, IlBYP*
Keith, Harold Verne 1903- *AmA&B, AuBYP, ConAu 5R, CurB 58, MorBMP, MorJA, NewbC 1956, SmATA 2, WNAA*
Keith, Louis *MnBBF*
Keith-Lucas, Alan 1910- *ConAu 5R, WWA 38*
Kelder, Diane 1934- *ConAu 25R*
Kelen, Emery 1896- *ConAu 9R, IlCB 1744, SmATA 13*
Kellaway, Frank 1922- *ConAu 9R, SingR 1*
Kelleam, Joseph Everidge 1913- *WWS 13*
Keller, Allan 1904- *ConAu 29*
Keller, Beverly L *SmATA 13*
Keller, Charles 1942- *ConAu 49, SmATA 8*
Keller, Frances Ruth 1911- *AuBYP*
Keller, Gail Faithfull *ConAu 57, SmATA 8*
Keller, Gail Faithfull *see* Faithfull, Gail
Keller, Helen *CurB 42, CurB 68*
Kelley, Reeve Spencer 1912- *AnCL*
Kellin, Sally Moffet 1932- *ConAu 61, SmATA 9*
Kelling, Furn L 1914- *ConAu 17R*
Kellner, Esther *ConAu 13R*
Kellogg, Elijah 1813-1901 *Alli Sup, AmA, AmA&B, BiD&SB, CarSB, DcAmA, DcNAA, OxAm, REnAL*
Kellogg, Gene 1916- *ConAu 9R, SmATA XR*
Kellogg, Jean 1916- *AuBYP, ConAu XR, SmATA 10*
Kellogg, Steven 1941- *ConAu 49, IlBYP, SmATA 8, WrD*
Kellogg, Vernon Lyman 1867-1937 *AmA&B, AmLY, CarSB, DcAmA, DcNAA, WNAA*

Kellow, Kathleen *ConAu XR, EncM&D,*
SmATA 2, WW 1974, WorAu
Kellow, Kathleen *see* Hibbert, Eleanor Burford
Kelly, Eric Philbrook 1884-1960 *AmA&B,*
AnCL, AuBYP, JBA 1934, JBA 1951,
Newb 1922, REnAL, WNAA, YABC 1
Kelly, Frank K 1914- *ConAu 1R*
Kelly, Margaret Ricaud *WrD*
Kelly, Martha Rose 1914- *ConAu 69*
Kelly, Martha Rose *see* Kelly, Marty
Kelly, Marty *ConAu XR*
Kelly, Marty *see* Kelly, Martha Rose
Kelly, Myra 1875-1910 *AmA&B, CarSB,*
DcAmA, DcNAA
Kelly, Ralph *ConAu XR, SmATA 7*
Kelly, Ralph *see* Geis, Darlene Stern
Kelly, Regina Z *ConAu 1R, CurB 56,*
ForWC 1970, SmATA 5
Kelly, Rosalie *ConAu 61*
Kelly, Walt 1913-1973 *AmA&B, AmSCAP 66,*
ArtCS, CelR 3, ConAu 45, CurB 56,
CurB 73, IlBYP, NYTBE 4, REnAL,
WWA 38
Kelsey, Alice Geer 1896- *AnCL, Au&Wr 6,*
AuBYP, ConAu 5R, ForWC 1970,
MorJA, SmATA 1, WrD
Kemp, Alec M *MnBBF, WWBWI A*
Kemp, Alec M *see* Richards, Frank
Kemp, Gene 1926- *ConAu 69, WrD*
Kemp, Lysander 1920- *AmA&B, ConAu 45*
Kempner, Mary Jean 1913-1969 *ConAu P-2,*
SmATA 10
Kempster, Bert *MnBBF*
Kempster, Bert *see* Gibbons, Harry Hornaby
Clifford
Kempster, Jim *MnBBF*
Kempton, Jean Welch 1914- *ConAu 49,*
SmATA 10
Kempton, Jean Welch *see* Welch, Jean-Louise
Kendal, Wallis 1937- *Prof*
Kendall, Carol Seeger 1917- *AuBYP,*
ConAu 5R, ForWC 1970, OhA&B,
SmATA 11, ThBJA
Kendall, Edward Augustus 1776?-1842 *Alli,*
BiDLA, CarSB
Kendall, Elaine 1929- *ConAu 17R*
Kendall, Lace *AmA&B, ConAu XR,*
SmATA 3, ThBJA, WWA 38
Kendall, Lace *see* Stoutenburg, Adrien
Kendall, Oswald *MnBBF, WWLA*
Kendrick, Michael *MnBBF*
Kenelski, Maurice *IlBYP*
Kennard-Davis, Arthur 1910- *ConAu P-1*
Kennedy, John Fitzgerald 1917-1963 *AmA&B,*
AnCL, ChPo, ConAu 1R, CurB 50,
CurB 61, CurB 64, NYTBE 3, OxAm,
REn, REnAL, SmATA 11
Kennedy, Joseph 1929- *ConAu 1R*
Kennedy, Joseph *see* Kennedy, X J
Kennedy, Paul Edward 1929- *IlCB 1957*
Kennedy, Richard 1910- *ArtsCL, IlBYP,*
IlCB 1946, IlCB 1957
Kennedy, Richard 1932- *ConAu 57*
Kennedy, W W *MnBBF, WWBWI A*
Kennedy, X J *AmA&B, ChPo, ChPo S2,*
ConAu XR, ConP 1970, ConP 1975,
DrAP 1975, Pen Am, WWA 38,
WWWor 2, WorAu, WrD
Kennedy, X J *see* Kennedy, Joseph

Kennedy-Bell, Douglas *MnBBF*
Kennell, Ruth Epperson 1893- *ConAu 29,*
SmATA 6
Kenny, Ellsworth Newcomb 1909- *AuBYP,*
ConAu 5R
Kenny, Ellsworth Newcomb *see* Newcomb,
Ellsworth
Kenny, Herbert Andrew 1912- *ConAu 41,*
SmATA 13, WWA 38, WWE 14
Kenny, Hugh *AuBYP*
Kenny, Stan *MnBBF*
Kenny, Stan *see* Giggah, K
Kent, Alexander 1924- *Au&Wr 6*
Kent, Arthur William Charles 1925- *MnBBF,*
WWBWI A
Kent, Beverley *MnBBF, WWBWI A*
Kent, Beverley *see* Gannon, E J
Kent, Elizabeth *WWBWI A*
Kent, Elizabeth *see* Rochester, George Ernest
Kent, Jack 1920- *AmA&B, WWA 38*
Kent, Louise *see* Tempest, Teresa
Kent, Louise Andrews 1886-1969 *AmA&B,*
AmNov, AuBYP, ConAu 1R,
ConAu 25R, JBA 1951, REnAL,
TwCA Sup
Kent, Margaret 1894- *Au&Wr 6, ConAu P-2,*
SmATA 2
Kent, Phillip *MnBBF*
Kent, Rockwell 1882-1971 *AmA&B, ChPo,*
ConAmA, ConAu 5R, ConAu 29,
CurB 42, CurB 45, DcCAA 2, IlBYP,
IlCB 1744, NYTBE 2, OxAm, REnAL,
SmATA 6, TwCA, TwCA Sup
Kent, Rockwell *see* Hogarth, Jr.
Kent, Sherman 1903- *AmMWS 12S,*
ConAu 53
Kenward, James Macara 1908- *Au&Wr 6,*
WrD
Kenworthy, Hugh *WWBWI A*
Kenworthy, Hugh *see* Walker, Rowland
Kenworthy, Leonard Stout 1912- *ConAu 1R,*
IndAu 1917, SmATA 6
Kenyon, Ley 1913- *Au&Wr 6, ConAu 13R,*
SmATA 6
Kenyon, Raymond G 1922- *AuBYP*
Keogh, Brian 1931- *ArtsCL*
Kepes, Gyorgy 1906- *AmA&B, AmPB,*
Au&Wr 6, CurB 73, DcCAA 2,
WWA 38, WWAA 1973
Kepes, Juliet 1919- *AmPB, AuBYP, ChPo,*
ChFB 1, ConAu 69, IlCB 1946,
IlCB 1957, SmATA 13, ThBJA
Kepple, Ella Huff 1902- *ConAu P-2*
Ker, David 1842-1914 *Alli Sup, BbD,*
BiD&SB, ChPo, DcAmA, DcNAA,
MnBBF, WWBWI A
Ker Wilson, Barbara 1929- *ConAu 5R*
Ker Wilson, Barbara *see* Wilson, Barbara
Kerigan, Florence 1896- *ChPo, ConAu 29,*
SmATA 12, WNAA, WrD
Kerigan, Florence *see* Kerry, Frances
Kerman, Gertrude Lerner 1909- *ConAu 5R,*
ForWC 1970
Kermond, Evelyn Carolyn Conway 1927-
Au&Wr 6, WrD
Kerner, Ben *AuBYP*
Kerr, James Stolee 1928- *ConAu 17R*
Kerr, Jessica 1901- *ConAu P-2, SmATA 13*
Kerr, Laura 1904- *AuBYP*

Kerridge, W T *MnBBF*
Kerrigan, Anthony 1918- *Au&Wr 6,*
 ConAu 49, ConLC 4, ConLC 6
Kerry, Frances *ConAu XR, SmATA XR*
Kerry, Frances *see* Kerigan, Florence
Kerry, Lois *ConAu XR, SmATA 1*
Kerry, Lois *see* Cardozo, Lois S
Kesler, Jay 1935- *ConAu 61*
Kessler, Leonard P 1921- *AmPB, AuBYP,*
 ChPo, IlCB 1946, IlCB 1957
Ketcham, Hank 1920- *ArtCS, ChPo*
Kettelkamp, Larry Dale 1933- *AuBYP,*
 ConAu 29, IlCB 1957, SmATA 2,
 ThBJA, WrD
Keveren, A G *MnBBF*
Keveren, A G *see* Veren, Gilbert
Kevles, Bettyann 1938- *ConAu 69*
Key, Alexander Hill 1904- *AuBYP, ConAu 5R,*
 SmATA 8, WrD
Key, Francis Scott 1779?-1843 *Alli, AmA,*
 AmA&B, BbD, BiD&SB, BiDSA, ChPo,
 ChPo S2, CnDAL, CyAL 1, DcAmA,
 DcLEnL, DcNAA, EvLB, OxAm, OxEng,
 PoCh, REn, REnAL
Keyes, Daniel 1927- *ConAu 17R, DrAS 6E*
Keyes, Fenton 1915- *AmMWS 12S, WWA 38*
Keyes, Nelson Beecher 1894- *AuBYP*
Keys, Ancel 1904- *CurB 66, IntWW 38*
Keyser, William R 1916- *ConAu 69*
Khanshendel, Chiron *ConAu XR,*
 SmATA XR
Khanshendel, Chiron *see* Rose, Wendy
Khayyam, Omar 1050?-1125? *BbD, BiD&SB,*
 ChPo S1, ChPo S2, DcOrL 3, NCHEL
Kherdian, David 1931- *ConAu 21R, ConLC 6,*
 DrAP 1975
Kiddell, John 1922- *Au&Wr 6, ConAu 29,*
 SmATA 3
Kiddell-Monroe, Joan 1908- *Au&Wr 6,*
 ConAu 13R, ConAu P-1, IlBYP,
 IlCB 1946, IlCB 1957, WWCL
Kidder, Barbara 1933- *ConAu 41*
Kiddle, Margaret Loch d1958 *SingR 1*
Kidwell, Carl 1910- *IlBYP, IndAu 1917*
Kiefer, Irene 1926- *ConAu 69*
Kielty, Bernardine *AuBYP, REnAL*
Kiene, Julia *AuBYP*
Kijima, Hajime *ConAu XR*
Kijima, Hajime *see* Kojima, Shozo
Killens, John Oliver 1916- *BlkAW,*
 ConNov 1972, ConNov 1976, DrAF 1976,
 LBAA, Pen Am, WWA 38, WWE 14
Killilea, Marie 1913- *ConAu 5R, SmATA 2*
Killingsworth, W *MnBBF*
Kilmer, Joyce 1886-1918 *AmA&B, AmLY,*
 AmSCAP 66, ChPo, ChPo S2, CnDAL,
 ConAmL, DcLEnL, DcNAA, LongC,
 OxAm, REn, REnAL, St&VC, TwCA
Kilner, Dorothy 1755-1836 *CarSB, ChPo*
Kilreon, Beth *ConAu XR, SmATA 4*
Kilreon, Beth *see* Walker, Barbara K
Kim, Yong-Ik 1920- *ConAu 17R*
Kimball, Dean 1912- *ConAu 69*
Kimball, Richard Laurance 1939- *ConAu 53,*
 LE 5
Kimball, Yeffe 1914- *IlCB 1957,*
 WWAA 1973
Kimble, George Herbert Tinley 1908- *AmA&B,*
 Au&Wr 6, CurB 52

Kimbrough, Emily 1899- *AmA&B, Au&Wr 6,*
 ConAu 17R, CurB 44, IndAu 1917,
 OxAm, REnAL, SmATA 2, WWA 38,
 WWAW 8, WWWor 2, WorAu
Kimbrough, Richard B 1931- *ConAu 41*
Kimmel, Eric A 1946- *ConAu 49, SmATA 13,*
 WrD
Kindred, Wendy Good 1937- *ConAu 37,*
 SmATA 7, WrD
Kinert, Reed Charles 1912?- *AuBYP,*
 IndAu 1917
Kines, Pat Decker 1937- *ConAu 65,*
 SmATA 12
Kines, Pat Decker *see* Tapio, Pat Decker
King, Arthur *ConAu XR, MnBBF,*
 SmATA 3
King, Arthur *see* Cain, Arthur H
King, Billie Jean 1943- *BiN 1974, CelR 3,*
 ConAu 53, CurB 67, NYTBE 1,
 NYTBS 5, SmATA 12, WWA 38
King, Charles 1844-1933 *Alli Sup, AmA&B,*
 AmLY, ArizL, BiD&SB, CarSB,
 DcAmA, DcNAA, OxAm, WNAA,
 WisW
King, Cynthia 1925- *ConAu 29, SmATA 7,*
 WrD
King, David Clive *WrD*
King, Edith *St&VC*
King, Frank L 1892-1958 *MnBBF*
King, Frank O 1883-1969 *AmA&B, ArtCS,*
 ChPo S1
King, Hilary *MnBBF, WWBWI A*
King, Hilary *see* Dickson, James Grierson
King, Hyam *MnBBF*
King, Kennedy *MnBBF*
King, Marian *AmA&B, Au&Wr 6,*
 ConAu 5R, ForWC 1970, WWA 38,
 WWAW 8, WWS 13,
 WrD
King, Martha Bennett *AuBYP*
King, Martin *ConAu XR*
King, Martin *see* Marks, Stan
King, Martin Luther, Jr. 1929-1968 *AmA&B,*
 BlkAW, ConAu 25R, ConAu P-2,
 CurB 57, CurB 65, CurB 68, NYTBS 5,
 OxAm, REnAL
King, Mary Louise 1911- *ConAu 21R*
King, Patricia 1930- *ConAu 5R*
King, Reefe *SmATA 8*
King, Reefe *see* Barker, Albert W
King, Reginald *MnBBF*
King, Reginald *see* Grosvenor, Mrs. Ian
King, Robert *MnBBF*
King, Robin 1919- *ConAu 5R,*
 IlCB 1946
King, Ruth *ConICB*
King, Seth S *AuBYP, WWE 14*
King, Stephen 1947- *SmATA 9*
King, T Staneyan *MnBBF*
King, Talbert *MnBBF*
King, Tom *MnBBF*
King-Hall, Stephen 1893-1966 *ChPo S2,*
 ConAu 5R, LongC, WWLA
Kingman, Dong 1911- *CelR 3, CurB 62,*
 IlCB 1946, IntMPA 1975, WWA 38,
 WWWor 2
Kingman, Lee 1919- *AuBYP, ChPo, ChPo S1,*
 ConAu 5R, ForWC 1970, MorJA,
 SmATA 1, WrD

Kings, Leslie *MnBBF*
Kingsford, Guy *MnBBF*
Kingsford, Guy *see* Murray, C Geoffrey
Kingsland, Leslie William 1912- *ConAu 69,*
SmATA 13
Kingsland, Peter *MnBBF*
Kingsley, Charles 1819-1875 *Alli, Alli Sup,*
AnCL, AtlBL, AuBYP, BbD, BiD&SB,
Br&AmS, BrAu 19, CarSB, CasWL,
Chambr 3, ChPo, ChPo S1, ChPo S2,
CriT 3, CyWA, DcBiA, DcEnA, DcEnL,
DcEuL, DcLEnL, EvLB, FamPYP,
JBA 1934, MouLC 3, NCHEL, OxEng,
Pen Eng, RAdv 1, REn, TelT, WEAL,
WWCL, YABC 2
Kingsley, Charles *see* Lot, Parson
Kingsley, Hamilton *MnBBF*
Kingsley, Hamilton *see* Martin, W
Kingsley, Henry 1830-1876 *Alli Sup, BbD,*
BiD&SB Sup, BrAu 19, CarSB, CasWL,
Chambr 3, ChPo S1, CyWA, DcBiA,
DcEnA, DcEnL, DcEuL, DcLEnL, EvLB,
HsB&A, NCHEL, OxEng, Pen Eng,
REn, WEAL
Kingsley, Horace *MnBBF*
Kingston, Brian *MnBBF, WWBWI A*
Kingston, Brian *see* Longhurst, Percy William
Kingston, Conrad *MnBBF*
Kingston, Kit *MnBBF*
Kingston, William Henry Giles 1814-1880 *Alli,*
Alli Sup, BbD, BbthC, BiD&SB,
BrAu 19, CarSB, CasWL, Chambr 3,
EvLB, MnBBF, OxEng, WWBWI A,
WWCL
Kingsway, Bradney *MnBBF*
Kinney, C Cle 1915- *ConAu 9R, SmATA 6*
Kinney, Harrison 1921- *ConAu 1R,*
SmATA 13
Kinney, Jean Stout 1912- *ConAu 9R,*
SmATA 12
Kinsella, E P *WWBWI I*
Kinsey, Elizabeth *ConAu XR, SmATA XR*
Kinsey, Elizabeth *see* Clymer, Eleanor
Kinsey-Jones, Brian *ConAu XR*
Kinsey-Jones, Brian *see* Ball, Brian N
Kinstler, Everett Raymond 1926- *ConAu 33,*
WWA 38, WWAA 1973, WWE 14
Kipling, John Lockwood 1837-1911 *ChPo,*
NCHEL
Kipling, Rudyard 1865-1936 *Alli Sup, AnCL,*
AtlBL,' AuBYP, BbD, BiD&SB, CarSB,
CasWL, Chambr 3, ChPo, ChPo S1,
ChPo S2, CnE&AP, CnMWL, CriT 3,
CyWA, DcAmA, DcBiA, DcEnA,
DcEnA Ap, DcEuL, DcLEnL, EncWL,
EvLB, FamAYP, FamSYP, JBA 1934,
LongC, MnBBF, ModBL, ModBL Sup,
NCHEL, OxAm, OxCan, OxEng,
Pen Eng, RAdv 1, RCom, REn, St&VC,
TelT, TwCA, TwCA Sup, TwCW,
WEAL, WWBWI A, WWCL, WWLA,
WWTwL, YABC 2
Kipniss, Robert 1931- *DcCAA 2*
Kipniss, Robert 1931- *IlBYP, WWAA 1973*
Kirby, Arthur *MnBBF, WWBWI A*
Kirby, Arthur *see* MacLean, Arthur George
Kirby, Douglas James 1929- *Au&Wr 6,*
ChPo S1, ConAu 25R
Kirby, Elizabeth 1823-1873 *CarSB*

Kirk, Ellen Warner Olney 1842-1928 *Alli Sup,*
AmA&B, BbD, BiD&SB, CarSB,
DcAmA, DcBiA, DcNAA
Kirk, Maria Louise 1860?- *ChPo S1, ConICB*
Kirk, Ruth Eleanor 1925- *AuBYP,*
ConAu 13R, SmATA 5, WWPNA
Kirk, Thomas Hobson 1899- *Au&Wr 6, WrD*
Kirkham, Reginald S *MnBBF, WWBWI A*
Kirkham, Reginald S *see* Clifford, Martin
Kirkham, Reginald S *see* Marlow, Hilary
Kirkham, Reginald S *see* Vincent, Frank
Kirkham, Reginald S *see* Vincent, Joan
Kirkland, Captain *MnBBF*
Kirkpatrick, Oliver 1911- *ConAu 49*
Kirkup, James 1927- *ConAu 1R, SmATA 12*
Kirkup, James *see* Falconer, James
Kirkup, James *see* James, Andrew
Kirkus, Virginia *AmA&B, ConAu XR,*
CurB 41, CurB 54
Kirkus, Virginia *see* Glick, Virginia Kirkus
Kirkwood, Ellen Swan 1904- *ConAu 25R*
Kirkwood, James 1930- *Au&Wr 6, AuNews 2,*
ConAu 1R
Kirmse, Marguerite 1885-1954 *ConICB, IlBYP,*
IlCB 1744, IlCB 1946
Kirn, Ann Minette 1910- *AuBYP, ChPo S1,*
IlCB 1957
Kirsch, Paul John 1914- *DrAS 6P*
Kirst, Hans Hellmut 1914- *CasWL,*
IntWW 38, ModGL, TwCW, WWWor 2,
WorAu
Kirtland, G B *ConAu XR, SmATA 2,*
ThBJA
Kirtland, G B *see* Hine, Sesyle Joslin
Kiser, Martha Gwinn *AuBYP*
Kishida, Eriko 1929- *ConAu 53, SmATA 12*
Kisinger, Grace Gelvin 1913-1960? *AuBYP,*
ConAu P-1, SmATA 10
Kissen, Fan 1904- *ConAu P-1*
Kissin, Eva H 1923- *ConAu 29, SmATA 10*
Kitchen, Fred *ChPo S2*
Kitson, Harry Dexter 1886- *CurB 51, CurB 59,*
IndAu 1816, WNAA
Kizer, Carolyn 1925- *ConP 1970, ConP 1975,*
CrCAP, DrAP 1975, Pen Am, WorAu
Kjelgaard, James Arthur 1910-1959 *AuBYP,*
JBA 1951, St&VC
Klaasse, Piet *ChPo S1*
Klagsbrun, Francine *ConAu 21R*
Klaperman, Gilbert 1921- *ConAu 49,*
WWWorJ 1972
Klaperman, Libby Mindlin 1921- *ConAu 9R*
Klass, Morton 1927- *AmMWS 12S,*
ConAu 1R, SmATA 11
Klausner, Abraham J 1915- *WWWorJ 1972*
Klebe, Charles Eugene 1907- *ConAu P-2*
Klebe, Charles Eugene *see* Klebe, Gene
Klebe, Gene *ConAu XR, WWAA 1973*
Klebe, Gene *see* Klebe, Charles Eugene
Kleberger, Ilse 1921- *ConAu 41, SmATA 5*
Kleeberg, Irene Cumming 1932- *ConAu 61*
Klein, Aaron E 1930- *ConAu 25R*
Klein, David 1919- *AmMWS 12S, AuBYP,*
ConAu 1R, IntWW 38, WWA 38
Klein, Deana Tarson 1925- *AmMWS 12P*
Klein, H Arthur *AuBYP, ConAu 13R,*
SmATA 8
Klein, Leonore 1916- *AuBYP, BiDL 5,*
ConAu 1R, SmATA 6

Klein, Mina C   *ConAu 37, SmATA 8*
Klein, Norma 1938-   *ChLR 2, ConAu 41, DrAF 1976, SmATA 7*
Klein, Richard M 1923-   *AmMWS 12P*
Klein, Stanley 1930-   *ConAu 57*
Klein, Suzanne Marie 1940-   *ConAu 57*
Klemke, Werner 1917-   *ArtsCL, WWGA*
Klemm, Edward G, Jr. 1910-   *ConAu 57*
Klemm, Roberta K 1884-   *ConAu 61*
Klimowicz, Barbara 1927-   *ConAu 21R, SmATA 10*
Kline, Morris 1908-   *AmMWS 12P, ConAu 5R, WWA 38*
Kline, Peter 1936-   *ConAu 25R*
Klink, Johanna L 1918-   *ChPo S1, ConAu 61*
Klose, Norma Cline 1936-   *ConAu 17R*
Klots, Alexander Barrett 1903-   *AmMWS 12P*
Kluwe, Mary Jean 1905-1975   *ConAu P-2*
Knatchbull-Hugessen, Edward Hugessen 1829-1893   *Alli Sup, ChPo, ChPo S1, DcEnL, NCHEL, TelT, WWCL*
Knatchbull-Hugessen, Edward Hugessen see Brabourne, Lord
Knebel, Fletcher 1911-   *AmA&B, Au&Wr 6, AuNews 1, BiN 1975, ConAu 1R, ConNov 1972, ConNov 1976, NYTBS 5, WWA 38, WWE 14, WWWor 2*
Knerr, Harold 1883-1949   *ArtCS*
Knew, George   *MnBBF*
Knickerbocker, Diedrich 1783-1859   *AmA&B, DcEnL, DcNAA, EvLB, OxAm, OxEng, YABC XR*
Knickerbocker, Diedrich see Irving, Washington
Knight, Anne Katherine   *WrD*
Knight, Arthur Lee   *MnBBF*
Knight, Bernard 1931-   *Au&Wr 6, ConAu 49, WrD*
Knight, Bertram 1904-   *Au&Wr 6, WrD*
Knight, Charles Robert 1874-1953   *IlCB 1946*
Knight, Charles W 1891-   *ConAu P-1*
Knight, Clayton 1891-1969   *AuBYP, ConAu P-1*
Knight, Damon 1922-   *ConAu 49, SmATA 9, WorAu*
Knight, David 1923-   *ArtsCL, AuBYP*
Knight, Derek   *MnBBF*
Knight, Eric Mowbray 1897-1943   *AuBYP, CnDAL, CurB 42, CurB 43, CyWA, REn, REnAL, TwCA, TwCA Sup, WWCL*
Knight, Frank 1905-   *SingR 2, WWCL*
Knight, Hilary 1926-   *AuBYP, ChPo, ChPo S1, ChPo S2, IlCB 1957, WWAA 1973*
Knight, Mallory T   *ConAu XR, SmATA XR*
Knight, Mallory T see Hurwood, Bernhardt J
Knight, Maxwell 1900-   *ConAu P-1*
Knight, Peter   *AuBYP*
Knight, Ruth Adams 1898-1974   *AuBYP, ConAu 5R, ConAu 49, CurB 43, CurB 55, ForWC 1970, MorJA, OhA&B*
Knightley, Miss D G   *MnBBF*
Knightley, Miss D G see Prior, Harry
Knightley, Phillip 1929-   *ConAu 25R*
Knipe, Alden Arthur 1870-1950   *AmA&B, AmLY, JBA 1934, JBA 1951, WNAA*
Knipe, Emilie Benson 1870-1958   *AmA&B, AmLY, ChPo, JBA 1934, JBA 1951, WNAA*

Knoepfle, John 1923-   *ConAu 13R, ConP 1970, ConP 1975, DrAP 1975, WrD*
Knollys, Bodley   *MnBBF*
Knopf, Mildred Oppenheimer 1898-   *WWAW 8*
Knott, Bill   *ConAu XR, SmATA 3*
Knott, Bill see Knott, William Cecil, Jr.
Knott, William Cecil, Jr. 1927-   *AmA&B, ConAu 5R, SmATA 3*
Knott, William Cecil, Jr. see Carol, Bill J
Knott, William Cecil, Jr. see Knott, Bill
Knotts, Howard 1922-   *ConAu 69*
Knowles, G H   *MnBBF*
Knowles, John 1926-   *AmA&B, Au&Wr 6, CasWL, ConAu 17R, ConLC 1, ConLC 4, ConNov 1972, ConNov 1976, DrAF 1976, RAdv 1, SmATA 8, WWA 38, WWWor 2, WorAu*
Knowles, Mabel Winifred 1875-   *MnBBF, WWLA*
Knowles, Mabel Winifred see Wynne, May
Knowles, Thomas E   *MnBBF*
Knowles, Thomas E see McLure, R
Knowlton, William H 1927-   *ConAu 17R, WrD*
Knox, Calvin M   *AuBYP, ConAu XR, SmATA XR, ThBJA*
Knox, Calvin M see Silverberg, Robert
Knox, Rose Bell 1879-   *AmA&B, JBA 1934, JBA 1951, WNAA*
Knox, Thomas Wallace 1835-1896   *Alli Sup, AmA, AmA&B, BbD, BiD&SB, CarSB, DcAmA, DcNAA, MnBBF, REnAL*
Knox-Johnston, Robin 1939-   *Au&Wr 6, ConAu 29*
Knudsen, Margrethe June   *WrD*
Knudson, R R   *ConAu XR, SmATA 7*
Knudson, R R see Knudson, Rozanne Ruth
Knudson, Rozanne Ruth 1932-   *ConAu 33, ForWC 1970, SmATA 7, WWAW 8, WrD*
Knudson, Rozanne Ruth see Knudson, R R
Kobayashi, Masako Matsuno 1935-   *AuBYP, ConAu 5R*
Kobayashi, Masako Matsuno see Matsuno, Masako
Kobrin, Janet 1942-   *ConAu 57*
Koch, Claude 1918-   *ConAu 9R*
Koch, Dorothy Clarke 1924-   *AuBYP, ConAu 5R, ForWC 1970, SmATA 6*
Koch, Kenneth 1925-   *AmA&B, ChPo S1, ChPo S2, ConAu 1R, ConDr 1, ConLC 5, ConP 1970, ConP 1975, CrCAP, DrAF 1976, DrAP 1975, DrAS 6E, NYTBE 1, Pen Am, RAdv 1, WEAL, WWA 38, WWWor 2, WorAu*
Koch, Thomas J 1947-   *ConAu 61, ConAu 69*
Kocsis, James C 1936-   *IlBYP, IlCB 1957*
Kocsis, James C see Paul, James
Koenig, Laird   *BlkAW, ConAu 29*
Koering, Ursula 1921-   *IlBYP, IlCB 1946, MorJA*
Koffler, Camilla d1955   *AuBYP*
Koffler, Camilla see Ylla
Koger, Earl, Sr.   *BlkAW*
Kohl, Marguerite   *AuBYP*
Kohler, Julilly H 1915?-1976   *AmA&B, ConAu 69, OhA&B*
Kohn, Bernice Herstein 1920-   *AuBYP, ConAu 9R, SmATA 4, WrD*
Kohner, Frederick 1905-   *AmA&B, Au&Wr 6,*

ConAu 1R, IntMPA 1975, SmATA 10, TwCW
Kojima, Shozo 1928- ConAu 69
Kojima, Shozo see Kijima, Hajime
Kolbrek, Loyal 1914- ConAu 29
Koller, Earl Leonard 1931- AmMWS 12P
Komisar, Lucy 1942- ConAu 33, ForWC 1970, SmATA 9
Komoda, Kiyo 1937- IICB 1957, SmATA 9
Komroff, Manuel 1890-1974 AmA&B, AmNov, AuBYP, CnDAL, ConAu 1R, ConAu 53, NYTBS 5, OxAm, REnAL, SmATA 2, TwCA, TwCA Sup, WWA 38, WWWor 2
Konigsburg, Elaine L 1930- AnCL, Au&ICB, AuBYP, ChLR 1, ConAu 21R, MorBMP, NewbC 1966, SmATA 4, ThBJA, WWA 38, WrD
Koning, Hans 1921- DrAF 1976, SmATA 5, WWA 38, WorAu
Koning, Hans see Koningsberger, Hans
Koningsberger, Hans 1921- AmA&B, Au&Wr 6, ConAu 1R, SmATA 5, WWWor 2, WorAu
Koningsberger, Hans see Koning, Hans
Konkle, Janet Everest 1917- ConAu 1R, ForWC 1970, SmATA 12
Konroff, Manuel 1890-1974 ConAu 1R, ConAu 53
Konwicki, Tadeusz 1926- WWWor 2
Konwicki, Tadeusz see Korwin-Rodziszewski, Audrey
Konwicki, Tadeusz see Korwin-Rodziszewski, George
Koob, Theodora 1918- AuBYP, ConAu 5R
Kopal, Zdenek 1914- AmMWS 12P, CurB 69, WW 1974, WWWor 2
Korach, Mimi 1922- SmATA 9
Koren, Edward 1935- ConAu 25R, SmATA 5
Korfker, Dena 1908- ConAu 1R, WrD
Korinetz, Yuri 1923- ConAu 61, SmATA 9
Korwin-Rodziszewski, Audrey see Konwicki, Tadeusz
Korwin-Rodziszewski, Audrey see Rodziszewski, Audrey Korwin
Korwin-Rodziszewski, George see Konwicki, Tadeusz
Korwin-Rodziszewski, George see Rodziszewski, George Korwin
Koshland, Ellen 1947- ConAu 33
Kossin, Sandy 1926- SmATA 10
Kossoff, David 1919- ConAu 61, WW 1974, WWT 15
Kostich, Dragos D 1921- AuBYP, ConAu 5R, DrAS 6H
Kotker, Norman 1931- ConAu 25R
Kotowski, Joanne 1930- ConAu 57
Kotzwinkle, William 1938- ConAu 45, ConLC 5
Koutoukas, H M see Rivoli, Mario
Kouts, Anne 1945- ConAu 29, SmATA 8
Kovalik, Nada 1926- AuBYP, ConAu 25R
Kowet, Don 1937- ConAu 57
Kowet, Don see Gell, Frank
Kozelka, Paul 1909- BiEnAT, ConAu P-2
Kraenzel, Margaret 1899- ConAu 1R
Kraenzel, Margaret see Blue, Wallace
Krahn, Fernando 1935- AmPB, AuBYP, ChLR 3, ChPo S1, ConAu 65

Kramer, Aaron 1921- ConAu 21R, DrAP 1975, DrAS 6E, WWE 14, WWWorJ 1972
Kramer, Edna Ernestine WWAW 8
Kramer, George AuBYP, ConAu XR
Kramer, Nora AuBYP, ForWC 1970, WWAW 8
Kramer, Rita 1929- ConAu 69
Kramer, Samuel Noah 1897- AmA&B, ConAu 9R, DrAS 6H, WWWorJ 1972
Kramon, Florence 1920- ConAu 25R
Krantz, Hazel 1920- SmATA 12, WrD
Kranzler, George G 1916- AmMWS 12S, ConAu 57
Kranzler, George G see Isaacs, Jacob
Kranzler, George G see Kranzler, Gershon
Kranzler, Gershon ConAu 57
Kranzler, Gershon see Kranzler, George G
Krasilovsky, Phyllis 1926- AuBYP, BkCL, ConAu 29, MorJA, SmATA 1
Krauch, Velma 1916- ConAu 37
Kraus, George 1912- WWMus 6
Kraus, Robert 1925- AmA&B, AuBYP, ConAu 33, IICB 1957, SmATA 4, ThBJA, WWA 38, WWE 14
Kraus, Robert see Hippopotamus, Eugene H
Krauss, Oscar IIBYP, IntMPA 1975
Krauss, Ruth Ida 1911?- AmA&B, AmPB, Au&ICB, Au&Wr 6, AuBYP, BkP, ChPo, ConAu 1R, ConDr 1, DrAP 1975, ForWC 1970, MorJA, SmATA 1, WWA 38, WrD
Krautter, Elisa ConAu 1R, SmATA 1
Krautter, Elisa see Bialk, Elisa
Kravetz, Nathan 1921- AmA&B, ConAu 9R, LE 5, WWA 38
Kredel, Fritz 1900-1973 ChPo, ConAu 41, IIBYP, IICB 1744, IICB 1946, IICB 1957, MorJA, WWAA 1973
Kredenser, Gail 1936- ConAu 21R
Krementz, Jill 1940- AuNews 1, AuNews 2, BiN 1975, ConAu 41, WWA 38, WWAW 8
Krentel, Mildred White 1921- ConAu 5R
Krents, Harold Eliot 1943- ConAu 37
Krevitsky, Nathan I 1914- ConAu 9R
Krevitsky, Nathan I see Krevitsky, Nik
Krevitsky, Nik ConAu XR
Krevitsky, Nik see Krevitsky, Nathan I
Krigstein, Bernard 1919- WWAA 1973
Kripke, Dorothy Karp ConAu 17R
Kristof, Jane 1932- ConAu 29, DrAS 6H, SmATA 8
Kristoffersen, Eva M 1901- AuBYP
Kroeber, Theodora Kracaw 1897- AmA&B, ConAu 5R, ForWC 1970, SmATA 1, WrD
Kroll, Francis Lynde 1904-1973 ConAu P-1, SmATA 10
Kroll, Steven 1941- ConAu 65
Kruess, James 1926- ConAu 53
Kruess, James see Kruss, James
Kruess, James see Polder, Markus
Kruess, James see Ritter, Felix
Kruif, Paul De CurB 42, CurB 63, NYTBE 2
Kruif, Paul De see DeKruif, Paul
Krum, Charlotte 1886- AuBYP
Krumgold, Joseph 1908- AuBYP, ConAu 9R,

EncM&D, FamMS, MorJA, Newb 1922, NewbC 1956, SmATA 1

Krummacher, Friedrich Adolf 1767-1845 *BiD&SB, CarSB*

Krusch, Werner E 1927- *AuBYP, ConAu 5R*

Krush, Beth 1918- *IlBYP, IlCB 1946, IlCB 1957, MorJA*

Krush, Joe 1918- *IlBYP, IlCB 1946, IlCB 1957, MorJA*

Kruss, James 1926- *AuBYP, SmATA 8, ThBJA*

Kruss, James *see* Kruess, James

Krutch, Joseph Wood 1893-1970 *AmA&B, Au&Wr 6, BiEnAT, CnDAL, ConAmA, ConAmL, ConAu 1R, ConAu 25R, CurB 59, CurB 70, DcLEnL, EvLB, NYTBE 1, OxAm, Pen Am, REn, REnAL, TwCA, TwCA Sup, WNAA*

Krythe, Maymie Richardson *ConAu 17R*

Kubert, Joe 1926- *ArtCS*

Kubie, Nora Gottheil Benjamin 1899- *AuBYP, ConAu 5R, WWAW 8*

Kubie, Nora Gottheil Benjamin *see* Benjamin, Nora

Kubinyi, Kalman 1906- *ConICB, IlCB 1744*

Kubinyi, Laszlo *ChPo S2, IlBYP*

Kublin, Hyman 1919- *ConAu 9R, DrAS 6H, WWWorJ 1972*

Kudian, Mischa *Au&Wr 6, WrD*

Kuenstler, Morton *see* Mutz

Kugelmass, Joseph Alvin 1910-1972 *AmA&B, AuBYP, ConAu 5R, ConAu 33, WNAA, WWA 38*

Kuh, Charlotte *AmPB*

Kuhlman, Kathryn *BiN 1974, ConAu 57, CurB 74, NYTBE 3*

Kuhn, Ferdinand 1905- *AmA&B, ConAu 5R, IntWW 38, WWA 38*

Kujoth, Jean Spealman 1935-1975 *ConAu P-2*

Kumin, Maxine Winokur 1925- *AmA&B, AnCL, AuBYP, AuNews 2, ChPo S1, ConAu 1R, ConLC 5, ConP 1975, DrAF 1976, DrAP 1975, ForWC 1970, SmATA 12, WWA 38, WWAW 8, WrD*

Kummer, Frederic Arnold 1873-1943 *AmA&B, AuBYP, DcNAA, WNAA*

Kummer, Frederic Arnold *see* Fredericks, Arnold

Kuner, M C 1922- *ConAu 41*

Kunhappa, Murkot 1905- *ConAu 69*

Kunhardt, Dorothy *AmPB*

Kunitz, Stanley 1905- *ConAu 41, CurB 43, CurB 59, DrAS 6E*

Kunstler, Morton 1927- *SmATA 10*

Kunz, Virginia B 1921- *ConAu 21R*

Kupferberg, Herbert 1918- *ConAu 29, WWWorJ 1972, WrD*

Kuppord, Skelton *MnBBF*

Kuratomi, Chizuko 1939- *ConAu 21R, SmATA 12*

Kurelek, William 1927- *ChLR 2, ConAu 49, SmATA 8, WWAA 1973*

Kurkul, Edward 1916- *ConAu 25R, ConAu 25R*

Kurland, Gerald 1942- *ConAu 41, DrAS 6H, SmATA 13*

Kursh, Harry 1919- *ConAu 9R*

Kurtis, Arlene Harris 1927- *ConAu 25R*

Kurtz, Edwin Bernard, Jr. 1926- *AmMWS 12P*

Kuruppu, D S C *MnBBF*

Kuruppu, D S C *see* Christie, Stephen

Kusan, Ivan 1933- *AuBYP, ConAu 9R*

Kuskin, Karla Seidman 1932- *AmPB, AuBYP, ChPo, ChPo S1, ConAu 1R, ForWC 1970, IlCB 1957, SmATA 2, ThBJA*

Kuskin, Karla Seidman *see* Charles, Nicholas

Kutcher, Ben 1895- *ChPo, ConICB, IlCB 1744, IlCB 1946*

Kutzer, Ernst 1880- *ConICB*

Kvale, Velma R 1898- *ConAu P-2, SmATA 8*

Kyle, Anne D 1896- *JBA 1934, JBA 1951*

Kyle, Elisabeth *AuBYP, ConAu XR, MorJA, SmATA 3, WW 1974, WWCL, WrD*

Kyle, Elisabeth *see* Dunlop, Agnes M R

L

LaBastille, Anne 1938- *ConAu 57*
LaBastille, Anne *see* Bowes, Anne LaBastille
LaBorde, Rene *ConAu XR*
LaBorde, Rene *see* Neuffer, Irene LaBorde
Laboulaye, Edouard R L De 1811-1883 *BbD, BiD&SB, CarSB, DcBiA, JBA 1934, JBA 1951*
Laboulaye, Edouard R L De *see* DeLaboulaye, Edouard R L
Lacher, Gisella Loeffler 1903- *IICB 1744*
Lacks, Cecilia 1945- *ConAu 69*
Lacks, Cecilia *see* Lacks, Cissy
Lacks, Cissy *ConAu XR*
Lacks, Cissy *see* Lacks, Cecilia
Lacy, Dan 1914- *BiDL 5, ConAu 37, CurB 54*
Lacy, Leslie Alexander 1937- *ConAu 33, LBAA, SmATA 6*
Lader, Lawrence 1919- *AmA&B, ConAu 1R, SmATA 38, WWA 38, WWE 14*
Lady Of Quality, A *ConAu XR, SmATA 1, TwCA, TwCA Sup*
Lady Of Quality, A *see* Bagnold, Enid
Ladyman, Phyllis *Au&Wr 6*
LaFarge, Oliver 1901-1963 *AmA&B, AmNov, AuBYP, CnDAL, ConAmA, CurB 53, CurB 63, DcLEnL, LongC, OxAm, Pen Am, REn, REnAL, TwCA, TwCA Sup, WNAA*
LaFarge, Phyllis *AuBYP*
Laffin, John 1922- *Au&Wr 6, AuBYP, ConAu 53, WWWor 2*
Laffin, John *see* Dekker, Carl
Laffin, John *see* Napier, Mark
Laffin, John *see* Sabre, Dirk
LaFontaine, Jean De 1621-1695 *AnCL, AtlBL, BbD, BiD&SB, CasWL, ChPo, ChPo S1, ChPo S2, CyWA, DcEuL, EuAu, EvEuW, NCHEL, OxEng, OxFr, Pen Eur, RCom, REn*
LaFontaine, M De 1621-1695 *CarSB*
Lagerlof, Selma O Lovisa 1858-1940 *CarSB, CasWL, ClDMEuL, CyWA, EncWL, EvEuW, JBA 1934, LongC, Pen Eur, REn, TwCA, TwCA Sup, TwCW, WWCL, WWLA, WWTwL*
LaGumina, Salvatore J 1928- *DrAS 6H*
Laidler, Thomas *WWBWI 1*
Laimgruber, Monika 1946- *SmATA 11*
Laing, R D 1927- *CelR 3, CurB 73, NYTBE 3*
Laird, Jean Elouise Rydeski 1930- *ConAu 9R,*

WWAW 8, WWMW 14
Laite, Gordon 1925- *IlBYP, IICB 1957*
Laklan, Carli *ConAu XR, ForWC 1970, SmATA 5*
Laklan, Carli *see* Clarke, John
Laklan, Carli *see* Laughlin, Virginia Carli
Lakritz, Esther *WrD*
Laliberte, Norman 1925- *AmA&B, WWA 38, WWAA 1973*
LaMare, Walter De *JBA 1951, TwCA, TwCA Sup*
LaMare, Walter De *see* DeLaMare, Walter
Lamb, Beatrice Pitney 1904- *ConAu 5R*
Lamb, Charles 1775-1834 *Alli, AtlBL, BbD, BiD&SB, BiDLA, BrAu 19, CarSB, CasWL, Chambr 3, ChPo, ChPo S1, ChPo S2, CriT 2, CyWA, DcEnA, DcEnL, DcEuL, DcLEnL, EvLB, MouLC 3, NCHEL, OxEng, Pen Eng, RAdv 1, RCom, REn, TelT, WEAL, WWCL*
Lamb, Elizabeth Searle 1917- *ConAu 33, WrD*
Lamb, G F *ConAu 53*
Lamb, G F *see* Balaam
Lamb, Geoffrey Frederick *Au&Wr 6, ConAu 53, SmATA 10, WrD*
Lamb, Harold Albert 1892-1962 *AmA&B, AuBYP, ChPo S2, JBA 1934, JBA 1951, OxAm, REn, REnAL, TwCA, TwCA Sup, WNAA*
Lamb, Harold M *MnBBF*
Lamb, Hugh 1946- *ConAu 49*
Lamb, J P *MnBBF*
Lamb, Lynton Harold 1907- *ArtsCL, Au&Wr 6, ConAu 1R, IlBYP, IICB 1946, IICB 1957, SmATA 10, WW 1974, WWGA*
Lamb, Mary Ann 1764-1847 *Alli, CarSB, ChPo, ChPo S2, DcEnA, DcEnL, DcLEnL, NCHEL, OxEng, TelT, WWCL*
Lamb, Robert 1941- *ConAu 29, SmATA 13*
Lamb, Ruth Stanton *ConAu 45, DrAS 6F, WWAW 8*
Lambe, F *MnBBF*
Lambe, Robert Justyn *MnBBF, WWBWI A*
Lambert, Janet Snyder 1894-1973 *AuBYP, ConAu 41, CurB 54, IndAu 1917, REnAL, ThBJA*
Lambert, Richard Stanton 1894- *CanWW 12, WW 1974*
Lambert, Saul *IlBYP*

Lambert, T H *MnBBF*
Lambert, T H *see* Lumberjack
Lambo, Don *IIBYP*
Lamburn, R C *WWBWI A*
Lamburn, R C *see* Lamburn, Richmal Crompton
Lamburn, Richmal Crompton 1890-1969
  *ConAu 9R, ConAu P-1, LongC, MnBBF,
  NCHEL, SmATA 5, WWCL*
Lamburn, Richmal Crompton *see* Crompton,
  William
Lamburn, Richmal Crompton *see* Crompton,
  Richmal
Lamburn, Richmal Crompton *see* Lamburn, R C
Lamm, Joyce 1933- *ConAu 57*
Lamond, Henry George 1885-1969 *ConAu 25R,
  SingR 1*
Lamont, Marianne *ConAu 57*
Lamont, Marianne *see* Rundle, Anne
Lamorisse, Albert *CurB 63, CurB 70,
  NYTBE 1*
Lamparski, Richard *ConAu 21R*
Lampell, Millard 1919- *AmA&B, AmNov,
  BiEnAT, ConAu 9R, EncFCW 1969,
  REnAL, WWA 38*
Lampen, Herbert Dudley *MnBBF*
Lamplugh, Lois 1921- *ConAu 13R*
Lampman, Evelyn Sibley 1907- *AuBYP,
  ConAu 13R, MorJA, SmATA 4,
  WWAW 8, WWPNA*
Lampman, Evelyn Sibley *see* Bronson, Lynn
Lamprey, Louise 1869-1951 *AmA&B, CarSB,
  ChPo, JBA 1934, JBA 1951, REnAL,
  WNAA, YABC 2*
Lancaster, Bruce 1896-1963 *AmA&B, AmNov,
  ConAu P-1, SmATA 9, TwCA,
  TwCA Sup*
Lancaster, Captain *MnBBF*
Lancaster, Captain *see* Hook, Samuel Clarke
Lancaster, Clay 1917- *ConAu 5R*
Lancaster, Jack *MnBBF*
Lancaster, Jack *see* Burrage, Alfred McLelland
Lancaster, Osbert 1908- *CurB 64, IICB 1946,
  IntWW 38, LongC, NCHEL, TwCA Sup,
  WW 1974, WWGA, WWWor 2*
Lancaster, Percival *MnBBF*
Lancaster, William Joseph Cosens 1851-1922
  Alli Sup, BiD&SB, MnBBF, WWCL
Lancaster, William Joseph Cosens *see*
  Collingwood, Harry
Lancaster Brown, Peter 1927- *Au&Wr 6, WrD*
Lance, James Waldo 1926- *Au&Wr 6*
Lance, John *MnBBF*
Lance, John *see* Bungay, E Newton
Land, Jane *ConAu XR, SmATA 8*
Land, Jane *see* Borland, Kathryn Kilby
Land, Jane *see* Speicher, Helen Ross
Land, Myrick 1922- *ConAu 13R*
Land, Ross *ConAu XR, SmATA 8*
Land, Ross *see* Borland, Kathryn Kilby
Land, Ross *see* Speicher, Helen Ross
Landau, Elaine 1948- *ConAu 53, SmATA 10*
Landau, Jacob 1917- *CurB 65, DcCAA 2,
  IIBYP, IICB 1946, IICB 1957, WWA 38,
  WWAA 1973, WWWor 2,
  WWWorJ 1972*
Landeck, Beatrice 1904- *AuBYP, LE 5*
Lander, Dane *WWBWI A*
Lander, Dane *see* Clarke, Percy A

Lander, Ernest McPherson, Jr. 1915-
  ConAu 1R, DrAS 6H, WrD
Landin, Les 1923- *ConAu 5R, SmATA 2*
Landis, Paul Henry 1901- *AmMWS 12S,
  ConAu 5R*
Landon, Herman 1882-1960 *AmA&B, MnBBF*
Landon, Margaret 1903- *ConAu 13R,
  CurB 45*
Landor, Owen *MnBBF*
Landry, Lionel 1919- *WWA 38*
Landsborough, G H *MnBBF*
Landsborough, G H *see* Cody, Stone
Landsborough, G H *see* McCracken, Mike
Landshoff, Ursula 1908- *ConAu 29,
  SmATA 13*
Lane, Carl Daniel 1899- *AmA&B, AuBYP,
  CurB 51*
Lane, Carolyn 1926- *ConAu 29, SmATA 10,
  WrD*
Lane, Ferdinand Cole 1885- *AmA&B,
  TwCA Sup*
Lane, Harry *WWBWI I*
Lane, Jane 1905- *Au&Wr 6, LongC, TwCW,
  WW 1974, WrD*
Lane, Marston *MnBBF*
Lane, Neola Tracy *AuBYP*
Lane, Rose Wilder 1887-1968 *AmA&B,
  REnAL, TwCA, TwCA Sup, WNAA*
Lane, Sheena Porter *ThBJA*
Lane, Sheena Porter *see* Porter, Sheena
Lanes, Selma Gordon 1929- *ConAu 25R,
  SmATA 3, WWAW 8*
Lanes, Selma Gordon *see* Gordon, Selma
Lang, A Ernest *WWBWI I*
Lang, Andrew 1844-1912 *Alli Sup, AnCL,
  AuBYP, BbD, BiD&SB, BiDPar,
  BrAu 19, CarSB, CasWL, Chambr 3,
  ChPo, ChPo S1, ChPo S2, DcBiA,
  DcEnA, DcEnA Ap, DcEuL, DcLEnL,
  EvLB, JBA 1934, LongC, ModBL,
  NCHEL, OxEng, Pen Eng, REn, St&VC,
  TelT, WEAL, WWCL*
Lang, Paul Henry 1901- *AmA&B, IntWW 38,
  REnAL, WWMus 6*
Lang, Peter *MnBBF*
Lang, Peter *see* Fearn, C Eaton
Lang, Robert 1912- *ConAu 41*
Lang, Stewart *MnBBF*
Lang, Stewart *see* Muir, Wardrop Openshaw
Langbridge, Frederick 1849-1922 *Alli Sup,
  ChPo, ChPo S1, ChPo S2, MnBBF,
  PoIre*
Lange, John *ConAu XR, SmATA XR*
Lange, John *see* Crichton, Michael
Lange, Suzanne 1945- *ConAu 29, SmATA 5*
Langhorne, Doctor 1735-1779 *CarSB*
Langley, Colin *MnBBF*
Langley, John *Alli, MnBBF*
Langner, Nola 1930- *ConAu 37, IIBYP,
  IICB 1957, SmATA 8*
Langone, John 1929- *ConAu 49*
Langstaff, John Meredith 1920- *AmA&B,
  ChLR 3, ChPo S2, ConAu 1R,
  SmATA 6, ThBJA, WWA 38*
Langstaff, Launcelot *Alli, DcEnL,
  YABC XR*
Langstaff, Launcelot *see* Irving, Washington
Langton, Charles *MnBBF*
Langton, Jane 1922- *AuBYP, ConAu 1R,*

SmATA 3, WrD
Langworthy, John Luther *CarSB*
Lanham, Urless Norton 1918- *AmMWS 12P,*
WWW 14
Lanier, Sidney 1842-1881 *Alli Sup, AmA,*
AmA&B, AtlBL, BbD, BiD&SB, BiDSA,
CarSB, CasWL, Chambr 3, ChPo,
ChPo S1, ChPo S2, CnDAL, CnE&AP,
CriT 3, CyWA, DcAmA, DcEnA Ap,
DcLEnL, DcNAA, EvLB, MouLC 3,
OxAm, OxEng, Pen Am, RAdv 1, REn,
REnAL, WEAL
Lanier, Sterling E *AuBYP*
Lankes, Julius J 1884-1960 *AmA&B, ChPo,*
ChPo S1, IICB 1744
Lansing, Alfred 1921-1975 *ConAu 13R,*
ConAu 61
Lansing, Elizabeth 1911- *AuBYP, ConAu 5R*
Lansing, Marion Florence 1883- *AmA&B,*
JBA 1934, JBA 1951, WNAA
Lantz, Paul 1908- *IICB 1744, IICB 1946*
Lapage, Geoffrey 1888- *Au&Wr 6,*
ConAu P-1
Lapicus, Elaine 1939- *ConAu 21R*
Lapidus, Elaine *see* Peters, Lane
LaPietra, Mary 1929- *ConAu 61*
LaPietra, Mary *see* Patanne, Maria
Lapp, Eleanor J 1936- *ConAu 69*
Lapp, Ralph Eugene 1917- *AmA&B,*
AmMWS 12P, CurB 55, WWA 38,
WWWor 2
Lappin, Peter 1911- *ConAu 57*
LaRamee, Louise De *BiD&SB, BrAu 19,*
DcEnA, JBA 1934
LaRamee, Louise De *see* DeLaRamee, Louise
LaRamee, Louise De *see* Ouida
Larcom, Lucy 1824?-1893 *Alli, Alli Sup,*
AmA, AmA&B, BiD&SB, Chambr 3,
ChP, ChPo, ChPo S2, DcAmA, DcLEnL,
DcNAA, OxAm, REnAL
Larkin, Sarah *ConAu XR*
Larkin, Sarah *see* Loening, Sarah Larkin
Larom, Henry V 1903?-1975 *AuBYP,*
ConAu 61
Larralde, Elsa *AuBYP*
Larrea, Jean-Jacques 1960- *ConAu 45*
Larrecq, John M *IIBYP*
Larrick, Nancy G 1910- *AuBYP, ChPo,*
ChPo S1, ChPo S2, ConAu 1R, LE 5,
MorBMP, SmATA 4, WWAW 8, WrD
Larsen, Egon 1904- *Au&Wr 6, ConAu 9R,*
WrD
Larsen, Johannes 1867- *IICB 1946*
Larsen, Peter 1933- *ConAu 1R, WrD*
Larsen, Ronald J 1948- *ConAu 41*
Larsen, Suzanne Kesteloo 1930- *IICB 1957*
Larson, Eve *ConAu XR, SmATA XR*
Larson, Eve *see* Saint John, Wylly Folk
Larson, Jean Russell 1930- *ConAu 21R,*
WWAW 8
Larson, William Herbert 1938- *ConAu 21R,*
SmATA 10, WWMW 14
Larue, Gerald Alexander 1916- *ConAu 21R,*
DrAS 6P
LaRue, Mabel Guinnip *AmA&B, ChPo S1,*
WNAA
LaSalle, Donald 1933- *ConAu 29*
Laschever, Barnett D 1924- *AuBYP,*
ConAu 1R

Lasell, Fen H *AuBYP, ConAu XR,*
IICB 1957
Lasell, Fen H *see* Calvert, Elinor H
Lasher, Faith B 1921- *ConAu 37, SmATA 12,*
WrD
Lasker, Joseph L 1919- *ConAu 49, IICB 1957,*
IIBYP, SmATA 9, WWA 38
Laskowski, Janina Domanska *ThBJA*
Laskowski, Janina Domanska *see* Domanska,
Janina
Laskowski, Jerzy 1919- *ThBJA*
Lasky, Kathryn 1944- *ConAu 69, SmATA 13*
Lassalle, C E *YABC 1*
Lassalle, C E *see* Ellis, Edward S
Lasson, Robert 1922- *AuBYP*
Lasswell, Fred 1916- *ArtCS*
Latham, Barbara 1896- *IICB 1744, IICB 1946,*
WWAA 1973
Latham, Frank B 1910- *ConAu 49, SmATA 6*
Latham, Jean Lee 1902- *AmA&B, Au&Wr 6,*
AuBYP, AuNews 1, ConAu 5R, CurB 56,
MorBMP, MorJA, NewbC 1956,
SmATA 2, St&VC, WWA 38,
WWAW 8
Latham, Mavis *ConAu XR, SmATA 8*
Latham, Mavis *see* Clark, Mavis Thorpe
Latham, Philip *AuBYP, ConAu XR,*
SmATA 8
Latham, Philip *see* Richardson, Robert S
Latham, Philip *see* Robinson, Robert Shirley
Lathrop, Dorothy Pulis 1891- *AmA&B,*
AuBYP, BkP, Cald 1938, ChPo,
ChPo S1, ConICB, IIBYP, IICB 1744,
IICB 1946, IICB 1957, JBA 1934,
JBA 1951, St&VC, WWAA 1973
Latourette, Kenneth Scott 1884-1968 *AmA&B,*
ConAu 21R, CurB 53, CurB 69, OhA&B,
TwCA Sup, WNAA
Lattimore, Eleanor Frances 1904- *AmA&B,*
AuBYP, ConAu 9R, IICB 1744,
IICB 1946, IICB 1957, JBA 1934,
JBA 1951, SmATA 5, SmATA 7
Lattin, Harriet Pratt 1898- *AuBYP, ConAu 33,*
WrD
Lauber, Patricia 1924- *AuBYP, ConAu 9R,*
SmATA 1, ThBJA
Laugesen, Mary E 1906- *ConAu P-2,*
SmATA 5
Laughbaum, Steve 1945- *SmATA 12*
Laughlin, Florence Young 1910- *ConAu 9R,*
ForWC 1970, SmATA 3, WrD
Laughlin, Ruth *AuBYP*
Laughlin, Virginia Carli 1907- *ConAu 1R*
Laughlin, Virginia Carli *see* Clarke, John
Laughlin, Virginia Carli *see* Laklan, Carli
Laumer, Keith 1925- *AmA&B, ConAu 9R*
Laurence *IIBYP*
Laurence, Ester Hauser 1935- *ConAu 29,*
SmATA 7, WrD
Laurie, A *MnBBF*
Lauritzen, Jonreed 1902- *ConAu 5R, CurB 52,*
SmATA 13, WrD
Laut, Agnes Christina 1871-1936 *AmA&B,*
CanNov, CanWr, DcAmA, DcNAA,
JBA 1934, JBA 1951, OxCan, REnAL,
WNAA
Laux, Dorothy 1920- *ConAu 61*
Lavell, Charles *MnBBF*
Lavell, Edith *CarSB*

Lavender, David 1910- *AuBYP, ConAu 1R*
Lavin, Mary 1912- *Au&Wr 6, CasWL,*
    CatA 1930, ConAu 9R, ConLC 4,
    ConNov 1972, ConNov 1976, EvLB,
    LongC, ModBL Sup, NCHEL, RAdv 1,
    TwCA Sup, WW 1974, WWWor 2,
    WrD
Lavine, David 1928- *AuBYP, WWE 14*
Lavine, Sigmund Arnold 1908- *AuBYP,*
    ConAu 1R, SmATA 3, WrD
Law, Stephen *MnBBF*
Lawn-Newark, J *MnBBF*
Lawrence, Chester *MnBBF*
Lawrence, Chester *see* Campbell, Sydney G
Lawrence, Christopher George Holman
    1866-1950 *MnBBF*
Lawrence, Christopher George Holman *see* Lynn,
    Escott
Lawrence, Christopher George Holman *see*
    Metcalfe, W C
Lawrence, Christopher George Holman *see*
    Abbott, Lawrence
Lawrence, D H 1885-1930 *AtlBL, CnE&AP,*
    CnMWL, CnThe, CyWA, LongC,
    ModBL, ModBL Sup, ModWD, NCHEL,
    OxAm, Pen Eng, RAdv 1, RCom, REn,
    REnAL, TwCW, WEAL, WWTwL
Lawrence, David Herbert 1885-1930 *CasWL,*
    Chambr 3, ChPo, ChPo S1, CnMD,
    DcLEnL, EncWL, EvLB, OxEng, TwCA,
    TwCA Sup
Lawrence, Herbert *MnBBF*
Lawrence, Isabelle *AuBYP, ForWC 1970,*
    WWAW 8
Lawrence, Jacob 1917- *AmPB, ChPo S1,*
    CurB 65, DcCAA 2, IlBYP, NYTBS 5,
    WWA 38, WWAA 1973, WWWor 2
Lawrence, Jerome 1915- *AmA&B,*
    AmSCAP 66, BiEnAT, ConAu 41,
    ConDr 1, ModWD, OhA&B, WWA 38,
    WWT 15, WWWor 2, WWWorJ 1972
Lawrence, Louise DeKiriline 1894-
    AmMWS 12P, ConAu 25R, SmATA 13
Lawrence, Louise DeKiriline *see* DeKiriline,
    Louise
Lawrence, Michael *MnBBF*
Lawrence, Mildred Elwood 1907- *AuBYP,*
    ConAu 1R, CurB 53, ForWC 1970,
    MorJA, SmATA 3, WWAW 8
Lawrence, R D *Prof*
Lawrence, W E *MnBBF, WWBWI A*
Lawrence, W E *see* Emmett Brothers
Laws, Percy *MnBBF*
Lawson, C G *MnBBF*
Lawson, Donald Elmer 1917- *AuBYP,*
    ConAu 1R, LE 5, SmATA 9, WWA 38,
    WWMW 14
Lawson, John *AuBYP*
Lawson, Marie Abrams 1894-1956 *AuBYP,*
    IlCB 1946, JBA 1951
Lawson, Patrick *AuBYP*
Lawson, Patrick *see* Eby, Lois Christine
Lawson, Robert 1892-1957 *Alli, Alli Sup,*
    AmA&B, AmPB, AnCL, Au&ICB,
    AuBYP, BkCL, Cald 1938, ChLR 2,
    ChPo, ChPo S2, CurB 41, CurB 57,
    FamAI, ForIl, IlBYP, IlCB 1744,
    IlCB 1946, JBA 1951, Newb 1922,
    St&VC, YABC 2

Lawson, Ted *CurB 43*
Lawson, Warren J *MnBBF*
Lawson, Warren J *see* Bobin, Donald E M
Lawton, Charles *ConAu XR*
Lawton, Charles *see* Heckelmann, Charles N
Lawton, Leslie *MnBBF*
Lawyer, Annabel Glenn 1906?-1974 *ConAu 53*
Laycock, George Edwin 1921- *AuBYP,*
    ConAu 53, SmATA 5, WWMW 14
Lazare, Gerald John 1927- *IlBYP, IlCB 1957*
Lazarus, Keo Felker 1913- *ConAu 41, WrD*
Lazarus, Mell 1927- *ArtCS, ConAu 17R*
Lea, Charlton *MnBBF, WWBWI A*
Lea, John 1871- *ChPo, ChPo S1, ChPo S2,*
    MnBBF, WWBWI A
Leach, Aroline Beecher 1899- *ConAu 61*
Leach, D *MnBBF*
Leach, Maria 1892- *AuBYP, ChPo S2,*
    ConAu 53
Leach, Owen *MnBBF*
Leacroft, Helen Mabel 1919- *Au&Wr 6,*
    ConAu 5R, SmATA 6
Leacroft, Richard V B 1914- *Au&Wr 6,*
    ConAu 5R, SmATA 6
Leaf, Munro 1905- *AmA&B, AmPB, AuBYP,*
    BkP, ChPo S2, JBA 1951, LongC,
    REnAL, TwCA, TwCA Sup, WWA 38,
    WWCL
Leaf, Russell Charles 1935- *AmMWS 12S,*
    ConAu 21R
Leaf, VaDonna Jean 1929- *ConAu 57*
Leamy, Edmund Stanislaus 1889- *ChPo,*
    ChPo S1, St&VC
Leaney, Alfred Robert Clare 1909- *Au&Wr 6,*
    ConAu 5R, WrD
Lear, Edward 1812-1888 *AmPB, AnCL,*
    AtlBL, AuBYP, BiD&SB, BrAu 19,
    CarSB, CasWL, Chambr 3, ChLR 1,
    ChP, ChPo, ChPo S1, ChPo S2,
    CnE&AP, CriT 3, DcEnL, DcEuL,
    DcLEnL, EvLB, FamAI, FamPYP,
    JBA 1934, MouLC 4, NCHEL, OxEng,
    Pen Eng, REn, St&VC, TelT, WEAL,
    WWCL
Lear, Melva Gwendoline Bartlett 1917-
    Au&Wr 6, ConAu 5R, SingR 1
Learmouth, D L *MnBBF*
Learsi, Rufus *AmA&B*
Leary, Lewis 1906- *ConAu 1R, DrAS 6E,*
    WWA 38
Leasor, James 1923- *Au&Wr 6, ConAu 1R,*
    WW 1974
Leatham, Moyra 1928- *IlCB 1946*
Leatherdale, G F *MnBBF*
Leavitt, Hart Day 1909- *ConAu 13R*
Leavitt, Jerome E 1916- *AuBYP, ConAu 1R,*
    LE 5
LeBaron, Grace 1845- *CarSB, DcNAA*
Lebedev, Vladimir Vasilievich 1891- *IlCB 1744,*
    WWGA
Leblanc, Georgette *CurB 41*
Leblanc, Maurice 1864-1941 *CasWL, CurB 42,*
    EncM&D, LongC, MnBBF, OxFr,
    TwCA
LeBreton, Thomas *MnBBF*
LeBreton, Thomas *see* Ford, T Murray
LeCain, Errol John 1941- *Au&Wr 6, ChPo S2,*
    ConAu 33, SmATA 6
LeCarre, John *ConAu XR, ConLC 3,*

*ConLC 5, ConNov 1972, ConNov 1976,
CurB 74, EncM&D, IntWW 38, NCHEL,
TwCW, NYTBS 5, WW 1974, WorAu*
Leckie, Robert 1920- *AuBYP, ConAu 13R*
Leckie, Robert *see* Barlow, Roger
Leckie, Robert *see* Porter, Mark
Lederer, William Julius 1912- *AmA&B,
Au&Wr 6, ConAu 9R, WWA 38,
WWWor 2, WorAu*
LeDoux, Harold *ArtCS*
Lee, Addison Earl 1914- *AmMWS 12P,
ConAu 9R, LE 5, WWA 38*
Lee, Albert 1855- *MnBBF*
Lee, Anne S *AmA&B, AuBYP*
Lee, Anne S *see* Murphy, Mabel Ansley
Lee, Carol *ConAu XR, SmATA XR*
Lee, Carol *see* Fletcher, Helen Jill
Lee, Carvel 1910- *ConAu P-1, MnnWr*
Lee, Charles H *WWBWI A*
Lee, Charles H *see* Woods, Ross
Lee, Dennis 1939- *ChLR 3, ConAu 25R,
Prof, WrD*
Lee, Doris Emrick 1905- *CurB 54, IlCB 1946,
WWA 38, WWAA 1973, WWAW 8*
Lee, Edgar *MnBBF*
Lee, Essie E 1920- *ConAu 49*
Lee, Harper 1926- *AmA&B, ConAu 13R,
DrAF 1976, OxAm, REnAL, SmATA 11,
TwCW, WWS 13, WorAu*
Lee, Holme *Alli Sup, DcEnL, TelT*
Lee, Holme *see* Parr, Harriet
Lee, Howard *ConAu XR*
Lee, Howard *see* Goulart, Ron
Lee, John R 1923- *ConAu 57*
Lee, Laurie 1914- *Au&Wr 6, CasWL,
ConP 1970, ConP 1975, IntWW 38,
LongC, ModBL, NCHEL, Pen Eng,
RAdv 1, REn, TwCW, WW 1974,
WWWor 2, WorAu, WrD*
Lee, Manfred B 1905-1971 *AmA&B,
Au&Wr 6, AuBYP, ConAu 1R,
ConAu 29, CurB 40, DcLEnL, EncM&D,
EvLB, LongC, Pen Am, NYTBE 2, REn,
REnAL, TwCA, TwCA Sup*
Lee, Manfred B *see* Queen, Ellery
Lee, Manfred B *see* Queen, Ellery, Jr.
Lee, Manfred B *see* Ross, Barnaby
Lee, Manning DeVilleneuve 1894- *ConICB,
IlBYP, IlCB 1744, IlCB 1946, MorJA,
WWA 38, WWAA 1973*
Lee, Mary 1949- *ConAu 29*
Lee, Mary Price 1934- *ConAu 57, SmATA 8*
Lee, Mildred *ConAu XR, ForWC 1970,
SmATA 6, ThBJA*
Lee, Mildred *see* Scudder, Mildred Lee
Lee, Norma E 1924- *ConAu 65*
Lee, Mrs. R 1791-1856 *Alli, CarSB*
Lee, Raymond *MnBBF, WWBWI A*
Lee, Raymond *see* Martin, E LeBreton
Lee, Robert C 1931- *ConAu 25R*
Lee, Robert Edwin 1918- *AmA&B,
AmSCAP 66, BiEnAT, ConAu 45,
ConDr 1, ModWD, OhA&B, REnAL,
WWA 38, WWT 15, WWWor 2*
Lee, Robert J 1921- *IlBYP, SmATA 10,
WWAA 1973*
Lee, Roy *AuBYP*
Lee, Roy *see* Hopkins, Clark
Lee, Stanhope *MnBBF*

Lee, Tanith 1947- *ConAu 37, SmATA 8,
WrD*
Lee, Tina *MorJA*
Lee, Virginia 1927- *ConAu 9R*
Leekley, Thomas Briggs 1910- *AuBYP,
ConAu 5R*
Leemans, H *MnBBF*
Leeming, Jill *WrD*
Leeming, Joseph 1897- *AuBYP, JBA 1951*
Leeper, John Joseph *WrD*
Lees, Captain *MnBBF*
Leeuw, Adele De *JBA 1951, WNAA*
Leeuw, Adele De *see* DeLeeuw, Adele
Lefebure, Molly *Au&Wr 6, ConAu 57, WrD*
LeFeuvre, Amy *CarSB*
LeFevre, Captain *MnBBF*
LeFevre, Felicite *WWLA*
Lefevre, Paul, Lieutenant *McGWD, MnBBF,
WWBWI A*
Lefebre, Paul, Lieutenant *see* Cooper, Charles H
St. John
Lefkowitz, R J 1942- *ConAu 45*
Lefler, Irene 1917- *ConAu 45, SmATA 12*
Leftwich, Joseph 1892- *Au&Wr 6, ConAu 5R*
LeGallienne, Eva 1899- *AmA&B, AuBYP,
BiEnAT, CurB 42, CurB 55, IntWW 38,
REn, REnAL, SmATA 9, WW 1974,
WWA 38, WWAW 8, WWT 15,
WWWor 2*
LeGallienne, Richard 1866-1947 *Alli Sup,
AnCL, BbD, BiD&SB, Chambr 3, ChPo,
ChPo S1, ChPo S2, DcAmA, DcEnA Ap,
DcLEnL, EvLB, LongC, MouLC 4,
NCHEL, OxAm, OxEng, Pen Eng,
TwCA, TwCA Sup, WEAL, WNAA*
Leger, Alexis Saint-Leger 1887-1975
ConAu 13R, ConAu 61
Leger, Alexis Saint-Leger *see* Perse, Saint-John
LeGrand *AuBYP, BkCL, IlCB 1946,
IlCB 1957, JBA 1951, SmATA XR*
LeGrand *see* Henderson, LeGrand
Legrand, Edy *AmPB, IlCB 1946*
Legrand, Edy *see* Edy-Legrand
LeGrand, Jack *MnBBF*
LeGuin, Ursula K 1929- *Au&Wr 6,
AuNews 1, BiN 1974, ChLR 3,
ConAu 21R, ConNov 1976, DrAF 1976,
SmATA 4, WWA 38, WWAW 8*
Legum, Colin 1919- *Au&Wr 6, ConAu 1R,
SmATA 10*
Lehane, Brendan 1936- *ConAu 21R*
Lehman, Celia 1928- *ConAu 49*
Lehn, Cornelia 1920- *ConAu 29*
Lehr, Delores 1920- *ConAu 17R, SmATA 10*
Lehr, Paul E 1918- *ConAu 65*
Lehrman, Robert L 1921- *ConAu 5R*
Leib, Amos Patten 1917- *ConAu 45, DrAS 6E*
Leicester, Henry *MnBBF*
Leichman, Seymour 1933- *ConAu 25R, IlBYP,
SmATA 5, WWAA 1973, WWE 14*
Leigh, Adrian *MnBBF*
Leigh, Arnold *MnBBF*
Leigh, Arthur, Captain *MnBBF*
Leigh, Arthur, Captain *see* Steffens, Arthur
Leigh, Brian *MnBBF*
Leigh, Felix *ChPo, ChPo S1, ChPo S2,
MnBBF*
Leigh, Percival 1813-1889 *BrAu 19, CarSB*
Leigh-Pemberton, John 1911- *WW 1974*

Leight, Edward *IIBYP*

Leighton, Clare Veronica Hope 1900?- *AmA&B, ChPo, ChPo S1, IIBYP, IICB 1946, IICB 1957, LongC, TwCA, TwCA Sup, WW 1974, WWAA 1973*

Leighton, Frances Spatz *ForWC 1970*

Leighton, Margaret Carver 1896- *AmA&B, Au&Wr 6, AuBYP, ConAu 9R, MorJA, OhA&B, SmATA 1, St&VC, WWA 38, WWAW 8, WrD*

Leighton, Marie Connor d1941 *LongC, MnBBF, WWLA*

Leighton, Robert 1859-1934 *CarSB, LongC, MnBBF, WWBWI A*

Leipold, L Edmond 1902- *ConAu 69*

Leisk, David Johnson 1906-1975 *AuBYP, ConAu 9R, ConAu 57, CurB 43, IICB 1946, IICB 1957, SmATA 1, ThBJA*

Leisk, David Johnson *see* Johnson, Crockett

Leister, Mary 1917- *ConAu 65*

Leitch, Adelaide *OxCan Sup, Prof*

Leitch, Patricia 1933- *ConAu 61, SmATA 11*

Leith, John Haddon 1919- *ConAu 5R, DrAS 6P*

Leithauser, Gladys Garner 1925- *ConAu 13R, ForWC 1970*

Lelland, Frank *MnBBF, WWBWI A*

Lelland, Frank *see* Burrage, Alfred McLelland

LeMair, H Willebeek 1889- *ChPo, IICB 1744*

Lembo, Diana L 1925- *ConAu 17R, DrLC 1969*

Lemke, Horst 1922- *IIBYP, IICB 1957*

Lemme, Janet E 1941- *ConAu 29*

Lemmon, Robert Stell 1885-1964 *AmA&B, AuBYP*

Lemoine, Georges *IIBYP*

Lenanton, C *ConAu XR*

Lenanton, C *see* Oman, Carola

Lenard, Alexander 1910- *ConAu 5R*

L'Engle, Madeleine 1918- *AmA&B, AmNov, AuBYP, AuNews 1, ChLR 1, ChPo, ChPo S1, ConAu 1R, MorBMP, MorJA, PiP, SenS, NewbC 1956, SmATA 1, WWA 38, WWAW 8, WWE 14, WrD*

Lengyel, Emil 1895- *AmA&B, AmMWS 12S, ConAu 9R, CurB 42, DrAS 6H, REnAL, SmATA 3, TwCA, TwCA Sup, WNAA, WWA 38, WWWor 2*

Lennig, Arthur 1933- *DrAS 6E*

Lennox, Henry *MnBBF*

Lens, Sidney 1912- *AuBYP, ConAu 1R, SmATA 13, WWA 38, WWWor 2*

Lenski, Lois 1893-1974 *AmA&B, AmPB, Au&ICB, Au&Wr 6, AuBYP, BkCL, BkP, CarSB, ChPo, ChPo S1, ChPo S2, ConAu 53, ConAu P-1, ConICB, FamAI, IICB 1744, IICB 1946, IICB 1957, JBA 1934, JBA 1951, NYTBS 5, Newb 1922, OhA&B, REnAL, SmATA 1, WNAA, WW 1974, WWA 28, WWAA 1973, WWAW 8*

Lent, Blair 1930- *AmPB, BkP, ConAu 21R, IIBYP, IICB 1957, NewbC 1966, SmATA 2, ThBJA, WWAA 1973, WWE 14, WrD*

Lent, Blair *see* Small, Ernest

Lent, Henry Bolles 1901- *AuBYP, JBA 1934, JBA 1951, St&VC*

Leodhas, Sorche Nic *ChPo, ChPo S1, ChPo S2, ThBJA*

Leodhas, Sorche Nic *see* Nic Leodhas, Sorche

Leonard, A Byron 1904- *AuBYP*

Leonard, Constance 1923- *ConAu 49, WrD*

Leonard, Henry *MnBBF, WWBWI A*

Leonard, Henry *see* Fennell, Hugh Wordsworth

Leonard, Jonathan N 1903-1975 *ConAu 61, WWA 38*

Leonard, V A 1898- *ConAu 37*

Leong, Gor Yun *SmATA 4*

LePage, Richard *MnBBF*

LeRei, David *WrD*

Lerner, Aaron Bunsen 1920- *AmMWS 12P, WWA 38*

Lerner, Marguerite Rush 1924- *AuBYP, ConAu 13R, SmATA 11, WWAW 8*

Lerner, Sharon 1938- *ConAu 5R, SmATA 11*

LeRoi, David 1905- *ConAu 9R*

Leroux, Gaston 1868-1927 *CasWL, EncM&D, LongC, MnBBF, OxFr, TwCA*

LeRoy, Miss *MnBBF*

LeRoy, Miss *see* Stuart, Esme

LeRoy, Douglas 1943- *ConAu 49*

LeSage, M 1668-1747 *CarSB*

LeShan, Eda J 1922- *ConAu 13R, NYTBE 4, WrD*

LeSieg, Theo *AuBYP, ConAu XR, SmATA 1*

LeSieg, Theo *see* Geisel, Theodor Seuss

Lesko, George 1932- *ConAu 17R*

Leslau, Wolf 1906- *DrAS 6F, WWA 38, WWWorJ 1972*

Leslie, Captain *MnBBF*

Leslie, Captain *see* Bradley, J J G

Leslie, Arthur Forbes *ChPo S2, MnBBF*

Leslie, Robert Franklin 1911- *Au&Wr 6, ConAu 49, SmATA 7*

LeSouef, Albert S *SingR 1*

Lesser, Milton 1928- *AuBYP, ConAu 13R*

Lesser, Milton *see* Frazer, Andrew

Lesser, Milton *see* Marlowe, Stephen

Lesser, Milton *see* Ridgway, Jason

Lesser, Milton *see* Thames, C H

Lessin, Andrew *AuBYP*

Lester, Julius B 1939- *AmA&B, Au&ICB, AuBYP, BlkAW, ChLR 2, ConAu 17R, LBAA, SmATA 12, WWA 38*

L'Estrange, James *MnBBF, WWBWI A*

L'Estrange, James *see* Strang, Herbert

LeStrange, W D L *MnBBF*

LeSueur, Meridel 1900- *ConAu 49, MnnWr, MorJA, SmATA 6*

Lethbridge, K G 1904- *Au&Wr 6, WrD*

LeTord, Bijou 1945- *ConAu 65*

Leuchtenburg, William Edward 1922- *AmA&B, ConAu 5R, DrAS 6H, WWA 38, WWWor 2*

Levenson, Dorothy 1927- *ConAu 9R*

Lever, Charles James 1806-1872 *Alli, Alli Sup, AtlBL, BbD, BiD&SB, BrAu 19, CarSB, CasWL, Chambr 3, ChPo S1, CyWA, DcBiA, DcEnA, DcEnL, DcEuL, DcLEnL, EvLB, HsB&A, MnBBF, MouLC 3, NCHEL, OxEng, Pen Eng, PoIre, REn, WEAL*

Levi, Herbert Walter 1921- *AmMWS 12P, WWA 38, WWE 14, WWWorJ 1972*

Levi, Riso *MnBBF*

Levin, Betty 1927- *ConAu 65*
Levin, Kristine Cox 1944- *ConAu 65*
Levin, Marcia Obrasky 1918- *AuBYP,*
 ConAu 13R, ForWC 1970, SmATA 13
Levin, Marcia Obrasky *see* Martin, Jeremy
Levin, Marcia Obrasky *see* Martin, Marcia
Levin, Meyer 1905- *AmA&B, AmNov,*
 Au&Wr 6, AuNews 1, BiEnAT,
 BiN 1974, CelR 3, CnMD, ConAu 9R,
 ConNov 1972, ConNov 1976, CurB 40,
 DcLEnL, ModAL, OxAm, Pen Am, REn,
 REnAL, TwCA, TwCA Sup, WWA 38,
 WWWorJ 1972
Levine, David 1926- *IlCB 1957*
Levine, Israel E 1923- *AuBYP, ConAu 1R,*
 SmATA 12, WWWorJ 1972, WrD
Levine, Joan Goldman *ConAu 61, SmATA 11*
Levine, Joseph *AuBYP, BkP*
Levine, Rhoda *AuBYP*
Levine, Sol 1914- *ConAu 9R, WWWorJ 1972*
Levinger, Elma Ehrlich 1887-1958 *AmA&B,*
 AuBYP, OhA&B, REnAL, WNAA
Levit, Herschel 1912- *WWAA 1973,*
 WWWorJ 1972
Levitin, Sonia 1934- *ConAu 29, SmATA 4*
Levy, Howard S 1923- *ConAu 17R, DrAS 6F*
Lewdrick, John *MnBBF*
Lewellen, John Bryan 1910-1956 *AuBYP,*
 IndAu 1917, MorJA
Lewesdon, John *ConAu XR*
Lewesdon, John *see* Daniell, Albert Scott
Lewin, Ted 1935- *ConAu 69, IlBYP*
Lewins, C A *MnBBF*
Lewins, C A *see* Rivers, Tex
Lewis, Alfred Henry 1858?-1914 *AmA&B,*
 AtlBL, AuBYP, BiD&SB, Chambr 3,
 CnDAL, DcAmA, DcLEnL, DcNAA,
 EncM&D, OhA&B, OxAm, REnAL
Lewis, Alice Hudson *AuBYP*
Lewis, Angelo J *see* Hoffman, Professor
Lewis, Angelo J *MnBBF*
Lewis, Anne *IlBYP*
Lewis, Anthony 1927- *ConAu 9R, CurB 55,*
 WWA 38
Lewis, Arthur Allen 1873-1957 *IlCB 1744,*
 IlCB 1946
Lewis, C S 1898-1963 *AnCL, ChLR 3,*
 ConLC 1, ConLC 3, ConLC 6, LongC,
 ModBL, ModBL Sup, MorJA, NCHEL,
 Pen Eng, RAdv 1, REn, SmATA 13,
 TwCW, WEAL
Lewis, C S *see* Clerk, N W
Lewis, C S *see* Hamilton, Clive
Lewis, C S *see* Lewis, Clive Staples
Lewis, Cecil Day 1904-1972 *CasWL,*
 Chambr 3, ChPo, ConLC 1, CurB 40,
 CurB 69, CyWA, DcLEnL, EncM&D,
 EvLB, LongC, ModBL, NCHEL, OxEng,
 Pen Eng, REn, TwCW, WWCL
Lewis, Charles *MnBBF, WWBWI A*
Lewis, Charles *see* Rowe, John Gabriel
Lewis, Claude A 1934- *ConAu 9R*
Lewis, Claudia Louise 1907- *ConAu 5R,*
 ChPo S2, ForWC 1970, SmATA 5, WrD
Lewis, Clive Staples 1898-1963 *Au&ICB,*
 AuBYP, CasWL, ChPo S1, ChPo S2,
 CurB 44, CurB 64, DcLEnL, EncWL,
 EvLB, OxEng, TelT, TwCA Sup,
 WWCL

Lewis, Clive Staples *see* Lewis, C S
Lewis, Edgar *MnBBF*
Lewis, Elizabeth Foreman 1892-1958 *AmA&B,*
 AuBYP, ChPo S1, JBA 1934, JBA 1951,
 Newb 1922, YABC 2
Lewis, Francine *ConAu XR, SmATA 2*
Lewis, Francine *see* Wells, Helen
Lewis, George Q 1916- *ConAu 21R*
Lewis, H M *WWBWI 1*
Lewis, Harold G *MnBBF*
Lewis, Harry *LE 5*
Lewis, Hilda 1896-1974 *Au&Wr 6, ConAu 49*
Lewis, J Morton *MnBBF*
Lewis, Jack *MnBBF, WWBWI A*
Lewis, Jack *see* Hood, Stephen
Lewis, Jack *see* Jackson, Lewis
Lewis, Jack *see* Lewis, Phylis
Lewis, Janet 1899- *AmA&B, AmNov,*
 AmSCAP 66, Au&Wr 6, ChPo,
 ChPo S1, CnDAL, ConAu XR,
 ConNov 1972, ConNov 1976,
 ForWC 1970, OxAm, TwCA Sup,
 WWA 38, WWAW 8, WrD
Lewis, Janet *see* Winters, Janet Lewis
Lewis, Judith Mary *WrD*
Lewis, June E 1905- *ConAu P-2*
Lewis, Leon 1833-1920 *MnBBF*
Lewis, Lucia Z *ConAu XR, ForWC 1970,*
 SmATA XR
Lewis, Lucia Z *see* Anderson, Lucia
Lewis, Matthew Gregory 1775-1818 *Alli, BbD,*
 BiD&SB, BiDLA, BrAu 19, CasWL,
 Chambr 2, ChPo, ChPo S1, ChPo S2,
 CriT 2, CyWA, DcBiA, DcEnA, DcEnL,
 DcEuL, DcLEnL, EvLB, MnBBF,
 MouLC 2, NCHEL, OxEng, Pen Eng,
 REn, WEAL
Lewis, Mildred D 1912- *AuBYP, ConAu 13R*
Lewis, Mildred D *see* DeWitt, James
Lewis, Milton *AuBYP*
Lewis, Naomi *ForWC 1970*
Lewis, Phylis *MnBBF*
Lewis, Phylis *see* Lewis, Jack
Lewis, Richard 1935- *AuBYP, BkP, ChPo S1,*
 ConAu 9R, DrAP 1975, OxCan Sup,
 SmATA 3
Lewis, Richard William 1933-1966 *IlCB 1957*
Lewis, Roger *AuBYP, ConAu XR*
Lewis, Roger *see* Zarchy, Harry
Lewis, Shari 1934- *CurB 58, WWA 38,*
 WWAW 8
Lewis, Thomas P 1936- *ConAu 29, WrD*
Lewiton, Mina 1904-1970 *AuBYP, ConAu P-2,*
 ConAu 29, MorJA, SmATA 2
Lewiton, Mina *see* Simon, Mina Lewiton
LeWitt, Jan 1907- *AuBYP, IlCB 1744,*
 IlCB 1946, WW 1974, WWGA
Lewites, Mordecai Henry *ConAu XR,*
 WWWorJ 1972
Lewittes, Mordecai Henry *see* Lewittes, Morton
H
Lewittes, Morton H 1911- *ConAu 25R, LE 5*
Lewittes, Morton H *see* Lewittes, Mordecai
Henry
Lewty, Marjorie 1906- *Au&Wr 6, ConAu P-1*
Lexau, Joan M *AuBYP, BkP, ConAu 17R,*
 SmATA 1
Lexau, Joan M *see* Nodset, Joan L
Ley, Willy 1906-1969 *AmA&B, Au&Wr 6,*

AuBYP, ConAu 9R, ConAu 25R,
CurB 41, CurB 53, CurB 69, REnAL,
SmATA 2, ThBJA, TwCA Sup
Ley, Willy see Willey, Robert
Leyda, Jay 1910- AmA&B, WorAu
Leyland, Éric 1911- MnBBF, WWCL
Leys, John K MnBBF
Leyson, Burr Watkins 1898- AuBYP
Lezra, Grizzella Paull 1934- ConAu 61
L'Heureux, Bill ConAu XR
L'Heureux, Bill see L'Heureux, W J
L'Heureux, W J 1934- ConAu 5R
L'Heureux, W J see L'Heureux, Bill
L'Hommedieu, Dorothy 1885-1964 AmA&B,
AuBYP
Liang, Yen 1908- ConAu 5R, IlCB 1946,
WWE 14
Libby, Bill ConAu XR, SmATA 5, WrD
Libby, Bill see Libby, William M
Libby, William M 1927- ConAu 25R,
SmATA 5
Libby, William M see Libby, Bill
Liberty, Gene 1924- ConAu 5R, SmATA 3
Lichello, Robert 1926- AuBYP, ConAu 13R
Liddell, Mary 1891- IlCB 1744
Liddell Hart, Basil Henry 1895-1970 CurB 40,
CurB 70, DcLEnL, EvLB, LongC,
NCHEL, TwCA, TwCA Sup
Lide, Alice AuBYP
Lidstone, F MnBBF
Lieb, Frederick George 1888- AuBYP, WNAA
Lieberg, Owen S 1896- ConAu P-2
Lieberman, Mark 1942- ConAu 29
Liebers, Arthur 1913- ConAu 5R, SmATA 12,
WrD
Liebers, Ruth 1910- ConAu P-1
Liebman, Arthur 1926- ConAu 57
Liebman, Oscar 1919- IlCB 1946
Liers, Emil Ernest 1890- AuBYP, BkCL
Lietz, Gerald S 1918- AuBYP, SmATA 11
Liffring, Joan Louise 1929- ConAu 17R
Lifton, Betty Jean 1926- AuBYP, ConAu 5R,
ForWC 1970, SmATA 6, ThBJA
Liggett, Clayton Eugene 1930- ConAu 29,
WWW 14
Liggett, Thomas 1918- ConAu 5R, WrD
Light, Walter H MnBBF, WWBWI A
Light, Walter H see Herrod, Walter
Light, Walter H see Wilson, Wingrove
Lightner, A M ConAu XR, SmATA 5
Lightner, A M see Hopf, Alice Lightner
Lignell, Lois 1911- IlCB 1946
Lillie, Amy Morris AuBYP
Lillie, Lucy Cecil 1855-1908? Alli Sup,
AmA&B, BbD, BiD&SB, CarSB,
DcAmA, DcNAA
Lillington, Kenneth James 1916- WrD,
Au&Wr 6
Lilly, Charles IlBYP
Liman, Ellen 1936- ConAu 61
Limburg, Peter R 1929- ConAu 33,
SmATA 13, WrD
Lincoln, C Eric 1924- AmA&B, AmMWS 12S,
ConAu 1R, DrAS 6P, LBAA, SmATA 5,
WWA 38, WWWor 2
Lincoln, Maurice MnBBF
Lincoln, Seymour MnBBF
Lincoln, Victoria 1904- ConAu 17R,
ForWC 1970, WWA 38, WWAW 8

Lind, Anton MnBBF, WWBWI A
Lind, Levi Robert 1906- DrAS 6F, WWA 38
Linday, Ryllis Elizabeth Paine 1919-
ConAu 13R
Lindbergh, Anne Morrow 1906- AmA&B,
AnCL, CelR 3, ChPo, ConAu 17R,
LongC, OxAm, REn, REnAL, TwCA,
TwCA Sup
Lindbergh, Charles A 1902-1974 AmA&B,
BiN 1974, ConAu 53, CurB 41, CurB 54,
CurB 74, IntWW 38, NYTBE 2,
NYTBS 5, OxAm, REn, REnAL,
WNAA, WW 1974, WWA 38,
WWWor 2
Linde, Gunnel 1924- ConAu 21R, SmATA 5
Lindeburg, Franklin Alfred 1918- ConAu 5R
Linden, A R MnBBF
Linden, Auguste CarSB
Linderman, Frank Bird 1868-1938 AmA&B,
DcNAA, JBA 1934, JBA 1951, OhA&B,
OxAm, REnAL, WNAA
Lindgren, Astrid 1907- Au&ICB, Au&Wr 6,
AuBYP, ChLR 1, ConAu 13R, FamMS,
MorJA, SmATA 2, WWAW 8,
WWWor 2
Lindman, Maj AuBYP, JBA 1951
Lindop, Edmund 1925- ConAu 5R, SmATA 5
Lindquist, Jennie Dorothea 1899-1977 AuBYP,
ConAu 69, MorJA, SmATA 13
Lindquist, Willis 1908- AuBYP, MorJA
Lindridge, James MnBBF
Lindsay, Edward MnBBF
Lindsay, Harold Arthur 1900- Au&Wr 6,
ConAu 5R, SingR 1
Lindsay, Maud McKnight 1874- AuBYP
Lindsay, Nicholas Vachel 1879-1931 AmLY,
BkCL, ChPo, ChPo S2, DcLEnL,
DcNAA, EvLB, FamPYP, SixAP
Lindsay, Norman Alfred William 1879-1969
ChPo S2, DcLEnL, LongC, Pen Eng,
REn, SingR 1, TwCA, TwCA Sup,
TwCW, WWCL
Lindsay, Vachel 1879-1931 AmA&B,
AmLY Xr, AnCL, AnMV 1926, AtlBL,
CasWL, Chambr 3, CnDAL, CnE&AP,
CnMWL, ConAmA, ConAmL, CyWA,
DcNAA, EncWL, LongC, ModAL,
OxAm, OxEng, Pen Am, RAdv 1, REn,
REnAL, St&VC, TwCA, TwCA Sup,
TwCW, WEAL, WNAA, WWTwL
Lindsay, Zaidee 1923- ConAu 29
Lines, Kathleen ChPo, ChPo S1
Liney, John J ArtCS
Ling, Jack 1930- ConAu 25R
Lingard, Joan 1932- Au&Wr 6, ConAu 41,
SmATA 8, WrD
Link, Ruth 1923- ConAu 29
Linklater, Eric 1899-1974 Au&Wr 6, CasWL,
Chambr 3, ChPo, ChPo S1, ChPo S2,
CnMD, ConAu 53, ConAu P-2,
ConNov 1972, DcLEnL, EvLB,
IntWW 38, LongC, ModBL, ModWD,
NCHEL, NYTBS 5, Pen Eng, REn,
TelT, TwCA, TwCA Sup, TwCW,
WW 1974, WWCL, WWWor 2
Linley, Julian MnBBF
Linley, Julian see Pearson, Alec George
Linley, Mark MnBBF
Linley, Mark see Samways, George Richmond

Linneman, Robert E 1928- *AmMWS 12S, ConAu 29, WWE 14*
Linton, Calvin Darlington 1914- *ConAu 13R, DrAS 6E, LE 5, WWA 38, WWWor 2*
Linton, Ralph 1893-1953 *AmA&B, TwCA Sup, WNAA*
Lionni, Leo 1910- *AmA&B, AmPB, Au&ICB, AuBYP, BkP, ChPo S2, ChFB 1, ConAu 53, FamAI, IlCB 1957, SmATA 8, ThBJA, WWA 38, WWAA 1973, WWGA*
Lipinsky DeOrlov, Lino Sigismondo 1908- *IlCB 1957, WWA 38, WWAA 1973, WWWor 2*
Lipkind, William 1904-1974 *AmPB, AuBYP, ConAu 53, MorJA, NYTBS 5*
Lipman, David 1931- *ConAu 21R, WWA 38, WWMW 14*
Lippard, Lucy Rowland 1937- *ConAu 25R, WWAA 1973, WWAW 8*
Lippincott, Joseph Wharton 1887-1976 *AmA&B, AuBYP, ConAu 69, CurB 55, MorJA, REnAL, WNAA*
Lippincott, Sara Jane 1823-1904 *Alli, AmA, AmA&B, BbD, CarSB, CyAL 2, DcAmA, DcEnL, DcNAA, FemPA, OxAm*
Lippman, Peter J 1936- *IlBYP, IlCB 1957*
Lipsey, Robert Edward 1926- *AmMWS 12S, ConAu 5R, WWA 38*
Lipsyte, Robert 1938- *ConAu 17R, SmATA 5*
Lipton, Lenny *WrD*
Lisker, Sonia O 1933- *ConAu 49*
Lisle, Seward D *YABC 1*
Lisle, Seward D *see* Ellis, Edward S
Lisowski, Gabriel *IlBYP*
Liss, Howard 1922- *AuBYP, ConAu 25R, SmATA 4*
Lissim, Simon 1900- *IlCB 1946, WWA 38, WWAA 1973, WWE 14, WWWor 2*
List, Ilka Katherine *ConAu XR, ForWC 1970, SmATA 6*
List, Ilka Katherine *see* Maidoff, Ilka List
Lister, Gladys *SingR 1*
Liston, Robert A 1927- *AuBYP, ConAu 17R, SmATA 5*
Litchfield, Ada B 1916- *ConAu 25R, SmATA 5*
Litchfield, Mary E *CarSB*
Litten, Frederic Nelson 1885-1951 *AmA&B, AuBYP, WNAA*
Little, Jack *ConAu 65*
Little, Jack *see* Little, John D
Little, Jean 1932- *AuBYP, ChPo S2, ConAu 21R, OxCan Sup, Prof, SmATA 2*
Little, John D 1894- *ConAu 65*
Little, John D *see* Little, Jack
Little, Mary E *AuBYP*
Little Owl *MnBBF*
Littledale, Freya *ConAu 21R, SmATA 2, WrD*
Littledale, Harold 1927- *ConAu 5R, LE 5*
Litvinoff, Barnet 1917- *ConAu 17R*
Lively, Penelope 1933- *Au&Wr 6, ChPo S2, ConAu 41, SmATA 7, WrD*
Livermore, Elaine *ChPo S2*
Liversidge, Douglas 1913- *ConAu P-1, SmATA 8*

Liversidge, Henry Douglas 1913- *Au&Wr 6, WrD*
Livesey, Claire Warner 1927- *ConAu 29*
Livingston, Myra Cohn 1926- *AmA&B, AnCL, BkCL, BkP, ChPo, ChPo S1, ChPo S2, ConAu 1R, SmATA 5*
Livingston, Richard R 1922- *ConAu 45, SmATA 8*
Llewellyn, Richard *ConAu XR, CurB 40, CyWA, DcLEnL, EvLB, LongC, NCHEL, RAdv 1, REn, SmATA XR, TwCA, TwCA Sup, TwCW, WW 1974, WWWor 2*
Llewellyn, Richard *see* Llewellyn Lloyd, Richard D V
Llewellyn Lloyd, Richard D V 1907?- *ConAu 53, CurB 40, SmATA 11, TwCA, TwCA Sup*
Llewellyn Lloyd, Richard D V *see* Llewellyn, Richard
Llewelyn, T Harcourt *MnBBF, SmATA XR*
Llewelyn, T Harcourt *see* Hamilton, Charles Harold St. John
Llewelyn Owens, Joan *WrD*
Lloyd, E M S *MnBBF*
Lloyd, Edward 1815-1890 *MnBBF, NCHEL, WWBWI A*
Lloyd, Everett 1881- *AmA&B, TexW, WNAA*
Lloyd, John Uri 1849-1936 *Alli Sup, AmA&B, BiD&SB, DcAmA, DcNAA, OhA&B, WNAA*
Lloyd, Marjorie 1909- *Au&Wr 6, ConAu 5R, WrD*
Lloyd, Norman 1909- *AmSCAP 66, ConAu 37, WWA 38*
Lloyd, Norris 1908- *ConAu 1R, ForWC 1970, SmATA 10*
Lloyd, Ronald *ConAu XR*
Lloyd, Ronald *see* Friedland, Ronald Lloyd
Lloyd, Tom *MnBBF*
Lobdell, Helen 1919- *ConAu 9R*
Lobel, Anita 1934- *BkP, ChPo S1, ConAu 53, IlBYP, IlCB 1957, SmATA 6, ThBJA*
Lobel, Arnold Stark 1933- *AuBYP, AuNews 1, BkP, ChPo S2, ConAu 1R, IlCB 1957, SmATA 6, ThBJA*
Loberg, Mary Alice 1943- *ConAu 29*
Lobley, Robert John 1934- *Au&Wr 6, ConAu 29, WrD*
Lobsenz, Amelia Freitag *AuBYP, ConAu 13R, ForWC 1970, SmATA 12*
Lobsenz, Norman Mitchell 1919- *AmA&B, ConAu 9R, SmATA 6*
Lochlons, Colin *ConAu XR, SmATA 6*
Lochlons, Colin *see* Jackson, C Paul
Lock, Anton 1893- *WWBWI 1*
Locke, Clinton W *ConAu P-2, SmATA 1*
Locke, Clinton W *see* Stratemeyer, Edward L
Locke, Elsie Violet 1912- *Au&Wr 6, ConAu 25R, WrD*
Locke, Lucie 1904- *ConAu 53, SmATA 10*
Locke, Lucie *see* Price, Lucie Locke
Locke, Margo *IlBYP*
Locke, Vance *IlBYP*
Lockley, Ronald Mathias 1903- *Au&Wr 6, ConAu 9R, WW 1974*
Lockwood, Myna *AuBYP*
Loeb, Robert H, Jr. 1917- *ConAu 29*

Loefgren, Ulf 1931- *ConAu 25R, SmATA 3*
Loening, Sarah Larkin 1896- *ConAu 45*
Loening, Sarah Larkin *see* Larkin, Sarah
Loeper, John J 1929- *ConAu 29, SmATA 10*
Loeper, John J *see* Lowe, Jay, Jr.
Loescher, Ann Dull 1942- *ConAu 61*
Loescher, Gil 1945- *ConAu 61*
Loewenstein, Bernice *IIBYP*
Lofting, Hugh 1886-1947 *AmA&B, AnCL,*
  AuBYP, ChPo, ChPo S1, ConICB,
  DcLEnL, DcNAA, EvLB, FamMS,
  IICB 1744, JBA 1934, JBA 1951, LongC,
  Newb 1922, REn, REnAL, St&VC, TelT,
  TwCA, TwCA Sup, WNAA, WWCL
Lofts, Norah 1904- *Au&Wr 6, AuNews 2,*
  ConAu 5R, LongC, SmATA 8, TwCA,
  TwCA Sup, WNAA, WW 1974,
  WWA 38, WWAW 8
Lofts, Norah *see* Curtis, Peter
Logan, Elizabeth D 1914- *ConAu 61*
Logan, John 1923- *AmA&B, ConLC 5,*
  ConP 1970, ConP 1975, CrCAP,
  DrAF 1976, DrAP 1975, OxAm, Pen Am,
  RAdv 1, WorAu, WrD
Logan, Rayford Whittingham 1897- *AmA&B,*
  ConAu 1R, DrAS 6H, WWA 38,
  WWWor 2
Logsdon, Lois Irene *AuBYP*
Logsdon, Richard Henry 1912- *AuBYP,*
  BiDL 5, ConAu 5R, DrLC 1969,
  WWA 38
Logue, Christopher 1926- *Au&Wr 6,*
  ChPo S2, CnMD, ConAu 9R, ConP 1970,
  ConP 1975, ModBL, ModWD, NCHEL,
  WW 1974, WorAu
Loh, Jules 1931- *ConAu 33*
Loisy, Jeanne 1913- *AuBYP*
Loken, Newton Clayton 1919- *ConAu 1R*
Lolli, Giorgio 1905- *ConAu 1R*
Lomas, Derek 1933- *ConAu 29*
Lomas, Peter 1923- *ConAu 21R*
Lomas, Steve *ConAu XR, SmATA 6*
Lomas, Steve *see* Brennan, Joseph Lomas
Lomask, Milton 1909- *AuBYP, BkC 6,*
  ConAu 1R
Lomax, Herbert *WWBWI A*
Lomax, Herbert *see* Maxwell, Herbert
Lomax, John A 1930- *ConAu 61*
Lomax, John Avery 1872?-1948 *AmA&B,*
  BiDSA, ChPo, CnDAL, DcNAA,
  EncFCW 1969, OxAm, REn, REnAL,
  St&VC, TexW, TwCA Sup, WNAA
Lomax, M *WWBWI A*
Lomax, W J *MnBBF*
Lomax, W J *see* Fulke, Commissioner
Lomax, W J *see* Maxwell, Herbert
Lombardi, Vince *CurB 63, CurB 70,*
  NYTBE 1
London, Carolyn 1918- *ConAu 57*
London, Jack 1876-1916 *AmA&B, AmWr,*
  AtlBL, AuBYP, AuNews 2, BiD&SB,
  CarSB, CasWL, Chambr 3, CnDAL,
  ConAmL, CyWA, DcAmA, DcBiA,
  DcLEnL, DcNAA, EncM&D, EncWL,
  FamAYP, JBA 1934, LongC, MnBBF,
  ModAL, ModAL Sup, OxAm, OxCan,
  OxEng, Pen Am, RAdv 1, RCom, REn,
  REnAL, St&VC, TwCA, TwCA Sup,
  TwCW, WEAL, WWBWI A, WWTwL

London, Jane *ConAu XR, SmATA 7*
London, Jane *see* Geis, Darlene Stern
London, Julius 1917- *AmMWS 12P*
Lonergan, Joy 1909- *AuBYP, ConAu 1R,*
  SmATA 10
Lonette, Reisie Dominee 1924- *IIBYP,*
  IICB 1946, IICB 1957
Long, Derek *MnBBF, WWBWI A*
Long, H W Shirley 1905- *MnBBF*
Long, Helen Beecher *ConAu P-2, SmATA 1*
Long, Helen Beecher *see* Stratemeyer, Edward L
Long, John Luther 1861-1927 *AmA&B,*
  BiD&SB, CarSB, CnDAL, DcAmA,
  DcLEnL, DcNAA, ModWD, OxAm,
  REnAL
Long, Judith Elaine 1953- *ConAu 65*
Long, Judith Elaine *see* Long, Judy
Long, Judy *ConAu 65*
Long, Judy *see* Long, Judith Elaine
Long, Nat *WWBWI 1*
Longfellow, Henry Wadsworth 1807-1882 *Alli,*
  Alli Sup, AmA, AmA&B, AmWr, AnCL,
  AtlBL, AuBYP, BbD, BiD&SB, CasWL,
  Chambr 3, ChPo, ChPo S1, ChPo S2,
  CnDAL, CnE&AP, CriT 3, CyAL 2,
  CyWA, DcAmA, DcBiA, DcEnA, DcEnL,
  DcLEnL, DcNAA, DcSpL, EvLB,
  FamAYP, FamPYP, MouLC 4, OxAm,
  OxEng, Pen Am, RAdv 1, RCom, REn,
  REnAL, St&VC, WEAL
Longhurst, Percy William 1874- *MnBBF,*
  WWBWI A
Longhurst, Percy William *see* Agent 55
Longhurst, Percy William *see* Hockley, Lewis
Longhurst, Percy William *see* Kingston, Brian
Longhurst, Percy William *see* Spence, Hubert
Longman, Harold S 1919- *ConAu 25R,*
  SmATA 5
Longmate, Norman Richard 1925- *Au&Wr 6,*
  ConAu 9R, WrD
Longo, Lucas 1919- *ConAu 25R*
Longstreet, Stephen 1907- *AmA&B, BiEnAT,*
  ConAu 9R, ConDr 1, IntMPA 1975,
  REnAL, TwCA Sup, WWA 38,
  WWAA 1973, WWWorJ 1972
Longstreth, Joseph 1920- *AuBYP, IndAu 1917*
Longstreth, Thomas Morris 1886- *ConAu 5R,*
  CurB 50, AmA&B, Au&Wr 6, AuBYP,
  MorJA, OxCan, WWA 38
Longsworth, Polly Ormsby *AuBYP*
Loomis, Frederic Brewster 1873-1937 *AmLY,*
  DcNAA, WNAA
Loomis, J Paul *AuBYP*
Loomis, Robert D *AuBYP, ConAu 17R,*
  SmATA 5
Loon, Hendrik Willem Van *JBA 1934, TwCA,*
  TwCA Sup
Loon, Hendrik Willem Van *see* VanLoon,
  Hendrik Willem
Loots, Barbara Kunz 1946- *ConAu 57*
Lopshire, Robert Martin 1927- *AuBYP, ChPo,*
  ConAu 5R, SmATA 6
Lorayne, Harry 1926- *ConAu 41*
Lord, Beman 1924- *AuBYP, ConAu 33,*
  SmATA 5
Lord, Douglas 1904- *ConAu P-1, SmATA 12,*
  WrD
Lord, John Vernon 1939- *ConAu 53, IIBYP,*
  WrD

Lord, Nancy *ConAu XR, SmATA 2, ThBJA*
Lord, Nancy *see* Titus, Eve
Lord, Walter 1917- *AmA&B, AmSCAP 66,*
ConAu 1R, CurB 72, REnAL, SmATA 3,
WWA 38, WorAu
Loree, Kate 1920- *ConAu 21R*
Lorentowicz, Irena 1910- *IIBYP, IICB 1744,*
IICB 1946
Lorenz, Ellen Jane 1907- *AmSCAP 66,*
WWMus 6
Lorenzini, Carlo 1826-1890 *AnCL, AuBYP,*
CasWL, EuAu, JBA 1934, JBA 1951,
WWCL
Lorenzini, Carlo *see* Collodi, Carlo
Lorenzo, Carol Lee 1939- *ConAu 53*
Lorimer, Lawrence T 1941- *ConAu 57*
Loring, Selden M *AuBYP*
Lorioux, Felix *IICB 1744*
Lorraine, Walter Henry 1929- *ChPo, ChPo S1,*
ChPo S2, IIBYP, IICB 1946, IICB 1957
Loss, Joan 1933- *SmATA 11*
Lossing, Benson John 1813-1891 *Alli, Alli Sup,*
AmA, AmA&B, BbD, BiD&SB, ChPo,
CyAL 2, DcAmA, DcNAA, EarAB,
EarAB Sup
Lot, Parson *DcEnL, OxEng, YABC XR*
Lot, Parson *see* Kingsley, Charles
Lothrop, Harriet Mulford Stone 1844-1924
Alli Sup, AmA, AmA&B, BbD, BiD&SB,
CarSB, ChPo, CnDAL, DcAmA,
DcNAA, OxAm, REnAL
Lothrop, Harriet Mulford Stone *see* Mulford,
Harriet
Lothrop, Harriet Mulford Stone *see* Sidney,
Margaret
Lounsberry, Lionel *MnBBF*
Louria, Donald Bruce 1928- *AmMWS 12P*
Lourie, Dick 1937- *ConAu 33*
Lourie, Helen *ConAu XR, SmATA XR*
Lourie, Helen *see* Storr, Catherine
Love, Adelaide 1889-1973 *ChPo, ChPo S1,*
ChPo S2
Love, Katherine Isabel 1907- *ChPo, SmATA 3*
Love, Sandra 1940- *ConAu 69*
Lovejoy, Bahija Fattuhi 1914- *AuBYP,*
ConAu 5R
Lovel, Vera *MnBBF*
Lovel, Vera *see* Murch, Mrs. N
Lovelace, Delos Wheeler 1894-1967 *AmA&B,*
AuBYP, ConAu 5R, ConAu 25R,
MnnWr, SmATA 7, TwCA, TwCA Sup,
WNAA
Lovelace, Maud Hart 1892- *AmA&B,*
Au&Wr 6, AuBYP, ConAu 5R,
JBA 1951, MnnWr, REnAL, SmATA 2,
TwCA, TwCA Sup, WNAA, WWAW 8
Lover, Samuel *MnBBF*
Lovett, Margaret Rose 1915- *Au&Wr 6,*
ConAu 61, WrD
Low, Alice 1926- *ConAu 61, SmATA 11*
Low, Elizabeth Hammond 1898- *AuBYP,*
ConAu P-2, SmATA 5
Low, Joseph 1911- *AmPB, AuBYP, ChPo,*
ChPo S1, ChPo S2, IICB 1946,
IICB 1957, ThBJA, WWA 38,
WWAA 1973, WWGA
Low, R D *MnBBF*
Lowbury, Edward 1913- *ConAu 29, WrD*
Lowe, A H *MnBBF*

Lowe, Claud D *MnBBF*
Lowe, Claud D *see* Clifford, Martin
Lowe, Claud D *see* Griffiths, Maurice
Lowe, Claud D *see* Hardy, Philip
Lowe, Jay, Jr. *ConAu XR, SmATA XR*
Lowe, Jay, Jr. *see* Loeper, John J
Lowe, T A *MnBBF*
Lowell, Amy 1874-1925 *Alli Sup, AmA&B,*
AmLY, AmWr, AtlBL, CasWL,
Chambr 3, ChPo, ChPo S1, CnDAL,
CnE&AP, ConAmA, ConAmL, DcLEnL,
DcNAA, EvLB, LongC, ModAL, OxAm,
OxEng, Pen Am, RAdv 1, REn, REnAL,
SixAP, St&VC, TwCA, TwCA Sup,
TwCW, WEAL
Lowell, James Russell 1819-1891 *Alli, Alli Sup,*
AmA, AmA&B, AtlBL, BbD, BiD&SB,
CasWL, Chambr 3, ChPo, ChPo S1,
ChPo S2, CnDAL, CnE&AP, CriT 3,
CyAL 2, CyWA, DcAmA, DcEnA,
DcEnA Ap, DcEnL, DcLEnL, DcNAA,
DcSpL, EvLB, MouLC 4, OxAm, OxEng,
Pcn Am, RAdv 1, REn, REnAL,
St&VC, WEAL
Lowenstein, Bernice *ChPo S1*
Lowenstein, Dyno 1914- *ConAu 9R,*
SmATA 6
Lowis, Geoffrey Lyttelton 1896- *Au&Wr 6,*
WrD
Lownsbery, Eloise 1888- *CurB 47, JBA 1951*
Lowrey, Janette Sebring 1892- *AmA&B,*
AuBYP, ChPo, ConAu 13R, TexW
Lowry, Henry Dawson 1869-1906 *ChPo,*
ChPo S1, MnBBF
Lowry, Lois 1937- *ConAu 69*
Lowry, Peter 1953- *ConAu 49, SmATA 7*
Lowther, Fred *MnBBF*
Lowther, George F 1913-1975 *ConAu 57*
Loxley, Raymond *MnBBF*
Loxley, Raymond *see* Murray, C Geoffrey
Lozier, Herbert 1915- *ConAu 49*
Lubell, Cecil 1912- *AuBYP, BkP, ConAu 9R,*
SmATA 6
Lubell, Winifred Milius 1914- *AuBYP, BkP,*
ConAu 49, IICB 1946, IICB 1957,
SmATA 6
Lucas, Edward Verrall 1868-1938 *CarSB,*
Chambr 3, ChPo, ChPo S1, ChPo S2,
DcLEnL, EvLB, LongC, ModBL,
NCHEL, OxEng, Pen Eng, REn, St&VC,
TelT, TwCA, TwCA Sup, TwCW,
WWCL, WWLA
Lucas, Jannette May 1885- *JBA 1951*
Lucas, John 1937- *ConAu 37, WrD*
Lucas, Mary Seymour 1912- *AnCL*
Luce, Celia 1914- *ConAu 61*
Luce, Willard 1914- *ConAu 61*
Luckhardt, Mildred Corell 1898- *ConAu 13R,*
ForWC 1970, SmATA 5
Luckock, Elizabeth 1914- *ConAu 21R*
Ludlum, Mabel Cleland *ConAu XR,*
SmATA 5
Ludlum, Mabel Cleland *see* Widdemer, Mabel
Cleland
Ludlum, Robert 1927- *BiEnAT, ConAu 33*
Ludovici, Laurence J 1910- *ConAu 21R*
Ludwig, Helen *IIBYP*
Lueders, Edward 1923- *ChPo S1, ConAu 13R,*
DrAP 1975

Lufkin, Raymond H 1897- *IIBYP, IICB 1744, IICB 1946*
Luhrmann, Winifred B 1934- *ConAu 61, SmATA 11*
Luis, Earlene W 1929- *ConAu 61, SmATA 11*
Lum, Peter *AnCL, AuBYP, ConAu XR, SmATA 6*
Lum, Peter *see* Crowe, Bettina Lum
Lumberjack *MnBBF*
Lumberjack *see* Lambert, T H
Lumley, Savile *WWBWI 1*
Lumn, Peter *AuBYP*
Lund, Doris Herold 1919- *ChPo S2, ConAu 17R, ForWC 1970, IndAu 1917, SmATA 12*
Lunn, Arnold 1888?-1974 *Au&Wr 6, BkC 4, CatA 1930, ChPo S2, ConAu 49, NYTBS 5, WW 1974, WWWor 2, WWCL, WWLA*
Lunn, Janet 1928- *ConAu 33, OxCan Sup, Prof, SmATA 4*
Lunt, Elizabeth Graves 1922- *ConAu 33*
Lupoff, Richard A 1935- *ConAu 21R*
Lustig, Arnost 1926- *IntWW 38, ModSL 2, TwCW, WWWor 2*
Luther, Martin 1483-1546 *AnCL, BbD, BiD&SB, CasWL, ChPo, ChPo S1, DcEuL, EuAu, EvEuW, NCHEL, OxEng, OxGer, Pen Eur, PoCh, RCom, REn*
Lutyens, Mary 1908- *Au&Wr 6, ConAu 25R, WW 1974, WWWor 2, WrD*
Lutz, Frank Eugene 1879-1943 *CurB 44, DcNAA*
Lutz, John 1939- *ConAu 65*
Lutzker, Edythe 1904- *ConAu 37, DrAS 6H, SmATA 5*
Luxemberg, Claude *MnBBF*
Luzzati, Emanuele 1921- *ConAu 29, IICB 1957, SmATA 7, WWWorJ 1972*
Lyall, Dennis *IIBYP*
Lydon, Michael 1942- *SmATA 11*
Lyford-Pike, Margaret Prudence *WrD*
Lyle, Katie Letcher 1938- *ConAu 49, SmATA 8*
Lyles, Vina Honish 1935- *ConAu 9R*
Lyman, Susan E *AuBYP*
Lynch, John Gilbert Bohun *MnBBF*
Lynch, John Gilbert Bohun *see* Bloomer, Jack
Lynch, Lorenzo 1932- *ConAu 29, SmATA 7*
Lynch, Patricia Nora 1898-1972 *Au&Wr 6, BkC 5, CatA 1952, ConAu P-1, SmATA 6, SmATA 9, WWCL*
Lynch, Patrick B 1927- *ConAu 9R*
Lyndon, Barre *MnBBF, WWBWI A*
Lyndon, Barre *see* Edgar, Alfred
Lynk, Warder *MnBBF*
Lynk, Warder *see* Bowman, Gerald
Lynn, Escott *MnBBF, WWBWI A*
Lynn, Escott *see* Lawrence, Christopher George Holman
Lynn, Mary *ConAu XR, SmATA XR*
Lynn, Mary *see* Brokamp, Marilyn
Lynn, Max *MnBBF*
Lynn, Max *see* Anderson, G J B
Lynn, Patricia *AuBYP, ConAu XR, SmATA XR*
Lynn, Patricia *see* Watts, Mabel Pizzey
Lyon, Elinor 1921- *ConAu 25R, SmATA 6, WrD*

Lyon, Jessica *AuBYP, ConAu XR, OhA&B*
Lyon, Jessica *see* DeLeeuw, Cateau
Lyon, Lyman R *ConAu XR, SmATA XR*
Lyon, Lyman R *see* DeCamp, L Sprague
Lyons, Arthur 1946- *ConAu 29*
Lyons, Dorothy Marawee 1907- *AmA&B, ConAu 1R, ForWC 1970, SmATA 3, WrD*
Lyons, Grant 1941- *ConAu 41*
Lyons, John *MnBBF*
Lyons, Ronald Samuel 1904- *MnBBF*
Lystad, Mary 1928- *SmATA 11*
Lytle, Ruby 1917- *ConAu P-1*
Lyttle, Richard B 1927- *ConAu 33*
Lytton, Baron Edward G E Lytton Bulwer- 1803-1873 *Alli, Alli Sup, BiD&SB, BrAu 19, CasWL, ChPo, ChPo S2, DcEnA, DcEuL, DcLEnL, EvLB, HsB&A, NCHEL, MnBBF, OxEng, Pen Eng, REn, TelT*
Lytton, Jane *WWBWI A*
Lytton, Jane *see* Clarke, Percy A

M

Maas, Julie *ChPo S1, IIBYP*
Maas, Peter 1929- *AmA&B, BiN 1974,*
  WWA 38
Maas, Selve *ConAu 69*
Maas, William Harold *MnBBF*
Mabie, Hamilton Wright 1845?-1916 *Alli Sup,*
  AmA&B, AnCL, BbD, BiD&SB, CarSB,
  ChPo, ChPo S1, ChPo S2, DcAmA,
  DcNAA, OxAm, REnAL, TwCA,
  TwCA Sup
Mac, Uncle, Of BBC *MnBBF*
Mac, Uncle, Of BBC see McCulloch, Derek Ivor
  Breashur
MacAgy, Douglas *AuBYP*
MacArthur, David Wilson 1903- *Au&Wr 6,*
  WW 1974, WrD
MacArthur, Douglas, II 1909- *CurB 54,*
  IntWW 38, WWA 38, WWWor 2
Macaulay, Doctor 1817-1902 *CarSB*
Macaulay, David 1946- *ChLR 3, ConAu 53*
MacBean, Dilla Whittemore 1895- *AuBYP,*
  ConAu 5R, ForWC 1970
MacBeth, George 1932- *ChPo S2,*
  ConAu 25R, ConLC 2, ConLC 5,
  ConP 1970, ConP 1975, ModBL Sup,
  RAdv 1, SmATA 4, WorAu, WrD
MacBride, Maud Gonne 1866- *IICB 1744*
MacClain, George *IIBYP*
MacClintock, Dorcas 1932- *ConAu 57,*
  SmATA 8
MacCloskey, Monro 1902- *ConAu 9R*
MacDonald, Alastair *MnBBF*
MacDonald, Alexander 1878- *MnBBF*
MacDonald, Anson *AuBYP, ConAu XR,*
  SmATA XR
MacDonald, Anson see Heinlein, Robert A
MacDonald, Betty Heskett 1908-1958 *AmA&B,*
  AuBYP, CurB 46, CurB 58, EvLB,
  LongC, REnAL, TwCA Sup, YABC 1
Macdonald, Blackie *ConAu XR, SmATA XR*
Macdonald, Blackie see Emrich, Duncan
MacDonald, Eric *MnBBF*
MacDonald, Eric see Allan, F Carney
MacDonald, George 1824-1905 *Alli, Alli Sup,*
  AuBYP, BbD, BiD&SB, BrAu 19,
  CarSB, CasWL, Chambr 3, ChPo,
  ChPo S1, ChPo S2, DcBiA, DcEnA,
  DcEnA Ap, DcEnL, DcEuL, DcLEnL,
  EvLB, FamSYP, JBA 1934, LongC,
  NCHEL, OxEng, Pen Eng, REn, TelT,
  WEAL, WWCL
MacDonald, George see MacDonald, Greville

MacDonald, Golden *AmPB, AuBYP,*
  JBA 1951, YABC XR
MacDonald, Golden see Brown, Margaret Wise
MacDonald, Greville see MacDonald, George
MacDonald, Greville Matheson 1856- *ChPo,*
  ChPo S1, JBA 1934
MacDonald, James *IIBYP*
Macdonald, Marcia *AmA&B, DcNAA,*
  WNAA, YABC XR
Macdonald, Marcia see Hill, Grace Livingston
Macdonald, R J d1955 *WWBWI I*
MacDonald, Roberta *ChPo*
Macdonald, Shelagh *WrD*
Macdonald, Zillah K 1885- *AuBYP,*
  ConAu P-1, ForWC 1970, SmATA 11
Macdonald, Zillah K see Zillah
MacDonough, Glen 1870-1924 *AmSCAP 66,*
  CarSB
MacDougall, Mary Katherine Slate *ConAu 29,*
  ForWC 1970, WrD
Mace, Jean 1815-1894 *BiD&SB, CarSB*
Mace, Katherine 1921- *AuBYP*
Mace, Wynn *AuBYP*
MacFall, Russell Patterson 1903- *ChPo S2,*
  ConAu P-1, IndAu 1917
Macfarlan, Allan A *AuBYP*
MacFarlane, Iris 1922- *SmATA 11*
MacFarlane, Stephen *WWCL*
MacFarlane, Stephen see Cross, John Keir
MacGibbon, Jean *WrD*
MacGill, Harold 1877-1952 *ArtCS*
MacGregor, A *MnBBF*
MacGregor, Ellen 1906-1954 *AuBYP, CurB 54,*
  MorJA
MacGregor, John *MnBBF*
MacGregor-Hastie, Roy 1929- *AuBYP,*
  ConAu 1R, SmATA 3
Machetanz, Frederick 1908- *AmA&B, IIBYP,*
  IICB 1744, IICB 1946, OhA&B,
  WWAA 1973
Machetanz, Sara Burleson 1918- *ConAu 1R,*
  ForWC 1970
Machlis, Joseph 1906- *Au&Wr 6, ConAu 1R*
Maciel, Judi 1942- *ConAu 33*
Maciel, Judi see Stewart, Judith Anne
MacInnes, Colin 1914-1976 *ConAu 69,*
  ConLC 4, ConNov 1972, ConNov 1976,
  LongC, ModBL, ModBL Sup, Pen Eng,
  RAdv 1, WW 1974, WWWor 2, WorAu
MacInnes, Helen 1907- *ConAu 1R, CurB 67,*
  ForWC 1970, IntWW 38, WWA 38,
  WWAW 8, WWE 14

MacIntosh, Sophiel *MnBBF*
MacIntyre, Elisabeth 1916- *ChPo, ConAu 9R, IICB 1744, IIBYP, IICB 1946, SingR 1*
MacIntyre, H *MnBBF*
MacIvor *MnBBF*
Mack, Jerry *ConAu XR*
Mack, Jerry *see* Johnson, Jerry Mack
Mack, Louise 187- *SingR 2*
Mack, Marjorie *ConAu XR*
Mack, Marjorie *see* Dixon, Marjorie
Mack, Stanley *IIBYP*
Mackay, Constance D'Arcy d1966 *AmA&B, ChPo, JBA 1934, JBA 1951*
MacKay, David *ChPo S1*
MacKay, Donald A *IIBYP*
MacKaye, Percy Wallace 1875-1956 *AmA&B, AnMV 1926, Chambr 3, ChPo, ChPo S1, ChPo S2, CnDAL, CnMD, CnThe, ConAmA, ConAmL, DcLEnL, McGWD, ModAL, ModWD, OxAm, REn, REnAL, REnWD Sup, St&VC, TwCA, TwCA Sup, WNAA*
MacKellar, William 1914- *AuBYP, ConAu 33, SmATA 4*
Macken, Walter 1915-1967 *CnMD, ConAu 25R, ConAu P-1, WorAu*
MacKenna, S J *MnBBF*
Mackenzie, Sir Compton 1883-1972 *Au&Wr 6, CasWL, CatA 1930, Chambr 3, ConAu 37, ConAu P-2, ConNov 1972, DcLEnL, EncWL, EvLB, LongC, ModBL, NCHEL, NYTBE 3, OxEng, Pen Eng, REn, TwCA, TwCA Sup, TwCW, WEAL, WWCL, WWLA, WWTwL*
MacKenzie, Garry 1921- *IIBYP, IICB 1946, IICB 1957*
Mackenzie, Jeanette Brown *AuBYP*
Mackenzie, Kathleen Guy 1907- *Au&Wr 6, ConAu 5R, WrD*
Mackenzie, Willard, Doctor *ConAu XR*
Mackenzie, Willard, Doctor *see* Stratemeyer, Edward L
Mackie, John 1862- *BbD, MnBBF, OxCan, WWBWI A*
Mackinlock, Duncan *ConAu XR*
Mackinlock, Duncan *see* Watts, Peter Christopher
Mackinrodd, Andrew *MnBBF*
MacKinstry, Elizabeth d1956 *ChPo, ChPo S2, ConICB, IICB 1744, MorJA*
Mackler, Bernard 1934- *AmMWS 12S, ConAu 21R, LE 5*
MacKnight, Ninon 1908- *IIBYP, IICB 1946*
MacKnight, Ninon *see* Ninon
Mackworth, John *MnBBF*
Maclaine, Shirley 1934- *WWAW 8*
MacLean, Alistair 1922- *ConAu 57, ConLC 3, IntWW 38, WW 1974, WorAu*
MacLean, Alistair *see* Stuart, Ian
Maclean, Angus *MnBBF*
MacLean, Arthur George *MnBBF, WWBWI A*
MacLean, Arthur George *see* Kirby, Arthur
MacLeod, Alan George *MnBBF*
MacLeod, Beatrice 1910- *AuBYP, ConAu P-1, SmATA 10*
MacLeod, Charlotte 1922- *ConAu 21R*
MacLeod, Ellen Jane 1916- *Au&Wr 6, ConAu 5R, WrD*

MacLeod, Fiona *MnBBF*
MacLeod, Fiona *see* Sharp, William
MacLeod, Walter A *MnBBF*
Macluire, David *MnBBF*
Maclure, David *WWBWI A*
Maclure, K *MnBBF*
MacMahon, Bryan Michael 1909- *Au&Wr 6, CatA 1952, ConAu 41, WrD*
MacManus, Seumas 1869-1960 *AmA&B, AnCL, AuBYP, BkC 5, CatA 1930, ChPo, ChPo S1, ChPo S2, JBA 1934, NCHEL, PoIre, TwCA, TwCA Sup, WNAA*
MacMillan, Annabelle *ConAu XR, SmATA 2*
MacMillan, Annabelle *see* Quick, Annabelle
MacMillan, William 1890- *MnBBF*
MacPeek, Walter G 1902-1973 *ConAu 41, ConAu P-2, SmATA 4, WNAA*
MacPeek, Walter G *see* Jumpp, Hugo
MacPherson, Angus, Captain *ChPo S2, MnBBF*
MacPherson, Angus, Captain *see* Colinski, A J
MacPherson, Barclay *MnBBF*
MacPherson, Margaret L 1908- *AuBYP, BrCA, ConAu 49, SmATA 9*
MacPherson, Thomas George 1915- *AuBYP, ConAu 1R*
MacQuoid, Percy d1925 *CarSB*
Macrae, Hawk *SmATA 8*
Macrae, Hawk *see* Barker, Albert W
MacRae, Herbert *MnBBF, WWBWI A*
MacRae, Herbert *see* Fearn, C Eaton
MacRae, Roy *MnBBF*
MacRae, Roy *see* Buley, Bernard
MacRae, Travis *ConAu XR, SmATA XR*
MacRae, Travis *see* Feables, Anita MacRae
Macrow, Brenda G Barton 1916- *ConAu 9R*
Macumber, Mari *ConAu XR, SmATA 5*
Macumber, Mari *see* Sandoz, Mari
MacVicar, Angus 1908- *Au&Wr 6, ConAu 13R, WrD*
Macy, William Hussey 1826-1891 *Alli Sup, CarSB, DcNAA*
Madden, Daniel Michael 1916- *ConAu 65*
Madden, Don 1927- *ConAu 25R, IIBYP, SmATA 3*
Madden, Mabra 1900- *AnCL*
Madden, Mabra *see* Bryan, Catherine
Maddison, Angela Mary 1923- *Au&Wr 6, ConAu 53, SmATA 10, WrD*
Maddison, Angela Mary *see* Banner, Angela
Madian, Jon 1941- *AuBYP, ConAu 61, SmATA 9*
Madison, Arnold 1937- *ConAu 21R, SmATA 6*
Madison, Steve *IIBYP*
Madison, Winifred *ConAu 37, SmATA 5*
Madlee, Dorothy 1917- *ConAu 17R, ForWC 1970*
Maestro, Betsy 1944- *ConAu 61*
Maestro, Giulio 1942- *ChPo S2, ConAu 57, IIBYP, SmATA 8*
Maeterlinck, Maurice 1862-1949 *AtlBL, BbD, BiD&SB, CasWL, ChPo, CIDMEuL, CnMD, CnThe, CyWA, EncWL, EvEuW, LongC, McGWD, ModRL, ModWD, NCHEL, OxEng, OxFr, Pen Eur, RCom, REn, REnWD, TwCA, TwCA Sup, TwCW, WWLA, WWTwL*

Magagna, Anna Maria *ChPo S1*
Mager, Gus Watso *ArtCS*
Magill, Frank Northen 1907- *AmAu&B,
   ConAu 5R, DrAS 6E, WWA 38,
   WWWor 2*
Magnus, Gerald *MnBBF*
Magnus, Gerald *see* Bowman, Gerald
Magoun, Francis Peabody, Jr. 1895- *AmAu&B,
   WWA 38*
Maguire, Harry *WWBWI 1*
Maher, John E 1925- *AmMWS 12S,
   ConAu 17R*
Maher, Ramona 1934- *ConAu 21R,
   SmATA 13*
Mahon, Julia C 1916- *ConAu 61, SmATA 11*
Mahony, Bertha *AmPB*
Mahony, Elizabeth Winthrop 1948- *ConAu 41,
   SmATA 8*
Mahony, Elizabeth Winthrop *see* Winthrop,
   Elizabeth
Mahy, Margaret 1936- *ChPo S2, ConAu 69*
Maidoff, Ilka List 1935- *ConAu 5R,
   SmATA 6*
Maidoff, Ilka List *see* List, Ilka Katherine
Maik, Henri *ConAu XR, SmATA XR*
Maik, Henri *see* Hecht, Henri Joseph
Mail, Audrey Maureen *WrD*
Mais, Stuart Petre Brodie 1885-1975 *Au&Wr 6,
   DcLEnL, EvLB, LongC, MnBBF,
   NCHEL, TwCA, TwCA Sup, WW 1974,
   WWLA*
Maitland, Antony Jasper 1935- *IlBYP,
   IlCB 1957, WWWor 2*
Maitland, H A *MnBBF*
Maitland, J A *MnBBF*
Maitland, Julia Charlotte *Alli, Alli Sup,
   CarSB*
Maitland, T G Dowling *MnBBF, WWBWI A*
Maitland, T G Dowling *see* Chandos, Herbert
Maitland, T G Dowling *see* Gale, H Winter
Maitland, T G Dowling *see* Hamilton, Cecily
Maitland, T G Dowling *see* Monck, Tristan K
Maizel, Clarice Matthews 1919- *ConAu 9R*
Majima, Setsuko *ChPo S1*
Major, Charles 1856-1913 *AmAu&B, BiD&SB,
   CarSB, DcAmA, DcBiA, DcLEnL,
   DcNAA, IndAu 1816, LongC, OxAm,
   REnAL, St&VC, TwCA*
Major, Dagney *MnBBF*
Major, Dagney *see* Major, J D
Major, Henriette 1933- *OxCan Sup, Prof*
Major, J D *MnBBF*
Major, J D *see* Hayward, Dagney
Major, J D *see* Major, Dagney
Makeba, Miriam 1932- *CurB 65,
   EncFCW 1969, WWE 14*
Makerney, Edna Smith 1921- *ConAu 61*
Maki, John McGilvrey 1909- *AmMWS 12S*
Makin, William James 1894- *MnBBF*
Makower, Addie 1906- *ConAu 65*
Malan, A N *MnBBF, WWBWI A*
Malavie, M J 1920- *ConAu 29*
Malcolm, Charles *MnBBF, WWBWI A*
Malcolm, Charles *see* Hincks, Cyril Malcolm
Malcolm, Margaret *ConAu 49*
Malcolmson, Anne Elizabeth 1910- *AnCL,
   AuBYP, ChPo S2, ConAu XR, MorJA,
   SmATA 1*

Malcolmson, Anne Elizabeth *see* VonStorch,
   Anne B
Malcolmson, David 1899- *ConAu 5R,
   SmATA 6*
Male, David Arthur 1928- *ConAu 57*
Malkus, Alida Wright Sims 1899?- *Au&Wr 6,
   AuBYP, ConAu 5R, OxCan*
Mallan, Lloyd 1914- *ConAu 5R*
Mallett, Anne 1913- *ConAu 49*
Malling, Acton *MnBBF*
Mallinson, Mavis *SingR 1*
Mallinson, R Russell *MnBBF*
Mallinson, R Russell *see* Stannard, Russell
Malloch, Douglas 1877-1938 *AmA&B, ChPo,
   ChPo S1, ChPo S2, DcNAA, St&VC,
   WNAA*
Mallory, Clare *SingR 1*
Malmberg, Carl 1904- *ConAu 33, SmATA 9*
Malmberg, Carl *see* Trent, Timothy
Malo, John W 1911- *ConAu 33, SmATA 4*
Malone, Mary *AuBYP, ConAu 1R*
Maloney, Pat *AuBYP, ConAu XR*
Maloney, Pat *see* Markun, Patricia Maloney
Malory, Sir Thomas d1471? *Alli, AnCL,
   AtlBL, BbD, BiD&SB, BrAu, CarSB,
   CasWL, Chambr 1, CriT 1, CyWA,
   DcEnA, DcEnL, DcEuL, DcLEnL, EvLB,
   MouLC 1, NCHEL, OxEng, Pen Eng,
   RAdv 1, RCom, REn, WEAL*
Malot, Hector Henri 1830-1907 *AuBYP, BbD,
   BiD&SB, DcBiA, EvEuW, OxFr*
Maltby, Peg *SingR 1*
Malvern, Corinne *IlBYP, JBA 1951*
Malvern, Gladys d1962 *AmA&B, AuBYP,
   JBA 1951*
Mammen, Edward William 1907- *AuBYP,
   DrAS 6E*
Manchel, Frank 1935- *ConAu 37, DrAS 6E,
   SmATA 10*
Manchester, Harland 1898- *ConAu 1R*
Mandel, Morris 1911- *ConAu 5R*
Mandel, Oscar 1926- *ConAu 1R, DrAF 1976,
   DrAS 6E, WWA 38*
Mandelkorn, Eugenia Miller 1916- *ConAu 9R*
Mandelkorn, Eugenia Miller *see* Miller, Eugenia
Mandell, Muriel 1921- *ConAu 9R*
Mandino, Og 1923- *WWA 38*
Manfield, Herbert *MnBBF*
Mangione, Jerre 1909- *AmA&B, AmNov,
   ConAu 13R, ConNov 1972, ConNov 1976,
   CurB 43, DrAF 1976, DrAS 6E, REnAL,
   SmATA 6, WWA 38*
Mango, Cyril Alexander 1928- *DrAS 6H,
   WW 1974*
Mangurian, David 1938- *ConAu 57*
Manicas, Peter Theodore 1934- *DrAS 6P*
Maniscalco, Joseph 1926- *ConAu 5R,
   SmATA 10*
Manley, Seon *ChLR 3*
Mann, Arthur 1922- *DrAS 6H, WWA 38*
Mann, Peggy *AmSCAP 66, ConAu 25R,
   SmATA 6, WrD*
Mannering, Melville *MnBBF*
Manners, Alexandra *ConAu 57*
Manners, Alexandra *see* Rundle, Anne
Mannheim, Grete 1909- *ConAu 9R,
   SmATA 10*
Mannin, Ethel 1900- *IntWW 38, WW 1974*
Manning, Jack 1920- *ConAu 69*

Manning, Rosemary 1911- *Au&Wr 6*, *AuBYP*,
  ConAu 1R, *SmATA 10*, *WorAu*, *WrD*
Manning, Rosemary *see* Voyle, Mary
Manning-Foster, Alfred Edge *MnBBF*
Manning-Sanders, Ruth 1895- *ChPo*, *ThBJA*
Manningham, Maurice *MnBBF*
Mansbridge, Norman *WWBWI 1*
Mansfield, Charles E *MnBBF*
Mansfield, George *MnBBF*
Mansfield, H T E *MnBBF*
Mansfield, Harold *MnBBF*, *WWBWI A*
Mansford, Charles J *MnBBF*, *WWBWI A*
Manson, A, Lieutenant *MnBBF*
Manson, A, Lieutenant *see* Pope
Mant, Richard *MnBBF*
Mant, Richard *see* Hearne, George Richard Mant
Mantel, S G *AuBYP*
Mantle, Mickey *BiN 1974*, *CurB 53*,
  NYTBS 5
Mantle, Winifred Langford 1911- *Au&Wr 6*,
  ConAu 13R, *WrD*
Manton, Jo 1919- *AuBYP*, *SmATA 3*
Manton, Jo *see* Gittings, Jo Manton
Manton, Peter *ConAu XR*, *LongC*,
  WWBWI A
Manton, Peter *see* Creasey, John
Manuel, Don Juan 1282-1347? *BiD&SB*,
  DcSpL
Manushkin, Frances 1942- *ConAu 49*,
  SmATA 7
Manville, George *MnBBF*
Manville, George *see* Fenn, George Manville
Mapes, Mary A *ConAu XR*, *SmATA 4*
Mapes, Mary S *see* Ellison, Virginia Howell
Maples, Evelyn Palmer 1919- *ConAu 5R*,
  ForWC 1970, *WrD*
Mara, Barney *ConAu XR*
Mara, Barney *see* Roth, Arthur J
Mara, Jeanette *SmATA XR*
Mara, Jeanette *see* Cebulash, Mel
Mara, Thalia 1911- *Au&Wr 6*, *ForWC 1970*,
  ConAu 9R, *WWAW 8*
Marabella, Madeline *AuBYP*
Marais, Josef 1905- *AmSCAP 66*, *AuBYP*,
  EncFCW 1969, *WWA 38*, *WWWor 2*
Marasmus, Seymour *SmATA XR*
Marasmus, Seymour *see* Rivoli, Mario
Marcatante, John 1930- *ConAu 25R*
Marceau, Marcel 1923- *BiEnAT*, *BiN 1974*,
  CurB 57, *IntWW 38*, *NYTBE 4*,
  WWA 38, *WWWor 2*
Marcelin, Pierre *CasWL*, *TwCA Sup*
Marcelino *ConAu XR*, *SmATA XR*
Marcelino *see* Agnew, Edith J
March, Dicky *MnBBF*
March, John *MnBBF*
March, William 1893-1954 *AmA&B*, *CnDAL*,
  ConAmA, *LongC*, *ModAL*, *OxAm*, *REn*,
  REnAL, *TwCA Sup*
Marchant, Bessie 1862-1941 *WWCL*, *YABC 2*
Marchant, Catherine *ConAu XR*,
  SmATA XR
Marchant, Catherine *see* Cookson, Catherine
Marchant, L S *MnBBF*
Marchant, R A 1933- *ConAu 13R*
Marcher, Marion Walden 1890- *ConAu 1R*,
  SmATA 10
Marcus, Rebecca Brian 1907- *AuBYP*,
  ConAu 5R, *WrD*, *SmATA 9*

Mare, Walter DeLa *Chambr 3*, *JBA 1934*,
  JBA 1951, *TwCA*, *TwCA Sup*
Mare, Walter DeLa *see* DeLaMare, Walter
Margenau, Henry 1901- *AmMWS 12P*,
  ConAu 37, *WWA 38*, *WWWor 2*
Margerison, John S *MnBBF*
Margerison, John S *see* Gray, Gilbert
Margerison, John S *see* Mellalieu, James S
Margolis, Ellen 1934- *ConAu 1R*,
  ForWC 1970
Margolis, Richard J 1929- *ChPo S1*,
  ConAu 29, *SmATA 4*, *WWWorJ 1972*
Mariana *AuBYP*, *IlCB 1946*, *IlCB 1957*,
  ThBJA
Mariana *see* Foster, Marian Curtis
Marino, Dorothy Bronson 1912- *AuBYP*,
  IlCB 1946, *IlCB 1957*
Mariotti, Marcello 1938- *ConAu 29*
Marisa *ConAu XR*
Marisa *see* Nucera, Marisa Lonette
Mark Twain 1835-1910 *AmA&B*, *BiD&SB*,
  CasWL, *CyAL 2*, *DcEnL*, *OxEng*,
  RCom, *St&VC*
Mark Twain *see* Clemens, Samuel Langhorne
Mark, Herman F 1895- *AmMWS 12P*,
  CurB 61, *IntWW 38*, *WWA 38*
Mark, Pauline 1913- *ConAu 17R*
Mark, Pauline *see* Mark, Polly
Mark, Polly *ConAu XR*
Mark, Polly *see* Mark, Pauline
Mark, Steven Joseph 1913- *ConAu 17R*, *LE 5*
Markam, Richard *CarSB*
Markandaya, Kamala 1924- *Au&Wr 6*,
  CasWL, *ConNov 1972*, *ConNov 1976*,
  DcOrL 2, *REn*, *WEAL*, *WWWor 2*,
  WorAu
Markins, W S *ConAu XR*, *SmATA 7*
Markins, W S *see* Jenkins, Marie M
Marko, Katherine D *ConAu 29*, *WrD*
Markoosie 1941- *Prof*
Marks, Edwin S 1926- *WWA 38*
Marks, Geoffrey 1906- *ConAu 33*
Marks, James Macdonald 1921- *ConAu 61*,
  SmATA 13, *WrD*
Marks, Mickey Klar 1914- *AuBYP*,
  SmATA 12, *ConAu 1R*
Marks, Peter *ConAu XR*, *SmATA XR*
Marks, Peter *see* Smith, Robert Kimmel
Marks, Stan 1929- *ConAu 29*, *WrD*
Marks, Stan *see* King, Martin
Markun, Patricia Maloney 1924- *AuBYP*,
  ConAu 5R, *WWA 38*, *WWAW 8*
Markun, Patricia Maloney *see* Forrest, Sybil
Markun, Patricia Maloney *see* Maloney, Pat
Markun, Patricia Maloney *see* Marroquin,
  Patricio
Marland, Bart *MnBBF*
Marlow, Hilary *WWBWI A*
Marlow, Hilary *see* Kirkham, Reginald S
Marlow, Joyce 1929- *ConAu 65*
Marlow, Stephen *MnBBF*
Marlowe, Amy Bell *ConAu P-2*, *SmATA 1*
Marlowe, Amy Bell *see* Stratemeyer, Edward L
Marlowe, Felix *MnBBF*
Marlowe, Francis *MnBBF*
Marlowe, Stephen 1928- *AuBYP*,. *ConAu 13R*
Marlowe, Stephen *see* Lesser, Milton
Marmur, Jacland 1901- *AmA&B*, *AmNov*,
  ConAu 9R, *MnBBF*, *REnAL*, *WNAA*,

WWWorJ 1972
Marne, Silas *MnBBF*
Marokvia, Artur 1909- *IIBYP, IICB 1946, IICB 1957*
Marokvia, Mireille 1918- *AuBYP, ConAu 29, SmATA 5*
Marquis, Don Robert Perry 1878-1937 *AmA&B, AmLY, BiDSA, CnDAL, CnE&AP, ConAmA, ConAmL, DcNAA, LongC, ModAL, OxAm, Pen Am, RAdv 1, REn, REnAL, St&VC, TwCA, TwCA Sup, TwCW, WNAA*
Marquis, M *MnBBF*
Marr, James *MnBBF*
Marr, Ray *MnBBF*
Marran, Ray J *AuBYP*
Marric, J J *ConAu XR, EncM&D, LongC, WWBWI A, WorAu*
Marric, J J *see* Creasey, John
Marriott, Alice Lee 1910- *AmA&B, AnCL, AuBYP, ConAu 57, CurB 50*
Marriott, Buck *MnBBF*
Marriott, Buck *see* Meagher, Miss M
Marriott, Pat 1920- *ChPo S2, IICB 1957*
Marroquin, Patricio *AuBYP, ConAu XR*
Marroquin, Patricio *see* Markun, Patricia Maloney
Marrow, Alfred J 1905- *AmMWS 12S, WWWorJ 1972*
Marryat, Francis Samuel 1826-1855 *CarSB, EarAB Sup*
Marryat, Frederick 1792-1848 *Alli, AtlBL, BbD, BiD&SB, BrAu 19, CarSB, CasWL, Chambr 3, ChPo, CyWA, DcBiA, DcEnA, DcEnL, DcLEnL, EvLB, HsB&A, HsB&A Sup, MnBBF, NCHEL, OxAm, OxCan, OxEng, Pen Eng, RAdv 1, REn, REnAL, TelT, WEAL, WWBWI A, WWCL*
Marryat, Hugh *MnBBF*
Mars, W T *ConAu XR, SmATA 3*
Mars, W T *see* Mars, Witold Tadeusz J
Mars, Witold Tadeusz J 1912?- *ConAu 25R, IIBYP, IICB 1946, IICB 1957, SmATA 3, WWE 14*
Mars, Witold Tadeusz J *see* Mars, W T
Marsh, Corinna *AuBYP, ChPo*
Marsh, Irving T 1907- *ConAu 9R*
Marsh, J E *ConAu XR, SmATA XR*
Marsh, J E *see* Marshall, Evelyn
Marsh, Jean *ConAu XR, SmATA XR*
Marsh, Jean *see* Marshall, Evelyn
Marsh, John *MnBBF*
Marsh, Ngaio Edith 1899- *Au&Wr 6, AuBYP, ConAu 9R, ConNov 1972, ConNov 1976, DcLEnL, EncM&D, EvLB, IntWW 38, LongC, NCHEL, OxEng, REn, TwCA, TwCA Sup, TwCW, WW 1974, WWWor 2*
Marsh, Reginald 1898-1954 *CurB 41, CurB 54, DcCAA 2, IIBYP, IICB 1946*
Marsh, Susan 1914- *ConAu 9R*
Marshak, Ilia Iakovlevich 1895- *AuBYP, JBA 1934, JBA 1951*
Marshak, Ilia Iakovlevich *see* Ilin, M
Marshall, Anthony Dryden 1924- *ConAu 29, WWA 38, WWWor 2*
Marshall, Archibald 1866-1934 *EncM&D, LongC, MnBBF, NCHEL, TwCA*

Marshall, Arthur C d1945 *MnBBF, WWBWI A*
Marshall, Arthur C *see* Brooke, Arthur
Marshall, Arthur C *see* Crane, Berkeley
Marshall, Arthur C *see* Steele, Howard
Marshall, Arthur C *see* Yorke, Carras
Marshall, Catherine 1914- *AuBYP, ConAu 17R, CurB 55, SmATA 2*
Marshall, Constance Kay 1918- *IIBYP, IICB 1946*
Marshall, D *MnBBF*
Marshall, Daniel *IIBYP*
Marshall, Dean 1900- *AuBYP*
Marshall, Douglas *ConAu XR, SmATA 3*
Marshall, Douglas *see* McClintock, Marshall
Marshall, Emma 1832- *Alli Sup, CarSB*
Marshall, Evelyn 1897- *Au&Wr 6, ConAu 5R, SmATA 11*
Marshall, Evelyn *see* Bourne, Lesley
Marshall, Evelyn *see* Marsh, J E
Marshall, Evelyn *see* Marsh, Jean
Marshall, H P *MnBBF*
Marshall, H P *see* Stark, Jonathan
Marshall, James *MnBBF*
Marshall, James 1896- *ConAu 41, WWWorJ 1972*
Marshall, James 1942- *ConAu 41, SmATA 6*
Marshall, James *see* Rister, Claude
Marshall, James Vance *ConAu XR*
Marshall, James Vance *see* Payne, Donald Gordon
Marshall, Jim 1891-1956 *St&VC*
Marshall, Joanne *ConAu 57*
Marshall, Joanne *see* Rundle, Anne
Marshall, John *MnBBF*
Marshall, John *see* Pepper, Frank S
Marshall, S P *MnBBF*
Marshall, Samuel L Atwood 1900- *AmA&B, AuBYP, CurB 53, WWA 38, WorAu*
Mart, Donovan *MnBBF, WWBWI A*
Mart, Donovan *see* Martin, E LeBreton
Martel, Jane G 1926- *ConAu 57*
Martel, Suzanne *Prof*
Martin, A L *MnBBF*
Martin, Alfred 1916- *DrAS 6P, LE 5*
Martin, April *ConAu XR*
Martin, April *see* Sherrill, Dorothy
Martin, Bernard 1905- *ConAu P-1*
Martin, Bernard 1928- *ConAu 53, DrAS 6P, WWA 38, WWWorJ 1972*
Martin, Charles E 1910- *WWA 38, WWAA 1973*
Martin, Charles Morris 1891- *AuBYP*
Martin, David 1915- *Au&Wr 6, WrD*
Martin, David Stone 1913- *IIBYP, IICB 1946, WWGA*
Martin, Dorothy 1921- *ConAu 57*
Martin, E LeBreton 1874-1944? *MnBBF, WWBWI A*
Martin, E LeBreton *see* Lee, Raymond
Martin, E LeBreton *see* Mart, Donovan
Martin, E LeBreton *see* Shaw, Martin
Martin, Ernest 1862- *MnBBF*
Martin, Eugene *ConAu P-2, SmATA 1*
Martin, Eugene *see* Stratemeyer, Edward L
Martin, Frances M 1906- *ConAu 61*
Martin, Frederick *ConAu XR, SmATA 2*
Martin, Frederick *see* Christopher, Matt
Martin, George Madden 1866-1946 *AmA&B,*

BiDSA, CarSB, ChPo S1, DcAmA,
DcNAA, WNAA
Martin, George Whitney 1926- *AmA&B,*
Au&Wr 6, AuBYP
Martin, Harold *MnBBF*
Martin, Harry W *MnBBF*
Martin, J P 1880?-1966 *WWCL*
Martin, James *MnBBF*
Martin, Janet *ConAu XR*
Martin, Janet *see* Garfinkel, Bernard
Martin, Jeremy *ConAu XR, SmATA XR*
Martin, Jeremy *see* Levin, Marcia Obrasky
Martin, John *MnBBF*
Martin, John S *MnBBF*
Martin, Joy 1922- *ConAu 57*
Martin, Joy *see* Crandall, Joy
Martin, Judith *AuBYP*
Martin, Lynne 1923- *ConAu 65*
Martin, Marcia *ConAu XR, SmATA XR*
Martin, Marcia *see* Levin, Marcia Obrasky
Martin, Marjorie *WrD*
Martin, Mary Steichen *AmPB*
Martin, Moyra 1898-1950 *SingR 1*
Martin, Moyra *see* Morell, Musette
Martin, Nancy *ConAu XR, SmATA XR*
Martin, Nancy *see* Salmon, Annie Elizabeth
Martin, P *MnBBF*
Martin, Patricia Miles 1899- *AuBYP,*
ConAu 1R, ForWC 1970, SmATA 1,
WWAW 8, WrD
Martin, Patricia Miles *see* Miles, Miska
Martin, Peter *ConAu XR, SmATA 1*
Martin, Peter *see* Chaundler, Christine
Martin, R D'O *MnBBF*
Martin, Radcliffe *MnBBF*
Martin, Ralph G 1920- *AmA&B, AuBYP,*
ConAu 5R, WWA 38, WWE 14
Martin, Rene *IIBYP*
Martin, Richard *Alli, ConAu XR, LongC,*
WWBWI A
Martin, Richard *see* Creasey, John
Martin, Stefan 1936- *ChPo S1, IIBYP,*
IICB 1957
Martin, Stuart *MnBBF*
Martin, Thomas *MnBBF, WWBWI A*
Martin, Thomas *see* Thomas, Martin
Martin, W *MnBBF*
Martin, W *see* Kingsley, Hamilton
Martin, Wendy 1940- *ConAu 37, DrAS 6E*
Martindale, Cyril Charlie 1879-1963 *BkC 4,*
CarSB, CatA 1930, LongC
Martineau, Harriet 1802-1876 *Alli, Alli Sup,*
BbD, BiD&SB, BrAu 19, CarSB,
CasWL, Chambr 3, ChPo, DcBiA,
DcEnA, DcEnL, DcEuL, DcLEnL, EvLB,
JBA 1934, MnBBF, MouLC 3, NCHEL,
OxAm, OxEng, Pen Eng, REn, TelT,
WEAL, WWBWI A, WWCL, YABC 2
Martinez, John *IIBYP*
Martini, Teri 1930- *AuBYP, ConAu 5R,*
ForWC 1970, SmATA 3, WWAW 8,
WrD
Martyn, Fred *MnBBF*
Martyn, Ivor *MnBBF*
Martyn, Ivor *see* Smith, Bernard
Martyn, Tom *MnBBF*
Marvel, Holt *MnBBF*
Marvel, Holt *see* Maschwitz, Eric
Marviss, Charles *MnBBF*

Marwick, J D *MnBBF*
Marx, Robert F 1934- *AuBYP, ConAu 9R*
Marx, Samuel *IntMPA 1975*
Marx, Wesley 1934- *ConAu 21R, WWA 38*
Marx, William James *MnBBF*
Mary Beth *ConAu XR, SmATA XR*
Mary Beth *see* Miller, Mary Beth
Marzani, Carl 1912- *Au&Wr 6, ConAu 61,*
SmATA 12
Masani, Shakuntala *AuBYP, IICB 1946*
Maschwitz, Eric 1901-1969 *LongC, MnBBF,*
WWLA, WWMus 6
Maschwitz, Eric *see* Marvel, Holt
Masefield, John 1878-1967 *AnCL, AuBYP,*
Br&AmS, CasWL, Chambr 3, ChPo,
ChPo S1, ChPo S2, CnE&AP, CnMD,
CnMWL, ConAu P-2, ConAu 25R,
DcLEnL, EncWL, EvLB, LongC,
McGWD, MnBBF, ModBL, ModBL Sup,
ModWD, NCHEL, OxEng, Pen Eng,
RAdv 1, REn, St&VC, TelT, TwCA,
TwCA Sup, TwCW, WEAL, WWBWI A,
WWCL, WWTwL
Masey, Mary Louise 1932- *ConAu 21R,*
WWAW 8
Masha *ChPo, ChPo S1, ConAu XR*
Masha *see* Stern, Marie
Maskell, Mrs. A E Anderson *Alli Sup, CarSB*
Mason, Alfred Edward Woodley 1865-1948 *BbD,*
BiD&SB, Chambr 3, DcLEnL, EncM&D,
EvLB, LongC, McGWD, ModBL,
NCHEL, OxEng, Pen Eng, REn, TelT,
TwCA, TwCA Sup, TwCW
Mason, Alpheus Thomas 1899- *AmA&B,*
AmMWS 12S, ConAu 1R, REnAL,
WWA 38, WWE 14, WWWor 2
Mason, Bernard Sterling 1896-1953 *AmA&B,*
OhA&B
Mason, Betty 1930- *ConAu 37*
Mason, Bower *MnBBF*
Mason, Douglas Rankine 1918- *Au&Wr 6,*
ConAu 49, WrD
Mason, E *MnBBF*
Mason, Edwin A 1905- *ConAu P-2*
Mason, F VanWyck 1901- *AmA&B, AmNov,*
Au&Wr 6, AuBYP, ConAu 5R, REnAL,
SmATA 3, WWWor 2
Mason, F VanWyck *see* Coffin, Geoffrey
Mason, F VanWyck *see* Mason, Frank W
Mason, F VanWyck *see* Mason, VanWyck
Mason, F VanWyck *see* Weaver, Ward
Mason, Frank W *AuBYP, ConAu XR,*
SmATA 3
Mason, Frank W *see* Mason, F VanWyck
Mason, George Frederick 1904- *AuBYP,*
IICB 1946, IICB 1957
Mason, Herbert Molloy, Jr. 1927- *ConAu 13R*
Mason, Miriam Evangeline 1900-1973 *AmA&B,*
AuBYP, ConAu 1R, IndAu 1917, MorJA,
SmATA 2, WWAW 8
Mason, Olive *SingR 1*
Mason, Philip 1906- *Au&Wr 6, ConAu 9R,*
IntWW 38, WW 1974, WWWor 2, WrD
Mason, Tally *ConAu XR, EncM&D,*
SmATA 5
Mason, Tally *see* Derleth, August
Mason, VanWyck *EncM&D, ConAu XR,*
WWA 38
Mason, VanWyck *see* Mason, F VanWyck

Mason, Zane Allen 1919- *DrAS 6H*
Mass, Nuri *SingR 1*
Massee, May *AmPB*
Masselink, Ben 1919- *ConAu 17R*
Masselman, George 1897- *ConAu 9R*
Massey, Erika 1900- *ConAu 61*
Massey, Erika *see* Zastrow, Erika
Massie, Diane Redfield 1930- *AuBYP, ChPo,*
  ChPo S1, IICB 1957
Masson, Michel 1800-1883 *CarSB*
Masterman, Dodie 1918- *IIBYP, IICB 1946*
Masterman, Rex *MnBBF*
Masteroff, Joe 1919- *AmA&B, BiEnAT,*
  ConDr 1, WWA 38
Masters, Bat *MnBBF*
Masters, Bat *see* Buley, Bernard
Masters, Elaine 1932- *ConAu 57*
Masters, Kelly Ray 1897- *Au&Wr 6,*
  ConAu 1R, CurB 53, AuBYP, SmATA 3
Masters, Kelly Ray *see* Ball, Zachary
Masters, Paul *MnBBF*
Masters, Paul *see* Samways, George Richmond
Masters, William *ConAu XR, SmATA 2*
Masters, William *see* Cousins, Margaret
Masterson, Val *MnBBF*
Masterson, Val *see* Wright, W George
Maston, T B 1897- *ConAu 5R*
Matchette, Katharine E 1941- *ConAu 53*
Mateaux, Clara L *Alli Sup, CarSB, ChPo*
Mates, Rudolf 1881- *IICB 1744*
Mathams, W J *MnBBF*
Mather, Kirtley Fletcher 1888- *ConAu 17R,*
  CurB 51, IntWW 38, REnAL, WNAA,
  WWA 38
Mathes, J C 1931- *ConAu 49*
Matheson, Duncan *MnBBF*
Mathews, Eliza Kirkham d1802 *CarSB*
Mathews, Evelyn Craw 1906- *ConAu P-2*
Mathews, Evelyn Craw *see* Cleaver, Nancy
Mathews, Joanna Hooe 1849-1901 *Alli Sup,*
  CarSB, DcAmA, DcNAA
Mathews, Marcia Mayfield *ConAu 9R,*
  ForWC 1970, WrD
Mathews, Mitford McLeod, Sr. 1891- *AmA&B*
Mathews, Sally *ChPo S1, ChPo S2*
Mathiesen, Egon 1907- *IIBYP, IICB 1946,*
  IICB 1957
Mathis, Sharon Bell 1937- *BlkAW, ChLR 3,*
  ConAu 41, DrAF 1976, DrAP 1975,
  LBAA, SmATA 7, WWA 38, WWAW 8
Matilda, Mackarness 1826-1881 *CarSB*
Matson, Emerson N 1926- *ConAu 45,*
  SmATA 12
Matsui, Tadashi 1926- *ConAu 41, SmATA 8*
Matsuno, Masako *AmPB, AuBYP, BkCL,*
  ConAu XR, SmATA 6, WrD
Matsuno, Masako *see* Kobayashi, Masako
  Matsuno
Matsutani, Mujoko 1925- *ConAu 69*
Mattam, Donald 1909- *ConAu 45*
Matthew, Eunice S *AuBYP*
Matthew, Jack 1911- *IICB 1946*
Matthews, C M 1908- *ConAu 25R*
Matthews, C M *see* Carrington, Molly
Matthews, Clayton 1918- *ConAu 53*
Matthews, Clayton *see* Brisco, Patty
Matthews, Herbert Lionel 1900- *AmA&B,*
  Au&Wr 6, AuBYP, ConAu 1R, CurB 43,
  IntWW 38, REnAL, WWA 38,

WWWor 2
Matthews, Leonard James 1914- *MnBBF*
Matthews, Patricia 1927- *ConAu 69*
Matthews, Patricia *see* Brisco, Pat A
Matthews, Patricia *see* Brisco, Patty
Matthews, William Henry, III 1919-
  AmMWS 12P, ConAu 9R
Matthiesen, Thomas *AuBYP*
Matthiessen, Peter 1927- *AmA&B, Au&Wr 6,*
  ConAu 9R, ConLC 5, ConNov 1972,
  ConNov 1976, DrAF 1976, WWA 38,
  WWWor 2, WorAu, WrD
Matulay, Laszlo 1912- *IIBYP, IICB 1946*
Matulka, Jan 1890- *DcCAA 2, IICB 1744,*
  NYTBE 3
Matus, Greta 1938- *SmATA 12*
Maugham, William Somerset 1874-1965 *AtlBL,*
  BiEnAT, CasWL, Chambr 3, CnMD,
  CnMWL, CnThe, ConAu 5R,
  ConAu 25R, ConLC 1, CyWA, DcBiA,
  DcLEnL, EncM&D, EncWL, EvLB,
  LongC, McGWD, ModBL, ModBL Sup,
  ModWD, NCHEL, OxEng, Pen Eng,
  RAdv 1, REn, REnWD, TwCA,
  TwCA Sup, TwCW, WEAL, WWTwL
Maughan, Joyce Bowen *WrD*
Maule, Hamilton Bee 1915- *AuBYP,*
  ConAu 1R, WWA 38
Maule, Hamilton Bee *see* Maule, Tex
Maule, Tex *ConAu XR*
Maule, Tex *see* Maule, Hamilton Bee
Maupassant, Guy De 1850-1893 *AtlBL,*
  BiD&SB, CIDMEuL, CyWA, DcEuL,
  EuAu, NCHEL, OxEng, OxFr, Pen Eur,
  RCom, REn
Maupassant, Guy De *see* DeMaupassant, Guy
Maureen, Sister Mary 1924- *ConAu 21R*
Maurelly, A R *MnBBF*
Maurer, Werner *IIBYP*
Maurice, Furnley 1881-1942 *DcLEnL, SingR 2,*
  WWLA
Maurice, Furnley *see* Wilmot, Frank
Maurier, Daphne Du *CurB 40, LongC,*
  TwCA, TwCA Sup
Maurier, Daphne Du *see* DuMaurier, Daphne
Maurois, Andre 1885-1967 *AtlBL, AuBYP,*
  CasWL, ChPo S2, CIDMEuL,
  ConAu 25R, ConAu P-2, EncWL,
  EvEuW, LongC, NCHEL, OxEng, OxFr,
  Pen Eur, RAdv 1, REn, TwCA,
  TwCA Sup, TwCW, WWLA, WWTwL
Maurois, Andre *see* Herzog, Emile Salomon
  Wilhelm
Maury, Inez 1909- *ConAu 61*
Maury, Jean West *WNAA*
Mauzey, Merritt 1898- *IIBYP, IICB 1946,*
  WWAA 1973
Maves, Mary Carolyn 1916- *ConAu 49,*
  SmATA 10
Maves, Paul Benjamin 1913- *ConAu 45,*
  DrAS 6P, LE 5, SmATA 10, WWA 38
Mawicke, Tran 1911- *WWAA 1973*
Mawson, Colin Ashley 1908- *AmMWS 12P*
Max, Peter 1937- *BiN 1974, CurB 71,*
  IIBYP, WWA 38, WWAA 1973
Maxey, Betty *IIBYP*
Maxey, Dale 1927- *ChPo S1, IICB 1957*
Maxon, Anne *ConAu XR, SmATA 2*
Maxon, Anne *see* Best, Allena Champlin

Maxon, Rex *ArtCS*
Maxwell, Allan *MnBBF*
Maxwell, Allan *see* Bayfield, William John
Maxwell, Allen *WWBWI A*
Maxwell, Arthur S 1896-1970 *ConAu P-1,
  SmATA 11*
Maxwell, Edith 1923- *ConAu 49, SmATA 7*
Maxwell, Gavin 1914-1969 *AuBYP,
  ConAu 5R, ConAu 25R, LongC,
  NCHEL, TwCW, WorAu*
Maxwell, Gordon *MnBBF, WWBWI A*
Maxwell, Gordon *see* Shute, Walter
Maxwell, Herbert *MnBBF, WWBWI A*
Maxwell, Herbert *see* Lomax, Herbert
Maxwell, Herbert *see* Lomax, W J
Maxwell, Jack *ConAu XR, MnBBF,
  WWBWI A*
Maxwell, Jack *see* McKeag, Ernest L
Maxwell, Thomas D *MnBBF*
Maxwell, William 1908- *AmA&B, AmNov,
  AuBYP, ConNov 1972, ConNov 1976,
  CurB 49, OxAm, REn, TwCA Sup,
  WWA 38, WWWor 2*
May, A H S *MnBBF*
May, Charles Paul 1920- *AuBYP, ConAu 1R,
  SmATA 4*
May, Ernest Richard 1928- *AmA&B,
  ConAu 1R, DrAS 6H, WWA 38,
  WWWor 2*
May, Frederick 1891- *WW 1974*
May, Harold *WWBWI A*
May, Julian 1931- *AuBYP, ConAu 1R,
  SmATA 11*
May, Julian *see* Feilen, John
May, Julian *see* Grant, Matthew G
May, Julian *see* Thorne, Ian
May, Lewis Victor, Jr. 1927- *IICB 1946*
May, Robert L *ChPo, ChPo S2*
May, W J *MnBBF*
Mayall, R Newton 1904- *ConAu P-1*
Mayberry, Florence V Wilson *ConAu 9R,
  SmATA 10*
Maycock, Sidney Arthur *MnBBF*
Mayer, Albert Ignatius, Jr. 1906- *OhA&B*
Mayer, Ann M 1938- *ConAu 57*
Mayer, Jane Rothschild 1903- *AmA&B,
  AmNov X, Au&Wr 6, AuBYP,
  ConAu 9R, CurB 54, ForWC 1970,
  WWA 38, WWAW 8, WWWorJ 1972*
Mayer, Jane Rothschild *see* Jaynes, Clare
Mayer, Jane Rothschild *see* Spiegel, Clara
Mayer, Joseph 1887- *AmMWS 12S,
  WWA 38*
Mayer, Mercer 1943- *IIBYP*
Mayerson, Charlotte Leon *ConAu 13R,
  ForWC 1970*
Mayhew, Henry 1812-1887 *Alli, Alli Sup,
  BiD&SB, BrAu 19, CarSB, ChPo,
  DcEnA, DcEnL, DcLEnL, OxEng,
  Pen Eng, WEAL*
Mayhew, Ralph *CarSB*
Mayland, W W *MnBBF*
Maylor, Phyllis 1933- *ConAu 21R*
Mayne, Arthur *MnBBF*
Mayne, Arthur *see* Batchelor, Richard A C
Mayne, Maurice *MnBBF*
Mayne, Talbot *MnBBF*
Mayne, William 1928- *AnCL, AuBYP,
  ConAu 9R, SenS, SmATA 6, ThBJA,*

WWA 38, WWCL, WWWor 2, WrD
Mayne, William *see* Carter, James
Mayne, William *see* Dynely, James
Maynes, J Oscar, Jr. 1929- *LE 5*
Mayo, Douglas *MnBBF*
Mayo, Edward Leslie 1904- *AnCL, ChPo,
  ConP 1970, ConP 1975, DrAS 6E*
Mayrocker, Friederike 1924- *OxGer*
Mays, Lewis Victor, Jr. 1927- *IIBYP,
  IICB 1957*
Mays, Victor 1927- *ConAu 25R, SmATA 5*
Mays, Willie 1931- *BiN 1974, BlkAW,
  CelR 3, CurB 55, CurB 66, NYTBE 1,
  NYTBE 4, NYTBS 5*
Mazer, Norma Fox 1931- *ConAu 69*
Mazonowicz, Douglas 1920- *ConAu 57*
Mazurkiewicz, Albert J 1926- *ConAu 9R,
  LE 5*
McAleavy, Henry 1912- *ConAu 21R*
McAllister, Mariana Kennedy *AuBYP*
McArdle, Brian *MnBBF*
McBain, Ed *AuBYP, ConAu XR,
  ConNov 1972, ConNov 1976, EncM&D,
  IntWW 38, Pen Am, TwCW, WWWor 2,
  WorAu*
McBain, Ed *see* Hunter, Evan
McBain, William Norseworthy 1918-
  AmMWS 12S
McBride, Mary Margaret 1899-1976 *AmA&B,
  ConAu 69, CurB 41*
McBride, Mary Margaret 1889-1976 *CurB 54*
McBride, Mary Margaret 1899-1976 *WWA 38,
  WWAW 8*
McBurney, Laressa Cox *WNAA*
McCabe, Joseph E 1912- *ConAu 17R, LE 5,
  WWA 38, WWMW 14*
McCabe, Olivia *CarSB*
McCaffery, Janet *IIBYP*
McCaffrey, Anne Inez 1926- *AuNews 2,
  ConAu 25R, SmATA 8, WWA 38,
  WWAW 8*
McCague, James 1909- *ConAu 1R*
McCahill, William Paul 1916- *AuBYP,
  WWA 38, WWS 13, WWWor 2*
McCaig, Robert Jesse 1907- *Au&Wr 6,
  ConAu 1R, WWPNA, WrD*
McCain, Murray David, Jr. 1926- *ChPo S1,
  ConAu 1R, SmATA 7*
McCaleb, Walter Flavius 1873-1967 *AmA&B,
  ConAu P-1, OhA&B, TexW*
McCall, Edith S 1911- *ConAu 5R, LE 5,
  SmATA 6, WrD*
McCall, Virginia Nielsen 1909- *ConAu 1R,
  ForWC 1970, SmATA 13, WWAW 8*
McCall, Virginia Nielsen *see* Nielsen, Virginia
McCallum, Phyllis 1911- *ConAu 53,
  SmATA 10, WrD*
McCann, Gerald 1916- *IIBYP, IICB 1946*
McCarthy, Agnes 1933- *ConAu 17R,
  SmATA 4*
McCarty, Rega Kramer 1904- *ConAu 5R,
  SmATA 10*
McCaslin, Nellie 1914- *ConAu 33, DrAS 6E,
  SmATA 12, WWAW 8*
McCay, Winsor 1869-1934 *ArtCS*
McClary, Jane Stevenson 1919- *ConAu 1R,
  ForWC 1970*
McClary, Jane Stevenson *see* McIlvaine, Jane
McClintock, Buck *MnBBF*

McClintock, Marshall 1906-1967 *AuBYP,*
ConAu P-1, SmATA 3
McClintock, Marshall *see* Duncan, Gregory
McClintock, Marshall *see* Marshall, Douglas
McClintock, Marshall *see* McClintock, Mike
McClintock, Marshall *see* Starret, William
McClintock, Mike *ConAu XR, SmATA 3*
McClintock, Mike *see* McClintock, Marshall
McClintock, Neil *MnBBF*
McClintock, Theodore 1902-1972 *AuBYP,*
ConAu 33
McClinton, Leon 1933- *ConAu 65,*
SmATA 11
McCloskey, Robert 1914-1969 *AmA&B,*
AmPB, AnCL, Au&ICB, AuBYP, BkP,
Cald 1938, ConAu 9R, CurB 42, FamAI,
IlBYP, IICB 1744, IICB 1946, IICB 1957,
JBA 1951, OhA&B, REnAL,
NewbC 1956, SmATA 2, St&VC,
WWA 38, WWAA 1973
McCloskey, Robert *see* Dangerfield, Balfour
McClung, Robert Marshall 1916- *AuBYP,*
AuNews 2, ConAu 13R, IICB 1957,
MorJA, SmATA 2, WrD
McClure, Darrell 1903- *ArtCS*
McClure, Gillian Mary 1930- *WWAW 8,*
WrD
McCluskey, John 1944- *BlkAW*
McColvin, Lionel Roy 1896- *Au&Wr 6,*
AuBYP, WW 1974
McConnell, James Douglas R 1915- *ConAu 9R*
McConnell, James Douglas R *see* Rutherford,
Douglas
McCord, Anne *WrD*
McCord, David 1897- *AmA&B, AnCL,*
BkCL, BkP, OxAm, REnAL, St&VC,
ThBJA, WNAA, WWA 38, WWWor 2
McCord, Jean 1924- *ConAu 49*
McCormack, James *MnBBF*
McCormack, James *see* Patrick, Max
McCormick, Alma Heflin *AuBYP*
McCormick, Arthur David 1860- *IICB 1744*
McCormick, Jack 1929- *ConAu 9R*
McCormick, Jo Mary 1918- *WWAA 1973*
McCormick, Wilfred 1903- *AuBYP,*
ConAu 1R, IndAu 1917, WWA 38
McCoy, Iola Fuller *BiDL 5, ConAu 13R,*
SmATA 3
McCoy, Iola Fuller *see* Fuller, Iola
McCoy, Joseph Jerome 1917- *AuBYP,*
ConAu 13R, SmATA 8
McCracken, Bullet *MnBBF*
McCracken, Glenn 1908- *ConAu 5R*
McCracken, Harold 1894- *AmA&B, AuBYP,*
CurB 49, JBA 1951, WWA 38,
WWAA 1973
McCracken, Mike *MnBBF*
McCracken, Mike *see* Landsborough, G H
McCrea, James 1920- *ConAu 5R, IICB 1957,*
SmATA 3
McCrea, Ruth 1921- *ConAu 5R, IICB 1957,*
SmATA 3
McCuaig, Ronald 1908- *ConP 1970,*
ConP 1975, WrD
McCue, Lillian Bueno 1902- *AuBYP,*
ConAu 1R
McCue, Lillian Bueno *see* DeLaTorre, Lillian
McCullagh, Sheila Kathleen 1920- *Au&Wr 6*
McCullers, Carson 1917-1967 *AmA&B,*

AmNov, AmWr, BiEnAT, CasWL,
CnDAL, CnMD, CnMWL, ConAu 5R,
ConAu 25R, ConLC 1, ConLC 4,
ConNov 1976, CurB 40, CurB 67,
CyWA, EncWL, LongC, McGWD,
ModAL, ModAL Sup, ModWD, OxAm,
Pen Am, RAdv 1, REn, REnAL, TwCA,
TwCA Sup, TwCW, WEAL, WWTwL
McCulley, Johnston 1883-1958 *AmA&B,*
MnBBF, REnAL, WNAA
McCulley, Johnston *see* Strong, Harrington
McCulloch, Derek Ivor Breashur 1897-1967
ChPo S1, MnBBF, WWCL
McCulloch, Derek Ivor Breashur *see* Mac, Uncle,
Of BBC
McCulloch, J H *MnBBF*
McCulloch, J H *see* Rawlings, James R
McCullough, Frances Monson 1938- *ConAu 41,*
ForWC 1970, SmATA 8, WWAW 8
McCully, Emily Arnold 1939- *IlBYP,*
IICB 1957, SmATA 5
McCurdy, Michael 1942- *ConAu 69,*
SmATA 13
McCutcheon, Hugh *MnBBF*
McDaniel, J W *IlBYP*
McDearmon, Kay *ConAu 69*
McDermott, Beverly Brodsky 1941- *ConAu 65,*
SmATA 11
McDermott, Gerald *AuNews 2, IlBYP,*
NewbC 1966
McDole, Carol 1936- *ConAu 21R, SmATA 4*
McDole, Carol *see* Farley, Carol
McDonald, Alex *MnBBF*
McDonald, Barbara Guthrie *AuBYP*
McDonald, F S *MnBBF*
McDonald, Forrest 1927- *ConAu 9R,*
DrAS 6H
McDonald, Gerald D 1905-1970 *BiDL 5, ChPo,*
ConAu P-1, OhA&B, SmATA 3
McDonald, Jill 1927- *ConAu 65, SmATA 13*
McDonald, Lucile Saunders 1898- *AuBYP,*
ConAu 1R, ForWC 1970, SmATA 10,
WWAW 8, WWPNA
McDonald, Mary Reynolds 1888- *ConAu P-1*
McDonald, Ralph J *IlBYP*
McDonald, William Colt *MnBBF*
McDonald, William Craik 1921- *AmMWS 12P*
McDonnell, Lois Eddy 1914- *ConAu 5R,*
SmATA 10, WrD
McDougall, Walt 1858-1938 *ArtCS*
McDowell, Elizabeth Tibbals 1912- *ConAu 5R*
McElderry, Margaret *AmPB*
McElfresh, Adeline 1918- *ConAu 1R*
McElwee, Andrew *MnBBF*
McEntee, Dorothy 1902- *IlBYP, IICB 1946*
McEnvoy, C N *MnBBF*
McEnvoy, C N *see* Strange, Kemble
McFadden, Dorothy Loa 1902- *AuBYP,*
ConAu 17R
McFadyen, Ella *SingR 1*
McFall, Christie 1918- *ConAu 5R,*
SmATA 12
McFarlan, Donald M 1915- *ConAu 65*
McFarland, Kenton D 1920- *ConAu 61,*
SmATA 11
McFarland, Marvin Wilks 1919- *DrAS 6H,*
WWA 38
McFarland, Wilma *AuBYP*
McFarlane, Harold *MnBBF*

McFerran, Ann *ChPo, ChPo S1*
McGavran, Grace Winifred *AuBYP*
McGaw, Jessie Brewer 1913- *ConAu 1R,
  DrAS 6F, ForWC 1970, IlCB 1957,
  SmATA 10, WWAW 8, WWS 13, WrD*
McGee, Barbara J 1943- *ConAu 25R,
  ChPo S1, SmATA 6*
McGee, Dorothy Horton 1913- *AuBYP,
  WWAW 8, WWE 14*
McGiffin, Lee 1908- *ConAu P-1, SmATA 1*
McGillicuddy, Mr. *ConAu XR*
McGillicuddy, Mr. *see* Abisch, Roslyn Kroop
McGinley, Phyllis 1905- *AmA&B, Au&Wr 6,
  AuBYP, BkP, CelR 3, ChPo, ChPo S1,
  ChPo S2, CnE&AP, CnMWL,
  ConAu 9R, ConP 1970, ConP 1975,
  CurB 41, CurB 61, EvLB, IntWW 38,
  JBA 1951, LongC, ModAL, OxAm,
  Pen Am, RAdv 1, REn, REnAL,
  SmATA 2, TwCA Sup, TwCW,
  WWA 38, WWAW 8, WWTwL,
  WWWor 2, WrD*
McGinn, Maureen Ann *ConAu 61*
McGinn, Maureen Ann *see* Sautel, Maureen Ann
McGovern, Ann *AuBYP, BkP, ConAu 49,
  SmATA 8*
McGowen, Thomas 1927- *ConAu 21R,
  SmATA 2*
McGowen, Thomas *see* McGowen, Tom
McGowen, Tom *ConAu XR, SmATA 2*
McGowen, Tom *see* McGowen, Thomas
McGrady, Mike 1933- *ConAu 49, SmATA 6*
McGrath, Edward 1901- *DrAS 6E*
McGrath, Thomas M 1916- *AmA&B,
  ConAu 9R, ConP 1970, ConP 1975,
  DrAP 1975, Pen Am, WWA 38, WrD*
McGraw, Eloise Jarvis 1915- *AmA&B,
  AuBYP, ConAu 5R, CurB 55, MorJA,
  SmATA 1, WWPNA*
McGraw, J H *MnBBF*
McGraw, J H *see* Jackson, Howard
McGraw, James 1913- *ConAu 1R*
McGraw, William Corbin 1916- *AuBYP,
  ConAu 29, MorJA, SmATA 3*
McGraw, William Corbin *see* Corbin, William
McGreal, Elizabeth *ConAu XR*
McGregor, Craig 1933- *Au&Wr 6,
  ConAu 21R, SmATA 8*
McGuffey, William Holmes 1800-1873 *AmA,
  AmA&B, ChPo, ChPo S1, ChPo S2,
  DcLEnL, DcNAA, OhA&B, OxAm,
  Pen Am, REn, REnAL*
McGuire, Edna 1899- *AuBYP, ConAu 5R,
  SmATA 13*
McGuire, Frances *AuBYP*
McGuire, James Dean 1936- *ConAu 21R*
McGurk, Slater *ConAu XR*
McGurk, Slater *see* Roth, Arthur J
McHargue, Georgess 1941- *ChLR 2,
  ConAu 25R, SmATA 4*
McHargue, Georgess *see* Chase, Alice
McHargue, Georgess *see* Usher, Margo Scegge
McIlvaine, Jane *AuBYP, ConAu XR*
McIlvaine, Jane *see* McClary, Jane Stevenson
McIlwraith, Maureen Mollie Hunter 1922-
  *Au&Wr 6, ConAu 29, SmATA 2, ThBJA,
  WrD*
McIlwraith, Maureen Mollie Hunter *see* Hunter,
  Mollie

McIntosh, Clarence Fredric 1922- *DrAS 6H*
McIntosh, Frank 1901- *ConICB, IlCB 1744*
McIntyre, Kevin *IlBYP*
McKay, Don 1932- *ConAu 33*
McKay, Donald 1895- *IlCB 1946*
McKeag, Ernest L 1896- *Au&Wr 6,
  ConAu P-1, MnBBF, WWBWI A*
McKeag, Ernest L *see* Grimshaw, Mark
McKeag, Ernest L *see* Haynes, Pat
McKeag, Ernest L *see* Maxwell, Jack
McKeag, Ernest L *see* McKeay, Eileen
McKeay, Eileen *ConAu XR, WWBWI A*
McKeay, Eileen *see* McKeag, Ernest L
McKee, David 1935- *ConAu 25R, IlBYP*
McKelvey, Gertrude Della *AuBYP*
McKemy, Kay 1924- *ChPo S2, ConAu 29,
  WrD*
McKendry, John Joseph 1933-1975 *ConAu 61,
  WWA 38*
McKenney, Kenneth 1929- *Au&Wr 6,
  ConAu 69*
McKenny, Margaret *AuBYP, WWAW 8*
McKeown, Martha Ferguson 1903- *WWPNA*
McKern, Sharon S 1941- *ConAu 37*
McKibbon, J E *MnBBF*
McKie, Roy *ChPo S1, ChPo S2*
McKillip, Patricia A 1948- *ConAu 49*
McKinnell, James 1933- *ConAu 61*
McKinney, A J *MnBBF*
McKinney, Harris D *ConICB*
McKinney, Roland Joseph 1898- *AuBYP*
McKinnon, Robert Scott 1937- *ConAu 37*
McKown, Robin *Au&Wr 6, AuBYP,
  ConAu 1R, SmATA 6, ThBJA*
McKuen, Rod 1938?- *AmA&B, AmSCAP 66,
  AuNews 1, BiN 1974, CelR 3,
  ConAu 41, ConLC 1, ConLC 3,
  ConP 1970, CurB 70, EncFCW 1969,
  IntWW 38, NYTBE 2, WWA 38,
  WWE 14, WWW 14*
McLachlin, Steve *IlBYP*
McLaren, J A *MnBBF*
McLaren, J A *see* Adams, John
McLaughlin, Charles Bernard 1937- *ConAu 61*
McLean, Allan Campbell 1922- *Au&Wr 6,
  BrCA, ConAu 1R, WrD*
McLean, Donald 1905?- *ConAu 1R, SingR 2*
McLean, Eric W *MnBBF*
McLean, Eric W *see* Rayle, Geoffrey
McLean, Eric W *see* Townsend, Eric W
McLean, Kathryn 1909-1966 *ConAu 25R,
  ConAu P-2, SmATA 9*
McLean, Kathryn *see* Forbes, Kathryn
McLean, Ruari 1917- *ChPo, ChPo S1,
  ConAu 21R*
McLean, Ruari *WW 1974*
McLeish, Kenneth 1940- *ConAu 29, WrD*
McLeod, Emilie Warren 1926- *ConAu 69*
McLeod, Margaret Vail *ConAu XR*
McLeod, Margaret Vail *see* Holloway, Teresa
McLeod, Philip *MnBBF*
McLin, Ruth 1924- *ConAu 61*
McLoughlin, Maurice 1918- *MnBBF,
  WWBWI A*
McLure, R *MnBBF*
McLure, R *see* Knowles, Thomas E
McManus, George 1884-1954 *ArtCS, REnAL*
McManus, Kay 1922- *Au&Wr 6, WrD*
McMeekin, Clark *AmA&B, AmNov, AuBYP,*

ConAu XR, CurB 57, SmATA 3
McMeekin, Clark *see* McMeekin, Isabel
McLennan
McMeekin, Isabel McLennan 1895- *AmNov X,*
AuBYP, ChPo, ConAu 5R, CurB 42,
CurB 57, MorJA, SmATA 3
McMeekin, Isabel McLennan *see* McMeekin,
Clark
McMillan, Priscilla Johnson 1928- *ConAu 41,*
ForWC 1970
McMillen, Neil Raymond 1939- *ConAu 33,*
DrAS 6H
McMillen, Wheeler 1893- *AmA&B, AuBYP,*
ConAu 33, OhA&B, WNAA, WWA 38,
WWS 13
McMullan, Frank 1907- *Au&Wr 6, BiEnAT,*
ConAu 5R
McMullan, James 1934- *IlBYP, IlCB 1957*
McMullen, Catherine *SmATA XR*
McMullen, Catherine *see* Cookson, Catherine
McMurtrey, Martin A 1921- *ConAu 69*
McNair, Kate 1911- *ConAu 17R, IndAu 1917,*
SmATA 3
McNally, E Evalyn Grumbine *AuBYP*
McNally, E Evalyn Grumbine *see* Grumbine, E
Evalyn
McNamee, James Owen 1904- *Au&Wr 6,*
AuBYP, ConAu 5R
McNaught, Harry *IlBYP*
McNeely, Jeannette 1918- *ConAu 41*
McNeely, Marian Hurd 1877-1930 *ChPo,*
DcNAA, JBA 1934, JBA 1951, WNAA
McNeer, May Yonge 1902- *AmA&B, AuBYP,*
BkCL, BkP, ConAu 5R, JBA 1934,
JBA 1951, SmATA 1, St&VC
McNeer, May Yonge *see* Ward, May McNeer
McNeill, Archibald *MnBBF*
McNeill, James 1925- *Prof*
McNeill, Janet 1907- *Au&Wr 6, ConAu 9R,*
SmATA 1
McNeilly, Wilfred Glassford 1921- *ConAu 29,*
MnBBF, WWBWI A
McNeilly, Wilfred G *see* Baker, William Arthur
Howard
McNeilly, Wilfred G *see* Ballinger, William A
McNeilly, Wilfred Glassford *see* Gregg, Martin
McNeilly, Wilfred Glassford *see* Reid, Desmond
McNeilly, Wilfred Glassford *see* Reid, D
McNickle, D'Arcy 1904- *AmMWS 12S,*
ConAu 9R, WWPNA
McNulty, Faith 1918- *ConAu 49, SmATA 12,*
WrD
McPhedran, Marie 1904- *AuBYP,*
CanWW 12
McPherson, James Munro 1936- *ConAu 9R,*
DrAS 6H, WWA 38
McPherson, Jock *MnBBF*
McPherson, Paul *MnBBF*
McQueen, Mildred Hark 1908- *ConAu P-1,*
SmATA 12
McQueen, Mildred Hark *see* Hark, Mildred
McRae, George *MnBBF*
McShean, Gordon 1936- *WWW 14*
McSwigan, Marie 1907-1962 *AuBYP, BkC 6,*
CurB 53, CurB 62, MorJA, WNAA
McVey, Ruth T 1930- *AmMWS 12S*
McWebb, Elizabeth Upham *ChPo, St&VC*
McWhirter, Millie *ForWC 1970*
Mead, Charles *MnBBF*

Mead, Margaret 1901- *AmA&B,*
AmMWS 12S, Au&Wr 6, AuBYP,
AuNews 1, BiN 1974, CelR 3,
ConAu 1R, CurB 40, CurB 51, DcLEnL,
EvLB, ForWC 1970, IntWW 38, LongC,
NYTBE 1, NYTBE 3, OxAm, Pen Am,
REn, REnAL, TwCA, TwCA Sup,
WNAA, WW 1974, WWA 38,
WWAW 8, WWWor 2
Mead, Matt *MnBBF*
Mead, Matt *see* Richards, Ross
Mead, Philip *MnBBF*
Mead, Russell 1935- *ConAu 9R, SmATA 10,*
WrD
Meade, Elizabeth Thomasina *TelT*
Meade, Elizabeth Thomasina *see* Meade, L T
Meade, Ellen 1936- *ConAu 41, SmATA 5*
Meade, L T *TelT*
Meade, L T *see* Meade, Elizabeth Thomasina
Meade, Lillie Thomas 1854-1914 *Alli Sup,*
Chambr 3, ChPo S1, ChPo S2, EncM&D,
WWCL
Meade, Marion 1934- *ConAu 49*
Meade, Ronald *MnBBF*
Meader, Stephen Warren 1892- *AmA&B,*
AuBYP, ConAu 5R, JBA 1934,
JBA 1951, REnAL, SmATA 1,
WWA 38
Meadow, Charles Troub 1929- *AmMWS 12P,*
ConAu 29, WrD
Meadowcroft, Enid LaMonte *AuBYP,*
ConAu XR, CurB 49, REnAL,
SmATA 3
Meadowcroft, Enid LaMonte *see* Wright, Enid
Meadowcroft
Meadows, Wilson *MnBBF*
Meagher, Miss M *MnBBF*
Meagher, Miss M *see* Marriott, Buck
Means, Elliott *IlBYP*
Means, Florence Crannell 1891- *AmA&B,*
AuBYP, BkCL, ConAu 1R, ForWC 1970,
JBA 1934, JBA 1951, SmATA 1,
WNAA, WWA 38, WWAW 8
Mecair, F C *MnBBF*
Medary, Marjorie 1890- *JBA 1951*
Medearis, Mary 1915- *ConAu 69, SmATA 5*
Mee, Arthur Henry 1875-1943 *ChPo, ChPo S1,*
ChPo S2, DcLEnL, EvLB, LongC,
WWCL
Mee, Charles L, Jr. 1938- *BiEnAT, ConAu 45,*
SmATA 8
Mee, Shirley *MnBBF*
Meech, Thomas Cox *WWBWI A*
Meech, Thomas Cox *see* Black, Ladbroke Lionel
Day
Meechan, Joseph *WWBWI A*
Meek, S P 1894- *AmA&B, ConAu 1R,*
WNAA
Meeker, Oden *AuBYP*
Meeks, Esther K MacBain 1921- *AuBYP,*
ConAu 1R, SmATA 1, WrD
Mehdevi, Alexander Sinclair 1947- *ConAu 49,*
SmATA 7
Mehdevi, Anne Sinclair 1922- *AmA&B,*
AuBYP, ConAu 5R, SmATA 8, WorAu
Meier, August 1923- *ConAu 9R, DrAS 6H,*
WWA 38, WWMW 14
Meigs, Cornelia Lynde 1884-1973 *AmA&B,*
AnCL, AuBYP, ChPo, ConAu 9R,

ConAu 45, ForWC 1970, JBA 1934,
JBA 1951, NYTBE 4, Newb 1922,
REnAL, SmATA 6, St&VC
Meigs, Cornelia Lynde *see* Aldon, Adair
Meigs, Elizabeth Bleecker 1923- *AuBYP*
Meigs, Mildred Plew 1894-1944 *BkCL, ChPo,*
ChPo S2
Meilach, Dona Zweigoron 1926- *ConAu 9R,*
ForWC 1970
Meillon, Claire *SingR 1*
Melancon, Claude *OxCan Sup*
Melbo, Irving Robert 1908- *AuBYP,*
ConAu 49, WWA 38, WWWor 2
Melbourne, Ida *WWBWI A*
Melbourne, Ida *see* Phillips, Horace
Melbourne, Ivor *MnBBF*
Melbourne, Ivor *see* Ransome, L E
Melcher, Marguerite Fellows 1879-1969
ConAu 5R, SmATA 10
Melin, Grace Hathaway 1892-1973 *ConAu 45,*
ConAu P-2, SmATA 10
Mellalieu, James S *MnBBF*
Mellalieu, James S *see* Margerison, John S
Mellen, Joan 1941- *DrAS 6E*
Mellersh, Harold Edward Leslie 1897-
Au&Wr 6, ConAu 53, SmATA 10, WrD
Mellin, Jeanne 1929- *AuBYP, ConAu 49*
Mellor, Kathleen *SingR 1*
Mellor, William Bancroft 1906- *ConAu 61*
Melton, David 1934- *ConAu 69*
Meltzer, Milton 1915- *ConAu 13R, DrAS 6H,*
MorBMP, SmATA 1, ThBJA, WWA 38
Melville, Herman 1819-1891 *Alli, Alli Sup,*
AmA, AmA&B, AmWr, AtlBL, BbD,
BiD&SB, CasWL, Chambr 3, Chambr 3,
ChPo, ChPo S2, CnDAL, CnE&AP,
CriT 3, CyAL 2, CyWA, DcAmA,
DcBiA, DcEnA, DcEnL, DcLEnL,
DcNAA, EvLB, MouLC 4, OxAm,
OxEng, Pen Am, RAdv 1, RCom, REn,
REnAL, WEAL
Melvin, A Gordon 1894- *ConAu 9R*
Melzack, Ronald 1929- *AmMWS 12S,*
ConAu 41, OxCan Sup, SmATA 5,
WWA 38, WrD
Memling, Carl 1918-1969 *AuBYP, ConAu 1R,*
SmATA 6
Mendel, Jo *ConAu XR*
Mendel, Jo *see* Bond, Gladys Baker
Mendoza, George 1934- *ThBJA*
Menen, Aubrey 1912- *ConAu 1R,*
ConNov 1972, ConNov 1976, EncWL,
LongC, ModBL, NCHEL, REn,
TwCA Sup, WWA 38, WWWor 2
Meng, Heinz 1924- *SmATA 13*
Menotti, Gian Carlo 1911- *AmSCAP 66,*
BiEnAT, CelR 3, ChPo S2, CurB 47,
IntWW 38, McGWD, NYTBS 5, OxAm,
REn, REnAL, WW 1974, WWA 38,
WWMus 6, WWWor 2
Mercer, Charles 1917- *ConAu 1R, WWA 38,*
WWE 14
Mercer, Diana *SingR 1*
Mercer, Jessie *AuBYP, ConAu 1R*
Mercer, Jessie *see* Shannon, Terry
Meredith, David *MnBBF*
Meredith, David William *AuBYP, ConAu XR,*
SmATA 1
Meredith, David William *see* Miers, Earl Schenck

Meredith, Geoffrey *MnBBF*
Meredith, Hal *EncM&D, MnBBF,*
WWBWI A, WWCL
Meredith, Hal *see* Blyth, Harry
Meredith, Nicolete *AuBYP, ConAu XR*
Meredith, Nicolete *see* Stack, Nicolete Meredith
Meredith, Robert 1923- *ConAu 5R*
Meredith, Tom *MnBBF*
Merida, Carlos 1891- *CurB 60, IlBYP,*
IlCB 1946, WWAA 1973, WWGA
Meriton, Peter *MnBBF, WWBWI A*
Meriton, Peter *see* Hunter, Alfred John
Merivale, J *MnBBF*
Merkling, Erica *IlBYP*
Merland, Oliver *MnBBF, WWBWI A*
Merland, Oliver *see* Collins, Colin
Merland, Oliver *see* Grant, Douglas
Merland, Oliver *see* Pound, Singleton
Mero, Lee *ChPo*
Merriam, Eve 1916- *AmA&B, AuBYP, BkP,*
ChPo, ChPo S1, ChPo S2, ConAu 5R,
DrAP 1975, ForWC 1970, SmATA 3,
ThBJA, WWA 38, WWAW 8, WWE 14
Merrick, Jim *MnBBF*
Merrick, Jim *see* Fearn, C Eaton
Merrill, Dean 1943- *ConAu 61*
Merrill, Jean Fairbanks 1923- *AuBYP,*
ConAu 1R, ForWC 1970, MorBMP,
SmATA 1, ThBJA, WWAW 8,
WWE 14
Merrill, Jean Fairbanks 1923- *WrD*
Merrill, Mary Ann 1930- *WWAW 8*
Merriman, Henry Seton 1862-1903 *BiD&SB,*
CarSB, Chambr 3, DcEnA Ap, DcLEnL,
EvLB, LongC, NCHEL, OxEng
Merriman, Maurice *MnBBF, WWBWI A*
Merriman, Maurice *see* Hook, Samuel Clarke
Merrion, Nick *MnBBF*
Merritt, Muriel 1905- *ConAu 69*
Merriweather, Magnus 1849?-1892? *CarSB,*
DcNAA
Merry, Malcolm James *HsB&A, MnBBF,*
WWBWI A
Merry, Malcolm James *see* Errym, Malcolm J
Merry, Malcolm James *see* Rymer, James
Malcolm
Mersand, Joseph 1907- *AmA&B, ConAu 1R,*
DrAS 6E, WNAA, WWE 14
Mertins, Louis 1885-1973 *AmA&B, ConAu 41,*
St&VC, WNAA
Merton, Alma *MnBBF*
Merwin, Decie 1894- *ChPo, IlBYP,*
IlCB 1946
Mesches, Arnold 1923- *WWAA 1973*
Meserole, Harrison Talbot 1921- *DrAS 6E*
Meshorer, Yaakov *WWWorJ 1972*
Messer, Ronald Keith 1942- *ConAu 57*
Messick, Dale 1906- *ArtCS, CurB 61,*
WWA 38
Metcalf, Suzanne *ThBJA*
Metcalf, Suzanne *see* Baum, L Frank
Metcalfe, Eric *MnBBF*
Metcalfe, Jane M *AuBYP*
Metcalfe, W C *MnBBF*
Metcalfe, W C *see* Lawrence, Christopher George
Holman
Metford, Lionel Seymour *MnBBF*
Methley, A A *MnBBF*
Methley, Noel T *MnBBF*

Methley, Violet M *MnBBF*
Methuen, John *MnBBF, WWBWI A*
Methuen, John *see* Bell, John Keble
Metos, Thomas H 1932- *LE 5*
Metzl, Ervine 1899- *ChPo*
Meyer, Carolyn 1935- *ConAu 49, SmATA 9*
Meyer, Edith Patterson 1895- *AuBYP,*
   ConAu 1R, SmATA 5
Meyer, Franklyn Edward 1932- *AuBYP,*
   ConAu 1R, SmATA 9, WrD
Meyer, Gerard Previn *AuBYP*
Meyer, Howard N 1914- *ConAu 13R,*
   WWWorJ 1972
Meyer, Jean Shepherd 1929- *SmATA 11*
Meyer, Jean Shepherd *see* Berwick, Jean
Meyer, Jerome Sydney 1895-1975 *Au&Wr 6,*
   AuBYP, ConAu 1R, SmATA 3,
   WWWorJ 1972
Meyer, Jerome Sydney *see* Jennings, S M
Meyer, June *BlkAW, ConAu XR, SmATA 4*
Meyer, June *see* Jordan, June Meyer
Meyer, Louis A 1942- *ConAu 37, SmATA 12*
Meyer, Mabel H 1890?-1976 *ConAu 61*
Meyer, Renate 1930- *ConAu 53, SmATA 6*
Meyer, Zoe 1888- *AmA&B*
Meyers, Joan Simpson 1927- *AuBYP,*
   ConAu 17R
Meyers, Robert William 1919- *IlBYP,*
   IlCB 1946, WWAA 1973
Meyers, Susan 1942- *ConAu 21R, WrD*
Meynell, Laurence 1899- *Au&Wr 6, WWCL*
Meynier, Yvonne *AuBYP*
Mezey, Robert 1935- *AmA&B, ConP 1970,*
   ConP 1975, CrCAP, DrAP 1975,
   DrAS 6E, Pen Am
M'Fall, Frances Elizabeth 1862-1943 *CarSB*
Miall, Derwent *MnBBF, WWBWI A*
Michael, John *MnBBF*
Michael, John *see* Sempill, Ernest
Michael, Manfred *ThBJA*
Michael, Manfred *see* Winterfeld, Henry
Michael, Paul *MnBBF*
Michael, Paul *see* Sempill, Ernest
Michaels, Kristin *ConAu XR*
Michaels, Kristin *see* Williams, Jeanne
Michaels, Ruth Gruber *ConAu XR*
Michaels, Ruth Gruber *see* Gruber, Ruth
Michelson, Florence B *ConAu P-2*
Michie, Allan Andrew 1915-1973 *AuBYP,*
   CurB 42, CurB 74, NYTBE 4
Mickey, Paul Albert 1937- *ConAu 49,*
   DrAS 6P
Micklewright, Robert 1923- *ArtsCL*
Micklish, Rita 1931- *ConAu 49, SmATA 12*
Micoleau, Tyler *IlBYP*
Middleton, Desmond *MnBBF*
Middleton, O E 1925- *ConNov 1972,*
   ConNov 1976, WrD
Miers, Earl Schenck 1910-1972 *AmA&B,*
   AuBYP, ChPo S2, ConAu 1R, ConAu 37,
   CurB 49, CurB 67, CurB 73, NYTBE 3,
   REnAL, SmATA 1, ·ThBJA, WWA 38
Miers, Earl Schenck *see* Meredith, David William
Mighels, Philip Verrill 1869-1911 *AmA&B,*
   DcNAA, MnBBF
Mikita, Stan 1940- *CurB 70, WWA 38*
Miklowitz, Gloria D 1927- *ConAu 25R,*
   SmATA 4, WrD
Mikolaycak, Charles 1937- *ConAu 61, IlBYP,*

SmATA 9
Mild, Warren 1922- *ConAu 21R*
Miles, Bebe 1924- *ConAu 61*
Miles, Betty 1928- *AuBYP, ConAu 1R,*
   SmATA 8, WrD
Miles, Cyril 1918- *WWAA 1973*
Miles, M E *MnBBF*
Miles, Mary Lillian 1908- *ConAu 13R*
Miles, Miska *AuBYP, ChPo S2, ConAu XR,*
   SmATA 1
Miles, Miska *see* Martin, Patricia Miles
Miles, Patricia 1930- *ConAu 69*
Miles, Stanley *MnBBF*
Milgram, Gail Gleason 1942- *ConAu 29*
Milgrom, Harry 1912- *AmMWS 12P,*
   ConAu 1R, LE 5
Milhous, Katherine 1894- *AmA&B, Au&ICB,*
   AuBYP, BkP, Cald 1938, ChPo, IlBYP,
   IlCB 1744, IlCB 1946, IlCB 1957,
   JBA 1951, St&VC, WWA 38,
   WWAW 8
Militant *ConAu XR, SmATA 8*
Militant *see* Sandburg, Carl
Mill, Eleanor *IlBYP*
Millar, Ashton *MnBBF*
Millar, Barbara F 1924- *ConAu 25R,*
   SmATA 12, WWAW 8
Millar, Harold Robert 1869-1939? *ChPo,*
   WWBWI I, WWCL
Millar, Jeff 1942- *ConAu 69*
Millard, Alice *WWBWI A*
Millard, Alice *see* Bullivant, Cecil Henry
Millard, C E *ChPo S1*
Millay, Edna St. Vincent 1892-1950 *AmA&B,*
   AmSCAP 66, AmWr, AtlBL, CasWL,
   Chambr 3, ChPo, ChPo S1, ChPo S2,
   CnDAL, CnE&AP, CnMD, CnMWL,
   ConAmA, ConAmL, CyWA, DcLEnL,
   EncWL, EvLB, LongC, McGWD,
   ModAL, ModWD, OxAm, OxEng,
   Pen Am, RAdv 1, REn, REnAL, SixAP,
   St&VC, TwCA, TwCA Sup, TwCW,
   WNAA
Millburn, Cynthia *ConAu XR*
Millburn, Cynthia *see* Brooks, Anne Tedlock
Millender, Dharathula Hood 1920- *IndAu 1917,*
   WWAW 8
Miller, Albert Griffith 1905- *ConAu 1R,*
   SmATA 12
Miller, Alice Patricia McCarthy *Au&Wr 6,*
   ConAu 29, ForWC 1970, WWAW 8,
   WWE 14
Miller, Arthur 1915- *AmA&B, AmNov,*
   AmWr, Au&Wr 6, AuNews 1, BiEnAT,
   BiN 1974, CasWL, CelR 3, CnDAL,
   CnMD, CnMWL, CnThe, ConAu 1R,
   ConDr 1, ConLC 1, ConLC 2, ConLC 6,
   CrCD, CurB 47, CurB 73, CyWA,
   DrAF 1976, EncWL, IntWW 38, LongC,
   McGWD, ModAL, ModAL Sup,
   ModWD, NYTBE 3, OxAm, OxEng,
   Pen Am, RCom, REn, REnAL, REnWD,
   TwCA Sup, TwCW, WEAL, WW 1974,
   WWA 38, WWT 15, WWTwL,
   WWWor 2, WWWorJ 1972, WrD
Miller, Barry 1946- *ConAu 33*
Miller, C N *MnBBF*
Miller, David William 1940- *ConAu 49,*
   DrAS 6H, WWMW 14

Miller, Donald George 1909- *Au&Wr 6,*
AuBYP, ConAu 5R, DrAS 6P
Miller, Doris R *ConAu XR*
Miller, Doris R *see* Mosesson, Gloria R
Miller, Eddie *ConAu XR, SmATA 8*
Miller, Eddie *see* Miller, Edward
Miller, Edna Anita 1920- *AuBYP, IlCB 1957*
Miller, Edward 1905-1974 *ConAu P-2,*
SmATA 8
Miller, Edward *see* Miller, Eddie
Miller, Edwin Haviland 1918- *DrAS 6E*
Miller, Elizabeth Cleveland 1889-1936
JBA 1934, JBA 1951, WNAA
Miller, Elizabeth Kubota 1932- *BiDL 5,*
ConAu 13R
Miller, Ethel Hull 1889- *OhA&B*
Miller, Eugene 1925- *WWA 38, WWMW 14*
Miller, Eugenia *AuBYP, ConAu XR*
Miller, Eugenia *see* Mandelkorn, Eugenia Miller
Miller, Floyd C 1912- *ConAu 1R, IndAu 1917*
Miller, Frank *ArtCS*
Miller, G M *MnBBF*
Miller, Grambs *IlBYP*
Miller, Harriet Mann 1831-1918 *Alli Sup,*
AmA, AmA&B, AmLY, BiD&SB,
CarSB, ChPo, ChPo S1, DcAmA,
DcNAA, OhA&B
Miller, Helen Knapp *AuBYP*
Miller, Helen Knapp *see* Miller, Helen Markley
Miller, Helen Louise *AuBYP*
Miller, Helen Markley 1899- *AmA&B,*
AuBYP, SmATA 5
Miller, Helen Markley *see* Miller, Helen Knapp
Miller, Helen Topping 1884-1960 *AmA&B,*
AmNov, AuBYP, WNAA
Miller, J *MnBBF*
Miller, Jane 1906- *WWAW 8*
Miller, Jay 1928- *ConAu 45*
Miller, Joaquin 1841?-1913 *Alli Sup, AmA,*
AmA&B, BiD&SB, CasWL, Chambr 3,
ChPo, ChPo S1, CnDAL, CriT 3,
CyAL 2, DcAmA, DcEnA Ap, DcEnL,
DcLEnL, DcNAA, EvLB, LongC, OxAm,
OxEng, Pen Am, REn, REnAL, St&VC
Miller, John *ConAu XR, SmATA 3*
Miller, John *see* Samachson, Joseph
Miller, John Chester 1907- *DrAS 6H*
Miller, Katherine *AuBYP*
Miller, Lawrence *MnBBF, WWBWI A*
Miller, Lawrence *see* Alais, Ernest W
Miller, Lisa *AuBYP*
Miller, M Hughes 1913- *WWA 38*
Miller, Margaret J *Au&Wr 6, ConAu XR*
Miller, Margaret J *see* Dale, Margaret J Miller
Miller, Marilyn Jean 1925- *IlCB 1957,*
WWAW 8
Miller, Mark *AuBYP*
Miller, Martha *AuBYP, ConAu XR*
Miller, Martha *see* Ivan, Gustave
Miller, Mary *ConAu XR*
Miller, Mary *see* Northcott, Cecil
Miller, Mary Beth 1942- *ConAu 61,*
SmATA 9
Miller, Mary Beth *see* Mary Beth
Miller, Mary Britton 1883-1975 *AmA&B,*
AmNov X, AuBYP, BkCL, ChPo,
ChPo S1, LongC, St&VC, TwCA Sup
Miller, Mitchell *ChPo S2, IlBYP,*
WWAA 1973

Miller, Shane 1907- *ConAu P-2, IlCB 1957*
Miller, Thomas 1807-1874 *Alli, Alli Sup,*
BiD&SB, BrAu 19, CarSB, Chambr 3,
ChPo, ChPo S1, ChPo S2, DcEnL,
DcLEnL, EvLB, NCHEL
Miller, Warren 1921-1966 *AmA&B,*
ConAu 25R, Pen Am, WorAu
Milligan, Spike *ChPo S1, ChPo S2,*
ConAu XR, WWT 15
Milligan, Spike *see* Milligan, Terence Alan
Milligan, Terence Alan 1918- *Au&Wr 6,*
ConAu 9R, WW 1974
Milligan, Terence Alan *see* Milligan, Spike
Milligan, W H *MnBBF*
Millington, Ernest *MnBBF*
Millington, T S *MnBBF*
Mills, Annette d1955 *WWCL*
Mills, Clifford *MnBBF*
Mills, George *MnBBF, WWBWI A*
Mills, Morris *MnBBF*
Mills, T Flower *MnBBF*
Mills, Yaroslava Surmach *IlCB 1957*
Mills, Yaroslava Surmach *see* Yaroslava
Milman, Constance *CarSB*
Miln, H Chrichton d1957 *MnBBF*
Miln, H Crichton d1957 *WWBWI A*
Miln, H Crichton *see* Crichton, Jack
Miln, H Crichton *see* Harper, Gillis
Milne, Alan Alexander 1882-1956 *AnCL,*
AuBYP, BkCL, CarSB, CasWL,
Chambr 3, ChLR 1, ChPo, ChPo S1,
ChPo S2, CnMD, DcLEnL, EncM&D,
EvLB
Milne, Alan Alexander 1882-1956 *FamMS*
Milne, Alan Alexander 1882-1956 *FamPYP,*
JBA 1934, JBA 1951, LongC, McGWD,
ModBL, ModWD, NCHEL, OxEng,
Pen Eng, RAdv 1, REn, St&VC, TelT,
TwCA, TwCA Sup, TwCW, WWCL,
YABC 1
Milne, Lorus Johnson 1912- *AmA&B,*
AmMWS 12P, Au&Wr 6, AuBYP,
CanWW 12, ConAu 33, SmATA 5,
WWA 38, WrD
Milne, Margery Joan Greene 1915- *AmA&B,*
AmMWS 12P, Au&Wr 6, ConAu 33,
SmATA 5, WWAW 8, WWE 14, WrD
Millotte, Alfred George 1904- *ConAu P-1*
Millotte, Alfred George 1904- *SmATA 11,*
WrD
Milsten, David Randolph 1903- *WWA 38*
Milton, Hilary H 1920- *ConAu 57*
Milton, John 1608-1674 *Alli, AtlBL, BbD,*
BiD&SB, BrAu, CasWL, ChPo,
ChPo S1, ChPo S2, CnE&AP, CnThe,
CrE&SL, CriT 2, CyWA, DcEnA,
DcEnA Ap, DcEnL, DcEuL, DcLEnL,
EvLB, HsB&A, MouLC 1, NCHEL,
OxEng, Pen Eng, PoCh, RAdv 1, RCom,
REn, REnWD, WEAL
Milton, John R 1924- *ConAu 33, DrAF 1976,*
DrAP 1975, DrAS 6E
Milton, Mark *ConAu XR, MnBBF*
Milton, Mark *see* Shepherd, S Rossiter
Mims, Sam 1887- *AuBYP*
Minale, Marcello 1938- *ChPo, IlBYP,*
IlCB 1957
Minarik, Else Holmelund 1920- *AuBYP, BkP,*
ChPo, ChPo S1, ThBJA

Mincieli, Rose Laura 1912- *ConAu 5R*
Miner, Irene Sevrey 1906- *AuBYP, ConAu 5R*
Miner, Lewis S 1909- *ConAu P-1, SmATA 11*
Minier, Nelson *ConAu XR, SmATA 3,*
ThBJA
Minier, Nelson *see* Stoutenberg, Adrien
Minja, Park *IlBYP*
Minshull, Evelyn 1929- *ConAu 37*
Mintonye, Grace *AuBYP, ChPo S1,*
ConAu 25R, SmATA 4
Mirsky, Jeannette 1903- *AmA&B, ConAu P-2,*
SmATA 8, WWA 38, WWAW 8
Mirsky, Reba Paeff 1902-1966 *AuBYP,*
ConAu 1R, SmATA 1
Mishima, Yukio 1925-1970 *Au&Wr 6, CasWL,*
CnMD, ConAu 29, ConLC 2, ConLC 4,
ConLC 6, DcOrL 1, EncWL, ModWD,
NYTBE 1, Pen Cl, RCom, REn,
WWTwL, WorAu
Miskovits, Christine 1939- *ConAu 53,*
SmATA 10
Miss Read *ConAu XR*
Miss Read *see* Saint, Dora Jessie
Mistral, Gabriela 1889-1957 *AtlBL, CasWL,*
CatA 1930, ChPo, CurB 46, CurB 57,
DcSpL, EncWL, Pen Am, REn,
TwCA Sup, TwCW, WWTwL
Mitchell, Allan *MnBBF*
Mitchell, Arthur A 1926- *ConAu 9R*
Mitchell, Barbara Anne 1939- *ConAu 25R,*
WWAW 8
Mitchell, Donald 1925- *Au&Wr 6, ChPo S1,*
ChPo S2, WWMus 6
Mitchell, Donald Grant 1822-1908 *Alli,*
Alli Sup, AmA, AmA&B, BbD,
BiD&SB, CarSB, Chambr 3, CnDAL,
CyAL 2, DcAmA, DcBiA, DcEnL,
DcLEnL, DcNAA, EvLB, OxAm, REn,
REnAL
Mitchell, Elyne Keith 1913- *ConAu 53,*
SingR 1, SmATA 10, WrD
Mitchell, Gladys 1901- *Au&Wr 6, ConAu 9R,*
EncM&D, LongC, WW 1974
Mitchell, Hutton *MnBBF, WWBWI 1*
Mitchell, Isla *AuBYP*
Mitchell, Jerry 1905?-1972 *ConAu 33*
Mitchell, Lucy Sprague 1878- *AmPB, ChPo*
Mitchell, Margaret 1900-1949 *AmA&B,*
CasWL, Chambr 3, CnDAL, CyWA,
DcLEnL, DcNAA, EvLB, LongC,
ModAL, OxAm, Pen Am, REn, REnAL,
TwCA, TwCA Sup, TwCW, WEAL,
WNAA
Mitchell, Minnie Belle Alexander 1863-
IndAu 1816
Mitchell, Ogilvy *MnBBF, WWBWI A*
Mitchell, Randolph *MnBBF*
Mitchell, Yvonne 1925- *Au&Wr 6,*
ConAu 17R, IntMPA 1975, WW 1974,
WWT 15, WrD
Mitchison, Naomi Margaret 1897-1964
Au&Wr 6, CasWL, Chambr 3, ChPo,
ChPo S2, ConNov 1972, ConNov 1976,
DcLEnL, EvLB, IntWW 38, LongC,
ModBL, NCHEL, Pen Eng, REn, TwCA,
TwCA Sup, WW 1974, WWCL, WWLA,
WrD
Mitford, Bertram d1914 *Alli Sup, CasWL,*
DcLEnL, MnBBF

Mitgang, Herbert 1920- *AmA&B, ConAu 9R,*
WWA 38, WWE 14, WWWor 2,
WWWorJ 1972
Mitson, Eileen N 1930- *ConAu 25R, WrD*
Mitsuhashi, Yoko *IlBYP*
Mitsui, Eiichi *IlBYP, IlCB 1957*
Mix, Paul E 1934- *ConAu 45*
Mix, Tom *MnBBF*
Mizner, Elizabeth Howard 1907- *AuBYP,*
ConAu 13R, CurB 51
Mizner, Elizabeth Howard *see* Howard, Elizabeth
Mizumura, Kazue *AmPB, ChPo S2, IlBYP,*
IlCB 1957, ThBJA
Mizzen *MnBBF*
Moat, John 1936- *Au&Wr 6, ConAu 33,*
ConP 1970, ConP 1975, WrD
Moberley, Lucy Gertrude 1860- *MnBBF*
Mochi, Ugo 1889- *WWAA 1973*
Mocniak, George *IlBYP*
Modell, Walter 1907- *AmMWS 12P*
Moderow, Gertrude *St&VC*
Moe, Barbara 1937- *ConAu 69*
Moe, Christian 1929- *ConAu 41*
Moe, Jorgen Engebretsen 1813?-1882 *CasWL,*
DcEuL, EuAu, EvEuW, WWCL
Moe, Louis Maria Niels Peder Halling 1859-
ChPo, ConICB, IlCB 1744
Moeri, Louise 1924- *ConAu 65*
Moeschlin-Hammar, Elsa 1879- *ConICB,*
IlCB 1744
Moffett, Martha 1934- *ConAu 37, SmATA 8*
Mofsie, Louis *IlBYP*
Mohn, Viola Kohl 1914- *SmATA 8*
Mohr, Nicholasa 1935- *ConAu 49, SmATA 8*
Molan, Dorothy Lennon 1911- *ConAu 9R,*
ForWC 1970
Molarsky, Osmond 1909- *ConAu 25R*
Moldafsky, Annie 1930- *ConAu 61*
Mole, Miss M *MnBBF*
Molesworth, Mary Louisa Stewart 1839?-1921
Alli Sup, BbD, BiD&SB, BrAu 19,
CarSB, Chambr 3, ChPo, DcLEnL,
EvLB, FamSYP, JBA 1934, LongC,
NCHEL, TelT, WWCL
Molloy, Anne Stearns Baker 1907- *AuBYP,*
ConAu 13R, ForWC 1970
Molloy, Paul 1920- *ChPo S2, ConAu 1R,*
SmATA 5
Molohan, Brew *MnBBF*
Mommens, Norman 1922- *IlBYP, IlCB 1946*
Monck, Tristan K *MnBBF, WWBWI A*
Monck, Tristan K *see* Hamilton, Cecily
Monck, Tristan K *see* Maitland, T G Dowling
Moncrieff, R Hope *MnBBF*
Moncrieff, R Hope *see* Prole, Ascott Robert
Mondale, Joan Adams 1930- *ConAu 41*
Monjo, Ferdinand N 1924- *ChLR 2*
Monk, Marvin Randolph 1921- *IlBYP,*
IlCB 1946
Monk, Richard *MnBBF*
Monka, Paul 1935- *ConAu 29*
Monro, A *WWBWI 1*
Monro, Harold Edward 1879-1932 *AnCL,*
ChPo, ChPo S1, ChPo S2, DcLEnL,
EvLB, LongC, ModBL, NCHEL, OxEng,
Pen Eng, REn, TwCA, TwCA Sup,
WEAL, WWLA, WWTwL
Monroe, Lyle *AuBYP, ConAu XR,*
SmATA XR

Monroe, Lyle *see* Heinlein, Robert A
Monroe, Lynn Lee 1935- *ConAu 53*
Monsell, Helen Albee 1895- *ConAu P-1*
Monsell, John Robert 1877- *ChPo, ChPo S1, IlCB 1744*
Monteith, Ewen *MnBBF*
Monteith, Ewen *see* Hook, Samuel Clarke
Monteith, Owen *MnBBF*
Monteith, Owen *see* Hook, Samuel Clarke
Montgomerie, Norah Mary 1913- *AuBYP, ChPo, ChPo S1, ChPo S2, IlCB 1946, IlCB 1957*
Montgomery, Elizabeth Rider 1902- *AuBYP, ConAu 1R, CurB 52, ForWC 1970, SmATA 3, WWAW 8, WWPNA*
Montgomery, John 1916- *Au&Wr 6*
Montgomery, John 1919- *ConAu 25R*
Montgomery, Lucy Maud 1874-1942 *CanWr, CarSB, CasWL, Chambr 3, ChPo, ChPo S1, ChPo S2, DcLEnL, DcNAA, EvLB, JBA 1934, LongC, OxAm, OxCan, REn, REnAL, TwCA, TwCW, WNAA, YABC 1*
Montgomery, Rutherford George 1894- *AmA&B, AuBYP, ConAu 9R, MorJA, WNAA, SmATA 3, WWA 38, WrD*
Montgomery, Rutherford George *see* Avery, Al
Montgomery, Rutherford George *see* Proctor, Everitt
Montgomery, Walter *Alli Sup, CarSB*
Montresor, Beni 1926- *AuBYP, BkP, ChPo, ConAu 29, CurB 67, IlBYP, IlCB 1957, NewbC 1956, SmATA 3, ThBJA, WWWor 2*
Montross, Lynn 1895-1961 *AmA&B, WNAA*
Monvel, Maurice Boutet De *AmPB*
Monvel, Maurice Boutet De *see* Boutet DeMonvel, Maurice
Monypenny, Kathleen *SingR 1*
Moody, Anne 1940- *ConAu 65, LBAA*
Moody, Ralph Owen 1898- *AuBYP, ConAu P-1, CurB 55, SmATA 1, WWA 38*
Moon, Carl 1879-1948 *AmA&B, AuBYP, ConICB, DcNAA, IlCB 1744, JBA 1934, JBA 1951, OhA&B, WNAA*
Moon, George P *MnBBF*
Moon, George P *see* Pembury, Montague
Moon, Grace Purdie 1877-1947 *AmA&B, AuBYP, ChPo, DcNAA, IndAu 1917, JBA 1934, JBA 1951, WNAA*
Moon, Sheila 1910- *ConAu 25R, SmATA 5*
Mooney, Elizabeth C 1918- *ConAu 61*
Moor, J Marston *MnBBF*
Moorcock, Michael 1939- *ConAu 45, ConLC 5, MnBBF*
Moore, Amos *MnBBF*
Moore, Anne Carroll 1871-1961 *AmA&B, AmPB, AuBYP, ChPo, ChPo S2, JBA 1934, JBA 1951, REnAL, SmATA 13, WNAA*
Moore, Barbara 1934- *ConAu 53, WWAW 8*
Moore, Carman Leroy 1936- *ConAu 61, LBAA*
Moore, Clement Clarke 1779-1863 *Alli, AmA, AmA&B, AnCL, BiD&SB, BkCL, CarSB, ChPo, ChPo S1, ChPo S2, CnDAL, CyAL 1, DcAmA, DcLEnL, DcNAA, EvLB, FamPYP, OxAm, REn,*

REnAL, St&VC
Moore, Clyde B 1886- *ConAu 1R, WNAA, WWA 38*
Moore, David William 1895-1954 *AuBYP, OhA&B*
Moore, Eva 1942- *ConAu 45*
Moore, Fenworth *ConAu P-2*
Moore, Fenworth *see* Stratemeyer, Edward L
Moore, Frank Gardner 1865- *WNAA*
Moore, Hilda F *MnBBF*
Moore, Janet Gaylord *IlBYP*
Moore, Jessie Eleanor 1886- *ConAu P-1*
Moore, John Alexander 1915- *AmMWS 12P, ConAu 45, IntWW 38, WWA 38*
Moore, John N 1920- *AmMWS 12P*
Moore, John Travers 1908- *ChPo, ChPo S1, ConAu 5R, SmATA 12, WWA 38*
Moore, L P *MnBBF*
Moore, Lamont 1909- *AuBYP*
Moore, Lilian *AuBYP, BkP*
Moore, Margaret Rumberger 1903- *ConAu 9R, SmATA 12, WWAW 8*
Moore, Marianne Craig 1887-1972 *AmA&B, AmWr, AnCL, AnMV 1926, CasWL, ChPo S2, CnDAL, CnE&AP, CnMWL, ConAmA, ConAmL, ConAu 33, ConLC 1, ConLC 2, ConLC 4, ConP 1970, DcLEnL, EncWL, EvLB, ForWC 1970, LongC, ModAL, ModAL Sup, OxAm, OxEng, Pen Am, RAdv 1, REn, REnAL, SixAP, SixAP, TwCA, TwCA Sup, TwCW, WEAL, WWTwL*
Moore, Marie Drury 1926- *ConAu 33*
Moore, Mona 1917- *ArtsCL*
Moore, Nancy *AuBYP*
Moore, Patrick Alfred 1923- *Au&Wr 6, AuBYP, ConAu 13R, WW 1974, WrD*
Moore, Regina *ConAu XR, SmATA XR*
Moore, Regina *see* Dunne, Mary Collins
Moore, Robert L, Jr., 1925- *ConAu 13R*
Moore, Robert L., Jr. *see* Moore, Robin
Moore, Robin *ArtCS, AuNews 1, BiN 1974, CelR 3, ConAu XR*
Moore, Robin *see* Moore, Robert L, Jr.
Moore, Rosalie *ChPo, ChPo S2, ConAu XR, DrAP 1975, SmATA XR, WrD*
Moore, Rosalie *see* Brown, Rosalie Moore
Moore, Roy Benjamin 1908- *LE 5*
Moore, Ruth 1908- *AmA&B, Au&Wr 6, ConAu 1R, CurB 54, WWA 38, WWAW 8*
Moore, Tony *MnBBF*
Moore, Tony *see* Morris, Tony
Moore, Vardine Russell 1906- *AuBYP, ConAu 41, IndAu 1917*
Moore, Virginia Dryden 1911- *ConAu 17R*
Moore, Wilfred George 1907- *Au&Wr 6, ConAu 9R*
Moorehead, Alan 1910- *Au&Wr 6, ConAu 5R, IntWW 38, LongC, NCHEL, REn, TwCA Sup, WWWor 2*
Moores, Dick 1909- *ArtCS*
Moos, Malcolm 1916- *IntWW 38*
Moran, Connie *IlBYP*
Moran, Eugene Francis 1872- *AuBYP*
Moran, James Sterling 1909- *ConAu 9R*
Moran, James Sterling *see* Moran, Jim
Moran, Jim *ConAu XR*

Moran, Jim see Moran, James Sterling
Moray, Dugald MnBBF, WWBWI A
Moray, Dugald see Cumming-Skinner, Dugald
    Matheson
Moray Williams, Ursula WrD
Mordaunt, Wilton MnBBF
Mordaunt, Wilton see Gill
Mordvinoff, Nicolas 1911-1973 AmPB, AuBYP,
    Cald 1938, ChFB 1, ConAu 41, IIBYP,
    IICB 1744, IICB 1946, IICB 1957,
    MorJA, WWAA 1973, WWE 14
Mordvinoff, Nicolas see Nicolas
More, Caroline AuBYP, ConAu XR,
    SmATA 1, ThBJA
More, Caroline see Cone, Molly Lamken
More, Caroline see Strachan, Margaret Pitcairn
More, George Alli
More, Hannah 1745-1833 Alli, AtlBL, BbD,
    BiD&SB, BiDLA, BrAu 19, CarSB,
    CasWL, Chambr 2, ChPo, ChPo S1,
    ChPo S2, DcBiA, DcEnA, DcEnL,
    DcEuL, DcLEnL, EvLB, NCHEL,
    OxEng, Pcn Eng, REn, WEAL
Morehead, Albert Hodges 1909-1966 AmA&B,
    AmSCAP 66, ConAu P-1
Morel MnBBF
Morell, Musette SingR 1
Morell, Musette see Martin, Moyra
Moremen, Grace E 1930- ConAu 45
Moreno, Martin ConAu XR
Moreno, Martin see Swartz, Harry
Morenus, Richard 1897- AuBYP
Moreton, John Alli, ConAu XR
Moreton, John see Cohen, Morton N
Morey, Charles ConAu XR, SmATA XR
Morey, Charles see Fletcher, Helen Jill
Morey, Walt 1907- Au&Wr 6, AuBYP,
    ConAu 29, SmATA 3, ThBJA
Morgan, Alfred Powell 1889- AuBYP, MorJA,
    WNAA
Morgan, Alison Mary 1930- ConAu 49, WrD
Morgan, Ava IIBYP
Morgan, Bryan Stanford 1923- Au&Wr 6,
    ConAu 5R, WrD
Morgan, Edmund Sears 1916-1966 AmA&B,
    Au&Wr 6, ConAu 9R, DrAS 6H,
    WWA 38
Morgan, F L MnBBF
Morgan, Geoffrey 1916- ConAu 21R, MnBBF
Morgan, Helen 1921- ConAu 57, WrD
Morgan, Sir Henry 1635?-1688 REn
Morgan, Henry 1825-1884 Alli Sup, CarSB,
    DcAmA, DcNAA
Morgan, James 1861-1955 Alli, Alli Sup,
    AmA&B, WNAA
Morgan, Lenore H 1908- ConAu P-2,
    SmATA 8, WrD
Morgan, Lionel WWBWI 1
Morgan, Paul 1928- ConAu 61
Morgan, Roy 1928- IIBYP, IICB 1946
Morgan, Sharon A 1951- ConAu 61
Morgan, Sharon A see Fufuka, Karama
Morgan, Shirley 1933- ConAu 37, SmATA 10
Morgan, Violet 1898- OhA&B
Morgenstern, Christian 1871-1914 CasWL,
    ChPo, ChPo S1, ChPo S2, ClDMEuL,
    CnMWL, EncWL, EuAu, EvEuW,
    ModGL, OxGer, Pen Eur, REn,
    WWTwL

Moriarty, Tim 1923- ConAu 61
Morin, Claude OxCan Sup
Morion, John MnBBF
Morison, Samuel Eliot 1887- AmA&B,
    Au&Wr 6, AuBYP, CelR 3, ConAu 1R,
    CurB 51, CurB 62, DcLEnL, DrAS 6H,
    IntWW 38, LongC, NYTBE 2, OxAm,
    OxCan Sup, Pen Am, REn, REnAL,
    TwCA Sup, WW 1974, WWA 38,
    WWWor 2
Morland, Bart MnBBF
Morland, Bart see Burrage, Edwin Harcourt
Morland, Nigel 1905- Au&Wr 6, ChPo S1,
    EncM&D, MnBBF
Morley, C MnBBF
Morley, Christopher Darlington 1890-1957
    AmA&B, AmNov, CarSB, CasWL, ChPo,
    ChPo S1, ChPo S2, CnDAL, ConAmA,
    ConAmL, DcLEnL, EvLB, LongC,
    ModAL, OxAm, OxEng, Pen Am, REn,
    REnAL, St&VC, TwCA, TwCA Sup,
    WNAA
Mornington, John MnBBF
Morrah, Dave ConAu XR, SmATA XR
Morrah, Dave see Morrah, David Wardlaw, Jr.
Morrah, David Wardlaw, Jr. 1914- ConAu 1R,
    SmATA 10
Morrah, David Wardlaw, Jr. see Morrah, Dave
Morrell, Dennis MnBBF
Morrell, Wallace MnBBF, WWBWI A
Morrell, Wallace see Garrish, Harold J
Morressy, John 1930- ConAu 21R,
    DrAF 1976, WrD
Morrill, Leslie IIBYP
Morris, David MnBBF
Morris, Desmond 1928- Au&Wr 6, CelR 3,
    ConAu 45, CurB 74, WWA 38,
    WWWor 2
Morris, Edita 1903- AmA&B, AmNov,
    Au&Wr 6, ConAu 1R
Morris, Henry MnBBF
Morris, John V ChPo
Morris, Loverne Lawton 1896- ConAu 5R
Morris, Mary 1913- ConAu 53
Morris, Patrick 1789-1849 BbthC, MnBBF,
    OxCan
Morris, Patrick 1868?- WWBWI A
Morris, Patrick see Mountmorres, Viscount
Morris, Richard Brandon 1904- AmA&B,
    AuBYP, ConAu 49, DrAS 6H, WWA 38
Morris, Robert Ada 1933- ConAu 49,
    SmATA 7
Morris, Ruth ConAu XR
Morris, Ruth see Webb, Ruth Enid Borlase
    Morris
Morris, Stanley MnBBF, WWBWI A
Morris, Tony MnBBF
Morris, Tony see Moore, Tony
Morris, William 1834-1896 Alli Sup, AtlBL,
    BbD, BiD&SB, BrAu 19, CasWL, ChPo,
    ChPo S1, ChPo S2, CnE&AP, CriT 3,
    DcBiA, DcEnA, DcEnA Ap, DcEnL,
    DcEuL, EvLB, MouLC 4, NCHEL,
    OxEng, Pen Eng, RAdv 1, RCom, REn,
    St&VC, WEAL
Morris, William 1913- AmA&B, ConAu 17R,
    WWA 38
Morris, William H MnBBF
Morris, Willie 1934- AuNews 2, CelR 3,

ConAu 17R, DrAF 1976, IntWW 38,
WWA 38, WWE 14, WWWor 2
Morrison, Dorothy Nafus *ConAu 61*
Morrison, Frank M 1914- *ConAu 37*
Morrison, Gert W *ConAu XR*
Morrison, Gert W *see* Stratemeyer, Edward L
Morrison, Lillian 1917- *AnCL, BiDL 5, BkP,*
ChPo, ChPo S1, ChPo S2, ConAu 9R,
DrAP 1975, SmATA 3
Morrison, Lucile 1896- *WNAA*
Morrison, Sean *ChPo S1*
Morrison, Theodore 1901- *AmA&B,*
ConAu 1R, DrAS 6E, OxAm, REnAL,
TwCA Sup, WWA 38
Morrison, Velma Ford 1909- *ConAu 9R*
Morrison, Velma Ford *see* Ford, Hildegarde
Morrison, Wilbur H *WrD*
Morrison, William *ConAu XR, SmATA 3,*
SmATA 3
Morrison, William *see* Samachson, Joseph
Morriss, Frank 1923- *ConAu 5R, WrD*
Morriss, James E 1932- *ConAu 57, SmATA 8*
Morrow, Albert 1863- *WWBWI 1*
Morrow, Barbara *IIBYP*
Morrow, Betty *ConAu XR, SmATA 3*
Morrow, Betty *see* Bacon, Elizabeth
Morrow, Elizabeth Reeve Cutter 1873-1955
AmA&B, AmPB, ChPo, OhA&B, REnAL,
St&VC
Morrow, George 1869- *ChPo, ChPo S1,*
ConICB, WWBWI 1
Morrow, Suzanne Stark *AuBYP*
Morse, Anne Christensen 1915- *ConAu 1R*
Morse, Anne Christensen *see* Head, Ann
Morse, Carol *ConAu XR, CurB 57*
Morse, Carol *see* Yeakley, Marjory Hall
Morse, David 1940- *ConAu 37*
Morse, Dorothy Bayley 1906- *IIBYP,*
IICB 1946
Mortimer, Derek *WrD*
Mortimer, Favell Lee 1802-1878 *Alli Sup,*
CarSB, ChPo, ChPo S1, ChPo S2
Morton, Anthony *ConAu XR, EncM&D,*
LongC, WWBWI A, WorAu
Morton, Anthony *see* Creasey, John
Morton, Brenda *WrD*
Morton, David 1886-1957 *AmA&B,*
AnMV 1926, ChPo, ChPo S1, REn,
REnAL, St&VC, WNAA
Morton, Marian *IIBYP*
Morton, Miriam 1918- *ChPo, ChPo S1,*
ChPo S2, ConAu 49, SmATA 9
Morton, N Douglas *MnBBF*
Morton, Paul *MnBBF*
Morton-Sale, Isobel 1904- *IIBYP, IICB 1744,*
IICB 1946, WWCL
Morton-Sale, Isobel *see* Sale, Isobel Morton
Morton-Sale, John 1901- *IIBYP, IICB 1744,*
IICB 1946, WWCL
Morton-Sale, John *see* Sale, John Morton
Moscati, Sabatino 1922- *Au&Wr 6*
Moscow, Alvin 1925- *AmA&B, AuBYP,*
ConAu 1R, SmATA 3
Moscow, Warren 1908- *ConAu 21R,*
WWE 14, WWWorJ 1972
Mosel, Arlene Tichy 1921- *AuBYP, ConAu 49,*
SmATA 7
Moseley, Elizabeth Robards *ForWC 1970*
Moses, Anna Mary 1860-1961 *AuBYP, ChPo,*

CurB 49, CurB 62, REn
Mosesson, Gloria R 1924- *ConAu 41,*
ForWC 1970, WWWorJ 1972
Mosesson, Gloria R *see* French, Kathryn
Mosesson, Gloria R *see* Miller, Doris R
Moskof, Martin Stephen 1930- *ConAu 29*
Mosley, Zack 1906- *ArtCS*
Moss, Don 1920- *SmATA 11*
Moss, Franklin 1909- *SingR 2*
Moss, Nancy *ConAu XR*
Moss, Nancy *see* Moss, Robert
Moss, Peter 1921- *Au&Wr 6, ConAu 49,*
WrD
Moss, R A *MnBBF*
Moss, Robert 1903- *Au&Wr 6, ConAu P-1*
Moss, Robert *see* Moss, Nancy
Moss, Robert *see* Moss, Roberta
Moss, Roberta *ConAu XR*
Moss, Roberta *see* Moss, Robert
Mossiker, Frances 1906- *ConAu 9R*
Mother Goose *ChP, FamPYP*
Mott, Michael 1930- *ConAu 5R*
Motz, Lloyd 1909?- *ConAu 9R, WWA 38,*
WWWorJ 1972
Moulton, Louise Chandler 1835-1908 *BiD&SB,*
CarSB, Chambr 3, ChPo, ChPo S1,
CyAL 2, OxAm, REnAL
Mountmorres, Viscount 1872-1936 *MnBBF,*
WWBWI A
Mountmorres, Viscount *see* Morris, Patrick
Moussard, Jacqueline 1924- *ConAu 61*
Moussard, Jacqueline *see* Cervon, Jacqueline
Mow, Anna Beahm 1893- *ConAu 9R*
Mowat, Farley McGill 1921- *AmA&B,*
Au&Wr 6, AuBYP, CanWW 12, CanWr,
CasWL, IntWW 38, OxCan, OxCan Sup,
SmATA 3, ThBJA, WWA 38,
WWCan 1973, WWE 14, WorAu,
WrD
Mowbray, John *MnBBF, WWBWI A,*
WWCL
Mowbray, John *see* Hadath, John Edward Gunby
Mowbray, Martin *MnBBF*
Mowbray, W J *MnBBF*
Mowbray, W J *see* Gascoigne, Eric
Mowery, Dee Dunsing *WrD*
Moxon, Stanley *MnBBF*
Moy, Seong 1921- *DcCAA 2, IIBYP,*
IICB 1957, WWA 38, WWAA 1973,
WWE 14
Moyers, William 1916- *ChPo, IIBYP,*
IICB 1946
Moyes, Patricia 1923- *Au&Wr 6, BiEnAT,*
ConAu 17R, EncM&D
Mozley, Charles 1915- *ArtsCL, ChPo S2,*
IICB 1957, WWGA
Muddock, Joyce Emerson Preston 1843-1934
Alli Sup, EncM&D, MnBBF, NCHEL
Muddock, Joyce Emerson Preston *see* Donovan,
Dick
Mude, O *ConAu XR*
Mude, O *see* Gorey, Edward St. John
Mudie, Ian 1911- *Au&Wr 6, ChPo S2,*
ConAu 25R, ConP 1970, ConP 1975,
DcLEnL, WrD
Muehl, Lois Baker 1920- *AuBYP, ConAu 1R,*
ForWC 1970, WrD
Mueller, Amelia 1911- *ConAu 57*
Mueller, Hans Alexander 1888- *IIBYP,*

IICB 1946
Mueller, Robert E 1925- *ConAu 1R*
Mueller, Virginia 1924- *ConAu 65*
Muenchen, Al 1917- *ConAu 49*
Mugford, J Trounsell *MnBBF*
Muhlenweg, Fritz *AuBYP*
Muhlhausen, John Prague 1940- *ConAu 61*
Muir, Augustus 1892- *Au&Wr 6, ConAu 13R,
MnBBF, WWBWI A, WrD*
Muir, Edwin 1887-1959 *AnCL, AtlBL,
CasWL, ChPo, ChPo S1, CnE&AP,
CnMWL, DcLEnL, EncWL, EvLB,
LongC, ModBL, ModBL Sup, NCHEL,
OxEng, Pen Eng, RAdv 1, RCom, REn,
TwCA, TwCA Sup, TwCW, WEAL,
WWTwL*
Muir, John 1838-1914 *AmA&B, BiD&SB,
DcAmA, DcLEnL, DcNAA, EvLB,
JBA 1934, OxAm, REn, REnAL, TwCA,
TwCA Sup, WisW*
Muir, Wardrop Openshaw 1878-1927 *MnBBF,
WWBWI A*
Muir, Wardrop Openshaw *see* Lang, Stewart
Muirden, James 1942- *Au&Wr 6*
Mukerji, Dhan Gopal 1890-1936 *AnCL,
AuBYP, BkCL, JBA 1934, LongC,
Newb 1922, TwCA*
Mulac, Margaret E 1912- *ConAu 5R,
ForWC 1970, WWAW 8*
Mulcahy, Lucille Burnett 1918- *AuBYP,
ConAu 5R, ForWC 1970, SmATA 12*
Mulcahy, Lucille Burnett *see* Hale, Helen
Mulford, Clarence Edward 1883-1956 *AmA&B,
EvLB, LongC, MnBBF, OxAm, REnAL,
TwCA, TwCA Sup, WNAA*
Mulford, Harriet *JBA 1934*
Mulford, Harriet *see* Lothrop, Harriet Mulford
Stone
Mulholland, Clara *MnBBF*
Mulholland, John 1898-1970 *AmA&B,
ConAu 5R, REnAL, WNAA*
Muller, Billex *HsB&A, YABC 1*
Muller, Billex *see* Ellis, Edward S
Muller, Charles G 1897- *ConAu 1R, WNAA,
WrD*
Mullin, Willard *NYTBE 2*
Mullins, Edward S 1922- *ConAu 17R, IIBYP,
SmATA 10*
Mullins, Vera Cooper 1903- *ConAu 61*
Mulock, Dinah Maria 1826-1887 *Alli Sup,
BiD&SB, BrAu 19, Chambr 3, CyWA,
DcBiA, DcEnA, DcLEnL, EvLB,
HsB&A, JBA 1934, NCHEL, OxEng,
PoIre, REn, TelT, WWCL*
Mulock, Dinah Maria *see* Craik, Dinah Mulock
Mulvihill, William Patrick 1923- *ConAu 1R,
SmATA 8, WWE 14*
Munari, Bruno 1907- *AuBYP, IICB 1946,
IICB 1957, ThBJA, WWGA*
Munce, Ruth Hill 1898- *ConAu P-1,
SmATA 12*
Munce, Ruth Hill *see* Hill, Ruth Livingston
Munch, Theodore W 1919- *ConAu 57*
Mundy, Talbot Chetwynd 1879-1940 *AmA&B,
CurB 40, DcNAA, MnBBF, REnAL,
TwCA, TwCA Sup*
Munn, Charles Clark 1848-1917 *AmA&B,
BiD&SB, CarSB, DcAmA, DcNAA*
Munoz, Rie 1921- *WWW 14*

Munro, A G *MnBBF*
Munro, Alice 1931- *AuNews 2, CanWW 12,
ConAu 33, ConLC 6, ConNov 1972,
ConNov 1976, OxCan, OxCan Sup*
Munro, Eleanor C 1928- *AuBYP, ConAu 1R*
Munro, George Colin 1907- *AmMWS 12P*
Munro, J *MnBBF*
Munroe, Kirk 1850-1930 *Alli Sup, AmA&B,
BbD, BiD&SB, BiDSA, CarSB, DcAmA,
DcNAA, JBA 1934, OxAm, TwCA*
Munsey, Frank Andrew 1854-1925 *Alli Sup,
AmA&B, CarSB, DcAmA, DcNAA,
REnAL*
Munshi, Shehnaaz *ConAu XR*
Munshi, Shehnaaz *see* Skagen, Kiki
Munson, Gorham Bert 1896-1969 *AmA&B,
AuBYP, CnDAL, ConAu P-1, OxAm,
Pen Am, REnAL, TwCA, TwCA Sup*
Munsterhjelm, Erik 1905- *ConAu 49, OxCan*
Munthe, Frances 1915- *ConAu 9R*
Munthe, Frances *see* Cowen, Frances
Munves, James 1922- *ConAu 5R*
Munz, Peter 1921- *ConAu 13R*
Munzer, Martha E 1899- *ConAu 1R,
SmATA 4, WrD*
Murai, Gensai *CarSB*
Murch, Mrs. N 1868- *MnBBF*
Murch, Mrs. N *see* Lovel, Vera
Murdoch, Temple *MnBBF*
Mure, Eleanor *ChPo S1, TelT*
Mure, Geoffrey *TelT*
Murfree, Mary Noailles 1850-1922 *Alli Sup,
AmA, AmA&B, BbD, BiD&SB, BiDSA,
CarSB, Chambr 3, CnDAL, DcAmA,
DcLEnL, DcNAA, OxAm, REn, REnAL*
Murphy, Barbara Beasley 1933- *ConAu 41,
SmATA 5*
Murphy, Beatrice M 1908- *BlkAW, ConAu 53,
LBAA*
Murphy, Beatrice M *see* Campbell, Beatrice
Murphy
Murphy, E Jefferson 1926- *ConAu 25R,
SmATA 4, WrD*
Murphy, E Jefferson *see* Murphy, Pat
Murphy, J M *MnBBF*
Murphy, Jimmy 1891-1965 *ArtCS*
Murphy, Mabel Ansley 1870- *AmA&B,
AuBYP*
Murphy, Mabel Ansley *see* Lee, Anne S
Murphy, Pat *ConAu XR, SmATA 4*
Murphy, Pat *see* Murphy, E Jefferson
Murphy, Richard 1927- *Au&Wr 6, CasWL,
ConAu 29, ConP 1970, ConP 1975,
ModBL Sup, NCHEL, WorAu*
Murphy, Richard William 1929- *WWA 38,
WWWor 2*
Murphy, Robert William 1902-1971 *AuBYP,
ConAu P-1, SmATA 10*
Murphy, Shirley Rousseau 1928- *ConAu 21R,
WWAW 8, WrD*
Murphy, Thomas Basil, Jr. 1935- *ConAu 69,
ConDr 1*
Murphy, Thomas Basil, Jr. *see* Murphy, Tom
Murphy, Tom *ConAu XR*
Murphy, Tom *see* Murphy, Thomas Basil, Jr.
Murray, A C *MnBBF, WWBWI A*
Murray, A C *see* Feveril, Hubert
Murray, A C *see* Gray, Andrew
Murray, Adrian *MnBBF*

Murray, Adrian *see* Gordon, Richard
Murray, Agatha *WWBWI A*
Murray, Agatha *see* Gibbons, Harry Hornaby
  Clifford
Murray, Albert 1916- *BlkAW, ConAu 49,*
  LBAA
Murray, Andrew 1880-1928 *WWBWI A*
Murray, Andrew *see* Gibbons, Harry Hornaby
  Clifford
Murray, Andrew Nicholas 1880-1929 *MnBBF*
Murray, Andrew Nicholas *see* Arnold, Malcolm,
  Captain
Murray, Andrew Nicholas *see* Deane, Vesey
Murray, Andrew Nicholas *see* Islay, Nicholas
Murray, C Geoffrey *MnBBF*
Murray, C Geoffrey *see* Gray, Geoffrey
Murray, C Geoffrey *see* Kingsford, Guy
Murray, C Geoffrey *see* Loxley, Raymond
Murray, Donald M 1924- *AmA&B, AuBYP,*
  ConAu 1R, WWA 38
Murray, Edgar Joyce 1878- *MnBBF,*
  WWBWI A
Murray, Edgar Joyce *see* Drew, Sidney
Murray, Edgar Joyce *see* Rover, Max
Murray, Frances *ConAu XR*
Murray, Frances *see* Booth, Rosemary Frances
Murray, Gladys Hall *AuBYP, WWAW 8*
Murray, John 1923- *ConAu 5R*
Murray, Marian *ConAu 41, SmATA 5*
Murray, Marr *MnBBF*
Murray, Sister Mary Verona 1909- *ConAu 17R*
Murray, Michele 1933-1974 *ConAu 49,*
  SmATA 7
Murray, Robert *MnBBF, WWBWI A*
Murray, Robert *see* Graydon, Robert Murray
Murray, Sidney *MnBBF*
Murray, William *MnBBF*
Murray, William *see* Graydon, William Murray
Murray, William Henry Harrison 1840-1904
  Alli Sup, AmA&B, BbD, BiD&SB,
  CarSB, DcAmA, DcNAA
Murrell, Elsie Kathleen Seth-Smith 1883-
  ConAu P-1
Musciano, Walter A *AuBYP*
Musgrave, Florence 1902- *AuBYP, ConAu P-1,*
  SmATA 3
Musgrave, Susan 1951- *ConAu 69, ConP 1975,*
  OxCan Sup, WrD
Musgrove, Margaret Wynkoop 1943- *ConAu 65*
Mussey, Virginia H *ConAu XR, SmATA 4*
Mussey, Virginia H *see* Ellison, Virginia Howell
Mussino, Attilio 1878-1954 *IlBYP*
Mutz *SmATA XR*
Mutz *see* Kuenstler, Morton
Myers, Arthur 1922- *ConAu 17R*
Myers, Bernice *ConAu 61, IlBYP,*
  SmATA 9
Myers, Caroline Clark 1887- *ConAu 29,*
  WWAW 8, WWE 14
Myers, Elisabeth Perkins 1918- *ConAu 5R,*
  ForWC 1970, WWAW 8, WrD
Myers, Gail E 1923- *ConAu 49, DrAS 6E,*
  LE 5
Myers, Garry Cleveland 1884- *ConAu 29*
Myers, Hortense 1913- *ConAu 1R,*
  ForWC 1970, IndAu 1917, SmATA 10,
  WrD
Myers, Madeline Neuberger 1896- *AuBYP*
Myers, Norman 1934- *ConAu 49*

Myers, Walter Dean 1937- *BlkAW, ConAu 33,*
  LBAA
Myles, Eugenie Louise 1905- *ConAu P-1*
Myller, Rolf 1926- *AuBYP, BkCL,*
  ConAu 5R
Mylne, W C R *MnBBF*
Myron, Robert 1926- *ConAu 13R, DrAS 6H*
Myrus, Donald 1927- *AuBYP, ConAu 1R*

N

Nadejen, Theodore *ConICB, IICB 1744*
Nadler, Robert *ChPo S2, IIBYP*
Nagenda, John 1938- *AfA*
Nagy, Al *IIBYP*
Nagy, Gil D 1933- *ConAu 25R*
Nailor, Gerald A 1917- *AmPB, IICB 1744*
Nakano, Hirotaka 1942- *ConAu 33*
Nakatani, Chiyoko *IIBYP*
Namioka, Lensey 1929- *ConAu 69*
Nandakumar, Prema 1939- *ConAu 9R*
Nankivel, Claudine *IIBYP*
Napier, Mark *ConAu XR*
Napier, Mark *see* Laffin, John
Nash, Linell *ChPo, ConAu XR, SmATA 2*
Nash, Linell *see* Smith, Linell Nash
Nash, Mary 1925- *AuBYP, ConAu 5R*
Nash, Ogden 1902-1971 *AmA&B,*
  AmSCAP 66, AnCL, Au&Wr 6, AuBYP,
  BkCL, CasWL, ChPo, ChPo S1,
  ChPo S2, CnDAL, CnE&AP, CnMWL,
  ConAmA, ConAu 29, ConAu P-1,
  ConP 1970, CurB 41, CurB 71, DcLEnL,
  EncWL, LongC, ModAL, NYTBE 2,
  OxAm, Pen Am, RAdv 1, REn, REnAL,
  SmATA 2, SmATA 2, TwCA,
  TwCA Sup, TwCW, WEAL, WWTwL
Nason, Thomas Willoughby 1889- *ChPo*
Nast, Elsa Ruth *ConAu XR, SmATA 3*
Nast, Elsa Ruth *see* Watson, Jane Werner
Nast, Thomas 1840-1902 *ChPo, EarAB,*
  EarAB Sup, OxAm, REn, REnAL
Nathan, Adele *AuBYP*
Nathan, Daniel *AuBYP, ConAu XR, LongC*
Nathan, Daniel *see* Dannay, Frederic
Nathan, Robert 1894- *AmA&B, AmNov,*
  AmSCAP 66, Au&Wr 6, ChPo,
  ChPo S1, CnDAL, ConAmA, ConAmL,
  ConAu 13R, ConNov 1972, ConNov 1976,
  IntWW 38, LongC, OxAm, REn,
  REnAL, SmATA 6, TwCA, TwCA Sup,
  WWA 38, WWW 14, WWWorJ 1972,
  WrD
Naughton, Bill 1910- *CnThe, ConDr 1,*
  ConNov 1972, ConNov 1976, CrCD,
  REnWD, WWT 15, WrD
Nava, Julian 1927- *ConAu 61, DrAS 6H*
Navarra, John Gabriel 1927- *AmMWS 12P,*
  ConAu 41, SmATA 8, WWE 14
Navarra, Toby *IIBYP*
Naylor, John Francis 1937- *DrAS 6H*
Naylor, Penelope 1941- *ConAu 37, IIBYP,*
  SmATA 10

Naylor, Phyllis Reynolds 1933- *IndAu 1917,*
  SmATA 12, WWAW 8, WrD
Nazaroff, Alexander I 1898- *ConAu 33,*
  SmATA 4
Neal, Charles Dempsey 1908- *ConAu 5R*
Neal, Harry Edward 1906- *AuBYP,*
  ConAu 5R, SmATA 5
Neavles, Janet Talmadge 1919- *ConAu 5R*
Nebel, Gustave E *IIBYP*
Nee, Kay Bonner *ConAu 49, SmATA 10*
Needleman, Jacob 1934- *ConAu 29, DrAS 6P,*
  SmATA 6
Neely, Kate J *CarSB*
Negri, Rocco 1932- *IIBYP, SmATA 12*
Neidlinger, William Harold 1863-1924 *CarSB,*
  ChPo
Neighbour, Ralph Webster, Sr. 1906-
  ConAu 1R, WrD
Neigoff, Anne 1911- *ConAu 41, ForWC 1970,*
  SmATA 13, WWAW 8, WWMW 14
Neigoff, Mike 1920- *ConAu 5R, SmATA 13*
Neilan, Sarah *ConAu 69*
Neill, John Rea 1878-1943 *ChPo S2, DcNAA*
Neilson *WWBWI I*
Neilson, Frances Fullerton 1910- *AuBYP,*
  CurB 55
Neilson, Vernon *MnBBF*
Neilson, Vernon *see* Clarke, Percy A
Neimark, Anne E 1935- *ConAu 29, SmATA 4*
Neinke, Peter *WrD*
Neish, Duncan *MnBBF*
Neish, Duncan *see* Allan, F Carney
Neish, R *MnBBF*
Nelson, Alix R 1938- *ForWC 1970*
Nelson, Barry *MnBBF*
Nelson, Barry *see* Thomas, Reginald George
Nelson, Cholmondeley M 1903- *AuBYP,*
  ConAu 5R
Nelson, Esther L 1928- *ConAu 69,*
  SmATA 13
Nelson, George *MnBBF*
Nelson, Gertrude *WWBWI A*
Nelson, Gertrude *see* Bobin, John William
Nelson, Marg Raibley 1899- *AuBYP,*
  ConAu 1R
Nelson, Marguerite *ConAu XR*
Nelson, Marguerite *see* Floren, Lee
Nelson, Mary Carroll 1929- *ConAu 49*
Nelson, Roy Paul 1923- *ConAu 17R,*
  DrAS 6E, WWW 14
Nelson, Stanley H *MnBBF*
Nelson, Steve *MnBBF*

Nelson, Steve *see* Bobin, John William
Nelson, T *MnBBF*
Nelson, T *see* Brown, Duncan
Nelson, Victor *MnBBF, WWBWI A*
Nelson, Victor *see* Bobin, John William
Nendick, Victor R *MnBBF*
Neolan, Ned *MnBBF*
Nephew, William *AuBYP*
Nerman, Einar 1888- *ConICB, IntWW 38, WWWor 2*
Nesbit, E *see* Bland, Edith Nesbit
Nesbit, E *see* Bland, Fabian
Nesbit, Edith 1858-1924 *Alli Sup, AtlBL, AuBYP, CarSB, CasWL, ChLR 3, ChPo, DcLEnL, EvLB, FamSYP, JBA 1934, LongC, MorJA, NCHEL, OxEng, Pen Eng, TelT, TwCA, TwCA Sup, WWCL, YABC 1*
Nesbit, Troy *AuBYP, ConAu XR, SmATA 5*
Nesbit, Troy *see* Folsom, Franklin
Nesbitt, Esta 1918- *IICB 1957*
Nesbitt, Rosemary Sinnett 1924- *WWAW 8*
Nesmith, Robert I 1891- *ConAu 1R*
Nespojohn, Katherine Veronica 1912- *ConAu 37, SmATA 7*
Ness, Evaline 1911- *AuBYP, BkP, ChPo, ChPo S1, ChPo S2, ConAu 5R, IIBYP, IICB 1957, NewbC 1966, SmATA 1, ThBJA, WWA 38, WWAW 8*
Netamuxwe *IIBYP*
Netamuxwe *see* Bock, William Sauts
Netherwood, Anne 1940- *IICB 1957*
Neuberger, Richard L *CurB 55, CurB 60*
Neufeld, John 1938- *AuBYP, ConAu 25R, SmATA 6*
Neufeld, Rose 1924- *ConAu 29*
Neuffer, Irene LaBorde 1919- *ConAu 61*
Neuffer, Irene LaBorde *see* LaBorde, Rene
Neumeyer, Peter F 1929- *ConAu 33, DrAS 6E, SmATA 13, WrD*
Neurath, Marie 1898- *Au&Wr 6, ConAu 13R, SmATA 1*
Neville, Emily Cheney 1919- *AuBYP, BkCL, ConAu 5R, ForWC 1970, MorBMP, NewbC 1956, SmATA 1, ThBJA, WWA 38, WWAW 8*
Neville, Mary *ConAu XR, SmATA 2*
Neville, Mary *see* Woodrich, Mary Neville
Nevins, Albert J 1915- *AuBYP, BkC 6, CatA 1952, ConAu 5R, WWA 38*
Nevins, Allan 1890-1971 *AmA&B, ConAu 5R, ConAu 29, CurB 68, CurB 71, LongC, NYTBE 2, OxAm, Pen Am, REn, REnAL, TwCA, TwCA Sup*
Newberry, Clare Turlay 1903-1970 *AmPB, AuBYP, ChPo, ChPo S1, ConAu P-2, IICB 1744, IICB 1946, JBA 1951, SmATA 1*
Newbery, John 1713-1767 *Alli, BrAu, ChPo, ChPo S1, DcLEnL, NCHEL, REn, REnAL, WWCL*
Newbolt, Sir Henry John 1862-1938 *CarSB, Chambr 3, ChPo, ChPo S1, ChPo S2, DcEnA Ap, DcLEnL, EvLB, LongC, ModBL, NCHEL, OxEng, Pen Eng, REn, TwCA, TwCA Sup*
Newby, P H 1918- *ConAu 5R, CurB 53, WrD*

Newcomb, Covelle 1908- *AmA&B, AuBYP, BkC 1, CatA 1930, ConAu P-2, JBA 1951*
Newcomb, Covelle *see* Brubank, Addison
Newcomb, Ellsworth *ConAu XR*
Newcomb, Ellsworth *see* Kenny, Ellsworth Newcomb
Newcomb, Franc J 1887- *ConAu 17R*
Newcomb, Harvey 1803-1863 *Alli, CarSB, DcAmA, DcNAA*
Newcombe, Jack *AuBYP*
Newcome, Colin *MnBBF*
Newcome, Colin *see* Young, Fred W
Newell, Crosby *IIBYP, ThBJA*
Newell, Crosby *see* Bonsall, Crosby Barbara Newell
Newell, Edythe W 1910- *ConAu 65, SmATA 11*
Newell, Homer Edward, Jr. 1915- *AmMWS 12P, AuBYP, CurB 54, IntWW 38, WWA 38*
Newell, Hope 1896-1965 *AmA&B, AuBYP, MorJA*
Newell, Peter 1862-1924 *AmA&B, CarSB, ChPo, ChPo S2, DcAmA, DcNAA, OxAm*
Newfeld, Frank 1928- *Prof*
Newlon, Clarke *ConAu 49, SmATA 6*
Newlon, Clarke *see* Clarke, Michael
Newman, Daisy 1904- *ConAu 37, WrD*
Newman, Kenneth E *MnBBF, WWBWI A*
Newman, Kenneth E *see* Clifford, Martin
Newman, Kenneth E *see* Conquest, Owen
Newman, Kenneth E *see* Richards, Frank
Newman, L J *MnBBF*
Newman, Robert 1909- *AuBYP, ConAu 1R, SmATA 4*
Newman, Shirlee Petkin 1924- *ConAu 5R, ForWC 1970, SmATA 10, WWAW 8, WWE 14*
Newman, Thelma Rita 1925- *ConAu 13R, ForWC 1970, LE 5*
Newsome, Arden J 1932- *ConAu 29*
Newsome, Arden J *see* Sebastian, Jeanne
Newton, David C *WWBWI A*
Newton, David C *see* Chance, John Newton
Newton, Suzanne 1936- *ConAu 41, SmATA 5, WrD*
Newton, Wilfred Douglas 1884- *MnBBF*
Neyhart, Louise Albright *AuBYP*
Nic Leodhas, Sorche 1898-1969 *AuBYP, ThBJA*
Nic Leodhas, Sorche *see* Alger, Leclaire G
Nic Leodhas, Sorche *see* Leodhas, Sorche Nic
Nicholas, A X 1943- *BlkAW*
Nicholls, Anthony *MnBBF*
Nicholls, Anthony *see* Parsons, Anthony
Nicholls, Frederick Francis 1926- *Au&Wr 6, WrD*
Nichols, Beverley 1899- *Au&Wr 6, ChPo, ChPo S1, IntWW 38, LongC, ModBL, NCHEL, TwCA, TwCA Sup, TwCW, WW 1974, WWCL*
Nichols, Beverley 1900- *WWWor 2*
Nichols, Cecilia Fawn 1906- *ConAu P-1, ForWC 1970, SmATA 12*
Nichols, Dale 1904- *ConAu P-2, IICB 1744, WWA 38, WWWor 2*
Nichols, Marie C 1905- *IIBYP, IICB 1946*

Nichols, Ruth 1948- *Au&Wr 6, ConAu 25R,*
OxCan Sup, Prof
Nichols, Spencer Baird 1875?- *ChPo,*
IICB 1744
Nicholson, Geoffrey 1929- *Au&Wr 6,*
ConAu 5R, WrD
Nicholson, Joyce *SingR 1*
Nicholson, Shirley J 1925- *ConAu 29*
Nicholson, Thomas Dominic 1922-
AmMWS 12P, WWA 38, WWE 14
Nicholson, Sir William 1872-1949 *AmPB,*
Br&AmS, ChPo, ChPo S2, IICB 1744,
IICB 1946
Nickel, Mildred Lucille 1912- *BiDL 5, LE 5,*
WWAW 8
Nickelsburg, Janet 1893- *ConAu 65,*
SmATA 11
Nickerson, Jan *AuBYP, ConAu 1R*
Nickerson, Jan *see* Smith, Jan
Nicklaus, Carol *IIBYP*
Nickless, Will 1902- *IICB 1957*
Niclas, Yolla 1900- *ConAu 25R*
Nicol, Ann *ConAu XR*
Nicol, Ann *see* Turnbull, Ann
Nicolas 1911-1973 *AmPB, AuBYP, BkP,*
IIBYP, IICB 1946, IICB 1957
Nicolas *see* Mordvinoff, Nicolas
Nicolay, Helen 1866-1954 *AmA&B, AmLY,*
AuBYP, JBA 1934, JBA 1951, REnAL,
YABC 1
Nicole *AmPB*
Nicole *see* Duplaix, Georges
Nicole, Christopher Robin 1930- *Au&Wr 6,*
ConAu 13R, ConNov 1972, ConNov 1976,
SmATA 5
Nicole, Christopher Robin *see* Grange, Peter
Nicole, Christopher Robin *see* York, Andrew
Niehuis, Charles C *AuBYP*
Nield, W A *CarSB*
Nielsen, Kay 1886- *CarSB, ConICB,*
IICB 1744
Nielsen, Virginia *ConAu XR, SmATA XR*
Nielsen, Virginia *see* McCall, Virginia Nielsen
Nielson, Vernon *WWBWI A*
Nielson, Vernon *see* Clarke, Percy A
Nightingale, Charles T 1878- *ChPo, ChPo S1,*
ConICB
Nimeth, Albert J 1918- *ConAu 25R*
Nimmo, Jenny *WrD*
Nimmo, John A *MnBBF*
Nimoy, Leonard 1931- *WWA 38*
Ninon 1908- *IIBY.P, IICB 1946*
Ninon *see* MacKnight, Ninon
Nisbet, Noel Laura 1887- *IICB 1744*
Nisenson, Samuel *IIBYP*
Nissman, Blossom Snoyer 1928- *ConAu 37,*
LE 5, WrD
Niven, Larry *ConAu XR, DrAF 1976,*
WWA 38
Niven, Larry *see* Niven, Laurence VanCott
Niven, Laurence Van Cott 1938- *ConAu 21R*
Niven, Laurence VanCott *see* Niven, Larry
Nivola, Claire A *IIBYP*
Nixon, F J *MnBBF*
Nixon, Joan Lowery 1927- *ConAu 9R,*
SmATA 8
Nixon, K *AuBYP*
Nixon, K *see* Nixon, Kathleen Irene
Nixon, Kathleen Irene *AuBYP*

Nixon, Kathleen Irene *see* Nixon, K
Noad, Frederick 1929- *ConAu 9R*
Noble, Iris 1922- *AuBYP, ConAu 1R,*
SmATA 5
Noble, Leonard M *WWBWI 1*
Nodset, Joan L *AuBYP, ConAu XR,*
SmATA 1
Nodset, Joan L *see* Lexau, Joan M
Noel, Hilda Bloxton, Jr. *ConAu XR*
Noel, Hilda Bloxton, Jr. *see* Schroetter, Hilda
Noel
Noel, Maurice *Alli Sup, CarSB*
Nohl, Frederick 1927- *ConAu 5R*
Nolan, Jeannette Covert 1897?-1974 *AmA&B,*
Au&Wr 6, AuBYP, ConAu 5R,
ConAu 53, ForWC 1970, IndAu 1917,
JBA 1951, SmATA 2, WWA 38,
WWAW 8
Nolan, Jeannette Covert *see* Tucker, Caroline
Nolan, John Vincent *MnBBF*
Nolan, Paul Thomas 1919- *ConAu 5R,*
DrAS 6E, WWA 38
Nolan, William Francis 1928- *ConAu 1R,*
EncM&D, WWW 14
Nolen, Barbara 1902- *ChPo S2, WWAW 8,*
WWE 14
Nolte, Elleta 1919- *ConAu 61*
Nonnast, Marie 1924- *IIBYP, IICB 1946,*
IICB 1957
Noonan, Julia 1946- *ConAu 33, IIBYP,*
SmATA 4
Noonan, Michael 1921- *SingR 1, WrD*
Norcross, Grace *ConICB*
Nordenskjold, Birgitta 1919- *IICB 1957*
Nordhoff, Charles 1830-1901 *Alli, Alli Sup,*
AmA, AmA&B, BbD, BiD&SB, CarSB,
CnDAL, CyAL 2, DcAmA, DcNAA,
OhA&B, OxAm, REnAL
Nordhoff, Charles Bernard 1887-1947 *AmA&B,*
AmNov, AuBYP, CnDAL, CyWA,
DcLEnL, DcNAA, JBA 1934, LongC,
MnBBF, OxAm, Pen Am, REn, REnAL,
TwCA, TwCA Sup
Nordstrom, Ursula *AmA&B, AmPB, AuBYP,*
ConAu 13R, ConAu 13R, ForWC 1970,
SmATA 3
Norfleet, Mary Crockett 1919- *ConAu 1R*
Norling, Ernest Ralph 1892- *AuBYP,*
WWPNA
Norling, Josephine Stearns 1895- *AuBYP,*
ConAu 1R, WWPNA
Norman, Charles 1904- *AmA&B, AuBYP,*
ChPo S2, REnAL, TwCA Sup, WWA 38
Norman, James *ConAu XR*
Norman, James *see* Schmidt, James Norman
Norman, Lilith 1927- *ConAu 45*
Norman, Marshall *MnBBF*
Norman, Philip *MnBBF*
Norman, Philip *see* Philips, George Norman
Norman, Victor *MnBBF*
Norman, Victor *see* Ransome, L E
Norris, Arthur *MnBBF*
Norris, Faith Grigsby *AuBYP*
Norris, Frank 1870-1902 *AmA&B, AmWr,*
AtlBL, BbD, BiD&SB, CasWL,
Chambr 3, CnDAL, CriT 3, CyWA,
DcAmA, DcBiA, DcLEnL, DcNAA,
EvLB, LongC, ModAL, OxAm, OxEng,
Pen Am, RAdv 1, REn, REnAL, TwCA,

TwCA Sup, TwCW, WEAL
Norris, Louanne 1930- *ConAu 53*
Norris, Margaret *St&VC*
Norris, Phyllis Irene 1909- *Au&Wr 6, WrD*
North, Andrew *AmA&B, ConAu XR,*
CurB 57, SmATA 1, WorAu
North, Andrew *see* Norton, Alice Mary
North, Colonel *MnBBF*
North, Colonel *see* Bullivant, Cecil Henry
North, George, Captain *MnBBF, WWBWI A,*
YABC XR
North, George, Captain *see* Stevenson, Robert
Louis
North, Jack *MnBBF, WWBWI A*
North, Jack *see* Pentelow, John Nix
North, James *MnBBF*
North, Joan Marian 1920- *Au&Wr 6,*
ConAu 13R, WrD
North, Pearson *MnBBF*
North, Pearson *see* Pearson, T E
North, Sterling 1906-1974 *AmA&B, AmNov,*
Au&Wr 6, AuBYP, ConAu 5R,
ConAu 53, CurB 43, CurB 75,
NYTBS 5, REnAL, SmATA 1, ThBJA,
TwCA, TwCA Sup, WWA 38, WWE 14
Northcott, Cecil 1902- *Au&Wr 6, ConAu 9R,*
WW 1974
Northcott, Cecil *see* Miller, Mary
Northcroft, George J H 1868- *ChPo S1,*
ChPo S2, MnBBF, WWBWI A
Northmore, Elizabeth Florence 1906-1974
ConAu P-2
Northmore, Elizabeth Florence *see* Stucley,
Elizabeth
Norton, Alice Mary 1912- *AmA&B, AuBYP,*
ConAu 1R, CurB 57, OhA&B,
SmATA 1
Norton, Alice Mary *see* North, Andrew
Norton, Alice Mary *see* Norton, Andre
Norton, Alice Mary *see* Norton, Andrew
Norton, Andre 1912- *AuBYP, ConAu XR,*
CurB 57, MorJA, OhA&B, SenS,
SmATA 1, WorAu, WrD
Norton, Andre *see* Norton, Alice Mary
Norton, Andrew *AuBYP*
Norton, Andrew *see* Norton, Alice Mary
Norton, Browning *ConAu XR, SmATA XR*
Norton, Browning *see* Norton, Frank R B
Norton, Charles Eliot 1827-1908 *Alli, Alli Sup,*
AmA, AmA&B, BbD, BiD&SB, CarSB,
Chambr 3, ChPo S1, CyAL 2, DcAmA,
DcNAA, EvLB, LongC, OxAm, Pen Am,
REn
Norton, Frank R B 1909- *ConAu 61,*
SmATA 10
Norton, Frank R B *see* Norton, Browning
Norton, Mary 1903- *AnCL, Au&ICB,*
Au&Wr 6, AuBYP, BkCL, CasWL,
FamMS, TelT, ThBJA, WWCL, WrD
Norton, Olive 1913- *ConAu 9R*
Norton, Olive *see* Norway, Kate
Norton, Victor *MnBBF*
Norton, Victor *see* Dalton, Gilbert
Norway, Kate *ConAu XR*
Norway, Kate *see* Norton, Olive
Notkin, Jerome J 1926- *LE 5*
Nourse, Alan Edward 1928- *Au&Wr 6,*
AuBYP, ConAu 1R, WWPNA
Nourse, Alan Edward *see* Edwards, Al

Nowell, Elizabeth Cameron *ConAu XR,*
SmATA 12
Nowell, Elizabeth Cameron *see* Cameron,
Elizabeth
Nowell, Elizabeth Cameron *see* Clemons,
Elizabeth
Nowell, Elizabeth Cameron *see* Robinson,
Elizabeth Cameron
Nowlan, Phil 1888-1940 *ArtCS*
Noyes, Alfred 1880-1958 *BkC 6, CatA 1930,*
Chambr 3, ChPo, ChPo S1, ChPo S2,
DcLEnL, EvLB, FamPYP, LongC,
ModBL, NCHEL, OxEng, Pen Eng, REn,
TwCA, TwCA Sup, TwCW, WWLA
Noyes, Nell Braly 1921- *ConAu 37*
Nucera, Marisa Lonette 1959- *ConAu 17R*
Nucera, Marisa Lonette *see* Marisa
Nugent, Frances Roberts 1904-1964? *AuBYP,*
ConAu 5R
Nugent, Frank *WWBWI I*
Nugent, Frank *see* Higgins, Lewis R
Nunan, Desmond James 1927- *ConAu 17R,*
WWE 14
Nura 1899-1950 *IlBYP, IlCB 1946*
Nura *see* Ulreich, Nura Woodson
Nurenberg, Thelma *AuBYP*
Nurnberg, Maxwell 1897- *ConAu 5R*
Nussbaumer, Paul Edmund 1934- *IlCB 1957*
Nutbrown, Maurice *MnBBF*
Nutbrown, Maurice *see* Denbigh, Maurice
Nuttall, Kenneth 1907- *ConAu 17R, WrD*
Nye, Robert 1939- *Au&Wr 6, ConAu 33,*
ConNov 1972, ConNov 1976, ConP 1970,
ConP 1975, SmATA 6, WrD
Nye, Whitworth *MnBBF*
Nyman, Ingrid Vang 1916- *IlBYP, IlCB 1946*

O

O-X-O *MnBBF*
Oakes, Vanya 1909- *ConAu 33, SmATA 6, WWAW 8, WWW 14*
Oakes, Virginia Armstrong *AuBYP*
Oakley, Don 1927- *ConAu 29, SmATA 8*
Oakley, Helen 1906- *ConAu 17R, SmATA 10*
Oakley, Thornton 1881- *ChPo S1, ConICB, IICB 1744*
Oates, Stephen Baery 1936- *ConAu 9R, DrAS 6H, WWA 38*
Obligado, Lilian Isabel 1931- *IICB 1957*
Obrant, Susan 1946- *IlBYP, SmATA 11*
O'Brian, Frank *ConAu XR*
O'Brian, Frank *see* Garfield, Brian Wynn
O'Brien, Captain *MnBBF*
O'Brien, Esse Forrester 1895?-1975 *ConAu 61, ForWC 1970, TexW*
O'Brien, Jack 1898-1938 *MorJA*
O'Brien, John Sherman 1898-1938 *AuBYP, DcNAA*
O'Brien, Robert C 1918-1973 *ChLR 2, ConAu XR, NewbC 1966*
O'Brien, Robert C *see* Conly, Robert L
O'Brien, Thomas Clement 1938- *LE 5*
O'Brine, Paddy Manning *MnBBF, WWBWI A*
O'Clery, Helen 1910- *AuBYP, ConAu 9R*
O'Connell, Peg *ConAu XR, SmATA XR*
O'Connell, Peg *see* Ahern, Margaret McCrohan
O'Connor, Patrick 1899- *AuBYP, BbthC, BkC 3, ChPo S1, ConAu XR, EncM&D, SmATA 2*
O'Connor, Patrick *see* Wibberley, Leonard
O'Connor, Richard 1915-1975 *AmA&B, ConAu 61, IndAu 1917, WWA 38, WWE 14*
O'Connor, Richard *see* Archer, Frank
O'Connor, Richard *see* Burke, John
O'Connor, Richard *see* Wayland, Patrick
O'Cuilleanain, Eilis Dillon *ThBJA*
O'Cuilleanain, Eilis Dillon *see* Dillon, Eilis
O'Daniel, Janet 1921- *ConAu 29, WrD*
O'Dare, Kerry *MnBBF*
O'Dare, Kerry *see* Starr, Richard
O'Dell, Scott 1903?- *AmA&B, AmNov, AnCL, Au&ICB, AuBYP, BkCL, ChLR 1, ConAu 61, MorJA, NewbC 1956, PiP, SenS, SmATA 12, St&VC, WWA 38, WWWor 2*
Odenwald, Robert Paul 1899-1965 *AuBYP, ConAu 1R, SmATA 11*
Odescalchi, Esther Kando 1938- *BiDL 5,*

ConAu 69
O'Donnell, Peter *MnBBF*
O'Donnell, Peter *see* Barnes, John
Oechsli, Kelly 1918- *ChPo, ChPo S2, IlBYP, IICB 1957, SmATA 5*
Oetting, Rae *MnnWr*
Offit, Sidney 1928- *ConAu 1R, DrAF 1976, SmATA 10, WWA 38, WWE 14, WrD*
Offord, Lenore Glen 1905- *AuBYP, CatA 1930, EncM&D, ForWC 1970, WWAW 8, WWW 14*
Offutt, Andrew Jefferson 1934- *ConAu 41*
O'Flynn, Jimmy *MnBBF*
O'Flynn, Jimmy *see* Graydon, Robert Murray
Ofosu-Appiah, L H 1920- *ConAu 33, SmATA 13*
Ogalvay, George *MnBBF*
Ogan, George F 1912- *ConAu 9R, SmATA 13*
Ogan, George F *see* Castle, Lee
Ogan, George F *see* Ogan, M G
Ogan, M G *ConAu XR, SmATA XR*
Ogan, M G *see* Ogan, George F
Ogan, M G *see* Ogan, Margaret E
Ogan, Margaret E 1923- *ConAu 9R, SmATA 13*
Ogan, Margaret E *see* Castle, Lee
Ogan, Margaret E *see* Ogan, M G
Ogburn, Charlton *CurB 55, CurB 62*
Ogburn, Charlton, Jr. 1911- *AmA&B, Au&Wr 6, ConAu 5R, SmATA 3, WWA 38, WWS 13*
Ogden, Brian John 1936- *Au&Wr 6, WrD*
Ogden, Ruth 1853-1927 *Alli Sup, AmA&B, CarSB, ChPo, ChPo S1, DcAmA, DcNAA*
Ogg, Oscar 1908-1971 *ConAu 33, NYTBE 2*
Ogilvie, Elisabeth 1917- *AmA&B, AmNov, AuBYP, CurB 51, TwCA Sup*
O'Gorman, Ned 1929?- *AmA&B, ChPo S2, ConP 1970, ConP 1975, DrAP 1975, WWA 38, WWE 14, WorAu, WrD*
O'Grady, Felix *MnBBF, WWBWI A*
O'Grady, Felix *see* Hadath, John Edward Gunby
O'Grady, Standish James 1846-1928 *Alli Sup, CasWL, EvLB, MnBBF, Pen Eng, PoIre, TwCA Sup*
O'Hara, Mary 1885- *AmA&B, AmNov, CatA 1952, ConAu XR, CurB 44, REn, REnAL, SmATA 2, TwCA Sup, WWA 38, WWAW 8*
O'Hara, Mary *see* Alsop, Mary O'Hara
O'Harris, Pixie *SingR 1*

Ohlsson, Ib 1935- *ChPo S1, ChPo S2, IIBYP, IICB 1957, SmATA 7*
Okun, Milt 1923- *EncFCW 1969*
Olatunji, Michael Babatunde *AuBYP*
Olcheski, Bill 1925- *ConAu 61*
Olcott, Frances Jenkins *AmA&B, JBA 1934, JBA 1951, REnAL*
Olcott, Henry Steel 1832-1907 *Alli, Alli Sup, AmA&B, BiDPar, DcNAA, OhA&B*
Olcott, Virginia *AmA&B, JBA 1934, JBA 1951*
Old Boy, An *MnBBF, WWBWI A*
Old Boy, An *see* Reed, Talbot Baines
Old Cap *MnBBF*
Old Fag *MnBBF, WWBWI A*
Old Fag *see* Bell, Robert Stanley Warren
Oldden, Richard *IIBYP*
Olden, Sam *AuBYP*
Oldham, Hugh R *MnBBF*
Oldham, Hugh R *see* Whitford, Joan
Oldrin, John 1901- *AuBYP*
Olds, Elizabeth 1896?- *AmA&B, AuBYP, ConAu 5R, IICB 1946, IICB 1957, SmATA 3, WWA 38, WWAA 1973, WWAW 8*
Olds, Helen Diehl 1895- *AuBYP, ConAu 1R, ForWC 1970, OhA&B, SmATA 9*
Oldstyle, Jonathan 1783-1859 *AmA&B, CnDAL, DcEnL, OxAm, REn, YABC XR*
Oldstyle, Jonathan *see* Irving, Washington
O'Leary, Brian Todd 1940- *AmMWS 12P, ConAu 33, SmATA 6, WWA 38, WWE 14*
Oleksy, Walter 1930- *ConAu 45*
O'Lincoln, Robert *CarSB*
Olivant, Alfred 1874-1927 *CarSB*
Oliver, Gertrude Kent *MnBBF*
Oliver, Gertrude Kent *see* Carr, Kent
Oliver, Jane *Au&Wr 6, AuBYP, ChPo, ConAu XR*
Oliver, Jane *see* Rees, Helen Christina Easson
Oliver, John Edward 1933- *AmMWS 12S, ConAu 33, WrD*
Oliver, Mark *ConAu XR*
Oliver, Mark *see* Tyler-Whittle, Michael Sidney
Oliver, Roland 1923- *IntWW 38*
Oliver, Tom *MnBBF*
Oliver, Tom *see* Olliver, Tom
Olivetti *WWBWI I*
Ollivant, Alfred 1798-1882 *Alli, Alli Sup*
Ollivant, Alfred 1874-1927 *BiD&SB, JBA 1934, LongC, NCHEL, REn, TwCA*
Olliver, Tom *MnBBF*
Olliver, Tom *see* Graydon, William Murray
Olliver, Tom *see* Oliver, Tom
Olmsted, Lorena Ann 1890- *ConAu 29, SmATA 13*
Olmsted, Robert Walsh 1936- *ConAu 41, WrD*
Olney, Ross Robert 1929- *AuBYP, ConAu 13R, SmATA 13, WrD*
Olschewski, Alfred Erich 1920- *ConAu 41, SmATA 7*
Olsen, Eugene E 1936- *ConAu 33*
Olsen, Eugene E *see* Steiger, Brad
Olsen, Ib Spang 1921- *ConAu 49, IICB 1957, SmATA 6, ThBJA*
Olsen, Ib Spang *see* Detine, Padre

Olsen, Ib Spang *see* Spang Olsen, Ib
Olson, David F 1938- *ConAu 49*
Olson, Gene 1922- *AuBYP*
Olugebefola, Ademola *IIBYP*
O'Malley, Mary Dolling 1889-1974 *ConAu 65, LongC*
O'Malley, Patricia *AuBYP*
Oman, Carola 1897- *ConAu 5R*
Oman, Carola *see* Lenanton, C
O'Mant, Hedley Percival Angelo 1899-1955 *MnBBF, WWBWI A*
O'Mant, Hedley Percival Angelo *see* Clifford, Martin
O'Mant, Hedley Percival Angelo *see* Conquest, Owen
O'Mant, Hedley Percival Angelo *see* Hawke, Robert
O'Mant, Hedley Percival Angelo *see* Owen, Hedley
O'Mant, Hedley Percival Angelo *see* Richards, Frank
O'Mant, Hedley Percival Angelo *see* Scott, Hedley
O'Mant, Hedley Percival Angelo *see* Scott, Hamilton
O'Meara, Walter 1897- *ConAu 13R, CurB 58*
Ommanney, F D 1903- *ConAu 13R*
Oncken, Clara *AuBYP*
Ondaatje, Michael 1943- *CanWW 12, ConP 1970, ConP 1975, OxCan Sup*
O'Neill, David P 1918- *ConAu 17R*
O'Neill, Eugene Gladstone 1888-1953 *AmWr, AtlBL, AuNews 1, CnDAL, CnMD, CnMWL, CnThe, ConAmA, ConAmL, CyWA, DcLEnL, EncWL, EvLB, LongC, McGWD, ModAL, ModAL Sup, ModWD, OxAm, OxEng, Pen Am, RCom, REn, REnAL, REnWD, TwCA, TwCA Sup, TwCW, WEAL, WWTwL*
O'Neill, Hester 1908- *AuBYP*
O'Neill, Lucas *MnBBF*
O'Neill, Mary Gibbons *BkCL*
O'Neill, Mary LeDuc 1908- *AuBYP, ChPo, ConAu 5R, ForWC 1970, SmATA 2, ThBJA*
Ono, Chiyo 1941- *ConAu 29*
Oosterman, Gordon 1927- *ConAu 49, LE 5*
Opdycke, John Baker 1878-1956 *AmA&B*
Openshaw, G H *MnBBF*
Openshaw, G H *see* Gale, John
Openshaw, G H *see* Shaw, Dick
Openshaw, G H *see* Shaw, Justin
Openshaw, G H *see* Sterne, Duncan
Opie, Iona 1923- *AnCL, Au&Wr 6, ConAu 61, SmATA 3*
Opie, Peter 1918- *AnCL, Au&Wr 6, ConAu 5R, SmATA 3*
Oppenheim, Edward Phillips 1866-1946 *Alli Sup, DcLEnL, EncM&D, EvLB, LongC, MnBBF, NCHEL, REn, TwCA, TwCA Sup, TwCW, WWBWI A, WWLA*
Oppenheim, Edward Phillips *see* Partridge, Anthony
Oppenheim, Joanne 1934- *ConAu 21R, SmATA 5*
Oppenheimer, Joan L 1925- *ConAu 37*
Oppenheimer, Lillian *AuBYP*
Opper, Frederick Burr 1857-1937 *AmA&B,*

ArtCS, AuNews 1, ChPo, DcNAA, OhA&B, REnAL, WNAA

Optic, Oliver *AmA, AmA&B, BiD&SB, ChPo, ChPo S2, CnDAL, ConAu XR, DcAmA, DcEnL, DcNAA, OxAm, REnAL*

Orbaan, Albert F 1913- *ConAu 5R, IlBYP, IlCB 1946*

Orbach, Ruth Gary 1941- *ConAu 65*

Orczy, Baroness Emmuska 1865-1947 *AuBYP, DcLEnL, EncM&D, EvLB, LongC, NCHEL, REn, TelT, TwCA, TwCA Sup, TwCW, WWLA*

Ord, Marion *WrD*

O'Reilly, John 1906- *AuBYP*

Orgel, Doris 1929- *AuBYP, AuNews 1, ConAu 45, SmATA 7*

Orgel, Doris *see* Adelberg, Doris

Orgill, Michael 1946- *ConAu 61*

Orleans, Ilo 1897-1962 *BkCL, ChPo, ChPo S1, ChPo S2, ConAu 1R, SmATA 10*

Orlob, Helen Seaburg 1908- *ConAu 5R, WWPNA*

Orme, K *MnBBF*

Orme, K *see* Clifford, Martin

Ormondroyd, Edward 1925- *AuBYP, ThBJA*

Ormsby, Virginia H *ConAu 9R, ForWC 1970, SmATA 11*

Orr, Bobby 1948- *CelR 3, CurB 69, NYTBE 2*

Orr, Munro Scott 1874- *IlCB 1744*

Orr, Robert Thomas 1908- *AmMWS 12P, ConAu 33, WWA 38, WWW 14*

Orr, William A *IlBYP*

Orrmont, Arthur 1922- *ConAu 1R*

Orton, Helen Fuller 1872-1955 *AmA&B, AuBYP, CarSB, ChPo S2, CurB 41, CurB 55, JBA 1934, JBA 1951*

Orton, Hugh *MnBBF*

Orwell, George 1903-1950 *AtlBL, CasWL, CnMWL, CyWA, DcLEnL, EncWL, EvLB, LongC, ModBL, ModBL Sup, NCHEL, OxEng, Pen Eng, RAdv 1, REn, TwCA, TwCA Sup, TwCW, WEAL, WWTwL*

Osborn, Merton B 1908- *ConAu 25R*

Osborn, Robert Chesley 1904- *AmA&B, CurB 59, IlBYP, IlCB 1957, WWA 38, WWGA*

Osborne, Adrian T *MnBBF, WWBWI A*

Osborne, Adrian T *see* Hamilton, Cecily

Osborne, Chester Gorham 1915- *ConAu 21R, SmATA 11, WWE 14, WrD*

Osborne, David *AuBYP, ConAu XR, SmATA XR, ThBJA*

Osborne, David *see* Silverberg, Robert

Osborne, Dorothy Gladys Yeo 1917- *Au&Wr 6, ConAu 9R, WrD*

Osborne, John 1907- *ConAu 61, WWA 38*

Osborne, Leone Neal 1914- *ConAu 21R, SmATA 2*

Osborne, Linda Barrett 1949- *ConAu 65*

Osborne, Mark *MnBBF, WWBWI A*

Osborne, Mark *see* Bayfield, William John

Osborne, Mark *see* Bobin, John William

Osgood, Mrs. M A *Alli Sup, CarSB*

Osgood, William E 1926- *AuBYP, BiDL 5, ConAu 33*

Osmond, Edward 1900- *Au&Wr 6, AuBYP,*

ConAu P-1, IlCB 1946, SmATA 10, SmATA 7

Osmond, Laurie *Au&Wr 6, WrD*

Ostendorf, Lloyd, Jr. 1921- *AuBYP, ConAu 1R, WWAA 1973*

Osterritter, John Ferdinand 1923- *AmMWS 12P, ConAu 45*

Ostman, Lempi 1899- *IlCB 1744*

Otchis, Ethel 1920- *ConAu 13R*

Otis, James 1848-1912 *Alli Sup, AmA&B, BiD&SB, DcAmA, DcNAA, JBA 1934, JBA 1951, OxAm*

Otis, James *see* Kaler, James Otis

Ottesen, Thea Tauber 1913- *ConAu 5R*

Ottesen, Thea Tauber *see* Bank-Jensen, Thea

Ottley, Reginald *Au&Wr 6*

Otto, Margaret Glover 1909-1976 *AuBYP, ConAu 61*

Ouida 1839?-1908 *BbD, BiD&SB, BrAu 19, CasWL, Chambr 3, CyWA, DcBiA, DcEnA, DcEnA Ap, DcEnL, DcEuL, DcLEnL, EvLB, HsB&A, JBA 1934, LongC, NCHEL, OxEng, Pen Eng, TelT*

Ouida *see* DeLaRamee, Louise

Ouida *see* LaRamee, Louise De

Ouida *see* Ramee, Louise DeLa

Oursler, Fulton 1893-1952 *AmA&B, AuBYP, CatA 1930, CurB 42, CurB 52, DcSpL, REn, REnAL, TwCA Sup, WNAA*

Ousley, Odille 1896- *ConAu P-1, SmATA 10*

Outcault, R F 1863-1928 *ArtCS*

Outhwaite, Ernest *MnBBF*

Overholser, Wayne D 1906- *AmA&B, Au&Wr 6, ConAu 5R*

Overman, Michael 1920- *Au&Wr 6*

Overton, Jenny Margaret Mary 1942- *Au&Wr 6, ConAu 57, WrD*

Overton, Robert *Alli Sup, ChPo S1, MnBBF, WWBWI A*

Ovington, Ray *AuBYP*

Owen, Benjamin Evan *WrD*

Owen, Betty Meek 1913- *ForWC 1970*

Owen, Caroline Dale *OhA&B, WNAA, YABC XR*

Owen, Caroline Dale *see* Snedeker, Caroline Dale Parke

Owen, Clifford *MnBBF, SmATA XR*

Owen, Clifford *see* Hamilton, Charles Harold St. John

Owen, Miss D E *MnBBF*

Owen, Miss D E *see* English, Don

Owen, Harold 1897- *ConAu 13R*

Owen, Hedley *MnBBF*

Owen, Hedley *see* O'Mant, Hedley Percival Angelo

Owen, Norman *MnBBF*

Owen, Norman *see* Walters, J

Owen, Russell 1889-1952 *AmA&B, AuBYP, REnAL*

Owen, Ruth Bryan 1885-1954 *AmA&B, AuBYP, ChPo S1, CurB 44, CurB 54*

Owen, Tom *ConAu XR*

Owen, Tom *see* Watts, Peter Christopher

Owen, Vincent *MnBBF, WWBWI A*

Owen, Vincent *see* Cook, Fred Gordon

Owen, Wilfred 1893-1918 *AtlBL, ChPo, ChPo S1, ChPo S2, CnE&AP, CnMWL, DcLEnL, EncWL, EvLB, LongC, ModBL, ModBL Sup, NCHEL, OxEng, Pen Eng,*

RAdv 1, REn, TwCA, TwCA Sup,
TwCW, WEAL, WWTwL
Owen, Wilfred 1912- *AmMWS 12S,*
ConAu 37
Owen, Will 1869- *WWBWI 1*
Owens, Jesse 1913- *BiN 1974, CurB 56*
Owens, Joan Llewelyn 1919- *ConAu 13R*
Owens, Thelma 1905- *ConAu 69*
Owens, Thelma *see* Grafton, Ann
Oxenbury, Helen 1938- *ChPo S2, ConAu 25R,*
IlBYP, SmATA 3, ThBJA
Oxenbury, Helen *see* Burningham, Helen
Oxenbury
Oxley, James Macdonald 1855-1907 *BiD&SB,*
DcLEnL, DcNAA, MnBBF, OxCan
Ozanne, C H *MnBBF*

P

Paasche, Carol L 1937- *ConAu 5R*
Pabke, Marie *Alli Sup, CarSB*
Pace, Mildred Mastin 1907- *ConAu 5R*
Pack, Robert 1929- *AmA&B, AuBYP, ChPo, ConAu 1R, ConP 1970, ConP 1975, DrAP 1975, Pen Am, REnAL, WorAu, WrD*
Packard, Andrew 1929- *ConAu 1R*
Packard, Frank Lucius 1877-1942 *AmA&B, AmLY, CanNov, CanWr, CurB 42, DcLEnL, DcNAA, EncM&D, MnBBF, NCHEL, OxCan, TwCA, TwCA Sup*
Packard, Vance 1914- *AmA&B, AuNews 1, BiN 1974, CelR 3, ConAu 9R, CurB 58, IntWW 38, LongC, REnAL, WW 1974, WorAu*
Packer, Joy 1905- *Au&Wr 6, AuBYP, ConAu 1R, TwCW, WW 1974*
Padgett, Henry J *MnBBF*
Page, Eileen *ConAu XR, SmATA 7*
Page, Eileen *see* Heal, Edith
Page, Eleanor *ConAu XR, SmATA 1, SmATA 1, WWAW 8*
Page, Eleanor *see* Coerr, Eleanor
Page, Grover, Jr. 1918- *ConAu 17R*
Page, Lou Williams 1912- *AuBYP, ConAu 5R*
Page, Richard *MnBBF*
Page, Thomas Nelson 1853-1922 *Alli Sup, AmA, AmA&B, AmLY, BbD, BiD&SB, BiDSA, CarSB, CasWL, Chambr 3, ChPo, CnDAL, CyWA, DcAmA, DcBiA, DcLEnL, DcNAA, JBA 1934, OxAm, Pen Am, REn, REnAL, St&VC, WEAL*
Page, Walter *MnBBF*
Pagels, Elaine Hiesey 1943- *ConAu 45, DrAS 6P*
Paget, Francis Edward 1806-1882 *Alli, Alli Sup, BiD&SB, BrAu 19, TelT, WWCL*
Paget, H M *WWBWI 1*
Paget, Sidney *WWBWI 1*
Paget, Walter *WWBWI 1*
Paget-Fredericks, Joseph E P Rous-Marten 1905?- *ChPo, ConICB, IIBYP, IICB 1946, St&VC*
Pahz, Cheryl Suzanne 1949- *ConAu XR, SmATA 11*
Pahz, Cheryl Suzanne *see* Goldfeder, Cheryl
Pahz, Cheryl Suzanne *see* Paz, Zan
Pahz, James Alon 1943- *ConAu XR, SmATA 11*
Pahz, James Alon *see* Goldfeder, Jim

Pahz, James Alon *see* Paz, A
Paice, Margaret 1920- *ConAu 29, SingR 1, SmATA 10*
Pain, Allison George Odell *ChPo, MnBBF*
Pain, Barry Eric Odell 1864-1928 *BbD, Chambr 3, ChPo, DcEnA Ap, DcLEnL, EncM&D, EvLB, LongC, MnBBF, NCHEL, OxEng, REn, TwCA, WWBWI A*
Pain, G O *MnBBF*
Paine, Albert Bigelow 1861-1937 *AmA&B, BiD&SB, CarSB, ChPo, ChPo S1, ChPo S2, CnDAL, DcAmA, DcNAA, JBA 1934, OxAm, REn, REnAL, TwCA, WNAA*
Paine, Hammond *MnBBF*
Paine, Hammond *see* Hook, H Clarke
Paine, Ralph Delahaye 1871-1925 *AmA&B, AmLY, DcNAA, JBA 1934, REnAL, TwCA*
Paine, Roberta M 1925- *ConAu 33, SmATA 13*
Painter, Sidney 1902-1960 *AmA&B*
Painton, Herbert *MnBBF*
Paisley, Tom 1932- *ConAu 61, SmATA XR*
Paisley, Tom *see* Bethancourt, T Ernesto
Palazzo, Anthony D 1905-1970 *ChPo, ChPo S1, ConAu XR, SmATA 3*
Palazzo, Anthony D *see* Palazzo, Tony
Palazzo, Tony 1905-1970 *AuBYP, ConAu 5R, ConAu 29, IICB 1946, IICB 1957, ThBJA*
Palazzo, Tony *see* Palazzo, Anthony D
Palder, Edward L 1922- *SmATA 5*
Paley, Alan L 1943- *ConAu 69*
Palgrave, Francis Turner 1824-1897 *Alli, Alli Sup, BiD&SB, BrAu 19, CasWL, Chambr 3, ChPo, ChPo S1, ChPo S2, DcEnA, DcEnA Ap, DcEnL, DcEuL, DcLEnL, EvLB, NCHEL, OxEng, Pen Eng, REn, WEAL*
Palk, Arthur J *MnBBF, WWBWI A*
Pallas, Dorothy Constance 1933-1971 *Au&Wr 6, ConAu 33*
Pallas, Norvin 1918- *ConAu 1R, WrD*
Pailenberg, Corrado 1912- *ConAu 13R*
Palmer, Bernard 1914- *ConAu 57*
Palmer, Bernard *see* Runyan, John
Palmer, C Everard 1930- *Au&Wr 6, ConAu 41*
Palmer, Candida 1926- *ConAu 61, SmATA 11*

Palmer, E Vance *MnBBF*
Palmer, E Vance *see* Palmer, Vance Edward
Palmer, Geoffrey *ChPo S2*
Palmer, Helen G 1911- *BiDL 5, SingR 1*
Palmer, Helen Marion 1898-1967 *AuBYP*
Palmer, John Leslie 1885-1944 *CurB 44,*
  DcLEnL, EncM&D, EvLB, LongC,
  MnBBF, NCHEL, TwCA, TwCA Sup
Palmer, John Leslie *see* Beeding, Francis
Palmer, Juliette 1930- *IlBYP, WrD*
Palmer, Marjorie 1919- *ConAu 57*
Palmer, Robin 1911- *AuBYP*
Palmer, Vance Edward 1885-1959 *ChPo,*
  LongC, MnBBF, Pen Eng, TwCW
Palmer, Vance Edward *see* Palmer, E Vance
Paltenghi, Madeleine *ConAu XR*
Paltenghi, Madeleine *see* Anderson, Madeleine
  Paltenghi
Panesis, Nicholas 1913- *IlCB 1744*
Panowski, Eileen Thompson 1920- *AuBYP,*
  ConAu 5R, WrD
Panowski, Eileen Thompson *see* Thompson,
  Eileen
Pansy *AmA&B, AmLY Xr, BiD&SB,*
  DcAMA, DcNAA, OhA&B, OxAm,
  YABC XR
Panter, Carol 1936- *ConAu 49, SmATA 9*
Panting, Arnold Clement d1917 *MnBBF,*
  WWBWI A
Panting, Arnold Clement *see* Arnold, Clement
Panting, James Harwood *MnBBF,*
  WWBWI A
Panting, James Harwood *see* Heathcote, Claude
Panting, Phyllis *MnBBF, WWBWI A*
Panzarella, Andrew 1940- *ConAu 25R*
Papas, William 1927- *ConAu 25R, IlCB 1957,*
  WrD
Papashvily, George 1898- *AmA&B, CurB 45,*
  REnAL, TwCA Sup, WWAA 1973
Papashvily, Helen 1906- *AmA&B, CurB 45,*
  REnAL, TwCA Sup
Pape, D L 1930- *ConAu XR, SmATA 2*
Pape, D L *see* Pape, Donna L
Pape, Donna L 1930- *ConAu 21R*
Pape, Donna L *see* Pape, D L
Pape, Eric 1870- *ChPo, ConICB*
Paperny, Myra 1932- *ConAu 69*
Paradis, Adrian Alexis 1912- *AuBYP,*
  ConAu 1R, MorJA, SmATA 1, WrD
Paradis, Marjorie Bartholomew 1886-1970
  AmA&B, AuBYP, ConAu 29, WNAA
Parbuckle, Lieutenant *MnBBF*
Pard *MnBBF*
Pardepp, R *MnBBF*
Paris, Jeanne 1918- *ConAu 1R, WWA 38,*
  WWAW 8, WWE 14
Paris, John 1912- *WW 1974*
Parish, James Robert 1944- *ConAu 33,*
  WWA 38
Parish, Margaret Holt *AuBYP*
Parish, Margaret Holt *see* Holt, Margaret
Parish, Peggy 1927- *AuBYP, ForWC 1970*
Park, Ruth *Au&Wr 6, CatA 1952, SingR 2,*
  TwCW
Park, Thomas Choonbai 1919- *AuBYP, LE 5*
Parke, Margaret Bittner *AuBYP, WWAW 8*
Parker, Alfred Eustace *AuBYP*
Parker, Arthur Caswell 1881-1955 *AmA&B,*

REnAL
Parker, Bertha Morris 1890- *AuBYP,*
  ConAu 5R, ForWC 1970, MorJA,
  WWA 38, WWAW 8
Parker, Edgar 1925- *ChPo, IlCB 1957,*
  ThBJA
Parker, Elinor Milnor 1906- *ChPo, ConAu 1R,*
  SmATA 3, WWA 38
Parker, Eric 1870- *ChPo, ChPo S1, ChPo S2,*
  MnBBF, WWBWI A, WWLA
Parker, Eric R 1897?- *WWBWI I, WWCL*
Parker, Fania M Pockrose *AuBYP*
Parker, Henry Webster 1822?-1903 *Alli,*
  CarSB, CyAL 2, DcAmA, DcNAA
Parker, John 1923- *BiDL 5, ConAu 5R,*
  DrAS 6H
Parker, K Langloh 1855-1940 *AnCL*
Parker, Kay Peterson 1901- *IlCB 1946*
Parker, Lois M 1912- *ConAu 69*
Parker, Martin *MnBBF*
Parker, Nancy Winslow 1930- *ConAu 49,*
  IlBYP, SingR 2, SmATA 10, WrD
Parker, Richard 1915- *AuBYP, WrD*
Parker, Robert Andrew 1927- *ChPo S2,*
  DcCAA 2, IlBYP, WWA 38,
  WWAA 1973
Parker, Rosa Abbott *Alli, Alli Sup, CarSB,*
  DcNAA
Parker, W H 1912- *ConAu 33*
Parkinson, C Northcote 1909- *ConAu 5R,*
  CurB 60, NYTBE 2
Parkinson, Ethelyn Minerva 1906- *ConAu 49,*
  SmATA 11, WWA 38, WWAW 8
Parkinson, Roger 1939- *Au&Wr 6*
Parkinson, Virginia *ChPo S1*
Parkman, Francis 1823-1893 *Alli, Alli Sup,*
  AmA, AmA&B, AtlBL, BbD, BbthC,
  BiD&SB, CasWL, CyAL 2, CyWA,
  DcAmA, DcLEnL, DcNAA, EvLB,
  MouLC 4, OxAm, OxCan, OxEng,
  Pen Am, REn, REnAL, WEAL
Parks, Aileen Wells 1901- *ConAu 5R*
Parks, David 1944- *ConAu 25R*
Parks, Edd Winfield 1906-1968 *AmA&B,*
  ConAu 5R, SmATA 10
Parks, Gordon 1912- *AmA&B, AuNews 2,*
  BlkAW, CelR 3, ConAu 41, ConLC 1,
  CurB 68, LBAA, SmATA 8
Parlett, George *WWBWI I*
Parlett, Reg *WWBWI I*
Parley, Peter 1793-1860 *Alli, AmA, AmA&B,*
  BiD&SB, BrAu 19, ChPo, ChPo S1,
  ChPo S2, DcAmA, DcEnL, DcNAA,
  OxAm, REn, REnAL, WWCL
Parlin, John *AuBYP, ConAu XR, SmATA 4*
Parlin, John *see* Graves, Charles Parlin
Parnall, Peter 1936- *ChPo S2, IlBYP,*
  IlCB 1957, ThBJA
Parr, Adolph Henry 1900- *AuBYP*
Parr, Harriet 1828- *Alli, Alli Sup, BbD,*
  DcEnL, PoCh, TelT
Parr, Harriet *see* Lee, Holme
Parr, Letitia Evelyn *WrD*
Parr, Lucy 1924- *ConAu 29, SmATA 10*
Parr, Lucy *see* Carroll, Laura
Parrish, Anne 1888-1957 *AmA&B, AmNov,*
  CnDAL, ConAmL, EvLB, IlBYP,
  IlCB 1744, IlCB 1946, LongC, OxAm,
  REnAL, TwCA, TwCA Sup, TwCW,

WNAA

Parrish, Mary *ConAu XR, SmATA 2*

Parrish, Mary *see* Cousins, Margaret

Parrish, Maxfield 1870-1966 *AmA&B, ChPo, ConICB, CurB 65, CurB 66, IIBYP, IICB 1744, JBA 1934, JBA 1951, OxAm, REnAL*

Parry, David Harold 1868-1950 *MnBBF, WWBWI A, WWCL*

Parry, David Harold *see* Blake, Wilton, Captain

Parry, David Harold *see* Pike, Morton

Parry, Marian 1924- *ConAu 41, SmATA 13*

Parry, Peter *MnBBF*

Parry, Reginald R *MnBBF*

Parry, Richmond *MnBBF*

Parsons, Anthony 1893-1963 *MnBBF, WWBWI A*

Parsons, Anthony *see* Nicholls, Anthony

Parsons, B *MnBBF*

Parsons, B *see* Hunt, Maurice

Parsons, B *see* Young, Warwick

Parsons, Harcourt *MnBBF*

Parsons, Kitty *ChPo, ChPo S1, ConAu 13R, WNAA, WWAA 1973, WrD*

Parsons, Virginia *IIBYP*

Parton, Ethel 1862-1944 *AmA&B, ChPo, DcNAA, JBA 1934, JBA 1951, REnAL*

Partridge, Anthony *EncM&D, WWBWI A*

Partridge, Anthony *see* Oppenheim, Edward Phillips

Partridge, Benjamin Waring, Jr. 1915- *ConAu 25R, WWE 14*

Pascal, David 1918- *ChPo S1, ConAu 9R, IICB 1957, WWA 38, WWAA 1973, WWE 14*

Paschal, Nancy *AuBYP, ConAu XR, ForWC 1970, SmATA XR*

Paschal, Nancy *see* Trotter, Grace V

Passingham, William John 1897- *MnBBF, WWBWI A*

Passos, John Dos 1896-1970 *CurB 40, CurB 70, Pen Am, TwCA, TwCA Sup*

Passos, John Dos *see* DosPassos, John

Patanne, Maria *ConAu XR*

Patanne, Maria *see* LaPietra, Mary

Patapoff, Elizabeth 1917- *ConAu 29*

Patch, Edith Marion 1876-1954 *AmA&B, AmLY, JBA 1934, JBA 1951, WNAA*

Patch, Olive 1839-1927 *Alli Sup, CarSB*

Patchen, Kenneth 1911-1972 *AmA&B, AmNov, Au&Wr 6, CasWL, ChPo, ChPo S1, CnDAL, ConAu 1R, ConAu 33, ConLC 1, ConLC 2, ConNov 1972, ConP 1970, ConP 1975, DcLEnL, ModAL, NYTBE 3, OhA&B, OxAm, Pen Am, RAdv 1, REn, REnAL, TwCA, TwCA Sup, WEAL, WWTwL*

Patchett, Mary Osborne Elwyn 1897- *Au&Wr 6, AuBYP, ConAu 5R, SingR 1, WrD*

Pate, Billie 1932- *ConAu 61*

Pateman, J S *MnBBF*

Patent, Dorothy Hinshaw 1940- *ConAu 61*

Paterson, Arthur Henry 1862-1928 *MnBBF, WWBWI A*

Paterson, Katherine 1932- *ConAu 21R, SmATA 13*

Paton, Alan Stewart 1903- *Au&Wr 6, AuBYP, CasWL, ConAu P-1, ConLC 4,*

ConNov 1972, ConNov 1976, CurB 52, CyWA, EncWL, IntWW 38, LongC, NCHEL, Pen Eng, REn, SmATA 11, TwCA Sup, TwCW, WEAL, WW 1974, WWTwL, WWWor 2

Paton, James *CarSB*

Paton, James, III 1923- *DrAS 6E*

Paton, Jane Elizabeth 1934- *Au&Wr 6, ChPo, ChPo S1, IIBYP, IICB 1957*

Paton Walsh, Gillian 1937?- *Au&Wr 6, SmATA 4, WWAW 8*

Paton Walsh, Gillian *see* Paton Walsh, Jill

Paton Walsh, Jill 1937?- *ConAu 21R, SmATA 4, WrD*

Paton Walsh, Jill *see* Paton Walsh, Gillian

Paton Walsh, Jill *see* Walsh, Jill Paton

Patrick, John *MnBBF*

Patrick, Max *MnBBF*

Patrick, Max *see* McCormack, James

Patten, Brian 1946- *ConAu 25R, ConP 1970, ConP 1975, WrD*

Patten, Lewis Byford 1915- *ConAu 25R, WWA 38, WWW 14*

Patten, William Gilbert 1866-1945 *AmA&B, CarSB, CnDAL, HsB&A, OxAm, REnAL*

Patterson, Emma L 1904- *ConAu P-2*

Patterson, Ewen K *MnBBF*

Patterson, Franklin 1916- *ConAu 45*

Patterson, George Andrew *MnBBF*

Patterson, Lillie G *AuBYP*

Patterson, Russell 1894- *ArtCS, WWA 38*

Patterson, Samuel White 1883-1975 *AmA&B, ChPo, ConAu P-2, DrAS 6H, WNAA*

Patton, Frances Gray 1906- *AmA&B, Au&Wr 6, CnDAL, ConNov 1972, ConNov 1976, CurB 55, REnAL*

Paul, Policeman *MnBBF, WWBWI A*

Paul, Policeman *see* Blyth, Harry

Paul, Aileen 1917- *ConAu 41, SmATA 12*

Paul, Grace 1908- *ConAu 17R*

Paul, James *IIBYP*

Paul, James *see* Kocsis, James C

Paulden, Sydney 1932- *ConAu 29, WrD*

Pauli, Hertha Ernestine 1909-1973 *AmA&B, AuBYP, BkC 5, CatA 1930, ConAu 1R, ConAu 41, ForWC 1970, NYTBE 4, SmATA 3, WWAW 8, WWE 14*

Paull, Grace A 1898- *AuBYP, IICB 1744, IICB 1946, JBA 1951*

Paull, Harry Major 1854-1934 *ChPo S1, MnBBF*

Paull, Harry Major *see* Blake, Paul

Paull, Mary Anna *Alli Sup, CarSB*

Paull, Minnie E 1859-1895 *CarSB, ChPo, DcNAA*

Paulson, Jack *ConAu XR, SmATA 6*

Paulson, Jack *see* Jackson, C Paul

Paulsson, Bjoern K 1932- *ConAu 61*

Paustovsky, Konstantin 1892-1968 *ConAu 25R*

Pavel, Frances K 1907- *ConAu 21R, SmATA 10*

Paxton, Alfred *MnBBF*

Payes, Rachel C 1922- *ConAu 49*

Payne, A B *WWBWI I*

Payne, Alan *ConAu XR, NYTBE 4*

Payne, Alan *see* Jakes, John W

Payne, Alma Smith *AuBYP, ConAu 17R, ForWC 1970*

Payne, Crutchley *MnBBF*
Payne, Crutchley *see* Evans, Frank Howel
Payne, Donald Gordon 1924- *ConAu 13R*
Payne, Donald Gordon *see* Marshall, James Vance
Payne, Emmy *AuBYP*
Payne, Emmy *see* West, Emily
Payne, G M *WWBWI I*
Payne, Joan Balfour 1923-1973 *ConAu 41, IlBYP, IlCB 1946, IlCB 1957*
Payne, Stephen *AmA&B*
Payson, Dale 1943- *IlBYP, SmATA 9*
Payzant, Charles *IlBYP*
Paz, A *ConAu XR, SmATA XR*
Paz, A *see* Pahz, James Alon
Paz, Zan *ConAu XR, SmATA XR*
Paz, Zan *see* Pahz, Cheryl Suzanne
Peabody, Josephine Preston 1874-1922 *AmA&B, BiD&SB, CarSB, ChPo, ChPo S1, CnDAL, ConAmL, DcAmA, DcNAA, EvLB, LongC, ModWD, OxAm, REnAL, TwCA*
Peacock, Lucy 1786-1815 *Alli, BiDLA, CarSB*
Peake, Mervyn Lawrence 1911-1968 *ChPo, ChPo S1, ChPo S2, ConNov 1976, IlCB 1946, LongC, REn, WWCL, WorAu*
Peake, Miriam Morrison 1901- *ConAu 57*
Peale, Norman Vincent 1898- *AmA&B, Au&Wr 6, AuBYP, AuNews 1, BiN 1974, CelR 3, CurB 46, CurB 74, OhA&B, REnAL, WWA 38, WWWor 2*
Pearce, Ann Philippa 1920- *Au&Wr 6, CasWL, WWA 38, WWAW 8, WWCL*
Pearce, C S *MnBBF*
Pearce, Charles Edward St. John *MnBBF, WWBWI A*
Pearce, Charles Louis St. John *MnBBF, WWBWI A*
Pearce, Charles Louis St. John *see* Fairbanks, Nat
Pearce, Charles Louis St. John *see* Pearce, St. John
Pearce, Philippa 1920- *AuBYP, ConAu 5R, SenS, SmATA 1, ThBJA, WWWor 2*
Pearce, St. John 1880- *MnBBF, WWBWI A*
Pearce, St. John *see* Pearce, Charles Louis St. John
Pearce, W E 1907- *AmMWS 12P*
Pearcy, G Etzel 1905- *ConAu 1R*
Peare, Catherine Owens 1911- *Au&Wr 6, AuBYP, ConAu 5R, CurB 59, MorJA, SmATA 9*
Pearl, Hal 1914?-1975 *ConAu 61*
Pearl, Jack *ConAu XR*
Pearl, Jack *see* Pearl, Jacques Bain
Pearl, Jacques Bain 1923- *ConAu 5R*
Pearl, Jacques Bain *see* Pearl, Jack
Pearl, Richard Maxwell 1913- *AmMWS 12P, AuBYP, ConAu 9R*
Pearlman, Moshe 1911- *ConAu 5R, WWWor 2, WWWorJ 1972*
Pears, Charles 1873- *ChPo, IlCB 1744*
Pears, John *MnBBF*
Pearse, Alfred 1856- *WWBWI I*
Pearse, Susan Beatrice *ConICB, IlCB 1744*
Pearson, Alec George *MnBBF, WWBWI A*
Pearson, Alec George *see* Howard, Bruce

Pearson, Alec George *see* Linley, Julian
Pearson, Alec George *see* Pearson, George
Pearson, Alec George *see* Scott, Russell, Captain
Pearson, B H 1893- *ConAu 65*
Pearson, E V *MnBBF*
Pearson, Edmund Lester 1880-1937 *AmA&B, CarSB, DcNAA, LongC, OxAm, REnAL, TwCA, WNAA*
Pearson, George *MnBBF*
Pearson, George *see* Pearson, Alec George
Pearson, Margaret M *SingR 1*
Pearson, Norman Holmes 1909-1975 *AmA&B, ConAu 61, DrAS 6E, WWA 38, WWWor 2*
Pearson, Shepperd *MnBBF*
Pearson, Shepperd *see* Hadath, John Edward Gunby
Pearson, Susan 1946- *ConAu 65*
Pearson, T E *MnBBF*
Pearson, T E *see* North, Pearson
Peary, Josephine Diebitsch 1863-1895 *AmA&B, CarSB, DcAmA, REnAL, WNAA*
Pease, Howard 1894- *AmA&B, AuBYP, ConAu 5R, JBA 1934, JBA 1951, REnAL, SmATA 2, WWA 38*
Pease, Josephine VanDolzen *AuBYP, ChPo, ChPo S1*
Pease, Lute 1869-1966 *ArtCS, CurB 49, CurB 63, REnAL*
Peattie, Donald Culross 1898-1964 *AmA&B, AuBYP, ConAmA, CurB 40, CurB 65, DcLEnL, MnBBF, OxAm, REnAL, TwCA, TwCA Sup, WNAA*
Peattie, Louise Redfield 1900-1965 *AmA&B, MnBBF, TwCA, TwCA Sup, WNAA*
Peck, Anne Merriman 1884- *AmA&B, AuBYP, ChPo, ChPo S1, IlCB 1744, IlCB 1946, JBA 1934, JBA 1951*
Peck, Anne Merriman *see* Johnson, Enid
Peck, Clara Elsene *ConICB*
Peck, Franklin M *MnBBF*
Peck, George Wilbur 1840-1916 *AmA, AmA&B, BbD, BiD&SB, CarSB, CnDAL, DcAmA, DcNAA, OxAm, Pen Am, REn, REnAL, WWCL, WisW*
Peck, Helen Estelle 1910- *ConAu 5R, ForWC 1970*
Peck, Richard *ChPo S2, DrAF 1976, DrAP 1975*
Peckham, Howard Henry 1910- *AmA&B, ChPo, ConAu 9R, DrAS 6H, WWA 38*
Peckinpah, Betty *AuBYP*
Peddie, Tom *ChPo, WWBWI I*
Pedersen, Elsa Kienitz 1915- *AuBYP, ConAu 1R, ForWC 1970*
Pedley, Ethel *SingR 1*
Peel, H M 1930- *ConAu 9R, WrD*
Peele, Ernest H *MnBBF*
Peeples, Edwin A 1915- *ConAu 9R, SmATA 6, WrD*
Peet, Bill 1915- *AmPB, Au&Wr 6, ChPo, ChPo S1, ChFB A, ConAu XR, IlCB 1957, IndAu 1917, SmATA 2, ThBJA, WrD*
Peet, Bill *see* Peet, William Bartlett
Peet, Creighton 1899- *AuBYP*
Peet, William Bartlett 1915- *AuBYP, ConAu 17R, SmATA 2*

Peet, William Bartlett see Peet, Bill
Pei, Mario Andrew 1901- AmA&B,
   ConAu 5R, DrAS 6F, REnAL,
   TwCA Sup, WWA 38, WWWor 2
Peirce, Waldo 1884-1970 CurB 44, CurB 70,
   DcCAA 2, IICB 1744
Pelaez, Jill Fletcher 1924- ConAu 33,
   SmATA 12, WrD
Pelking, Kirk WrD
Pelletier, Ingrid 1912- ConAu 29
Pellowski, Anne 1933- BiDL 5, ChPo S1,
   ConAu 21R, WWAW 8
Pels, Gertrude Jaeckel AuBYP
Peltier, Leslie C 1900- AmMWS 12P,
   ConAu 17R, SmATA 13
Peltz, George A CarSB
Pemberton, Sir Max 1863-1950 BbD, BiD&SB,
   Chambr 3, DcBiA, DcEnA Ap, EncM&D,
   EvLB, LongC, MnBBF, NCHEL,
   WWBWI A, WWCL, WWLA
Pembroke, Richard MnBBF
Pembroke, Ronald MnBBF
Pembury, Bill ConAu XR, SmATA XR
Pembury, Bill see Groom, Arthur William
Pembury, Grosvenor MnBBF
Pembury, Grosvenor see Haydon, N G
Pembury, Montague MnBBF
Pembury, Montague see Moon, George P
Pender, Lydia Podger 1907- AuBYP,
   ConAu 5R, SingR 1, SmATA 3, WrD
Pendery, Rosemary Schmitz ConAu 53,
   SmATA 7
Pendexter, Hugh 1875-1940 AmA&B, MnBBF,
   REnAL, WNAA
Pendle, George 1906- Au&Wr 6, ConAu 5R
Pendleton, Don 1927- ConAu 33, WWMW 14
Pendleton, Louis 1861-1939 AmA&B, BbD,
   BiD&SB, BiDSA, CarSB, DcAmA,
   DcNAA, WNAA
Pendower, Jacques 1899- Au&Wr 6,
   ConAu 9R, MnBBF, WWBWI A
Pendower, Jacques see Jacobs, T C H
Pene DuBois, William AmPB
Pene DuBois, William see DuBois, William Pene
Penfield, Thomas 1903- ConAu 5R
Penn, Ruth Bonn ConAu XR, SmATA 3
Penn, Ruth Bonn see Rosenberg, Ethel
Pennage, E M ConAu XR, SmATA 8
Pennage, E M see Finkel, George
Penney, Grace Jackson 1904- AnCL,
   ConAu 5R
Penney, Richard L 1935- AmMWS 12P
Pennington, Eunice 1923- ConAu 57
Pennington, Howard 1923- ConAu 49
Penrose, Margaret ConAu P-2
Penrose, Margaret see Stratemeyer, Edward L
Pentelow, John Nix 1872-1931 MnBBF,
   WWBWI A
Pentelow, John Nix see Clifford, Martin
Pentelow, John Nix see Graham, Armitage
Pentelow, John Nix see Huntingdon, Harry
Pentelow, John Nix see Hustington, Harry
Pentelow, John Nix see North, Jack
Pentelow, John Nix see Randolph, Richard
Pentelow, John Nix see Richards, Frank
Pentelow, John Nix see Ryle, Randolph
Pentelow, John Nix see West, John
Pepe, Phil 1935- ConAu 25R
Peppe, Rodney Darrell 1934- ChPo S2,

ConAu 33, SmATA 4, WrD
Pepper, Curtis G 1920- ConAu 21R
Pepper, Frank S MnBBF, WWBWI A
Pepper, Frank S see Marshall, John
Pepper, Frank S see Wilton, Hal
Peppercorn, E L MnBBF
Peppler, Alice Stopler 1934- ConAu 53
Perard, Victor Semon 1870- IICB 1744
Perceval, Don 1908- IIBYP, IICB 1946
Percival, John 1927- ConAu 33
Percival, Thomas 1740-1804 Alli, CarSB
Percy, Charles Harting 1919- BiN 1974,
   CelR 3, ConAu 65, CurB 59, IntWW 38,
   WWA 38, WWMW 14, WWWor 2
Percy, Charles Henry ConAu XR, SmATA 4
Percy, Charles Henry see Smith, Dodie
Perera, Thomas Biddle 1938- AmMWS 12S,
   ConAu 37, SmATA 13
Peretz, Don 1922- AmMWS 12S, ConAu 9R,
   WWWorJ 1972
Pergarth, Peter MnBBF
Pergarth, Peter see Goddard, Norman Molyneux
Perkins, Al ChPo S1
Perkins, Lucy Fitch 1865-1937 AmA&B,
   CarSB, ChPo, ChPo S2, ConICB,
   DcNAA, IndAu 1816, JBA 1934,
   JBA 1951, OxAm, REnAL, WNAA
Perkins, Marlin WWA 38
Perkins, Marlin see Perkins, Richard Marlin
Perkins, Nancy ChPo S2
Perkins, Richard Marlin 1905- AmMWS 12P,
   AuBYP, CurB 51
Perkins, Richard Marlin see Perkins, Marlin
Perkins, Steve ConAu 49
Perkins, Wilma Lord 1897- WWA 38
Perl, Lila AuBYP, ConAu 33, SmATA 6
Perl, Susan 1922- ChPo, ChPo S2,
   ConAu 17R, IIBYP, IICB 1957,
   WWE 14
Perlman, Raymond 1923- WWAA 1973
Perlmutter, O William 1920-1975 ConAu 57,
   SmATA 8
Perowne, Barry 1908- EncM&D, MnBBF,
   WWBWI A
Perowne, Barry see Atkey, Philip
Perrault, Charles 1628-1703 AnCL, BbD,
   BiD&SB, CarSB, CasWL, ChPo, DcEuL,
   EuAu, EvEuW, NCHEL, OxEng, OxFr,
   Pen Eur, REn, St&VC, WWCL
Perrin, Blanche Chenery 1894-1973 ConAu 5R,
   ConAu 41
Perrine, Mary 1913- ConAu 25R, SmATA 2
Perrott, Jennifer IIBYP
Perry, Bill 1905- ArtCS
Perry, George B MnBBF
Perry, John 1914- AuBYP, ConAu 5R
Perry, Nora 1831-1896 Alli Sup, AmA,
   AmA&B, BbD, BiD&SB, CarSB, ChPo,
   ChPo S1, ChPo S2, DcAmA, DcNAA,
   REnAL
Perry, Richard ConAu 41
Perry, Shauneille BlkAW, NYTBE 2
Perry, Vincent MnBBF
Perse, Saint-John 1887-1975 AnCL, CnMWL,
   ConAu XR, ConLC 4, CyWA, EncWL,
   EvEuW, IntWW 38, ModRL, Pen Eur,
   REn, TwCW, WWTwL, WWWor 2
Perse, Saint-John see Leger, Alexis Saint-Leger
Person, William Thomas 1900- AuBYP

Pesek, Ludek 1919- *ConAu 29*
Pete, Lariat *MnBBF*
Peter, John 1921- *ConAu 1R, DrAS 6E*
Peterkin, Julia 1880-1961 *AmA&B, CnDAL, ConAmA, LongC, OxAm, REn, REnAL, TwCA, TwCA Sup*
Peters, Alexander *ConAu XR*
Peters, Alexander *see* Hollander, Zander
Peters, Caroline *ConAu XR, SmATA XR*
Peters, Caroline *see* Betz, Eva Kelly
Peters, Donald Leslie 1925- *ConAu 21R, WWW 14*
Peters, Elizabeth 1927- *ConAu 57*
Peters, Elizabeth *see* Michaels, Barbara
Peters, Ken 1929- *ConAu 17R*
Peters, Lane *ConAu XR*
Peters, Lane *see* Lapidus, Elaine
Peters, Margaret Evelyn 1936- *ConAu 53*
Peters, Maureen 1935- *Au&Wr 6, ConAu 33, WrD*
Peters, S H *YABC XR*
Peters, S H *see* Porter, William Sydney
Petersham, Maud 1889-1971 *AmA&B, AmPB, AnCL, AuBYP, BkP, Cald 1938, ChPo, ChPo S1, ConAu 33, ConICB, IlBYP, IlCB 1744, IlCB 1946, IlCB 1957, JBA 1934, JBA 1951, REnAL, St&VC*
Petersham, Miska 1889-1960 *AmA&B, AmPB, AnCL, AuBYP, BkP, Cald 1938, ChPo, ChPo S1, ConICB, IlBYP, IlCB 1744, IlCB 1946, JBA 1934, JBA 1951, St&VC*
Peterson, Betty Ferguson 1917- *IlCB 1957*
Peterson, Hans 1922- *ConAu 49, SmATA 8*
Peterson, Harold Leslie 1922- *ConAu 1R, DrAS 6H, SmATA 8*
Peterson, Helen Stone 1910- *ConAu 37, SmATA 8, WrD*
Peterson, James *AuBYP, ConAu XR*
Peterson, James *see* Zeiger, Henry Anthony
Peterson, Ottis 1907- *ConAu 21R*
Peterson, Roger Tory 1908- *AmA&B, CelR 3, ConAu 1R, CurB 59, IntWW 38, NYTBS 5, REnAL, TwCA Sup, WWA 38, WWWor 2*
Peterson, Russell Francis *AuBYP, IlCB 1957*
Petie, Haris 1915- *ConAu XR, IlBYP, SmATA 10*
Petie, Haris *see* Petty, Roberta
Petrich, Patricia Barrett 1942- *ConAu 61*
Petrides, Heidrun 1944- *IlCB 1957*
Petrovich, Michael Boro 1922- *DrAS 6H*
Petrovskaya, Kyra 1918- *ConAu 1R, SmATA 8*
Petrovskaya, Kyra *see* Wayne, Kyra Petrovskaya
Petry, Ann Lane 1912- *AmA&B, AmNov, AnCL, AuBYP, BlkAW, ConAu 5R, ConLC 1, ConNov 1972, ConNov 1976, CurB 46, DrAP 1975, LBAA, LBAA, REn, REnAL, SmATA 5, ThBJA, TwCA Sup, WWAW 8, WrD*
Pettit, Mary P *AuBYP*
Petty, Roberta 1915- *ConAu 61*
Petty, Roberta *see* Petie, Haris
Pevsner, Sir Nikolaus 1902- *Au&Wr 6, ConAu 9R, DcLEnL, IntWW 38, LongC, WW 1974, WorAu*
Pevsner, Stella *ConAu 57, SmATA 8*
Peyton, K M 1929- *AuBYP, ChLR 3,*

ConAu XR, PiP, SenS, ThBJA, WrD
Peyton, K M *see* Peyton, Kathleen Wendy
Peyton, Karen 1897-1960? *ConAu P-1*
Peyton, Kathleen Wendy 1929- *Au&Wr 6, BrCA, ConAu 69*
Peyton, Kathleen Wendy *see* Herald, Kathleen
Peyton, Kathleen Wendy *see* Peyton, K M
Pfeffer, Susan Beth 1948- *ConAu 29, SmATA 4, WrD*
Phares, Ross 1908- *ConAu P-1*
Phelan, Joseph A *IlBYP*
Phelan, Josephine 1905- *AuBYP, BkC 5, CanWW 12, OxCan, OxCan Sup, Prof*
Phelan, Mary Kay 1914- *ConAu 1R, ForWC 1970, SmATA 3, WWAW 8, WWMW 14, WrD*
Phelps, Elizabeth Stuart 1815-1852 *Alli, AmA, AmA&B, CarSB, Chambr 3, CyAL 1, DcAmA, DcNAA, OxAm, REnAL*
Phelps, Elizabeth Stuart Ward 1844-1911 *Alli, Alli Sup, AmA, AmA&B, BbD, BiD&SB, CarSB, ChPo, ChPo S1, CyAL 2, DcAmA, DcBiA, DcEnL, DcLEnL, DcNAA*
Phelps, Margaret *AuBYP*
Philbrook, Clem 1917- *AuBYP*
Philips, George Norman 1888- *MnBBF, WWBWI A*
Philips, George Norman *see* Fremlin, Victor
Philips, George Norman *see* Norman, Philip
Philips, George Norman *see* Skene, Anthony
Philipson, Morris 1926- *WWA 38*
Philipson, Susan Sacher 1934- *ChPo, ConAu 9R*
Phillips, Alfred R *MnBBF*
Phillips, Derek *MnBBF*
Phillips, Ethel Calvert d1947 *AmA&B, DcNAA, JBA 1934, JBA 1951, WNAA*
Phillips, Forbes A *MnBBF*
Phillips, Forbes A *see* Forbes, Athol
Phillips, Horace 1880- *MnBBF, WWBWI A*
Phillips, Horace *see* Duke, Derek
Phillips, Horace *see* Hope, Walter
Phillips, Horace *see* Melbourne, Ida
Phillips, Horace *see* Stanton, Marjorie
Phillips, Irv *SmATA XR*
Phillips, Irv *see* Phillips, Irving W
Phillips, Irving W 1908?- *SmATA 11, WWAA 1973*
Phillips, Irving W *see* Phillips, Irv
Phillips, Irving W *see* Sabuso
Phillips, Jack *ConAu XR, SmATA 8*
Phillips, Jack *see* Sandburg, Carl
Phillips, Jo *NYTBS 5*
Phillips, Loretta 1893- *ConAu 13R, ConAu P-1, SmATA 10*
Phillips, Louis 1942- *ConAu 49, SmATA 8*
Phillips, Marie Tello 1874-1962 *AmA&B, AnCL 1926, ChPo S1, WNAA*
Phillips, Mary Geisler 1881-1964 *AuBYP, CarSB, ConAu 5R, SmATA 10, WNAA*
Phillips, Michael Joseph 1937- *ConAu 49*
Phillips, Prentice 1894- *ConAu 13R, ConAu P-1, SmATA 10*
Phillpotts, Eden 1862-1960 *BbD, BiD&SB, CarSB, Chambr 3, ChPo, ChPo S1, ChPo S2, DcBiA, DcEnA Ap, DcLEnL, EncM&D, EvLB, LongC, MnBBF, ModBL, NCHEL, REn, TwCA,*

*TwCA Sup, TwCW, WWBWI A,
WWCL, WWLA*
Phipps, Sidney Arnold *MnBBF*
Phipps, William Eugene 1930- *ConAu 29,
DrAS 6P*
Phipson, Joan *WrD*
Phipson, Joan 1912- *AuBYP, ConAu XR,
SingR 1, SmATA 2, ThBJA, WWA 38,
WWAW 8, WWWor 2*
Phipson, Joan *see* Fitzhardinge, Joan Margaret
Phiz 1815-1882 *ChPo, NCHEL, REn,
WWBWI 1*
Phiz *see* Browne, Hablot Knight
Phleger, Frederick B 1909- *AmMWS 12P,
AuBYP, ConAu 1R, WWA 38,
WWWor 2*
Phleger, Marjorie Temple 1909- *ConAu 9R,
ForWC 1970, SmATA 1*
Piaget, Jean 1896- *ConAu 21R, CurB 58,
IntWW 38, WW 1974, WWWor 2*
Piatti, Celestino 1922- *AuBYP, ChPo S1,
ChFB 1, IICB 1957, ThBJA, WWGA*
Picard, Barbara Leonie 1917- *Au&Wr 6,
AuBYP, BrCA, ConAu 5R, SmATA 2,
ThBJA, WrD*
Piccard, Joan Russell *ConAu 29*
Pick, Robert 1898- *ConAu 17R*
Pickard, Charles *IIBYP*
Pickard, Dorothea Wilgus 1902- *ConAu 21R*
Picker, Ingrid 1932- *ConAu 25R*
Pickering, Edgar *CarSB, MnBBF,
WWBWI A*
Pickering, James Sayre 1897- *ConAu 1R*
Pickering, Wilhelmina *TelT*
Pickering, Wilhelmina *see* Stirling, Mrs. A M W
Pickett, Carla 1944- *ConAu 37*
Pickford, Charles *MnBBF*
Pienkowski, Jan 1936- *ConAu 65, SmATA 6*
Pier, Arthur Stanwood 1874-1966 *AmA&B,
AmLY, BiD&SB, CarSB, ChPo,
ConAu 25R, DcAmA, JBA 1934,
JBA 1951, REnAL, WNAA*
Pierce, Edith Gray 1893- *ConAu 61*
Pierce, Edith Gray *see* Gray, Marian
Pierce, Frank Richardson 1887- *AmA&B,
MnBBF*
Pierce, Katherine *ConAu XR, SmATA XR*
Pierce, Katherine *see* Saint John, Wylly Folk
Pierce, Mary Cunningham 1908- *AuBYP*
Pierce, Mary Cunningham *see* Cunningham,
Mary
Pierce, Philip Nason *AuBYP*
Pierce, Ruth Ireland 1936- *ConAu 29,
SmATA 5*
Pierik, Robert 1921- *ConAu 37, SmATA 13*
Pierson, Clara Dillingham *CarSB*
Pierson, Sherleigh G *AuBYP*
Pike, E Royston 1896- *ConAu 9R*
Pike, Morton *MnBBF, WWBWI A, WWCL*
Pike, Morton *see* Parry, David Harold
Pike, Norman 1901- *ConAu 25R*
Pike, William Ernest *MnBBF, WWBWI A*
Pike, William Ernest *see* Conquest, Owen
Pike, William Ernest *see* James, Ernest
Pike, William Ernest *see* Richards, Frank
Pike, William Ernest *see* Stuart, W E
Pilarski, Laura P 1926- *ConAu 29,
SmATA 13, WrD*
Pile, D W *MnBBF*

Pile, D W *see* Webber, Stawford
Pilgrim, Anne *AuBYP, ConAu XR,
SmATA 5*
Pilgrim, Anne *see* Allan, Mabel Esther
Pilkington, Francis Meredyth 1907- *ConAu P-2,
SmATA 4, WrD*
Pilkington, Roger Windle 1915- *Au&Wr 6,
AuBYP, SmATA 10, WW 1974, WrD*
Pilot, John *MnBBF*
Pimlott, Douglas H 1920- *AmMWS 12P*
Pincus, Harriet *AmPB, IIBYP*
Pine, Tillie Schloss 1896- *AuBYP, BkP,
ConAu 69, SmATA 13*
Pines, Maya *Au&Wr 6, ConAu 13R*
Pinkerton, Kathrene Sutherland 1887-1967
AuBYP, CurB 40, CurB 67
Pinkney, Jerry 1939- *IICB 1957*
Pinkwater, Manus 1941- *ConAu 29,
SmATA 8*
Pinney, Roy 1911- *ConAu 5R*
Pinson, William Meredith, Jr. 1934-
ConAu 17R, DrAS 6P, WWS 13
Pinto, Jacqueline 1927- *Au&Wr 6, WrD*
Pinto, Ralph *IIBYP*
Pintoff, Ernest 1931- *ConAu 17R*
Pippet, Gabriel Joseph 1880- *ChPo S1,
IICB 1744*
Pirani, Leila *SingR 1*
Pirbright, Robert *MnBBF*
Piro, Richard 1934- *ConAu 49, SmATA 7*
Pirsig, Robert M 1928- *ConLC 4, ConLC 6,
NYTBS 5*
Pissarro, Lucien 1863-1944 *IICB 1744,
IICB 1946*
Pistorius, Anna *AuBYP*
Pitcairn, John *MnBBF*
Pitcher, Robert Walter 1918- *AmMWS 12S,
ConAu 29, LE 5, WWMW 14*
Pitkin, Dorothy 1899?-1972 *ConAu 37*
Pitrone, Jean Maddern 1920- *ConAu 17R,
ForWC 1970, SmATA 4, WWAW 8*
Pitt, David *MnBBF*
Pitt, Sarah *Alli Sup, CarSB*
Pitz, Henry Clarence 1895-1976 *AmA&B,
ChPo, ChPo S1, ConAu 9R, ConAu 69,
ConICB, ForII, IIBYP, IICB 1744,
IICB 1946, IICB 1957, MorJA,
SmATA 4, WWA 38, WWAA 1973*
Piussi-Campbell, Judy *IIBYP*
Pizer, Vernon 1918- *AuBYP, ConAu 1R,
WrD*
Place, Marian Templeton 1910- *AuBYP,
ConAu 1R, IndAu 1917, SmATA 3,
WWAW 8, WWPNA*
Place, Marian Templeton *see* White, Dale
Place, Marian Templeton *see* Whitinger, R D
Plagemann, Bentz 1913- *AmA&B, AmNov,
ConAu 1R*
Plaidy, Jean 1906- *Au&Wr 6, ConAu XR,
SmATA 2, TwCW, WW 1974, WorAu*
Plaidy, Jean *see* Hibbert, Eleanor Burford
Planche, James Robinson 1796-1880 *Alli,
Alli Sup, BbD, BiD&SB, BrAu 19,
CarSB, CasWL, Chambr 3, ChPo,
ChPo S1, DcEnA, DcEnL, DcEuL, EvLB,
NCHEL, OxEng, REn, TelT*
Plant, John 1914- *ArtsCL*
Plasencia, Peter P *IIBYP*
Plate, Robert 1918- *AuBYP, ConAu 17R*

Plath, Sylvia 1932-1963 *AmA&B, CasWL, ChPo S1, ConAu 17R, ConLC 1, ConLC 2, ConLC 3, ConLC 5, ConP 1975, CrCAP, EncWL, LongC, ModAL Sup, NYTBS 5, OxAm, Pen Am, RAdv 1, TwCW, WEAL, WWTwL, WorAu*

Platt, Charles 1945- *ConAu 21R*

Platt, Edward *MnBBF*

Platt, Kin 1911- *ConAu 17R, WWA 38*

Platt, Rutherford 1894-1975 *ConAu 61*

Player, Eddie *MnBBF*

Pletsch, Oskar 1830-1888 *CarSB, ChPo S2*

Plimpton, George 1927- *AuNews 1, CelR 3, ConAu 21R, CurB 69, NYTBE 1, SmATA 10*

Plimpton, Ruth Talbot 1916- *ConAu 13R*

Plinius Secundus, Caius 023?-079 *CarSB*

Pliss, Louise *AuBYP*

Plowden, Alison 1931- *ConAu 33, WrD*

Plowden, David 1932- *ConAu 33*

Plowhead, Ruth Gipson 1877- *AmA&B*

Plowman, Stephanie 1922- *ConAu 53, SmATA 6, WrD*

Pluche, Noel-Antoine 1688-1761 *CarSB, OxFr*

Pluckrose, Henry 1931- *ConAu 33, SmATA 13*

Pluckrose, Henry *see* Cobbett, Richard

Pluff, Barbara Littlefield 1926- *ConAu 5R*

Pluff, Barbara Littlefield *see* Clayton, Barbara

Plummer, Margaret 1911- *ConAu 25R, SmATA 2*

Plummer, T Arthur *MnBBF*

Plummer, William Kirtman *IlBYP*

Plutarch 046?-125? *AtlBL, BbD, BiD&SB, CasWL, CyWA, DcEnL, NCHEL, OxEng, Pen Cl, RCom, REn*

Plympton, Almira George 1852-1939 *Alli Sup, AmA&B, CarSB, ChPo, DcAmA, DcNAA*

Pocklington, Geoffrey Richard 1879- *ChPo S1, ChPo S2, MnBBF, WWBWI A*

Pocock, Doris Alice *MnBBF*

Pocock, Guy Noel 1880- *ChPo, ChPo S1, MnBBF*

Pocock, H E D *MnBBF*

Pocock, Roger 1865-1941 *MnBBF, OxCan, WWLA*

Podmore, Charles T *MnBBF*

Poe, Charlsie 1909- *ConAu 21R*

Poe, Edgar Allan 1809-1849 *Alli, AmA, AmA&B, AmWr, AnCL, AtlBL, BbD, BiD&SB, BiDSA, CasWL, Chambr 3, ChPo, ChPo S1, ChPo S2, CnDAL, CnE&AP, CriT 3, CyAL 2, CyWA, DcAmA, DcBiA, DcEnA, DcEnL, DcLEnL, DcNAA, EncM&D, EvLB, MnBBF, MouLC 3, OxAm, OxEng, Pen Am, RAdv 1, RCom, REn, REnAL, St&VC, WEAL*

Pogany, Willy 1882-1955 *ChPo, ChPo S1, ChPo S2, ConICB, IlBYP, IlCB 1744, JBA 1934, JBA 1951, REn*

Pohl, Frederik 1919- *ConNov 1972, ConNov 1976, DrAF 1976, Pen Am, WWA 38, WorAu*

Pohlmann, Lillian 1902- *AuBYP, ConAu 9R, SmATA 11, SmATA 8, WrD*

Poindexter, David 1929- *ConAu 29*

Pointon, Robert *ConAu XR, SmATA XR*

Pointon, Robert *see* Rooke, Daphne Marie

Polatnick, Florence T 1923- *ConAu 29, SmATA 5*

Polder, Markus 1926- *ConAu XR, SmATA 8*

Polder, Markus *see* Kruess, James

Polese, Marcia Ann 1949- *ConAu 65*

Polgreen, John *IlBYP*

Politi, Leo 1908- *AmPB, Au&ICB, AuBYP, BkP, Cald 1938, CatA 1952, ConAu 17R, IlBYP, IlCB 1744, IlCB 1946, IlCB 1957, JBA 1951, SmATA 1, St&VC*

Polk, Dora 1923- *ConAu 49*

Polking, Kirk 1925- *ConAu 29, ForWC 1970, SmATA 5, WWMW 14*

Pollack, Cecelia 1909- *ConAu 29, LE 5*

Pollack, Peter 1911- *WWWA 1973*

Pollack, Reginald Murray 1924- *ConAu 37, DcCAA 2, IlCB 1957, WWA 38, WWAA 1973, WWWor 2, WrD*

Pollak, Felix 1909- *BiDL 5, ConAu 25R, WWMW 14*

Polland, Madeleine Angela Cahill 1918- *AuBYP, ConAu 5R*

Polland, Madeleine Angela Cahill 1918- *SmATA 6, ThBJA*

Pollard, Alfred *CarSB*

Pollard, Eliza F *MnBBF*

Pollard, Jack 1926- *ConAu 29*

Pollock, Dean 1897- *WWPNA*

Pollock, William *MnBBF*

Polmar, Norman 1938- *Au&Wr 6, ConAu 49*

Polo, Eddie *MnBBF*

Polo, Marco 1254?-1324? *BbD, BiD&SB, CasWL, CyWA, DcEuL, EuAu, EvEuW, NCHEL, OxEng, Pen Eur, RCom, REn*

Polonsky, Arthur 1925- *WWAA 1973, WWWorJ 1972*

Polseno, Jo *IlBYP*

Polykoff, Shirley *ForWC 1970, WWAW 8, WWE 14*

Pomeroy, Pete *ConAu XR*

Pomeroy, Pete *see* Roth, Arthur J

Pomeroy, Wardell Baxter 1913- *AmMWS 12S, ConAu 1R, CurB 74, IndAu 1917, WWA 38*

Pond, Alonzo William 1894- *AmMWS 12S, ConAu 1R, SmATA 5, WWA 38*

Pond, S T R *MnBBF*

Pond, S T R *see* Reay, Trevace

Pond, Seymour Gates 1896- *AuBYP*

Ponsot, Marie Birmingham 1922- *ConAu 9R, ForWC 1970*

Pont, Clarice Holt 1907- *ConAu 5R*

Ponting, Clarence *MnBBF*

Poole, Frederick King 1934- *ConAu 25R*

Poole, Gray Johnson 1906- *AuBYP, ConAu 5R, SmATA 1*

Poole, Josephine 1933- *Au&Wr 6, ConAu 21R, SmATA 5, WrD*

Poole, Lynn D 1910-1969 *AmA&B, AuBYP, ConAu 5R, CurB 54, CurB 69, MorJA, SmATA 1*

Poole, Michael 1885- *MnBBF, WWBWI A*

Poole, Michael *see* Poole, Reginald Heber

Poole, Peter Andrews *AmMWS 12S*

Poole, Reginald Heber 1885- *MnBBF*

Poole, Reginald Heber *see* Heber, Austin

Poole, Reginald Heber *see* Heber, Reginald

Poole, Reginald Heber *see* Poole, Michael
Poole, Reginald Heber *see* Thomas, Anthony
Poole, Reginald Heber *see* Valentine, Henry
Pope *MnBBF*
Pope *see* Manson, A, Lieutenant
Pope, Clifford Hillhouse 1899- *AmA&B,*
AmMWS 12P, Au&Wr 6, AuBYP,
ConAu 1R, WWA 38
Pope, E Legh *MnBBF*
Pope, Elizabeth Marie 1917- *ConAu 49,*
DrAS 6E
Pope, F W *MnBBF*
Pope, F W *see* Hulbert, Lloyd
Pope, Ray 1924- *ConAu 29*
Pope, Travers *WWBWI 1*
Popescu, Christine 1930- *ConAu 13R*
Popescu, Christine *see* Keir, Christine
Popescu, Christine *see* Pullein-Thompson,
Christine
Popham, Hugh 1920- *Au&Wr 6, ConAu 5R*
Poppleton, Marjorie 1895- *Au&Wr 6,*
ConAu P-1, WrD
Porchat, J J 1800-1864 *Alli, CarSB*
Portal, Colette 1936- *ConAu 53, IlCB 1957,*
SmATA 6
Porteous, Richard S 1897- *SingR 1*
Porter, Admiral *CarSB*
Porter, Eleanor Hodgman 1868-1920 *AmA&B,*
AmLY, CarSB, DcLEnL, DcNAA, EvLB,
LongC, OxAm, REn, REnAL, TwCA,
TwCA Sup, TwCW, WWCL
Porter, Ella Blodwen *AuBYP*
Porter, Frederick 1871- *MnBBF*
Porter, Frederick *see* Watson, Frederick
Porter, Gene Stratton 1868-1924 *AmA&B,*
AmLY, CarSB, ChPo, CnDAL, DcLEnL,
DcNAA, EvLB, IndAu 1816, LongC,
OxAm, Pen Am, REn, REnAL, TwCA,
TwCA Sup, TwCW, WWCL
Porter, George *IlBYP*
Porter, Horace 1863- *CarSB*
Porter, Jane 1776-1850 *Alli, BbD, BiD&SB,*
BiDLA, BrAu 19, CarSB, Chambr 2,
CyWA, DcBiA, DcEnA, DcEnL, DcEuL,
DcLEnL, EvLB, HsB&A, NCHEL,
OxEng, REn
Porter, Jean Macdonald 1906- *IlBYP,*
IlCB 1946
Porter, Katherine Anne 1890- *AmA&B,*
AmWr, AuNews 2, CasWL, CelR 3,
CnDAL, CnMWL, ConAmA, ConAu 1R,
ConLC 1, ConLC 3, ConNov 1972,
ConNov 1976, CurB 40, CurB 63,
CyWA, DcLEnL, DrAF 1976, EncWL,
EvLB, ForWC 1970, IntWW 38, LongC,
ModAL, ModAL Sup, NYTBE 1, OxAm,
OxEng, Pen Am, RAdv 1, REn, REnAL,
TwCA, TwCA Sup, TwCW, WEAL,
WW 1974, WWA 38, WWAW 8,
WWE 14, WWTwL, WWWor 2
Porter, Mark *ConAu XR*
Porter, Mark *see* Leckie, Robert
Porter, Sheena 1935- *ThBJA*
Porter, Sheena *see* Lane, Sheena Porter
Porter, William Sydney 1862-1910 *AmA&B,*
AtlBL, CasWL, CnDAL, DcLEnL,
DcNAA, EncM&D, EvLB, LongC,
OhA&B, OxAm, OxEng, Pen Am, REn,
REnAL, TwCA, TwCA Sup, WEAL,

YABC 2
Porter, William Sydney *see* Henry, O
Porter, William Sydney *see* Henry, Oliver
Porter, William Sydney *see* Peters, S H
Portinari, Candido 1903-1962 *CurB 40,*
CurB 62, IlCB 1744
Portisch, Hugo 1927- *ConAu 21R,*
WWWor 2
Posell, Elsa Zeigerman *ConAu 1R, SmATA 3,*
WWAW 8
Posey, Anita E *ChPo S1*
Posner, Richard *WrD*
Post, Elizabeth Lindley 1920- *ConAu 49,*
WWAW 8
Post, Henry 1948- *ConAu 61*
Post, Henry *see* Spot, Ryhen
Posten, Margaret L 1915- *ConAu 29,*
SmATA 10
Poston, Martha Lee *AuBYP*
Pothecary, Raymond *MnBBF, WWBWI A*
Pothecary, Raymond *see* Ford, Quentin
Potok, Chaim 1929- *AmA&B, Au&Wr 6,*
AuNews 1, AuNews 2, BiN 1974,
ConAu 17R, ConLC 2, DrAF 1976,
WWA 38, WWE 14, WWWor 2,
WWWorJ 1972
Pott, Charles L *WWBWI 1*
Pott, William H *CarSB*
Potten, Phil *MnBBF*
Potter, Beatrix 1866-1943 *AnCL, AuBYP,*
CarSB, CasWL, ChLR 1, ChPo,
ChPo S1, ChPo S2, CurB 44, DcLEnL,
EvLB, FamAI, JBA 1934, JBA 1951,
LongC, NCHEL, OxEng, Pen Eng, REn,
St&VC, TelT, WWCL, YABC 1
Potter, Edna *ConICB*
Potter, Margaret 1926- *Au&Wr 6,*
ConAu 13R, WrD
Potter, Marian 1915- *ConAu 49, SmATA 9*
Potter, Miriam Clark 1886-1965 *AmA&B,*
AuBYP, ChPo, ConAu 5R, SmATA 3,
WNAA
Potter, Robert Ducharme 1905- *AmMWS 12P,*
AuBYP, WWE 14
Potter, Stephen 1900-1969 *AuBYP,*
ConAu 25R, DcLEnL, EvLB, LongC,
ModBL, NCHEL, Pen Eng, RAdv 1,
REn, TwCA Sup, TwCW
Potts, Mrs. Arthur *CarSB*
Pough, Frederick Harvey 1906- *AmMWS 12P,*
AuBYP, WWA 38
Pough, Richard Hooper 1904- *AmMWS 12P,*
WWA 38
Poulsson, Emilie 1853-1939 *AmA&B, CarSB,*
JBA 1934, JBA 1951, WNAA
Poultney, S Vic *MnBBF*
Pound, Singleton *MnBBF, WWBWI A*
Pound, Singleton *see* Merland, Oliver
Pournelle, Jerry *DrAF 1976*
Powell, Barclay *MnBBF*
Powell, David *ChPo S1*
Powell, Fern 1942- *ConAu 25R*
Powell, Frank *MnBBF, WWBWI A*
Powell, Lawrence Clark 1906- *AmA&B,*
BiDL 5, ChPo, ConAu 21R, CurB 60,
WWA 38, WorAu
Powell, Meredith 1936- *ConAu 37*
Powell, William Stevens 1919- *BiDL 5,*
DrAS 6H

Power, Anthony *MnBBF*
Power, Effie Louise 1873- *AuBYP, OhA&B*
Power, Jules 1921- *IndAu 1917, WWA 38*
Power, Nelson *MnBBF*
Power, Nelson *see* Judd, Alfred
Power, Phyllis M *SingR 1*
Powers, Anne 1913- *AmA&B, Au&Wr 6,*
ConAu XR, MnnWr, SmATA XR,
WWA 38, WWAW 8
Powers, Anne *see* Schwartz, Anne Powers
Powers, David Guy 1911- *ConAu P-2*
Powers, Margaret *ConAu XR, NYTBE 3,*
SmATA 7
Powers, Margaret *see* Heal, Edith
Powers, Richard M 1921- *ConAu 21R, IlBYP,*
IlCB 1946, IlCB 1957
Powers, Richard M *see* Gorman, Terry
Powers, William K 1934- *ConAu 25R,*
OxCan Sup
Powledge, Fred 1935- *ConAu 21R, WWE 14*
Pownall, Eve *SingR 1*
Pownall, Eve *see* Pownall, Marjorie Evelyn
Sheridan
Pownall, Marjorie Evelyn Sheridan *SingR 1*
Pownall, Marjorie Evelyn Sheridan *see* Pownall,
Eve
Prago, Albert 1911- *ConAu 29*
Prater, Ernest *WWBWI 1*
Pratt, Fletcher 1897-1956 *AmA&B, AuBYP,*
CurB 42, CurB 56, REnAL, TwCA Sup,
WNAA
Pratt, Hugo *WWBWI 1*
Pratt, John 1931- *ConAu 1R*
Pratt, John *see* Winton, John
Pratt, John Lowell 1906- *ConAu 1R*
Pratt, Laura Maria Loring *Alli Sup, CarSB,*
ChPo S2
Pratt, Leonard E *MnBBF, WWBWI A*
Pratt, Leonard E *see* Smith, Fenton
Pratt, Viola Leone *WrD*
Prelutsky, Jack *ChPo S1, ChPo S2*
Prentiss, Elizabeth Payson 1818-1878 *Alli Sup,*
AmA&B, BbD, BiD&SB, CarSB, ChPo,
ChPo S1, DcAmA, DcBiA, DcNAA,
OxAm, PoCh
Presberg, Miriam Goldstein 1919- *ConAu 1R,*
WWWorJ 1972, WrD
Presberg, Miriam Goldstein *see* Gilbert, Miriam
Prescott, G *MnBBF*
Prescott, Gerald Webber 1899- *AmMWS 12P,*
Au&Wr 6
Prescott, Orville 1906- *AmA&B, AuBYP,*
ConAu 41, CurB 57, REnAL, WWA 38
Prest, Thomas Peckett 1810?-1879? *MnBBF,*
WWBWI A
Preston, Alice Bolam 1889- *IlCB 1744*
Preston, Edna Mitchell *ChPo S2*
Preston, Walford *MnBBF*
Preston, Walford *see* Townley, Houghton
Preston, Whyatt *MnBBF*
Preussler, Otfried 1923- *AuBYP*
Prevert, Jacques 1900-1977 *CasWL, CnMWL,*
ConAu 69, EncWL, EvEuW, OxFr,
Pen Eur, REn, TwCW, WorAu
Price, Beverley *WrD*
Price, Christine Hilda 1928- *Au&Wr 6,*
AuBYP, ChPo S1, ConAu 5R,
IlCB 1946, IlCB 1957, MorJA,
SmATA 3, WWAW 8, WrD

Price, Derek John DeSolla 1922- *AmMWS 12S,*
ConAu 1R, WWA 38, WWE 14,
WWWor 2
Price, Edith Ballinger 1897- *AmA&B, ChPo,*
JBA 1934, JBA 1951, WNAA
Price, Evadne *Au&Wr 6, MnBBF*
Price, Evadne *see* Smith, Helen Zenna
Price, Garrett 1896- *ChPo, IlBYP, IlCB 1957*
Price, Harold 1912- *IlBYP, IlCB 1946*
Price, Hattie Longstreet 1891- *ConICB,*
IlCB 1744
Price, Jennifer *ConAu XR, SmATA XR*
Price, Jennifer *see* Hoover, Helen
Price, Lillian L *CarSB*
Price, Lucie Locke 1904- *ConAu XR,*
SmATA XR
Price, Lucie Locke *see* Locke, Lucie
Price, Luxor *ConICB*
Price, Margaret Evans 1888- *AmA&B,*
IlCB 1744, WNAA
Price, N Penton *MnBBF*
Price, Norman Mills 1877-1951 *IlBYP,*
IlCB 1744, IlCB 1946
Price, Olive 1903- *AuBYP, ConAu 41,*
SmATA 8
Price, Olive *see* Cherryholmes, Anne
Price, Olive *see* West, Barbara
Price, Roger 1921- *ConAu 9R, IntMPA 1975*
Price, Steven D 1940- *ConAu 49*
Price, Susan *WrD*
Price, Willadene Anton 1914- *AuBYP,*
ConAu 5R, ForWC 1970
Price, Willard DeMille 1887- *AmA&B,*
Au&Wr 6, AuBYP, ConAu 1R,
IntWW 38, WNAA, WW 1974,
WWA 38, WWWor 2, WrD
Prichard, Katharine Susannah 1884?-1969
CasWL, ConAu P-1, DcLEnL, EvLB,
NCHEL, Pen Eng, REn, TwCW,
WWLA, WorAu
Priddy, Frances Rosaleen 1931- *AuBYP,*
ConAu 1R
Pride, Merlin *MnBBF*
Priess, Byron *ConAu 69*
Priest, Christopher 1943- *ConAu 33, WrD*
Priestley, J B 1894- *BiEnAT, CnThe,*
ConAu 9R, ConDr 1, ConLC 2,
ConLC 5, ConNov 1972, ConNov 1976,
CrCD, CyWA, EncM&D, IntMPA 1975,
LongC, McGWD, ModBL, ModBL Sup,
ModWD, NCHEL, NYTBS 5, Pen Eng,
REn, REnWD, TwCW, WEAL,
WWT 15, WWTwL
Priestley, Lee Shore 1904- *AuBYP, ConAu 5R*
Prieto, Mariana Beeching 1912- *Au&ICB,*
AuBYP, BkP, ConAu 5R, ForWC 1970,
SmATA 8, WrD
Priley, Margaret Hubbard 1909- *ConAu 1R*
Priley, Margaret Hubbard *see* Hubbard,
Margaret Ann
Prime, C T 1909- *ConAu 49*
Prime, Derek James 1931- *Au&Wr 6, WrD*
Primrose, Jean Logan 1917- *ChPo S1,*
IlCB 1957
Prince, Alison 1931- *ConAu 29*
Prince, Leonora E *IlBYP*
Pringle, Laurence 1935- *ConAu 29,*
SmATA 4
Pringle, Laurence *see* Edmund, Sean

Pringle, Patrick 1917- *Au&Wr 6*
Priolo, Pauline Pizzo 1907- *ConAu 1R*
Prior, Harry *MnBBF*
Prior, Harry *see* Knightley, Miss D G
Prior, Vivian *MnBBF*
Procter, Adelaide Ann 1825-1864 *Alli, BbD,*
   BiD&SB, BrAu 19, CarSB, CasWL,
   Chambr 3, ChPo, ChPo S1, ChPo S2,
   DcEnA, DcEnL, DcEuL, EvLB, NCHEL,
   OxEng
Proctor, Everitt *AuBYP, ConAu XR,*
   SmATA 3
Proctor, Everitt *see* Montgomery, Rutherford
   George
Proctor, H G *MnBBF*
Proctor, John *Alli, WWBWI 1*
Proctor, John *see* Puck
Proctor, Paul *MnBBF*
Proctor, Paul *see* Samways, George Richmond
Proctor, Samuel DeWitt 1921- *LE 5, LBAA,*
   NYTBE 3, WWA 38
Prohaska, Ray 1901- *WWAA 1973*
Prokoficff, Serge 1891-1953 *AnCL*
Pronzini, Bill 1943- *ConAu 49*
Protheroe, Charles *MnBBF*
Protheroe, Ernest *MnBBF*
Protheroe, Ernest *see* Henley, P A
Proudfit, Isabel 1898- *AuBYP, MorJA*
Proudfoot, John *MnBBF*
Proujan, Carl 1929- *WWA 38, WWE 14*
Prout, Geoffrey 1894- *ChPo S2, MnBBF,*
   WWBWI A
Prout, Geoffrey *see* Spencer, Roland
Prout, Geoffrey *see* Valentine, Henry
Provensen, Alice 1918- *ChPo, ConAu 53,*
   IlBYP, IlCB 1946, IlCB 1957, SmATA 9,
   ThBJA, WWCL
Provensen, Martin 1916- *ConAu 53, IlBYP,*
   IlCB 1946, IlCB 1957, SmATA 9,
   ThBJA, WWCL, WWGA
Prowse, Robert *WWBWI 1*
Prud'hommeaux, Rene *AuBYP*
Prusina, Katica 1935- *ConAu 69*
Pruszynska, Aniela 1888- *IlCB 1744*
Pryor, Helen Brenton 1897-1972 *ConAu P-2,*
   SmATA 4
Pucci, Albert John 1920- *WWA 38*
Puck *WWBWI 1*
Puck *see* Proctor, John
Pudney, John Sleigh 1909- *Au&Wr 6, ChPo,*
   ChPo S1, ChPo S2, ConAu 9R,
   ConNov 1972, ConNov 1976, ConP 1970,
   ConP 1975, IntMPA 1975, IntWW 38,
   LongC, ModBL, NCHEL, Pen Eng,
   WW 1974, WWCL, WWWor 2, WorAu,
   WrD
Pugh, Ellen Tiffany 1920- *BiDL 5, ConAu 49,*
   SmATA 7, WWAW 8
Pugh, Mabel 1891- *ChPo, ConICB*
Pugh, Roger *MnBBF*
Pugh, Roger *see* Rogers, Ben
Puleo, Nicole *ConAu 49*
Pullein-Thompson, Christine 1930- *Au&Wr 6,*
   ConAu XR, SmATA 3, WWCL, WrD
Pullein-Thompson, Christine *see* Keir, Christine
Pullein-Thompson, Christine *see* Popescu,
   Christine
Pullein-Thompson, Diana *Au&Wr 6,*
   ConAu XR, SmATA 3, WWCL, WrD

Pullein-Thompson, Diana *see* Farr, Diana
   Pullein-Thompson
Pullein-Thompson, Josephine M Weddenburn
   Au&Wr 6, ConAu 5R, SmATA 3,
   WWCL, WrD
Pumphrey, F M *MnBBF*
Pumphrey, George Henry 1912- *Au&Wr 6,*
   WrD
Puncher *MnBBF*
Pundt, Helen Marie *AuBYP, ConAu 5R,*
   ForWC 1970
Puner, Helen W 1915- *ConAu 5R*
Punshon, Ernest Robinson 1872-1956 *EncM&D,*
   MnBBF
Purcell, J S *MnBBF*
Purcell, J S *see* Stapleton, Maurice
Purcell, John Wallace *AuBYP*
Purchase, Walter H *MnBBF, WWBWI A*
Purdy, Claire Lee 1906- *AuBYP, WNAA*
Purdy, Susan Gold 1939- *AuBYP, ChPo,*
   ChPo S1, ConAu 13R, ForWC 1970,
   IlCB 1957, SmATA 8, WWAW 8
Purley, John *MnBBF, WWBWI A*
Purley, John *see* Thomas, Reginald George
Purnell, Idella 1901- *AnMV 1926, ChPo,*
   ChPo S1, ConAu 61, WNAA
Purnell, Idella *see* Stone, Idella Purnell
Purnell, Idella *see* Stone, Ikey
Purscell, Phyllis 1934- *ConAu 25R,*
   SmATA 7
Pursell, Weimer *IlBYP*
Purton, Rowland W 1925- *Au&Wr 6,*
   ConAu 53
Purves, E Eric *MnBBF*
Putnam, David Binney 1913- *CarSB*
Putnam, Peter Brock 1920- *WWA 38*
Putnam, Samuel 1892-1950 *AmA&B, REnAL,*
   TwCA Sup
Putzu *WWBWI 1*
Puzo, Mario 1920- *AmA&B, CelR 3,*
   ConAu 65, ConLC 1, ConLC 2,
   ConLC 6, ConNov 1972, ConNov 1976,
   DrAF 1976, WWA 38, WrD
Pye, Clifford H *MnBBF*
Pye, David 1932- *ConAu 25R*
Pye, Virginia 1901- *WWCL*
Pyk, Jan *IlBYP*
Pyke, Helen Godfrey 1941- *ConAu 29*
Pyle, Howard 1853-1911 *Alli Sup, AmA,*
   AmA&B, AnCL, AuBYP, BbD, BiD&SB,
   CarSB, ChPo, ChPo S1, ChPo S2,
   DcAmA, DcLEnL, DcNAA, FamSYP,
   IlBYP, JBA 1934, OxAm, REnAL,
   WWCL
Pyle, Katharine d1938 *AmA&B, AnCL,*
   ChPo, ChPo S1, DcAmA, DcNAA,
   JBA 1934, JBA 1951, WNAA
Pym, J H *MnBBF*
Pyne, Mable Mandeville 1903-1969 *AuBYP,*
   ConAu 1R, IlCB 1744, IlCB 1946,
   SmATA 9
Pyrnelle, Louise Clarke 1852- *AmA&B*

Q

Quackenbush, Robert Mead 1929- *ConAu 45,*
ChPo S2, IlBYP, IlCB 1957, SmATA 7
Quaife, Milo Milton 1880-1959 *AmA&B,*
REnAL, WNAA, WisW
Quammen, David 1948- *ConAu 29, SmATA 7*
Quarles, Benjamin 1904- *ConAu IR,*
DrAS 6H, SmATA 12
Quarrie, Bruce 1947- *WrD*
Quayle, Eric 1921- *Au&Wr 6, ChPo S1,*
ChPo S2, WrD
Queen, Ellery *AmA&B, CelR 3, ConAu XR,*
ConLC 3, CurB 40, DcLEnL, EncM&D,
EvLB, IntWW 38, LongC, OxAm,
Pen Am, REn, REnAL, TwCA,
TwCA Sup, TwCW, WW 1974
Queen, Ellery *see* Dannay, Frederic
Queen, Ellery *see* Lee, Manfred B
Queen, Ellery, Jr. *AuBYP, ConAu XR,*
SmATA 3
Queen, Ellery, Jr. *see* Dannay, Frederic
Queen, Ellery, Jr. *see* Holding, James
Queen, Ellery, Jr. *see* Lee, Manfred B
Quennell, Charles Henry Bourne 1872-1935
LongC, MorJA, TwCA, TwCA Sup
Quennell, Marjorie 1884- *DcLEnL, EvLB,*
JBA 1934, LongC, MorJA, TwCA,
TwCA Sup
Quennell, Peter 1905- *IntWW 38, WW 1974*
Quibell, Agatha Hunt 1921- *Au&Wr 6, WrD*
Quick, Annabelle 1922- *ConAu 21R,*
SmATA 2, WWAW 8
Quick, Annabelle *see* MacMillan, Annabelle
Quigley, John 1927- *Au&Wr 6, ConAu 17R*
Quiller-Couch, Sir Arthur Thomas 1863-1944
BbD, BiD&SB, CasWL, Chambr 3, ChPo,
ChPo S1, ChPo S2, CurB 44, DcBiA,
DcEnA, DcEnA Ap, DcLEnL, EvLB,
JBA 1934, LongC, ModBL, MnBBF,
NCHEL, OxEng, Pen Eng, RAdv 1,
REn, TwCA, TwCA Sup, TwCW
Quiller-Couch, Lilian M *ChPo, MnBBF*
Quilter, Eddie *MnBBF*
Quilter, Eddie *see* Woodman, Thomas
Quimby, Myrtle 1891- *ConAu P-2*
Quin, Tarella *SingR 1*
Quinn, John Paul 1943- *ConAu 33*
Quinn, Vernon 1881-1962 *AmA&B*
Quinn, Zdenka 1942- *ConAu 33*
Quintanilla, Luis 1900?- *AmA&B, CurB 40,*
IlBYP, IlCB 1946, IntWW 38, WNAA,
WWWor 2
Quintin, Paul *MnBBF*

Quintin, Paul *see* Wright, W George
Quintin, Peter *MnBBF*
Quintin, Rex *MnBBF*
Quintin, Rex *see* Hardinge, Rex
Quirk, Leslie W 1882- *AmA&B, CarSB,*
WNAA, WisW
Quirroule, Pierre 1892- *MnBBF, WWBWI A*
Quirroule, Pierre *see* Sayer, Walter William
Quittenton, Bertram *MnBBF*
Quittenton, Bertram *see* Quiz, Roland, Jr.
Quittenton, R M H *WWBWI A*
Quittenton, R M H *see* Quittenton, Richard
Martin Howard
Quittenton, Richard Martin Howard 1833-1914
MnBBF
Quittenton, Richard Martin Howard *see*
Quittenton, R M H
Quittenton, Richard Martin Howard *see* Quiz,
Roland
Quiz, Roland 1833-1914 *AlLi, MnBBF,*
WWBWI A, WWCL
Quiz, Roland *see* Quittenton, Richard Martin
Howard
Quiz, Roland, Jr. *MnBBF, WWBWI A*
Quiz, Roland, Jr. *see* Quittenton, Bertram

R

Raab, Robert Allen 1924- *ConAu 29*
Rabalais, Maria 1921- *ConAu 61*
Rabe, Berniece Louise 1928- *ConAu 49,
    SmATA 7*
Rabe, Olive H 1887-1968 *AuBYP, ConAu P-2,
    SmATA 13*
Rabinovitz, Rubin 1938- *ConAu 21R,
    DrAS 6E*
Raboy, Mac 1914- *ArtCS*
Rachleff, Owen Spencer 1935- *ConAu 21R,
    WWE 14*
Rachlis, Eugene 1920- *ConAu 5R*
Rackham, Arthur 1867-1939 *CarSB, ChPo,
    ChPo S1, ChPo S2, ConICB, JBA 1934,
    JBA 1951, LongC, St&VC, WWBWI I,
    WWCL*
Radcliffe, Arthur *MnBBF*
Radford, Ruby Lorraine 1891-1971 *ConAu 1R,
    ForWC 1970, SmATA 6*
Radford, Ruby Lorraine *see* Bailey, Matilda
Radford, Ruby Lorraine *see* Ford, Marcia
Radlauer, Edward 1921- *AuBYP, ConAu 69*
Rae, Gwynedd 1892- *ConAu 65, WWCL*
Rae, John 1882-1963 *AmA&B, ChPo,
    ChPo S1, IlCB 1744, WNAA*
Rae, John Malcolm 1931- *ConAu 1R,
    WW 1974, WrD*
Rae, Scott *MnBBF*
Rae, Scott *see* Hamilton, Cecily
Rae, William Shaw *MnBBF, WWBWI A*
Raebeck, Lois 1921- *ConAu 13R, SmATA 5*
Raeburn, David *WWBWI A*
Raeburn, David *see* Herring, Paul
Raef, Laura C *ConAu 29*
Raftery, Gerald 1905- *ChPo S1, ConAu P-1,
    SmATA 11*
Ragozin, Zenaide Alexeievna 1835?-1924
    *Alli Sup, BiD&SB, CarSB, DcAmA,
    DcNAA*
Rahn, Joan Elma 1929- *AmMWS 12P,
    ConAu 37*
Rahv, Philip 1908-1973 *AmA&B*
Raible, Alton Robert 1918- *IlBYP, IlCB 1957*
Raife, Raymond *MnBBF*
Raiff, Stan 1930- *ConAu 61, SmATA 11*
Raine, William MacLeod 1871-1954 *AmA&B,
    AmLY, EvLB, MnBBF, REnAL, TwCA,
    TwCA Sup, WNAA*
Rainey, W 1852-1936 *ChPo S1, WWBWI I*
Ralston, Jan *AuBYP, ConAu XR, SmATA 3*
Ralston, Jan *see* Dunlop, Agnes M R
Rama Rau, Santha 1923- *AmA&B, BiEnAT,*

*ConAu XR, CurB 45, CurB 59, NCHEL,
    WWAW 8, WWWor 2, WorAu*
Rama Rau, Santha *see* Rau, Santha Rama
Ramee, Louise DeLa 1839-1908 *BiD&SB,
    BrAu 19, Chambr 3, DcEuL, EvLB,
    HsB&A, JBA 1934*
Ramee, Louise DeLa *see* DeLaRamee, Louise
Ramee, Louise DeLa *see* Quida
Ramsay, William M 1922- *ConAu 13R*
Ranadive, Gail 1944- *ConAu 53, SmATA 10*
Rand, Addison 1896- *AuBYP*
Rand, Ann *AuBYP, ChPo, ThBJA*
Rand, Paul 1914- *AmPB, AuBYP,
    ConAu 21R, IlCB 1946, IlCB 1957,
    SmATA 6, ThBJA, WWA 38,
    WWAA 1973, WWGA*
Randali, W C B *MnBBF*
Randall, Blossom E *AuBYP*
Randall, Christine *IlBYP*
Randall, Florence Engel 1917- *BlkAW,
    ConAu 41, SmATA 5*
Randall, Homer *CarSB*
Randall, Janet *AuBYP, ConAu XR, PoIre 3,
    SmATA 3*
Randall, Janet *see* Young, Janet Randall
Randall, Janet *see* Young, Robert W
Randall, Kenneth Charles *AuBYP*
Randall, Robert *AuBYP, ConAu XR,
    SmATA XR, ThBJA*
Randall, Robert *see* Silverberg, Robert
Randall, Ruth Elaine Painter 1892-1971
    *AmA&B, Au&Wr 6, AuBYP, ConAu 1R,
    CurB 57, SmATA 3*
Randolph, J H, Lieutenant *HsB&A, YABC 1*
Randolph, J H, Lieutenant *see* Ellis, Edward S
Randolph, Richard *MnBBF, WWBWI A*
Randolph, Richard *see* Pentelow, John Nix
Rands, William Brighty 1823-1882 *Alli,
    Alli Sup, BrAu 19, ChPo, ChPo S1,
    ChPo S2, DcEnL, DcLEnL, NCHEL,
    OxEng, TelT*
Ranger, Ken *ConAu XR, WWBWI A*
Ranger, Ken *see* Creasey, John
Rankin, Louise S 1897?-1951 *MorJA*
Rankin, Robert Harry 1909- *WNAA*
Ranney, Agnes V 1916- *ConAu 5R,
    SmATA 6*
Ranney, Agnes V *see* Reeves, Ruth Ellen
Ransohoff, Doris *AuBYP*
Ransome, Arthur Michell 1884-1967 *Alli Sup,
    AuBYP, CarSB, CasWL, ChPo,
    ChPo S1, DcLEnL, EvLB, JBA 1934,*

JBA 1951, LongC, NCHEL, Pen Eng,
REn, TelT, TwCA, TwCA Sup, WWCL,
WWLA
Ransome, Charles A *MnBBF, WWBWI A*
Ransome, Charles A *see* Rowe, John Gabriel
Ransome, L E *MnBBF, WWBWI A*
Ransome, L E *see* Clifford, Martin
Ransome, L E *see* Hayes, Ivor
Ransome, L E *see* Melbourne, Ivor
Ransome, L E *see* Norman, Victor
Ransome, L E *see* Richards, Frank
Ransome, L E *see* Stirling, Tom
Ranucci, Renato 1921- *AuBYP*
Ranucci, Renato *see* Rascel, Renato
Rapaport, Stella F *ConAu 1R, SmATA 10*
Rappaport, Eva 1924- *ConAu 29, SmATA 6*
Rascel, Renato *AuBYP*
Rascel, Renato *see* Ranucci, Renato
Raskin, Edith Lefkowitz 1908- *ConAu 9R,
ForWC 1970, SmATA 9*
Raskin, Ellen 1928- *AmPB, BkP, ChLR 1,
ChPo, ChPo S1, ChPo S2, ConAu 21R,
IlBYP, IlCB 1957, SmATA 2, ThBJA*
Raskin, Joseph 1897- *ConAu 33, SmATA 12,
WWWorJ 1972*
Raspe, Rudolf Erich 1737-1794 *CarSB, CasWL,
Chambr 2, DcEuL, EvEuW, EvLB,
HsB&A, OxGer*
Ratcliffe, E *ChPo, WWBWI I*
Ratcliffe, Frederic *MnBBF*
Ratcliffe, Mary Joan *WrD*
Rathbone, St. George 1854-1928 *CarSB,
DcAmA*
Rather, Dan 1931- *AuNews 1, BiN 1974*
Rathjen, Carl H 1909- *ConAu 5R,
SmATA 11*
Rathjen, Carl H *see* Russell, Charlotte
Rattray, Simon *ConAu XR*
Rattray, Simon *see* Trevor, Elleston
Rau, Margaret 1913- *ConAu 61, SmATA 9*
Rau, Santha Rama 1923- *CelR 3, CurB 45,
CurB 59, IntWW 38, Pen Eng, TwCW,
WW 1974, WWWor 2*
Rau, Santha Rama *see* Rama Rau, Santha
Raucher, Herman 1928- *ConAu 29,
SmATA 8*
Raven, G *MnBBF*
Raven, G *see* Wood, Samuel Andrew
Ravenglass, Hal *MnBBF, WWBWI A*
Ravenglass, Hal *see* Hook, H Clarke
Ravenglass, Hal *see* Wood, Samuel Andrew
Raverat, Gwendolen Mary 1885-1957 *ChPo,
IlBYP, IlCB 1744, IlCB 1946, LongC*
Ravielli, Anthony 1916- *Au&Wr 6, AuBYP,
ConAu 29, IlCB 1946, IlCB 1957,
SmATA 3, ThBJA, WWE 14*
Rawlings, Clyde *MnBBF*
Rawlings, James R *MnBBF*
Rawlings, James R *see* McCulloch, J H
Rawlings, Marjorie Kinnan 1896-1953 *AmA&B,
AmNov, CnDAL, CurB 42, CurB 54,
CyWA, DcLEnL, EvLB, LongC, ModAL,
OxAm, Pen Am, REn, REnAL, ThBJA,
TwCA, TwCA Sup, TwCW, YABC 1*
Rawlins, Margaret Grace *ChPo S2*
Rawls, Wilson 1919- *AuNews 1, BiN 1974,
ConAu 1R*
Rawson, T W *MnBBF*
Ray, Anna Chapin 1865-1945 *AmA&B, CarSB,*

DcAmA.
Ray, Carl 1943- *Prof*
Ray, Deborah 1940- *ConAu 57, IlBYP,
SmATA 8*
Ray, Irene *ConAu XR, SmATA 1*
Ray, Irene *see* Sutton, Margaret Beebe
Ray, JoAnne 1935- *ConAu 61, SmATA 9*
Ray, Mary Eva Pedder 1932- *Au&Wr 6,
ConAu 29, SmATA 2, WrD*
Ray, Ophelia *AuBYP*
Ray, Ralph 1920-1952 *IlBYP, IlCB 1946*
Ray, Rena *CarSB*
Ray, Saxon *MnBBF*
Ray, Stacey *MnBBF*
Rayle, Geoffrey *MnBBF*
Rayle, Geoffrey *see* McLean, Eric W
Raymond, Alex 1909-1956 *ArtCS*
Raymond, John *AuBYP*
Raymond, Margaret Thomsen *AuBYP*
Raymond, N G *MnBBF*
Raymond, Robert *ConAu XR, SmATA XR*
Raymond, Robert *see* Alter, Robert Edmond
Raymond, Rossiter Worthington 1840-1918 *Alli,
Alli Sup, AmA&B, CarSB, ChPo,
ChPo S1, DcAmA, DcNAA, OhA&B*
Rayne, Clifford *MnBBF*
Rayner, Guy *MnBBF, WWBWI A*
Rayner, Guy *see* Clarke, S Dacre
Rayner, Mary 1933- *ConAu 69*
Rayner, William 1929- *Au&Wr 6*
Raynes, John 1929- *ArtsCL, IlBYP*
Raynes, Robert *MnBBF*
Rayson, Steven *WrD*
Razzell, Arthur 1925- *SmATA 11*
Razzi, James 1931- *ConAu 53, SmATA 10*
Read, Miss 1913- *SmATA XR, WorAu*
Read, Alfred *MnBBF*
Read, Brian 1927- *Au&Wr 6, WrD*
Read, Charles Anderson 1841-1878 *MnBBF,
PoIre*
Read, Elfreida 1920- *Au&Wr 6, ConAu 21R,
SmATA 2, WrD*
Read, Sir Herbert 1893-1968 *ConAu 25R,
CurB 62, CurB 68*
Read, Piers Paul 1941- *Au&Wr 6,
ConAu 21R, ConDr 1, ConLC 4,
ConNov 1976, WW 1974*
Reade, Sidney *MnBBF*
Reading, Val *WWBWI I*
Reading, Val *see* Val
Reading, Willis *WWBWI I*
Reaney, James Crerar 1926- *Au&Wr 6,
CanWW 12, CanWr, CasWL, ChPo S1,
CnThe, ConAu 41, ConDr 1, ConP 1970,
ConP 1975, DrAS 6E, McGWD, OxCan,
OxCan Sup, Pen Eng, REnAL, REnWD,
WEAL, WrD*
Rearden, Jim 1925- *ConAu 65*
Reay, Trevace *MnBBF*
Reay, Trevace *see* Pond, S T R
Rechnitzer, Ferdinand Edsted 1894- *AuBYP*
Reck, Alma Kehoe 1901- *AuBYP, ConAu 1R,
ForWC 1970, IndAu 1917*
Reck, Franklin M 1896- *MnBBF, WNAA*
Redding, Robert Hull 1919- *ConAu 21R,
SmATA 2*
Redford, Lora Bryning *AuBYP*
Redknapp, E E *MnBBF*
Redman, Ben Ray 1896-1961 *AmA&B,*

AnMV 1926, Au&Wr 6, REnAL
Redman, Lister Appleton 1933- Au&Wr 6,
WrD
Redmond-Howard, Louis G 1884- MnBBF
Redmond-Howard, Louis G see Howard, Louis G
Redmond
Redway, Ralph LongC, MnBBF,
SmATA XR, . WWBWI A, WWCL
Redway, Ralph see Hamilton, Charles Harold St.
John
Redway, Ridley MnBBF, SmATA XR
Redway, Ridley see Hamilton, Charles Harold St.
John
Reed, A W WrD
Reed, A W 1908- ConAu 9R
Reed, Betty Jane 1921- ConAu 29, SmATA 4
Reed, Gwendolyn Elizabeth 1932- AuBYP,
ChPo S1, ConAu 25R, SmATA 7,
WWAW 8
Reed, Ivy Kellerman ChPo
Reed, Kit 1932- AmA&B, Au&Wr 6,
ConAu XR, WWA 38, WrD, WWAW 8
Reed, Kit see Reed, Lillian Craig
Reed, Lillian Craig 1932- ConAu 1R
Reed, Lillian Craig see Reed, Kit
Reed, Lucas MnBBF
Reed, Mary 1880?-1960 AmA&B
Reed, Philip G 1908- ChPo, IlBYP,
IlCB 1744, IlCB 1957, ThBJA,
WWMW 14
Reed, Stanley 1912- Au&Wr 6, WrD
Reed, Talbot Baines 1852-1893 Alli Sup,
CasWL, ChPo S2, EvLB, LongC,
MnBBF, TelT, WWBWI A, WWCL
Reed, Talbot Baines see Old Boy, An
Reed, Veronica IlBYP, IlCB 1946
Reed, Veronica see Sherman, Theresa
Reed, W Maxwell 1871- JBA 1951
Reeder, Red, Colonel 1902- AuBYP,
ConAu XR, SmATA 4
Reeder, Red, Colonel see Reeder, Russell P, Jr.
Reeder, Russell P, Jr. 1902- AuBYP,
ConAu 1R, SmATA 4
Reeder, Russell P, Jr. see Reeder, Red, Colonel
Reely, Mary Katharine 1881- AuBYP
Rees, David MnBBF, WWBWI A
Rees, David see Wignall, Trevor C
Rees, Edward MnBBF
Rees, Ennis 1925- AuBYP, ChPo S1,
ConAu 1R, DrAP 1975, DrAS 6E,
SmATA 3
Rees, George MnBBF, WWBWI A
Rees, Helen Christina Easson 1903- AuBYP,
ConAu 5R
Rees, Helen Christina Easson see Oliver, Jane
Rees, J Roger MnBBF
Rees, Jean Sinclair 1912- ConAu 1R
Rees, Leslie 1905- Au&Wr 6, SingR 1
Rees, Walter MnBBF
Reese, John Henry AuBYP
Reese, Lizette Woodworth 1856-1935 Alli Sup,
AmA&B, AnCL, BiD&SB, BiDSA,
ChPo, ChPo S2, CnDAL, ConAmA,
ConAmL, DcAmA, DcLEnL, DcNAA,
LongC, OxAm, REn, REnAL, TwCA,
TwCA Sup
Reese, M M 1910- ConAu 9R
Reese, Terence 1913- WW 1974
Reesink, Maryke 1919- ConAu 25R

Reeves, James 1909- AnCL, Au&Wr 6,
AuBYP, BkCL, ChPo, ChPo S1,
ChPo S2, ConAu 5R, ConP 1970,
ConP 1975, Pen Eng, ThBJA, WW 1974,
WWCL, WWTwL, WorAu, WrD
Reeves, Marjorie Ethel 1905- Au&Wr 6,
ConAu 13R, WW 1974, WrD
Reeves, Martha Emilie 1941- ConAu 65
Reeves, Percy MnBBF
Reeves, Ruth Ellen 1902- ConAu XR,
DrAS 6E, SmATA 6
Reeves, Ruth Ellen see Ranney, Agnes V
Regehr, Lydia 1903- ConAu 45
Reginald, F MnBBF
Regli, Adolph Casper 1896- AuBYP
Reid, Alastair 1926- AuBYP, ChPo, ChPo S1,
ChPo S2, ConAu 5R, ConP 1970,
ConP 1975, WorAu, WrD
Reid, Barbara 1922- ConAu 25R
Reid, Bill IlBYP
Reid, Desmond ConAu XR, MnBBF,
WWBWI A
Reid, Desmond see McNeilly, Wilfred Glassford
Reid, Dorothy M OxCan, OxCan Sup, Prof
Reid, Eugenie Chazal 1924- ForWC 1970,
SmATA 12
Reid, George K 1918- AmMWS 12P
Reid, J Dougall MnBBF
Reid, James 1907- ChPo, ChPo S2, ConICB
Reid, John Calvin ConAu 25R
Reid, Mayne 1818-1883 Alli, Alli Sup,
AmA&B, BbD, BiD&SB, BrAu 19,
CarSB, Chambr 3, DcAmA, DcEnL,
EvLB, HsB&A, MnBBF, NCHEL,
OxAm, Pen Am, REn, REnAL,
WWBWI A, WWCL
Reid, Mayne see Reid, Meta Mayne
Reid, Meta Mayne Au&Wr 6, ConAu 13R,
WrD
Reid, Meta Mayne see Reid, Mayne
Reid, Stephen 1873-1934 ChPo, ChPo S1,
IlCB 1744
Reid, Sybil MnBBF
Reid, Vic WrD
Reidy, John Patrick 1930- ConAu 17R
Reiley, Catherine Conway AuBYP
Reilly, Robert Thomas 1922- ConAu 5R, WrD
Reilly, William K ConAu XR, MnBBF,
WWBWI A
Reilly, William K see Creasey, John
Reinach, Jacquelyn 1930- AmSCAP 66
Reincheld, Bill 1946- ConAu 57
Reinecke, Esther E MnnWr
Reiner, William B 1910-1976 ConAu 45,
ConAu 61, LE 5
Reinfeld, Fred 1910-1964 AuBYP, ConAu P-1,
SmATA 3
Reinfeld, Fred see Young, Edward
Reiniger, Lotte 1899- IlCB 1946
Reitici, Rita Krohne 1930- ConAu 5R
Reitici, Rita Krohne see Ritchie, Rita
Remarque, Erich Maria 1898?-1970 AmA&B,
CasWL, CIDMEuL, ConAu 29, CyWA,
EncWL, EvEuW, LongC, ModGL,
NYTBE 1, OxEng, OxGer, Pen Eur,
REn, REnAL, TwCA, TwCA Sup,
TwCW, WWTwL
Rembadi, Gemma Mongiardini 1856- CarSB
Remi, Georges 1907- ConAu 69, SmATA 13

Remi, Georges *see* Herge
Remington, Barbara *ChPo S1*
Remington, Ella-Carrie 1914- *ConAu 69*
Remington, Ella-Carrie *see* Alden, Carella
Remington, Frederic 1861-1909 *AmA,*
    AmA&B, AtlBL, CnDAL, DcAmA,
    DcLEnL, DcNAA, OxAm, REn, REnAL
Remington, Rex *MnBBF*
Remini, Robert Vincent 1921- *ConAu 9R,*
    DrAS 6H, WWA 38
Renault, Mary 1905- *Au&Wr 6, AuBYP,*
    ConLC 3, ConNov 1972, ConNov 1976,
    CurB 59, IntWW 38, LongC,
    ModBL Sup, NCHEL, RAdv 1, REn,
    TwCW, WW 1974, WWWor 2, WorAu,
    WrD
Rendell, Joan *Au&Wr 6, WrD*
Rendina, Laura Cooper 1902- *AuBYP,*
    ConAu 9R, MorJA, SmATA 10
Renich, Jill 1916- *ConAu 25R*
Renick, Marion Lewis 1905- *AuBYP,*
    ConAu 1R, MorJA, OhA&B, SmATA 1
Renin, Paul *WWBWI A*
Renin, Paul *see* Goyne, Richard
Renken, Aleda 1907- *ConAu 21R*
Renlie, Frank H 1936- *SmATA 11*
Renstrom, Moiselle *ChPo S1*
Renvoize, Jean 1930- *Au&Wr 6, ConAu 41,*
    SmATA 5
Resnick, Seymour 1920- *AuBYP, DrAS 6F*
Ressler, Theodore Whitson *AuBYP*
Ressner, Philip 1922- *AuBYP, ConAu 13R*
Rethi, Lili 1894- *IlBYP*
Retla, Robert *ConAu XR, SmATA XR*
Retla, Robert *see* Alter, Robert Edmond
Retner, Beth A *ConAu XR*
Retner, Beth A *see* Brown, Beth
Reuter, Carol 1931- *ConAu 21R, SmATA 2*
Revel, Harry *MnBBF*
Revel, Harry *see* Floyd, Gilbert
Rexroth, Kenneth 1905- *AmA&B, CelR 3,*
    ChPo, CnE&AP, ConAu 5R, ConDr 1,
    ConLC 1, ConLC 2, ConLC 6,
    ConP 1970, ConP 1975, DrAP 1975,
    EncWL, IndAu 1917, IntWW 38,
    ModAL, ModAL Sup, OxAm, Pen Am,
    RAdv 1, REn, REnAL, TwCA Sup,
    WEAL, WWA 38, WWTwL, WWW 14,
    WWWor 2
Rey, Hans Augusto 1898- *AmPB, Au&ICB,*
    AuBYP, BkP, ChFB A, ConAu 5R,
    FamAI, IlCB 1744, IlCB 1946,
    IlCB 1957, JBA 1951, SmATA 1,
    WWAA 1973
Rey, Hans Augusto *see* Uncle Gus
Rey, Lester Del *ThBJA*
Rey, Lester Del *see* DelRey, Lester
Rey, Margaret *AmPB, Au&ICB, AuBYP,*
    BkP
Reyna, Marilyn De *IlBYP*
Reyna, Marilyn De *see* Hafner, Marilyn
Reynolds, Basil *MnBBF, WWBWI A,*
    WWBWI 1
Reynolds, Christopher 1911- *Au&Wr 6*
Reynolds, E Cockburn *MnBBF*
Reynolds, Frank 1876- *IlCB 1744*
Reynolds, George William Macarthur 1814-1879
    Alli, BrAu 19, DcLEnL, MnBBF,
    WWBWI A

Reynolds, Helen Mary Greenwood Campbell
    1884- *ConAu 5R, WNAA*
Reynolds, Malvina 1900- *AmSCAP 66,*
    EncFCW 1969, WWA 38, WWAW 8,
    WWW 14, WWWor 2
Reynolds, Marjorie Harris 1903- *AuBYP,*
    ConAu 5R
Reynolds, Quentin James 1902-1965 *AmA&B,*
    AuBYP, CurB 41, CurB 65, LongC,
    REnAL, TwCA Sup
Reynolds, Warwick *MnBBF, WWBWI A,*
    WWBWI 1
Rhinehart, Susan Oneacre *WrD*
Rhinehart, Susan Oneacre 1938- *ConAu 1R*
Rhoades, Walter C *MnBBF, WWBWI A*
Rhoads, Dorothy Mary 1895- *AuBYP,*
    ConAu 17R
Rhodes, Evan H 1929- *ConAu 57*
Rhodes, Frank Harold Trevor 1926-
    AmMWS 12P, WWA 38
Rhodes, Oakmead *MnBBF*
Rhodes, Oakmead *see* Burke, Thomas
Rhys, Megan *SmATA 5*
Rhys, Megan *see* Williams, Jeanne
Ribalow, Harold U 1919- *ConAu 5R,*
    WWWorJ 1972, WrD
Ribbons, Ian 1924- *IlBYP, IlCB 1946,*
    IlCB 1957
Ricciuti, Edward R 1938- *ConAu 41,*
    SmATA 10
Rice, Alice Caldwell Hegan 1870-1942 *AmA&B,*
    AmLY, BiDSA, CarSB, ChPo, CnDAL,
    ConAmL, CurB 42, DcAmA, DcBiA,
    DcNAA, EvLB, LongC, OxAm, REn,
    REnAL, TwCA, TwCA Sup, TwCW,
    WNAA
Rice, Charles D *AuBYP*
Rice, David Talbot 1903- *Au&Wr 6,*
    ConAu 9R, LongC
Rice, Dorothy 1916- *BiDL 5*
Rice, Elizabeth 1913- *ConAu 21R,*
    ForWC 1970, IlBYP, SmATA 2
Rice, Eve 1951- *ConAu 53*
Rice, Inez 1907- *AuBYP, ConAu 29,*
    SmATA 13
Rice, James 1934- *ConAu 61*
Rice, Ruth Little Mason 1884-1927 *AnCL 1926,*
    DcNAA, WNAA
Rich, Elaine Sommers 1926- *AuBYP,*
    ConAu 17R, IndAu 1917, SmATA 6,
    WrD
Rich, Gibson 1936- *ConAu 57*
Rich, Henry K *MnBBF*
Rich, Henry K *see* Goddard, Norman Molyneux
Rich, Josephine Bouchard 1912- *AuBYP,*
    ConAu 5R, SmATA 10
Rich, Louise Dickinson 1903- *AmA&B,*
    AuBYP, CurB 43, REnAL, TwCA Sup
Richard, Adrienne 1921- *ConAu 29,*
    SmATA 5
Richards, Christine-Louise 1910- *WWAW 8,*
    WWE 14, WrD
Richards, Dorothy *CarSB*
Richards, Frank 1875-1961 *LongC, MnBBF,*
    SmATA XR, WWBWI A, WWCL
Richards, Frank *see* Austin, Stanley E
Richards, Frank *see* Barnard, Richard Innes
Richards, Frank *see* Barrie, S
Richards, Frank *see* Brooks, Edwy Searles

Richards, Frank *see* Catchpole, William Leslie
Richards, Frank *see* Cook, Fred Gordon
Richards, Frank *see* Davies, A W
Richards, Frank *see* Down, C Maurice
Richards, Frank *see* Duffy, Michael Francis
Richards, Frank *see* Gibbons, William
Richards, Frank *see* Hamilton, Charles Harold
St. John
Richards, Frank *see* Herman, Julius
Richards, Frank *see* Hinton, Herbert Allan
Richards, Frank *see* Hook, H Clarke
Richards, Frank *see* Hope, William Edward
Stanton
Richards, Frank *see* Kemp, Alec M
Richards, Frank *see* Kirkham, Reginald S
Richards, Frank *see* Newman, Kenneth E
Richards, Frank *see* O'Mant, Hedley Percival
Angelo
Richards, Frank *see* Pentelow, John Nix
Richards, Frank *see* Pike, William Ernest
Richards, Frank *see* Ransome, L E
Richards, Frank *see* Samways, George Richmond
Richards, Frank *see* Shepherd, S Rossiter
Richards, Frank *see* Wood-Smith, Noel
Richards, George Mather 1880- *ChPo,*
IICB 1744
Richards, Gordon *MnBBF*
Richards, Hilda *LongC, SmATA XR,*
WWBWI A, WWCL
Richards, Hilda *see* Hamilton, Charles Harold St.
John
Richards, Ivor Armstrong 1893- *AmA&B,*
CasWL, Chambr 3, ConP 1970,
ConP 1975, DcLEnL, DrAP 1975,
EncWL, EvLB, IntWW 38, LongC,
ModBL, ModBL Sup, NCHEL, OxAm,
OxEng, Pen Eng, RAdv 1, REn, TwCA,
TwCA Sup, TwCW, WEAL, WW 1974,
WWA 38, WWLA
Richards, Jack *OxCan Sup*
Richards, Jane 1934- *ConAu 33*
Richards, John Paul *IlBYP*
Richards, Larry *ConAu XR*
Richards, Larry *see* Richards, Lawrence O
Richards, Laura Elizabeth 1850-1943 *Alli Sup,*
AmA&B, AmLY, AnCL, BiD&SB,
BkCL, CarSB, ChP, ChPo, ChPo S1,
ChPo S2, CnDAL, CurB 43, DcAmA,
DcNAA, FamPYP, JBA 1934, OxAm,
REnAL, St&VC, TwCA, TwCA Sup,
WNAA, YABC 1
Richards, Lawrence O 1931- *ConAu 29*
Richards, Lawrence O *see* Richards, Larry
Richards, Ross *MnBBF*
Richards, Ross *see* Mead, Matt
Richards, Walter *MnBBF*
Richards, William Carey 1818-1892 *Alli,*
Alli Sup, BiDSA, CarSB, ChPo, DcAmA,
DcNAA
Richardson *MnBBF*
Richardson *see* Haggerston, Scrope
Richardson, Dorothy *WrD*
Richardson, Flavia *MnBBF*
Richardson, Flavia *see* Thomson, Christine
Campbell
Richardson, Frank Howard 1882-1970 *AmA&B,*
WNAA
Richardson, Frederick 1862- *ChPo, ConICB*
Richardson, Gladwell 1903- *ArizL, MnBBF*

Richardson, Gladwell *see* Grant, Maxwell
Richardson, Grace Lee *ConAu XR, SmATA 8*
Richardson, Grace Lee *see* Dickson, Naida
Richardson, Midge Turk 1930- *ConAu 65*
Richardson, Robert *MnBBF*
Richardson, Robert S 1902- *ConAu 49,*
SmATA 8
Richardson, Robert S *see* Latham, Philip
Richey, David 1939- *ConAu 57*
Richey, David *see* Davey, John
Richey, David *see* Johnson, Richard
Richey, Dorothy Hilliard *ConAu 9R,*
ForWC 1970, WWAW 8
Richler, Mordecai 1931- *Au&Wr 6,*
AuNews 1, BiN 1975, CanWW 12,
CanWr, CasWL, ConAu 65, ConLC 3,
ConLC 5, ConNov 1972, ConNov 1976,
EncWL, IntWW 38, OxCan, OxCan Sup,
Pen Eng, REnAL, TwCW, WEAL,
WW 1974, WWTwL, WWWor 2,
WorAu
Richmond, Court *MnBBF*
Richmond, George *MnBBF*
Richmond, George *see* Samways, George
Richmond
Richmond, Grace 1866-1959 *AmA&B, CarSB,*
EvLB, TwCA
Richmond, H B *MnBBF*
Richmond, H B *see* Bungay, E Newton
Richmond, Legh 1772-1827 *Alli, BbD,*
BiD&SB, BiDLA, CarSB, ChPo S2,
DcEnL, OxEng
Richmond, Robert Price 1914- *ConAu 21R,*
WWE 14, WrD
Richoux, Patricia 1927- *ConAu 25R,*
SmATA 7
Richter, Conrad Michael 1890-1968 *AmA&B,*
AmNov, CnDAL, ConAu 5R,
ConAu 25R, CurB 51, CurB 68, CyWA,
DcLEnL, ModAL, OxAm, Pen Am,
RAdv 1, REn, REnAL, SmATA 3,
TwCA, TwCA Sup, WNAA
Richter, Dorothy 1906- *ConAu 29*
Richter, Hans Peter 1925- *ConAu 45,*
SmATA 6
Rickert, Corinne Holt *ConAu XR*
Rickwood, E *MnBBF*
Rideing, William Henry 1853-1918 *Alli Sup,*
AmA, AmA&B, AmLY, BiD&SB,
CarSB, DcAmA, DcNAA
Rideout, Harold *MnBBF*
Rider, John Russell 1923- *ConAu 25R,*
DrAS 6E, WWMW 14
Ridge, Antonia Florence *Au&Wr 6, ChPo S1,*
ConAu 9R, SmATA 7, WrD
Ridge, Martin 1923- *DrAS 6H*
Ridge, William Pett 1860?-1930 *BiD&SB,*
Chambr 3, DcLEnL, EvLB, LongC,
MnBBF, NCHEL, WWBWI A
Ridgway, Jason *AuBYP, ConAu XR*
Ridgway, Jason *see* Lesser, Milton
Ridgway, John *WrD*
Ridle, Julia Brown 1923- *ConAu 1R*
Ridley, Anthony 1933- *Au&Wr 6*
Ridley, Nat, Jr. *ConAu P-2*
Ridley, Nat, Jr. *see* Stratemeyer, Edward L
Ridout, Albert K 1905- *ConAu P-2*
Riedesel, C Alan 1930- *ConAu 25R, LE 5*
Riedman, Sarah Regal 1902- *AuBYP,*

ConAu 1R, ForWC 1970, SmATA 1
Riedman, Sarah Regal *see* Gustafson, Sarah
  Regal
Rieger, Shay 1929- *ConAu 29*
Rienow, Leona Train *AuBYP, WWAW 8,*
  WWE 14
Rieseberg, Harry E 1892- *ConAu 5R*
Riesenberg, Felix, Jr. 1913- *AuBYP, CurB 57*
Rietveld, Jane 1913- *AuBYP*
Rieu, Emile Victor 1887- *AnCL, AuBYP,*
  ChPo, ChPo S1
Rifkin, Lillian *AuBYP*
Rigby, Arthur *MnBBF*
Rigby, Hugh *MnBBF*
Riggs, Ida Berry *AuBYP*
Rigot, Sebastian *MnBBF*
Riis, Jacob August 1849-1914 *AmA&B, BbD,*
  BiD&SB, DcAmA, DcNAA, OxAm,
  REn, REnAL
Rikhoff, Jean 1928- *ConAu 61, SmATA 9*
Rikon, Irving 1931- *ConAu 29*
Riley, James Whitcomb 1849-1916 *Alli Sup,*
  AmA, AmA&B, AmSCAP 66, BbD,
  BiD&SB, BlkAW, CarSB, CasWL,
  Chambr 3, ChP, ChPo, ChPo S1,
  ChPo S2, CnDAL, DcAmA, DcEnA Ap,
  DcLEnL, DcNAA, EvLB, FamPYP,
  IndAu 1816, JBA 1934, LongC, OxAm,
  Pen Am, RAdv 1, REn, REnAL,
  St&VC
Riley, Tex *ConAu XR, WWBWI A*
Riley, Tex *see* Creasey, John
Rimanelli, Giose *OxCan*
Rinehart, Mary Roberts 1876-1958 *AmA&B,*
  AmNov, ConAmL, DcBiA, DcLEnL,
  EncM&D, EvLB, LongC, ModWD,
  OxAm, Pen Am, REn, REnAL, TwCA,
  TwCA Sup, TwCW, WNAA
Ringi, Kjell *SmATA XR*
Ringi, Kjell *see* Ringi, Kjell Arne Sorensen
Ringi, Kjell Arne Sorensen 1939- *ConAu 45,*
  IlBYP, SmATA 12
Ringi, Kjell Arne Sorensen *see* Ringi, Kjell
Ringi, Kjell Arne Sorensen *see* S-Ringi, Kjell
Rink, Paul 1912- *AuBYP*
Rinkoff, Barbara Jean 1923-1975 *AuBYP,*
  ConAu 57, ConAu P-2, MorBMP,
  SmATA 4, WrD
Riordan, James 1936- *ConAu 69*
Rios, Juan Antonio 1888-1946 *CurB 42,*
  CurB 46
Rios, Tere *ConAu XR, ForWC 1970,*
  SmATA 2
Rios, Tere *see* Versace, Marie Teresa Rios
Ripley, Dillon 1913- *ConAu 57*
Ripley, Elizabeth Blake 1906-1969 *AuBYP*
Ripley, Elizabeth Blake 1906-1969 *ChPo S2*
Ripley, Elizabeth Blake 1906-1969 *ConAu 1R,*
  CurB 58, SmATA 5
Ripley, S Dillon 1913- *AmMWS 12P, CelR 3,*
  CurB 66, IntWW 38, WWS 13
Ripper, Charles L 1929- *ConAu 1R, IlBYP,*
  IlCB 1946, IlCB 1957, SmATA 3
Riser, Wayne H 1909- *AmMWS 12P,*
  ConAu P-1
Rishton, William *MnBBF*
Rishton, William *see* Wright, W George
Rist Arnold, Elisabeth 1950- *ConAu 65*
Rister, Claude *MnBBF*

Rister, Claude *see* Marshall, James
Riswold, Gilbert *ChPo S2, IlBYP, IlCB 1957*
Ritchie, Lady Anne Isabella Thackeray
  1837-1919 *Alli Sup, BbD, BiD&SB,*
  BrAu 19, CarSB, ChPo, DcEnA,
  DcEnA Ap, EvLB, LongC, NCHEL,
  OxEng, REn
Ritchie, Balfour *MnBBF, WWBWI A*
Ritchie, Balfour *see* Baldwin, Basil
Ritchie, Barbara Gibbons *AuBYP*
Ritchie, C T 1914- *ConAu 9R, WrD*
Ritchie, Jean 1922- *AmSCAP 66, CurB 59,*
  EncFCW 1969
Ritchie, Paul 1923- *ConAu 21R*
Ritchie, Rita 1930- *AuBYP, ConAu XR*
Ritchie, Rita *see* Reitici, Rita Krohne
Ritchie, Trekkie 1902- *ChPo, ChPo S1,*
  ChPo S2, IlBYP, IlCB 1946
Rittenberg, Max 1880- *MnBBF, WWBWI A*
Rittenhouse, Mignon 1904- *ConAu 41,*
  WWAW 8
Ritter, Felix *ConAu XR*
Ritter, Felix *see* Kruess, James
Rivera, Carlos 1916- *WWS 13*
Rivers, Tex *MnBBF*
Rivers, Tex *see* Lewins, C A
Riverside, John *AuBYP, ConAu XR,*
  SmATA XR
Riverside, John *see* Heinlein, Robert A
Riviere, Bill *ConAu XR*
Riviere, Bill *see* Riviere, William Alexander
Riviere, William Alexander 1916- *ConAu 5R*
Riviere, William Alexander *see* Riviere, Bill
Rivoli, Mario 1943- *IlBYP, IlCB 1957,*
  SmATA 10
Rivoli, Mario *see* Koutoukas, H M
Rivoli, Mario *see* Marasmus, Seymour
Riwkin-Brick, Anna 1908-1970 *AuBYP*
Rix, Witton *MnBBF*
Roach, Marilynne K 1946- *ConAu 57,*
  SmATA 9
Robbins, Frank 1917- *ArtCS, IlBYP,*
  WWAA 1973
Robbins, Leonard Harman 1877-1947 *MnBBF*
Robbins, Raleigh *MnBBF, SmATA XR,*
  WWBWI A
Robbins, Raleigh *see* Hamilton, Charles Harold
  St. John
Robbins, Ruth 1917- *AuBYP, IlCB 1957,*
  ThBJA
Roberson, Peter 1907- *ArtsCL*
Robertiello, Richard C 1923- *ConAu 9R*
Roberts, Bruce 1930- *ConAu 9R*
Roberts, Catherine Christopher 1905- *AuBYP*
Roberts, Sir Charles George Douglas 1860-1943
  Alli Sup, BbD, BiD&SB, CanNov,
  CanWr, Chambr 3, ChPo, ChPo S1,
  ChPo S2, ConAmL, CurB 44, DcAmA,
  DcBiA, DcNAA, EvLB, JBA 1934,
  LongC, OxAm, OxCan, OxEng, Pen Eng,
  REn, REnAL, TwCA, TwCA Sup,
  WEAL
Roberts, D H *MnBBF*
Roberts, David *ConAu XR, SmATA XR*
Roberts, David *see* Cox, John Roberts
Roberts, Doreen 1922- *IlCB 1957*
Roberts, Elizabeth Madox 1886-1941 *AmA&B,*
  AnCL, BkCL, ChPo, ChPo S1, CnDAL,
  ConAmA, ConAmL, CurB 41, CyWA,

DcLEnL, DcNAA, EncWL, LongC,
ModAL, OxAm, Pen Am, REn, REnAL,
St&VC, TwCA, TwCA Sup
Roberts, Elliott B 1899- *ConAu 1R, WrD*
Roberts, Eric B 1914- *Au&Wr 6, ConAu 5R,*
WrD
Roberts, Franklin *MnBBF*
Roberts, Holt *MnBBF*
Roberts, Holt *see* Draper, Ben
Roberts, Jack 1894- *IICB 1744*
Roberts, Jim *ConAu XR, SmATA XR*
Roberts, Jim *see* Bates, Barbara S
Roberts, John *ConAu XR*
Roberts, John *see* Bingley, David Ernest
Roberts, John G 1913- *ConAu 49*
Roberts, John H 1861- *WWBWI I*
Roberts, John Llewellyn *MnBBF, WWBWI A*
Roberts, John Morris 1928- *Au&Wr 6,*
WW 1974, WrD
Roberts, Lee *MnBBF*
Roberts, Louis *MnBBF*
Roberts, Lunt *WWBWI I*
Roberts, Murray *MnBBF, WWBWI A*
Roberts, Murray *see* Graydon, Robert Murray
Roberts, Ralph 1915- *AmMWS 12P, MnBBF*
Roberts, Terence *ConAu XR, SmATA 6,*
SmATA 6
Roberts, Terence *see* Sanderson, Ivan T
Roberts, Theodore Goodridge 1877-1953
MnBBF
Roberts, Virginia *ConAu XR*
Roberts, Virginia *see* Dean, Nell Marr
Roberts, Willo Davis 1928- *ConAu 49*
Robertshaw, Denis 1911- *ConAu 65*
Robertshaw, Denis *see* Gaunt, Michael
Robertson, Barbara Anne 1931- *ConAu 25R,*
OxCan Sup, SmATA 12, WWAW 8,
WrD
Robertson, Colin 1906- *Au&Wr 6, ConAu 9R,*
MnBBF
Robertson, Don 1929- *ConAu 9R, SmATA 8*
Robertson, Dorothy Lewis 1912- *ConAu 25R,*
SmATA 12
Robertson, Frank Chester 1890- *AmA&B,*
ConAu 1R, MnBBF, REnAL, WNAA,
WWPNA
Robertson, G E *ChPo S1, ChPo S2,*
WWBWI I
Robertson, Henry *MnBBF*
Robertson, J B *MnBBF*
Robertson, J G *MnBBF*
Robertson, James *MnBBF*
Robertson, Jennifer Sinclair 1942- *ConAu 53,*
SmATA 12
Robertson, Keith Charlton 1914- *Au&Wr 6,*
AuBYP, ConAu 9R, MorBMP, MorJA,
SmATA 1
Robertson, Keith Charlton *see* Keith, Carlton
Robeson, Kenneth *ConAu XR*
Robeson, Kenneth *see* Goulart, Ron
Robinet, Harriette Gillem 1931- *ConAu 69*
Robins, Fenton *MnBBF*
Robins, Fenton *see* Gammon, D J
Robins, Patricia *WrD*
Robins, Seelin *HsB&A, YABC 1*
Robins, Seelin *see* Ellis, Edward S
Robinson, Adjai 1932- *ConAu 45, SmATA 8*
Robinson, Anthony 1931- *AmA&B,*
ConAu 1R

Robinson, Barbara Webb 1927- *AuBYP,*
ConAu 1R, SmATA 8
Robinson, Barry 1938- *ConAu 25R*
Robinson, Ben Carl 1890- *MnBBF*
Robinson, Bill *ConAu XR*
Robinson, Bill *see* Robinson, William Wheeler
Robinson, Boardman 1876-1952 *AmA&B,*
ChPo, CurB 41, CurB 52, DcCAA 2,
IICB 1744
Robinson, C A, Jr. 1900- *ConAu 1R*
Robinson, Chaille Howard Payne *ConAu 13R*
Robinson, Chaille Howard Payne *see* Robinson,
Kathleen
Robinson, Charles 1870-1937 *ChPo, ChPo S1,*
ChPo S2, WWCL
Robinson, Charles 1931- *ConAu 49, IIBYP,*
SmATA 6, WWBWI I
Robinson, Charles Alexander, Jr. 1900-
AmA&B
Robinson, Charles Alexander, Jr 1900- *AuBYP*
Robinson, David 1929- *AmMWS 12P*
Robinson, Earl 1910- *AmSCAP 66, ConAu 45,*
EncFCW 1969
Robinson, Edith 1858- *Alli Sup, AmA&B,*
BiD&SB, CarSB, DcAmA, DcNAA
Robinson, Elizabeth Cameron *ConAu 1R*
Robinson, Elizabeth Cameron *see* Nowell,
Elizabeth Cameron
Robinson, Ernest Herbert 1880-1947 *MnBBF,*
WWBWI A
Robinson, Florine 1920- *LBAA, WrD*
Robinson, Frank M 1926- *ConAu 49*
Robinson, Gunner *MnBBF*
Robinson, Hubert J *MnBBF*
Robinson, Irene Bowen 1891- *IIBYP,*
IICB 1744, IICB 1946, JBA 1951
Robinson, Jackie 1919-1972 *CurB 47, CurB 72,*
NYTBE 2, NYTBE 3
Robinson, Jan M 1933- *ConAu 61, SmATA 6*
Robinson, Jan M *see* Flood, Flash
Robinson, Jean O 1934- *ConAu 29, SmATA 7*
Robinson, Jerry *IIBYP*
Robinson, Joan G 1910- *Au&Wr 6,*
ConAu 5R, SmATA 7, WWCL
Robinson, Joan G *see* Thomas, Joan Gale
Robinson, Kathleen *ConAu XR*
Robinson, Kathleen *see* Robinson, Chaille
Howard Payne
Robinson, Mabel Louise d1962 *AmA&B,*
AmNov, JBA 1951, WNAA
Robinson, Matt 1937- *ConAu 45*
Robinson, Maudie Millian Oller 1914-
ConAu 61, SmATA 11
Robinson, Paul 1898- *ArtCS*
Robinson, Ray *AuBYP*
Robinson, Richard 1945- *ConAu 57*
Robinson, Robert Shirley 1902- *AuBYP*
Robinson, Robert Shirley *see* Latnam, Philip
Robinson, Rowland Evans 1833-1900 *Alli Sup,*
AmA, AmA&B, CarSB, CnDAL,
DcAmA, DcLEnL, DcNAA, OxAm,
REnAL
Robinson, Sondra Till 1931- *ConAu 53*
Robinson, Spider 1948- *ConAu 65*
Robinson, Stuart 1936- *BiEnAT*
Robinson, Thomas Heath 1869-1950 *IICB 1744,*
WWBWI I, WWCL
Robinson, Thomas Pendleton 1878- *AuBYP,*
ChPo, ChPo S1

Robinson, Thomas Pendleton *see* Robinson, Tom
Robinson, Timothy Michael 1934- *Au&Wr 6,*
WrD
Robinson, Tom 1878- *BkCL, JBA 1951,*
St&VC
Robinson, Tom *see* Robinson, Thomas Pendleton
Robinson, W L *Alli*
Robinson, W W 1891- *JBA 1951, St&VC*
Robinson, William Heath 1872-1944 *ChPo,*
ChPo S1, ChPo S2, ConICB, CurB 44,
WWBWI 1, WWCL
Robinson, William Wheeler 1918- *ConAu 5R*
Robinson, William Wheeler *see* Robinson, Bill
Robison, Bonnie 1924- *ConAu 57, SmATA 12*
Robison, Mabel Otis 1891- *ConAu P-1,*
MnnWr
Robottom, John Carlisle 1934- *Au&Wr 6,*
ConAu 29, SmATA 7, WrD
Robson, Ralph *MnBBF*
Roche, A K *ConAu XR, SmATA XR*
Roche, A K *see* Abisch, Roslyn Kroop
Roche, Arthur Somers 1883-1935 *AmA&B,*
DcNAA, MnBBF, TwCA
Roche, Eric *MnBBF, WWBWI A*
Roche, Eric *see* Rochester, George Ernest
Roche, Hester *WWBWI A*
Roche, Hester *see* Rochester, George Ernest
Roche, Regina Maria 1764?-1845 *Alli, BbD,*
BiD&SB, BiDLA, BrAu 19, CarSB,
DcBiA, NCHEL
Rochefort, Julian *MnBBF*
Rochefort, Julian *see* Stevens, Christopher
Rochester, George Ernest 1895?- *MnBBF,*
WWBWI A
Rochester, George Ernest *see* Beresford, John
Rochester, George Ernest *see* Chatham, Frank
Rochester, George Ernest *see* Frazer, Allison
Rochester, George Ernest *see* Furze, Barton
Rochester, George Ernest *see* Gaunt, Jeffrey
Rochester, George Ernest *see* Hale, Martin
Rochester, George Ernest *see* Kent, Elizabeth
Rochester, George Ernest *see* Roche, Eric
Rochester, George Ernest *see* Roche, Hester
Rochester, George Ernest *see* Smith, Hamilton
Rochester, George Ernest *see* West, Mary
Rochester, W F *MnBBF*
Rocker, Fermin 1907- *IICB 1957*
Rockowitz, Murray 1920- *ConAu 25R,*
WWE 14
Rockwell, Anne 1934- *ConAu 21R, IIBYP*
Rockwell, Gail *ChPo S1, IIBYP*
Rockwell, Harlow *IIBYP*
Rockwell, Jane 1929- *ConAu 65*
Rockwell, Norman 1894- *CelR 3, ChPo S2,*
CurB 45, ForII, IIBYP, IICB 1744,
NYTBE 2, REn, REnAL, WWA 38,
WWAA 1973, WWGA, WWWor 2
Rockwell, Thomas 1933- *ChPo S1, ConAu 29,*
SmATA 7, WrD
Rockwood, Joyce 1947- *ConAu 57*
Rockwood, Roy *ConAu P-2, HsB&A,*
SmATA 1
Rockwood, Roy *see* Stratemeyer, Edward L
Rodd, Kylie Tennant 1912- *ConAu 5R*
Rodd, Kylie Tennant *see* Tennant, Kylie
Rodgers, Mary 1931- *AmSCAP 66, BiEnAT,*
ConAu 49, SmATA 8, WWAW 8
Rodman, Emerson *HsB&A, YABC 1*

Rodman, Emerson *see* Ellis, Edward S
Rodman, Maia *ConAu XR, SmATA 1*
Rodman, Maia *see* Wojciechowska, Maia
Rodman, Selden 1909- *AmA&B, ChPo,*
ChPo S1, ConAu 5R, OxAm, REn,
REnAL, SmATA 9, TwCA Sup,
WWA 38, WWAA 1973, WWWor 2
Rodowsky, Colby F 1932- *ConAu 69*
Rodway, Roland *MnBBF*
Rodway, Roland *see* Hamilton, Charles Harold
St. John
Rodziszewski, Audrey Korwin *see*
Korwin-Rodziszewski, Audrey
Rodziszewski, George Korwin *see*
Korwin-Rodziszewski, George
Roe, Edward Payson 1838-1888 *Alli Sup, AmA,*
AmA&B, BbD, BiD&SB, CarSB,
Chambr 3, DcAmA, DcLEnL, DcNAA,
MnBBF, OxAm, REnAL
Roe, Harry Mason *ConAu P-2*
Roe, Harry Mason *see* Stratemeyer, Edward L
Roethke, Theodore 1908-1963 *AmA&B,*
AmWr, AnCL, AtlBL, CasWL, ChPo,
ChPo S1, ChPo S2, CnDAL, CnE&AP,
ConLC 1, ConLC 3, ConP 1975, CrCAP,
EncWL, LongC, ModAL, ModAL Sup,
OxAm, Pen Am, RAdv 1, REn, REnAL,
TwCA Sup, TwCW, WEAL, WWPNA,
WWTwL
Roever, J M *IIBYP*
Roger, Mae Durham *ConAu 57*
Roger, Mae Durham *see* Durham, Mae
Rogers, Mister *see* Rogers, Fred
Rogers, Alan 1937- *ConAu 25R,, SmATA 2*
Rogers, Ben *MnBBF*
Rogers, Ben *see* Pugh, Roger
Rogers, Bertha *ChPo*
Rogers, Carol *IIBYP*
Rogers, Cedric *AuBYP*
Rogers, Dale Evans 1912- *AmA&B, CurB 56*
Rogers, Frances 1888-1974 *ConAu 5R,*
SmATA 10
Rogers, Fred 1928- *AmSCAP 66, WWE 14*
Rogers, Fred *see* Rogers, Mister
Rogers, Fred Baker 1926- *AmMWS 12P,*
WWA 38
Rogers, G M *MnBBF*
Rogers, James T 1921- *ConAu 45*
Rogers, Joe *ChPo S2*
Rogers, Julia Ellen 1866- *AmA&B*
Rogers, Matilda 1894- *ConAu 29, SmATA 5*
Rogers, Pamela 1927- *ConAu 49, SmATA 9*
Rogers, Robert *MnBBF, SmATA XR,*
WWBWI A
Rogers, Robert *see* Hamilton, Charles Harold St.
John
Rogers, Steve *MnBBF*
Rogers, Steve *see* Clarke, Percy A
Rogers, Tom *MnBBF*
Rogers, Tom *see* Edgar, Alfred
Rogers, William Garland 1896- *AmA&B,*
AuBYP, ConAu 9R
Rohmer, Sax 1883-1959 *EncM&D, EvLB,*
LongC, MnBBF, NCHEL, Pen Eng,
TwCA, TwCA Sup, TwCW, WWBWI A,
WWLA
Rohmer, Sax *see* Ward, Arthur Sarsfield
Roizel, Albert *MnBBF*
Rojankovsky, Feodor Stepanovich 1891- *AmPB,*

AuBYP, BkP, Cald 1938, ChPo,
ChPo S1, IlBYP, IlCB 1744, IlCB 1946,
IlCB 1957, JBA 1951, NYTBE 1,
NewbC 1956, WWCL
Roland, Albert 1925- *ConAu 61, SmATA 11*
Roland, Betty *SingR 2, WrD*
Roland Smith, Gordon *WrD*
Rolerson, Darrell A 1946- *ConAu 49,*
SmATA 8
Rolfsrud, Erling Nicolai 1912- *ConAu 65*
Roll, Winifred 1909- *ConAu 49, SmATA 6*
Rollem, John W *MnBBF*
Rollington, Ralph *MnBBF, WWBWI A*
Rollington, Ralph *see* Allingham, John W
Rollins, Charlemae Hill 1897- *AuBYP, BlkAW,*
ChPo S1, ConAu 9R, LBAA, MorBMP,
SmATA 3
Rollo, Vera Foster 1924- *WrD*
Rolls, Eric Charles 1923- *Au&Wr 6,*
ConAu 33, ConP 1970, WrD
Rolt-Wheeler, Francis W 1876-1960 *AmLY,*
JBA 1934, JBA 1951, WNAA, WWLA
Rolt-Wheeler, Francis W *see* Wheeler, Francis W
Rolt
Romano, Clare 1922- *ConAu 41*
Romano, Louis G 1921- *ConAu 17R, LE 5,*
WrD
Romany *WWCL*
Romany *see* Evens, George Bramwell
Rombauer, Irma S 1877-1962 *CurB 53,*
CurB 62
Rome, Stewart *MnBBF*
Romulo, Carlos Pena 1899- *AmA&B,*
CatA 1930, ConAu 13R, CurB 43,
CurB 57, IntWW 38, WNAA,
WWWor 2
Ronald, Grayling *MnBBF*
Ronald, Grayling *see* Gray, R E
Ronald, Guy *MnBBF*
Ronald, James *MnBBF*
Ronan, Colin Alistair 1920- *Au&Wr 6,*
ConAu 5R, WrD
Rongen, Bjoern 1906- *ConAu P-2, SmATA 10*
Rongione, Louis Anthony 1912- *BiDL 5,*
WWA 38
Ronne, Finn 1899- *AmMWS 12S, ConAu 1R,*
CurB 48, WWA 38, WWWor 2
Rood, Ronald N 1920- *ConAu 21R,*
SmATA 12
Rooke, Daphne Marie 1914- *Au&Wr 6,*
AuBYP, ConAu 53, ConNov 1972,
ConNov 1976, SmATA 12, TwCW,
WW 1974, WorAu, WrD
Rooke, Daphne Marie *see* Pointon, Robert
Roos, Ann *AuBYP, MorJA*
Roose-Evans, James 1927- *ConAu 29,*
WWT 15, WrD
Roosevelt, Eleanor 1884-1962 *AmA&B,*
AuBYP, BiN 1974, CurB 40, CurB 49,
CurB 63, LongC, OxAm, REn, REnAL
Roosevelt, Elliott 1910- *AmA&B, AuNews 1,*
CurB 46, WWA 38
Roosevelt, Wyn *CarSB*
Root, Frederick Stanley 1853-1906 *CarSB,*
DcNAA
Root, Waverley 1903- *ConAu 25R, CurB 43*
Roper, Archibald G *MnBBF*
Roper, Laura Wood 1911- *ConAu 57, WrD*
Roper, Laura Wood *see* Wood, Laura N

Roper, Mary E *MnBBF*
Roscoe, William 1753-1831 *Alli, BbD,*
BiD&SB, BiDLA, BrAu 19, CasWL,
Chambr 2, ChPo, ChPo S1, ChPo S2,
DcEnL, DcEuL, DcLEnL, EvLB,
NCHEL, OxEng, TelT
Rose, Anne *CqnAu 49, SmATA 8*
Rose, Carl 1903-1971 *ChPo, ConAu 29,*
NYTBE 2
Rose, Charles E *MnBBF*
Rose, Elizabeth Jane 1933- *ConAu 5R,*
ThBJA
Rose, Florella *ConAu XR*
Rose, Florella *see* Carlson, Vada F
Rose, Gerald 1935- *ChPo S2, ConAu 65,*
IlBYP, IlCB 1957, ThBJA
Rose, Nancy A 1934- *ConAu 37*
Rose, Nancy A *WrD*
Rose, Richard 1933- *Au&Wr 6, ConAu 21R,*
WW 1974
Rose, Wendy 1948- *DrAP 1975, SmATA 12*
Rose, Wendy *see* Edwards, Bronwen Elizabeth
Rose, Wendy *see* Khanshendel, Chiron
Roselli, Luciana *AuBYP*
Rosen, Sidney 1916- *AmMWS 12P,*
ConAu 9R, LE 5, SmATA 1, WrD
Rosen, Winifred 1943- *ConAu 29, SmATA 8*
Rosenbaum, Eileen 1936- *ConAu 21R*
Rosenbaum, Jean 1927- *ConAu 17R*
Rosenbaum, Maurice 1907- *ConAu 17R,*
SmATA 6
Rosenberg, Arthur D 1939- *ConAu 61*
Rosenberg, Ethel *ConAu 29, SmATA 3*
Rosenberg, Ethel *see* Clifford, Ethel
Rosenberg, Ethel *see* Penn, Ruth Bonn
Rosenberg, Nancy Sherman 1931- *AmA&B,*
ConAu 1R, ForWC 1970, SmATA 4,
WWA 38, WWAW 8, WWE 14
Rosenberg, Nancy Sherman *see* Sherman, Nancy
Rosenberg, Sharon 1942- *SmATA 8*
Rosenblatt, Suzanne Maris 1937- *ConAu 69*
Rosenblum, Richard 1928- *ConAu 65, IlBYP,*
SmATA 11
Rosenburg, John M 1918- *AuBYP,*
ConAu 21R, SmATA 6
Rosendall, Betty 1916- *ConAu 49*
Rosenfeld, Sam 1920- *ConAu 9R*
Rosenthal, Harold 1914- *AmMWS 12P,*
WWWorJ 1972
Rosenthal, Jules M 1924- *ConAu 17R*
Rosewall, Ken 1934- *CelR 3, CurB 56*
Rosmond, Babette 1921?- *AmA&B, AmNov,*
ConAu 5R, ForWC 1970, WWAW 8,
WWE 14
Rosner, Joseph 1914- *ConAu 57*
Rosner, Lynn 1944- *ConAu 61*
Rosoman, Leonard 1913- *ArtsCL*
Ross, Alan *MnBBF*
Ross, Alan 1922- *WrD, Au&Wr 6, ChPo,*
ConAu 9R, ConP 1970, ConP 1975,
LongC, ModBL, NCHEL, TwCA Sup,
WW 1974
Ross, Alan *see* Warwick, Alan Ross
Ross, Alex 1909- *WWA 38*
Ross, Anne 1925- *Au&Wr 6*
Ross, Barnaby *AmA&B, AuBYP,*
ConAu XR, CurB 40, DcLEnL,
EncM&D, EvLB, LongC, Pen Am,
REnAL, TwCA, TwCA Sup

Ross, Barnaby *see* Dannay, Frederic
Ross, Barnaby *see* Lee, Manfred B
Ross, Charles Henry 1842-1897 *Alli, Alli Sup, ChPo, ChPo S2, HsB&A, HsB&A Sup, MnBBF*
Ross, Clare Romano 1922- *IlCB 1957*
Ross, David 1896-1975 *ChPo S2, ConAu 61, WWA 38*
Ross, Edgar *MnBBF*
Ross, Eulalie Steinmetz 1910- *ConAu 17R*
Ross, Frances Aileen 1909- *ConAu P-1*
Ross, Frank, Jr. *ChPo S1*
Ross, Ishbel 1897-1975 *AmA&B, AmNov, ConAu 61, ForWC 1970*
Ross, John 1921- *IlBYP, IlCB 1957*
Ross, Leonard Q 1908- *AmA&B, ConAu XR, CurB 42, LongC, OxAm, Pen Am, REnAL, TwCA, TwCA Sup, WW 1974*
Ross, Nancy Wilson 1907- *AmA&B, AmNov, CurB 52, TwCA Sup, WWA 38, WWAW 8*
Ross, Patricia Fent 1899- *AnCL, AuBYP*
Ross, Phillip *MnBBF*
Ross, Wilda *WrD*
Ross, Z H *ConAu XR*
Ross, Z H *see* Ross, Zola Helen
Ross, Zola Helen 1912- *AuBYP, ConAu 53, WWPNA*
Ross, Zola Helen *see* Arre, Helen
Ross, Zola Helen *see* Iles, Bert
Ross, Zola Helen *see* Ross, Z H
Ross Williamson, Hugh 1901- *Au&Wr 6, ConAu 17R, IntWW 38, LongC, WW 1974*
Ross Williamson, Hugh *see* Rossiter, Ian
Rossel, Seymour 1945- *ConAu 53, WrD*
Rosselli, Colette 1916- *ChPo, IlCB 1957*
Rossetti, Christina Georgina 1830-1894 *Alli, Alli Sup, AnCL, AtlBL, BbD, BiD&SB, BrAu 19, CarSB, CasWL, Chambr 3, ChP, ChPo, ChPo S1, ChPo S2, CnE&AP, CriT 3, CyWA, DcEnA, DcEnA Ap, DcEnL, DcEuL, DcLEnL, EvLB, FamPYP, JBA 1934, MouLC 4, NCHEL, OxEng, Pen Eng, RAdv 1, REn, St&VC, WEAL*
Rossi, Mario 1916- *ConAu 5R*
Rossini, Gioacchino Antonio 1792-1868 *AtlBL, OxFr*
Rossiter, Ian *ConAu XR*
Rossiter, Ian *see* Ross Williamson, Hugh
Roth, Arnold 1929- *ConAu 21R, IlBYP, WWE 14*
Roth, Arthur 1920- *ConAu 1R*
Roth, Arthur J 1925- *ConAu 53, DrAF 1976*
Roth, Arthur J *see* Mara, Barney
Roth, Arthur J *see* McGurk, Slater
Roth, Arthur J *see* Pomeroy, Pete
Roth, June 1926- *ConAu 9R*
Roth, Mary Jane 1913- *ConAu 21R, ConAu 21R, WWAW 8, WWMW 14*
Rothberg, Abraham 1922- *AmA&B, ConAu 33, WWA 38*
Rothenberg, Lillian 1922- *ConAu 9R*
Rothery, Agnes Edwards 1888- *AmA&B, AmLY, AuBYP, CatA 1952, WNAA*
Rothery, Guy Cadogan 1863- *MnBBF, WWLA*
Rothkopf, Carol Zeman 1929- *ConAu 25R, SmATA 4, WWAW 8*

Rothman, Joel 1938- *ConAu 37, SmATA 7, WrD*
Rothman, Milton A 1919- *AmMWS 12P, ConAu 41*
Rothweiler, Paul R 1931- *ConAu 65*
Roucek, Joseph S 1902- *AmMWS 12S, ConAu 9R*
Roueche, Berton 1911- *AmA&B, Au&Wr 6, ConAu 1R, CurB 59, DrAF 1976, REnAL, WWA 38, WWWor 2*
Rounds, Glen H 1906- *AmPB, AuBYP, ChPo, ChPo S1, ChPo S2, ConAu 53, IlCB 1744, IlCB 1946, IlCB 1957, JBA 1951, REnAL, SmATA 8*
Rountree, Harry 1878-1950 *ChPo S1, ChPo S2, IlCB 1744, WWBWI 1, WWCL*
Rourke, Constance Mayfield 1885-1941 *AmA&B, AnCL, CnDAL, ConAmA, CurB 41, DcNAA, ModAL, MorJA, OhA&B, OxAm, Pen Am, REn, REnAL, TwCA, TwCA Sup, YABC 1*
Rouse, Parke, Jr. 1915- *ConAu 17R*
Rousselet, Louis *MnBBF*
Routh, Jonathan *WrD*
Routledge, Edmund 1843-1899 *Alli, Alli Sup, ChPo, ChPo S1, ChPo S2, HsB&A, MnBBF*
Roux, Georges 1914- *ConAu 17R, WWBWI 1*
Rover, Max *MnBBF*
Rover, Max *see* Murray, Edgar Joyce
Rowan, Deirdre *ConAu XR*
Rowan, Deirdre *see* Williams, Jeanne
Rowan, Jack *MnBBF*
Rowand, Phyllis *IlBYP, IlCB 1946*
Rowe, Alice E *WWBWI A*
Rowe, Alice E *see* Rowe, John Gabriel
Rowe, Dorothy 1898- *JBA 1934, JBA 1951*
Rowe, H M *MnBBF*
Rowe, Jeanne A 1938- *ConAu 29*
Rowe, John Gabriel 1873- *MnBBF, WWBWI A*
Rowe, John Gabriel *see* Austin, Mortimer
Rowe, John Gabriel *see* Bright, James
Rowe, John Gabriel *see* Dunstan, Gregory
Rowe, John Gabriel *see* Ferris, Arthur
Rowe, John Gabriel *see* Gabriel, John
Rowe, John Gabriel *see* Lewis, Charles
Rowe, John Gabriel *see* Ransome, Charles A
Rowe, John Gabriel *see* Rowe, Alice E
Rowe, John Gabriel *see* Walters, T B
Rowe, Viola Carson *AuBYP, ConAu 1R*
Rowe, W *MnBBF*
Rowe, W *see* Bingham, Arthur, Major
Rowe, W I *MnBBF*
Rowland, Florence Wightman 1900- *ConAu 5R, SmATA 8*
Roy, Cal *ChPo*
Roy, Liam *ConAu XR, SmATA 2*
Roy, Liam *see* Scarry, Patricia
Roy, Michael 1913- *ConAu 61*
Roy, Michael *see* Roy, Mike
Roy, Mike *ConAu XR*
Roy, Mike *see* Roy, Michael
Royal, Rex *MnBBF*
Royston, Olive *WrD*
Rozek, Evalyn Robillard 1941- *ConAu 61*
Rubenstone, Jessie 1912- *ConAu 69*
Rubicam, Harry Cogswell, Jr. 1902- *AuBYP,*

ConAu 17R
Rubin, Eva Johanna 1926- *ChPo Sl,*
IlCB 1957
Rubin, Mark 1946- *ConAu 53*
Rubin, Theodore Isaac 1923- *AmA&B,*
AuNews 1, BiN 1974, WWA 38,
WWWor 2
Ruchlis, Hyman 1913- *AuBYP, ConAu 1R,*
SmATA 3
Rudolf, R DeM *MnBBF*
Rudolph, L C 1921- *BiDL 5, ConAu 5R*
Rudolph, Marguerita 1908- *AuBYP, ChPo S2,*
ConAu 33, LE 5
Rudomin, Esther *ConAu XR, SmATA 4*
Rudomin, Esther *see* Hautzig, Esther Rudomin
Rudwick, Elliott 1927- *DrAS 6H*
Rue, Leonard Lee, III 1926- *ConAu 1R*
Ruedi, Norma Paul *ConAu XR, SmATA XR*
Ruedi, Norma Paul *see* Ainsworth, Norma
Ruffo, Vinnie *ConAu 25R*
Rugh, Belle Dorman 1908- *Au&Wr 6, AuBYP,*
ConAu P-1, ForWC 1970, ThBJA
Ruhen, Olaf 1911- *Au&Wr 6, ConAu 1R,*
SingR 2
Ruiz, Ramon Eduardo 1921- *ConAu 25R,*
DrAS 6H, WWA 38
Rukeyser, Muriel 1913- *AmA&B, AuBYP,*
CasWL, ChPo, ChPo Sl, CnDAL,
ConAu 5R, ConLC 6, ConP 1970,
ConP 1975, CurB 43, DcLEnL,
DrAP 1975, DrAS 6E, ForWC 1970,
ModAL, ModAL Sup, OxAm, Pen Am,
RAdv 1, REn, REnAL, SixAP, SixAP,
TwCA, TwCA Sup, TwCW, WEAL,
WWA 38, WWAW 8, WWWor 2, WrD
Rumbelow, Donald 1940- *ConAu 49*
Rumsey, Marian 1928- *ConAu 21R, St&VC*
Rundle, Anne *Au&Wr 6, ConAu 57, WrD*
Rundle, Anne *see* Lamont, Marianne
Rundle, Anne *see* Manners, Alexandra
Rundle, Anne *see* Marshall, Joanne
Rundle, Anne *see* Sanders, Jeanne
Runyan, John *ConAu 57*
Runyan, John *see* Palmer, Bernard
Runyon, Catherine 1947- *ConAu 61*
Rus, Vladimir 1931- *ConAu 17R*
Rush, Philip 1908- *Au&Wr 6, WrD*
Rush, Stanley *MnBBF*
Rush, William Marshall 1887-1950 *AuBYP*
Rushmore, Arthur *AmPB*
Rushmore, Helen 1898- *AuBYP, ConAu 25R,*
SmATA 3
Rushmore, Robert 1926- *ConAu 25R,*
DrAF 1976, SmATA 8
Rushton, William *WrD*
Ruskin, Ariane 1935- *AuBYP, ConAu 13R,*
SmATA 7
Ruskin, John 1819-1900 *Alli, Alli Sup, AtlBL,*
BbD, BiD&SB, BrAu 19, CarSB,
CasWL, Chambr 3, ChPo, ChPo Sl,
ChPo S2, CriT 3, CyWA, DcEnA,
DcEnA Ap, DcEnL, DcEuL, DcLEnL,
EvLB, FamSYP, MouLC 4, NCHEL,
OxEng, Pen Eng, RCom, REn, TelT,
WEAL, WWCL
Russ, Lavinia 1904- *ConAu 25R*
Russ, Lavinia *see* Faxon, Lavinia
Russ, Richard P *MnBBF*
Russan, Ashmore *MnBBF, WWBWI A*

Russell, C *MnBBF*
Russell, C *see* Clifford, Martin
Russell, C *see* Wood, Geoffrey
Russell, Charlotte *SmATA XR*
Russell, Charlotte *see* Rathjen, Carl H
Russell, Don 1899- *ConAu 1R, WrD*
Russell, Francis 1910- *Au&Wr 6, ConAu 25R,*
WWA 38
Russell, Franklin Alexander 1926- *AmA&B,*
Au&Wr 6, AuBYP, ConAu 17R, OxCan,
SmATA 11, WrD, WWA 38
Russell, George Hansby 1895- *MnBBF*
Russell, Helen Ross 1915- *AmMWS 12P,*
ConAu 33, SmATA 8, WrD
Russell, Herbert 1869- *MnBBF*
Russell, Ivy Ethel 1909- *Au&Wr 6, ChPo Sl,*
ConAu 5R
Russell, John 1919- *Au&Wr 6, ConAu 13R,*
WW 1974
Russell, Patrick *ConAu XR, SmATA 4*
Russell, Patrick *see* Sammis, John
Russell, Philip *MnBBF*
Russell, Sinclair *MnBBF*
Russell, Solveig Paulson 1904- *AuBYP,*
ConAu 1R, SmATA 3, WWPNA
Russell, Spike *MnBBF*
Russell, William Clark 1844-1911 *Alli Sup,*
BbD, BiD&SB, BrAu 19, Chambr 3,
CyWA, DcBiA, DcEnA, DcEnA Ap,
DcLEnL, EncM&D, EvLB, MnBBF,
NCHEL, OxEng, REn, WWBWI A,
WWCL
Russon, Mary Georgina 1937- *IlCB 1957*
Rust, Doris *Au&Wr 6, ConAu 13R*
Rutgers VanDerLoeff-Basenau, An 1910-
ConAu 9R
Ruth, Babe 1895-1948 *BiN 1974, CurB 44,*
CurB 48
Ruth, Rod 1912- *IlBYP, SmATA 9*
Rutherford, Douglas 1915- *Au&Wr 6,*
ConAu XR
Rutherford, Douglas *see* McConnell, James
Douglas R
Rutherford, Meg 1932- *ConAu 29*
Ruthin, Margaret *SmATA 4*
Ruthven, Jack *MnBBF*
Rutledge, Archibald Hamilton 1883-1973
AmA&B, AmLY, BiDSA, ChPo,
ChPo Sl, ChPo S2, MnBBF, REnAL,
WNAA
Rutstrum, Calvin 1895- *ConAu 1R,*
IndAu 1917, MnnWr
Rutz, Viola Larkin 1932- *ConAu 21R,*
SmATA 12
Ruzic, Neil Pierce 1930- *ConAu 17R,*
WWA 38, WWWor 2
Ruzicka, Rudolph 1883- *IlBYP, IlCB 1744,*
IlCB 1946, WWA 38
Ryan, Betsy *ConAu XR*
Ryan, Betsy *see* Ryan, Elizabeth
Ryan, Elizabeth 1943- *ConAu 61*
Ryan, Elizabeth *see* Ryan, Betsy
Ryan, John Gerald Christopher 1921-
Au&Wr 6, ConAu 49, WrD
Ryan, Nolan 1947- *CurB 70, NYTBE 1,*
NYTBE 4, WWA 38
Ryan, Peter 1939- *ConAu 61*
Ryback, Eric 1952- *ConAu 37*
Rydberg, Ernest E 1901- *ConAu 13R, WrD*

Rydberg, Louisa Hampton 1908- *ConAu 69*
Rydell, Wendell 1927- *ConAu XR, SmATA 4*
Rydell, Wendell *see* Rydell, Wendy
Rydell, Wendy 1927- *ConAu 33, SmATA 4, WrD*
Rydell, Wendy *see* Rydell, Wendell
Ryden, Hope *ConAu 33, SmATA 8*
Ryder, Steve *MnBBF*
Ryder, Steve *see* Edgar, Alfred
Ryland, Lee *ConAu XR*
Ryland, Lee *see* Arlandson, Leone
Ryle, Randolph *MnBBF, WWBWI A*
Ryle, Randolph *see* Pentelow, John Nix
Rymer, James Malcolm *HsB&A, MnBBF, WWBWI A*
Rymer, James Malcolm *see* Merry, Malcolm James

S

S-Ringi, Kjell *ConAu XR, SmATA XR*
S-Ringi, Kjell *see* Ringi, Kjell Arne Sorensen
Sabatini, Rafael 1875-1950 *DcBiA, DcLEnL,*
    EvLB, LongC, MnBBF, NCHEL, REn,
    TwCA, TwCA Sup, TwCW
Sabin, Edwin Legrand 1870-1952 *AmA&B,*
    AmLY, ChPo S2, DcAmA, JBA 1934,
    JBA 1951, REnAL, WNAA, YABC 2
Sabin, Francene *ConAu 69*
Sabin, Louis 1930- *ConAu 69*
Sabre, Dirk *ConAu XR*
Sabre, Dirk *see* Laffin, John
Sabuso *SmATA XR*
Sabuso *see* Phillips, Irving W
Sachs, Marilyn Stickle 1927- *ChLR 2,*
    ConAu 17R, SmATA 3, WrD
Sack, John 1930- *ConAu 21R, WWE 14*
Sackett, S J 1928- *ConAu 1R, SmATA 12*
Sackson, Sid 1920- *ConAu 69*
Sader, Lillian *IlBYP*
Sadie, Stanley 1930- *ConAu 17R, WW 1974*
Sadler, Glenn Edward *ChPo S1, ChPo S2*
Sadler, S Whitechurch d1890 *Alli Sup,*
    MnBBF, WWBWI A
Sagan, Carl 1934- *AmMWS 12P, ConAu 25R,*
    CurB 70
Sagarin, Edward 1913- *AmMWS 12S,*
    ConAu 5R
Sage, Juniper *AmPB, ConAu XR, SmATA 2,*
    YABC XR
Sage, Juniper *see* Brown, Margaret Wise
Sage, Juniper *see* Hurd, Edith Thacher
Sagon, Amyot *MnBBF*
Sagsoorian, Paul 1923- *IlBYP, SmATA 12*
Saint, Dora Jessie 1913- *Au&Wr 6,*
    ConAu 13R, SmATA 10, WorAu, WrD
Saint, Dora Jessie *see* Miss Read
St. Aubyn, Giles 1925- *ConAu 5R*
St. Briavels, James *SmATA 1*
St. Briavels, James *see* Wood, James Playsted
St. Clair, A *MnBBF*
Saint-Exupery, Antoine De 1900-1944 *AnCL,*
    AtlBL, CasWL, ClDMEuL, CnMWL,
    CurB 40, CurB 45, CyWA, EncWL,
    EvEuW, LongC, ModRL, OxFr, Pen Eur,
    REn, TwCA, TwCA Sup, TwCW,
    WWTwL
Saint-Exupery, Antoine De *see* DeSaint-Exupery,
    Antoine
St. George, Judith 1931- *ConAu 69,*
    SmATA 13
St. John, Arthur *MnBBF*

St. John, Henry 1869-1926 *MnBBF,*
    WWBWI A
St. John, Henry *see* Cooper, Charles Henry St.
    John
St. John, Henry *see* Saint John, Mabel
St. John, Mabel *WWBWI A*
St. John, Mabel *see* Saint John, Henry
St. John, Patricia Mary 1919- *Au&Wr 6,*
    ConAu 5R, WrD
St. John, Percy Bolingbroke 1821-1889 *Alli,*
    Alli Sup, BbD, BiD&SB, DcEnL,
    HsB&A, MnBBF, WWBWI A
St. John, Philip *AuBYP, ConAu 65*
St. John, Philip *see* DelRey, Lester
St. John, Primus 1939- *BlkAW, DrAP 1975*
St. John, Robert 1902- *AmA&B, Au&Wr 6,*
    ConAu 1R, CurB 42, WWA 38,
    WWWor 2
St. John, Vane *MnBBF, WWBWI A*
St. John, Wylly Folk 1908- *ConAu 21R,*
    ForWC 1970, SmATA 10, WWAW 8,
    WrD
St. John, Wylly Folk *see* Fox, Eleanor
St. John, Wylly Folk *see* Larson, Eve
St. John, Wylly Folk *see* Pierce, Katherine
St. John, Wylly Folk *see* Vincent, Mary Keith
St. John, Wylly Folk *see* Williams, Michael
St. Johnston, Alfred *MnBBF*
St. Lawrence, J *MnBBF*
St. Mars, Florence *MnBBF, WWBWI A*
St. Mervyn, Guy *MnBBF*
St. Myer, Ned *ConAu XR*
St. Myer, Ned *see* Stratemeyer, Edward L
Saintsbury, Noel, Jr. 1884- *CarSB*
Sala, George Augustus Henry 1828-1895 *Alli,*
    Alli Sup, BbD, BiD&SB, BrAu 19,
    CasWL, Chambr 3, ChPo, DcEnA,
    DcEnA Ap, DcEnL, DcEuL, DcLEnL,
    EvLB, MnBBF, NCHEL, OxEng, REn,
    REnAL
Salamanca, Lucy *ConAu XR*
Salamanca, Lucy *see* DelBarco, Lucy Salamanca
Sale, Isobel Morton- *IlCB 1946*
Sale, Isobel Morton *see* Morton-Sale, Isobel
Sale, J Kirkpatrick 1937- *ConAu XR*
Sale, J Kirkpatrick *see* Sale, Kirkpatrick
Sale, John Morton *IlCB 1946*
Sale, John Morton *see* Morton-Sale, John
Sale, Kirkpatrick 1937- *ConAu 13R*
Sale, Kirkpatrick *see* Sale, J Kirkpatrick
Sale-Barker, Mrs. *CarSB*
Saletan, Alberta L *WrD*

Salinger, J D 1919- *AmA&B, AmWr,*
  Au&Wr 6, CasWL, CelR 3, CnMWL,
  ConAu 5R, ConLC 1, ConLC 3,
  ConNov 1972, ConNov 1976, DrAF 1976,
  EncWL, IntWW 38, LongC, ModAL,
  ModAL Sup, OxAm, Pen Am, RAdv 1,
  REn, REnAL, TwCA Sup, TwCW,
  WEAL, WWTwL
Salkey, Andrew 1928- *CasWL, ChPo S2,*
  ConAu 5R, ConNov 1972, ConNov 1976,
  LongC, Pen Eng, WEAL, WrD
Salmon, Annie Elizabeth 1899- *Au&Wr 6,*
  ConAu 69, SmATA 13, WrD
Salmon, Annie Elizabeth *see* Ashley, Elizabeth
Salmon, Annie Elizabeth *see* Martin, Nancy
Salmon, Edward G 1885- *MnBBF*
Salten, Felix 1869-1945 *AuBYP, ClDMEuL,*
  CurB 45, CyWA, LongC, OxGer, TwCA,
  TwCA Sup, WWCL
Salten, Felix *see* Salzman, Siegmund
Salzman, Siegmund 1869-1945 *AuBYP*
Salzman, Siegmund *see* Salten, Felix
Salzmann, Alice *MnBBF*
Salzmann, C G 1744-1811 *CarSB*
Samachson, Dorothy 1914- *AuBYP,*
  ConAu 9R, SmATA 3
Samachson, Joseph 1906- *AmMWS 12P,*
  AuBYP, ConAu 17R, SmATA 3
Samachson, Joseph *see* Miller, John
Samachson, Joseph *see* Morrison, William
Sammis, John 1942- *ConAu 29, SmATA 4*
Sammis, John *see* Russell, Patrick
Sampson, Emma Speed 1868-1947 *AmA&B,*
  DcNAA, WNAA
Samson, Anne Stringer 1933- *ConAu 25R,*
  SmATA 2, WWAW 8
Samson, Joan 1937-1976 *SmATA 13, WrD*
Samstag, Nicholas 1903-1968 *AuBYP,*
  ConAu 5R, ConAu 25R
Samuel, Helen Jo 1909- *SingR 1*
Samuels, Charles 1902- *ConAu 1R,*
  SmATA 12
Samuels, Gertrude *AuBYP, ConAu 9R,*
  ForWC 1970, WWWorJ 1972
Samways, George Richmond 1890?- *MnBBF,*
  WWBWI A
Samways, George Richmond *see* Clifford, Martin
Samways, George Richmond *see* Linley, Mark
Samways, George Richmond *see* Masters, Paul
Samways, George Richmond *see* Proctor, Paul
Samways, George Richmond *see* Richards, Frank
Samways, George Richmond *see* Richmond,
  George
Sanborn, Duane 1914- *AuBYP, ConAu 1R*
Sanborn, Duane *see* Bradley, Duane
Sancha, Sheila 1924- *ConAu 69*
Sanchez, Carlos 1908- *ChPo, ConICB,*
  IICB 1744
Sanchez, Sonia 1934- *CrCAP, BlkAW,*
  ConAu 33, ConLC 5, ConP 1975,
  DrAP 1975, LBAA, LBAA, WrD
Sanchez-Silva, Jose 1911- *ThBJA*
Sand, George X *ConAu 13R*
Sandberg, Harold W *MnnWr*
Sandberg, Inger 1930- *ConAu 65, ThBJA*
Sandberg, Karl C 1931- *ConAu 49, DrAS 6F,*
  WWA 38
Sandberg, Lasse E M 1924- *IIBYP, IICB 1957,*
  ThBJA

Sandberg, Margaret M 1919- *ConAu 61*
Sandburg, Carl 1878-1967 *AmA&B,*
  AmSCAP 66, AmWr, AnCL, AtlBL,
  AuBYP, CasWL, Chambr 3, ChPo,
  ChPo S1, ChPo S2, CnDAL, CnE&AP,
  CnMWL, ConAmA, ConAmL,
  ConAu 5R, ConAu 25R, ConLC 1,
  ConLC 4, CurB 40, CurB 63, CurB 67,
  CyWA, DcLEnL, EncWL, EvLB,
  FamPYP, LongC, ModAL, ModAL Sup,
  OxAm, OxEng, Pen Am, RAdv 1, REn,
  REnAL, SixAP, SmATA 8, St&VC,
  TwCA, TwCA Sup, TwCW, WEAL,
  WWTwL, WisW
Sandburg, Carl *see* Militant
Sandburg, Carl *see* Phillips, Jack
Sandburg, Carl *see* Sandburg, Charles August
Sandburg, Charles August *AuBYP, ConAmA,*
  ConAu XR, SmATA 8
Sandburg, Charles August *see* Sandburg, Carl
Sandburg, Helga 1918- *AuBYP, ConAu 1R,*
  ConP 1970, ForWC 1970, SmATA 3,
  ThBJA, WWA 38, WWAW 8
Sandell, Courtney *MnBBF*
Sanderlin, George 1915- *ConAu 13R,*
  SmATA 4
Sanderlin, Owenita 1916- *ConAu 17R,*
  SmATA 11, WrD
Sanders, Jack Thomas 1935- *ConAu 37,*
  DrAS 6P, WWW 14
Sanders, Jeanne *ConAu 57*
Sanders, Jeanne *see* Rundle, Anne
Sanders, Sol 1926- *ConAu 49*
Sanderson, Ivan T 1911-1973 *AmA&B,*
  AmMWS 12P, AuBYP, ConAu 37,
  ConAu 41, IICB 1744, IICB 1946,
  REnAL, SmATA 6, TwCA, TwCA Sup
Sanderson, Ivan T *see* Roberts, Terence
Sandford, Nell Mary *WrD*
Sandham, Elizabeth *CarSB*
Sandin, Joan 1942- *IIBYP, SmATA 12*
Sandoz, Edouard 1918- *IIBYP, IICB 1946*
Sandoz, Mari 1901-1966 *AmA&B, AuBYP,*
  CnDAL, ConAu 1R, ConAu 25R, OxAm,
  REn, REnAL, SmATA 5, ThBJA,
  TwCA, TwCA Sup, WNAA
Sandoz, Mari *see* Macumber, Mari
Sandri *WWBWI I*
Sandstrom, George F *IIBYP*
Sandstrom, Marita *IIBYP*
Sanford, Agnes 1897- *ConAu 17R*
Sanger, Frances Ella *AuBYP*
Sanger, Marjory Bartlett 1920- *ConAu 37,*
  SmATA 8, WrD
Sankey, Alice 1910- *ConAu 61*
Santalo, Lois *AuBYP*
Santee, Ross 1888?-1965 *AmA&B, ArizL,*
  REnAL, TwCA Sup
Sapieha, Christine *IIBYP*
Sapt, Arkus *MnBBF, WWBWI A*
Sapte, W *MnBBF*
Sapte, W *see* Edwards, Robert Hamilton
Sara, Dorothy *ForWC 1970*
Sarac, Roger *SmATA XR*
Sarac, Roger *see* Caras, Roger A
Sarasy, Phyllis Powell 1930- *AuBYP,*
  ConAu 13R
Sarg, Anthony Frederick 1880-1942 *ChPo,*
  ChPo S1, DcNAA, YABC 1

Sarg, Anthony Frederick *see* Sarg, Tony
Sarg, Tony 1880-1942 *AmA&B, ChPo S2, ConICB, CurB 42, DcNAA, JBA 1934, JBA 1951, REnAL, YABC 1*
Sarg, Tony *see* Sarg, Anthony Frederick
Sargent, George Etell 1808?-1883 *Alli, Alli Sup, CarSB, ChPo S1*
Sargent, Maud Elizabeth *ChPo, ChPo S1, ChPo S2, MnBBF, PoIre*
Sargent, Pamela *ConAu 61, DrAF 1976*
Sargent, Robert Edward 1933- *ConAu 21R, IICB 1957, SmATA 5*
Sargent, Shirley 1927- *AuBYP, ConAu 1R, ForWC 1970, SmATA 11*
Sari *IIBYP, IICB 1946*
Sari *see* Fleur, Anne
Sarnoff, Jane 1937- *ConAu 53, SmATA 10*
Sarnoff, Paul 1918- *ConAu 5R*
Saroyan, William 1908- *AmA&B, AmNov, Au&Wr 6, BiEnAT, CasWL, CelR 3, CnDAL, CnMD, CnMWL, CnThe, ConAmA, ConAu 5R, ConDr 1, ConLC 1, ConNov 1972, ConNov 1976, CurB 40, CurB 72, CyWA, DcLEnL, DrAF 1976, EncWL, EvLB, IntWW 38, LongC, McGWD, ModAL, ModAL Sup, ModWD, NYTBE 3, OxAm, Pen Am, RAdv 1, REn, REnAL, REnWD, TwCA, TwCA Sup, TwCW, WEAL, WW 1974, WWA 38, WWT 15, WWTwL, WWWor 2, WrD*
Sarton, May 1912- *AmA&B, ConAu 1R, ConLC 4, ConNov 1972, ConNov 1976, ConP 1970, ConP 1975, DrAF 1976, DrAP 1975, DrAS 6E, ModAL, ModAL Sup, OxAm, Pen Am, RAdv 1, REnAL, TwCA Sup, WWA 38, WWWor 2*
Sasaki, Tazu 1932- *ConAu 25R*
Sasek, Miroslav 1916- *Au&Wr 6, BkP, IICB 1957, ThBJA*
Sattler, Helen Roney 1921- *ConAu 33, SmATA 4*
Sauer, Julia L 1891- *MorJA*
Saunders, Allen 1899- *ArtCS*
Saunders, Blanche 1906-1964 *Au&Wr 6, AuBYP, ConAu P-1*
Saunders, Caleb *AuBYP, ConAu XR, SmATA XR*
Saunders, Caleb *see* Heinlein, Robert A
Saunders, Charles Wesley *MnBBF*
Saunders, D M *MnBBF*
Saunders, Hilary Aidan St. George 1898-1951 *CatA 1930, DcLEnL, CurB 43, CurB 52, EncM&D, EvLB, LongC, MnBBF, NCHEL, TwCA, TwCA Sup*
Saunders, Hilary Aidan St. George *see* Beeding, Francis
Saunders, Jean *WrD*
Saunders, Keith 1910- *SmATA 12*
Saunders, Margaret Marshall 1861-1947 *BiD&SB, CarSB, DcAmA, DcNAA, OxAm*
Saunders, Marshall 1861-1947 *CanNov, CanWr, DcAmA, DcNAA, JBA 1934, OxCan, TwCA, TwCA Sup, WNAA*
Saunders, Rubie 1929- *ConAu 49*
Sautel, Maureen Ann 1951- *ConAu 61*
Sautel, Maureen Ann *see* McGinn, Maureen Ann

Sauter, Edwin Charles Scott, Jr 1930- *ConAu 13R*
Sauvage, Sylvain 1888- *IICB 1744*
Sauvain, Philip Arthur *WrD*
Savage, Blake *ConAu XR, SmATA XR*
Savage, Blake *see* Goodwin, Harold Leland
Savage, Katharine James Sanford 1905- *Au&Wr 6, ConAu 13R*
Savage, Steele 1900- *IIBYP, IICB 1946*
Savery, Constance Winifred 1897- *Au&Wr 6, AuBYP, ConAu 9R, CurB 48, JBA 1951, SmATA 1, WrD*
Saville, Malcolm 1901- *ChPo S1, MnBBF, TelT, WrD, WW 1974, WWCL*
Saville, Ray *MnBBF*
Saviozzi, Adriana Mazza 1918- *ConAu 1R, IICB 1957*
Savitt, Sam 1917- *AuBYP, ConAu 1R, SmATA 8, WrD*
Savitz, Harriet May 1933- *ConAu 41, SmATA 5*
Savoldi, Gloria Root *AuBYP*
Sawyer, Corinne Holt 1924- *ConAu 17R, DrAS 6E*
Sawyer, Mark *ConAu XR*
Sawyer, Mark *see* Greenhood, David
Sawyer, Ruth 1880-1970 *AmA&B, AmLY, AnCL, AuBYP, BkCL, CarSB, ChPo, JBA 1951, Newb 1922, TwCA, TwCA Sup, WNAA*
Saxby, Argylle *MnBBF, WWBWI A*
Saxby, Jessie Margaret Edmondston 1842- *ChPo, ChPo S1, ChPo S2, MnBBF, WWLA*
Saxe, John Godfrey 1816-1887 *Alli, Alli Sup, AmA, AmA&B, AnCL, AuBYP, BbD, BiD&SB, Chambr 3, ChPo, ChPo S1, ChPo S2, CnDAL, CyAL 2, DcAmA, DcEnL, DcLEnL, DcNAA, OxAm, REnAL*
Saxon, Gladys Relyea *ConAu 5R*
Saxon, Gladys Relyea *see* Borden, M
Saxon, Gladys Relyea *see* Seyton, Marion
Saxon, Peter *MnBBF, WWBWI A*
Saxon, Peter *see* Baker, William Arthur Howard
Say, Allen 1937- *ConAu 29*
Sayer, W W *WWBWI A*
Sayer, W W *see* Sayer, Walter William
Sayer, Wal *MnBBF*
Sayer, Wal *see* Sayer, Walter William
Sayer, Walter William 1892- *MnBBF*
Sayer, Walter William *see* Quirroule, Pierre
Sayer, Walter William *see* Sayer, W W
Sayer, Walter William *see* Sayer, Wal
Sayers, Charles Marshall 1892- *AuBYP*
Sayers, Dorothy Leigh 1893-1957 *CasWL, Chambr 3, CnMD, DcLEnL, EncM&D, EncWL, EvLB, LongC, ModBL, ModBL Sup, ModWD, NCHEL, OxEng, Pen Eng, REn, TwCA, TwCA Sup, TwCW*
Sayers, Edgar *MnBBF*
Sayers, Edgar *see* Edgar, Alfred
Sayers, Frances Clarke 1897- *AuBYP, ChPo, ChPo S2, ConAu 17R, JBA 1951, SmATA 3, WWW 14*
Sayers, Gale 1943- *NYTBE 1, NYTBE 3, WWA 38*
Sayers, James Denson *MnBBF*

Sayers, James Denson *see* Bardwell, Denver
Sayers, Wilfred *WWBWI 1*
Sayler, Harry Lincoln 1863-1913 *AmA&B,*
  CarSB, DcNAA, IndAu 1816, OhA&B
Sayles, E B 1892- *ConAu P-2*
Sayles, E B *see* Sayles, Ted
Sayles, Ted *ConAu XR*
Sayles, Ted *see* Sayles, E B
Sayre, Anne 1923- *ConAu 61*
Sazer, Nina 1949- *ConAu 69, SmATA 13*
Scabrini, Janet 1953- *SmATA 13*
Scagnetti, Jack 1924- *ConAu 49, SmATA 7*
Scalzo, Joe 1941- *ConAu 49*
Scanlon, Marion Stephany *ConAu 5R,*
  ForWC 1970, MnnWr, SmATA 11, WrD
Scarborough, Alma May C 1913- *ConAu 5R*
Scarf, Maggi *ConAu XR, SmATA 5*
Scarf, Maggi *see* Scarf, Maggie
Scarf, Maggie 1932- *ConAu 29, SmATA 5*
Scarf, Maggie *see* Scarf, Maggi
Scarry, Patricia 1924- *ConAu 17R, SmATA 2*
Scarry, Patricia *see* Roy, Liam
Scarry, Patricia *see* Scarry, Patsy
Scarry, Patsy *ConAu XR, SmATA 2*
Scarry, Patsy *see* Scarry, Patricia
Scarry, Richard 1919- *AuBYP, ChLR 3,*
  ConAu 17R, FamAI, IICB 1957, PiP,
  SmATA 2, ThBJA, WrD
Scarth, Paul *MnBBF*
Schaaf, Martha Eckert 1911- *ConAu 1R,*
  IndAu 1917
Schachner, Erwin *IIBYP*
Schaefer, Charles E 1933- *ChPo S2,*
  ConAu 37
Schaefer, Jack Warner 1907- *AmA&B,*
  Au&Wr 6, AuBYP, ConAu 9R,
  IntMPA 1975, OhA&B, SmATA 3,
  ThBJA, WWA 38, WWW 14
Schaeffer, Elizabeth 1939- *ConAu 45*
Schaeffer, Mead 1898- *IICB 1744*
Schaeffer, Susan Fromberg 1941- *ConAu 49,*
  ConLC 6, DrAF 1976, DrAP 1975,
  DrAS 6E
Schaeren, Beatrix 1941- *ConAu 29*
Schaller, George B 1933- *ConAu 5R*
Scharl, Josef 1896-1954 *IICB 1744, IICB 1946*
Schary, Dore 1905- *AmA&B, BiEnAT,*
  ConAu 1R, ConDr 1, CurB 48,
  IntMPA 1975, ModWD, NYTBE 1,
  REnAL, WWA 38, WWE 14, WWT 15,
  WWWor 2, WWWorJ 1972, WorAu
Schealer, John Milton 1920- *AuBYP,*
  ConAu 5R
Schechter, Betty Goodstein 1921- *AuBYP,*
  ConAu 5R, SmATA 5
Scheele, William E 1920- *AuBYP, IICB 1946,*
  IICB 1957, ThBJA, WWA 38
Scheer, Julian Weisel 1926- *AmA&B, AuBYP,*
  SmATA 8, ConAu 49, WWA 38
Scheffer, Victor Blanchard 1906- *ConAu 29,*
  SmATA 6, WWA 38
Scheib, Ida *AuBYP*
Schein, Clarence J 1918- *AmMWS 12P,*
  WWWorJ 1972
Schell, Orville H 1940- *ConAu 25R,*
  SmATA 10
Schemm, Mildred Walker 1905- *ConAu 1R,*
  DrAS 6E
Schemm, Mildred Walker *see* Walker, Mildred

Scherf, Margaret Louise 1908- *AmA&B,*
  Au&Wr 6, ConAu 5R, EncM&D,
  SmATA 10, WWAW 8, WWPNA,
  WWW 14
Scherman, Katharine 1915- *AuBYP,*
  ConAu 5R
Schick, Eleanor 1942- *ChPo S2, ConAu 49,*
  IICB 1957
Schickel, Richard 1933- *AuNews 1, BiN 1974,*
  ConAu 1R, WWA 38, WWE 14
Schiff, Kenneth Roy 1942- *ConAu 49,*
  SmATA 7
Schiller, Andrew 1919- *ConAu 41, DrAS 6F*
Schiller, Barbara 1928- *AuBYP, ConAu 17R*
Schilling, Betty *IIBYP*
Schimel, John L 1916- *ConAu 25R*
Schindelman, Joseph 1923- *ChPo, IIBYP,*
  IICB 1957, ThBJA
Schisgall, Oscar 1901- *ConAu 53, MnBBF,*
  SmATA 12
Schisgall, Oscar *see* Cole, Jackson
Schisgall, Oscar *see* Hardy, Stuart
Schlein, Miriam 1926- *AmPB, AuBYP,*
  ConAu 1R, CurB 59, MorJA, SmATA 2
Schlein, Miriam *see* Weiss, Miriam
Schloat, G Warren, Jr. 1914- *ConAu 21R,*
  SmATA 4
Schmandt-Besserat, Denise 1933- *ConAu 69*
Schmid, Eleonore 1939- *ConAu 53,*
  SmATA 12
Schmiderer, Dorothy *ChPo S2*
Schmidt, Harvey 1929- *BiEnAT, BiN 1974*
Schmidt, James Norman 1912- *ConAu 1R*
Schmidt, James Norman *see* Norman, James
Schmitt, Gladys 1909-1972 *AmA&B, AmNov,*
  Au&Wr 6, ConAu 1R, ConAu 37,
  CurB 43, CurB 72, NYTBE 3, OxAm,
  REnAL, TwCA Sup, WWAW 8
Schmitt, Marshall L 1919- *ConAu 13R*
Schmitz, Dennis 1937- *ConAu 29, ConP 1970,*
  ConP 1975, DrAP 1975
Schmitz, Joseph William 1905-1966 *ConAu 5R*
Schnaubelt, Franz Joseph 1914- *ConAu 65*
Schnaubelt, Franz Joseph *see* Joseph, Franz
Schneider, Herman *AmPB*
Schneider, Herman 1872-1939 *DcNAA,*
  OhA&B
Schneider, Herman 1905- *Au&Wr 6, AuBYP,*
  ConAu 29, MorJA, SmATA 7
Schneider, Laurie *ConAu XR*
Schneider, Laurie *see* Adams, Laurie
Schneider, Leo 1916- *ConAu 5R*
Schneider, Nina 1913- *AmPB, Au&Wr 6,*
  AuBYP, ConAu 29, MorJA, SmATA 2
Schoen, Barbara 1924- *ConAu 21R,*
  SmATA 13
Schoenherr, John Carl 1935- *IIBYP,*
  IICB 1957, WWE 14
Schoffelmayer, Victor H *TexW*
Scholastica, Sister Mary *ConAu XR,*
  SmATA 7
Scholastica, Sister Mary *see* Jenkins, Marie M
Scholefield, Edmund O *ConAu XR,*
  SmATA 5
Scholefield, Edmund O *see* Butterworth, W E
Scholes, Percy Alfred 1877-1958 *LongC,*
  TwCA Sup, WWLA
Scholz, Jackson Volney 1897- *AuBYP,*
  ConAu 5R, MorJA

Schongut, Emanuel *IIBYP*

Schooling, Geoffrey Holt *MnBBF*

Schoolland, Marian M 1902- *ConAu 5R*, *WrD*

Schoonover, Frank Earle 1877- *ConICB*, *IICB 1744*, *MorJA*

Schoor, Gene 1921- *AuBYP*, *ConAu 29*, *SmATA 3*

Schosberg, Paul A 1938- *ConAu 13R*

Schosberg, Paul A *see* Allyn, Paul

Schraff, Anne E 1939- *ConAu 49*

Schramm, Ulrik 1912- *IICB 1957*

Schrank, Joseph 1900- *AuBYP*, *ConAu 5R*, *WrD*

Schranz, Karl 1938- *CurB 71*, *WWWor 2*

Schreiber, Elizabeth Anne 1947- *ConAu 69*, *SmATA 13*

Schreiber, Georges 1904- *AmA&B*, *CurB 43*, *IIBYP*, *IICB 1946*, *WWA 38*, *WWAA 1973*, *WWWorJ 1972*

Schreiber, Hermann 1920- *ConAu 25R*

Schreiber, Hermann *see* Bassermann, Lujo

Schreiber, Hermann *see* Buehnau, Ludwig

Schreiber, Ralph W 1942- *ConAu 69*, *SmATA 13*

Schreiter, Rick 1936- *ChPo S1*, *ConAu 21R*, *IIBYP*, *IICB 1957*

Schreivogel, Paul A 1930- *ConAu 25R*

Schroetter, Hilda Noel 1917- *ConAu 29*

Schroetter, Hilda Noel *see* Noel, Hilda Bloxton, Jr.

Schubert, Delwyn George 1919- *ConAu 9R*, *LE 5*

Schuberth, Christopher J 1933- *ConAu 25R*

Schucker, James *IIBYP*

Schule, Clifford H *IIBYP*, *IICB 1946*

Schull, Joseph 1916?- *CanWr*, *ConAu 53*, *DcLEnL*, *OxCan*, *OxCan Sup*, *WNAA*

Schulman, L M 1934- *ConAu 33*, *SmATA 13*

Schultz, Barbara 1923- *ConAu 21R*

Schultz, Gwendolyn *ConAu 65*

Schultz, Harry Pershing 1918- *AmMWS 12P*, *WWA 38*

Schultz, James Willard 1859-1947 *AmA&B*, *AuBYP*, *JBA 1934*, *JBA 1951*, *WNAA*, *YABC 1*

Schultz, Pearle Henriksen 1918- *ConAu 49*

Schultze, Bunny 1866-1939 *ArtCS*, *REnAL*

Schulz, Charles Monroe 1922- *AmA&B*, *ArtCS*, *AuBYP*, *CelR 3*, *ConAu 9R*, *CurB 60*, *MnnWr*, *SmATA 10*, *ThBJA*, *WWA 38*, *WWAA 1973*, *WWWor 2*

Schulz, Florence 1908- *ConAu P-2*

Schumann, Elizabeth Creighton 1907- *ConAu P-1*

Schuon, Karl Albert 1913- *AuBYP*, *ConAu 13R*, *WWS 13*

Schurfranz, Vivian 1925- *ConAu 61*, *SmATA 13*

Schurr, Cathleen *ConAu 9R*

Schutzer, A I 1922- *ConAu 25R*, *SmATA 13*

Schuyler, Remington 1884-1955 *IIBYP*, *IICB 1744*, *IICB 1946*

Schwabe, Randolph 1885- *IICB 1744*, *WWLA*

Schwalberg, Carol 1930- *ConAu 69*

Schwalje, Earl G 1921- *AuBYP*

Schwalje, Marjory C *AuBYP*

Schwartz, Alvin 1927- *ChLR 3*, *ConAu 13R*, *SmATA 4*

Schwartz, Anne Powers 1913- *ConAu 1R*,

SmATA 10

Schwartz, Anne Powers *see* Powers, Anne

Schwartz, Charles Walsh 1914- *ConAu 13R*, *AuBYP*, *SmATA 8*

Schwartz, Elizabeth Reeder 1912- *AmMWS 12P*, *AuBYP*, *ConAu 13R*, *SmATA 8*

Schwartz, Julius 1907- *AuBYP*

Schwartz, Lieselotte *ChPo S2*

Schwartz, Sheila Ruth 1929- *ConAu 25R*, *DrAS 6E*, *LE 5*, *WrD*

Schwarz, Frank 1924- *AmMWS 12P*

Schwatka, Frederick 1849-1892 *Alli Sup*, *AmA*, *AmA&B*, *BbD*, *BiD&SB*, *DcAmA*, *DcNAA*, *OxCan*

Schwebell, Gertrude C *ConAu 9R*

Schweitzer, Byrd Baylor *AuBYP*, *ChPo*

Schwiebert, Ernest George 1895- *ConAu P-1*, *DrAS 6H*, *OhA&B*

Scism, Carol K 1931- *ConAu 41*

Scobey, Joan 1927- *ConAu 57*

Scoggin, Margaret C *CurB 52*, *CurB 68*

Scoppettone, Sandra 1936- *ConAu 5R*, *SmATA 9*

Scortia, Thomas N 1926- *ConAu 1R*

Scotland, Jay *ConAu XR*

Scotland, Jay *see* Jakes, John W

Scotland, Kennedy *MnBBF*

Scott, Alex 1882- *SingR 1*

Scott, Angus, Captain *MnBBF*

Scott, Angus, Captain *see* Colinski, A J

Scott, Ann Herbert 1926- *BkP*, *ConAu 21R*

Scott, Barbara Ann *CanWW 12*, *CurB 48*

Scott, Cora Annett 1931- *AuBYP*, *ConAu 17R*, *SmATA 11*

Scott, Cora Annett *see* Annett, Cora

Scott, Dan *ConAu XR*, *ConAu P-2*, *SmATA XR*

Scott, Dan *see* Barker, S Omar

Scott, Dan *see* Stratemeyer, Edward L

Scott, Digby *MnBBF*

Scott, Ernest *MnBBF*

Scott, Ernest *see* Groves, William E

Scott, Evelyn 1893- *AmA&B*, *CnDAL*, *ConAmA*, *ConAmL*, *DcLEnL*, *OxAm*, *REnAL*, *TwCA*, *TwCA Sup*, *WNAA*

Scott, G Firth *MnBBF*

Scott, George A *MnBBF*

Scott, Hamilton *MnBBF*

Scott, Hamilton *see* O'Mant, Hedley Percival Angelo

Scott, Harold Richard 1887- *ConAu 5R*

Scott, Hedley *MnBBF*, *WWBWI A*

Scott, Hedley *see* O'Mant, Hedley Percival Angelo

Scott, Hedley *see* Young, Fred W

Scott, J Irving E *ConAu 21R*

Scott, John 1912- *AmA&B*, *Au&Wr 6*, *ConAu 5R*, *WWA 38*

Scott, John Anthony 1916- *ConAu 9R*, *DrAS 6H*

Scott, John M 1913- *ConAu 65*, *SmATA 12*

Scott, Joseph 1917- *ConAu 57*

Scott, Judith Unger 1916- *ConAu 5R*, *ForWC 1970*

Scott, Kingsbury *MnBBF*

Scott, Lenore *ForWC 1970*

Scott, Maxwell 1862-1927 *MnBBF*, *WWBWI A*

Scott, Maxwell *see* Staniforth, John William
Scott, Michael *MnBBF*
Scott, Natalie Anderson 1906- *AmA&B,*
  AmNov, ConAu P-2, REnAL, WWAW 8
Scott, Nigel *MnBBF*
Scott, Reginald Thomas Maitland 1882-
  AmA&B, MnBBF, WNAA
Scott, Robert Falcon 1868-1912 *AnCL,*
  NCHEL, OxEng, REn
Scott, Russell, Captain *MnBBF, WWBWI A*
Scott, Russell, Captain *see* Pearson, Alec George
Scott, Tom 1918- *Au&Wr 6, ChPo S2,*
  ConAu 9R, ConP 1970, ConP 1975,
  WrD
Scott, Sir Walter 1771-1832 *Alli, AnCL,*
  AtlBL, BbD, BiD&SB, BiDLA,
  BiDLA Sup, BrAu 19, CarSB, CasWL,
  Chambr 3, ChPo, ChPo S1, ChPo S2,
  CnE&AP, CriT 2, CyWA, DcBiA,
  DcEnA, DcEnA Ap, DcEnL, DcEuL,
  DcLEnL, EvLB, FamAYP, HsB&A,
  MnBBF, MouLC 3, NCHEL, OxEng,
  Pen Eng, PoCh, RAdv 1, RCom, REn,
  St&VC, WEAL, WWCL, YABC 2
Scott, Sir Walter *see* Cleishbotham, Jebediah
Scott, Warwick *ConAu XR*
Scott, Warwick *see* Trevor, Elleston
Scott Moncrieff, Martha Christi 1897-
  ConAu 61
Scovel, Myra 1905- *ConAu 5R, WrD*
Scoville, Samuel, Jr. 1872-1950 *AmA&B, ChPo,*
  JBA 1934, JBA 1951, REnAL, WNAA
Scratton, Howel *MnBBF*
Scribe, The *MnBBF*
Scribner, Charles, Jr. 1921- *AmA&B, CelR 3,*
  ConAu 69, IntWW 38, SmATA 13,
  WWA 38, WWWor 2
Scrimsher, Lila Gravatt 1897- *AuBYP,*
  ConAu 1R
Scudder, Horace Elisha 1838-1902 *Alli,*
  Alli Sup, AmA, AmA&B, BbD,
  BiD&SB, CarSB, ChPo, DcAmA,
  DcNAA, JBA 1934, OxAm, REn,
  REnAL
Scudder, Mildred Lee 1908- *ConAu 9R,*
  ThBJA
Scudder, Mildred Lee *see* Lee, Mildred
Scull, Florence Doughty 1905- *ConAu P-1,*
  WrD
Scuro, Vincent 1951- *ConAu 53*
Seaborg, Glenn Theodore 1912- *AmMWS 12P,*
  ConAu 49, CurB 48, CurB 61,
  IntWW 38, NYTBE 1, WW 1974,
  WWA 38, WWWor 2
Seabrook, William Buehler 1886-1945 *AmA&B,*
  CurB 40, CurB 45, DcNAA, MnBBF,
  REnAL, TwCA, TwCA Sup, WNAA
Sealey, Leonard George William 1923-
  Au&Wr 6, WrD
Seaman, Augusta Huiell 1879-1950 *AmA&B,*
  AuBYP, ChPo, JBA 1934, JBA 1951,
  REnAL, WNAA
Seaman, David M *AuBYP*
Seaman, Louise *AmPB*
Seaman, Louise *see* Bechtel, Louise Seaman
Seaman, Mary Lott *ConICB*
Seamands, Ruth 1916- *ConAu 45, SmATA 9*
Seamark *MnBBF*
Seamark *see* Small, Austin J

Seamer, H St. John *MnBBF*
Searight, Mary W 1918- *ConAu 29*
Searle, Kathryn Adrienne 1942- *ConAu 29,*
  SmATA 10
Searle, Kathryn Adrienne *see* Kathryn
Searle, Ronald 1920- *Au&Wr 6, ChPo S2,*
  ConAu 9R, IlBYP, IlCB 1946,
  IntWW 38, NCHEL, WWA 38, WWGA,
  WWWor 2
Sears, Paul Bigelow 1891- *AmA&B,*
  ConAu 17R, CurB 60, IntWW 38,
  OhA&B, WWA 38
Sears, Paul M 1920- *ConAu 1R*
Sears, Stephen W 1932- *ConAu 33,*
  SmATA 4
Seawell, Molly Elliot 1860-1916 *AmA&B,*
  BiD&SB, BiDSA, CarSB, DcAmA,
  DcBiA, DcNAA, TwCA
Seawrack *MnBBF*
Sebastian, Jeanne *ConAu XR*
Sebastian, Jeanne *see* Newsome, Arden J
Sebastian, Lee *SmATA 5, ThBJA*
Sebastian, Lee *see* Silverberg, Robert
Sebrell, William Henry, Jr. 1901- *WWA 38,*
  WWWor 2
Sechrist, Elizabeth Hough 1903- *AmA&B,*
  AuBYP, ChPo, ConAu 5R, SmATA 2,
  WWA 38, WWAW 8
Secunda, Sheldon 1929- *AmSCAP 66*
Sedges, John *ConAu XR, SmATA 1*
Sedges, John *see* Buck, Pearl
Sedgwick, Catherine Maria 1789-1867 *Alli,*
  CarSB, ChPo, DcEnL, DcLEnL, DcNAA
See, Ruth Douglas 1910- *ConAu 1R,*
  ForWC 1970
Seed, Cecile Eugenie *WrD*
Seed, H A *MnBBF*
Seed, Jenny 1930- *ConAu 21R, SmATA 8*
Seeger, Elizabeth 1889-1973 *ConAu 45*
Seeger, Pete 1919- *BiN 1974, CelR 3,*
  CurB 63, EncFCW 1969, SmATA 13,
  WWA 38, WWWor 2
Seeger, Ruth Porter Crawford 1901-1953
  AuBYP, ChPo
Seeman, Bernard 1911- *Au&Wr 6,*
  ConAu 21R, WWE 14
Segal, Erich 1937- *AmA&B, AmSCAP 66,*
  CelR 3, ConAu 25R, ConLC 3, CurB 71,
  DrAS 6F, NYTBE 2, WWA 38,
  WWE 14, WWWorJ 1972
Segal, Lore Groszmann 1928- *AmA&B,*
  ConAu 13R, DrAF 1976, SmATA 4,
  WWA 38, WrD
Segal, S S 1919- *ConAu 25R, WrD*
Segar, Elzie 1895-1938 *ArtCS*
Segar, James *MnBBF*
Segawa, Yasuo 1932- *IlBYP*
Segraves, Kelly L 1942- *ConAu 61*
Segur, Sophie Rostopchine, Comtesse De
  1799-1874 *CarSB, OxFr*
Seidelman, James Edward 1926- *AuBYP,*
  ChPo S1, ConAu 25R, SmATA 6
Seidler, Ann 1925- *ConAu 25R, WrD*
Seigel, Kalman 1917- *ConAu 25R,*
  SmATA 12
Seignobosc, Francoise 1900-1961 *AmPB, AnCL,*
  IlBYP, IlCB 1744, IlCB 1946, IlCB 1957,
  MorJA
Seignobosc, Francoise *see* Francoise

Seitz, Patricia *IIBYP*

Sejima, Yoshimasa 1913- *ConAu 33,*
   SmATA 8

Selby, John 1897- *ConAu 1R*

Selden, George *AuBYP, ConAu XR,*
   MorBMP, SmATA 4

Selden, George *see* Thompson, George Selden

Selden, Samuel 1899- *AuBYP, BiEnAT,*
   ConAu 1R, DrAS 6E, WWA 38

Self, Margaret Cabell 1902- *AmA&B, AuBYP,*
   ConAu 5R, OhA&B, WWA 38,
   WWAW 8, WWS 13, WrD

Selig, Sylvie 1942- *IIBYP, SmATA 13*

Selinko, Annemarie 1914- *Au&Wr 6,*
   CurB 55

Selkirk, Jane *AmA&B, AuBYP, TwCA Sup,*
   WWA 38

Selkirk, Jane *see* Chapman, John Stanton

Sellew, Catharine Freeman 1922- *AuBYP*

Sellick, G Godfrey *MnBBF*

Selsam, Millicent Ellis 1912- *AmPB, AnCL,*
   AuBYP, BkP, ChLR 1, ConAu 9R,
   MorJA, SmATA 1

Seltzer, Charles Alden 1875-1942 *AmA&B,*
   AmLY, DcNAA, MnBBF, OhA&B,
   TwCA

Selvin, David F 1913- *ConAu 25R*

Selwyn, Jack *MnBBF*

Sempill, Ernest d1909 *MnBBF, WWBWI A*

Sempill, Ernest *see* Coles, Detective Inspector

Sempill, Ernest *see* Gale, Alan

Sempill, Ernest *see* Michael, John

Sempill, Ernest *see* Michael, Paul

Sempill, Ernest *see* Storm, Michael

Sempill, Ernest *see* Storm, Rupert

Senarens, Luis Philip 1863?-1939? *AmA&B,*
   CurB 40, DcNAA, MnBBF, REnAL,
   WWBWI A

Sendak, Jack *AuBYP*

Sendak, Maurice 1928- *AmA&B, AmPB,*
   ArtsCL, Au&ICB, AuBYP, BkP,
   ChLR 1, ChPo, ChPo S1, ChPo S2,
   ChFB A, ConAu 5R, CurB 68, FamAI,
   IIBYP, IICB 1946, IICB 1957, MorJA,
   NYTBE 1, NYTBE 4, PiP, NewbC 1956,
   SmATA 1, St&VC, WrD

Sender, Ramon 1902- *ConAu 5R*

Sendler, David A 1938- *ConAu 65*

Senior, Charles *MnBBF*

Senior, Margaret *SingR 1*

Senior, Walter *MnBBF*

Sennett, Tertia *MnBBF*

Sentman, George Armor *AuBYP*

Serage, Nancy 1924- *ConAu 65, SmATA 10*

Serebriakoff, Alexandre 1907- *IICB 1744*

Seredy, Kate 1899?-1975 *AnCL, Au&ICB,*
   AuBYP, BkCL, ChPo, ConAu 5R,
   ConAu 57, CurB 40, IICB 1744,
   IICB 1946, JBA 1951, Newb 1922,
   SmATA 1, St&VC, WWAA 1973

Serif, Med 1924- *ConAu 17R*

Serjeant, Escort *MnBBF*

Serling, Rod 1924-1975 *AmA&B, AuNews 1,*
   CelR 3, ConAu 65, ConDr 1, CurB 59,
   IntMPA 1975, REnAL, WWA 38,
   WWWor 2

Seroff, Victor I 1902- *Au&Wr 6, ConAu 25R,*
   SmATA 12, WWMus 6

Serraillier, Ian Lucien 1912- *Au&Wr 6,*

   ChLR 2, ChPo, ChPo S1, ChPo S2,
   ConAu 1R, SmATA 1, ThBJA, WrD

Servello, Joe 1932- *SmATA 10*

Serventy, Vincent Noel *Au&Wr 6, WrD*

Service, Robert William 1874?-1958 *CanNov,*
   CanWr, CasWL, Chambr 3, ChPo,
   ChPo S1, ChPo S2, CnDAL, CnE&AP,
   DcLEnL, EvLB, LongC, NCHEL, OxAm,
   OxCan, Pen Eng, REn, REnAL, TwCA,
   TwCA Sup, TwCW, WEAL, WNAA,
   WWLA

Serwer, Blanche L 1910- *SmATA 10*

Sesshu 1420-1506 *REn*

Seth, Ronald 1911- *Au&Wr 6, AuBYP*

Seton, Anya 1916- *AmA&B, AmNov,*
   Au&Wr 6, ConAu 17R, CurB 53, LongC,
   OxAm, Pen Am, REn, REnAL,
   SmATA 3, TwCA Sup, WW 1974,
   WWA 38, WWWor 2, WrD

Seton, Ernest Thompson 1860-1946 *AmA&B,*
   AmLY, CanWr, ChPo, ChPo S1,
   ConAmL, CurB 43, CurB 48, DcNAA,
   EvLB, IICB 1744, JBA 1934, LongC,
   OxAm, OxCan, REn, REnAL, TelT,
   TwCA, TwCA Sup, TwCW, WNAA,
   WWCL

Seton-Thompson, Ernest 1860-1946 *CarSB,*
   Chambr 3, DcLEnL

Settle, Mary Lee 1918- *CurB 59, WorAu*

Setton, Kenneth M 1914- *AmA&B,*
   ConAu 9R, DrAS 6H, WWA 38

Setzekorn, William David 1935- *WWW 14*

Seuling, Barbara 1937- *ConAu 61,*
   SmATA 10

Seuss, Dr. 1904- *AmA&B, AmPB, AuBYP,*
   BkP, ChPo, ChPo S1, IICB 1946,
   IICB 1957, MorJA, PiP, REn, REnAL,
   SmATA 1, St&VC, TwCA, TwCA Sup,
   WWA 38, WWCL, WrD

Seuss, Dr. *see* Geisel, Theodor Seuss

Severin, Mark 1906- *ChPo S2, IIBYP,*
   IICB 1946, WWGA

Severn, Bill 1914- *AuBYP, ConAu XR,*
   SmATA 1

Severn, Bill *see* Irving, Nancy

Severn, Bill *see* Irving, William

Severn, Bill *see* Severn, William Irving

Severn, David *AuBYP, ConAu XR,*
   WW 1974

Severn, David *see* Unwin, David Storr

Severn, Sue 1918- *AuBYP, ConAu 5R,*
   ForWC 1970

Severn, William Irving 1914- *ConAu 1R,*
   SmATA 1

Severn, William Irving *see* Severn, Bill

Sewall, Marcia 1935- *ConAu 45*

Seward, Prudence *IIBYP*

Sewell, Anna 1820-1878 *BrAu 19, CarSB,*
   CasWL, DcLEnL, EvLB, JBA 1934,
   NCHEL, OxEng, REn, WWCL, TelT

Sewell, Elizabeth 1919- *CatA 1952,*
   ConAu 49, DrAF 1976, DrAP 1975,
   TelT, WorAu

Sewell, Helen Moore 1896-1957 *AmA&B,*
   AmPB, AuBYP, ChPo, ChPo S2,
   ConICB, IICB 1744, IICB 1946,
   JBA 1951, St&VC

Sewell, William G *MnBBF*

Sexton, Anne Harvey 1928-1974 *AmA&B,*

CasWL, ChPo SI, ConAu IR, ConAu 53,
ConLC 2, ConLC 4, ConLC 6,
ConP 1970, ConP 1975, CrCAP,
DrAS 6E, ForWC 1970, ModAL,
ModAL Sup, NYTBS 5, Pen Am,
RAdv 1, SmATA 10, WEAL, WWA 38,
WWW 8, WWE 14, WWTwL, WorAu
Sexton, Irwin 1921- *WWA 38, WWS 13*
Seyfert, Ella Maie *AuBYP*
Seymour, Alta Halverson *ConAu P-1,*
SmATA 10
Seymour, Brenda Meredith *ChPo S2*
Seymour, Flora Warren 1888-1948 *AmA&B,*
CurB 42, OhA&B, WNAA
Seymour, Mary *Alli Sup, CarSB*
Seymour, W J *MnBBF*
Seyton, Marion *ConAu XR*
Seyton, Marion *see* Saxon, Gladys Relyea
Shackleford, Martin *MnBBF*
Shadwell, Detective Inspector *MnBBF*
Shafer, Robert Eugene 1925- *DrAS 6E, LE 5,*
SmATA 9, WWW 14
Shaffer, Paul Raymond 1910- *AmMWS 12P,*
WWA 38
Shaftner, Dorothy 1918- *ConAu 25R*
Shah, Amina 1918- *ConAu 49*
Shah Ali Ikbal *MnBBF*
Shah Ali Ikbal *see* Abdullah, Ahmed, Sheikh
Shahar, David 1926- *CasWL, ConAu 65,*
WWWorJ 1972
Shahn, Ben 1898-1969 *AtlBL, ChPo SI,*
CurB 54, CurB 69, DcCAA 2,
IlCB 1957, OxAm, REn, WWGA
Shahn, Bernarda Bryson *ConAu 49,*
SmATA XR
Shahn, Bernarda Bryson *see* Bryson, Bernarda
Shakespeare, William 1564-1616 *Alli, AnCL,*
AtlBL, BbD, BiD&SB, BrAu, CarSB,
CasWL, Chambr 1, Chambr 2,
Chambr 3, ChPo, ChPo SI, ChPo S2,
CnE&AP, CnThe, CrE&SL, CriT 1,
CyWA, DcEnA, DcEnA Ap, DcEnL,
DcEuL, DcLEnL, EvLB, FamAYP,
McGWD, MouLC 1, NCHEL, OxEng,
OxFr, OxGer, Pen Eng, RCom, REn,
REnWD, WEAL
Shallard, E F *MnBBF*
Shanan, C H *MnBBF*
Shand, Captain *MnBBF*
Shand, Captain *see* Floyd, Gilbert
Shane, Harold Gray 1914- *ConAu 9R, LE 5,*
WWA 38
Shanks, Ann Zane Kushner *ConAu 53,*
SmATA 10, WWAW 8
Shannon, A Donnelly *MnBBF*
Shannon, A Donnelly *see* Aitken, A Donnelly
Shannon, Monica *AmA&B, AuBYP, ChPo,*
JBA 1951, Newb 1922, St&VC
Shannon, Terry *AuBYP, ConAu XR*
Shannon, Terry *see* Mercer, Jessie
Shapiro, Irwin 1911- *AuBYP, ChPo SI,*
JBA 1951
Shapiro, Karl Jay 1913- *AmA&B, AnCL,*
CasWL, ChPo, ChPo S2, CnDAL,
CnE&AP, ConLC 4, ConP 1970,
ConP 1975, CrCAP, DcLEnL,
DrAF 1976, DrAP 1975, DrAS 6E,
EncWL, EvLB, IntWW 38, ModAL,
ModAL Sup, OxAm, Pen Am, RAdv 1,

REn, REnAL, SixAP, SixAP,
TwCA Sup, TwCW, WEAL, WWA 38,
WWTwL, WWWorJ 1972
Shapiro, Milton J 1926- *AuBYP*
Shapiro, Rebecca *AuBYP*
Shapiro, William E 1934- *ConAu 25R*
Shapp, Charles M 1906- *ConAu 57*
Shapp, Martha Glauber 1910- *ConAu IR,*
SmATA 3, WWA 38, WWAW 8
Sharfman, Amalie *AuBYP*
Sharmat, Marjorie Weinman 1928- *ConAu 25R,*
SmATA 4, WrD
Sharoff, Victor *AuBYP*
Sharp, Adda Mai *AuBYP*
Sharp, Dallas Lore 1870-1929 *AmA&B,*
ConAmL, DcAmA, DcNAA, JBA 1934,
REnAL, TwCA
Sharp, Edith Lambert 1917- *CanWW 12,*
ConAu 5R
Sharp, Margery 1905- *Au&Wr 6, AuBYP,*
ConAu 21R, ConNov 1972, ConNov 1976,
DcLEnL, EvLB, IntWW 38, LongC,
NCHEL, RAdv 1, REn, SmATA 1,
ThBJA, TwCA, TwCA Sup, WW 1974,
WWAW 8, WWWor 2, WrD
Sharp, William 1855-1905 *Alli Sup, AnCL,*
BbD, BiD&SB, BrAu 19, CasWL, ChPo,
ChPo SI, ChPo S2, DcBiA, DcEnA,
DcEnA Ap, DcLEnL, EvLB, LongC,
MnBBF, NCHEL, OxEng, Pen Eng
Sharp, William 1900- *IlBYP, IlCB 1744,*
IlCB 1946
Sharp, William *see* MacLeod, Fiona
Sharpe, Caroline *IlBYP*
Sharpe, Mitchell R 1924- *Au&Wr 6,*
ConAu 29, SmATA 12
Sharpe, Stella Gentry *AmPB*
Shaw, Arnold 1909- *AmSCAP 66, ConAu IR,*
SmATA 4, WWA 38, WWE 14
Shaw, Charles Green 1892-1974 *AmA&B,*
AmPB, ConAu P-1, DcCAA 2, IlBYP,
SmATA 13, WWA 38, WWAA 1973
Shaw, Dick *MnBBF*
Shaw, Dick *see* Openshaw, G H
Shaw, Edward Richard 1850-1903 *Alli Sup,*
CarSB, DcNAA
Shaw, Evelyn 1927- *AmMWS 12P*
Shaw, Flora Louise 1851-1929 *Alli Sup,*
BrAu 19, JBA 1934, NCHEL, TelT
Shaw, Frank H 1878- *MnBBF, WWBWI A*
Shaw, Frank H *see* Cleveland, Frank
Shaw, Frank H *see* Guthrie, Archibald
Shaw, Frank H *see* Hammerton, Grenville
Shaw, Frank H *see* Hubert, Frank
Shaw, Gordon *MnBBF, WWBWI A*
Shaw, Gordon *see* Shaw, Stanley Gordon
Shaw, Herbert *MnBBF*
Shaw, John Mackay 1897- *BiDL 5, ChPo,*
ChPo SI, ChPo S2, ConAu 29, WrD
Shaw, Justin *MnBBF*
Shaw, Justin *see* Openshaw, G H
Shaw, Martin *MnBBF, WWBWI A*
Shaw, Martin *see* Bridges, Thomas Charles
Shaw, Martin *see* Martin, E LeBreton
Shaw, Ray *ConAu 33, ForWC 1970,*
SmATA 7, WWAW 8, WrD
Shaw, Reeves 1886- *MnBBF, WWBWI A*
Shaw, Richard 1923- *ChPo S2, ConAu 37,*
DrAP 1975, SmATA 12, WrD

Shaw, Stanley Gordon 1884-1938? *MnBBF,*
WWBWI A
Shaw, Stanley Gordon *see* Dare, Captain
Shaw, Stanley Gordon *see* Gordon, S S
Shaw, Stanley Gordon *see* Gordon, Stanley
Shaw, Stanley Gordon *see* Heritage, John
Shaw, Stanley Gordon *see* Shaw, Gordon
Shaw, Stanley Gordon *see* Strange, Harry
Shaw, Stanley Gordon *see* Wallace, Gordon
Shawn, Frank S *ConAu XR*
Shawn, Frank S *see* Goulart, Ron
Shay, Arthur 1922- *ConAu 33, SmATA 4,*
WWA 38, WWMW 14
Shay, Frank 1888-1954 *AmA&B, ChPo S1,*
ChPo S2, CurB 52, CurB 54, REnAL,
St&VC, WNAA
Shea, Victor *MnBBF*
Shead, Isobel Ann *SingR 1*
Sheahan, Henry Beston *AmA&B, JBA 1934,*
JBA 1951
Sheahan, Henry Beston *see* Beston, Henry
Shecter, Ben 1935- *AuBYP, ChPo S1,*
IlCB 1957, ThBJA
Shecter, Ben 1935- *WrD*
Shedd, Charlie W 1915- *ConAu 17R*
Sheean, Vincent 1899-1975 *AmA&B, AmNov,*
CnDAL, ConAmA, ConAu 61, CurB 41,
NYTBS 5, OxAm, REn, REnAL, TwCA,
TwCA Sup
Sheed, Wilfrid 1930- *ConAu 65*
Sheehan, Ethna 1908- *AuBYP, ConAu 61,*
SmATA 9
Sheffield, Janet N 1926- *ConAu 65*
Shefter, Harry 1910- *ConAu 9R*
Shekerjian, Haig *IlBYP*
Shekerjian, Regina *ChPo S2, IlBYP*
Sheldon, Ann *ConAu P-2, SmATA 1*
Sheldon, Ann *see* Stratemeyer, Edward L
Sheldon, Aure 1917-1976 *ConAu 61,*
SmATA 12
Sheldon, Walter J 1917- *AuBYP, AuNews 1,*
ConAu 25R
Sheldon, William Denley 1915- *ConAu 17R,*
WWA 38
Sheldrake, S *MnBBF*
Shellabarger, Samuel 1888-1954 *AmA&B,*
AmNov, CnDAL, CurB 45, CurB 54,
OhA&B, REn, REnAL, TwCA Sup
Shelley, Mary Wollstonecraft Godwin 1797-1851
Alli, AtlBL, BbD, BiD&SB, BrAu 19,
CasWL, Chambr 3, ChPo, ChPo S1,
CyWA, DcBiA, DcEnA, DcEnL, DcEuL,
DcLEnL, EncM&D, EvLB, MouLC 3,
NCHEL, OxEng, Pen Eng, RAdv 1,
·REn, WEAL
Shelley, Noreen *SingR 1*
Shelley, Percy Bysshe 1792-1822 *Alli, AtlBL,*
BbD, BiD&SB, BrAu 19, CasWL,
Chambr 3, ChPo, ChPo S1, ChPo S2,
CnE&AP, CnThe, CriT 2, CyWA,
DcEnA, DcEnL, DcEuL, DcLEnL, EvLB,
McGWD, MouLC 2, NCHEL, OxEng,
Pen Eng, RAdv 1, RCom, REn, REnWD,
WEAL
Shelton, William Roy 1919- *AuNews 1,*
ConAu 5R, SmATA 5
Shemin, Margaretha 1928- *ConAu 13R,*
SmATA 4
Shenton, Edward 1895- *AmA&B, IlBYP,*

IlCB 1744, IlCB 1946
Shepard, Ernest Howard 1879- *Au&Wr 6,*
ChPo, ChPo S1, ChPo S2, ConAu 9R,
ConICB, IlBYP, IlCB 1744, IlCB 1946,
IlCB 1957, MorJA, REn, SmATA 3,
WW 1974, WWCL
Shepard, Mary Eleanor 1909- *IlBYP,*
IlCB 1946, IlCB 1957, WWCL
Shephard, Esther 1891-1975 *ConAu 57,*
ConAu P-2, DrAS 6E, SmATA 5
Shepherd, Catherine *SingR 2*
Shepherd, Elizabeth *ConAu 33, SmATA 4*
Shepherd, James Affleck 1867-1946 *IlCB 1744*
Shepherd, S Rossiter *MnBBF, WWBWI A*
Shepherd, S Rossiter *see* Milton, Mark
Shepherd, S Rossiter *see* Richards, Frank
Shepherd, William Robert 1871-1934 *DcAmA,*
DcNAA
Sheppard, Harold Lloyd 1922- *AmMWS 12S,*
ConAu 45
Sheppard, Raymond 1913- *IlCB 1946*
Sheppard, Sally 1917- *ConAu 69*
Sheppard-Jones, Elisabeth 1920- *ConAu 13R,*
WrD
Sherburne, Zoa Lillian Morin 1912- *AuBYP,*
SmATA 3, WWPNA
Sheret, Rene 1933- *ConAu 29*
Sheridan, James Edward 1922- *ConAu 21R,*
DrAS 6H, WWA 38
Sherie *WWBWI I*
Sheriff, Katherine E *MnBBF*
Sherin, Ray 1926- *IlCB 1957*
Sherliker, James *MnBBF*
Sherlock, A B *MnBBF*
Sherlock, Sir Philip Manderson 1902- *AnCL,*
Au&Wr 6, AuBYP, ConAu 5R,
ConP 1970, WWWor 2
Sherman, Allan 1924-1973 *AmSCAP 66,*
AuBYP, ChPo S1, ConAu 45, CurB 66,
CurB 74, NYTBE 4
Sherman, D R 1934- *ConAu 13R*
Sherman, Diane 1928- *ConAu 9R,*
SmATA 12
Sherman, Elizabeth *AuBYP, ConAu XR,*
SmATA 5
Sherman, Elizabeth *see* Friskey, Margaret
Richards
Sherman, Emalene 1920- *ConAu 21R*
Sherman, Frank Dempster 1860-1916 *Alli Sup,*
AmA, AmA&B, BbD, BiD&SB, ChP,
ChPo, ChPo S1, CnDAL, DcAmA,
DcNAA, OxAm, REn, REnAL
Sherman, Harold Morrow 1898- *BiDPar,*
WNAA, WWS 13
Sherman, Nancy *ConAu XR, SmATA 4*
Sherman, Nancy *see* Rosenberg, Nancy Sherman
Sherman, Theresa 1916- *IlBYP, IlCB 1946*
Sherman, Theresa *see* Reed, Veronica
Sherrard, Philip 1922- *ConAu 13R*
Sherriff, Robert Cedric 1896-1975 *Au&Wr 6,*
Chambr 3, CnMD, CnThe, ConAu 61,
ConDr 1, CrCD, CyWA, DcLEnL, EvLB,
IntMPA 1975, IntWW 38, LongC,
McGWD, ModBL, ModWD, NCHEL,
OxEng, Pen Eng, REn, TwCA,
TwCA Sup, TwCW, WW 1974,
WWT 15, WWWor 2
Sherrill, Dorothy 1901- *AmPB, ConAu 69*
Sherrill, Dorothy *see* Martin, April

Sherrington, Alf *MnBBF, WWBWI A*
Sherrington, Alf *see* Burrage, Alfred Sherrington
Sherrington, Richard Wallace *WrD*
Sherrod, Jane *ConAu XR, SmATA 4*
Sherrod, Jane *see* Singer, Jane Sherrod
Sherry, Sylvia 1932- *Au&Wr 6, ConAu 49, SmATA 8, WrD*
Sherwan, Earl 1917- *ConAu 5R, SmATA 3*
Sherwood, Mrs. 1775-1851 *CarSB*
Sherwood, Captain *MnBBF*
Sherwood, Debbie *ConAu 25R, WWAW 8*
Sherwood, L *MnBBF*
Sherwood, Mary Martha 1775-1851 *Alli, BiD&SB, BrAu 19, CarSB, CasWL, Chambr 3, DcEnL, DcEuL, EvLB, NCHEL, OxEng, WWCL*
Sherwood, Merriam 1892- *AnCL*
Shick, Eleanor 1942- *SmATA 9*
Shiefman, Vicky 1942- *ConAu 57*
Shiel, Matthew Phipps 1865-1947 *BbD, DcLEnL, EncM&D, LongC, MnBBF, NCHEL, TwCA, TwCA Sup, WWLA*
Shields, Brenda Desmond 1914- *ConAu 5R*
Shields, Charles 1944- *SmATA 10*
Shields, Karena *AuBYP*
Shields, Leonard 1876-1949 *WWBWI I*
Shields, Rita *AuBYP*
Shikes, Ralph E 1912- *ConAu 29*
Shillabeer, Mary Eleanor 1904- *IlCB 1957*
Shillaber, Benjamin Penhallow 1814-1890 *Alli, Alli Sup, AmA, AmA&B, BbD, BiD&SB, CarSB, ChPo, ChPo S2, ChDAL, DcAmA, DcEnL, DcLEnL, DcNAA, OxAm, REnAL*
Shilstone, Arthur *IlBYP*
Shimer, John A 1913- *AmMWS 12P*
Shimin, Symeon 1902- *BkP, ChPo S1, ChPo S2, IlBYP, IlCB 1946, IlCB 1957, SmATA 13, ThBJA*
Shindler, H L *WWBWI I*
Shinn, Everett 1876-1953 *ChPo, ChPo S2, CurB 51, CurB 53, DcCAA 2, IlBYP, IlCB 1744, IlCB 1946*
Shipley, Nan 1904- *ConAu 9R, OxCan Sup, Prof*
Shippen, Katherine Binney 1892- *AnCL, AuBYP, ConAu 5R, CurB 54, MorJA, SmATA 1, St&VC*
Shipton, Eric Earle 1907- *Au&Wr 6, SmATA 10, WW 1974*
Shirer, William Lawrence 1904- *AmA&B, Au&Wr 6, AuBYP, ConAu 9R, CurB 41, CurB 62, IntWW 38, OxAm, REn, REnAL, TwCA Sup, WW 1974, WWA 38, WWWor 2*
Shirk, Jeanette Campbell 1898- *AuBYP, ChPo, ChPo S1*
Shirley, Mostyn *MnBBF*
Shirley-Smith, Richard *see* Smith, Richard Shirley
Shirreffs, Gordon D 1914- *AuBYP, ConAu 13R, SmATA 11, WrD*
Shirreffs, Gordon D *see* Donalds, Gordon
Shirreffs, Gordon D *see* Flynn, Jackson
Shirreffs, Gordon D *see* Gordon, Stewart
Shirts, Morris A 1922- *LE 5*
Shirvanian, Rose *ChPo*
Shirvell, Michael *MnBBF*
Shissler, Barbara Johnson *ConAu 29,*

WWAW 8
Shoberg, Lore 1949- *ConAu 33*
Shockley, Robert Joseph 1921- *LE 5*
Shoemaker, Hurst Hugh 1907- *AmMWS 12P, IndAu 1917*
Shoemaker, Mrs. J W *DcNAA*
Shoesmith, Kathleen A 1938- *Au&Wr 6, ConAu 49, WrD*
Shor, Pekay 1923- *ConAu 45*
Shore, June Lewis *AuNews 1*
Shore, Robert 1924- *IlBYP, IlCB 1957*
Shore, Wilma 1913- *ConAu 13R, ForWC 1970*
Short, Alison 1920- *ConAu 61*
Short, Lester L, Jr. 1933- *AmMWS 12P*
Short, Robert Lester 1932- *WWMW 14*
Shortall, Leonard *IlBYP, IlCB 1946, IlCB 1957*
Shorter, Bani *AuBYP*
Shostak, Jerome 1913- *ConAu 17R*
Shotwell, Louisa Rossiter 1902- *ConAu 1R, MorBMP, SmATA 3, ThBJA, WrD*
Showalter, Jean B *ConAu 21R, SmATA 12*
Showers, Paul *AmPB*
Shrand, David *WrD*
Shriver, Donald Woods, Jr. 1927- *ConAu 45, DrAS 6P*
Shub, Elizabeth *ChPo S2, ConAu 41, SmATA 5*
Shulevitz, Uri 1935- *AuBYP, BkP, ChPo S1, ConAu 9R, IlBYP, IlCB 1957, NewbC 1966, SmATA 3, ThBJA, WWA 38*
Shulman, Alix Kates 1932- *ConAu 29, ConLC 2, DrAF 1976, SmATA 7, WWAW 8*
Shulman, Irving 1913- *AmA&B, AmNov, Au&Wr 6, ConAu 1R, CurB 56, SmATA 13, WWA 38, WWE 14, WWWorJ 1972*
Shulman, Milton 1913- *Au&Wr 6, WW 1974, WWT 15, WrD*
Shultz, Gladys Denny 1895- *ConAu 49*
Shultz, James Willard 1859- *MnBBF*
Shumsky, Zena Feldman 1926- *ConAu 1R*
Shumsky, Zena Feldman *see* Collier, Zena
Shura, Mary Francis 1923- *ConAu XR, ForWC 1970, SmATA 6, ThBJA*
Shura, Mary Francis *see* Craig, Mary Francis
Shuster, Joe *ArtCS*
Shute, Henry Augustus 1856-1943 *AmA&B CarSB, DcNAA, OxAm, REnAL, WNAA*
Shute, Nevil 1899-1960 *CurB 42, CurB 60, DcLEnL, EvLB, LongC, ModBL, NCHEL, Pen Eng, REn, TwCA, TwCA Sup, TwCW, WWTwL*
Shute, Walter d1940? *MnBBF, WWBWI A*
Shute, Walter *see* Edwards, Johnson
Shute, Walter *see* Edwards, Walter
Shute, Walter *see* Maxwell, Gordon
Shute, Walter *see* Wentworth, Charles
Shuttlesworth, Dorothy Edwards 1907- *AuBYP, ConAu 1R, ForWC 1970, SmATA 3*
Shyer, Marlene Fanta *ConAu 69, SmATA 13*
Sibal, Joseph *IlBYP*
Siberell, Anne *ChPo S1, IlBYP*
Sibley, Don 1922- *IlBYP, IlCB 1957, SmATA 12*

Sibley, Mulford Quickert 1912- *AmMWS 12S*,
  ConAu 5R, *DrAS 6H*
Sichel, Harold M 1881- *ChPo, ChPo S1*,
  ConICB
Sickles, William Russell 1913- *AmMWS 12P*,
  ConAu 57
Siculan, Daniel 1922- *SmATA 12*
Siddiqui, Ashraf 1927- *ConAu 5R*, *St&VC*
Sidjakov, Nicolas 1924- *AuBYP*, *ChFB I*,
  IlBYP, *IlCB 1957*, *MorJA*, *NewbC 1956*,
  WWA 38
Sidney, Frank *MnBBF*
Sidney, Frank *see* Warwick, Alan Ross
Sidney, Frank *see* Warwick, Francis Alister
Sidney, Frank *see* Warwick, Sidney
Sidney, Margaret 1844-1924 *Alli Sup*, *AmA*,
  AmA&B, *ChPo S2*, *DcAmA*, *DcNAA*,
  FamSYP, *JBA 1934*, *OxAm*
Sidney, Margaret *see* Lothrop, Harriet Mulford
  Stone
Siebel, Fritz 1913- *ChPo, IlBYP, IlCB 1957*
Siedel, Frank 1914- *OhA&B*
Siegel, Bertram M 1936- *ConAu 25R*
Siegel, Eli 1902- *AmA&B, ChPo*,
  ConAu 17R, ConP 1970, ConP 1975,
  REnAL, WWA 38, WWE 14,
  WWWorJ 1972
Siegel, William 1905- *ChPo, ChPo S2*,
  ConICB, IlCB 1744
Siegl, Helen 1924- *ChPo, IlCB 1957*
Siegmeister, Elie 1909- *AmA&B*,
  AmSCAP 66, Au&Wr 6, AuBYP,
  BiEnAT, ConAu 1R, WWA 38,
  WWMus 6, WWWorJ 1972
Sienkiewicz, Henryk 1846-1916 *AtlBL, BbD*,
  BiD&SB, CasWL, CIDMEuL, CyWA,
  DcBiA, DcEuL, EncWL, EuAu, EvEuW,
  LongC, ModSL 2, Pen Eur, REn
Sigourney, Lydia Howard Huntley 1791-1865
  Alli, AmA, AmA&B, BbD, BiD&SB,
  CarSB, CasWL, Chambr 3, ChPo,
  ChPo S1, ChPo S2, CnDAL, CyAL 1,
  DcAmA, DcEnL, DcLEnL, DcNAA,
  EvLB, FemPA, OxAm, PoCh, REnAL
Siks, Geraldine Brain 1913?- *BiEnAT*,
  ConAu 25R, DrAS 6E
Silas, Ellis *MnBBF*
Silber, Irwin 1925- *ConAu 9R*,
  EncFCW 1969
Silcock, Sara Lesley 1947- *SmATA 12*
Silliman, Leland 1906- *AuBYP*
Silvaroli, Nicholas Joseph 1930- *ConAu 29*,
  LE 5, WWW 14
Silver, Isidore 1906- *DrAS 6F*,
  WWWorJ 1972
Silver, Ruth *ConAu XR, SmATA 7*
Silver, Ruth *see* Chew, Ruth
Silver, Samuel Manuel 1912- *ConAu 21R*,
  WWA 38, WWE 14, WWWorJ 1972
Silverberg, Robert *AmA&B, AuBYP*,
  ConAu 1R, SmATA 13, ThBJA,
  WWA 38
Silverberg, Robert *see* Chapman, Walker
Silverberg, Robert *see* Drummond, Walter
Silverberg, Robert *see* Jorgenson, Ivar
Silverberg, Robert *see* Knox, Calvin M
Silverberg, Robert *see* Osborne, David
Silverberg, Robert *see* Randall, Robert
Silverberg, Robert *see* Sebastian, Lee

Silverman, Al 1926- *AuBYP, ConAu 9R*,
  WWA 38
Silverman, Burton Philip 1928- *IlBYP*,
  IlCB 1957, WWAA 1973
Silverman, Melvin Frank 1931-1966 *ConAu 5R*,
  IlBYP, IlCB 1957, SmATA 9
Silverman, Morris 1894-1972 *AmA&B*,
  ConAu 33, WWWorJ 1972
Silverman, William Bertram 1913- *ConAu 49*,
  WWMW 14, WWWorJ 1972
Silvers, Vicki *WrD*
Silverstein, Alvin 1933- *ConAu 49, SmATA 8*
Silverstein, Alvin *see* Doctor A
Silverstein, Virginia B 1937- *ConAu 49*,
  SmATA 8
Simak, Clifford D 1904- *ConAu 1R, ConLC 1*,
  MnnWr, WorAu
Simbari, Nicola 1927- *AuBYP, ConAu 1R*,
  WWGA
Simbori *WWBWI 1*
Simister, Florence Parker 1913- *ConAu 5R*,
  ForWC 1970, WrD
Simmonds, Ralph *MnBBF*
Simmons, Anthony 1922- *Au&Wr 6, WrD*
Simmons, Dawn Langley 1937- *ConAu 29*
Simmons, Dawn Langley *see* Hall, Gordon
  Langley
Simmons, Patricia Anne 1946- *WWAW 8*
Simon, Charlie May 1897- *AmA&B, AuBYP*,
  ConAu XR, JBA 1951, SmATA 3,
  WWA 38, WWAW 8
Simon, Charlie May *see* Fletcher, Charlie May
  Hogue
Simon, Edith 1917- *Au&Wr 6, ConAu 13R*,
  CurB 54, WorAu, WrD
Simon, George Thomas 1912- *ConAu 25R*,
  WWA 38
Simon, Henry 1921- *WWA 38*
Simon, Hilda Rita 1921- *AuBYP, IlCB 1957*
Simon, Howard 1903- *ChPo, ConAu 33*,
  IlBYP, IlCB 1744, IlCB 1946, IlCB 1957,
  MorJA, WWAA 1973
Simon, Joe *ConAu XR, SmATA 7*
Simon, Joe *see* Simon, Joseph H
Simon, Joseph H 1913- *ConAu 29, SmATA 7*
Simon, Joseph H *see* Simon, Joe
Simon, Martin P 1903-1969 *ConAu P-1*,
  SmATA 12
Simon, Mina Lewiton 1914- *ChPo, ConAu XR*,
  ForWC 1970, SmATA 2
Simon, Mina Lewiton *see* Lewiton, Mina
Simon, Norma 1927- *AuBYP, ConAu 5R*,
  SmATA 3
Simon, Paul 1928- *WWA 38, WWMW 14*
Simon, Ruth Corabel 1918- *AuBYP*
Simon, Seymour 1931- *ConAu 25R*,
  SmATA 4, WrD
Simon, Shirley 1921- *ConAu 5R, SmATA 11*
Simon, Solomon 1895- *WWWorJ 1972*
Simon, Tony 1921- *AmA&B, ConAu 5R*
Simons, Barbara Brooks 1934- *WWAW 8*
Simonson, Mary Jane *ConAu 29*
Simont, Marc 1915- *AmA&B, AmPB*,
  AuBYP, BkP, Cald 1938, ChPo S1,
  ChPo S2, ConAu 61, IlBYP, IlCB 1946,
  IlCB 1957, MorJA, NewbC 1956,
  SmATA 9, WWA 38, WWAA 1973
Simpich, Frederick, Jr. 1911-1975 *ConAu 61*,
  WWA 38

Simpson, Horace J *MnBBF*
Simpson, Jean *WrD*
Simpson, Margaret 1935- *AmMWS 12P*
Simpson, Maxwell Stewart 1896- *IlCB 1744, WWAA 1973*
Simpson, Myrtle Lillias 1931- *Au&Wr 6, ConAu 21R, WrD*
Sims, Agnes 1910- *WWAA 1973*
Sims, George Robert 1847-1922 *Alli Sup, BbD, BiD&SB, BrAu 19, Chambr 3, ChPo, ChPo S1, ChPo S2, EncM&D, EvLB, LongC, MnBBF, NCHEL*
Sims, Lydel *AuBYP*
Sinbad *MnBBF*
Sinbad *see* Dingle, Aylward Edward
Sinclair, Captain *MnBBF, WWBWI A*
Sinclair, Captain *see* Blyth, Harry
Sinclair, Catherine 1800-1864 *Alli, BiD&SB, BrAu 19, DcEnL, NCHEL, OxEng, TelT, WWCL*
Sinclair, Harold 1907-1966 *ConAu 5R*
Sinclair, Harry *MnBBF*
Sinclair, Olga Ellen 1923- *Au&Wr 6, ConAu 61, WrD*
Sinclair, Upton Beall 1878-1968 *AmA&B, AmNov, AuBYP, BiDPar, CasWL, Chambr 3, ChPo S1, CnDAL, ConAmA, ConAmL, ConAu 5R, ConAu 25R, ConLC 1, CurB 62, CurB 69, CyWA, DcAmA, DcLEnL, EncWL, EvLB, LongC, ModAL, OxAm, OxEng, Pen Am, RAdv 1, REn, REnAL, SmATA 9, TwCA, TwCA Sup, TwCW, WEAL, WNAA, WWTwL*
Sinclair, Upton Beall *see* Fitch, Clark
Sinclair, Upton Beall *see* Garrison, Frederick
Sinclair, Upton Beall *see* Stirling, Arthur
Sinclaire, Gavin *MnBBF*
Singer, Isaac Bashevis 1904- *AmA&B, AmWr, AnCL, Au&Wr 6, AuBYP, AuNews 1, AuNews 2, CasWL, CelR 3, ChLR 1, ConAu 1R, ConLC 1, ConLC 3, ConLC 6, ConNov 1972, ConNov 1976, CurB 69, DrAF 1976, EncWL, IntWW 38, ModAL Sup, MorBMP, NYTBE 1, Pen Am, SmATA 3, NYTBE 3, ThBJA, TwCW, WEAL, WWA 38, WWE 14, WWTwL, WWWor 2, WorAu, WrD*
Singer, Isaac Bashevis *see* Bashevis, Isaac
Singer, Isaac Bashevis *see* Warshofsky, Isaac
Singer, Jane Sherrod 1917- *ConAu 25R, ForWC 1970, SmATA 4, WWAW 8, WWW 14*
Singer, Jane Sherrod *see* Sherrod, Jane
Singer, Julia 1917- *ConAu 65*
Singer, Marilyn 1948- *ConAu 65*
Singer, Samuel Loewenberg 1911- *WWA 38*
Singer, Susan 1941- *ConAu 61, SmATA 9*
Singmaster, Elsie 1879-1958 *AmA&B, AmNov, ChPo, ConAmL, CyWA, JBA 1934, OxAm, REnAL, TwCA, TwCA Sup, WNAA*
Sisson, Rosemary Anne 1923- *Au&Wr 6, ConAu 13R, SmATA 11, WrD*
Sitwell, Edith 1887-1964 *AnCL, AtlBL, CasWL, Chambr 3, ChPo, ChPo S1, ChPo S2, ClDMEuL, CnMWL, ConAu 9R, ConLC 2, DcLEnL, EncWL,*

EvLB, LongC, ModB̈L, ModBL Sup, NCHEL, OxEng, Pen Eng, RAdv 1, REn, TwCA, TwCA Sup, TwCW, WEAL, WWTwL
Sivulich, Sandra Stroner 1941- *ConAu 61, SmATA 9*
Sizer, Kate T *MnBBF*
Sjoberg, Leif 1925- *ConAu 65, DrAS 6F*
Sjowall, Maj *EncM&D, NYTBE 2*
Skaar, Grace Brown 1903- *AmPB, ConAu 69*
Skagen, Kiki 1943- *ConAu 37*
Skagen, Kiki *see* Munshi, Shehnaaz
Skeel, Dorothy June *ConAu 61, LE 5, WWAW 8*
Skelton, Charles L *St&VC*
Skelton, Red 1913- *CelR 3, CurB 47, IntMPA 1975*
Skelton, Robin 1925- *Au&Wr 6, AuNews 2, CanWW 12, ChPo S1, CnE&AP, ConAu 5R, ConP 1970, ConP 1975, DrAP 1975, DrAS 6E, OxCan Sup, WW 1974, WWW 14, WorAu*
Skene, Anthony 1888- *MnBBF, WWBWI A*
Skene, Anthony *see* Philips, George Norman
Sketchley, Sidney *MnBBF*
Skilton, Charles *MnBBF, WWBWI A*
Skinner, Constance Lindsay 1882?-1939 *AmA&B, CanNov, ChPo, DcLEnL, DcNAA, JBA 1934, MorJA, OxAm, OxCan, St&VC, TwCA, TwCA Sup, WNAA, YABC 1*
Skinner, Cornelia Otis 1901- *AmA&B, Au&Wr 6, BiEnAT, CelR 3, ChPo, CurB 42, ConAu 17R, CurB 64, DcLEnL, EvLB, IntWW 38, LongC, OxAm, Pen Am, REn, REnAL, SmATA 2, TwCA Sup, TwCW, WW 1974, WWA 38, WWAW 8, WWT 15, WWWor 2*
Skinner, Elliott Percival 1924- *AmMWS 12S, ConAu 13R*
Skinner, James T *MnBBF*
Skipper, Mervyn 1886?-1959 *SingR 1*
Skolnik, Peter L 1944- *ConAu 57*
Skorpen, Liesel Moak 1935- *ConAu 25R, SmATA 3*
Skurzynski, Gloria 1930- *ConAu 33, SmATA 8*
Slackman, Charles B 1934- *ChPo, SmATA 12*
Slade, Gurney d1956 *MnBBF*
Slade, Richard 1910-1971 *Au&Wr 6, ConAu P-2, SmATA 9*
Sladen, Kathleen 1904- *ConAu 69*
Slater, Mary Louise 1923- *ConAu 29*
Slaughter, Jean *ConAu XR*
Slaughter, Jean *see* Doty, Jean Slaughter
Sleator, William 1945- *ConAu 29, SmATA 3*
Sleigh, Barbara DeRiemer 1906- *Au&Wr 6, ConAu 13R, SmATA 3, WWCL, WrD*
Sleigh, Stanton *MnBBF*
Slicer, Margaret O 1920- *ConAu 25R, SmATA 4*
Sloan, Irving J 1924- *ConAu 17R*
Sloane, Eric 1910- *AmA&B, CurB 72, IlCB 1957, WWA 38, WWAA 1973*
Sloane, William, III 1906- *WWE 14*
Slobodkin, Florence Gersh 1905- *ConAu 1R, SmATA 5*
Slobodkin, Louis 1903-1975 *AmA&B, AuBYP,*

BkCL, BkP, Cald 1938, ChPo,
ConAu 13R, ConAu 57, CurB 57, IIBYP,
IICB 1744, IICB 1946, IICB 1957,
JBA 1951, REnAL, SmATA 1,
WWA 38, WWAA 1973, WWWorJ 1972
Slobodkina, Esphyr 1909- *AmPB, AuBYP,*
ChPo, ConAu 1R, ForWC 1970,
IICB 1946, SmATA 1, ThBJA
Slocum, Rosalie 1906- *IICB 1744*
Slote, Alfred 1926- *SmATA 8*
Small, Austin J *MnBBF*
Small, Austin J *see* Seamark
Small, Ernest *ConAu XR, SmATA 2,*
ThBJA
Small, Ernest *see* Lent, Blair
Small, William *ConAu XR*
Small, William *see* Eversley, David Edward
Charles
Smalley, Janet 1893- *ConICB*
Smaridge, Norah 1903- *AuBYP, ConAu 37,*
SmATA 6
Smart, Hegan *MnBBF*
Smeaton, Fred *MnBBF, WWBWI A*
Smeaton, Fred *see* Cook, Fred Gordon
Smedley, Francis Edward 1818-1864 *Alli,*
CarSB, CasWL, Chambr 3, ChPo,
DcEnL, DcEuL, DcLEnL, EvLB,
NCHEL, OxEng
Smiles, Sam *MnBBF*
Smiley, Lavinia 1919- *IICB 1946*
Smiley, Virginia Kester 1923- *ConAu ·29,*
SmATA 2
Smith, Agnes *AuBYP, WWA 38, WWAW 8*
Smith, Al 1902- *ArtCS*
Smith, Alvin 1933- *IIBYP, IICB 1957,*
WWAA 1973
Smith, Beatrice S *ConAu 57, SmATA 12*
Smith, Bernard *MnBBF*
Smith, Bernard *see* Campbell, Harry
Smith, Bernard *see* Heath, Bernard
Smith, Bernard *see* Martyn, Ivor
Smith, Bernard *see* Smith, Jack
Smith, Bernard *see* Williams, Fred J
Smith, Betty 1896-1972 *AmA&B, AmNov,*
CnDAL, ConAu 5R, ConAu 33, CurB 43,
CurB 72, CyWA, LongC, OxAm,
Pen Am, REn, REnAL, SmATA 6,
TwCA Sup
Smith, Bradford 1909-1964 *AmA&B, ChPo,*
ConAu 1R, SmATA 5
Smith, C W 1940- *ConAu 61*
Smith, Caesar *ConAu XR, EncM&D*
Smith, Caesar *see* Trevor, Elleston
Smith, Catherine C 1929- *ConAu 29*
Smith, Catherine C *see* Smith, Kay
Smith, D M Percy *MnBBF*
Smith, Datus Clifford, Jr. 1907- *SmATA 13,*
WWA 38, WWWor 2
Smith, David Eugene 1860-1944 *AmA&B.*
DcAmA, DcNAA, REnAL.
WNAA
Smith, Dodie 1896- *Au&Wr 6, BiEnAT,*
Chambr 3, ConAu 33, DcLEnL,
IntWW 38, LongC, McGWD, NCHEL,
REn, SmATA 4, WW 1974, WWT 15,
WWWor 2, WorAu, WrD
Smith, Dodie *see* Anthony, C L
Smith, Dodie *see* Percy, Charles Henry
Smith, Don 1909- *ConAu 49*

Smith, Donald G 1927- *AuBYP, ConAu 13R*
Smith, Doris Buchanan 1934- *ConAu 69*
Smith, Dorothy Stafford 1905- *ConAu 21R,*
SmATA 6
Smith, Dorothy Stafford *see* Smith, Sarah
Stafford
Smith, Dorothy Valentine 1908- *ConAu 29*
Smith, E Boyd 1860-1943 *AmPB, CarSB,*
ConICB, YABC 1
Smith, E Brooks 1917- *ConAu 5R*
Smith, Elizabeth Thomasina Meade 1854-1914
Alli Sup, CarSB, EncM&D
Smith, Elva Sophronia 1871- *WNAA*
Smith, Emma 1923- *AuBYP, ConNov 1972,*
ConNov 1976, LongC, WW 1974, WrD
Smith, Eunice Young 1902- *AuBYP,*
ConAu P-1, ForWC 1970, IndAu 1917,
SmATA 5, WWAW 8
Smith, Fenton *MnBBF*
Smith, Fenton *see* Pratt, Leonard E
Smith, Fowler *MnBBF*
Smith, Frances C 1904- *ConAu 1R,*
ForWC 1970, SmATA 3, WWAW 8
Smith, Frances C *see* Smith, Jean
Smith, Francis Hopkinson 1838-1915 *Alli Sup,*
AmA, AmA&B, BbD, BiD&SB, BiDSA,
CarSB, Chambr 3, ChPo, ChPo S2,
CnDAL, DcAmA, DcBiA, DcLEnL,
DcNAA, OxAm, REnAL
Smith, Fredrika Shumway *AuBYP*
Smith, Garry 1933- *ConAu 5R*
Smith, George *MnBBF*
Smith, George Harmon 1920- *ConAu 49,*
SmATA 5
Smith, Hamilton *MnBBF, WWBWI A*
Smith, Hamilton *see* Rochester, George Ernest
Smith, Harriet Lummis d1947 *AmA&B,*
DcNAA
Smith, Helen Catharine 1903- *ChPo S1,*
WWAW 8, WWMW 14, WrD
Smith, Helen Zenna *MnBBF*
Smith, Helen Zenna *see* Price, Evadne
Smith, Hobart Muir 1912- *AmMWS 12P,*
ConAu 65, WWA 38
Smith, Howard E, Jr. 1927- *ConAu 25R,*
SmATA 12, WrD
Smith, Howard Godwin 1910- *WWA 38*
Smith, Howard Kingsbury 1914- *AmA&B,*
BiN 1974, CelR 3, ConAu 45, CurB 43,
IntMPA 1975, IntWW 38, WWA 38,
WWS 13, WWWor 2, WrD
Smith, Hugh L 1921-1968 *ChPo S1,*
ConAu P-2, SmATA 5
Smith, Imogene Henderson 1922- *AuBYP,*
ConAu 5R, SmATA 12
Smith, Irene 1903- *AuBYP, WrD*
Smith, Jack *MnBBF*
Smith, Jack *see* Smith, Bernard
Smith, Jan *AuBYP*
Smith, Jan *see* Nickerson, Jan
Smith, Janet A *WW 1974*
Smith, Jean *ConAu XR, SmATA 3*
Smith, Jean *see* Smith, Frances C
Smith, Jean Pajot 1945- *ConAu 53,*
SmATA 10
Smith, Jessie Willcox 1863-1935 *AuBYP, ChPo,*
ChPo S1, ChPo S2, ConICB, DcNAA,
JBA 1934, JBA 1951
Smith, Joe *MnBBF*

Smith, John 1924- *Au&Wr 6, ConP 1970, ConP 1975, WrD*
Smith, Johnston 1871-1900 *AmA, DcNAA, REnAL, YABC XR*
Smith, Kay *ConAu XR*
Smith, Kay *see* Smith, Catherine C
Smith, Kenneth Danforth 1902- *ConAu 45, WWA 38*
Smith, Kenneth Homan 1928- *AmMWS 12S*
Smith, Lacey Baldwin 1922- *AmA&B, ConAu 5R, DrAS 6H, WWA 38*
Smith, Lafayette *ConAu XR, SmATA 4*
Smith, Lafayette *see* Higdon, Hal
Smith, Lawrence Beall 1909- *ChPo, IIBYP, IICB 1957*
Smith, Lee *IICB 1957*
Smith, Lee *see* Albion, Lee Smith
Smith, Linell Nash 1932- *ConAu 5R, SmATA 2*
Smith, Linell Nash *see* Chenault, Nell
Smith, Linell Nash *see* Nash, Linell
Smith, Lynwood S 1928- *AmMWS 12P*
Smith, Marion Hagens 1913- *ConAu 17R, SmATA 12*
Smith, Marion Jaques 1899- *ConAu 69, SmATA 13*
Smith, Mary 1918- *Au&Wr 6*
Smith, Mary *WrD*
Smith, Mary Ellen *ConAu 69, ForWC 1970, SmATA 10*
Smith, Mary Ellen *see* Smith, Mike
Smith, Mary Prudence Wells 1840-1930 *Alli Sup, AmA&B, AmLY, CarSB, DcAmA, DcNAA, OhA&B, TwCA, WNAA*
Smith, Mike *ConAu XR, SmATA XR*
Smith, Mike *see* Smith, Mary Ellen
Smith, Moishe 1929- *WWAA 1973*
Smith, Moyne Rice *AuBYP*
Smith, Nancy Covert 1935- *ConAu 57, SmATA 12*
Smith, Ned *IIBYP*
Smith, Neville 1897- *SingR 2*
Smith, Nila Banton *ConAu 21R, LE 5, WWAW 8, WWW 14, WrD*
Smith, Nora Archibald 1859?-1934 *AmA&B, AmLY, ChPo, ChPo S1, ChPo S2, DcAmA, DcNAA, JBA 1934, REnAL*
Smith, Norman David 1923- *Au&Wr 6, WrD*
Smith, Norman F 1920- *ConAu 29, SmATA 5*
Smith, Pauline C 1908- *ConAu 29*
Smith, Philip M 1927- *AuBYP*
Smith, Ralph Lee 1927- *AmA&B, AuBYP, ConAu 1R, WWA 38*
Smith, Richard 1931- *IntWW 38*
Smith, Richard Harris 1946- *ConAu 41*
Smith, Richard Shirley *ChPo S1*
Smith, Richard Shirley *see* Shirley-Smith, Richard
Smith, Robert Kimmel 1930- *ConAu 61, SmATA 12*
Smith, Robert Kimmel *see* Marks, Peter
Smith, Robert Paul 1915-1977 *AmA&B, AmNov, AuBYP, BiEnAT, ChPo, ConAu 69, CurB 58, WWA 38, WorAu*
Smith, Ruth Leslie 1902- *ConAu P-2, SmATA 2*
Smith, Sally Liberman 1929- *ConAu 21R*
Smith, Sarah *Chambr 3, DcLEnL, NCHEL,*

TelT
Smith, Sarah *see* Stretton, Hesba
Smith, Sarah Stafford *ConAu XR, SmATA 6*
Smith, Sarah Stafford *see* Smith, Dorothy Stafford
Smith, Sidney 1877-1935 *Alli, AmA&B, ArtCS, DcNAA*
Smith, Stan 1946- *CelR 3, NYTBE 4*
Smith, Stewart *MnBBF*
Smith, Susan Carlton 1923- *SmATA 12*
Smith, Vesta 1933- *ConAu 5R*
Smith, Vian 1920-1969 *ConAu 1R, SmATA 11*
Smith, Vivian 1933- *ConAu 61, WrD*
Smith, W V *MnBBF*
Smith, William Arthur 1918- *ChPo, IIBYP, IICB 1946, SmATA 10, WWA 38, WWAA 1973, WWE 14, WWWor 2*
Smith, William Jay 1918- *BkCL, ChPo, ChPo S1, ChPo S2, ConAu 5R, ConLC 6, ConP 1970, ConP 1975, CurB 74, DrAP 1975, DrAS 6E, Pen Am, SmATA 2, WWA 38, WorAu, WrD*
Smithies, Richard H R 1936- *ConAu 21R*
Smyth, Sir John 1893- *Au&Wr 6, ConAu 61, WW 1974*
Smythe, Ernest *WWBWI I*
Smythe, J Louis 1880- *WWBWI I, WWCL*
Snedeker, Caroline Dale Parke 1871-1956 *AmA&B, AnCL, AuBYP, IndAu 1816, JBA 1934, JBA 1951, OhA&B, WNAA, YABC 2*
Snedeker, Caroline Dale Parke *see* Owen, Caroline Dale
Snell, E L *MnBBF*
Snell, E L *see* Ellison, Ellis
Snell, E L *see* Ellson, Ellis
Snell, Edmund 1889- *MnBBF*
Snell, Roy Judson 1878- *AmA&B, MnBBF, WNAA*
Sneve, Virginia Driving Hawk 1933- *ChLR 2, ConAu 49, SmATA 8*
Sneve, Virginia Driving Hawk *see* Driving Hawk, Virginia
Sniff, Mr. *ConAu XR, SmATA XR*
Sniff, Mr. *see* Abisch, Roslyn Kroop
Snodgrass, Thomas Jefferson *YABC XR*
Snodgrass, Thomas Jefferson *see* Clemens, Samuel Langhorne
Snow, Dorothea J 1909- *ConAu 1R, SmATA 9*
Snow, Dorothy Mary Barter 1897- *Au&Wr 6, ConAu P-1, WrD*
Snow, Edward C *MnBBF*
Snow, Edward Rowe 1902- *Au&Wr 6, ConAu 9R, CurB 58*
Snow, Phil *MnBBF*
Snyder, Anne 1922- *ConAu 37, SmATA 4, WrD*
Snyder, Dick *AuBYP*
Snyder, Gerald S 1933- *ConAu 61*
Snyder, Jerome 1916- *IIBYP, IICB 1957, WWGA*
Snyder, Louis Leo 1907- *AuBYP, ConAu 1R, DrAS 6H, WWA 38, WWE 14, WWWor 2, WrD*
Snyder, Zilpha Keatley 1927- *AuBYP,*

ConAu 9R, MorBMP, SmATA 1, ThBJA
Snyderman, Reuven Kenneth 1922- *ConAu 29,*
SmATA 5, WWE 14
Sobel, Robert 1931- *ConAu 5R, DrAS 6H*
Sobol, Donald J 1924- *AuBYP, ConAu 1R,*
SmATA 1
Sobol, Harriet Langsam 1936- *ConAu 61*
Sobol, Ken *WrD*
Sockman, Ralph Washington 1889-1970
AmA&B, ConAu 5R, CurB 46, CurB 70,
NYTBE 1, OhA&B, WNAA
Sofia 1926- *IIBYP, IICB 1946, IICB 1957*
Sofia see Zeiger, Sophia
Softly, Barbara 1924- *SmATA 12, WrD*
Soglow, Otto 1900-1975 *AmA&B, ArtCS,*
ChPo, ConAu 57, CurB 40, REnAL,
WWA 38, WWAA 1973
Sohl, Frederic John 1916- *ConAu 21R,*
SmATA 10, WrD
Sohn, David Albert 1929- *ConAu 9R,*
IndAu 1917, WWMW 14
Sokol, Bill 1925- *ChPo, ChFB 1, IICB 1957,*
WWGA
Sokol, Bill see Sokol, William
Sokol, William 1925- *AuBYP*
Sokol, William see Sokol, Bill
Solbert, Romaine G 1925- *ConAu 29,*
SmATA 2
Solbert, Romaine G see Solbert, Ronni G
Solbert, Ronni G 1925- *ChPo S2, ConAu XR,*
IIBYP, IICB 1946, IICB 1957, SmATA 2
Solbert, Ronni G see Solbert, Romaine G
Solem, Alan 1931- *AmMWS 12P, ConAu 57*
Solley, Charles Marion, Jr. 1925-
AmMWS 12S, ConAu 1R
Soloman, David R *MnBBF*
Solomon, Louis *AuBYP*
Solot, Mary Lynn 1939- *ConAu 49,*
SmATA 12
Soltes, Avraham 1917- *WWWorJ 1972*
Somerfield, Thomas S 1870?- *WWBWI 1*
Somers, Boston *MnBBF*
Somerville, Elizabeth *Alli, BiDLA, CarSB*
Somerville, Hugh 1922- *ConAu 9R*
Somerville, Lee 1915- *ConAu 69*
Sommer, Elyse 1929- *ConAu 49, SmATA 7*
Sommer, Joellen 1957- *ConAu 45*
Sommer, Robert 1929- *AmMWS 12S, BiDPar,*
ConAu 9R, SmATA 12
Sommerfelt, Aimee 1892- *AuBYP, ConAu 37,*
SmATA 5, ThBJA
Sommerschield, Rose *IIBYP*
Soni, Welthy H *AuBYP*
Sonnabend, Roger Philip 1925- *WWA 38,*
WWE 14, WWWorJ 1972
Sonneborn, Ruth A 1899-1974 *BkP, ConAu 49,*
ConAu P-2, SmATA 4
Sootin, Harry *AuBYP*
Soper, Eileen Alice 1905- *Au&Wr 6,*
ConAu 9R, IIBYP, IICB 1744,
IICB 1946, WrD
Soper, George 1870- *WWBWI 1*
Sophocles 496?BC-406?BC *AtlBL, BbD,*
BiD&SB, CasWL, ChPo S2, CnThe,
CyWA, DcEnL, McGWD, NCHEL,
OxEng, Pen Cl, RCom, REn, REnWD
Sorden, L G 1898- *ConAu 1R*
Sorel, Edward 1929- *ConAu 9R, IIBYP,*
IICB 1957, WWA 38, WWE 14,

WWWor 2
Sorell, Walter 1905- *WWE 14*
Sorensen, Theodore Chaikin 1928- *AmA&B,*
ConAu 45, IntWW 38, WWA 38,
WWWor 2
Sorensen, Virginia 1912- *AmA&B, AmNov,*
Au&Wr 6, AuBYP, ConAu 13R,
CurB 50, MorBMP, MorJA,
NewbC 1956, SmATA 2, TwCA Sup,
WWA 38, WWAW 8, WWWor 2, WrD
Sorley Walker, Kathrine *Au&Wr 6,*
ConAu 5R, WrD
Sorrell, Alan 1904- *Au&Wr 6, WW 1974*
Sorrell, Lucian *MnBBF*
Sorrells, Dorothy C *ConAu 9R*
Sorrentino, Joseph N 1930?- *ConAu 49,*
SmATA 6
Sortor, June Elizabeth 1939- *ConAu 61,*
SmATA 12
Sortor, June Elizabeth see Sortor, Toni
Sortor, Toni *ConAu XR, SmATA XR*
Sortor, Toni see Sortor, June Elizabeth
Soskin, V H *ConAu XR, SmATA 4*
Soskin, V H see Ellison, Virginia Howell
Sotomayor, Antonio 1902- *ConAu 25R, IIBYP,*
IICB 1946, IntWW 38, SmATA 11,
WWW 14, WWWor 2
Soudley, Henry *ConAu XR, SmATA 1*
Soudley, Henry see Wood, James Playsted
Soule, Gardner 1913- *ConAu 5R*
Soule, Jean Conder 1919- *ConAu 5R,*
ForWC 1970, SmATA 10
Soutar, Andrew 1879-1941 *ChPo S2, MnBBF,*
NCHEL, WWBWI A
Southall, Ivan Francis 1921- *Au&Wr 6,*
AuBYP, ChLR 2, ConAu 9R, SenS,
SingR 1, SmATA 3, ThBJA, WWWor 2,
WrD
Southey, Robert 1774-1843 *Alli, AtlBL, BbD,*
BiD&SB, BiDLA, BrAu 19, CasWL,
Chambr 3, ChPo, ChPo S1, ChPo S2,
CnE&AP, CriT 2, CyWA, DcEnA,
DcEnA Ap, DcEnL, DcEuL, DcLEnL,
EvLB, MouLC 3, NCHEL, OxEng,
Pen Eng, PoLE, REn, WEAL, WWCL
Southgate, Vera *Au&Wr 6, WrD*
Southwick, David *MnBBF*
Southworth, John VanDuyn 1904- *Au&Wr 6,*
ConAu 5R, WNAA, WWA 38
Sowerby, Amy Millicent *ChPo S1, ConICB,*
IICB 1744, WW 1974
Sowerby, Temple *MnBBF*
Sowers, Phyllis *AuBYP*
Sowman, Gordon *MnBBF*
Spache, George Daniel 1909- *AmMWS 12S,*
AuBYP, ConAu 5R
Spanfeller, James John 1930- *ChPo S1,*
ChPo S2, IICB 1957
Spang Olsen, Ib *ThBJA*
Spang Olsen, Ib see Olsen, Ib Spang
Spangenberg, Judith Dunn 1942- *ConAu 29,*
SmATA 5
Spangenburg, Judith Dunn see Dunn, Judy
Spangler, Earl 1920- *ConAu 5R, DrAS 6H,*
LE 5, MnnWr, WWMW 14
Spar, Jerome 1918- *AmMWS 12P,*
ConAu 25R, SmATA 10
Sparks, James Calvin, Jr. 1925- *WWE 14*
Sparrowhawk *MnBBF*

Spaull, Hebe 1893- *Au&Wr 6, ConAu 9R*
Speare, Elizabeth George 1908- *AmA&B,*
  Au&Wr 6, AuBYP, ConAu 1R, CurB 59,
  ForWC 1970, MorBMP, MorJA,
  NewbC 1956, SmATA 5, WWA 38,
  WWAW 8, WrD
Spearing, Judith 1922- *SmATA 9*
Specking, Inez 1890-1960? *AmA&B, BkC 1,*
  CatA 1930, ConAu 5R, SmATA 11,
  WNAA
Speckter, Otto 1807-1871 *CarSB, ChPo*
Spector, Robert Donald 1922- *ConAu 13R,*
  DrAS 6E, WWA 38
Spector, Robert Melvyn 1926- *DrAS 6H*
Spector, Shushannah 1903- *ConAu 9R*
Speed, H Fiennes *MnBBF*
Speed, Lancelot *ChPo, ChPo S2*
Speevack, Yetta *AuBYP*
Speicher, Helen Ross 1915- *ConAu 5R,*
  ForWC 1970, IndAu 1917, SmATA 8
Speicher, Helen Ross *see* Abbott, Alice
Speicher, Helen Ross *see* Land, Jane
Speicher, Helen Ross *see* Land, Ross
Speiser, Jean *ConAu 69*
Spellman, John Willard 1934- *ConAu 13R,*
  DrAS 6H
Spence, Eleanor 1928- *ConAu 49, SingR 1,*
  WrD
Spence, Geraldine 1931- *ArtsCL, IlCB 1957*
Spence, Hubert *MnBBF*
Spence, Hubert *see* Longhurst, Percy William
Spencer, Captain *MnBBF*
Spencer, Captain *see* Tuite, Hugh
Spencer, Ann 1918- *ConAu 29, SmATA 10*
Spencer, Cornelia 1899- *AmA&B, AmNov,*
  AuBYP, ConAu XR, JBA 1951,
  SmATA 5
Spencer, Cornelia *see* Yaukey, Grace
  Sydenstricker
Spencer, John *MnBBF*
Spencer, John *see* Vickers, Roy C
Spencer, Roland *MnBBF, WWBWI A*
Spencer, Roland *see* Prout, Geoffrey
Spencer, Roland *see* Warwick, Francis Alister
Spencer, William 1922- *AuBYP, ConAu 17R,*
  DrAS 6H, SmATA 9, WrD
Spender, Stephen 1909- *Au&Wr 6, CasWL,*
  Chambr 3, ChPo, ChPo S2, CnE&AP,
  CnMD, CnMWL, ConAu 9R, ConLC 1,
  ConLC 2, ConLC 5, ConP 1970,
  ConP 1975, CurB 40, CyWA, DcLEnL,
  EncWL, EvLB, IntWW 38, LongC,
  ModBL, ModBL Sup, ModWD, NCHEL,
  OxEng, Pen Eng, RAdv 1, REn, TwCA,
  TwCA Sup, TwCW, WEAL, WW 1974,
  WWTwL, WWWor 2
Sperry, Armstrong W 1897- *AmPB, AnCL,*
  AuBYP, ConAu P-1, CurB 41,
  IlCB 1744, IlCB 1946, JBA 1951,
  Newb 1922, SmATA 1, St&VC
Sperry, J E *ConAu XR*
Sperry, J E *see* Eisenstat, Jane Sperry
Sperry, Margaret 1905- *ConAu 37, WrD*
Sperry, Raymond, Jr. *ConAu P-2, SmATA 1*
Sperry, Raymond, Jr. *see* Stratemeyer, Edward L
Speyer, Leonora 1872-1956 *AmA&B, AnCL,*
  ChPo, ChPo S1, CnDAL, DcLEnL,
  OxAm, REn, REnAL, TwCA,
  TwCA Sup, WNAA

Spicer, Dorothy Gladys *AuBYP, ConAu 1R,*
  ForWC 1970
Spicer, Howard Handley 1872- *MnBBF*
Spiegel, Clara *AmA&B, AmNov X,*
  Au&Wr 6, AuBYP, ConAu XR,
  CurB 54
Spiegel, Clara *see* Mayer, Jane
Spiegelman, Judith M *ConAu 21R, SmATA 5*
Spielmann, Mabel Henrietta 1862-1938 *CarSB,*
  ChPo S2, WWLA
Spier, Peter 1927- *BkP, ChPo S1, ChPo S2,*
  ConAu 5R, IlBYP, IlCB 1946,
  IlCB 1957, SmATA 4, ThBJA
Spiers, C L *MnBBF*
Spilhaus, Athelstan 1911- *ConAu 17R,*
  CurB 65, SmATA 13, WWA 38,
  WWS 13, WWWor 2
Spilka, Arnold 1917- *AuBYP, ChPo S1,*
  ChPo S2, ConAu 49, IlCB 1957,
  SmATA 6, ThBJA
Spiller, Leonard *MnBBF*
Spink, Reginald 1905- *Au&Wr 6, ConAu 53,*
  SmATA 11, WrD
Spinner, Stephanie 1943- *ChPo S2, ConAu 45*
Spiro, Jack D 1933- *ConAu 9R*
Splaver, Sarah *WWAW 8, WWE 14,*
  WWWorJ 1972
Spock, Benjamin McLane 1903- *AmA&B,*
  Au&Wr 6, AuNews 1, REnAL,
  WW 1974, WWA 38
Spollen, Christopher 1952- *SmATA 12*
Spot, Ryhen *ConAu XR*
Spot, Ryhen *see* Post, Henry
Sprague, Gretchen 1926- *AuBYP, ConAu 13R*
Sprague, Rosemary 1922?- *AuBYP,*
  ConAu 17R, DrAS 6E, OhA&B,
  WWAW 8
Sprigg, T Stanhope *MnBBF*
Sprigg, William Stanhope 1867-1932 *MnBBF,*
  WWBWI A
Sprigge, Elizabeth Miriam Squire 1900-1974
  Au&Wr 6, BiEnAT, ConAu 13R,
  SmATA 10, TwCA, TwCA Sup,
  WW 1974
Spring, Howard 1889-1965 *ConAu P-1,*
  CurB 41, CurB 65, DcLEnL, EvLB,
  LongC, NCHEL, Pen Eng, REn, TwCA,
  TwCA Sup, TwCW, WWCL
Spring, Norma 1917- *ConAu 61*
Springer, L Elsinore 1911- *ConAu 69*
Springer, Marilyn Harris 1931- *ConAu 21R*
Springer, Marilyn Harris *see* Harris, Marilyn
Sprunt, Alexander 1898-1973 *ConAu 37*
Spykman, Elizabeth C d1965 *MorJA,*
  SmATA 10
Spyri, Johanna Heusser 1827?-1901 *AnCL,*
  AuBYP, CarSB, JBA 1934, JBA 1951,
  OxGer, WWCL
Squire, C B *see* Squire, Elizabeth D
Squire, Elizabeth D *see* Squire, C B
Squire, Peter *MnBBF*
Squires, James Duane 1904- *AmA&B,*
  Au&Wr 6, ConAu 5R, DrAS 6H,
  WW 1974, WWA 38
Squires, Phil *ConAu XR, SmATA XR*
Squires, Phil *see* Barker, S Omar
Stables, William Gordon 1840-1910 *Alli Sup,*
  BrAu 19, ChPo, ChPo S1, EvLB,
  MnBBF, NCHEL, WWBWI A, WWCL

Stack, Nicolete Meredith 1896- *AuBYP,*
ConAu 13R, ForWC 1970, WWMW 14
Stack, Nicolete Meredith *see* Meredith, Nicolete
Stacpoole, Henry DeVere 1863-1951 *ChPo S2,*
EvLB, MnBBF, PoIre, TwCW,
WWBWI A
Stacy, Donald L 1925- *ConAu 29*
Stadtler, Bea 1921- *ConAu 65*
Stafford, Arthur *MnBBF*
Stafford, Jean 1915- *AmA&B, AmNov,*
CnDAL, ConAu 1R, ConLC 4,
ConNov 1972, ConNov 1976, CurB 51,
DrAF 1976, EncWL, ModAL, OxAm,
Pen Am, RAdv 1, REn, REnAL,
TwCA Sup, WWA 38, WWAW 8,
WWE 14, WWTwL, WWWor 2, WrD
Stagg, J Cecil *MnBBF*
Stagg, J R *MnBBF*
Stagg, J R *see* Barnett, John
Stagg, J R *see* Harte, Oliver
Stagg, James 1918- *Au&Wr 6, MnBBF,*
WWBWI A
Stagg, James *see* Johns, Gilbert
Stahl, Ben 1910- *ConAu 29, IlBYP,*
IlCB 1957, SmATA 5, WWA 38,
WWAA 1973, WWS 13
Stahl, L C *CarSB*
Stainforth, Frank *MnBBF*
Stainforth, Martin *WWBWI I*
Stair, Gobin 1912- *WWA 38*
Stalder, Valerie *ConAu 41*
Stall, Dorothy *AuBYP*
Stallybrass, Óliver 1925- *ConAu 29*
Stamaty, Mark Alan 1947- *ConAu 61,*
SmATA 12
Stambler, Irwin 1924- *AuBYP, ConAu 5R,*
SmATA 5
Stamper, Joseph 1886- *MnBBF, WWBWI A*
Stanbury, David 1933- *Au&Wr 6*
Standish, Burt L *AmA&B, CurB 45, DcNAA,*
OxAm, REnAL, TwCA, TwCA Sup
Standish, Evelyn *WWBWI A*
Standish, Evelyn *see* Goyne, Richard
Standish, J O *MnBBF*
Standish, J O *see* Horler, Sydney
Standish, Richard *MnBBF, WWBWI A*
Standish, Richard *see* Goyne, Richard
Standon, Anna 1929- *ConAu 17R*
Standon, Edward Cyril 1929- *IlBYP,*
IlCB 1957
Standring, Heather 1928- *ArtsCL*
Standring, Robert *MnBBF*
Stanford, Don 1918- *ConAu 53*
Stanford, Ernest Elwood 1888-1966 *MnBBF,*
WNAA
Stang, Judit 1921- *ConAu 5R*
Stang, Judit *see* Varga, Judy
Stanhope, Eric *MnBBF, SmATA XR,*
WWBWI A
Stanhope, Eric *see* Hamilton, Charles Harold St.
John
Staniforth, John William 1863-1927 *MnBBF,*
WWBWI A
Staniforth, John William *see* Scott, Maxwell
Stankevich, Boris 1928- *ConAu 21R,*
SmATA 2
Stanley, Diana 1909- *IlBYP, IlCB 1946,*
WWCL
Stanley, Sir Henry Morton 1841-1904 *Alli Sup,*

AmA&B, BbD, BiD&SB, BrAu 19,
CarSB, Chambr 3, DcAmA, DcEnA,
DcEnA Ap, EvLB, OxAm, OxEng, REn,
REnAL
Stanley, Robert *MnBBF, SmATA XR,*
WWBWI A
Stanley, Robert *see* Hamilton, Charles Harold St.
John
Stanley, Warwick *ConAu XR*
Stanley, Warwick *see* Hilton, John Buxton
Stanley-Brown, Rudolph *ConICB*
Stanley-Wrench, Margaret 1916- *Au&Wr 6,*
ConAu 9R
Stannard, Russell *MnBBF*
Stannard, Russell *see* Mallinson, R Russell
Stanovitch, Boris *MnBBF*
Stansky, Peter 1932- *ConAu 17R*
Stanstead, John *ConAu XR, SmATA XR*
Stanstead, John *see* Groom, Arthur William
Stanton, James *MnBBF*
Stanton, John *MnBBF, WWBWI A*
Stanton, John *see* Bridges, Thomas Charles
Stanton, John *see* Wallis, George C
Stanton, Marjorie *WWBWI A*
Stanton, Marjorie *see* Phillips, Horace
Stanton, Schuyler *ThBJA, TwCA,*
TwCA Sup
Stanton, Schuyler *see* Baum, L Frank
Stanton, William *MnBBF, WWBWI A*
Stanton, William *see* Hope, William Edward
Stanton
Stanton-Hope, W E *WWBWI A*
Stanton-Hope, W E *see* Hope, Stanton
Stapler, Harry 1919- *ConAu 61*
Stapleton, Maurice *MnBBF*
Stapleton, Maurice *see* Purcell, J S
Stapp, Arthur Donald 1906-1972 *AuBYP,*
ConAu 1R, ConAu 33, MorJA,
SmATA 4
Star, Martin *MnBBF*
Starbird, Kaye 1916- *AuBYP, ChPo,*
ChPo S1, ConAu 17R, SmATA 6
Starbird, Kaye *see* Jennison, C S
Stark, Jack *ConAu XR*
Stark, Jack *see* Stark, John H
Stark, James *ConAu XR, SmATA 6*
Stark, James *see* Goldston, Robert Conroy
Stark, John H 1914- *ConAu 49*
Stark, John H *see* Stark, Jack
Stark, Jonathan *MnBBF*
Stark, Jonathan *see* Marshall, H P
Starkey, Marion L 1901- *ConAu 1R,*
ForWC 1970, SmATA 8, SmATA 13,
WrD
Starkie, Walter Fitzwilliam 1894- *Au&Wr 6,*
CarSB, CatA 1930, IntWW 38, LongC,
NCHEL, TwCA, TwCA Sup, WW 1974,
WWA 38, WWMus 6
Starr, Frank *MnBBF*
Starr, John *MnBBF*
Starr, Leonard 1925- *ArtCS*
Starr, Richard *MnBBF, WWBWI A*
Starr, Richard *see* Essex, Captain
Starr, Richard *see* Essex, Lewis
Starr, Richard *see* Essex, Richard
Starr, Richard *see* Godwin, Frank
Starr, Richard *see* O'Dare, Kerry
Starret, William *ConAu XR, SmATA 3*
Starret, William *see* McClintock, Marshall

Starrett, Charles Vincent Emerson 1886-1974
  *AmA&B, AuBYP, ChPo, ChPo S2,
  DcLEnL, EncM&D, REn, REnAL,
  TwCA, TwCA Sup, WNAA*
Stashin, Leo *NYTBE 4*
Staudacher, Rosemarian Valentiner 1918-
  ConAu 5R, ForWC 1970, WrD
Steadman, Ralph 1936- *ChPo S2, WWCL*
Steahly, Vivian Eugenia Emrick 1915-
  *ConAu 61, DrAS 6E, WWAW 8,
  WWMW 14*
Stearns, John Newton 1829-1895 *Alli, AmA&B,
  CarSB, ChPo, ChPo S1, DcNAA*
Stearns, Monroe 1913- *ConAu 5R, SmATA 5*
Stearns, Pamela Fujimoto 1935- *ConAu 65*
Stebbing, G *MnBBF*
Stebbins, George S *CarSB*
Steedman, Marguerite Couturier 1908-
  ConAu 1R
Steegmuller, Francis 1906- *AmA&B,
  Au&Wr 6, ChPo, ConAu 49,
  ConNov 1972, ConNov 1976, REnAL,
  TwCA Sup, WW 1974, WWA 38*
Steel, Flora Annie 1847-1929 *BbD, BiD&SB,
  CarSB, Chambr 3, DcBiA, LongC,
  NCHEL, OxEng, REn, St&VC, TwCA*
Steele, Chester K *ConAu XR*
Steele, Frank *MnBBF*
Steele, George P 1924- *ConAu 1R*
Steele, Howard *MnBBF, WWBWI A*
Steele, Howard *see* Brooks, Leonard Harold
Steele, Howard *see* Edgar, Alfred
Steele, Howard *see* Hayter, Cecil Goodenough
Steele, Howard *see* Marshall, Arthur C
Steele, Howard *see* Symonds, Francis Addington
Steele, Mary Quintard Govan 1922- *AuBYP,
  ConAu 1R, SmATA 3, ThBJA, WrD*
Steele, Mary Quintard Govan *see* Gage, Wilson
Steele, Max 1922- *AmA&B, ConAu 25R,
  DrAF 1976, SmATA 10, WWS 13, WrD*
Steele, S *MnBBF*
Steele, William Owen 1917- *AmA&B,
  ConAu 5R, Au&Wr 6, AuBYP, BkCL,
  MorJA, SmATA 1, WWA 38, WrD*
Steen, Colin *MnBBF*
Steevens, G W *MnBBF*
Stefansson, Evelyn Baird 1913- *AuBYP,
  ConAu 49*
Steffan, Alice Kennedy 1907- *ConAu 5R,
  WWPNA*
Steffan, Alice Kennedy *see* Steffan, Jack
Steffan, Jack *ConAu XR*
Steffan, Jack *see* Steffan, Alice Kennedy
Steffanson, Con *ConAu XR*
Steffanson, Con *see* Goulart, Ron
Steffens, Arthur 1873- *MnBBF*
Steffens, Arthur *see* Cooper, Freemont
Steffens, Arthur *see* Dee, Dare
Steffens, Arthur *see* Glyn, Harrison
Steffens, Arthur *see* Hale, Clement
Steffens, Arthur *see* Hardy, A S
Steffens, Arthur *see* Hardy, Arthur Steffens
Steffens, Arthur *see* Hardy, E S
Steffens, Arthur *see* Leigh, Arthur, Captain
Steffens, Arthur *see* Walters, W G
Steffens, Arthur *see* Wentworth, Charles
Steffens, Lincoln 1866-1936 *AmA&B, LongC,
  ModAL, OxAm, Pen Am, REn, REnAL,
  TwCA, TwCA Sup, WEAL*

Stefferud, Alfred Daniel 1903- *AuBYP,
  WWA 38, WWE 14*
Steichen, Paula 1943- *ChPo S1, ConAu 25R*
Steig, William H 1907- *AmA&B, AmPB,
  AuBYP, AuNews 1, CelR 3, ChLR 2,
  CurB 44, IlBYP, NYTBE 3, REnAL,
  NewbC 1966, ThBJA, WWA 38,
  WWAA 1973, WWE 14, WWWor 2*
Steiger, Brad *ConAu XR*
Steiger, Brad *see* Olsen, Eugene E
Stein, Evaleen 1863-1923 *AmA&B, AmLY,
  ChPo, DcAmA, DcNAA, IndAu 1816,
  JBA 1934, JBA 1951*
Stein, Gertrude 1874-1946 *AmA&B, AmPB,
  AmWr, AtlBL, CasWL, Chambr 3,
  ChPo S1, CnDAL, CnE&AP, CnMD,
  CnMWL, ConAmA, ConAmL, CurB 46,
  DcLEnL, DcNAA, EncWL, EvLB,
  LongC, ModAL, ModAL Sup, ModWD,
  OxAm, OxEng, Pen Am, RAdv 1,
  RCom, REn, REnAL, SixAP, TwCA,
  TwCA Sup, TwCW, WEAL, WNAA,
  WWAW 8, WWTwL*
Stein, Harve 1904- *IlBYP, IlCB 1946,
  WWAA 1973*
Stein, J H *MnBBF*
Stein, J H *see* Dixon, Don
Stein, M L *ConAu 17R*
Stein, Meyer Lewis 1920- *AmMWS 12S,
  AuBYP, DrAS 6E, SmATA 6, WWE 14*
Stein, Mini *AmSCAP 66, ConAu 29,
  SmATA 2*
Stein, R Conrad 1937- *ConAu 41*
Stein, Walter 1924- *ConAu 25R,
  WWAA 1973, WWWorJ 1972*
Steinbeck, John 1902-1968 *AmA&B, AmNov,
  AmWr, BiEnAT, CasWL, CnDAL,
  CnMD, CnMWL, CnThe, ConAmA,
  ConAu 1R, ConAu 25R, ConLC 1,
  ConLC 5, CurB 40, CurB 63, CurB 69,
  CyWA, DcLEnL, EncWL, EvLB, LongC,
  McGWD, ModAL, ModWD, OxAm,
  OxEng, Pen Am, RAdv 1, RCom, REn,
  REnAL, SmATA 9, TwCA, TwCA Sup,
  TwCW, WEAL, WWTwL*
Steinberg, Alfred 1917- *AuBYP, ConAu 5R,
  SmATA 9*
Steinberg, David Joel 1937- *ConAu 25R,
  DrAS 6H*
Steinberg, David Michael *IlBYP*
Steinberg, Fred J 1933- *ConAu 37, SmATA 4*
Steinberg, Rafael 1927- *ConAu 61*
Steinberg, Saul 1914- *AmA&B, CelR 3,
  CurB 57, DcCAA 2, IntWW 38, OxAm,
  REn, WWA 38, WWGA, WWWor 2*
Steiner, Barbara A 1934- *SmATA 13*
Steiner, Barbara A *see* D'Andrea, Annette Cole
Steiner, Barbara A *see* Daniel, Anne
Steiner, Charlotte *AuBYP*
Steiner, Rudolf 1861-1925 *LongC, OxGer*
Steiner, Stan 1925- *ConAu 45, WWA 38*
Steinmetz, Eulalie *ConAu XR*
Stembridge, Frank *MnBBF*
Stenner, Thomas Robert 1886- *MnBBF,
  WWBWI A*
Step, Edward 1855-1931 *Alli Sup, LongC,
  MnBBF, WWBWI A*
Stephen, David 1910- *Au&Wr 6*
Stephen, Handley *MnBBF*

Stephen, Roy *MnBBF*
Stephens, Alice Barber 1858-1932 *ChPo,*
  ConICB
Stephens, Arthur *MnBBF*
Stephens, Arthur *see* Agnew, Stephen Hamilton
Stephens, Charles Asbury 1844-1931 *Alli Sup,*
  AmA&B, BiD&SB, CarSB, ChPo,
  ChPo S1, DcAmA, DcNAA
Stephens, Donald Ryder *MnBBF*
Stephens, Henry Louis 1824-1882 *Alli,*
  ChPo S1, ChPo S2, DcNAA, EarAB,
  EarAB Sup
Stephens, Jack *MnBBF*
Stephens, James 1882-1950 *AnCL, CarSB,*
  CasWL, Chambr 3, ChPo, ChPo S1,
  ChPo S2, CnE&AP, CyWA, DcLEnL,
  EncWL, EvLB, LongC, ModBL,
  ModBL Sup, NCHEL, OxEng, Pen Eng,
  PoIre, RAdv 1, REn, St&VC, TwCA,
  TwCA Sup, TwCW
Stephens, Kenneth *MnBBF*
Stephens, Kenneth *see* Agnew, Stephen Hamilton
Stephens, Mary Jo 1935- *ConAu 37,*
  SmATA 8
Stephens, Peter John *AuBYP*
Stephens, William M 1925- *ConAu 57*
Stephenson, Marjorie *ChPo S1*
Steptoe, John Lewis 1950- *BlkAW, ChLR 2,*
  ConAu 49, IlBYP, LBAA, LBAA,
  SmATA 8, WWA 38
Sterling, Chandler Winfield 1911- *ConAu 21R,*
  WWA 38, WrD
Sterling, Dorothy 1913- *AuBYP, BkCL,*
  ChLR 1, ConAu 9R, ForWC 1970,
  MorBMP, SmATA 1, ThBJA
Sterling, Helen *AuBYP*
Sterling, Helen *see* Hoke, Helen L
Sterling, Philip 1907- *ConAu 49, SmATA 8*
Stern, Ellen Norman 1927- *ConAu 37, WrD*
Stern, Madeleine Bettina 1912- *AuBYP, ChPo,*
  ConAu 17R, ForWC 1970, WWAW 8,
  WWE 14, WWWorJ 1972, WrD
Stern, Marie 1909- *ConAu 45, IlCB 1744*
Stern, Marie *see* Masha
Stern, Philip VanDoren 1900- *AmA&B,*
  AmNov, Au&Wr 6, ConAu 5R,
  DrAS 6H, REnAL, SmATA 13,
  TwCA Sup, WNAA, WWA 38
Stern, Philip VanDoren *see* Storme, Peter
Stern, Simon *ChPo S2*
Sterne, Duncan *MnBBF*
Sterne, Duncan *see* Openshaw, G H
Sterne, Emma Gelders 1894-1971 *AmA&B,*
  ConAu 5R, MorJA, SmATA 6, TwCA,
  TwCA Sup
Sterne, Emma Gelders *see* Broun, Emily
Sterne, Emma Gelders *see* James, Josephine
Sterne, Laurence 1713-1768 *Alli, AtlBL, BbD,*
  BiD&SB, BrAu, CasWL, Chambr 2,
  CriT 2, CyWA, DcBiA, DcEnA, DcEnL,
  DcEuL, DcLEnL, EvLB, MouLC 2,
  NCHEL, OxEng, OxGer, Pen Eng, PoIre,
  RAdv 1, RCom, REn, WEAL
Sterrett, Cliff 1883- *ArtCS*
Sterrett, Virginia Frances 1900- *ConICB*
Steurt, Marjorie Rankin 1888- *ConAu 13R,*
  SmATA 10, WrD
Stevens, Lieutenant *MnBBF*
Stevens, Alden Gifford 1886- *AuBYP*

Stevens, Arthur *MnBBF*
Stevens, Beatrice 1876- *ChPo, ConICB*
Stevens, C L McLuer *MnBBF*
Stevens, Carla McBride 1928- *AuBYP,*
  ConAu 69, SmATA 13, WWAW 8
Stevens, Charles *MnBBF, WWBWI A*
Stevens, Christopher *MnBBF, WWBWI A*
Stevens, Christopher *see* Rochefort, Julian
Stevens, Fae *SingR 2*
Stevens, Franklin 1933- *ConAu 29, SmATA 6*
Stevens, Franklin *see* Franklin, Steve
Stevens, Leonard A 1920- *ConAu 17R*
Stevens, Lucile Vernon 1899- *ConAu 61*
Stevens, Lucy Beatrice 1876- *IlCB 1744*
Stevens, Mary E 1920-1966 *IlBYP, IlCB 1946,*
  IlCB 1957
Stevens, Patricia Bunning 1931- *ConAu 53*
Stevens, Peter *ConAu XR, SmATA 7*
Stevens, Peter *see* Geis, Darlene Stern
Stevens, S Smith 1906- *AmA&B, NYTBE 4*
Stevens, William Oliver 1878-1955 *AmA&B,*
  AmLY, AuBYP, BiDPar, ChPo, WNAA
Stevenson, Anna 1905- *SmATA 12*
Stevenson, Augusta *AuBYP, ConAu 1R,*
  IndAu 1816, MorJA, SmATA 2
Stevenson, Burton Egbert 1872-1962 *AmA&B,*
  BiD&SB, ChPo, ChPo S2, DcAmA,
  EvLB, OhA&B, REn, REnAL, TwCA,
  TwCA Sup, WNAA
Stevenson, Gloria 1945- *ConAu 61*
Stevenson, Janet 1913- *ConAu 13R,*
  ForWC 1970, SmATA 8
Stevenson, Lionel 1902-1973 *AmA&B,*
  Au&Wr 6, ConAu 45, NYTBE 4,
  OxCan, St&VC, WWS 13
Stevenson, Mabel Rose 1875-1953 *ChPo S1,*
  ChPo S2, St&VC
Stevenson, Robert Louis 1850-1894 *Alli Sup,*
  AnCL, AtlBL, AuBYP, BbD, BiD&SB,
  BrAu 19, CarSB, CasWL, Chambr 3,
  ChP, ChPo, ChPo S1, ChPo S2, CriT 3,
  CyWA, DcBiA, DcEnA, DcEnA Ap,
  DcEuL, DcLEnL, EncM&D, EvLB,
  FamAYP, FamPYP, JBA 1934, MnBBF,
  MouLC 4, NCHEL, OxAm, OxEng,
  Pen Eng, RAdv 1, REn, REnAL,
  St&VC, TelT, WEAL, WWBWI A,
  WWCL, YABC 2
Stevenson, Robert Louis *see* North, George,
  Captain
Stevenson, William 1925- *ConAu 13R*
Stever, H Guyford 1916- *AmMWS 12P*
Steward, Colin *MnBBF*
Stewart, Allan 1865- *IlCB 1744*
Stewart, Allan 1939- *ConAu 1R*
Stewart, Anna Bird 1880- *AmA&B, AuBYP,*
  ChPo S2, CurB 48, OhA&B
Stewart, Arvis L *IlBYP*
Stewart, Charles *ConAu XR, SmATA XR*
Stewart, Charles *see* Zurhorst, Charles
Stewart, Charles William 1915- *IlBYP,*
  IlCB 1946
Stewart, Desmond 1924- *Au&Wr 6,*
  ConAu 37
Stewart, Donald Ogden 1894- *AmA&B,*
  BiEnAT, CarSB, CurB 41, DcLEnL,
  OhA&B, OxAm, Pen Am, REnAL,
  TwCA, TwCA Sup, WNAA, WWA 38
Stewart, Elizabeth Laing 1907- *AuBYP,*

ConAu 49, SmATA 6
Stewart, George Rippey 1895- *AmA&B,*
AmNov, Au&Wr 6, CnDAL, ConAu 1R,
CurB 42, OxAm, REnAL, SmATA 3,
TwCA Sup, WNAA, WWA 38
Stewart, Hubert *MnBBF*
Stewart, John 1920- *ConAu 33*
Stewart, Joy Eleanor 1931- *Au&Wr 6, WrD*
Stewart, Judith Anne *ConAu XR*
Stewart, Judith Anne *see* Maciel, Judi
Stewart, Katharine Jeanne 1914- *Au&Wr 6,*
ConAu 9R
Stewart, Mary 1916- *ConAu 1R, PoIre,*
SmATA 12, WW 1974, WrD
Stewart, Ora Pate 1910- *ForWC 1970,*
WWAW 8, WWW 14
Stewart, Paul *MnBBF*
Stewart, Ramona 1922- *ConAu 1R,*
ForWC 1970
Stewart, Robert Neil 1891-1972 *ConAu 9R,*
SmATA 7
Stewart, Ronald *MnBBF*
Stewart, Stuart *MnBBF*
Stidworthy, John 1943- *Au&Wr 6*
Stiles, Martha Bennett *ConAu 37, SmATA 6*
Still, James 1812- *BlkAW*
Still, James 1906- *AmA&B, ConAu 65,*
CyWA, DrAF 1976, REn, REnAL,
TwCA, TwCA Sup
Stillerman, Robbie 1947- *SmATA 12*
Stilley, Frank 1918- *ConAu 61*
Stillman, Myra Stephens 1915- *AuBYP,*
ConAu 5R, ForWC 1970
Stilwell, Alison 1921- *IlCB 1946*
Stine, G Harry 1928- *ConAu 65*
Stine, G Harry *see* Correy, Lee
Stine, George Harry 1928- *AuBYP,*
SmATA 10
Stinetorf, Louise A 1900- *ConAu 9R,*
ForWC 1970, SmATA 10
Stirling, Mrs. A M W *TelT*
Stirling, Mrs. A M W *see* Pickering, Wilhelmina
Stirling, Arthur *ConAu XR, OxAm,*
SmATA XR
Stirling, Arthur *see* Sinclair, Upton Beall
Stirling, Bruce *MnBBF*
Stirling, Jack *MnBBF*
Stirling, John *MnBBF*
Stirling, Lilla *AuBYP*
Stirling, Monica 1916- *ConNov 1972,*
ConNov 1976, WrD
Stirling, Nora Bromley *AuBYP, ConAu 5R,*
SmATA 3, WrD
Stirling, Tom *MnBBF*
Stirling, Tom *see* Ransome, L E
Stirnweis, Shannon 1931- *IlBYP, SmATA 10*
Stobart, Ralph *IlBYP*
Stobbs, William 1914- *ArtsCL, ChPo,*
ChPo S2, IlBYP, IlCB 1946, IlCB 1957,
ThBJA, WWCL
Stock, Ralph 1881- *CarSB, MnBBF*
Stockton, Frank Richard 1834-1902 *Alli, AmA,*
AmA&B, AuBYP, BbD, BiD&SB,
CarSB, CnDAL, CyAL 2, DcLEnL,
EncM&D, EvLB, FamSYP, JBA 1934,
OxAm, OxEng, RAdv 1, REn
Stockton, Wallace *MnBBF*
Stoddard, Edward G 1923- *AuBYP,*
ConAu 9R, SmATA 10

Stoddard, Hope 1900- *AuBYP, ConAu 49,*
SmATA 6
Stoddard, William Osborn 1835-1925 *Alli Sup,*
AmA, AmA&B, BiD&SB, CarSB, ChPo,
DcAmA, DcNAA, OxAm, REnAL
Stoddart, Isabella *CarSB*
Stoiko, Michael 1919- *ConAu 9R*
Stoker, Bram 1847-1912 *Alli Sup, CyWA,*
DcLEnL, EncM&D, EvLB, LongC,
Pen Eng, REn, TwCA, TwCA Sup,
WWCL
Stokes, Jack 1923- *ConAu 29, SmATA 13*
Stokes, Olivia Pearl 1916- *ConAu 37*
Stokley, James 1900- *AmA&B, WWA 38*
Stolper, Joel *IlCB 1744*
Stolz, Mary Slattery 1920- *AmA&B,*
Au&Wr 6, AuBYP, AuNews 1,
BiN 1974, ConAu 5R, CurB 53,
ForWC 1970, MorBMP, MorJA, REnAL,
SmATA 10, WWA 38, WWAW 8,
WWE 14
Stone, Alan *ConAu P-2, SmATA 1,*
SmATA 2
Stone, Alan *see* Stratemeyer, Edward L
Stone, Alan *see* Svenson, Andrew E
Stone, David K 1922- *ChPo S2, IlBYP,*
SmATA 9
Stone, Elaine Murray 1922- *WWAW 8*
Stone, Eugenia 1879-1971 *ConAu 9R,*
SmATA 7
Stone, Eugenia *see* Stone, Gene
Stone, Gene *ConAu XR, SmATA 7*
Stone, Gene *see* Stone, Eugenia
Stone, George K *AuBYP*
Stone, Helen 1904- *ChPo, ChPo S2,*
ConAu 25R, ForWC 1970, IlBYP,
IlCB 1744, IlCB 1946, IlCB 1957,
MorJA, SmATA 6
Stone, Idella Purnell *ConAu XR*
Stone, Idella Purnell *see* Purnell, Idella
Stone, Ikey *ConAu XR*
Stone, Ikey *see* Purnell, Idella
Stone, Irving 1903- *AmA&B, AmNov,*
Au&Wr 6, AuNews 1, CelR 3,
ConAu 1R, ConNov 1972, ConNov 1976,
CurB 67, DrAS 6E, IntWW 38, LongC,
Pen Am, REn, REnAL, SmATA 3,
TwCA, TwCA Sup, TwCW, WNAA,
WWA 38, WWWor 2, WWWorJ 1972
Stone, James Champion 1916- *ConAu 17R,*
WWW 14
Stone, Marcus *WWBWI 1*
Stone, Martin *MnBBF*
Stone, Ralph A 1934- *ConAu 37*
Stone, Raymond *CarSB, ConAu P-2,*
SmATA 1
Stone, Raymond *see* Stratemeyer, Edward L
Stone, Richard A *ConAu XR*
Stone, Richard A *see* Stratemeyer, Edward L
Stoneham, Charles Thurley 1895- *MnBBF*
Stonehouse, Bernard 1926- *Au&Wr 6,*
ConAu 49, SmATA 13
Stoneman, Elvyn Arthur 1919- *AmMWS 12S,*
ConAu 17R
Stong, Philip Duffield 1899-1957 *AmA&B,*
AmNov, AuBYP, CnDAL, ConAmA,
CyWA, MnBBF, MorJA, OxAm,
REnAL, St&VC, TwCA, TwCA Sup
Storey, Basil 1909- *MnBBF*

Storey, Margaret 1926- *ConAu 49, SmATA 9*
Storey, Robert Gerald 1893- *CurB 53,*
IntWW 38, WWA 38, WWS 13,
WWWor 2
Storm, Duncan *MnBBF, WWBWI A*
Storm, Duncan *see* Floyd, Gilbert
Storm, Duncan *see* Storm, Julie
Storm, Harold *MnBBF*
Storm, Ivan *MnBBF*
Storm, Ivan *see* Thomas, Reginald George
Storm, Julie *WWBWI A*
Storm, Julie *see* Storm, Duncan
Storm, Leslie *MnBBF*
Storm, Michael d1910? *MnBBF, WWBWI A*
Storm, Michael *see* Sempill, Ernest
Storm, Rupert *MnBBF*
Storm, Rupert *see* Sempill, Ernest
Stormalong, Rex *MnBBF*
Storme, Peter *ConAu XR, SmATA XR*
Storme, Peter *see* Stern, Philip VanDoren
Storr, Catherine 1913- *Au&Wr 6,*
ConAu 13R, SmATA 9, WrD
Storr, Catherine *see* Adler, Irene
Storr, Catherine *see* Lourie, Helen
Storrie, J A *MnBBF*
Story, Alfred Thomas *MnBBF*
Story, Jack Trevor 1917- *ConAu 29, MnBBF,*
WWBWI A
Story, Rosamund *MnBBF, WWBWI A*
Story, Rosamund *see* Woods, Ross
Stoutenburg, Adrien 1916- *AmA&B,*
Au&Wr 6, AuBYP, ChPo S2,
ConAu 5R, ConP 1970, ConP 1975,
DrAP 1975, MnnWr, SmATA 3, ThBJA,
WWA 38, WWAW 8, WWW 14, WrD
Stoutenburg, Adrien *see* Arden, Barbi
Stoutenburg, Adrien *see* Kendall, Lace
Stoutenburg, Adrien *see* Minier, Nelson
Stovell, Dennis H *MnBBF*
Stover, Allan C 1938- *ConAu 69*
Stover, Jo Ann 1931- *ConAu 37, IlBYP*
Stover, Marjorie Filley 1914- *ConAu 45,*
SmATA 9
Stow, Fred G *MnBBF*
Stowe, Harriet Beecher 1811-1896 *Alli,*
Alli Sup, AmA, AmA&B, AtlBL, BbD,
BiD&SB, CarSB, CasWL, Chambr 3,
ChPo, ChPo S1, ChPo S2, CnDAL,
CriT 3, CyAL 2, CyWA, DcAmA,
DcBiA, DcEnA, DcEnL, DcLEnL,
DcNAA, EvLB, JBA 1934, MouLC 4,
OhA&B, OxAm, OxEng, Pen Am,
RAdv 1, REn, REnAL, WEAL, WWCL,
YABC 1
Stowe, Harriet Beecher *see* Crowfield,
Christopher
Strachan, Margaret Pitcairn 1908- *ConAu 5R,*
WWPNA, WrD
Strachan, Margaret Pitcairn *see* More, Caroline
Stradling, Arthur *MnBBF*
Strain, Frances Bruce 1892- *AmA&B,*
ConAu 29, OhA&B
Strand, Sidney *MnBBF*
Strang, Herbert 1866-1958 *ChPo S1, ChPo S2,*
LongC, MnBBF, WWBWI A, WWCL
Strang, Herbert *see* Ely, George Herbert
Strang, Herbert *see* L'Estrange, James
Strang, Ruth May *ConAu 1R, CurB 60,*
CurB 71, NYTBE 2

Strange, Harry *MnBBF, WWBWI A*
Strange, Harry *see* Shaw, Stanley Gordon
Strange, Kemble *MnBBF*
Strange, Kemble *see* McEnvoy, C N
Strange, Oliver *MnBBF*
Strange, Robert *WWBWI I*
Stranger, Joyce *ConAu XR*
Stranger, Joyce *see* Wilson, Joyce M
Stratemeyer, Edward L 1862-1930 *AmA&B,*
BiD&SB, CarSB, ConAu P-2, DcAmA,
DcNAA, EncM&D, HsB&A, OxAm,
REn, REnAL, SmATA 1
Stratemeyer, Edward L *see* Abbott, Henry,
Manager
Stratemeyer, Edward L *see* Adams, Harrison
Stratemeyer, Edward L *see* Appleton, Victor
Stratemeyer, Edward L *see* Appleton, Victor II
Stratemeyer, Edward L *see* Barnum, Richard
Stratemeyer, Edward L *see* Bartlett, Philip A
Stratemeyer, Edward L *see* Barton, May Hollis
Stratemeyer, Edward L *see* Beach, Charles
Amory
Stratemeyer, Edward L *see* Bonehill, Ralph,
Captain
Stratemeyer, Edward L *see* Bowie, Jim
Stratemeyer, Edward L *see* Calkins, Franklin
Stratemeyer, Edward L *see* Carson, James,
Captain
Stratemeyer, Edward L *see* Chadwick, Lester
Stratemeyer, Edward L *see* Chapman, Allen
Stratemeyer, Edward L *see* Charles, Louis
Stratemeyer, Edward L *see* Cooper, James A
Stratemeyer, Edward L *see* Cooper, John R
Stratemeyer, Edward L *see* Daly, Jim
Stratemeyer, Edward L *see* Davenport, Spencer
Stratemeyer, Edward L *see* Dawson, Elmer A
Stratemeyer, Edward L *see* Dixon, Franklin W
Stratemeyer, Edward L *see* Duncan, Julia K
Stratemeyer, Edward L *see* Edwards, Julie
Stratemeyer, Edward L *see* Emerson, Alice B
Stratemeyer, Edward L *see* Ferris, James Cody
Stratemeyer, Edward L *see* Forbes, Graham B
Stratemeyer, Edward L *see* Ford, Albert Lee
Stratemeyer, Edward L *see* Gordon, Frederick
Stratemeyer, Edward L *see* Hamilton, Robert W
Stratemeyer, Edward L *see* Hardy, Alice Dale
Stratemeyer, Edward L *see* Harkaway, Hal
Stratemeyer, Edward L *see* Hawley, Mabel C
Stratemeyer, Edward L *see* Henderley, Brooks
Stratemeyer, Edward L *see* Hicks, Harvey
Stratemeyer, Edward L *see* Hill, Grace Brooks
Stratemeyer, Edward L *see* Hope, Laura Lee
Stratemeyer, Edward L *see* Hunt, Francis
Stratemeyer, Edward L *see* Judd, Frances K
Stratemeyer, Edward L *see* Keene, Carolyn
Stratemeyer, Edward L *see* Locke, Clinton W
Stratemeyer, Edward L *see* Long, Helen Beecher
Stratemeyer, Edward L *see* Mackenzie, Willard,
Doctor
Stratemeyer, Edward L *see* Marlowe, Amy Bell
Stratemeyer, Edward L *see* Martin, Eugene
Stratemeyer, Edward L *see* Moore, Fenworth
Stratemeyer, Edward L *see* Morrison, Gert W
Stratemeyer, Edward L *see* Optic, Oliver
Stratemeyer, Edward L *see* Penrose, Margaret
Stratemeyer, Edward L *see* Ridley, Nat, Jr.
Stratemeyer, Edward L *see* Rockwood, Roy
Stratemeyer, Edward L *see* Roe, Harry Mason
Stratemeyer, Edward L *see* Saint Myer, Ned

Stratemeyer, Edward L *see* Scott, Dan
Stratemeyer, Edward L *see* Sheldon, Ann
Stratemeyer, Edward L *see* Sperry, Raymond, Jr.
Stratemeyer, Edward L *see* Steele, Chester K
Stratemeyer, Edward L *see* Stone, Alan
Stratemeyer, Edward L *see* Stone, Raymond
Stratemeyer, Edward L *see* Stone, Richard A
Stratemeyer, Edward L *see* Strayer, E Ward
Stratemeyer, Edward L *see* Thorndyke, Helen
  Louise
Stratemeyer, Edward L *see* Warner, Frank A
Stratemeyer, Edward L *see* Webster, Frank V
Stratemeyer, Edward L *see* West, Jerry
Stratemeyer, Edward L *see* Wheeler, Janet D
Stratemeyer, Edward L *see* White, Ramy Allison
Stratemeyer, Edward L *see* Winfield, Arthur M
Stratemeyer, Edward L *see* Winfield, Edna
Stratemeyer, Edward L *see* Woods, Nat
Stratemeyer, Edward L *see* Young, Clarence
Stratford, Philip 1927- *CanWW 12,*
  ConAu 9R, OxCan Sup
Stratton, Helen *ChPo*
Stratton, William David 1896- *AuBYP,*
  ConAu P-1
Straus, Jacqueline Harris *AuBYP*
Strayer, E Ward *ConAu XR*
Strayer, E Ward *see* Stratemeyer, Edward L
Streano, Vince 1945- *ConAu 53*
Streatfeild, Noel 1897- *AuBYP, ChPo S2,*
  JBA 1951, LongC, TelT, WW 1974,
  WWCL, WrD
Street, Alicia 1911- *ConAu 5R*
Street, F *MnBBF*
Street, James 1903-1954 *AmA&B, AmNov,*
  CnDAL, CurB 46, CurB 54, REnAL,
  TwCA Sup
Street, Julia Montgomery 1898- *ConAu 5R,*
  ForWC 1970, SmATA 11, WrD
Streeter, Floyd Benjamin 1888- *WNAA*
Streeter, James *ConAu 61*
Stretton, Hesba 1832-1911 *Alli, Alli Sup,*
  Chambr 3, DcEnL, DcLEnL, LongC,
  NCHEL, TelT
Stretton, Hesba *see* Smith, Sarah
Strickland, Agnes 1796?-1874 *Alli, Alli Sup,*
  BbD, BiD&SB, BrAu 19, CarSB,
  Chambr 3, ChPo, ChPo S1, ChPo S2,
  DcEnL, DcEuL, EvLB, NCHEL, OxEng,
  Pen Eng, REn
Stringer, Arthur John Arbuthnott 1874-1950
  AmA&B, BiD&SB, CanNov, CanWr,
  CasWL, ChPo, ChPo S2, DcAmA,
  DcLEnL, EncM&D, MnBBF, OxCan,
  REn, TwCA, TwCA Sup
Stringer, Ruth M Pearson 1905- *ConAu 5R*
Strong, Charles 1909- *AuBYP, ConAu XR,*
  SmATA 1
Strong, Charles *see* Epstein, Samuel
Strong, Charles Stanley 1906-1962 *AmA&B,*
  AuBYP, CatA 1952, WNAA
Strong, Harrington *AmA&B, MnBBF,*
  WNAA
Strong, Harrington *see* McCulley, Johnston
Strong, Jack *MnBBF*
Strong, James *MnBBF*
Strong, James *see* Hervey, Hedley
Strong, Stephen *MnBBF*
Strother, Elsie W 1912- *ConAu 65*
Stroud, Len *MnBBF*

Stroyer, Poul 1923- *SmATA 13*
Struan, Lesley *MnBBF*
Struble, Virginia *ConAu XR*
Struble, Virginia *see* Burlingame, Virginia
Strutton, Bill 1918- *Au&Wr 6*
Stuart, Donald *MnBBF, WWBWI A*
Stuart, Donald *see* Stuart, Ronald
Stuart, Donald *see* Verner, Gerald
Stuart, Esme *Alli Sup, BbD, BiD&SB,*
  MnBBF
Stuart, Esme *see* LeRoy, Miss
Stuart, Forbes 1924- *ConAu 69, SmATA 13,*
  WrD
Stuart, Ian *ConAu 57, WorAu*
Stuart, Ian *see* MacLean, Alistair
Stuart, Jesse 1907- *AmA&B, AmNov,*
  Au&Wr 6, ChPo, ChPo S1, ConAu 5R,
  ConLC 1, ConNov 1972, ConNov 1976,
  CurB 40, CyWA, OxAm, RAdv 1, REn,
  REnAL, SixAP, SixAP, SmATA 2,
  TwCA Sup, TwCW, WrD
Stuart, Michael *MnBBF*
Stuart, Michael *see* Thomas, Reginald George
Stuart, Morna 1905- *Au&Wr 6*
Stuart, Oliver *MnBBF*
Stuart, Ronald *MnBBF*
Stuart, Ronald *see* Stuart, Donald
Stuart, Sheila *Au&Wr 6, ChPo S2,*
  ConAu XR, SmATA XR
Stuart, Sheila *see* Baker, Mary Gladys Steel
Stuart, W E *MnBBF*
Stuart, W E *see* Pike, William Ernest
Stubis, Talivaldis 1926- *ChPo S1, IlBYP,*
  SmATA 5
Stucley, Elizabeth *ConAu XR*
Stucley, Elizabeth *see* Northmore, Elizabeth
  Florence
Studd, Burton F J *MnBBF*
Studdy, George E 1878- *WWBWI I*
Sture-Vasa, Mary Alsop Parrot *CatA 1952,*
  CurB 44, SmATA 2, TwCA Sup
Sturges, Patricia P 1930- *ConAu 69*
Sturmer, Dudley *MnBBF*
Sturtevant, Wallis H *ConICB*
Sturton, Hugh *ConAu XR*
Sturton, Hugh *see* Johnston, H A S
Sturtzel, Howard A 1894- *ConAu 1R,*
  SmATA 1
Sturtzel, Howard A *see* Annixter, Paul
Sturtzel, Jane Levington 1903- *ConAu 1R,*
  SmATA 1
Sturtzel, Jane Levington *see* Annixter, Jane
Sturtzel, Jane Levington *see* Comfort, Jane
  Levington
Styles, Frank Showell 1908- *ConAu 1R,*
  SmATA 10
Styles, Frank Showell *see* Carr, Glyn
Styles, Frank Showell *see* Howell, S
Styles, Frank Showell *see* Styles, Showell
Styles, Showell 1908- *Au&Wr 6, AuBYP*
Styles, Showell *see* Styles, Frank Showell
Styron, Rose 1928- *ConAu 17R*
Suba, Susanne 1913- *ChPo S2, ConAu 29,*
  IlBYP, ForWC 1970, IlCB 1744,
  IlCB 1946, IlCB 1957, MorJA,
  SmATA 4, WWAA 1973
Sublette, Clifford MacClellan 1887-1939
  AmA&B, JBA 1934, JBA 1951
Subond, Valerie *SmATA 7*

Subond, Valerie *see* Grayland, Valerie
Sudbury, Rodie *WrD*
Suddaby, Donald 1901?-1964 *LongC, WWCL*
Sugarman, Daniel Arthur 1931- *AmMWS 12S, ConAu 21R*
Sugarman, Tracy 1921- *ConAu 21R*
Suggs, Robert Carl 1932- *AuBYP, ConAu 9R*
Sugimoto, Etsu Inagaki 1874-1950 *JBA 1934, TwCA, TwCA Sup*
Suhl, Yuri 1908- *ChLR 2, ConAu 45, SmATA 8, WWWorJ 1972*
Sullivan, A M 1896- *AnCL, BkC 3, ConAu 29, CurB 53, REnAL*
Sullivan, Edward D *MnBBF*
Sullivan, George Edward 1927- *AuBYP, ConAu 13R, SmATA 4, WrD*
Sullivan, Jake *MnBBF*
Sullivan, James F 1853-1936 *CarSB*
Sullivan, Mary W 1907- *SmATA 13*
Sullivan, Navin 1929- *Au&Wr 6, ConAu 5R*
Sullivan, Pat 1888-1933 *ArtCS*
Sullivan, Peggy Anne 1929- *ConAu 29*
Sullivan, Walter 1906- *ConAu 13R*
Sully, Francois 1927-1971 *ConAu 29, ConAu P-2*
Sulzberger, C L 1912- *CelR 3, ConAu 53, CurB 44*
Summerlin, Sam 1928- *ConAu 45, WWA 38, WWE 14*
Summers, Colin *MnBBF*
Summers, Colin *see* Agnew, Stephen Hamilton
Summers, James L 1910- *AuBYP, ConAu 13R, MorJA*
Summers, Somers John 1876?-1905? *MnBBF, WWBWI A*
Summers, W Lloyd *MnBBF*
Sumner, Aurea *WrD*
Sung, Betty Lee *ConAu 25R*
Super, Arthur Saul 1908- *Au&Wr 6, WWWorJ 1972*
Supraner, Robyn 1930- *ConAu 69*
Supraner, Robyn *see* Frost, Erica
Supraner, Robyn *see* Warren, Elizabeth
Supree, Burton 1941- *ConAu 65*
Surany, Anico *AuBYP*
Surge, Frank 1931- *ConAu 69, SmATA 13*
Surplus, Robert W 1923- *ConAu 5R, LE 5*
Surrey, G *MnBBF*
Susac, Andrew 1929- *ConAu 49, SmATA 5*
Suskind, Richard 1925- *ConAu 13R*
Sutcliff, Rosemary 1920- *Au&Wr 6, AuBYP, BrCA, CasWL, ChLR 1, ChPo, ConAu 5R, MorJA, PiP, SenS, SmATA 6, TelT, WW 1974, WWAW 8, WWCL, WWWor 2, WrD*
Suter, Harry *MnBBF*
Sutherland, Efua Theodora 1924- *AfA, BlkAW, ConDr 1, RGAfL, WWWor 2, WrD*
Sutherland, Margaret *WrD*
Sutherland, William Colin *MnBBF*
Sutton, Ann 1923- *AuBYP, ConAu 5R*
Sutton, Eve 1906- *ConAu 65*
Sutton, Felix *AuBYP*
Sutton, Jeff *ConAu XR*
Sutton, Jeff *see* Sutton, Jefferson H
Sutton, Jefferson H 1913- *ConAu 21R*
Sutton, Jefferson H *see* Sutton, Jeff
Sutton, Margaret Beebe 1903- *AuBYP, ConAu 1R, ForWC 1970, SmATA 1*

Sutton, Margaret Beebe *see* Ray, Irene
Sutton, Myron Daniel *AuBYP*
Sutton-Smith, Brian 1924- *AmMWS 12S, ConAu 29*
Svenson, Andrew E 1910-1975 *ConAu 5R, ConAu 61, SmATA 2, WWE 14*
Svenson, Andrew E *see* Dixon, Franklin W
Svenson, Andrew E *see* Stone, Alan
Svenson, Andrew E *see* West, Jerry
Swados, Harvey 1920-1972 *AmA&B, ConAu 5R, ConAu 37, ConLC 5, ConNov 1972, ModAL, NYTBE 3, OxAm, Pen Am, REnAL, WorAu*
Swain, Suzan Noguchi 1916- *ConAu 5R, IlCB 1957*
Swainson, Fred *MnBBF, WWBWI A*
Swainson, Leslie R *MnBBF*
Swann, Peter Charles 1921- *CanWW 12, ConAu 5R, WWWor 2*
Swanson, Anne *AuBYP*
Swanson, Arlene Collyer 1913- *AuBYP, ConAu 5R*
Swanson, Neil Harmon 1896- *AmA&B, AmNov, AuBYP, REnAL, TwCA, TwCA Sup*
Swarthout, Glendon 1918- *AuBYP, ConAu 1R, ConNov 1972, ConNov 1976, WrD*
Swarthout, Kathryn 1919- *AuBYP, ConAu 41, SmATA 7*
Swartz, Harry 1911- *AmMWS 12P, ConAu 57, WWWorJ 1972*
Swartz, Harry *see* Moreno, Martin
Swartz, Harry *see* Valcoe, H Felix
Swayne, Zoa Lourana 1905- *IlBYP, IlCB 1946*
Sweat, Lynn *IlBYP*
Sweeney, James B 1910- *ConAu 29*
Sweet, John W *MnBBF*
Sweet, Sophie *CarSB*
Sweetser, Mary 1894- *ConAu 41*
Sweney, Frederic 1912- *IlBYP, IlCB 1957, WWAA 1973*
Swenson, May 1919- *AmA&B, AnCL, ChPo S1, ChPo S2, ConAu 5R, ConLC 4, ConP 1970, ConP 1975, CrCAP, DrAP 1975, Pen Am, RAdv 1, WWA 38, WWAW 8, WWWor 2, WorAu*
Swetenham, Violet Hilda *WrD*
Swezey, Kenneth M 1905?-1972 *ConAu 33*
Swift, Edd 1943- *ConAu 37*
Swift, Helen Miller 1914- *AuBYP, ConAu 1R*
Swift, Hildegarde Hoyt 1890?-1977 *AuBYP, ChPo S2, ConAu 69, JBA 1951*
Swift, Jonathan 1667-1745 *Alli, AtlBL, BbD, BiD&SB, BrAu, CarSB, CasWL, Chambr 2, ChPo, ChPo S1, CnE&AP, CriT 2, CyWA, DcBiA, DcEnA, DcEnA Ap, DcEnL, DcEuL, DcLEnL, EvLB, HsB&A, MouLC 2, NCHEL, OxEng, Pen Eng, PoIre, RAdv 1, RCom, REn, WEAL, WWCL*
Swiger, Elinor Porter 1927- *ConAu 37, SmATA 8*
Swinburne, Algernon Charles 1837-1909 *Alli, Alli Sup, AtlBL, BbD, BiD&SB, BrAu 19, CarSB, CasWL, Chambr 3, ChPo, ChPo S1, ChPo S2, CnE&AP, CriT 3, CyWA, DcEnA, DcEnA Ap, DcEnL, DcEuL, DcLEnL, EvLB,*

MouLC 4, NCHEL, OxEng, Pen Eng,
RAdv 1, RCom, REn, WEAL
Swinburne, Laurence 1924- *ConAu 61,*
SmATA 9
Swindler, William Finley 1913- *ConAu 13R,*
DrAS 6P, WWA 38
Swinford, Betty 1927- *ConAu 5R*
Swinnerton, James Guilford 1874- *ArtCS*
Swinnerton, Phillipe Charles 1879-1963 *MnBBF,*
WWBWI 1
Swinton, William Elgin 1900- *AmMWS 12P,*
ConAu 13R, Au&Wr 6, AuBYP,
CanWW 12
Switzer, Ellen 1923- *ConAu 45*
Swortzell, Lowell 1930- *ConAu 49*
Sydney, Frank *MnBBF, WWBWI A*
Sydney, Frank *see* Warwick, Alan Ross
Sydney, Frank *see* Warwick, Francis
Sydney, Frank *see* Warwick, Sidney
Sydney, George *MnBBF, WWBWI A*
Syers, William Edward 1914- *ConAu 1R*
Sykes, Jo 1928- *AuBYP, WWPNA*
Sykes, Pamela 1927- *Au&Wr 6*
Sylvester, John 1901- *MnBBF, WWBWI A*
Sylvester, John *see* Hawton, Hector
Syme, Ronald 1913- *Au&Wr 6, AuBYP,*
ConAu 9R, MorJA, SmATA 2
Symeoni *WWBWI 1*
Symonds, Francis Addington 1893- *Au&Wr 6,*
MnBBF, WWBWI A
Symonds, Francis Addington *see* Danesford,
Earle
Symonds, Francis Addington *see* Steele, Howard
Symons, Geraldine *WrD*
Synge, Ursula 1930- *ConAu 49, SmATA 9,*
WrD
Sypher, Lucy Johnston 1907- *ConAu 45,*
SmATA 7, WrD
Syred, Celia Mary 1911- *ConAu 29, SingR 2*
Szasz, Suzanne Shorr 1919- *AuBYP,*
ConAu 5R, SmATA 13
Szasz, Thomas *CurB 75, NYTBE 2*
Sze, Mai-Mai *AuBYP*
Szekeres, Cyndy 1933- *IIBYP, SmATA 5*
Szulc, Tad 1926- *AmA&B, ConAu 9R,*
WWA 38, WWWor 2
Szyk, Arthur 1894-1951 *ChPo, CurB 46,*
CurB 51, IIBYP, IICB 1946

T

Taback, Simms *ChPo S1*
Tabrah, Ruth Milander 1921- *ConAu 13R,*
  ForWC 1970, LE 5, WWAW 8
Taffrail 1883-1968 *DcLEnL, LongC, MnBBF,*
  TwCW
Taffrail *see* Dorling, Henry Taprell
Tait, Agnes 1897- *ChPo, IlBYP, IlCB 1946*
Tait, Douglas 1944- *IlBYP, SmATA 12*
Tait, George Edward 1910- *Au&Wr 6,*
  CanWW 12, ConAu 5R, LE 5
Tait, W *MnBBF*
Takashima, Shizuye 1928- *ConAu 45,*
  OxCan Sup, SmATA 13
Talbert, Ansel Edward McLaurine 1912-
  AuBYP, WWA 38, WWS 13
Talbot, Charlene Joy 1928- *ConAu 17R,*
  ForWC 1970, SmATA 10, WrD
Talbot, Charles Remington 1851-1891 *Alli Sup,*
  AmA&B, BiD&SB, CarSB, ChPo,
  DcAmA, DcNAA
Talbot, E *MnBBF*
Talbot, Toby 1928- *ConAu 21R*
Tallant, Robert 1909-1957 *AmA&B, AmNov,*
  AuBYP, CurB 53, CurB 57, REnAL,
  TwCA Sup
Tallcott, Emogene *ConAu 29, SmATA 10*
Tallon, Robert 1940- *ConAu 9R*
Talmadge, Marian *AuBYP*
Tamarin, Alfred H 1913- *ConAu 29, MorBMP,*
  IntMPA 1975, SmATA 13
Tamburine, Jean 1930- *AuBYP, ChPo S1,*
  ConAu 9R, SmATA 12, WWAW 8
Tamulaitis, Vytas 1913- *ConAu 17R*
Tanizaki, Jun'ichiro 1886-1965 *CasWL,*
  CnMWL, ConAu 25R, DcOrL 1, EncWL,
  Pen Cl, REn, WWTwL, WorAu
Tannehill, Ivan Ray 1890-1959 *AuBYP,*
  OhA&B
Tannenbaum, Beulah Goldstein 1916- *AuBYP,*
  ConAu 5R, ForWC 1970, SmATA 3
Tanner, James M 1920- *Au&Wr 6,*
  ConAu 13R
Tanner, Louise S 1922- *ConAu 69, SmATA 9*
Tanobe, Mujuki 1937- *ConAu 69*
Tanous, Helen Nicol 1917- *AuBYP*
Tanyzer, Harold Joseph 1929- *ConAu 9R*
Tapio, Pat Decker *ConAu 65, SmATA XR*
Tapio, Pat Decker *see* Kines, Pat Decker
Tappan, Eva March 1854-1930 *AmA&B,*
  AmLY, BiD&SB, CarSB, ChPo,
  ChPo S1, DcAmA, DcNAA, JBA 1934,
  REnAL, TwCA, WNAA

Tarkington, Booth 1869-1946 *AmA&B, AtlBL,*
  CarSB, ChPo S2, CnDAL, ConAmA,
  ConAmL, CurB 46, CyWA, DcAmA,
  DcLEnL, DcNAA, JBA 1934, LongC,
  McGWD, ModAL, ModWD, OxAm,
  OxEng, Pen Am, REn, REnAL, TwCA,
  TwCA Sup, TwCW, WEAL, WNAA,
  WWCL
Tarkington, Booth *see* Tarkington, Newton Booth
Tarkington, Newton Booth 1869-1946 *BbD,*
  BiD&SB, CasWL, Chambr 3, DcBiA,
  EvLB, IndAu 1816, MnBBF
Tarkington, Newton Booth *see* Tarkington, Booth
Tarrant, Margaret W *ChPo, ChPo S1,*
  ChPo S2, ConICB
Tarry, Ellen 1906- *AmPB, AuBYP, BkP,*
  BlkAW, LBAA
Tarshis, Jerome 1936- *ConAu 61, SmATA 9*
Tashjian, Virginia A 1921- *AnCL, ConAu 29,*
  ForWC 1970, SmATA 3
Tasker, James 1908- *ConAu 49, SmATA 9*
Tate, Allen 1899- *AmA&B, AmWr,*
  Au&Wr 6, CasWL, CatA 1952, ChPo,
  ChPo S2, CnDAL, CnE&AP, ConAmA,
  ConAu 5R, ConLC 2, ConLC 4,
  ConLC 6, ConNov 1972, ConNov 1976,
  ConP 1970, ConP 1975, CurB 40,
  DrAF 1976, DrAP 1975, DrAS 6E,
  EncWL, IntWW 38, LongC, ModAL,
  ModAL Sup, OxAm, Pen Am, RAdv 1,
  REn, REnAL, SixAP, TwCA,
  TwCA Sup, TwCW, WEAL, WWA 38,
  WWS 13, WWTwL, WWWor 2
Tate, Carole *ChPo S2*
Tate, Elizabeth *AuBYP*
Tate, Ellalice *Au&Wr 6, ConAu XR,*
  EncM&D, SmATA 2, WW 1974, WorAu
Tate, Ellalice *see* Hibbert, Eleanor Burford
Tate, Joan 1922- *ConAu 49, SmATA 9,*
  WrD
Tate, Nahum 1652-1715 *Alli, AnCL, BrAu,*
  CasWL, Chambr 2, ChPo, DcEnA,
  DcEnL, DcEuL, DcLEnL, EvLB,
  NCHEL, OxEng, Pen Eng, PoCh, PoIre,
  PoLE, REn
Tatham, Campbell *AuBYP, ConAu XR,*
  MorJA, SmATA 2
Tatham, Campbell *see* Elting, Mary
Tattersall, M 1931- *ConAu 9R*
Tattersall, M *see* Waud, Elizabeth
Tattersall, Muriel Joyce 1931- *Au&Wr 6,*
  ConAu P-1, WrD

Taves, Isabella 1915- *ConAu 21R, WWAW 8*
Tavo, Gus *AuBYP, ConAu XR*
Tavo, Gus *see* Ivan, Martha Miller Pfaff
Tawse, Sybil *IlCB 1744*
Taylor, Allan M *MnBBF*
Taylor, Ann 1782-1866 *Alli, BrAu 19, CarSB,
    ChP, ChPo, ChPo S1, ChPo S2, DcEnL,
    DcEuL, EvLB, FamPYP, NCHEL,
    OxEng, St&VC, TelT, WWCL*
Taylor, Arthur *AuBYP*
Taylor, Barbara J 1927- *ConAu 53,
    SmATA 10*
Taylor, Bernard 1937- *ConAu 69*
Taylor, Carl *AuBYP*
Taylor, David 1900-1965 *ConAu 1R,
    SmATA 10*
Taylor, Dawson 1916- *ConAu 13R*
Taylor, Duncan 1912- *Au&Wr 6, ConAu 25R*
Taylor, Edgar 1793-1839 *Alli, ChPo, St&VC*
Taylor, Elizabeth 1912-1975 *Au&Wr 6,
    ConAu 13R, ConLC 2, ConLC 4,
    ConNov 1972, ConNov 1976, LongC,
    NCHEL, RAdv 1, SmATA 13,
    TwCA Sup, TwCW, WW 1974,
    WWAW 8, WWWor 2*
Taylor, Eric *MnBBF*
Taylor, Ethel Stoddard 1895?-1975 *ConAu 57*
Taylor, Florance Walton *ConAu 37*
Taylor, Florance Walton *SmATA 9*
Taylor, Florence Walton *MnBBF*
Taylor, Florence M 1892- *ConAu 13R,
    SmATA 9*
Taylor, George Boardman 1832-1907 *Alli,
    Alli Sup, BiDSA, CarSB, DcAmA,
    DcNAA*
Taylor, Gordon Rattray 1911- *Au&Wr 6,
    WW 1974*
Taylor, Isaac 1759-1829 *Alli, BiD&SB,
    BiDLA, BkIE, BrAu 19, CarSB, ChPo,
    ChPo S1, DcEuL*
Taylor, James *MnBBF*
Taylor, Jane 1783-1824 *Alli, CarSB, ChP,
    ChPo, ChPo S1, DcEnL, DcEuL, EvLB,
    FamPYP, OxEng, PoCh, St&VC, TelT,
    WWCL*
Taylor, Jefferys 1792-1853 *Alli, BrAu 19,
    CarSB, ChPo, ChPo S1*
Taylor, John G 1931- *Au&Wr 6, ConAu 29*
Taylor, Kenneth Nathaniel 1917- *Au&Wr 6,
    AuNews 2, ConAu 17R, WWA 38*
Taylor, Margaret *ConAu XR, AuBYP*
Taylor, Margaret *see* Burroughs, Margaret
    Taylor
Taylor, Norman *MnBBF, WWBWI A*
Taylor, Norman *see* Wood-Smith, Noel
Taylor, Rebe Prestwich 1911- *Au&Wr 6,
    ConAu 13R*
Taylor, Reginald S *MnBBF*
Taylor, Robert Lewis 1912- *AmA&B,
    Au&Wr 6, ConAu 1R, ConNov 1972,
    ConNov 1976, CurB 59, OxAm, REnAL,
    SmATA 10, WWA 38, WWE 14,
    WWWor 2, WorAu*
Taylor, Sydney Brenner 1904- *AuBYP, BkCL,
    ConAu 5R, MorBMP, MorJA, SmATA 1,
    WrD*
Taylor, Theodore 1924- *ConAu 21R,
    SmATA 5*
Taylor, W T *MnBBF*

Taylor, W T *see* Bredon, John
Taylor, W T *see* Gregory, Dave
Taylor, W T *see* Whitehouse, Arch
Tazewell, Charles 1900-1972 *ConAu 37,
    NYTBE 3*
Teague, Bob *BlkAW, LBAA*
Teague, Donald 1897- *ConICB, ForII,
    IlCB 1744, WWA 38, WWAA 1973,
    WWW 14*
Teal, Val 1903- *AmA&B, AmNov,
    ConAu 61, SmATA 10*
Teale, Edwin Way 1899- *AmA&B, Au&Wr 6,
    AuBYP, ConAu 1R, CurB 61, REnAL,
    SmATA 7, St&VC, ThBJA, TwCA Sup,
    WNAA, WWA 38, WWWor 2*
Teasdale, Sara 1884-1933 *AmA&B, AnCL,
    AnMV 1926, BiDSA, BkCL, CasWL,
    ChPo, ChPo S1, ChPo S2, CnDAL,
    ConAmA, ConAmL, DcLEnL, DcNAA,
    EvLB, LongC, OxAm, RAdv 1, REn,
    REnAL, SixAP, St&VC, TwCA,
    TwCA Sup, TwCW, WNAA*
Tebbel, John 1912- *AmA&B, CurB 53,
    WWA 38*
Techter, David 1932- *BiDPar*
Tee-Van, Helen Damrosch 1893-1976 *ConAu 49,
    ConAu 65, IlBYP, SmATA 10,
    WWAA 1973*
Tee-Van, Helen Damrosch *see* Damrosch, Helen
    Therese
Teed, George Hamilton 1878-1939 *MnBBF*
Teed, George Hamilton *see* Teed, George Heber
Teed, George Heber 1878-1939 *MnBBF,
    WWBWI A*
Teed, George Heber *see* Brittany, Louis
Teed, George Heber *see* Hamilton, George
Teed, George Heber *see* Hamilton, Murray
Teed, George Heber *see* Teed, George Hamilton
Tegner, Bruce 1928- *ConAu 61*
Temkin, Sara Anne Schlossberg 1913- *AuBYP,
    BiDL 5, ConAu 1R*
Temko, Florence *ConAu 49, SmATA 13*
Temperley, W H *MnBBF*
Tempest, Alan *MnBBF*
Tempest, E Dudley *MnBBF*
Tempest, Jack *MnBBF*
Tempest, Margaret *WW 1974*
Tempest, Teresa *AuBYP*
Tempest, Teresa *see* Kent, Louise
Templar, John *MnBBF*
Templar, John *see* Garbutt, John L
Templar, Maurice *ConAu XR, SmATA XR*
Templar, Maurice *see* Groom, Arthur William
Temple, Nigel Longdale 1926- *ChPo S2, WrD*
Temple, William *MnBBF*
Tench, C V *MnBBF*
Tenenbaum, Samuel 1902- *AmMWS 12S*
Tenggren, Gustaf 1896- *AmPB, IlBYP,
    IlCB 1744, IlCB 1946, MorJA*
Tennant, Kylie 1912- *Au&Wr 6, CasWL,
    ConAu XR, ConNov 1972, ConNov 1976,
    DcLEnL, EvLB, REn, SingR 1,
    SmATA 6, TwCW, WWWor 2, WorAu*
Tennant, Kylie *see* Rodd, Kylie Tennant
Tenney, Mrs. Sanborn 1836- *Alli, CarSB*
Tenniel, Sir John 1820-1914 *Alli, ChPo,
    ChPo S1, ChPo S2, IlBYP, JBA 1934,
    JBA 1951, LongC, NCHEL, REn,
    St&VC, WWCL*

Tennissen, Anthony Cornelius 1920-
  AmMWS 12P
Tennyson, Alfred 1809-1892 *Alli, Alli Sup,*
  AnCL, AtlBL, AuBYP, BbD, BiD&SB,
  BrAu 19, CasWL, Chambr 3, ChPo,
  ChPo S1, ChPo S2, CnE&AP, CnThe,
  CriT 3, CyWA, DcEnA, DcEnA Ap,
  DcEnL, DcEuL, DcLEnL, EvLB,
  McGWD, MouLC 4, NCHEL, OxEng,
  Pen Eng, PoLE, RAdv 1, RCom, REn,
  REnWD, St&VC, WEAL
Tensen, Ruth Marjorie 1905- *AuBYP,*
  ConAu 5R, ForWC 1970, WrD
Ter Haar, Jaap 1922- *ConAu 37, SmATA 6*
Ter Haar, Jaap *see* Haar, Jaap Ter
Terhune, Albert Payson 1872-1942 *AmA&B,*
  AmLY, AuBYP, BiD&SB, ChPo,
  CnDAL, CurB 42, DcAmA, DcNAA,
  EvLB, JBA 1934, OxAm, REnAL,
  TwCA, TwCA Sup, WNAA
Terhune, Mary Virginia 1830?-1922 *Alli,*
  Alli Sup, AmA, AmA&B, BbD,
  BiD&SB, BiDSA, CarSB, ChPo, CnDAL,
  CyAL 2, DcAmA, DcNAA, LFWS,
  OxAm, REnAL
Terkel, Studs 1912- *AmA&B, AuNews 1,*
  ConAu 57, CurB 74, WWMW 14
Terraine, John 1921- *ConAu 5R*
Terrell, John Upton 1900- *AmA&B, AmNov,*
  AuBYP, ConAu 29, OxCan Sup,
  WWW 14
Terrien, Samuel 1911- *DrAS 6P*
Terrill, G Appleby *MnBBF*
Terris, Susan 1937- *ConAu 29, SmATA 3,*
  WrD
Terry, Luther Leonidas 1911- *AmMWS 12P,*
  ConAu P-2, CurB 61, IntWW 38,
  SmATA 11, WWA 38
Terry, Noel *MnBBF*
Terry, Noel *see* Wood-Smith, Noel
Terry, Walter 1913- *AmA&B, AuBYP,*
  ConAu 21R, WWA 38
Tether, Graham 1950- *ConAu 57*
Tetlow, George 1934- *SingR 2*
Teuffel, Blanche Willis Von 1847-1898 *BiD&SB,*
  CarSB, DcAmA, DcNAA
Thacher, Alida McKay 1951- *ConAu 69*
Thacher, Edith *AmPB*
Thacher, Edith *see* Hurd, Edith Thacher
Thacher, Mary McGrath 1933- *SmATA 9*
Thackeray, William Makepeace 1811-1863 *Alli,*
  AtlBL, BbD, BiD&SB, BrAu 19, CarSB,
  CasWL, Chambr 3, ChPo, ChPo S1,
  ChPo· S2, CriT 3, CyWA, DcBiA,
  DcEnA, DcEnA Ap, DcEnL, DcEuL,
  DcLEnL, EvLB, FamSYP, HsB&A,
  MouLC 3, NCHEL, OxAm, OxEng,
  Pen Eng, RAdv 1, RCom, REn, TelT,
  WEAL, WWCL
Thackray, Derek Vincent *WrD*
Thames, C H *AuBYP, ConAu XR*
Thames, C H *see* Lesser, Milton
Thane, Adele 1904- *BiEnAT, ConAu 25R*
Thane, Elswyth 1900- *AmA&B, AmNov,*
  Au&Wr 6, ConAu 5R, ForWC 1970,
  REnAL, WWA 38, WWAW 8,
  WWE 14
Tharp, Louise Hall 1898- *AmA&B, Au&Wr 6,*
  AuBYP, ChPo, ConAu 1R, CurB 55,

ForWC 1970, MorJA, RAdv 1,
  SmATA 3, WorAu
Thatcher, Alice Dora 1912- *Au&Wr 6, WrD*
Thatcher, Dora 1912- *ConAu 13R*
Thaxter, Celia 1835-1894 *ChP*
Thayer, Emma 1842-1908 *BiD&SB, CarSB,*
  DcAmA, DcNAA
Thayer, Ernest Lawrence 1863-1940 *AuBYP,*
  ChPo, ChPo S1, CurB 40, EvLB
Thayer, Jane *AuBYP, ConAu XR, MorJA,*
  SmATA 3
Thayer, Jane *see* Woolley, Catherine
Thayer, Peter *ThBJA*
Thayer, Peter *see* Ames, Rose Wyler
Thayer, William Makepeace 1820-1898 *Alli,*
  Alli Sup, AmA&B, BbD, BiD&SB,
  CarSB, DcAmA, DcNAA
Thayne, Emma Lou 1924- *ConAu 65*
Thayne, Mirla Greenwood 1907- *ConAu 21R*
Theiner, George 1927- *ConAu 29*
Theiss, Lewis Edwin 1878-1963 *AmA&B,*
  AuBYP, WNAA
Themerson, Stefan 1910- *Au&Wr 6,*
  ConAu 65
Theriault, Yves 1915- *CanWW 12, CanWr,*
  CasWL, OxCan, OxCan Sup, Pen Eng,
  Prof, REnAL
Thieda, Shirley Ann 1943- *ConAu 69,*
  SmATA 13
Thiele, Colin 1920- *ConAu 29, SingR 1,*
  WrD
Thiele, Margaret Rossiter 1901- *ConAu 21R,*
  WrD
Thistle, Mel 1914- *ConAu 53*
Thistle, Mel *see* Bohr, Theophilus
Thistlethwaite, Miles 1945- *SmATA 12*
Thoborn-Clark, L B *MnBBF*
Thoby-Marcelin, Philippe 1904-1975 *CasWL,*
  ConAu 61, DcCLA, TwCA Sup
Thollander, Earl Gustave 1922- *IlBYP,*
  IlCB 1957
Thomas, Annie 1838-1918 *Alli, Alli Sup,*
  DcEnL, HsB&A, MnBBF
Thomas, Annie *see* Cudlip, Mrs. Pender
Thomas, Anthony *MnBBF, WWBWI A*
Thomas, Anthony *see* Poole, Reginald Heber
Thomas, Arline 1913- *ConAu 49, NYTBE 2*
Thomas, Benjamin Platt 1902-1956 *AuBYP*
Thomas, Bill 1934- *ConAu 61*
Thomas, Colin F *MnBBF*
Thomas, D *MnBBF*
Thomas, Dylan 1914-1953 *AnCL, AtlBL,*
  CasWL, ChPo, ChPo S1, ChPo S2,
  CnE&AP, CnMD, CnMWL, ConP 1975,
  CyWA, DcLEnL, EncWL, EvLB, LongC,
  McGWD, ModBL, ModBL Sup, ModWD,
  NCHEL, OxEng, Pen Eng, RAdv 1,
  RCom, REn, TwCA, TwCA Sup, TwCW,
  WEAL, WWTwL
Thomas, Edward 1878-1917 *AnCL, AtlBL,*
  ChPo, ChPo S1, ChPo S2, CnE&AP,
  CnMWL, DcLEnL, LongC, ModBL,
  ModBL Sup, NCHEL, OxEng, Pen Eng,
  REn, TwCA, TwCA Sup, TwCW,
  WEAL, WWTwL
Thomas, Estelle Webb 1899- *ArizL,*
  ConAu 21R, WrD
Thomas, Evan *MnBBF*
Thomas, Glen *IlBYP*

Thomas, H C *AuBYP*, *ConAu XR*
Thomas, H C *see* Keating, Lawrence A
Thomas, Henry 1886-1970 *ConAu 29*,
 NYTBE 1
Thomas, Henry 1888-1970 *WNAA*
Thomas, Ivan *MnBBF*
Thomas, J F *ConAu XR*, *SmATA 8*
Thomas, J F *see* Fleming, Thomas J
Thomas, Joan Gale *ConAu XR*, *SmATA 7*
Thomas, Joan Gale *see* Robinson, Joan G
Thomas, John 1890- *ConAu 49*
Thomas, Lowell Jackson 1892- *AmA&B*,
 Au&Wr 6, *AuBYP*, *AuNews 1*,
 AuNews 2, *BiN 1974*, *CelR 3*,
 ConAu 45, *CurB 40*, *CurB 52*,
 IntMPA 1975, *JBA 1934*, *MnBBF*,
 NYTBE 1, *OhA&B*, *OxCan*, *REnAL*,
 TwCA, *TwCA Sup*, *WNAA*, *WW 1974*,
 WWA 38
Thomas, Lowell Jackson, Jr. 1923- *AmA&B*,
 AuBYP, *WWA 38*, *WWW 14*
Thomas, Martin *MnBBF*, *WWBWI A*
Thomas, Martin *see* Martin, Thomas
Thomas, May *SingR 1*
Thomas, P R *MnBBF*
Thomas, Patricia J 1934- *ConAu 37*
Thomas, R S *WrD*
Thomas, Reginald George 1899-1958? *MnBBF*,
 WWBWI A
Thomas, Reginald George *see* Nelson, Barry
Thomas, Reginald George *see* Purley, John
Thomas, Reginald George *see* Storm, Ivan
Thomas, Reginald George *see* Stuart, Michael
Thomas, Reginald George *see* Wilson, Reg
Thomas, Ruth *AuBYP*
Thomas, W Fletcher *WWBWI I*
Thomas, W Jenkyn *CarSB*
Thompson, Blanche Jennings 1887- *BkC 1*,
 BkP, *CatA 1930*, *ChPo*, *ChPo S1*,
 ConAu 5R
Thompson, Brenda *WrD*
Thompson, Charles K *SingR 1*
Thompson, Christine Pullein *SmATA 3*
Thompson, Corrie 1887- *ConAu 61*
Thompson, Daniel Pierce 1795-1868 *Alli*, *AmA*,
 AmA&B, *CarSB*, *CnDAL*, *CyAL 1*,
 CyWA, *DcAmA*, *DcBiA*, *DcLEnL*,
 DcNAA, *OxAm*, *REn*, *REnAL*
Thompson, D'Arcy Wentworth 1829-1902 *Alli*,
 ChPo, *ChPo S1*, *TelT*
Thompson, David Hiram 1897- *WNAA*
Thompson, Diana Pullein *SmATA 3*
Thompson, E W *MnBBF*
Thompson, Eileen 1920- *AuBYP*, *ConAu XR*,
 ForWC 1970
Thompson, Eileen *see* Panowski, Eileen
 Thompson
Thompson, George Selden 1929- *AuBYP*,
 ConAu 5R, *SmATA 4*
Thompson, George Selden *see* Selden, George
Thompson, Harlan H 1894- *AuBYP*,
 ConAu P-1, *SmATA 10*, *St&VC*
Thompson, Harlan H *see* Holt, Stephen
Thompson, Hildegard Steerstedter 1901-
 AuBYP, *ConAu 17R*, *IndAu 1917*,
 WrD
Thompson, J H *MnBBF*, *WWBWI A*
Thompson, Josephine Pullein *SmATA 3*
Thompson, Joyce Blaikie 1920- *Au&Wr 6*,

 WrD
Thompson, Kay 1912- *AmA&B*, *CelR 3*,
 ChPo, *CurB 59*, *WWA 38*, *WWAW 8*
Thompson, Mary Wolfe 1886- *AmA&B*,
 AuBYP, *CurB 50*
Thompson, Maurice 1844-1901 *AmA*, *AmA&B*,
 BbD, *BiD&SB*, *BiDSA*, *CarSB*, *ChPo*,
 ChPo S1, *CnDAL*, *DcAmA*, *DcLEnL*,
 DcNAA, *OxAm*, *REnAL*
Thompson, Mozelle *IlBYP*
Thompson, N D *WrD*
Thompson, Paul Devries 1939- *AmMWS 12P*
Thompson, Philip Duncan 1922- *AmMWS 12P*,
 WWA 38
Thompson, Ralph *IlBYP*, *IlCB 1946*
Thompson, Reginald George *MnBBF*
Thompson, Ruth Plumly 1895- *AmA&B*, *ChPo*,
 WWA 38, *WWAW 8*, *WWCL*
Thompson, Stephen *Alli*, *MnBBF*
Thompson, Stephen *see* Dell, Draycot Montagu
Thompson, Stith 1885-1976 *AmA&B*, *AnCL*,
 Au&Wr 6, *IndAu 1917*, *OxCan*
Thompson, Vivian Laubach 1911- *AuBYP*,
 ConAu 1R, *ForWC 1970*, *SmATA 3*,
 WWAW 8, *WrD*
Thompson, W Harold *MnBBF*
Thompson, William E, Jr. 1923- *ConAu 13R*
Thomson, Arline K 1912- *IlBYP*
Thomson, Sir Arthur 1861-1933 *LongC*
Thomson, Christine Campbell *MnBBF*
Thomson, Christine Campbell *see* Richardson,
 Flavia
Thomson, David 1914- *Au&Wr 6*, *WrD*
Thomson, Hugh 1860-1920 *ChPo*, *ChPo S1*,
 ChPo S2, *WWBWI I*
Thomson, Joan *ConAu XR*
Thomson, Joan *see* Charnock, Joan
Thomson, Karline 1912- *IlCB 1946*
Thomson, Neil *MnBBF*
Thomson, Neil *see* Johnson, Henry T
Thomson, Peter 1913- *Alli*, *AuBYP*,
 ConAu 5R
Thoreau, Henry David 1817-1862 *Alli*, *AmA*,
 AmA&B, *AmWr*, *AnCL*, *AtlBL*, *BbD*,
 BbthC, *BiD&SB*, *CasWL*, *Chambr 3*,
 ChPo, *CnDAL*, *CnE&AP*, *CriT 3*,
 CyAL 2, *CyWA*, *DcAmA*, *DcEnA*,
 DcLEnL, *DcNAA*, *EvLB*, *MouLC 3*,
 OxAm, *OxCan*, *OxEng*, *Pen Am*,
 RAdv 1, *RCom*, *REn*, *REnAL*, *WEAL*
Thorndike, Susan 1944- *ConAu 41*
Thorndyke, Helen Louise *ConAu P-2*,
 SmATA 1
Thorndyke, Helen Louise *see* Stratemeyer,
 Edward L
Thorne, Diana 1894- *AmA&B*, *IlBYP*,
 IlCB 1744, *IlCB 1946*
Thorne, Ian *SmATA XR*
Thorne, Ian *see* May, Julian
Thorne, Rushden *MnBBF*
Thorne-Thomsen, Gudrun 1873- *JBA 1934*,
 JBA 1951
Thornhill, C *MnBBF*
Thornhill, J *MnBBF*
Thornicroft, J *MnBBF*
Thornton, Dorothy K *MnBBF*
Thornton, Edward *MnBBF*, *WWBWI A*,
 WWCL
Thornton, Edward *see* Brooks, Edwy Searles

Thornton, Norman *MnBBF*
Thornycroft, Rosalind 1891- *ChPo, IICB 1744*
Thorpe, E G 1916- *ConAu 9R*
Thorpe, P J *MnBBF*
Thorsen, Harry D, Jr. 1913- *WWA 38, WrD*
Thorvall, Kerstin 1925- *ConAu 17R, SmATA 13*
Thrasher, Crystal 1921- *ConAu 61*
Throckmorton, Peter 1928- *AuBYP, ConAu 17R*
Throneburg, James *AuBYP, ConAu 5R*
Thum, Gladys 1920- *ConAu 41*
Thum, Marcella *ConAu 9R, SmATA 3, WrD*
Thundercloud, Katherine *ConAu XR*
Thundercloud, Katherine *see* Witt, Shirley Hill
Thurber, James 1894-1961 *AmA&B, AnCL, AtlBL, AuBYP, BkCL, CasWL, CnDAL, CnMWL, ConAmA, ConLC 5, CurB 40, CurB 60, CurB 62, CyWA, DclEnL, EncWL, EvLB, LongC, McGWD, ModAL, MorJA, OhA&B, OxAm, OxEng, Pen Am, RAdv 1, REn, REnAL, SmATA 13, TwCA, TwCA Sup, TwCW, WEAL, WWGA, WWTwL*
Thurman, Judith 1946- *ConAu 49, DrAP 1975*
Thurman, Wallace 1902-1934 *AmA&B, BlkAM, REnAL*
Thwaite, Ann Barbara 1932- *Au&Wr 6, ConAu 5R, WrD*
Tibber, Robert *ConAu XR*
Tibber, Robert *see* Friedman, Eve Rosemary Tibber
Tibble, Anne 1912- *Au&Wr 6, ChPo S2, ConAu 9R*
Tice, George A 1938- *ConAu 61*
Tichenor, Tom 1923- *BiEnAT, ConAu 29, WrD*
Tickle, Phyllis 1934- *ConAu 65*
Tiddeman, Lizzie Ellen *MnBBF*
Tietjens, Eunice 1884-1944 *AmA&B, ChPo, ChPo S1, ChPo S2, ConAmL, CurB 44, DclEnL, DcNAA, JBA 1934, OxAm, REn, REnAL, TwCA, TwCA Sup, WNAA*
Tiltman, Hugh Hessell 1897- *MnBBF*
Tiltman, Hugh Hessell *see* Davenport, Tex
Tiltman, Hugh Hessell *see* Hessell, Henry
Timmins, William Frederick *SmATA 10, WWAA 1973*
Timmis, Norman L S *MnBBF*
Timoney, Francis 1938- *ConAu 61*
Tindall, Gillian 1938- *ConAu 21R, WrD*
Tinkelman, Murray 1933- *SmATA 12*
Tinkle, Lon 1906- *AmA&B, WWS 13*
Tippett, James Sterling 1885-1958 *AnCL, BkCL, ChPo, St&VC*
Titcomb, Margaret 1891- *ConAu 5R, ForWC 1970*
Tittle, Y A *CurB 64, NYTBE 1*
Titus, Eve 1922- *AuBYP, ConAu 29, SmATA 2, ThBJA*
Titus, Eve *see* Lord, Nancy
Tobias, Tobi 1938- *ConAu 29, SmATA 5*
Todaro, John *AuBYP*
Todd, Alden 1918- *ConAu 1R, WWE 14*
Todd, Anne Ophelia *AuBYP, ConAu XR, SmATA 7*

Todd, Anne Ophelia *see* Dowden, Anne Ophelia
Todd, Barbara Euphan 1890?- *Au&Wr 6, ChPo, ChPo S1, ChPo S2, WWCL*
Todd, Barbara K 1917- *ConAu 61, SmATA 10*
Todd, Herbert Eatton 1908- *Au&Wr 6, ConAu P-1, SmATA 11, WrD*
Todd, James *MnBBF*
Todd, Mary Fidelis *AuBYP*
Todd, Ruthven 1914- *AuBYP, ChPo, ChPo S2, ConP 1970, ConP 1975, LongC, ModBL, MorJA, TwCA Sup, WrD*
Toepfer, Ray Grant 1923- *ConAu 21R*
Toffler, Alvin 1928- *AmA&B, ConAu 13R, WWA 38*
Tolchin, Martin 1928- *WWE 14*
Tolford, Joshua 1909- *IlBYP, IICB 1946*
Tolkien, John Ronald Reuel 1892-1973 *AnCL, Au&Wr 6, AuBYP, AuNews 1, CasWL, CelR 3, ChPo, ChPo S1, ChPo S2, CnMWL, ConAu 45, ConAu P-2, ConLC 1, ConLC 2, ConLC 3, ConNov 1972, ConNov 1976, CurB 57, CurB 67, CurB 73, DclEnL, EncWL, LongC, ModBL, ModBL Sup, MorJA, NCHEL, NYTBE 4, OxEng, Pen Eng, RAdv 1, REn, SmATA 2, TelT, TwCW, WEAL, WWCL, WWTwL, WWWor 2, WorAu*
Tolles, Martha 1921- *ConAu 49, SmATA 8*
Tolmie, James *MnBBF*
Tolmie, Kenneth Donald 1941- *ConAu 69*
Tolstoy, Serge *AuBYP*
Tomalin, Miles 1903- *Au&Wr 6, WrD*
Tomfool *ConAu XR, SmATA 2*
Tomfool *see* Farjeon, Eleanor
Tomkins, Calvin 1925- *ConAu 13R*
Tomlinson, Everett Titsworth 1859-1931 *AmA&B, BiD&SB, CarSB, DcAmA, DcNAA, MnBBF, REnAL, WNAA*
Tomlinson, Jill 1931- *Au&Wr 6, ConAu P-2, SmATA 3, WrD*
Tomlinson, Paul Greene 1888- *AmA&B, CarSB, WNAA*
Tompert, Ann 1918- *ConAu 69*
Tompkins, Alan 1907- *WWAA 1973*
Tompkins, Jane 1898- *AuBYP*
Tompkins, Malcolm *WWBWI 1*
Tompkins, Walker Allison 1909- *AuBYP, ConAu 5R*
Toner, Raymond John 1908- *ConAu 5R, SmATA 10*
Tonkin, Humphrey 1939- *ConAu 41*
Tonks, Rosemary *ConNov 1972, ConNov 1976, ConP 1970, ConP 1975, WrD*
Tonn, Martin *WrD*
Tonn, Maryjane Hooper 1927- *WWAW 8*
Toonder, Martin *ConAu XR, SmATA XR*
Toonder, Martin *see* Groom, Arthur William
Toothaker, Roy Eugene 1928- *ConAu 65*
Tooze, Ruth 1892-1972 *AuBYP, ConAu 5R, SmATA 4*
Topolski, Feliks 1907- *IlBYP, IICB 1946, IntWW 38, WW 1974, WWGA, WWWor 2*
Toppin, Edgar Allan 1928- *ConAu 21R, DrAS 6H, LBAA, LBAA*
Topping, Anne *Au&Wr 6, ConAu 25R*

Topping, Audrey R 1928- *ConAu 41*
Tor, Regina *AuBYP*
Torbet, Laura 1942- *ConAu 69*
Torok, Lou 1927- *ConAu 49*
Torrey, Helen 1901- *IIBYP, IICB 1946*
Torrey, Marjorie 1899- *ChPo S1, IIBYP,*
    IICB 1946, MorJA
Toschik, Larry 1922- *IIBYP, IICB 1946*
Totham, Mary *SmATA XR*
Totham, Mary see Breinburg, Petronella
Toto, Joe *IIBYP*
Tottle, John *AuBYP*
Tournier, Michel 1924- *ConAu 49, ConLC 6,*
    EncWL, IntWW 38
Tourtel, Mary *ChPo S1, WWCL*
Tousey, Sanford *AuBYP, JBA 1951*
Townley, Houghton *MnBBF, WWBWI A*
Townley, Houghton see Preston, Walford
Townley, Langton *MnBBF*
Townsend, Eric W *MnBBF, WWBWI A*
Townsend, Eric W see McLean, Eric W
Townsend, J David 1888- *ConAu 5R*
Townsend, John Rowe 1922- *Au&Wr 6,*
    ChLR 2, ChPo S2, ConAu 37, PiP,
    SmATA 4, WWWor 2, WrD
Townsend, Lee 1895- *ChPo S1, IIBYP,*
    IICB 1946
Townsend, Richard F *IIBYP*
Townsend, W T *MnBBF*
Townshend, Richard Baxter *MnBBF*
Towry, M H *Alli Sup, CarSB*
Toye, William Eldred 1926- *ConAu 1R,*
    OxCan, OxCan Sup, SmATA 8
Tracey, Hugh 1903- *ConAu P-2*
Trachsel, Myrtle Jamison *AmA&B, AuBYP,*
    WNAA
Tracy, Horace Ernest Humphrey 1883- *MnBBF*
Traherne, Michael *ConAu XR, SmATA 6*
Traherne, Michael see Watkins-Pitchford, Denys
    James
Trahey, Jane 1923- *ForWC 1970, ConAu 17R,*
    WWAW 8, WWE 14
Train, Arthur Cheney 1875-1945 *AmA&B,*
    CarSB, DcNAA, EncM&D, OxAm, REn,
    REnAL, TwCA, TwCA Sup, WNAA
Tranter, Nigel 1909- *Au&Wr 6, AuBYP,*
    ConAu 9R, WW 1974
Trapp, Maria Augusta Von 1905- *AmA&B,*
    CatA 1952, CurB 68, WWA 38,
    WWAW 8, WWE 14, WWWor 2
Traudl *ConAu XR*
Traudl see Flaxman, Traudl
Travaglini, Barbara Carlson 1925- *WWAW 8*
Travanion, Tracy *MnBBF*
Traven, B 1890?-1969 *AmA&B, ConAu 25R,*
    ConAu P-2, EncWL, OxAm, OxGer,
    REnAL, TwCA, TwCA Sup, WEAL
Traven, Beatrice *ConAu 49*
Travers, Pamela Lyndon 1906- *AnCL, AuBYP,*
    ChLR 2, ConAu 33, FamMS, JBA 1951,
    LongC, MorBMP, NCHEL, REn,
    SmATA 4, TelT, TwCA, TwCA Sup,
    WWCL
Treadgold, Mary 1910- *Au&Wr 6,*
    ConAu 13R, WWCL, WrD
Trease, Geoffrey 1909- *AuBYP, ConAu 5R,*
    DcLEnL, MnBBF, MorJA, SmATA 2,
    TelT, WW 1974, WWBWI A, WWCL,
    WrD

Treat, Roger L *AuBYP*
Treaves, Norman *MnBBF*
Trebing, Harry Martin 1926- *AmMWS 12S,*
    ConAu 29, WWMW 14
Tredez, Alain *IICB 1957, ThBJA*
Tredez, Alain see Trez, Alain
Tredez, Denise 1930- *ConAu 5R, ThBJA*
Tredez, Denise see Trez, Denise
Tree, Travers *MnBBF*
Treece, Henry 1911?-1966 *AuBYP, CatA S1,*
    ConAu 1R, ConAu 25R, DcLEnL, EvLB,
    LongC, ModBL, MorJA, NCHEL,
    Pen Eng, REn, SmATA 2, TwCA Sup,
    TwCW, WWCL
Treeton, Ernest A *MnBBF, WWBWI A*
Treeves, Norman *WWBWI A*
Tregaskis, Richard 1916-1973 *AmA&B,*
    Au&Wr 6, AuBYP, ConAu 1R,
    ConAu 45, CurB 73, NYTBE 4,
    SmATA 3, WWA 38, WWWor 2
Tregellis, John *MnBBF, WWBWI A*
Tregellis, John see Gowing, Sydney
Treichler, Jessie *AuBYP*
Trelawney, Hubert *MnBBF*
Trelawney, Hubert see Tuite, Hugh
Trelease, Allen William 1928- *DrAS 6H,*
    WWA 38
Trelease, Harold *MnBBF*
Trell, Max 1900- *ConAu 41*
Tremaine, Roger *MnBBF*
Tremayne, Hartley *MnBBF, WWBWI A*
Tremayne, Hartley see Armour, R Coutts
Tremellan, Wilfred *MnBBF, WWBWI A*
Tremellan, Wilfred see Webber, Stawford
Trent, James *MnBBF*
Trent, Jeffrey *MnBBF*
Trent, Robbie 1894- *AuBYP, ConAu P-1*
Trent, Timothy *ConAu XR, SmATA XR*
Trent, Timothy see Malmberg, Carl
Tresilian, Cecil Stuart 1891- *IIBYP,*
    IICB 1744, IICB 1946, IICB 1957
Tresselt, Alvin 1916- *AmPB, AuBYP, BkP,*
    ConAu 49, MorJA, SmATA 7
Tressider, G *WWBWI I*
Trevelyan, Julian *WrD*
Trevelyan, Pauline 1905- *ChPo, IICB 1744*
Trevino, Elizabeth Borton De 1904- *AuBYP,*
    ConAu 17R, NewbC 1966, SmATA 1,
    ThBJA, WWA 38, WWAW 8, WWS 13
Trevino, Elizabeth Borton De see Borton,
    Elizabeth
Trevor, Edward C *MnBBF*
Trevor, Elleston 1920- *Au&Wr 6, ConAu 5R,*
    EncM&D, MnBBF, WW 1974, WWA 38,
    WWWor 2, WrD
Trevor, Elleston see Black, Mansell
Trevor, Elleston see Burgess, Trevor
Trevor, Elleston see Fitzalan, Roger
Trevor, Elleston see Hall, Adam
Trevor, Elleston see Rattray, Simon
Trevor, Elleston see Scott, Warwick
Trevor, Elleston see Smith, Caesar
Trevor, Gordon *MnBBF*
Trevor, Meriol 1919- *Au&Wr 6, ConAu 1R,*
    SmATA 10, WW 1974, WWAW 8,
    WWWor 2, WrD
Trevor, Sid *MnBBF*
Trew, Dighton *MnBBF*
Trew, Dighton see Jones, J G

Trez, Alain 1926?- *IICB 1957, ThBJA*
Trez, Alain *see* Tredez, Alain
Trez, Denise 1930- *ConAu XR, ThBJA*
Trez, Denise *see* Tredez, Denise
Trier, Walter 1890-1951 *IIBYP, IICB 1744, IICB 1946*
Trimble, Joe *AuBYP*
Trimble, Louis P 1917- *ConAu 13R*
Trimble, Louis P *see* Brock, Stuart
Trimmer, Ellen *WrD*
Trimmer, Sarah Kirby 1741-1810 *Alli, BrAu, CarSB, CasWL, DcEnL, DcLEnL, OxEng*
Tripp, Eleanor B 1936- *ConAu 29, SmATA 4*
Tripp, Paul 1911- *AmSCAP 66, ConAu 21R, SmATA 8, WWE 14*
Tripp, Wallace *ChPo S2, IIBYP*
Trippett, Frank 1926- *ConAu 21R*
Trnka, Jiri 1912-1969 *IICB 1957, ThBJA, WWGA*
Troop, Miriam 1917- *ConAu 13R*
Tropp, Martin 1945- *ConAu 65*
Trost, Lucille Wood 1938- *ConAu 61, SmATA 12*
Trotta, John 1936- *ConAu 45*
Trotter, Grace V 1900- *AuBYP, ConAu 1R, SmATA 10*
Trotter, Grace V *see* Paschal, Nancy
Trowbridge, G T *MnBBF*
Trowbridge, John Townsend 1827-1916 *Alli, Alli Sup, AmA, AmA&B, BbD, BiD&SB, CarSB, ChPo, ChPo S1, CyAL 2, CyWA, DcAmA, DcBiA, DcEnL, DcLEnL, DcNAA, OxAm, REnAL*
Troy, Hugh 1906-1964 *IIBYP, IICB 1744, IICB 1946, IICB 1957*
Troy, Una 1913- *Au&Wr 6, ConAu 1R, WrD*
Troyer, Johannes 1902- *ChPo, IIBYP, IICB 1946, IICB 1957*
Trudeau, Garry *AuNews 2, WrD*
Trupin, James E 1940- *ConAu 37*
Trusler, John 1735-1820 *Alli, BiDLA, BiDLA Sup, CarSB*
Truss, Leslie Seldon 1892- *MnBBF, WW 1974*
Tsireh, Awa *AmPB*
Tubb, E C *MnBBF*
Tuchman, Barbara Wertheim 1912- *AmA&B, Au&Wr 6, CurB 63, DrAS 6H, IntWW 38, OxAm, WWA 38, WWAW 8, WWE 14, WWWor 2, WWWorJ 1972, WorAu*
Tuck, A L *MnBBF*
Tucker, Caroline *AuBYP, ConAu XR, SmATA 2*
Tucker, Caroline *see* Nolan, Jeannette Covert
Tucker, Charlotte Maria 1821-1893 *Alli, Alli Sup, BrAu 19, CarSB, ChPo S1, ChPo S2, NCHEL, WWCL*
Tucker, Charlotte Maria *see* A L O E
Tucker, Ernest Edward 1916-1969 *AuBYP*
Tucker, Nicholas 1936- *ChPo S2, ConAu 65*
Tucker, Sterling *LBAA*
Tucknor, R I *MnBBF*
Tudor, Bethany *AuBYP*
Tudor, Tasha 1915- *AmA&B, AuBYP, ChPo, IICB 1744, IICB 1946, IICB 1957, JBA 1951, WWAA 1973, WWAW 8*

Tuer, Andrew White 1838-1900 *Alli Sup, CarSB, ChPo, ChPo S1*
Tuffs, J Elsden 1922- *ConAu 5R*
Tufts, Anne *AuBYP*
Tufts, Georgia *AuBYP*
Tufty, Barbara 1923- *ConAu 37*
Tuite, Hugh *MnBBF*
Tuite, Hugh *see* Spencer, Captain
Tuite, Hugh *see* Trelawney, Hubert
Tully, John 1923- *ConAu 69*
Tung, Shih-Tsin 1900- *ConAu 5R*
Tunis, Edwin Burdett 1897-1973 *AuBYP, ChLR 2, ConAu 5R, ConAu 45, IICB 1946, IICB 1957, MorJA, SmATA 1, WWAA 1973*
Tunis, John Roberts 1889-1975 *Au&ICB, AuBYP, ConAu 57, ConAu 61, MorJA, REnAL, TwCA, TwCA Sup*
Tunnicliffe, Charles Frederick 1901- *IIBYP, IICB 1946, WW 1974*
Turk, Midge 1930- *ConAu 33*
Turkle, Brinton Cassaday 1915- *BkP, ChPo S2, ConAu 25R, FamAI, IIBYP, IICB 1957, SmATA 2, ThBJA*
Turley, Charles 1871?- *MnBBF, WWBWI A*
Turlington, Bayly 1919- *ConAu 29, DrAS 6F, SmATA 5, WWA 38*
Turnbull, Agnes Sligh 1888- *AmA&B, AmNov, Au&Wr 6, AuBYP, ConAu 1R, REnAL, TwCA, TwCA Sup, WNAA, WWA 38, WWAW 8*
Turnbull, Ann 1943- *ConAu 65*
Turnbull, Ann *see* Nicol, Ann
Turnbull, Bob 1936- *ConAu 37*
Turnbull, Patrick *MnBBF*
Turner, Alice K 1940- *SmATA 10*
Turner, Ann W 1945- *ConAu 69*
Turner, Elizabeth 1775?-1846 *Alli, BrAu 19, ChPo, ChPo S1, TelT, YABC 2*
Turner, Eloise Fain 1906- *AuBYP, ConAu 5R*
Turner, Ernest Sackville 1909- *Au&Wr 6, MnBBF, WWBWI A, WorAu*
Turner, Ethel Sybil 1872-1958 *CarSB, ChPo S1, ChPo S2, DcLEnL, SingR 1, SingR 2*
Turner, John Victor *MnBBF*
Turner, John Victor *see* Hume, David
Turner, Josie *SmATA 3*
Turner, Josie *see* Crawford, Phyllis
Turner, Morrie 1923- *ConAu 29*
Turner, Nancy Byrd 1880- *AmA&B, BkCL, ChPo, ChPo S2, St&VC, WNAA*
Turner, Philip 1925- *ConAu 25R, SmATA 11*
Turngren, Annette 1902- *AuBYP, ConAu 9R, MnnWr, MorJA*
Turngren, Annette *see* Hopkins, A T
Turngren, Ellen d1964 *AuBYP, ConAu 5R, MnnWr, SmATA 3*
Turska, Krystyna *ChPo S1*
Turville, Henry *MnBBF, WWBWI A*
Turville, Henry *see* Bullivant, Cecil Henry
Tusiani, Joseph 1924- *AmA&B, AuBYP, BkC 6, ChPo S2, ConAu 9R, DrAS 6F, WWA 38*
Tuska, George *ArtCS*
Tute, Warren 1914- *Au&Wr 6, ConAu 1R, WrD*
Tuthill, Louisa Caroline 1798-1879 *Alli, CarSB, ChPo S1, CyAL 2, DcAmA, DcNAA*

Tutt, Kay Cunningham *AuBYP*
Tutton, Barbara 1914- *Au&Wr 6, WrD*
Twain, Mark 1835-1910 *Alli, Alli Sup, AmA,*
  AmA&B, AmWr, AtlBL, AuBYP,
  BiD&SB, BiDPar, BiDSA, CasWL,
  Chambr 3, CnDAL, CriT 3, CyWA,
  DcAmA, DcEnA, DcEnA Ap, DcEnL,
  DcLEnL, DcNAA, EncM&D, EncWL,
  EvLB, FamAYP, JBA 1934, ModAL,
  ModAL Sup, OxAm, OxEng, Pen Am,
  RAdv 1, RCom, REn, REnAL, WEAL,
  WWCL, WWTwL, YABC XR
Twain, Mark *see* Clemens, Samuel Langhorne
Tweedsmuir, Baron *DcLEnL, EncM&D,*
  EvLB, NCHEL, TwCA, TwCA Sup,
  YABC XR
Tweedsmuir, Baron *see* Buchan, Baron John
  Tweedsmuir
Twidle, Arthur *WWBWI 1*
Twiner, J V *MnBBF*
Twist, John C *MnBBF*
Tworkov, Jack 1900- *CurB 64, DcCAA 2,*
  WWA 38, WWAA 1973, WWWor 2,
  WWWorJ 1972
Twyman, Harold William 1898- *MnBBF,*
  WWBWI A
Twyman, Harold William *see* Cartwright, A
Twyman, Harold William *see* Forge, John
Tylee, E S *MnBBF*
Tyler, Anne 1941- *ConAu 9R, ConNov 1972,*
  ConNov 1976, DrAF 1976, SmATA 7,
  WWAW 8, WWE 14
Tyler, Charles W *MnBBF, WWBWI A*
Tyler, William Royall 1910- *ConAu 37,*
  IntWW 38, WWA 38
Tyler-Whittle, Michael Sidney 1927- *Au&Wr 6,*
  ConAu 5R, WrD
Tyler-Whittle, Michael Sidney *see* Oliver, Mark
Tyler-Whittle, Michael Sidney *see* Whittle, Tyler
Tyrer, Walter 1900- *MnBBF, WWBWI A*
Tyson, Wallace *MnBBF*

U

Ubell, Earl 1926- *ConAu 37, SmATA 4, WWA 38*

Uchida, Yoshiko 1921- *AuBYP, BkCL, ConAu 13R, MorJA, SmATA 1*

Udall, Jan Beaney 1938- *ConAu 65, SmATA 10*

Udall, Jan Beaney *see* Beaney, Jan

Udry, Janice May 1928- *AmPB, AuBYP, BkP, ConAu 5R, SmATA 4, ThBJA*

Ueno, Noriko *ConAu 49*

Uhl, Melvin John 1915- *ConAu 5R*

Ullerton, Herbert *MnBBF*

Ullman, James Ramsey 1907-1971 *AmA&B, Au&Wr 6, AuBYP, ConAu 1R, ConAu 29, CurB 45, CurB 71, LongC, NYTBE 2, REn, REnAL, SmATA 7, TwCA Sup, WNAA*

Ulreich, Nura Woodson 1899-1950 *IlBYP, IlCB 1744, IlCB 1946*

Ulreich, Nura Woodson *see* Nura

Ulrich, Betty Garton 1919- *ConAu 29*

Ulrich, Homer 1906- *AmA&B, Au&Wr 6, AuBYP, ConAu 5R, DrAS 6H, LE 5, WWA 38*

Ulyatt, Kenneth 1920- *ConAu 61*

Unada *ConAu XR, SmATA 3*

Unada *see* Gliewe, Unada G

Uncle Gus *ConAu XR, SmATA 1*

Uncle Gus *see* Rey, Hans Augusto

Uncle Ray *AmA&B, ConAu XR, SmATA 4*

Uncle Ray *see* Coffman, Ramon Peyton

Underhill, Alice Mertie 1900-1971 *ConAu 1R, SmATA 10*

Underhill, Ruth Murray 1884- *AmA&B, Au&Wr 6, ConAu 1R, CurB 54, OxCan Sup, WrD*

Underwood, F *MnBBF*

Underwood, Leon 1890- *ConICB, IlCB 1744, WW 1974*

Undset, Sigrid 1882-1949 *AtlBL, AuBYP, CasWL, CatA 1930, CIDMEuL, CurB 40, CurB 49, CyWA, EncWL, EvEuW, LongC, OxEng, Pen Eur, REn, TwCA, TwCA Sup, TwCW*

Unger, Marvin H 1936- *ConAu 29*

Ungerer, Jean Thomas 1931- *AmA&B, Au&Wr 6, ConAu 41, SmATA 5, WWA 38*

Ungerer, Jean Thomas *see* Ungerer, Tomi

Ungerer, Tomi 1931- *AmPB, AuBYP, BkP, ChLR 3, ChPo, ConAu XR, FamAI, IlCB 1957, SmATA 5, ThBJA, WWGA*

Ungerer, Tomi *see* Ungerer, Jean Thomas

Ungermann, Arne 1902- *ChPo S2, IlBYP, IlCB 1946, WWGA*

Ungermann, Kenneth Armistead 1916- *ConAu 9R*

Unitas, John 1933- *CelR 3, CurB 62, NYTBS 5*

Unkelbach, Kurt 1913- *ConAu 21R, SmATA 4, WWE 14*

Unnerstad, Edith Totterman 1900- *Au&Wr 6, AuBYP, ConAu 5R, SmATA 3, ThBJA*

Unpunga *MnBBF*

Unrau, Ruth 1922- *ConAu 61, SmATA 9*

Unstead, Robert John 1915- *Au&Wr 6, ConAu 9R, SmATA 12, WW 1974, WrD*

Unsworth, Walt 1928- *SmATA 4*

Unsworth, Walt *see* Unsworth, Walter

Unsworth, Walter 1928- *ConAu 29*

Unsworth, Walter *see* Unsworth, Walt

Unterecker, John 1922- *AmA&B, Au&Wr 6, AuBYP, ConAu 17R, DrAP 1975*

Untermeyer, Louis 1885- *AmA&B, AmLY, AnCL, AnMV 1926, Au&Wr 6, AuBYP, CelR 3, Chambr 3, ChPo, ChPo S1, ChPo S2, CnDAL, ConAmA, ConAmL, ConAu 5R, ConP 1970, ConP 1975, CurB 67, DcLEnL, EvLB, IntWW 38, LongC, OxAm, REn, REnAL, SmATA 2, TwCA, TwCA Sup, TwCW, WNAA, WW 1974, WWA 38, WrD*

Unthank, Luisa-Teresa 1924- *ConAu 33*

Unthank, Luisa-Teresa *see* Unthank, Tessa Brown

Unthank, Tessa Brown *ConAu XR, WrD*

Unthank, Tessa Brown *see* Unthank, Luisa-Teresa

Unwin, David Storr 1918- *Au&Wr 6, AuBYP, ConAu 9R, WW 1974, WrD*

Unwin, David Storr *see* Severn, David

Unwin, Nora Spicer 1907- *AmA&B, AuBYP, ChPo, ChPo S1, ChPo S2, ConAu 21R, IlCB 1744, IlCB 1946, IlCB 1957, MorJA, SmATA 3, St&VC, WW 1974, WWA 38, WWAA 1973, WWAW 8*

Upchurch, Boyd 1919- *ConAu 25R*

Upchurch, Boyd *see* Boyd, John

Updike, John 1932- *AmA&B, AmWr, AnCL, Au&Wr 6, AuBYP, CasWL, CelR 3, ChPo, ConAu 1R, ConLC 1, ConLC 2, ConLC 3, ConLC 5, ConNov 1972, ConNov 1976, ConP 1970, ConP 1975, CurB 66, DrAF 1976, EncWL, ModAL,*

ModAL Sup, OxAm, Pen Am, RAdv 1,
REn, REnAL, TwCW, WEAL, WWTwL,
WorAu, WrD
Upington, Marion *AuBYP*
Upton, Florence K 1873-1922 *ChPo, ChPo S2,*
LongC, WWCL
Uris, Leon 1924- *AmA&B, Au&Wr 6,*
AuNews 1, AuNews 2, CelR 3,
ConAu 1R, ConNov 1972, ConNov 1976,
CurB 59, REn, REnAL, TwCW,
WWA 38, WWWor 2, WorAu
Urmston, Mary 1891- *MorJA*
Urquhart, Paul *MnBBF, WWBWI A*
Urquhart, Paul *see* Black, Ladbroke Lionel Day
Uschold, Maud E *AnMV 1926, ChPo,*
St&VC
Usher, Margo Scegge *SmATA 4*
Usher, Margo Scegge *see* McHargue, Georgess
Uttley, Alice Jane 1884-1976 *ConAu 53,*
ConAu 65, SmATA 3
Uttley, Alice Jane *see* Uttley, Alison
Uttley, Alison 1884-1976 *Au&Wr 6, AuBYP,*
ChPo, ConAu XR, DcLEnL, LongC,
SmATA 3, TelT, WW 1974, WWCL,
WrD
Uttley, Alison *see* Uttley, Alice Jane
Utz, Lois 1932- *ConAu 25R, SmATA 5*

V

Vachell, Horace Annesley 1861-1955 *BbD*, *BiD&SB*, *DcAmA*, *DcLEnL*, *EncM&D*, *EvLB*, *LongC*, *MnBBF*, *ModBL*, *NCHEL*, *REn*, *TwCA*, *TwCA Sup*, *TwCW*, *WWBWI A*, *WWLA*
Vaeth, J Gordon 1921- *ConAu 5R*
Vaizey, John 1929- *Au&Wr 6*, *ConAu 5R*, *CurB 64*, *IntWW 38*, *WW 1974*, *WWWor 2*
Val *WWBWI I*
Val *see* Reading, Val
Val Baker, Denys *AuBYP*
Valcoe, H Felix *ConAu XR*
Valcoe, H Felix *see* Swartz, Harry
Valda, John Harris d1940? *WWBWI I*
Valen, Nanine 1950- *ConAu 65*
Valens, Evans G, Jr. 1920- *AuBYP*, *ChPo S2*, *ConAu 5R*, *SmATA 1*
Valentine, Henry *MnBBF*
Valentine, Henry *see* Poole, Reginald Heber
Valentine, Henry *see* Prout, Geoffrey
Valentine, James Cheyne 1935- *ConAu 45*
Valentine, James Cheyne *see* Valentine, Tom
Valentine, Tom *ConAu XR*
Valentine, Tom *see* Valentine, James Cheyne
Vallence, Peter *MnBBF*
Valli *IIBYP*
Valli *see* VanDeBovencamp, Valli
Valmiki *BiD&SB*, *CasWL*, *CyWA*, *DcOrL 2*, *Pen Cl*
Valpy, Judith *ChPo S1*, *IIBYP*
VanAbbe, Salaman 1883?-1955 *IIBYP*, *IICB 1946*
VanAnrooy, Francine 1924- *ConAu 21R*, *SmATA 2*
VanAnrooy, Francine *see* VanAnrooy, Frans
VanAnrooy, Frans *ConAu XR*
VanAnrooy, Frans 1924- *SmATA 2*
VanAnrooy, Frans *see* Anrooy, Frans Van
VanAnrooy, Frans *see* VanAnrooy, Francine
Vance, Eleanor Graham 1908- *ConAu 9R*, *ForWC 1970*, *SmATA 11*, *WWAW 8*, *WrD*
Vance, F T *CarSB*
Vance, Marguerite 1889-1965 *AmA&B*, *AuBYP*, *CurB 51*, *CurB 65*, *MorJA*, *OhA&B*
VanCoevering, Jack 1900- *AuBYP*
VanCoevering, Jack *see* VanCoevering, Jan Adrian
VanCoevering, Jan Adrian 1900- *AuBYP*, *ConAu P-1*

VanCoevering, Jan Adrian *see* VanCoevering, Jack
VanDeBovencamp, Valli *IIBYP*
VanDeBovencamp, Valli *see* Valli
Vandegrift, Margaret *Alli Sup*, *AmA&B*, *BiD&SB*, *CarSB*, *ChPo*, *ChPo S2*, *DcAmA*, *DcNAA*
VanDerBoom, Mae M *AuBYP*
Vandercook, Margaret 1876- *CarSB*
VanDerHaas, Henrietta *AuBYP*
VanDerHorst, Brian 1944- *ConAu 41*
VanDerPost, Laurens 1906- *ConAu 5R*
VanDersal, William R 1907- *AmMWS 12P*
VanDerVeer, Judy 1912- *ChPo*, *ChPo S1*, *ConAu 33*, *SmATA 4*, *WNAA*
VanDerVeldt, James A 1893- *AuBYP*, *CatA 1952*
Vandivert, Rita 1905- *ConAu 5R*
Vandivert, William *CurB 63*
VanDoren, Margaret 1917- *IICB 1744*
VanDruten, John William 1901-1957 *Chambr 3*, *CnMD*, *CnThe*, *CurB 44*, *CurB 58*, *DcLEnL*, *LongC*, *McGWD*, *MnBBF*, *ModAL*, *ModBL*, *ModWD*, *NCHEL*, *OxAm*, *Pen Am*, *REn*, *REnAL*, *TwCA*, *TwCA Sup*, *TwCW*, *WWBWI A*
VanDuyn, Janet 1910- *ConAu 69*
VanDyke, Henry Jackson, Jr. 1852-1933 *Alli Sup*, *AmA&B*, *BbD*, *BiD&SB*, *ChPo*, *ChPo S1*, *ChPo S2*, *ConAmL*, *DcAmA*, *DcNAA*, *EvLB*, *JBA 1934*, *LongC*, *REnAL*, *St&VC*, *TwCA*, *TwCA Sup*, *WNAA*
VanDyne, Edith 1902- *AmA&B*, *AuBYP*, *DcNAA*, *ThBJA*
VanDyne, Edith *see* Baum, Lyman Frank
Vane, Derek *MnBBF*
VanEssen, W *WrD*
VanEveren, Jay *ConICB*, *IICB 1744*
VanGelder, Richard George 1928- *AmMWS 12P*, *WWA 38*, *WWWor 2*
VanHorn, Grace *AuBYP*
VanLeeuwen, Jean 1937- *ConAu 25R*, *SmATA 6*, *WWAW 8*
VanLhin, Erik *ConAu 65*
VanLhin, Erik *see* DelRey, Lester
VanLoon, Hendrik Willem 1882-1944 *AmA&B*, *AnCL*, *AuBYP*, *ChPo S2*, *ConAmA*, *ConAmL*, *CurB 44*, *DcLEnL*, *DcNAA*, *JBA 1934*, *LongC*, *Newb 1922*, *OxAm*, *REn*, *REnAL*, *TwCA*, *TwCA Sup*, *WNAA*

VanOort, Jan 1921- *ConAu 29*
VanOort, Jan *see* Dulieu, Jean
VanOrden, M D 1921- *ConAu 37, SmATA 4*
VanRensselaer, Alexander 1892- *AuBYP*
VanRiper, Guernsey, Jr. 1909- *ConAu 5R,
    IndAu 1917, SmATA 3, WrD*
VanSchaick, George Gray 1861-1924 *CarSB,
    DcNAA*
VanScott, Glory *BlkAW*
Vansittart, Peter 1920- *Au&Wr 6, ConAu 1R,
    WWA 38, WWWor 2, WorAu, WrD*
VanStockum, Hilda 1908- *AuBYP, BkC 2,
    CatA 1930, ChPo, ConAu 9R, IlCB 1744,
    IlCB 1946, IlCB 1957, JBA 1951,
    SmATA 5*
VanTuyl, Barbara 1940- *ConAu 53,
    SmATA 11*
VanVogt, A E 1912- *ConAu 21R*
VanWoerkom, Dorothy O 1924- *ConAu 57*
VanWormer, Joe *ConAu XR*
VanWormer, Joe *see* VanWormer, Joseph
    Edward
VanWormer, Joseph Edward 1913- *ConAu 9R*
VanWormer, Joseph Edward *see* VanWormer,
    Joe
VanWyck Mason, F *SmATA 3*
Varga, Judy *ConAu XR*
Varga, Judy *see* Stang, Judit
Varley, Dimitry V 1906- *ConAu P-1,
    SmATA 10, WrD*
Varner, Velma *AmPB*
Vasiliu, Mircea 1920- *ChPo S2, ConAu 21R,
    IlBYP, IlCB 1946, IlCB 1957, SmATA 2,
    WWE 14*
Vass, George 1927- *ConAu 37*
Vaughan, Anne 1913- *IlBYP, IlCB 1744,
    IlCB 1946*
Vaughan, Dudley *MnBBF*
Vaughan, Dudley *see* Johnson, Dudley Vaughan
Vaughan, Harold Cecil 1923- *ConAu 29*
Vaughan, Sam 1928- *ConAu 13R*
Vaughan-Jackson, Genevieve 1913-
    ForWC 1970, IlBYP, IlCB 1946
Vaughan-Jackson, Genevieve *see* Jackson,
    Genevieve Vaughan
Vavra, Robert James 1935- *ConAu 25R,
    SmATA 8*
Vecsey, George 1939- *ConAu 61, SmATA 9*
Veglahn, Nancy Crary 1937- *AuBYP,
    ConAu 17R, SmATA 5*
Venable, Alan 1944- *ConAu 45, SmATA 8*
Venn, Mary Eleanor 1908- *AuBYP*
Venn, Mary Eleanor *see* Adrian, Mary
Venn, Mary Eleanor *see* Jorgensen, Mary Venn
Ventura, Piero *IlBYP*
Venturo, Betty Lou Baker 1928- *AuBYP,
    ConAu 1R, ThBJA*
Venturo, Betty Lou Baker *see* Baker, Betty
VerBeck, Frank 1858-1933 *DcNAA, WNAA*
Veren, Gilbert *MnBBF*
Veren, Gilbert *see* Keveren, A G
Vergara, William Charles 1923- *AmMWS 12P,
    ConAu 1R*
Vermes, Hal G *AuBYP*
Vermes, Jean C *AuBYP*
Verne, Jules 1828-1905 *AtlBL, AuBYP, BbD,
    BiD&SB, CarSB, CasWL, CyWA,
    DcBiA, DcEnL, DcEuL, EuAu, EvEuW,
    JBA 1934, JBA 1951, LongC, MnBBF,*

*NCHEL, OxEng, OxFr, Pen Eur, REn,
    WWBWI A, WWCL*
Verner, Gerald *MnBBF, WWBWI A*
Verner, Gerald *see* Stuart, Donald
Verney, Sir John 1913- *Au&Wr 6, AuBYP,
    ChPo S2, ConAu 65, IlCB 1957,
    WW 1974*
Vernon, Louise A 1914- *ConAu 53*
Vernor, D *ConAu XR, SmATA 4*
Vernor, D *see* Casewit, Curtis
Verral, Charles Spain 1904- *AuBYP,
    ConAu P-1, SmATA 11, WrD*
Verral, Charles Spain *see* Eaton, George L
Versace, Marie Teresa Rios 1917- *ConAu 17R,
    SmATA 2*
Versace, Marie Teresa Rios *see* Rios, Tere
Vesey, Paul *BlkAW, ConAu XR,
    SmATA XR*
Vesey, Paul *see* Allen, Samuel
Vessel, Matthew F 1912- *AmMWS 12P, LE 5*
Vestal, Edith Ballard 1884- *ConAu P-2*
Vestal, Herman B *IlBYP*
Vetter, Carole 1939- *ConAu 25R*
Vicker, Angus *AuBYP, ConAu XR,
    SmATA 1*
Vicker, Angus *see* Felsen, Henry Gregor
Vickers, Roy 1889?-1965 *Au&Wr 6,
    EncM&D, MnBBF*
Vickers, Roy C *see* Spencer, John
Vickery, William Paul *MnBBF, WWBWI A*
Victor, Edward 1914- *ConAu 1R, LE 5,
    SmATA 3*
Victor, J *MnBBF*
Victor, Joan Berg 1937- *IlBYP, IlCB 1957*
Victor, Joan Berg *see* Berg, Joan
Viereck, Ellen K 1928- *AuBYP, ConAu 53*
Viereck, Phillip R 1925- *AuBYP, ConAu 5R,
    SmATA 3, WWE 14, WrD*
Viertel, Janet 1915- *ConAu 53, SmATA 10*
Viguers, Ruth Hill 1903-1971 *AuBYP, BiDL 5,
    ChPo, ChPo S1, ConAu 29, ConAu P-1,
    SmATA 6*
Viguers, Ruth Hill *see* Hill, Ruth A
Viksten, Albert 1889- *AuBYP*
Viles, Edward *MnBBF*
Viles, Walter *MnBBF*
Viles, Walter *see* Beaumont, Brenchley
Villiard, Paul 1910-1974 *ConAu 53*
Villiers, Alan John Murray 1903- *Au&Wr 6,
    AuBYP, ConAu 1R, DcLEnL, EvLB,
    IntWW 38, LongC, SingR 1, SmATA 10,
    TwCA, TwCA Sup, TwCW, WNAA,
    WW 1974, WWA 38, WWWor 2*
Villiers, Walter *MnBBF*
Vimar, A 1851-1916 *CarSB*
Vincent, Frank *MnBBF, WWBWI A*
Vincent, Frank *see* Kirkham, Reginald S
Vincent, Joan 1920- *ConAu 21R, WWBWI A*
Vincent, Joan *see* Kirkham, Reginald S
Vincent, Mary Keith *ConAu XR,
    SmATA XR*
Vincent, Mary Keith *see* Saint John, Wylly Folk
Vining, Elizabeth Gray 1902- *AmA&B,
    AuBYP, ConAu 5R, JBA 1951,
    SmATA 6, WWA 38, WWAW 8*
Vining, Elizabeth Gray *see* Gray, Elizabeth Janet
Vinson, Kathryn 1911- *ConAu 5R*
Vinton, Iris *AuBYP, ForWC 1970*
Viorst, Judith *ChLR 3, ConAu 49,*

SmATA 7, WWS 13
Vipont, Charles 1902- ConAu XR, WWCL
Vipont, Charles see Foulds, Elfrida Vipont
Vipont, Charles see Vipont, Elfrida
Vipont, Elfrida 1902- Au&Wr 6, ChPo S1,
    ConAu XR, WWCL
Vipont, Elfrida see Foulds, Elfrida Vipont
Vipont, Elfrida see Vipont, Charles
Viscott, David S 1938- AuNews 1, ConAu 29,
    WrD
Vise, Toye MnBBF
Visser, W F H 1900-1968 ConAu 25R,
    SmATA 10
Vittengl, Morgan John 1928- AuBYP,
    ConAu 5R
Vivian, Evelyn Charles MnBBF
Vlahos, Olivia 1924- ConAu 21R
Vogel, Helen Wolff 1918- ConAu 17R,
    ForWC 1970
Vogel, Ilse-Margaret 1918- ChPo, ConAu 13R
Vogelsinger, Hubert 1938- ConAu 25R,
    WWE 14
Vogt, Esther Loewen 1915 ConAu 17R,
    ForWC 1970, WWAW 8
Vogt, Marie Bollinger 1921- ConAu 57
Voight, Virginia Frances 1909- AuBYP,
    ConAu 5R, MorJA, SmATA 8
Voils, Jessie Wiley 1900- ConAu P-2, WNAA,
    WWAW 8
Volgyes, Ivan 1936- AmMWS 12S
VonAlmedingen, Martha Edith ConAu XR,
    SmATA 3
VonAlmedingen, Martha Edith see Almedingen,
    M E
VonDaeniken, Erich 1935- ConAu 37
VonDaeniken, Erich see VonDaniken, Erich
VonDaniken, Erich 1935- AuNews 1,
    BiN 1975, ConAu XR
VonDaniken, Erich see VonDaeniken, Erich
VonDumzene, Anneliese Freifrau ConICB
VonHagen, Christine AuBYP
VonHagen, Victor Wolfgang 1908- AmA&B,
    Au&Wr 6, AuBYP, CurB 42, REnAL,
    TwCA Sup, WW 1974, WWA 38,
    WWWor 2
VonHoffman, Nicholas 1929- AmA&B,
    CelR 3, WWA 38, WWS 13
VonLewinski, Anneliese Freifrau ConICB
VonSchmidt, Eric 1931- AuBYP, ChPo,
    ConAu 17R, IICB 1957
VonStorch, Anne B 1910- ConAu P-2,
    SmATA 1
VonStorch, Anne B see Malcolmson, Anne
    Elizabeth
Vorspan, Albert 1924- ConAu 21R,
    WWWorJ 1972
Vorwald, Alan AuBYP
Vosburgh, Leonard IlBYP
Voss, Carl Hermann 1910- AmA&B,
    ConAu 21R, WWA 38
Voss, George L 1922- ConAu 57
Voute, Kathleen 1892- IlBYP, IICB 1946
Vox, Maximilien IICB 1744
Voyle, Mary AuBYP, ConAu XR,
    SmATA XR, WorAu
Voyle, Mary see Manning, Rosemary
Vroman, Mary Elizabeth 1923-1967 BlkAW

W

W, S *CarSB*

Waaland, J Robert 1943- *AmMWS 12P*

Wabbes, Maria *IIBYP*

Wabbes, Maria *see* Florence

Waber, Bernard 1924- *AmPB, AuBYP, ConAu 1R, IICB 1957, ThBJA*

Wackerbarth, Marjorie *ConAu 13R, ConAu P-1, MnnWr*

Waddell, Evelyn Margaret 1918- *SmATA 10, WrD*

Waddell, Evelyn Margaret *see* Cook, Lyn

Waddell, Helen Jane 1889-1965 *AnCL, Chambr 3, ChPo S2, DcLEnL, EvLB, LongC, NCHEL, REn, TwCA, TwCA Sup, TwCW*

Waddy, Stacy *MnBBF*

Wade, George Alfred 1863- *MnBBF*

Wade, John Reed *MnBBF*

Wade, Mary Hazelton Blanchard 1860-1936 *AmA&B, AmLY, CarSB, DcAmA, DcNAA, WNAA*

Wadowski-Bak, Alice *IIBYP*

Wadsworth, Wallace Carter 1894-1933 *IndAu 1917, St&VC*

Wagenheim, Kal 1935- *ConAu 29*

Wagenknecht, Edward 1900- *AmA&B, ConAu 1R, DrAS 6E, REn, REnAL, TwCA Sup, WWA 38*

Wagenvoord, James 1937- *ConAu 41*

Wagner, Frederick 1928- *AuBYP, ConAu 5R*

Wagner, Glenn A *AuBYP*

Wagner, Ken 1911- *ConAu 37*

Wagner, Margaret D 1949- *ConAu 5R, ForWC 1970*

Wagner, Margaret D *see* Wagner, Peggy

Wagner, Peggy *ConAu XR*

Wagner, Peggy *see* Wagner, Margaret D

Wagner, Sharon Blythe 1936- *ConAu 25R, SmATA 4, WWAW 8, WrD*

Wagoner, David 1926- *AmA&B, ConAu 1R, ConLC 3, ConLC 5, ConNov 1972, ConNov 1976, ConP 1970, ConP 1975, CrCAP, DrAF 1976, DrAP 1975, WWPNA, WorAu*

Wagoner, Jean Brown 1896- *IndAu 1917*

Wahl, Jan 1933- *AuBYP, ConAu 25R, SmATA 2, ThBJA*

Wahl, Robert 1948- *ConAu 49*

Wahloo, Per 1926-1975 *EncM&D*

Wain, Louis 1861?-1939 *ChPo, ChPo S1, ChPo S2, WWBWI I, WWCL*

Waite, Helen Elmira 1903- *ConAu 1R*

Wakefield, Connie LaVon 1948- *ConAu 65*

Wakefield, George William *WWBWI I*

Wakefield, Priscilla 1750?-1832 *Alli, BiDLA, BrAu 19, CarSB*

Wakefield, Terence *WWBWI I*

Wakeman, Marion Freeman 1891-1953 *IIBYP, IICB 1946*

Wakin, Edward 1927- *ConAu 5R, WWE 14*

Walcott, Fred George 1894- *ConAu 37, DrAS 6E*

Walcutt, Charles Child 1908- *ConAu 1R, DrAS 6E, WrD*

Wald, Carol 1935- *ConAu 65*

Waldeck, Jo Besse McElveen *JBA 1951*

Waldeck, Theodore J 1894- *AuBYP, JBA 1951*

Walden, Amelia Elizabeth 1909- *AuBYP, ConAu 1R, CurB 56, ForWC 1970, MorJA, SmATA 3, WWA 38, WWAW 8, WWE 14, WWWor 2, WrD*

Walden, Howard T, II 1897- *ConAu 45*

Waldman, Frank 1919- *AuBYP*

Waldman, Frank *see* Webster, Joe

Waldrop, W Earl 1910- *ConAu 5R*

Walford, Astrid 1907- *ChPo, IIBYP, IICB 1946*

Walford, Astrid *see* Cumpston, Astrid Kate Oatelaye

Walker, A B *MnBBF*

Walker, Alice 1944- *BlkAW, ConAu 37, ConLC 5, ConLC 6, DrAF 1976, DrAP 1975, LBAA, WWA 38, WWAW 8*

Walker, Barbara K 1921- *ConAu 33, SmATA 4*

Walker, Barbara K *see* Kilreon, Beth

Walker, Braz 1934- *ConAu 69*

Walker, Charles W 1911- *ConAu 17R*

Walker, Charles W *IIBYP*

Walker, Charles W 1911- *WrD*

Walker, David Harry 1911- *CanWW 12, CanWr, CasWL, ConAu 1R, ConNov 1972, ConNov 1976, LongC, OxCan, OxCan Sup, Prof, REnAL, SmATA 8, WW 1974, WWCan 1973, WorAu, WrD*

Walker, Diana 1925- *SmATA 9*

Walker, Dugald Stewart 1888?-1937 *ChPo, ChPo S1, ChPo S2, ConICB, DcNAA*

Walker, Frank 1930- *ConAu 69*

Walker, James Perkins 1829-1868 *Alli, AmA&B, CarSB, DcAmA, DcNAA*

Walker, Kathrine Sorley *AuBYP*
Walker, Martin *MnBBF*
Walker, Mildred 1905- *AmA&B, AmNov, Au&Wr 6, ConAu XR, CurB 47, REnAL, TwCA Sup, WWA 38, WWAW 8, WrD*
Walker, Mildred *see* Schemm, Mildred Walker
Walker, Mort 1923- *ConAu 49, SmATA 8, WWA 38, WWAA 1973, WWE 14, WWWor 2*
Walker, N Bradbury *MnBBF*
Walker, Nedda *IlBYP, IlCB 1946*
Walker, Richard Louis 1922- *AmMWS 12S, ConAu 9R, WWA 38*
Walker, Robert Harris 1924- *ConAu 13R, DrAS 6E*
Walker, Rowland *MnBBF, WWBWI A*
Walker, Rowland *see* Blair, Anthony
Walker, Rowland *see* Kenworthy, Hugh
Walker, Stephen J 1951- *SmATA 12*
Walker, W H *MnBBF*
Walkey, Samuel 1871?-1950? *MnBBF, WWBWI A, WWCL*
Wall, Charles *Alli, CarSB*
Wall, Gertrude Wallace *AuBYP*
Wallace, Alfred *MnBBF*
Wallace, Barbara Brooks *ConAu 29, SmATA 4, WrD*
Wallace, Bill *ConAu XR*
Wallace, Bill *see* Wallace, William N
Wallace, Bryan Edgar *Au&Wr 6, MnBBF, WWBWI A*
Wallace, Carlton *MnBBF*
Wallace, Dillon 1863-1939 *AmA&B, AmLY, CarSB, DcNAA, JBA 1934, JBA 1951, MnBBF, OxCan, REnAL, WNAA*
Wallace, Edgar 1875-1932 *CasWL, DcLEnL, EncM&D, EvLB, LongC, MnBBF, ModBL, NCHEL, OxEng, Pen Eng, REn, TwCA, TwCA Sup, TwCW, WWBWI A, WWTwL*
Wallace, Gordon *MnBBF, WWBWI A*
Wallace, Gordon *see* Shaw, Stanley Gordon
Wallace, John Adam 1915- *AuBYP, ConAu 5R, SmATA 3*
Wallace, Lewis 1827-1905 *Alli Sup, AmA, AmA&B, BbD, BiD&SB, CarSB, CasWL, Chambr 3, ChPo, CnDAL, CyWA, DcAmA, DcBiA, DcEnA Ap, DcLEnL, DcNAA, EvLB, IndAu 1819, JBA 1934, OxAm, Pen Am, RAdv 1, REn, REnAL*
Wallace, Sister M Imelda 1884- *BkC 4*
Wallace, May Nickerson 1902- *AuBYP*
Wallace, Nigel *MnBBF, SmATA XR, WWBWI A*
Wallace, Nigel *see* Hamilton, Charles Harold St. John
Wallace, William N 1924- *ConAu 13R, MnBBF*
Wallace, William N *see* Wallace, Bill
Wallas, Ada Radford d1934 *CarSB, ChPo*
Waller, Leslie 1923- *AmA&B, AmNov, Au&Wr 6, ConAu 1R*
Wallerstedt, Don *IlBYP*
Walley, Clive Phillips *MnBBF*
Wallhauser, Henry T 1930- *ConAu 29*
Wallis, G McDonald *ConAu XR*

Wallis, G McDonald *see* Campbell, Hope
Wallis, George C *MnBBF*
Wallis, George C *see* Stanton, John
Wallner, John C 1945- *SmATA 10*
Wallower, Lucille *AuBYP, BiDL 5, ConAu 21R, SmATA 11, WWAW 8, WrD*
Walmsley, Leo 1892-1966 *ConAu P-1, DcLEnL, LongC, NCHEL, TwCA, TwCA Sup, TwCW*
Walpole, Sir Hugh Seymour 1884-1941 *CasWL, Chambr 3, ChPo S2, CurB 41, CyWA, DcBiA, DcLEnL, EvLB, LongC, MnBBF, ModBL, NCHEL, OxEng, Pen Eng, REn, TwCA, TwCA Sup, TwCW, WEAL, WWCL, WWBWI A, WWLA, WWTwL*
Walser, Richard 1908- *ConAu 5R, DrAS 6E*
Walsh, Chad 1914- *AmA&B, Au&Wr 6, ConAu 1R, ConP 1970, ConP 1975, CurB 62, DrAP 1975, DrAS 6E, WWA 38, WorAu, WrD*
Walsh, Frances Waggener *AuBYP, ChPo*
Walsh, George Ethelbert *CurB 41, MnBBF*
Walsh, Gillian Paton 1939- *ConAu 37*
Walsh, Gillian Paton *see* Walsh, Jill Paton
Walsh, Jill Paton 1939- *ChLR 2, ConAu XR, SmATA 4*
Walsh, Jill Paton *see* Paton Walsh, Jill
Walsh, Jill Paton *see* Walsh, Gillian Paton
Walsh, John 1927- *ConAu 17R*
Walsh, Richard John 1886-1960 *AmA&B, AuBYP*
Walshe, Douglas *MnBBF*
Walshe, Douglas *see* Carr, Adams
Walter, Frances *IlBYP*
Walter, Nina Willis 1900- *ConAu 5R, ForWC 1970, WrD*
Walter, Villiam Christian *YABC 1*
Walter, Villiam Christian *see* Andersen, Hans Christian
Walters, Audrey *IlBYP*
Walters, Hugh *AuBYP*
Walters, J *MnBBF*
Walters, J *see* Owen, Norman
Walters, Leonard *MnBBF*
Walters, Marguerite *AuBYP*
Walters, T B *WWBWI A*
Walters, T B *see* Rowe, John Gabriel
Walters, Thomas N 1935- *ConAu 65, DrAP 1975*
Walters, W G *MnBBF*
Walters, W G *see* Steffens, Arthur
Waltner, Elma 1912- *AuBYP, ConAu 17R, ForWC 1970*
Waltner, Willard *AuBYP*
Walton, Bryce 1918- *ConAu 21R*
Walton, Cecile 1891- *ChPo, IlCB 1744*
Walton, Elizabeth Cheatham *ConAu 5R, ForWC 1970, WrD*
Walton, Izaak 1593-1683 *Alli, AtlBL, BbD, BiD&SB, BrAu, CarSB, Chambr 1, CrE&SL, CyWA, DcEnA, DcEnL, DcEuL, DcLEnL, EvLB, NCHEL, OxEng, Pen Eng, REn, WEAL*
Walton, L L *MnBBF*
Walton, Mrs. Octavius Frank *WWCL*
Walton, Richard J 1928- *ConAu 25R, OxCan Sup, SmATA 4*
Walton, Robin *MnBBF*

Waltrip, Lela 1904- *BkCL, ConAu 5R, SmATA 9*
Waltrip, Mildred 1911- *IlBYP*
Waltrip, Rufus 1898- *BkCL, ConAu 5R, SmATA 9*
Walworth, Jane *IlBYP*
Walworth, Nancy Zinsser 1917- *ConAu 5R*
Wangle, Captain *MnBBF*
Warbler, J M *ConAu XR, SmATA 7*
Warbler, J M *see* Cocagnac, Augustin Maurice
Warburg, Sandol Stoddard 1927- *AuBYP, BkP, ChPo S1, ConAu 5R, ForWC 1970*
Ward, Arthur Sarsfield 1883?-1959 *EncM&D, EvLB, LongC, MnBBF, Pen Eng, WWBWI A*
Ward, Arthur Sarsfield *see* Rohmer, Sax
Ward, Bill G *WWBWI I*
Ward, Bill G *see* Ward, William G
Ward, Colin 1924- *ConAu 57*
Ward, Don 1911- *ConAu 17R*
Ward, Elizabeth Honor 1926- *Au&Wr 6, ConAu 9R, WrD*
Ward, Evelyn *WWCL*
Ward, Evelyn *see* Everett-Green, Evelyn
Ward, G Whiteley *MnBBF*
Ward, Herbert *MnBBF*
Ward, Herman Matthew 1914- *ChPo, ConAu 5R, DrAS 6E*
Ward, John 1917- *IlBYP, IICB 1946*
Ward, Leighton *MnBBF*
Ward, Lynd Kendall 1905- *AmA&B, Au&ICB, AuBYP, BkP, Cald 1938, ChPo, ChPo S2, ConAu 17R, ConICB, IlBYP, IICB 1744, IICB 1946, IICB 1957, JBA 1934, JBA 1951, SmATA 2, St&VC, WWA 38, WrD*
Ward, Martha Eads 1921- *BiDL 5, ConAu 17R, SmATA 5, WWAW 8*
Ward, Mary Augusta 1851-1920 *Alli Sup, CarSB, DcBiA, DcEnA, DcEnA Ap, DcLEnL, EvLB, OxEng, TwCA, TwCA Sup*
Ward, May McNeer *Au&ICB*
Ward, May McNeer *see* McNeer, Mat Yonge
Ward, Nanda Weedon 1932- *AuBYP*
Ward, Ralph T 1927- *ConAu 49*
Ward, William G 1929- *ConAu 21R, WWMW 14*
Ward, William G *see* Ward, Bill G
Ward-Thomas, Evelyn Bridget Patricia 1928- *ConAu 9R*
Ward-Thomas, Evelyn Bridget Patricia *see* Anthony, Evelyn
Wardell, Phyl 1909- *ConAu 9R*
Ware, Jean 1914- *ConAu P-1, WrD*
Ware, Leon Vernon 1909- *AuBYP, ConAu 1R, SmATA 4*
Warmke, Roman Francis 1929- *ConAu 17R, LE 5, WWMW 14*
Warner, Anna Bartlett 1827?-1915 *Alli, Alli Sup, AmA, AmA&B, BiD&SB, CarSB, ChPo, ChPo S1, BiD&SB, CyAL 2, DcAmA, DcEnL, DcLEnL, DcNAA, REnAL*
Warner, Edythe Records 1916- *ConAu 5R, IICB 1957*
Warner, Frank A *ConAu P-2, SmATA 1*
Warner, Frank A *see* Stratemeyer, Edward L
Warner, Gary 1936- *ConAu 21R*

Warner, Gertrude Chandler 1890- *AmA&B, AuBYP, ConAu 1R, ForWC 1970, SmATA 9, WNAA*
Warner, Lucille Schulberg *ConAu 69*
Warner, Matt *ConAu XR*
Warner, Matt *see* Fichter, George S
Warner, Oliver 1903- *Au&Wr 6, ConAu 1R, LongC, OxCan Sup, WW 1974*
Warner, Peter 1939- *IICB 1957*
Warner, Priscilla Mary 1905- *IICB 1946*
Warner, Rex 1905- *ChPo, ChPo S1, ConNov 1972, ConNov 1976, ConP 1970, ConP 1975, DcLEnL, IntWW 38, LongC, ModBL, NCHEL, Pen Eng, REn, TwCA, TwCA Sup, TwCW, WEAL, WW 1974*
Warner, Susan Bogert 1819-1885 *Alli, Alli Sup, AmA, AmA&B, BbD, BiD&SB, CarSB, Chambr 3, ChPo, ChPo S1, ChPo S2, CyAL 2, DcAmA, DcBiA, DcEnL, DcLEnL, DcNAA, EvLB, OxAm, REnAL, WWCL*
Warner, Susan Bogert *see* Wetherell, Elizabeth
Warren, Betsy *ConAu XR*
Warren, Betsy *see* Warren, Elizabeth Avery
Warren, Billy *AuBYP, ConAu XR, SmATA XR*
Warren, Billy *see* Warren, William Stephen
Warren, Elizabeth *ConAu XR*
Warren, Elizabeth *see* Supraner, Robyn
Warren, Elizabeth Avery 1916- *ConAu 5R*
Warren, Elizabeth Avery *see* Warren, Betsy
Warren, Francis H 1886-1960 *WWBWI I*
Warren, George A *CarSB*
Warren, John Russell 1886- *MnBBF*
Warren, Mary Crowninshield *CarSB*
Warren, Mary Phraner 1929- *ConAu 53, SmATA 10*
Warren, Maude Lavinia Radford 1875-1934 *AmA&B, CarSB, DcNAA*
Warren, Nathan Boughton 1815?-1898 *Alli, CarSB, CyAL 2, DcAmA, DcNAA*
Warren, Robert Penn 1905- *AmA&B, AmNov, AmWr, Au&Wr 6, AuNews 1, CasWL, CnDAL, CnE&AP, CnMD, ConAmA, ConAu 13R, ConLC 1, ConLC 4, ConLC 6, ConNov 1972, ConNov 1976, ConP 1970, ConP 1975, CurB 70, CyWA, DcLEnL, DrAF 1976, DrAP 1975, EncWL, EvLB, IntWW 38, LongC, ModAL, ModAL Sup, ModWD, OxAm, Pen Am, RAdv 1, RCom, REn, REnAL, SixAP, TwCA, TwCA Sup, WEAL, WNAA, WW 1974, WWA 38, WWTwL, WWWor 2*
Warren, William Stephen 1882-1968 *AuBYP, ConAu P-2, SmATA 9*
Warren, William Stephen *see* Warren, Billy
Warri, K *MnBBF*
Warrick, Patricia Scott 1925- *ConAu 61*
Warshaw, Jerry 1929- *ConAu 37*
Warshofsky, Fred 1931- *ConAu 9R, WWE 14*
Warshofsky, Isaac *ConAu XR, SmATA 3*
Warshofsky, Isaac *see* Singer, Isaac Bashevis
Warwick, Alan Ross *MnBBF, WWBWI A*
Warwick, Alan Ross *see* Ross, Alan
Warwick, Alan Ross *see* Sidney, Frank
Warwick, Alan Ross *see* Sydney, Frank
Warwick, Clifford *WWBWI A*

Warwick, Clifford *see* Gibbons, Harry Hornaby
   Clifford
Warwick, Dolores *ConAu XR*
Warwick, Dolores *see* Frese, Dolores Warwick
Warwick, Francis Alister *MnBBF,*
   WWBWI A
Warwick, Francis Alister *see* Clifford, Martin
Warwick, Francis Alister *see* Jardine, Warwick
Warwick, Francis Alister *see* Sidney, Frank
Warwick, Francis Alister *see* Spencer, Roland
Warwick, Francis Alister *see* Sydney, Frank
Warwick, Sidney 1870-1953 *MnBBF,*
   WWBWI A
Warwick, Sidney *see* Drayson, A W
Warwick, Sidney *see* Sidney, Frank
Warwick, Sidney *see* Sydney, Frank
Warwick, Stanley *ConAu XR*
Washburn, Bradford 1910- *ConAu 49*
Washburne, Heluiz Chandler 1892- *AmA&B,*
   Au&Wr 6, AuBYP, ConAu P-1, OhA&B,
   SmATA 10, WNAA
Washington, Booker Taliaferro 1856-1915
   AmA&B, BiD&SB, BiDSA, BlkAW,
   CasWL, Chambr 3, DcAmA, DcLEnL,
   DcNAA, LongC, OxAm, OxEng,
   Pen Am, REn, REnAL, WEAL
Wasserman, Burton 1929- *WWAA 1973,*
   WWE 14
Wasserman, Selma 1929- *ConAu 5R*
Wassersug, Joseph David 1912- *AuBYP,*
   ConAu 17R, WWWorJ 1972
Wassersug, Joseph David *see* Bradford, Adam, M
   D
Waterhouse, Charles 1924- *ConAu 29*
Waters, Eddie *MnBBF*
Waters, Eddie *see* Fryars, Austin
Waters, John Frederick 1930- *ConAu 37,*
   SmATA 4, WrD
Waters, Sheila *IlBYP*
Watkins-Pitchford, Denys James 1905-
   Au&Wr 6, ChPo Sl, ConAu 9R,
   IlCB 1946, SmATA 6, ThBJA, WWCL,
   WrD
Watkins-Pitchford, Denys James *see* B B
Watkins-Pitchford, Denys James *see* Traherne,
   Michael
Watson, Aldren Auld 1917- *ChPo, ChPo S2,*
   ForIl, IlBYP, IlCB 1744, IlCB 1946,
   IlCB 1957, WWAA 1973
Watson, Clyde 1947- *ChLR 3, ChPo S2,*
   ConAu 49, SmATA 5, WrD
Watson, Emily *AuBYP*
Watson, Frederick 1871- *MnBBF,*
   WWBWI A
Watson, Frederick *see* Porter, Frederick
Watson, H B Marriott 1863-1921 *Alli Sup,*
   CarSB, Chambr 3, LongC, NCHEL
Watson, Helen Orr 1892- *AmA&B, AuBYP,*
   ConAu 5R
Watson, Henry Clay 1831-1869 *Alli, AmA&B,*
   BbD, BiD&SB, BiDSA, CarSB, ChPo,
   DcAmA, DcNAA
Watson, Howard N *IlBYP*
Watson, Ina *SingR 1*
Watson, James 1936- *Au&Wr 6, ConAu 53,*
   SmATA 10, WrD
Watson, Jane Werner 1915- *ConAu 5R,*
   SmATA 3
Watson, Jane Werner *see* Bedford, A N

Watson, Jane Werner *see* Bedford, Annie North
Watson, Jane Werner *see* Hill, Monica
Watson, Jane Werner *see* Nast, Elsa Ruth
Watson, Jane Werner *see* Werner, Jane
Watson, Julia 1943- *Au&Wr 6, ConAu 41,*
   WrD
Watson, Lyall 1939- *ConAu 57*
Watson, Matt *MnBBF*
Watson, Nancy Dingman *ConAu 49*
Watson, Pauline 1925- *ConAu 69*
Watson, Philip *MnBBF*
Watson, Saint John *MnBBF*
Watson, Saint John *see* Clarke, Percy A
Watson, Sally 1924- *ConAu 5R, SmATA 3*
Watson, Sara Ruth 1907- *AuBYP, ConAu 37,*
   DrAS 6E
Watson, Spencer *MnBBF*
Watson, T C *MnBBF*
Watson, Wendy 1942- *ChPo Sl, ChPo S2,*
   ConAu 49, IlBYP, SmATA 5
Watson, Sir William 1858-1935 *AnCL, BbD,*
   BiD&SB, Chambr 3, ChPo Sl, ChPo S2,
   DcEnA, DcEnA Ap, DcLEnL, EvLB,
   LongC, ModBL, NCHEL, OxEng,
   Pen Eng, TwCA, TwCA Sup
Watt, J E *MnBBF*
Watt, Thomas 1935- *ConAu 37, SmATA 4*
Watts, Bernadette 1942- *ChPo Sl, ConAu 29,*
   IlBYP, SmATA 4
Watts, Bernadette *see* Bernadette
Watts, Franklin 1904- *Au&Wr 6, ConAu P-2*
Watts, Isaac 1674-1748 *Alli, Alli Sup, AnCL,*
   BbD, BiD&SB, BrAu, CarSB, CasWL,
   Chambr 2, ChPo, ChPo Sl, ChPo S2,
   CnE&AP, DcEnA, DcEnL, DcEuL,
   DcLEnL, EvLB, NCHEL, OxEng,
   Pen Eng, PoCh, REn, St&VC, WEAL
Watts, John Francis 1926-. *Au&Wr 6,*
   ConAu 25R
Watts, John Francis *WrD*
Watts, Mabel Pizzey 1906- *AuBYP, ChPo Sl,*
   ConAu 1R, ForWC 1970, SmATA 11,
   WrD
Watts, Mabel Pizzey *see* Lynn, Patricia
Watts, May Theilgaard 1893- *ConAu 41*
Watts, Peter Christopher 1919- *ConAu 69*
Watts, Peter Christopher *see* Chisholm, Matt
Watts, Peter Christopher *see* James, Cy
Watts, Peter Christopher *see* Mackinlock,
   Duncan
Watts, Peter Christopher *see* Owen, Tom
Watts-Phillips, E *MnBBF*
Waud, Elizabeth *ConAu XR*
Waud, Elizabeth *see* Tattersall, M
Waugh, Alec 1898- *Au&Wr 6, ConAu XR,*
   ConNov 1976, DcLEnL, IntWW 38,
   LongC, ModBL, NCHEL, RAdv 1, REn,
   TwCA, TwCA Sup, TwCW, WW 1974,
   WWBWI A, WWWor 2
Waugh, Alexander Raban 1898- *ConAu 17R,*
   EvLB, MnBBF, Pen Eng
Waugh, Dorothy 1896- *AmPB, Au&Wr 6,*
   ConAu 1R, IlCB 1744, IlCB 1946,
   SmATA 11, WNAA
Way, H J *MnBBF*
Wayland, Patrick *ConAu XR*
Wayland, Patrick *see* O'Connor, Richard
Wayman, Vivienne *WrD*
Wayne, Donald 1913- *ConAu XR, WWA 38,*

WWWor 2
Wayne, Donald *see* Dodd, Wayne D
Wayne, Jenifer 1917- *Au&Wr 6*
Wayne, Kyra Petrovskaya 1918- *ConAu XR,*
SmATA 8
Wayne, Kyra Petrovskaya *see* Petrovskaya, Kyra
Wayne, Richard *AuBYP, ConAu XR,*
MnBBF, SmATA 5
Wayne, Richard *see* Decker, Duane
Weafer, Elizabeth *CurB 58*
Weales, Gerald 1925- *BiEnAT, ConAu 5R,*
SmATA 11
Weart, Edith Lucie 1898?-1977 *AuBYP,*
ConAu 69
Weary, Ogdred *ConAu XR*
Weary, Ogdred *see* Gorey, Edward St. John
Weatherbee, Donald E 1932- *AmMWS 12S*
Weaver, Jack 1925- *IIBYP, IICB 1946*
Weaver, John Downing 1912- *AmA&B,*
AmNov, AuBYP, ConAu 9R
Weaver, Robert Glenn 1920- *DrAS 6E, IIBYP*
Weaver, Ward *AmNov X, AuBYP,*
ConAu XR, SmATA 3
Weaver, Ward *see* Mason, F VanWyck
Webb, Cecil S *AuBYP*
Webb, Christopher *EncM&D, SmATA 2*
Webb, Christopher *see* Wibberley, Leonard
Webb, Clifford Cyril 1895- *AuBYP, ChPo S1,*
IICB 1744, IICB 1946, IICB 1957
Webb, Francoise *IIBYP*
Webb, Harry *MnBBF*
Webb, Jean Francis 1910- *ConAu 5R*
Webb, Jean Francis *see* Hamill, Ethel
Webb, Marion St. John 1890-1930 *ChPo S1,*
ChPo S2, WWCL, WWLA
Webb, Nancy 1915- *ConAu 1R*
Webb, Robert N *AuBYP*
Webb, Ruth Enid Borlase Morris 1926-
Au&Wr 6, ConAu 9R, WrD
Webb, Ruth Enid Borlase Morris *see* Morris,
Ruth
Webb, T C P *MnBBF*
Webb, W S K *MnBBF, WWBWI A*
Webb, Walter Prescott 1888-1963 *AmA&B,*
OxAm, REnAL, TexW
Webber, Irma Eleanor Schmidt 1904-
AmMWS 12P, AmPB, ConAu 69, IIBYP,
IICB 1744, IICB 1946
Webber, Stawford *MnBBF, WWBWI A*
Webber, Stawford *see* Pile, D W
Webber, Stawford *see* Tremellan, Wilfred
Weber, Alfons 1921- *AmMWS 12P,*
ConAu 29, SmATA 8, WWA 38
Weber, Alice *CarSB*
Weber, Lenora Mattingly 1895-1971 *AmA&B,*
AuBYP, BkC 3, ConAu 29, ConAu P-1,
MorJA, SmATA 2
Weber, Walter Alois 1906- *IICB 1744*
Weber, William John 1927- *ConAu 69*
Webster, David 1930- *ConAu 29, SmATA 11*
Webster, Frank V *CarSB, ConAu P-2,*
SmATA 1
Webster, Frank V *see* Stratemeyer, Edward L
Webster, Frederick Annesley Mic 1886- *MnBBF*
Webster, Gary *ConAu XR*
Webster, Gary *see* Garrison, Webb B
Webster, Jean 1876-1916 *AmA&B, CarSB,*
ChPo, CnDAL, DcNAA, EvLB,
JBA 1934, LongC, OxAm, REn, REnAL,

TwCA, TwCW, WWCL
Webster, Joe *AuBYP*
Webster, Joe *see* Waldman, Frank
Webster, Ronald *MnBBF*
Wechsberg, Joseph 1907- *AmA&B, Au&Wr 6,*
CurB 55, OxAm, REnAL, WWA 38,
WWMus 6, WWWor 2
Wechsler, Herman J 1904-1976 *ConAu 65,*
WWAA 1973
Wechter, Nell Wise 1913- *ConAu 57*
Weddle, Ethel Harshbarger 1897- *AuBYP,*
ConAu 9R, ForWC 1970, SmATA 11
Weddle, Ferris 1922- *ConAu 17R*
Wedel, Leonard E 1909- *ConAu 21R*
Wedgewood, Eric *MnBBF*
Wedgwood, Cicely Veronica 1910- *DcLEnL,*
IntWW 38, LongC, ModBL, REn,
WW 1974, WWA 38, WWWor 2
Weekes-Wylde, Oliver *MnBBF*
Weeks, Thelma E 1921- *ConAu 57*
Weems, John Edward 1924- *ConAu 1R*
Wees, Frances Shelley 1902- *AuBYP,*
CanWW 12, CanWr, ConAu 5R,
ForWC 1970
Wegner, Fritz 1924- *ChPo S2, IIBYP,*
IICB 1946
Wehen, Joy DeWeese 1926- *AuBYP,*
ConAu 5R, WrD
Weik, Mary Hays 1898- *ConAu 21R,*
IndAu 1917, MorBMP, SmATA 3,
WWA 38
Weil, Ann Yezner 1908-1969 *ConAu 5R,*
IndAu 1917, SmATA 9
Weil, Lisl 1910- *ConAu 49, CurB 58, IIBYP,*
IICB 1946, IICB 1957, SmATA 7,
WWA 38
Weilerstein, Sadie Rose 1894- *ConAu 5R,*
SmATA 3, WWWorJ 1972
Weinberger, Betty Kiralfy 1932- *ConAu 65*
Weiner, Sandra 1922- *ConAu 49*
Weingarten, Violet 1915- *ConAu 9R,*
SmATA 3
Weingartner, Charles 1922- *ConAu 49,*
DrAS 6E, LE 5, SmATA 5
Weingast, David E 1912- *AuBYP, ConAu 5R*
Weinheimer, George *IIBYP*
Weinstock, Herbert 1905-1971 *AmA&B,*
AuBYP, ConAu 1R, ConAu 33,
NYTBE 2
Weir, LaVada *ConAu 21R, SmATA 2, WrD*
Weir, Rosemary 1905- *Au&Wr 6, AuBYP,*
ConAu 13R
Weisberger, Bernard A 1922- *ConAu 5R,*
DrAS 6H
Weisgard, Leonard Joseph 1916- *AmPB,*
AuBYP, BkP, Cald 1938, ChPo,
ChPo S1, ConAu 9R, IIBYP, IICB 1744,
IICB 1946, IICB 1957, JBA 1951,
REnAL, SmATA 2, WWAA 1973
Weisgard, Leonard Joseph *see* Green, Adam
Weisheit, Eldon 1933- *ConAu 29*
Weiss, Ann E 1943- *ConAu 45*
Weiss, Elizabeth S 1944- *ConAu 61*
Weiss, Emil 1896-1965 *IIBYP, IICB 1957*
Weiss, Harvey 1922- *AuBYP, ConAu 5R,*
IICB 1946, IICB 1957, SmATA 1,
ThBJA, WWAA 1973
Weiss, Leatie 1928- *ConAu 65*
Weiss, Malcolm Earl 1928- *ConAu 25R,*

SmATA 3, WWE 14

Weiss, Miriam 1919- *BiDL 5, ConAu XR, SmATA 2*

Weiss, Miriam *see* Schlein, Miriam

Weiss, Peter 1916- *ConAu 45, CurB 68, IntWW 38, WW 1974, WWT 15, WWWor 2*

Weiss, Renee Karol 1923- *ConAu 41, SmATA 5, WWAW 8*

Weitz, Joseph Leonard 1922- *AmMWS 12P*

Weitzman, Alan 1933- *ConAu 29*

Welch, Ann Courtenay Edmonds 1917- *Au&Wr 6, ConAu 9R, WrD*

Welch, Jean-Louise *ConAu XR, SmATA XR*

Welch, Jean-Louise *see* Kempton, Jean Welch

Welch, June Rayfield 1927- *ConAu 41*

Welch, Mary Scott Stewart *WWAW 8*

Welch, Pauline *ConAu XR, SmATA XR*

Welch, Pauline *see* Bodenham, Hilda Esther

Welch, Ronald *ConAu XR, SmATA 3, WWCL*

Welch, Ronald *see* Felton, Ronlad Oliver

Welcher, Rosalind 1922- *ConAu 45, WWAW 8, WrD*

Weldon, Martin 1913- *AuBYP*

Weldon, Pat *MnBBF*

Weller, George 1907- *ConAu 65*

Welles, Samuel Paul 1907- *WrD, WWA 38*

Welles, Winifred 1893-1939 *AmA&B, AnMV 1926, BkCL, ChPo, ChPo S1, ConAmA, REnAL, St&VC*

Wellman, Henry Q 1945- *ConAu 37*

Wellman, Manly Wade 1903- *AuBYP, ConAu 1R, CurB 55, EncM&D, MorJA, SmATA 6*

Wellman, Paul Iselin 1898-1966 *AmA&B, AmNov, Au&Wr 6, AuBYP, ConAu 1R, ConAu 25R, SmATA 3, REn, REnAL, TwCA Sup*

Wells, Ann *SingR 2*

Wells, Carolyn 1869?-1942 *AmA&B, AmLY, BiD&SB, CarSB, ChPo, ChPo S1, ChPo S2, CurB 42, DcAmA, DcNAA, EncM&D, EvLB, REn, REnAL, TwCA, TwCW, WNAA*

Wells, Evelyn *ConAu 53*

Wells, H G 1866-1946 *AtlBL, BbD, BiD&SB, CnMWL, CyWA, EncM&D, LongC, ModBL, ModBL Sup, NCHEL, Pen Eng, RAdv 1, RCom, REn, TwCW, WEAL, WWTwL*

Wells, H G *see* Wells, Herbert George

Wells, Harford *MnBBF*

Wells, Helen 1910- *AuBYP, ConAu 29, SmATA 2, WWAW 8, WrD*

Wells, Helen *see* Lewis, Francine

Wells, Herbert George 1866-1946 *CasWL, Chambr 3, CurB 46, DcBiA, DcEnA Ap, DcLEnL, EncWL, EvLB, MnBBF, OxEng, TwCA, TwCA Sup, WWBWI A, WWLA*

Wells, Herbert George *see* Wells, H G

Wells, J Wellington *ConAu XR, SmATA XR*

Wells, J Wellington *see* DeCamp, L Sprague

Wells, Maie Lounsbury *AuBYP*

Wells, Peter 1912- *CurB 42, IlCB 1744*

Wells, Rhea 1891- *AmA&B, ConICB, IlCB 1744, JBA 1934, JBA 1951*

Wells, Robert L 1913- *AuBYP*

Wells, Rosemary *ChPo S1, ChPo S2, IlBYP*

Wells, William *MnBBF*

Wels, Byron G 1924- *ConAu 61, SmATA 9*

Welty, Eudora 1909- *AmA&B, AmNov, AmWr, CasWL, CelR 3, ChPo, CnDAL, ConAu 9R, ConLC 1, ConLC 2, ConLC 5, ConNov 1972, ConNov 1976, CurB 42, CyWA, DrAF 1976, EncWL, IntWW 38, LongC, ModAL, ModAL Sup, OxAm, Pen Am, RAdv 1, REn, REnAL, TwCA Sup, WEAL, WW 1974, WWA 38, WWAW 8, WWTwL, WWWor 2, WrD*

Welty, S F *ConAu XR, SmATA XR*

Welty, S F *see* Welty, Susan F

Welty, Susan F 1905- *ConAu P-2, SmATA 9*

Welty, Susan F *see* Welty, S F

Wende, Philip 1939- *ConAu 29, IlBYP*

Wender, Dorothea 1934- *ConAu 45*

Wennerstrom, Genia Katherine 1930- *IlBYP, IlCB 1957*

Wennerstrom, Genia Katherine *see* Genia

Wenning, Elizabeth *AuBYP*

Went, Frits W 1903- *IntWW 38*

Wentworth, Charles *HsB&A, MnBBF, WWBWI A*

Wentworth, Charles *see* Bradley, Albert W

Wentworth, Charles *see* Clarke, Percy A

Wentworth, Charles *see* Shute, Walter

Wentworth, Charles *see* Steffens, Arthur

Wentworth, Herbert *MnBBF, WWBWI A*

Wentworth, Herbert *see* James, Herbert Wentworth

Wernecke, Herbert Henry 1895- *AuBYP, ConAu 5R*

Werner, Jane *ChPo, ConAu XR, SmATA 3*

Werner, Jane *see* Watson, Jane Werner

Werner, K *ConAu XR, SmATA 4*

Werner, K *see* Casewit, Curtis

Werner, Pat *AuBYP*

Werner, Victor 1894- *ConAu 29*

Wersba, Barbara 1932- *AuBYP, ChLR 3, ConAu 29, SmATA 1, ThBJA*

Werstein, Irving 1914?-1971 *AuBYP, ConAu 29, NYTBE 2*

Werth, Kurt 1896- *ChPo, ChPo S1, ChPo S2, IlBYP, IlCB 1946, IlCB 1957, MorJA, WWAA 1973*

Wescombe, Charles *MnBBF*

Wescombe, Charles *see* Carr, Gordon

Wesley, Mary 1912- *ConAu 49*

West, Anthony 1914- *AmA&B, Au&Wr 6, ConAu 45, ConNov 1972, ConNov 1976, LongC, ModBL, NCHEL, REn, TwCA Sup*

West, Avonmore *MnBBF*

West, Barbara *ConAu XR, SmATA 8*

West, Barbara *see* Price, Olive

West, Betty 1921- *Au&Wr 6, AuBYP, ConAu 5R, SmATA 11*

West, Betty *see* Bowen, Betty Morgan

West, Edgar *MnBBF, WWBWI A*

West, Edgar *see* Bayfield, William John

West, Edgar *see* Carr, Gordon

West, Emily *AuBYP*

West, Emily *see* Payne, Emmy

West, Fred 1918- *ConAu 5R*

West, James *AuBYP*

West, James *see* Withers, Carl

West, Jerry *ConAu XR, SmATA 2*
West, Jerry *see* Stratemeyer, Edward L
West, Jerry *see* Svenson, Andrew E
West, Jerry 1938- *CelR 3, NYTBS 5,*
    WWA 38
West, Jessamyn 1907- *ChPo, ConAu 9R,*
    ConNov 1972, ConNov 1976, DrAF 1976,
    IndAu 1917, OxAm, REnAL, TwCA Sup,
    WWA 38
West, John *MnBBF, WWBWI A*
West, John *see* Pentelow, John Nix
West, Marvin 1879-1917 *CarSB, DcNAA*
West, Mary *WWBWI A*
West, Mary *see* Rochester, George Ernest
West, Montague *MnBBF*
West, Paul 1930- *AmA&B, ChPo,*
    ConAu 13R, ConNov 1972, ConNov 1976,
    DrAF 1976, WorAu
West, Peter *MnBBF*
West, Walter Richard 1912- *IIBYP,*
    IICB 1946
West, Ward *AmA&B, ConAu XR,*
    SmATA 5, WorAu
West, Ward *see* Borland, Hal
Westell, William *MnBBF*
Westerberg, Christine 1950- *ConAu 61*
Westerman, J F C *MnBBF, WWBWI A*
Westerman, Percy Francis 1876-1960? *MnBBF,*
    WWBWI A, WWCL
Western, Barry *MnBBF*
Western, Barry *see* Evans, Gwyn
Westervelt, Virginia Veeder 1914- *ConAu 61,*
    SmATA 10, WWAW 8
Westmacott, Bernard 1887- *ConICB*
Westmacott, Mary *ConAu XR, EncM&D,*
    EvLB, LongC, TwCA Sup
Westmoreland, Lesley *SingR 2*
Weston, Cedric *MnBBF*
Weston, G A *MnBBF*
Weston, John 1932- *ConAu 17R*
Westover, Russ 1896-1966 *ArtCS*
Westphal, Barbara Osborne 1907- *ConAu P-1,*
    WWAW 8
Westphal, Clarence 1904- *ConAu 17R*
Westwood, Gwen 1915- *ConAu 25R, WrD*
Westwood, Jennifer 1940- *ConAu 65,*
    SmATA 10
Wetherby, John *MnBBF*
Wetherell, Elizabeth 1819?-1885 *Alli, AmA,*
    AmA&B, BiD&SB, Chambr 3, ChPo S1,
    DcAmA, DcEnL, EvLB, OxAm, REnAL,
    WWCL
Wetherell, Elizabeth *see* Warner, Susan Bogert
Weygant, Sister Noemi *AuBYP, ConAu 45,*
    MorBMP
Weyman, Louis *MnBBF*
Weyman, Stanley John 1855-1928 *BbD,*
    BiD&SB, CarSB, Chambr 3, DcBiA,
    DcLEnL, EvLB, LongC, NCHEL,
    OxEng, TelT, TwCA
Whadcoat, Gordon Cuming 1873- *MnBBF*
Whalen, Philip 1923- *ConAu 9R, WrD*
Whalley, George H *MnBBF*
Wheatcroft, John 1925- *ConAu 37*
Wheelan, Ed 1888- *ArtCS*
Wheeler, Captain *Alli, HsB&A, HsB&A Sup,*
    YABC 1
Wheeler, Captain *see* Ellis, Edward S
Wheeler, Edmund L *MnBBF*

Wheeler, Francis W Rolt- *JBA 1934,*
    JBA 1951
Wheeler, Francis W Rolt *see* Rolt-Wheeler,
    Francis W
Wheeler, Harvey 1918- *AmMWS 12S,*
    ConAu 45
Wheeler, Janet D *CarSB, ConAu P-2,*
    SmATA 1
Wheeler, Janet D *see* Stratemeyer, Edward L
Wheeler, Keith 1911- *ConAu 5R*
Wheeler, Molly 1920- *ConAu 29, WrD*
Wheeler, Sir Mortimer 1890- *CurB 56,*
    IntWW 38, LongC, WW 1974,
    WWWor 2
Wheeler, Opal 1898- *ChPo S1, ChPo S2,*
    MorJA
Wheeler, Paul 1934- *Au&Wr 6, ConAu 25R*
Wheeler, Penny Estes 1943- *ConAu 33*
Wheeler, Post 1869-1956 *AmA&B, AmLY,*
    AnCL, AuBYP, DcAmA, REnAL,
    WNAA
Wheeler, Sessions S *AuBYP, ConAu 17R*
Wheelhouse, M V *ConICB, IICB 1744*
Wheeling, Lynn *AuBYP*
Wheelock, John Hall 1886- *AmA&B, AmLY,*
    AnMV 1926, Au&Wr 6, ChPo, ChPo S1,
    ChPo S2, CnDAL, ConAmA, ConAmL,
    ConAu 13R, ConP 1970, ConP 1975,
    DcLEnL, DrAP 1975, IntWW 38,
    ModAL, OxAm, RAdv 1, REn, REnAL,
    TwCA, TwCA Sup, WNAA, WWA 38,
    WWWor 2
Wheelright, John Tyler 1856-1925 *CarSB*
Wheelwright, Jere Hungerford, Jr. 1905?-1961
    AmA&B, AuBYP
Whempner, Verna Huber *MnnWr*
Wheway, John W *MnBBF, WWBWI A*
Wheway, John W *see* Armitage, Vincent
Whipple, Chandler 1905- *ConAu 25R*
Whishaw, Fred *MnBBF, WWBWI A*
Whistler, John *MnBBF*
Whistler, Theresa 1927- *IICB 1946*
Whitaker, David 1930- *ConAu 21R*
Whitaker, Evelyn *CarSB*
Whitaker, George O *AuBYP*
Whitcomb, Jon 1906- *ConAu 13R,*
    ConAu P-1, SmATA 10, WWA 38,
    WWAA 1973
White, Alan *Au&Wr 6, ConAu 45*
White, Alice Violet 1922- *Au&Wr 6,*
    ConAu 61
White, Anne Terry 1896- *AuBYP, ConAu 9R,*
    MorJA, SmATA 2
White, Antonia 1899- *Au&Wr 6, BkC 5,*
    CatA 1952, ConNov 1972, ConNov 1976,
    LongC, NCHEL, REn, WW 1974,
    WorAu, WrD
White, Arthur *WWBWI I*
White, Bessie 1892- *AuBYP*
White, Claude Graham *MnBBF*
White, Dale *AuBYP, ConAu XR, SmATA 3*
White, Dale *see* Place, Marian Templeton
White, David Omar 1927- *ConAu 17R, IIBYP*
White, Dori 1919- *ConAu 37, SmATA 10*
White, E B 1899- *Au&ICB, BkCL, CelR 3,*
    ChLR 1, CnDAL, ConAu 13R, FamMS,
    LongC, ModAL, MorBMP, MorJA,
    OxAm, Pen Am, PiP, RAdv 1, REn,
    REnAL, SmATA 2, TwCW, WrD

White, E B see White, Elwyn Brooks
White, Edgar B 1947- BlkAW, ConAu 61,
   LBAA
White, Edward Lucas 1866-1934 AmA&B,
   BiDSA, DcNAA, JBA 1934, OxAm,
   REn, REnAL, TwCA, WNAA
White, Eliza Orne 1856-1947 AmA&B, AmLY,
   BbD, BiD&SB, CarSB, DcAmA,
   DcNAA, JBA 1934, JBA 1951, YABC 2
White, Elwyn Brooks 1899- AmA&B, AuBYP,
   AuNews 2, ChPo, ChPo S1, ChPo S2,
   CurB 60, DcLEnL, EvLB, IntWW 38,
   TwCA, TwCA Sup, WW 1974,
   WWA 38, WWCL, WWWor 2
White, Elwyn Brooks see White, E B
White, Florence M 1910- ConAu 41
White, Fred M MnBBF
White, J Harrington MnBBF
White, Jean MnBBF
White, Joan MnBBF
White, JoAnn 1941- ConAu 53
White, John S 1847-1922 Alli Sup, DcAmA,
   DcNAA
White, Jon Manchip 1924- ConAu 13R,
   ConNov 1972, ConNov 1976, ConP 1970,
   DrAF 1976, DrAS 6E
White, Laurence B, Jr. 1935- ConAu 65,
   SmATA 10
White, Mary CarSB
White, Nancy Bean 1922- AuBYP,
   ConAu 13R, ForWC 1970
White, Patrick Cecil Telfer 1924- DrAS 6H
White, Pauline AuBYP
White, Percival 1887- AuBYP, ConAu 1R
White, Ramy Allison CarSB, ConAu P-2,
   SmATA 1
White, Ramy Allison see Stratemeyer, Edward L
White, Robb 1909- AmA&B, AuBYP,
   ChLR 3, ConAu 1R, JBA 1951,
   SmATA 1, WNAA, WWA 38
White, Stewart Edward 1873-1946 AmA&B,
   ArizL, BiDPar, CarSB, CnDAL,
   ConAmA, ConAmL, CurB 46, DcAmA,
   DcLEnL, DcNAA, LongC, OxAm,
   REnAL, TwCA, TwCA Sup, WNAA
White, T H 1906-1964 CnMWL, LongC,
   ModBL, Pen Eng, RAdv 1, REn,
   SmATA 12, TwCW
White, T H see White, Terence Hanbury
White, Ted . ConAu XR
White, Ted see White, Theodore Edwin
White, Terence Hanbury 1906-1964 CasWL,
   DcLEnL, OxEng, TelT, TwCA,
   TwCA Sup, WWCL
White, Terence Hanbury see Aston, James
White, Terence Hanbury see White, T H
White, Theodore Edwin 1938- ConAu 21R
White, Theodore Edwin see White, Ted
White, William, Jr. 1934- ConAu 37,
   DrAS 6H
White, Zita 1933- ConAu XR, SingR 1
White, Zita see Denholm, Therese Mary Zita
   White
Whitebead, Baida IlBYP
Whitechurch, Victor Lorenzo 1868-1933 ChPo,
   ChPo S1, EncM&D, MnBBF, WWLA
Whitefield, Raoul MnBBF
Whiteford, Andrew Hunter 1913-
   AmMWS 12S, ConAu 45, WWA 38

Whitehead, Don F 1908- AmA&B, ConAu 9R,
   SmATA 4
Whitehead, Robert John 1928- ChPo S1,
   ConAu 37, IndAu 1917, LE 5
Whitehill, Dorothy CarSB
Whitehouse, Arch 1895- AuBYP, ConAu XR,
   MnBBF
Whitehouse, Arch see Taylor, W T
Whitehouse, Arch see Whitehouse, Arthur
   George
Whitehouse, Arthur George 1895- AuBYP,
   ConAu 5R
Whitehouse, Arthur George see Whitehouse,
   Arch
Whitehouse, Elizabeth S 1893-1968 ConAu P-1
Whitehouse, F Cowley MnBBF
Whitelaw, David MnBBF
Whiteman, L MnBBF
Whitford, Joan 1922- MnBBF
Whitford, Joan see Ford, Barry
Whitford, Joan see Oldham, Hugh R
Whitinger, R D AuBYP, ConAu XR,
   SmATA 3
Whitinger, R D see Place, Marian Templeton
Whitley, Reid MnBBF, WWBWI A
Whitley, Reid see Armour, R Coutts
Whitlock, Charles MnBBF
Whitlock, Herbert Percy 1868-1948 AmA&B,
   DcNAA
Whitlock, Judith SingR 2
Whitlock, Pamela ChPo
Whitlock, Ralph 1914- Au&Wr 6
Whitlock, Ralph WrD
Whitman, Edmund Spurr 1900- ConAu 17R,
   WWA 38
Whitman, Walt 1819-1892 Alli, Alli Sup,
   AmA, AmA&B, AmWr, AnCL, AtlBL,
   BbD, BiD&SB, CasWL, Chambr 3,
   ChPo, ChPo S1, CnDAL, CnE&AP,
   CriT 3, CyWA, DcAmA, DcEnA,
   DcEnA Ap, DcEnL, DcLEnL, DcNAA,
   EvLB, MouLC 4, OxAm, OxCan, OxEng,
   Pen Am, RAdv 1, RCom, REn, REnAL,
   St&VC, WEAL
Whitney, Adeline Dutton Train 1824-1906 Alli,
   Alli Sup, AmA, AmA&B, BbD,
   BiD&SB, CarSB, ChPo, ChPo S1,
   CyAL 2, DcAmA, DcNAA
Whitney, Alex 1922- ConAu 53
Whitney, Charles Allen 1929- AmMWS 12P,
   WWA 38
Whitney, David Charles 1921- ConAu 9R,
   DrAS 6H, WWA 38
Whitney, Elinor 1889- AmA&B, ChPo,
   ChPo S1, JBA 1934, JBA 1951
Whitney, Leon Fradley 1894- AmA&B,
   AuBYP, ConAu 5R, WNAA, WWA 38
Whitney, Phyllis Ayame 1903- AmA&B,
   AuBYP, AuNews 2, ConAu 1R, CurB 48,
   EncM&D, ForWC 1970, JBA 1951,
   SmATA 1, WWA 38, WWAW 8, WrD
Whitney, Thomas Porter 1917- WWA 38,
   WWE 14, WWWor 2
Whitridge, Arnold 1891- AmA&B, Au&Wr 6,
   ConAu 9R, DrAS 6H, WWA 38
Whittaker, Otto 1916- ConAu 25R
Whittam, Geoffrey William 1916- IlBYP,
   IlCB 1946
Whittemore, Constance ConICB

Whittier, John Greenleaf 1807-1892 *Alli,*
Alli Sup, AmA, AmA&B, AnCL, AtlBL,
BbD, BiD&SB, CarSB, CasWL,
Chambr 3, ChPo, ChPo S1, ChPo S2,
CnDAL, CriT 3, CyAL 2, CyWA,
DcAmA, DcEnA, DcEnL, DcLEnL,
DcNAA, EvLB, MouLC 4, OxAm,
OxEng, Pen Am, RAdv 1, REn, REnAL,
St&VC, WEAL
Whittingham, Richard 1939- *ConAu 37*
Whittle, Tyler *ConAu XR*
Whittle, Tyler *see* Tyler-Whittle, Michael Sidney
Whittlesey, Susan 1938- *ConAu 29*
Whitwell, T M R *WWBWI 1*
Whymper, Edward 1840-1911 *Alli, BbD,*
BiD&SB, BrAu 19, Chambr 3, EvLB,
OxEng, WWBWI 1
Whyte, H *MnBBF*
Whyte, Melton *MnBBF, WWBWI A*
Whyte, Melton *see* Anderson, G J B
Whyte-Melville, George John 1821-1878 *BbD,*
BiD&SB, Br&AmS, BrAu 19, Chambr 3,
ChPo, ChPo S2, CyWA, DcEnA,
DcEnA Ap, DcLEnL, EvLB, MnBBF,
NCHEL, OxEng, REn, WEAL
Wibberley, Leonard 1915- *AuBYP, ChLR 3,*
ChPo, ConAu 5R, EncM&D, MorJA,
REn, SmATA 2, WorAu
Wibberley, Leonard *see* Holton, Leonard
Wibberley, Leonard *see* O'Connor, Patrick
Wibberley, Leonard *see* Webb, Christopher
Wiberg, Harald Albin 1908- *IlCB 1957*
Wicker, Ireene 1905- *ConAu 69, CurB 43,*
ForWC 1970, WWA 38, WWAW 8,
WWE 14, WWWor 2
Widdemer, Mabel Cleland 1902-1964 *AuBYP,*
ConAu 5R, SmATA 5
Widdemer, Mabel Cleland *see* Cleland, Mabel
Widdemer, Mabel Cleland *see* Ludlum, Mabel
Cleland
Widder, Robert B *WrD*
Widell, Helene 1912- *ConAu 37, OxCan Sup*
Widerberg, Siv 1931- *ConAu 53, SmATA 10*
Widmer, Eleanor Rackow *WrD*
Wier, Ester 1910- *AuBYP, ConAu 9R,*
SmATA 3, ThBJA
Wiese, Kurt 1887-1974 *AmA&B, AmPB,*
AuBYP, ChPo, ConAu 9R, ConAu 49,
ConICB, IlCB 1744, IlCB 1946,
IlCB 1957, JBA 1934, JBA 1951,
REnAL, SmATA 3
Wiesner, William 1899- *ChPo, ConAu 41,*
IlBYP, IlCB 1946, IlCB 1957, SmATA 5
Wiggin, Kate Douglas 1856-1923 *Alli Sup,*
AmA&B, BbD, BiD&SB, CarSB,
Chambr 3, ChPo, ChPo S1, ChPo S2,
CnDAL, ConAmL, DcAmA, DcLEnL,
DcNAA, EvLB, FamAYP, FamSYP,
JBA 1934, LongC, OxAm, REn, REnAL,
TwCA, TwCA Sup, WWCL, YABC 1
Wiggin, Maurice 1912- *Au&Wr 6, ConAu 9R*
Wiggins, Archibald Raymond *WrD*
Wigginton, Eliot *AuNews 1, BiN 1974*
Wightman, Francis P *BiDSA, CarSB*
Wightman, Warren *MnBBF*
Wighton, Rosemary Neville 1925- *ConAu 9R*
Wignall, Trevor C 1883-1958 *MnBBF,*
WWBWI A
Wignall, Trevor C *see* Dene, Alan

Wignall, Trevor C *see* Rees, David
Wikland, Ilon 1930- *IlCB 1957*
Wilber, Donald Newton 1907- *ConAu 5R,*
AuBYP
Wilbur, C Keith 1923- *ConAu 25R*
Wilbur, Richard Purdy 1921- *AmA&B,*
Au&Wr 6, BiEnAT, CasWL, ChPo S1,
ChPo S2, CnDAL, CnE&AP, CnMWL,
ConAu 1R, ConLC 3, ConLC 6,
ConP 1970, ConP 1975, CrCAP,
CurB 66, DrAF 1976, DrAP 1975,
DrAS 6E, EncWL, IntWW 38, ModAL,
ModAL Sup, OxAm, Pen Am, RAdv 1,
REn, REnAL, SmATA 9, TwCA Sup,
TwCW, WEAL, WWA 38, WWE 14,
WWT 15, WWTwL, WWWor 2, WrD
Wilcox, Daniel 1941- *ConAu 53*
Wilcox, Don *AuBYP*
Wilcox, R Turner 1888-1970 *BiEnAT,*
ConAu 5R, ConAu 29
Wilcox, W M *MnBBF*
Wilde, D Gunther *ConAu XR, SmATA XR*
Wilde, D Gunther *see* Hurwood, Bernhardt J
Wilde, Oscar 1854?-1900 *Alli Sup, AtlBL,*
BbD, BiD&SB, BrAu 19, CarSB,
CasWL, Chambr 3, ChPo, ChPo S2,
CnE&AP, CnMD, CnThe, CriT 3,
CyWA, DcBiA, DcEnA Ap, DcEuL,
DcLEnL, EncWL, EvLB, LongC,
McGWD, ModWD, MouLC 4, NCHEL,
OxEng, OxFr, Pen Eng, PoIre, RAdv 1,
RCom, REn, REnWD, TelT, WEAL,
WWCL
Wilder, Alec 1907- *AuBYP, BiEnAT,*
WWA 38, WWWor 2
Wilder, Laura Ingalls 1867-1957 *AnCL,*
AuBYP, BkCL, CasWL, ChLR 2,
ChPo S1, CurB 48, CurB 57, FamMS,
JBA 1951, REnAL, St&VC, WWCL
Wilder, Thornton 1897-1975 *AmA&B, AmNov,*
AmWr, Au&Wr 6, AuNews 2, BiEnAT,
CasWL, CelR 3, Chambr 3, CnDAL,
CnMD, CnMWL, CnThe, ConAmA,
ConAmL, ConAu 13R, ConAu 61,
ConDr 1, ConLC 1, ConLC 5, ConLC 6,
ConNov 1972, CrCD, CurB 43, CurB 71,
CyWA, DcLEnL, EncWL, EvLB, LongC,
ModAL, ModAL Sup, ModWD, OxAm,
OxEng, Pen Am, PiP, RAdv 1, RCom,
REn, REnAL, REnWD, TwCA,
TwCA Sup, TwCW, WEAL, WNAA,
WWTwL, WisW
Wildsmith, Brian Lawrence 1930- *ArtsCL,*
Au&ICB, BkP, BrCA, ChLR 2, ChPo,
ChPo S1, IlBYP, IlCB 1957, ThBJA,
WW 1974, WWCL
Wiley, Karla H 1918- *AuBYP, ConAu 61*
Wilhelm, Kate 1928- *ConAu 37*
Wilk, Max 1920- *ConAu 1R*
Wilkes, W *MnBBF*
Wilkes, W *see* Evelyn, A W
Wilkie, Katharine Elliott 1904- *AuBYP,*
ConAu 21R, ForWC 1970
Wilkin, Eloise Burns 1904- *IlBYP, IlCB 1744,*
IlCB 1946
Wilkin, Robert *WWBWI 1*
Wilkins, Hugh Percival 1896- *AuBYP*
Wilkins, Mary Eleanor 1862- *Alli Sup,*
AmA&B, AmLY Xr, BbD, BiD&SB,

CasWL, Chambr 3, ChPo, DcAmA,
DcEnA Ap, DcNAA, OxAm, REn,
REnAL, TwCA, TwCA Sup
Wilkins, Mary Huiskamp Calhoun *ThBJA*
Wilkins, Mary Huiskamp Calhoun *see* Calhoun,
Mary
Wilkins, Vaughan 1890-1959 *LongC, WWCL*
Wilkinson, Brenda 1946- *BlkAW, ConAu 69*
Wilkinson, Burke 1913- *AuBYP, ConAu 9R,*
SmATA 4
Wilkinson, Charlotte Jefferson *ConAu 69*
Wilkinson, Ernest *WWBWI 1*
Wilkinson, Frederick 1891- *WW 1974*
Wilkinson, Marguerite Ogden 1883-1928 *AnCL,*
ChPo, ChPo S1, ConAmL, DcNAA,
REnAL, TwCA, WNAA
Wilkinson, T W *MnBBF*
Wilkinson, Tom *WWBWI 1*
Wilkon, Jozef 1930- *IIBYP, IICB 1957*
Wilks, Brian 1933- *ConAu 69*
Wilks, Brian *see* Hughes, Sam
Willard, Barbara Mary *Au&Wr 6, BrCA,*
WrD, ChLR 2
Willard, Charlotte 1914- *WWA 38,*
WWAA 1973, WWAW 8
Willard, Frank 1893-1958 *ArtCS*
Willard, Mildred Wilds 1911- *ConAu 21R,*
WrD
Willard, Nancy 1936- *AmA&B, ConP 1975,*
DrAP 1975, WrD
Willcox, Sandra *IIBYP*
Willetts, R F 1915- *ConAu 5R*
Willey, Robert *AuBYP, ConAu XR,*
SmATA 2
Willey, Robert *see* Ley, Willy
Williams, Barbara 1925- *ConAu 49,*
SmATA 11, WW 1974
Williams, Barry 1932- *ConAu 29, ConAu 29*
Williams, Bert 1930- *Prof*
Williams, Beryl 1910- *ConAu XR, OhA&B,*
SmATA 1
Williams, Beryl *see* Epstein, Beryl
Williams, Brad 1918- *ConAu 1R*
Williams, Byron 1934- *ConAu 29*
Williams, Carol *WrD*
Williams, Charles *ConAu XR, SmATA 8*
Williams, Charles *see* Collier, James Lincoln
Williams, Clyde C 1881- *ConAu P-2,*
SmATA 8
Williams, Clyde C *see* Williams, Slim
Williams, Dorian 1914- *Au&Wr 6,*
ConAu 9R, WW 1974
Williams, E Neville 1917- *ConAu 9R*
Williams, Edgar *AuBYP*
Williams, Effie M *WNAA*
Williams, Eric Ernest 1911- *Au&Wr 6,*
AuBYP, BiN 1975, ConAu 9R, CurB 66,
WW 1974
Williams, Frances B *SmATA 5*
Williams, Frances B *see* Browin, Frances
Williams
Williams, Frances B *ConAu XR*
Williams, Fred J *MnBBF*
Williams, Fred J *see* Smith, Bernard
Williams, Garth Montgomery 1912- *AmA&B,*
AmPB, AuBYP, ChPo, ChPo S1,
IICB 1744, IICB 1946, IICB 1957,
MorJA, REnAL, St&VC, WWA 38,
WWAA 1973

Williams, Graeme *MnBBF*
Williams, Graeme *see* Dent, Denis
Williams, Gurney, III 1941- *ConAu 69*
Williams, Guy Richard 1920- *Au&Wr 6,*
ConAu 13R, SmATA 11, WrD
Williams, H J *MnBBF*
Williams, Hawley *YABC 1*
Williams, Hawley *see* Heyliger, William
Williams, Herbert Darkin 1802- *ChPo S1,*
ChPo S2, MnBBF
Williams, J R *ConAu XR, SmATA 5*
Williams, J R *see* Williams, Jeanne
Williams, Jay 1914- *ConAu 1R, CurB 55,*
SmATA 3, WorAu, WrD
Williams, Jay *see* Delving, Michael
Williams, Jeanne 1930- *ConAu 25R,*
SmATA 5, WrD
Williams, Jeanne *see* Crecy, Jeanne
Williams, Jeanne *see* Michaels, Kristin
Williams, Jeanne *see* Rhys, Megan
Williams, Jeanne *see* Rowan, Deirdre
Williams, Jeanne *see* Williams, J R
Williams, Jenny 1939- *ChPo S1, IICB 1957*
Williams, Jerome 1926- *AmMWS 12P,*
ConAu 49, WWE 14
Williams, John Alfred 1925- *AmA&B,*
Au&Wr 6, BlkAW, ConLC 5,
ConNov 1972, ConNov 1976, DrAF 1976,
LBAA, Pen Am, RAdv 1, WWA 38,
WorAu
Williams, Kathryn Vinson 1911- *ForWC 1970,*
WrD
Williams, Leslie *MnBBF*
Williams, Margery *JBA 1934*
Williams, Martin 1924- *ConAu 49, WWA 38*
Williams, Maureen 1951- *SmATA 12*
Williams, Michael 1908- *ConAu XR,*
SmATA XR
Williams, Michael *see* Saint John, Wylly Folk
Williams, Patrick J *SmATA 5*
Williams, Patrick J *see* Butterworth, W E
Williams, Richard *MnBBF, WWBWI A*
Williams, Richard *see* Baker, William Arthur
Howard
Williams, Richard *see* Francis, Stephen D
Williams, Richard *see* Janson, Hank
Williams, Richard Lippincott 1910- *WWA 38*
Williams, Ruth C *SingR 1*
Williams, Selma R 1925- *ConAu 49*
Williams, Slim *ConAu XR, SmATA 8*
Williams, Slim *see* Williams, Clyde C
Williams, T Harry 1909- *ConAu 1R,*
WWA 38, WWS 13
Williams, Ted *CurB 47, NYTBE 1,*
NYTBS 5, WWS 13
Williams, Ursula Moray 1911- *Au&Wr 6,*
ConAu 13R, SmATA 3, WWCL, WrD
Williams, Valentine 1883-1946 *CatA 1930,*
EncM&D, LongC, MnBBF, NCHEL,
TwCA, TwCA Sup, WWLA
Williams, W H *MnBBF*
Williams, William Lloyd 1902?- *SingR 2*
Williams-Ellis, Amabel 1894- *Au&Wr 6,*
EvLB, IntWW 38, LongC, REn, TwCA,
TwCA Sup, TwCW, WW 1974
Williamson, C H *MnBBF*
Williamson, Henry 1897- *Au&Wr 6, CasWL,*
ConNov 1972, ConNov 1976, DcLEnL,
EvLB, IntWW 38, LongC, ModBL,

NCHEL, REn, TwCA, TwCA Sup,
TwCW, WW 1974, WWCL, WWWor 2
Williamson, Jack 1908- *ConAu XR, MnBBF,*
WNAA
Williamson, Jack *see* Williamson, John Stewart
Williamson, Jane 1920- *LE 5*
Williamson, Joanne Small 1926- *AuBYP,*
ConAu 13R, ForWC 1970, SmATA 3,
ThBJA
Williamson, John Stewart 1908- *ConAu 17R*
Williamson, John Stewart *see* Williamson, Jack
Williamson, Kay *MnBBF*
Williamson, Margaret 1886- *ChPo*
Williamson, Margaret 1924- *AuBYP*
Williamson, Thomas *MnBBF*
Williamson, William Alan 1893- *MnBBF,*
WWBWI A
Willis, Anthony Armstrong 1897- *MnBBF,*
WW 1974
Willis, Anthony Armstrong *see* Armstrong,
Anthony
Willis, Irene 1929- *ConAu 65*
Willis, Priscilla D *AuBYP*
Willis, Robert J *AuBYP*
Willis, Ted 1918- *ConAu 9R, IntMPA 1975,*
WW 1974, WWT 15
Willis, Thomas John *MnBBF*
Willock, Ruth *ConAu 13R*
Wills, Jonathan 1947- *ConAu 69*
Willson, Dixie *AuBYP, ChPo*
Willson, Wingrove *WWBWI A*
Wilma, Dana *ConAu 49, SmATA XR*
Wilma, Dana *see* Faralla, Dana
Wilmot, Frank *SingR 2*
Wilmot, Frank *see* Maurice, Furnley
Wilms, Barbara 1941- *ConAu 57*
Wilson, Andy *MnBBF*
Wilson, Barbara Ker *ConAu XR, SingR 2,*
WrD
Wilson, Barbara Ker *see* Ker Wilson, Barbara
Wilson, Beth P *ConAu 49, SmATA 8*
Wilson, Carter 1941- *ConAu 17R, SmATA 6,*
WrD
Wilson, Charles 1932- *ConAu 65*
Wilson, Charles Banks 1918- *IlBYP,*
IlCB 1946, WWAA 1973
Wilson, Charles Morrow 1905- *AmA&B,*
Au&Wr 6, AuBYP, ConAu 5R, REnAL,
TwCA Sup, WWA 38
Wilson, Colin 1931- *Au&Wr 6, CasWL,*
ConAu 1R, ConLC 3, ConNov 1972,
ConNov 1976, CurB 63, LongC, ModBL,
ModBL Sup, NCHEL, RAdv 1, REn,
TwCW, WWWor 2, WorAu
Wilson, Dagmar 1916- *ChPo S2, WWAW 8*
Wilson, David Henry *WrD*
Wilson, Dorothy Clarke 1904- *AmA&B,*
AmNov, Au&Wr 6, ConAu 1R, CurB 51,
ForWC 1970, WWA 38, WWAW 8,
WrD
Wilson, Edward Arthur 1886- *ChPo, ChPo S1,*
ChPo S2, IlBYP, IlCB 1744, IlCB 1946
Wilson, Eleanore Hubbard *AuBYP*
Wilson, Ellen *ConAu 49, SmATA 9*
Wilson, Erica *NYTBE 2*
Wilson, Erle 1898- *ConAu 5R, SingR 1*
Wilson, Forrest 1918- *ConAu 53,*
WWMW 14
Wilson, Gahan 1930- *ConAu 25R, IlBYP*

Wilson, Granville 1912- *ConAu 69*
Wilson, Hazel 1898- *AuBYP, ConAu 1R,*
SmATA 3, WrD
Wilson, Holly *AuBYP*
Wilson, Jeanne 1920- *ConAu 69*
Wilson, John *IlBYP*
Wilson, John 1922- *WWA 38*
Wilson, John Park 1867-1932 *WWA 38,*
WWBWI A
Wilson, John Park *see* Jackson, Julian
Wilson, Joyce M *ConAu 17R*
Wilson, Joyce M *see* Stranger, Joyce
Wilson, Julia 1927- *BkP, ConAu 21R*
Wilson, Jumbo *WWBWI I*
Wilson, Katharine M *WrD*
Wilson, Kenneth Lee 1916- *ConAu 29,*
WWA 38
Wilson, Matt *MnBBF*
Wilson, Maurice *ChPo*
Wilson, Mitchell 1913-1973 *AmA&B, AmNov,*
Au&Wr 6, ConAu 1R, ConAu 41,
ConNov 1972, NYTBE 3, NYTBE 4,
OxAm
Wilson, Peggy *ChPo S1, IlBYP, IlCB 1957*
Wilson, Reg *MnBBF, WWBWI A*
Wilson, Reg *see* Thomas, Reginald George
Wilson, Rex *MnBBF*
Wilson, Robert *MnBBF*
Wilson, Ruth *AuBYP*
Wilson, Sarah *Alli Sup, CarSB, ChPo,*
ChPo S1
Wilson, W Harmon 1905- *ConAu 37*
Wilson, Wingrove *MnBBF*
Wilson, Wingrove *see* Light, Walter H
Wilton, Elizabeth M 1937- *ConAu 69,*
SingR 2
Wilton, Hal *MnBBF, WWBWI A*
Wilton, Hal *see* Pepper, Frank S
Wilwerding, Walter Joseph 1891-1966
ConAu P-1, IlCB 1744, MnnWr,
SmATA 9
Wimbury, Harold *MnBBF*
Wimmer, Helmut Karl 1925- *IlCB 1957*
Winchester, Clarence *ChPo S1, MnBBF,*
WW 1974, WWBWI A
Winchester, James Hugh 1917- *AmA&B,*
ConAu 17R, WWA 38
Winchester, M E *Alli Sup, CarSB*
Winchester, Mark *MnBBF, WWBWI A*
Winder, Blanche *ChPo, ChPo S1, ChPo S2*
Winder, Viola Hitti *AuBYP*
Winders, Gertrude Hecker 1897- *ConAu 1R,*
ForWC 1970, IndAu 1917, SmATA 3
Windham, Basil *ConAu XR, MnBBF,*
WWBWI A
Windham, Basil *see* Wodehouse, Pelham
Grenville
Windolph, F Lyman 1889- *AmA&B,*
ConAu 41
Windsor, Frank *MnBBF*
Windsor, Frank *see* Birnage, Derek A W
Windsor, Patricia 1938- *ConAu 49*
Windsor-Richards, Arthur Bedlington 1904-
Au&Wr 6, ConAu P-1, WrD
Winfield, Arthur M *ConAu XR, DcNAA,*
REn, REnAL
Winfield, Arthur M *see* Stratemeyer, Edward L
Winfield, Edna *ConAu XR*
Winfield, Edna *see* Stratemeyer, Edward L

Wing, Helen *ChPo*
Wingate, Gifford Wendell 1925- *ConAu 65,*
    DrAS 6E
Wingate, John 1920- *Au&Wr 6, WrD*
Winkler, Rolf 1884- *ConICB*
Winn, Charles S 1932- *ConAu 69*
Winokur, Joan Gelman 1935- *ConAu 41*
Winship, Florence Sarah *WWAA 1973*
Winston, Richard 1917- *ConAu 25R*
Winter, Charles A 1902- *AmMWS 12P*
Winter, Elmer Louis 1912- *ConAu 13R,*
    WWA 38
Winter, Ginny Linville 1925- *AuBYP,*
    ConAu 1R, ForWC 1970, IndAu 1917
Winter, Klaus 1928- *ConAu 29, WWGA*
Winter, Milo Kendall 1888-1956 *ChPo S2,*
    ConICB, IIBYP, IICB 1744, IICB 1946
Winter, R R *ConAu XR, SmATA XR*
Winter, R R *see* Winterbotham, R R
Winter, William John 1912- *AuBYP*
Winterbotham, R R 1904-1971 *ConAu 1R,*
    SmATA 10
Winterbotham, R R *see* Addy, Ted
Winterbotham, R R *see* Bond, J Harvey
Winterbotham, R R *see* Hadley, Franklin
Winterbotham, R R *see* Winter, R R
Winterfeld, Henry 1901- *ThBJA*
Winterfeld, Henry *see* Michael, Manfred
Winters, Janet Lewis 1899- *ConAu P-1,*
    DrAF 1976, DrAP 1975, WWA 38
Winters, Janet Lewis *see* Lewis, Janet
Winters, Yvor 1900-1968 *AmA&B, AnCL,*
    AtlBL, CnDAL, CnE&AP, ConAmA,
    ConAu 25R, ConAu P-1, ConLC 4,
    DcLEnL, EncWL, LongC, ModAL Sup,
    OxAm, Pen Am, RAdv 1, REn, REnAL,
    SixAP, SixAP, TwCA, TwCA Sup,
    TwCW, WEAL, WWTwL
Winthrop, Elizabeth *ConAu XR, SmATA 8*
Winthrop, Elizabeth *see* Mahony, Elizabeth
    Winthrop
Winton, John *ConAu XR*
Winton, John *see* Pratt, John
Wintterle, John 1927- *ConAu 29*
Winwar, Frances 1900- *AmA&B, Au&Wr 6,*
    AuBYP, OxAm, REn, REnAL, TwCA,
    TwCA Sup, WWA 38, WWAW 8
Wirt, Mildred A 1905- *AmA&B, AuBYP,*
    CarSB
Wirtenberg, Patricia Z 1932- *ConAu 61,*
    SmATA 10
Wisbeski, Dorothy G 1929- *ConAu 9R*
Wise, Daniel 1813-1898 *Alli, Alli Sup,*
    AmA&B, BiD&SB, CarSB, DcAmA,
    DcNAA
Wise, William 1923- *AuBYP, ChPo,*
    ConAu 13R, SmATA 4
Wise, Winifred E *AuBYP, ConAu 25R,*
    ForWC 1970, SmATA 2
Wiseman, Ann 1926- *ConAu 65*
Wiseman, Ann *see* Denzer, Ann Wiseman
Wiseman, B 1922- *ConAu 5R, SmATA 4*
Wiseman, B *see* Wiseman, Bernard
Wiseman, Bernard 1922- *SmATA 4, WrD*
Wiseman, Bernard *see* Wiseman, B
Wiser, Guy Brown 1895- *ChPo*
Wiskur, Darrell *IIBYP*
Wisner, William L *AuBYP*
Wissmann, Ruth H 1914- *AuBYP*

Wister, Owen 1860-1938 *Alli Sup, AmA&B,*
    AmLY, ArizL, BiD&SB, CarSB, CasWL,
    Chambr 3, ChPo, ChPo S2, CnDAL,
    ConAmA, ConAmL, CyWA, DcAmA,
    DcLEnL, DcNAA, LongC, OxAm,
    Pen Am, RAdv 1, REn, REnAL, TwCA,
    TwCA Sup, WEAL, WNAA
Withers, Carl *AnCL, AuBYP*
Withers, Carl *see* West, James
Witker, Jim *AuBYP*
Witt, Shirley Hill 1934- *AmMWS 12S,*
    ConAu 53
Witt, Shirley Hill *see* Thundercloud, Katherine
Witte, Betty J *AuBYP*
Wittenbach, Henry August *WrD*
Witton, Dorothy *AuBYP*
Witty, Paul Andrew 1898- *AuBYP,*
    IndAu 1917, WWA 38
Witzen, A E *MnBBF*
Wizard, Mr. *SmATA 2*
Wizard, Mr. *see* Herbert, Don
Wodehouse, P G 1881-1975 *AmA&B,*
    AmSCAP 66, BiEnAT, CelR 3,
    ConAu 45, ConAu 57, ConDr 1,
    ConLC 2, ConLC 5, ConNov 1972,
    ConNov 1976, CurB 71, LongC,
    McGWD, ModBL, ModBL Sup, NCHEL,
    Pen Eng, RAdv 1, REn, TwCW, WEAL,
    WWTwL
Wodehouse, P G *see* Wodehouse, Pelham
    Grenville
Wodehouse, Pelham Grenville 1881-1975
    AmSCAP 66, Au&Wr 6, AuNews 2,
    CasWL, Chambr 3, DcLEnL, EncWL,
    EvLB, IntWW 38, MnBBF, OxEng,
    TwCA, TwCA Sup, WW 1974,
    WWA 38, WWCL, WWBWI A,
    WWWor 2
Wodehouse, Pelham Grenville *see* Wodehouse, P
    G
Wodehouse, Pelham Grenville *see* Windham,
    Basil
Wodge, Dreary *ConAu XR*
Wodge, Dreary *see* Gorey, Edward St. John
Wohlberg, Meg 1905- *ChPo S1, IICB 1957*
Wohlrabe, Raymond Adolph 1900- *AuBYP,*
    ConAu 1R, SmATA 4, WWPNA,
    WWW 14, WrD
Wojciechowska, Maia 1927- *AmA&B,*
    Au&ICB, AuBYP, ChLR 1, ConAu 9R,
    MorBMP, PiP, NewbC 1956, SmATA 1,
    ThBJA
Wojciechowska, Maia *see* Rodman, Maia
Wolberg, Lewis Robert 1905- *ConAu 45,*
    WWA 38
Wolcott, Carolyn Muller *AuBYP*
Wolcott, Elizabeth Tyler 1892- *ConICB*
Wolcott, Leonard Thompson *AuBYP,*
    ConAu 13R, DrAS 6P
Wolcott, Patty 1929- *ConAu 57, WrD*
Wold, JoAnne 1938- *ConAu 61*
Wolf, Arnold Jacob 1924- *ConAu 29*
Wolfe, Burton Harold 1932- *ConAu 25R,*
    SmATA 5, WWW 14
Wolfe, Cedric *MnBBF, WWBWI A*
Wolfe, Cedric *see* Alais, Ernest W
Wolfe, Humbert 1885-1940 *AnCL, ChPo,*
    ChPo S1, ChPo S2, CurB 40, DcLEnL,
    EvLB, LongC, ModBL, NCHEL,

Pen Eng, REn, St&VC, TwCA,
TwCA Sup, TwCW, WWLA
Wolfe, Josephine Brace 1917- *ConAu 5R,*
WWAW 8
Wolfe, Louis 1905- *AuBYP, ConAu 5R,*
SmATA 8
Wolfert, Jerry *AuBYP*
Wolff, Janet L 1924- *ConAu 5R,*
ForWC 1970, WWAW 8
Wolff, Leslie 1912- *Au&Wr 6, WrD*
Wolff, Robert Jay 1905- *ConAu 25R,*
DcCAA 2, SmATA 10, WWA 38,
WWAA 1973, WrD
Wolff, Ruth 1909?-1972 *ConAu 37*
Wolfson, Victor 1910- *BiEnAT, ConAu 33,*
TwCA Sup, WWWorJ 1972
Wolfson, Victor *see* Dodge, Langdon
Wolitzer, Hilma 1930- *ConAu 65, DrAF 1976,*
WrD
Wolkstein, Diane 1942- *ConAu 37, SmATA 7*
Wollheim, Donald Allen 1914- *AuBYP,*
ConAu 1R, WWE 14
Wollheim, Donald Allen *see* Grinnell, David
Wondriska, William Allen 1931- *AuBYP,*
ConAu 1R, IICB 1957, SmATA 6,
ThBJA
Wong, Jeanyee 1920- *IIBYP, IICB 1946*
Wonsetler, John Charles 1900- *IIBYP,*
IICB 1744, IICB 1946
Wood, Andrew *MnBBF*
Wood, Andrew *see* Wood, Samuel Andrew
Wood, Clement 1888-1950 *AmA&B,*
AmSCAP 66, AnMV 1926, ChPo,
ChPo S1, ChPo S2, REn, REnAL,
TwCA, TwCA Sup, WNAA
Wood, Dorothy Carrico *AuBYP*
Wood, Edward *MnBBF*
Wood, Elizabeth L *MnBBF*
Wood, Eric *MnBBF, WWBWI A*
Wood, Eric *see* Campling, F Knowles
Wood, Esther 1905- *JBA 1951, OhA&B*
Wood, Geoffrey *MnBBF*
Wood, Geoffrey *see* Russell, C
Wood, George *MnBBF*
Wood, Harrie 1902- *ConICB, IICB 1744*
Wood, Innis *MnBBF*
Wood, J Claverdon *MnBBF, WWBWI A*
Wood, J G *WWBWI A*
Wood, James Playsted 1905- *AmA&B,*
Au&Wr 6, AuBYP, ChPo S2,
ConAu 9R, SmATA 1, WWA 38, WrD
Wood, James Playsted *see* Saint Briavels, James
Wood, James Playsted *see* Soudley, Henry
Wood, John George 1827-1889 *Alli, Alli Sup,*
BiD&SB, BiDLA, CarSB, DcEnL, EvLB,
MnBBF
Wood, Joyce 1928- *ConAu 25R*
Wood, Kenneth 1922- *ConAu 69*
Wood, Kerry 1907- *OxCan Sup, Prof*
Wood, Laura N 1911- *AuBYP, ConAu 57*
Wood, Laura N *see* Roper, Laura Wood
Wood, Lawson 1878- *IICB 1744, WWBWI I*
Wood, Leslie 1920- *IIBYP, IICB 1946*
Wood, Lorna 1913- *Au&Wr 6, ConAu 69,*
WWCL, WrD
Wood, Nancy 1936- *ConAu 21R, SmATA 6*
Wood, Paul W 1922- *ConAu 61*
Wood, Phyllis Anderson 1923- *ConAu 37,*
WrD

Wood, Ray *ChPo*
Wood, Robert Williams 1869?- *ChPo,*
ChPo S1, WNAA
Wood, Rodney *MnBBF*
Wood, Ruth C *ConAu 37*
Wood, Samuel Andrew 1890- *MnBBF,*
WWBWI A
Wood, Samuel Andrew *see* Cross, Thomson
Wood, Samuel Andrew *see* Raven, G
Wood, Samuel Andrew *see* Ravenglass, Hal
Wood, Samuel Andrew *see* Wood, Andrew
Wood, Stanley L *WWBWI I*
Wood, Theodore 1862- *Alli Sup, CarSB*
Wood, Walter 1886- *MnBBF*
Wood-Smith, Noel d1955? *MnBBF,*
WWBWI A
Wood-Smith, Noel *see* Clifford, Martin
Wood-Smith, Noel *see* Conquest, Owen
Wood-Smith, Noel *see* Richards, Frank
Wood-Smith, Noel *see* Taylor, Norman
Wood-Smith, Noel *see* Terry, Noel
Woodberry, Joan Merle 1921- *Au&Wr 6,*
ConAu 9R, SingR 1, WrD
Woodburn, John Henry 1914- *ConAu 1R,*
LE 5, SmATA 11
Woodcock, George 1912- *Au&Wr 6,*
CanWW 12, CanWr, CasWL, ConAu 1R,
ConP 1970, ConP 1975, ModBL, OxCan,
OxCan Sup, WW 1974, WWA 38
Wooden, John *NYTBE 4, CelR 3*
Woodford, Cecile *WrD*
Woodgate, Mildred Violet *Au&Wr 6,*
ConAu 9R, WrD
Woodhouse, Lawrence *MnBBF*
Woodhouse, Martin 1932- *ConAu 21R*
Woodman, George D *MnBBF, WWBWI A*
Woodman, Thomas *MnBBF*
Woodman, Thomas *see* Quilter, Eddie
Woodress, James 1916- *ConAu 5R, DrAS 6E*
Woodrich, Mary Neville 1915- *ConAu 25R,*
SmATA 2
Woodrich, Mary Neville *see* Neville, Mary
Woodroffe, Paul Vincent 1875- *ChPo,*
ChPo S2, IICB 1744
Woodruff, Anne Helena 1850- *AmA&B,*
CarSB, ChPo S1, DcNAA
Woodruff, Peter *MnBBF*
Woods, George A 1926- *ConAu 29*
Woods, James *MnBBF*
Woods, Kate Tannatt 1838-1910 *Alli Sup,*
AmA&B, BiD&SB, CarSB, ChPo,
ChPo S2, DcAmA, DcNAA
Woods, L H *MnBBF*
Woods, Loren P 1913- *AmMWS 12P*
Woods, Margaret 1921- *ConAu 21R,*
SmATA 2
Woods, Margaret Staeger 1911- *LE 5,*
WWAW 8
Woods, Nat *ConAu XR*
Woods, Nat *see* Stratemeyer, Edward L
Woods, Ross *WWBWI A*
Woods, Ross *see* Lee, Charles H
Woods, Ross *see* Story, Rosamund
Woods, W O *MnBBF*
Woodson, Jack *SmATA XR*
Woodson, Jack *see* Woodson, John Waddie, Jr.
Woodson, John Waddie, Jr. 1913- *SmATA 10*
Woodson, John Waddie, Jr. *see* Woodson, Jack
Woodville, Richard Caton 1856- *WWBWI I*

Woodward, Alice Bolingbroke 1862- ChPo,
   ChPo S1, ChPo S2, ConICB, IlBYP,
   IlCB 1744
Woodward, C Vann 1908- ConAu 5R,
   WW 1974, WWWor 2
Woodward, Cleveland 1900- SmATA 10
Woodward, Edward MnBBF
Woodward, Hildegard 1898- AuBYP,
   ConAu 5R, ForWC 1970, IlCB 1744,
   IlCB 1946
Woodworth, Francis Channing 1812-1859 Alli,
   AmA&B, CarSB, ChPo, ChPo S1,
   DcNAA
Woody, Regina Llewellyn Jones 1894- AuBYP,
   ConAu 5R, ForWC 1970, MorJA,
   SmATA 3, WWAW 8, WWE 14, WrD
Wooldridge, Rhoda AuBYP
Woolgar, Jack 1894- ConAu 17R
Woolley, Catherine 1904- Au&Wr 6, AuBYP,
   ConAu 1R, ForWC 1970, MorJA,
   SmATA 3, WWAW 8
Woolley, Catherine see Thayer, Jane
Woolley, Horace A MnBBF
Woolsey, Janette 1904- ConAu 1R,
   ForWC 1970, SmATA 3
Woolsey, Sarah Chauncey 1835?-1905 Alli Sup,
   AmA, AmA&B, BiD&SB, CarSB,
   Chambr 3, ChPo, DcAmA, DcLEnL,
   DcNAA, EvLB, JBA 1934, OhA&B,
   REnAL, WWCL
Woolsey, Sarah Chauncey see Coolidge, Susan
Wooton, Edwin MnBBF
Worcester, Donald Emmet 1915- AmA&B,
   AuBYP, ConAu 1R, DrAS 6H,
   WWA 38, WWS 13, WrD
Worden, Alfred Merrill 1932- IntWW 38,
   NYTBE 2, WWA 38, WWS 13
Wordsworth, William 1770-1850 Alli, AnCL,
   AtlBL, BbD, BiD&SB, BiDLA, BrAu 19,
   CasWL, Chambr 3, ChPo, ChPo S1,
   ChPo S2, CnE&AP, CriT 2, CyWA,
   DcEnA, DcEnL, DcEuL, DcLEnL, EvLB,
   MouLC 3, NCHEL, OxEng, Pen Eng,
   PoLE, RAdv 1, RCom, REn, St&VC,
   WEAL
Worline, Bonnie Bess 1914- AuBYP,
   ConAu 69
Worm, Piet 1909- Au&Wr 6, IlBYP,
   IlCB 1946
Wormser, Sophie 1897- ConAu 65
Worsleigh, David MnBBF
Worstell, Emma Vietor ChPo
Worth, Kathryn 1898- AuBYP, ChPo,
   JBA 1951
Worth, Richard MnBBF
Worth, Valerie 1933- ChPo S2, ConAu XR,
   SmATA 8
Worth, Valerie see Bahlke, Valerie Worth
Worthing, Jack MnBBF
Worthing, Jack see Worthing, John
Worthing, John MnBBF
Worthing, John see Worthing, Jack
Worthington, R CarSB
Worthylake, Mary Moore 1904- ConAu 1R,
   ForWC 1970, WWPNA
Wortis, Avi ConAu 69
Wortis, Avi see Avi
Wortley, Beatrice MnBBF
Wouk, Herman 1915- AmA&B, AmNov,

Au&Wr 6, BiEnAT, CnMD, ConAu 5R,
   ConLC 1, ConNov 1972, ConNov 1976,
   CrCD, CurB 52, EncWL, IntWW 38,
   LongC, ModAL, ModWD, OxAm,
   Pen Am, REn, REnAL, TwCA Sup,
   TwCW, WW 1974, WWA 38,
   WWWor 2, WWWorJ 1972
Wray, Reginald MnBBF, WWBWI A
Wray, Reginald see Home-Gall, William
   Benjamin
Wren, Ellaruth ConAu XR
Wren, Ellaruth see Elkins, Ella Ruth
Wren, Percival Christopher 1885-1941 CurB 42,
   DcLEnL, EvLB, LongC, MnBBF,
   NCHEL, OxEng, Pen Eng, REn, TwCA,
   TwCW
Wrexe, Charles MnBBF
Wrexe, Charles see Hardinge, Rex
Wright, Anna Rose CurB 52
Wright, Blanche Fisher ChPo, ChPo S1
Wright, Dare AuBYP
Wright, David 1806-1877 DcNAA, WWBWI I
Wright, Enid Meadowcroft 1898-1966 AuBYP,
   ConAu P-2, SmATA 3
Wright, Enid Meadowcroft see Meadowcroft,
   Enid LaMonte
Wright, Esmond 1915- Au&Wr 6, ConAu 1R,
   SmATA 10, WW 1974
Wright, Frances Fitzpatrick 1897- AuBYP,
   ConAu P-1, SmATA 10
Wright, Franklin MnBBF, WWBWI A
Wright, Franklin see Farmer, Henry
Wright, Gordon 1912- ConAu 9R, DrAS 6H,
   WWA 38, WWWor 2
Wright, H Philpott MnBBF, WWBWI A
Wright, Harold Tomlinson WWBWI A
Wright, Harold Tomlinson see Grant, Howard
Wright, Helen 1914- AmA&B, ConAu 9R,
   CurB 56, WWA 38, WWAW 8
Wright, Henrietta Christian d1899 Alli Sup,
   AmA&B, BiD&SB, CarSB, ChPo,
   DcAmA, DcNAA
Wright, James 1927- ConAu 49
Wright, Judith Arundell 1915- AnCL, CasWL,
   ChPo, CnMWL, ConAu 13R, ConP 1970,
   ConP 1975, IntWW 38, LongC, Pen Eng,
   SingR 1, TwCW, WEAL, WW 1974,
   WWTwL, WWWor 2, WorAu, WrD
Wright, Louis Booker 1899- AmA&B,
   Au&Wr 6, BiEnAT, ChPo S1,
   ConAu 1R, CurB 50, DrAS 6H,
   IntWW 38, REnAL, WW 1974,
   WWA 38
Wright, Mabel Osgood 1859-1934 AmA&B,
   AmLY, BiD&SB, CarSB, DcAmA,
   DcNAA
Wright, Nathan, Jr. 1923- BlkAW, ConAu 37,
   DrAS 6H, LBAA, WWE 14
Wright, Philip Mercer MnBBF
Wright, R H 1906- ConAu 17R, SmATA 6
Wright, Richard 1908-1960 AmA&B, AmNov,
   AmWr, BlkAW, CasWL, CnDAL,
   ConLC 1, ConLC 3, ConLC 4,
   ConNov 1976, CurB 40, CurB 61,
   CyWA, DcLEnL, EncWL, EvLB, LongC,
   ModAL, ModAL Sup, OxAm, Pen Am,
   RAdv 1, REn, REnAL, TwCA,
   TwCA Sup, TwCW, WEAL, WWTwL
Wright, Robert H 1906- AmMWS 12P

Wright, W George *MnBBF*
Wright, W George *see* Bouchard, William
Wright, W George *see* Bryant, Bruce
Wright, W George *see* Grant, Howard
Wright, W George *see* Masterson, Val
Wright, W George *see* Quintin, Paul
Wright, W George *see* Rishton, William
Wright, Walter B *MnBBF*
Wright, Warwick *MnBBF*
Wright, Wendell William 1893-1961
 IndAu 1917
Wright, Wynna *ConICB*
Wrightson, Patricia 1921- *AuBYP, ConAu 45,*
 SenS, SingR 1, SmATA 8
Wrigley, Denis *ChPo S1, ChPo S2*
Wronker, Lili Cassel 1924- *IIBYP, IICB 1957,*
 SmATA 10
Wronker, Lili Cassel *see* Cassel, Lili
Wroth, Lawrence Counselman 1884-1970
 AmA&B, ConAu 29, NYTBE 1, OxAm,
 REnAL, WNAA
Wroxham, Cecil *MnBBF*
Wroxham, Cecil *see* Belfield, Harry Wedgwood
Wulff, Edgun Valdemar 1913- *IIBYP,*
 IICB 1946
Wulff, Edgun Valdemar *see* Edgun
Wulff, Lee 1905- *ConAu 61*
Wunder, George 1912- *ArtCS*
Wunsch, Josephine McLean 1914- *AuBYP,*
 ConAu 1R, ForWC 1970, WrD
Wuorio, Eva-Lis *ThBJA*
Wyatt, Ben *MnBBF*
Wyatt, Ben *see* Young, Fred W
Wyatt, Edgar *AuBYP*
Wyatt, Geraldine 1907- *AuBYP*
Wyatt, Isabel *AuBYP*
Wyatt-Brown, Bertram 1932- *ConAu 25R,*
 DrAS 6H
Wyckoff, James M 1918- *AuBYP,*
 ConAu 17R
Wyeth, N C 1882-1945 *CurB 45, ForII*
Wyeth, N C *see* Wyeth, Newell Convers
Wyeth, Newell Convers 1882-1945 *AmA&B,*
 ChPo, ChPo S2, ConICB, IIBYP,
 JBA 1934, JBA 1951, REnAL
Wyeth, Newell Convers *see* Wyeth, N C
Wylde, Anson *MnBBF*
Wylde, Jack *MnBBF*
Wyler, Rose 1909- *AuBYP, BkP, ThBJA*
Wyler, Rose *see* Ames, Rose Wyler
Wylie *MnBBF*
Wylie, Elinor Hoyt 1885-1928 *AmA&B, AnCL,*
 AtlBL, CasWL, Chambr 3, ChPo,
 ChPo S1, ChPo S2, CnDAL, CnE&AP,
 ConAmA, ConAmL, CyWA, DcLEnL,
 DcNAA, EvLB, LongC, ModAL,
 ModAL Sup, OxAm, OxEng, Pen Am,
 RAdv 1, REn, REnAL, SixAP, St&VC,
 TwCA, TwCA Sup, TwCW
Wylie, Philip 1902-1971 *ConAu 33,*
 ConAu P-2, NYTBE 2
Wyllie, Crichton *MnBBF*
Wymer, B O *WWBWI I*
Wymer, Norman 1911- *Au&Wr 6, AuBYP*
Wynants, Miche 1934- *IICB 1957*
Wynard, Talbot *WWBWI A*
Wynard, Talbot *see* Hamilton, Charles Harold St.
John
Wyndham, John 1903-1969 *LongC, REn,*

TwCW, WEAL, WorAu
Wyndham, John *see* Harris, John Wyndham
Parkes Lucas Beynon
Wyndham, Lee 1912- *AuBYP, ConAu 5R,*
 ForWC 1970, MorJA, SmATA 1,
 WWE 14, WrD
Wyndham, Lee *see* Hyndman, Jane Lee
Wyndham, Robert 1906?-1973 *ChPo S1,*
 ConAu 41
Wyndham-Gittens, Herbert *MnBBF*
Wynne, Annette 1885- *ChPo, ChPo S1,*
 ChPo S2, St&VC
Wynne, John Huddlestone 1743-1788 *Alli,*
 CarSB, ChPo, PoIre
Wynne, May 1875- *MnBBF, WWLA*
Wynne, May *see* Knowles, Mabel Winifred
Wynnton, Patrick 1899- *MnBBF*
Wynter, Edward 1914- *ConAu 69*
Wynyard, Talbot *MnBBF, SmATA XR*
Wynyard, Talbot *see* Hamilton, Charles Harold
St. John
Wyss, Johann David Von 1743-1818 *CarSB,*
 CasWL, OxGer, St&VC, WWCL
Wyss, Johann Rudolf 1781-1830 *BbD,*
 BiD&SB, CasWL, CyWA, DcBiA,
 EvEuW, WWCL
Wyss, Thelma Hatch 1934- *ConAu 29,*
 SmATA 10

X

Xavier, Father *ConAu XR, SmATA XR*
Xavier, Father *see* Hurwood, Bernhardt J
Ximenes, Ben Cuellar, Jr. 1911- *ConAu 5R*

Y

Y, Viscount *MnBBF*
Y, Viscount *see* Anderson, G J B
Yalon, Reuven 1935- *WWWorJ 1972*
Yamaguchi, John Tohr 1932- *ThBJA*
Yamaguchi, Marianne Illenberger 1936-
   ConAu 29, IIBYP, IICB 1957, SmATA 7,
   ThBJA
Yang, Jay 1941- *IIBYP, SmATA 12*
Yangtzepoo *MnBBF*
Yap, Weda 1894- *IIBYP, IICB 1946*
Yarbro, Chelsea Quinn 1942- *ConAu 65*
Yare, Edmund *MnBBF*
Yarmolinsky, Avrahm 1890-1975 *AmA&B,*
   Au&Wr 6, ConAu 5R, ConAu 61,
   DrAS 6F, TwCA, TwCA Sup, WNAA,
   WWA 38, WWWor 2, WWWorJ 1972
Yaroslava 1925- *IICB 1957*
Yaroslava *see* Mills, Yaroslava Surmach
Yashima, Taro 1908- *AmPB, BkP, ChPo S2,*
   ChFB I, IIBYP, IICB 1946, IICB 1957,
   MorJA
Yates, Brock Wendel 1933- *AuBYP,*
   ConAu 9R
Yates, Elizabeth 1905- *AmA&B, AmNov,*
   Au&ICB, Au&Wr 6, AuBYP, ChPo,
   ConAu 1R, CurB 48, JBA 1951,
   MorBMP, Newb 1922, REnAL,
   SmATA 4, TwCA Sup, WWA 38,
   WWAW 8
Yates, H S *MnBBF*
Yates, Raymond Francis 1895- *Au&Wr 6,*
   AuBYP, MorJA, WNAA
Yaukey, Grace Sydenstricker 1899- *AmA&B,*
   AmNov X, AuBYP, JBA 1951,
   SmATA 5
Yaukey, Grace Sydenstricker *see* Spencer,
   Cornelia
Yeakley, Marjory Hall 1908- *ConAu 1R,*
   CurB 57
Yeakley, Marjory Hall *see* Blair, Lucile
Yeakley, Marjory Hall *see* Hall, Marjory
Yeakley, Marjory Hall *see* Morse, Carol
Yeats, Jack Butler 1871-1957 *AtlBL, CarSB,*
   ChPo, CnMD, IICB 1744, IICB 1946,
   NCHEL, WWBWI 1
Yeats, William Butler 1865-1939 *Alli Sup,*
   AnCL, ArizL, BbD, BiD&SB, CasWL,
   Chambr 3, ChPo, ChPo S1, ChPo S2,
   CnE&AP, CnMD, CnMWL, CnThe,
   CyWA, DcEnA, DcEnA Ap, DcLEnL,
   EncWL, EvLB, LongC, McGWD,
   ModBL, ModBL Sup, ModWD, NCHEL,

OxEng, Pen Eng, Polre, RAdv 1, RCom,
   REn, REnWD, TwCA, TwCA Sup,
   TwCW, WEAL, WWTwL
Yeo, Wilma 1918- *ConAu 25R*
Yeoman, John 1934- *Au&Wr 6*
Yep, Laurence Michael 1948- *ChLR 3,*
   ConAu 49, SmATA 7
Yerby, Frank 1916- *CurB 46, LBAA,*
   WWA 38
Yezback, Steven A 1943- *AuBYP*
Ylla d1955 *AmPB, MorJA*
Ylla *see* Koffler, Camilla
Yolen, Jane H 1939- *AuBYP, ChPo S2,*
   ConAu 13R, ForWC 1970, SmATA 4
Yomes, Margot Ladd 1917- *ChPo S1,*
   ChPo S2, IIBYP, IICB 1957
Yonge, Charlotte Mary 1823-1901 *Alli,*
   Alli Sup, BbD, BiD&SB, BrAu 19,
   CarSB, CasWL, Chambr 3, ChPo S1,
   DcBiA, DcEnA, DcEnA Ap, DcEnL,
   DcEuL, DcLEnL, EvLB, FamSYP,
   JBA 1934, NCHEL, OxEng, Pen Eng,
   REn, TelT, WWCL
Yoo, Grace S *ConAu XR*
Yoo, Grace S *see* Yoo, Young Hyun
Yoo, Young Hyun 1927- *ConAu 41*
Yoo, Young Hyun *see* Yoo, Grace S
Yorick 1871- *OhA&B, WWBWI 1*
Yorick *see* Hodgson, Ralph
York, Andrew *ConAu XR, ConNov 1972,*
   ConNov 1976, SmATA 5
York, Andrew *see* Nicole, Christopher Robin
York, Carol Beach 1928- *ConAu 1R,*
   ForWC 1970, SmATA 6
York, Harrison *MnBBF*
York, Jeremy *ConAu XR, EncM&D, LongC,*
   WWBWI A
York, Jeremy *see* Creasey, John
Yorke, Carras *MnBBF, WWBWI A*
Yorke, Carras *see* Marshall, Arthur C
Yorke, Edward G *MnBBF*
Yorke, Sidney *MnBBF*
Yost, Edna 1889- *AuBYP, ConAu 1R*
Young, Bernice Elizabeth 1931- *ConAu 37,*
   WrD
Young, Bob *ConAu XR, SmATA 3*
Young, Bob *see* Young, Robert W
Young, Charles *MnBBF*
Young, Chesley Virginia Barnes 1919-
   AmSCAP 66
Young, Chesley Virginia 1919- *ConAu 33*

Young, Chesley Virginia Barnes 1919-
 WWAW 8, WWE 14
Young, Chic 1901- *ArtCS, ConAu XR,*
 NYTBE 4, WWA 38
Young, Chic *see* Young, Murat Bernard Chic
Young, Clarence *ConAu P-2, SmATA 1*
Young, Clarence *see* Stratemeyer, Edward L
Young, Dick *MnBBF*
Young, Dorothea Bennett 1924- *ConAu 13R*
Young, Dorothea Bennett *see* Bennett, Dorothea
Young, Ed 1931- *ChPo S1, IlBYP,*
 SmATA 10, ThBJA
Young, Edward 1910-1964 *AuBYP,*
 ConAu XR, SmATA 3
Young, Edward *see* Reinfeld, Fred
Young, Eleanor R 1918- *ConAu 37, WrD*
Young, Ella 1867?-1956 *AnCL, AuBYP,*
 ChPo, ChPo S1, ChPo S2, JBA 1934,
 JBA 1951, TwCA, TwCA Sup
Young, Ernest 1869- *CarSB*
Young, Evelyn *AmPB*
Young, Frank W *MnBBF*
Young, Frank W *see* Young, Fred W
Young, Fred W *MnBBF*
Young, Fred W *see* Arnold, Frank
Young, Fred W *see* Newcome, Colin
Young, Fred W *see* Scott, Hedley
Young, Fred W *see* Wyatt, Ben
Young, Fred W *see* Young, Frank W
Young, Frederica *AuBYP*
Young, Jan *AuBYP, ConAu XR, SmATA 3*
Young, Jan *see* Young, Janet Randall
Young, Janet Randall *WrD*
Young, Janet Randall 1919- *AuBYP,*
 ConAu 5R, ForWC 1970, SmATA 3
Young, Janet Randall *see* Randall, Janet
Young, Janet Randall *see* Young, Jan
Young, John Richard *AuBYP*
Young, Lois Horton 1911- *ConAu 9R*
Young, Louise B 1919- *ConAu 25R, WrD*
Young, Margaret Buckner 1922- *BkP,*
 ConAu 21R, SmATA 2, WWAW 8,
 WWE 14
Young, Miriam 1913-1974 *AuBYP, ConAu 37,*
 ConAu 53, NYTBS 5, SmATA 7, WrD
Young, Morris N 1909- *AmMWS 12P,*
 ConAu 33
Young, Murat Bernard Chic 1901-1973
 ConAu 41
Young, Murat Bernard Chic *see* Young, Chic
Young, Patrick 1937- *AuBYP, ConAu 69*
Young, Percy Marshall 1912- *Au&Wr 6,*
 AuBYP, ConAu 13R, WWMus 6
Young, Robert W 1916-1969 *AuBYP,*
 ConAu 5R, SmATA 3
Young, Robert W *see* Randall, Janet
Young, Robert W *see* Young, Bob
Young, Scott Alexander 1918- *ConAu 9R,*
 OxCan, OxCan Sup, SmATA 5,
 WWA 38
Young, Stewart *MnBBF*
Young, Stewart *see* Burrage, Alfred McLelland
Young, Virginia Brady 1921- *ConAu 61,*
 DrAP 1975
Young, Warwick *MnBBF*
Young, Warwick *see* Parsons, B
Young, Will *MnBBF, WWBWI A*
Young, Will *see* Home-Gall, William Bolinbroke
Youngs, Betty F 1928- *ConAu 33, WrD*

Yuill, Phyllis Jean 1941- *ConAu 65*
Yuki *ConAu XR*
Yuki *see* Inoue, Yukitoshi
Yung, Leong Gor *see* Ellison, Virginia Howell
Yurchenco, Henrietta 1916- *ConAu 37*

Z

Zabransky, Adolf 1909- *IlCB 1957, WWGA*
Zacks, Irene *AuBYP*
Zaffo, George J *AmPB, AuBYP*
Zagoren, Ruby 1922- *AuBYP, ForWC 1970, WWAW 8*
Zaidenberg, Arthur 1903?- *AmA&B, AuBYP, WWA 38*
Zalben, Jane Breskin 1950- *ConAu 49, SmATA 7, WrD*
Zallinger, Jean Day 1918- *IlBYP, IlCB 1957*
Zander, Hans 1905- *WWMus 6*
Zappler, Lisbeth 1930- *ConAu 49, SmATA 10*
Zarchy, Harry 1912- *AuBYP, ConAu 1R, MorJA*
Zarchy, Harry *see* Lewis, Roger
Zarem, Lewis *AuBYP*
Zastrow, Erika *ConAu XR*
Zastrow, Erika *see* Massey, Erika
Zaturenska, Marya 1902- *ChPo, CnDAL, ConAu 13R, ConLC 6, ConP 1970, ConP 1975, DrAP 1975, ForWC 1970, OxAm, Pen Am, REn, REnAL, SixAP, TwCA, TwCA Sup, WWA 38, WWAW 8*
Zebrowski, George 1945- *ConAu 41, DrAF 1976*
Zei, Alki *AuBYP*
Zeiger, Henry Anthony 1930- *AuBYP, ConAu 9R*
Zeiger, Henry Anthony *see* Peterson, James
Zeiger, Sophia 1926- *IlBYP, IlCB 1946, IlCB 1957*
Zeiger, Sophia *see* Sofia
Zemach, Harve 1933-1974 *AmA&B, AmPB, ConAu XR, SmATA 3, ThBJA, WWA 38*
Zemach, Harve *see* Fischtrom, Harvey
Zemach, Kaethe 1958- *ConAu 57*
Zemach, Margot 1931- *AmPB, IlBYP, IlCB 1957, NewbC 1966, ThBJA, WWA 38, WWAW 8*
Zemach, Margot *see* Fischtrom, Margot Zemach
Ziegler, Ursina *AuBYP*
Ziel, Ron 1939- *ConAu 21R*
Ziemienski, Dennis 1947- *SmATA 10*
Zillah *ConAu XR, SmATA XR, WNAA*
Zillah *see* Macdonald, Zillah K
Zim, Herbert Spencer 1909- *AmA&B, AmPB, Au&Wr 6, AuBYP, BkP, ChLR 2, ConAu 13R, CurB 56, JBA 1951, SmATA 1, WWA 38*

Zimelman, Nathan *AuBYP*
Zimmerman, Eleanor 1916- *ConAu 61*
Zimmerman, Naoma 1914- *ConAu 1R, SmATA 10, WrD*
Zimmerman, Velma E 1902- *ConAu 29*
Zimnik, Reiner 1930- *ChLR 3, ChFB 1, IlBYP, IlCB 1946, IlCB 1957, ThBJA*
Zindel, Paul 1936- *AuBYP, CelR 3, ChLR 3, CnThe, ConDr 1, ConLC 6, CurB 73, McGWD, WWA 38, WWT 15*
Ziner, Feenie 1921- *SmATA 5*
Ziner, Florence Feenie Katz 1921- *AuBYP, ConAu 1R, SmATA 5*
Zinkin, Taya *WrD*
Zinkoff, Dave *AuBYP*
Zinsser, Hans 1878-1940 *AmA&B, CurB 40, DcNAA, LongC, REnAL, TwCA, TwCA Sup*
Zion, Eugene 1913?-1975 *Au&Wr 6, ConAu 61*
Zion, Gene 1913?-1975 *AmPB, AuBYP, MorJA, WrD*
Zirbes, Laura *AuBYP*
Zistel, Era *ConAu 25R*
Zollinger, Gulielma 1856-1917 *ChPo, DcAmA, DcNAA, JBA 1934, JBA 1951*
Zolotow, Charlotte Shapiro 1915- *AmPB, AuBYP, BkP, ChLR 2, ConAu 5R, ForWC 1970, MorJA, PiP, SmATA 1, WWAW 8, WrD*
Zulli, Floyd, Jr. 1922- *ConAu 37, CurB 58, DrAS 6F*
Zumwalt, Eva 1936- *ConAu 65*
Zurhorst, Charles 1913- *ConAu 45, SmATA 12*
Zurhorst, Charles *see* Stewart, Charles

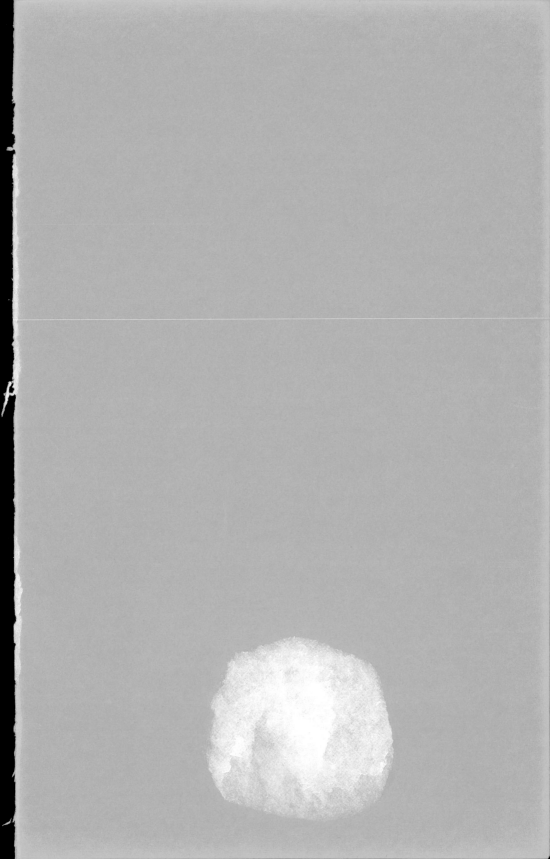

KEY TO TITLE CODES FOR USE IN LOCATING SOURCES

Detailed bibliographical information about the sources
listed below appears on pages vii-xxiii

AfA	African Authors
Alli	Allibone: Critical Dictionary
AmA	American Authors, 1600-1900
AmA&B	American Authors & Books
AmLY	American Literary Yearbook
AmMWS	American Men & Women of Science
AmNov	American Novelists of Today
AmPB	American Picturebooks
AmSCAP	ASCAP Biographical Dictionary
AmWr	American Writers
AnCL	Anthology of Children's Literature
AnMV	Anthology of Magazine Verse
ArizL	Arizona in Literature
ArtCS	The Art of the Comic Strip
ArtsCL	Artists of a Certain Line
AtlBL	Atlantic Brief Lives
Au&ICB	Authors & Illustrators of Children's Books
Au&Wr	Authors & Writers Who's Who
AuBYP	Authors of Books for Young People
AuNews	Authors in the News
BbD	Bibliophile Dictionary
BbthC	Bibliotheca Canadensis
BiD&SB	Biographical Dictionary & Synopsis of Books
BiDL	Biographical Directory of Librarians
BiDLA	Biographical Dictionary of Living Authors
BiDPar	Biographical Dictionary of Parapsychology
BiDSA	Biographical Dictionary of Southern Authors
BiEnAT	Biographical Encyclopedia & Who's Who of the American Theatre
BiN	Biography News
BkC	Book of Catholic Authors
BkCL	Book of Children's Literature
BkIE	Book Illustrators of 18th Century England
BkP	Books Are by People
BlkAW	Black American Writers
Br&AmS	British & American Sporting Authors
BrAu	British Authors before 1800
BrAu 19	British Authors of the 19th Century
BrCA	British Children's Authors
Cald	Caldecott Medal Books
CanNov	Canadian Novelists
CanWW	Canadian Who's Who
CanWr	Canadian Writers
CarSB	Carolyn Sherwin Bailey Historical Collection
CasWL	Cassell's Encyclopaedia of World Literature
CatA	Catholic Authors
CelR	Celebrity Register
Chambr	Chambers' Cyclopaedia of English Literature
ChFB	The Child's First Books
ChLR	Children's Literature Review
ChP	The Children's Poets
ChPo	Childhood in Poetry

CLDMEuL	Columbia Dictionary of Modern European Literature
CnDAL	Concise Dictionary of American Literature
CnE&AP	Concise Encyclopedia of English & American Poets
CnMD	Concise Encyclopedia of Modern Drama
CnMWL	Concise Encyclopedia of Modern World Literature
CnThe	Concise Encyclopedia of the Theatre
ConAmA	Contemporary American Authors
ConAmL	Contemporary American Literature
ConAu	Contemporary Authors
ConDr 1	Contemporary Dramatists
ConICB	Contemporary Illustrators of Children's Books
ConLC	Contemporary Literary Criticism
ConNov	Contemporary Novelists
ConP	Contemporary Poets
CrCAP	Crowell's Handbook of Contemporary American Poets
CrCD	Crowell's Handbook of Contemporary Drama
CrE&SL	Crowell's Handbook of Elizabethan & Stuart Literature
CriT	The Critical Temper
CurB	Current Biography
CyAL	Cyclopaedia of American Literature
CyWA	Cyclopedia of World Authors
DcAmA	Dictionary of American Authors
DcBiA	Dictionary of Biographies...Authors Digest Series
DcCAA	Dictionary of Contemporary American Artists
DcCLA	Dictionary of Contemporary Latin American Authors
DcEnA	Dictionary of English Authors
DcEnL	Dictionary of English Literature
DcEuL	Dictionary of European Literature
DcLEnL	Dictionary of Literature in the English Language
DcNAA	Dictionary of North American Authors
DcOrL	Dictionary of Oriental Literatures
DcRusL	Dictionary of Russian Literature
DcSpL	Dictionary of Spanish Literature
DrAF	Directory of American Fiction Writers
DrAP	Directory of American Poets
DrAS	Directory of American Scholars
DrLC	Directory of Library Consultants
EarAB	Early American Book Illustrators
EncFCW	Encyclopedia of Folk, Country & Western Music
EncM&D	Encyclopedia of Mystery & Detection
EncWL	Encyclopedia of World Literature
EuAu	European Authors
EvEuW	Everyman's Dictionary of European Writers
EvLB	Everyman's Dictionary of Literary Biography